MANASĀ AND NETA

MYTH AND MAGICK OF EAST INDIA'S SERPENT GODDESSES

Picture 1: Manasā Neta.

Manasā and Neta

Myth and Magick
of East India's Serpent Goddesses

Related truthfully
and innovated with amazing extras
by

Jan Fries

Published by Avalonia
www.avaloniabooks.co.uk

Published by Avalonia

BM Avalonia, London, WC1N 3XX, England, UK

www.avaloniabooks.co.uk

MANASĀ AND NETA

First published by Avalonia

ISBN 978-1-910191-14-9 (PB)

Typeset and designed by Satori

Cover image by Astrid Bauer

Illustrations by Jan Fries

Dedication

This book is dedicated to you and everyone who believes in the future, and makes it happen, better than expected, each and every day.

Table of Contents

ACKNOWLEDGEMENTS

1. A Swift Introduction ---- 12
2. In the Evening ---- 22
3. A Fairy Tale: Manasā's Brata Story ---- 25

PART ONE: ŚIVA

4. Creation, traditional ---- 42
5. Creation, Bengal Style ---- 46
6. Gaṅgā ---- 58
7. Courtship ---- 64
8. Married Life ---- 72

PART TWO: MANASĀ

9. Lotusborn ---- 85
10. Outside ---- 98
11. Tigerfight ---- 104
12. Milkocean ---- 108
13. Husbands ---- 118
14. Over There ---- 125
15. Duel ---- 133
16. Cowherds ---- 142
17. Hāssan and Hussein ---- 148

PART THREE: CĀNDO

18. Power ---- 154
19. Fishermen ---- 160
20. Sonakā's Conversion ---- 165
21. Conflict ---- 171
22. Dhanvantari ---- 179
23. Journey to Anupāma Pāṭana ---- 186
24. Journey to Dakṣiṇ Pāṭana ---- 192
25. Return ---- 197
26. Coming Home ---- 202

PART FOUR: BEHULĀ

27. Heaven ---- 215
28. Beans ---- 220
29. Plans ---- 230
30. Marriage ---- 233
31. Iron-House ---- 245
32. Water's Edge ---- 253
33. Downstream ---- 258
34. Dark Waters ---- 271
35. Back ---- 292
36. Thanksgiving ---- 299

PART FIVE: FUN WITH SNAKES

37: SNAKE CHARMING ---------- 304

38. THE NĀGA CULTS ---------- 317

39. KUṆḌALINĪ: THE TANTRIC FIRE SNAKE ---------- 329

PART SIX: VENOMS AND ELIXIRS

40. DRUGS AND SPICES ---------- 339

41. CĀNDO'S PARADISE ---------- 345

42. AUSPICIOUS SONGS ---------- 359

43. MANASĀ MAṆGALS ---------- 363

44. BRATA RITUALS ---------- 365

PART SEVEN: THE CULT OF MANASĀ

45. PRACTICAL WORSHIP ---------- 376

46. LIVE PERFORMANCE ---------- 389

47. SEASONS OF THE SNAKE ---------- 392

48. WEST BENGAL ---------- 399

49. EAST BENGAL ---------- 404

50. TRIPURA AND BIHAR ---------- 407

51. ASSAM ---------- 409

PART EIGHT: MEDITATION AND RITUAL

52. DHYĀNA INSTRUCTIONS ---------- 413

53. A TANTRIC GODDESS ---------- 420

54. FIRST PŪJĀ INSTRUCTION ---------- 426

55. MANTRAS ---------- 430

56. SECOND PŪJĀ INSTRUCTION ---------- 438

57. THIRD PŪJĀ INSTRUCTION ---------- 440

58. FAST PŪJĀ INSTRUCTION ---------- 443

59. DIVINE NAMES ---------- 444

60. OUROBOROS ---------- 449

APPENDIX: THE SOURCES ---------- 452

BIBLIOGRAPHY ---------- 473

INDEX ---------- 477

Picture Legends

Picture 1: Manasā Neta. *(frontispiece)*
Picture 2: Manasā rising.
Picture 3: Gardens of Darksome Delight.
Picture 4: The Descent of Gaṅgā.
Picture 5. Durgā as Mahiṣamardinī (the Slayer of the Buffalo Demon of Arrogance), based loosely on a wooden carving.
Picture 6: The Wisdom of the Heart.
Picture 7: Splatterbrain Sunrise.
Picture 8: Kadrū: Mysteries of Forest and Water.
Picture 9: Blinded.
Picture 10: Mountain Guardian.
Picture 11: Sisters.
Picture 12: Fishermen.
Picture 13: "We worship Manasā."
Picture 14: Mangroves.
Picture 15: Crocodile Madness.
Picture 16: Cotton Venom.
Picture 17: Jagged Edges (Pandanus pristis).
Picture 18: Lost (Pandanus balsamifera).
Picture 19: Yakṣa Forest.
Picture 20: Reincarnation (Bollywood Metempsychosis).
Picture 21: Vīṇā Dreaming.
Picture 22: Flowers of the Night.
Picture 23: Banana Blossom Serpentine.
Picture 24: A Haze of Toxic Berries.
Picture 25: Call of the Koel.
Picture 26: Downstream.
Picture 27: Worms.
Picture 28: Between Worlds.
Picture 29: Neta Savage.
Picture 30: Beyond Exhaustion.
Picture 31: Facing the Truth.
Picture 32: Shore Guardian.
Picture 33: Yama Deathlord (based on Bengal Folk Art).
Picture 34: Death and Disease Spirits (based on Bengal Folk Art).
Picture 35: Neta: That's me!
Picture 36: Manasā Temple.
Picture 37: Manasā, traditional.
Picture 38: Three Snakes, engraved on a piece of mammoth ivory, Mal'ta, Siberia.
Picture 39: Göbekli Tepe: Animals grace Standing Stones.
Picture 40: Göbekli Tepe: T-shaped megalith with serpent pattern and unidentified animal (ram?). Photo in Schmidt, 2006:121.
Picture 41: Turkey. Top right: back of a stone head with rising snake, Nevalı Çori, 8,500-7,900 BCE. Photo in *Die Ältesten Monumente der Menschheit,* 2007:289
Top left: polished stone from Göbekli Tepe (4cm), 8,800-8,000 BCE). Photo in *Die Ältesten Monumente der Menschheit*, 2007:306

Bottom: Körtik Tepe. Fragment of a stone bowl graced with serpents, centipedes and tiny birds. Pre-Ceramic period, 9,500-8,500 BCE. After Schmidt, 2006:188.

Picture 42: Going East: Top right: snake woman or goddess, from Bahrain, c. 2000 BCE (after Bibby). At the time, the Sumerians and the Indus Valley people were trading with each other. A few centuries later it stopped, when the Indus Valley Culture disappeared. Bahrain was an important trade point in between. Indeed, the Sumerians considered it a holy land, blessed by the influence of Enki.

Top left: Terracotta fragment from Susa (Iran), late 3rd millennium BCE, showing an unidentified serpent goddess (After Koch, 2007:153).

Bottom right: Seal of a vessel, Susa, late fifth millennium BCE (after Koch, 2007:33).

Picture 43: Mesopotamia: an all-time favourite, the horned serpent. Top: a horned serpent from a kudurru stone, presented by Melik-Šipak to his son, Marduk-Apla-Iddina, ca. 1,200 BCE (BKR # 32). The stone shows the emblems of twenty-four deities; the horned serpent is at the bottom.

Bottom: horned serpent head, c. 7-6th century BCE, Babylon (photo in Margueron, 1965:128).

Picture 44: Chinese serpents. Top: from a bronze zun vessel, late Shang Dynasty or early Zhou (c. 1100-1000 BCE), after Yang, 2000:124.

Centre: from a bronze gui vessel, Early Western Zhou Dynasty, after Yang: 2000:124.

Bottom: Snake image from the bottom of a theriomorphic ritual vessel, late Shang Dynasty, after Yang, 2000:121.

Picture 45: Dragon head, copper, treated with tin and gold. 3rd century. Originally mounted on a pole and carried by an officer of the Roman cavalry. A tube of thin cloth (silk?) was attached to the head, which swung and twisted. From Niederbieber (Neuwied). An image of its use appears on the Ludovisian sarcophagus, Rome.

Picture 46: Tombstone of a Frankish Warrior with Pagan Imagery (note the serpents), Niederdollendorf, photo in Schneider: 1951: plate 15.

Picture 47: Nāga goddess, wooden statue from Tamilnadu, after Chandra and Bose, 1984:358.

Picture 48: Unidentified snake goddess with child, from Tundara, Balasor, in Orissa. The image has been identified with Manasā (and the child with Āstika), but there are no convincing reasons for this assumption. In this region, Manasā was probably unknown, but the Buddhist serpent goddess Jāṅgulī was worshipped. After photo in Maity, 2001:298).

Picture 49: Nāga girls, Down in the Seventh Underworld.

Picture 50: Nāga talisman. Sorry, the image I worked from was rather wanting. I'm sure the spelling is wrong.

Picture 51: Clay head of Śiva, emphasising his relationship to the serpent world, Nadia, West Bengal. Photo in Bussabarger & Robbins, 1968:35.

Picture 52: Mask of Śiva, used in folk dances, papier-mâché, West Bengal. Note Gaṅgā in his hair. Photo in Bussabarger & Robbins, 1968:157.

Picture 53: Gaṅgā in a fierce mood. Statuette, made for the festival season, Nadabwib, West Bengal, photo in Bussabarger & Robbins, 1968:134.

Picture 54: Gaṅgā reclining on her crocodile-dolphin-fish. After a kalighat print from 19th Century Calcutta, after Zbavitel, 1976.

Picture 55: Ālpanā painting for Manasā's brata ritual, Bengal, after Mode and Chandra, 1984:195.

Picture 56: Ālpanā painting for Lakṣmīs's brata ritual, Bengal, after Mode and Chandra, 1984: 22.

Picture 57: Footsteps of the Goddess: Ālpanā painting for Lakṣmīs's brata ritual, Bengal, after Mode and Chandra, 1984: 23.

Picture 58: Top: Ālpanā painting for safe travel on sea, bottom: brata painting for unknown ritual, Bengal, after Mode and Chandra, 1984:195 & 226.

Picture 59: Manasā, kālīghāt print, 19th century.

Picture 60: Manasā pot. Very unusual, shaped as the head of the goddess with cobra headdress (some missing). Midnapore, West Bengal, photo in Bussabarger & Robbins, 1968:45.

Picture 61: Ālpanā painting for Subachani, the Mother of Ducks brata ritual, Bengal, after Mode and Chandra, 1984: 227.

Picture 62: Top: Ālpanā painting for the Chariot of the Gods; bottom: for marriage ceremonies, Bengal, after Mode and Chandra, 1984: 226 & 227.

Picture 63: Top: Ālpanā painting for Ganeṣa's brata ritual, bottom: feet of a goddess, Bengal. Picture 64: Top left: Ālpanā paintings for Tārā's brata ritual, Bengal. Note that Tāra is not just the Chinese goddess of alchemy but also a star. Photo in Maity, 1989: plate X a & b, and Maity 1988.

Picture 65: Happy lunacy: Kāmākhya, refining the kalās of the gods.

Picture 66: Black Manasā. Temple statue.

Picture 67: Unidentified Snake Goddess. Women's painting on paper, Madhubani, Bihar, after Mode and Chandra, 1984:219.

Picture 68: Two pictures of Manasā. These come from the picture scrolls used by travelling Paṭuā singers. Photos in Kaiser, 2012:142 (detail from a painting of Bakha Chidrakal & 46 detail from a painting by Manimala Chitrakar).

Picture 69: Manasā and Neta, Behulā and Lakhindār. Start of a picture scroll by Madhab Chitrakar of Ghuli, inscription omitted. After Kaiser, 2012: 64.

Picture 70: Manasā Mask made of plant fibres, Goalpara, Assam. Photo in Mode & Chandra, 1984:118.

Picture 71: Behulā and Neta wash the clothes of the gods. Detail from a picture scroll by Bakhar Chidrakar in Kaiser, 2012:150.

Picture 72: Bare Bones. The Sources of the Epic (python, tiger with missing canine, cobra and gavial).

Picture 73: Nirṛti, Lack of Cosmic Order, Destroyer, Owl-Goddess of the Dark.

Acknowledgements

As I write these lines, I feel deeply grateful. The sun drenches the freshly sprouting green in light and warmth, and it's good to be alive. Trees unfold their foliage, photosynthesis kicks in, the stomata open, moisture evaporates and from the roots, an incessant stream of water rises, carrying minerals delivered courtesy of mycorrhiza enterprises. Plantain sprouts, mosses gleam, ferns unwind their tentacles, here and there a dandelion raises its head, looks at the purple nettles nearby, and watches a brave yarrow blossoming in mid-April freshness. The elders unfold new leaves, the whitethorn blossoms and yes, at last, the warm season has returned and serpents emerge from their lairs. Soon grass snakes go hunting near the sparkling Taunus brooks, and relax on the lower branches of spruce trees, their scales shimmering in the sun. Smooth snakes start the day sunbathing on the warm rocks of the Rhine valley vineyards, and when they are warm and wide awake, go after lizards. Aesculapian snakes, almost two metres long, climb trees, and explore the nests of birds and squirrels. Elsewhere, an adder may raise its head out of the heather and stare into the wide and colourful world through slanted pupils. And there are dice snakes, very rare, these days, and on a bare few kilometres, in the Black Forest, asp vipers. Sadly, they have almost disappeared. It's not much: Central Europe is far from snake-lovers paradise. But it is a start, and may improve as the climate gets warmer. Happy snakes are an excellent reason for gratefulness.

Let me thank all snakes, and those who participated, laughed, and contributed ideas and inspiration, listened, agreed, disagreed, and confused me, those who played the divine as the divine plays us, and made this book so much better:

Tina B. & H.H.F. my parents; my dear and wonderful friends Julia H. (favourite painter; see her page Medea: Magick Art), Volkert V.(hard-core Druid), Astrid B. (who made the cover such a treat) & Gavin S.(Musician and Spareologist), Nidaba (Mesopotamian Mysteries), Asenath Mason (all the way around the tree), Sorita & Lokabandhu of Avalonia (Publishers extraordinaire), Mogg & Kym M. of Mandrake (Egyptian delights), Holger & Christiane K. of Edition Roter Drache, Ruth K. (who manages anything), Jing & Xinyue L. (who remind me of what matters in life), Mike and the late Nema of the Maat Current, Dagmar B. (resolute optimiser), Norbert of the Zeil Antiquaritat, the local Bengali Community and all those weird and wonderful people who read my books and explore consciousness, life, and joy.

Extra blessings for all who respect the work of authors and publishers and refrain from stealing books on the net.

You all helped, you all supported this project, in those days when I worried about everything while I corrected passage after passage, fifteen, twenty, thirty times, and thought I would go crazy. Indeed I did. It was worth the effort.

Thank you!

1. A Swift Introduction

The wild, bizarre and epic tale of the serpent goddess Manasā has inspired poets for more than five hundred years. It's not really much. Five hundred years are practically yesterday. However, we are talking about literary works. Before them, an oral tradition existed, and before that, rituals, prayers and offerings, and yearning for the divine. Serpent worship is an ancient faith. In India, it can be traced to at least 1,000 BCE. But that's only serpent cults in general. Here, our question is: how old is Manasā? In a text called *Rājamārtaṇḍa* , allegedly composed by King Bhoja (c. 1040-1060), goddess Manasā is briefly mentioned. Sadly, King Bhoja had no sense of priorities and failed to provide details. A few centuries earlier, an anti-serpent spell naming Manasā was included in the *Garuḍa Purāna*. It introduces her as Śiva's daughter and provides useful mantras. You'll read it further on. How about something earlier? A Buddhist text of the sixth century mentions a goddess called Manasā who expels toxins. Here's the story. One day, a Buddhist monk called Svāti was bitten by a serpent. Undaunted, the Buddha improvised a spell to cure his follower. The charm was called *Mayūrīvidyā (Wisdom/Magic /Science of the Peacocks)*. Peacocks, as everyone knew, are snake-killers and immune to their poison. The spell made it into Buddhist literature and was used to cure snakebite. Here is the passage, quoted by Maity (2001:154), slightly amended:

> Hail Buddha. Hail Dharma. Hail Saṅga.
> Thus it is: (O Goddess) who are pure, blameless, devoid of impurities, auspicious,
> of golden complexion, the female energy of the Golden Egg, good, very good;
> who art characterised by all-round goodness, marked by prosperity;
> who art a means to achieve all objects,
> an instrument to the realisation of the Ultimate End,
> a pacifier of all evils and a means to bring about all kinds of goodness,
> Manasā, broadminded, unshaken, wonderful, most wonderful, free, the releaser, the liberator,
> devoid of the rajas 'element' (the quality of fierce passion),
> (full of) nectar, immortal, divine,
> manifesting thyself as the Sound of Brahman, perfect;
> who fulfils all kinds of desires, liberated, living;
> protect Svāti from all calamities, fears and diseases.
> I salute you.

The setting is Buddhist. The contents are not. Our spell is far from the stern creed which the historical Buddha taught in the fifth or fourth century BCE. Indeed, it is much closer to Hinduism and early Tantra. Let's explore this. Historically, the great achievement of the Buddha was to blend the teachings of several early *Upaniṣads*, like world-rejection, rebirth, Karman and the omnipresence of suffering and delusion, with another philosophical school, which preached Anātman (*Not-Self*). The Nāstikas (*deniers*) insisted that the self, universal consciousness, the existence of gods, spirits etc. are impossible to prove, hence, they do not exist. They also taught that there is no life after death and that Karman is a fable. Buddha agreed with them regarding the non-reality of the self, or any self, but he insisted that rebirth and Karman exist. What people, spirits, gods etc. experience as 'self' is a painful delusion that continues life after life, until Karman is exhausted. Liberation, in his opinion, meant to destroy all bondage and to blot out every notion of identity. His creed aimed at Nirvāṇa, a term that used to mean *cessation, dissolution, disappearance*. No doubt you have heard that Nirvāṇa is bliss. That's a wonderful idea based on reformed Mahāyāna and tantric Buddhism; it was invented centuries later, and has very little to do with what the historical Buddha taught. Our spell calls on a goddess (or several). The Buddha wasn't much into gods, let along goddesses, and believed that deities are just as illusionary as you and me and everything. And it mentions Brahman, Absolute Reality, the All-Self, a favourite Upaniṣadic concept the historical Buddha passionately disliked.

The seers of the Upaniśad Period (c. 800 BCE-400 BCE) and most of the Hindu seers, who came after them, believed that Brahman is formless, shapeless, nameless, indefinable and totally passive consciousness. It is not male or female, not here or there, not alive or dead. It is Absolute Reality, the fundamental ground of all being. This formless consciousness desires to experience itself. It utters the great mantra:

Āhaṁ bahu syam: May I be Many.

From Brahman, all gods, spirits, people, beings, elements, energies, ideas and things arise. According to some, the first emanation of Brahman is Śabda-Brahman, that is, the pure sound-vibration of the All-Self. In this stage, reality is pulsation. Out of this consciousness (manas), audible sound, energy, form, thought, emotion, melody, colour, name, identity, and everything appear (not necessarily in that order).

Whoever composed this spell was fond of the All-Self and its primal sound-vibration, and identified it with Manasā. The first line is a standard phrase of Buddhism. The rest looks like an effort to integrate ancient Nāga/Serpent worship into reformed Mahāyāna or even innovative tantric Buddhism. This spell allows us to trace the cult of Manasā to the fifth century. It could indicate that her cult is older than the cult of the minor Buddhist serpent goddess Jāṅgulī, who appeared in the late sixth century, and never really made it. That's because the Buddhist Jāṅgulī remained specialised on serpent spells, while the Hindu Manasā was identified with all mental activity, and invoked for lots of boons. It turned her into a major high goddess. Nowadays, the name Jāṅgulī is mostly used as a title of Manasā.

But are we really talking about Manasā? At this point, a few scholars voice their doubts. They point out that it isn't certain whether we should understand the word Manasā as a name or as a description. Manas means mind, awareness, thought, imagination and so on. Hence, the name of the goddess is also a descriptive title, meaning: *'Thinking One, Conscious One, Aware One, Imaginative One'*.

It seems that our spell invokes Manasā. However, life is complicated. In Saṁskṛta, there are no distinguishing marks indicating whether we are dealing with a name or adjective. Each descriptive term in that line, i.e. *Awareness* (Manasā), *Broadminded, Unshaken, Wonderful* etc, could be the name of a deity. Maybe the spell doesn't invoke a single Manasā but an entire series of deities. And maybe all of them are her.

Please go back to the spell. Recite, taste, drink and breathe every word, and consider that, apart from referring to a specific serpent goddess, it relates to everything you are aware of. Outside, inside, in between and beyond. Consciousness is Manasā; yours, mine, that of every being, energy, and thing.

Outside of consciousness, nothing can exist.

Even when you sleep, trance or die and shed your names and identity, you remain Manasā. Manasā is subject and object and the process of perception. And Manasā is the dance of awareness, between memory, imagination, identification, participation and dis-association, the Krama-Mudrā (*Seal of Continuity*) which celebrates the great Upaniṣadic formula: You are That and That is You.

Stop a moment, smile, take a deep breath and wake up. Take a look around. Wherever you may be: You are that and that is you. Introvert. You are that and that is you. Between inside and outside is consciousness. You are that and that is you.

Well, that's the gist. It will help you understand the *Manasā Epic*, her rituals and meditations, and to enjoy sheer consciousness. For wherever you are and whatever you do: your awareness is Manasā. You dance her and she dances you. And serpents, I'm sure you know, are really good at dancing.

Things might be much older. Let me introduce the earliest known serpent/dragon goddess of history. She is the *Lady of Serpents*. I wrote about her in *The Seven Names of Lamaštu*. For full detail, check it out. Here, a brief summary should suffice. Meet the Sumerian goddess Ningirima, *the Conjurer of the Gods, Lady of the Pure House/Temple, Lady Whose Conjuration is Life, Lady of Heaven, Lady of Uruk*, (the greatest metropolis of early history), and, her major title, *Lady of the Girima*, a special, heavenly water, kept in a divine agubba vessel, which *'breeds/feeds snakes/ dragons'* and was used in purification rites. The Akkadians, Babylonians and Assyrians called her Goddess Min, but the Sumerian version of the name can be traced to c. 2,700 BCE; it is much older and was generally preferred. Min might remind you of Manasā. Ningirima was a major player in early third millennium BCE Sumerian literature, i.e. the period when the Sumerians and the Indus Valley people were happily trading with each other.

Manasā's major ritual item is her sacred pot, a jar filled with holy water. Sacred pots are more than holy vessels. They can be understood as metaphors for the mind; the energy/consciousness zones brain, heart, and belly; the entire human being, the divine in all of its manifestations and indeed the world each of us be-lives. In tantric literature, the vessel, jar, or pot is an essential symbol. Here is a passage from the *Tripurā Rahasya*:

Likewise, after appearances of duality are removed, pure consciousness alone remains. Just as an image is seen in a jar of water, similarly, an image is seen in the mirror of pure consciousness. That state of freedom is pure consciousness, the absolute state. There is no sorrow in it; therefore, it is full of everlasting bliss. Because that state is essentially bliss, everyone desires to attain it. The very nature of the self is joy. (22, 90-92)

Or try this passage. It comes from the famous *Vijñāna Bhairava Tantra* and describes, in a few brief words, two methods of meditation:

58. O great goddess! One should meditate about the universe as totally void. Within this (idea) all thought dissolves and one becomes part of the absorption into this (voidness).

59. One should gaze into the inside of an empty jar, leaving out the limiting walls. In the same instant one is absorbed and through being absorbed, one unites.

Let's quote Kashmir's universal genius, Abhinavagupta.

Of manifestation, the delightful form of the energy of the natural, innate mantra known as parā vāk (the Supreme divine utterance) is I (ahaṁ). As has been said: "The repose of all manifested phenomena in the Self is said to be I-consciousness." (APS 22) i.e. the real I-feeling is that in which in the process of withdrawal, all external objects like a jar, clothes etc., being withdrawn from their manifoldness come to rest or final repose in their eternal, uninterrupted Anuttara (Supreme, Absolute) aspect. This Anuttara aspect is the real I-feeling (ahaṁ-bhāva). This is a secret, a great mystery. (*Parātrīśikā-Vivaraṇa, The Secret of Tantric*

Mysticism, trans. Singh, 2002:54-55, slightly amended).

Knotty revelations like these ensured that the jar, full or empty, became a favourite metaphor for the pioneers of Kashmir Tantra. Like Manasā, Ningirima/Min has power over life and death. Her word *'means life'* (recovery) and her blessing makes magic spells come true. *'This is not my conjuration, it is the conjuration of Ningirima, Mistress of Magic'* is a common formula. Maybe she connects with India. There is a South Indian serpent goddess called Mañchā, or Mañchā-Ammā (*Mañchā the Woman/Mother*), who has a cult but, as far as I know, no epic. Mañchā sounds much like Manasā when you pronounce the 's' as a 'sh', as people in East India usually do.

Our topic is the *'Manasā Epic'*. It is such an inconvenient term. The word epic is well and good, as our story starts with the creation of the cosmos and extends through the ages. The term 'Manasā Epic', however, creates the illusion that we are dealing with a single story or composition. This is not the case. The 'epic' is a stream of stories. Maity names more than fifty important poets who played with the material as they liked. There must have been more. Our poets wanted to create great art, but they also knew about the preferences of their customers, and where the money comes in. Not that these were the only influences. Just as important was spiritual effort: some poets worshipped the goddess and did their best to support her cult. A few were tantric practitioners and hinted at deeper meanings. Some were disgusted by the way women were treated in traditional Indian society, and hoped to raise their status. They created Behulā, and the story of her odyssey; to this day the most popular section of the tale. By and large, all writers adhered to a basic structure, though they were quite capable of omitting essential episodes or putting them in different places. Apart from this, they extended the material, ornamented it with fancy ideas, jokes, proverbs, tales from classic Indian literature or turned things upside down. None of these authors were traditionalists or fundamentalists. In their worldview, unalterable scripture was unthinkable. Each poet was blessed (or cursed) by personal visions and preferences; many had original or bizarre ideas and improved the story by including prayers, personal insights and comedy. To liven up the material, they included elements from folk tales, stories that belonged to specific vrata/brata rituals, verses from ballads and introduced episodes from sacred literature, such as the Mahābhārata, the Śrimad Devī Bhāgavatam Purāṇa and the Brahmā Vaivarta Purāṇa, the Devī Mahātmya episode of the Mārkāṇḍeya Purāṇa, the popular story of Śiva and Satī, and the rebirth of Satī as Pārvatī/Umā/Durgā.

Our poets wrote and sang as they liked. Their audience appreciated originality. The results, if we call them the *'Manasā Epic'*, are astonishingly creative. I doubt there was an 'original version'. In all likeliness, a bundle of tales came together in a complicated weaving, a 'Tantra' (*weft, textile, treatise, scientific manual*) with major local differences. Some of the material is recent; some goes back to much earlier periods. In this case, we are talking about the eleventh or tenth century. All earlier material is lost.

The literary tradition of East India is comparatively young, full of gaps and tragic interruptions. If you want to relate the hymns and rituals of the Vedic seers (c. 1,200-800 BCE), the Upaniṣadic philosophers (c. 800-400 BCE) and the poets of early Hinduism (c. 400 BCE-400 CE) to the literature of Bengal and Assam, you are in for a disappointment. East India had very little contact with the mainstream of Indian faiths up to the tenth century, when Hinduism gradually became the dominant religion. Before this period, Buddhism, Jainism and a wide range of local cults, many of them shamanic, were superior. For a while, Hinduism proved to be the most powerful creed, but didn't remain so. When invaders enforced Islam, it lost its dominance. Simultaneously, Buddhism disappeared from India. While Islam became the major religious creed, Hinduism continued in a subservient role. Sure, some Hindus remained rich and powerful. They sponsored rituals and encouraged culture. Nevertheless, most regents were Muslims.

Among the Hindus, now somewhat degraded, the Brahmins were the highest class. The Hindu warrior class (Kṣatriya) lost its importance. In a society dominated by Islam, Hindu warriors were unemployable, unless they converted. The result was a social vacuum. It was filled by traders. Generally, in the Indian class systems, traders (plus peasants, servants, employees and moneylenders) belong to the Vaiśya class: *those who obey orders*. In the Vedic world-order, they were in the lower third of society and the Brahmins and warriors despised them. Nevertheless, some East Indian traders amassed wealth, and became more influential than the rulers of tiny kingdoms, who depended on businessmen and moneylenders to keep up a semblance of respectability. Great traders had their own networks of influence, power and information. In our story, you will meet a perfect specimen. Manasās greatest opponent is not a deity or a king but Cāndo, the most powerful trader of East India. He is the perfect representative of the money makers who ravage our planet nowadays.

In spite of Islam, most of the population remained Hindus. The middle and top segments of Hindu society approved of a rigid form of Brahmanism. The lower segments of society were also influenced by local and tribal traditions. There were no rigid frontiers between them. Indeed, Islam and Hinduism merged in several respects. Many Hindu festivals and cults were popular with Muslims, and vice versa. The same syncretistic attitude appears in Bengali ballads. Famous poets had no qualms about praising Allah and the Hindu goddess Gaṅgā in the same poem. Indeed, some Muslim emperors, like Akbar the Great (1556-1605), did their best to promote both faiths. Most people only know Akbar as an amazingly successful conqueror, a descendant of the Mongols, who extended his realm from Afghanistan to East India. The powerful warlord, however, was just one side of his fascinating character. Akbar was fond of Sufism and was raised by a teacher who insisted on religious tolerance. Earlier Muslim regents made the Hindus pay special taxes. Akbar abolished them, wore his hair long, in Hindu fashion, and occasionally painted a red tilak mark on his brow. He served all guests water from the sacred Ganges, had the *Upaniṣads* translated into Persian, and preferred them to the *Qur'an*. During his reign, the Hindus regained the right to build and renovate temples. His descendant, Jahāngīr (1605-1627), continued a policy of religious tolerance. Unlike them, Shāh Jahān (1628-1658) reverted to the intolerance and brutality of earlier regents.

Dinesh Chandra Sen mentions similar cases of religious tolerance: *The Dewans of Jangalbari were sometimes very friendly to the Hindus who elected them as judges and arbitrators even in their own social matters. Dewan Ibrahim Khan who died about a century ago, spent Rs. 50,000 at Mymensing for getting the whole of the Mahābhārata read and explained before the public by competent Hindu pundits* (1923:LXXIII).

East Indian literature is rarely older than five hundred years. The *Manasā Epic* is among the earliest surviving material. In the damp, hot, fungus- and insect-infected climate, books soon go to rot. An unknown amount of elder literature is irrevocably lost. The same fate awaited the ballads, which were frequently performed by several professional singers of either sex. The ballads are long, elaborate and hard to memorize, so they never passed into the repertoire of folk singers. Around the start of the twentieth century, Chandra Kumar and Dinesh Chandra Sen managed to record four volumes of ballads. It was a rescue at the last moment. When Dušan Zbavitel searched Bengal for ballads in the early 1960's, the art of the professional singers had disappeared.

Another source of the Manasā 'Epic' is the special stories told at vrata/brata rituals. Vrata (Bengal pronunciation: brata) means *will*, and is an oath to perform a religious practice for several years. It can be a ceremony, a series of offerings, an act of asceticism or a pilgrimage. Such rituals were and are accompanied by simple stories. In this context, the story is essential. It allows the audience to participate in the original event, to witness how gods work miracles and human protagonists triumph. The majority of worshippers who undertook (and undertake) such a vow were women. They continued a magical and religious tradition, based on oral transmission that survived mostly outside of the influence of the Brahman orthodoxy.

Similar stories were in the domain of popular entertainers. Some told the Manasā tales, some sang and performed them. Groups of professional singers and actors (some included women) were hired for the feast days of the goddess. We also encounter professional storytellers and puppet players, making the great events come alive on public holidays, near temples, markets and fairs.

Finally, more than five hundred years ago, poets began to turn the Manasā tales into books. These, handwritten and expensive, were just the beginning. When the British introduced printing presses, the *Manasā Epic,* in many versions, became available to a larger audience.

A few years ago, while I wrote a book on Lamaštu and Mesopotamian Magick, I needed a bit of entertainment. Two of my favourite studies, books on the *Manasā Epic* by Pradyot Kumar Maity and W. L. Smith, inspired me. Earlier, I had written a lengthy essay on Chinese Serpent Cults (privately published by Asenath Mason) and wanted to extend the material into a book on Asian snake cults plus fun, rituals and exciting trance adventures. I had plenty of stuff on China, Mesopotamia and the Fertile Crescent. In my naivety, I assumed that a chapter on the Indian Nāga cult and a summary of the Manasā tale would be a fine addition. But what I knew of the *Manasā Epics* was far from satisfactory. Maity and Smith provided dry-as-dust summaries of the rudimentary structures of the tale. Maity, starting with the assumption that the *Epic* by Bipradās would be the earliest, provided a short outline (2001:77-107) and devoted the next pages (107-128) to what he considered variations by other poets. Smith tackled the *Epic* by dividing it into episodes. Each of them offers a minimal synopsis with a few notes. It was enough to get a basic idea, but as most events were summed up in just one or two sentences, they lacked the flesh and bone that makes a truly epic story come to life.

For each section, I selected the ideas and variations that seemed spiritually relevant. The result was a sparse and scholarly summary and not much fun. At long last (as I'm naive and stupid) I realised that I neglected the essence of the epic: stories should inspire. A summary, no matter how good, is never good enough. Like many poets and performers, I expanded the material by adding material from classical Indian literature (*Mahābhārata*, *Śrīmad Devī Bhāgavatam Purāṇa, Brahmā Vaivarta Purāṇa, Devī Mahātmya)*, the *Purāṇas*, Bengal ballads, ethnographic studies and the like. For the fun of it, I collected a few hundred Bengal metaphors, proverbs and sayings, and used them where appropriate. These, of course, did not suffice. Like it or not, I had to compose my own version of the epic. Luckily, I had plenty of help. Manasā supplied fascinating extras and Neta made me laugh. They got into my meditations, my trances and my dreams. They made me get up at three in the morning to jot down a few funny ideas and made me stagger back to bed at five. Getting up at six, I felt more dead than alive, while I did my early morning meditation and zombied off to work. Truth to tell, that's what you get with goddesses who do birth, life, death, transcendence and rebirth.

It wasn't easy at all. Being used to writing serious, practical, no-funny-business handbooks, I began to struggle with fiction, and worked my way through a dozen guidebooks.

But writing fiction wasn't enough. After all, I was re-inventing a tale that would be unfamiliar to people living far from Bengal. The East Indian authors had an easy life. They addressed a well-informed audience of deeply religious people, who needed no explanations regarding exotic cults and early mythology. They sang, accompanied by gorgeous music, they acted and joked and improvised. In short, their performance was playful and spontaneous.

By contrast, I sat in front of a screen (the dullest place in the universe), naively assuming that a flood of adjectives and adverbs would improve the situation. I explained one hell of a lot, until I realised that things should explain themselves. Eventually plenty of waste material got kicked out. The first version was around eighty pages in length and a moribund mutant hovering between dry scholarship and flowery extras. It got rewritten again and again. Luckily, I had plenty of material to enliven it. Smith provided several useful quotations. So did Sabita Baishya Baruah, whose PhD thesis deals with the linguistic aspects of the Bengal and Assamese variations. Fascinating material on East Indian folk religion can be found in Maity's other books and in June McDaniel's admirable studies. I discovered fragments of the *Epic* in several versions, and am especially indebted to the last part of the tale, as related by Ketakādās, a passionate worshipper of the serpent goddess. A translation of Bipradās' version is available in French. I had French in school and mostly left it there. In 2015, when my version was approaching 350 pages, I came upon Kaiser Haq's admirable treatment. His translation blends material from five versions of the *Epic*. I was delighted that he chose a range of variations which I neglect, mainly, as they are too close to the traditional body of upper-class Hindu myths. If you want a different version of the Manasā tale, please read his composition.

By then, I had given up any pretensions of scholarship. I remained true to the basic themes and episodes, to the characters and what happened to them. You will encounter traditional metaphors and elements from Indian lore and ritual, but I described the incidents as they appeared to me. This Epic is a new interpretation, and it is only traditional in that it describes vivid experience. The major deities emerged in my daily meditations and rituals and eventually I heard them talking, laughing and arguing in my head. They invaded my dreams, meditations and danced through daily life. Finally, I had to abridge. The book you hold in your hands (producing strong arm and shoulder muscles) was streamlined as I deleted roughly a hundred fifty pages.

Let me apologise to all well-educated people who treasure complicated prose and sophisticated references: I simplified and simplified and simplified.

It wasn't enough.

Richard Bandler posed the wonderful question: Are you serious? Are you serious enough about what you are doing to laugh about it?

I am damned serious. So are my personal deities. That's why we keep joking.

This not a bone-dry study. The *Manasā Epic* is alive, like you and me and the goddesses who made it happen; and they love bottomless swamps, dripping wet rainforests, inaccessible mountains, spiky plants, rotting flesh, bleached bones and any amount of fireworks.

Some may find my treatment disrespectful. Where is the serious, academic transmission of the sacred tradition? It's a great question. Someone should answer it someday. I'd love to see scholars translating every known version of the *Manasā Epic* into European languages. However, you and I will have to wait until our next incarnation to see it happen.

Hereabouts, interest in traditional Bengali literature is sadly limited. Manasās cult is widely popular, ranging over Bihar, Orissa, West Bengal (Pashimbanga), Tripura, Meghalaya, Jharkhand, Orissa and Bangladesh. For Europeans and Americans, it sounds like a couple of no-account spots on the other side of the world. Need I mention that these are the most densely populated parts of Planet Earth? Every seventh person lives near the Ganges! Manasā's home territory ranges from east to west for more than a thousand kilometres. From north to south it extends from the Himalayas (province Darjeeling) to the tangled mangrove forests at the Sundarbans, where the countless tributaries of the Ganges and Brahmaputra meet the open sea. Calcutta is part of it, the former capital of the British Raj, famous for trade, wealth, classical European architecture, endless slums, overpopulation, violence, plague and poverty.

Culturally, this part of South East Asia is eminently important. Sadly, first impressions mislead. India is famous for the palaces, temples and fortifications of its dry landscapes. In East India, much of the countryside is flat and barely above sea level. Cyclones and floods are common, the climate is moist and hot and the monsoon is devastating.

The palaces of Rājasthān, the fortifications of the Thar Desert, the temples of Khajuraho and the Taj Mahal would go to rot under East Indian conditions. As a foreigner, you look at East India and wonder where the great cultural achievements are. You have to take a closer look to realise how short-lived, changeable and intense life can be.

Just like the poets and singers of East India, I believe that a story can only stay alive when it is reinterpreted. The similarity to classical Indian music is obvious. A musician playing a rāga (a multipurpose word meaning: *musical theme, colour, delight, passion, love, joy,* and *nasalisation*) does more than perform a song or a symphony. The Indian approach is **strict and flexible**. Each rāga is based on specific, narrowly defined scales, rhythms and short melodic elements. It is associated with distinct moods, emotions, and possibly with seasons, times of day, occasions, deities or famous persons. Some rāgas invoke gods; others are played to bless a marriage, to make the monsoon rains come or to commemorate important historical figures like the Emperor Akbar.

The *Manasā Epics* are related to a range of rāgas. In most cases, the associations are lost. Few poets left notes on the performance of their works. Unlike them, Bipradās was precise and specified more than thirty rāgas to accompany his poem. To liven up each rāga, musicians introduce a range of melodic structures. They are short and playful. Some of them are traditional; others are gifts by the guru or freely invented. These elements provide a basic plan, a foundation for free, mind-blowing improvisation. Classical Indian music is not suitable for orchestras. The performance is limited to a few musicians, who enjoy playing, and improvising. They usually know each other and take their time to explore and transform a given piece of music. The audience is in for a surprise. Nobody knows whether a given rāga will last for ten minutes or for three hours. Compared to classical rāgas, Western music is dull and predictable. A rāga, just like the dance of the gods, is ever old and ever young. It isn't played but spontaneously re-created. This isn't music from sheets or out of the can. Performers and audience allow themselves to be carried away. It turns music into a unique spiritual experience. It's no surprise that so many leading tantric innovators were passionate musicians. When Abhinavagupta lectured, so legend claims, he had a vīṇā lute on his lap and played as he went along. Let's quote the instructions to the worship of Śiva, from the *Skanda Purāṇa*, 2, 41, 112: *Even if a person pretends to perform dance, vocal music and instrumental music, the Lord (Śiva) will be pleased with him, since the benefit of vocal music and instrumental music is infinite.*

You don't have to be an expert. Even if you pretend that you make music, you are going in the right direction.

When you make sounds, and listen, and delight in them, you are manipulating the limbic system of your brain. That's where feelings come from. Music is the sound vibration of the All-Self encountering itself. Classical Indian music blends rigid specifications and free improvisation. Similar rules apply to Indian ritual and worship.

As spiritual effort without humour is futile, I added bizarre dialogues and jokes. Spoilsports may disapprove. Churchgoers in retarded Europe are used to a form of worship that makes a clear distinction between the 'sacred' and the 'profane', between 'spirit' and 'matter', between 'soul' and 'body'. René Descartes (1596-1650) introduced this dichotomy in order to further the development of science. In his time, it was a grand idea. Thanks to this division, the church remained in control of the 'sacred' parts of life while the 'secular' realm was, at long last, open for scientific study. It was a major improvement. Nowadays, it has become a serious limitation. Western people discriminate between matter and mind where other, more inspired cultures, recognize continuity. Indian religion does not approve of narrow-minded distinctions. When you participate in a genuine, large Bengali pūjā, you meet people who worship passionately while others chat, laugh, check their mobiles, discuss shopping opportunities, arrange matches and do business. Some men sneak away to have a drink. Children play while the ritualists recite sacred verses or intone mantras. At times, the ritual becomes intense, and the audience is caught up; at others, attention wavers and people enjoy life. The whole event pulses, it surges like waves against the shore, and there is never a moment that is fully 'serious' or 'frivolous'. If you want to meet Manasā and Neta, you need a similar approach to the divine. Their rituals are ecstatic, wild and joyous. They are not separate from daily life but infuse it.

Observe small children. They learn while they play. For them, learning and laughter are a way of life. Indeed, they try to learn everything at once. It makes them accident prone. However, it also accelerates their learning. Adults, by contrast, like to break skills into fragments, practice them separately, and try to put them together later on. It's a much slower process.

As we grow older, we limit ourselves. Adult personalities are controlled and predictable. They are restricted to a special selection of skills, trance states and definitions of identity. In short, we become funny figures. We see more limits than possibilities. The more we assume to know what is real and important, the funnier we get. The gods enjoy our antics. They play with us, and they play us as we play them. If you retain the ability to laugh, about yourself, your world, and your beliefs and, of course, your deities, the divine will manifest everywhere. In this mindset, profanity and blasphemy are impossible. Honestly, how could a human being insult a deity? And why should a god or goddess feel insulted, instead of, sadly misunderstood? Serious people get it wrong. Religion should be fun. You encounter this happy attitude in the *Manasā Epic*, and in such rare gems of spiritual literature as the *Eddas*, the Enki poems of Mesopotamia, the parables of Zhuangzi and Liezi, and the stories of Anansi and Coyote. Whenever a religion promotes trickster figures, humour creeps in.

Let's have some examples. In classic Indian literature, such as the *Upaniṣads*, the *Purāṇas, the Niyamas, Agamas* and *Tantras*, Śiva tends to appear as a respectable high god who represents (at least to his worshippers) the ultimate principle, the nameless, formless, incomprehensible All-Self Brahman (*Extension*). This Śiva is Pure Consciousness and Absolute Reality. It has no shape, no name, no gender, no attributes, no past or future. It is and it is not. Śiva is imminent, transcendent, transcendent/immanent and totally incomprehensible; it is the formless awareness, the sense of 'I-am' (*Āhaṁ*) indwelling every being and thing. That's the sophisticated point of view, founded on years of deep thought and daily meditations. In short, it is miles away from the statue in the temple, the figure in the puppet play and from the half-naked ascetic, the wild dancer at the edge of reality, of folk worship.

Our East Indian poets preferred a simple, crazy figure. In the *Manasā Epic,* in the *Caṇḍī Maṅgal* and similar folk epics, we meet a Śiva who, just like all important men, is supposed to own a palace, a garden, large fields and many cows. He is married, and has a family. Sadly, he tends to forget them. Instead of working he walks around nude, smears ashes on his body, hangs around at street crossings, and watches pretty girls walk by. He relaxes on cemeteries, drinks terrifying amounts of alcohol and smokes dope all day; he goes to the brothel to worship the prostitutes and makes friends with ascetics, artists, beggars and lunatics. His entire life revolves around sex, drugs and meditation. At night, when he is asleep, his good-for-nothing sons steal his drugs.

In the traditional Umā songs (McDermott 2001 and 2011) things are even more extreme. Here Śiva is a nude old man who owns next to nothing. Property is meaningless to him. His wife complains, so he promises to work, but goes begging. When he gains money, he wastes it on drugs. In plain fact, he is crazy. But he is also devoted to his wife. Quite literary, she is his one and all. This old man Śiva has a terrifying side. In some districts of Bengal, his annual pūjā requires the devotees to unearth corpses on the cemetery. During the festivities, they smear themselves with the ashes of the burning ground and dance with half-rotten heads, limbs and infant corpses (Basu, 2005:142-153). While he goes on endless walks across India, his wife Umā/Pārvatī/Durgā lives in a dismal hut. She wears rags, her hair is filthy and full of snakes, she has lost her sense of shame, and she doesn't care. For all her poverty, she loves her husband and spends her days with ascetic exercises and meditation. Or she gets drunk with him. When she visits her parents, they have a nervous breakdown.

In the *Manasā Maṅgals*, Śiva's wife Umā/Pārvatī/Durgā is stunningly beautiful, but she is also spiteful, jealous and given to fits of temper. We should forgive her, as she had a terrible childhood. Unlike him, she dresses well. She shape-changes to tempt him, just as he assumes different personalities to seduce her. Whenever possible, they ignore their divine duties and spend centuries in bed.

Then there's Brahmā, the small god of creation. Call him a grandfather, as he was there fairly soon after the cosmos began, and did a lot to improve it. In a good mood, he invents anything. In folk tradition, he tends to spurt whenever he gets excited. None of the gods takes him seriously. What about Viṣṇu, the Maintainer of the Cosmos? For his worshippers, he is Brahman, the All-Self, an abstract, all-pervading sentience; or the grandiose, impeccable epitome of absolute virtue and joy, the good god, who receives offerings and cares for those who love him. Viṣṇu's cult thrives on Bhakti, on passionate devotion and emotional dedication. For the poets of the *Manasā Epics*, he is a slightly neurotic CEO with a tendency to regulate things nobody cares about.

Manasā, as a hot-blooded serpent goddess, is naive, innocent and lethal. And she is a fact of life. Everyone in East India, especially poor people out in the fields, knew that serpents lurk anywhere. You walk through muddy rice flats, with bare feet, and use your hands to harvest? It can be lethal. In some versions of the *Epic,* Manasā devastates entire armies, cities and provinces. It does not upset her; in fact, she doesn't comprehend why people worry about death. That's because death is a prelude to life, and birth is the beginning of death. On request, she brings the corpses back to life.

Her sister Neta is a high goddess, a funny, clever counsellor, but as a washerwoman, she performs tasks which are absolutely polluting, and generally left to the lowest classes.

Holy men, when they appear, are either difficult or ridiculous and the major sorcerer of the *Epic*, the almost-divine Dhanvantari, is caught up in his own ego-cult.

The 'Merchant King', Cāndo, is a power craving, narrow-minded fanatic and his wife Sonakā has problems facing life. The only truly virtuous person of the *Epic*, Behulā, has to learn and endure a lot. She undergoes the most terrifying ordeals, faces dangers and horrors and insanity. No matter how awful it got: she retained her sense for the divine, for justice, for the wonders of East India. Let's hear the famous poet Jibananda Das:

> Behulā once on a raft upon the river-
> when the moon's sliver died away behind some sandy shoal-
> had seen many an aśvattha and a banyan (fig) beside the golden paddy,
> had heard the śyamā (black) bird's soft song, once had gone to Amara and when
> she danced like a clip-winged wagtail bird at Indra's court, Bengal's
> rivers, fields, bhāṭ blossoms wept like ankle bells upon her feet (Radice, 2010:317).

It turned her into an all-time heroine of East Indian literature.

Many poets admired her independence, and her stubborn dedication. Others, obsessed by upper-class brahmanical fundamentalism, gave her a shameful reputation or forced her to undergo a series of divine ordeals to prove her virtue.

No, I did not invent this. For good or bad, this is life. The poets of Bengal and Assam were much closer to reality than the literati who composed 'high' literature. Those who want to know about the authors and sources that inspired each chapter will find an account in the appendix.

Primal Blessing

Salutations to Gaṇeśa, the Elephant-Headed Lord, brother of Manasā, who, riding on a mouse, blesses all beginnings, destroys obstacles and grants the typing fingers swiftness.

Blessings to Sarasvatī, river goddess, weaver of spells, mistress of songs, melodies and arts, queen of speech and creatrix of the Universe.

Praise to Manasā, Thinking One, serpent lady, Mahādevī, all-consciousness, pure awareness. Without you: no book, no mind, no miracle of experience.

Devotion to Neta, watchful one, washerwoman at the Dark Waters. Grant purification, liberation, laughter and a bit of space on the washing line so we can dry in peace.

Classical Invocation

This invocation is based loosely on the *Manasāvijaya* (*Triumph of Manasā*) by Vipradās/ Bipradās.

It was recorded or composed around 1495-1496. My comments appear in brackets.

> Victory, Victory for Viṣahari (Full of Poison, or: Destroyer of Poison, or: Custodian of Poison.)
> whose entire body is graced by serpents,
> and (victory) for the servant of the goddess,
> whose appearance is beautified
> by the serpents who dwell in her hair as jewellery,
> unmoving (in trance, in Absolute Reality. A title of Śiva),
> with Nāgas (snake deities) who rest in her full hair as ornaments.
> Nāga Udyakāla transformed into the five blossoms in her chignon,
> Nāga Citra beautified her locks,
> like shining stars in a black sky,
> Nāga Sinduriyā (vermillion) turned into the cinnabar line (which adorns the hairline of married women),
> like the red sun of the Eastern Mountain,
> the ash-coloured viper turned into the plaits of the goddess,
> the Kuilā serpent into the excitement of her face,
> and the Nāgas with many names became the jewels at her hairline.
> As a lightning flash cuts through dark clouds,
> the Nāga Kālaciti graces the eyebrows of the goddess,
> like the elephant within Kālindi, within the Mountain of Gold,
> the Nāginī Kāli (Dark One. Not necessarily identical with the goddess Kālī),
> turned into the makeup of her eyes,
> like two wagtails on blue lotus blossoms.
> The Nāga Kankaciti gleamed from the nose of the goddess,
> the Nāga Kuṇḍaliyā became the eyelet of her earrings,
> the cinnabar-coloured Nāga beautified her lips,
> the white Nāga was the row of her teeth.
> Slithering reptiles adorned her skin,
> just like the mighty snakes on her body.
> The Nāga Śvetkarṇa was the pandanus (-tree) necklace around her throat,
> flowing like river Bhāgirathī (goddess Gaṅgā, the Ganges) around the Yellow Mountain,
> her throat shone with the serpent Maṇināga (Nāga of the Magic Jewel),
> gleaming gold like the rays of the rising sun.
> As a garland, the Nāga Haliyā graced the breasts of the goddess,
> and appeared like flickering lightning on Mount Sumeru (seat of Viṣnu, centre of the universe).
> The royal serpent became the bracelets on her wrists,
> ornamented like the golden stem of the lotus flower.
> The snake Saṅkaniyā transformed into her shell-bracelets,
> and Aḍiyāla, the curvaceous, was the finery of her upper arms.
> The viper Bighatiyā (finger ring) transformed into her finger ring,

the Nāga Gandha-Citi was her musk perfume and colourful makeup.
Her skin was adorned with sandalwood:
it was the Nāga Malayaja,
whose sweet scent extended through the ten directions.
The viper Maṅgaliyā was the bodice of the goddess,
the Nāga Dhaniyāhuli the rim of her silken costume,
the Nāga Ulobodā settled on her feet,
and Beta-Āchāḍa (girdle ornament) encircled her waist.
Nāga Lāuḍugi transformed into the dress of the goddess,
her anklets were made of Nāgas,
Kālaciti became her toe-rings,
and all the other Nāgas the jewels of her feet.
The goddess appeared terrifying in her serpent jewellery,
and the Nāginī Kāli held a royal sceptre above her head.
To both sides (of the goddess), the Nāga-troops lined up,
Vāsuki (her brother) recited scripture from the Śastras and Purāṇas,
Ananta (Eternal) and Takṣaka (a flying serpent) danced,
Saṅka and Mahāsaṅka cheered passionately:
"(Goddess) come to earth, and grant your servant,
the twice-born Vipradāsa (Bipradās),
the grace of your neighbourly hands

Picture 2: Manasā rising.

2. In the Evening

Our world is full of light and shadow. Illumination extends as far as our senses reach, and we can touch it, see it, hear it, and imbue it with meaning, in this instant, this terrifying, gorgeous moment of reality, when we realise that this is now and it will never be the same again. Like a miniature cosmos, an island in the current, brightened by hope and dreams and happiness, the courtyard glows, surrounded by an eternity of darkness, ablaze with stars.

Brazen lamps, one next to the other, scores of them, gleam in a golden haze. Their soft radiance attracts, enchants and comforts. The thick smell of burning butterfat drifts by. Several generations of women sit in the clean, well-swept yard. The ground is purified with water and cow manure, the sky is open and clear, under the stunning glory of the Milky Way. The air feels nice and cool and we are lucky, it isn't raining for a change. The women wear their best clothes, red, pink, emerald green and honey yellow. Embroidery sparkles in the lamplight. Their arms are laden with bracelets, of gold, silver, iron and glass. They laugh; they chime and tinkle as they move. Children run and play; they buzz with excitement, for tonight they are up and about. At the edge of the crowd, a few men sit; their pipes bubble and they listen. The others are out in the night, and there is merriment everywhere.

The day had been long, and exhausting. The women had risen early, before sunrise; they had done their work and never complained of hunger, though they abstained from food. Before noon, they had visited the makeshift shrine on the marketplace. The image of the goddess resided in a bamboo contraption, clad in bright cloth, agleam with shiny ornaments. A Brahmin with a bushy beard and a paunchy belly had conducted the pūjā; the man was drenched in sweat, but his voice rang out, the air was full of incense, and there were heaps of fruit and vegetables, plenty of bananas and dishes full of milk. Worshippers and visitors got down and knelt before the figure. They prayed; they gave their thanks, they gazed into the eyes of the goddess until time stopped and silence reigned. Some wept, some laughed, and some bowed, placed a few blossoms at her feet, sighed with relief and went their way. Around the figure and her shrine, human life swirled and circled, people met, talked and laughed, they discussed business and marriages and gossiped. Children chased each other through the crowd. Young men, clustered in groups, talked loud and tough. They cast shy glances at the girls, who remained, far away and adorable, and delighted in the furtive attention of their worshippers. The goddess loved each moment and showed her painted smile.

In the late afternoon, the women made their offerings, returned home and delighted in a meal. Now, well fed and comfortable, they sit back and relax. The best part of the day is yet to come. "The goddess is satisfied," they say, "it will be a good year".

The night is dedicated to their guest. She has come from far away. It could be from her home on Sij Mountain, far above the clouds, or from the shore of the Dark Waters, where lotus blossoms sway, or from the depths of the sea, where unknown monsters lurk. You never know with gods. They are in your heart and home, and can be anywhere. Their guest is young. She has long, coiling hair, sits on a lotus flower, and holds writhing cobras in her hands. For the occasion, she has put on a brightly coloured sari. She grins happily, for tonight the villagers show their devotion. The flickering lights and the bright colours fascinate her. There is joy and laughter, the fragrance of blossoms and the soothing smell of burning sandalwood. So many people! Humans get her confused. The goddess does her best. She tries to understand their talk, but there is too much subtext. Even their body language is a mess! Should she relate to personal expression, to studied gestures, or to animal signals? Each of them is a language in itself! Humans! Why don't they show what they feel? She sighs and relaxes into her statue. People are enigmatic. Snakes are so much easier. At least, they don't confuse the message with so many limbs. People point one way with their heads, another with their torsos, and a third way, mostly unconscious, with their feet. In between, their hands flutter or freeze and their pelvis points, or shies away. They squirm or hold themselves erect; they signal strength or gracious fragility. Who can make sense of them? The goddess shows a smile and tries to appear friendly. The worshippers smile back. It's good to approach the goddess as a friend. For whether you like it or not, the serpents writhing in her hair, sliding over her arms and gracing her ankles, are everywhere: in the paddy fields, at the riverside, in the thick, high grasses, in spiky growth at dusty roadsides and in your home. When the rains come, serpents appear out of nowhere. You can't exclude them. You watch your step and take your time; you walk with caution, and you praise their goddess. Now, in the season of the snake, her ritual can last a day, a week, or longer. There will be puppet plays, songs, scripture, boat races and country fairs. For three long months the monsoon rains soak the world; they cover walls with algae, make rivers flood and roads disappear in mud. The villagers delight: the stunning heat of summer is over and the world turns green. Plants, damp with moisture, verdant and vigorous, sigh with relief. It is good to remain at home, with family and friends, and celebrate.

From the street, voices ring: "Jai Devī!" Yes, *Victory to the Goddess*. There are men on the road, on the marketplace, feasting and laughing. Some are drunk. "Jai Devī! Jai Viṣahari!" *Triumph for the Destroyer of Poison*!

Their noise will continue until morning. Clouds of incense swirl through the dark. Far away, drums thunder and temple-gongs chime loud and shrill.

The gods of Bengal are generous and friendly. The serpent goddess grants protection from snakebite, smallpox, cholera and skin diseases. She provides heavy, enduring rainfall, rich fields, fruits in orchards, four harvests annually, safe travel across land and water, many children, a happy marriage and the joy of sheer being which gives meaning to life. She makes flowers blossom in fantastic hues, she fills the air with brightly shining dragonflies and turns the vegetation soft and verdant. The world gleams in a million colours, and many of them are in your mind. To some, she grants scholarship, eloquence, poetic inspiration, innocence and insight. A very few, dear to her heart, acquire magic power, yoga and the art of serpent charming. Her closest friends find joy, laughter and liberation.

Many women and a few men swore brata-oaths. They would perform the worship of the goddess on her special feast days, four years, and the goddess would fulfil their wishes, if they were reasonable. Some would go on pilgrimages; others would feed the poor, care for orphaned kids, aid the sick and helpless and do their service to the community. Others would paint and write and perform the rites of true thanksgiving. And they would tell the brata story of the goddess, again and again, and pass it to their children and the children of their children.

Snake Preview: Our Brata Story

Unlike the *Manasā Epic*, with its highbrow standard of true literature, brata stories are innocent fairy tales. Call them a folk tradition, if you like, a ritual enjoyed by the uncultured and illiterate, the people who know reality, 'cause it gets them out of bed before sunrise and makes them work long after dark. Brata stories are plain and simple and, like you and me, wonderfully naive. Naiveté is an art form. Children do it naturally, and explore a world of joy and miracles. They see possibilities where older people expect disappointment. Truly, the mind, loaded with life experience, ages much faster than the body does. Naiveté allows you to remember what your life is all about, and to delight in the glory of this moment. People tell brata stories because they are fun, and holy, and traditional. But these tales are more than simple entertainment. Simple or complicated, they work their magick. Year after year they imbue the rituals and offerings with enchantment. Without the brata story, the ritual is meaningless. For when you tell and listen, you participate...

Picture 3: Gardens of Darksome Delight.

3. A Fairy Tale: Manasā's Brata Story

In a small, dusty village, of which there are thousands in East India, close to the great stream of coming and going, lived a trader. The man, paunchy, bearded, and self-important, was wealthy by village standards; he owned a house with several rooms, a terrace, and a derelict brick wall that circled his property. He had a small well, a shed full of cows, a pond for daily baths, a garden and a scattering of palm trees, banyans, mangos, and jackfruit, providing shade and comfort when the sun came down like fire. True, his property was small. But for a village merchant, in the middle of nowhere, he had done well, and could afford to look down on the lower classes who didn't own a thing, and never would. That's because of Karman: the rich are rich and the poor are poor, 'cause they deserve it. Of course our man was married; and just like her husband, his wife had gained weight, and delighted in bossing everyone around. In fact, she did her best and he did as he was told. The gods smiled on them: the man had fathered seven sons, and each was the very image of his father: strong, proud and hardworking. They walked tall and self-important, sported oiled, twisted moustaches; were well clad and overweight. They smiled with satisfaction; their women were young and healthy, they had wide hips, large breasts and good teeth and they looked neither too ugly nor too good. When men discussed business, their spouses bowed and left the room. By village standards, they were rich. They owned jewellery, much of it gold, enjoyed lavish meals and were rarely beaten. Of course they had to work. It wasn't much. The merchant employed servants, who improved their bad Karman by sweeping dust, washing clothes, and cleaning the latrine. Life was easy and each meal dripped with sugar, butterfat and spices. What more could a young woman expect?

Meet the youngest. In Manasā's Brata story, she has no name. But people deserve names. We all do, and we can change them as we like. Let's call her Vidyā. Vidyā was different. Hers was a love marriage. It was against tradition and almost disgusting. Love, as the elders repeated in their squeaking, nasal voices, was delusive. "A marriage", they said, "is not an instant thing. It has to grow and ripen. It must be based on duty. A husband is wise to be suspicious of his wife, and to beat her once in a while, until she proves her value and gives him many sons. A wife is sure to love her husband eventually, when he fulfils his duties to his family, the gods and ancestors."

Thus spoke the elders, with their shrivelled faces and their bitter, restless eyes.

To no avail. The youngest son was lost. God Kāma had whisked his mind and pierced him with the arrows of desire. His brothers cursed, his parents complained, and all the neighbours laughed. The girl was unacceptable. The merchant believed in wealth and business opportunities. His wife understood social class. They said 'no' and kept repeating it. It didn't work. He was the youngest son, the chubby little nestling, the boy who would never grow up. Youngest sons are stuffed with sweets and dainties until they are ready to burst. They are forgiven everything. Our boy lingered on the road, hoping to catch sight of his adored, and almost fainted in the heat. He tried to compose poetry, tore the paper, broke the pen, chewed his fingernails, spilt ink and, after much despair, burned the lot. He sweated and wept and ranted. Finally he confronted his parents.

"We were united by Prajāpati! How can you defy the creator?"

"You were united by insanity! You ought to work and work some more, and leave it to your parents to find a match for you!"

"There can never be another one!"

"Of course there will be!"

"I won't marry! I will abstain and become a recluse!"

"Don't be stupid! You will take the girl we select, and she'll be a crore times better than this wretched thing!"

"She is my one and all!"

"In a few years, you'll forget her!"

"I'd rather kill myself!"

"Go ahead! You won't like it!"

"I will!"

And so it went on.

Baby boy yowled, cursed, and threatened suicide.

His parents barked and argued in the bedroom, late at night; their voices carried far and made the neighbours laugh. The weeks went by, painfully slow, the villagers smirked, and the merchant hated each of them. Ultimately, after much grumbling, the matchmaker was consulted, and the bride's clan was approached. With due ceremony, the families met, exchanged gifts, and consulted astrologers; they worried, squabbled and agreed.

Marriages are made on earth, but they can go to hell anytime.

Vidyā's parents were poor folk, who lived in a mud hut with a grass-covered bamboo roof. Sure, they were pious. They made a point to pray and worship every day, which can't be said about the groom's family, and they lived on a basically vegetarian diet, as poor people often do, in the hope that suffering and malnutrition will produce a better life next time.

Finally, the Brahmins sang their verses, the newlyweds were tied together, and when the traditional exchange of gifts between the families was to happen, the ceremony became unspeakably painful.

That was months ago and much better forgotten. Look at Vidyā. She is young, much younger than you would expect a bride. She has a pretty face and a nose that points to heaven. Her skin is clean, her posture upright, and her hair is dark and long and wonderful. Having married into a rich household, her costume has improved. She has finger and toe rings, if only cheap material, and a hairpin with a gleaming pearl. Imagine her pretty, by village standards. You would have to employ a poet to praise her properly. It would have been expensive. Her lips were hardly shaped like lotus blossoms, her curls unlike blue lilies, her eyes not like the eyes of antelopes, her breasts not vast enough to feed the universe and her walk by no means as elegant as an elephant cow in heat. She didn't even waddle like a goose.

Vidyā tried to do her best, and hurried. All through the long and weary day she worked as much as three women. Sadly, those who work and achieve much, make mistakes. Day in day out, her mother-in-law reclined on her thickly padded velvet cushions, as if she were the queen of all Hind, and lashed out with her bitter tongue "Rotten child! Can't you listen? Don't you know that your mother-in-law is the goddess?"

She turned to her youngest son. "The proverb says: a man can leave his wife without committing a sin. The man who leaves his mother commits the greatest sin."

She smiled, like a self-satisfied toad, all fat and wobble and success.

"Yes, mother," whispered her youngest, as he sneaked away.

"Come here," she grinned at Vidyā. "You must be punished."

Vidyā rose earlier than the others and went to bed later. In the cowshed, far from the eyes of others, she wept. Her husband, slightly inebriated, waited for her in the bedroom, twisting his grandiose moustache, and wondered why his little cuckoo looked so worn and wretched.

The wives of his brothers had a nicer life. Their families sent presents that made the merchant and his wife chortle with delight. In the years after a marriage, gifts are expected almost every month. Those who can afford it send jewellery, cash, clothes, sashes, golden embroidery, hair-pins, shoes, towels, soap, brushes, combs, ribbons, spices, sandal, perfume, betel and the best food the market has to offer. There is a schedule for these offerings. Rich people make their servants send the gifts; poor people shy away and feel ashamed. Vidyās parents could only afford fruit and vegetables. They were hardly noticed. Her life became darker every day. And at this point, slap bang in the midst of total misery, good fairy tales invite a miracle.

The hot season, to everyone's relief, ended in mid-summer. Heaven turned dark; the black clouds came rolling from the sea like a stampeding herd of elephants. Angry, nervous gales shook the palms, they tore at leaves, broke branches and alarmed the frogs, who croaked by day and night. Thick drops of rain splattered like missiles as the clouds opened their floodgates and turned the air into a waterfall. Few things are as stunning, overwhelming and exhilarating as the East Asian monsoon. Traffic dwindles, roads turn into rivers and families stay at home.

The wives sat under the covering of the veranda and listened to the rain. It drummed on the roof and surged down the walls. The whitewash was coated with algae and in the garden, rivulets foamed and danced. Vidyā squatted at the edge of the group. She was pregnant, and extended her belly, as if to prove her right to exist. So far, hardly a bulge was visible. She folded her hands under her abdomen and glanced to the others. Her stomach grumbled and it made her reckless. "I'm starving. How about you? Shall we have a snack?"

The eldest wife tilted her head. "Our chicken is famished. You dirty little fledgeling. Come on, is your belly swelling? I guess it will be a girl."

The women giggled.

"Honestly," said the eldest, "what can we expect from her?" She faced Vidyā and there was no humour in her smile. "Tell us. What's your favourite? What do your people eat?"

Vidyā stared at the floor. She was angry, but she didn't dare to show it. "I like cold rice. Watered. With sour fish."

"You will abort your baby!" said the eldest, and all broke out in laughter.

Vidyā had been taught about the gods. Her parents believed, and worshipped every day. They did pūjā, invited the gods into their homes, and had little to offer but water, paddy and flowers. As everybody knew, poverty came from the sins of past lives. Poor people are poor because they deserve it. The same goes for foreigners, cripples, idiots and women. That's Karman. Those who suffer much get a better life next time. Her father worshipped Viṣṇu, the Lord of the Universe, whose statue, adorned with flowers, stood in a corner of the hut. Viṣṇu was clad in gorgeous finery. His silken coat was studded with jewels and peacock feathers shone above his turban. Her father said so. The statue was made of plaster, it had four arms and the jewels were painted. He held a club and a conch trumpet, a lotus blossom and made the entire cosmos spin around his index finger.

"He is the great god", said her father, "who maintains the universe. He blesses and protects us."

His wife Lakṣmī sat next to him. Her costume was even brighter, in sky blue, plant green and psychic magenta, and her four arms scattered fertility, wealth, beauty and success.

"They are our guests and we are grateful," said her father, "it's not befitting to ask, demand or plead. They give us so much."

Vidyā nodded and learned. Her father taught her ritual gestures, a few mantras; he made her wave lamps in circles, sprinkle water and sound the cheap brass bell. To buy incense for the gods, the family fed on paddy. The girl offered fruit and flowers, water for washing face and feet, and the finest of every meal. The gods are guests: they receive the best a family can offer. Viṣṇu and Lakṣmī accepted the offerings. They presided, in their sacred niche, over family life and smiled their painted smiles.

In the morning, she vomited. In the evening her back ached. Her hands shook when she retired to bed, and her nails were broken. She tried to pray. Her voice shook, and her words drifted along like empty shells. She thought of Viṣṇu, but he wouldn't come. She prayed to Lakṣmī, but she didn't listen. Someone else did.

She was dark and terrifying.

Vidyā knew her.

Crunch! Down came the cleaver, as she split heads on the battlefield! "Kriṁ!" screeched the goddess of liberation and transcendence, as she disembowelled enemies, "Hūṁ!" she roared, as she cut down war elephants and devoured armies of demons and monsters. Kālī, nude and radiant, roared with lust and savagery. Blood splattered and limbs flew, heads rolled and bones crunched. Vidyā opened her eyes and gasped. Her face was coated in sweat. Nearby, her husband snored. It's shameful, she thought. Good girls shouldn't have such dreams. Today, she would fast and purify herself, and work until exhausted.

In the evening, the air was warm and thick with moisture; grey mist crept from the sodden earth and drifted through the banana grove. The seven wives seized the opportunity.

"We'll get water", they said, and jammed large earthenware pots against their hips. At the edge of the settlement, close to the riverside, a thin line of forest and vegetation flourished. The way was muddy, the trees glistened, and from the leaves, thick drops cascaded to the ground. The women lifted the rims of their saris and stepped over the rich, slippery soil. The river was faster than usual, and on the sparkling surge, foam and bubbles danced. Cautiously, the women looked around. They were alone. Each discarded as much of her clothing as she dared and stepped into the current.

The youngest held her belly. Ah, Vidyā. Most of the afternoon she had dreamed of sour fish. And no matter what the others said, yesterday's rice, if properly watered, is a delicacy.

Setting her feet with caution, Vidyā waded into the stream. The mud felt slippery. The water, hip-high, tore at her and made the fabric of her sari swirl.

Vidyā paused behind a large rock. Here, the water was less turbulent. Slowly, she bent and extended her hand. A sudden move, one grab, and she held a fish. Her prey wriggled and jerked. Vidyā smiled. She struggled up the river bank, where she had left her jug. Cautiously, she dropped the fish in the vessel, and waded back into the stream. Vidyā knew where to look. She approached the next rock, slid into the current and caught another. The other wives screeched with laughter. None of them had known poverty, had learned to dig roots, catch fish and collect manure on the meadow. Soon, Vidyā had trapped eight fishes. They twisted and wriggled in her water pot. That would be enough. Tomorrow, no matter what anyone said, she would have old watered rice and sour fish. And while the other wives carried their water to the kitchen, Vidyā took her pot into her chamber, and sealed it with a heavy lid.

Eight fishes, no matter their size, are pretty much. The pot was full to its capacity. First, the fishes circled. Again and again, they bumped their heads against the lid, which sat where it was and didn't move. When they realised that flight was impossible, they began to elongate. Fins disappeared into flesh; gills closed and when they had extended to the limit, there were eight snakes within the pot.

When Vidyā opened the lid in the early light of dawn, they were ready for her. Eight terrifying serpents, their bodies twisted and coiled, with sharp faces and merciless eyes, each one of them more toxic than the other! She leapt back. The snakes seemed to grin. We are your fate. Be honest. You seek release. Life doesn't offer much? Come closer; we will free you. This could be your lucky day.

Then it got dark. Vidyā had dropped the lid on them.

Much later, the light returned. The serpents raised their heads. Their jailor knelt before them, her head low, her hands folded, and mumbled. Vidyā had prepared an offering and prayed. The snakes faced a plate of small bananas and a bowl of warm milk. All snakes, as everyone in Bengal knows, love small bananas and warm milk. Our snakes were hungry. They shot forward and fell to. The food was perfect and life was happiness. What did it matter that the girl mumbled mantras and spells and knotted her fingers? They graciously allowed the young women to bow, to pray and to remain alive.

Each morning, Vidyā lifted the lid and made her offering. While the serpents fed, their worshipper knelt and praised them. After a few weeks, they were used to the routine. They did not even hiss when the girl called them her brothers. Day in and day out the serpents grew. Life among people wasn't as bad as they had thought. Out there, the monsoon drenched villages and flooded fields, while storks, peacocks and mongooses waded through the morass and hunted snakes. In Vidyā's company, they enjoyed peace, protection and fat meals. Occasionally, to liven up their diet, they slid through the house and ate rats.

But life isn't all milk, bananas and rats. They heard the merchant's wife screaming, and Vidyā weep. It doesn't take much to make a serpent angry. Our sister is unhappy, they thought, and her mother-in-law is a nightmare. It would be fun to kill her.

Vidyā disagreed. Leaning over the pot, her eyes red and her hands shaky, she pleaded forgiveness for her oppressors. The snakes watched her with cold eyes. She couldn't hide her bruises.

Deep in the night, when her husband, asleep, was grunting like a hog, Vidyā dreamed. Maybe, by chance or by fate, one day the merchant would be bitten by a serpent. His wife would be a widow. Some widows were burned with their husbands. Or she would crop her hair and wear white, unadorned clothes. She would be forbidden almost every food. No salt, no spices, no sugar. She would subsist in a hut at the rim of the property, living on leftovers. Eventually, she might walk away. Vidyā could see her tottering, another dusty, impoverished pilgrim, like a million others, struggling from one sacred place to the next, begging for alms. Some widows starve. Others end in a ditch, racked by cholera, and shit themselves to death. Vidyā tensed. Her heart pounded and her breath came in short grasps. Hopefully, it wouldn't happen. Tomorrow she would pray for the health of everyone. She rolled over and the dreams went on.

One night, when Vidyā had stopped weeping, the serpents assumed their cosmic form. They pierced the ceiling, passed through the roof and soared into the heights. They surged through rain showers, howling gales and lightning flashes. When they emerged from the clouds, heaven opened and revealed its glory. A fat, buttery moon soaked the night with liquid gold. Way beyond, the river of stars continued to eternity.

Far above the world of coming and going, Sij Mountain rears its crest into the sky. Its lower flanks are rich with pastures and fields, gurgling streams, with settlements and verdant forests. Further up, the vegetation is tougher. Here, trees only grow into dwarf forms, and herbs clutch the naked rock. Only snow leopards and ibex dare to climb this high. Beyond, the rock disappears under a coat of snow and ice. Above the frosty bleakness, another world begins. Where the snowfields end, fortifications emerge. In their centre, a magick palace rises, with domes, turrets and towers that almost touch the stars. The serpent brothers had never flown that high. Their lungs laboured, the air was bitterly cold and weak. It was beautiful and pure; but it felt threatening.

Sharp edges excite, jagged angles upset, cragged rocks, pointed stones and icicles signal danger, as they resemble teeth and claws. Everything pointed and spiky is trouble. Welcome to the home of Manasā, the serpent goddess, the place where realities connect and consciousness extends in all directions. And watch your mind; it could go twisted. Moonlight shone on the massive wall, gleaming like polished bone.

The eight serpents, duly humbled, landed in the snow and slid towards the gate.

"Piss off! We don't buy anything! And we've got a religion."

The serpents stopped.

Dhāmāi Rat Snake faced them.

He had assumed human shape and wore a pretty pink turban topped by a bundle of peacock feathers.

The eldest of the serpents bowed. It wasn't easy. The guy was evidently low-class trash. His clothes were badly patched and there were spots and stains all over. And look at the headdress! He tries to look like Viṣṇu!

"Honourable guardsman. We greet you with due respect. My name is Āṛona, and these are my brothers Pāṛona, Dhonṛa, Boṛā, Bunye, Ārul, Pārul and Keuṭe. We come on a quest of virtue, as we want to turn a bad Karman into a better one."

He lowered his head, lest his face betray disgust.

Dhāmāi spat. "You are beggars, and your Karman is a mess."

"We are eight royal Nāga princes. In our home world, we are feared and worshipped."

"Worshipped like my ass. It doesn't count up here. What justifies your existence?"

"We serve a greater good! This is the truth!" The eldest serpent glanced at his brothers, those dumb slow worms, who nodded fervently.

"We don't care about truth. Here, on Sij Mountain, we do Absolute Reality. It comes in all sizes. It suits anyone and anything."

"My dear Lord Guardian! Respect our high standing."

"Never."

"King! Be kind and listen to our story."

Dhāmāi bared his yellow teeth. "Go ahead. Make me laugh."

"One fine day" the eldest brother began, "one fine and fated day we embarked to amuse ourselves on earth. We chose a hunting trip. My high born brothers and I were rushing through the forest when a bushfire arose. Lord Agni, great is his fame, devoured the vegetation. He was inordinately hungry. We threw ourselves into a stream and transformed into fishes. The fire roared across the water, while we hid beneath a waterfall. We remained in the deep while the forest turned to ashes."

Dhāmāi grinned. "Fish is stupid. Fish is food."

"Permit me to elaborate, your honour", the eldest brother said, "It's a blessing to be a fish. Long ago, great Viṣṇu assumed the form of a fish to save the world." His brothers nodded. "We wandered up and down the stream; we sported in the waves. Until, one fated day, we were caught."

"Of course you were. Did someone try to eat you?"

"By no means." The eldest serpent raised its head. "We were caught by a virtuous and pious girl, a maiden in the flower of her prime, who took us home in a jug. She recognised the divine in us, dropped to her knees and worshipped us every day."

"I can see it. Gods, you are fat!"

"Our benefactress is suffering. She leads a terrible life. They abuse and beat her, though she is quite an excellent lass. We want to return her generosity. Maybe, we thought, our lady, the goddess, would allow us to do something good for her."

"Something good?" Dhāmāi sniggered. "Oh yes. Come in. Let's see what good she does to you."

Their heads bowed, one after the other, the brothers slid into the palace. The silence was immense. They slithered down the corridor, past pillars, alcoves and closely shut doors, and hardly dared to raise their eyes.

The great entrance hall was almost empty. In its centre rose a pool, framed with marble. Next to it, a woman crouched. She was young and almost naked. Long curls cascaded down her shoulders, and her ankles and wrists were wrapped in serpents. The woman gazed into the pool, as if she were in trance. The serpent brothers stopped and pushed the eldest to the front.

"Hello?" he squeaked, "I greet the divine in you!"

"Shut up." The woman hissed. "I know you lot." She watched the sparkle on the water.

The serpent brothers bowed. "Lady of All Serpents," they hissed, "Queen of the World, Light of Awareness, please forgive our intrusion. We are humble knights on a mission of mercy."

"I don't understand mercy. It's a human thing." The woman whispered. The waters in the pool began to spiral.

"May we speak?"

"I hear you do."

"Lady, we have a benefactress, a human girl called Vidyā. She feeds and worships us."

"Maybe she is crazy. Most people are."

"Of course not!"

"So maybe she is lonely."

"She calls us her brothers. She leads a life of hardship. Her mother-in-law abuses her."

The goddess sighed. "Most of them do."

"We want to do her a favour."

"You want to be favoured?"

"She favours us. She admires us. So we thought..."

"You thought?"

"Your Highness; let me apologise. We thought that we thought."

"Oh that. Thinking. It's overestimated. I do it all the time. It makes me dizzy."

"We could make her happy. It would be a good deed. It would improve our Karman. Wouldn't it be nice to release her from her suffering?"

"Are you thinking what I think you think?"

"Maybe she wants to go to heaven. We could make her wish come true."

The goddess raised her face. Her three eyes burned red.

"Stop it!" she hissed. "You fools! Go away! I'll take care of it."

"But we could..."

"You can't."

"But we would..."

"You won't."

The serpents flinched. They dropped their heads, turned around and hurried away. The goddess watched them. What imbeciles! To send that girl to heaven.

There were screams in the distance, and laughter. Dhāmāi rat-snake was having fun.

Manasā smiled. Death is rarely a solution. Next life, same problems, sometimes worse.

The serpent goddess gazed into the deep. Her eyes followed the serpent brothers, as they hurried through the gate, got stuck in the snow, squeaked, leapt and flew. She smiled. They were too self-important, too serious, too fat. But every character, no matter how weird, was an asset. They would make excellent performers in the play.

She leaned over the pool, and watched the waters swirl. The currents and eddies cleared her mind. An image formed before her. She had been over there before.

Reflected in the vortex, East India gleamed. The green was wonderful. The land was full of beauty. Wide rivers carried fertility across the land. She saw fields, juicy with rice and sugarcane, throbbing with happiness and nourishment, under an azure sky. Pastures with tall grasses fed herds of cattle, each bovine fat and sacred, a blessing from the gods. Ah, the goddess thought, this is the place. A village, like so many others; it pretends to be a town, and it's richer than the hamlets surrounding it. Houses cling together, different classes converge, a settlement appears, and feeds on the wealth of the countryside. She smiled. A miniature universe. The gardens are full of vegetables, shaded by figs and mangos and banana trees. Small rectangular pools dot the scenery. Those people have two baths each day. And they fear spiritual pollution: most Hindus have pools north to south; and Muslims east to west. Tiny cottages sparkle like gems; there are shrines and a few muddy roads. The monsoon is almost over; soon, it would be time to travel.

Manasā rose. It was time for a miracle. She clapped her hands and a wardrobe appeared.

A blaze of colours shone into her face. The serpent goddess reeled backwards, shook her head and bared her teeth.

"Neta!" she yelled, "could you come for a moment? I have no idea what I can wear!"

"A dress up?" the voice was young and cheerful. The girl who entered the room was barely past puberty. She had a terrifying grin on her face. Of course she had been listening.

"Clothes? For you? This will be a nightmare!" She laughed. "Let's try to make it simple. Who is your target?"

Manasā scowled. "I want to boss a merchant's wife. She is plainly horrible." She turned to Neta. "Say what you think, please, and be honest. Will this suit me?"

The serpent goddess lifted a piece of silk so pink it could make your vision blur. Her eyebrows rose hopefully. "With a little gold and a few bells?"

Neta frowned. "No," she said, "It's tiny. It wouldn't cover anything. When you visit respectable people, seem impressive. This means layers."

Manasā sighed and dropped the piece. "I hate it."

Neta held out a sari. It was an endless piece of cloth.

"You could conceal a continent in it," Manasā complained. "Why do these monkeys wrap themselves?"

Neta laid her head to the side and tried a smile. This was going to take a while.

Manasā sighed. "Why can't everybody walk nude?"

By daybreak, Manasā and Neta were high above the village. They stood in an invisible flying chariot. It was pulled by six invisible swans, which flapped their wings and struggled to keep the vehicle in place. Manasā was wrapped to her neck. Four tons of cloth, she thought, I'm dying. Neta had only allowed her a little bit of gold. She had to leave her favourite serpents at home.

I feel like a respectable housewife, Manasā thought, suffocated and boring. Well, the day is young. Maybe I'll kill someone.

"No, you won't," said Neta and grinned.

Manasā hissed at her.

In the village, doors opened and women emerged; they were tired, but ready to face the chores of the day. The air was wonderfully fresh. There was no need to hurry, as the morning was much too young to make an effort. They greeted each other and talked. A reddish hue unfolded like a blossom in the eastern sky. It raised the insects from their slumber. They sang, droned, buzzed and made the village hum. Dogs lifted their heads and barked. Cows in their stables got restless and began to call. Red turned to turmeric, and then the sun appeared, in a haze of honey and promise.

Manasā shook her head in disbelief. "Why did they get up so early? And what are they waiting for?"

"No idea," said Neta, "I guess they are totally lost. That's what being human is all about."

"Over there," Manasā pointed, "that's the house of the merchant. He's got walls and a roof and rooms, and his very own latrine."

Neta grinned. "He must be a happy, happy man."

"See, there she comes. That's our girl." Manasā clapped her hands.

In the fresh light of dawn, a young woman emerged. Her belly bulged, but her posture was upright.

"Look, she is proud. She doesn't give in." Manasā smiled. "She could be a fighter. Maybe we could inspire her."

"She can't stay here," Neta said, "see the bruise near her eye. That was a fist. And look at her forearms. Dark spots all over. She tried to shield her face."

"She's up early," said Manasā. "Someone should admire her."

Neta shrugged. "Not me. I guess she gets milk for her serpent brothers."

"Lazy creeps," said Manasā. "They can wait and hunger. I can't."

The serpent goddess adjusted her sari.

"I'll go down and fix everything. Tell me, how should I treat her?"

"Don't be too nice." Neta raised her eyebrows. "This girl isn't used to nice."

An instant later, Vidyā heard a sound, spun around and faced a stranger. Outsiders rarely made it to the village. The main road was far away. The stranger stood like a pillar, like a queen from foreign lands. Her clothes, of finest cotton and embroidery, showed wealth and taste, her hair was tied back in a bun, on her arms jingled golden bracelets, and her face was fair and slim. The fine lines around her eyes and mouth, Vidyā saw, showed that she had endured much. She wondered why her left eye was shut.

Cautiously, she glanced down. The stranger had slim feet; they were encased in expensive sandals and pointed forward.

"I'm not a ghost" the lady said, "and I have a shadow. You can look me in the eyes. Come on! Face me! Smile! What's your name?"

"They call me Vidyā."

The stranger beamed. "A lucky name. I'm glad to see you. But we lack time. Village people make me nervous. So let's come to the point. Stop gawking! And believe in yourself!"

"Did I do anything wrong?"

"Not yet. But you will."

Vidyā dropped her bucket.

The stranger smiled. "Relax. This is magic. I'm your aunt, and now you remember me." She snapped her fingers.

"My aunt?" Vidyā said, and her eyes widened. "My aunt!" she laughed and fell into her arms.

Manasā grinned. She grabbed Vidyā by her shoulders and held her back. "Let me have a look at you."

She shook her head. "Last time we met, you were tiny. Now you are a grown woman. You are pregnant. And you are up too early."

"There's so much work."

Manasā tilted her head. "Don't apologise. There always is. Work is a drug. People get hooked. They drive themselves like slaves. They abuse others. And they complain. But my clothes itch. Let's get this over with." She pointed at the door. "Take me to your mother-in-law."

"She won't receive visitors at this time."

"She'll receive me," said Manasā, "tell her that I bear presents from our family."

Mother-in-law was surprised. Her face elongated like an owl regurgitating a package of fur and bones. The magic word 'presents' changed everything. The aunt, a new and unexpected miracle, was politely asked to enter. Vidyā introduced her and stepped back. Mother-in-law, residing on a sofa like a rotten piece of roadkill, examined the visitor. Indeed, aunty made a good impression. She wore refined costume, not flashy but subtly imposing, used excellent language, knew when and how much to laugh and kept unwrapping gifts. Bracelets, finger rings, golden chains, nose ornaments, and a splendid lacquer casket from far away China. The merchant's wife hardly dared to trust her eyes. Who would have thought that a member of this family could afford so much! Auntie was worth more than the lot of them!

Manasā inspected her just as carefully. She saw a lazy, oily sausage, spoiled by life, who had to be right in every instance and loved to watch others toiling for her. This woman, as everyone could see, was a success. She had married the right man and given him plenty of sons.

"Vidyā has always been my favourite", said Manasā, and made the next present appear. Another bracelet. The merchant's wife laughed and her chins wobbled.

A face like a bowl of yoghurt, thought Manasā, and look at these feisty stubbly fingers.

"Indeed, you are right", said the merchant's wife. "Vidyā is a good girl. She has gained a place in my heart."

The goddess smiled and offered another necklace. This one was studded with pearls and looked like something from the belly of a fish. Neta had packed a lot. Where did she get the stuff from?

Another bracelet followed. It was laden with coral ornaments and looked like a bad case of measles.

"For me? Oh dear!" the woman gave a coy smile. "I don't deserve it!"

The woman forced her chubby hand through the ring.

Manasā felt as if she was stuffing a sacrificial animal. She produced the next package. It jingled. Enough, she thought, it's time to come to the point.

"Dear lady," said the serpent goddess, "my little darling Vidyā is pregnant. Her parents are worried. Allow me to voice a small request. May I take her to her family for the duration of the pregnancy? She would be with her parents, and I will pay the midwife."

The merchant's wife grinned like a swollen cat.

"Pregnant women are difficult. When they give birth, they contaminate everyone. There's blood, there's filth and fluids. Purification rituals are a must, and the Brahmins are a bunch of greedy thieves."

Manasā bowed a little. "I promise that she will be safe. After she has given birth, I will return her to your home."

She waited while the merchant's wife deliberated. The woman stared at her fingers, with all those gleaming rings, at her bracelets, each of them worth a fortune, and at her new gilded sandals. Her pudgy feet had never been so beautiful.

"You have my consent," said the mother-in-law, flashing a marzipan smile, "my husband will hardly notice she is away and her husband can't use her anyway. Nor is she up to proper work. You know what young women are like, these days. They demand so much and are never satisfied. And their hunger is immeasurable. Vidyā is a good girl, but we have spoiled her. She tries to gobble up the household. Do take her along and keep her in health." The woman raised her eyes to the ceiling. "May Viṣṇu the Maintainer give her a son."

It made the goddess smile. Viṣṇu had better stay out of this.

Auntie gave the girl a stern look. "You heard her. Pack your things and hurry up. We leave now. And remember to bring your pot."

"Her pot?" the merchant's wife seemed confused.

"That's what we say in our family."

Vidyā carried a bundle of clothes and the serpent pot, jammed tight against her hip. Her face was tense. Manasā looked worse. Her poison glands had swollen; she swallowed hard and was glad to leave before an accident occurred. The day had turned scorching hot.

The women reached the forest edge and settled in the shade. Sunlight flickered through the foliage and shadows danced. Manasā gazed into the distance. She didn't seem to care for anything.

"What's next?" Vidyā wiped her brow. "What are we waiting for? I can't go on much further. Auntie, have you ordered a palanquin?"

"Something better," said her aunt, "let me show you." She unwrapped a strip of black cloth.

"What's that?" asked the young woman. She pressed both hands against her belly.

Auntie lifted the item. "Let me cover your eyes. The darker it gets, the brighter it will be."

Vidyā protested. "Auntie, you talk nonsense!"

"Sit still. You'll be better soon."

She knotted the blindfold and clapped her hands. "Neta! We need you!"

Vidyā startled. She heard the flapping of large wings and the crunch of carriage wheels.

"Everybody does," a girlish voice said. Someone young and carefree laughed and took hold of her hands. Vidyā was raised, moved and pushed.

"Get up! Here is our chariot. Lift your foot. Higher! That's fine, step on it. Now for the other one. Excellent. Sit down. And feel comfortable."

"How could I?"

"Just do it."

The carriage tilted sideways, then stabilised. "Now for the pot. Hey, you! Stay in there!"

Vidyā grabbed her seat. It felt as if the carriage was alive.

"What are you doing?"

"We are off into your future," Auntie said, "relax and enjoy."

"I'm scared!"

"Stop it," said Manasā, "it's a bright, happy day, the sky is blue, the birds sing, you are going for a holiday and I am Auntie who makes you feel safe."

She snapped her fingers and Vidyā relaxed. The vehicle jolted, and fresh wind hit her face. She almost screamed. The carriage shook, swayed and stabilised. Soon, it got really cold.

The wheels crunched as the vehicle came to a halt. The air was almost frozen and Vidyā shivered. Manasā opened the knot of Vidyā's blindfold. The goddess smiled. "Have a look. You are home now."

Vidyā rubbed her eyes to wipe away the tears. Her breath stopped. They were surrounded by crystal brightness. Before her rose a pale wall with a wide gateway, decorated with serpents, swans, spiders and elephants. Behind the entrance, under a swirl of sparkles, appeared a garden. Beyond the trees and flower beds rose a moonbleak palace, with towering halls and jagged towers, sky high, incomprehensible, and nameless colours cascaded down the walls. Vidyā lowered her gaze; everything was far too big.

"Step down" said Auntie, "the white stuff is snow. You can trust it. One foot after another, that's fine. Keep breathing. You are home. And relax, take your time, and you'll be fine."

Vidyā shook her head. I'm mad, she thought, how can I handle this? She heard a giggle and turned her head. Next to her stood a brightly clad girl, who seemed to be her age. She shows her navel, Vidyā thought, and most of her breasts! The girl flashed the most insolent smile that Vidyā had ever seen. It seemed to extend from one ear to the other, and it was teeth, teeth, teeth, far more than people ought to have.

"Welcome. I'm Neta. I do the weird stuff. And the woman who got you here is the Goddess of Snakes, the Light of the World, the Mistress of the Multiverse and pretends to be your aunt."

Vidyā stared at Auntie, who was much younger now. She struggled to get out of her clothes. One foot caught in the sari and she swayed dangerously. Vidyā heard cloth ripping. Auntie cursed, and trampled her dress into the snow. She was totally nude now. "What a piece of rubbish!" From the palace, serpents came sliding. They wrapped themselves around her legs and arms.

Vidyā sank to her knees. She reached for the feet of her patron, but Manasā stepped aside, caught her hand and pulled her up.

"Get over it. Stand straight. We are here, so let's go in. "

Vidyā raised her eyes.

"Stop looking like a rodent," Auntie said, "And don't you dare to whimper. Get your pot."

"And my clothes?"

"Take them or throw them away." Manasā forced a smile. The girl needed encouragement. "Who needs them?"

After a march through empty corridors, Vidyā received a bedroom. That's what Neta called it. In plain fact, it was huge enough to stable a herd of elephants. Her bed was as large as a house, the ceiling as high as the clouds and her bathroom shimmered like the inside of a shell. Carefully, she placed her serpent pot in a corner. She lifted the lid and the serpent brothers raised their heads. They had been tossed around, and now they showed their teeth and hissed.

"Hi there," Neta said, "you are back again. Let me suggest something." She bared her teeth. "You stay in there and behave." Her eyes sparkled. "I don't want to step on you."

"Where am I?" Vidyā asked.

"That's a strange question," Manasā said, "you are here, of course. Where else?"

"Questions are never strange," Neta said, "it's always here." She raised her hands apologetically, "at least, for her. And for me, no matter where it is. But I agree, some places are more here than others. For you, of course, it might be anywhere."

Vidyā clasped her hands to hide the tremors. "Why am I here?"

"Why. That's useless. Forget about the why. You should ask how." Manasā raised her eyebrows. "Listen: Your question is: How am I here? Or is it: Who am I here?"

"Auntie!"

"Calm down. Keep breathing. This place is made for happiness." Manasā looked dead serious.

"Ignore her, girl. Cheer up!" Neta laughed. "She isn't half as lethal as she seems. And she thinks of serpent happiness. Or plant happiness. You know what I mean. The easy ones. A lotus blossom. Or a Venus flytrap. A strangler vine. A moist bit of moss. Can you do that?"

Vidyā chewed her lower lip.

The serpent goddess patted her shoulder. She wasn't used to patting. "Listen, I understand you are a human ape female. It's not an easy role. But you are welcome. We love you. There's just one task for you."

Vidyā could have wept. It didn't help that Neta sniggered.

The serpent goddess turned to Neta: "How can I deal with her? I'm not used to visitors. She's too damn timid!"

"And angry." Neta smiled. "It'll come out. See how she tries to be nice."

"I'm sure it hurts." Manasā tilted her head and forced a smile. "Look at me, girl! This is your great adventure. It'll change everything! And try to laugh! You are alive, so pay attention. Here is your new home. That's the easy bit. It can be heaven, and it can be hell. You decide."

"Nonsense." Neta laughed, "It's too complex. You confuse our crazy chick." She winked at Vidyā. "You know what? My sister is mad. Completely insane. Her head is full of toxins. That's 'cause she thinks so much. This place is simple. Life is simple. I'll tell you a secret: Everything is you."

"What?"

"Stop it! Don't listen. Neta has no idea. She lacks complexity." Manasā clapped her hands. "Let me explain. I'll make it really easy. There's just one duty. Make a meal for your serpent brothers. The usual: bananas and warm milk. Every morning, punctually."

Vidyā nodded. Her face was pale and she didn't dare to raise her eyes.

Manasā seemed satisfied. "I'm glad we settled this. And you may never look north."

"Warm milk and bananas? And one forbidden direction?" The girl was close to fainting. "Is that all? Is it really all?"

Neta shook her head. "Sweetheart, it's quite enough. We don't want to stress you. Breathe slowly, from the belly. Make your navel move. You'll be much closer to your feelings. We don't want to see you hit the floor."

Manasā smiled. "Vidyā, we like you. You are our guest, our joy, our entertainment. The guest is god, if you are up to it. Relax! Feel happy. Today is fine, the world is great and all is well. No one will hit you. Unless you want it. Neta, do you think she wants to be hit?"

"Not really. But you never know with monkeys."She turned to Vidyā, "This is the happiest day of your life. And you'll be proud of yourself, once we are through with you."

"You keep confusing her!" Manasā shook her head.

Neta sighed. "She's human. She needs confusion."

Vidyā raised her head. Her voice was frail. "I'm not a servant or a slave?" she asked, "You won't beat me? Or lock me up? I don't have to clean anything?"

"Of course not," Auntie said. "We want you to relax and think. If you are up to it. You'll get your meals. They happen. And cleaning isn't needed. No matter where you go, no matter what you do, everything remains pure."

"Who does the housework?" Vidyā asked. Her voice trembled.

Neta laughed. Two of her three bunches bobbed. "No one."

Life in Manasās palace wasn't trouble-free. Each morning when Vidyā woke, she took care of her serpent brothers. Bananas and warm milk, day after day, punctually. It didn't seem much. They liked their fare and got fatter. Vidyā wasn't that easy. Out of sheer ennui she began to explore the palace. She walked through passages that led on and on forever. She hurried up staircases, leaving her breathless and exhausted, almost too scared to gaze out of the windows. She descended stairs that reached into the bowels of the mountain, as far as she dared. She heard screams and laughter, and hurried back in panic. Outside, life was easier.

Manasās palace lay enclosed by snow drifts. But the gardens within the enclosure were always warm and sunny. Some sections seemed carefully groomed. The hedges were cut in ornamental shapes, surrounding spaces of rest and meditation. Vidyā loved the flower beds, the precisely cut hedgerows, the sparkling arrays of blossoms. Bushes were aflame with magenta petals, releasing stunning scents and haunting melodies. Brooks sparkled as they surged through the green, water gurgled as it danced under arched bridges, where she could gaze into the distance, and dream. Jewel encrusted pavilions, small and inviting, made her rest and doze. Thousands of blossoms released their stunning scents and whispered in the gentle breeze. Elsewhere, different rules applied. Here, the serpent goddess allowed nature to have its way. Spikes! Vidyā thought. Thorns, needles, toxic berries! The growth went unhindered, bearing down on paths, embracing benches, suffocating resting spaces. Tendrils, vines, brambling horrors swooped down on her, ketakā trees raised their foliage, each leaf jagged, like a saw, hungry for blood and madness. Between them, in the shade, wet mosses sucked her feet into the depth.

Fungi raised their cheerful caps. "Eat us and blow your mind away!" they giggled, and Vidyā ran.

Rocks revealed eroded ornaments; they sported serpents with broadly gaping mouths, dragons, their wings wide open, eyes mad with rapture, and spiders residing in dewdrop gleaming yantra patters, scorpions studded with black pearls and monsters that defied description. Under dripping ferns she discovered bones, and rotting flesh, throbbing with maggots.

Wherever she walked, she encountered a special emblem: the black serpent. Neta explained that this was Manasā's personal crest of arms. Vidyā shuddered. And Neta smiled, all-knowing, and went her way, leaving the girl alone.

Vidyā stuck to the easy parts of the enclosure, and sought the places where she could relax. Life wasn't bad when she rested on a padded swing, stretched, eased her belly, and watched emerald birds fluttering through the branches. She sighed, touched her belly, closed her eyes and gave in to sleep. This was life, of sorts, she thought, but was it worth living?

Halls, corridors, staircases. Most of life, she realised, is passages. And most of them were bleak. Vidyā found it hard to get used to them. In her village, everything was bright, colourful and noisy. She began to miss sounds. Silence followed her, enclosed her like a mantle, and made her hear her own thoughts. Many of them were terrifying. Meanwhile, Auntie and the incomprehensible Neta went their own ways.

Manasā, as Vidyā knew, was always busy. She had given her a stern glance and told her to make herself at home. Then she slid away, totally nude, except for a few serpents draped across her skin, as if she had all the work in the world to do. Neta, too, was busy. Occasionally Vidyā saw her walk, laden with baskets, across the empty halls. When Vidyā asked, Neta mumbled something about the washing, and disappeared through doors that hadn't been there a moment ago, and faded as soon she was gone. Washing! Vidyā didn't believe it. Why should she wash a thing? Her clothes cleaned themselves. Manasā didn't use any. And Neta never seemed to change her clothes. She wore a bit of red across her bulging breasts and another tiny piece across her hips, with plenty of gold as ornamentation. When she laughed, and she laughed a lot, everything chimed. Vidyā shuddered. It was worse than nude. The villagers would have stoned her to death.

Her moods got worse. Sometimes she talked to herself. She tried to sing, but the tunes went awry and the lines were full of gaps. Moving from hall to hall, she could hear her heart beat and her lungs pump. One day she met Manasā. Vidyā ran and tried to touch the feet of the goddess. But Manasā stepped back, and when Vidyā showered her with questions, the goddess raised an eyebrow, smiled like a razor and disappeared. Vidyā sank to the ground and began to weep. And Neta. Her laughter chimed through wide and empty halls. Vidyā followed the sound, and tried to find her. But the corridors were empty, the halls silent, and Neta's laughter died away.

She would have loved to meet a visitor. Someone kind and human, someone to laugh and chat with, someone who cared.

But in the gardens there were only birds and butterflies, and colourful spiders building truly complicated nets.

When you stand outside the gate, where the snowfields begin, you can see as far as the haṁsa bird can fly. Vidyā almost shut her eyes. The snow was just too bright. Far away, there were mountain peaks, encrusted in snow and ice, just as cold and desolate as the one she was standing on. Snow, she thought, it's lifeless. It kills everything. She tried to glimpse a sign of life. The mountaintops remained empty. She knew that each of them was populated. I wonder how the other gods make it, she thought. They dwell surrounded by ice and desolation. Or are they always busy in the mortal realm, in their temples and shrines, in the coming and going of the human world? Why don't we ever have a visitor?

"I'm doing well" Vidyā repeated to herself, "I eat, I sleep and my baby grows." She chewed her lower lip. How could anyone lead such a lonely life?

But maybe she was wrong. Gods exist everywhere and nowhere. Maybe Manasā was happy, doing her duty in the human world. Plenty of shrines and temples served her. Day in and day out, visitors walked in, rang the bell to announce their coming, knelt at her feet and told her of their plight. She listened to a stream of worries and complaints and smiled.

Religion is a chore. Day in and day out, people ask much and give little; they think the divine is there to accommodate them. And as they bow before the goddess, they humble themselves to make a greater profit. Who has a heart for her? Poor people, cow herders, fishers, peasants, those who walk with naked feet through high grasses, through flooded paddy fields, through thickets and tangled undergrowth. Fishers dread the coming of the storm, and feel blessed when they return home with their catch, and feed their family. What of the travellers, the mendicants and pilgrims, who brave the roadsides and the wilderness? And poor Brahmins, perfectly educated, who cook food at the street side, exposed to snakes like everyone. What gives them the strength to do their task, to fulfil the duties of their class? Maybe Manasā needs an empty home, thought Vidyā. Maybe she only comes here when she is tired of the world.

When Vidyā woke, the morning sun shone into her chamber. She rubbed her eyelids. One day like any other day. Why get up? Why live? Taking her time, she raised herself. "Why me?" she exclaimed. Her voice echoed. It sounded sad and bitter. She ambled to the kitchen, prepared the bananas, warmed the milk and fed her serpent brothers. Returning to the kitchen, Vidyā found her breakfast ready. It always was. She chewed without tasting, and her thoughts were far away. She recalled the hut of her parents. It seemed so vast when she was small. Life had been easier. Is this the meaning of the past, she thought, that you begin to value what you lost? She got up, trembling with anger. Things couldn't go on like this. She stalked out of the room and hurried along the corridor. North. She could feel it in her belly. She would go north, into the dark direction, into the realm of Kālī. North is trouble, north is dangerous, and no traditional Bengal Hindu would dream of sleeping with his head pointing north. Vidyā rushed through empty passages, descended staircases, crossed chambers, ran up stairs and finally, when no other way remained, she reached a small black door. This is it; she thought and pulled it open. Darkness greeted her, and took her breath away. The room was gigantic. Somewhere in a corner stood a tiny, narrow bed. There was a window next to it, shut by a black curtain. In a corner she could see a bookshelf, a small wardrobe, a plain writing table and a rickety chair. Each piece of furniture was black. The table was almost empty. A few sheets of palm leaf paper, an inkstand with a pen, a tiny lamp and a reed flute. Next to the bookshelf leaned a vīṇā lute. The room was a hall, it was far too big, and there was next to nothing in it. Was this Neta's bedroom? Or Manasā's? Slowly, Vidyā approached the window. This is it, she thought, this will decide my fate. The curtain felt heavy and velvety, it smelled of dust and long forgotten memories. Vidyā hesitated. Right now she would have loved to run away. But sometimes, no matter how much you try to be good, you have to misbehave. With a jerk she tore the curtain aside. Vidyā faced north, the cold direction, the dark corner of reality.

Out on the terrace stood the goddess. She was nude, magenta sunlight seemed to suffuse her body and a gentle breeze played with her hair. Manasā stood still, her feet close together, and swayed. In soft, rolling motions her pelvis began to shift. Gently, like a blossom opening to the day, she extended her arms and raised her head. A small step followed, then another. Moving to an inaudible rhythm, the goddess shifted her feet, tilted her hips, and bowed her torso to the sides, drifting, swaying, meandering, as her head moved up and down. Her steps accelerated, her toe rings sparkled and Manasā, aglow with yearning, began to twist, to spin under a mind-wide sky. She smiled and her teeth flashed. Vidyā choked: this world lacked space for two. There was just room for the goddess, dancing with devotion, committing herself to the universe. Her naked limbs shook with a lust that could never be fulfilled. The rhythm accelerated. Vidyā raised her eyes and saw cloud fragments spinning. Cruel, bloody red, contrasted with kingfisher blue, and cirrus, wind-crazy, scattered in all directions. In the garden, the trees took up the rhythm, stems groaned, branches rattled, and foliage hissed like a flood. The gale increased, it came howling from the sky, grasping and clutching, tearing at the dancer. A shower of blossoms cascaded through the air. Vidyā staggered back. The goddess radiated a brightness that stunned her. She lowered her head. The marble under her feet rippled. Vidyā clutched her hair. She saw algae and mosses creep across the polished stone, the vegetation studded with eyes, looking up at her. The plants, they see me all the time! She grabbed the window sill. In the garden, the trees hurled their crowns in a frenzy. On the black lakes, lotus blossoms were tossed around. The reeds danced, bent, hissed, and snarled. The motions of the goddess blurred. Her body was hardly visible, her garden, all spikes and claws, howled like a raging beast. Plants are animals, though Vidyā, animals are people and people are gods. I never knew, and now I have to live with it, or fade away. The walls of the chamber curved and bulged. Out there, straight avenues knotted themselves, pavilions throbbed and black birds were snatched into the cyclone sky.

The goddess stopped. She was silence personified, rest and clarity, all in one, the only stable point in a vortex of chaos. Around her, lighting flashes zigzagged like mad bats, foam-crested waves rose from the pools and sizzled into steam. Then, just like the goddess, everything stopped, and the world held its breath. The rivulets and brooks froze, their fluids crystallising like obsidian. For one brief moment, anything could have happened. When the water melted, it surged backwards, cascaded uphill, and rushed away. The dawn sky turned to hazy gloom, the sun reversed its course, dropped under the horizon, and night embraced the firmament. Stars, the sky was full of stars! The firmament melted, and constellations rotated backwards. Vidyā collapsed. She stared at the ground, at good, solid ground, and saw the pictures come. The marble was full of imagery. Gods, animals and people rushed across the floor. Here, lovers embraced. There, armed men impaled each other on long, wicked swords. Next to them, a peasant led a goat to a tree. It was struck by lightning, the trunk burst and dropped on both. Traders with heavily laden camels forced their way through the desert. Before them danced spirits that were living flame; luring, tempting, hungry, leading them onward into emptiness. Between them rushed a flood of serpents. From a jungle clearing rose a house, a village, a town, a city, gained glory and everlasting fame, where traders met and elegance was celebrated. Tanelorn! It comes and goes, from age to age. A moment later, rivers shifted, the fields went to waste, the trees died, dust storms danced, walls crumbled and the metropolis became a myth. Where kings had walked, monkey troops screeched at each other in the peachy early morning haze. The sun scorched the ground, the soil cracked, the winds blew the fertility way. Where civilisation had reigned, bleak rocks and barren ground remained.

Vidyā wept for the city, for the people, for the animals, and for the vegetation. Plants can't run away. People force them, rape them, and suppress them. But when the people are gone, they return. Inevitably, like a green tide, silent, patient, hungry, slithering like a host of serpents, devouring the past, obliterating the future. Return to soil, the plants call, return to fertile earth. It may take thousands of years, but we'll be back. The soil is your future; the humic acids are your sacrament. And turn your face to heaven, like a blossom emerging from dark water, eat sunlight and drink wind. Look at yourself: your eyes are like aparājitā blossoms; dark like a thunderstorm, your lips open and your breath is full of jasmine. There are lotus blossoms everywhere. They gleam, they shine, and they make me want to die.

Vidyā curled up, pressed her hands against her face and whimpered. A huge crocodile dragged itself past, crushed the shore vegetation and slid into the water. It looked like Neta.

When Vidyā opened her eyes, everything had changed. The floor was calm, moderately horizontal and remained where it belonged. The call of birds and frogs turned into music. She was crouching in the centre of the great entrance hall. The stone framed pool gurgled happily, its water brilliant like a rainbow. The air was full of sparkles, each of them a bell, a star, a point of sheer good luck. Near one wall played an orchestra of beings composed of heavenly essence. Next to them danced a group of beauties, shaking veils of multicoloured emotion. Near a large buffet crowded a cluster of gods with too many heads and hands, whose lustre made her vision blur.

"Hands off!" a bright voice chimed, "This is mine. And take your trunk out of the cream cake!"

A lion strode past, talking with a bull. Next to them ran a mouse, squeaking angrily. Hungry seers with emaciated faces struggled through the melee. They returned, holding bowls full of curry, their hands and beards dripping with oily turmeric. Loud laughter, a jumble of voices, and a crash as a plate full of titbits met the ground. "Was that yours? Have some more!"

A lightning flash tore across the hall.

"Sorry! Just an accident!" said a deep voice, "any heads or arms gone missing?"

But Vidyā didn't listen. She had fainted.

She woke on the floor. Her back and shoulders ached. The hall was in twilight and silence reigned. She raised herself and groaned. She turned her head, winced, got up and stumbled to her bedroom.

It was dawn, as ever, and it could have been dawn forever. Softly, she raised the lid from the pot, and looked at the serpent brothers. They faced her, all teeth and eyes and hunger. I must have been gone for ages, Vidyā thought. They are angry with me! I forgot to feed them!

Vidyā hurried to the kitchen. She set a pot of milk on the stove, worked the bellows, and grabbed the bananas. Tearing off the peels, she arranged them on a platter. By then, the milk was beginning to boil. Gods, thought Vidyā, I'm too late and everything is wrong! My hands shake!

Vidyā filled a bowl with hot milk, set it on a tray, and got up in a hurry.

"The bitch is late", the serpents whispered, "she forgot us!"

Vidyā slammed the tray to the ground. She bowed before her serpent brothers, again and again, and tears welled from her eyes, as she pleaded their forgiveness.

"The slut pretends!" the serpents hissed, "She tried to starve us!"

My goddess, thought Vidyā, how long have I neglected them?

Eight serpents dipped their heads into the milk.

Ouch! Ouch! Ouch!

Vidyā knocked her head against the ground and her face was wet with tears. Everything is wrong, she thought, they got burned and now the world comes crashing down on me!

I wasn't there for them. I was selfish! And I watched the serpent goddess dance!

"Forgive me! Forgive me!" She wept, as if that would change a thing.

Her serpent brothers glared at her.

She is out of reach, they thought. Soon, very soon, we will bite her and see her twitch. She will swell like a pumpkin and burst apart.

Manasā knew her serpents, especially these eight.

"Just look at them! They are proud and hurt and ready to kill!"

"Too damn stupid" said Neta.

"What shall we do with them?" Manasā raised an eyebrow. She had practised before a mirror and thought it would make her seem inquisitive.

Neta knew the expression. She had watched Manasā practising it. "They are primed and ready. There is no way back."

Manasā tilted her head. That's supposed to show concern, thought Neta. It's meant to look genuine. But there is too much deliberation behind it. I wonder how long she'll take to sort her body language out.

Manasā tried to look benevolent. "Neta, dear. I've got a solution. Could you milk their toxins?"

"Are you crazy?"

"That's hardly productive."

"You tempted her! You told her not to look north!"

"Well, maybe I did. A little bit. But let's face facts." Manasā reached for a rat. The rodent was paralyzed with fear. She bit, swallowed, and relocated her jawbones. "How will Vidyā survive? She did fine when she watched me dancing. I liked it. I thought her eyes would fall out. "

"She went absolutely out of her head! And the assembly of the gods didn't help one bit."

"Vidyā is young and strong. I trust her. She'll learn."

"Provided she lives long enough. Just look at the snakes in her pot. They are ready to kill her."

"These snakes? They are fat and dumb. She'll find a way. Just give her time to relax."

"She needs to return, just like her stupid 'brothers'."

"To monkey village?"

"That's where she belongs."

"To the house of misery?"

"She will change it."

"All by herself?"

"What could be better?"

The bushes throbbed with cicadas and the sky burned. Weeks had passed. The monsoon floods were over and the showers were getting rare. The countryside had acquired a fresh emerald coat and the earth was soft and juicy. The village, a tiny microcosm, appeared like an enchanted jewel, set into a frame of lush and happy green.

The settlement was quiet. Midday heat had sent the villagers into the shade. The air near the river seemed to shiver. A young woman emerged from the shade. She carried a pot, pressed against her hip. Around her shoulders, she was draped in cloth. Before her breasts, a bundle stirred and a soft whimper emerged.

"Be silent, darling," said the woman. "We are almost home."

One step after another, she advanced. Vidyā raised her eyes to the clear blue sky. The heat was incredible. There was much to think about and very little time. Only a few days ago, she gave birth to her child.

Manasā had watched. "What's that wriggly thing? I thought there would be an egg!"

"It's a baby." Neta smiled. "It's messy, but that's the way they do it."

"On dry land? They are crazy."

"Relax," Neta turned to Vidyā, "your child is wonderful."

"We have to decide the name," said Manasā, "names are important. They shape the way a person thinks about itself."

Vidyā stared at the goddess in amazement. She was the mother, and she had assumed that naming was her choice. It turned out to be wrong. There is a science of naming. The first letter of a name counts. That's because each phoneme, and there are more than fifty, has its own vibration and significance. So does the position of the planets, the day of the week and the lunar day. Manasā and Neta ignored her. They discussed astrology, numerology, musical scales, mantras, calendar science and categories of reality.

"Saturn matters," said Neta, "he is always causing problems."

"He never did with me," said Manasā, "and he can screw off and leave us alone. This isn't about superstitions."

"These ain't superstitions," Neta declared, "Astrology is based on maths and observations; it is a science, albeit a stupid one."

"Who cares about a stupid science?"

"People do," Neta was getting edgy, "no matter how stupid, what people believe is real. Especially if it's stupid."

"If the planets ain't happy they can come round and complain." Manasā smiled. "I'll kick their asses anytime. Just look at this wretched little thing. It needs help. It's so sweet. Let's give it a name that scares the shit out of everyone."

"No way. How about a name that is loveable?"

"Loveable. I heard about that." Manasā frowned. "It's useless. My name isn't loveable either. And look at me. Everybody likes me."

Neta sighed. Her sister was a nuisance.

Manasā gesticulated. "Look at this poor little ape. Next thing, you'll make it seem cute!"

"Why not?"

"It never works! Cute is for losers."

"Let's settle on a name that doesn't upset everyone."

"Nonsense. Look at Bhairavī. She's an honest, hardworking goddess like you and me. Her name means the *Fear-Inspiring-One*. People love and worship her. She gets blossoms and blood and everything."

"They are scared out of their heads!"

"So what? It's good for them. People need drama. They love it."

Vidyā listened. She, as the mother, wasn't worth consulting. "Let me..."

"Not now. We are busy."

"It's my baby. I name it."

"Nonsense."

"I insist!"

Manasā and Neta shared a glance.

"Are you sure? We are good at naming."

"You simply quarrel."

"Will you fight for it?"

"Of course I will!" Vidyā raised herself. "I call her Prītī."

Neta smiled. *"Beloved, Pleasure. Joy. Satisfaction."*

Manasā shook her head. "It won't do. You'll get your fight."

As soon as Vidyā was strong enough to walk, the goddesses wrapped her baby up. Prītī looked like a colourful gift package. Vidyā was awkwardly hugged by Manasā and with more feeling by Neta. Mother and daughter were dragged to the chariot, the swans were harnessed, and the pot was ready, the angry serpent brothers having been confined by Neta, who had slammed the lid on top of them. Manasā stood like a pillar. Vidyā saw her mouth twitch, as if she wanted to say something. Instead, the goddess turned and walked away. Neta waved a piece of cloth.

"Come here," she said, "we are late. Let me ensure you won't see a thing"

Vidyā felt the blindfold and Neta, holding her arm, helped her into the chariot.

"You'll be on earth in a blink."

"What about Prītī?"

"She'll love it. Children like sudden motions. How about you?"

Vidyā felt herself pushed into a seat. The chariot rocked, shuddered, and seemed to drop into nothingness. She heard her daughter gurgle happily.

Down on earth, Neta took off the blindfold.

"You are home".

Vidyā could have wept. This was the world. It was full of limits, edges, corners and wicked, spiky things. It wasn't home and it would never be.

"Smile," said Neta, "the gods love happiness. And relax. You learned a lot."

"I learned nothing."

"It'll do."

That's how Vidyā returned. The settlement was smaller than before. Even the rich houses seemed derelict, with their dusty walls, their crumbling terraces and their worm-eaten doors. Nobody was in sight. The noontime heat had smothered everything. Only plants can endure this place, thought Vidyā. The village is worn out, wasted, and heading towards ruin. We live in the middle of the void. If she could, she would have run away. Setting one foot in front of the other, with much deliberation, she returned to the merchant's house. At this time of the day, her husband, like his father and his brothers, would be out. Her mother-in-law would be there. Oh yes, she would be snoring like an overfed sow; but she would wake and resent the intrusion. Not that it mattered. Vidyā looked at her daughter. Nobody would like her. Cautiously, she opened the door.

"Worthless!" The merchant's wife screeched. "A useless mouth, a parasite, a daughter! The gods must have been angry. They cursed us!"

Her face was red and her chins wobbled. Given such a piece of bad luck, the aunt should have paid up. Vidyā should have arrived in tears, laden in presents, in gold and valuables, to make up for her shame!

"Your wife is rubbish! She is good for nothing!"

Vidyā's husband had heard it all. His brothers, coming home, one after the other, were told and told again. He glanced at his wife, gave his freshly born daughter a twisted smile, and tried to hurry away. His mother's voice stopped him. Actually, the baby looked cute, and he was glad his wife was well. He would have loved to hug them. But there was no way to admit it. His mother was screaming at full volume and outside, in the garden, doves were dropping from the mango trees.

"Who is she, to feast in our house like a leech? Boy, listen to me! Your wife is worthless; she is just a hungry mouth! Her parents are poor, the gods have cursed them! If we keep her, we will suffer!"

She pointed at her youngest son. "You! Do your duty! Throw her out!"

He did not dare to meet her eyes. His mother grabbed him by the shoulders. "You are a man, you must divorce her!"

"But mom..."

"Don't give me that! We'll find you a proper girl."

Vidyā raised her face, her hands shook and her eyes were red with tears. She placed the baby on a cushion and got up.

"Stay where you are!" The merchant's wife spat at her. She pushed her son. "You should beat her!"

He didn't move. His eyes were fixed to the ground.

She turned to her husband, "Tell your son to obey!"

Vidyā trembled. The room was spinning, her head reeled and all those people seemed far away. The ground under her feet began to wobble. Vidyā knew the feeling. She had felt like that, when her world came crashing down. Then, when Manasā danced, she had collapsed, and fainted. Now, the heat welled up from the ground, contorted her face and made her vision blur.

The room filled with a haze. Rage flooded her and all of a sudden she seemed to watch herself, standing there, trembling, almost mindless in her anger. This Vidyā was new, she was hot with rage.

Her mother-in-law recoiled. "Back! Go back! I tell you!"

Vidyā snarled, as she advanced like a cobra, her pupils moved up and everything went black and white.

Somewhere in the distance, she heard Neta giggle and a pot burst apart.

The universe changed course.

Through the open door, eight fat snakes slid.

Their eyes were fierce and their teeth gleamed. Oh yes, they were full of hate. Since Sij Mountain they had been confined. No attention, no veneration, no food. Again and again, they had vowed to kill that stupid, useless girl.

And there she was, Vidyā, reeling, crazy, drunk on madness and divinity.

The serpents slowed. She looked so wrong.

Vidyā sensed them. They seemed so fat and cuddly. She laughed "This is the hour of truth. This is pūjā for us all. Welcome my brothers Āṛona, Pāṛona, Dhonṛa, Boṛā, Bunye, Ārul, Pārul and Keuṭe! Blessings on their ways, their deeds, their killings; fat meals, leisure, a life of joy and a happy rebirth!"

The snakes stopped and stared.

Vidyā bowed. "My brothers, you are family." She opened her arms, "Please come to me."

The snakes shuddered. They circled around Vidyā, spiralled up her legs and drew themselves up until they covered her entire left side.

She shook and jerked and tears ran down her face. This was the end. It broke her apart, and made her giggle. Her belly lost its tension, her ribs moved and deep breaths made her sway. Somewhere, out there, people made a scene. Vidyā smiled at herself, she stepped aside, and allowed the change to happen. The Nāga wind surged through her frame. At last! She relaxed and trembled with relief.

The merchant's wife regained her voice. "The witch is possessed! She is an evil spirit! Throw her out! Kill her! Call an exorcist!"

Vidyā grabbed hold of her, dug her nails into her shoulders and hissed.

"I am Manasā!" She bared her teeth, and I am welcome. Today, Auntie has different gifts for you. They are much better, you little piece of scum!"

She turned around. "Look at me, apes! Who wants my embrace? Come on, speak up before you die!"

The merchant dropped behind the divan. His sons pressed themselves against the walls. Their faces shone with sweat. The crazy woman was close and the door was far away.

"Meet me. I am the goddess of snakes and my home is in the sij tree. Listen, I live between thorns!"

Vidyā released her mother in law, who sank to the ground.

"Worship me in the tree, as the tree and under the tree. I am the tree between the worlds and my twigs bear spikes and poisons."

She grinned. "Strike me and you bleed."

She pointed at the merchant. "You there, face me!"

The man pressed his head into the carpet. "Forgive us, goddess! Forgive our errors! We don't deserve to live."

The goddess seized the hair of his wife and pulled her up. "Fat slob!" she laughed, "I am your future. Look at Vidyā. How do you like her ornaments?"

"Mercy!" The woman was white with fear.

"Nāgdevī!" called her husband. "We will worship you!"

The goddess stepped back, lowered her eyebrows and pouted. She had practised that expression and it seemed to work. "I'm hungry. Ask Vidyā. Would you like poor people's fare? Watered rice from yesterday? And sour fish? I like what she likes. And I like the world. Maybe, one day, I'll even like you."

She pointed at the merchant. "My worship is simple. Vidyā will do it. So will her daughter. I don't demand much. Worship me every fifth of the bright and the dark half of the month. And on full moon, and new moon. Remember me in the morning, and when you go to bed. Dawn is excellent for worship. That's when serpents laze in the sun. And midnight, when we sleep in the Underworlds. Set up a pot of water and a twig of sij. Celebrate me when the monsoon comes, when the sky goes black, when the rains fall and the rivers swell. Make music in my honour. Sing and dance and say happy things. And when Vidyā wants sour fish and your obedience, you will perform!"

The whole family was on the ground, their heads bobbing up and down like ducks in a pond. People are funny, thought Manasā. Religion is so simple. I've got their attention, they behave, and now I'll make them love me.

"It's your lucky day," she smiled, "I like this place. Actually, I am fond of primates. My little demons! You should be laughing, as you are alive!"

Here begins The Manasā Epic.

Part One:

Śiva

4. Creation, traditional

All good epics require a beginning.

Unlike a lot of crazy seers, we start with clear and rational reasoning. That's because we are modern people, with electronic devices that keep us awake in the middle of the night. We won't be fooled by ancient superstitions. This chapter is about science. Speculation, I ask you. Who needs it? The world you inhabit didn't appear out of a vacuum. Any mouse baby knows that something does not come from nothing. Something comes from something, and this, the original something, is huge, confusing and wonderfully mind-blowing. Call it totally chaotic and perfectly organised. When it is unthinkable, and way beyond comprehension, it will naturally make sense. People like us make sense of anything.

Maybe, Monday morning, under the shower, you don't really care how everything began. But Mondays, showers, a schedule 24/7 and everyone goes bonkers all the time all share a divine origin. The seers of ancient India asked the crucial question.

Where did the world come from?

Welcome in ancient northern India, Vedic Period, around 1,000 BCE. East India, with its fertile plains, is far away and undiscovered. We are in the middle of the night. It's been a tough day.

The great pyre has burned down and the embers gleamed. A small group of hairy seers squatted at the edge of the sacrificial space. The men, each of them a formidable authority on things divine and mundane, had painted their brows, wore very little and some were coated with ashes. All day long they had swilled the heavy, intoxicating Soma broth, and sung their hymns with passion. They had sacrificed and intoned mantras, guaranteeing their regent, the sponsor of the ritual, a life of wealth and blessings, and as a collateral bonus, granted fertility and happiness to his kingdom. It was pretty good going. Sure, the preparation had taken weeks. The sacred Soma plants had to be obtained, their seller was ritually beaten up, there were sacrifices, chants and offerings, there was a mock dispute between a prostitute and a scholar, a ritual copulation involving low-class people, exorcisms of all directions, and plenty of offerings demanding precision and dedication. The plants (or was that fungi?) were crushed and mixed with milk, they were prepared and blessed, enchanted and transformed, until their juice, running through a cloth, mingled in a forest, which, as it happened, was a wooden tub. Whether you like it or not, the schedule was exasperating. Nevertheless, everything had worked out. The Vedic seers were a tough bunch: their deeds exceeded what the gods could do.

Finally, the ritual had come to an end. An hour ago, the sponsor had collapsed in his high seat, and began to snore. Days of ceremony had worn him out. Next to him, his wife was sleeping. The two had done their best, but they weren't young and the ritual had taken its toll. Vedic ceremony is exhausting. Before the sponsor and his wife were pure enough to participate, they had to spend more than a day in a tiny shed, close to a sacred fire. They were wrapped in the skins of black antelopes, tied up, so they could hardly breathe or move. The heat of the fire and the heat of the sun produced a savage combination. Ritual demanded that the couple could not speak until the Dikṣā was over. As a small blessing, they were allowed to scratch, using the horns of an antelope, and to utter their requests in nonsense-language. The rules were extreme: no talk, no food and no water. Only a few sips of milk when they were close to breakdown.

The seers observed them closely. They watched how the sponsors lost weight, how their faces became lined and their expression wearied. Finally, they ended the ordeal and dragged them to the river. Truth to tell, the sages were worried. The sponsor and his wife were scorched, and Agni, the god of fire, was in them. That's more divinity than anyone should manifest. Especially, if they are mere regents, and not Brahmins. The river swept the excess away. The royal couple drank their fill and were helped to the ritual space. And while the seers had their fill of Soma, and saw the true rituals and heard the true songs, the sponsors received a nice and harmless substitute which made them dizzy and sent them to sleep.

The seers huddled around a fire. Their eyes gleamed, their hands twitched and they were altogether too much awake. How do you relax when your mind is ablaze with drugs? When they closed their eyes, everything spun brighter and faster.

A cough. A respectable elder lifted his hand. "Right. We are awake and it's going to be a long night. We are out of our heads, but that's no reason to go slack. Let's get the facts sorted out. I want to hear serious reasoning. Anyone with funny ideas had better keep quiet."

He gave his colleagues the look. They knew what it meant.

"How did the universe begin?" He lifted a branch and stirred the coals. "Long ago, the seers had an easy life. They sacrificed and made the gods do what they wanted. Origins? They didn't worry. But times have changed." A shower of sparks flew into the sky. "These days, we want reasons."

"I can tell you." A seer scratched his beard. Small things rained down. "My ancestors knew everything.

Their words are eternal. Listen! My grandfather sang this:

In the beginning rose the Golden-Sprout, born as the only lord of all created beings. He stabilized and suspended earth and heaven. What god shall we adore with our offerings? Giver of vital breath, of power and liveliness, he, whose orders all gods recognize: the Lord of Death, whose shade is immortal life. What god shall we adore with our offerings?"

The man bowed his head. For him, things were settled. The Lord of Death fixed anything. Life was simple and easy, tradition a must, grandfather had used a stick and he was always right.

"It ain't good enough." Another seer rose. His back was bent with age; he rubbed his frosty hands and extended them towards the fire. His eyes were almost invisible under bushy brows. He frowned at his colleagues. "A few centuries ago, seers didn't go for such nonsense. New ideas are rubbish. A Golden Sprout? Who needs it? And a Lord of Death. That's sheer extravagance. Life isn't fancy or romantic. If this went on, practically anything could become a deity." He pointed to the ground.

"You personify the world. But honestly, the world is but a dream. Without painful ascetic practice, nothing is worth anything. You, my young friends, don't suffer enough. Pain is your teacher, ache is your initiator, anguish is your salvation. These are the real gods. Good things have to hurt. That's what Indra, the Lord of Thunder, told me."

"Come on! When did he talk with you?"

"When I was young, idiot. Many hundred rainy seasons ago."

Loud laughter.

The seer grinned. "You have no idea! In those days, the Soma juice was stronger than today! The offerings were greater and striplings didn't dare to laugh. They listened and obeyed! We sacrificed; we drank and went crazy with insight! Real insight! Let me reveal reality:

Eternal law and truth were born from painful abstinence; from it arose the Night and the billowy flood of the sea arose. From the same billowy flood appeared the Year, O Lord of all who close their eyes, establisher of the day's nights, Dhātar, the great creator, formed first the sun and then the moon. He formed heaven first and earth second, then the regions of the air, and light."

"Rubbish!" A seer leapt up. "Painful asceticism is great for our sponsors. And they deserve it! Why should we suffer? We are Brahmins, we are seers, we are greater than the gods!"

The elder wouldn't give in. "I saw the truth! Pain is universal! Everything is pain! Everyone needs pain! And when it hurts, when your body aches and your mind bleeds, great blessings will be gained! Painful exercises, I tell you, are the gate to greater joy."

"You make us ache! Go home, granddad! Pain is for low-class scum!"

"I ask your attention." A small, emaciated seer called from the background. His voice was faint, the man seemed starved, and his ribs were clearly visible. Obviously, nobody had given many cows to him. "We should solve problems with reason and logic. This is a new age: we perform experiments, draw up statistics, and derive reasonable conclusions from them. So let us ask ourselves a few questions. I prefer the difficult ones, the sort that can't be answered. How did painful ascetic exercises develop? Who performed them? Where did anything begin? Stop laughing! This is serious. How started the night? From where did the sea appear? And how did Dhātar turn up?" Slowly, he waggled his head. "Don't try to be so clever. Dhātar means *'Creator, Establisher, Founder and Supporter'*. Who is he? Where did he come from? I can tell you. My friends, we should show dignity. We come from excellent families. We are here to set an example. And where it comes to creation, let me tell you, it happened like this:

He cleared his throat and raised his hands to the sky.

"In the first age of gods, existence arose from non-existence. Afterwards, the regions of space were established. The creator god Dakṣa was born of Aditi, the goddess, who is a primal cow, and Aditi was Dakṣas child. From Aditi, oh Dakṣa, she who is thy daughter, was indeed brought forth. After her, the immortal gods were born, the sharers of immortal life. When you, oh gods, stood in yonder deep, closely embracing one another, thence, as from dancers, a thickening cloud of dust arose from your feet. When, oh you gods, like devotees, caused all existing things to grow, then you brought Sūrya, the sun, forth, who had been resting hidden in the sea. Eight are the sons of Aditi, who sprang forth from her body into life, with seven she went to meet the gods, but she cast Mārtāṇḍa, the sun, far away. So with her seven sons Aditi went to meet the earlier age; she brought Mārtāṇḍa here, to come to life and die again."

Our seer bowed. "It's simple. I hope you listened. It explains everything."

"It doesn't! There's not s shred of logic in your tale!" A young, ambitious seer gesticulated. In his age, excitement was a way of life. Unlike the elder seers, he had coloured his tangled locks with henna, and hoped to achieve a dashing look. "None of this makes sense. A cow gives birth to Dakṣa and then Dakṣa creates that cow. Sure, they are both deities, they are primordial and crazy. We have to make allowances. But I ask you, who was there first? Do you think that cause and effect can be twisted any way you like?"

"We used to get it up. In the old days. Sometimes several times each night!" An old seer, who could hardly keep his eyes open, giggled and revealed a mouth devoid of teeth. "We did as we liked. And it was huge, and jingled." He scratched his hairy belly and collapsed.

"This can't be true," Another seer stood straight and adjusted his dhoti. This man was shaved, in medium age, and wore a serious expression. Had he lived a few thousand years later, he might have been a banker. "Young people should listen and behave. They have no idea what is good for them. I have this vision on the highest authority.

In the beginning there was Puruṣa, the ancient spirit, the primordial being, the man. He had a thousand eyes and a thousand feet. He pervaded the entire earth and extended beyond it for ten fingers width. This Puruṣa is all that had been and is to be, the very lord of immortality, who grows by food incessantly. So mighty is his greatness, and even greater than that, he is Puruṣa. Puruṣa raised three-fourths of himself and one-fourth of him remained here. He strode over everything he eats and everything he won't eat. From him, Viraj, the Universal Sovereignty, was born, and he was born from Viraj. As soon as he was born he extended across the earth to east and west. When the gods performed the sacrifice, they made Puruṣa their offering. The sacrificial oil was spring, the holy gift was autumn and the wood was summer. They laid Puruṣa as the victim on the sacred grass, with him, the deities, the celestial sacrificers and the seers sacrificed. The dripping fat was raised, and from it, the creatures of the air were made, all animals, both wild and tame. From this great sacrifice, the chants and hymns and spells were born. Horses were born from it, and cattle with two rows of teeth, the cows, the goats and sheep. When they cut Puruṣa apart, how many sections did they make? What did they call his mouth, his arms, his thighs and feet? The Brahmans were his mouth, the Warrior class was his arms, the thighs became Those, Who Obey Orders and from the feet the Śūdra class was made. The Moon was created from Puruṣa's mind; the Sun was born from his eye, thunder-god Indra and fire-god Agni from his mouth, and wind-god Vāyu from his breath. Mid-air appeared from his navel, his head was turned into the sky, his feet became the earth and his ears became the regions of space. Thus they formed the worlds. Seven sticks were used to make the fence; seven layers of fuel were prepared, when the gods, to make their sacrifice, bound Puruṣa as the offering. The gods, sacrificing, sacrificed the victim, and these were the first holy ordinances. The Mighty Ones attained the height of heaven, the region where the celestial sacrificers, the ancient gods are dwelling."

The seer raised his eyebrows and bowed. "That's how you do creation. It's all about order, control, resources and hierarchies. You need consultants, agents, executives and public relations officers. They work, you gain. When things go wrong, you delegate. You keep the profits far above the costs, and wages at a minimum. And, of course, no matter what you do: someone has to be sacrificed." The man tried a grin. "Don't let it be you."

"Gods, this is sick!" croaked a seer whose beard was clotted with drool. "But it works. I admire you. Here, have another drink. I liked the bit with the thousand hands best. Provided they ain't mine. Or get under my dhoti."

Another seer agreed. He had pierced his cheeks with a bronze spike. It showed his holiness. "Great!" His voice was hard to understand. "That's how vision is done. Full blast bonkers and bang your head against the sky. We need visionaries; we need achievers who make the gods go 'ouch'!" He gazed at his colleagues. "Are we done?"

A dry cough. This seer had a shiny bald head, shaking hands and a dripping nose. His time was long past. With great effort, he got to his feet.

"My children, my little innocents," he said, and raised laughter.

"You believe to know and yet you don't know anything. Your visions are so certain. But in reality, they ain't. Nothing is certain. Not your mind or mine, not even the Soma juice. Who could trust anything? The world is made of questions and errors. Have you embraced doubt? Can you delight in ignorance? You see me standing here. But can you know that I exist, or you? Ah, you striplings. You think you know so much and try to rule the world. Be ashamed. None of you understands anything. Everything began in doubt and crisis.

In the beginning, there was not non-existence and not existence. There was no realm of air, and no sky extended from it. What covered it, and where? And what provided shelter? Was water there, an unfathomable abyss of water? Death did not exist nor was there immortality, there was no measure dividing night and day. The One Thing, breathless, breathed by its own nature; and apart from it, there was nothing whatsoever. Darkness was there, and within the darkness was the All, as undifferentiated chaos. All that existed then was void and formless, but finally, by the great power of heat, was the Unit created. Then arose Desire, god Kāma; in the beginning, appeared Desire, the primal seed and germ of spirit. Sages who searched with the thoughts of their hearts discovered the kinship of the existent in the non-existent. The dividing line extended crosswise: what lay above and what lay below? There were begetters; there were mighty forces, free action here and energy over there. Who really knows it and who can declare it here, whence was it born and whence comes this creation? The gods appeared after the creation of this world.

Who may know from whence the world came into being? He, the first origin of creation, whether he formed it or didn't form it, whose eye controls this world in highest heaven; truly, he knows it, or perhaps he knows it not."

The seer winked at his audience. "None of us does. We just pretend. We try to look good. For money, for fame, for girls." He laughed and his last teeth gleamed in the firelight. "But maybe you think that I am wrong. Of course I am. I am more wrong than any of you wimps, and I am proud of it" He grinned at the assembly. "Let me tell you a secret of the gods: questions are better than answers. They last much longer, year after year, life after life, and you can rely on them."

His companions applauded. Agreed, his hymn was incomprehensible. Maybe he was inspired, crazy or senile. But granddad was happy.

"Attention!" called a seer. "We are not done yet. I am sure there is a final truth we need to hear."

Finally, one sage arose. The man was a renouncer. His face was lined by starvation, his cheekbones stood out, his hair was a tangle of filth and his eyes were red. But he was serious, and tears ran down his cheeks.

"What I reveal is all about emotions."

The seers cheered him; 'cause emotions are reliable when reason is wanting.

"Listen, my friends," he said, and his voice trembled. "It's not easy, nor will it ever be. Nothing is. None of us should be happy we were born. Life, death, and everything, these things can really take it out on you. We do our duty and it does us in. You ask about the beginning? Or a beginning before the beginning? Or before that? Alas, the mind fails and the heart stops; indeed, we are not made to understand. I will tell you what was there before earth and heaven, before the gods and the Asuras came into being.

What was the ancient germ that was received where all the gods assembled?

The waters, they received the original seed, wherein the gods were all assembled.

It rested on the Unborn's navel, that One, wherein all things of existence reside.

Oh, you will not find him, who produced these creatures,

for another thing has risen up amongst you.

Enclosed in a misty cloud, with stammering lips,

hymn-chanters wander and are malcontent."

He gave a grim nod and sat. "That's it."

Excellent. The seers grinned. They came closer to the fire and filled their bowls. Time for the next shot. The night was excellent and could only get better. The visions were juicy, mad and crazy. Each was undeniably true. Someone, they thought, ought to memorize the lot. One day, they ought to be published as a proper book.

5. Creation, Bengal Style

The seers of the Vedic Period didn't have the foggiest idea. Though they composed the 1028 Hymns of the *Ṛg Veda* (you just read a selection from the tenth book) they only agreed where it came to lavish offerings and payments. One healthy, fat cow per Brahmin, as a minimum. Plus extras, expenses and tips. The gods could wait.

By contrast the much later seers and poets of Bengal were badly paid. People hardly cared for them. Nor did they do hard drugs, like Soma. However, they were much better informed.

The Universe didn't start with a great emptiness. The vacuum is a stupid idea, as any nuclear scientist will tell you. Wherever holes seem to appear, other things get sucked in. Some are molecules, some are atoms, some are ideas and some are simply crazy. But what existed, long before creation, was and remains incomprehensible. It had no shape, no meaning, function or name. It was conscious, but it couldn't comprehend what it was conscious of. Meet Anāndi Deb, the *Endless Deity*. It had no beginning and no end. Resting in the inexplicable, nameless and unfathomable, alone and undefined, it felt bored.

Anything, Anāndi thought, would be better than this. He, she or it, whatever it was, decided to do something. That's because consciousness is not just a state but an activity. It only took one magnificent gesture, a bit of visualisation and a certain drone (you always need vibration) and four brothers appeared. If we trust scripture (Neta says you shouldn't) the four brothers were perfectly dressed. They wore shiny turbans on their heads, their bellies bulged and their moustaches were oiled and twisted. They were clad in silk, adorned with jewels, they radiated divinity and were proud of it. These four brothers started everything. Or so they say. Sadly, they had no idea what they were supposed to do, and what it would do to them. There was just one directive: Anāndi Deb wanted them to get a move on, and start creation.

The four brothers stared into the huge, chaotic totality. There was neither here nor there, no today, yesterday or tomorrow. All things were formless and nameless and the brothers didn't know what to do with them. If possible, they would have gone home and had an early night.

Finally, one had an idea. "We need a basic principle."

The others nodded.

"A basic principle tells us what we have."

"A basic principle reveals how to proceed!"

"A basic principle allows us to measure the development!"

"Unless there is a principle, we can't boast how great we are!"

The brothers smirked. One day or another, they would make a principle. It would be short, neat and convincing. And it shouldn't require more than, say, three paragraphs.

"Thirty seconds," they decided, "should be enough to explain anything."

Their brand new universe would be amazing.

"Great!" said one brother, "We are doing well. But what is our basic principle?"

"We need something real."

"We need something close to our hearts."

"We need something worth to live and die for."

"We need something like us."

Four brothers held hands. In their midst, a fantastic idea congealed.

In case you want to try this, here are the instructions. They thought of everything that seemed essential, everything they would miss, if it disappeared or re-emerged when you didn't expect it, or that was plainly unthinkable. They imagined home, warmth, friends, family, good literature, uplifting classical music, seven-course meals, whirlpools, girls clad in next to nothing, drinks made of bananas and rum with little umbrellas, holiday cruises, in-door trampolines and most important, plenty of excitement and someone to drive them home. Whatever this universe would turn out like, it would be amazingly flexible. It would be primordial, ancient, old, contemporary, parallel, enigmatic, incomprehensible, futuristic, real, unreal, reasonable, logical, irrational, mysterious, ever young, ever old, now and then, forever and absolutely perfect. Their dreams became passionate, detailed, gained weight and congealed. If you want to imagine what the brothers imagined, you have to make your visions really large, colourful, and very touching. In fact, they wrapped themselves up in them.

Manasā says: "Hey you! This is a secret of the Universe. Great visions should be intense, huge, overwhelming, and dramatic, if they are any good. Emotion is everything! Those who reduce their imagination to small, pale, distant pictures will never create a universe."

Neta stands nearby. She gives a crooked smile and shrugs. "Don't be so serious. Universes just happen. I found one in the bin today. My sister makes too much of this. She likes important stuff. I don't. Let's face it. New worlds appear all the time. Every baby creates dozens, every day. Tadpoles do it. Their world is a pond, and damn it, that pond is the universe. People are like tadpoles. Their pond ain't much bigger. You create your world, whether you are a tadpole, a frog, or a baby. Or just you. And you can change it, anytime. Change yourself, and keep changing as you go along. Or change your pond."

Manasā frowns. It sounds too simple. "What if a person doesn't want to change?"

"They stay as they are. And drop dead. Everybody does. There's always another life," says Neta, "people die all the time. They are good at it. I like it. It's fun to watch. Today, enormously important. Tomorrow: twitch, die and rot. Or burn. Say welcome to the humus. Feed the soil and start again. Or stay alive. Not that I care. It can happen many times, in each lifetime."

"You make it sound so trivial!"

"It is. And people are. You change the personality. Everything's different. Or you change the world. It transforms the personality. Same thing, new game. What's so hard to understand?"

"You are! We are talking creation! That's big business! And you make it sound like something people do each morning!"

"They could, if they wanted to. I do." Neta grins. "You can choose who you want to be. Get a new set of underwear, make a fresh start, feel young and new and loveable. Or realise this ain't the world that you were used to. Reality happens. That's nature, whether you know it or not."

Neta shrugs. She has said her piece and leaves. A lot of stuff needs to be washed. Some of it is crusty. "You simply do it. Like everything. Or you are done. That's all. Sorry, I'll be off to the river."

Her river. It's dark. Let's return to the beginning.

The four brothers got it right. They muttered, argued, agreed and disagreed. Finally, when they had enough, they put everything into a major effort. From their dreams, their desires, their fears and limitations, they created Dharma. Then they departed for paradise elsewhere, to have pizzas with everything and lots of heavy drinks.

Meet Dharma. You have known him as long as you live. Dharma is *truth, virtue, justice, care, compassion, structure, commandments, religion, duty, the configuration of the world, the order of society, limitation* and *dissolution*. That's quite a lot for a single deity. He lifted his head and heaven appeared. He wriggled his toes and the earth extended everywhere. He surrounded earth with an infinite world-ocean, and supported it on many underworlds. To give the whole thing a bit of zest he added matter, antimatter, black matter, elements, strings, quarks, bits of quantum, loads of neutrinos and totally occult substances, such as abstrusium, stringentium, realium, irrationalium, ultimativum, coherencium, causalium, coincidencium, insanium plus error, fun and irresponsibility. He stuffed theodiversium into the gaps, 'cause that stuff, though difficult to handle, and strongly psychedelic, gives sense to everything, no matter how insane.

"Order is chaos, enigmas refresh the mind, paradoxes nourish, the impossible is real, irresponsibility creates obligations and anything crazy makes sense," he said. "Freedom and bondage are the same." It was his first insight and the four brothers were shocked. Dharma clapped his hands. It started space and told time to accelerate. A shudder went through everything. It has been shuddering ever since. Over the freshly created matter, pulsating incessantly, shone a cosmic light, the fresh energy of the newly created sun. Deep down at the bottom of the ocean, in boiling hot volcanic chutes, life began. The black waves of the primal sea broke against bleak rocky coasts, and, in the foam of the breakers, algae, lichens, mosses and horsetail crept to land. They met fungi, blushed, embraced and grew twice as strong. In their wake arose the plants, they sprouted, grew, scattered pollen and withered, covering jagged rock with layers upon layers of slime, fertility and humus. Wherever plants grow the serpent goddess lurks. Like the plants, she is intelligent and very observant. However, unlike her sister Neta, she was only there in potential, waiting, restless, unfulfilled and getting jumpy.

Dharma stood at the shore of the primal ocean. The winds whipped up the salty froth and hurled it into his face. He laughed. This was creation, this was life, and it developed perfectly! Up and down, here and there, yesterday, today, tomorrow, they all began to make sense. The whole universe appeared out of Dharma; all parts were full of Dharma, and followed the rules of Dharma, who kept it perfectly balanced.

"I care for you!" he shouted, "I care for everything!"

"Those who violate Dharma will be destroyed by it, those who support Dharma will be protected by it" said Manu, the mythical law-giver, or really one of them, as every world age needs a new Manu to update or retard society. For good reason he added that Dharma accompanies people through life and death. Saint Vasiṣṭha added: *"Proper, acceptable conduct is Dharma. He, who violates Dharma, is doomed in this world and outside of it; ascetic exercises and offerings will fail to redeem him."*

Dharma had a fantastic time. He created the world, the directions of space, up and down, the waters, countries and airs, the plants and animals, with all their bizarre characteristics. His task was wonderful, as every single being and thing was unique. Each time he got something done he stepped back, smiled from ear to ear and felt proud of his achievement.

"I like you!" he said, to whatever it was. "You are me and I am you and we are wonderful." His spirit extended through the moving and the unmoving parts of the universe, and whatever he created and perceived made him laugh with joy. Soon, space was filled by rough, young mountains, and fertile valleys, by sparkling rivers, soggy swamps, lakes that shimmered like turquoise eyes under a mind-wide sky, dark forests, churning oceans, red-golden deserts and wide, inhabitable plains.

One of his favourites was time. He invented twelve months and built special effects into each of them. It would only take a few million years to get them sorted out. In the beginning, the months were crude and difficult. They influenced a rough and almost lifeless world. But there were seeds of hope in each of them. Much later, when things had sorted themselves out, the poets of Bengal couldn't stop to praise the Twelve Sisters. **December** was mild, as fresh winds blew and rice turned the fields green. The air was frosty and the distant mountains shone blue, serrated and jagged. Many were crested with snow. No matter how happy you were, you had to use thick blankets. While the lotus withered, the fig was budding. **January** was colder and cloaked the land in fog and gloom. More blankets were needed. Hoarfrost encrusted the foliage and rhinos clustered in their hives, high up in the trees, and beat their wings to preserve warmth. I'm sure it was rhinos. Or was that elephants? In **February**, the cold froze the buds and the cranes began to call. They announced the coming of spring, and filled all beings with hope. The goats went crazy, searching for new green, and feasted. In **March**, queen of all months, the warmth awoke, the trees stood bright, the leaves gleamed and blossoms opened everywhere. The air was full of stunning scents. Young people went mad on hormones, thought with their bellies and somewhat underneath, and craved each other. Lord Kāma, the ancient deity, laughed as he scattered flowers over meadows and plains and shot his five arrows of desire, lust and love at anything that moved. **April** turned the vegetation golden; the winds were hot, and filled all hearts with longing. The honey bees went swarming, the lotus flowers welcomed them; the cuckoos called and the swallows drank the water of the clouds. The heat of spring began in **May**, when new leaves unfolded to delight the eye. Crows and ravens croaked from the treetops all day long. The days were hot and stunning, and everyone was restless in the night. Mango blossoms opened and the meadows, covered by flowers, were aflame with lust. Jasmine radiated perfume and in the forests, the trees danced in delight. **June** ripened the mangos, the blackberries and the jackfruit, while the great drought advanced, bitter and merciless, hardening ground and shattering the soil. The days were scorching; the quivering air was clogged with dust. The nights were stifling hot, and tempted the restless to bathe in the stream. In overheated bedrooms, lovers were coated in sweat and panted with exhaustion. At last, in **July**, the sky turned black with clouds. Indra's herd of madly surging elephants came rolling in from the east. Thunderbolts tore through the height; rain turned into a waterfall, and rivers, swollen, angry, left their beds. The rains were like a maiden with a golden pitcher in her hands. The peacocks danced and frogs were drunk on downpour. There was no dry place on earth! In **August**, the sky was black with rain; you could not tell the bright or dark fortnight of the moon. Each day, each night, was dripping wet. The forest robed itself in emerald, as buds appeared on every branch, young grasses sprouted from the muddy ground, algae and juicy mosses painted house walls green. Brooks turned into rivers, rivers became lakes, and fields disappeared under the deluge. From muddy waters, the lotus blossoms raised their heads. Howling storm winds stung like needles. Carts were stuck in the morass, travellers and oxen, stranded in mud, struggled to the nearest settlement. **September** gave the rivers rest and eventually, their waters cleared. The mountains shone in radiant azure, lilies opened their blossoms; the air, at last, was cool and fresh. **October** raised gentle winds and made the lotus gleam. The pandanus trees filled the air with striking scents; lianas flowered, the lavish land was clad in green, so young, so fresh and innocent. In **November**, a happy sun laughed. The grains ripened, the night sky was full of stars, and the moon drifted in a haze of molten butter. The world was blessed and wonderful. Then, at last, the dry cold returned.

In the divine play, everything acted just as Dharma did. Space and time appear thanks to awareness, and Dharma was full of it. He experienced the world as himself and could have burst with love and joy and pride. It was so inexpressibly beautiful! And there was far more detail than he had expected. Each pebble was unique, each drop of water right, each cloud, no matter how, was perfect. The algae were Dharma as they swayed in the waters and crept to the shore as they struggled for the light. Animals were moved by the wild, reckless heart of Dharma; Dharma aroused joy and wonder, and delighted in meeting and recognising itself. This will go on, he thought, life after life, rebirth after rebirth, through all ages, all worlds, all realms of existence! Dharma recognised and remembered himself in beings, things and ideas, in animals, plants and fungi, and each of them was good.

"See this!" he shouted to the elder gods, "I care for everything! This is the world, I made it, I love it and it is me!"

The four brothers scrutinized the world and it was good. They cast a glance at Dharma, who was standing there, in love with himself and proud of his achievement, and he wasn't good.

They shook their heads and cursed him.

"As you are great, you will meet your limits. As you are high, you will drop low. As you are proud, you will be damned. As you created virtue, you will die of it.

Your corpse will drift on the waters of infinity. You will rot and disintegrate and anyone nearby will choke and vomit!"

Dharma was shocked.

He clenched his fists. This was wrong; it was unjust and outrageous! How could these nut-crackers pass judgement on him? Wasn't the world good enough? A craftsman is worth his wage! Hadn't he done enough?

The brothers gazed into the distance.

Dharma turned and walked away.

"You are the fossils of the past," he muttered. "You are frogs in a well, talking about heaven. Do your own thing, if you can. I know I'm good, and I'm the future."

He walked through his creation, and gave it up like a piece of rubbish; he cursed, and spat, he crossed the otherworlds and left everything behind.

It was time for a new start. Dharma had visions. "I am excellent," he thought, "and my next world will be better."

His new reality needed new gods. Courageous, self-confident, happy gods. Gods with ambitions and visions, who would lead the universe into a better future. Dharma would boss them around and they would love him.

He gave a sigh of relief. Those four brothers? Who cares? They were history.

It happened on a mountain peak. That's as high as you can get without losing contact to the ground. Dharma sat down, and relaxed. He took a deep breath, focussed his energy, exhaled and created three new gods.

First of all, an artist. Let's call him **Brahmā**: the creative, spontaneous and thoroughly unpredictable Lord of Creation. Brahmā was young, but he was born old. In fact, he appeared as a grandfather. True, he is a small guy. In a reliable universe, creativity has to be limited. However, he is proud, self-centred, smokes spiced cigarettes and wears all sorts of funny hats and scarves on his four heads. Originally he had five. After a scrabble with Śiva, only four remained. His costume tells the world: I am an artist. I am special. Feel proud that you know me, and tell your friends. I have great visions, I start amazing projects, but as I feel vulnerable and insecure, I only want to hear your praises. Say something nice, say it again, admire me, buy me a drink, or leave me alone.

Next came **Viṣṇu**: dependable, reasonable and heroic. He has a trustworthy, orderly character and is perfectly suited to maintain the universe 24/7 without getting bored or going home early. "Holidays are for weaklings", he says, "I do my duty all the time." In his book, Law and Order come first, and hardly anything second. Excellent, thought Dharma, he's so devoted that it hurts. He worries. He thinks and worries even more. He advances; he goes back, he sidesteps and finally he walks around. It doesn't make him happy. His employees moan. They never understand his policies. The guy is just too complicated. Viṣṇu examines, stops, and reconsiders. And he does progress: one small step after the other. That's how it works. For when things go wrong, after a small step, you have time to reconsider. Viṣṇu says: "Those who hurry, fail." And he won't go away on weekends 'cause there is always something to do. His wife Lakṣmī complains. She pouts and looks at him with antelope eyes. Her bosom heaves. It's quite impressive. Her patchouli perfume makes him dizzy. He shakes his head; he has his duty and can't help it. "This is about the cosmos," he says, "the word means 'beautiful order'. You don't get order for free, let alone beauty. I wish I had some time off, but honestly, when I'm not on the job, my employees go slack and the world is overrun by Anti-Gods." Lakṣmī sighs. She's heard it all before. Duty, responsibility and self-surrender. Viṣṇu is Mr. Altruism. She goes out with her girlfriends and buys shoes until the sun goes down. She hangs around in bars and chats with passing strangers. Viṣṇu stays in his office, reads reports, writes memos, and has a bowl of cold rice.

Last, we need someone totally different. Dharma took a deep breath, as this one was difficult, and he created crazy, unpredictable **Śiva**, who loves change, chaos, coincidence; who disagrees with everyone and with himself, turns reality upside down and dissolves whatever isn't needed any more. He is destruction and liberation, thought Dharma: when people are stuck, when rules fail and principles cease to matter, he will kick ass and liberate them. But let's get real. Transcendence is more than enough for anyone, and it is far too much for him. Dharma nodded sympathetically. "Hi there," he said, "My poor crazy loony. You've got an awful task. Please do it any way you like!"

Let's face it: Reality is enigmatic and people are insane. That's why Śiva spends his life, when he isn't blissful, cosmic, and incomprehensible, with sex and drugs and rāg 'n roll. He staggers through the spiky sij trees, blots his mind out, and falls asleep on the cremation place.

Great! Three extremes and each of them perfect! Dharma laughed. His world was governed by gods who got things done!

Dharma told his triplets to organise the world. I'm sure you noticed: they do an excellent job. There is creation, maintenance and dissolution, in your world, your district, your house and in your mind. But Dharma felt a tinge of doubt. Something was missing in his wonder-world. Things were just too primitive. For a while, he closed his eyes. Let's reconsider, he thought. How did it all begin? We started out with rocks. Then followed water; most of it dropping from the skies. The deep filled up; we had oceans, and rivers, and life began, somewhere in the deep. The oceans were a perfect habitat. But eventually, the primordial sea wasn't enough. Some beings wanted to escape. The mosses emerged from water, made friends with fungi, and were thriving on wet ranges, covered by barren rock and crusty lichens. But while the lichens, a wonderful symbiosis of algae and fungi, were flat and hard and leathery, the mosses seemed like a promise of the forests of the times to come. They were so soft, so innocent and flexible. They had no proper roots, sure, that would be the future, but for the moment their underside was coated with fungi who gained them water and extracted minerals from rocks. Meanwhile, the plants create sugars and starches from sunlight. That's it, he thought. It's sharing. They support each other. What a great idea! I did it again! Symbiosis is the future, and we need more of it.

Dharma thought long and deep, and encouraged every little doubt and every weird idea. Come here, he thought, make me uneasy. Point out my flaws! I need doubt and worry to turn things upside down. Show me my limits and my errors. He watched his mind for a long time, and finally, he understood. The missing ingredient was art. "The world lacks love, and elegance. Call it beauty, if you like, for beauty is truth and perfection." Dharma scratched his head, dislodging gritty stuff and parallel universes.

"What use is a world without astonishment and wonder?" he asked. "I'll do it, it'll blow my mind, and it will be the best I ever did." He took a deep breath containing the self-essence of everything. When he exhaled, a goddess appeared. It was **Ādyā**, the *Original, Primordial One*. She seemed shy and modest, but was much prettier and stronger than her brothers.

Understand this: Ādyā is sheer energy, and energy is form. And she has the skill to transform into millions of goddesses, powers and shapes.

Dharma scratched his hairy belly. "I did it!" he whispered "I'm so damn good!" He leaned back and the beads of his rosary trailed slowly through his fingers. "It's been so long. But it's done. I can calm down and relax. Maybe I'll even have a holiday. Everything will work out. Problems will solve themselves and I can stop meddling. It's great to let go." His work, the Multiverse, was getting along perfectly. Everything worked. Prehistory was past. The elder gods had had their chance, and blew it.

The sun speeded across the sky, day followed day, year on year and soon we could count the aeons, cycles and megacycles, heavy like lead, that every project needs to get anywhere. The young gods grew up and their skills multiplied. Dharma watched and was amazed: they were so dexterous, so talented, so amazingly unique.

"I'm a miracle," he said, "they are my kids, they do reality and everything, and I am proud of them."

Boys were boys, and Dharma saw himself in each of them, without noticing how different they had turned out. "My seed!" he said. His daughter was different. She grew, she radiated like a rose on a summer's day, and when her brothers quarrelled, she sorted them out without raising her voice.

"I made her," thought Dharma, "and she is much nicer than I am." Her face, her graceful bearing, her enchanting voice bedazzled him. His eyes followed her, wherever she walked, and he couldn't get enough of her. He loved her laughter, her song, the delicate motions of her hands and the elegant curve of her waist. One day he noticed that her breasts had grown, that her hips swayed when she walked and that the cheerful child had become a woman. Her hair had the lustre of a blue-black cloud rolling in from the ocean, the dark curls promising relief from heat and drought. Her face shone peacefully like the moon. Her eyes sparkled like the jewels of the Underworlds, her legs were sturdy like banana stalks and her walk was as graceful as a swan. When she greeted him, the earth and sky were lit by her beauty. "You are the summit of perfection," he said, and she blushed and looked away.

It took a while, but finally, he understood. Dharma fought for breath and his face went wet with sweat. This is Karman: first realization, then insight, followed by doom. His sin. It was desire. Whether he liked it or not, under his dhoti things began to stir. He watched his daughter as a lover would. That simply didn't do. The world stopped and held its breath. So did Dharma. He wasn't stupid. I'm prey to my lust, he thought, I can't fight it, I can't exorcise it, and it will finish me. It's the end of my journey and the grand finale of my existence. His hands bulged into fists, his eyes closed and tears streamed down his face. The misery of everything came over him. Dharma had made the cosmos, and the cosmos ran on laws. The god of truth, rightness and virtue is not allowed to lust after his daughter. Dharma dropped into the abyss within himself and faced depravity, vanity, boundless narcism and insatiable greed. At last, he recognised himself. Who was he, really? Good? Just good? Or only barely good enough? His world, was it worth anything? The curse seized him, and burst into his mind with claws that ripped his mind to shreds. Dharma discovered disgust. I am this, he thought, and this is me. It isn't good enough! With a scream that made heaven and earth convulse and echoed all the way into the Serpent Underworld, he gave up his ugly, tattered being and died. His corpse tumbled down the cliffs that divide earth from the primal sea, where it was caught by breakers, slammed against rocks and tossed about recklessly. Bones broke, blood spurted, flesh tore and fishes arrived to feast and swarm and multiply. Without aim or purpose, the dead carcase of order, virtue and right floated on the waves, and aimless was the pattern of the world.

High up on a mountain ridge, Ādyā crouched. Her hands clutched the naked rock, her hair was tangled, her clothes in tatters, and she wept. A while ago, she had noticed that her dad was acting strange. He seemed restless, and hungry, and quite beside himself. As soon as she could, she disappeared into the hills. Finally, between rocks and snow, she tried to relax. It didn't work. Her mind whirled and her body trembled. I need to climb further, she thought; I need to leave it all behind.

The very moment that Dharma fell into the sea, Ādyā was squatting on a mountaintop. The air was frosty and the rock coated with ice. She paled and her breath stopped. Her posture froze; her face ceased moving, and her fingers dug into the moss. Ādyā wept. It's all about attraction and desire, she thought. It's empathy that keeps the world together.

Empathy was over.

Dharma was dead. She felt it in her bones.

Her eyes filled with tears. She had loved him as a child loves a parent, and for her he was a good, if somewhat childish father, with all his pride and arrogance, his unreasonable ideas and silly fancies. Imagine someone crazy enough to create a stegosaurus! Equipped with a brain the size of a walnut and a secondary brain in his ass! It could become a politician! Her father had done his best. He had assumed that he was truth and virtue. He cared for anyone and anything.

And then he went weird. Whatever: he was gone. Her fingers clutched the growth and tore it out. The mosses died. She hardly noticed. Now she was scratching bare rock. Her dad, for all his weirdness, was reliable. Sure, he was crazy. It's not easy to manifest the cosmic order. The more it develops, the weirder it gets. Evolution is the same. When you see one species develop into a hundred, each of them with its own bizarre idiosyncrasies, each screaming for attention and support, you realize the working day is far too short make them happy. In large districts, with major communities, the gene pool keeps itself on average. In tiny, isolated communities, it goes for crazy permutations, each of them stunningly unique. And when a being is badly stressed, it produces an extra helping of mutations. Most of them are insignificant. Some turn into cancer. A few are crazy, weird or brilliant. Maybe they'll be the future.

But just how much can a deity do, no matter how grand and universal, before things grind her or him down? She wished that he could have taken a few weeks off, relaxed somewhere, unknown, unnamed, and returned in a better mood. Now, without him, the world forgot its meaning. The universe lost order, virtue, and structure. Ādyā wept and her nails broke. Her eyes searched the storm-torn sky, and saw bright blue transform to bile. Above her head, a vortex began to churn. Sun and moon trembled; they staggered and lost their course. Stars fell into neverness; seasons chased each other without sense and purpose and nameless creatures ran insane. That's us, she thought, it's my brothers and me, we are pointless, aimless, driven by blind urges. Look at poor, exhausted planet earth! Here there was drought, over there the rivers turned to oceans, clouds raced across the sky and dust storms suffocated the vegetation. On the high mountains seers staggered, blinded by the madness of the sky, and in the settlements people killed each other for a few grains of rice. Ādyā saw everything. She saw the present and the future, and it turned her tears to blood. It was the end of order. Her fingernails were gone, she was tearing out her hair, and her body shook in madness and hurled itself at naked rock.

"You brothers of the beginning!" she screamed, "can you hear me? You damned bystanders, watchers, spectators, you are responsible! Do you realise what's going on? Do you care? Are your hearts dead? Have you ever dared to live?"

She lifted her fists to the sky, "I curse you!" she screamed, "I curse you!" But she received no answer.

"My father was rightness and virtue. He wasn't perfect, but he did his best. Now the world is governed by ignorance, by cruelty and greed! All beings are ruled by fear. Fear, you scumbags, creates hate. That's what the world is like. It's your world and you will be held responsible!"

Ādyā collapsed, and tears ran down her face. "Hate kills anything. Look at me, you creatures without feeling! What happened to love? What happened to forgiveness?" Her fists struck the rock. They were covered in blood, but Ādyā didn't notice.

"Look at me! I am your granddaughter! What can I give to the world? What is my place in it?"

Ādyā collapsed on her black antelope skin. Her breath was heavy and laboured. In-breath: excitation, out-breath: relaxation, the eternal cycle of being. Ādyā wanted none of it. She drove her fingers into the fur. Her eyes were firmly shut. The whole wide world was far too much. It was time to end it all.

She closed her eyes, her nose, her mouth and ears. Giving up the periphery of her body, she shrank and fell into the vastness of her inner self. Sure, out there, misery was on the rampage. In here, the world was quiet, peaceful, and everlasting. Ādyā shrank as she dropped into the vastness of her inner self. Her life, her thoughts and passions faded away, they made their way to the periphery and disappeared like dew in the sunshine. Within the greatest cave in the world, between being and non-being, Ādyā found her peace. She recited the mantra that causes death.

From the bottom of her body, near the perineum, a flame surged upwards. The hungry fire rose, devouring organs, intestines and bones. Her mouth opened and oily smoke emerged. Finally, when the blaze reached the top of her skull, hope disappeared. Ādyā screamed. It was the End of Time. From the crown of her skull, a shower of combustion, madness and delight flew into heaven. So ended Ādyā, the Primal One, and her blackened, charred corpse lay under a bleary-minded sky and became a feasting place of vultures, ravens, crows, of jackals and hyenas, of swarming flies and creeping maggots.

The waves came in; hungry, gurgling, incessantly. Near the waterline, where fish and algae go to rot, the sons of Dharma stood. They gazed over a leaden ocean, they stared into eternity. The breakers crashed and with a hiss, the foaming water swept across the sand. The sky was full of cloud fragments, scattered by mighty storms, like mindless birds and empty dreams. The waves were greedy, their sparkling crests advanced, and sucked at feet and legs.

Brahmā, Viṣṇu and Śiva stood in the flood. The wet air seemed to suffocate their breath. It was cold; the whole world had gone cold. Their father was dead. It was time to honour him. The grey waters tore at them. Life had become misery: it would have been so easy, to give in, to disappear into the waters. Out of the haze, Dharma's corpse appeared, supported by the waves. The ocean and the cliffs had not been kind to him. Rocks had crushed his face, and fishes had feasted on his flesh.

The corpse drifted past Brahmā. Brahmā loves everything that is young, new and original, and he creates the things that give hope and rejuvenate the world. Ask me! He just inspired great wax moths to eat plastic bags! On a global scale, it doesn't get much better than this. Brahmā loves youth and promise. And he needs hope. The tiny, vulnerable grandfather god of beginnings hopes for a better future. Right then, there wasn't any. He watched the corpse of his father and saw nothing but despair and pain. Tears glazed his eyes. He gave the corpse a kick and the rotten carcase drifted on.

Dharma's corpse reached Viṣṇu. He faced torn skin, bare bone, and bloated flesh, crawling with pestilence. Viṣṇu recoiled; he couldn't recognise his father any more. Were these the eyes that had encouraged him to maintain the cosmos? Was this the mouth that told him that the world was good, and always worth sustaining? Viṣṇu thrives on things that are constant, reliable and supportive. He encourages rules and symmetries, he knows that boundaries provide safety, and loves the order of the world. What happened to regulations, to laws of science, to conventions? None of them were apparent in the corpse. Watersnakes and fishes had fed on Dharma's flesh. His abdominal cavity was wide open and his guts, a garland of putrification, were tossed about by the waves. There was no order in the rot and the stench was unbearable. Viṣṇu closed his nose and staggered to the shore.

The corpse drifted to Śiva. He had consumed so many drugs that he was hardly capable of thought. The raging breakers tore and pulled at his legs. The god of transcendence giggled. This was crazy, he thought, am I standing, am I floating? He looked for Brahmā, but he had run away. He saw Viṣṇu, way up on the beach, bent over, vomiting. Śiva shook his head. You've got no idea, he thought, and neither have I.

He grinned from ear to ear. Call me insane, he thought, but reason is a dream. The corpse of Dharma came close. He looked at pale, frayed flesh, into empty eye-sockets and gaping ribs. Śiva took a deep breath, enjoyed the scent, and sighed with relief. Let's breathe, he thought, that's enough, one breath after another. No one can expect more. Breath. It's life. It's reality. One after the other, and I'm happy. So this is Dharma. Hey daddy! You are virtue, order, structure. You care for anyone and everything. And you are totally, absolutely dead.

Śiva had never seen anything like this. This wasted flesh, this wave torn carcass was an object of beauty. Structure dissolved, tissue went to rot and something wonderfully new emerged. Hey, he thought, this is food for birds! He laughed. The gulls would take their fill, and the eels, the fishes, and the crabs! Worms and maggots crept through the organs, microbes feasted; what seemed dead was throbbing with life. Dharma, Śiva realised, will live forever. The carcass bursts with vitality! Śiva laughed. Dharma wasn't dead, he was simply transforming. Everything was perfect! There was life everywhere, and more and more of life.

"Everything is holy," Śiva mumbled; he staggered, as the waves pushed him. "I love it, I love everything!" Tears surged down his cheeks. It's so crazy, he thought. Yes. Everything is crazy. Everyone is a fool. His brothers were insane, and he was worse. Come on, he thought, understand me! Damn it! He couldn't understand himself! The world began to spin. Śiva exhaled, again and again, found his centre in the middle of the cyclone, in his belly, and relaxed. Very slowly, he bowed.

It was all that he could do. And Dharma came alive.

The icy wind, the twisted trees and the grey sky showed the way. Empty branches, withered grasses and bleak rocks, this was reality, and it extended everywhere. Brahmā, Viṣṇu and Śiva followed the track to total misery. Carrion birds indicated how close they were. Up on the mountain, the gods found what they had searched for. Screeches echoed, as the scavengers took to the air. How incredibly small and fragile their sister seemed. Her corpse, sheltered by rocks, was in tatters. Her flesh was torn by teeth and beaks. Swarms of flies had ripened in her corpse. The gods gazed into empty eyeholes and saw that her inside was scorched. The heat of despair had turned her core to coal. In the Fire of the End of Time, she had found release.

Brahmā, Viṣṇu and Śiva lifted her empty shell. They carried her corpse to the shore of the world ocean. From nearby, they dragged dry wood, broken branches, splintered trees, growth that had supported the sky and stabilised the soil. Trees that had never felt such pain, had never suffered from anguish, worry or betrayal.

On the long shore, under a bleak sky, they erected the pyre. They drenched the trunks with butterfat. They laid the tattered corpse on top of the pile; they adorned her body with red blossoms. To the sound of the waves, they chanted mantras. Finally, they lightened the pyre, and Agni, Firelord, greedy, restless, ever hungry, rose like a blossom and devoured the corpse. All through the night the flames danced and thick, oily smoke ascended. By daybreak, most of the wood had turned to cinders and from the gleaming embers a soft voice sounded. The gods gazed into the ashes and saw a baby. She was a girl and she laughed with joy.

Brahmā staggered back. He had been lost in sadness; now, fresh life, uncreated by him, was gurgling with pleasure.

Viṣṇu shuddered. The Lord of Maintenance buried his hands in his hair. His perfect haircut emerged twisted; his diamond crown slipped and fell. This was altogether too much.

Śiva, totally high and beside himself, was perfectly reasonable. I am sure you treasure the moment; it won't happen often. He shook his head and smiled at his brothers with compassion.

"No, folks," he said, "let's face reality. You ain't up to raising a child and neither am I."

He grinned in an immensely provocative way. "We are too busy running the universe. Raising a child is far more difficult."

"What do you mean?" said Brahmā. "We are almighty. And children are simple."

"No way," said Śiva. "They learn anything. We would have to set an example."

"I'm the perfect example," said Viṣṇu, "and the world is welcome to copy me."

"That's bloody terrifying."

"By no means. Everybody would be perfect."

"You dumb moron," said Śiva, "have you ever been awake all night? And done a full working day afterwards? Night after night, after night? Let's get real. And, for that matter, do any of your mantras mention 'diapers'?"

"I don't believe they have to. It's not even Saṁskṛta."

"It should be."

The brothers looked at the little girl, who was happily sucking her foot.

Like you and me, gods have limits. Unlike most people, they are perfectly aware of them. Indeed, (cool hint, says Neta) if you want to understand your divinity, explore your restrictions. They tell you everything. In ecology, the rarest commodity defines the dominant species. Knowing limits is what keeps you from becoming demonic.

The gods raised their voices and invoked Viśvakarman, the Divine Architect. He's the guy you never really think about. Unless you need a divine palace on a mountaintop, pretty fast, with plumbing, central heating and trans-dimensional gateways leading anywhere. He shows up late, shrugs, looks at you through horn-rimmed spectacles, as if you were an imbecile, and gives a gentle smile. You smile in response. At least, you do, until you see his bill.

This time, the job was simple. "Viśva, we need an iron box," said Śiva.

"It will banish evil spirits," said Viṣṇu.

"And it has to be solid," said Brahmā, "'cause she will struggle and fight."

"No problem," said Viśvakarman, "but it won't be cheap. Look at this babe. She's a real beauty. So young, so innocent, so damned powerful. This box needs experience and skill." He grinned and rubbed his hands.

There's a moment when you face Absolute Reality. It tends to present an invoice.

Very slowly, they nodded, and kept their faces bland.

Viśvakarman delighted. This was a one of a kind opportunity. When he returned from his forge, he carried an iron box. It was simply gorgeous. Auspicious mantras graced each side, and pictures of lions, blossoms and weapons, just perfect for a baby embodying the energy and beauty of the Universe. Here gleamed a dead buffalo, there rose nine sacred plants, and in the middle shone a pool of blood. The whole thing was rimmed with skulls.

"It will be her home. She'll love it," he said, "and so will you, provided you pay up."

The gods stared at the chest. Its power was evident. With a bit of luck, it would last as long as their sister needed.

With great caution, the gods lifted the girl and placed her in the iron chest. They closed the lid and breathed a sigh of relief. Her screams were muted. At last, they could listen to their thoughts again.

Tenderly, the gods placed the chest on a boat. In the evening, when the sun sank through the blood-red clouds, the flood rose. Boat and chest went floating across the sea. The screams of the baby faded away and soon, only the gulls could be heard.

The gods stood at the shore and watched her disappear into the horizon.

One day, holy Hemanta went to the beach to meditate. Hemanta was a simple guy. Unlike other saints, he did not do his meditations in the centre of the city, right next to the royal palace, the stock exchange and the opera, where people have fat pouches, and give a few cents to demonstrate how spiritual they are. That's where the cheats hang out, the con-artists who impress the vulgar and the guilty. Hemanta had seen it all and cursed it. He had a little hermitage, right in the middle of a lonely forest, where only ascetics, and quite a lot of them, bothered to live. In fact, the forest was crammed full of them. You couldn't walk a step without running into a crusty singing "holy, holy". For his peace of mind, Hemanta preferred the seaside. He loved the screeching gulls, the smell of rotting algae and the thunder of the breakers. Also, and attend closely, for this is a special sport of saints, he loved to collect pretty shells and pebbles. He laid them out in patterns, and was delighted when a passerby stopped in amazement, and picked up a few. He got the laugh, they got the Karman and everything was perfect.

The saint placed his black antelope skin on the ground, sat down, crossed his legs and set up the arm support. Very slowly, for this was a moment worth treasuring, he got out his rosary. Suspending his right arm on the support, he allowed the beads to stream through his hands. He had plenty of time, and before long, the motion of the beads, and his fingers, slowed down, his eyes almost closed and his breathing became inaudible.

One after another, the beads slipped. Just as slowly, mantras drifted across his mind. He relaxed into them. Their meaning faded away. Who cares about mantras? Who gives a damn for words? This was just about the seaside, and reality, and him. The gulls called and Hemanta smiled. Bliss was everywhere.

When he raised his eyelids, he saw a boat close to the shore. The vehicle had seen better days. The wood was sun-scorched and splintered; the colour had almost faded away. A miracle, that the thing was still afloat. When the breakers pushed the boat against the sand, he heard a voice. It was high pitched, angry and very much alive. Hemanta got up and staggered into the froth. He saw an iron box within the boat. Cautiously, he lifted the item. Maybe, he thought, it was a gift of the gods. Scripture says that a devotee of Śakti may receive anything. That's quite a perk. Hemanta carried the box up the beach and set it down on the wet sand. Behind him; not that he bothered to notice, the boat broke apart and was swallowed by the waves.

Very cautiously, the seer opened the box. Facing him was an excited little girl who screamed as if she wanted to make heaven fall in.

"My darling," said Saint Hemanta, "calm down. I'll get you out."

He reached into the iron box, but the baby fought him, and the rest of the world, until he got hold of her. Cautiously, he rested her against his shoulder. The baby calmed.

"You are home now," said Hemanta, "and I hope you don't pee on me."

"You will be called Durgā," he said, as this name means *the Inaccessible, the One Who Can't Be Touched*.

Hemanta carried the baby to his sagging hut. Each day, he walked to the main road, where he stopped people leading cows, and asked them for a little milk.

The girl drank as if she would never get enough.

"You are my little sponge", laughed Hemanta, "one day you will swallow the world!"He patted his child and smiled. "My little monster. How you are kicking! How you hunger for life!" Hemanta grinned at his daughter, "Will you ever be satisfied?"

In one day, she grew as much as a normal baby did in one month. Her hair sprouted like the wings of a crow, her teeth gleamed like pearls and the grasp of her fingers was like iron. Whatever the girl saw, fascinated her, and she wanted to have it. In a few weeks she learned to raise herself, to stand, and to walk wherever she liked. Hemanta was out of his head with pride. His daughter was a miracle! By the time she could run, and got into everybody's way, he trained her to read and write, explained scripture, taught grammar and etymology, enthused her to tell the difference between right and wrong, told fables, related histories and encouraged her to meditate. The girl learned everything. In fact, Hemanta merely had to mention something and little Durgā mastered the concept and applied it to life. Had she been a human child, he would have taught her how to pray and make offerings to the gods. But this child, Hemanta was painfully aware, was a goddess already. He hardly understood how anyone as simple as he could have earned the honour of raising her!

Durgā ran, screamed, romped, she tossed the furniture around (luckily, Hemanta owned very little, and that was solid or replaceable), made her father laugh and had fits of divine wrath when the ice cream supply failed. In those painful moments, sacred Hemanta went for long walks in the forest, to cultivate his sanity and to return late at night, when his little girl was sleeping peacefully.

"Spare my home! Oh goddess, be kind to us!" said Hemanta, all too often, "I need these shelves, these walls and very much that door!" he shook his head. "My little darling. You had your fun. The wood was really expensive!"

Soon enough, all ascetics, wandering denouncers, begging nuns, yogīnīs and total-deniers had realised that Hemanta's freshly discovered daughter was a deity. Day in and day out they pressed their brows into the dirt and tried to please the child with little offerings. Durgā laughed. She forgave any misdeed, no matter what, and without hesitation, as the very idea of sin was incomprehensible to her. In return, she received juicy fruit, fluffy animals (I wonder where the ascetics got them from) and any amount of over-sugared sweets. They made her go crazy.

Soon, the divine child turned into a voluptuous young woman. Puberty can be a nightmare and lead to savage side-effects. Teenagers are on the weirdest mixture of neurotransmitters that anyone could imagine. Seers, keen to retain their sanity (or chastity) refrained from visiting. As Neta comments, it saved them from masturbating to death. Hemanta didn't notice. No matter how much his daughter bulged (and she bulged into more dimensions than you or I could imagine), she was his happy little girl. The neighbours talked. They told the tale of Hemanta's daughter, who had become a formidable young woman.

As usual, Śiva was hanging around on the road. He loved to squat at dusty street corners, to watch the world revolving around him, to see things happen as they liked, not that he was supposed to interfere or improve anything, and to have peaceful, leisurely chats with crazy people, like beggars, poets, artists, tantrics, ascetics, travelling sorcerers, dancers, prostitutes, children, scientists, historians and lunatics. These people were close to his heart. Before long, he heard that Saint Hemanta was raising a veritable goddess, beautiful beyond description, mind-blowing in her learning, as bright as the mid-day sun and as wise as a scholar of scripture.

"Her lotus-brow gleams like the dawn, her mouth is shaped like a bimba blossom; she smells like the blossom of bakula and is lively and joyous as a kokila-bird." The traveller was perfectly informed.

"That's amazing," said Śiva. He offered his waterpipe. "Take a drag. And now, tell me, are you a poet or a lunatic?"

"I'm a pilgrim," said the man, "can't you see?"

He inhaled deeply. The water in the coconut shell bubbled. The pilgrim coughed. This was far stronger than he had imagined. "The goddess isn't simply beautiful. I ask you, you get beauty anywhere. It's strong in the teens, tones down in the twenties and becomes a memory by the age of thirty." He raised his eyebrows. "This girl, I tell you, is different. She isn't only beautiful. She is also sacred. And, so they say, she tends to be a little wild."

The waterpipe gurgled.

She's passionate, Śiva thought and his dhoti twitched.

"Her splendour is beyond description," said the traveller, "and that, which cannot be described, is exactly what makes us crave for more."

He collapsed. Śiva smiled. Great, he thought, this is my kind of girl.

When Śiva returned to Mount Kailāsa, he was jittery with mad emotions. All the way from the plains up the slopes, past mountain forests and heath, across snowfields and ice-encrusted rocks, he felt utterly alone. He faced himself and wondered. What kind of girl, he thought, would love a guy who hardly ever wore clothes? Or one who rubbed ashes all over himself? She might think that he was poor, helpless, a total failure! Why should she choose to inhabit the crest of a mountain that was just as high and jagged as her husband's mind? When he reached the summit, the stars were so close he might have touched them. The air was thin and icy. Sure, it was the highest mountain in the world. But what did he, crazy Śiva, have to offer? There was his little mud-hut, roofed with the husks of rice-straw. The sun shone in and lightened up the day. Life had been so simple, and, comparatively happy, up to now. The floor was made of pounded earth. He, personally, had danced it solid. The walls bulged, the door hung askance. To keep out blizzards, he had to slam it, and tie the damn thing shut. The only thing that held the contraption together was hope. A few beams, thick bamboo rods from the plains, a woven mat, and just enough space to allow his bull, Nandi (the *Joyous One*), to lay down for sleep. Interior decoration? Shelves leaning dangerously, a pot full of grains, another vessel for vegetables and a few smaller ones for spices. They filled themselves, and Śiva never wondered where the stuff came from. And some raw meat, fat and juicy, and ready for the fire. He owned a water pot and a pile of dung cakes for heating. In one corner, his trident leaned, a wonderfully dramatic item full of symbolic import, but quite useless, as there were no fishes to spear. Śiva had acquired it when, ages ago, he had met the Greek god Poseidon near the Indus River, and spent a night dicing. On a nail sticking from a wall, his hourglass-shaped drum hung. It could make hearts beat faster. Not that he needed it; his pulse was faster than a human heart could handle. Nearby, an array of bottles gleamed. Each of them had been full of rum; now they were, as he noticed, utterly empty.

This, he realised, was his life. He never needed anything else. And on the ground, he discovered, was everything he never really thought about. Śiva sighed. For good reason, he usually came home when it was dark. He lit a small fire, or an oil lamp, which is perfect when you want to ignore cobwebs, puddles and rubbish. Śiva looked at the floor, and the fresh, enthusiastic sunlight revealed wonder weapons, scripture (much of it too weird for human eyes), crumbs, leftovers, bones, tissues, socks and underwear. Things couldn't stay like this. His first idea was to blot out the sun. It would have helped a lot.

The Lord of Ascetics sat down and faced the tiny window. He took a few deep breaths. Groaning, he extended his arms (there were quite a lot of them at the moment) and opened his three eyes. He exhaled "Hā", which is great to release anything you might keep knotted up in your guts, and things became ecstatic, crazy and complicated. His hut bulged, grew and extended in all dimensions at once; it raised its roof, like a mighty dome, into the sky and shifted its boundaries to contain the universe. From Śiva's vision rose gigantic walls of polished marble, huge portals, halls, staircases, towers and balconies. The floors were smooth, inlaid with precious stones, and wonderfully cool during the summer months. The corridors extended, leading to any world or time. The windows were elegantly curved, the stairs reached across eternity. Śiva smiled. Around his palace he scattered mighty gardens, maintaining their own pleasant microclimate, with playful rivulets dancing beneath rounded bridges and converging in lakes that invited you to bathe in them. Śiva invented ornamental pavilions, their pillars crusty with rubies and emeralds, shady arcades, mysterious grottoes and romantic ruins, for peace and meditation. Between them, he made a hundred thousand multi-coloured roses blossom; their perfume would have made a human visitor collapse. On the walls, fat lizards baked in the sun; between the flowerbeds and drug plantations, butterflies danced, and birds, impossibly coloured, warbled with happiness. In ornamental pools and unlimited lakes, water lilies blossomed and lotus plants raised gleaming heads. The whole assortment of magickal haṁsa birds sported on the water: geese, ducks, swans and flamingos. Each of them was, individually considered, a representation of the spirit of pure consciousness and free breath that extends through all worlds and all dimensions. This is liberty, he thought, mine and theirs, they look silly, as they waddle along, and their chatter is funny. But damn it, so am I. He surrounded the gardens with a wall.

I invent my paradise! No matter how high we are, I'll have fertile meadows with tall grasses, where fat bovines graze in the heat. And I want fields of grains, of rice and paddy, I want sugarcane standing in the sun, and any amount of hemp. In nature, four metres is the limit; I'll double that and make it grow all through the year! Śiva scratched his locks. This was getting better all the time. Let's invent a bit of comfort, he thought. I want huge banyan trees with snakelike roots. They cast a pleasant shade. And I want diversity. With one exhalation (and a perfectly trained imagination) he created groves of banana, mango, guavas, figs, jackfruit, tall coconut palms and huge vakula trees, full of singing, chattering and screeching birds, plus shady bamboo groves, where you might rest all day unbothered. Privacy, he thought, is essential. His new domain would amaze visitors, and it would be irresistible to the girl of his dreams. But, honestly, a little seclusion is a must. And as Śiva is quite brilliant, provided he has a sober moment, he was aware of the things that make life worth living: hidden, shady corners where lovers could enjoy themselves on huge, comforting beds and padded swings. Again and again. Śiva knew what mattered. He thought in terms of eternities.

Before long, the crazy Lord of the Dance had transformed his desolate mountaintop into a paradisiacal miracle, sparkling in a thousand colours that made his brothers shake their many heads with amazement. Who would have thought that that the God of Transcendence could enjoy such trivia?

Picture 4: The Descent of Gaṅgā.

6. Gaṅgā

Mount Kailāsa was freshly renovated, wiped, polished, decorated and gleamed at all edges, where Śiva had scrubbed enthusiastically. It was a onetime effort, as he knew. She will love me, he thought, for what I am. That will be enough. Afterwards, housework won't be needed. When one room is littered, we'll create a few more. His palace, he knew, was sheer infinity.

Mountain paradise stood in painful contrast to the rest of the world. Down there, in the wide plain, things weren't perfect at all. In a moment of total madness, Brahmā had created mankind, and given everyone a station in life. It had seemed so easy, so simple, and almost inevitable. However, existence is tough and there are limits all over the place. We have to make allowances. Even the greatest artists can't get things right every time. Mankind, as Brahmā came to realise, was neither this nor that. It had amazing potential and a stunning failure rate. Some people were wonderful. Most were mediocre and some were nightmares incarnate. These, of course, bossed everybody around. Other creator gods might have eliminated humans, and invented updated human beings with common sense, ethics, and a friendly character. Plus four arms, three eyes and a dozen sets of wildly inventive genitals, just to keep them busy. But Brahmā liked those silly little creeps, provided they sang and danced, didn't get under his feet, stayed out of his hut and worshipped him.

People got the message. They settled in villages and towns, they built huts, just as shabby and derelict as that of Brahmā, they worried and fought, they copulated like mad, but they had no children. The same happened among the animals. They ate and excreted, just like human beings, but (this is a bonus point when you are a higher lifeform) they didn't whine or squabble.

Life had appeared, gone to a certain point and got stuck. Things neither moved nor developed. And while no offspring came forth, neither was there death. No coming, no going, just the same dreary day, recycled forever. Kāma, the ancient god of lust, love and desire, gave a deep sigh and went home. He leaned the bow of longing to the wall and tossed the five arrows of infatuation into a corner. In case you wish to know, each arrow is a divine power: the Fascinating, Exciting, Stunning, Feverous and Total-loss-of-sense. There was no need for them. "People are like cattle," Kāma said, "only less exciting. The regurgitate reality."

The world had begun with so much passion. By now, all emotions had faded. The dopamine level had sunk below recognition, the nucleus accumbens had shut shop 'cause of no customers and no-one seemed to care. Kāma shook his head, had a glass of warm milk and went to bed.

With furrowed brow, his eyes fixed to the ground, Brahmā, the Creator ambled along. The road was dusty, and the scenery dull. Each pebble seemed offensive. Once, it had been unique, meaningful and great. Now it was simply pointless. Grandfather did not care. Who cares about pebbles? Who cares about anything? It was his early morning routine, as walking aids digestion. Digestion, Viṣṇu lectured, was essential. Brahmā had his doubts. Bowel movements, and indeed the world had been fun, for a while. Now, they were just boring. Occasionally he stopped. In the distance, the Himalayas gleamed, a range of jagged peaks, all fresh and new and snow-clad, and he thought, well, I did a good job with them. But frankly, was it worth the effort? Or water. Once, it seemed so great. Take two highly combustible elements, like hydrogen and oxygen. You get a mixture that isn't explosive at all. And it behaves unlike all other fluids. Water had been a miracle. You get it started and it goes around, through every landscape, through every being, through all ages. That's reincarnation. But honestly, reincarnation is stupid and it ain't worth the effort.

He stuck a betel leaf roll into his mouth and began to chew. The sixty-four spices didn't taste like anything. It would be great to invent something new. But damn it, what would be the use? Everything was there already. And frankly, he hadn't had a good idea in ages. Maybe tomorrow, he thought, tomorrow I will have an inspiration. Or the day after. He cursed.

Bells tingled and Brahmā raised his head. Mohinī (*Enchanting, Spell-Binding, Fascinating*), the Heavenly Dancer approached. Brahmā had heard about her. Everyone had. Some minor gods and nature spirits salivated at the mere mention of her name. They screeched and squirmed and hit their heads against palm trees, to stop the fire in their underwear. For Mohinī was more than divine, she was in a class all of her own. Everyone knew her as the great Celestial Prostitute. Mohinī wore hardly anything, and was adorned with gold and silver and tingling bells. Her tiny bra strained to hide her breasts, and if you looked closely you could see that it was ornamented with embroidery, pearls, and sacred jewels, showing the major events of history, all influential rulers and the important deities. They were under her spell. That, however, was nothing compared to her slip. Mohinī was a high goddess and she knew it. Nevertheless, she lowered her eyes and smiled. That smile could have made the moon fall from the sky. "Brahmā!" she cooed like a kokil bird in honey, "You look great today! I'm so glad to meet you. Did you create anything new?"

Brahmā stopped in his tracks "How dare you speak to me?"

"Oh darling Granddaddy," Mohinī pouted, and the sun began to tremble, "don't be rude. You are a high god, and the creator of everything." She winked. "Let me show you something beautiful."

"You are a whore," he exclaimed, as his belly knotted, "a rotten, evil creature! Your presence means pollution." He sneered. "Why do you approach me? I am far above your class."

"True lovers know no class. There is just desire, and laughter, and recognition!"

"Go away! Desire is a lie!"

"Desire moves the world!"

"I hate this dipshit universe!"

The Lord of Creation was in a rage. "The world is finished! It's worthless! Everything is done!

I don't desire you! I don't desire anything!" His four heads shone crimson. "You decorate your body with tinsel and expose your flesh. The body is a thing of vileness and disgust. The self is not the body, and the world is worthless!"

"Grandfather", said Mohinī. She didn't look that charming any more. "You hate yourself. Your balls must be as big as watermelons."

Brahmā barely restrained himself from hitting her.

"I am a high god. It is my duty to instruct you. Listen to the regulations of the *Śāstra*. There are only three female virtues: chastity, obedience and submission. Lust and sex are aberrations of the mind. They should be restricted to occasions where they cannot be avoided. For procreation, according to the purity rites and the regulations of the sages, and only on the days declared by scripture. They serve to produce children."

"Where are those children?" asked Mohinī, "Do you have any? Why isn't there anything new?"

"Creation is over. I did it and it's done."

The Lord of Creation glared at her. "Mohinī", he declared, "you are a slut; you have no useful function in the world. Sex without marriage is for animals. Those, who enjoy it, are cursed and bound for hell." Brahmā raised his hands. "You should fast, purge your rotten, sinful flesh and find release in starvation."

The Lord of Creation wiped his brow. He had lost his temper. That was pretty bad for a high deity. But it wasn't his fault. The bitch deserved it.

Mohinī trembled. "I'm a high goddess and that's my Karman!" she spat.

"Some" she said, trying to keep her voice steady, "are born to be Brahmā and some are born to be heavenly prostitutes. You, the god of creation, were born from the lotus sprouting from Viṣṇu's navel. It's not much, but it isn't little either. Your brothers laugh about you. Whenever you try to create something big, you have to ask them for permission. Sure, long ago, you did your job. Now you are obsolete. You haven't come up with a fresh idea for ages."

She shook her head and happy chimes tinkled. "My dear little grandfather, you ain't so special. There's a Brahmā in every world. Most of them have better manners. You are redundant! Soon, someone else will take over."

"I am unique! Without my contribution, the world would stop!"

"Do something, you dumb squirt!" Mohinī snarled. "What do you think I was sent here for?"

She pointed at him. "Look at yourself! Once, you had five heads. As you boasted so much, Śiva chopped one off! Did you learn anything? You remain proud and vainglorious! Why do you stare at me like an imbecile! Do you fancy my breasts? Here, come on, touch them! They will scorch your hands! In other worlds, there are Brahmās who have ten or a hundred heads, and far more sense. Baby, I tell you, I get around. I do my thing in any universe. And this world, which you find so enchanting, is just a backwater, compared to the worlds that celebrate me!"

"I am who I am. The best there is. That's Karman. And Karman is based on merit." Brahmā screeched, "You are filthy! That's why you were born as a woman!"

Mohinī laughed "You arrogant twat! Women are the foundation of life and the seed of the world. Slight me, and you slight nature. Those who curse lust, curse themselves!"

"Lust is the seed of evil. In the entire world," foamed Brahmā, "there is no woman who defiles her race as much as a woman who yearns for fornication. You are the only one!"

"What do you know about that, you tired old man?"

The heavens trembled; sun and moon veiled their faces. Mountains shuddered, rivers left their beds, lightning struck, fishes sank into the deep and birds dropped from the sky.

The gods and sages appeared.

Brahmā saw them coming. He squeaked. "Hello!" and his voice gave in.

"Enough." Viṣṇu commanded. "Whatever it is, stop it. You upset the world."

"Did we miss anything?"Śiva grinned.

The seers were excited. "Did you do the weird stuff?"

"Nothing happened!" said Brahma. "You can go away."

"Why are you quarrelling? What's going on between you?" The gods seemed concerned.

So were the seers. "Did you fail to get it up?"

"Women are stupid by nature. She exhausted herself with her dancing; now she is weak and asks me for advice. Leave me alone with my daughter."

The gods laughed.

Mohinī didn't. Her eyes burned like a firestorm.

"Brahmā! How dare you insult me?" She raised her hands. "I will teach you to fear the curse of a whore! As you damn lust, your cult will disappear. Your devotees will leave you and join other faiths! Your talk is full of lies, for you, like everyone, are embedded in a net of desire!"

Mohinī faced the gods. "That's it. You need a new Lord of Creation. I used this one up."

The path was steep. Viṣṇu and Śiva had been climbing for ages. Viṣṇu lead; he had a busy schedule and worried about being late. Śiva came after him, groaning. "We should have flown," he muttered, "that's how gods do it."

"Wrong," said Viṣṇu, "We must show devotion. Great Rituals have to hurt."

They do, Śiva thought, every bit of them. Getting up in the morning, of all times. With a hangover. Climbing this mountain on bare feet. They were pretty raw by now.

"We will save the universe," said Viṣṇu. "It's a crucial task demanding major sacrifices and I would appreciate a positive outlook, achievement orientation and less grumbling."

"I would appreciate my bed," said Śiva, "and the girl of my dreams."

"Nonsense." said Viṣṇu, "take a look at yourself. You need a haircut and some attitude. Girls don't fall for guys who think that ashes are smart."

"Screw your peacock feathers," said Śiva, "you may fancy trash, but my future wife likes me honest and nude."

They stumbled along. It wasn't easy. Saving the world rarely is.

Brahmā should have been with them. He had caused this mess, and should have made up for it. But grandfather Brahmā, the Lord of Creation, crouched in his hut and refused to come out. "Go away!" he whined, "you know I'm worthless. I can't do anything."

"You can, if you want. Fresh air will do you good."

"It's not fresh," complained Brahmā, "it's the same old stuff as ever."

"That's not a healthy mindset." Viṣṇu shook his head, "You have to face reality. Have a bath, think positive, organise your time-table, and stop being such a nuisance."

"Or drop dead," said Śiva.

Well, that was ages ago. The gods had left their brother in his gloom. The plan was simple. They needed the biggest mountain in the world, and they had to ascent on foot.

By sunset, the horizon flamed like the blossoms of a mango tree. Then night fell, beautiful, gorgeous and incomparably new. High up on the mountain, the air was fresh and clear. The gods looked out into the sky, and saw a haze of stars sparkling across the multiverse.

"It's so amazing," said Viṣṇu, "imagine getting some order into that. You could make the worlds work twice as fast."

"Imagine enjoying it as it is," said Śiva, "and you could stop worrying about efficiency."

He reached for his water pipe. It was a coconut shell with two pieces of bamboo. He stuffed the chillum. "And imagine we call it a day and go home. I've got better things to do."

"Better than saving the universe?"

"If the universe is as great as they say, it can look after itself. And so can I, if you leave me alone."

He gazed into space. The flow of stars was continuous. It connected worlds upon worlds in a garland of glamour.

The pipe bubbled. "Hey," said Śiva, and coughed. "see those twinkly bits. I like them. Purple and green. They get anywhere. Why can't we have a few?"

Viṣṇu frowned. Śiva, in his deluded way, seemed to be right. "It looks like a river of stars."

Śiva laughed. "O man," he said, "this is more than lights. It's love and change." He shook his head. "And it's way too heavy."

His brother stared. Maybe this was it. Śiva was crazy, but he sure had intuitions. Viṣṇu raised himself and lifted his arms in a majestic gesture.

Śiva giggled. "You look like a toddler who wants to be picked up"

"Stand up, idiot!" Viṣṇu insisted. "This is serious."

"You are. I'm not."

Viṣṇu raised his voice.

"Hail to thee, thou River of the Stars, Stream of Transformation, Flow of all Realities, Current of Change, Torrent of Life and Death! Greatest Power in the Universe! We praise thee, Essence of Being and Transformation. And my silly brother over there, who has trouble getting up, is also praising thee!"

"Is he?" asked Śiva, "I wonder why."

"He is!" Viṣṇu insisted."That's because he knows his duty and is a responsible senior citizen of the divine world."

"What a dumb twit." Śiva reached for his satchel. "Let me have another pipe. I can't make sense of what you say."

"Celestial Deity!" called Viṣṇu, "the earth is hungry for your blessings! This tiny planet, drifting aimlessly through space, appeals for your help. Come to us, River of Stars. Give us your blessing! Touch the peaks and flow across the plains. You are fertility! You are transformation! You are the wheel of life. Grant prosperity to us. We ask you, we implore you, to make things change!"

"Yea." said Śiva. His pipe gurgled. "I agree. Whatever. Who cares. Let's call it a night."

Viṣṇu had done his best. Now he could only wait. Śiva had also done his best. Indeed, he had done far more than that. If only he knew, he would have run away. But what was coming from the sky was more than a pair of gods could handle.

The goddess had listened. Planet Earth. It's tiny, she thought. At the edge of nothing. A ball of minerals, water, air and make-believe. No wonder everyone overlooks it. But it is full of the most amazing things. She turned her full attention on the planet. And she began to swell and surge and flow.

Viṣṇu heard the sound; he looked up and the sky was full of light. He closed his eyes. It was the last thing he could recall. Śiva also looked up. Wow, he thought. This stuff is hot. I wonder where I can get more of it?

The glare came down like a waterfall. It scorched and gleamed and embraced the mountaintop. Within the shimmer stood the Lady of the Stream of Life, on a crocodile-dragon-dolphin (cryptozoologists call it a makara). Her third eye was wide open, her head almost shaved, except for the highest point of her skull, where a thick sprout of hair erupted like a geyser, black, gleaming, tangled, and cascading to the ground. Viṣṇu stood trembling and Śiva cleared his throat. "Honestly," he giggled, "I had expected someone more complicated."

"I am Gaṅgā" said the goddess, "I am the Current of Change. My waters are pure like milk, clear like crystals; my body pulses in huge waves. One bath in my river is like a visit to Vaikuṇṭha heaven. Just as fire devours wood, I destroy sins. My fluids fertilise the fruits of good deeds, of virtue and compassion, and bring the consequences of each evil deed. Those who die at my shore are released from their misdeeds. I bring changes, life, death, rebirth and final liberation!"

"We greet and honour you", called Viṣṇu, "noble lady, great goddess, feel welcome and grant your blessings to this world!"

Heaven tore apart and the earth shook. Then the torrent came down. Mountains were smashed to pieces; plains disappeared under water, continents were ripped apart. Viṣṇu almost fell over. This was more than he had expected! Śiva wasn't into falling. That's because he was on the ground already.

The cosmic waters hit his head. The goddess, in all her joy and fury, surged through his tangled locks. The fluids slowed; they divided, turned into brooks and rivulets, tore down chutes, and thundered as waterfalls. They crashed against cliffs, uprooted trees, crushed boulders, stripped the hillsides of their vegetation and fell in glittering cascades. Finally, they met and slowed, turned into pools and lakes, into rivulets and rivers, and united as a stream. The goddess laughed and wept with relief as she relaxed and streamed into the wide and fertile plain.

Viṣṇu nodded. This was almost perfect. With a bit of discipline and better organisation (he had made some notes already), everything would be fine. The timing was essential. The flood should be precise and punctual.

Śiva could have smiled, but didn't. The goddess kept thundering over his head.

Viṣṇu, the Maintainer, straightened his robes, adjusted his crown and clapped his hands. That's how you get the attention of Indian gods should you lack a bell or a plate gong.

"Wake up, Brahmā! The Goddess of Change has come to earth! Hear me! And stop sulking! Our planet has joined the stream of coming, going and returning."

Brahmā didn't react. He squatted in a corner of his hut and chewed his fingernails. That's what creative people do when everything is far too late.

"Brahmā!" called Viṣṇu. "Come out! You should be ashamed!"

"I can't hear you," said Brahmā, "go away. I'm happy."

"Brahmā! Don't make me cross with you!"

"I don't care. You don't need me. Run your stupid universe any way you like."

"I want you here now!"

"Leave me alone. Let me tell you: everything's an illusion!"

"Brahmā! Stop it! I made you the Creator and now I'm telling you to have a bath!"

Brahmā bared his teeth. What rubbish, he thought. One day soon I'll drop everything.

He would leave his dumb brothers to their stupid schemes and walk and walk and walk away. That would teach them. Where's the creator? They would say. For all he cared, the universe could fall to pieces.

Viṣṇu's voice got louder.

Grandfather grabbed a towel, put on his flip-flops, threw the door open and, ignoring his two damn-stupid brothers, walked down to the river. The water looked cold. Brahmā cursed. Ritual purity, he thought, is overvalued. And so is water. Who needs it?

He knew his brothers were watching, and that he was making a fool of himself. As if he needed purification!

Mohinī is a good-for-nothing bitch! Why don't they bathe her?

He didn't get much further. Goddess Gaṅgā rose; she seized him, sank him, and pulled him into the deep. Brahmā struggled and fought and swallowed water. He was submerged and scraped across the river bed. Again.

Hours later, the Lord of Creation crawled out of the waves. He staggered up the slope, spitting and sneezing, and his knees gave in. His face fell into the sand, his breath laboured, and he retched. Aching all over, he raised himself. He hated everything. Some things needed improvement. The world needs softer sand, he thought, and padded riverbeds. It needs soundproof houses and brothers that leave you alone. It needs knees that don't give in and bigger bathing towels. Water, he decided, is too wet. And it isn't solid enough. He could have drowned! How about bladders, he thought. You could blow up a cowhide and float on it. "Let me fix a few things..." he mumbled.

Viṣṇu and Śiva watched. Nearby, leaning against a willow, stood Kāma, the God of Desire. He raised his bow and aligned his five arrows.

"Boy," said Kāma, "you'll be horny!" and shot.

Gaṅgā keeps streaming though Śiva's locks. She gurgles, bubbles, foams and thunders across his head. That's how she became Śiva's first wife. And she is really special.

Twice a year, Gaṅgā swells and makes him crazy.

When winter ends and the glaciers and snowfields of the Himalayas melt in the sunshine, the goddess wakes. Laughing wildly, she surges through ravines and rushes down stony slopes. She races along, young, happy, reckless; she dances as a thousand waterfalls, gleaming in the light, fills turquoise lakes, carries mud and nourishment and grants the world her blessing.

Soon, spring begins and the meadows are ablaze with flowers. In May, the air turns suffocating hot. When summer advances, and rain is just a memory, the fertile topsoil turns into a hardened crust. For months on end, the sunlight bites and hurts. People lower their heads and the merciless blue heavens make their eyes water. Plants shrivel, wither and die. The days go on endlessly. When summer has become an ordeal, the winds change their directions. Above the sea, wet air turns into clouds. Like a herd of elephants, they thunder inland, and cross the subcontinent until they meet the Snow Mountains and burst. Gaṅgā comes down in her passion. She turns into a tantric goddess, into Nityaklinnā, *She-Who-is-Always-Wet*. The goddess thunders down the mountainsides. Roaring in ecstasy she surges across pastures and hurls herself down slopes, dislodging trees and rope bridges, rousing animals to panic flight and clothes herself in muddy brown. Her gifts cannot be denied: she carries devastation and fertility, the seeds of life, of death and liberation. When she reaches the lowlands, her fury abates. Her stream, swollen from a thousand brooks and rivulets, begins its leisurely journey across the plains. The river rises, the flood widens, devouring the mud banks at the shore, snatching buildings and turning farmlands into lakes. People laugh and celebrate; they sing and revel in the cool air. In her happiness, Gaṅgā extends across the world. Finally, she journeys through the mangrove swamps and salt marshes of the Sundarbans and meets the open sea. The goddess gives a sigh of relief. She relaxes, loses the configurations of shape, force, and identity, and finds her freedom in the cosmic ocean. Light sparkles on her waves and gulls glide on the breeze. Autumn follows and it is juicy, happy, and green.

Picture 5. Durgā as Mahiṣamardinī (the Slayer of the Buffalo Demon of Arrogance), based loosely on a wooden carving.

7. Courtship

Whether Śiva liked it or not, he had found a wife. Night and day she cascaded down his head. She numbed him, paralysed his thoughts and made him reel. His face dripped, his hands shook and lighting a pipe became a major effort. And she brought change, incessant, mindless change. When the whole thing became too much for him, Śiva consumed all the drugs he could lay his hands on and complained they didn't work.

His marriage was ecstatic, miraculous and a total failure. Sure, by divine standards, he tried hard. When the goddess arrived, and life seemed new and hopeful, he created the river dolphin to make her happy. "You'll be the friend of the fishers and the bearer of good tidings" he told the grey swimmer. "Go and jump with joy." The dolphin gave him a toothy grin and slid into the deep.

Śiva leaned back and felt happy. His happiness didn't last.

It could have been so good. He had expected hot nights and dreamy days in large, well-padded beds, on ornamental swings and in turquoise swimming pools. They never happened. To be sure, Gaṅgā moved into his palace. She occupied chambers, halls and an entire series of bathrooms. But she was never home. The goddess stowed her things away, glared at the mountain scenery and departed to her riverbed.

From the peak of Kailāsa, far in the bluish haze, he could see her sparkle in the distance. Marriage, he thought. What is it good for? He shook his head. It must be one of those Viṣṇu things.

"Whatever you do," he muttered, "I'll do my thing. I'm a major god and have important tasks." He thought long and hard and invented several. On very rare occasions, when he was up at sunrise, he went to visit his cows. They were happy, munching away at the tall, tough grasses. Śiva gazed into their dark, understanding eyes, listened to their thundering digestion, smelled their farts and felt useless. Or, when he was seized by a sudden attack of motivation, he grabbed his plough and tried to make a furrow. It wasn't long, it wasn't deep and he didn't know what it was good for. He sat down in the shade of a tree and let the world go on without him. Slowly, his eyelids sank. It's great to let go, he thought. I'm best at relaxing. That's my contribution to the universe. Breathing softly, he loosened his face muscles, eased his neck, and allowed the tension to seep into the ground. His hands settled in his lap. Śiva withdrew from his cattle and his fields, from the tree and its shade, from the periphery of his body. Exhaling softly, he sank into himself, fell inwards, into the vast empty core of himself, and floated deeper and deeper into formless consciousness. His thoughts slowed, his breath became faint. Ideas passed by, like shoals of tiny fish; they travelled to the periphery of the body, and disappeared. Śiva smiled. It's easy, he thought, everything is, and that mantra, word by word, syllable by syllable, letter by letter, took ages to develop, and before it ended, he had forgotten himself.

But when he came back, once in a century, the world was far too bright and noisy.

Squinting, his hands trembling, he reached for his pouch. For those of you who like to know (I have no idea why), the little leather sack contained an inexhaustible supply of hashish, opium, fungi, long pepper, black pepper, betel nut, betel leaves, Withania, ginger, nutmeg, madhūka blossoms, Indian nightshade, henbane, thorn-apple seeds, galangal, water lily blossoms, rhododendron, sweet oleander, coriander, cardamom, snakeweed, turmeric, acacia bark, sweet sedge, myrrh, asafoetida, juniper, shrubby horsetail, Indian poke, scorpion juice pellets, dried centipedes, toad skins and, if none of them helped, limes, chilli and bitter oranges. Śiva treasured the lot. Indeed, he had created most of them. Like all higher plants, each of his favourites could produce between a hundred and a thousand toxic substances, and combine them in endless ways. That's because plants are fighters. They fought him, and he loved them for it. Psychedelic, aphrodisiacal, deeply symbolic, tasty, beautiful, magical, medical, noxious, or lethal; go ahead, shake me, knock me, clear my sinuses, flush my bowels, make my hair stand on end, smash my skull and murder me; the God of Yoga smiled and consumed another handful.

Reckless, he thought. And irresponsible. That's me. And a terrible example for the ten-thousand worlds. That's what Viṣṇu would say. Śiva giggled. His brother was addicted to his own drugs. You only had to listen how he praised the class-system.

Śiva as a married man, abandoned by his cosmic wife, fled into the mountains, danced on crags and pinnacles, and spaced off into oblivion. And when the meditations became dull and the drugs failed to work, 'cause habituation is as merciless as gravitation, he drank. Rice wine, palm wine, fermented blossoms, grain-beer and sugarcane rum, the stronger the better.

Each night, he tried to get smashed. By daybreak, he vomited gall, ate headache tablets, and vowed to remain sober for the rest of his life. He sauntered across the dusty plain, lurked at waysides and cremation grounds until his head cleared up, had laughing fits in temples, drummed with beggar-musicians, worshipped the prostitutes in their bordellos and refused to come home, or to his senses, forever.

One fresh and cheerful spring morning, as Śiva was trying to sober up by banging his head against a wall, he remembered the beautiful adopted daughter of Saint Hemanta. It had all started with her! Her wishful fantasy had made him build a palace of delight!

Aching all over, he staggered to a mountain spring. The brilliant morning sparkle on the snowfields made tears run down his cheeks. The spring looked at him like a hungry beast. The water was almost frozen and, in its own way, wonderfully and terribly true. "And now for reality!" he muttered, clenched his teeth and immersed his head.

"Everything is the epitome of everything else," Saint Abhinavagupta had told him. Well, you can't understand seers, let alone trust them. If you want to understand reality, try ice-water. Or get sober any way you like. It isn't the epitome of anything.

After his bath, he dried himself, and rubbed himself with ashes. He took a piece of string and tied his hair into a disorderly tangle. Not good enough, yet. For a man of the world, a few extras were needed. I want a cool head. Something white will do the job. He stuck a lunar crescent and a thorn-apple blossom into the mess. That's it, he thought, she'll be stunned. Now for my erotic appeal. Watching his reflection in a puddle, he applied eyeliner. I look smashing, he thought, she'll be out of her head and we'll go straight to bed. A sudden thought struck him. "Do I need clothes?"

Attire, as everybody agrees, is either wonderful or trouble. In old rural Bengal, men who did not belong to the urban upper classes traditionally wore two items. The dhoti is a length of white cloth, approximately four meters by one, which is wrapped around the hips. The other piece, the gāmchhā, is three ells in length and one and a half ells across. After your morning bath it functions as a towel. As you go about your business, you may wear it across your shoulders, or around your neck, or wrap your head with it, if you want to look fashionable. Śiva did not. He was proud of his hair, no matter what it was up to. A dhoti would do. It would make him appear sophisticated. I'll look like an achiever, he thought, and wrapped a tattered piece of tiger hide around his hips.

"Class matters." That's what Viṣṇu always said. "By dressing well, you honour other people." That's why he walks around in silk, with golden ornaments and peacock feathers. His sacred thread is adorned with diamonds. As if he needs one! Most men of the upper three classes underwent the ritual of the 'second birth' and acquired the right to wear a loop, a sacred thread, across the body from neck to flank. Śiva grabbed a fat cobra, told the reptile to behave, and knotted the ends together. The rest of his outfit was easy. Drum, trident, meditation rosary (bone beads are lucky!), armrest, water vessel, drug pouch, coconut hookah, spittoon. And plenty of fresh blossoms.

It hardly took an instant to reach the dusty, sun-baked plains. A small, secluded forest, he sensed, near the horizon, seemed to throb with energy. The place felt dangerous. That would be her.

He arrived at the clump of trees. It was a late, hazy afternoon, the sun shone in a golden hue, and the atmosphere was uniquely spiritual. The air buzzed with mantras, the sky was bluer than blue, and a cooling breeze drifted through trees whose fruit-laden branches touched the ground. Between them nested birds, sparkling like jewels, reciting the *Tripurā Rahasya*.

"The true self is Pure Consciousness devoid of objects! Consciousness is the object of its own awareness. I am consciousness, I am the entire universe. Oh you worldly people, cast off the shackles of delusion by focusing on consciousness alone!"

Nearby sat wise monkeys and took notes. A brook danced through the growth. In the shade of vast trees rose huts made of bamboo, mud and reeds, each of them inhabited by a hermit, devoting her- or himself to the well-being of the universe. The huts were surrounded by tiny gardens, full of shiny vegetables, and nearby were small rectangular pools, where recluses, or at least some of them, could have a morning and an evening bath. It must be heavenly bliss to live in solitude, Śiva thought, and that's why there are so many.

The Lord of the Dance opened his third eye and stared through the vegetation. Right, he thought, that's the hut. No better or worse than the others, but, whew, the aura is orange and red. It practically burns!

Śiva closed his third eye and shook his head. This girl is something different, he thought. Totally divine. One hell of a temperament. Cautiously, he stepped closer. I wonder what she's like. I've heard so much. Maybe it isn't true. Well, it can't be completely true, he thought, but it would be nice to know what to expect. She is a great goddess. It doesn't say anything about her looks. Maybe she has jutting fangs, a hump, eight bloody eyes and her face is full of bristles. Śiva exhaled. For an instant, time seemed to stop. It's just fate, he thought, fate is easy, even babies can handle it, and bit his lip. Would she like him? Would they get along? How do you say 'Hello, I'm your future' to a goddess?

"When she screams, trees fall over", a mendicant had told him, long ago. "Her glance can make an elephant faint." The guy had a dirty laugh. So had Śiva, then, but now it didn't seem funny at all. The Lord of Transcendence twirled his twisted locks.

The aura was sheer power. What, if she is stronger than me?

Durgā sat in the hut and felt bored. She had been raised as a good girl and she tried to be one, no matter how much it hurt. Just like Hemanta she meditated every day. She knew the essential spiritual exercises, the gestures, the sacred verses, and the important offerings. It took all of her patience to remain humble and devout when, in her core, she felt vibrantly beautiful, gorgeous and stunningly divine. With admirable patience she had studied the *Vedas*, the *Classical Upaniṣads* and the *Forest Books*. Many hymns were truly beautiful. Sadly, she wasn't mentioned in any of them. Other items seemed odd, impractical, or crazy. A few passages were totally revolting. But Durgā, like a good girl, had kept her temper. She had improved the lines with her strong handwriting or simply torn offensive pages out. Sure enough, Hemanta noticed, but it was not his habit to say anything. And she had gone for walks, day in and day out, in the wonderful enchanted forest. Before long, she knew every tree personally. She knew which plant would blossom in each season, and did her best to encourage it. She pulled on branches to make them grow faster and kicked the trees to toughen their roots. And she had come to know each hermit, ascetic nun and dropout. They were her family. Durgā knew the interior of every shabby hut and what each crusty had for dinner. As a little girl, she had slept in their arms and puked on their shoulders. No-one, she acknowledged, could have as many wonderful parents as she had. She greeted them, they bowed and she received their worship.

One day, a lion cub strayed into the forest. It was cute and fluffy and Durgā took it home. Her adopted father was surprised. Luckily, he was a saint, and used to surprises. He did not take offence when the little darling chewed his sandals, provided he got his feet out of them fast enough.

Durgā grew and her lion grew more. Eventually, both reached maturity and the lion barely fitted through the door. Grown up, the goddess felt restless, impatient and difficult. It worried her. Yes, she was tall and well built. Almost everyone would have called her beautiful. Hemanta tried to ignore the change. He smiled blissfully, evaded quarrels and went for long walks. Durgā talked with her lion. The furry beast watched her with soulful eyes, it never said a thing, nor was it supposed to. Durgā had listened to the stories the ascetics told, most of them ending with a sticky moral. They made her nervous. What was her place in the world? Would she go for walks forever? Should she shave her hair and become a renouncer? What was there to renounce? Something was missing in her life. She was sure the ascetics didn't tell her everything. When asked, they blushed and hurried away. The missing bit would have a name. It didn't appear in scripture, and it made her itch all over.

This fine sunny day, Durgā looked out of the window. Something unusual was going on. From a nearby thicket, clouds of smoke were rising. They were accompanied by a bubbling sound and coughs. Someone is hiding, she thought, it can't be a hermit, 'cause they have nothing to hide. She opened her third eye and stopped thinking. A fierce aura radiated from the shadows. It has to be a god! Durgā stepped back. Maybe he hadn't seen her. Moving soundlessly, she opened her iron box and got out the essentials. She adorned herself with jewels, blackened her eyelids, put rings on fingers and toes, stuck a diamond tiara into her hair and, just to be sure, took off all superfluous clothing. Cautiously, she peered through the door. The shrubs were cloaked in a haze. She lifted a hand; her lion rose and stretched.

"Over there, baby" she whispered, "get him!"

Like a sleek ochre nemesis, her lion slid through the door. Pressing itself to the ground, it sneaked through vegetables and shrubs. In front of the thicket, it seemed to freeze. The gargling sounded and another cloud rose. The lion bared its fangs and pounced.

Durgā grinned. Beasts like a bit of fun. Let's see who is in shock now.

The thicket remained calm. Then she heard her lion cough. Durgā ran through the door and into the garden. She parted branches and blossoms and stared into a mist.

In the clouds sat an incredibly good-looking god who gazed at her with dreamy, half-closed eyes. With one hand, he stroked the lion, who stretched on the ground, belly exposed, and purred. In his other hand he held something that smoked.

"Would you like a drag?"

"Yes," said Durgā, feeling terribly brave, "yes, I will."

It took a few days to agree about the marriage. If you want to get the picture, imagine frantic discussions, conducted by silly hermits, virtuous monkeys and birds with university degrees. The lion had the last word, and everyone was happy. Is this for real? I see you shake your head. So do I. For an Indian marriage, a couple of days is incredibly fast.

However, as Hemanta observed, before he retired to a corner and went to sleep, there was hardly anything to plan. When gods marry, matchmakers are not required. Astrologers can safely stay at home. No one needs to settle a dowry, as every god owns everything. It takes a monkey to mention social class. Durgā's lion growled, and that settled it.

When he wasn't asleep, or mysteriously absent, Hemanta was beside himself to make his son-in-law feel at home. Agreed, the young man was a little strange. He walked almost nude, but nowadays, as Hemanta was careful not to notice, so did Durgā. The seer knew he was facing a high god. He tried to discuss scripture and religious ordinances, but when he recommended traditional virtue, abstinence and painful self-mortification; his visitor disappeared into a cloud of smoke and refused to come out. Hemanta watched him through the haze and wondered why he coughed and spat so much. The saint scratched his bushy beard. He did not ask the groom which deities he worshipped. The question was superfluous. Day in and day out, Śiva stared into Durgā's eyes, and when she turned, his gaze dropped elsewhere.

The groom had moved into the small hut that Hemanta and Durgā shared. He sat on the seat of honour, a bleached pillow made of fibres and cotton, and fidgeted. All through the day, his pipe bubbled. Occasionally, he grinned, and it seemed as if the moon would rise in milky happiness, when he offered his pipe, seeds, berries and fungi to his fiancée. Durgā blushed and tried everything. They made her stagger and giggle in a most unladylike sort of way. Hemanta coughed and the lion had tears in its eyes. Around him, hermits argued, birds screeched and monkeys tried to mediate. Śiva smiled, exhaled and his eyelids drooped. He focussed on his breath, and felt his belly move, while the world sorted itself out. Inhalation and exhalation, soft, inaudible, let it all out, and everything is fine.

Śiva knew when he wasn't needed. It's a wise god, he realised, who refrains from meddling. The less he did, the wiser he became. But people complicate everything. They've got opinions, they make rules and then they break them. Hey, folks, Śiva thought, this is all about love and lust and millions of years in bed! He marvelled at the assembly. These loners, he thought, are shrivelled long before their time. They hide behind their wrinkles! And now they lecture me!

Indeed they did. There were so many rules and regulations. Indian scripture is immense, sages disagreed with each other and anything, and Śiva, who had missed most of the Vedic period by hiding in the forest, exploring weird plants and talking to trees, was keen to ignore it. Had he been a warrior, he could have done the easy thing, and carried his future wife away. That's an honourable sort of marriage in the warrior class, provided one doesn't mind retaliation. But Śiva is a high deity (in more senses than one), worshipped, feared and occasionally loved by a few daring loonies since the dawn of time. Given such a formidable age, he was supposed to respect customs. That's what the literati and the monkeys said.

"I do," Śiva smiled and reached for his pouch, "these are my customs. You wouldn't like them. My habits would kill most people in a few days."

"Indeed", said Hemanta, and shuddered. "That's why I abstain."

"Have it your way," said Śiva, and smiled. "I like you for being high on sobriety."

"Some rules must be observed," the seers declared.

"Fine," said Śiva, "I'll tell you when I come upon them."

"Young man," the ascetics insisted, "even gods have to follow Dharma."

"I'd rather not," said Śiva, "last time I saw him, he went from rot to health in three seconds, and ran away into the hills." He laughed. "I wonder why he screamed."

"Let me apologise," said holy Hemanta, "but in this world, you are a god, but we, the seers, make the rules."

"Make them well," said Śiva and knocked the ashes out of his chillum, "or I won't listen."

"They are easy," Hemanta said. "Custom says that the bride has to travel to the house of the groom."

"And that's all?"

"Under the circumstances, it is."

"No extra regulations?"

"Certainly not. The goddess would get angry."

"I'm sure she would." Śiva packed his pipe away. "I like your proposal. Imagine I left early. Like now. Would she follow me?"

"As sure as the sun is hostile and the moon is friendly, "replied Hemanta, "as milk is sacred and cow dung brings blessings. She will come to you and your marriage will be auspicious."

"I can live with that," said Śiva, "and I'll leave you now. Cheer up! But tell her to hurry."

He clapped his hands and disappeared.

No matter what you do, the essential part is preparation. The Lord of Ascetics came home and realised that everything was wrong. Mount Kailāsa could do with more buildings, a new sky and plenty of fresh paint. The snowfields, he was sure, were pretty much all right. Snow is wonderful, he thought, you can depend on it. The same went for the walls and gates. But he would have to distance the main halls from the apartments occupied by the usually absent Gaṅgā. He needed more bathrooms and beds and, as far as he could judge, a little space for clothes. That'll be easy, he thought, just like me, she likes to be nude. But we need some order. Maybe he should do a little housework. With a shudder, Śiva remembered the garbage cans. They were flowing over. Whenever one was full he simply created another. Some were brimming with new lifeforms, with creatures that had never been tried out before. Microbes, he knew, could be a problem. Most of them lacked a sense of humour. Viruses were worse. They didn't even live. Well, I'll dump them in the cities. And there was stuff in every corner. Half-eaten pizzas, underwear, empty bottles and full ashtrays. Maybe, he thought, I have to clean up. Before she appears with that oversized pussy, drags me to bed, smashes my pelvis and eats my heart out. He grinned.

In Hemanta's hut, the hermits shook their heads. Here one moment, gone the next. Gods may be necessary, but the way they buzz around is unhealthy.

The next step required planning. The bride, as tradition demands, departs in a palanquin. She has to be accompanied by friends, relations, musicians, guests, an honour guard, and anyone who fancies fun, food, music or a fight. Plus beggars, dope addicts and drunks. It adds a gritty realism to the scene.

The ascetics shuddered and those who still had hair on their head, scratched it frantically. Most of them were far beyond the age where you go for extended walks. Mount Kailāsa, they thought? That's almost on another continent!

Hemanta bowed before Durgā.

"My dear daughter," he sighed, "life is difficult and age is cruel. We would have loved to accompany you."

"Would you?" Durgā was shocked.

"Alas," her father continued, "the road is far too long. We would have to beg our way, would have to rest, make pauses, visit sacred sites, write postcards, buy souvenirs and get our ageing joints set. Some of us are not as young as I am."

"I can't believe it."

"My dear, we all love you. You are our happy little girl. Forgive our trembling feet, our staggering gait, our empty eyes and dripping noses. Forgive us for failing you. Once, we were young and strong. We could toss elephants around."

Hemanta shook his head, and his eyes glistened. "Mont Kailāsa is high and far away. I ask for your forgiveness. Could you travel on your own?"

"On my lion? I'll be there in no time at all."

She grinned while she inspected her nails. It's easy to find Kailāsa; the highest mountain in the world can't be missed. And she was getting jittery. However, Durgā forced herself to remain patient. These people had been wonderful to her.

Hemanta gathered his courage. It wasn't much. His daughter seemed more grown-up than ever. "May we give you a ceremonial goodbye? We have prepared something special for you."

Durgā nodded her agreement. This would take time, but time didn't matter. Gods, just like humans, can make time any way they like. Soon, she would spend eternities in bed.

She went to her room, stuffed her things into the iron box and cast a last look at her former life. A small cot, some pillows and a dusty fireplace. The sun shone through the cracks and dust motes danced. It had been her home and it would be her past.

When she emerged, the forest philosophers, wretchfolk, gunkgirls, world-deniers, abstainers, crazies and crackers had assembled along the roadside. Most wore nothing except long hair and tangled beards. They were sacred, and all of them were family. Durgā knew she would miss them.

Holy Hemanta did his best to appear happy, but his eyes were damp. He's such a brave guy, she thought, as she watched him scratch his beard, bringing me up wasn't easy.

"I thank you; daddy," she said, "and I thank all of you. You are my family, my friends, and my roots."

She realised that her eyes were getting wet. Her voice squeaked like a folded frog. Not now! Let's do this fast and get it over with.

"My blessings will always be with you. You are brave, braver than warriors. You taught me all that I need. I love you."

Hemanta wiped his eyes. "Today, my little darling, knowing you are a real, grown-up goddess, we want to do something for you. We have composed a sacred hymn which celebrates your 108 divine names."

"One hundred and eight?" said Durgā and blushed, "so many? Oh, you shouldn't have!"

Her face went red and she felt as if she could burst apart. At last, at long last, they respected her!

The forest dwellers raised their hands in supplication. Hemanta took a deep breath and the chant began.

"Oṁ! Chaste One! Virtuous One!"

Durgā glared at them. What an awful start!

"Beloved of Bhāva-Śiva! Spouse of Bhāva-Śiva!"

Things were improving.

"Manifest Brahman!"

At last. Only high deities, serene, supreme and over the top, could manifest Brahman, the Absolute Ground of All Being.

"Liberator from the World of Births and Deaths. Destructress of Distress!"

Durgā smiled. This was exactly what she wanted.

"Jayā! Victorious One! Ādya! Primordial One! Trinetrā! Three Eyed One!

Holder of the Spear! Spouse of Him who holds the Pināka Bow!

Wonderful One! Whose Bell sounds Fearfully!

Of Great Austerities! Manas! Thinking One! Buddhi! Intellectual One! Āhaṁkāra! Principle of Self!

You Form of Awareness!"

It got her. Durgā wanted to lie down, purr and melt in sunshine, honey and affection.

"Funeral pyre!"

What?

"Knowledge! Substance of All Mantras! Reality!

You Whose Nature is Pure Bliss! Endless One! Vessel of All Three Temperaments!

Accessible by Devotion! Auspicious! Pervading All things!

Spouse of Śiva-Śambhu!"

It reminded her. That guy, her future husband. He was so cute! She ought to be with him, right now, dig her claws into his dhoti and tear the thing apart.

The itch was there again. She would hurl herself on her husband and then...

"Mother of the Gods!"

Durgā took a deep breath. The word 'mother' sobered her. Motherhood could wait. She envisioned millennia of red-hot heat, broken beds, sweaty pillows and wet floors. I'll spew like a fountain, she thought. I'll drench him with delight!

She mounted her lion. For the time being, this was enough. "Thank you! Thank you" The goddess beamed. "You are doing a wonderful job. Please keep going. I promise blessings and rewards, in this and other lifetimes. One day I'll come and visit you. But now I must be going."

She slapped her lion, the great savage cat yowled and the two disappeared towards the horizon.

The recluses stared at the dust cloud indicating her trail.

"She's a fast girl" a crusty said. "That's young people nowadays."

"We shouldn't have mentioned motherhood," said Hemanta, "it makes her nervous."

He shrugged and gave the assembly a crooked smile. "Still, we have plenty of time to think of something better."

It's easy to cross India when you are in a hurry. Truth to tell, India isn't very big. As this story requires scientific precision (Hello, academics, I hope you are attending!) I have looked it up in the atlas, and as it happens, India, from east to west, measures 43cm. It's not a lot, considering that the same book grants the Netherlands 23cm. In case you've never been there, the Netherlands are barely bigger than your living room. They consist of five cows, three windmills, the van Gogh Museum, a pony farm and thirty-eight coffee shops. The rest is dunes and water. You could do it in an afternoon, on foot, without breaking sweat. By contrast, India has a ten modern airports, a hundred discotheques, several war zones, the Taj Mahal, five temples full of erotica, Varanasi (where elders go to grumble and regret), Poona (drive-through-enlightenment), Goa (where Indian tourists study stranded hippies), and several lakes where toxic sewage burns. In between, and indeed, covering two-thirds of the subcontinent, resides the movie industry. It's much larger, but hardly large enough.

Before long (actually, within instants, as Durgā was speeding), the goddess reached a river. It was huge and bleak and gloomy. She could barely see the opposite shore. The river, she realised, extended from one end of the cosmos to the other. Most of it happened in outer space. From one shore to the other there swirled turbid, muddy water, and not a bridge in sight. Her lion came to a halt. The huge, auburn cat glared at the waves and snarled. This stream was far too big to be leapt. Tigers, I am sure you know, love to swim, but lions have a different stuffing, and prefer to remain dry.

Durgā glanced at the flood and smiled. Yes, she thought, this is a goddess. She is mighty and strong and easily excited. People would call her indefatigable. Pity them.

At the shore, next to their boat, stood two fishermen. She flashed a diamond smile and they dropped their nets.

They had seen much, but never such a woman.

Durgā tried to appear charming, and succeeded.

"My friends, "she said, "I am a goddess." She winked at them. "Could I be yours?"

The fishermen paled.

"Would you carry me, and my little darling to the other side?"

The fishers bowled over and pressed their brows into the sand. Like all low-class folk, they had a sound head for reality. They bowed again and again. Eventually, they got up, dragged their boat into the waves and asked the goddess and her lion to be seated.

The river wasn't friendly. Soon, waves hurled themselves against the boat, restless, chaotic, angry, while winds howled, and the waters began to churn. On their crests they carried foam, and the heavens went grey, then dark. The lion leaned over the railing and retched. The great wild beast slunk to the bottom of the boat and hid its head between its paws. Durgā, however, smiled and pretended that she had taken boat rides for eternities.

The fishers knew that something was wrong. In the distance, lightning flashed like serpents. "Mother Gaṅgā!" They prayed. "Mother of all brooks, all rivers, all streams, let us reach the other shore!"

"Ḍākur! Mahānanada!" the waters called, "you are my sons!"

The fishermen paled. The goddess talked to them. Unless you are a dedicated tantric or a total lunatic, this isn't supposed to happen.

"Prove your loyalty!" the waves hissed, and rocked the boat, "your goddess demands obedience!"

The fishermen clung to the railings.

"If you want to stay alive, make the boat turn over and drown your passenger!"

Foam crashed against the boat. The vehicle was tossed about; heaven turned from lead to nightmare and pressed on them like a wall of iron. Forgive us, lady, the fishers thought, and guided their vehicle into a whirlpool. The flood surged, the boat shook, and the fishermen leant to tilt the craft. The goddess kept her balance. "Who would have thought that boat journeys are so much fun?"

The stream roared. The fishermen were terrified. They made the vessel lurch.

"More!" Durgā was getting excited. With a final jerk, the boat turned over, and floated, the keel pointing to the sky. The fishermen, immersed in churning water, held on to its sides and prayed. Goddess and lion were tossed into the flood. The lion, relying on its instincts, made a frantic leap and stuck its claws into the wood. Yelping, it dragged itself out of the water. Durgā clung to its tail. She grabbed the mane, scrambled up and took her seat on top of the keel.

"This is fun", Durgā said, as she arranged her hair; "but you two need to learn a lot about boat-rides." She pointed at them. "Honestly, I have no idea how you remain alive."

Picture 6: The Wisdom of the Heart.

8. Married Life

Śiva had dropped into bed, burrowed his head into a pillow, gone asleep and was now, for his terms, terribly awake. Gaṅgā, his dear wife, towered above him. She looked like thunder, storm and total deluge, seized him by his shoulders and shook. Śiva tried to look cute. His teeth rattled.

"What do you mean to grin like that? I met your bride!"

"What bride?" he asked, "who are you talking about?"

"The girl who comes to marry you!"

Damn, she thought, he's out of his mind. He's a dope-head! A total failure! "You know who I mean! Feminine, almost nude, wears cheap jewellery and rides a huge smelly lion! A divine slut!"

"Really?"

Gaṅgā stopped. The evening had taken its toll. During the storm, while the boat tossed around but would not sink, she had faced her Karman. She looked at Śiva and shook her head. Her husband seemed so strange, so remote, as he was lying on his cot, almost absent-minded, never here and never there. Gaṅgā stepped back. She saw herself, in the middle of the night, making a scene. It was all over. And it had never been much.

Her husband. He wasn't bad, just weird. But could you blame him? His magick was dissolution, dance and transcendence. Mr. Total Destruction. Mr. Bleach-Bone-Cemetery-Friend-Blow-Your-Mind-to-Liberation. A wonderful guy, and totally chaotic.

"I won't complain," she whispered. "We only met by chance. I came down from heaven and your head was in the way. Your hair and my juices. And it was never really easy."

She raised her eyebrows. "Stop. Don't say a thing. Don't make me weep or slap you. This girl suits you. She is just as lazy and reckless as you are."

Gaṅgā looked down at him. He seemed continents away.

"Marry her, if you like. Waste your days. Blow your heads off. You have my blessings. Copulate for eternity, if that's what you want. I don't complain. And should you want to see me; I'm in every riverbed."

The goddess disappeared. Śiva exhaled. His eyes were wet. He wouldn't sleep for the rest of the night. In her riverbed, sure, she was busy as ever. That meant pretty far away. But she wouldn't get out of his mind.

By daybreak, Śiva pushed his sadness into the past and did his best to make Durgā's arrival glorious. When the bride moves into her new home, everything has to be perfect. The god of ascetics leaned back on his tiger skin and stared at the ceiling. Cobwebs! He thought. I'm sure she'll love them.

What do you need for a proper marriage? Śiva had never really thought about it. Some worshippers asked him for a partner and plenty of children, but none consulted him as a god of ceremony.

"I tell you what," he said to a spider, "The rules are simple. Marriage is fun. Anyone can do it, and I can do it best of all."

For the perfectly executed Indian marriage, in case you want to have one, you need marriage planners who arrive accompanied by a platoon of decorators, equipment specialists, architects, lighting-engineers, flower-binders, costume designers, seamstresses, carpenters, cable-layers, photographers, a film crew, seat-order coordinators, topologists, invitation writers, drivers, mediators, insurance specialists, reality designers, soothsayers, astrologers, wonder healers, singers, musicians, choreographers, chefs, barkeepers, waiters, talisman pedlars plus at least three tame elephants, and the sweepers that follow them. For the ceremony, you have to hire ritualists of high class, the more the better and good luck to all of you. Everyone needs accommodation, consideration and huge tips. A typical must-have are insect suppliers: when bride and groom circle the sacred fire, millions of butterflies have to flutter around them. And, of course, someone has to keep an eye on children, drunkards, lunatics, academics and potential suicide victims. Professional staff have to handle the major families, run the carousel, bowling alley, discotheque, wrestling arena, roller coaster and provide emergency surgery. The representatives of the major banks must be invited, as a marriage without a massive credit is impossible nowadays. And you need glamour, so you should have a couple of pop- and movie stars flown in. That, Śiva knew, were the bare essentials. For the day after, he would require professionals to handle garbage removal, recycling, renovation, therapy, criminal investigation, arrests and autopsies. Some marriages require Special Forces commandoes to escort the guests, politely but firm, and if necessary in chains, to their homes. In rare cases, newlyweds hire a crane with a demolition ball.

People, Śiva thought, are great at simple entertainment. They enjoy the bare essentials. Gods, however, are a lot harder to please.

He leaned against the cushions and thought. In case you didn't notice, Śiva is the Lord of All Awareness, the Light of Experience and the Fountain of True Insight. It says so on his door plate. He can think faster and deeper than all inhabitants of the subcontinent at once. That's what his devotees say; at least, those devotees who can still articulate themselves before they walk into the next palm tree, and fall over.

Picture 7: Splatterbrain Sunrise.

Sacred matrimony is a divine challenge. Fascinated by the complexity of the task, Śiva explored the possibilities of non-deterministic logic, multi-dimensional accounting, and, a vital extra, the amount, size and originality of the presents. Their price wouldn't matter; he was out of money anyway. It's the idea that counts, for gods, as we all know, own everything, and what they haven't got, they create, or borrow elsewhere. Male gods do much of their creating in tiny garden sheds, while goddesses have accidentally created entire planetary systems to store their shoes, wigs and padded bras. Someone was needed to select the gifts, to wrap and drag them around. Someone tough would have to stop the quarrels. Yes, he thought, for security I'll hire some Asuras. They do anything if the drinks are free.

How about interior decoration? Pretty lights won't be enough. I'll amaze them with rainbow twisters, neutrino-compensators, interference-amplifiers, colourful strings, quantum, spin-factors, unknown constants, lots of artificial flavours, Bayesian probability accelerators, n-dimensional toilets, drinks with little umbrellas and funny hats with bells. One chaos-generator for each deity should do. After all, you never know if a guest has stocked up on coincidences. It's a terrible truth: most gods are boring and predictable. They recycle the same dull miracles. That's why people fascinate them, the less responsible the better. The rule is: the more rational, the duller is life. Apes. Śiva sighed. It wasn't his problem. They rule the world and screw it up. Let Viṣṇu worry. He's the Maintainer, and it serves him right. Everything else would be settled at the bar. He would fill it up with stuff that makes the neurons wriggle. And he would create a new drink for the occasion: the Heisenbomb. Either you knew where you are or who you are.

This is fun! Śiva had never realized that marriages could be so exciting. Creating a galaxy is simple by comparison: divine marriage requires genius! He would amaze his guests and his wife would tremble with admiration. And then, while the guests were occupied, to the bedroom.

He grinned from ear to ear as he reached for his pipe. I'll give you the perfect marriage. You'll be stunned. Indeed, maybe I should give you several marriages. It doesn't really matter if, what or how often we marry. There would be one ceremony after the other, each better than the last! He took a deep drag, held the smoke and exhaled slowly. His marriage would be the talk of the world-age. Provided his guests remembered anything. He giggled and took another drag. Then his expression became serious. Life was more than fun and fornication.

"Let's remain humble. The greatest artists restrain themselves."

Thinking hard, he eliminated inessentials, tightened the schedule, added a wide range of extravagances, sighed, dropped his pipe, collapsed and fell asleep.

When, in the afternoon, Durgā, dusty, with tangled hair, and panting mightily, arrived at Mount Kailāsa, Śiva had not even lit the sacred fire. Nothing was prepared and nobody invited. The divine palace stood silent and empty. Durgā didn't know what to say, and Śiva was speechless.

So what? The lovebirds grinned at each other and held hands, while they ran around the sacred fire, seven times as custom demands, as fast as they could. As far as ceremony was concerned, this was it. Nobody poured yoghurt on Śiva's hands or feet or struck rice plants into his hair. No one offered the bride to the groom. There was no exchange of gifts. Durgā and Śiva ripped their clothes off and were entangled before they even reached the bedroom. They tumbled across the floor, through the bed, over the sofa, into the pool, across the kitchen table, into the swing, over the trampoline and ended up in the chandelier.

By early evening, some 10,000 years later, the newlyweds woke. The night had been long and demanding. Śiva was direly challenged to get his eyes open. Durgā fought her sweat encrusted locks. Within the tangle, she discovered a bottle opener and sticky pastries. Śiva stared at his hands. They were shaking. Over there, on the ground, was the chandelier. Above, there was a hole in the ceiling, and there was plenty of plaster everywhere. Durgā looked for her underwear but gave up. Presumably, her husband had eaten it.

"I'll go and look after the cattle", Śiva stuttered, as he got up, groaned, and pressed his hands into his back to relocate the vertebra. His loins ached, the connective tissue felt badly stretched and further down everything had gone raw. He grabbed his satchel of drugs and tottered through the door. Durgā nodded absentmindedly and disappeared into the bathroom. When she reappeared, much prettier, a few decades later, her husband was still out of sight.

When you are a goddess, you know what you want and usually you get it. Durgā was a humble girl who had been raised in a forest hermitage. Her needs were hardly worth mentioning. She snapped her fingers and created a few dozen rooms full of costumes and mirrors, plus a storage hall full of shoes. Observing her reflection, she turned this way and that, and decided on her costume for the night. First she chose her clothes. Just a few of them; one shouldn't hide too much, when textiles simply mean delay. Then she chose the jewellery for the costumes. The result was stunning. Durgā admired herself. Then she frowned. The selection did not match. I need different clothes for the jewellery, she thought. She chose a better dress for the ornaments, and then better ornaments for the dress. It didn't do. She cursed and dropped the stuff. Soon, the floor was covered in textiles. Where do I find a sari for these sandals? A girl like me has absolutely nothing to wear. She restarted and tried to remain optimistic. What would her husband appreciate? Something missing, something blue, something tattered, something true? She shook her head. Probably he wouldn't even notice. I'll take something that rips easily, she decided, 'cause it won't be such an obstacle. Purring like a happy cat, she started again.

By nightfall, several years later, she was ready and felt wonderful. She reclined on a divan and stretched. I wonder, she thought, how long he needs to get his cattle organised. Then, counting her breath, she relaxed and waited for several minutes.

That's enough! Durgā got up. What had happened to her guy? Why did he take so long? It was outrageous. Of course, we have to be reasonable. Some gods are, and Durgā tried to be. Maybe he had been held up. Well, there's no problem you can't sort out in less than five minutes when you're a deity and eager to drop into bed with your beloved.

Mortals might wonder why Durgā didn't use divine omniscience. Here's a secret of the gods: omniscience is impossible. To be omniscient, you have to know everything. That includes you. And as you know everything, you have to know yourself as you know everything. Obviously, this means you have to know yourself as you know everything as you know everything. It goes on forever, for, while you are trying to know what you know, while you know it, the knowing grows. Call it infinite regression, if you like difficult words. Honestly, it's not only stressful, it's impossible. 'Omniscience' is only claimed by primitive monotheistic gods. Real gods don't claim to know everything. Indeed, some are delighted when the universe surprises them. Durgā was not and her dark eyes shone like a thundercloud. Like so many women, she began to realise that her partner had his own little habits, and Śiva's were more peculiar than most.

The Lord of Ascetics, eyes watering, knees trembling and loins aching, had wandered into the wide, fertile plains that surrounded his mountaintop palace. He had started out with clear objectives. He would look after the cattle. It sounded reasonable. Well, one excuse was as good as any other. Or relax and rest his frayed member. Oh heavens. If only his legs would stop shaking. Then, reality caught up with him. Or this reality, which isn't too bad, unless you are in his state, and meet the morning after head-on. Life is a dream and reality a fable. We shouldn't be too fussy, there are realities in all sizes and qualities; they are common as sand at the seaside, and honestly, most of them are pretty cheap and don't last long. Some fall apart as soon as the warranty is over. Others are not even delivered with batteries.

It's too damn bright, was his first thought. The second: it's far too loud. Cicadas can be stunning. The hotter they get the noisier they become. Śiva pressed a hand against his brow. He lurched to the forest edge. Between the trees and the damp meadow, tall grasses grew. His cattle seemed fine. They had gotten along for ten thousand years without anyone who cared for them. They had fed, chewed, regurgitated, chewed again, had barfed and farted and, in between, bred new cattle. Śiva smiled as he looked into their deep, soulful eyes. They hadn't missed him. As a drop-out god lacking a proper education and certificate, he appreciated creatures that didn't need his help.

He walked to a lone bilva tree and collapsed in its shade. The tree was his best friend. It was strong, reliable, and silent. The firm stem, the sturdy branches, and the wide, thickly leafed crown radiated peace. The tree has all the time in the world, he thought, and the same goes for me. Slowly, his lids dropped. He listened to his breath, as it moved in, creating the world in its fullness, and moved out, dissolving it. The in-breath sounded like 'sa' and the out-breath like 'ha'. Let's make this a mantra. No-one will understand. These fools, he thought, all they want is mystical formulae. Complicated letters, weird associations, spiritual fall-out and promises of profit and a better afterlife. Light-bearers, guru figures, white-robed prattlers, bankers of holiness. The cream of the workshop industry, regents of enclaves, exploiters of the dull and insecure. Curse the lot! My friends are simple, they live at the edge of reality, they are crazy, like me and they get along just fine. Everything could be so easy. Just shut up and listen to your breath, as it fades and slows and drifts away. In-breath and out-breath. It's the totality of the cosmos. What more could anybody want? Slowly, his breath calmed and faded away, just like the breaths of the foliage, into the sky. Eventually, there was just breathing, not mine or yours but a pulse of the universe, sustaining every being and everything. Śiva sighed with relief and relaxed, as he forgot himself. The last couple of thousand years had been slightly demanding. But for now, the cattle, the tree and the broken chandelier could get along as well as they could. A smile rose from the deep. Cosmic rule number one: make it feel good. Very slowly, his eyes closed, and his attention sank into the abysmal inner universe. The God of Yogīs grinned as he became smaller and smaller, and dropped into the void of the heart.

He shrank to the size of a thumb, of a molecule, an atom, a particle, and disappeared.

Durgā examined the nails of her feet. 52 layers of varicoloured nail polish gleamed at her, one for every phoneme of the alphabet. It had taken a while to apply them, and by now they were pretty dry and solid. Anyone bowing to my feet, she thought, will be stunned. She snarled. It had been a long, long time and her husband was still gone. Even as a deity, she thought, you don't have all the time in the world.

First, she paid a visit to the kitchen, where she devoured, in a most unladylike fashion, anything she could lay her hands on, provided it was fat, sugary and dripping with blood. Then she packed a couple of saris, sandals, ornaments and perfumes and went her way, across the snow, down the mountain and into the human realm, where gods are seriously disadvantaged 'cause they are not mad enough.

Just where, she thought, would Śiva keep his cattle?

The answer was easy: where plenty of bovines grazed, in the wet meadows of Bengal. Durgā sauntered through rich fields and plantations of sugar cane. She kept her eyes open for cattle that looked a) rather divine and b) totally neglected. She crossed plantations full of trees bearing juicy fruit, strayed through villages like a shadow and encountered people who, seeing her, shut their eyes and tottered away as if they were drunk. She followed sparkling brooks, dreamy rivers and mighty streams, and discovered larger settlements. Cities, she thought, are amazing. People live together in huge congregations, but essentially, they are hermits. That's 'cause their brains can't handle more than a hundred fifty persons. They don't speak with one another. They greet their neighbours, they pass each other, like ghosts on the cemetery, and everyone remains alone. Human life, she realised, is all about territory. For people, territory means a hiding place, a wide view, resources, procreation and a chance to run away. Give them a home space and they perform. Take it away and they go to pieces. It doesn't even have to be real: academics fight for intellectual territory, and are just as crazy as everybody else. But honestly, why should a warrior goddess care?

Before long, Durgā discovered miracles that really blew her mind. Let me mention markets, boutiques, bazaar streets, jewellery shops and special sales. And shoe shops. I don't have to emphasise them: shoe shops are cosmic, universal and self-evident. She bought what she liked and ordered the deliveries to the crest of Mount Kailāsa.

The quest for Śiva drove her onwards. One day, sometime, she would find him. Durgā wasn't really used to the world, so she assumed, like simple people do, that reason, logic and virtue would help her find her way. She was aware that Śiva loved street crossings, cremation places, dark forests, dangerous mountains, riversides, bordellos and pubs. With a lion at your side you can handle any of them. Reason told her she would find him there. But reason is overestimated. Experienced deities know the Law of Cosmic Uncertainty, which states that weird coincidences, errors, misunderstandings, painful shortcomings, general incompetence, absolute chaos and personal delusion must be added and multiplied, and subsequently forgotten, when the damage is done. The result isn't much, when you wake in the middle of the night, feeling cold and lonely, but it's all there is.

After a few months of futile search Durgā felt totally fed up. She had wasted millions of rupees on costumes and ornaments which she couldn't wear, 'cause they had been delivered to her home, in the faraway Himalayas. Her husband was still absent. Just you wait, she thought, you bastard. When I catch you I will seize you by the upper lip and drag you to bed. And I will wear all of my new clothes and shoes and jewellery, and I won't be available no matter how much you plead and howl and weep.

It was a noble thought, but, as her lion remarked, totally unrealistic.

Honestly, who could predict where Śiva was?

It would be better to focus on her interests. And Durgā did. With a bitchy smirk, she created a lengthy, red, four-sided dice (the first in history!), and used it to decide which way to go. It freed her from useless planning and allowed her to focus on places of interest, such as luscious gardens, mighty palaces, cultural institutions, museums, temples, wellness spas and exclusive boutiques.

Month after month, Durgā explored India. Eventually, she learned how to appear to people without leaving their brains in tatters. Humans, she realised, are simple. Most of them are driven by two forces: lust and death. Or call them desire and fear. It amounts to the same. She gave them what they could handle, and laughed about their ignorance. Deluded like any other type of apes, they realised that she was the most gorgeous woman in the world and that her merest whim had to be obeyed. They also learned to forget her afterwards, as too much perfection is poison for the human mind.

Durgā had a wonderful time. She laughed a lot, flirted with any better-looking guy, allowed men to pay for her drinks and show her the tourist sites. When she felt lonely, she went to see the movies. Bollywood movies are a panacea; they provide great feelings, for three hours or more, and help against winter-depressions. She laughed and wept and felt herself alive. Her journey continued. She sailed on the great rivers, circled Sri Lanka on an air mattress and learned to go skiing in the cleanest of all Indian provinces, Switzerland.

Śiva, aching all over, woke, and regretted it. Moments ago, he had been a subatomic particle, so small that even a scientist would have no word for it.

His limbs tingled, his joints were stiff and this scorching thing up there was far too bright.

"Ouch!" he said, which is not a holy manta (yet) and squinted at the world. It wasn't that different from what it had been before. There were big things with horns, who were patiently chewing. On the ground, there were slender things in green and yellow. And there was a complicated thing above him, which seemed to shelter him.

Heavens, he thought, I'm totally burned out.

Nothing amplifies reality like a mouthful of rum. It reduced his perception to a small and controllable focus: sun, cattle, meadow and tree.

Fine, he thought, it's just four items, and I hope they won't mess me up.

Three eyes wide open, he stared into the universe. Damn it, he thought, sometimes it's vast and sometimes too narrow. Apart from those wrinkly, twisted bits. And, honestly, it's silly. Śiva leaned backwards until he fell over. Reality, he giggled, is wonderful as long as you remained at right angles to it.

He closed his eyes.

When he opened them again, someone stood before him.

At first glance, the creature seemed huge. It seemed to extend to the height of heaven and extended across all continents of the earth.

She was exceptionally beautiful and seemed to wear hardly anything.

Her eyes were as deep as maelstroms and her skin was pure and free from scars. Maybe she is a cowgirl, he thought, they get infected with a virus which vaccinates them against the pox.

This woman was a stunner. Somehow, he realised, she seemed familiar. It felt important but wasn't: as a deity, you are acquainted with anyone and anything. Each person, tree or bug is an old acquaintance. Whoever you meet is yourself. It makes life confusing.

The wave of energy got him by the most sacrosanct, made his balls tingle and shot up into his head. "You are my goddess, you are my snake!"

Her eyes caught him, sucked him into vortices beyond comprehension, and made him sigh, shake and disintegrate. Her entire body seemed to consist of curves, bents and voluptuous delights that transcended physical reality. You are beyond anything, he thought, as he marvelled at her incredible dimensions, which would have put hardened mathematicians into straitjackets. I know you, thought Śiva, but maybe I know you from another world, the past, or from the future.

"Have we met before?" Śiva muttered and felt like an idiot. That's the dumbest line in the universe. The girl laughed and offered a bowl of milk. The Lord of Ascetics, milk-hungry like all gods, couldn't refuse. He bowed, gave her a fiery look, and drank. The girl giggled and tried to turn away. Śiva lowered the bowl, grinned like a tiger, and took her hand.

"Goddess!" he said, and meant it.

"My lord, you shame me!" The girl lowered her head and pretended to depart.

"Your fingers are slim like fresh sprouts, your hand gleams like the rays of the moon as it emerges from dark clouds, and grants bliss to all worlds," and before she knew, Śiva had put a silver ring with a huge diamond on her finger. "Let this be a testimony of our eternal love".

She stared at the sparkling crystal, transfixed, and gasped. Playfully, she reached for Śiva's necklace, which consisted of happy laughing skulls, and pulled him closer. Her breath was hot and her eyes were infinite. Śiva dropped the bowl. We will never learn what happened to it.

Words fail me. Some things are mysteries: you have to be there and experience them for yourself. Preferably several times a day, over weeks, months, years and all the way through cosmic cycles. That's what Jñāna (*direct spiritual experience*) and Karman (*appropriate deeds*) are all about. In Tantra, Śraddhā (*belief, faith*) is a tool, not a virtue. Blind trust may make followers of Viṣṇu happy, but for hard-core ascetics it won't do. No matter how your loins feel afterwards, and whether you can still walk without ouching. Let's limit our account to the bare essentials, and they were bare indeed, while the lovers embraced and squirmed, their steady rhythmic pulse driving the Indian continental plate under the Himalayas, which shook and trembled and rose by several metres every minute. And that was just the start. Our lovers had eternity at their disposal. The sun shot like a gleaming trail of fire across the sky, the moon pursued him, as day and night flickered, the monsoon came and went and constellations shifted. After a series of cataclysms, Śiva gave a happy sigh and reached for his drug pouch. He took a deep breath. When he looked up, the girl was gone.

Did I imagine her? For a human girl, she was amazing. Maybe she was wishful thinking. But can a god imagine something that isn't real? He shook his head. Let's test this, he thought. We need an impossible idea. While his hookah burbled, he visualised swarms of blue pigs fluttering through the sky, and would you believe it, they manifested instantly, circled around their creator and departed for distant mountaintops to build nests and lay eggs. That was easy, he thought. Point proved. For centuries to come, the heavens would be full of flying pigs. Of course the airlines would cover it up.

He giggled and leaned back. Exhale, he thought, simply exhale. With this happy thought, he sank into a trance. The seasons flew by like panicked birds; the tree behind him reached its height, aged, leaned backwards, shed its branches, was eaten by fungi and crashed. The wood went to rot while a new shoot rushed towards heaven. Śiva didn't notice. Until, eternities later, someone touched him. With much effort, he managed to raise an eyelid. Another girl. She, too, seemed familiar. Young, amazingly beautiful and clad like a girl from Cooch-Behar. Her mouth was soft like a lotus blossom, her nose ring sparkled like a supernova and her eyes concealed a hidden sadness.

"Have we met before?" Oh no. The same dumb line. But it seemed to work, the girl smiled at him, as if he were someone special, and said something he couldn't comprehend.

With eternity at his disposal, he reached out to her and pulled her to his lap, he felt her warmth, heard her heartbeat and melted into her.

Things became narrow, then wet and wild and loud.

Śiva shook his head, to get some sense into it. The world was full of mysteries. He urgently needed more dope. Or something less refined. By the time he had found the rum bottle, he heard a scream that shook heaven and earth. It sounded very angry.

"What?" he said. Then his wife pulled his hair and shook his head so that his teeth clattered.

Durgā had spent 36 terrestrial years searching for her husband. It's not very long, by divine standards, for a young and enthusiastic goddess who likes plenty of fun, has her hair and nails done once in a while and explores every better disco on the subcontinent. Nevertheless, when she got up in the late afternoon, she occasionally felt a little lonely. Married life, she thought, should be more exciting. One fine day, as she was on her way to a jumble sale, she noticed her absent husband sitting in a meadow. He seemed like a mirage, obscured by the shadow of a lone tree, and totally oblivious of the world. Heavens, she thought, he's spaced out, and he doesn't recognise me. So, just for the fun of it, she transformed into a cowgirl and offered him a bowl of milk. Instants later she was on top of him, and remained there, sweaty and trembling, screeching in delight, for divine centuries. When they finished, he fought for air, but he hadn't recognised her. Durgā shook her head. It would take ages, or a hammer, to get any sense into him. The goddess stood up, rearranged her costume and left. She didn't have the time to waste. In her belly was a spark of life. It wouldn't do to have a baby in a soggy meadow with a husband who was less attentive than a water buffalo.

She felt a divine sentience developing in her womb. It was hungry for sweets.

The goddess flew to Mount Kailāsa. It would be fun to create a nursery, a playground and a swimming pool. Before long, she gave birth to her first son, a beautiful boy with deep brown eyes, dark locks and an insatiable craving for sticky, honeyed cream pies. He's wonderful, she thought, and he looks almost as gorgeous as his mother.

"You will be the Leader of the Armed Troops, the Gaṇas," she said, "Your name is Gaṇeśa."

The boy was tough. He had a fierce temperament and he screamed a lot. She swaddled him, nursed him, rocked him and gave him, as custom demands, his first firm food at the age of six months. It suited him. Before long, his diet consisted of anything sweet. Most of it would have made your teeth shrivel, it dripped perfumed oil and scorched its way through marble. The boy ate and ate, but he hardly gained weight. That's what Durgā thought; my darling, you are hungry, while she stuffed him.

"He looks like a pig" said Viṣṇu, "you overdo it."

"No way," said Durgā, "he has a healthy appetite. He's not really fat. He is simply well padded. And he will lose his extra weight when he grows up to be a hero."

When her little jewel wasn't eating, he played with his mouse. The little rodent had appeared in the hour of his birth and the two couldn't be separated.

Durgā, reclining on a divan, did her foot nails, and watched them play. She was immensely proud of her sweetheart, who grew so well and who would squeak with joy (he spoke mousish perfectly), provided there was sugar involved. Only one thing was missing in her domestic paradise. Her husband was still absent.

A goddess has to do what a goddess has to do. She put her son and his furry companion to sleep with a magic spell and left Mount Kailāsa. With a bit of luck, her damnstupid husband would still be under that tree. And she was almost right. It was just that the tree had died and there was a different one.

Durgā studied her husband. What a blissful smile, she thought, he has all the fun in the world, but damn it, I have to do the mothering by myself.

And look at all those bottles. Well, most of them are empty. Maybe he'll come home soon.

She grinned. I'll need plenty of silver, to demonstrate my wealth, a folksy costume, and I'll jingle and clatter, as loud as possible, until he comes to. And now for a magick trick. She had invented it all on her own. Please don't call her cruel. It could help, if your partner snores. She clasped one hand over his mouth and the other shut his nose. Hello my love, she thought, let's see what happens.

Śiva shook, turned purple and almost exploded. When he had one eye open, she released him. Of course he didn't recognise her. "Have we met before?" he stuttered, "are you from Cooch-Behar?"

Not again, thought Durgā. He's an idiot, but he sure looks nice. And wow, his underwear is rising.

"I'm a humble girl from the countryside," said Durgā, "who never had an evil thought."

She came over him like a dark monsoon cloud.

It was almost like the first time. Again and again.

After a few aeons, she realised that her husband wasn't really attentive. Sure, he kept the rhythm and did his best. Only that the pupils of his eyes went up, leaving only the white, while his face went blank and little galaxies spun around his brow.

Then he stopped breathing. What's next, she thought, will he fall over and pretend to be a corpse?

She rose, adjusted her costume, and scowled at him.

The Lord of Transcendence collapsed and began to snore.

She took hold of his head and shook.

Śiva hardly seemed to notice. He reached for a bottle. Durgā slapped it out of his hand. He looked at her; his eyes glazed, and said, "Hey, who are you?"

"You damn loser!" She hit him until his eyes were open.

"I know you," he stuttered, "just give me a moment..."

"You idiot!" she screamed, "I'm your wife!"

Śiva smiled. "That explains everything."

Durgā. The Untouchable. Warrior goddess. Fire of the End of Time. "I'd recognize you anywhere."

She slapped him again.

He swayed. "You look wonderful," he said, "how come you wear that costume? I liked you better without. "

"Idiot! Drug-Head!" Durgā was in a rage. "You let yourself be laid by any village beauty!"

"Not any." Śiva raised a hand to soothe her. "They are all you."

Heaven went dark, mad winds howled, and the firmament began to boil. In the distance, lighting flickered and thunder rolled. The universe held its breath.

"Do you know what it means to be a single mother?"

The clouds burst and rain came down in torrents.

Before Śiva could think of a good reply, Durgā had disappeared to Mount Kailāsa. She reclined on her divan, cursed all men, read women's magazines, ordered multi-bladed steel weapons on the internet and watched 'Sex in the Sundarbans', 'Desperate Deities' and 'How I Met Your Mammoth'.

Her laughter was bitter and loud.

In the nursery nearby, her boy grew up. For all she cared, the mouse would look after him.

Far away, the Lord of Ascetics sat in the rain and watched the ashes washing down his limbs.

He wondered what had happened.

But no matter how fast you think (and Śiva really didn't) the world is faster. Eventually, all bottles were empty and his drugs didn't seem to work. This stuff is crap, he thought, as he glared into his pouch. Maybe I should try placebos. He got up, groaned, stretched his tingling legs and faced the universe.

"OK," he said. "We had a wonderful time and I'm sure I had some cosmic insights. Let's go home and sober up." I'm a god, he thought, I have duties, and my schedule is pretty tight. One day I'll amaze everyone.

He tightened the tiger skin around his hips, gathered drum, trident, arm-rest, bone-mālā, emptied the spittoon and shook his head. Home. It wasn't really far away. He could be there in an instant. He reached for his hookah. No reason to hurry. Let's sit under the banana leaves and have another one for the road. The rain came down like a waterfall.

When Śiva staggered up Mount Kailāsa, the monsoon was past. The mountain meadows were agleam with blossoms and butterflies danced in the sunshine. Happy brooks rushed into the valleys, and Śiva sat down to watch them, as he wasn't eager to come home.

Weeks later he reached the summit, saw his palace gleaming against the fresh blue sky, and his heart seemed to open. He walked into the courtyard and faced a pretty lad sitting in front of the bathhouse. Thick fumes of perfumed steam drifted from the window.

The boy held a comic book with his right hand, and read, while his left hand kept stuffing sweets into his mouth.

Gods, Śiva thought, he doesn't even unwrap them.

The Lord of Enlightenment knew that with children you have to be friendly, as otherwise they won't like you and all sorts of terrible things happen, especially when their mothers are involved.

"Hey youngster," he said, "who are you and what the hell are you doing here?"

"I guard the bathhouse," said the boy, without raising his eyes, "my mother doesn't want to be disturbed. Not by me, not by my mouse and not by a beggar like you."

"Watch it," Śiva scowled, "this is my mountain, my palace and my bathhouse, and I don't take cheek by a piece of snot."

"Screw off," said the boy, "and drop dead."

"That's my wife in there!" Śiva exclaimed. "I married her!"

"In that case I should know you," said the boy, "but I'd rather not."

He looked at the filthy ascetic, and laughed.

"Piss-pot! You look wasted."

Śiva paled. "I have no idea where she got you from, but in my house you had better shut up!"

"Go away, loser! This is Durgā's palace. We don't need trash like you!"

The divine child laid his book aside and took out a catapult.

Śiva slapped him.

He hadn't meant to. At least, not that hard. But there's this thing about gods, they get carried away.

The boy's head flew off.

O damn, Śiva thought. I didn't mean to!

From the bathhouse, Durgā's voice called. "My pet! Who's there?"

Śiva paled under his ashes.

The ultimate cataclysm.

Total annihilation. The Fire of the End of Time.

He looked at the boy. Where his head used to be, blood spurted.

Śiva plunged through the mountain forest. He crushed trees, smashed boulders, tore through tickets and raced through waterfalls. Until he saw the forest elephant. He was huge. His scarred grey hide stretched as if it could contain the universe. His benign glance told of irresistible power, of years of divine monsoons, and might and fertility.

Śiva grinned, said "Sorry!" and tore his head off.

Instants later he was back on the peak. He grabbed the twitching torso of the boy, slammed the elephant head on top of the neck and fixed it with emergency mantras.

Then he sat back and held his breath. The boy came back to life.

Śiva didn't know what to do. Say hello? Remain and wait for his mom to emerge? Or simply run for it? The kid had tusks and a trunk!

I can only hope, he thought, that Durgā won't notice.

The door of the bathhouse flew open. Durgā, Warrior Goddess, Fate of Kingdoms, Demon Slayer, Destroyer of Universes, stood before him, wrapped in a towel which, as he noticed, left quite a bit in sight. It could have been promising, but it wasn't.

"You look like an angry silkworm," he said, before common sense told him not to.

Durgā glanced at her boy and that was enough.

Heaven turned black, earth trembled, and cosmic harmony went down the drain.

"What did you do?" she roared and the hurricane roared with her.

Śiva fell backwards.

"I want an explanation!"

"Dear...I mean, sweet-heart...."

Śiva stopped. Absolute Reality has many faces and some of them were totally out of control. "You want my honest opinion? He's a godrotten little brat!"

That didn't explain anything. He raised his hands. His brow was wet with sweat. "Forgive me darling. Please try to understand."

Durgā didn't. Śiva would have loved to sink into the earth. Through the humus, past roots and rocks and down seven underworlds. Down under, life was supposed to be wonderful. In the deepest heart of the depth, in Nāgaloka, the serpent underworld, where awareness is joy, things would be much easier. By all accounts you could spend days in meditation and no questions asked. Śiva had heard the tales of travellers. The sky is turquoise, they said, and the forests are emerald. You will enjoy rosy palaces and gardens full of magenta blossoms, the very colour that human eyes can't see but have to make up, and caves of delight and wells where inspiration foams to the surface and all those serpent girls, truth to tell, he had always fancied serpents, well, they could keep a god busy, if not in shreds, and there was ancient wisdom everywhere. Śiva swallowed. Eventually, if he tried hard, he would get used to their toxic fangs. But that wasn't an option.

When things are really bad, even gods have to take a stand.

He looked at his wife. She was screaming at full volume and looked ravishing.

And she had an amazingly thick belly.

"Another child?" he pointed, "by me?"

"Right!" Durgā was in a frenzy. "This babe will be a warrior god! And do you know why?"

The Lord of Enlightenment could hazard a guess.

Feeling embarrassed, he patted his son Gaṇeśa on his dear, grey head and barely missed being stabbed by a tusk. He's full of bristles, he thought, but I'll get used to them. And his trunk is impressive. What a lad!

This was the moment to demonstrate cosmic insight. "Children," he said, "are our chance to rediscover the miracle of the world. Love them and they will love you. And they are Karman, so we can't help it. I'll do my best. Maybe I'll read a book on education."

And so it happened, as the storytellers say (and these people never lie) that Śiva and Durgā had two sons. Both of them grew up to be tough, impressive lads, a delight to their parents and a terror to their little friends. Before long, their courage and holiness made them famous. To be sure, they had a bad start with their father, but he made up for it by ignoring everything he didn't really want to know about. And though he did his best, he wasn't made for fatherhood.

While he contemplated the blinding white purity of the snowfields and his eyes went wet as he watched the flight of blue pigs, his sons romped around, unwatched, uncared for and without a good example. Gaṇeśa ran around like a bulldozer on the rampage, and made rocks burst, cliffs fall and trampled anything that got into his way. There was one thing, and only one thing that got his attention and that was sugar. His younger brother Kārrtikeya was an incredible war god, a conqueror, a master of all lands. In the hour of his birth a peacock appeared, who became his vehicle and advisor, as he scaled mountains, wielded spears, crushed districts and danced across the glaciers. His mother was so proud. To be sure, he wasn't easy. Nor was his sacred animal. The peacock kept hacking at the snakes which Śiva wore around his neck.

I love my little boy, but his vehicle is a nuisance, Śiva thought, 'cause where would I be without serpents? And when the Lord of Ascetics fell asleep, Gaṇeśa sent his mouse into his bedroom. The crafty rodent gnawed its way into Śiva's pouch and stole drugs. His sons spent many smoky nights, bombed out of their skulls and up to no good, without their parents noticing.

Śiva stood on the balcony and looked out into the warm, black night. It felt inviting, and tempted him to drop everything, to forget his shape and nature and go roaming in infinity. Let me embrace the dark, he thought, let me pace the void. By his standards, he was relatively sober. It was a challenge, and a surprise.

And it made him think. Gods have deep thoughts, even if they are rather simple. Durgā had seduced him, in altered shape, twice. He had not noticed. Hell, how can you be cosmic when you are supposed to take in every tiny little detail?

Now, she made him suffer for it.

She pretended that he had wronged her twice! It simply wasn't true!

Why did she make a fuss? She had enjoyed plenty of orgasms and in between, conceived two wonderful kids!

Luckily, he thought, in this world of madness, things tend to adjust. You only have to wait a while. Or take the initiative and form the world according to your wishes. It was time for a neat, funny revenge. For a start, he would shame her. What if the straps that held her bra would burst? The goddess would withdraw, and she would order a tailor. That would be him. The best looking tailor in the world. In changed shape, he would measure her breasts. He would marvel at her proportions, feel stunned by her beauty, and faint at her feet. One thing would lead to the next. He would sport a well-oiled moustache. He would show his belly muscles. Before long, she would undress. And I wonder what, he thought, would develop next. He looked at his dhoti. It would be impressive.

Śiva grinned. Durgā was easy. She was almost predictable. Take her to a dance performance; give her a few drinks, a hot night and a new weapon with curved blades, chains and poisoned spikes and she's almost perfectly at ease. And, face it; the games that people play are pretty much the same.

Early in the morning, when the wind was fresh and the sunlight merciless, Śiva woke and realised his brain had shrunk. It had been all too much. Especially the alcohol. His glial cells told him they would move out and find a better future elsewhere. No matter how much water he consumed during the night, they had barely washed the toxins out. Who cares how much you moan, they told him: if you want to think a thought worth thinking, send us a postcard or simply drop yourself into the sea. We don't care.

Śiva sighed. He knew it; he knew it all too well. Even small amounts of alcohol interrupt the sleep phases and mess up the nocturnal cleansing routines in the cerebrum. So what? Life can be cruel. He would have loved to weep. Theoretically, he was a wonderful father. He had a wife embodying sheer energy and their two boys were sure to be heroes, one day or another, no matter how much it hurt.

That was a thought worth thinking. Did it help? It didn't.

Squinting from swollen eyelids, he watched his sons at the breakfast table. They were tired, their eyes were bloodshot and obviously they hadn't slept much. From time to time they coughed and spat, and hardly touched their food. "You look like a bunch of addicts!"

Absentmindedly, he grinned at his wife, tempestuous Durgā, who was fighting a pan of rice with lentils. They fought back. The goddess snarled and added a handful of spices. That should teach them.

Śiva got up. My Durgā, he thought. I'm sure, one day, you'll educate our boys.

Smiling blissfully, he drifted out of the room. Let anybody else face breakfast. Let breakfast face itself. He had better things to do.

Out there, on the balcony, he inhaled. The universe stopped. In all leisure, he exhaled, and relaxed. It was like coming home. This is a world of wonder, he thought, except in there, at the breakfast table.

High up in the sky, cirrus clouds moved. Ice crystals, gorgeous, crunchy, glittering like diamond curls. He loved them, he loved the day, and he loved the future, no matter what it involved.

Śiva smiled. While he straightened his spine, high up, in the cold perfection of Mount Kailāsa, his temples were full of worshippers. They poured milk and yoghurt, they pleaded and whined. Come on, thought Śiva, am I your piggy bank? You ask me to hurt your enemies? To raise your bank account? Are you too stupid to solve your problems?

I don't care. If you love me, go ahead, and love yourselves. Love the sky, the earth, the underworlds and anything in-between. Love the people around you. Love the animals and plants and fungi. Love slime mould and microbes. Recognise your place in the net of food-chains. You eat, and you are eaten. It's perfect. And if you fail to get the message, screw off. Worship Viṣṇu, or anything. I'm not going to clean your snotty noses or resolve your daily bickering. I don't do stupid wishes; I do transcendence.

Durgā sighs, she looks at her juvenile delinquents; she shakes her head and says the same.

Part Two:

Manasā

Picture 8: Kadrū: Mysteries of Forest and Water.

9. Lotusborn

By daybreak, the sky had cleared, the clouds were gone and geese passed the peak of Mount Kailāsa, honking happily. Their wings gleamed in the early morning light. Śiva watched their flight and sighed. Waterbirds, he thought, are my breath, my mind, my freedom. The air was fresh and wonderfully cold. It was just the day to wander around aimlessly. Geese, like all water birds, promised auspicious events. They were at home in all worlds; in water, on earth, in the sky and could pass across the otherworlds with ease. If something blocked their path, like the Himalayas, they simply flew higher.

The Lord of Ascetics wiped the curd from his mouth, ran his soggy fingers through his locks, smiled at Durgā and announced he would go for a walk.

Durgā mirrored his smile; like him, she had plans for the day, and husband or children did not feature in them.

"I'll be off to Lotus-Lake," said Śiva, as he checked his pouch. I wonder why the stuff disappears so fast. "For a bit of meditation."

"Fine," said Durgā, as she reached for her hairbrush (reinforced steel hiding a stiletto), "but don't stay so long. And be a dear and pluck a basket full of flowers. It's Brahmā's pūjā later on."

She handed him a tiny, tightly woven basket. It had been crafted by Viśvakarman, the Architect of the Gods. The elegant little contraption weighed absolutely nothing and had enough holding space to transport entire flowerbeds, plus anything that came with them - trees, walks, ponds, pavilions, artificial hills, the odd temple building plus personnel.

Like all refined technology it made no sound, produced no waste and practically carried itself.

Flowers for Brahmā? You might ask what for. But Śiva merely raised an eyebrow and shrugged. Brahmā may be the creator, when Viṣṇu and I let him, but, let's be honest, anyone can do the job.

Śiva tied his pouch to his belt, and stowed a couple of bottles of palm wine (soft) and rum (hard) in the basket. The day was untarnished by worry, the world was young and innocent and anything could happen. "Maybe I'll surprise myself", he said. "Meditation might suffice. Maybe I'll stay sober".

Durgā raised her eyebrows and sighed. She could have made predictions.

"Boys! Obey your mum and make me proud of you!"

Geese, he through, as he ambled down the frosty slope, his feet crunching through the icy crust, are a lot nicer than adolescents. They don't stuff themselves with chocolate all day. Or protein bars. They traverse the sky with graceful wing beats, show perfect posture and turn the day into a miracle.

The Lotus Forest surrounds a lake, and the lake is part of a tangle of dark waterways, deep in the heart of the jungle. Indian forests are pretty light during most of the year. Most of them are dry and the sun gleams through the dusty foliage. Unless the forests are close to a river or a swamp, or grace the monsoon-drenched, cloud-veiled peaks of the Western Ghats, they wither, and take on the colour of leather. The Lotus Forest is different. Everybody has heard of it, but no-one seems to know where it is. Maybe it lies hidden in the wet mountains along India's western coast, where the ferns abound and moisture is a way of life. Or it extends in some lonely valley in the Himalayas, where no sane person ever goes, except for ascetics, and no one takes them seriously. It might be concealed in the mangrove swamps of the Sundarbans, where Gaṅgā and Brahmaputra meet and mangy, life-hardened tigers, the last of their kind, stalk buffaloes, honey-collectors and fishermen. If you enquire at the tourist office, they might direct you to the 'real' lotus lake. It's on the map somewhere. After you have left, they will shake their heads. Tourists are crazy. In real life, the Lotus Forest could be anywhere. Call it a mystery. In its centre is the bottomless black Lotus Lake, gleaming like the eye of a crow. Some find it by accident. They stumble along, slip down its banks, and get stuck hip-deep in mud. The air smells of fungi and decay. That's the moment travellers begin to ask questions. An all-time favourite is: are there crocodiles around? Hey, you are lucky, there are.

Śiva loves the Lotus Forest. It was there, dark and inviting, before the earth congealed around it. Vast shadowy trees, as old as the cycles of the universe, rose to a sky that disappeared in multicoloured mists. They were covered in mosses and succulents, their sinewy roots extending like lianas to the ground. On the branches, gaudy blossoms shone, and radiated perfumes that could stun a bird in flight. A rotten tree, an open space at the shore, invited him to rest. Black butterflies fluttered through the dripping foliage, each wing adorned with a red spot, stunning, gorgeous and as big as bats. Śiva exhaled and the universe settled around him. The Lord of Ascetics smiled when he spotted a pair of scarlet birds. They copulated in a flurry of wings, feathers and screeching ecstasy.

Fumes coiled above the surface of the lake. He watched the flying frogs, clinging to each other, as they disappeared into the tangled branches. Cautiously, he moved his head, eased the tightness in his neck, and heard the vertebra click into place. The lake seemed calm; as far as he could look, there wasn't a ripple in sight. Much of it was dense with lotus, white, red, pink, magenta, blue, yellow, in amazing shades and bizarre combinations. Between the blossoms appeared a tangle of rounded leaves and twisted stalks, of pointed, still unopened buds and spindly seed capsules, a blue seed staring through each hole. Unlike most gods (especially the modern ones: digital, mass-produced and a total waste of time) he remembered the age when the lotus was worshipped as a serpentine goddess.

How can a plant be so bizarre! The lotus ascends from thick, fertile mud, like a cobra raising its head. The plant feeds on the rot, on carcases of plants and animals, on bones and shit of bygone ages. It reaches for the light, for air and freedom, unfolding leaves as large as plates, coated by wax, so not a trace of dirt can cling to them. The buds rise, and open, sighing, like a yonī. The blossoms unfold, they shine and laugh and gleam. Insects come humming; then, fertilised, the petals fade and fall, and hardened seed capsules remain. All faiths of India celebrate the lotus. But hardly any worshipper is aware of the nameless lotus goddess of prehistory, who started it all, millions of years ago, when water plants were just beginning to develop blossoms, and learned to entice insects as their lovers, partners and friends.

Far away, he heard the amphibian chorus, the squeaking, rattling, scraping, clicking and roaring of a million frogs. A dark fish with golden fins rose to the surface, gulped air, and disappeared. I'll follow you anywhere, thought Śiva, as the beads of his mālā slipped through his fingers, for this is life: a brief emergence from the deep, a glimpse of air and light and blessings, and then we're off into the dark again. His eyes closed, his mind slowed, his breath went faint and silence extended everywhere. The frogs stopped calling, the birds came to a rest and only the crocodile bulls, far away, roared.

The Lord of Ascetics smiled. Horny like a plated reptile, he thought, as he drifted into the deep within. He became smaller and smaller, shrank to the size of a thumb, a mustard seed, a molecule, and dropped into the inner void. In the depth of his heart, your heart, all hearts, where form and emptiness make love, he cast away the veils of self-definition, forgot about his aims, and faded. The lotus blossoms followed him into the deep; intensely colourful and moist with lust.

Flowers! Their scent is stunning and their nectar everything.

Quite by coincidence, he thought of Durgā. The thought was huge, bright and six-dimensional. It caught Śiva by the holy-of-holies, and within instants his loins were on fire, his tiger dhoti rose, and he ejaculated.

Milk-seed, lunar essence, cosmic consciousness: whatever you may call it: the stuff shot out, described a graceful arch and landed on a lotus blossom.

The universe held its breath. Gods trembled, cities shook, but Śiva didn't even notice. He gave a sigh, and disappeared into the depths where mind and identity fade into oblivion and even gods can't tell what's going on, or can't be bothered.

The seed was boiling hot. It fumed, as it burned its way into the blossom, and disappeared into the depth. It travelled down veins, migrated through roots, penetrated earth and stone, passed through the mineral crust of the continental shelf and flamed, brimming with vitality, into the deep.

There are plenty of underworlds. The Indians count seven, which is a pretty good estimate, considering that you can only know about an underworld when you return from it alive. Śiva's seed passed through the lot. Nothing could stop it: the pale elixir was far too hot to rest.

The soil of every underworld has a specific colour. The juice seared its way through white, black, purple, yellow, ochre and stone-coloured grey. In the lowest level, Pātālā, otherwise known as Nāgaloka (*Serpent Realm*), the ground is gold and the sky is green, and things are truly weird.

Just as Śiva's sperm congealed in the dome of the Nāga Sky, old serpent woman Kadrū passed by. It could have been fate, or, as I suspect, on purpose, because Kadrū is wise, and doesn't believe in fate. "I shape my fate" she says, "agree, or get out of my way." Kadrū is a stunner. Sometimes she seems to be an ancient cobra, a king's cobra, far bigger than anything you know from earth. In the early morning, she lazes in the sun like a gigantic python. Or she slides, her top half shaped like a comely dancer. She may be nude, or fully clothed, or clad in radiance and madness, or all of these at once. She is old and young, her hair is black or grey or white or golden, it turns red with the sunrise and violet with sunset, she is soft and powerful, gentle and vicious, a thunderstorm, a hurricane, and far beyond definition. Kadrū, Mother of All Serpents, has been around forever, in the depths of the deep, and here on earth, and up in the skies, before the gods appeared. "I'm still young," she says, "barely a girl, and hardly worth calling the Mother of All Serpents. Honestly, my age is inconceivable." She winks, but there is sadness in her eyes, "it's bad luck to ask a girl how old she is."

Kadrū, wise in the Long-Forgotten and the Soon-to-Come, looked at the gleaming, greenish sky, and grinned. High above, the glob of sperm was ripe for vintage. "Come down," she crooned, and quivered with excitement.

The fluid fell and Kadrū, underneath, caught the lot in her mouth.

In her long and youthful life, the Mother of Serpents had swallowed more than was good for her, but this, whatever it was, was plainly too much. Her eyes bulged as she fought to gulp it down.

She tossed her head around, tightened and extended her throat, gasped, coughed and fought. She spat and choked and tossed, her tail whipped through the air; it toppled trees and smashed boulders.

In her belly, something grew, knotted, and twisted. It made her nauseous and mad and almost killed her. She screamed, and her cry shook heaven and earth. It was too vast, too hot, too crazy! Kadrū moaned, as she collapsed and twisted. The something was big. It was full of madness, full of awareness, far stronger than anything she had experienced before. Sure, you don't die, when you are far beneath the Realm of Death. Occasionally, you might wish you could. She retched and vomited; she shifted her four rows of teeth, and expelled something incredible.

In her puke lay a gleaming, slimy lump.

What are you, Kadrū thought, a deity or a nightmare horror?

The thing seemed misshapen. It didn't even have a proper shell. A baby, she thought; I just had the craziest child ever. And I can' tell if it is male or female, or whatever.

The thing began to struggle. "Calm down," Kadrū said, "Quiet, darling. Let me see what you are."

She shook her head. What a mess! It didn't look like a snake at all. It had limbs, imagine that, like a monkey or a human being and it was covered in long, slimy hair.

"My dear, "said Kadrū, "my little nightmare. You look horrible, but mummy is here for you."

She forced a smile. The baby opened its eyes, vast like the Lotus Lake and just as black. It hissed, tossed around, and yelled.

The earth began to tremble. "We can't have that," Kadrū muttered, as she embraced her newborn daughter in smooth, shiny coils, "shut up and grow!"

Within instants, the Dikpālas assembled. They are the cosmic guardians of the six directions, the great dragon-serpents who keep the worlds in balance.

The Nāga lords studied their little sister with intense fascination.

They smiled, as was their duty. For good, bad or worse, the girl was family. In Absolute Reality, they would have wished to plug their ears.

"What a fine baby," said Vāsuki. "She looks healthy and happy. And she has a strong voice. How amazing! None of us would have guessed you would have another child."

"I'm young," said Kadrū, "no matter what you think. I can have plenty of children."

She held the baby up, and smiled.

"Look at her! So cute! She doesn't look much like a serpent. But see her poison fangs!" She kissed her little darling. "One day you'll kill an elephant!"

Vāsuki frowned. He had been in a hurry to assume a human form. If you had seen his magnificent turban, the peacock plumes, the golden ornaments and diamonds, had looked into his dark, soulful eyes, had marvelled at his eyebrows and the proud, shiny moustache, you would have taken him for a prince. Underneath, below his red vest, emblazoned with gold thread and ornamented with rubies and emeralds, his body remained that of a serpent.

Vāsuki bowed before his mother.

Kadrū raised her baby.

"See my youngest daughter," declared Kadrū, the Mother of all Serpents, "she belongs to the serpent world, to the realm of plants and of course, to the world of gods."

"Mother, I have to ask you, on behalf of all the serpents here. Who is her father?"

Kadrū blushed. "The Incredible, Absolute, Most Supreme of All Gods. The Auspicious Śiva, the blissful Śaṅkara, the fierce Rudra. He is One-in-All and All-Over-the-Top. Pay homage to my daughter: she is the child of Absolute Consciousness!"

Kadrū looked immensely proud.

Vāsuki shook his head. "Forgive me. I beg your pardon: You had this child with Total Reality?" He seemed to pale. "Have you been to Mount Kailāsa? Have you met Him, with the Matted Locks, the Lord as White as Jasmine?"

"My boy," said Kadrū and shyly averted her eyes, "don't ask. It was a hot night."

Vāsuki bowed again, much deeper than before. He was a good son and took his office seriously. Kadrū kept her face under control. She could have had a laughing fit.

"This, my daughter, "she said, "is the child of all serpents, but her essence comes directly from the All-Consciousness of the Universe, the Auspiciousness-Of-All-Being. That's why I name her Manasā, the Conscious One, the Thinking One, the Imaginative One; the One Who is Sheer Awareness!"

"Oṁ Manasāyaī namaḥ!" sang the serpent lords and bowed their heads in rhythm. Their voices fused in a stream of fluid sound and buzzing overtones. The moment was sheer bliss: the world would never be the same again.

The baby gurgled and drooled: she seemed to acknowledge the veneration of the world. Kadrū could barely keep it in her grip. With two legs and four arms you can wriggle as you like. She needs food, thought her mother, or she'll scream again. Will she prefer frogs or rats?

Time is flexible. It can be as fast or slow as any serpent wishes. People, being sort of dense, hardly ever use the chance. Any serpent could tell them: speed up your thoughts, your inner voice, your inner imagery, your breathing and your motions, and the world slows down. Or do the opposite and relax. Serpents are masters of time management. When they lurk in ambush, they quiet down, and the world speeds up. Give them a juicy rodent and they stretch the experience. The taste goes on forever. They will relax in the sun, watch hot-blooded mammals hurry by, wonder if it's worth the effort, shake their heads and smirk. The next meal will happen in a few weeks. They pity dumb hairy beings with a fast metabolism, like us, who stuff themselves with food, sensations and thoughts, and are never satisfied.

Children, and young serpent goddesses, are fast. For them, each day is an eternity. They run when they can and experience so much that the adults scratch their heads, give a strained smile and wish it were time to put them to bed.

Kadrū's girl was a romping, stomping, multi-dimensional catastrophe. Clever serpents shuddered when they sensed the hectic pattern of her feet. She ran, she jumped, she climbed on things, fell down, she screamed, laughed and accelerated. She had two of these forky things, let's call them legs, which got anywhere and stepped on anything. A wise serpent, as many thought, had better hide, or travel to some other world. And the child grew. From day to day, she extended, stretched, and became more of a nuisance. For heaven's sake, they whispered, Kadrū may be her mother, and maybe she got around a bit, but this brat is impossible. She never clambered from an egg nor did she have a tail.

Kadrū loved her daughter. She admired anything her little tornado did and wouldn't have dreamed of interfering. "When snakes grow up," she said, "they shouldn't be disciplined or educated, but accompanied."

The girl grew. Before long, her figure changed. Bits that had seemed straight began to bulge. Her gait, which had been tempestuous, turned into an elegant saunter. Even Kadrū, who, as her mother, was the last to realise what happened, had to admit: her baby had grown up.

How can we describe Manasā as a young woman? I wouldn't ask the snakes. They were glad to keep their opinion to themselves. But maybe we should employ a poet. The guy grins, as he takes the cash in advance, gets out a reed pen and a stalk of palm-leaf paper and starts composing. It seems to be an easy job. Her hair shines like the blue-black clouds surrounding the full moon; her eyelashes are as long as the wings of celestial haṁsa birds; her lips radiate like red berries, throbbing with forbidden delights. Her teeth gleam like pearls, but, bloody hell, they are fangs, and drip with toxins.

Or poet wipes his brow, stuffs his wage into his pouch and runs. We shouldn't blame him. The deepest underworld isn't really meant for tourists.

Even muckworms, groundcreeps and scalewrigglers noticed the change. Earlier, the girl used to stampede about in a threatening way. Now she walked with sensuous grace and asked questions.

It was almost worse.

"Who is my father?"

"No idea," hissed the serious cobras, averted their heads and slithered away. The question ought to be answered by her mother, or her relations, or anyone else, and they were welcome to it.

"Kadrū, who is my father?"

"You are too young to understand."

"I want to know!"

"One day you will. Have another egg."

Manasā braced herself. It takes determination to swallow them whole.

"Vāsuki, who is my father?"

The serpent prince shuddered. Agreed, the query was significant. Nevertheless it involved tactful references to Kadrū's careless love life. As Manasā's elder brother he couldn't simply slink away.

He blushed. "Listen closely," he said," and stop jittering. What I have to relate is very, very important."

Manasā's eyes widened.

Vāsuki took a deep breath. His body seemed to swell.

"Your father is a high god, maybe the highest of them all." He knotted his brow in due humility, "that's what the great seers say. He is transcendent, as he is outside of all form and being, he is immanent, as he is within everything, and he is transcendent-immanent, meaning both at once and incomprehensible." He took a closer look at his little sister. Sure, she was grown up now. But big thoughts were new to her.

"He contains the entire multiverse. But he did not start that way. In the Vedic period, they called him Rudra. He was a wild and crazy god, a dweller in the forest, a hunter, a robber, a destroyer, an expert on poisons and healing plants. We remember him well. He liked us and we liked him. At the great sacrifices, when he got the carcase of an animal, we got the entrails and plenty of blood. It was a perfect deal. Normal people were afraid. They wouldn't have dreamed of inviting him into their huts. But they made offerings so he would stay away."

Vāsuki shook his head. "Well, sister, things change. Religion isn't reliable. True believers are anything but true. And you can't trust people. Rudra was scary, so they tried to be nice. They gave him the name Śiva, which means the *Auspicious One, the Benevolent One, the Giver of Blessings*. He liked it. And he tries his best to be kind to them, or to understand them, though it almost drives him mad."

Manasā scratched her head, dislocating serpents from her locks.

Vāsuki continued. "It's not all. It isn't even half of it. To some people, he is much more than that. They believe he is Formless Consciousness, Absolute Reality, and the Awareness of the Cosmos."

Vāsuki hissed. "The word 'Cosmos' means '*Beautiful Order*'. I wish he knew. Alas, he doesn't really care."

Manasā stuffed the serpents back into her hair. "Tell me," she said, "who is he?"

Vāsuki lifted his head, bowed deeply, and sang an ancient hymn:

"*Oṁ namaḥ Śivāya! Oṁ namaḥ Mahādevāya! Let me praise the greatness of the God of Gods, from whose sentience everything appeared. Those who want to understand the All-Consciousness, the Supreme, Primordial Brahman, the Absolute Ground of All Reality, should listen with devotion.*

He cannot be understood by humans, nor can he be attained by ascetic practices, through generous gifts or sacrificial offerings. Lacking deep and exceptional devotion, it is impossible to know him. Indeed, he dwells in all beings everywhere. But the highest sages are those who do not know him, the Cosmic Consciousness.

He is their creator and the Distributor of Fate, of Time, and the Lord of Fire, who glances in all directions. The entire universe exists in him and he is the transcendent Destroyer of All. The saints, the spirits of the ancestors and the dwellers of heaven cannot perceive him. Nor can the others recognise him, whose deeds are extolled, like Brahmā, the seers, and Indra, King of the Gods.

The Vedas praise him incessantly, as the single, highest lord. The Brahmins worship him with many Yajña and Makha sacrifices.

All worlds, and even Brahmā, the grandfather of the world, cannot comprehend him. Nevertheless, the yogīs meditate on him, the Bright God, the Lord of All Beings.

As All is dissolved in him and he is the Breath-Soul of All, he assumes the shape of all gods and turns into the enjoyer of all sacrificial offerings, and the provider of the fruits that arise therefrom.

His worshippers will never die. His devotees cannot commit a sin.

Whether it is a leaf, a blossom, a fruit or simply water: when a devotee makes regular offerings to delight him, he will receive his love.

He releases the yogīs from their worldly fetters. He is the primal cause of the creation of the world, but he is not attached to it.

He alone is the Destroyer, the Creator and Maintainer of the Universe. Māyā, Magical Illusion, the Enchantress of the Worlds, is his personal energy.

What is claimed to be transcendental knowledge is his power.

He rests in the heart of yogīs and dissolves their delusion.

There can be no doubt that one, who experiences him as such, becomes a lord of yogīs and will be one with him, through the reliable path of Meditative Yoga.

Thus, he is the God who makes everything happen. His refuge is the highest joy, and he dances within it, the Yogī, eternally. Who understands this, becomes a master of yoga."

Manasā was stunned. "And that's my daddy?"

It couldn't be worse. That's what the serpents said. At any time of day or night, Manasā buzzed around, and unnerved them.

Small children ask an average of four hundred questions a day. Manasā managed four thousand. She didn't even listen to the answers. Kadrū told her to be quiet; Vāsuki recommended patience and ascetic exercises, but Manasā couldn't be stopped. Why did these people treat her like a newly hatched slow-worm?

"Your body is adult," they said, "but your brain isn't fully developed. You have access to adult feelings and urges, but the frontal lobes aren't ready."

"So what?"

"It means you can't control yourself!"

"That's a lame excuse!" Manasā shouted, "You are all against me!" She slammed doors, smashed things and hurled furniture around. "If I wait until my brain is ripe, I've missed half of my life!"

The wiser serpents nodded. You have to make mistakes early in life, if you want funny stories later on.

"I want to meet my daddy!" She trampled in a rage and the underworlds shook.

"You unfeeling creeps. You don't understand a thing. I have to say goodbye to you now. I hate you and I love you."

The serpents looked at each other, grinned uneasily, and agreed.

Vāsuki had described him, as best as he could. It sounded quite unlikely. Why should the highest of the high stagger around in a rancid tiger hide? Why should he plaster his body with ashes from the cremation place? I'm not going to dress like that, she thought, I'm different. Vāsuki, hinting at Śiva's nudity, had gone red in his face. Unlike Vāsuki, she liked the idea. He wears a serpent around his neck. So will I. Quite a lot of them, everywhere, with plenty of open skin in between. A proper hairdress? He doesn't bother. Nor do I. The snakes would mess it up.

But now for something pretty. He darkens his eyelids with kohl. That's so cool! I'll do the same. What else is there? He has divine attributes. Vāsuki had listed the items. Manasā rolled her eyes. For the time being, I can do without a tiger skin, an armrest, a rosary, a noose, an axe, a deer, a dwarf, a spear, a bag full of drugs or a basket full of bottles. Let alone a moon, a river in my hair and a spittoon. Maybe I'll pick up drumming later on, she thought, and tridents look great. I wonder what they are good for.

And that, she decided, was enough. You can't plan the unexpected. No matter what you assume, the uncertainties multiply with coincidences, errors and miracles. Preparation is superior to planning. I've got what I need and am who I am. Watch it, universe, here I come.

Look at the sky of the Serpent Underworld. Here and there, thick roots reach to the ground. They connect to sacred trees and flowers, thriving millions of miles above, in other worlds and other times, no matter how crazy or unthinkable.

The fibres are tough and easy to grasp. Manasā took hold of a root and pulled herself up. The strands were moist and clung to her body. Soon, they turned into thicker tubes. By then, our girl was halfway up to heaven, and looked down on her former home. I never knew you're all so small, she thought, as she waved at the serpents who watched her. "Hey you!" she called, "I'm happy!"

The Nāgas cheered. They were in high spirits. Except for Kadrū, who struggled to hide her tears. But that's life: children grow up and eventually, with a bit of luck, their parents too.

When she reached the dome of heaven, the roots had become trunks. Manasā made herself small, she squeezed through a pore and found herself within a stream of fluids. Giggling, she shot upwards, through world after world, past the volcanic rock, and quartz, and younger minerals. Finally, the roots emerged in the wet and muddy realm where sediments congeal, turned into stems and rose through the Dark Waters. The lotus flowers emerged, fresh and wonderful, high above the surface, crowned with huge, oval leaves and blossoms of stunning complexity. So did Manasā. One moment, she was twisting through a narrow bit of stalk, next, she was inside a capsule and last, she emerged on a platform surrounded by multi-coloured petals.

She sat down and relaxed. New places are exciting, but it's good to take your time. To her sides, there were unfamiliar pinks and blues, whites and magentas that took her breath away. I'm in a forest, she thought, and everything is full of detail. But when she looked down, through the tangle of leaves and stalks, she saw Dark Waters swirl, as old as time and thrice as wonderful. Under the glittering surface, shadows moved. Manasā stared in awe. Are these fishes, she thought? Or giant amphibians, or reptiles?

Far away, the shore was veiled by mists. In the twilight haze, she discerned a divine aura. Here was a god, albeit a very passive one, who had found peace and lost himself in it.

Adult people plan, think and consider. Manasā did not. She leapt from leaf to leaf, from blossom to blossom, and adjusted her size as she went along. Within instants she had reached the water margin and waded through muck and slime of untold ages. The mud reeked. Behind her, she heard crocodiles roar.

Śiva sat, at peace, his body barely upright and his breath was faint.

Occasionally, a shudder ran through him. His body swayed, his eyes were firmly closed. Around his neck, a fat cobra lazed. Like her master, the reptile seemed to sleep.

Manasā stopped. That's him, she thought. And he is just as I imagined.

Her mind went into overdrive. My daddy. He looks so holy.

The Lord of Yoga, Awareness of the Universe, began to snore.

Cautiously, Manasā advanced. She reached out and touched his arm. Śiva did not notice.

She tapped his shoulder. No use. A third try. This one was stronger. He almost fell over. Manasā grabbed his shoulders and rattled him.

The Lord of Ascetics moaned.

What time, what age, what planet? Oh damn! He was late and Durgā would be waiting. And he hadn't collected a single flower. It was time to get a move on.

Manasā stared at her father. He hadn't even noticed her.

She shook him again. He opened his eyes and gasped with amazement.

Before him stood a woman. She was young and almost nude. Oh my goddess! What a beauty, he thought, and under his dhoti Absolute Reality began to twitch.

Stop. Śiva grinned. Not again. My dear Durgā, this time you won't fool me. I've seen through your little tricks. But how should he react? Stay sovereign and distant, and make her mad with desire? Or reach out, seize her hips, pull her close and cover her face with burning kisses?

Should he laugh and tell her that she couldn't fool him?

Or pretend that she was just a normal, innocent, you-meet-them-anywhere serpent girl, straying in the Lotus Forest and obviously lost? Leave me alone, thought Śiva, you are too damn complicated. And why do you stare like that?

Manasā had expected a warm welcome. Instead, while he gawked like an idiot, his underwear rose. Gods, she thought, this guy is a cripple! He only has one penis!

Śiva beamed and touched her nipple.

"Hands off!" she screamed. "I'm your daughter!"

The Lord of Ascetics recoiled.

A daughter?

He couldn't remember having one. In fact, there were loads of things he couldn't remember. It made his life exciting.

"Who is your mother?"

"I was born by Kadrū," said Manasā, and kept her eyes away from his dhoti.

"Nonsense." Śiva tried to radiate supernatural self-control. It cost enormous effort. With trembling fingers, he stuffed his hookah. "I would remember Kadrū. She is a sizzling snake, and she's got lots of curves, but honestly, we never got as far as that."

"She had a hot night with you, and swallowed your seed."

"That's a lie." He leaned forwards, lit a flame, sucked on the bamboo tube and made the pipe gurgle.

"Kadrū and I? We have never been in bed. She couldn't have my sperm."

Manasā showed her teeth. "Stop acting! You are my daddy."

Śiva grinned. The dope hit him and he relaxed. Motherhood, fatherhood, what did it matter? "Well and good, my pretty little loony. If you are my daughter, show your divine nature."

Manasā hissed at him. She stood, stretched and transformed. The Lord of Ascetics paled, his pipe sank, and so did something else.

Before his eyes, the Lotus-Born revealed her essence. It transcended heaven, the mortal realm and all seven underworlds, and cast a shadow over Lotus Lake. From all corners of the universe, serpents emerged. They travelled on the breath of the winds, swam through black waters, writhed through wet foliage, wriggled through roots and mosses and swaying ferns. From holes, caverns, and cracks, they came slithering. They assembled, heaped and clustered around her feet, they clutched and coiled and copulated, they bowed their heads and offered blossoms, fruit and jewels.

How shall I describe it? Let me pass the pen to the famous poet Dvija Rasik. True enough, he wasn't there. That saved his life. However, he had his little visions:

The snake Śaṅkhinī hangs on her head, a conch-shell ornament,

the snake Kāśurihyā ties the hair knot on her head,

Karkaṭiyā is her ear pins.

The rings of her bodice are finer than the crest-jewels of the cobra.

The Sindūriyā snake is the vermillion mark on the goddess's head,

the Khañjaniyā serpent the anklets on the goddess's feet,

Kajjoliyā the collyrium of the goddess Padmāvatī,

and the neck ring on her throat is the serpent Gaganiyā.

The Tāṛuyā snake is her four beautiful ear-ornaments,

the serpent Sitaliyā is the seven-stranded necklace of the goddess.

Having put on her snake-ornaments, her joy is incomparable.

Ananta spread his five hoods over her head.

In all directions are the thick bodies and hoods of serpents.

Everywhere clusters of snakes glisten.

It was more than enough. Śiva, who only takes reality for real when things get really desperate, was convinced. With a groan, he averted his eyes.

"Please assume a simple form."

Manasā had been holding her breath; she exhaled and relaxed.

The serpents paled and faded into imagination.

Śiva glanced at her. She looked much smaller now, and vulnerable. A few thin snakes remained, here and there on her body. He shook his head. The Brahmins will never allow her into a temple in this outfit.

"Forgive me, daughter. I'll keep my hands to myself. Promised!"

The serpent goddess raised an eyebrow.

Śiva grinned. "Please take my greeting as a compliment."

Side by side, father and daughter sat and stared into the fog, while the sun sank and the birds began the evening chorus. Suddenly, Śiva remembered. He was supposed to be home early, with flowers, for Brahmā's pūjā.

"Daughter," he said, as he rose, "Sorry, but I have to hurry. It was good to meet you. I would have stayed longer, but if I'm not home by sunset, the world will face a cataclysm."

Manasā rose and blushed. "Take me with you!"

"Impossible," Śiva exclaimed, "forget it."

Picture 9: Blinded.

"I've never seen a mountain," said Manasā, "I heard Kailāsa is the greatest of them all."

"Of course it is. They all are."

"What is it like?"

"Well, it's my home. Nothing much really. Plenty of rocks, some snow, a little palace, the usual stuff."

"You must take me!"

"I can't" said Śiva, "'cause life is complicated."

"But you are the highest of all gods!"

"I have divine problems."

"But I can't stay here."

"Sure you can. It's the world. I like it and so will you. Have a look around, make yourself at home, and if there's trouble, your snakes will sort it out."

"I want to meet my family!"

"Family life is never easy. It's not my decision. And if it were, it might be re-decided."

"Why?"

"Well, for a start, you have two brothers, and they are really difficult." He kept his voice steady. "One of them rides a huge, divine peacock, and that damn bird is an enemy of snakes."

Manasā was amazed.

"And your other brother is stubborn, and lazy and stuffs himself with sweets."

"Does he also ride a bird?"

"No, he's got a mouse."

"I like mice."

Śiva closed his eyes and shuddered. "And finally, there's your stepmother. Her name is Durgā, the *Untouchable*, and she is slightly emotional. Rides a lion; a typical warrior goddess. And now, I'm late, I have to pluck my flowers and be off!"

He reached for his basket. "Daughter, forgive me. I have no idea how I can bring you home."

"But I want to meet my stepmother."

"You must be out of your mind."

"But I'm family!"

"Maybe another time. I have to explain this with great caution."

"What?"

"That I've got a daughter all of a sudden. And that I never spent a night with Kadrū, no matter how it looks!"

"I'll explain," said Manasā, "and she'll understand." She looked at him with sad, dark, antelope eyes and pouted.

The Lord of Cosmic Awareness felt shaken. Luckily, in this instant, the fat old cobra which he wore around his neck raised its head and hissed: "Take her along in transformed shape and tell Durgā when she feels happy and relaxed."

'Relaxed'. What a wonderful word. Śiva smiled. He had no idea that his innocent little daughter had just spoken through the cobra's mouth.

"Fine, he said, "help me pick flowers. Any colour will do."

Manasā was happy. She waded hip-deep through the water, picked lotus blossoms and Śiva taught her a mantra to bless them. "It's for Brahmā. We have to cheer him up."

"How can I give him flowers?" she said, "I've never met this guy."

"You are lucky," Śiva mumbled.

"Why do you look like that?"

"Don't get me wrong. Brahmā is pretty much all right. He knows his limits."

"I thought he is a high god?"

"Sure he is. That's why we honour him. He is creative, and has a friendly character, most of the time. But be a clever girl and keep your distance."

"Why?"

"He drips and drools and squirts."

When the basket was moderately full, Manasā showed her magick skill and transformed into a white spider. She seemed as delicate as glass, looked at Śiva with eight beautiful and highly intelligent eyes and gave him a cheerful grin, which isn't easy if you lack mandibles.

Śiva nodded, dropped her into the basket and closed the lid.

Travelling at the speed of thought, the Lord of Ascetics arrived on the peak of Mount Kailāsa. He was in a hurry. Nevertheless, he stopped in front of the gate, knee-deep in the snow, and pulled a bottle of sugarcane mindwarp-overcloud-buzzrock-splatterhead out of the flower basket. It was empty within seconds. He dropped the bottle, heard the glass smash and exhaled very slowly, while his eyes watered and tremors racked his frame.

Durgā waited. She had had a busy day; much of it devoted to changing her costume and make-up, and was reclining on a blood-red divan. Apart from her underwear and a few dozen ornaments she wore a translucent red veil.

Śiva strode into the hall, placed the basket on a table in a corner and grinned like a tiger. "My dear, you look glamorous!"

"Of course. And you have been drinking."

"Not really," Śiva advanced, reached for his wife and pulled her close. His kiss was stunning, and Durgā forgot what she intended to say.

Śiva kissed her throat, her nipples, her mouth and when she finally got a chance to breathe, he was coiled around her like a python. Durgā screeched with delight as her veil ripped and her sandals (gold with rubies) went flying.

If you think this is about sex I have to disappoint you. Many sober thinkers have announced that Indian religion may look, feel or sound like sex, but in truth it isn't. Any sane observer had better ignore the moans, the sweaty limbs and the world-shaking tremors: Consciousness-Without-Form and Consciousness-Within-Form were in total embrace and exchanged breath, fire and body fluids. The sage philosophers wiped their sweaty brows and agreed: it simply didn't happen. Except in a symbolic fashion they didn't really approve of. Nevertheless it was damned loud and the furniture shook.

Manasā sat in the basket. She rested between scarlet java, yellow campaka, white, red and yellow ghanda, blue aparājitā, pink padmā, the small, pale bakulā with its sweet scent, the choice mallikā and the soft and fragrant mālatī. It was dark and stuffy. She waited and hardly dared to breathe. Had she arrived? Would this be her new home? Out there, she heard grunts and groans while things fell over, and crashed. She tried to look out, but the basket was perfectly tight. The screams got higher and louder. Was this her stepmother? She didn't sound untouchable at all. And what, for heaven's sake, were they doing?

She patiently counted to one hundred thousand. She tried to stretch, wriggled her eight legs, shook her head, twisted her belly, and pissed into a blossom. This was taking far too long!

Durgā and Śiva were pretty much knotted up when a young and cheerful voice announced: "I greet the Divine within you!"

The Untouchable twisted around and Śiva paled. Not now!

Manasā trembled. Her daddy was totally nude and the ashes from his skin were all over the divan, the floor and the beautiful woman in his arms. All three gleamed with sweat.

Durgā jumped up and screamed. Śiva stuttered. Before he could say anything, Durgā grabbed a stick of firewood and hit her rival.

Manasā staggered back.

Durgā hurled the thing and caught Manasā's left eye.

The eye went blind and Manasā howled in anguish.

The socket filled with pain and poison.

Durgā raised another stick.

The poison erupted; it hit Durgā and knocked her over.

Manasā stared, through a haze of tears, at this beautiful woman, writhing and twisting on the floor.

Śiva leapt up and Manasā's gaze caught him in mid-motion and sent him sprawling. Her stepmother and her daddy twitched, blanched and went rigid.

Everything was pain. Her left eye was closed and swollen. The right could see, but failed to understand. Before her lay her father and that strange, beautiful woman. Neither of them moved. Around her, the world was coming apart. Stone groaned as faint cracks ran across the pillars and walls. The air was full of shadows.

Is this death? She had seen old, respectable snakes die, when they were done with life and gladly released their bodies. They chose their time, they said goodbye and left. It was a good way to depart. And she knew the everyday death of mice, frogs, grass snakes and small birds. Most died of heart failure before she gulped them down. That, too, was a good way to go. But her new parents? How could the universe be so cruel?

Tears ran down her face.

Death! It had to be an error, a delusion!

Her limbs twisted and her breath wheezed.

She stared at the corpses and understood reality.

Consciousness and power. This, she realised, isn't about divine actors. It's about principles and ideals.

"Hear me, you idiots!" she exclaimed, "I'm alive, and so are you. Gods can't die! I love you and I hate you. Get up! You make me feel ashamed!"

The corpses began to twitch; they stretched and shook, lifted their heads and groaned. Śiva, totally burned out, raised his head. His lungs rattled, he retched and giggled.

He must be used to moments like these, she thought, and he loves them! The Lord of Ascetics knelt; he touched her feet and worshipped her.

The Lion Rider raised herself and vomited. Her hair was tangled, her face shone with sweat. She bared her teeth, pulled her top over her head and stowed her breasts away. Manasā averted her eyes.

Durgā cursed, ran to her apartments, and slammed doors.

Thunder shook the palace and brightness filled the hall. The very ceiling seemed to disappear, a wide sky opened as the worlds aligned and a shower of blossoms cascaded from the height. Conch shell trumpets sounded: the gods assembled in their glory.

Gaṇeśa and Kārrtikeya, her brothers, hurled themselves to the ground and worshipped her.

"I am the Lord of All Heroes!" said the muscular one, with the shiny teeth, the oily locks and the peacock feather costume.

"And I am hungry," said the stocky one, with the elephant head.

Before Manasā could say a thing, cymbals thundered, trumpets roared, drums made the walls tremble and rainbows flashed across the marble. A huge man, clad like an emperor, entered.

"Hail Indra, Lord of the Gods!" chanted her brothers, and bowed again.

The newcomer twirled his moustache. "I greet you, Goddess of Thought and Consciousness" said the Thunderer, and the thousand warriors of his entourage cheered. Slowly, like a mountain, he got down on his knees and touched her feet.

"Hail to the Feet of the Goddess!" chanted the celestial musicians, as they paraded into the hall, playing their gleaming instruments.

"Hail to the Lady of True Insight" sang the heavenly nymphs, waved fluorescent veils and filled the air with perfume.

A shadow dropped from the heavens and the dancing girls scattered. It was Garuḍa, the terrifying firebird, the famous enemy of snakes. Manasā stepped back and felt her poison glands swelling. But the bird landed before her and bowed his head, revealing riders on his back. On a golden throne, shaped like a seven-headed serpent, sat Viṣṇu, the Maintainer, the Lord of Rules and Regulations, Master of the Avatar Succession, clad in rainbows, and at his side reclined Lakṣmī, the Divine Essence of Brightness, Beauty, Wealth, Love and Fertility. From her hands cascaded pink blossoms and golden coins. To their sides, elephants lined up, went up on their hind legs and showered the congregation with the rain of affluence and happiness.

"We greet and worship you, Goddess of Serpents, Mistress of Awareness!" Viṣṇu opened his vest and revealed his navel. From its centre appeared a spark, a stalk sprouted, unfolding leaves and a singular bud. A blossom opened, and in its centre sat a tiny god with four heads, bushy eyebrows, hairy ears and long, matted beards.

"Hi sweetheart!" he squeaked, "I'm Brahmā, the Creator of Everything!"

"Don't believe him," Viṣṇu laughed, "I created him."

"Got any plans for the evening?" Brahmā grinned, but Viṣṇu grunted, and stowed him away.

A rain of stars came falling, cosmic vapours spiralled, galaxies were born, swirled, flared up and collapsed into themselves. The hall expanded into new dimensions, room enough for any amount of gods.

Four hundred millions, Manasā realised, and the number seemed incomprehensible.

Rotation drums rattled and Śiva's host came running, hairy, ash-smeared and totally insane, their eyes red from smoking bhaṅg, bearing sticky cakes, spongy pastries, lumps of butterfat, and sugarcane brandy spiced with honey, ginger, pepper, Withania, opium, hashish, fly-agaric, and toad skins. Through the floor, the goddesses of the deep arose, the river ladies, custodians of lakes and ponds and sacred wells, raising golden chalices, and Soma, milky, foaming and deceptively sweet, geysered into the height. The heavenly musicians made their strings yowl, blew flutes and hammered temple-gongs, the heavenly nymphs danced, swayed and scattered jewellery, the Garuḍa bird screeched and Manasā simply wished she could turn into a spider and creep into a hole.

"Hail to the Mistress of the Universe!" they chanted, "Hail to the Light of the World, the Great Goddess, the Queen of All Thoughts!"

A hand touched her shoulder. She spun around and halted in mid-strike. It was just her daddy, smiling softly, who looked at her with understanding.

"It's always like that," he said, "don't take it personally. They simply play."

Manasā glared at the turbulent crowd, bit her teeth and fought to keep the tears back.

Late in the night, things calmed down. The food was eaten, spilt and wasted, the chalices empty and the last guests staggered away, unless they were carried. Manasā crouched in a corner. The floor was full of clothes. Between them, fruit and yoghurt floated in puddles of strong alcohol. A deep groan made her turn. But it was only her brother Gaṇeśa. His face was full of cream and he snored. Squeaking with the strain, his mouse dragged him away. Manasā waited. She felt relieved that things were quiet again. Noiselessly, her bare feet on the marble, she slid through the hall. Here was a broken lute; presumably someone had sat on it. There a pair of smashed cymbals, next to the underwear of a heavenly dancer. Nearby, soaked with milk and juice, her sari. I wonder how she travelled home. The snake goddess slipped through empty corridors, through arcades and colonnades, a shadow in the gloom, ascended staircases that extended through eternity and found her destination. She stopped before an ornate door. The musky scent of lion filled the air. On the other side, someone was weeping. Manasā knocked. The weeping stopped.

She knocked again and waited. The quiet extended forever.

"Durgā?"

No reply.

"Durgā?"

Deadly silence. Manasā leaned against a wall and waited. After a while, she turned. The ceiling had disappeared into flickering shadows. The great hall was vast and desolate, a cracked shell, an empty skull. She wouldn't find her peace in it. She slid to the balcony and emerged high above the clouds, under a canopy of frosty stars. The air tasted like ice, but it felt real. Manasā shivered. In the moonlight, a series of towering peaks, each clad in snow and frost, appeared, too small for heaven and too huge for earth, in-between worlds, desolate, foreign, forbidden, the homes of the gods.

Her ears roared. How could the gods survive such feasts! Nothing but noise and turmoil! They sang and danced, struggled, feasted, worshipped and groped each other, fell into the food and made a total mess of everything. Will I ever understand them?

"No-one can understand them."

She turned her head. Śiva stood next to her, pale by moonlight, his eyes burning with sobriety.

"Why did they worship me?" The goddess raised her hands. "We don't know each other."

Śiva grinned like a corpse. "They sense your poison and they fear you."

"I am nothing and can't do anything! They are the wonder workers!"

"You are thought and imagination." His laugh was dry and cruel. "Without you, religion disappears. So do the world and everything."

"What about Durgā?" Manasā whispered. "She locked her door."

The Lord of Ascetics raised an eyebrow. "That's another mystery no-one can understand. Go to sleep, it will be dawn soon."

"And you?"

"I'll stay. Just look, how beautiful the mountains are. Today I died. And I was reborn."

"Forgive me."

"Gladly." Śiva smiled as he sat down. "Do you feel it? The night is wonderful to be alive."

Picture 10: Mountain Guardian.

10. Outside

"Why do they call me the power of awareness?"

Śiva glanced at his daughter. The early morning light made her body gleam, woke the serpents and made her locks shine like gilded obsidian. He stifled a yawn. The night had been long and he was in no mood for philosophical excurses. The day could see how it got along. Preferably without him.

"They worship me as Absolute Consciousness, the formless force behind all manifestation. Don't blame me, I didn't do it. Your essence is my essence. Only that you are younger, look better, are wonderfully naive and I have more experience." His eyes sparkled. "I can see you got involved with a lotus blossom. There's plenty of plant life in your system. Consider this. In the age before ages, the trees were mostly conifers. They gave their pollen to the wind. You need a lot of pollen to procreate. It's pretty wasteful. A little later, a few plants learned to blossom. The water plants were among the first. They set up a partnership with insects and other animals, and look how successful they are. They made it. Success requires symbiosis."

"But I was born from a serpent."

"Sure. Kadrū played her part. It's a crazy mixture. You are plant and serpent and divine awareness. And you are fated to control the toxins of the world."

He smiled. "It means you are a killer."

Manasā chewed her lip. Śiva waited for her reaction.

She lowered her head. "Sorry. I'll learn to handle it."

"You will need peace of mind."

"How do I get it?"

"It's simple. But I have to admit, it isn't perfect. You don't get peace by being peaceful. Pacifists ooze frustration and hate. You get it by enjoying the parts of yourself which are never fully satisfied."

"Do you have peace?"

"Of course not." He seemed amused. "I'm too chaotic for that sort of thing. That's my nature. But you could."

"How?"

"Just as a formality, you could worship a deity who is really different."

"I won't worship Brahmā!"

Śiva burst out laughing. "No one really does. Oh daughter! You are far too serious! And serious means stupid. It has to be someone who balances who you are."

"I don't know who I am!"

"Try Kṛṣṇa. He can teach you a lot."

She remembered Kṛṣṇa. He was young and attractive, his eyes glowed like embers and when he played his reed flute the gods wept with sadness and joy. Unlike many others, and no matter how drunk, he remained courteous and respectful. Indeed, most of the time he was on the lookout, and only relaxed when his girlfriend Rādhā arrived. At first glance she appeared like a simple cowgirl. Until you saw her eyes, shimmering like aparājitā blossoms. Those who met her gaze would consider thunderclouds bright, for the rest of their lives. Great, Manasā thought, he is in a steady relationship, he is true and reliable, a god with a sense of honour, and will keep his hands to himself.

Manasā chose an empty room. There were plenty of them around, her dad had created a series of spaces, halls, corridors and swimming pools, just for her, as far from Durgā's premises as possible. She got down on the ground and stretched, moved her muscles in tiny motions; she yawned and swayed until she found her bodycenter. The silence was immense and the room seemed emptier than ever. She had never been known her breath was loud. Maybe, she thought, I should burn some sandalwood. Or ring a bell. Or chant some hymns.

"You won't need to" said a melodious voice. Like a flash of lightning against a turquoise summer sky, the Dark Lord stood before her. He wore less jewellery than the night before, but his sparkling eyes were lined with kohl and he held his reed flute as if couldn't wait to play. His smile was diamonds and gold. "I am glad to be invited."

Manasā raised her hands in greeting, and bowed formally. "I am glad you answered my call."

"Don't thank me. I'm there for everyone." Kṛṣṇa tilted his head. He looked stunningly good, and knew it.

"Daddy said I should worship someone who is different."

"A pleasure." The god of herders settled down in front of her and reverently laid his flute aside. "Everyone worships me. Especially the women. The whole world lies in my embrace."

He winked playfully. "I'll make it easy for you. You have to make feelings. Passion, craving, self-surrender; a desire that burns you up, and makes the ashes spiral in the wind. You should see my worshippers. Some weep. Some laugh. Many sway, shake, sing and dance. Some roll on the ground. And they forget themselves in their yearning for the divine."

"I don't understand the divine! The more I think, the crazier it gets."

"Consider it a game. You play with me, and I will play with you. Focus your attention on my shape. Everything is highly symbolic. You could start by admiring my looks. Observe my ornaments, my expensive costume, my clean skin, the long, curly hair, my noble countenance, the radiant smile, my passionate, full lips, my athletic body, my sensitive, manly hands..."

Manasā stared at him and her inner voice went silent. It was like running into a waterfall. She surged into the dark god and Kṛṣṇa's smile faded. His eyes went wide as Manasā flooded his mind; he was seized and whirled and tossed about, as she bathed herself in his darkness and laughed at the melodies spiralling through his soul.

They remained like statues, frozen, unable to move, and locked into each other.

Then Kṛṣṇa broke out laughing, and the sound cascaded through her mind like silver fountains. He shook his head and beamed. Ceremoniously, he leaned forwards and bowed. Manasā could hardly get her head together. She looked at the god, whom she was meant to worship, and saw him prostrate on the ground, his face pressed against the marble, praying for her blessing.

"Kṛṣṇa?" she whispered.

He lifted his head, and touched her feet. Like a happy cat he got up, circled her as the sun moves, gave her a wicked grin, and disappeared.

The world is ice, thought Manasā, as she raised her foot. Leaning forward, she broke through the crust and sank in to her knee. A biting wind swept across the whiteness, spiralling crystal clouds. In the distance, frost spirits swirled and scattered. Eternity feels like this, everything is cold, beautiful, meaningless, and her eyes stung. Each step the same: lift a foot, set it down vertically, shatter the crust and find a foothold, then raise the other, hour after hour, no matter how much it aches. Next to her Śiva crunched along. She refused to follow in his tracks.

"Soon we've made it through the pass."

Manasā bit her lips. He treated her like a child. Just over this ridge, down that slope, careful in the ravine, let's wade this stream, then up the other side, painful, numbing, until her legs were raw and her feet felt like stumps. Occasionally she got stuck in snow drifts that reached her navel. They clambered through thickets of dwarf birches, coated in ice, their fine branches gleaming like crystal spider webs, struggled through snow-laden pines, and staggered down the next path, into a valley, where the wind calmed. At the end of each path: another tiny settlement.

"This one will be great!" Her father seemed so optimistic. She could see it strained him. But long before they reached paddocks and huts and the dogs began to bark, they faced a red-orange gleam, shielding the village and its inhabitants with angry magic.

The travellers turned, gave fields and houses a wide berth, crossed the brook, struggled up another slope and fought their way to another valley, somewhere far away, and surely much better than the last.

Durgā had done what she could. In the nights after Manasā's arrival, she had appeared to her priests and worshippers.

"The serpent demon is coming. She is shameless and evil. Her worshippers will feel my wrath."

Manasā didn't understand. She had done her best to placate her stepmother. But Durgā refused to listen. When Manasā entered a room, Durgā made bitter remarks, insulted Śiva, smashed a few things and departed like an empress, furious and untouchable. Śiva looked away and pretended everything was fine. Night after night, their quarrels echoed through the corridors. Manasā would have loved to run away, or to visit her brothers, who hid somewhere else and smoked more dope than ever. Only her father, increasingly strained, remained friendly and encouraging. One night she heard Durgā scream "I'll go away, I'll pack my stuff, and I will take my sons! We will move to Hemanta, where people respect us!"

One morning, chewing on a frog that tasted like cardboard, she had enough.

"Daddy," she said, "I need a place for myself."

His eyes were moist, but he smiled.

"We'll find you a divine mountain and you will be happy. It'll be the highest of them all."

Heaven wore a rosy tinge, like banners in the wind, when they left. She thought that the colour hinted at good luck. Shortly afterwards, snow began to fall. That had been long ago. Before she left, Manasā gave Durgā a golden ring, studded with four jewels. Each gem was the essence of Krama, the Way of Going: birth, being, re-absorption and the indescribable. That's the cycle of reality. They were balanced and bound by the fifth: the continuity of formless awareness. The ring had appeared from Manasā's mind, and she had infused it with love.

Durgā studied the item and showed her teeth. Nobody could mistake it for a smile.

"It's cheap."

"Mother!" Manasā bowed and tried to touch her feet. Durgā stepped back.

"Perhaps you don't like this ring. I'm sure it isn't good enough. You deserve much better. But if you or Śiva are in trouble, hold it and send a call! I'm always there for you."

Durgā tossed the ring into the snow. "That day will never come."

Father and daughter left. They climbed peak after peak and were repelled by so many settlements that Manasā lost hope. This was Durgā's realm, harsh, cold and spiteful, and they were not welcome. Months later, they reached the rim of the high mountain range and saw the hills and plains below. Their path took them downhill, into warmer and wealthier lands. The travellers descended through rhododendron forests, where birds fluttered, shining like flying jewels; they crossed the tracks of musk deer and red pandas, and struggled down chutes where glacier water sprayed. Manasā laughed when she saw a sloth bear, carrying her offspring on her back. Śiva sighed with relief; it was the first time his daughter showed a sign of happiness. He plucked a blue poppy blossom for her. It almost made her weep. Further down, the landscape flattened out and fields appeared. Here, barley grew, and further down the slopes they saw terraces where rice was cultivated, and a grimy little town. For an experienced god like Śiva, it was just a cluster of weather-savaged huts, glued to each other and stacked to the hillside with sheer hope and desperation, but Manasā was amazed. So many houses, so many gardens! There must be fifty, perhaps a hundred of them! These people were rich! She counted in amazement: four major roads, five shops, a smithy, a potter, two temples, five shrines, a tiny mosque and three inns. Thirty-four social classes inhibited the village. The upper classes did not. Here, many gods were worshipped, but no matter whether she looked at shrines or into houses, there was Durgā reclining on her lion, illuminated by the golden light of butterfat lamps, swathed in sandalwood fumes, smug and satisfied.

At the foothills of the Himālayas, turbulent brooks merged into streams that glittered as they cascaded to the plains. In the trees, golden monkeys jumped and high above, kora birds circled on the hot air currents. Below them, herds of cattle grazed on swampy meadows, watched by herders whose long and lazy days were devoted to talk, sleep and fluting. The village people wore lighter garments than those in the hills: a white cotton dhoti and a smaller piece across the shoulders sufficed. In the morning they bathed in small rectangular ponds at the edges of their gardens and allowed the sun to dry them.

Warmth is a state of mind, and suits snakes perfectly. Given enough heat, even humans relax and slow and take their time.

"Heat is a drug," said Śiva, "it stimulates the parasympathetic nervous system."

"The what?" Manasā shook her head.

"The parts of you that calm you down. Cold does the opposite. It makes you active and restless."

He grinned. "And like all good things, both are addictive."

Manasā disagreed. "I'm a snake!" she said, "Human rules don't apply to me."

Snakes don't get edgy in the cold; they go stiff. For them, heat is food and joy and energy. But that's no reason to disagree with a god who knows everything about states that leave you inspired or dead.

Manasā liked the sun-bathed hills, she relaxed, her eyelids drooped and her legs became heavy. She's tired, Śiva thought, my little girl, it's time for sleep.

Manasā rolled up under a sij tree and snoozed. Her father sat in silence, the beads of his rosary, one skull after another, slipping, like world-ages, as he relaxed into the motion. His breath faded into nothingness. Finally, his fingers rested. There was perfect silence. No diversions, no distractions, just plain reality. He had dreaded this moment.

It was time to say goodbye. From now on, his little girl, hissing in her sleep, would have to face the world alone. It wouldn't be easy. And honestly, he would miss her. A tear ran down his face. Śiva smiled, caught it in his shoulder cloth and dropped it to the ground. He spoke a mantra, made a gesture, and clapped his hands. The cloth convulsed, transformed, and a goddess emerged. She was a happy girl, maybe sixteen years old, clad in a tiny red bra that hardly covered the bulges underneath and an even smaller slip. Both were encrusted with golden ornaments: Śiva spotted tigers, reptiles, plants, blossoms and plenty of bones between them. Her face was all eyes, sparkling, gleaming, glittering with fascination, and her hair, divided into three bunches, leapt as she laughed. She has wider cheekbones, thought Śiva, and is a little overdressed. What a lot of gold. Look at those bangles and garlands, I'm sure she jingles.

"Hi, daughter!" He grinned from ear to ear. "Blossoms and snakes. They are great. I like the skulls best," he said, "they chortle with delight."

He felt so proud of himself. Manasā was born from thoughts and semen; this daughter was born from love and compassion. And she is just as deadly.

"You are Neta", he declared, and touched her brow, "as you were born from my eye (netra) and a piece of cloth (netā). Feel blessed. Yours are the tears of joy and sorrow, of tension and release. You are liberation, death and rebirth."

Neta laughed. It seemed so funny and so true.

"Please look after your big sister," Śiva said, "she is a thinker, not a knower, and she needs your help."

He bowed, and touched the feet of the girl. She giggled. The Lord of Ascetics rose, winked, clapped his hands, and disappeared. Neta squatted next to Manasā and watched the serpents in her hair. What a lazy bundle. Hello big sister, she thought, you look so young and innocent. How will you face the world?

Important poets report that Śiva returned to Mount Kailāsa in a hurry, where he calmed Durgā's temper, praised her divinity, massaged her feet and made her happy in bed. He did his duty as a good husband, ignored his sons, spent eternities in altered states and kept the universe spinning, twisting and going upside down. Other poets disagree. Their accounts rest on the yarns of monkeys and giant squirrels. You know our furry friends: they tell their lies to anyone who buys them nuts and drinks.

Before going home, Śiva gazed at the horizon where the snowy peaks disappeared into the sky, and gave a sigh of relief. He could be home in a second. But what if something happened to the girls? This was the world, and not a children's playground, the very place where life is difficult and dangerous. Forests, he recalled, are full of tigers, leopards and sloth bears. Such a bear seems like a moth-eaten bag, snoring in a thicket. You wake it by mistake and its paw goes straight through your eye socket and into the brain. There are red dogs, merciless hunters, that make leopards and tigers clamber into trees. There are striped hyenas. Sure they are pretty, and some of my best friends are hyenas, they are wonderful company, and always ready for a laugh, but mind you, each can crush the leg-bone of a tiger and send a pack of wolves running. There are short-sighted, choleric rhinos with fewer brains than a sofa and male elephants, mad on hormones, their eyes dripping juices, going bonkers. Worst of all, the world is full of humans. I know it was a mistake; Brahmā shouldn't have created them. Some are moderately all right, a few are nice and great and wonderful; the rest are simply there. Like them or not, you can't trust people. My cute little girls, they are hardly adult, almost nude and have no life-experience! I should have stayed with them. Neta, I'm sure, can handle anything. But Manasā, my dear, innocent serpent girl, is a thinker! I should have cast a protection-spell on them. I should have loaded them with weapons! I should have roused an army of blood drinking ghosts as their honour guard!

Śiva shuddered. None of these were good enough. He wiped his clammy brow and scattered the drops. The earth fumed and a young god rose. Earth, water and salt, an excellent mixture, provided you don't expect too much. The lout who slouched before him didn't bother to bow. His clothes didn't fit; his teeth were yellow, but his sneer revealed cunning and sarcasm. He is salt and filth and greed, thought the Lord of Ascetics, he has shifty eyes and he thinks like a thief. That's perfect.

"I name you Dhāmāi."

The fellow knotted his eyebrows. Nobody likes to be a 'ratsnake'. Among biologists, the dhāmanā is known as Pytas mucosis; the villagers are fond of it, as it eats rodents in the attic. It looks large and dangerous, but has, so I am told, a good heart, underneath the rest, which is pretty much a lot, and plainly terrible. Śiva rubbed his hands: for royal cobras, like his darling girls, a ratsnake is no problem. If it fails to behave, it constitutes breakfast.

"You will be the guardsman for my two girls, and serve them in all ways."

Dhāmāi gave a dirty grin. He had his own ideas about 'serving'.

"Follow this path and you will find them. Take good care of them; be wary and paranoid, for you were born from my suspicions and doubts."

That should suffice. Why explain everything? His other sons had received less fatherly attention, and got along perfectly. Someone should pity the world. It wouldn't be him.

And with this happy thought, Śiva clapped his hands and disappeared.

We can't trust our literary sources. Historians quarrel, poets disagree and monkeys ask for more nuts, before they invent anything new. One evening, sharing a bowl of rodents, I asked Manasā for the truth.

"It was easy. We walked in a haze and I kept inventing things." She smiled and picked bits of fur from her teeth. "I made the dream like the world and the world like the dream. I mean, look at all this stuff, mountains, houses, trees, people, they are basically awareness. Everything is. That's me. You can shape it any way you want. And it shapes you.

When everything fit, I knew where we were. The land was so peaceful: no inhabitants, just a bit of vegetation, and silence. Sure, there were rivers, swamps, wetlands, and my mountain. Many thousand metres high, just like those of other gods. The peak crusted with eternal snow, down the slopes herbs and growth and further down stunted trees, conifers, then forests, thickets, fruit trees, spikes, thorns, nightmares and anything you like. That's what it looked like when we arrived."

She reached for another rat. "You know, once I start I can't stop. I love the crunchy bits. The sauce is fabulous. A touch of chilli, some ginger, long pepper, turmeric for colour, cardamom and cumin, some vinegar and honey, I mean, I don't need much to be happy. The world was new and huge and amazing. I visualised something, and all of a sudden it existed, in more detail than I could have imagined, and had a head of its own. Or several. And it was fresh, as if I had invented it a moment ago. Or like it had been there for aeons, waiting for me to remember. Believe me; I remember a lot, life after life after life. I came home, and it was great, but it wasn't good enough. I wanted more spikes and blossoms, and toxic animals. So I re-dreamed the lot." She shook her head. "I tried and tried again. It isn't perfect. Neta says, it will never be. In her opinion, that's excellent."

Dhāmāi Ratsnake has a different tale.

"It was just us, we three, and I had to look after my sisters. They were totally helpless. Difficult, demanding, no idea about reality. I mean, we are talking about girls. It was damned obvious why Śiva needed me to handle them. Without male help they were lost. The elder dreamed as she moved along. She was out of her mind for days, sleepwalking like an idiot. She talked with trees, ate earth, fell over rocks and asked spiders for the way. Hopeless. Occasionally she fell into a thorn bush and didn't even notice. I had to scout, find food, water, shelter and scare predators. The younger one was even worse. All right, nothing against Neta, she's a fine girl, but awfully bossy. Sure, if you look like that, you can behave any way you like. But, honestly, her mouth wouldn't stand still. Do this, do that, behave, hands off, you touch my bottom and I'll break your arm...all the time, day in and out. Finally, we arrived. In the middle of nowhere, Manasā opened a door. I doubt she noticed what she did. We walked through and were home. If you could call it home. There was nothing but a wasteland, pretty, if you like stuff with spikes on it, but too damn boring. A gigantic mountain and zero occupants. No city, no nightlife, no fun. The girls insisted that we climb, all the way up, well, you can't say no to them. We waded through swamps, crept through thorns, struggled through cedars, then over rocks and finally across the snow. Really, I hate the stuff. It's rubbish. When we reached the top, the girls left me alone. No idea why. Honestly, they were as crazy as headless chickens. It was awfully cold. I sat on a stone until my ass went blue. Nothing there, just rocks and ice. The girls ascended to the peak. They invoked this god who builds stuff. He created the palace for them, out of nothing and hopes, just like Manasā's ideas, no matter how crazy they are. Within minutes the thing was done, huge, with a wall and all sorts of stuff inside and I looked forward to a good night in bed and Neta said "another remark like that and I'll stuff your tailbone into your mouth". I mean, I'm Śiva's son, and people respect me, when I kill rodents, but they won't take me seriously. As a rat snake you have to eat a lot of shit. I got a few rooms near the entrance and they suit me fine. I guard the gate and I kick ass. It's the least that I can do. Well, that's the tale. It's true, no matter what they say. That'll be six hundred rupees, cash."

Neta disagrees: "Just listen. I don't have much time. See this basket here? The stuff is filthy. I've got a job to do. Śiva said, "Hey, would you like a hobby? Being a counsellor isn't everything. Manasā needs your help, but you need something special, something all for yourself, and you should have a bit of fun." I say, yes, and he says "Do you like the river?" I say, sure, it's shady, and cool at noontime and the forest is gorgeous and damp and he says, "That's where you'll get your temple!"

Next thing I'm busy. Have you noticed? The gods are perfectly dressed. It's an illusion. In real life, the gods get filthy. They fight Anti-Gods and Monsters, they hang around with ascetics and crusties; they rescue people in the wilderness. Gods go sweaty and goddesses have their days. And they have a lovelife. It leaves stains. In the temples, people pour milk over their statues, push cheese and yoghurt into their faces and spill flowers and goat-blood over them. It all goes to rot. Call it filth, if you like. That's the story of my life.

Let's hurry. Yes, we climbed Sij Mountain. Manasā picked the name, she loves sij plants and anything that bites and stings and disagrees. Especially if it's toxic. Euphorbias, small and nasty; or large and towering, and ketakā trees, mango, figs, creepers, crawlers, winders and stranglers, you name it. We performed a ceremony, up on the mountaintop. Without Dhāmāi Ratsnake, of course. He can do a lot, and some of it is useful, but he won't do holy. That guy was made from dirt and sweat and that's his approach to life. I don't want to nag. He is my brother and he has his good sides, though they are hard to find. And sure, Śiva created him, don't ask me why. But the same goes for tapeworms and lampreys.

Well, we stood there, hip deep in the snow and sang mantras. In the meantime, and it was mean, Viśvakarman, the Divine Architect built this palace for us. And the rest of it, like gardens, streams, bridges, grottoes, lakes and pavilions. More dimensions than you can imagine. It was a start. Manasā made some improvements. "It's too perfect," she said, "I can't stand so much order!"and turned parts of it into a wilderness. That's how she thinks. Then we opened the doors and sent out invitations. The guests arrived, and we got seers, ascetics, nuns, yoginīs, poets, singing girls, prostitutes and artists. People of all 36 classes, most of them crazy, but no matter, we accept anyone who can find the way to us. They built settlements around the slopes. Some work fields, most herd cattle, keep bees, hunt, fish, write epic ballads, paint, carve, sculpture, sing, dance, make love, hang around or celebrate all day. A few total nutters write books or do 'pure science'. That's fine, don't blame me, I try to agree with everyone. We've got plenty of magicians and witches; you can't exclude them when food and drinks are free.

It was a start. Then the dead came travelling, hordes of them, swollen, rotten, and falling apart. People out there, in the world, they got the news that there's a serpent goddess in business. The world, a silly place, if you ask me, that's where people die of snakebite, ten-thousands of them, each year. They twitch and go stiff and look pretty much done, but in reality, their relations say, they ain't dead. It wouldn't do to burn or bury them. They put the corpse on a raft of banana logs, add sacrificial gifts, you know, trinkets, food, water, milk, blossoms and vegetables, and let it drift downriver. Sooner or later, they say, a sorcerer will restore the dead to life. That's what they hope. It doesn't work. Good sorcerers are rare. They find no students. Nowadays there are computer games and smartphones and more idiots than ever. I say: chatty, stupid, lonely. They invest in gadgets instead of brains. We are stuck with a generation of spectators. Hardly anyone bothers to meditate, to do ritual, to transform thought and belief and personality. People watch zombie movies. I've seen a few. In real life, zombies are everywhere. So where should the magic come from? But you can trust the river. I do. It takes you all the way. And baby, I love it. The flood is deep and dark. It cares for everyone. The dead go floating, for days and weeks. They forget their worries, their hopes and dreams, they rot and putrefy. Some slip into the river, some get eaten in the swamps; some make it to the sea. A few end up with us. Yes, I know it sounds insane. Here on Sij Mountain we are up in the sky. But we are also down there, where the Dark Waters flow. We are under the sea, and in the human world, all at once. Don't ask me to explain. I didn't do it.

Well, you can find me at the river. I do the washing. I handle pollution. And you should come and see my temple. You've never seen anything like it.

I do the washing for the gods; and when the dead come floating by, I pull the corpses out of the river and Manasā revives them, if they are worth it. We examine them. We test them. You don't get anything for free, not even when you're dead. Have you seen the crocodiles? I like them. They are fat, and they laugh all day.

Go for a walk on Sij Mountain and you meet plenty of dead people. Most of them are happier than before. When you have left it all behind, life can only get better. Right, that's enough for now, evening comes, there's a lot to do. Will you help me wash?"

The sun rose like a globe of honey, drenching mountain slopes and the rivers in the valleys with golden sweetness. The air was fresh and inviting. Manasā, Neta and friends met at the riverside to have an early morning bath. High above, Princess Vinālatā leaned over her celestial balcony and watched. The princess was a Gandharva; she belonged to the class of divine singers, musicians and sorcerers, and as she heard the shouts and laughter and saw the glitter on the waves, she simply couldn't resist. Vinālatā undressed as far as she dared, and descended graciously. In case you wonder, in East India, celestial spiders weave golden webs connecting the heavens, worlds and underworlds. She was a figure of beauty, a flame of eternity, clad in rainbows, hope, and promise, and allure. Brahmā the Creator sat in the company of a few minor gods hip-deep in the current, telling them how wonderful he was, and when he saw Vinālatā's perfect dream figure, he couldn't hold back. He spurted high into the air and hit the wet sand at the shoreline, where his semen hissed and burned and smoked. Vinālatā was used to involuntary compliments. She granted him a shy but inviting smile that made Brahmā blush and chew his beard, before she gracefully turned away, to other, more important matters. Deeply ashamed, Brahmā looked at his friends. Most of them tried to keep their expression under control. Oh damn! They'll laugh about me later! And look at the shore! The sand boiled, bubbled, foamed and gave birth. Not again, he thought, heaven help, I wish I were far away, unconscious or dead. For good or bad, and help me tell the difference, creativity is unstoppable. From the sizzling sands arose seven hundred divine seers. They were nude, smeared with ashes, had long, filthy hair and glared at the world with loathing. Well and good, in Manasā's realm anyone is welcome, provided she or he is mad enough. Next arose two seven-headed monsters, their torso human and their hips and legs bestial, furry and clawed. They seemed confused, and whether they joined the bath or ran away screaming wasn't recorded. Brahmā tried to hide his twitching, rock-hard penis and thought fiercely of all things which didn't turn him on. The range of subjects was tiny. Uncertain what to do with the damned thing; he hurled himself into the current and submerged himself where the water was icy.

It doesn't end our story. After the bath, a sacrificial ceremony followed, and one of the officiating priests spilt holy water from his jug, directly on the spot where Brahmā's seed was fuming.

"You did it on purpose!" hollered Brahmā, "You cheat! It's not fair!"

From the wet sand rose a bunch of giant tigers. They had claws as sharp as razors, eyes full of fire and gaping mouths that reached from the underworlds into the height of heaven. If you think the dark is scary, think again. These tigers were the scorching heat of noon, when forests go up in flame, and they left nothing to the imagination. Brahmā paled. They would be trouble, and he would be blamed. Furtively, he glanced at Manasā, and was relieved that she was giggling. Neta grinned from one ear to the other; she showed more teeth than anyone should have, and looked much like the crocodiles that keep her company.

Brahmā had an inspiration. "Don't be deluded! It's Karman, folks! It's fate and higher forces and so on! I couldn't help it. I know, don't tell me, this is trouble. And of course, I sympathise with everyone. But I prophecy that the tigers will be defeated by the bull calf of the divine cow Kapilā!"

The tigers bared their teeth and slunk away. They wandered into the mountain wilderness and led a wild and uninhibited life.

11. Tigerfight

High gods have a hard time. That's why they complain, should you ask, particularly at four in the morning, when they roll around in bed and can't return to sleep, as their thoughts are far too big and loud and colourful. Śiva, for instance, worries whether the trances, drugs and fits of divine lovemaking will keep the universe in perfect harmony, or catapult him into outer space. Or he wakes up thirsty as his throat is parched and his emblem feels raw and hurt and overused.

Durgā smiles. "My little darling," she says," I see you need a rest." She snuggles up against him. "Just hold me tight."

"I love you," he says, "but, honestly, I want a holiday." It never really happens.

Viṣṇu knows his duty. Running the universe is one hell of a job. At times he wishes he could recline on his serpent bed and drift away in dreamless sleep. Reality catches up with him. He dreams of schedules and meetings and important matters on the agenda. He wakes when he fears he might forget an important point. On his bedside table rests a pocket calculator, a pad of stickers and a large notebook, with the heading 'My Rules'.

"You don't care!" he tells the assembly of gods, "I am totally worn out! And you are lazy, undisciplined and useless. Without my effort, the universe would simply fall apart! I do my work and I do your work and all you do is laugh!"

At five a.m. he realises that all hopes for sleep are gone, slips out of bed without waking Lakṣmī, has a cold shower, tip-toes into his office, drinks several cups of strong coffee, counts his paperclips, orders his pencils by size, colour and density, writes memos, sends emails and waits for the sunrise. It arrives, bleary, disheartening, and he says hello to another day of chores and duties. "It's all about limitations," he mutters. "Ecology is defined by possibilities and limits. The potential makes you hope, the limits grind you down. The rarest resource within each biosphere defines who thrives and who is blotted out." He sighs. "That's my job. It isn't easy. I do the game board, the players, the playing figures, heaven, earth and underworld. And I make rules. Some break them. Some are foolish. Like Śiva. He's all for chaos and doing your own thing. It happens, within the limits that I set. And it keeps changing, as Brahmā introduces chance mutations." He snaps a pencil, looks at it, and drops it in the basket. "Brahmā," he sighs, "has no conscientiousness whatsoever. He mucks around, he plays, he messes things up and goes hot with desire. He is wise and stupid and plainly irresponsible. For some reason, people admire him. Frankly, I wish I were more popular."

Brahmā, of course, has the hardest fate. He's a small guy with four heads and four silly beards, each in a different colour. People laugh when he walks by. But he is an artist. He's got the hat, the scarf, and smokes bindies. He can't control himself, or anything. On bad days, he squirts all over the place, as creativity can't be stopped, and this can go on all through the night. His bed turns into a puddle, and when he rises, he scrubs and curses, while his emissions turn the cosmos purple and green. Once a month, the high goddesses have similar problems, so I've been told, but as I respect them, and their function, their grace, joy, and perfection and as they could squash me like a bug, I prefer to shut up and pretend that nothing happens.

Let us return, no matter how slimy it may get, to Brahmā.

One fine day he was a guest on Mount Kailāsa. Śiva, Durgā and he celebrated almost until dawn and when morning came, unwelcome and grey, none of them felt really happy. Śiva mumbled something about "looking after the cattle" and staggered away across the snow, where he hoped, eventually, to sober up a little. Durgā, looking wrinkled and frayed, declared that she needed at least two days of beauty sleep and swayed to her bedroom. Brahmā, feeling anything but fresh, remained alone. His head buzzed and his hands shook, but try as he might, he couldn't go to sleep. He sat on the couch, feeling miserable, and wondered whether vomiting is allowed when you are the Creator and anything might happen. Finally, he rose and looked out of the window. High mountains, peaks without number, craggy rocks, glistening ice, the odd avalanche here and there, is this the life, he thought, everything is cold and bright and makes my eyes water. No matter how far I look, hardly anything happens. Feeling bored, he walked through the palace. Quite by coincidence, he chanced to walk into Durgā's bedroom. There she was, heroine of all worlds, champion of truth and justice, warrior goddess, untouchable and inviting, lying on her bed, with just a thin veil covering this and that, and there was plenty of it. Brahmā froze. The goddess was terrifying in her beauty. Below her couch slept her lion, a huge, smelly cat, and snored. Brahmā felt deeply touched. The sight woke the poet in him. I wish I could capture this in a rhapsody, he thought. And then he saw her hand. It emerged from the veil and her little finger was so gracious, so slim, so delicate, well, our poet, stuck by divine perfection, grasped for air and spurted all across the bedroom.

That's what Durgā says, who was in deep and happy slumber, believe it who will. Her lion agrees and grumbles, for the dear beast is wise and knows what is good for him.

The ways of the gods are miraculous. Quite by coincidence, Durgā found herself pregnant. Dear reader! Don't criticize her; it could have happened to any of us. She didn't have the slightest idea how it had happened, so in her innocence, she walked down the slope to river Balluka and washed the embryo into the foaming waters. She purified herself, muttered a mantra to avert bad luck, and hurried home. The embryo drifted on the sparkling flood, helpless, and innocent, until it reached a sandy beach. Standing in the torrent, the divine cow Kapilā was drinking; a happy, motherly bovine, with a shiny pelt, proud horns and never a bad thought in her whole life. Kapilā swallowed the embryo and, from one moment to the next, she was pregnant.

Let me introduce Kapilā. A long time ago, Brahmā wanted to celebrate a ritual. For the offering, he needed a special bouquet, consisting of forty-two wonderful blossoms. The number was important to the seers who composed the *Manasā Epics*, but gained international importance when Saint Douglas Adams immortalized it, and countless followers of Śiva had it tattooed on their bums. Collecting forty-two blossoms was a major effort. As Brahmā wasn't just creative but also rather lazy, he walked to Indra's garden. The Thunderer, former King of all Worlds (retired) raised the most wonderful flowers. Indra, as Brahmā was glad to notice, was absent. It would have been easy to steal the lot. But Karman, as Brahmā knew, cannot be ignored. He didn't want to plunder the garden. That would be theft, and lead to retribution. Someone else should do the job for him.

Brahma approached a woman whose shape was wonderfully rounded and whose eyes were deep and dark. She was watering the flowerbeds; a happy horticulturist, or the wife of one, and surely not of much account.

"My lady," he addressed her, and when she turned to him, and Brahmā saw her heaving bosom, he staggered, stared at the ground and fought to keep his dhoti under control.

"Lady Gardener," he stuttered, "Mistress of curves and milky fountains. I am Brahmā the Creator, which means that I am practically the Boss of Everything. I need the forty-two most magical plants you can pick. Meet me near the gate. Hurry up, for I'm waiting for you."

He staggered away, his face wet with sweat, his loins thumping.

A little later, the woman stood before him. Meanwhile, Brahmā had found some relief, and hoped the woman would overlook the puddle.

With a charming smile, he accepted the bundle of plants. It looked so lush and wonderful.

"I feel grateful," he said, "and forever in your debt."

It didn't last. It never does.

"You picked thistles!" he yelled, as his hands and face turned red, "and stingy barbweed, porcupine's ass, eyeburn, skinscorcher, nettleflame, blisterface and bloat-my-bum!"

"But they are precious", said Lady Gardener, in her deep, velvety voice, "just look at the blossoms! So rich and wet and wonderful." She blushed and her eyes were deep like autumn lakes. "They are much like me."

Brahmā fell over. "A spider! Yeuch! Are you trying to kill me?"

"I didn't pick it." The gardener shook her head. "But notice how it gleams and sparkles."

"I curse you!" screamed Brahmā, whose face was hot and swollen, "I curse you for your stupidity!" He choked, coughed and snarled, "You are a cow and will turn into one!"

Lady Gardener did. The gods laughed, but as they liked her, and were happy to see Brahmā swollen like a pumpkin, they made her a divine, celestial cow; the very measure of holiness, a cow who loves all plants, insects, worms and spiders, provided they are edible.

Kapilā, the *Brown Like Ochre*, embarked on a happy, careless life. Indra's garden? Who needs it? The place was just too limited. She walked right through those heavy iron doors and into the wide world. There were shrubs at the wayside, flowers on the meadows, and thick, nourishing growth at the crossroads. Food, wonderful food, was everywhere. From time to time, she devastated gardens. They might belong to you or me, or anybody else. When you are a celestial cow, and full of holiness, you don't care. In the warm, velvet nights, while her stomachs thundered, she gazed into the stars and laughed. Other cows, she thought, may jump over the moon. I'll stay here and be happy, and make the moon jump over me. For whatever reason (Brahmā wasn't there, couldn't have done it and refuses to comment), she was pregnant. Her baby grew, and made her hungry. Day in and day out, Kapilā munched grasses and herbs and fed the bacteria and fungi in her stomachs. There were quite a lot of them, in a climate of low acidity, a colony of devourers, digesters and transformers. One fine day she was ready. Her belly had swollen to alarming dimensions. She gave birth to a bull-calf, under a sky full of stars, and she called her baby Manorath, *'Joy of the Heart'*.

Kapilā was a happy cow. She yielded plenty of milk and her dear little bull-calf drank her empty and roared for more. Before long, our happy cow felt weak and hungry. Where, in all heavens and all hells, would she find food to keep herself in shape?

Luckily, there are many solutions for every problem; most of them are funny and tragic and a few may even work. Her best friend (another respectable cow with a divine background) told her that the best flowers and vegetables grow in Brahman's garden. Kapilā listened; she left her baby bull snoring at the shore of River Ballukā and was off.

Brahman, the word means *Extension*, is the Great Cosmic, All-Pervading All-Self, the Formless, Indescribable, Absolute Ground of All Being, or as the crazy seers of the Upaniṣadic period declared, Absolute Reality. Out of Brahman, everything appears, and into Brahman it disappears again. This Brahman is Pure Consciousness. It should not be confused with the minor god of creation, four-headed Brahmā, who squeaks and spews wherever he goes. As the garden of the All-Self is indescribably vast, I won't bother to give a description. Go for a walk: it's here and there and everywhere. The door was wide open; Kapilā strolled in and stuffed her cosmic belly. By the time Brahman realised what was going on, she had devoured half of the vegetation and was going strong. Luckily, the All-Self is impartial to everyone and everything. Kapilā, no matter how greedy, was a manifestation of itself. So Brahman greeted the cosmic cow with due politeness, took her by her horns and forced her, gently but firmly, out. Before she knew, the gates slammed shut. Kapilā stood there, re-urgitating, and wondered what had happened. There was no way to get back in. So, like all wise cows, she accepted the inevitable and waddled homewards. On her way she passed through Manasā's land. Feeling daring and a little wicked; she nibbled the spiky sij and decided against it.

All of a sudden a bunch of tigers faced her. They were much larger than the usual sort, and like all divine or demonic beings, they could speak.

"Hello moo-cow," said the leader, "we greet the divine in you. You are respectable, holy and fat, and that's why we'll eat you alive."

Kapilā stood and bowed. She was a cow of good family, and her manners were impeccable. "My dear tigers, I greet the divine in you and ask your pardon. Could you eat me later on? I've got a happy little baby bull at home, and he is hungry. I promise to return when I have suckled him."

"Great." The tigers were delighted. "We, too, have children and can understand your worries. But we insist, when you return to us, you'll bring your little darling."

Kapilā's eyes widened. "Why?"

"We just want to have a look."

"It would be such an honour. I'm sure you'll love him. He's sweet and cuddly, I could lick him all day."

Our happy cow walked on, and hummed a happy song. At the shore of River Balluka, she saw her little pet sleeping. What she did not see, was the river. Her calf had been thirsty: it had walked down the shore and drunk the river up. Nothing but a muddy riverbed remained.

"My darling!" she smiled, and laid down.

By evening, her baby had drunk its fill and Kapilā took it for a walk.

Manorath was slightly cleverer than his mom.

When he saw the tigers, he charged ahead, his knobbly horns extended, and roared like an avalanche. The fight was wild and mad, and much of it happened in a cloud of dust that prevents me, as other writers, to give an accurate description. When the sun sank, the earth was red: Manorath had torn the tigers apart and trampled them into the ground. Thus, Brahmā's prophecy came true.

The cow herders heard the story. They've been worshipping Manorath and Kapilā ever since.

While the evening faded into twilight, the white egrets left the sandbanks and departed to their trees. Fruit bats emerged from their caves and swarmed across the velvet sky. The air cooled and the aged creator god Prajāpati sat on his doorstep and felt itchy. Some gods are old but stay young. Prajāpati was born old and wrinkled, with an incomparably restless organ, and the liberal use of his creative semen had wasted him. This evening he met a few friends and walked to River Balluka.

They were in for a surprise.

The river was gone, the riverbed dry, and the fishes had stopped twitching hours ago. The gods stood at the shore, stared into the emptiness, chewed betel leaves and quarrelled. Eventually, they marched downstream. Somewhere, down there, used to be the ocean. But when they emerged at the shore they found a great gaping chasm that reached to the horizon. Not a drop of water in sight.

"It wasn't like this when I was young" said Prajāpati. He sighed. "Nothing really is." His friends agreed. Landscapes ought to be reliable. Not here one day and gone the next. These days, nothing seems to last. And everyone is in a hurry.

What do you do, when things go wrong? The solution is timeless and simple. You delegate the problem. Prajāpati had a special character in mind. Not that he liked him much. The snotty boy lacked manners.

He clapped his hands and called "Śiva! God of Drop-Outs! Failure of the Universe! Wake up, get your head out of the ashtray, and attend!"

His friends shook their heads. "Not him! He's a loafer! A splatter-brain. He's useless!"

"He is all that. But he has the Eye of Absolute Insight," said Prajāpati, "though he doesn't deserve it."

"I'm here," yawned Śiva, and got up. "No need to scream."

He grinned at the assembly. Angry, furry men in bathing trunks, with diving goggles, snorkels, and inflatable rubber animals.

Maybe he had overdosed.

"Young man! Stand straight! We need a prophecy."

Śiva sighed. "You are gods. Make your own."

Prajāpati snarled. "It's not my choice, boy. My friends insist you do the job."

"I could. If I wanted to."

"Then do it!"

"For you? You are a crazy fossil. And stop shouting. You are far too loud." The Lord of Ascetics shook his head. "Say please."

"Please, and damn you."

Śiva laughed and opened his third eye. For a moment, time stood still. He shuddered. "Oh no. This is too much. You won't believe it. It's incredible."

"Speak up!"

"I won't tell."

"You have to!"

"Says who?"

"My dear youngster." Prajāpati tried a fatherly grin, revealing age-worn blackish stumps. "I know you ain't really such a failure, no matter what everyone says. Do it for your elders and betters."

"I'm older than you."

"So it might appear to be. Maybe you are right. But I was born older."

Śiva kept his face straight. He had seen the future. It was fun. He just needed to add a little spin. In a sonorous voice, he proclaimed:

"Listen and learn, you mighty ones! Great seers, sages of the dawn of time, I had a vision. I beheld the cosmic cow Kapilā. She has a cosmic calf; it drank the river and the ocean."

"Rubbish!"

"Trust me, it's the truth, and nothing but the truth. You just don't like it. To prove my point, I will send Nārada to get her here."

"That's the most stupid thing I ever heard!"

"You won't believe what happens next." Śiva raised his hands. "My friends, my venerable elders, do not despair. Soon you can have your bath."

The Lord of Ascetics struggled to keep his face straight. His words were true, and now he simply had to wait. After much encouragement, Kapilā appeared. Nārada pushed her, Śiva pulled her, and there she stood, her legs apart, complained bitterly, strained her udders, and created a new ocean, a vast, primordial sea of milk and curds and cream with yoghurt and cheese bobbing in the waves. It was thick and yucky.

Śiva bowed, "Illustrious Prajāpati," he announced, "master of creation, lord of the immeasurable thing, your bath is ready." He smiled and stepped back. He knew the future. Soon, the gods would trample their bathing gear into the sand.

12. Milkocean

Old tales are wired into our minds. And they are recalled with a vengeance. This myth was crafted by generations of inspired, enlightened and totally irresponsible poets, before several versions were blended in the *Mahābhārata*. And even this was not enough. They found their way into the *Purāṇas*, where they became the heart and guts of Hinduism. In the elder versions, Śiva is a mere bystander, while Viṣṇu has the centre of the stage. It's not a coincidence. Religion is business and legends don't come for free: Viṣṇu Enterprises paid large sums to the storytellers. Most Indians are used to it. Not so the poets and seers of Bengal and Assam, who were crazy, drugged and inspired. Here is the truth. Hear Neta laugh, and see what it does to you.

It was a fine and happy morning. The sun shone from the skies and here on earth insects buzzed, spiders snared, lizards scrambled and people went about their business, stupid, insensible and totally beside themselves, as ever. In short, life was much like today, only that there weren't so many zombies around.

"Let's do something new" said the Holy Seer Durvāsā. He grinned as he twisted his whiskers and began to ascend Mount Kailāsa. Our seer, a remarkable specimen of the moth-eaten, more-than-holy variety, was keen to pay a visit to Śiva and Durgā, see the sights and be admired for his saintliness. As he travelled at the speed of thought, he only needed an instance, and no effort, to reach the pinnacle, where he came to a sudden halt and realized that standing waist high in crunchy snow is not recommended for extended periods. It was a clear day and he could see forever. Neta says, "So can you, anywhere".

Bells rang, lights flashed, and while the alarm went on, Śiva and Durgā realised that an exceptionally holy man had come for a visit, and disentangled. Holy men can be spiteful and difficult, so they rushed to invite him. Within instants, Durvāsā found himself hugged, fed, loaded with presents and hurried across the frozen waste. The seer had no experience with heights that were more demanding than, say, a thick cushion. The towering mountains, gleaming in crystal perfection, blew his mind. He laughed when avalanches thundered into the valleys, marvelled at the pristine beauty of vast ice crusts under a blue sky that made his eyes water, giggled when he fell into the snow, showed deep reverence at the source of River Gaṅgā and worshipped the cosmic goddess with such intensity that Durgā bared her teeth (if only to Śiva). Most of the time, he leapt across rocks and pinnacles like a young goat. When he watched a snow leopard seize a blue sheep, he was quite beside himself. And he delighted to witness the famous seers Bhṛgu and Parāśara, who sat in a deep trance, in their underwear, on exposed rocks, and seemed pretty well frozen. They didn't seem to breathe, nor did he expect them to. This was sheer holiness and Durvāsā couldn't get enough of it. Śiva guided him around, one glittering snowfield after another, and pointed out the great peaks in the distance, where the great gods reside. Durvāsā squinted, saw nothing specific, nodded happily and was ready to believe anything. Śiva fed him cookies and Durgā announced that their guest would surely enjoy something exciting, and made him ride her lion.

As everybody loves the drama curve, the last evening called for a spectacular finale. Śiva and Durgā had discussed this for an entire evening, while their guest lay on a sofa, knocked out of his skull, and drooled. When he finally got up, and after being rescued from the n-dimensional toilet, he was led to the grand plateau in front of the palace. Celestial music sounded and the heavenly Vidyāharīs descended.

"These are our celestial ladies," said Śiva, "Each of them is a science, and art and a branch of magic."

"And they hardly feel the cold," said Durgā, "did you notice they are almost naked?"

"They assist the greatest adepts." Śiva looked proud. It was expensive to hire the troupe. "Heroes of Left-Hand-Path Tantra love and venerate them, and try to embark on a meaningful relationship with them. Those who belong to the Right-Hand-Path, however, flee for their homes, nail the doors and windows shut and hide in the wardrobe."

The god of ascetics shrugged apologetically. "Let me quote Abhinavagupta: *the Right-Hand-Path is full of terrible practices*."

Durgā grinned. "I'm sure you noticed how holy they are."

Durvāsā had. The saint tried to keep his hands (and other things) under control.

"I wasted my life!" he whispered, "I never knew that abstinence is stupid! Oh, I should have climbed this mountain in my youth, when things were going strong and stiff, and sought for true enlightenment..."

Tears ran down his face. "My friends, I wasted decades. I denied myself, and everyone. Now I regret. Wisdom, virtue and quivering whatnots are Anuttara, the Supreme."

Śiva nodded in agreement and patted his shoulder.

"This," he said, "is the real thing."

Durgā would have loved to kick her husband, but kept her temper. "Stop staring," she muttered, "or else."

With an easygoing smile she led Durvāsā by the hand. The guy was close to burn-out, and whatever happened, he would talk about it everywhere. "My dears," she addressed the Vidyāharīs, "you have come a long way. Say hello to our guest."

The heavenly girls curtseyed and blushed. With decorous shame, they presented a flower garland to the holy man. The scent was overwhelming. While Durvāsā sank to his knees and fainted, the divine Vidyāharīs waved goodbye and floated away from Mount Kailāsa, their highly spiritual behinds swaying mightily.

By sunrise next morning, Saint Durvāsā was on his way downhill. His eyes were reddish, his hands shook and his steps faltered. Occasionally he stumbled, touched his groin, ouched, and proceeded in pain. All through the night, no matter what he did, and he had done a lot, his emblem throbbed. The flower garland was in his pack, and whenever the scent caught up with him, he bared his teeth and whimpered. The thing was far too hot for him.

A few weeks later, Saint Durvāsā went to visit Indra's heaven. After surviving Mount Kailāsa, it seemed a little more relaxing. Indra, as everyone knows, is the King of All Gods. He had a mighty reputation in the early Vedic period, when there was quite a demand for lighting and thunder and heroic derring-do. Sadly, times change and superheroes are not always fashionable. Before Indra really understood what happened, Viṣṇu was there with his notebook, adjusted his tie and crown and handkerchief, spun the universe a few times, smiled faintly, congratulated Indra to his amazing and inspiring career as a thunder god, gave him a golden (really goldish) watch and sent him away to his retirement home.

"You'll love it," he said, "you did an excellent job and we are proud of you."

Indra went into retreat, accompanied by a host of heroic warriors and an exceptional troupe of celestial dancers and musicians. "If you ever need me," he said, but Viṣṇu pursed his lips. "We don't". That was it. The thunderbolts were set up on the mantelpiece. The Vedic thunder god, for good or bad, was out of it. But he still had amazing All-Night-Discotheques.

And he was delighted when Saint Durvāsā came for a visit. More so, he was astonished that the saint had such a hypnotic, pleasing scent.

"It's this garland." Durvāsā exclaimed, as he pulled the item out of his dhoti.

Indra felt the power in the faded blossoms. "If you stay a while," he said, "the heavenly Apsaras girls will dance for you. Some say that they are much prettier than the Vidyāharīs."

"Do you?"

"As a thunder god, I wouldn't dream of having an opinion."

"It would be a great boon." Durvāsā blushed. In his embarrassment, he extended the garland. "Take this as a present!"

"I am deeply honoured." Indra bowed. He stuck the garland into his sash and mounted his largest elephant. The dear beast was as dark as a monsoon cloud and as tall as cumulonimbus going incus, and bang.

"See you again" said Indra, as he lifted his prod. At this fateful moment, the garland slipped. It tumbled from the height (more than a ten-thousand metres, in case you want to know) and fell into the mud.

Saint Durvāsā gasped. In general, hardcore ascetic saints suffer from low blood sugar levels, and lack animal fats, tryptophan, serotonin, dopamine, zinc, niacin, and vitamins B_1 and B_{12}. In other words, they are a.) Occasionally blissful, b.) Generally gaga and c.) Less than a millisecond from howling misery and/or world-destructive rage. And they are sugar junkies. That's because sugar stimulates a short-lived kick involving adrenalin, endorphins, tryptophan, and serotonin. Provided tryptophan and serotonin are available. On a purely vegetarian diet, they are rare. I'm sure you guessed: saintliness and idealism come at a price. The saints pay it, as they wither away, and take it out on the people in their company.

Durvāsā shook in holy wrath. "No god may abuse the offerings of a saint! Indra! You careless bastard! Hear my word and feel my curse! Goddess Kamalā-Lakṣmī will leave you! This is your divorce! Your prosperity fades away!"

Indra froze; his face went as pale as his dhoti. "My lord!" he pleaded, as he leapt from his elephant, and went down on his knees. "Forgive my errors, forgive my lack of manners. I am a spark at your feet, a glow worm in the rain." He knocked his face into the mud, but Durvāsā didn't care.

Holy men are Always Right, and what they say is Law Eternal.

Lakṣmī-Kamalā screamed in despair. She pleaded for mercy, and tears, as thick as autumn rains, cascaded down her face. But no-one is as narrow-minded as a starving saint.

Lakṣmī ran into the forest. "Save me!" she called. The bilva trees shuddered, "Go your way. The saint will destroy us!"

Lakṣmī ran into the mountains. "Save me!" But Himavat, Lord of the Snow Peaks, shook his head and avalanches roared down the cliffs. "What can a hill of eight thousand metres do against the curse of a saint?"

"Save me!" Lakṣmī called, as she reached the shore of the Milk Ocean.

The pale flood lapped at her feet. It wasn't afraid of anything. "Come to me" sighed the foam, "relax and feel at home". Lakṣmī waded into the flood, disappeared, and the waves rejoiced.

The earth went grey and ugly. With Lakṣmī, joy and happiness, virtue and value disappeared. So did rice, grains, the moon, Indra's favourite elephant Airāvata, his favourite horse Uchchaśravā, the patijāta plant with its divine blossoms and the Elixir of Immortality.

From one instant to the next, the universe was practically defunct.

Gods, plants, animals and people stood in a daze.

Heaven turned slate, then black, then lethal. The planets buzzed around in confusion, sun and moon paled, the temperature dropped and the great dying began. Diplodocus staggered and collapsed, pterodactyls fell from the sky; tyrannosaurus gave a last, loud shriek and buried their faces in the sand, out there, on the long shore, where land-life began and almost ended, and the waves came hissing, without aim or purpose, unrelenting, merciless. Only crocodiles remained, hidden, in deep trance, and waited for the reappearance of the sun. The gods lost their glamour; they staggered, cursed and their joints screamed with pain. Whole world ages came bearing down on them. Śiva coughed and reached for his pouch. "Let's get into the habit again," he said, as he stuffed his chillum and blotted out his mind. Durgā barely managed to paint her toenails and Indra, lacking his rain-elephant, was forced to walk, or reel, like a lost soul.

At the shore of the Milk-Ocean, where angry gales howled, the gods stood and shuddered. Their bodies had lost lustre, and their heads were grey.

Lakṣmī had to be recovered, no matter the cost. She, and all the blessings of the universe, were somewhere in the balmy sea, in the deep, out of reach, too far for comfort or hope.

"Do get a grip on yourselves and stop yowling. Any positive contributions will be welcome."

"Lakṣmī is gone!" Indra was in a rage. "The universe is finished!" It didn't help that he couldn't stand straight.

"You exaggerate. Lakṣmī exists, down there. And face it: it's just milk," Viṣṇu said, "The stuff comes from cows. I agree, there's a lot of it. But there's no need to worry. With a bit of discipline and effort we can handle it. It just needs to be buttered." His eyes were inflamed and his nose dripped. "I'm sure you don't mind working overtime. We turn this silly ocean into butter and all the good stuff comes up."

"You expect a lot," Brahmā squeaked, "why don't you do it?" He stared at his wrinkled hands. "Gods, I'm ugly. It's your fault. You should have stopped the seer. You are a failure. And now you ask us to work. Are you totally mad? We are gods, remember? We don't work. People work, we have fun."

"We need help," Śiva seemed resolute. His hair was white. Before long, his teeth would fall out. "We need the Asuras."

"What rubbish!" Brahmā complained. "The Asuras are Anti-Gods! You can't trust them! They will try to steal our divine powers!"

"Silence! The world is based on agreements and contracts." Viṣṇu tried to straighten his aching back, and groaned. "Anything can be negotiated. I am sure, deep in their rotten hearts, the Asuras are trustworthy and helpful."

Brahmā gasped. "Trustworthy and helpful! That goes for gods, and not for demons!"

"I say we give them a chance!"

"I say you are an idiot!"

"Relax, old man." Śiva grinned from ear to ear, "Eat your four beards and come up with something better. Churn the milk ocean on your own."

Viṣṇu gave Śiva a stern glance. "Silence, now. We won't have insults. I am glad to tell the board that everything is settled. Our volunteer, Śiva, will be our representative. He will lead the negotiations, and bring them to success."

The gods applauded, as well as they could.

Śiva glared. In the good old age of prehistory, when huge populations migrated, he had been a member of the Asura family. Just like the Devas, the Asura were just another bunch of gods, no better or worse than anyone. Maybe they were related to the Nordic Aesir and they certainly inspired the Persian Ahura. They supplied respectable deities: fire god Agni, sun god Savitar, moon god Soma, sky-god Dyaus, river-goddess Sarasvatī, Uṣas, goddess of dawn, her sister Ūrmyā, goddess of the night, Indra, the Thunderer, and the lord of justice and healing, Varuṇa. And Rudra, or better Śiva, as he was called nowadays, the crazy guy from the forest. The Deva clan, of course, offered better opportunities. Asuras with a sense of priority left their tribes and joined the Deva group. It was a career move, and improved their ranking enormously. Nowadays, thanks to the ascent of narrow-minded Hinduism, the remaining Asuras had been turned into a horde of Anti-Gods. What about you, Varuṇa? You made it to Greece, where they called you Uranus! Nowadays you hang around with quacks and administer multi-vitamin treatments! With a bit of effort, you could have become the All-Self, the Yakṣa, and then you failed and gave up. The 'Yakṣa' became a minor nature deity! You loser! Aren't you ashamed? How about you, Indra? You paid the fees, became a naturalised citizen, and have pretended to be a Deva ever since!

A curse on you Devas, you *Shining Ones*! How about you, Agni, Fire-God? No matter your family background, you remain in power. Your flames take sacrifices to the height. And you are holy, holy, holy. Curse those idiots! And curse the followers of Zarathustra, who invented the battle between 'good and evil'. Dumb ideas are successful, Śiva thought, and now I have to negotiate with the Asuras, all night through.

Clouds of oily smoke rose from the Asura camp. Śiva could hear them drinking and quarrelling. He would go there, but not just now. He got out his pouch and stared into the waves. The Milk Ocean shone like the belly of a putrefying fish and leaden clouds sealed the sky. A bitter wind scattered sand; the cold advanced, and stunned.

Late at night, Śiva sighed, stretched his limbs and raised himself. His knees hurt. But there was no use delaying it. By now, the Asuras would have reached a level that was plainly indescribable. Many of them followed a new fashion, and looked partly bestial. Others were greedy, and chaotic, or plainly insane. It would be a tough party. The Lord of Ascetics was in no hurry to join them. Here and there he stopped for a pipe and a drink, to get his head together. Almost delirious, he entered the Asura camp, carrying an armful of bottles, and spent the night singing bawdy songs and swearing vows of eternal friendship. The morning found him, more dead than alive, near the Deva settlement. He was badly hung-over, bitter and cynical. Oh yes, he had been optimistic. He had laughed and joked and praised the Anti-Gods. They were mistrustful, not that he could blame them.

His pipe gurgled and he coughed until tears ran down his face. The stuff was rubbish. It didn't work.

"A hard night?" Viṣṇu stood nearby, pale and wretched, and daring anyone to mention it.

"I made them agree. But they don't like it."

"Well, neither do I. But times are bad and we need them."

"They made me swear all sorts of oaths."

"That shouldn't be a problem. You were under the influence of whatever."

"You leech! I feel responsible."

"And so you should. I'm glad to hear it."

"Shut up!"

"The way I see it, you made promises. With the best of intentions. We didn't. That leaves a few options open."

"You cheat!"

Viṣṇu shook his head. "That's uncalled for. I do my duty, as every deity should."

By noon, Viṣṇu had organised the parties. He had drawn up a long and complicated list, had noted the priorities, and called for a meeting. First of all, he invoked the great serpent lord Vāsuki and made him volunteer. You met him: he is Manasā's elder brother. Next, he plucked the Mandāra Mountains from the Landscape. They would serve as a whisk. And last, as a boss has to do all the difficult stuff himself, he transformed into a giant turtle, waddled across the beach and disappeared into the depths. Down at the bottom of the Milk Ocean, he sank his claws into the muck and waited, while the gods settled the mountains on his back. Vāsuki curled around the peaks and extended from one shore to the other. It was a simple contraption, but huge.

"We'll hold the head," said Brahmā.

"Forget it," the Asuras replied. "The head is the seat of the soul. We'll hold the head or we go home."

"Anything you like," said Brahmā, and grasped the tail. So did the gods.

The gods chanted, and on command, they pulled the tail. Vāsuki, coiled around the Mandāra Mountains, twisted and ached. The mountains turned one way, and a huge wave surged across the beach. Then, on command, the Asuras pulled, with less enthusiasm, as their end had teeth. The mountains spun again, and Viṣṇu, in the deep, acted as the pivot and grunted, as he was pushed into the murk.

The Mountains rotated, this way and that, the gods cheered, the Asuras cursed, and Vāsuki felt stretched beyond repair. Another heave, another pull. One way, then the other, again and again. The waters roared, the waves crested to heaven, and the fluids churned, getting denser and tighter, they congealed, foamed, and turned to butter.

Out of the milky foam, all blessings appeared. First Kamalā Lakṣmī arose, the manifestation of joy and lustre, the essence of love, beauty and wealth. The clouds tore apart and hazy sunlight soaked the world in gold. The gods cheered and so did the Asura. They fell to and pulled, their rhythmic calls echoing over the churning deep. Lakṣmī smiled, waved at her fans and showed the gestures that dispel fear and grant boons. Even Vāsuki gave a strained smile. A divine horse emerged, then a thundercloud elephant, then grains and gems and blessings. The Gandharvas made music, the Apsarases danced. Soon, everything would be well. While the waves calmed, an imposing figure rose to the surface. It was Dhanvantari, a young ascetic, who held a treasure beyond belief: the Elixir of Immortality. He was greeted by applause. Well aware of his importance, he strode through the yucky foam, ascended the shore and bowed, as he offered his treasure to the gods. Brahmā chortled with happiness and did a little dance, his paunchy belly wobbling. He reached into nothingness, created a magic scarf and a talisman pouch, and handed both to Dhanvantari.

"You are my favourite, my boy!" the God of Creation could hardly keep himself contained, "you don't know how much you mean to me!"

Dhanvantari lowered his glance. "My merits are negligible, my actions faulty and my offerings worthless."

"And how humble you are!" Brahmā fought to keep himself under control, "You are a darling! And what a prim beard you have. You watch it! I'll make you a wonder-doctor, you'll be successful, no matter what you do, and your life extends through the ages! Maybe, one day, you'll be a saint or a deity."

"I remain speechless," muttered Dhanvantari.

"But we need limits. There have to be conditions. I'll make this easy for you. You can only die when goddess Viṣahari steals your scarf and pouch, or when the snake Udyakāl bites you."

"I never heard of them."

"That's because they don't matter."The Lord of Creation grinned. "For a clever boy like you, they shouldn't be a problem." He winked at the gods. "See, here! The elixir! We won!"

Dhanvantari looked up. "Brahmā! What shall I do if I am bitten?"

"That's easy." Brahma was generous. He loved these little games. "Take some śali-biśali herb. Or foam of this ancient sea. Both are fine. Life will return to you."

Dhanvantari pressed his brow into the sand. As he got up, he saw Brahmā handing the elixir to Viṣṇu.

I'll better be gone, thought Dhanvantari. Gratefulness has limits. On the other side of the Milk Ocean, the Asuras screamed with rage. They had realised that all treasures had appeared, and they wouldn't get a thing.

Śiva sat on the beach and refused to participate. Around him, the gods shared the elixir. Viṣṇu had dropped his notebook. In a moment of crazy cheerfulness, he assumed the shape of a heavenly courtesan. Dancing through the assembly, he offered elixir to the gods. His antics were hilarious.

He is out of his mind, Śiva thought, his tits are terrifying and look how he tilts his hips. It's a caricature. No woman would walk like that.

The Asuras, on the other shore, brandished their weapons.

"They are damn right." He reached for his mālā.

"Agreements," giggled Viṣṇu, "are tricky. They contain fine print, no matter how simple they seem."

"You made me break my word!"

"It was never yours to give."

"And now they hate me!" Śiva glared at the deities. Most of them were totally out of their heads. Immortality can do this to you. "The Asuras are my relations. And they are your relations, too!"

The gods stared. This was in pretty bad taste. Viṣṇu swayed like a drunken rhino cow. "Don't be so cruel. Take it easy. Have a drink!"

"I won't!"

"Don't spoil the fun."

"I won't drink unless the Asuras get their share!"

He could hear the gods muttering.

Viṣṇu frowned. "Get yourself together. This is important! Old age isn't funny at all. You will ache all over. Your joints will be stiff, your vertebra will slip and your breath will rattle. Your eyes will blur, your ears ring and you won't get it up, no matter how hard you try."

"So I grow old," the Lord of Ascetics grinned at the assembly, "I wither and shrivel and drop dead. I'm used to it. It happens every weekend! So what? I like decay. You can see how you get along. Without me."

From the other shore, he heard the Asuras cheering.

"They appreciate divine justice. What about you?"

Viṣṇu shook his head. "It's impossible. There's not enough elixir for them. I know, we are partial. But we are the good guys. We have to keep the lot."

"I insist," said Śiva, "that we churn the ocean again. Let's make some more. Let's show virtue."

"It's a bad idea!" Brahmā complained. "The elixir is finite. You crazy boy! Forget your ethics. The next churning will produce poison!"

"I agree," said Viṣṇu. "Virtue is fine, if you can afford it. But let's be sensible. We can't. Don't be sentimental. We have the lot, they haven't. That's life. It runs on cruelty."

Brahmā was excited, "We are good, they are evil, and that's why the future belongs to us."

Śiva raised a hand and smiled like a tiger. "Do you want to lose another head?"

Rhythmic shouts, hissing waves, churning fluids, you've been there before. The Asura did their best and the gods did what was needed. None of them invested much faith in their effort. Vāsuki, badly stretched and raw, could hardly hiss. The Mandāra Mountains twirled and in the pale murk, deep undersea, sat Viṣṇu in turtle shape and felt himself screwed into the ground.

The result should have been great. It wasn't. The churning produced toxins, like wrath, and madness, hate and fury. It distilled insane desire and deadly longing and heart-numbing acedia, brainless addiction, lethal intoxication and cataclysmic greed. Clouds of insanity rose to the sky.

Eventually, the gods lost their strength, and the Asuras stumbled back. Vāsuki collapsed into the broth, screamed, and slithered to the shore. His scales blistered, he yowled and crept into a hole.

When the worst rose to the surface, the beach was almost empty.

"This is absolute destruction" said Hanumān, the monkey god, Friend of All Beings. He was brave enough to remain. Śiva sat where he was. He had demanded the second churning, and the result was nightmarish. He faced the ultimate challenge.

Hanumān shook his head. "If you try that, you are gone. Do you hear me? You'll disintegrate. No future, no hope, not even shreds of memory. This stuff is lethal."

"If I don't do it, you can forget the world."

He rose, and shook his legs to get the numbness out. "If anyone can do it, it's me."

Hanumān would have loved to run away. He stayed.

Śiva grinned like a skull. He had been through a lot. He had survived any drug or poison the plant kingdom had invented, and rounded off his studies with toad skins, fungi, serpent venoms and Spanish Fly in Tora Fugu Zombie Juice. The Milk Ocean promised nightmare. This might be the climax or the end. Not that it mattered.

He sighed and waded into the broth. His legs burned and the stench took his breath away. He went down on his knees, bent over, and drank.

Hanumān was scared. He saw Śiva gulp and swallow, saw his hands twitch, his eyes bulge and his throat turn blue. Wave after wave disappeared into Śiva's belly. The Lord of the Dance went red, like the blossoms in a funeral ceremony, and white, like an aged, long-forgotten bone. When he collapsed into the waves, Hanumān was ready. He ran into the surge, and pulled his friend to the beach. Behind him, the waves calmed.

It took a while before the gods returned. They saw the Lord of Ascetics, lifeless, a carcase on the shore of eternity. Śiva the Destroyer was destroyed. His belly was swollen, his throat discoloured and his eyes were red with blood.

Hanumān sat next to him. He rose when the gods appeared, and glared at them. "You weaklings!" he spat, "none of you helped him!"

Nārada approached. The seer had acted as Śiva's messenger, on numerous occasions. "I like him," the Lord of Ascetics used to say, "He's unreliable and nasty, he cheats and steals and you can trust him to make a mess of everything. Pretty girls? He chats them up. And then he comes to me and lies. Compared to him, I'm the virgin blossom of virtue."

Hanumān didn't like him. But he was ready to enlist his help. "Go and travel, my friend," he said, "and tell the gods and Anti-Gods that Śiva, the Liberator, is dead. Go to Durgā. Tell her what happened, and that her husband died to save us all."

Nārada swallowed. He would have preferred to stay home. Indeed, he would have preferred anything.

"Go, do your duty. Bring Durgā here. We will prepare the pyre."

Nārada left in a hurry. As soon as he was out of sight, he slowed. In the past, he had carried plenty of bad messages. That's why the gods kept choosing him: no matter how awful the news, he had survived. The gods laughed about him, they sneered, and they abused him. Not Śiva. The Lord of Drugs and Madness was always friendly (or incoherent).

You can rely on me, Nārada thought, damn you. I'll tell Durgā. For good or bad. I owe you that much. And I'll be off before she kills me.

In his absence, the gods went to work. They crossed the barren plain and walked into the withered forests. Here and there a tree remained alive, here and there fresh green fought toxins and despair. When gods and people fail, you can rely on plants. They collected the noble woods, the true timbers, the plants that offered scent and joy and hope. With a mighty effort, they dragged them to the beach. There, at the shore of eternity, where milky waves hissed across the sand, in the bleak hours between night and day, they built the pyre.

Some wept. Some cursed. Others wondered about their careers. A major cosmic function had turned vacant. There might be job opportunities; there might be chances to be big and powerful, and to receive the veneration of the masses.

By the time they dragged Śiva's corpse to the pyre, Durgā had arrived. Her knees gave in; she fell, buried her hands in the wet sand and howled with anguish. The waves sucked at her sari, but the goddess didn't notice.

What would her life bring? What future did she face?

What good was morning? What good was evening? And how could she survive the lonely, frozen nights? Her sons would grow and grunt and drift away. Her husband was a memory.

And her life would go on. On earth, where things were really dense, people would appeal to her. As a goddess, she would listen to their cries, and do her best to make them happy. Durgā knew her duty, and right then, she hated it, and every worshipper. Scum, parasites, opportunists! I curse your feeble oaths, your pointless sacrifices. I loathe your self-inflicted sufferings. Where is your pride, your joy, your backbone? Dare you stand up? Are you ready to fight?

Your prayers are lies and your offerings bribes. Goat's blood, chicken peas and pumpkins. I refuse your butterfat! I spit into your milk, your cream, your curds and yoghurt! Your ceremonies leave the evils as they are.

None of your offerings creates a world worth living in.

None of them brings him back.

Durgā howled in anguish.

No matter what she did, her innocence was gone.

Manasā. That bitch. She had left a ring. And smiled into her face.

As if she knew what would happen. Maybe she even planned it.

One eye? It wasn't enough. I should have killed her.

And now?

A promise. A vague hope. A dream of better days. Durgā was ready to try anything.

You creep! I know that you are good with toxins!

The gods watched in amazement, as the Lion Goddess raised herself and clapped her palms. The sound echoed through eternity.

The ring appeared.

"Come here, Nārada," she called, "I need you. Take this piece of trash. Go and get Manasā. No matter the cost, no matter what she says. Just get her."

Nārada bowed. There wasn't much of a choice.

"Get her here," Durgā whispered, "or her father burns and I will claw you to pieces."

Nārada hurried. It was bad enough to inform Durgā of her husband's death. Getting Manasā was worse. Should he survive, he promised himself a long and luxurious holiday. Somewhere on earth where different gods were worshipped. Or among atheists. He approved of hot-blooded un-believers. They burned in their religious fervour, they proselytised and punished the faithful, they were proud of their ignorance and, best of all, they left him alone. Within instants, he flew through heaven, earth and all seven underworlds. He almost missed Manasā's realm. You need leisure, a playful attitude, a love of life, a longing for death and the freedom that comes from not taking yourself seriously, to enter her realm. Nārada, like so many seers, was stressed, totally beside himself and altogether lost. Luckily, Neta sensed he was coming, kept all gates wide open, and snatched him when he hurried by.

Nārada rushed up Mount Sij like a whirlwind, shot through the palace gate, before Dhāmāi Rat-Snake could demand a fee, hurled himself down the corridor, slipped, slid into the grand hall and almost slammed into the serpent goddess.

She looked so small, before the well, where black waters churned, so young and vulnerable. Far away, in the gloom, Nārada espied a throne. High gods should be seated, where they belong, he thought. This throne was covered with dust and cobwebs. It was almost as if the goddess wasn't home.

"Lady", he whispered, "Nāgdevī, Serpent Goddess."

Manasā stared into the well. She nodded.

"Durgā sends me."

"I'm glad to hear it."

"She is unhappy."

"Indeed."

"Goddess, let me apologise. I bear bad news. Forgive me. Your father, Śiva the Incomprehensible, has swallowed all Toxins of the World and lies dead on the pyre, at the shore of the Milk Ocean."

Manasā didn't raise her face. "My father. Overdosed. Again."

Nārada bowed. "Durgā sends her greetings. Would you come and revive him?"

"Certainly." Manasā remained seated. Her eyes were full of tears.

"Please hurry!"

"Of course." Manasā wiped her face and forced a charming smile. "I should apologise. I'm a shy girl who hasn't anything to wear."

That, indeed, was obvious. Manasā blushed. "Perhaps, maybe, Durgā could help me dress?"

"I'll inform her!" Nārada got up and ran. He was gone in an instant. Manasā shook her head. He would be faster, she thought, if he took his time.

"Durgā!" Nārada screamed, as he stumbled across the beach. "Manasā will come. But she has nothing to wear. She asks you to dress her!"

Durgā's face went dark. Over many years, she had remarked on Manasā's nudity, and pointed out that a piece of scum shouldn't be seen in public as long as she wore nothing but reptiles. "Snakes," she kept saying, "should hide in holes. They do not constitute a costume. And nudity is cheap and shameful."

Nārada knelt before her. "Goddess, your contribution is essential."

Durgā bit her lips. All the gods were watching her! It made her mad with rage. She would have loved to screw Nārada head first into the sand. Sadly, that sort of thing isn't allowed when you are a deity. Only Asuras can behave as they like.

"I'm sure you've got a sari for her." Nārada barely dared to murmur. "Please make her come. I know you can do it."

Durgā opened her third eye and visualised her wardrobes. At the time, they consisted of 36 large rooms, for the better stuff. Plus the halls containing shoes, boots and sandals, and the great subterranean storage rooms for ornaments, crowns and glittery stuff. And the palaces for umbrellas, fans, handbags, sunglasses, hair ornaments and, her favourite, the weapon arsenals. Spears, lances, sabres, cleavers, chain-saws, flame-throwers, nuclear missiles, anything a classy girl might need, out in the city, to make it through the night.

Durgā glared. "I lead a simple life. You know me, I'm humble. I haven't got much, and I can't spare a thing," she declared. "Maybe I'll chance upon a bargain somewhere."

She mounted her lion and was on her way. As she passed a rice-field, she noticed a frayed jute sack. Someone had thrown it away. "This will do!" The thing was in tatters, and still too nice for Missy Scaly-Slut.

By the time she reached Sij Mountain, her mood was terrifying. The lower slopes were full of stingy stuff. Her lion yowled as it tore through bristly euphorbias and spiky pandanus, the growth scratched her legs and drew blood, she cursed and snarled but she kept herself under control. Further up, she rode through twisted forests and along craggy mountain slopes, until finally; she crossed the realm of ice and snow. The crust was sheer pain.

Manasā's palace gleamed. It's overdone, Durgā thought, just look at the gate, what a trashy proletarian look, this girl has no sense or taste and I wish I could crush her.

She waited until her breath had calmed, and adjusted her sari.

"I'm the Empress of All Worlds," Durgā repeated to herself, as she walked into the palace. For very good reasons, Dhāmāi-Rat-Snake did not appear to greet her.

The Lion-Goddess strode down the corridor. She had an instinct for power, and appeared in the throne room like the ruler of all worlds.

Manasā didn't face her. The Serpent Goddess, young, nude and obviously helpless, leaned over a well. She watched the waters spiralling.

This place is but an empty vault, Durgā thought. No furniture, no extras, not a bit of glamour. Look at the cobwebs! How will she impress a paying audience? No matter. It's her life, it's worthless and it suits her. I will show class, and I will shine. That's what makes one deity higher than the others.

Durgā showed her teeth. "Here is your sari, dear. I am sure it will improve your looks." She offered the item. "Hurry up! Put it on! Your father's corpse rots and we lack time."

Manasā accepted the gift, bowed deeply, and retired to her dressing room.

Durgā hardly trusted her eyes, when, much later, the Serpent Goddess emerged. Manasā, as she realised, wore the sack. However, the faded piece of bygone ages had turned into a magenta miracle, bordered with gold and turquoise, brimming with pearls and black obsidian, a stunning pattern showing the worlds, the realms of reality, the gods and all World Ages, plus symbols, blossoms, and toxic animals. Durgā stared and her eyes watered. She could still sense the dusty old sack, behind the mirages, but what appeared before her eyes transcended art and love and inspiration. It still has holes, Durgā thought; it is frayed and cheap and damn it, wherever a hole appeared, some part of the goddess allured. Naked flesh, bordered with diamonds. I hate her, Durgā thought, I hate this sari and I wish I could strangle her with it.

Manasā appeared demure. "Dear stepmother." She bowed deeply. "You make me want to faint. This is the most wonderful dress I ever had."

Durgā snarled. "No time for that! Let's hurry!"

"You are so generous." Manasā seemed close to tears. "Please accompany me. We can take my air-chariot and be there in an instant."

"I trust my lion" Durgā replied, "and I'll be there before you!"

"Forgive me." Manasā bowed. The sack suited her perfectly.

An instant later, she was at the shore of the Milk Ocean. Her swans wheezed, the carriage wheels crunched across the sand, and the serpent goddess faced the gods.

As everyone could see, she was clad in a stinky old jute bag.

"My dear, dear gods," Manasā apologised. "My friends, I am sorry if I'm late. Please don't glare at me. You make me feel ashamed. I had no time. This costume is a gift of Durgā. She wanted me to hurry."

"This costume is outrageous." Viṣṇu said, "it is poor and trashy and an insult to good taste. Deities should be shining examples. We have style; we do not dress in filth. But let me apologise. Your intentions are recommendable. Young people should know their duty. It's just your stepmother. She makes us feel ashamed."

A few minutes later, Durgā appeared. She had plunged through snowfields, had stumbled down slopes, had fought her way through thickets of thorns and survived avalanches and dust storms. Her lion was close to collapse. The great beast panted, it was bleeding and in an evil mood. His rider wasn't much better. Her legs were torn; her costume was in tatters.

"You look sweaty," said Viṣṇu, "and embarrassing."

"O Durgā" exclaimed Manasā, "you poor dear! What happened to your hair?"

"I expect an explanation," said Viṣṇu, "on behalf of the Divine Congregation. This is official, and everything you say will be recorded. What, exactly, did you intend, when you clothed your stepdaughter in a rancid jute bag?"

The gods nodded. The bag was beyond compare. Worse yet, it revealed some juicy bits.

"Don't nag her." Manasā raised her eyebrows, "she only meant well. And she did the best she could."

"You evil slut!" Durgā erupted.

"Dear stepmother, I am just a humble virgin," said Manasā, and did not get further. Durgā screamed and hurled herself at her.

What do you do when cat-lady claws your face?

Manasā had been waiting for it.

She opened her Evil Eye. Durgā froze and collapsed.

The gods trembled.

Manasā advanced gracefully, one step after the other, as if she had all time in the world. She faced the pyre, and on top, her father. He looked paler than ever, except for his throat, which had turned bluish black. Manasā tapped a finger against his brow.

"Hi Daddy. I'll take you home."

She turned him, raised his head, and leaned over him. This would be extreme. With an effort, she forced his mouth open. The toxins filled him to the rim. She lowered her mouth to his, and sucked.

Next to her stood the sacrificial vessels. All of them were empty. Manasā spat into them. Bending over Śiva, she filled her mouth again. It made her head spin. Again, she vomited. The vessels brimmed with evil. And they were not enough.

"My friends!" the goddess called. Her lips were numb, her tongue was almost paralysed. The creatures heard her call. Snakes raised their heads, spiders left their nets, scorpions emerged from holes and centipedes came creeping from crevices. Toxic frogs hopped and lethal toads clambered. They emerged from slopes and hills, from forests, swamps and riversides, the slid and crawled and pounced, they swarmed over the beach and surrounded her. Myriads of shiny eyes gleamed, thousands of mouths opened, hungry for toxins, hungry for power, greedy for recognition and love. Manasā spewed into their midst. Her body was racked by cramps, her limbs shook and her pupils went up, so her eyes went white, then crimson. Her little friends hurled themselves into the juice; they fed, they feasted and they swarmed. But however much they were, they were not enough. The serpent goddess leaned over her father and drank again. Three times, she thought, fix any spell. She pressed the poison into her evil eye, where it churned and swirled and congealed. She forced it into her belly, into her guts, and stored it in the cakras along her spine. The quintessence went into her head, and to the top of her brow, where the Manascakra is situated. That's the place where good ideas come from, if you treat them nicely, and imbue them with joy. Right now, the good ideas shook with terror, closed the shop and went home for the weekend.

Cold sweat ran down her face, her legs trembled and the world began to spin.

My centre, she thought, I must hold on to my centre, and tried to breathe into her belly. That's a splendid idea if you have too much of anything. Your belly can stabilise the universe. Right now, it didn't help. Sweat ran down her face, she raised her head and stared into a sky where lethal lights were spinning. Around her, the grasses swayed with alien winds, each strand a-throb with the greenest sap, its tip graced with a pearl of icy diamond dew. The pebbles rose, and swirled like hornets. The scenery turned into geometry, plain and stark lines, angles and vortices. Someone said "Did you know the world is made of hexagons?" and when she realised it was herself, she had a laughing fit and doubled over. The pain twisted her. I have to stop this, she thought, or I will die like him. She exhaled, again and again. The slopes transformed into flesh, they bulged and heaved, and stringy veins ran across the beach. They carried force and nutrients. She saw the gods and had a laughing fit. "Don't be so serious. I die. It's fun."

What a bunch of idiots. So many arms and hands. And all the junk they carry. Here's the sword of justice, there's the celestial sardine can opener and over there the thing you need to dislodge the other thing should it ever get stuck. It would, she knew. If it can, it will. Everything gets stuck, one time or another. That's reality, folks, and none of us has enough hands or tools to handle everything.

Brahmā was funny. Four heads, each with a fluffy beard, and not a single brain between them. Gaṅgā was delirious, as she foamed and rolled over the sand. I guess this is anguish, Manasā thought, but it looks hilarious. Viṣṇu was a joke, as he tried to call the gods to order. Nobody listened. Drop your notebook, baby, she thought, and be what you are. It isn't much, but it is good enough. Here's to reality: you're right and you are wrong. We all are, all the time. And we learn. That's what makes us divine.

Best of all was Durgā. She had stopped twitching and lay with her face in the sand.

She heard a moan. Who is this, she thought, hey, it's Daddy, and he is coming to! What is he doing on this heap of logs? And why does he stink of butterfat?

Daddy opened his three eyes. They were incredibly huge.

"You are my cute little toddler," said Manasā, and pulled off her jute sack. "Have a drink and shut up." She stuffed a nipple into his mouth. "Hey gods," she called, "I've got a baby now!"

Śiva tried to evade her, but she slapped him, hard. "Shut up and drink!"

The gods averted their faces. This was incredibly shameful. Śiva, too, tried to resist.

"You dumb little thing!" Manasā tightened her grip, "grow up. You look famished. Are you sure you lead a healthy life?"

Śiva struggled, but the goddess held him tight. He twisted, turned his head and saw Durgā, motionless, dead on the beach.

"What..." he exclaimed, and choked.

"It's Durgā," said Manasā, "she died."

He wrenched himself free, dropped from the pyre, and crawled across the sand.

Like him, the gods and goddesses wept.

Manasā felt amazed. The moaning sounded like an orchestra. She listened to the resonances, to the overtones, and to the blend of infratones. They merged with the roll of the breakers. The gulls, she thought, are perfect. They fill the gaps. I wonder how they do it. Then, a tiny thought raised its head. Hello, it said, you are the Goddess of Awareness, and maybe you should listen to me.

No way, Manasā replied, thoughts have never made me happy. They creep up like weeds and fungi. They get me confused. Well, said the thought, did you notice that the Power of the Universe is dead?

So what, thought Manasā, she's been a nightmare.

I know, said the thought, but pay attention, 'cause without Śakti, the Universe goes down the drain.

Will it? asked Manasā.

Sure, said the thought, it's holding on by its fingertips.

O damn, you mean she's important?

She certainly is.

And I should resurrect her?

Great idea, said the thought, and hurry up.

Manasā looked at the gods. Most of them were howling. "You are ridiculous," she declared, "and a shame to your vocation. Stop snivelling! You make me want to kill you."

She approached the corpse.

"Well, if I really have to, I'll save the world. That includes all of you, no matter how stupid, so stop whining and behave."

She turned towards Durgā. I'm going to regret this, she thought.

I'm sure you will, her thought said.

You be silent! Manasā thought, I can't stand my own opinions.

She raised her hands to heaven and opened her third eye.

"Śakti can't die. So get up, you, down there, and pull yourself together!"

The corpse of Durgā, the Untouchable, began to tremble.

"I'm doing this for Daddy," Manasā said, "'cause he would be lonely and edgy and constantly horny without you furry bitch. And for all of you imbeciles and silly figures."

Coughing and vomiting, the warrior goddess came to her senses.

Her face contorted with hate.

Manasā pulled the jute sack over her breasts. "I liked you better when you were dead."

13. Husbands

Marriage matters. Sacred scripture says so, and married people agree, whether they like it or not, 'cause it says so in the contract. It's a god given structure, a social norm and a pillar of the community. Matrimony stabilises the class system, ensures legal protection, provides tax cuts, gives children a name and legislates ownership and inheritance. And it's an investment in the future. Gods with a head for business agree. They are the successful ones. Anything that's good for profit suits them fine. You guessed it: Śiva raises an eyebrow, laughs and reaches for his bone mālā. He doesn't understand wealth. Whatever you own, owns you. "I don't have anything," he says, "I only borrow. And I return everything." He is a great god and knows more than most. However, as many Tantrics learned the hard way: How can a god make you rich who can't even afford clothes?

Śiva shrugs. Who needs clothes? They only interfere with sex.

"Listen!" Viṣṇu appeared, with his date planner and his notebook. "Your daughter is grown up! She has to marry!"

Śiva yawned. He had been nicely in trance and Viṣṇu was too loud. "My child? She barely appeared on earth."

"Women need to have a master. Male and female unite, that's cosmic balance."

"She's young. Let her take her time, let her build up a cult."

"She's got no time. I'm sure she's over twelve already."

"How should I know?"

"Listen, dope-head. When girls grow, they get ideas. Like all fathers, you have to choose a husband."

"I won't."

"And like all daughters she has to obey."

"In my family, nobody does."

"Stop laughing. This is serious. And sober up. Young women are dangerous. They have too much heat. They need a man to cool them."

"What was that?" Śiva raised an eyebrow. "I didn't listen."

"It's all about order! Girls will be wives, have children, and the ancestors are happy."

"About what? They weren't happy when they were alive."

"I hate to explain this, 'cause you never listen."

"That's right. I don't."

"Do pay attention. It's simple. It's cosmic and divine. Submission and fidelity are foundations of society. A woman worships her husband and obeys. She is chaste and virtuous. She gives herself to him, and only him. One husband, one life. And the husband is god to her. It's her duty, her Karman and her reason to exist."

"Don't be silly. Your wife had plenty of husbands. Agni, Kubera, Soma, Dharma, Indra..."

"Leave Lakṣmī out of this!"

"...and you reincarnate all the time to keep her satisfied."

"I reincarnate to save the world."

"Sure Mr. Hero. Be the avatāra; she is your religion, your all. Cling to her feet like silver anklets; chime her praise all day. Go to earth, save the world, come back for dinner. Punctually. And she says, wow, baby, you are so exciting, who will you be this time, a turtle or a pig?"

"Shut up! You should be ashamed. Gods are ideals. We have to set an example."

"Maybe I'll ask Manasā, one day." Śiva reached for his pipe, "Sit down. Relax. Have a drag. Blow your head off. We have to set an example."

The legend comes in many shapes. Each of them combines propaganda, misinformation and human stupidity. Let's start at the top: the *Mahābhārata*. I hope you feel awed. This is world-literature in 100,000 double verses. Take a deep breath and stop squirming. Listen to the true story, attested by the greatest seers, and hardly improved at all.

Long ago, King Janamejaya announced: "I will kill all serpents on earth, and their friends, and their associates, and all of the Nāga-race. I will hold a great sacrifice and burn the lot."

The king was angry. And he was stupid, for angry makes you stupid. His father had ridiculed a seer, and, Karman being what it is, he was bitten by a snake. The father did what people do under the circumstances: he ouched, twitched, and died. Janamejaya was outraged. He would have his revenge. He would kill all serpents on Planet India, and anyone who sympathised with them. Normal serpents tried to hide. They were caught. The great Nāgalords hid in the underworld. Deep down, rock bottom, King Janamejaya couldn't get them. But he could stop their worship. Deities need attention. When their cult fades away, they wither and go comatose. Or worse yet, they become 'aspects' of another deity. Up there, on earth, Janamejaya hollered in anger while his men scurried through plains, swamps and forests and filled huge baskets with snakes. Down in the deep, the Nāga Lords met in conference. It would have been wonderful to bite King Janamejaya. Sadly, the king was surrounded by wizards and Brahmins, people who could kill a serpent with a glance and exterminate its clan with a talisman.

The Nāgas were close to despair, and so were their friends. Over the ages, many Vedic gods had come to like the serpent lords, and to party in their realm 'til sunrise. Nāga girls, everyone knew, had more curves than anyone, and Nāga drinks, full of weird toxins, could make your head open up like a lotus blossom. Indra, the Thunderer, was deeply worried. He had a friend in the serpent world, the mighty Takṣaka. "When all serpents burn," King Janamejaya had promised, "Indra will burn with them."

"Attention!" hissed a weary old serpent, "I recall a prophecy." It glared at its companions. "Listen and stop fidgeting. One day, when all serpents are threatened, a hero called Āstika will save them. That boy will be a noble Brahmin youth. His father will be the mighty seer Jaratkāru."

"We have a chance!" The serpents were delighted. It didn't stay like that.

Jaratkārū was a bitter, angry loner. He had spent centuries mortifying himself. His flesh was wasted, his bones stuck out and his belly was full of red-hot tapas energy. For a hundred years, he had stood on just one toe, which had swollen way beyond recognition. Of course he was a fanatic vegetarian, and he lived in chastity. His loins were almost withered and his head was full of hate. "Why should I waste my sperm to save a lot of worms?"

The serpents were shocked. Then the ancestors woke. They came after Jaratkārū by day, at night and in his visions. Jaratkārū faced them, serious, hairy men with bushy eyebrows and hordes of fat, oily women, who hung from a rope like spiders and demanded obedience. That rope, of course, was their last descendant. Should it break, the ancestors were lost. A man has to bear sons, they screeched, to continue the sacrifices, and if he didn't, all spiritual achievements would be in vain.

Jaratkārū cursed them. He walked away; he tried to think of other things. But the ancestors gave him no rest. Finally, the seer gave in. Nevertheless, he made demands. "I will only sleep with a woman who bears my name. That's the first condition." The Serpent lords cheered. There was a Nāga princess called Jaratkārū and she was young, beautiful, and unmarried.

"I won't pay a bride-price, or care about her upkeep, her interests or feelings."

The ancestors nodded. The serpents paled.

"And third, she must obey."

Serpents and ancestors went quiet. A serpent princess, they knew, will never be a little housewife.

Jaratkārū cheered up. The marriage wouldn't last.

Let's get this over. The scene is short and brutal. At the first opportunity, and without much ceremony, the seer straddled his young wife. He heaved, spurted, grunted, adjusted his dhoti, curled up on the ground and went to sleep. Princess Jaratkārū was stunned. It hadn't been much of a wedding and she wasn't sure if she liked Mr. Smellybum-Bristleface. But she believed that she had duties to fulfil. When evening came and the sun sank, she became restless. It was time for the sunset ritual. A seer who misses this ritual incurs enormous shame and misery. She whispered "My lord, it is time to rise and do the ritual."

The guy kept snoring.

Soon, the sun reached the blue mountains on the horizon and goddess Ūrmyā, Lady Night, began to drape her cloak of velvet, blue and black, across the sky.

The princess nudged him.

"Husband! Get up! If you miss the ritual, the world will lose its Dharma!"

She grabbed his shoulders and shook.

The seer raised himself and hit her. "How dare you wake me!"

The princess recoiled. "Forgive me. I just did my duty."

"You didn't trust me!"

"Husband! The sun is almost down."

"So what? It will stay like that." He stood up. "The sun is nothing. It won't sink without permission!"

"I can't believe this!" said the serpent princess.

"It's true!" squeaked the sun, "Very sorry. I can only leave when I'm allowed to."

The seer raised his fists to heaven. "Sun and Moon, Heaven and Earth! Wind and Water, Forest and Scripture, hear my words, and be my witnesses! A bitch who doubts her husband cannot be my wife."

He turned around and slapped her. "Our marriage is over. It's your fault. You will never see me again."

And so he walked away, and out of the story, to grump in lonely, dusty wildernesses, where seers of his ilk truly belong. He lived on air, he never slept and he was angry, angry, angry.

Princess Jaratkārū sighed. It wasn't quite what she expected. But as the moons flew by, her belly grew. One day, her son was born. He went to the court of King Janamejaya and ended the serpent sacrifice. Thanks to his deed, there are snakes in many countries. What happened to him afterwards is not related.

This tale is part of the frame story of the *Mahābhārata* and was recorded more than two thousand years ago. It's part of the upper-class tradition of Hinduism, and venerably holy.

The seers of Bengal and Assam had different ideas. In their opinion, the serpent princess Jaratkārū was Manasā. It was a surprising thought, as the *Mahābhārata* never mentions Manasā. Nor is Jaratkaru's son, Āstika, an important character in *Manasā's Epics*. Difficult people, like academics, would tell you that the whole episode was pruned on top of the Manasā legend like an alien growth. Deep in their inner hearts, the storytellers agreed. They referred to the episode, got it over with, and hurried to the next event.

Once in a while, a sober moment may be healthy. In real life, all the way through the epic, Manasā and Neta live alone. They are childless goddesses, and they have other interests. Apart from their doorkeeper, there isn't a man in sight. He is a rat-snake, so he doesn't count. Her worshippers invoke Manasā as *'Without Husband'*, a state which seems terrifying to traditional Hindus, and almost blasphemous to the fundamentalist Brahmins. Her connection to the *Mahābhārata* was inconvenient, but immensely important. In stratified Hindu society, the goddess made a career move. She became Princess Jaratkārū, and this turned her into a protagonist in one of India's earliest and most important pieces of high-brow literature. All of a sudden, Manasā had it made: aristocrats and Brahmins could worship her. That, of course, provided the impulse to incorporate her short and unhappy marriage with Saint Jaratkāru in the *Manasā Epics*. Many poets of East India were well educated. They knew their sacred literature, no matter whether they liked it or not. They had read the original story of the Nāga princess and her angry husband. Or they (like Neta) preferred to watch the *Mahābhārata* on eight extremely long and boring low-quality DVDs without jokes, special effects and far too little dancing. But they insisted on giving an extra spin to it.

To begin with, they decided that the seer Jaratkāru was born without a pregnancy: the poor guy was a mental cripple who had never known the womb. It might explain a lot. Nor did they approve of his ancestors, who did not appear in several versions.

Jaratkāru was a tough guy. Like the Vedic seers, he devoted much of his life to heat-generating spiritual exercises (tapas). For a start he spent several millennia standing on his head. That, of course is something anyone can do. It gives you a flat head. To make it more painful, he never closed his eyes. "Spirituality," he snarled, "is pain and greater pain is greater merit".

Jaratkāru stood on his head, never daring to blink, when Śiva appeared, looked at the performance, sighed, sat down, and got out his bone mālā. This, he knew, wouldn't be easy.

He snapped his fingers and Jaratkāru fell over.

"The Nāgas sent me," said the Lord of Ascetics. "Listen, stupid. This is important. Let me use simple words, 'cause you are dumb. You are to marry my daughter, give her a fun night and save the Nāgas."

He evicted a few small animals from his dhoti. "You will have a bath, or I guess, a dozen. You'll be kind and well behaved. And, what's more, you should say 'yes' or keep your mouth shut."

The seer raged and cursed. Śiva sat unperturbed, ignored the noise, glanced into the distance and waited. Eventually, the holy man gave up.

"That's better" said Śiva, "I like saints when they are funny. Or silent. Have it your way."

A moment later, the two arrived on top of Sij Mountain. That, of course, was a terrible deviation from tradition. Normally, the bride moves to the house of the groom and forgets her family. If she is lucky, she may visit them for a few days, once a year, in autumn.

Manasā was excited. She was to marry, to have a child, and to save all Nāgas everywhere!

What followed wasn't up to her expectations. Jaratkāru was a lot of things, but 'charming' didn't feature. Nor did 'moderately well behaved' or 'friendly', or even 'tolerable'.

Well-meaning poets claim that the two underwent a brief and irrelevant marriage ceremony. The groom tied a holy piece of string around the wrist of the bride. That, of course is next to nothing. Śiva had expected as much. He closed his eyes halfway and tried to think happy thoughts, one after the other, no matter how hard it seemed, and hoped to appear supportive and transcendental while the demons and corpse-spirits in his retinue grew restless.

This was all about duty and conception. Companionship, love and lust didn't turn up. God Kāma remained at home and watched TV. The couple departed to the bridal chamber where they conceived, without much enthusiasm, the heroic and wonderful Āstika.

Some Poets disagreed. A marriage is a wonderful opportunity to elaborate. Especially an Indian marriage, which ranks among the most complicated, if not impossible ceremonies in the universe. So here we have Viṣṇu, who knows what matters, 'cause he said so in his guidebook.

"All things have to follow order, Dharma and tradition" he recited, and many gods, knowing what was good for them, applauded. Except for Śiva, who sighed and reached for his satchel. He would have preferred his mālā, his mediation necklace, one happy skull after the other, but he knew, better than anyone, that he wouldn't be allowed to fade away.

Maybe he should have a drink, or a dozen. He glared at the guests. Free food and booze, he thought, that's their idea of spirituality. Sij Mountain was crowded with gods. They filled the palace, cluttered the gardens, trampled the vegetation, drank, screwed and fell into the pools. Most stood outside, in the snow, and tried to get in. Why give a party for the newlyweds? Śiva knew that their union wouldn't last. So did the major gods. Why perform a stupid ceremony, knowing that it couldn't, shouldn't, wouldn't last?

"I'll celebrate the divorce," Śiva said. "Divorces are reliable."

"That's a terribly negative idea", said Viṣṇu, "sure, I know the odds. Nowadays, with longer life-expectations, and education, marriages don't seem to last. Especially in the cities. But we should hope for the best."

"I do" said Śiva, "I believe in learning. After a divorce, everyone is happier and wiser."

"I'll ignore your comment, for the moment, and ask you to attend in silence, "said Viṣṇu, "as we have to conduct a ceremony." He raised his voice, "Hear me! Deities, Anti-deities, spirits, serpents, ghosts and whoever, we have assembled to perform a sacred ritual. We are happy to have among us the most impressive seer, the holy Jaratkāru, stronger than the gods, mightier than the Universe, a masterful renouncer of everything. And we greet, as his pleasant, cheerful bride, the Light of the World, the glorious Manasā! May they spend eternities together, have millions of children and grant their blessings to everyone! Come on folks! I want to see you laugh! You drank, you ate; it's time to applaud!"

Śiva glared at him. "Fuck you."

The ceremony wasn't easy. Gaṇeśa and Kārrtikeya had to pull the holy man out of his pillows. Jaratkāru was angry. He had just fallen asleep. They put him on his feet, drenched him with yoghurt, put flower garlands around his neck, stuck blossoms in his hair and tied him to his bride.

And now he was supposed to go around the sacrificial fire, seven times, and happy ever after, damn it, what did these upstart gods demand? Why should he marry a girl who wasn't much better than a worm?

"You are sick!" he muttered, while they made him act, "you are delusions! I impregnated her. That's enough. I hate the lot of you!"

And why did they expect him to dance?

You can't help it. People in India dance all day. I've seen it; so have the gods; Bollywood movies are full of dancing. In fact, no respectable Indian would dare to leave home without choreography. Śiva agrees, he has seen all Bollywood movies ever made. Most of them, several times. He gobbles down buckets of tandoori popcorn, he swills curried rum, he laughs and weeps and collapses. Provided they feature Juhi Chavla, Mallika Sheravat, Kajol, Priyanka Chopra, Madhuri Dixit, Kareena Kapoor, and, sure, some of these guys, with the sad eyes and the bushy eyebrows, hey, he likes the one with the big nose who pretends to play the mandolin; they ain't too bad, ah, he can't remember their names.

Neta has her own opinion, which is merciless, she writes the critiques, and has columns in all major newspapers and internet sites, where she harasses gormless screen-writers, bad actors, cowardly producers and lousy composers. "Surprise your audience. Entertain them, keep them salivating for more. Digital effects are rubbish, if you notice them as such. Cut the sentimental slob. Explosions don't improve anything. Gunfights are a waste of time. Blood and guts are boring. I get to see them every day. The dead and the undead; who cares? The river carries anyone. Most of them meet the crocodiles. A few end up with me. Everyone can use a cleaning. You and me, no matter how wonderful you are. That cleaning is the drama curve. It's not simple, life never is. It says so in the brochure. You want excitement? Use dialogue. Real people talking with each other. It has worked for millennia. 'Cause dialogue is action. It needs a pace, a rhythm, and it has to push things ahead. Protagonists should learn and change. If they don't, they are just flotsam on my river. We are here to learn. If we don't move, we are stuck. Your story needs well defined, unique characters. Good versus evil is for people with smaller brains than cockroaches. Genuine characters are complex. They experience conflicts. It makes them real. Good guys get things wrong for the best of reasons. Bad guys don't know they are bad; most of them think they are doing something wonderful. Each character, no matter how unimportant, has a tale, a reason to be there. No-one is really simple, no one is decoration. You tell a story? Everyone and everything has a story. Bricks and ducks and slime mould have a story. Each is dramatic. Life means conflict. It happens within you, it happens everywhere. You want a good story? Look for trouble. You want laughs? Look for pain and humiliation. Don't be kind to your favourite actors. Make them suffer. The audience will love it. I just say what has to be said, and sorry folks, I can't help it. Actors, screenwriters, directors and producers: face the truth." She grins, "That's me."

Manasā's marriage was a feast. A thousand flames gleamed; a million butterflies rose to the sky, transformed, and cascaded in a shower of blossoms. The heavenly musicians played, the Apsarases danced, night turned to day, the gods stuffed themselves, got drunk, cheered, embraced, lost their clothes, crashed through the furniture and collapsed. The renouncers ate until their bellies were swollen, their guts obstructed and their countenances turned grim, and finally the holy seer Jaratkāru was forced, amidst much laughter, to go to the bridal chamber.

The guests were cheerful. Everyone knew that in the first night, no congress would happen. Traditional Bengali believe that in the first night of a wedding, bride and groom get to know each other. It's a great idea. After all, the parents decided about the marriage. They didn't consult their children. Often, the happy couple had just met during the ceremony, had dared a shy look and wondered what the future would bring. In many cases, plenty of people were present. And if they were not, the happy couple was expected to keep dressed and well behaved. Instead of sex, there was dicing, and talk, and shy advances. The chastity of the bride was necessary to keep the groom protected. In case you didn't know: malignant forces lurk everywhere, and husbands are weak, shy and vulnerable.

Of course there are exceptions. Mainly among crazy gods, like Durgā and Śiva, who didn't give a damn for marriage rules and ancient traditions, and who couldn't wait until they fell into bed, and crashed it.

Saint Jaratkāru hated to hear himself praised, and the compliments of the guests made him sick. They are idiots, he thought, they don't understand anything! And why should I bother to visit the girl? I impregnated her. It was yucky and sweaty and I'd hate to do it again. He opened the door of the bridal chamber and stopped.

Manasā, perfectly nude, was sitting on the bed. She was surrounded by clusters of writhing serpents. Her face pointed up, her mouth was open and she was eating frogs alive. Head first, so they wouldn't get stuck.

Jaratkāru whimpered and ran.

The guest searched for the groom, all through the night and well into the morning. No matter where they looked, the guy had disappeared.

A few days later, Śiva discovered the seer. He was crouching under the shell of a sea-snail, deep in the ocean. And he wasn't coming back.

"Your daughter has to have a husband." Viṣṇu looked serious. Or constipated.

"Leave me alone." Śiva was in no mood for sermons.

"You get it wrong" he said, "Dharma isn't about power and hierarchies and control. It's about self-nature and adaptation. Everything has to change. That's the fabric of life. Brahmā won't understand, and you can't stop it. That's why Dharma is hiding."

"Rubbish," said Viṣṇu, "Dharma, our creator, relies on order and clear definitions. He insists on ritual, on hierarchy, on social classes, on the god-given-order of society."

"No way," said Śiva, "you refused him and I didn't. Remember how you threw up? I know him better than you or anyone. Dharma means that you care. For people, gods, for every being and thing."

Viṣṇu didn't give in. "Limits are important. Things cannot run any way they want. She has a son and she lives alone. It's shameful. She isn't even a widow."

"Who cares? I don't. Jaratkāru was a total idiot. He disappeared. I'm glad he did. And I hope he died."

"The son did his duty. And he left. She has to re-marry. That's bad enough."

"Maybe Āstika is happy elsewhere. Let's think positive. Maybe he doesn't want a family. That's fine with me. I'm not sure I want one, either. As long as my daughter is happy, I'm happy, too."

"Your daughter is unmarried."

"So what? She's not a widow. For all I know, she's almost a virgin. She can do as she likes. And she won't stand another stupid seer."

Viṣṇu scowled. Reality has limits. Everything has. If you don't understand the limits, you can't understand the whole. Without a strictly defined game board and clear regulations, how can the play proceed? What would happen if everyone did what they liked? Manasā was young and dangerous. Her hips were wide, her waist slim, her breasts bulged and her eyes were so deep and dark a worshipper could suffocate in them. Worst of all, she walked nude and she was full of toxins. The girl needed a mate, damned soon.

Her father, as usual, wasn't seeing sense. Viṣṇu would have loved to send him to rehab. But that, he knew from experience, would multiply his troubles. Śiva, when sober and sane, was simply terrifying. He dissolved anything that got in his way. In his wake followed total chaos. He even seemed to like it.

Viṣṇu did what all managers do when they can't solve a problem: he invited the divine assembly and tried to delegate. The conferences lasted for hours; everyone got mad on coffee and finally drifted away. Viṣṇu lay awake, in the early hours, as the pictures in his mind were too big, the voices too loud and the feelings too intense. I hate this job, he thought. I never wanted to maintain anything. The universe is too big, one day it'll kill me. He gritted his teeth. A holiday would be perfect. Just him and Lakṣmī, somewhere at the seaside, relaxing on the beach and having drinks with weird fruit and tiny umbrellas stuck in them. Afterwards, a hotel suite, seven stars, a nice cool bedroom, and ecstasy till morning. Room service would provide meals. The world? Forget it. It could maintain itself until he was back. Only, he knew, it wouldn't. Not if he entertained standards of excellence, and ambitions, and wanted to achieve something divine. Responsibility is a curse, and work is a drug. Like it or hate it, someone has to do it. That someone was he. And honestly, the other gods were a bunch of spineless loafers. They couldn't be trusted to get anything right.

Viṣṇu sighed; he wiped his brow, adjusted his dhoti and called for another meeting. He reminded everyone of their duties and obligations, discoursed on punctuality and thrift, the necessity to sort desktop equipment by size, colour and shape, and to use pencils until the stubs made fingers falter. "Right now, you may think I'm a bad boss," he said, "but one day you will come to understand that I am doing my best. I am always ready to point out your flaws. True, it hurts. But I am also here to inspire you." He placed a pen on the table. "Watch this. It is perfectly aligned with the eraser and the notepad. That's clarity. A clean desk is a clean mind." He raised his hands, "Right and left, up and down. Clear angles, clear thoughts. There's nothing strange, and nothing inessential. It'll make your life much easier. Order beats chaos anytime. Remember this: Little things cause great things."

The gods nodded. Viṣṇu loved little things. They were not as frightening as the big things.

Finally, the assembly agreed on a candidate.

Here is our saint: applaud the seer Maṇirāja. The poor guy lived on his own, he did his yoga in the middle of nowhere, and fed on worms, grasshoppers and flies. He was a lucky guy, as flies surrounded him. The gods appeared, in their mind-blowing beauty and luminosity. They ordered him to gird his loins, or at least to wrap up everything hanging out, and told him to get married.

The seer was amazed. Female company? He had plenty. Most of it hovered in the scorching midday heat, and put his loins on fire. His hands were jittery, his wrists were strained, and Neta says she wouldn't wash his underwear, no matter what.

That doesn't mean he was a fool. You don't get to be a great seer without realising a thing or two. Lust, he knew, was an illusion. It kept him crazy all day. Women? There were loads of them, all over the place. They followed him around. Damn it, he thought, and wiped his brow. Round things. Like boobs. The world was full of them, and they got bigger all the time.

Maṇirāja had a problem. Let's call it Viṣṇu. The Maintainer of the Universe took him for a walk. He lectured, about duty and marriage, all day.

"Leave me alone" thought Maṇirāja. He thought it very silently.

Viṣṇu didn't care. He dragged him to the sky. He put him on top of Sij Mountain. He forced him into an icy pool, made him wear clean clothes and burned the old ones.

Our seer worried. All the signs were bad. The raven croaked, the lizard chirped and the entire world opposed him. One night, when he was asleep, Durgā appeared to him. The seer, in his dream, dropped to his knees. "O Goddess! Your legs are sturdy as banana stalks, your arms are like lotus stems, your navel could contain the universe, when the moon sees your face, it goes hiding, your lips are red like jujube fruit, elephants faint when they see your beauty, swans drop from the sky..."

"Shut up and listen." The goddess was in no mood for metaphors. "They will marry you to Manasā, the filthy serpent slut. She is irresponsible, evil, nasty, worthless, deadly, disgusting, and polluting; a shame and a disgrace. Did you get this? Would you like more adjectives? Hello! I'm speaking to you. Stop whimpering! If you marry her, you are doomed. I'll curse you, everyone will curse you, and finally, she'll poison you. Do you hear me?"

Maṇirāja did. He dared a question. "Viṣṇu says I must marry her. What happens if I do?"

"Either she kills you or I do. I do it worse. What do you prefer?"

The holy man woke. Sure, the marriage was fixed. As he recalled, everything was prepared. Plenty of gods and ascetics would come. All sorts of celestial creatures would grant their blessing, accept fresh clothes and presents and stuff themselves with food. The astrologers had determined the perfect date, which was today, and he, the groom, was desperate.

Without a noise, he slid out of the bed. On bare feet, he crept through the room. His staff, his bundle, his little bookcase; they could stay behind. Maybe they would gain him a few minutes when his absence was discovered. Clinging to the walls, he sneaked through shady corridors. Finally, the grand gate was in sight. A few steps and he would be outside, in the cold starry night. His path would lead through crusty snowfields. Maybe he would lose a few toes. They hardly mattered.

"Who's there?"

Maṇirāja froze. Before him stood Dhāmāi Ratsnake, armed with round shield and heavy sabre, and blocked the door.

"My lord!" the seer stuttered, "What a wonderful night it is."

"You look like a criminal." Dhāmāi smirked. It wasn't nice.

"Please, please, venerable sire, lord of all worlds, I need some fresh air."

"To run away?"

"My god, my salvation, you know everything. Please let me go."

"You dumb loser. Why should I?"

"I would be grateful forever. I would pray for you and do my austerities in your name."

"Rubbish. You want to leave, you pay."

"I'm poor."

"I can see that." Dhāmāi twisted his moustache. "So you stay."

"I will give you all I have!"

"What's that? Your underwear?"

"You can have my dhoti. You can have my shawl. Here is my mālā. Take my begging bowl."

"That's all?"

"They keep me alive."

"You are a failure." Dhāmāi fondled his sabre. "I'd love to see you running down the glacier, nude."

"Yes, sir."

"But I've got a heart of gold. There's one thing you can offer. You won't miss it."

"Anything!"

"That's excellent. You've got a deal. Step into my rooms. I am sure you can write?"

In the faint light of the false dawn, when drunken bats walk home, Dhāmāi Ratsnake marched into Manasā's bedroom. He was in his finery: a purple turban with peacock feathers, an embroidered orange vest (slightly patched), a greenish girdle and a dhoti turned inside out, 'cause that side looked better. His feet were in yellow slippers. They were dashing.

"Arise, wife, it's our wedding day."

"What?"

Manasā was slow. Serpents are sluggish when the day begins; they need warmth to come to their senses.

"Your groom ran away. He had the grace to set up this document."

Dhāmāi pulled a palm-leaf out of his dhoti. The goddess took the page and read

"Herewith and in all truth and honesty, the honourable, high-born, supremely wonderful and thoroughly divine Dhāmāi Rat-Snake gains the god-given and irrevocable right to take the maiden Manasā as his lawful wife, plus as many other wives as he would ever wish for, to retain them, to abuse them, and to kick them out if this should strike his fancy. They are to serve him any way he likes. Granted by the former groom (retired), now once again the holy, abstinent and chaste seer Maṇirāja, living somewhere really far away, where you won't find him, and attested with his signature, oath and three drops of blood."

Manasā raised her eyes. "Three drops?"

"I helped."

The goddess grinned. "I'm amazed," she said. "This is our lucky day. Come closer."

The sunrise was amazing. Well, truly, every sunrise is. As the gods rose, and marvelled at the rosy clouds (only Śiva knew that they portended rain and storm), Dhāmāi slunk to his post. His face was badly swollen and he had lost two teeth. His mouth bled and he wondered how he could get drunk in this condition.

Manasā remained in bed. She needed time to consider. By noon she rose, did her nails, brushed her fangs, put on a few serpents, and walked into the assembly hall. "The marriage is off," she declared, "please eat as much as you can. Have a few drinks, dance and celebrate. I want you to be happy. And do excuse my absence. I'm busy."

She walked out to the north terrace, and cursed Maṇirāja.

In his next life, he would be a snake.

Let's explore an idea from the anonymous Assamese version. After two attempts to marry Manasā had failed, the gods were in despair. Viṣṇu called for emergency conferences, got out his coloured pencils and sketched diagrams with arrows and exclamation marks. He snapped his laser pointer and absentmindedly ate a box of paper clips. Śiva gave his brother a cheerful 'thumbs up' and handed him another package. The poor guy was totally lost.

That, of course was no reason to help him. Śiva packed his stuff and went for a long walk.

Eventually, the divine assembly decided on the perfect husband for Manasā. Not a seer, this time, as seers didn't make it. They chose the gigantic python Ajagara, and sent Saint Nārada to invite it. Nārada, they should have guessed, wanted to get away from everything. Our guy spent months visiting gambling houses, bars, discotheques and brothels; he lost his money, his reputation and his clothes, and caught several exciting sexual diseases before he sobered up and remembered his mission. By that time, Ajagara had heard what had happened to the first two candidates. The python did the sensible thing. He disappeared into the dark heart of the forest and hid under a waterfall. The gods searched, called and cursed. The python won't come out.

14. Over There

In the late afternoon, the countryside gleamed like a wonderful, golden work of art. Most of it consisted of honey. Sweetness drifted on the breeze, gilded the trees, the ascetics and the gloriously spiky plants. It drenched the ground and promised anything. Manasā could have hugged the world. It was her favourite state of mind. My own country, she thought, it's like me, so weird and wonderful. My plants, my fungi, my animals and people. They do as they like, but they are sweet. They don't snivel or plead; they walk with a straight back and hardly ever remember me. I can't understand any of them. That's how it should be. I'm proud of them.

Then the cramps set in. The goddess clutched her belly and almost bent over. She retched and spat. Nothing but gall and slime.

Śiva raised his eyelids. He sighed. "Hi, daughter. You have made a start. Look at yourself. It's nice but it ain't enough."

"How would you know?" She pressed her teeth together.

"You are pale and jittery. You think honey."

"I'm not hungry." She tried a grin. "I keep my figure."

"You're almost starved."

"I eat well. And I like being slim."

"You eat nothing but rodents and frogs."

"And small snakes."

"That's not enough for a goddess."

"It's all I need."

"Your ribs show. Your hands twitch. You need something stronger."

"I won't drink with you."

"You wouldn't last. What you need is emotion."

"I make my own emotions."

"You need stronger stuff. Worshippers, who love you, fear you, hate you. People with serious problems, believers and unbelievers. Even atheists. Hey, atheists are great. They release plenty of energy. 'Cause they believe in disbelief. Wake up, daughter! There's more than toads and lizards. You need fat! Imagine shrines, temples, and sacred cities. Imagine congregations. Feast on belief! When you see thousands bowing, living, dying, reborn in your name, you'll know what I mean."

"My people treasure me."

"They are great. They love you and you love them. They are your family. They are you. But they don't supply enough emotion to cause miracles."

"Who needs miracles?"

"Everyone does."

"These other people, whoever they may be. Where do I find them?"

"Out there. It's easy. In the World of Delusions, where people are full of anger, greed, and fear."

"Daddy, I won't have it. Don't you understand? I'm a thinker. I think. I am aware. I am sheer consciousness and no extras. I don't do party tricks. Why should these idiots worship me?"

Śiva laughed. "They will love you. If they don't, scare them to death."

"You there!" Manasā stood at the roadside. The seer lifted his head. He didn't seem stupid. The man used a stick to scratch a mathematical formula into the ground. "What's up?"

"Do you worship any deity?"

"No, why should I?" said the holy man.

"But deities are everything. They could bless you, inspire you, or grant you visions. That's what gods do. You look a bit worn. Maybe you need a healing?"

"No." The seer looked at his formula. "I'm here, on Sij Mountain. It's got height, width, length and duration. It can be calculated. I can think all day. What should I ask for?"

"Maybe fresh insights."

"No need. I make my own."

"How about the truth?"

"There isn't any. Really, my girl, truth is old-fashioned. It's almost a superstition. Nowadays we have science. Real science cites probabilities."

"And that's enough for you?"

The seer scratched his beard. "Personally, I like question marks. They are much better than 'facts'. That's 'cause people who believe in 'facts' stop thinking. I don't. And I can see you are crazy. You ask weird questions. Hey, I like it. That makes you a scientist."

"Is that any good?"

"Of course it is. Doubts are perfect. Facts come and go. Just like beliefs. Doubts are forever."

"Well, who helps you doubt?"

"Some sort of goddess, I heard. Nutcase Chandra, the physicist, says she is called Manasā. *The Thinking One*. That's a stupid name. But I can live with that, as long as she leaves me alone."

He scratched another row letters and numbers. "See this? That's what I call divine. What we need are convergent, self-replicating and constantly mutating numeral systems that won't self-destruct when they transcend infinity and bite their own tail. Easy, reliable stuff. Like twelvefourtyhexagesimalady-times halfsixprimeperioddoubletransgressrootfactormulticlo neexplosion-deducted-by-itself." He shrugged. "Inverted of course, and mirrored in n-dimensions. That's what I call reasonable."

Manasā bowed her head. "I'm sorry I asked. I greet the divine in you."

The seer laughed. "And I greet the divine in you, whatever it may be. Forgive me. You seem a bit simple. Are you new here? If you ever need my help, doing accounts, or adding things up, please ask."

Chaos, this has been proved, is perfectly organised and badly limited. The Law of the Great Numbers, as Hanumān, the monkey god explained, says that millions of unpredictable chaotic impulses boil down to a very boring average. "Those who praise chaos start as rebels and end up voting liberal."

It sounded terrible. Manasā didn't understand.

"It's easy," he said. "You want to understand mankind. It seems complicated. Every person is unique and unpredictable. That's what makes it simple. You have a billion insane weirdoes, you know, butchers, bureaucrats, shop-girls, artists, florists, scientists, lunatics, chain-saw murderers, geniuses, movie directors, prostitutes, bankers, beggars, werewolves, taxi drivers and stamp collectors. And a few politicians, but they don't count. They do as they are told, if they do anything at all. We talk about real people. They are all over the place. Wherever you go, they get under your feet. Some have a job, some have a family. Some work and some waste their days chatting on the internet. They are all crazy. Each of them goes off on her or his tangent. People weird their way, that's natural. The results should be unpredictable. That's what simple people think. But in reality, they won't. If you have three chaotic geniuses, you can't foresee their actions, or their effects. If you have three million of them, they will cancel each other out."

"What?"

"Let's have an easy example. It's about animals."

Manasā relaxed. Animals, she thought, are easy. Some are cute and fluffy; others are fat and juicy. Her stomach knotted and she gritted her teeth.

"There's a famous butterfly. It sits in Sri Lanka, on a branch, flaps its wings and causes a flood wave in the Himalayas."

"You make this up."

"No way. I've studied at all better universities, and I have read everything there is. Ask me anything, I know it. Well, this butterfly flaps its wings, in the wrong moment, and accidentally influences one of these amazingly rare air fluctuations. It's a chaotic effect. Well, one air molecule goes this way and another that way, and they interfere with what-do-you know; the whole thing spans continents and within a few minutes you have a roaring storm in another climatic zone and the yetis have to put on helmets and diving goggles."

"Really?"

"Sure. It's proved. And it happens all the time. Theoretically, the Himalayas are under water most of the year. Or they explode. Or dry up. Or fly away to the moon."

Manasā shook her head. Here she was, sitting on boring old Sij Mountain, and over there, in the World of Delusion, the most amazing stuff happened.

"I feel so stupid."

"You shouldn't. Science will enlighten you. You see, the point is, there are many butterflies. And they all flutter their wings. So when one flutter causes a flood, another causes drought, or primes a volcano. In real life, you can't have everything. So when a thousand million butterflies flutter, none of them gets its head. The weather stays as it is."

"And you can prove this?"

"Easy. Take a look around. Over there, on the other side. The people. And hear them grumbling."

Manasā raked her hair. "Right. People complain. About the weather. Hanumān, I'm confused."

"That's perfect. Religion gives you certainty, and causes doubts. Science causes confusion, and gives you degrees."

"But what if one of those butterflies goes home and says, no more, I have enough, flutter as much as you like, I'll have a few drinks and curse the lot of you!"

Hanumān wrinkled his famous washboard brow. "Then, my dear, we might expect the end of the world. It's inevitable. Worlds have a short shelf-life. They happened before, they will happen again."

"And that's how the universe works? By Chaos Theory?"

"Honestly, it only works in computer programs. On a tiny scale, with very few variables, under strictly controlled conditions." Hanumān shrugged. "Chaos is overestimated. It's just a concept, a way of looking at things. And it's by no means the only one. Some years ago, it seemed so glorious, and nowadays it's almost embarrassing. Forgive me. I didn't make it."

Manasā felt stunned. It was obvious that Hanumān, though a large monkey, spent much of his time at universities, talked with important professors, and loved to read thick books full of quotations in foreign languages, with diagrams and mathematical formula.

He even made notes.

I wish I were that clever, she thought, but all I do is think and doubt. What happened to reality? It doesn't make me happy. Sometimes I wish I were Neta. Hanumān is scared of her.

"If you study hard, you will understand anything." That's what Hanumān said. "You'll be as wise as me."

Her father said the same, when he was totally out of his head, absolutely bonkers, and had to be carried to bed. "I'm the intelligence of the multiverse," he mumbled. Before twilight he would eat sodium to settle his stomach and declare he would never touch anything in future, no matter what. And he would be serious, deadly serious. It's not easy to be a high god.

"Manasā," Hanumān was solemn. "Let me apologise. As your, let me call myself your mentor, well, over here, in Absolute Reality, you have a fine time, and enjoy divine inspiration and theorems and overwhelming freedom. Numbers go anywhere you like, liberty just needs a few fresh breaths and you are at home anywhere. Behold your mind: it's cosmic. Your people are happy and they get along as they like. They simply don't need you. It's their choice, and their nature, and you guarantee it. You are their goddess, invisible, incredible, unsurpassable and in the background.

Over there, in the human realm, where life consists of limits, edges and sharp corners, things are different. Remember this: people are stupid. Among humans, you have to get up damn early to get anywhere at all, and you can only do so by stepping on toes, elbowing competitors, ignoring misery and kicking the ass of anyone who appears weak or slow or innocent. You do your best, fight as much as you can, savage the naive, trample the weak, exploit the stupid and feel wasted by afternoon. That's because humans worship Progress."

"I never heard of him."

"He ain't much of a god. Some say he is moving ahead, others claim he is running away. He's blind and stupid. Anyway, he doesn't do blessings, joy or liberation."

"You mean, he's an Asura?"

"An anti-god? No way. He wouldn't be up to it. He is an error, a madness, a senseless machine." Hanumān looked troubled. "Sorry about this. Want to know a secret? He hasn't got worshippers. He has addicts, workaholics, executives, warlords and terminal failures."

Manasā stared at her fingernails. This is too much, she thought, people are crazy and I'll never understand them. Whatever you think you think, it turns out to be too much. Let's forget people and focus on something simple and useful. My fingernails. Really, how should I paint them? In blood red, 'cause that's how I feel, with a black fringe and a bit of green for hope, and sparkles? Yes, sparkles. I love them. They improve anything.

"Sorry," she said, "I didn't listen. The human world is incredibly complicated."

"It is. If you want to make a compliment, say 'you look overworked'. They love it."

The monkey god scratched his ass. He seemed sad and weary. "In the human world, and I talk about long-time observations with follow up interviews under ideal test-conditions, people work from dawn to dusk. They worry, co-operate, quarrel, fight, give-in, calm down and go mad again. They organise in top-down hierarchies, which never works, but provides great laughs. People, in theory, should be noble. Some do great deeds. Some are virtuous. Some set an example by doing simple things in a wonderful way. That's real magick: something done perfectly well. Like raising the kids, or living an honest life, or being there for other people. You don't have to read occult books, or get yourself a degree in some sour-faced order. Life is wonderful and death is a relief. Both are real magick, if you do them right. Some people are friendly. That's a major art form. Some are happy and inspire others. Some focus on science. Or on art, or magick, or they perfect daily life. I love them. It's great. It's glorious, and it's rare. Some people are geniuses. Some are simply good. Good is enough, no, good is wonderful. There isn't enough goodness around. People could be amazing. We should love and admire them, if only we could. And some make life hell for everyone."

Manasā hugged him. "My wonderful monkey. We have to be brave."

The monkey god struggled to hold back his tears. "Evolution is overestimated. It went totally wrong. The selection of the fittest? It's a nightmare, just like everything. I say, stay on your tree, eat your fruit, enjoy the sun and shut up about progress."

"I agree."

"You wouldn't know. You are too young. But I thank you." He wiped his tears away. "Banana?"

Manasā shook her head.

"You look hungry."

"I'm fine. I get along without nourishment. That's because food is an illusion. But, Hanumān, I understand that people are unhappy. Why are they? Why don't the gods solve their problems?"

"Are you crazy? You solve a problem, they invent three, just to get attention."

"But they could be happy!"

"They ain't. And they never will be."

"Why don't we make them happy?"

"Nobody can. It's impossible. There's a hole in them that can't be filled. Every person carries a begging bowl. Some do it openly; some hide it, some hate to be reminded that they do and some threw it away. We face the universe as beggars. Everyone lacks something. And everyone has something to offer. Well, ask me, do we offer it to each other? Do we share any damn thing?"

"Well, do we?"

"Why share when you can sell or steal?"

"Hanumān, you make me crazy. The way you tell it, life is insanity."

"It is, over there. But it makes sense when you live like that. Humans like it narrow and suffocating. There are laws and regulations everywhere. You have to fight to remain alive. And that's just the start. Every lost soul is obsessed with profit."

"But how can I find worshippers out there?"

The monkey god raised his brows and tried a toothy smile. His eyes were still wet. "That's easy. They'll adore you, as long as you deliver. No matter who you are, or what they are. Over there, they worship anything. Almost everyone is unhappy."

"I lost weight" said Manasā. She stood facing a mirror. "I'm almost slim. That's great, isn't it? See how my cheekbones come out."

"You jitter and shake," said Neta.

"That's just 'cause I'm excitable."

"Your new diet is rubbish."

"I live on air. There's power in each breath. That's what our father says, in all the better Tantras."

"Our dad is so crazy, he can turn anything divine." Neta grinned. "Yesterday you blacked out and fell down the stairs."

"I was just tired."

"How come? You sleep most of the day."

"Life exhausts me."

"You don't do anything."

"Neta! I contemplate! I reflect! I think all day!"

"You worry and doubt and harass yourself."

"How do you know?"

Neta laughed. "It starts with worry and continues with depression. Next, it's resignation. Then stupor, indifference, collapse and slow death. I've seen it thousands of times. That's what starvation is like. Poor people do it all the time."

"Well, it's not true. I have light and happy moments when I feel as if I could float."

"You don't. That's just when you drown your frogs in sugar."

"They are better that way. And I believe they like it, too."

Neta clapped her hands. A door appeared. "Let me show you something."

"Why should I?"

"It may solve your problems."

"I don't have problems." Manasā fought the hunger cramps. Her belly knotted. "My life is excellent. I guess I'm just going through this stage where I transcend body and become totally cosmic. Honestly, Neta, I have left all illusions behind."

"Don't weep. We all need a bit of help, from time to time." Neta offered a tissue. "There, that's good. Have another one. Just take a look. Can you see the light on the horizon?"

"No."

"Come closer, there, that's great, can you see it now?"

"Not really."

Neta shoved.

The river ran narrow and deep, between the mudflats, and herons rose in flight. Manasā landed on the shoreline and almost lost her balance. The ground was slippery. She stared at the brown flow and shook her head. Then she turned around. Neta, she thought, I'll get you. The door, of course, had disappeared.

The serpent goddess went down on her knees and buried her face in her hands. She wept. This world, any world, it was all too much.

Much later, she stood up. There was a woman at the shore. Her clothes were old and frayed and her arms were bare. She had a basket next to her and she was busy hitting a soggy piece of fabric against a stone. Manasā approached cautiously. The woman wasn't young. She must be a washer! Just like Neta! Only that Neta was much better dressed, if hardly at all, and laughed. She could open the washing basket of the gods, pull out a random item and reveal its history. It was great fun. There was drama, and romance and much to giggle about. Neta knew everything, and enjoyed the nasty bits. This washerwoman looked weary. She had a thin mouth and her face seemed shrivelled.

Manasā stared at the fabric. It was hard to tell its difference from the mud.

The woman turned and gasped.

"O washerwoman. I greet the divine within you. Whose clothes do you wash?"

"Lady." The washerwoman bowed, "they are simple things from simple people. Most people are poor. The village is poor."

"You must have a good life," said Manasā, "you know, my sister is a washer, too. She loves it."

The woman kept her face down. The stranger was mad. And she was terrifying. Sometimes her outlines seemed to swirl. She seemed to wear a rich blue sari, and then she appeared nude, before another dream in silk and embroidery floated across her. Luckily, she had a shadow. That's a good sign. Her feet pointed in the right direction. Maybe she's an Apsaras. When they get into trouble, they get exiled on earth, no matter how stupid they are. But Apsaras don't have sisters who wash things.

"Look at me!" Manasā commanded. "Washerwoman. Face me like an equal. Look into my eyes. I like you. And relax. What's your name?"

The washerwoman bowed. "Serūyā, my lady." The stranger wore plenty of gold. She had no guards, no palanquin, no husband to protect her. Maybe she is an enchanted queen? But why would a queen address her?

"I'm new here," said Manasā, "and this is terribly exciting. This place has so much texture. I never knew there were more than fifty shades of brown! Serūyā, you must have a wonderful life. May I watch you work?"

When dusk came, the women walked to the village. The washerwoman led the way, swaying, as she struggled with her basket. The odd one, clad like an empress, followed her. Manasā had learned amazing things. She could hardly get her head around them. People were so much stranger than she thought. The washerwoman had told her of her life, had spoken of work and hunger, of obedience, the daily chores, and the need to work off the bad Karman of so many other lives. She was lucky, she said, she had a husband and two sons, and there was always washing to do. It gained her a few coins. That's more than what most people earn.

The hut was at the edge of the village. At night, Serūyā heard the half-starved wolves howl in the jungle, and she was glad that her husband did not even own a cow. Bandits and beggars ignored her. Poverty can be a blessing. Serūyā knew she had to do her duty. She was lucky, she had been born as a human being, if only a woman, and she stood a chance to gain a better rebirth if she bore her load, obeyed her husband, and worshipped the gods. Suffering, she knew, is the key to liberation. Two sons were excellent good luck.

"I live a good life," she said, "and of course I never eat meat or touch drink. On many evenings, I fast. The gods are demanding, but I can't offer much. Just a bit of paddy, a few lentils. It's all we have."

She opened a flimsy door. "Be welcome, lady. The guest is god."

Manasā stood and stared. There was just one room. The floor was dry earth, and filthy. On a bamboo bed sat two young men. Unlike their mother, they did not bother about their appearance. Their hair was tangled, their beards soiled and their eyes were red from smoking bhaṅg. One held an open bottle.

"Make space, children. And behave; we have a noble visitor."

The boys grunted. They knew they would spend the night in the shed. Serūyā invited her guest to sit on the bed. Manasā stared at the contraption. The washerwomen apologised and bowed. Cautiously, the serpent goddess took her seat. The bed squeaked like a tortured creature. She looked around. There wasn't much to see. The roof was reeds, the walls were made of bamboo and woven mats, there was a fireplace, a dark pot, and a strong wooden chest, chained to the bed. On one wall, above a cheap brass lamp was a monochrome print showing Viṣṇu and Lakṣmī. Manasā was astonished. The Maintainer of the World and the Goddess of Wealth.

Manasā turned to her host. The bed wobbled and made her feel out of balance. This place is insane, she thought. Why do people live like this?

She pressed a fist into her stomach to ease the cramps. Are these people renouncers? She couldn't believe it. There were plenty of renouncers on Sij Mountain. Even a stupid one would have fixed the bed!

Long after dark, Serūyā's husband walked in. His wife dragged him aside and whispered urgently. The man approached the guest and greeted the divine in her. It felt good. Manasā granted him a smile. Then he withdrew into a corner, where his water pipe gurgled until his wife had the food ready. It was simple fare, watered rice from yesterday, slightly warmed, as fuel is expensive.

Manasā ate a small bowl. It was more than her hosts had. The sons withdrew; husband and wife rolled up on the floor, and the goddess wondered how to spend the night. As a guest, she had the bed all to herself. And all the little beasts that lived in there.

Serūyā filled a bowl of cold rice for her husband and another for herself. Her man departed early; the Thakur had ordered all low-class men to his building site. Payment was not an option. Serūyā left for a bath and her washing duties. Manasā remained and tried to sleep. Each time she turned, her bed tried to get away. Her back ached. Finally, she opened her eyes. Sunlight shone through the walls. There were plenty of holes in the bamboo, and the floor was agleam with amazing patterns. That's why they do it, Manasā thought, this is glorious.

The door squeaked and she watched, from the corners of her eyes, as Serūyā's sons sneaked in.

Manasā pretended to be asleep. Maybe they would go away.

The elder moved first. He scratched his head and his bum, put on an oily grin and advanced. The whore was waiting for it. Manasā read his thoughts. It wasn't difficult.

She raised her head, bared her fangs and opened her evil eye. One glance sufficed: both tumbled to the ground.

The goddess relaxed. She watched the patterns. Slowly, the sun moved, and she observed the brightness as it shifted across the floor. Dust motes danced. It was the most wonderful thing the hut had to offer. Out there, the human realm, she thought, is amazing. No matter where you look, there is a miracle. Her belly ached and it was hard to fight the hunger.

As evening came, she heard steps. Sure, this is Serūyā. She carries her basket, and it's heavy. She'll want to prepare a meal. Manasā remembered the corpses. They are rubbish, she thought, but Serūyā loves them. I have no idea why. Maybe Neta could explain. And I guess she wants them alive, no matter how stupid they are. She granted them a life-restoring glance. Groaning and spitting, the brothers recovered. Serūyā walked in. She saw them waking and cursed them for being such a lazy lot.

The next morning, Manasā felt worse. When night fell, and all the family was asleep, she had tried the stuff Serūyā's sons were smoking. It was bitter and beastly and stung her eyes. Her father wouldn't touch that sort of trash. "Better sober than wasted," that's what he said, "Sober is divine, and much better than trashed. As a god, you insist on quality."

She had a coughing fit, and as her mood didn't improve, she tried the stuff they drank. There were plenty of bottles around. Cheap sugarcane rum, distilled on homemade apertures by craftsmen who courted death and traded in souls. It made her cough and retch and spit. Her eyes watered. She tried more and it got worse. Finally, she gave up. The stuff was strong, but strong wasn't good enough. Who needs this sort of consciousness? My head feels like a piece of roadkill. Let's be sensible. It's time for bed, I say goodbye to the world and hello to my little friends.

Her sleep was uneasy, and it ended when one brother sniggered and the other groped her breast. Ouch! Her evil eye opened, she heard them drop, turned around and went to sleep again.

When she woke, the sun was setting. Serūyā was in the hut, and screamed.

Manasā tried to open her eyes. They felt like glued. The light was far too bright. Manasā raised her head. It was far too heavy.

Serūyā leaned over the corpses of her sons and made a scene. What the hell, thought Manasā, it's nothing special. Death happens all the time. It happens to people who are much nicer than these. Why worry? Maybe they'll have a good rebirth. They could be cockroaches, if they tried extra hard.

Serūyā wouldn't stop.

"You are too loud!" Manasā rose. "Shut up and have them back again!"

She opened her third eye. The brothers twitched and groaned and spat. Eventually, they got up. The washerwoman collapsed in tears.

"Serūyā! Look at them. They ain't better than before. Why do you want them? Can't you make some better kids?"

Manasā felt her head. It ached. The whole damn hut ached. The universe did. It's too narrow in here, I need air, I need space to breathe!

While the brothers shambled away, Serūyā cowered before the goddess and touched her feet.

"Forgive me, lady. I did not recognise you. I'm your humble servitor. Take my life, accept my offerings! All I have is yours."

"I don't want it."

"Are you an Apsaras? A Yakṣī? A Yogīnī? Or a witch?"

Manasā shook her head. It hurt. "No, Serūyā. I'm just a goddess."

The washerwoman paled. She did what all her ancestors had done. Her head hit the ground, again and again. It hurt to watch. Manasā could have screamed. But there was something amazing. Her stomach filled, her limbs tingled, her head seemed light and easy. I feel good, she thought, I feel better than I have for months. Is this worship? Is this how gods survive?

"Serūyā. Get up. Keep your dignity. Stop howling. You are too loud, too sad, too miserable!" Manasā felt tears running down her cheeks. A sneaky part of her mind watched herself, and delighted at how she got stronger.

"Serūyā. I am your guest. You took me in. You told me all those stories. I'm indebted to you. I like you, I love you. Be yourself. You are wonderful."

Her husband opened the door. Serūyā turned and hissed at him. A moment later, he, was on his knees.

"I am filth, I am useless, a toy of fate, a mindless thing, a worthless sinner. I abase myself. I am wretched, and do not deserve your blessings. Let me kiss your feet. Goddess, bless us."

Manasā would have loved to run away. But here she was, facing these weirdoes, feeling happy and alive. I am a parasite, she thought, I'm worse than they are. "Stop it!" the serpent goddess had enough. "I can't stand your whining!"

Husband and wife froze. Something was wrong. They had complained their whole lives through. It was a simple thing. When you grumble incessantly, you get things for free. People sympathise with you. Some offer advice, attention and support. Others provide free food, drinks and loans. Everybody hopes that eventually, you'll shut up. More complaints get more benefits. Misery can be a way of life. And their new goddess wouldn't listen.

The husband raised his face. "Great goddess, mistress of the universe, we humble ourselves; we are dirt beneath your feet."

"What do you want? I mean, what do you really want?"

"Give us wealth and power, destroy our enemies and rivals, make our lives a success, give us palaces and fields, many descendants, and grant eternal happiness."

"And that's all?" Manasā felt her toxic glands swell.

"It's all for the beginning" said the man. "There might be more."

Manasā rose. She threw her hair back and tried to appear divine. She looked much better than before. Her face had regained colour and her hands were steady. "I am grateful. You did your best. But I can't take this any longer. Let's come to a conclusion, 'cause I have to leave. I am the serpent goddess Manasā. You can worship me every day, provided you stop yowling, 'because I can't stand that, and might kill you. Leave me alone with your wishes. They are extreme. I don't do miracles unless they are really needed. Look after your own interests. Be responsible. Whiners don't get anything."

She glared at her worshippers. They knelt; their faces were pressed into the dirt.

"I want to see some attitude. Raise your heads. Where is your spine? Fight for your goals. Be accountable for yourself."

She grinned, and her fangs gleamed. "And call me when your sons make trouble."

Picture 11: Sisters.

15. Duel

East India is full of snake conjurers and serpent doctors. The first variety is obvious: you see them on the marketplace, where they abuse a squeaky drone instrument and force a weary reptile to lift its head out of a basket. Most of these snakes are defanged. They die, one day at a time. The conjurers demonstrate their power, they smirk and bless; they collect coins and sell talismans.

As Neta says, they are booked for hell.

The snake doctors, by contrast, wouldn't be caught in such an embarrassing situation. Many of them are ohjās, and fulfil the tasks of shamans, sorcerers, astrologers and house priests. A few are from the upper classes; in Maṅgal literature you meet ohjās who are low-class Brahmins. Or they pretend to be; forgive my naïveté; it's not my job to doubt everything.

Some ohjās handle toxic reptiles. They drag baskets of snakes around and drape the terrifying reptiles around their necks. It can be risky: many snakes bite, when they are mishandled, and most of them shit. It's almost worse. Some ohjās, I was told, are swindlers. Others treat their serpents with religious awe and consider their profession a vocation.

Meet the most famous one: Manir from Kanirbanir. He lived a poor, ascetic life, was close to starvation most of the time, and healed people of all classes without accepting payment or gifts. He even refused the gift of a single betel nut. That's because healing was his way of worship. The gods were his friends. He knew the spells of the snake-killing Garuḍa bird. He blessed water in bamboo tubes and gave it away for free. His power was so intense that he could wake corpses six months after their death! Six months is an enormously long time, in a hot climate where bodies have to be buried fast, because rot happens instantly. Manir did the trick, most of the time. When a body was way beyond resurrection, he could still make it wake and speak. The dead could say goodbye to their families, or curse them as they liked.

Manir lived in iron-cast chastity. He never allowed a lewd thought to cross his mind. He did not care for the beauty of women, nor did he respect the ancient law that requires men to have sons, so that the ancestors would receive offerings. Manir went his way and healed anyone, anywhere, for free.

One day, as he was walking down the road, he found an infant. Her parents had died of snakebite and left their little girl orphaned and hungry. Manir scratched his head. He never had a wife, or tried to have a family. But here, sent by the gods, was a toddler in need. Manir picked up the girl. He went to his patient and worked a cure. He carried the girl home and raised her.

People talked. Sure, people talk all the time. Most of it is rubbish. Manir didn't care. They stopped gossiping when they needed help.

Meanwhile, the girl grew up. Manir educated her, as best as he could. At the age of six, the girl was literate. She knew her basic prayers, the major mantras, the ritual gestures, and had heard more myths and legends than anyone could handle. She could do the house pūjā, when Manir was away, healing people in distant villages, and she kept their hut a place of light and beauty. Manir loved his daughter. He had never known how lonely he was. His work took him across fields and fords, and sometimes he was away for weeks. When he came home, he found the fire burning, and there was his little girl, who made him feel at home.

"She's different," Manir told his friends, "most women are unreliable. They are just like men, and other animals. But my little girl is saintliness in person."

The years went by. Manir hardly noticed how she grew. She turned eight, the perfect age for marriage, as the Kanoj Brahmins insisted. Manir didn't care. She turned nine, and ten, and eleven. A marriage at eleven is dangerous, the Brahmins said, the girl feels her sexuality and tries to get her head. Manir didn't listen. "Look at the Kanoj Brahmins," he said, "They are spiteful and arrogant. They glut themselves on riches and power. And when a little serpent bites them, they whimper like puppies."

The girl turned twelve. By that age, the Kanoj Brahmins proclaimed, a girl must be wed and leave her house. Manir didn't care. He had no idea what happens during puberty. His daughter was a pleasure. She cleaned and swept, she cooked and laughed; she recited sacred literature and performed the daily offerings. Manir was proud she was so much brighter than her girlfriends. Who disappeared, as, one by one, they were married off.

The neighbours talked. The families gossiped. Here was Manir, the saintly healer, and he had failed to marry his daughter at the age of twelve! The gods would curse him, and he would go to hell.

The Kanoj Brahmins said so. The neighbours remained polite and dropped hints.

One fine day Manir looked at his daughter, and realised she wasn't a child any more. She talked like an adult, she held herself like a heavenly nymph, and her breasts had started to grow. When she walked, her hips swayed like a swan. Manir sighed. He felt old and wretched. The years had taken their toll. He had walked thousands of miles, all over the country, to cure his patients. His back ached and his knees hurt. His eyes were dim and his ears had lost their acuity. I'm getting old, he thought. One day, I'll be alone, right here, in this hut. The roof will leak, but I'll be too weak to repair it. People will ask for healings. But once they are healed, they'll forget me. It's just Manir, they'll say. Sure, he's a great ohjā, maybe the best there ever was. He heals anyone for free. Well, the gods will repay him. He will be happy, one way or another.

By then, he would be alone. He would be squatting in his hut, eating cold rice, watching the rain form puddles on the floor, following the call of duty, until he was done.

Manir knew everything about death. His would happen on a lonely road, and days later, they would find his corpse, swollen and green, covered with flies, rotting in a ditch.

"I have saved the lives of thousands," he said, "but will they care for me, when I am wretched and old?" Manir knew that gratitude lasts a few days, before it turns into embarrassment. People are scum, he thought. They'll hate me, he thought, especially those who owe me everything. He stirred the embers, and sparks rose. Soon, he would be alone. There would be a marriage. His daughter would join the family of the groom. She would fade away, and he would face a cold fireplace, in the early morning twilight, and a garden overgrown with weeds. The dowry would cost him everything he had; it would indebt him, and cripple him forever. Perhaps he would have to sell his property.

Staring into the future, a remarkably stupid idea appeared. What, he thought, if I should marry my daughter? We are not related by blood, she is an orphan, I adopted her, she owes me everything and when I grow old and destitute, she'll be here to warm my soup and push my vertebrae where they belong. Manir smiled. He wouldn't decay, forgotten in his hut, or rot in a ditch on some forgotten mountain path.

His girl was clever and obedient. She understood her adoptive father's fears, and realised her duty. Marriage, she knew, would be a formality. It wouldn't change a thing. The old guy didn't care about sex. One day soon I'll be a widow, and find a man who longs for me. Truth to tell, she loved Manir. He had saved her life and raised her; he had given her an education and a purpose in life. He understood her, and forgave her, no matter what she did.

The neighbours laughed and gossiped. Manir pretended not to notice. He walked, as was his custom, from village to village, and healed the poor, the lonely, and the hopeless. Snake-bite, stroke or pestilence, Manir could cure anything. At times he was away for weeks. He acted as well as he could, and the gods acted through him. The monsoon rains came and went. His young wife sat at home. She read the *Vedas* and the *Upaniṣads*, recited hymns, did rituals, tended the garden and kept the hut clean. Her husband, she knew, was away on a mission. He did the work of the gods, and she was proud of him.

One day she noticed a young man. He looked smooth, and golden, and muscular, like Kārrtikeya. His eyes were deep and dark, like those of Kṛṣṇa. He stood, near the gate, shining like the early morning sun, and made her burn with desire. The boy came and went, and he remained in her thoughts. He was greater, better and lovelier than all five Pāndava brothers combined. He caught her eyes, her heart, and he inflamed her loins. By day and night, his image scorched her mind.

The girl fought. She struggled, she abused herself, and finally, nature being stronger than ethics, she gave in. She met him, unobserved, near the water tank. She talked like an innocent, while he pretended to have higher things in mind. That's young people. Each of them is busy with her or his personal myth. And each of them is unique, no matter how often it's repeated. The next day, she was waiting for him. On the third day, she gave him a garland of blossoms, just as newlyweds do.

While Manir was gone, far away, across a dozen rivers, she ran away with her beloved. We shouldn't blame her: her instincts forced her, and each of them was divine. The girl tried to do her best. Before she disappeared, she cleaned the hut, prepared everything, to make Manir feel at home, and locked the door thrice. Days later Manir came home. He felt tired, and was astonished that the door was locked. He had to ask his neighbours to break it open. He walked into the hut and emptiness embraced him. "No matter," he told his neighbours, "My wife is gone but I'll be fine. She will be back soon."

The ohjā sat, in a corner of his hut, on the earth floor, and prayed. Manir, of course, was familiar with the *Rāmāyana*. His wife, just like the wife of Rāma, had been abducted by monsters, by Asuras or dacoits. He knew her: she was good, she was true, and she wouldn't have left him, no matter what.

"She's my wonderful girl, and a true saint," he kept saying.

But, whatever the reason and whoever had carried her away, she had found time to clean the floor, do the dishes and lock the door three times. Manir was not an idiot, he understood Karman and he knew the world. He said, "She needs my help. I have to find her. I will search for her in the bright forest. I'll trace her across the snowy mountains. I'll find her in the dark heart of the jungle." He nodded to the neighbours. "All will be well. It'll be a long journey. I hope I'm strong enough. At my age, nothing is easy. But I'm not dead yet. And before I go, I will find her in my heart."

He walked to the river. The water rushed by, dark, dangerous and uncaring. Bubbles danced on the waves. He threw himself into the flood and drowned. That's what the poets sing. They were not present, sure; they are never around when they are needed, but they have a clear idea about reality and the songs that people weep and pay for. Give them a story, and they turn it into tragedy.

In our *Epic*, things are slightly different. Sure, like everybody else, we have a mighty serpent doctor. It says so on his dhoti. Ours has an almost cosmic format. He is well dressed, keeps his beard trimmed, and looks formidable. Also, he has bushy eyebrows, and dark eyes; he is young and carries himself like an emperor.

Women faint when they see him. He doesn't even notice.

This guy, I am sure you'll understand, wouldn't have dreamed of curing anyone for free. "People don't appreciate things that are free," he observed. His eyebrows rose with regret. "The living take life for granted. They waste it all the time. We ohjās have to deal with reality. Whether I like it or not: I charge as much as I can. When people die of snakebite, they are keen to pay. So are their relations. I say: let them beg for my services. Let them indebt themselves. It makes the magic so much stronger."

It's not that Dhanvantari was a miser. Had he met an orphaned toddler, he would have shared his food with her. He would have wished her well (one day she might be a customer) and walked on.

Since Dhanvantari rose from the Milk Ocean, and received the victory scarf and the all-healing medicine pouch from Brahmā, and got the cottage cheese out of his hair, he had had the time of his life. It's great to be a winner and an all-time success, especially if you look good and everyone admires you. One day, he knew, he would surpass the gods. It would be easy. Gods, after all, are old-fashioned misfits, the ideals and fears of bygone ages. Dhanvantari wasn't an atheist. It's silly to deny the gods, when they are everywhere. But he was so much better.

The ohjā fingered his magic scarf. It was a nice gift, but he wasn't grateful. Trinkets are like talent, he thought, they make you lazy. On the long run, talent runs dry but determination continues. It means practice, every day. He had travelled far. It wasn't far enough. And he was keen to learn.

The fog was almost everywhere. The sorcerer could hardly see the rocks beneath his feet, and the water between them. The air was moist, but the sound drew him on. Here it came again, a loud 'slosh!" as textiles hit a stone. In the distance, he heard a female voice. He couldn't make out words, nor was he sure if she was laughing, grumbling or both.

Another 'Slosh!' Dhanvantari advanced. The stones were slippery. He could have used a spell to dispel the fog. That, however, would have ruined everything. With the mist, the mystery would disappear. He would face clarity, and limits, and another dead end.

'Slosh!" it went again. The voice got clearer. He could hear the woman. "Stay there, stop it! I'll see you clean or dead!"

A silhouette emerged. The woman was young, and almost nude. She turned in his direction.

"There you are. You took your time. What's your excuse? I've been waiting for ages."

Dhanvantari stopped. She's a girl, he thought, and these bunches are silly. She can't be the woman that I heard about.

The girl laughed. "Your thoughts are pretty loud," she said, "and you are quite a fool. Never believe anything you hear, unless I tell you."

"Why should I believe you?"

"See this?" the woman grinned. She held a moth-eaten tiger skin in her hands. The bundle was dripping wet. One sweep and it hit the rocks. 'Slosh!'

Her teeth gleamed. "This could be you."

Dhanvantari stared in amazement. He recognised Śiva's dhoti, and wondered what the god was wearing now.

"Ashes," said Neta, "and nothing else. He feels better that way."

"How dare you insult the Lord of Dissolution?"

"How dare I speak of my dad? It's easy. I just do it. 'Cause I know him and you don't. I say to him, stop meddling; sit back, relax, I'll get it sorted out. He grins and slips into alternative realities. Sure, he is nude. I'm used to it. I do my thing."

"My lady!" Dhanvantari went down on his knees. The stones hurt his knees. "Forgive me. I did not recognise you."

"Don't play humble. You are proud and you pretend, and I won't fall for it."

Dhanvantari bowed, "forgive my lack of manners."

"Get up. I want to see you stand." Neta grinned. "You look smashing. I know you came on purpose. Show me how good you are."

Dhanvantari raised himself. His mind was reeling. He was a seer, a high born Brahmin and a demi-god. He had officiated at the Milk Ocean. The girl before him was a washerwoman. Washers are low-class-trash. They deal with filth. It doesn't get much worse than this. By right and tradition, she should have knelt before him. And here he was, trying to impress here.

"I know my limits. You are a goddess. I have heard of you."

"And you seek initiation. That's really bold, you know. Look at this stuff. I wash the garments of the gods. They are full of sweat and filth and blood and juices. Come and join me. Get your hands dirty. But realise: alive or dead, you'll be polluted. It could make you a real healer. It could destroy your reputation."

Dhanvantari hesitated.

Neta giggled; her mouth held more teeth than it should. Quite a few were pointed. "Watch out, Mr. Celestial Career. I could kill you anytime."

"You won't. You are far too glad to see me."

"That's true. You're not quite stupid. You seem eager to learn. It won't be easy. So show me what you've got, Baby Saint. They say you seek to surpass the gods. Here is the washing. It's filthy. I want to see you work."

When the evening sky went rosy, the mist faded and the egrets flapped to the other shore. Neta and Dhanvantari sat on the rocks and watched the crocodiles. They were gavials, huge lizards with slim snouts.

"Don't worry," said Neta, "they only eat fish. Stop wriggling or they'll give you a try."

"Goddess," said Dhanvantari. His voice was deep, and he kept his eyes on the ground.

"Don't flatter me!" Neta laughed, "I know your aspirations. You are a career addict. You found me, and that was pretty good. You might relax and enjoy. You could see a sunset like it had never happened before. You could enjoy the crocodiles, and the birds, and know that this is the best moment of your life."

"But I do."

"You don't. All you think about is profit. You hurry for a goal and lose yourself. And you believe you are wonderful. Come on, adept. You look great and your beard is perfectly trimmed. You want to be better than us? Then start learning."

"I helped to do the washing."

"Not very well. Baby, you're just a beginner. Too shy, too timid, too proud. You need practice and plenty of hard work. You need to get your hands filthy! Durgā's slips aren't made for the faint hearted. They have teeth, and almost ate your fingers. But you managed to hang them up. That's not bad," she knocked an elbow into his ribs and laughed, "for a mortal."

"Teach me," he whispered.

When Dhanvantari woke, his head spun and his belly gurgled. Rain lashed his face. The riverside had disappeared. He seemed to be surrounded by sij. There were spikes everywhere.

Neta had done her best. He only wished he could forget the scene. Aching all over, he raised himself. What had happened to his dhoti? Why did his connective tissue screech? And what had she mumbled, while she cooked that cauldron full of snakes?

"I'll tell you once. If you can't remember, well, that ain't my problem."

Gods, yes, there had been mantras. Lots of them. They made his head spin. Neta recited them, or invented them, as she went along, and some were in languages that Dhanvantari had never heard before. "I'll pierce your mind," she giggled, "and guess what I'm going to find?"

When the broth was ripe and its stench blazed his sinuses and made his eyes water, she told him to open his mouth and poured so much into his face and down his throat that he choked.

"Great," said the goddess, while she pounded his back. "You poor deluded thing! Keep it down. Hey, you look funny! Relax! Feel happy! The cramps will pass, and now you're full of serpent sorcery. One day you'll understand how much you learned today. I'll drink the rest."

She gurgled as the stuff ran down her chin and splattered over her breasts.

"That's it. "She announced. "You had your share. And now I want a bit of fun. Show me how you surpass the gods."

The time: days later. The place: the middle of nowhere. See Dhanvantari staggering across the desert landscape. He is hungry and thirsty and quite beside himself. There are sij plants everywhere, the river is far away, that's his good luck, 'cause his twitches might invite all fish-eating crocodiles. The spikes have taken their fill; his legs and arms are scratched and bleeding. He is nude and sun-scorched, his hair is full of debris, his hands jitter, and his mind is a thing of patchwork and insanity. "I know how the gods feel" he announces to a thorny shrub, "Worship me, little plant. I am ultimate reality! I have drunk from the cauldron and my mind is everywhere."

The plant sighs, and its spikes shudder. It's seen it all. Neta's initiates usually don't make it. A few laugh; most of them go crazy or die.

"Obey my command!" Dhanvantari looks imposing.

The plant bristles. Five-inch spikes can bristle perfectly.

"Get down on your knees!" hollers Dhanvantari, "I demand respect!"

"Little darling," says the growth, "shut up. You are making a scene. Come close. Embrace me."

Dhanvantari does.

That was years ago, and is better forgotten. Since then, Dhanvantari had learned a lot. It wasn't enough.

He conjured the mighty Garuḍa bird, the special enemy of all snakes, and made it reveal its sorceries. He made grandiose offerings for Śiva and Durgā, and forced them to disclose their healing secrets. His reputation spread all across India, and even to the dark and distant north, near the source of the Seven Oceans, where sun and moon are unknown and eternal darkness reigns. Bandits, robbers, destroyers, bears and tigers heard of great Dhanvantari, and went down on their knees.

He became famous, and students appealed to him. "I don't teach losers," he said, "no matter how rich. You have to prove your merit every day!" He grinned as he raised his diamond mālā. "The best isn't good enough. That means: Perform or disappear. One day, I want you to surpass the gods. That's a lot of hard work. And it's expensive."

One sunny day Dhanvantari was travelling through the mountains. He was accompanied by a thousand students from the best families. They cooked for him, they clothed him, and they obeyed his merest whims.

The congregation made its way between towering cliffs and twisted waterways. As they negotiated a narrow track, they were stopped by a serpent. The reptile was huge. It could have swallowed an elephant in a bite, and topped it off by three rhinos and half a village.

"This is your chance," he announced. "Students, your life was far too easy. You learned a lot but you never had to use it."

The sorcerer snarled, "Go and kill the beast!"

His students stood like frozen.

"You there!" Dhanvantari addressed his best pupil, "listen, 'cause this is your fight. Take this knife. It's magical. Go for the serpent. There's a weak spot at the back of its head."

The student was pale, and wished he could have fainted. "Go on," the master grinned, "I'll stun the beast with mantras!"

The serpent heaved. The sound made its head spin. The next moment, someone was slashing at it with a knife. The snake tried to bite, but its mind was far away. Another mantra echoed, and hurt. The snake twisted and writhed. A moment later, this fuzzy, irritating human was labouring at its head. He reached into the brain, and pulled.

"I've got it!" he called, "Guru, I've got the wish-fulfilling jewel."

He raised the gory trophy.

Dhanvantari laughed. "Throw it away!'

"Master, it can work miracles"

"The maṇi stone is nothing!" Dhanvantari raised himself, and made sure everyone heard him, "The serpent's jewel is garbage compared to my arts!"

He faced the other students. "You idiots! You feared and doubted. But now I'll separate the losers from the winners. Anyone with wet pants is dismissed!"

The sorcerer raised his hands to heaven, "You scum! Run away before I curse you! Go to your parents and weep! Kneel before the gods! Snivel and complain! Find another vocation. And know that you are rubbish!"

"He dismissed half of them." Vāsuki shrugged. "They are trying to find their way home. The hills are full of aimless wanderers. Some of them collapse. They are too stupid to find water. And, honestly, without a leader they are lost."

"That's excellent!" Manasā appeared relieved.

"It isn't. There's always a little snake around. It saw the big snake die, and came straight to me. I called the other Nāga lords. We elected generals, amassed troops and dispatched an army of snakes to the hillside."

Vāsuki stopped. "I feel guilty," he whispered. "We underestimated him."

"You wanted to shock him."

"He shocked us. Truly, as the seers say, the greatest weakness of the Nāgas is their anger. I acted too fast. When the mountain flank erupted with snakes, Dhanvantari's students screamed."

Vāsuki reached for his drink. It was made of pink rum with sugar and a newt floated in it.

"We lost. That man is a nightmare. He used a few mantras, some gestures, a bit of blessed water. Some of our snakes died, many others fainted. Dhanvantari ordered his students to bash their heads in."

"Is that why you called me?"

"You might be strong enough to handle him. Serpent mantras won't affect you. And maybe Śiva will help."

"I'll do this on my own," said Manasā, "My dad won't be needed."

Vāsuki bowed to his sister. She looked so young and vulnerable, and tried to be so brave.

"You'll find his camp on the mountain slope, right next to a brook. Look for the dead tree. And be careful. He has hundreds of students with him."

"They'll spread the story of his shame."

She turned to the Nāga assembly and faced the many snakes who had watched her grow up. "My friends, companions, children of Kadrū. I will defeat the sorcerer."

"He's too strong", hissed the serpents. "Neta taught him mighty spells."

"Neta likes to have a laugh. It's like a game. She loves it. She teaches anyone who looks promising, gets them totally confused, turns their heads upside down, enjoys a wild night and leaves them worn out before daybreak. Few have the skill and discipline to use her knowledge. To apply Neta's spells, you have to forget the words, forget yourself and embrace death with a laugh."

"He learned from the Garuḍa bird!" The assembly hissed. Garuḍa, the primal fire-bird, is the eternal enemy of snakes.

"What did the bird teach him? How to scrape jackals from the lane? Has he equipped the fool with wings? My friends! Bird magic is for birds!"

"Dhanvantari learned from Śiva."

"Only the basics. Do you think my father taught him anything that I wouldn't know?"

Manasā held her head high and allowed the tension to build. One moment, two moments, three moments. And now.

"Dhanvantari is arrogant. But his skills are limited. Look at him. Sure, he keeps his beard trimmed. He wears fancy clothes and he has many students. That's a sign of weakness. He exploits them and they eat him alive! Karman will grind him down. I hardly need to do a thing."

"You are arrogant, too!" the serpents complained.

Manasā held herself like an empress. She had practised that posture before the mirror, until Neta wept with laughter.

"Arrogance? Never. I am humility in person. I will show him that the world is vast and wonderful."

She bowed, turned, and walked away.

Behind her, she heard a voice. "She's such a baby."

In the faint light of dawn, the grasses glistened. Here and there, spiderwebs gleamed, studded with dew-drop jewellery. Between them were serpents. Many of them were dead. A few students staggered through the twilight. They held blood encrusted rocks, and used them to bash heads in. On the large rock under the dead tree, Dhanvantari sat. He had wrapped himself in blankets; the air was chilly, and it would be a while before his breakfast was ready. The sorcerer made his pipe bubble. His students were scared to meet his eyes.

The ohjā felt greatly satisfied. Down the slope, he heard cattle calling. In the distance, there were cow herders huddling around fires, waiting for the first rays of the sun.

"Bring me water," Dhanvantari commanded, and a student ran for the nearby pond. He returned, his dhoti wet, and dropped to his knees. The master accepted the bowl. The demonstration had worked well. Dismiss the loafers and the survivors are twice as keen to please. One day, he would transform a selected few into master magicians. Provided they gave everything.

Manasā, in serpent form, emerged from an earth hole. The dead tree stood out against the twilight sky. That's where Dhanvantari sat. His aura was painful.

She reached the stream, slid into the water and made her way down the mountainside. A little pool provided shelter. Lotus, she thought, that's all I need, and picked one.

With great caution, she raised her head. There were no students nearby. But there were snakes, as far as she could see, hundreds and thousands of them. None of them moved. Some had been killed by stones. The others had died from mantras. Many were stunned. That's fine, she thought, it's time for celebration. She changed her shape and spoke the mantra that revives the dead.

Above the campsite stood a woman, silhouetted against the morning sky. She hissed mantras, and dead snakes raised their heads. The students screamed.

"Little whore," the sorcerer whispered, as he stood up. This would be fun. "Come here, mountain spirit, let me grind you down. When your head is crushed, your spells will fail."

Manasā remained where she was. She knew that she looked splendid, before the rosy clouds of dawn. "Dhanvantari, you don't know me. Are you a man or a frog? How long did you live in a well? Isn't it narrow in there, with so many idiots?"

She pointed at him. "Come on, sorcerer! Show me your skill. What did you learn from my sister Neta? And what did you learn from my father Śiva?"

The sorcerer paled. "Who are you, demon?"

"The daughter of Rudra."

"You filthy liar!"

"Answer my questions, guru! I want to hear you loud and clear. Your students have a right to learn! Your initiations, I hear, were granted by a washerwoman, and by a filthy carrion bird! Śiva fed you ashes from the burning place!"

Dhanvantari glared at her. "You gods!" He raised his hands to the sky, "You owe me! Remember the Milk Ocean. You are indebted! I humiliated myself a thousand times! Kill the snakes! I command you, kill the snakes!"

Manasā laughed. Nothing happened. No god appeared, no serpent found its end.

The ohjā felt bitterly alone. Further down the slope, he could see his students running.

Manasā beamed at him. "Little frog, do you give up?"

"I fight."

"See this blossom." The goddess raised the lotus. It gleamed white and pink, and seemed so fresh and soft. "Observe the petals. The whole world is within them. The flower is your heart. Today, it will be your fate!"

She hurled the blossom at the sorcerer.

Dhanvantari raised his hands and cast a spell. In mid-air, the lotus flamed and fell. The sorcerer forced a laugh, but his hands trembled, shudders racked him, and his heart went numb.

"I seek refuge with Śiva, Lord of all Magic, Destroyer of the Multiverse!" he exhaled slowly, and his breath was bitter poison. Icy cold crept up the hillside. His stomach knotted, and he bared his teeth.

"God of Ascetics! Kill this slut!"

Manasā grinned. "Śiva hates you. Take this!"

She hurled a handful of mustard seeds.

Dhanvantari lifted a hand full of dust and threw it. Mustard seeds met dust. Dhanvantari almost stumbled. His world turned grey and meaningless.

"I hate you, bitch" he mumbled, "and I will kill you and tear out your guts and hang you from the branches of this tree!"

His face twisted. "Mahādeva, great god, Śiva, hear my prayer! I order you, come here and help!"

Manasā towered over him. "You call on my father? Let me curse you! Here are the mantras that Śiva taught me! Each is a dagger in your guts!"

The goddess snarled and hissed.

The sorcerer felt his belly cramp. He didn't understand a word.

"Do you give up?"

"Never!"

"Dhanvantari" Manasā shouted, "Face me! Man without a heart, man without a future! You are a frog and I will eat you alive!"

She raised a spear.

"My father Śiva gave this spear to me! It destroys the three worlds!"

The shaft was ornamented with pictures and sigils that burned like molten metal. The point was decorated with the mountaintops, and the palaces of the high gods. The bottom showed all seven underworlds. The middle section showed the world, not as it seems, but as it really is. Plants throve and tangled, animals went their way and people tried to make a living, best as they could. People, ah, people. So close to divinity, so lost in their delusions. He saw himself, with his students, a fool among many.

The ohjā shrieked in pain. He reached into his dhoti and produced a knife.

An icy wind went swept down the mountainside. It was too cold for dawn; it was too icy for the future. The gods appeared.

And they were in a hurry.

Śiva arrived first.

"Daughter! Stop it! Don't use the spear!" He caught her arm. "The three worlds must continue. Have compassion for their inhabitants. Most of them are nicer than this guy. Remember algae and dragonflies and vultures! There are bananas and hemp! Think of trees and rivers and cremation places."

"I'll cremate everything!"

"Most gurus are stupid. The world isn't. It doesn't deserve to end."

Brahmā came next. "Please, darling, you can't do this. It's the multiverse. I made most of it. Keep it, protect it, and love it. Kill that idiot, if you like, smear his brains across the rocks, but let the worlds go on!"

Then Viṣṇu appeared, and he was really angry. He grabbed Dhanvantari's head and knocked it against a rock. "You fool! You idiot! A thousand students! You are a failure! Be ashamed! How could you kill so many serpents! How could you endanger the three worlds?"

"Mercy," squeaked the sorcerer.

Manasā grinned. "I can't hear you!"

"Forgive me, goddess!" the ohjā pleaded. "I give up, I accept your punishment. Kill me, torture me, let me suffer for my sins."

Viṣṇu nodded. That's how it should be. Dhanvantari was on his knees, his nose was bleeding, and no matter his misdeeds, he promised to better himself. That surely counted for something.

"Right," said the Maintainer of the Universe, "let's be objective. Our offender has led an evil, greedy life, but he is keen to learn humility. We should show mercy. But words ain't good enough. We want to see a different attitude and a much better performance."

"I'll do anything. Anything you say, anything you want."

The gods nodded. Dhanvantari, they knew, had a future. Provided he remained meek and worshipped them with many sacrifices.

Brahmā laughed. The dawn was glorious. Red and blue and cirrus clouds floated across the sky. Ice crystals, as faint as feathers, each of them a glitter of eternity. He loved them.

Dhanvantari had coiled up like an embryo. What a slimy little loser, thought Brahmā, he tries to wriggle back into the womb. Well, people are like that.

"Hello, Mr. Ohjā," he said. "I hear you are better than anyone and anything."

Dhanvantari sobbed.

"Raise your head, you little idiot. After all, you look good. What a wonderful beard! You ain't stupid, you are just deluded. Your students made you feel important. They didn't last." Brahmā grinned. "Do you want to keep learning?"

"May I?"

"Of course you may. The gods smile, 'cause you are a happy little tadpole. I greet the divine in you. It had better make an effort." Brahmā slapped the sorcerer on his shoulder. "Your pool is much larger than before. And you are lucky. Look up, you wretched little innocent and get the blood out of your face. I'll tell you a secret and I only tell it once. You want to cure snake bite? Worship Manasā. She'll like it, no matter how dumb you perform."

The rock radiated heat, and it was nice to sit upon, while the sun disappeared under the horizon. Twilight blossomed in rose and purple. Manasā and Śiva shared the silence.

They were alone. Brahmā and Viṣṇu had left early. So had Dhanvantari. He was keen to reach the plains. Preferably someplace where no one knew him. He had been lucky to survive. It had cost him dearly. The great Dhanvantari had pressed his brow into the dirt and pleaded for mercy. The goddess had laughed, gave him a slap on his head and another on his bottom and told him to run. He did.

Down in the valley, the herders gathered their cattle.

"You had a wonderful day, daughter." Śiva was happy. "You look healthier than before. The Nāgas will worship you. The story will be told. Snakes in all worlds will seek your refugee."

The Lord of Ascetics stretched. She heard his vertebra click into place. "But do explain one thing. You said I taught you mantras. I can't remember. Which mantras would that be?"

Manasā glanced at him sideways. "You told me many mantras."

"Speak up!" the Lord of Cremation lifted a bottle and drank. He offered the vessel to his daughter. Manasā recoiled.

"What you always say. 'Wake me next Saturday.' 'Disagree with yourself before others do.'"

"These are fabulous mantras." Śiva took another drag. "They helped me through the centuries. One day, maybe, I'll find out what they mean." He upended the bottle. Yes, it was empty now. "I could teach you a few."

"Any good ones?"

"Sure. There are loads. 'Young pigs become old goats.' 'It takes a snail to slide across a razor.' 'The pebble laughs when morning comes.'"

"Why?"

"No idea. Ask the pebble."

"And these are magic spells?"

"Of course. They are reliable. They function almost anytime."

"They are too complicated."

"That's just because you never were a pebble. They have an amazing life. It goes by in thousands of years. But I know what you mean. Philosophers want simple stuff, like 'All beings are pots.' That's because pots have an inside, an outside, and a wall in-between. Just like humans. But here is something better: 'Reality is blue.'"

Śiva snapped his fingers. The bottle filled again. He grinned. "It's nonsense. Reality is magenta and green."

"You make them up."

"So do you."

Manasā bit her lower lip.

Her father gazed into the distance. He sounded apologetic. "Long ago, I invented something serious. I thought it would change the world. Yes, I know, I was young and stupid. One day, I met this forest dweller. He was totally insane. But he did wonderful lamb kebab from nothing but mud and bushrat shit. I wanted to give him something in return. I said, 'Repeat this mantra: **You are This**.'

A child could handle it, though it's the greatest mystery in the world. I thought it would make him happy."

Śiva stowed the bottle away and sighed. "I'll keep this for later. Durgā wants her share. Well this seer, he was totally insane, but he started a mass movement. Thousands of students followed him. Plants, trees, whatever, were trampled into the ground. By people who believed in divine harmony and spiritual refinement and some such crap. The forest died. There's a pharmaceutical plant there, these days. And fields of corn and wheat and soy, I tell you, they are evil. Agriculture destroys everything. And say hello to skyscrapers and nuclear plants and the biggest parking lot in Asia." Śiva sighed. "All right, I thought, let's turn it around. Last time I got it wrong. I got hold of another seer and said: 'Here, fuzzy boy, is your new mantra: **This is You**.'

He says, 'What is me?' and I say,

"The world. Feel responsible. He says, 'For what?'

And I reply, 'For everything.'

The guy was happy. He could start his own sect! His students walked around in a daze. They were worried. 'Here's a tree,' they went, 'but I'm not a tree. I don't have leaves. And I can walk.'

The tree shook its crown. 'I wish you would.'

I apologised. To the tree."

"But these mantras are brilliant!"

"People are too complicated. In future, I stuck to simple stuff. 'The happy cow finds a way.' 'Run fast, die soon.'" The Lord of Ascetics grinned. "'Drop the Cactus!'"

He got up. "A lot of people need that one. But it's getting dark, I'm late and Durgā is waiting. So tell me. What did you hiss and snarl?"

Manasā lowered her head. She whispered, "People are funny".

"And what did you use for a spear?"

Manasā raised a broken greenish something.

The thing looked wretched.

"Thank you." Śiva took the lotus stalk.

"Be careful," Manasā smiled, "it might destroy the worlds."

16. Cowherds

The cow raised her head and swished her tail. Flies scattered, buzzed and returned. Our cow hardly knew what a fine life she had. In her last lifetime, she had been a guru. Just by coincidence, she had accepted too many presents. Now she stood on a swampy meadow and fought flies who had been her students.

Indian cows enjoy a leisurely life which is fundamentally based on avoiding vermin and people.

Our cow gazed into the bushes, right, there were her herders, resting under a banyan tree. They smoked something terrible.

Here was her family, and her relations, all of them dutiful, respectable bovines, whose entire existence revolved around keeping their stomachs gurgling. Grasses are tough and contain little nourishment. That's why cows eat any worm, insect, snail, egg or young animal that can't get away. Her belly thundered. Cows leave their digestion to microbes and fungi. Her tenants thrive in the low-acidity climate of her stomachs. That means 200 trillion bacteria, four billion protozoan plus fungi, yeasts and extras, having the time of their lives in a digestive system that never, ever empties. They convert low-quality vegetable fat into high-value animal fat. The cow eats them.

The gods decreed that cows are scared. Sure, they had taken their time about it. In the Vedic periods, cows were sacrifices and ended up in curry sauce. There were different colours for different gods. With the advent of Hinduism, this shameful custom was outlawed. The cows, as everyone delighted, produce milk. Milk means cheese and curds and yoghurt, and wonderful butterfat, all of them favourites of the gods. Also, a household cow is perfect heating during the winter monsoon when the cold winds from Central Asia come howling. The cow is a member of the family. It gurgles, burps and farts and gives you the feeling that you are really home.

Our cow did not notice that she was closely watched, analysed, and dismissed.

"Just as I thought," said Neta, "their lives are boring. They don't mind, 'cause they are stupid. And so are the guys who watch them."

"Nonsense." Manasā straightened the snakes in her hair. "I have also thought, and my thoughts are better. Cows are sacred and their herders are a priesthood."

"They are hopeless. Just look at them. They sleep under the tree. They get up, drink, piss, eat some fruit and lie down again."

"They have mastered tranquillity. It's close to perfection."

"It's close to total stupor. I call them dumb."

"I call them wilderness philosophers. They have seen through the illusionary nature of life. They delight to be poor, and happy, and they love sunshine and open air."

"They are stuck with it."

"They are much like me. And let me tell you, they'll be my worshippers."

"Appeal to the cows. They are wiser." Neta stuffed the washing basket. "The moment you go over there, you'll be in trouble."

"Why should I? I'll simply appear and they'll love me."

"'Simply,'" said Neta, "you have no idea what that means."

"Don't take me for a fool. I'm not stupid! Of course I'll change my shape. And I'll buy a little milk."

Oh yes, thought Neta, you are the thinking one. But what the hell. She wouldn't dream of stopping her sister. Thinkers deserve what they think up.

Cow herders, she knew, are coarse. They spend their days on the edge of the forest, near swampy ground and dusty meadows. They carry responsibility, as most of their cattle don't belong to them. They scare predators, should any be around, and keep the cows from other people's gardens.

There are massive differences between the life of the farmer and the herder. The peasant has to plan his life, and the poorer he is, the more he worries. He frowns at the weather and counts the days, he indebts himself and struggles to cull the harvest in time. Bad dreams haunt him. The hard, bitter earth disfigures his spine, ruins his joints and makes his head droop. When he comes home, by nightfall, his muscles ache and his body is coated with sweat and dust. His diet is poor. He eats a little rice, a few lentils, and falls asleep.

The herder has plenty of leisure. He rests in the shade, chats with his cronies and dreams of the day when he'll be lucky and rich and have more wives than he can count.

That's how Kṛṣṇa lived, the happy god, when he herded cows near Gokula. He wouldn't have dreamed of ruining his posture with field work. Occasionally he looked after the cows. Usually, they looked after him. And they behaved. Meanwhile, he told stories and swam in the river; he played ball with the boys, sneaked up on bathing cowgirls, stole their clothes, and spent the evening performing soulful tunes on his reed flute. The sad melodies enchanted the hearts of the girls and made them run, their faces flushed, to embrace the dark god whose eyes shone like lotus blossoms. Each of them gained all of his heart and his entire love, but honestly, deep within himself he was totally lost to his beloved Rādhā. She, of course, struggled with yearning, hope, despair and rage.

Rādhā is divine, but she is also jealous. It's damn hard to be the special sweetheart of a god who boasts of having 16,000 wives. Kṛṣṇa remained tactful and didn't mention it in her presence. But Rādhā was aware that 15,999 drooling rivals hated her. The dark flute player, whose smile shows brightly shining teeth and wonderful dimples, has a heart for almost any woman because a) cosmic love is unlimited and b) social conventions are rubbish. It made him declare that fast, reckless action is best and you can think about Karman afterwards. That's how he steered his war chariot, at the battle of Kurukṣetra, and how Indians drive their cars.

Rādhā with her hypnotising midnight eyes wept, pouted, cursed and forgave him. You can't reprimand a high god for infidelity. Nor would he blame her. Rādhā was married to the grumpy old cowherd Ayanghoṣa, surely a good, if boring man, who was dumb enough to let her escape to the forest edge, and her lover, every evening.

If you suspect that high gods are not always true to their spouses, you misunderstand the sheer impact of spiritual symbolism. "We have divine functions," Kṛṣṇa explains to any philosopher, "and no time to be examples. We do our best. Anyone who dislikes our conduct should understand it as an abstract metaphor with no connotations to love, sex or anything. Promised!"

The cow herders entertained similar thoughts. Sure, They wouldn't have noticed a metaphor, abstract or not, if it had eaten them alive. But they understood sex, 'cause their cattle taught them how.

The dust devil danced through the meadow. Bleached grasses flew, leaves were tossed about and the herders touched their talismans for safety. The air shimmered with heat, and a woman rose. She was an old rose; long past her prime, her face was eroded like a mountainside and her greasy hair was full of debris. She had not bothered to veil herself. Her spotted face was crusty with filth and when she laughed and blushed, like a young girl, she revealed teeth which leant in all directions.

That's how Neta described her, to me. "I don't exaggerate. This is cold realism."

But had we asked a real poet, we would have received a double helping of superlatives: her eyes were red like coals, her crooked neck wrinkly like that of a tortoise, her hands like crippled branches, covered with greenish lichen, her knees as thick as watermelons, her breasts hung to her ankles and her ass was bony like the bum of a zebu cow. That, Manasā says, it's simply not true. "I never had a zebu bum. But keep the passage, 'cause I think it's dramatic and readers like that sort of stuff."

I agree. Let's give our poet a few rupees and ask him to leave. Neta sends her regards, and he should never, ever try to write a love letter.

The woman stood and stared. The herders stared back. She raised her open hands and swayed like a sāl tree in the storm.

"My dear philosophers! I'm so glad to meet you!"

The herders paled.

The woman giggled like a girl. Now she had the full attention of herders and bovines, and the former began to scream.

"A witch! An evil spirit!"

Some grabbed sticks, others bent for stones.

"My lords, I greet the divine in you!"

"Away! Be off!" A stone flew past her. The women didn't even seem to notice. She simply flickered sideways.

"Let's kill her!" More stones flew. "Kill the witch!"

Manasā had thought long and hard, and talked about her thoughts, and what she thought she thought, or ought to think, or might think if she thought otherwise, and Neta left the room.

The serpent goddess had a plan. She was proud of it. It dealt with every eventuality. That's what good plans do. In case you want to know Neta's opinion, plans are fantasy. Have one by all means, be nice to it, keep it warm, but forget it when you meet reality. That's what all washerwomen, artists, military experts, and brain surgeons say. Take care of your plan and it will take care of you. When you are cold and lonely in the middle of the night. Or better, go to sleep again.

When Neta returned (somewhat drunk), Manasā was fighting with her wardrobe. It wasn't easy. The wardrobe fought back.

"I want khaki and slime-green. And a touch of diarrhoea."

The wardrobe shuddered and tried to sneak away.

"And I want patches and frayed spots and gaps where you can see flesh gleam. That's because it's sexy."

The wardrobe looked at Neta and Neta bared her teeth. The wardrobe gave up.

"Great!" Manasā danced before the mirror. "O Neta, you came at the right moment. Admire me! I have to show you a few combinations!"

Neta forced a smile. "Sorry, no time. I'm in a hurry."

"You can't be. Look, should I use bile yellow or twilight vomit?"

"I never heard of these colours. Nor has my basket."

"Don't be a spoilsport. I need you. Dear, dear little sister!"

"Don't 'little sister' me. I'm older than you by aeons."

"Only 'cause you were born long ago. It doesn't count. But you are still my little sister and I love you!"

"All right, make it fast. The river screams for me."

"It always does. Now look, I need to change my body- should I have bigger feet?"

"Bigger ones than these?"

"Ah! You noticed. You are so clever! I enlarged them already. But, you see, everybody loves ducks. I thought, if I could..."

"You don't."

"Right. How about a badly crooked spine? They might pity me."

"It works. I do."

"And swollen, dripping eyes?"

Manasā seemed so happy. "The thing is, among monkeys, you don't want to look good. Anyone can look good, especially people in their twenties. They really don't deserve it. But, you see, for sages, like cow-herders, you have to go deep."

"I wish I could. Look, I really have to leave now!"

"Just listen. You'll love this. Real people want you to look like them. It raises sympathy."

"In bile yellow?"

"It's an early morning colour that reminds you of a happy night. So Śiva says. I asked him."

Neta picked up her basket. "Well, we settled that. I'm sure you can do the rest without me."

"I have studied the herders and I think I understand them. They are quite simple, for philosophers."

Like you, thought Neta. Maybe I should drop the basket and run.

"Most people love wrinkles. They collect them. Old people have plenty. I can beat them anytime!"

Deep silence.

"Are you listening?"

Manasā pushed her fingers through her hair.

"Shall I make my hair slimy or fill it up with little animals?"

Neta bit her teeth.

"Or should I get rid of my hair?"

Right, thought Neta, let's do this like a pro. "Have you considered pimples?"

Manasā froze.

"Pimples! Blackheads, redheads, purple bloats and greenish blisters!" her eyes gleamed. "Neta, you're a genius! I almost forgot them!"

She drew her hands across her face and transformed. Neta winced.

"Ready! See this! I'm done!"

Neta shook her head. She should say something. Maybe, one day, Manasā would listen. But not today.

Manasā gleamed. She was so happy. "Hello, herders! Here I come! I look just like your mothers!"

"Noble lords! I'm a customer! I only want a tiny drop of milk!"

The noble lords did not listen. From far away, the stones came flying. None of them hit its target.

"I know you love a bit of fun. But I'm a normal old lady, like millions of others, and the day is hot. Please give me a drink!"

The serpent goddess tried to look cute. She made her eyes grow and turned her tangled hair into three bunches. They looked so good on Neta.

"Begone, witch! You won't curse our cows!"

"I only want a drink." She raised a basket. "Could you fill this thing? I'll give you gold and diamonds and all sort of stuff."

She tried a charming smile and her teeth gleamed. "You want to see something funny? I can drink upside down!"

The herders got their hatchets out.

"Neta! I need you here! Right now!"

The air shimmered and another woman appeared. This one was worse than the first. She was a little smaller than the crone and almost nude. Her age? She wouldn't be above sixteen. Neta was in her usual outfit, which was a tiny bit of red silk and plenty of gold across her breasts and a slip so small you'd need a microscope to find it. It's a practical costume for a girl who spends much of her time in the Dark Waters, surrounded by crocodiles.

Neta smiled, and the diamond ring in her nose gleamed.

"Look at the whore!" a herder shouted, "she's another witch! Kill them!"

"First we kill the crone, then we take the young one and later we kill her too. And we share her jewellery. You hear this? We share!"

Neta snarled at them. It stopped them in their tracks. "Right," she said to Manasā, "Think and think fast. I'm sure you've got plenty of plans. These are your philosophers. Go ahead. Convert them!"

The herders sat in the grass and flies buzzed. The day had been exhausting. First, they had met two witches. That was bad enough. No one had told them that cow herding would involve witches. Then, when they were ready to kill them, the earth broke open and a million snakes emerged. They surged through the grasses, made the herders freeze and the cows stampede. The witches laughed. Damn them, they thought it's funny! There were snakes on the ground, snakes in the trees, snakes round their legs and snakes in their dhotis!

And then, one moment to the other, the witches were gone. So were the snakes. The herders had a lot of trouble getting the cows together. Finally, they settled down and waited for the twilight. Cows recover fast, but people need more time. The herders smoked and argued. They glared and cursed and decided to keep the story to themselves.

Finally, as twilight fell, they began the trek home. One herder remained. He had hidden in the bushes, when the others hurled their missiles, and watched. He couldn't have thrown, even had he wanted to. His aim was off, as he had a twisted frame, a crooked spine and a hunched back. When the meadow was almost empty, except for his cows, he knelt. He plucked long grasses and wove a tiny basket. He placed the item in the middle of a heap of cow dung. That; in his opinion, was a perfect altar. With great reverence, he poured milk into the contraption. It doesn't get much holier.

"Hear me, great ladies. I don't know if you are goddesses or witches. I'm stupid and I can't tell the difference." He raised his gaze to the twilight sky. The evening star shone in a greenish haze; in a few minutes, it would be dark. "I believe that my colleagues misbehaved. Maybe they sinned. I apologise for them. Listen, ladies, we are just herders. We don't understand anything. Forgive our errors and our ignorance."

The hunchback bowed. When he raised his face, the witches stood before him.

"I like him. He's sort of cute. But twisted. I like twisted." This was the taller one.

"Cute? That's the big eyes. And actually, he doesn't like twisted." That was the wicked young one. The herder tried to ignore her bulges.

"Do you think he's a worshipper? I could do with another one."

"Give him a try."

"How should I?"

"Straighten him out!" The little witch laughed while the tall one approached. She looked much younger now. The herder bowed. She grabbed his jaw and leaned on his back. There was a twist, a stabbing pain, a lot of clicks, a terrible ouch, and she was off again.

The herder raised his head. The witches had disappeared. His spine felt strange. When he got up, he realised his hump was gone.

"Mahādevī!"

He gathered his stuff and got his cows together. It was getting dark and he would follow the others, but not too fast, cause there would be questions.

Sometimes it's lucky to be slow, or lazy, or somewhere else. Fast people are disadvantaged. They get into trouble even faster. The herders were eager to go home and get drunk. The former hunchback took his time. He was busy making up a story that would convince the others. It should involve respectable gods. And it should be reasonable. Only that it wouldn't. Try as he might, that story didn't want to happen. It gave him a wonderful chance to watch what happened next.

The herders, in their hurry, didn't see it coming. Right beneath the hooves of their cows, the earth fell in. Cattle and herders dropped into a chasm that shouldn't have been there.

Up on the ridge, outlined against the sky, stood the two witches. By now, the elder one had lost her pimples. Her figure looked much better. Mind you, she wore serpents, and that didn't really help.

Down there, in the earth hole, reactions differed. The cows, once they got up, regurgitated. They can keep this up much longer than most people would like to know. Unlike them, Neta is sure you will. "Brilliant people," she says, "are just like small children: they are interested in everything." So here are the facts: a cow regurgitates an average 500 times a day, for eight hours, which amounts to 25,000 chewing motions. That's what you need, plus horizontally moving jaws, to break down plant matter until its ready for microbe consumption. I'm sure you are amazed and will mention this when you meet business acquaintances, lovers, and celebrities. "Facts," Neta says, "make everybody happy."

The herders were in a frenzy. Some went down on their knees and cried for mercy, while others screamed abuse.

Manasā opened her evil eye and glared. "Stop being rude! I could be your sister!" Down in the pit, herders dropped and died, while others doubled the intensity of their prayers "That'll teach you. Next time, you behave."

The survivors howled all the louder.

"Let's reconsider." Neta calmed her sister. "If you want a next time, resurrect them."

"Why should I?"

"People like that sort of thing."

"But they might have a better rebirth."

"Trust me. They liked being what they were."

"If you say so." The serpent goddess shook her head. "I wonder why." She opened her wisdom eye and revived their corpses. "Get up, if you really have to."

She glanced at Neta. "I got everything right. They live, I'm sure they'll love me, and Śiva will be amazed. I've got a religion and a lot of happy followers."

"They ain't happy. They are scared to death!"

"Why? I mean, listen. They are on the ground, and they say nice things about me."

"It's no fun for them. It's survival."

"That's great! I'm survival!"

"And you are death. If you want to be popular, get them out of the hole and make them happy."

Manasā frowned. Being popular was complicated. She clapped her hands. Herders and cows returned to the plain.

"All right, stop nagging. Everyone dead is back to life. Be twice as grateful."

"They ain't. The story isn't complete."

"We like bananas" said Neta. The herder ran away into the dark.

Neta arranged her hair. The fire was nicely warm and she enjoyed the sparks.

Another guy approached, dropped to his knees and offered fruit. Manasā took one.

"Say 'thank you'", Neta hissed.

Manasā did. She had no idea why.

By now, the goddess looked much happier than before. She had shed her clothes, her filth, the twisted teeth and paddle-shaped feet.

The men did their best to make the deities feel at home. One produced a reed flute and haunting tones swirled through the dark-night firmament. He was a coarse, ugly guy, but his music made hearts melt and tears flow over stubbly cheeks.

A moment later, the goddesses were treated to bananas. The man carried as many as he could.

"You are spoiling us". Neta was all charm.

The herder laughed, bowed, and ran away, to the other side of the fire.

"Do they?"Manasā shook her head. "How could they? I'm unspoiltness in person."

"It's a metaphor. It means a thing it isn't, but could be. Most of the time, a metaphor is literally true, though never really real."

"So it's a lie?"

"Yes, but a good one. It functions. No one gets really spoiled, though we all should. We are goddesses, and when they make offerings they delight themselves."

"I don't understand. Surely they expect something in return."

"Just the usual." Neta chewed, "Trifles. The bare essentials. Life, money, power, health, love, offspring, in short, everything."

"Then," declared Manasā, "they should provide more than food."

She stood up. The herders stared in silence.

"I've been told to thank you. Milk and bananas are splendid. And the music was delightful. But here is something far more important. I am sure you wondered how I should be worshipped."

The herders had not. Worship was conducted by Brahmins, and they were born to it and needed special training. As a herder, you wouldn't be allowed into the temple.

"My worship is simple.

On the tenth lunar day of the month Jyaiṣṭha (May/June) my feast shall be celebrated with many different offerings. Gifts shall be excessive: many sweets, and ten sorts of good fruit. Small bananas, karkatī, coconuts, phuti-cucumbers, betel nuts, dates, jackfruit, mangoes, black jām berries, and the fruit of palm trees. Plus betel nuts and bēl leaves, a wealth of fresh blossoms, incense, bright lights and sandalwood paste. A lot of musical instruments shall be played with great pleasure. The offerings shall be blessed with holy water; then a golden pot is set up, full of holy water, and across its mouth a twig of spiky sij shall rest. Within that pot, I will receive your worship.

Listen and remember: I will appear in this vessel; I will fulfil the wishes of my worshippers and bless them with wealth, children and fame.

That should suffice. Please continue."

The goddess bowed. The herders bowed back. Then they began to laugh.

"Jai ho!" It was simple. It required no wealth, no birthright, nor an education. It was so wonderfully easy that even they could do it.

Neta and Manasā sat near the fire and ate one banana after the other. In between, they gulped down bowls of milk. Around them swirled beetles, moths, glow worms and bats. It could be wonderful on earth. Everything was so direct, so gritty, so intensely genuine.

The herders did their best. They sang and fluted, they danced and told stories that made Neta laugh and Manasā ask for explanations. Finally, they got out their dice. They tossed their little toys across the ground, they cheered and screamed and cursed. Manasā was awed.

"Why do they do it? They don't own much, they are crazy! Just watch them risk and lose everything."

"They are addicts," said Neta, "and dreamers. Each is the hero of his own tale."

She grinned. "Watch this!"

Neta whispered to the man who shook the dice. "If you want to win, you have to invoke Manasā's pot."

The herder frowned. It was another new idea. He wasn't sure he could handle any more.

"Go ahead, do it!"

The herder rattled the dice. "I invoke Manasā's pot!"

The dice fell and he laughed while he raked his winnings in.

"Did you get that?" Neta faced the herders. "He won. So could you. I'm sure you know that life is a game."

The herders didn't. Their life wasn't even playful.

"Go ahead. Do as you're told!"

"I invoke Manasā's pot!" The player tossed and won. The next one did the same.

"They stop! Neta! You've ruined their fun!"

"I started a different game. It's on another level. Look at them. Do they seem unhappy?"

The herders were beside themselves with joy. They called and won and won and won. Sure, it wasn't worth the effort any more. But tomorrow, in the village, they would find some idiots and dice them to ruin.

"That's how you do religion." Neta leaned back. "Being alive isn't enough. They got life for free and they take it for granted. People want to win."

17. Hāssan and Hussein

Gorā Mina stared at the marble. He had never really looked at it before. It was finely textured, with amazing lines and colourations that seemed to blur and melt and drift. His head was bent, his neck ached and he had trouble breathing. Before him rose stairs, and quite a lot of them. On top of them was the throne that Gorā wouldn't want to face. He was the head of the royal watch, and he had awful news.

"Lord, there is no milk. Neither butter, yoghurt of ghī."

He waited. One day, he thought, I'll have a home with a marble floor. But until then, I'll be as humble as I can.

"You idiot! I should take your head!"

"Yes, lord."

"Why didn't you get them elsewhere?"

"Lord, there is none to be head. In the city, in the suburbs, even in the country."

"Explain!"

"The herders didn't deliver any. They are lazy and blasphemous. They have been celebrating for three days!"

"Why? It's not the time for Hindu festivals! Are they crazy?"

"My lord, I spied on them. I went to their settlements, I peeked into their huts. They've got plenty of milk. They don't deliver it."

The king groaned. Gorā Mina explained. "They are infidels. They have a new goddess. In each hut, I saw a pot full of water. Crude pottery, painted red or yellow. And a spiky twig on top of each. Before them, lights, incense, fruit, meat and anything."

"That's new," said the king, "why do they keep inventing deities?"

"They are filth," said a deep voice. No, Gorā did not move his head. The marble at his feet was comforting. The new speaker was not. Had he looked, he would have seen a fat man with a beard that looked like an exploded octopus. He sat next to the king, on a much smaller throne, and he was angry.

"Why seek an explanation? The Hindus worship anything. Their heads are full of sins and they never mean what they say. I do: There is no god except Allah and Muhammad is his prophet. Gorā, you should know this. Didn't you embrace the true faith when you were raised to your position?"

"I did, my lord."

The head of the royal watch had been a Muslim for three years. He had seen the old king die and his eldest son, Hāssan, take the throne. Hāssan was, by and large, a friendly character. He was pot-bellied and spent too much time in the harem. It made him jittery. And he showed the astonishing kindness of leaving his brother Hussein alive. Gorā Mina didn't know how to explain. As a born Hindu, he accepted reality. There were many faiths, and a man in his position didn't mess with any. King Hāssan, long may he live, was a philanthropist and an enlightened ruler, who only ordered executions on special occasions and, of course, on Saturdays. His younger brother Hussein was angry with him. The king, as everyone could see, was one huge softie. And he was far too nice to everyone.

King Hāssan tried to sound interested. "Who is their new idol?"

"My lord, she is a new goddess. They call her the daughter of Śiva. She rules all snakes."

Hussein shook his head. Four hundred million idols and devils are worshipped in Hindustan, one worse than the next, and there's a new one every day! She's a goddess of vermin and her father is a useless lout. "The cult must be destroyed!"

King Hāssan cleared his throat. "My brother, you mean well. But I'm the king and I give orders here. Let me remind you. We are Moguls. Emperor Akbar the Great established his empire. He taught that Hindus and Muslims should live in peace. Of course we have the One True Faith. Akbar gave peace to the Hindus; he resolved their court cases, promoted their music and tolerated their rituals. He even stopped their pilgrimage taxes. We reintroduced them, as they should pay for their evil, but in general, unless it means a loss of income, we should follow his example."

"Akbar was a spineless loser! He lived like a coward, he wore his hair like a Hindu, and he died as a blasphemer. He failed to enforce the True Faith!"

"Our ancestor Akbar conquered the greatest empire under the sun, and he governed in peace and justice."

"He bribed the Brahmins and he studied their scripture! He praised the *Upaniṣads*! I'm sure he burns in hell!"

"Brother, we are not Akbar. Our realm is small and our funds are limited. Look at our army. It barely suffices for parades. We are glad to live in peace. Let the heathens worship as they want."

Hussein leapt from his throne, and roared. "This is no cult. They are unbelievers, so how can they have a faith? They fail to deliver our milk. This is a revolt, and it has to be crushed."

Hāssan looked at his dear, impulsive brother. His face is red, he thought, and one day he'll overstep all limits. Maybe he'll even try to murder me. It would be so traditional. But let it be another day. He raised the corners of his mouth. It almost looked friendly.

"We are forced to act. Gorā, take the guard and crush this cult. I expect milk tomorrow. You may go now."

By daybreak, Gorā and his troops returned. The men were sweaty, heavily laden and in a cheerful mood. The night had been profitable. For a start, the guards had marched to the settlement where the new faith was celebrated. When they saw the earthen throne which the herders had erected for their new goddess, they had a laughing fit. Instead of a statue, they had placed a pot full of water on it. A spiky twig lay across its mouth. Is that all, they thought? No glamour, no glitter, no Brahmins to chant the hymns?

Gorā smashed the vessel. He trampled the throne into the ground, and the guards cheered. Then, his men swarmed into the huts, and they took everything. They broke the sacred pots and threw the sij twigs into the fire. They beat up the men and made the women flee. Cow herders, of course, are low-class trash. They didn't own much. It was hardly worth the effort to break some bones. Their neighbours were different. A few poor Brahmins had joined the cult. The guards laughed. This was a night of entertainment! But Gorā calmed them. "King Hāssan," he said, "will not allow us to kill his subjects. Even a poor Brahmin is a taxpayer. Make them suffer! Take what they have, and beat them up, but leave them alive." The guards did. They smashed open the heavy wooden chests that held the valuables. Most of them were scripture. Well, books are rubbish, but they are better than nothing. Someone would buy them, and sell them for more. But Gorā had higher goals. Ever since he converted to the True Faith, he had hated the Brahmins. These were poor and simple, and they could not fight back. He forced them to eat filth, to destroy their spiritual purity, and sent them running. They would need many rituals and offerings to regain their former sanctity. The guards roared with laughter.

Finally, they burned the houses to the ground.

When Gorā faced the king, he dared to raise his eyes. He had done his duty, and he had done it well. King Hāssan showed his gratitude, and allowed the men to keep their booty. He gave Gorā Mina a few gleaming trinkets and sent him home. Gorā bowed, but not as deeply as before, and walked out of the palace in the early morning light, feeling like a conqueror. Today, he thought, I'm just the captain of the guard. Tomorrow I will lead the army. It's a small army, but it will do for a start. The king needs me. One day I might be his advisor. I could eliminate his brother, well, sooner or later, someone has to, and I would wield real power. Gorā twisted his moustache and his teeth shone.

Close to his house, a snake was waiting. Before the scorching noontime heat, Gorā was dead.

The herders faced a bleary dawn. The cold wind was full of smoke. Their wives were busy, cutting long grasses. A few lengths of bamboo would keep the woven walls in place. The roof was straw, as it had ever been. Houses, they knew, are easily rebuilt. And there were always cows to look after. Their goddess, they knew, would help them. Now they would fight for their faith. The persecution had only increased their fervour. Meanwhile, the poor Brahmins packed what was left of their possessions, and walked away. As Bijay Gupta tells us, they left the kingdom of King Hāssan and found new homes in distant lands, where they established the creed of the serpent goddess.

When King Hāssan woke from his noontime sleep, he heard the news, and his face went cold and hard like a stone cliff when the winter monsoon comes howling. There was no doubt: Gorā Mina, head of the guard, was dead. He had been trustworthy, he had done his duty, and the serpent was his fate. It did not help that Cāmpā Bibi, the queen, was on her knees and wept.

"You are a convert," said her husband, "you were a Hindu before the One True Faith saved your soul. Stop whining! The snake bitch is a demon. She killed a good man. I will erase her cult."

"My Lord!" his wife was in tears, "how can you fight snakes?"

"In Allah's name, I will fight anyone!"

Leaning back on his throne, he glanced at his younger brother. Sure, Hussein wasn't tired. He had that special, dreamy look indicating he was inventing new tortures. There would be pain and horror. King Hāssan would have loved to retire. A nice, padded divan, a few girls, one could sit on his face, another explore his groin, yes, as a king one had the right, no, the duty to cultivate leisure. That's because leisure makes you smarter. His brother wouldn't allow him.

He hardly noticed when the ground began to wobble. The vibrations began softly, and took their time to build up pressure. Then the tremor increased, and finally it got loud. A table moved across the audience hall, the guards gasped, the servants screamed. Prince Hussein just got angrier. King Hāssan clutched the armrests of his throne. The thing was heavy, but it began to shift. When the chandeliers began to swing and a candle stand fell over, he knew that something was wrong.

Hāssan pulled up his robes and prepared to run for it. His brother eyed the ceiling with suspicion. It was old, under repair, and had never been quite trustworthy. Their father had tried to cut costs. Minor kings have to. The ground broke open with a dry and painful crash. The marble split and tore apart, as you would rip a piece of paper, and with it, reality went sideways. Hāssan stared and almost forgot to breathe. From underneath, serpents erupted, gleaming, shining, their mouths wide open, their tongues tasting the air. Their teeth were clearly visible. The king was a survivor. He knew he couldn't run. Instead, he climbed up the backrest of his throne, as far as he could. His brother was just as fast. He took a jump and managed to reach his brother's throne. Both of them yelled for help. The reptiles poured across the audience chamber like a wave. The guards ran, but a few were too slow. Their twitching bodies fell, and the serpents slithered over them. They came as if the monsoon had swept them out of their holes; they burst from cellars and crevices, they clogged canals and drainage pipes, they broke down doors and sent the king's men running for their lives.

Hāssan and Hussein clung to the backrest of the throne and stared into the writhing madness at their feet. Hāssan reacted first. He turned and leapt to an ornamented pillar. A few seconds later, he had reached the balustrade of the first storey. His brother came after him. The regents looked down; the reptiles lifted their heads and sniffed the air. Their tongues flickered and they identified their prey. Within instants they began to climb the pillars and slithered up the stairs. The brothers squeaked with fear. They ran along the passageway and discovered a stairway to the roof. On a normal day, they could have admired the view. They would have felt proud of their city, and its inhabitants and the plantations and fields that surrounded it. They would have smoked their pipes and planned a little war. Today, snakes came after them. People, as Manasā likes to remark, are apes. They are better at climbing than elephants. But serpents beat them any day.

The brothers ran across the roof. No way down and no way up.

When things are really bad, alternative realities appear.

Our brothers did the impossible: they climbed into the sky.

Let me remind you: in East India, huge golden spiders craft webs that connect the underworlds, the earth and heavens. They are real, at least in fairy tales; they function anytime, and, like all better technology, they are silent, energy efficient, strong, flexible and stunningly beautiful. Proteins are simply amazing. And they can be recycled: before a spider makes a new web, it eats the old one up.

The brothers didn't appreciate any of these miracles. They just made use of them, as fast as they could, and cursed as they clambered along.

First, along this strand, and up this cloud, next, a big leap, then up another hazy vapour. It takes a lot of effort. However, in some mind-states, clouds are just as solid as magick spider webs. The snakes came after them.

High up in the sky, resting halfway up a cumulus, the brothers went down on their knees. They wheezed and fought for breath as they implored Mohammed to help.

The Prophet remained silent.

The brothers ran on, they climbed, they jumped, up and ever upwards, through towering clouds, along the gleaming silken strands, until they were far above the earth, where the air is thin and frosty cirrus makes eyes water.

"Help us, Allah!" the brothers squealed.

It might have helped to rest a while. It would have been useful to remember what the divine is all about. Our brothers had no time for it.

They rushed on, their lungs ached, and their steps faltered. Drenched in sweat, they reached a different plane. Hussein grit his teeth and King Hāssan did the unforgivable, and implored the Hindu gods to help them.

Śiva heard their call; he smiled, and closed all doors and windows. Mount Kailāsa disappeared in a haze. Viṣṇu reclined on his serpent couch and raised an eyebrow. "Go, Hanumān," he told the Monkey God, "and tell them that I'm busy." He wrapped an arm around Lakṣmī, who blushed, as he opened her bra.

Hanumān glared at them. "You just want to get rid of me," he observed. "That's fine. Have a messy afternoon. Be hot and sweaty, blow your heads off, do the hormone roundabout, while I go to earth and do some research."

Brahmā refused to listen. He hid underneath the cosmic lotus blossom that emerges from Viṣṇus navel, and did crossword puzzles. Eventually, he knew, these people would stop screaming. They always did.

"We implore you, goddesses;" Hāssan was in a frenzy; he looked down and realised that some serpents fly. "Damn you," shouted his brother Hussein, "you are a bunch of useless bitches, and when we need you you won't come."

"That's right" said Pārvatī, "you understand us perfectly well." And she disappeared behind a fog of ice crystals. Gaṅgā gurgled in her rage, and even Durgā, untouchable warrior queen, got angry. Before the brothers could complain, her lion faced them. The beast was bigger than a whale, bared yellow fangs the size of palm trees, and roared. The brothers ran.

Within instants, they were somewhere else. Within a multiverse that curves on itself and is far bigger inside than outside (don't be deluded by the cheerful blue colour, it flakes off) somewhere else is practically the same as here, and extends all over the place. Now they stumbled across an uninhabited desert where thorny plants grew a hundred meters high and spikes, the size of lances, tore at their clothes and skin. They hardly noticed that heaven turned magenta and the horizon gleamed in painful yellow-green merging to black. Darkness came, and with it came relief.

The brothers saw a well. It seemed the only option. Behind them, they heard the lion running. They clambered, leapt and dropped. Far below the surface, they hit the water. It wasn't deep. The brothers looked around. The stonework was slimy, but happily the water just went to the breasts. There were cracks in the walls, covered by mosses, and with a bit of luck, they could climb out again.

For the time being, they were safe. Far above them, they could see a tiny bit of sky. It went dark as the twilight advanced.

They heard the lion roar.

And they saw spiders, high above, who built their nets across the well.

"They'll hide us," said Hāssan, "no one will guess we are down here."

"We will wait," his brother whispered. "In a few hours, the lion will be far away."

The brothers looked at each other. Their clothes were torn, their limbs bloody, but they were alive.

Far above, a little lizard climbed the stones. Lizards are harbingers of evil, when they make a clicking sound, and warn the world of bad Karman. This one didn't. It kept silent while it scrambled across the mortar and disappeared. The lizard sighed: it faced an awful journey. The crest of Sij Mountain is a challenge for a little reptile.

The night went on, and the brothers looked up and watched the stars rotate. The water turned cold. Each of them could have wept, but as they were men, and tough, they didn't.

Eventually, the stars disappeared. A dark form blocked their view and three red eyes glared down on them.

"Hello my heroes," said a female voice, "I'm glad you waited. Say 'thank you' to the spiders. They didn't hide but jail you!"

Deep in the night, faint steps echoed through the palace. The rooms were empty: all servants, guards, and concubines had run away. Here and there, corpses lay. They had stopped moving long ago. By nightfall, the serpents disappeared into the deep.

An elderly woman appeared. Before the throne, she found the corpses. Her sons: Hāssan and Hussein.

She fell down on her knees, she caressed their faces and she wept.

It was hard to recognise them. They were swollen beyond recognition and their trousers stank of piss and excrement. They had died without honour, alone, an evil death.

The crone wept and sobbed. Her life had lost its meaning.

When she looked up, she faced a woman. Her hair was full of writhing snakes and her sari shone like the blood moon.

The queen mother hit her head against the ground and yowled. She clawed her fingers into her hair and tore, while her whine turned into a scream.

Manasā stared at her in amazement.

"Goddess, take my life! How can I live now that my sons are dead? I should have died before them!"

"O no," said Manasā, "you won't get away so easily."

"They were my little boys. The never did an evil deed. Their death destroys the dynasty."

"They were spoiled and greedy and stupid." Manasā snarled at the woman. "You taught them to be tyrants!"

"I did my best!"

"It wasn't good enough."

"Goddess, be merciful! Kill me, or give them life!"

"Why should I? The two are worthless!"

"We will pray to you, and worship you every day!"

"Will you?" Manasā scrutinized the crone. "Are you allowed to? I thought you only believe in Allah?"

The queen mother did not dare to raise her eyes.

"Of course we do. There is only one god, who is all and everything."

"Sure," said Manasā, "I can live with that. That god is me."

Hāssan and Hussein bowed. They snivelled and whined and bowed again. Neta says that they looked cute. Finally, Manasā laughed.

"My little headbangers," she chirped, "life is a gift for high performance. It has to be cherished, and used for something really good. You've got a second try. I'll bless you, provided you perform

"Goddess, tell us..." King Hāssan sounded eager. His brother echoed him.

"I won't. Think for yourself."

"But how can we..."

"You will. And I will grant a very special bonus."

She clapped her hands and all corpses came to life again.

"Here are your guards, your women and your stupid little bureaucrats. They were dead, but maybe they learned something. Neta says that death is educational. And I'm sure you'll learn a lot."

"But we lack scripture!"

"Write your own."

She clapped her hands and disappeared.

The kings remained prostrate, their heads on the ground, and silent, for several minutes.

The whole court, alive or freshly revived, got the message.

Hāssan and Hussein had a new temple built, with extra large gates, shiny bells and a high domed roof, inlaid with semi-precious stones. The walls were ornamented with snakes and spiders. It stood right across the main square and faced the royal mosque. They set up a huge pot, which was thoroughly gilded, and employed a whole cast of Brahmins to perform the sacrifices. The Brahmins were astonished, but as the king paid well, they improvised a couple of high-class rituals for the new goddess. Each day six Brahmins chanted mantras and scattered holy water over the congregation. Hāssan and Hussein were keen to learn. They made lavish gifts, and the Brahmins educated them, until they saw the light. Before long King Hāssan and his brother could do the offerings themselves, according to the Śastra, in perfect Saṁskṛta, and they even understood what they were saying. They performed the celebrations on every Tuesday and Saturday, and on every fifth of the dark and the bright fortnight, and of course during all three monsoon months; they studied the Vedas and Upaniṣads, gave alms to the poor, and punished exploiters and evildoers. Under their rule, there were country fairs and boat races in Manasā's name, and they sent holy men to distant provinces to preach the truth and extol the glory of the serpent goddess.

And when they bowed before her pot and tears of joy ran down their cheeks, Manasā felt as happy as she had never been before. Bipradās, the famous poet, tells us that Hāssan and Hussein worshipped Manasā with true fervour, and they were blessed with children, wealth, power and fame.

Part Three:

Cāndo

18. Power

Sij Mountain lay gleaming and frosty in the early morning light and a thick coat of snow veiled crags and crevices under its pure, crystalline beauty. The air was still, but bitterly cold; it numbed her face and paralysed her fingers. Manasā rubbed her hands. She stood at a window and gazed into the frosty wilderness. So cold, so clean, so lifeless! She had woken long before sunrise, and had taken care to dress and make-up properly. It didn't take long; her costume consisted of a few selected serpents. It was early, far too early, and she didn't know what to do. She walked through halls and corridors, tried to relax in the gardens, stretched out on an ornamental swing, and hurried back, to stalk through her palace, uneasy, nervous and restless, like a homeless ghost. She stared out of each window, and when that didn't help, she climbed a tower to have a better view. It was much colder up here. She glared into all directions, and still no motion anywhere. How time slows down when you are in a hurry!

Around midday, her father, Śiva appeared. His bull, Nandi (the *Joyous One*) plunged through the snow and Manasā could have screamed with impatience.

Śiva reclined on his bull and seemed absent-minded. Bull and rider took their time.

The serpent goddess watched them. She hid in the shadow and did her best to remain invisible. No matter how long this would take, she would appear calm and in control of everything.

Her fingers twitched. But apart from this, she was relieved that her father had arrived. Manasā knew Śiva. It was a miracle he remembered her invitation. Under normal circumstances, he might have been in deep trance, and forgotten everything, or he might have overdosed on whatever, and spent an exciting day with Hanumān, getting his stomach pumped out.

And Śiva knew his daughter. He had done his best to remain temperate and responsible and indeed he was so sober that heaven bulged and the sun jittered.

When the Lord of Dissolution slid from his bull and led the great, steaming animal into the courtyard, Manasā couldn't wait any longer. She ran into his arms and laughed, and Śiva was amazed to see how healthy she looked. Taking him by the hand, she dragged him up the stairs and to a window.

"Look at this!" she exclaimed, and leaned over the balustrade. She pointed at something in the distance. "Over there, no, to the right, almost at the horizon, see this, dwells the great King Hāssan! He is my strongest worshipper! His whole kingdom believes in me. Day in and day out, they sacrifice and pray, and it gets twice as strong on festival days!"

She jumped up and down and clapped her hands.

Śiva squinted. "Where is this place?"

"Back there, far away; can you see the little blot? That's his palace."

"It's a little blot."

"Of course it ain't! I've been there. It's a real palace and you would be astonished. Daddy! Don't make me angry. I can tell the difference between a hut and a palace. It's made of stone. It has pillars. The floor is marble and there are fifteen, maybe twenty rooms! And towers, turrets, balustrades, balconies, cellars and storage rooms. I counted four bedrooms, a treasure chamber, a kitchen, two bathrooms and four toilets! And a stable with six horses, one mule and two elephants, but they don't like to go out, 'cause they are old."

Śiva squinted. It was hard to discern anything. Far away, the hot air quivered. He saw dust and a greyish something that might be a settlement.

The blot was and remained a blot, embedded in the ochre plains, and clearly very poor.

He tried a happy smile. It signalled a positive attitude and occasionally saved his life, when Durgā had her days.

"Great, I hear you. And sure, it's a palace. You've achieved something wonderful."

"Don't drown me in honey. I'm not Durgā. I think, I think a lot, and I doubt all sorts of stuff, so watch it."

"Right." Śiva appeared carefree, "indeed you do. And you are wonderful. But let's get to the point. Is it good enough?"

He waited. Some ideas have to sink in. And thinkers, he knew, are much slower than those who simply react. "Daughter, you won a victory. I can see how happy you are. But I am sure you want to face reality."

"What do you know about reality?"

"More than enough. I tell you it's a blot. A godforsaken settlement in the middle of nowhere. Kings of that sort; well, there are hundreds of them, on every inch of fertile ground. They come, they go, and nobody cares. They are governed by an emperor, who squeezes them until they squeak. Each little king is proud and wonderful, and makes just enough to pay a hundred guards and warriors, a dozen bureaucrats, plus a few servants, slaves and concubines. His girls are barely above average; they drain his loins and empty his purse. And he has administrators. They know what they are doing. Usually, they are twice as rich as the king."

"King Hāssan is wealthy! I saw it. He built a temple for me."

"And now he prays to you for profit, 'cause he wants to get out of debt. I am sure your king wears silk. And goldish stuff, and ornaments, and a rusty sword with fake jewels on the sheath. He has to. But look at his palace. I bet that half the buildings haven't been repaired for centuries. There will be worm-eaten doors, and an empty treasury. You say two ageing elephants? Why hasn't he got younger ones, and more?"

"Maybe he likes the old ones. He is very sentimental."

"They all are. They dream of the golden age that never was. And look how they behave. Each year in autumn, when Durgā Pūjā is over, they invade the kingdom of a neighbour and chop down his sacred tree. They steal some cattle, burn a few villages and are off again."

Śiva stopped, his face was serious. "Daughter, this is history. You have no idea how tedious it is."

Manasā grabbed his arm. "Daddy! You've never been there. I was. I fought and won. The royal family makes offerings. The guards are converted, and I have hundreds of worshippers who herd cows!"

"Will they be enough? Come on, tell me." Her father looked sad. "People come and go. Souls and bodies, they are like foam on the waves, like pollen in the wind." He wiped his brow. This would be painful. "People live, die and their life essence is reborn. They differ from what they were, so hardly any of them remembers. Life after life, as soon as they grow up, they feel special. Each pretends to be the centre of the multiverse. How can you trust them? A small cult is easily forgotten. Look at your worshippers and tell me: do they like, or love you? Are they afraid, or do they wish to make a profit? They pray to many gods and they expect results. If you don't deliver, they will curse you. And let me tell you, most of their desires are stupid anyway."

Manasā stood like a pillar. "How could this be?"

"It's always been like that. And maybe it's good for us. We may be gods, but we have to make an effort." He raised an eyebrow. "Please, daughter, keep yourself controlled. Don't tell me that you want to kill them all."

Manasā exhaled and tried to keep her temper. Stay calm, she thought, life isn't easy, and here is my dad and I'm not going to make a scene 'cause that's what Durgā does every other day.

"You mean, this king won't get me far?"

"He'll do his best. Just like you and me. But see, it's a blot. You can't expect much."

Obviously, his daughter was struggling. Her toxic glands were swollen and her evil eye kept twitching. But she made an effort, and he was proud of her.

Manasā hissed "I am hungry. I could devour anything. Tell me, where do I get more worshippers?"

"Do you want them terrified or affectionate?"

"I am a great goddess; I want them to love me."

"That's tough. Terrified would be easier. But neither of them is enough. You need patience, and cunning, and compassion, and most of all, political acumen.

"A skin disease?"

"It's a special game. People invented it, more than a million years ago, when they began to play with fire, and it's complicated."

"What's complicated about fire?"

"Fire is energy, and light, and warmth, and digestible meat. It means food, and bigger brains, and families and clans and property." Śiva shrugged. "Without money and power, your cult is doomed."

"You mean I take bribes and grant favours?"

"I mean, you appeal to everyone who cares. You know, there are wonderful people out there. Ascetics, lunatics, artists, writers, dancers, you name it, who love you with a whole heart. Some will devote their lives to you. They are the ones who count. They are your awareness: through them, you delight in the world. Only, they are very few. And the more they love you, the more they will be ridiculed." Śiva stared into emptiness. A tear ran down his cheek. He shook his head. "Brahmā has a lot to account for. The world is great and full of stupid people. Most of them are scared and greedy. If you want your cult to thrive, you have to convert the mightiest person of them all."

"Another king? Or an emperor?"

Manasā leaned on the window sill. She seemed quite relaxed. Śiva wasn't fooled, he could see she had driven her fingernails into the stone. I am tranquil, she thought, and I can handle anything. My father might think I'll go mad any moment, but I can think what he would think, and so I won't.

"Let me show you." Śiva opened his eye of Absolute Reality, the one that makes his life so exasperating, and touched his daughter's hand to share the vision. A network of colourful lines crisscrossed the country. "The red stuff is power. Some is wealth, some dominance, and a lot is hope and fear. Can you see where the lines converge?"

Manasā almost fainted. Before her eyes unfolded East India in all its beauty and wealth. It was so intricate, so full of detail. The land, she saw was enormously rich. It grew rice and produced fruit, sugar cane, indigo, jute, hemp, cotton and tea, the earth was full of minerals and crystals, and there was plenty of food for the middle classes and wealth for the unscrupulous. And iron! How could anyone forget it? It shaped the history of the subcontinent! The rivers and the seashore were rimmed with gleaming settlements, and there were traders from all over the world, who came to make a profit and would return to their homes as rich as princes. And there were poor people lining the roadsides, losers who slept on pavements, beggars who starved without a funeral. It could have made her weep. Across it all, like a scarlet spider web, ran money, power and influence. A few people grew rich and many others worked themselves to death or starved. It wasn't just. It was far from anything that Dharma represented. She could see the convergence of the net. It throbbed and pulsed like an angry, bloated ulcer.

"There's a trader who makes all lines of power meet. It looks like blood, but its commerce."

"A trader?" Manasā glared. "Since when do traders matter?"

"Nowadays, traders control everything. They make the peasants starve and squeeze the customers to the limit. They are the middlemen, and they control all prices."

"Daddy, you talk nonsense. I've read plenty of scripture. Traders belong to the Vaiśya class. It means they have to follow orders."

"They don't. Not anymore."

"The *Vedas* say they are almost at the bottom of society! The farmer produces rice, the herder milk, the fisher catches fish. Warriors protect and Brahmins guarantee the blessing of the gods. Builders build and craftsmen carve and paint. Some dance and sing and entertain. Some burn the dead, some sweep the streets. They do something for society. Traders don't produce anything. They buy cheap and sell expensive."

"They make money. And they control everyone."

"Brahmins are holy! Warriors rule!"

"These days, both are indebted. The Muslims rule the land. And they rely on trade and credit."

"How can we allow this?"

"We have to. We are gods, we set an example. We don't force; we inspire."

"How can merchants be so strong?"

"They travel and they distribute. You want something? They get it. And they sell dreams. Most people don't want what they really need. They yearn for glamour and illusions. They can go on little food, but when their dreams fade, they wither and die."

Śiva wiped his face. His eyeliner was running. "I apologise. Life has turned into a nightmare. Maybe it shouldn't be this way. Small traders have a place in the world. They are valuable. They move goods and ideas to places where they are needed. They take great risks when they travel, and should be respected. Big merchants are different. The richer they are, the worse they get. Their hearts are hungry, hungry, hungry. They find no peace by day or night."

"Stop it!" Manasā bared her teeth, "This is nonsense. Merchants don't count."

"They count. They count all the time."

"I won't believe it. Who is this trader? Tell me!"

"His name is Cāndo. Like his father and his grandfather, he loves to take and hates to give. He goes for rare products, for things that bedazzle, and cause addiction. He comes from the class of spice merchants. Spices are huge business, and there's enormous profit in them. That's because people think with their stomachs. But he also does works of art, rare items, luxury articles, jewels, embroidered silks, perfumes, incenses, medicines, aphrodisiacs, chemicals and, of course, plenty of opium. He is the true regent of East India."

Śiva raised his hand and pointed. "It's a rich country. The rivers fertilise the soil. The people could be happy and content. A few are. Most of them are close to starvation. Everything really expensive goes through Cāndo's hands."

"Why don't the kings take his wealth away?"

"Cāndo knows everything. His spies are in every province, on every island, in every city, on every road. Before a king could move against him, Cāndo knows. He smiles and stops to finance him. Then he supports another regent. One against each other, the game is simple. The kings learned fast. They are all in debt. Cāndo gives credit or denies it; he decides who wins and fails."

"And how can I gain his favour?"

"That's the problem. Cāndo claims to be devout. He makes offerings to the 330 million gods of Hind, and he supports Islam. He feeds ascetics, and makes lavish gifts to priests and Brahmins. And he likes to appear humble and devout. His friends call him 'the sāddhu'."

"You make this up. A sāddhu is an ascetic; he owns nothing but a filthy robe, a begging bowl and a water pipe. He tends a fire and begs for alms."

"Right. A true sāddhu, male or female, is a renouncer. Most of them are crazy and some are sacred. A few are my friends. Cāndo wants to appear spiritual. It's good for business. Among his friends, he boasts he is a beggar, and complains about his poverty. His servants have to call him 'king'."

Manasā frowned. "Daddy, this is insane. Why do you allow it?"

"Rich merchants appear naturally. They eat up the small traders. He isn't worse than others of his kind. And, in bygone days, he was much better. You met him, long ago."

Many, many lifetimes ago, Śiva had created Cāndo. Of course he wasn't called 'Cāndo' in those days. Then, he was a wise and noble seer, and as his ascetic exercises could make earth tremble and the sky turn crimson, the gods allowed him to attend when the Milk Ocean was churned and the man felt honoured. When the gods quarrelled with the Asuras, he did his best to support the gods. It gained him Viṣṇu's favour. For his courage and selfless effort, the divine assembly granted him mighty magick.

Śiva took a liking to him. "Hey, scruffy man, you are ambitious and disciplined," he said, "you never miss a ritual and you do your meditations punctually every day. That's amazing. I admire you. Mainly as, honestly, I couldn't do it. Not even if I wanted to. Hell, I've got a wife, two loutish sons, I drink a lot, smoke more, go to bed late, and even getting up can be a problem."

"Not for me," said the ascetic, "that's 'cause I never go to bed."

"You are incredible," said Śiva, "and I'm glad that there are people like you. You are a shining example for everyone. One day, I predict, you might become immortal."

"I was stupid," said Śiva, "I gave him ideas. They made him crazy."

The saint was mad about perfection. And he expected everyone to be the same.

Life after life, his soul made progress. In each new incarnation he gained power, wisdom and ambition. In the meantime, he forgot laughter, and happiness, and the great joy of being funny and fallible. In one lifetime, he was the seer Paśuakhā. That's a nice name, it means *Friend of Animals*. Of course he lived a strictly vegetarian life. Śiva laughed, and called him 'Enemy of Plants'. Our seer lived in the wilderness. He couldn't stand people and their incessant chattering. In his opinion, animals were much better than humans, mainly as he didn't understand them. He built himself a tiny hut of bamboo and grasses. It contained a bed, a yoga seat and a fireplace. That was it. The seer practised self-denial. Whenever he encountered a desire, he denied it. Beauty? Forget it. Company? No way. Comfort? Never. Before long he stopped to go for walks, he ceased to meditate and he loathed food and sleep.

Before his hut grew a banyan tree, with coiling, twisting roots, like snakes. A bird mother built her nest on a branch, right opposite Paśuakhā's hut. The seer had nothing to do. He spent days staring at the nest. Alas, Karman is terrible. The monsoon came; the seer sat in his hut and hated everything. The roof leaked and the floor was under water. Other people would have fixed the roof. Paśuakhā didn't. In the night, the storm gales toppled the tree. The branches crashed, the bird mother flew in panic and was swept away by the gales. The nest landed softly and the eggs rolled out. The seer gathered them, and warmed them. Two chicks hatched. Paśuakhā was beside himself with delight. "You are my children! You are my followers!" he chuckled, and went out to gather worms.

While he was gone, a serpent crept into the hut. It was hungry.

The seer returned, muddy and wet, and saw the snake slither away. His children were gone. The seer had a fit of rage. He hurled the worms into the thicket; he raised his fists to the sky and screamed with rage. "Śiva!" he yelled, "Attend!"

There's no arguing with a mad and undernourished saint. Śiva gave a sigh, apologised to Durgā, put on his dhoti, left Mount Kailāsa and appeared.

"Snake vermin ate my chicks!"

Śiva stood in the rain and wondered how to explain. Let's give this pathos, he decided; the guy is insane, but maybe it will shut him up.

"Behold, I, the great lord Mahādeva, Sadāśiva the Eternal, answer your call."

"You must kill all serpents!"

"Great seer, accept the truth. Listen and learn: for these are cosmic mysteries. Big snakes eat little birds. Big birds eat little snakes. It's nature."

"They weren't any stupid birds! They were mine!"

"Property is a mirage. You own nothing. Not even your body. You borrowed it, when you were born. It changes all the time. Food goes in, excrement goes out. Cells come and go. You grow, you live, and you wither. When you die, you give it back."

"Don't give me holy shit!" The seer was mad with anger, "I know what I own. It isn't much, but it's mine. The birds were my children. I loved them. From now on, in all lifetimes, I will hate serpents and do my best to kill them all!"

"Great", said Śiva, "go into your hut, be miserable, you silly idiot, and stop wasting my time."

The seer screamed abuse, but when he realised the god had left; he crept into his hut and wept. For the rest of his life, he mortified his flesh. The gods shunned him.

Next, he was born into the royal house of Kāśī. He was a prince. One day, with a bit of luck, he might have become king. But he was proud and he had better things to do. His intellect was astonishing. As a small child, he learned to read and write. As a youth, he knew the *Vedas* and the better *Upaniṣads* by heart. True, he was not satisfied with them. There was plenty of space for progress. But improvements were other people's business. The man who would be Cāndo, desired power, no matter how much it cost. In this lifetime, he gave up his rights to the royal succession, called himself Saṅkha Gāṛurī, and travelled across India to learn magick and healing. His skill was stunning, and the greatest doctors accepted him as their student. He needed only a few weeks to master every skill. Then he moved on, and his greed of knowledge surpassed the limits of the universe. Saṅkha Gāṛurī collected truths and mysteries. He kept them, locked up in his head and never revealed a thing. Secrets, he knew, were power. Let others envy him. There was only one passion in his life: he killed serpents.

One day he met beautiful Manasā. It was in Jayantinagar. The goddess was young and innocent, and just getting used to Planet Earth. People, she knew, were difficult. Most of them were tied up in knots. Their body language was a mess, their minds were warped and their customs colourful and incomprehensible. To understand living beings, she needed something simple. So maybe she should start with fungi, plants, mosses, slime mould and insects. She had chosen a wonderful landscape, a lavish mountain meadow where, under a pure blue sky, countless blossoms raised their heads towards the sun; where lizards relaxed on warm rocks, where bees swarmed and butterflies hovered, and there was warmth and joy and fullness everywhere. The world was wonderfully detailed. Each blade of grass stood out against its background, each spider web promised hours of amazement. She made her great serpent throne appear, and reclined, clad in a few snakes, in the sunshine. A light breeze ruffled the herbs, the flowers trembled, and Manasā could have hugged the world for being real. She sipped her rodent smoothie and gave a sigh of relief.

Saṅkha Gāṛurī appeared. His clothes were filthy, his medicine bag bulged and he carried a huge stick. He stuck the bushes, parted tall grasses, and turned stones over.

Then he beheld the goddess. "Are you real?" he said, and came closer. "Curse you. Are you a reptile or a girl?"

Renunciation had equipped him with diamond radiance. His aura touched the snakes that made up Manasā's costume. The reptiles hissed and fled. The saint stared at the goddess and had a laughing fit. What a cheap girl. She was totally nude.

Manasā didn't understand. The gods appeared, and like the seer, they doubled up with laughter. Loudest of them was Durgā. She screeched with delight and her voice made stones split and storm winds howl. Manasā tried to laugh with them. She simply didn't get the joke. When she realised they laughed about her, she cursed the seer. "Saṅkha Gāṛurī, from now on, you are cursed. You will become a merchant!"

He did. But his magickal power was strong. He became the lord of all merchants and before him, kings and emperors prostrated themselves and kissed the dust.

"That makes it easy," said Manasā, "he never apologised, so he owes me. I'll appear to him, all right, I'll wear some clothes so he won't get excited; he worships me, I bless him, we'll be friends forever and everything is fine."

Śiva shook his head. "Cāndo controls kings. He doesn't care for cults that come straight out of the jungle."

It was too much. Manasā's head went red and her fangs emerged. "So what? I'll bite him to death and speak with his successor!"

"You can't. Great gods have to behave. We are not allowed to kill those who fight our cult."

Manasā raked her hair. "I hate it!" she hissed, "Life was so much better in the Underworlds!"

"If you kill him, you have lost your chance. You can only be a Great Goddess when Cāndo supports your cult."

"Why do you protect him?"

"He has a right to live and learn."

"Come on, daddy. You don't have to pretend. I'm sure he offers in your temples."

"He is generous. I admit, one day, I gave him a magick scarf and Durgā gave a lucky pouch."

Manasā tilted her head. Her teeth gleamed. "Let me guess. I should spare him, so you can make a profit?"

Śiva grinned. "No. You will spare him 'cause he will be useful. For you."

"Get out!"

Picture 12: Fishermen.

19. Fishermen

By late afternoon, the sky became restless. Wild gusts of wind swept across the land like forgotten souls, they tore at branches and leaves and made trees shudder. Clouds appeared on the horizon, leaden and foreboding and heaven went dark. The river was agitated. Small waves swirled, scattered, rippled and sudden gales hurled spray across the shore. What do you do when the weather goes bad? Most fishermen went home. Only two remained, hidden in the wind shadow of their boat, on the long, bleak shore, and waited.

Meet Jālo and Mālo; they are brothers. One day they would be famous ritualists. Right now they tried to get their pipes to burn. They sucked at the bamboo tubes and the water bubbled, but the sparks were swept out of the chillums and flew across the empty waste. The day was as good as over. A storm was coming, and it would be terrible. The fishes would hide in the deep, where nets couldn't reach them, and they could forget their catch, and be happy to stay alive. Alas, the King of Merchants, Cāndo the Greedy, had ordered a delivery for his palace. He was a man who did not accept 'no' for an answer. The fishers worried. Out there, on the river, they might gain a catch or lose their lives. But when Cāndo's men came and found no catch, they would be lucky if they were simply beaten up.

"Let's wait and pray," said the elder.

"I greet the divine in you." The woman looked old but she held herself straight. Her clothes and class marks indicated high rank; surely she was a wealthy Brahmin, and used to order everyone around.

The fishermen stared. What did she do, here, on the storm-swept beach, at this time of the day?

"We have no catch," said Jālo, and his brother grinned agreement. Maybe the stranger would go away.

"I ask for passage." Her voice was astonishing young.

Jālo got up and the wind tore at his clothes. "We won't go out in this weather. The wind is too strong."

"I offer great rewards."

"Not even the King of Merchants can pay for our lives." Mālo stood next to his brother, and spat. This woman might be evil. What did she do, out here, on a day like this? Where was her husband, her brother or her retinue?

"I am sure we will be safe." The woman smiled. "Take me to the other shore. You will be rich, and I will bless you."

"Your blessings ain't enough." Jālo was firm and his brother bared his teeth. "I guess you are a witch."

"Of course not." The woman seemed surprised, "look closely. I could be a respectable woman, or your mother. That's what Neta said."

"Our mother has more brains. Can't you see how the water churns?"

"With me, you are safe."

"How can you say so? The river is a goddess, and she's angry!"

"I know Gaṅgā. She's a good woman and very busy. She does life and death, all of the time, and I guess we should be grateful. Her husband is my father, so I am related, though mind you, she ignores me, and him. In my company, you will be safe."

The fishers reached for the amulets that dangled from their necks.

"When we meet her, I'll have a good word for you."

That was it. The fishers took hold of their boat and pushed it into the water. They clambered aboard and rowed, to keep it steady. A few metres would be enough. Everyone knows: witches can't cross running water, demons are bad swimmers and ghosts have to stay close to their graves. It was hard work, their vessel shook, and they struggled to keep it in the shallow range.

"You started without me. That's disappointing," said the woman, "give me a hand and take me aboard."

The fishermen mumbled their prayers. The words were torn from their lips and scattered by the gales.

Like them, Manasā prayed. Her words, like all good mantras, were simple. They went: "Maruts, wind gods, singers, make the storm stronger! Indra, my friend, make lightning flash and thunder roar! Aditi, primordial cow, turn the rain into a waterfall!"

"There. That was easy. I was sure you would come back. 'Cause you remembered your manners and that I'm a respectable Brahmin woman." Manasā reclined in the boat. The rain had stopped and the wind was gentle. "You came back as you saw sense. That means you get good Karman. And look, life is wonderful, and you ain't dead."

The fishermen kept their heads down. The storm had forced them to the shore. The woman had smiled and stepped aboard. She didn't even seem to get her feet wet. And now she lay there, on the hard planks, in all comfort, and talked about the weather.

"I told you, our journey would be wonderful. You know, it's the first time I get to ride a boat. And I am so excited."

So were Jālo and Mālo. They rowed their craft across a river that was so smooth you could watch your reflection watching you. The wind faded, the clouds did not move. Sure, the sky was black, but it was also silent.

"Let's do something funny," said the woman. "Cast your nets and see what you get."

The fishermen did. A moment later, they were full. They dragged their catch aboard and didn't trust their eyes. They bowed their heads and mumbled praise.

"I'm glad you come to your senses. Sure, I am a goddess. And I like to hear you babble nonsense, provided you do it with good feelings." She rubbed her hands. "But this was just the start. I'm sure you want to know that I'm the serpent goddess Manasā. Maybe you heard of me. I'm getting famous these days."

She passed her hands across her face. Her cheeks gleamed. "And I can't tell you how happy I am, to get rid of these wrinkles." She snapped her fingers, "and of these clothes."

The fishermen pressed their heads into their catch. They didn't dare to look.

"Come on, I order you to laugh! You'll have plenty of food tonight. You can sell a lot and dry the rest tomorrow."

No reaction.

"Let me give you an office. You may worship me. And you will conduct a boat race, every year, in my honour!"

When the keel crunched into the sand, the serpent goddess rose, refreshed and happy. She clapped her hands and time set in. Above the river, heaven cleared and the stars sparkled in diamond glory. The fishermen were pale but, she was glad to see, they were breathing. It was time for the grand finale. If only Neta could see this!

"My dear, dear fishermen, I like you. And that's why I'll work a miracle for you!"

The goddess clapped her hands. The boat turned to solid gold.

Instantly, the men were on their knees. "O goddess!" they complained, "Reverse your curse. A boat of gold will never swim!"

"It won't?"

"We need our old boat back!"

"What for? This one is much nicer."

"It would sink!"

"Have it your way. If you think you know better than I, you have to live with it!"

The goddess snapped her fingers. The boat transformed, and the brothers kissed the aged wood and wept with joy.

"Well, that went wrong. It's your fault. But now I want you to row away. And when you reach the middle of the river, cast out your nets again."

"We can't handle more fishes!"

"You'll get something better," the goddess winked, "my naughty boys."

In midstream the brothers cast their nets. What they pulled up was heavy, big, and golden.

"These are my sacred pots" Manasā called from the shore, "use them for worship."

"How should we do that?" called Jālo.

"Fill them with water, place a sij twig across, and have a jolly evening. If you are happy, I am happy. Invite your friends, pray, dance, make music, offer fruit and milk, and that's enough."

"How about fish?"

"I enjoy anything you like."

The brothers hardly dared to trust their ears.

"What about Brahmins?"

"Do you like them?"

"No," said Jālo, and his brother grinned like the moonrise, "we don't."

To travel at night is wonderful, for when dawn arrives the world is fresh and you have no idea how you got there. For a few precious moments, everything is new and miraculous. You can enjoy innocence, and wonder, and feel as if you were a child again. The light of the early morning sun bathed the palm plantations and the sugarcane fields in amber. Before her rose the city Campaka. A campaka, in the natural world, is a gorgeous yellow blossom. Please look it up; the plant is called *Michelia champaka*. Just like the blossom, the city was lush, wealthy and beautiful. It rested, in the heart of the wealthy Gangetic Plain, close to the river, and though nobody agrees where the location may have been, we can be sure it was in the best place anywhere. That's because Cāndo chose it as his home. You can trust him to get business right. If there's a profit to be made, there will be a river and a city. To him, the city, was just a convergence of labour, profit and dues. More important, it provided access to all vital trade routes, by land and water, and it throve as it was in the right place in the right time, with the right guy who owned everything and got the money coming in. As Manasā stood staring, the heavy, ironclad city gates opened and groups of traders led their pack animals inside. The guards had a stern expression and took their business seriously. Nobody noticed the young woman with her trailing black hair and her poppy-red sari, who drifted past the guards without attracting attention.

Manasā kept her eyes on the ground. It was good, dry earth, and that's as good as anything you might imagine. It was easy. The wall was something different. She didn't like the look of it. The goddess stepped aside, allowed a herd of goats to pass her, and glared. The thing was huge, and made of bricks. They were of equal size, but different ochre colours, and when she faced the rows and rows of neatly structured rectangles, her vision blurred and her head began to spin. Vertical and horizontal, these bricks said: order and organisation are the law of the world. Everything here is man-made. Obey, consume, behave, pay bribes, get on your knees and pray. Anyone who tries to enter will be overwhelmed.

There were proud men around, in gleaming armour, with heavy curved swords. Their faces gleamed like oil and their beards were orange with henna. They strutted around like emperors and chased the beggars away. It doesn't get much worse.

Within minutes, the air was full of dust. The snake goddess shook her head; she coughed, tried to clear her throat, and made her way, past a palanquin and accompanied by camels, through the second gate. Two gates, she thought. These people understand war. Is this civilisation?

Beyond the inner gate, our serpent goddess, much confused, found herself on a wide and terrifying open space. Campaka was a truly metropolitan city, where people of all ethnic backgrounds lived. You could meet citizens of a thousand social classes. You could buy anything your heart desired, legal, illegal and plainly impossible, if you were rich, cautious, well armed, and ready to take a risk. Here, the markets began. In spite of the early hour, the city throbbed with noise.

Manasā passed stands where simple traders sold their goods. You call them simple? Forget it. They knew everything about psychology, and used it to the limit. Some sold spices, and foodstuffs, some sold fowl or pets or scorpions on a stick, coated with pepper juice. Strangers might ask "What do they taste like?" The answer is "Like pepper."

Manasā walked past stands where hot dishes were prepared, looked into alleys dedicated to crafts, here smiths and artisans, woodcarvers, jewellers, goldsmiths, stone polishers, and ebony carvers; there embroiderers, tailors, butchers, spice merchants, vegetable sellers, and traders in spices, perfumes, drugs, and hopes. She smelled the thick, enchanting scent of curry herbs, and listened to a tangle of voices. It was more than enough for a young, innocent and lethal serpent goddess: Manasā staggered through the crowd. Hardly anyone noticed her.

A fountain spurted, cascades of glittering water released themselves into a bowl ornamented with elephants and lotus blossoms, and that, all by itself, would have been enough to occupy her attention for hours. Inevitably, the trickle soothed her. Water, no matter how you meet it, takes care of everyone and everything. The air was moist and pleasant. She looked at the city wall, in the distance, gleaming red, with battlements, loaded with archers, and laughed; it looked like the back of a crocodile. Underneath were stands catering to any needs. Between them walked low-class hucksters. Their goods came from cloth bags and were produced from belts and pockets. They were homeless; they had goods to sell, and they were cheap. Manasā felt like fainting. The world surrounded her, the voices were too loud, the colours too bright, and everything began to spin. She breathed; she breathed into her belly, and focussed on a tiny empty space within herself, her heart, her mind, sheltered, peaceful and easy to comprehend. Breathe in and breathe out. Belly moves. That's enough. Her eyes closed half-way; a trick she had learned from Śiva. Outside, in huts and tents and market stands, donkeys, horses, camels, even elephants found their place, were estimated, priced and sold. Manasā focussed on the air. Air is good, air is simple, air is easy. It's shared by everyone and anything. Plants and animals and people: you breathe it and it breathes you. Honestly, she thought, the city was insane. In spite of the early hour, business was over the top. While merchants screamed, customers pleaded, bargained and complained. Between the booths, sorcerers and yogīs walked through the crowd. Their talismans, not really cheap, but worth every anna, could cure anything. She stared at entertainers who dragged bears on chains; their fur was filthy and their eyes had turned a milky grey. But ask anyone: the moment, the bear trainer struck up a tune on his fiddle, the animal howled in long-remembered pain and began to dance. Not far away, a puppet player demanded attention. Manasā felt relieved; at least this guy did honest business. He charmed his audience, and promised drama, true love and great feelings.

A spicy scent made her head swivel; someone was baking grain cakes in a pan; they smelled of sugar and butterfat, of cumin and cardamom. The man had clean hands, but his body was clothed in tattered linen; he sported a huge moustache, the ends twisted upwards, and praised his merchandise. People gave him tiny metal pieces and departed with a steaming piece of cake. Manasā was amazed, while her stomach gurgled and twisted. I should buy a piece of cake, with oil and meat and everything. It seemed so simple, but it wouldn't work. She had no metal pieces.

I wish I could eat some rats. But they are hiding. I can't blame them.

Wherever she looked, people exchanged bits of metal. I hate you, she thought. People should exchange something of value, like sheep, vegetables, grains, and frogs. Or drugs; I don't mind, my father thrives on them. And a few luxury items for those who feel ugly and insecure. Or happen to be Durgā. That's how a market makes sense. It's all about real value. Anything else is just weird.

Manasā watched, her stomach knotted and her fangs showed. People are insane, she thought, they fell from the trees, got used to the savannahs, carried themselves upright, made flint tools, fed on fruit and meat and anything, and the more animal fat they ate, the bigger their brains went. Then, one day to the other, they built settlements, ruined their health on grains, destroyed landscapes and sold their souls for symbols!

It's a religion, she thought. Metal pieces are their idea of salvation.

Normal people didn't notice she was there. They were far too crazy with their own concerns. Most of them were in a hurry and scuttled across the marketplace like frenzied crabs. Manasā had heard it from Hanumān. "The early bird gets the worm." That's because the early worm got up too early and didn't wait for Mister Beetle to get up earlier. Hanumān knew everything. He could have warned the early worm. And he could have told the early bird to get up late. That's because early birds are wretched and angry and miserable. That's life. Even thinking about it can ruin your day.

Let's face it, Manasā thought, early birds and early worms are total failures. And honestly, no matter how it works out, it's going to hurt. Reality does. It's forced by evolution. That's a no-fun business if ever there was. And birds and worms had better stay in bed, or go on a holiday, or fall in love, and sleep as long as they can, for in the real world, there are few laughs for anyone.

Crooked figures approached the well. Each carried a bamboo pole across his back, with buckets dangling from the ends. They must be true ascetics, thought Manasā, just look how starved they are. Nothing but bones and muscles on a twisted frame! And they belong to a cult. They wear similar rags and they carry water for the world. I'm sure they swore an oath. As sick as they seem, it must have been mighty.

"A flower for a flower". They oily voice came right from behind. Manasā spun around, her hands raised, ready to stab a throat or blind the eyes. She faced a hairy guy, clad in rags that must have been classy and fashionable a decade ago. The man had a smile like Neta when she wanted to devour someone. Unlike Neta, he kept bowing. Manasā stepped back. This guy shouldn't have seen her! But the man was a pedlar, or trader, if you felt generous, and wanted to pay a compliment. Those who have been kicked out of society, the fringe people, get a gift from Śiva. It's the ability to see some things as they are. That's why some go enlightened, some make shifty business and others drink themselves to death.

The guy pushed a bunch of flowers into her face. Yellow, red, purple and blue; Manasā recoiled.

"My queen, you are the jewel of my heart. Enjoy the scent, inhale the mystery, feel the tinge of yearning! Great empress! I am sure; if I may be that bold, to predict that somewhere resides a lord, a king or a rich Brahmin, who aches for your loins! He can't eat, he can't drink, and he dreams of you. One whiff of this bouquet and he will drop to his knees and slide to the ground, and beg you to sit on his face!"

Manasā walked backwards. "How can you see me?"

"Call me a good genie, a divine messenger to fulfil your fated love!"

"I'm not in love!"

"But you should be. Everybody should. These flowers, queen of the night, are the key to eternal fulfilment. Buy the bouquet and give it to the man of your heart. He will be bound by the chains of desire and live, sucking your feet, as your slave for evermore!"

"Stop it! I don't want a man!"

"Oh, I have things to make a woman yearn for you. Here is a powder. Drop it into the drink of a lady, say, your best girlfriend, and she will drown in your eyes, lick your breasts and nevermore go straying. This powder is attachment! A child will never leave you; a pet will fight to stay at your side, or die for you, oh mistress of the universe."

"Go away!"

"How could I, mediocre me, who am your faithful servant, ready to turn your world into a dream of bliss, depart from your side?"

The man is a sorcerer. Or a demon! Manasā pressed herself into a house wall and blended into the whitewash. Cow urine gives a nice, pale colour and protects from evil, no matter what. Her face and contours faded.

The trader stood and gasped. His customer was gone! He looked around, spat, to avert ill fortune, and walked across the market space, holding his bouquet like a weapon.

Manasā didn't dare to breathe. She watched how he approached a lady in stunning colours and bowed so deep he almost fell over. He pressed the bouquet into her face; the lady giggled and reddened, and looked at him with antelope eyes. Her hands fluttered, as she flirted, and the peddler danced like a love-mad cockerel.

Manasā shook her head. It's all magick, she thought. It's magick that makes the bricks so uniform, so similar, and stunning. Magick moves those guards; magick makes metal pieces addictive. The traders deal in magick! And people buy it, crave it, need it, all the time!

She emerged from her hiding place, and took a deep breath. She smelled food and sweat, fear and loathing, dust and exhaustion, desire and greed. That's it, she thought, it is driven by delusion. I wish I were home. I could sit with Neta at the Dark Waters, and we would hang up the washing and she would take me to her temple for a snack. Life could be so easy.

Look at these buildings! Some were several storeys high. Some had domes and turrets and towers, and some were set within gardens so lush that it took a hundred slaves to water the flower beds!

These people are sorcerers and one day they will try to be gods.

And honestly, Manasā stopped, and exhaled, I admire them. Their madness makes them wonderful. A city like this, well, on Sij Mountain, we don't have anything the like. My people don't make much of an effort. They like sunshine and drinks and discuss theorems or compose ballads. And they dance the night away. By next morning, they are weary and have a hangover. They get up late, and call it great. But people here are driven. They have ambition and they make things happen. Maybe I should kill them all. I could carry them, and this wonderful place, away, and put it on Sij Mountain. They would be happy and all gods would come visiting and Durgā would go pale with envy and daddy would say, 'hey, I like this place, may I come visiting when I need a bit of entertainment' and I would say 'anytime you like, you know where the action is, and people here are simply crazy to meet you'.

The goddess sighed. Neta would laugh. She would say, 'Killing the population of a city is a pretty bad form. It's your job to establish your cult, in plain, dumb, damn stupid reality. Go and meet Cāndo. Convert him or kick his ass, and make things happen'.

20. Sonakā's Conversion

Karman means that things have consequences. Like it or not, whatever you do or avoid changes the world. Changes mean responsibility. Moral evaluations come later. Watch Jālo and Mālo, the fishermen, return to the huts near the shore. They carry a net that seems to burst. Their catch is unique, their wives laugh, their children screech with delight, and it takes many mats to lay out the fishes. Finally, the brothers show their pots and tell their tale. The light of true faith shines in their eyes, and anyone who appreciates religion and a handsome profit agrees with them.

Each day, the brothers and their families assembled. They prayed to the new goddess, caught an enormous amount of fish, and danced and celebrated every evening. Before long, the neighbours and the communities upstream and downstream joined the cult. They set up crude altars, big pots and sij twigs, arranged vegetables and fruit, incense, milk and yoghurt, they prayed and laughed and sang and worshipped. The drums and the hammering of the plate gongs echoed across through the night. The goddess attended, if invisible, and showed her grace. Day in and out, larger catches were taken to the market. What couldn't be sold locally was dried in the sun and carried inland. The demand for fish was immense, and before long, the fishermen needed bigger boxes to store their wealth, chained to the pillars of their huts so thieves couldn't drag them away. And look at the women! All of a sudden, they wore multicoloured saris. The bracelets on their arms clattered and chimed, and no, we are not just talking of glass, but of real gold and silver, set with precious stones or rimmed with pearls. Their children had earrings and amulets of red gold. In the old days, a bit of fish with rice had been a frugal meal. Now there were courses, with spices and sweets, and thick steaming curries with lamb and fowl and bubbling sauces.

The Brahmins cursed. They learned about the cult, made some shrewd guesses regarding its income, and were not admitted, unless they were poor and devout and just as unpopular as the fishers had been.

The new goddess, the leaders of the faiths declared, was a dangerous delusion.

"That's fine," said the fishers, "she fills out nets and the high classes pay up to marry our girls. We have boat races in her honour. We sing her songs as we paddle along."

"Who taught you these songs?" asked the rich Brahmins.

"We made them up ourselves."

"They are blasphemous and vulgar."

"Our goddess," said Jālo and Mālo, now high priests of the cult, "likes them."

Cāndo's agents acted everywhere, they controlled the markets; they bought dried fish and traded it to distant provinces. In turn, they supplied the fishers with milk and spices and delicacies, and aphrodisiacs for hot and passionate nights. Cāndo's doctors took care of the sick, and Cāndo's pharmacists were ready when a fisher needed medicine. The sandalwood incense burned at Manasā's pūjās went through Cāndo's hands. So did the jewellery that adorned the women, so did the silks they wore, when they paraded through the streets, colourful and noisy, with their coarse dialects, each of them rich like a landowner.

The King of Merchants gained a fat profit, but as he was busy controlling trade routes over thousands of kilometres, he didn't notice much. Well trained accountants with sour faces watched the local markets. His wife, Sonakā, thought different. What happened in foreign countries was none of her concern. But every day, when she went shopping, accompanied by her daughters-in-law, her servants and guards, she saw the fisherwomen. Each day they seemed richer. Their crude remarks were loud; and when they laughed, all women of true breeding bit their lips and looked askance.

Meet Cāndo's wife. Sonakā Śaśurī came from a high-level family, which wouldn't have dreamed of marrying her to a mere merchant. But Cāndo wasn't any other trader. He could have bought up the property of Sonakā's clan, and all their neighbours, without a second thought. But, as a cunning man, he appealed for her hand, bowed to her parents and showed his generosity. As a small token of respect, he bought up their debts, and cancelled them. Within a few months, the happy couple had the most expensive marriage that East India had ever seen. Sonakā, as Cāndo knew, was a priceless gem. Her background was perfect, her clan had excellent connections, and she was young, stunningly beautiful, healthy and, what was more, educated. He needed a woman who was more than a plaything, a clever, capable bride who would run the household, supervise the employees and slaves and give him many sons. Sonakā, of course, was aware that she was a business investment. Her husband was much older than she was, and, by all accounts, neither a romantic, nor much at home. It didn't trouble her. In her world, men married when they had achieved something, while women married when they reached puberty. Over the years, while Cāndo's beard went grey, Sonakā gave him six sons. Six is a perfect number, a lucky number, and Cāndo, who made immense offerings in the temples and donated huge amounts to the building of mosques, was a lucky man. His sons, each of them strong and healthy, had the best training that teachers could supply, and went through the rigorous training that Cāndo devised to make them merchants, just as good as him.

Their first lesson was simple: anything is negotiable. The second: every person has a price. The sons watched their father grinding suppliers into the ground, before he relaxed, smiled and granted them the tiny profit that kept them alive.

Cāndo was proud of his sons, but he didn't show it. Let them struggle, he thought, I've had a hard life and theirs was far too easy. When I seem kind and grateful, they take this for weakness and go slack.

As soon as each boy sported a well-kept beard, he let them do trial deals. Of course he kept them supervised by experts. One after the other, Cāndo made his sons marry. He chose brides who were not only well connected, and excellent business investments, but also well behaved and beautiful.

The money came in, and that means, as everyone knows, that the major gods are happy.

But no matter how much Cāndo prayed, and offered at the temples, none of his sons had a child.

Outside his citadel, people talked. They stared at the domes of Cāndo's palace, behind fortifications higher than the city wall, and manned by much better fighters. They imagined the storehouses and treasure rooms, the gardens and the guest residences, the ceremonial avenues and the stables for horses, donkeys, elephants and unicorns.

"He has a racetrack in there," Rām, the shoemaker said, "and a pool with boats and girls for evening parties."

"Are you sure?" Kumar, the blacksmith, raised his head in wonder. "I wish I had."

"These girls are special. They can dislocate their legs and twist their spines so their tits are on their backs. They coil around you and they eat your mind."

"Rubbish. Nobody can have girls like that."

"If you have money, you can."

"I don't believe a word."

"Relax, my friend. I know it from the niece of a friend of the cousin of a gardener."

"But Cāndo is not the type to go boating."

"Of course not. He lacks the time. He simply uses luxury to soften up his guests."

"I think he is cursed."

"But he is filthy rich!"

"Look at him, when you see him riding. He isn't happy. He rarely laughs. He hates himself, and everyone. And his boys, they are proud and arrogant, and sterile. The whole family is doomed."

"I'm sure he has an evil secret."

"That's it. A spirit eats his heart, so he is never satisfied. Sorcery made him rich, and now his family will die and fade away."

Sonakā rose early. You have to, if you wish to keep a large household under control. She had a bath, prayed, made offerings, and when the sun was up, she walked downhill to the market. Walking, as she knew, indicated humility. You can afford to appear humble when you are wealthier than any queen in the neighbourhood. As ever, her six daughters-in-law, each of them clad in much richer clothes than she, accompanied her. Down at the market, they made their ways along the rows of stands, the huts and stalls, where the girls looked for the finest cloth, the stunning colours and the newest line in jewellery. Sonakā, who rarely bought a thing to improve her appearance, observed them closely. The girls were good at detecting bargains. She let them barter and buy, as everything they acquired would end up in the family. Long ago, Sonakā had learned to keep her expression under control. Sure, when she was younger, her head was full of dreams. She was keen on the love of her husband, and failed. Instead, she found duty, responsibility and faith. Her man wasn't bad, in fact, he was far better than most. Cāndo was a provider. It wasn't his fault that his heart and his hopes were buried in the depth, under a million pages of accounts.

Young wives have to be watched and supervised. It's only when they have given birth to a son that their lives settle down. Then, at last, their husband's family is satisfied: the ancestors will get their offerings, and the future is blessed.

She never said a thing. They knew it anyway, and when Sonakā wasn't watching, they bought obscure aphrodisiacs and fertility powders, and fed them to their husbands.

Sonakā, herself, preferred muted tones. Her clothes were rich, but didn't say so. Wealth, she thought, should be owned, not demonstrated. She wore a modest sample of exquisite golden jewellery, enough to show she came from a good family. She was proud of her finely lined face, her upright gait; her nose had an elegant curve and her high brow was graced by the red sinduri dot. I am as young as I feel, she thought; it's not my fault that Cāndo has no time for me. My skin is almost free of wrinkles.

Sonakā walked from stand to stand, she got the best prices, and made her servants carry the goods home. The eager chatter of her daughters-in-law amused her; silly girls; of course they tried to make up for their shortcomings.

She watched the fisherwomen. A few months ago, they had been at the bottom of society. Nowadays, they radiated wealth. Just look at their faces, the make-up was overpowering and the perfume stunning. And consider the setting. Women, who had been below comprehension, wore gold and jewels, and pretended to be empresses or Apsaras or anything.

Look at their mascara. And see those lips, gleaming like poppies in the sun! They talked vulgar, they laughed vulgar. They wore their wealth and made men stutter. These women were happy, and she, who owned more than thousands of them, was not.

Since when, Sonakā thought, may silly women show betel reddened teeth?

Sonakā scrutinised the goods of a merchant. The man had silk from China and embroidery from Assam, expensive carvings in black ivory and jewellery that made her daughters-in-law giggle. She picked up a pretty box carved with images from the *Mahābhārata*. It was made of ivory and showed the Pāndava brothers dicing. That, of course, was a crucial moment in the epic. The dice game decided everything. The brothers lost, they lost their freedom and they lost their wife, Draupadī, and it was only thanks to the generosity of the winner, that they were exiled into a forest, where they built a city beyond compare. She laid down the casket and gave the trader a fierce look and walked on. She knew who she was, and she disapproved of the Pāndava brothers. Sure, each of them was an incarnate deity. They were the major characters of India's greatest epic! And just as sure, all five had married the same woman. Draupadī, as far as Sonakā was concerned, was a filthy slut, who had one brother each night, and never complained about lack of affection. That woman dripped with pleasure! It was outrageous that some people worshipped her as a goddess, and equated her with Lakṣmī.

Warriors! She thought. Their class is overestimated. No sense or virtue, and no subtlety. Give them a woman with breasts that bulge to the horizon and they die a hero's death! If high-class people, like bureaucrats or, or for that matter, wealthy merchants, had composed the *Mahābhārata*, such idiots wouldn't have appeared!

She stopped. Before her, and totally unaware of their true position in society, a bunch of fisherwomen converged. They bought whatever they liked, and they didn't bother to haggle.

This, Sonakā thought, is the end of the world. Bargaining is culture. Real people talk, they exchange offers and take their time about it. With your purchase, you got an extra helping of gossip. You learned about providers, and about the market situation, about fashions and about politics. No matter what you bought or how badly you were cheated, you remained perfectly informed.

Sonakā sent their escort home. A few guards, she estimated, would be enough. They would accompany her and her daughters-in-law, down to the shore, where things got filthy and rebellious.

From far away, she heard the throbbing of drums and the hard chime of plate gongs. Simple instruments, to be sure, but what could you expect from a bunch of fishermen? They had just turned rich; it would take them years to gain culture. A flute joined in, and the sound touched her heart. These people, she knew, were primitives, but that flute was divine.

The fishermen lived close to their boats. If a flood rose, their houses would be lost. They would rebuild them higher up the shore.

Today, the settlement was full of life. The music was loud, the worshippers chanted and some clapped complex rhythms. Clapping, thought Sonakā, is poor people's music. But there were variations that amazed her. How can two hands produce so many distinct sounds?

"Stop! I want to speak with you."

The woman shook with fright; she faced the Queen of East India, the wife of Cāndo, the Merchant King.

"Forgive me, Lady! I am dust under your feet!"

"What's your name, child?" Sonakā raised her chin. The woman, to be sure, was of her age, but that was no reason to respect her.

"I am Sardāi."

"A fisherwoman. Tell me, what's happening here?"

"Lady, I apologise. We worship the daughter of Mahādev, the Lord of Lords, the daughter of the highest, eternal Sadaśiva. Please forgive the noise, we are simple people, and we worship the gods."

"You fool! Who taught you about religion? My husband worships Śiva; he gives offerings to Durgā, and to their heroic sons. Tell me, who is this daughter of Śiva?"

The fisherwomen shrunk. Her voice was hardly audible. "She is Manasā, the serpent goddess, the Lady of Awareness."

"Explain. Did you invent her? Why have I never heard of her?"

"The lord of ascetics fathered her, and a lotus took his seed. She was born from Kadrū, in the seventh underworld. You should meet her. In Manasā, Śiva's awareness is realised!"

The woman shook with fright. "My lady, she grants boons without measure!"

"I can see that. You should be ashamed to show yourself in public, wearing so much gold! So tell me, upstart. What's the charm of your new goddess?"

"Come with me," said the woman, "the serpent goddess has a heart for everyone."

Sonakā stopped before the largest hut. Here, the music was loud, the fumes intense, and she could smell the sweat and madness of the worshippers. Women screamed "Ulululululu" as if they were furies, their tongues going right and left, in total frenzy. The metal plates chimed, the drums thundered and her head went dizzy.

The fisherwoman opened the door. Sonakā stared into the gloom. The fumes scorched her eyes and the scent of smouldering butterfat clogged her nostrils. Inside, she glimpsed a congregation of lunatics. They had assembled around a golden vessel, with a spiky twig across. Around the vessel, there were vegetables, fruit, bananas, rice, paddy, hemp, flowers, bowls of milk and choice pieces of meat, on platters. She saw a piece of cloth, far too expensive for this simple crowd, which was to clothe the goddess. And there were pastries and sweets. No image was in sight. Apart from the gold this was low-class, to say the least.

"Come in," said her guide. "The guest is god." Sonakā grit her teeth and advanced into the gloom. The music stopped. Everyone knew who she was. Her daughters-in-law followed her. Within instants, people cleared a space, and offered cushions, so their new guests sat in comfort. Show me; thought Sonakā, I want to see the glory of this deity. Otherwise I'll have the settlement burned down.

The day before, Cāndo had had a tough schedule. There were the callers, the reports, too many letters and accounts and scribes, all of them calling for attention. Several ships had arrived, full of goods, and their captains demanded an audience. The King of Traders ground his teeth. They are a bunch of boys, he thought, they deliver a few trifles and make a big scene, as if their effort was special! Everyone calls for attention! But people are replaceable. And it's just cargo! You may think of ivory and jewels and opium, but in the end there's just a number! It's a damn nuisance to run half a continent, and these idiots are full of envy. They think I live a life of ease. In reality, I have no leisure. And I hate it! One day I will retire. One day I will relax and find peace and meditate and the world will go away.

My sons will run my business empire.

That's when his doubts showed their claws. Doubts are merciless. None of his sons was good enough. None had the guts, the daring and the greed to get things organised.

I will have to help them, Cāndo thought; I will have to set them right. I will have to hurt and punish them until they see the light.

There was no peace and there would never be.

He, personally, had to go to the storage halls. He had to break seals, open boxes, had to examine sacks of spices, had to count barrels of perfumes and tusks of elephants. It was embarrassing. But if he didn't, at least twenty percent would go missing. Cāndo knew his employees. He instinctively realised what was wrong, and he was good at reprimanding anyone. For most of the day, he criticized, and doubted, and found errors. He confronted his employees and nagged. Why didn't you do this, why did you overlook that and why are you such a failure? They squirmed and hated him. But what could he do? They were so hopelessly inferior, and not even worth their wages. When he returned to his residence, he felt wasted. Accounts kept him awake. Finally, it was too late to go home, he went to the spare bed in his main office, but sleep evaded him. He got up, had a cup of water, went to the toilet, swung his arms, twisted his painful back, and tried to go to sleep again. His shoulders ached and his neck was tense. So what! If he couldn't rest, well, he would get up early. He would go on inspection and shock his guards, so they would tell the world their master never slept. It suited him fine. Eventually, and almost beside himself, he dropped asleep. A glaring light shook him awake. Heaven gleamed; stars fell in cascades, divine vibrations shook his couch and before him rose a woman clothed in radiance.

Cāndo dropped to his knees. He saw her feet, miraculously perfect; he saw the trident and the staff. Beside her stalked a lion. Cāndo knew who faced him and kept his head down.

"Cāndo!" her voice echoed. "My darling! My slave!"

"Goddess! Without you, and your husband, I am nothing." The King of Merchants knocked his head against the marble floor.

"And what is a deity without its greatest worshipper?" the goddess seemed to flirt. "My juicy servant, raise your face."

"Durgā! I will do anything for you!"

"Cāndo, dear Cāndo. You are so attentive to numbers and percentages. You understand accounts better than people. This is your grace and your glory. Alas, it makes you blind to many things. You failed to notice what has happened. An evil cult has come to your kingdom. A demon goddess tries to wreak my rule!"

"My lady, tell me. I am ignorant, I am a fool, I never noticed anything."

"That's why I am here, my little mouse." Durgā radiated her smile and Cāndo almost fainted. "You are such a sweetie. I love you. And I have a task for you." The goddess patted his head. "My sāddhu, my true believer. You are the defender of my faith. In you, alone, I place my trust."

Cāndo was close to breakdown. Tears ran down his cheeks.

"An evil cult has risen. It corrupts the people, it threatens law and order, and it blinds people with promises of indecency and freedom. Of course, my dear, you know that freedom is insane. Society needs rules and punishments. Cowherds and fishers must remain where they are. The gods made the world, and gave it to the wealthy and important. You are the true King of East India and you will make it stay the way it is."

The goddess fluttered her lashes. Cāndo shook with emotion.

"My merchant! Fight the serpent woman. She is a bastard, a creature of filth, a goddess of the lowest classes!"

Cāndo looked up. "Great Devī. How can I fight her?"

"Take this staff. It is made of black hemtāla wood, and it will cripple and destroy her! I promise she will come to you. Be prepared, and show no mercy. Break her bones! Crush her skull and kill her!"

Cāndo woke and felt wretched. His limbs shook and his blanket was drenched with sweat. He felt as if half of his brain was out of order. Just let me die, he thought, but very silently. His employees must never notice that their boss was plainly wasted.

He worked through morning, noon and afternoon. He hammered numbers, signed papers and cursed the world. Then his wife returned. She was excited, and Cāndo had no patience for her silly chatter.

Sonakā was in a frenzy. "Cāndo," she called. "I have been to the most amazing cult! And look at this, I bought a golden vessel!"

"What did you pay for it?"

"Hardly anything. I got it from the fishermen, and they don't understand money at all."

"So," Cāndo said, "what is it good for?"

"It's the vessel of the serpent goddess, Manasā. And look at this; I got her sij twig for free!"

Cāndo scowled.

"I was at the worship. I can't tell you how wonderful it was. I sat there, and the girls chanted, and I wept and thought, I feel at home, and life will go better, and the goddess is with me and everything is wonderful."

"Oh." Cāndo raised an eyebrow. "Is it?"

"Of course it is!" Sonakā was beside herself. "I haven't felt so much alive in years!"

"That," Cāndo said, "is wrong. You worshipped a demon. Her cult is sinful and her servants are filth. Of course, I'll forgive you. You are a woman, and will never understand what's what. But you must denounce this evil spirit."

"But darling," said Sonakā.

"Don't 'darling' me." Cāndo glared. "Let me show you how I deal with this." He raised his staff of black hemtāla wood and smashed the vessel to bits. "Go to your rooms!" he commanded. "And the same goes for your flock of silly birds!" He was red in his face. "You are deluded and you ought to repent! The great gods ordered me to crush this sect!"

Cāndo, the Kings of Merchants, called for his guards. "Go to the fishermen. They have a new cult. They worship an evil serpent demon. Destroy their vessels, smash their altars, and erase all traces of their faith. I want to hear no more of them!"

Cāndo leaned back on his throne and smiled. The air was damp with the early morning rain and the work of the night was done. Yes, tonight he had slept well. It was a welcome relief. No dreams, no worries, no supernatural visitations. There were good reasons to feel grateful. His guards had done their duty. This morning, the chief officers assembled, each of them proud like a peacock. They were keen to report and gain merit. Merit, as Cāndo knew, meant profit. Their profit was his loss. It would have worried him on other days. But this morning, sure that they had done the work of the gods, he smiled. His henchmen could keep their plunder. Whatever the campaign might have cost, the gods would pay him back six times.

His guards had come over the fishermen like a wave of devastation. They had thrown them out of their huts and set the settlement on fire. And in between, they had broken the treasure boxes and stripped the women and made the men, naked, kneel in the sand and eat filth. It had been profitable. The gods smiled on them. The Manasā pots were broken, smashed or flattened. Her twigs were burned, just like everything. Cāndo was satisfied. His little project had been a success. Of course he had ordered that the boats and nets were spared. Fishers have to make a catch. In a few days they would improvise shelters. That would take them out of the rain. A month or two were needed to weave walls. Their huts would rise again. Then they were back to being fishers. Without the wealth that, by rights, wasn't theirs. Of course they had been splendid customers. However, he thought, they served a demon. They paid the price and should be happy they were still alive. They would come to their senses, provided they suffered enough. And they would bless him for his mercy.

Cāndo stroked his beard which showed, no matter how much it bothered him, streaks of white. Other men would have dyed it. But Cāndo was too proud to oblige the crowd. Let them see I'm old, he thought, and better than any of them.

He clapped his hands. The guards stood at attention. His administrators, bookkeepers, archivists and servants lined up. Sonakā, his sons and their wives appeared. He had an announcement to make.

The merchant king rose. He stood, leaning on a black staff no one had seen before.

"You are here to learn the decision of the gods. I, Cāndo, convey what Durgā told me.

The new cult of the serpent-whore is prohibited. Those who dare to worship her, break Cāndo's Law, violate the god-given order of society and will be punished. All cultic items will be destroyed and there will be heavy fees. Those who cannot pay will be employed for forced labour or they may sell their children. There will be no exceptions. This is Dharma; this is the law of Cāndo's Land."

He scrutinised the faces. Who is guilty, who is in sympathy with the serpent demon? Who dares to doubt my mission? The guards were evidently on his side. His sons were uneasy; while their wives let their heads hang. Women. Well, let them.

Cāndo cleared his throat. He had been severe, now it was time to demonstrate his justice. He turned to the guards. "You are not allowed to kill the followers of the serpent-witch. You may mete out my punishment; you will arrest those who err in their ways. However, we are not murderers. There will be no rule of terror. I will not allow torture or mutilation. We must demonstrate virtue."

He walked to his throne, sat, and relaxed. "You have heard my words. Everyone is dismissed."

That moment, the air flickered, lights danced and thunder echoed.

Facing Cāndo stood a young woman who wore nothing but serpents. Her three eyes shone red.

"Cāndo! You tyrant! How dare you act like a beast!"

The women screamed, the brothers paled and the guards raised their weapons.

Cāndo grinned. "I hoped you would come, but I wasn't sure you'd dare the sunlight."

"I'm no demon! I'm a goddess and I demand obedience."

"I'm glad to hear it. Yes, we should talk about this." He raised himself and advanced, leaning on his staff. "I am sure you will see reason. So, little girl, take this!"

The staff described an arc and struck.

Manasā screamed. She barely kept herself on her feet. It felt as if her hip was broken.

"Right," said Cāndo and raised the staff again. "Here's another one, with greetings from Durgā."

Manasā reeled and stumbled. The staff barely missed her face. She would have loved to open her poison eye.

It wasn't allowed. Gritting her teeth, she evaded the old man, who came after her, laughing like a fanatic. He swung his staff, again.

"Eat fire!" she shouted and exhaled. Cāndo staggered back; his face and beard were badly scorched.

"Is this all you can do, demon slut?" He aimed for her head. "Your journey is over!"

The air froze. Cāndo stood like a statue, and so did his people. None of them moved, none of them breathed.

Facing them stood a tiny guy. His skin was dark, like some low-life aborigine, he had a pot belly, and wore a filthy rag across his hips. No shoes, no ornaments, not even a caste mark on his brow. The man sported a beard that reached to his knees, with bright red spots, indicating the tandoori chicken he had been eating.

The little man stared at him. His hair was full of ashes and his eyebrows bushy.

"You criminal!" he squeaked. "No one may hit my daughter!"

He stabbed Cāndo with his index finger, right in the solar plexus.

"You sneaky little money-maker, down you go. You may ask for her pardon."

Cāndo collapsed. He coughed and retched. "Beggar, I will kill you!"

The ascetic looked at him, scratched his hairy belly and spat betel juice. His teeth were almost black. "You are really silly."

He turned to Manasā. "Come on, girl. The party is over. We ain't wanted anymore."

The guy spun on his heels and disappeared. Cāndo glared: like him, the serpent–bitch was gone.

Slowly, the merchant king raised himself. His body ached. In his age, swinging a staff was just too stressful. He bared his teeth and glared at the congregation: wife, sons, daughters-in-law, officials, guards, everyone. They must think he was a fool.

"Right," he snarled, "while you did nothing, I fought the demons. And I won!"

He raised a fist. "It's all your fault. And let me tell you one thing! This has never happened. And it won't be talked about. Understood? Repent, make up for your sins and wash the court with cow manure. I want all walls whitened with the stuff. I'll go and purify myself. So should you."

He walked away as best as he could. In the bathroom, he cleaned himself with the five jewels of the cow. He repeated the Gāyatrī a hundred times. For the rest of the day, he would fast and sacrifice to Durgā. A little later, the adrenaline wore off and he collapsed. Cāndo tried to pray to his benefactress, but his words were empty, and his mind confused. While Cāndo whimpered, his men went through the city. They broke open houses, smashed serpent pots, raped women and plundered as they liked.

21. Conflict

Manasā crouched on the ground, right in the central hall of her palace and tried to focus on her breath. It takes a while to heal a broken hip, even if you are a goddess. And as she felt her body healing, her hunger grew. Over there, in the world of mortals, her cult was disappearing.

Occasionally Neta walked by. She was always busy. That's how she kept her energy. You can have a cult, on earth, with untrustworthy human worshippers. Or you can do the washing of the gods. They are indebted, and pay up.

Śiva had resumed his shape and carried her up Sij Mountain. At first, it had been fun to fool Cāndo. But when he saw his daughter's injuries, and recognised the black hemtāla staff, he knew that Durgā was involved. What do you do as a high god? Go and confront your wife? Have a terrible row, and spend your days worrying? Śiva had learned much from the animal world. He understood the basic options: to fight, to freeze, and to flee. The last was the all-time favourite: when you stress an animal or a person, it will eventually go away. Mobility promotes evasion. Plants, by contrast, have to stay where they are. They gather more information than animals can hope to handle, and they find solutions. His daughter had plenty of plant life in her. She wouldn't run. Manasā would adapt herself, or adapt her world, no matter how much it hurt.

When he was sure that Manasā was recovering, Śiva mounted his bull Nandi and ambled down the slope. First crunchy ice, then shrubs and herbs, tough and small, next dwarf pines and twisted evergreens, then birches, and flowers and rhododendrons. He took his time. It would be nice to remain in the forest, like in the good old days of Vedic sacrifice, when marriage was not a problem and he could bloody well do as he liked. The conifers would welcome him. They would provide shelter, and silence, and time to relax. Once recovered, or drunk, or whatever, he would rage through the mountain passes, howl with the storm winds, and rush, like a cyclone, accompanied by hordes of madwomen and delirious serpent girls, through the wilderness. People would bar their doors and pray for mercy. Rudra, they would plead, spare our homesteads, spare our cattle, aim your lethal arrows at somebody else! And he would eat every toxic plant, fungus and animal he could lay his hands on, provided they were strong and promised forgetfulness.

Gods heal faster than humans do. That's because no matter how bleak the future seems, they think happy thoughts, and happy thoughts promote healing. Also, they sleep a lot. Manasā felt weak but tried to keep a smile on her face. Eventually, she got up, had a bath, oiled her body, put on a new set of toxic reptiles, organised her hair around them and left her palace. Out There, in the human world, that godforsaken realm of greed and insanity, there was plenty to do.

Cāndo had been mortifying his flesh. He had fasted, he had denied himself comfort and he had evaded his wife and her obnoxious prattle. His dreams were terrifying and his mornings felt like lead.

The guards woke him. "The ground broke open," they whined, "and a million snakes erupted from the deep!"

Indeed they had. The serpents had overrun Cāndo's plantations like a surge of destruction, they had eaten all fruit, they had torn down trees, and crushed the grains. Their toxic breath made the herbs wither and left the soil barren and dead.

The merchant king hurried, and faced annihilation. What had been the finest residence in Asia was just as merry as a burning ground. There was death in the air.

Cāndo took his time. The yarn, of course was already being told. Let them gossip, he thought, I'll give you something to talk about. This would be a story, and it would celebrate him.

He had drawn the horizontal marks of a Śiva devotee across his brow. His dhoti was plain, clean and very expensive. I am the sāddhu, he thought, I am the renouncer, the poor, faithful beggar, and I'll show you how to wield power and make an income. In his hands, he held sheer magick.

He called for his family, his administrators and guards.

It would do them good to learn how humble he could be.

When everyone was ready, Cāndo circled his property. Like a Vedic King he walked deosil, as the sun does, and muttered mantras. From time to time, he raised his victory scarf and his bag of magick power. "Śiva and Durgā", he prayed, "I am your humble servant. Let me remind you of your promises. You gave these gifts to me. I trust in you, now make them work!"

The servants had erected a plain earth altar. They set up the statues of the major gods. Cāndo stood in silence, watching like a hawk. First Śiva and Durgā, his favourites. They had the greatest debt to him. Next Gaṇeśa, with his friendly elephant head, yes, Cāndo mistrusted him, because that guy never did a decent day of work, but he was the son of his personal gods, and his favour counted. Then, Kārrtikeya, the warrior lord. Well, nothing against warriors; if they gain profit or protect the treasury. On a special seat of honour, he had the statue of Gandheśvarī set up, the sweet-smelling goddess who guards the class of spice and perfume merchants, his special benefactress. She had received many offering; it was time that she got out of her perfumed bathtub and performed.

Finally, two low-class men appeared, dragging a pair of sacrificial goats. In general, sacrificial animals should be treated with love and care. They should be fed with juicy morsels and soothed with mantras. If they accepted their fate, in their next life, they might be born as human beings. An unwilling victim is bad luck. Cāndo had no time for nonsense. At his words, the men lifted their cleavers and chopped. Blood splattered, and incense fumes swirled to the heavens.

Cāndo prayed. He was serious, angry, and demanding. When the fog lifted, he clapped his hands and bowed. A divine wind arose, swept across the fields and lifted up the fallen trees. It set the grains upright; it made the blossom raise their heads. Wherever he looked, Cāndo delighted in wealth and fertility and the greatness of the gods. There was fresh green in the bushes, the sugar cane stood like an army, the indigo blossomed and the herbs gleamed in the sun. On the pools, new lotus blossoms raised their heads, each one prettier than the other, the onions sprouted, the lentils laughed, the beans climbed up the poles.

Cāndo clapped his hands. "The ritual is finished." He glared at his employees. "Stop lazing. The pause is over, you had your fun and there is work to do. We lost enough time. I want to speak with my accountants."

"How do I look?" Manasā stood before a mirror. For the occasion, she had selected a tiny piece of something, faintly magenta coloured and almost translucent. It barely fit across her hips. Add a bra, almost invisible, encrusted with gold ornaments, which left the nipples free, 'cause that's where her serpents were supposed to sit. And sandals, with high heels, studded with diamonds.

Neta shook her head. The serpent goddess was starving. Her ribs were coming out and her pelvis had acquired a sharp edge.

"Look at this!" Manasā gleamed, and pointed at her skirt, "it's embroidered with lotus flowers."

She reached for her makeup.

"Neta, say something. I want to look desirable. Like a classy courtesan."

She rotated her hips. "Will this blow his mind?"

Neta forced a grin, the sort that you reserve for senile hamsters and bank accountants. "Who is your target?"

"Come on. You know."Manasā reached for the rouge. Her face was pale and her cheekbones hollow, but with a bit of colour it wouldn't really show. "My future worshipper; Cāndo, the Merchant King."

Neta's mouth tightened. She could have said a lot. It wouldn't have helped one bit.

"You are the Thinking One!" she snapped. "So think. And for a change, think, as ordinary, stupid people do. You are almost nude. That's fine among the wilder gods. It won't do on Planet Idiot!"

"I've clad some bits. The rest looks good!"

And it is simply too thin, thought Neta. You are starving, your serotonin is out of balance, your dopamine is fading, and you are high on endorphins and adrenaline. It won't last, no matter how many honey rats you devour.

"But I want to be gorgeous. If I were human, I might be famous."

"For what? Looking starved?"

"For being a perfect dancer, or a lady of the night. You know; an expensive concubine or whatever they call their therapists."

"You are too nude." Neta dragged her to the wardrobe. It was surprisingly easy. "You need more clothes!"

"But men like nude women," Manasā complained. "Hanumān told me. He read it in a book."

"Only when they can unwrap them themselves."

"I make it easy." Manasā struggled. "One or two motions and all textiles are gone."

"You'll scare him."

Neta loaded her with saris. Red, pink, magenta, even blue. "You'll try the lot."

"But they are plain! I want gold embroidery! And pearls! And emerald studded edges!"

"That's too expensive. It signals wealth. Wealth means independent, and demanding. That's another thing which scares men."

"But he's rich!"

"He's still a man. An old man. He can hardly keep it up, and he will feel inferior. And he will prefer you exclusive, but dependant on him."

Neta was devastating. Gold jewellery was replaced by bronze. Sapphires made way for glass. Finally, she rolled her sister into a red sari with just a little embroidery at the fringes, barely enough to spread glamour, but not enough to upset a Merchant King. Next followed mascara. Black lines around the eyes.

"I want more!"

"You'll look like a panda!"

And finally, a daring touch. While her sister stood, almost wrapped up, and tried to breathe, Neta took hold of the fabric and tore. Just a small hole. Enough to allow a tiny bit of flesh to gleam. "That's the Forbidden," she said, "a hint of what should not be revealed."

Manasā stared. "It's a hole."

"Men love holes."

"Why?"

"Don't ask me. I didn't create mankind. And if I had, it would be better."

The day hadn't been too bad. Cāndo went to his favourite guest house. It also functioned as a high-class restaurant, an exclusive hotel and, if need be, as a refined brothel. Of course Cāndo wasn't a guest. Like so much in Campaka, Cāndo owned the place. The guards bowed, and so did the waiters. Within instants, word was around: the owner was there, and everyone was on their toes. The Merchant King retired to a private cubicle. The walls were carved of chosen timbers, the cushions thick, the light muted. The manager appeared and bowed. Cāndo greeted him, respectfully. He was a trader, and a realist, he knew his limits; and running a high-class establishment was not his forte. He left it to a man who was addicted to the company of pop stars, wealthy idiots and criminals.

The first drinks arrived. The merchant king intended to relax. It was still early and he was in no hurry. At home, his accountants would stay awake over the books. His wife could sit and worry. His guards were busy. And here he was, suave, successful, the winner of the day. The story, of course, had gone around. Cāndo, whom many considered a blood-sucker, had demonstrated spiritual grace. Śiva's victory scarf and Durgā's magick pouch had revived the devastated land.

The Brahmins would envy him. He's a mere trader, they would think, and he works miracles. Yes, Cāndo thought, believe it or not, but there is something spiritual in money making. It pleases my gods, and all the other gods. 330 millions of them, what rabble. Plus Allah, Christ, Buddha and Mahāvīra. And who knows whatever low-life-spirits the untouchables believe in. Religion is business.

I won't have any talk of 'universal love'. My priests know numbers, they understand me, and I understand them. I donate, they preach, and there is a profit for everyone.

Cāndo leaned back. His alcove was special. There were lucky symbols in the carved panelling, inlaid in gold, and in one corner stood a statue of dancing Gaṇeśa, prancing on one leg, holding an umbrella. That, Cāndo thought, is what religion really means. A pot-bellied monstrosity doing pirouettes for the gullible.

A servant appeared with a platter of light snacks. The merchant king smiled. His food would take a moment. Unlike the stuff served to the wealthy and important, his meal was truly fresh.

He nodded at Lakṣmī. Her statue was of choice teak, well oiled, and almost nude. That's because wealth is naked; it reveals its beauty. Gaṇeśa and Lakṣmī, Cāndo didn't trust either of them. But they influenced the few, special guests whom he invited into the privacy of his alcove.

The lamb curry was simple and perfect. The cook was excellent, and almost worth his pay. Here, at last, he could find peace. His wife, at home, would weep and worry, and scold him through the evening. She got upset, just because he slapped her, and when he left, she yowled to her sons, who did their best to get away.

The merchant king chewed, slowly and deliberately. Food, like customers and suppliers, has to be masticated. There was just one thing that annoyed him. That serpent slut. He should have crushed her skull.

In the central hall of the restaurant, admired by a hundred wealthy guests, a woman danced. She was accompanied by a tempura, four strings that repeated a droning chord, a sitar, whose passionate melodies made the sky melt and hearts flutter, a deep, weeping bansuri flute and a tabla player whose soft hands fluttered over his drums like bird wings. Had Cāndo understood anything about music, he would have appreciated their mastery. To learn an instrument, you need at least five lifetimes. In the first, you learn to relax, and gain true softness in your hands. In the second, you practice. Best, if you start before daybreak; that's what the masters say, 'cause before dawn the world is fresh and virgin, and you can truly hear what you are doing. Maybe your neighbours will complain. Who cares; they can move away if they don't like it. Good music, they insist, is a blessing for the universe, it's a religious duty. In the third lifetime, you really learn what can be done. And in the fourth, you develop your own style. In the fifth, if you are any good, you transcend all limits. In between, you have to undergo an initiation. It requires you to play your instrument for three days, or to sing its rhythms, from dawn to dusk and deep into the night, while the whole family and your teacher pray for you. Few people and few families can take the strain. Drums are hard, but slightly lower-class. That's because you touch the skin of a dead animal. Playing the sitar isn't really simple, either. The word means *Three Strings*, and refers to the basic tuning of the major strings, which, in modern terminology, would be F, C and G, before we start with c again. Provided we chose C as the tonic. Most sitar masters have their own ideas; they spend years admiring their gurus, and decide on a basic tone that may be one or two semitones in each direction, to suit the spirit of each rāga. The thin metal strings are sharp; they cut into the fingertips. Dedicated players develop calluses and deep grooves; the posture makes their shoulders harden, the neck goes rigid and the scales require decades of daily practice. And reed flutes: the longer they are, the more they strain the hands and wrists. Some players go to a surgeon. He makes a few cuts, so the fingers can spread wider. Truly, all musical instruments twist and distort the human body, and each demands its price in pain. And yet, musicians laugh and give their best. They create sublime feelings and make the world a better place.

Cāndo didn't know and wouldn't have cared. He didn't know he heard Rāga Asāwarī, one of the sacred scales of India (it corresponds, in European terms, to C minor or Eb major), a tune sure to bedazzle snakes and deer and peacocks, with reverberations reaching from the height of heaven to the depths of Nāga Underworld.

A servant appeared, with bowls of hot water, to wash his fingers, and spices to chew, to freshen up his breath. Cāndo took the hot, damp towel and wiped his face and hands. The cardamom tasted excellent. He watched the dancer in the centre of the hall. She was new; he had never seen her face. Her motions were superb, her gestures to the point. And when she swayed, she seemed as light and nubile as grasses in the wind.

Very slowly, he stroked what was left of his beard. It still smelled scorched. How her hips quivered! How she thrust her pelvis, as if it were a weapon, and how her breasts shook, like waves crashing against a stony shore. Her lips burned like red poppy and her eyes were like hibiscus blossoms. She did not look at him. Cāndo bared his teeth, look at me, he thought, see me, I'm here!

The woman didn't seem to care.

She dances like Sonakā used to dance, long ago, before she gave birth to our six sons. Time demands a price. But what is a price when you own everything. The merchant king made a gesture, and within instants, the manager was at his side. This woman, he knew, was special. He would enjoy her, would delve into her navel, would bury his head in her breasts, would forget himself within her. She would be the special reward of a perfect day.

It hurt. Everything did. Slowly, Cāndo came to his senses. He raised his head and moaned. Yes, he was at the wayside, in the bleak light of early morning. The sun was about to rise, the insect chorus began and soon the birds would set in, and wake the world. The merchant king realised that his legs were in a ditch, and glared into the blood red sunrise. The day would bring evil weather. His head hurt, his hands shook, and when he touched his brow, he realised his turban was gone. So was the golden needle, with the diamonds, that held the thing together. Cāndo groaned and placed his weight on his right arm. He tried to raise himself. Maybe, he thought, I drank too much. I don't know, in fact, I can't remember anything. His feet were wet, his silk shoes, with the silver inlay, ruined forever. Groaning, he sat up and faced abject misery.

His memory was in fragments. Sure, he had had his meal. It was pretty good, and worth its price. He had watched the woman who danced like a cobra. The manager came round, Cāndo gave his orders, and soon she stepped into his alcove. O yes, the girl was shy. She blushed and hardly knew where to cast her eyes. They were damned black, he remembered. Like the eyes of antelopes, like the monsoon clouds, before the world turns into a waterfall.

Of course he had been charming. As an experienced older man, not really old but mature, he had flattered her with compliments, and made her sit at his side. He had smiled generously, he had made her drink from a golden cup, and then he had a drink, and another one. Accidentally, she touched his arm. It felt like fire. Cāndo would have given anything to embrace her. That, however, was impossible. The alcove was open, and people would have noticed. So he grinned like an oily leech, and when the servants came round to bring more drinks and sweets, he had ordered them to make the Emperor Suite ready. Tonight, Cāndo knew, he wouldn't go home.

And now, with an aching head under the blood red morning sky, he saw black clouds rising and wondered why he was lying in the dirt. He reached into his jacket. His purse was there: evidently, the woman was no thief. He reached for his neck: the scarf was gone. Śiva's present! Another check. Durgā's pouch had disappeared.

Cāndo contorted and his breath went shallow. He would have howled, had he remembered how to howl, and he would have screamed, had he been less controlled. His face turned white and froze; that was it.

Twisted by ache, the merchant king got up. His gait was unsteady, his sight blurred. He would find a palanquin, and he would pay the bearers thrice, so that they kept their mouths shut. He would not scream or worry or curse. Emotions were for lesser beings.

Much later, when he slipped out of the palanquin and faced the grand gate, all hell was going on. Behind the high wall that protected his palace, oily smoke spiralled to the sky. All warehouses were on fire, and his treasure house had burst aflame. Sparks flew to heaven, ashes smudged his face. Cāndo coughed and pressed a few coins into the hands of the bearers and ran. His guards barely managed to catch him. Without their effort, the Merchant King would have darted into the blaze.

"He tore her blouse apart. It almost killed him. I tell you, her tits were brighter than the sun. If you see mangos like that, you simply want to die."

"That's crap, man. What do you know?"

The bazaar scribe was agitated. He was a Kayastha, and hardly anyone believed his tale. Most people called him a crow or a jackal, and that in spite of the fact that he was the highest class a Śūdrā could belong to. The whole world discussed the events of the night. His friend Mustapha, who sold sweet pasties dripping with oil, shook his head. "You know the proverb? A dead Kayastha floated down the river. A crow came close. It said: 'Brother, why do you pretend?'".

"I've got the tale from my good friend Arjun. The storyteller. You know him from the market. And his friend Raj was almost present."

"Almost? Was he or wasn't he?"

"He has the tale from first-hand witnesses. And he would have been there, but he was delayed on the way. His donkey went lame."

"Do you believe everything?"

"Everything? You insult me! It's the truth! Sun and moon, deities of the forest, trees and plants and Yama himself, Lord of the Underworlds: be my witnesses! You call me a liar?"

"Of course I don't. Leave Yama out of this. He can remain where he is. Calm down, my friend. No need to argue or fight. We have known each other for years. The stars in the sky, the moon, the sun, and the planets are the guardians of virtue; they know what happened in the four ages. I believe what you say. Please go on."

"Well, he pulled them out. They gleamed like the peaks of the Snow Mountains, and they were just as large. Cāndo slobbered over them. I could hardly believe it. He pretends to be so rational. Can you imagine what a goat he is? She couldn't get enough. She moaned and squirmed, I tell you, that woman oozed like a waterfall. A man could suffocate in her groin."

"Yes, I agree. Go on!"

"So she opened his sash. He grunted like a pig. And his magick pouch dropped into the pillows. He didn't notice."

"That's typical. The guy has nothing in his head but numbers. And when life grabs him by his balls, he loses control."

"Right. Agni put his underwear on fire. It made his brain shut down."

"Same thing would have happened to us!"

They laughed.

"And then she reached for his pouch and took the scarf from his neck. And this idiot says: 'Thank you, I was getting too hot!'"

More laughter.

"Arjun, the storyteller, says after one night with her a man dies blissfully. And then, of course, she pulled down his pants."

The pastry seller disagreed. "I thought they were in his tavern. People would have watched."

"Agreed. They would have. But let's assume there was nothing worth seeing. She looks at his shrimp and grins. And then she says, 'I need to piss.'"

"Nonsense. A goddess would have used better language."

"Fine. Let's assume she said 'I want to powder my nose'. She strokes his thing, he goes insane with lust, then she gets up, gives him a smile that makes him fight for breath, he thinks his head explodes, and she walks off. Once through the door she calls 'Goodbye, dead rat. I've got your magick power. You'll never be immortal!'"

"What, Cāndo wants to be immortal?"

"Sure. They all do. The richer they get, the more they fear death, 'cause that means giving up everything."

"Really!"

"It's disgusting. So she laughs, 'Cāndo, you are a pile of shit and if I see you again I'll tear off your balls and feed them to the hyenas!'"

"She didn't. That's vulgar."

"Well, maybe not exactly in these words. But she meant it."

"And then?"

"Cāndo leapt up and ran. Or he tried to. His trousers interfered. He fell flat on his face and broke his nose. I swear; it was divine justice."

"You swear?"

"Everybody knows it's true. Arjun told me."

"And next?"

"He staggered outside and saw her taking off! She flew, I tell you!"

"Did Arjun see this too?"

"Not Arjun. It was his friend. Or somebody. Anyway, she was in the air, in an invisible chariot, pulled by six swans. Cāndo tried to grab her. She kicked him in the face. Hard. Cāndo fell backwards and spat. Six teeth gone."

"Six teeth!"

"Everybody knows. And she flew off. To Sij Mountain or wherever. Cāndo remained on the ground. Unconscious. Without trousers. In the middle of the night. Well, some people take advantage. They robbed everything."

"I can imagine. Drop rich, wake as a beggar."

"In the morning, he woke up again. His clothes had disappeared. He was nude, except for his dhoti. And I tell you, that thing was in tatters. One hole next to the other. It had been mended a hundred times!"

"Rich men are mean. Why waste money on underwear?"

"That proves it. And when he came home, on foot, totally worn out, his storehouses were on fire. His residence was in a panic. Everybody screamed and hollered and ran around without aim or sense. And Cāndo was happy, 'cause his wife didn't ask where he was overnight."

"Mine would have asked."

"Sure she would. She's real. But Sonakā? She doesn't understand a thing. She didn't even notice he had lost his teeth."

"I can't believe that. Arjun, or maybe his friend, made it up."

"Arjun would never tell a lie. And Cāndo has a beard. It covers everything."

"Man, you are crazy."

"I swear it is the truth. And I can prove it."

"How?"

"Look at his beard."

"I can't see anything."

"Right!"

You don't get to be the Merchant King without being organised. Cāndo had lost his magick toys and self-esteem, but his trousers, his money and teeth were not on the list.

He retired for a bath. When he came back, he examined the damage and told his scribes to estimate the loss. Meanwhile, he would raise money.

Like so many rich men, Cāndo had no faith in the world. He spent a busy morning exploring the flowerbeds with a shovel, where he unearthed sealed vessels full of golden coins. In a shrine, he had the Śiva statue moved. Underneath, locked in a casket, was a hoard of documents recording contracts and credits. Residing like the emperor of Hindustan in the central hall of his palace, he called in his business associates, fed them sugary snacks and made them pay up. Next, he reduced the wages of his employees. "Of course this is just temporary," he said, "when you work twice as hard and we are out of trouble, your wages might be raised." Those who didn't approve could seek employment elsewhere. Cāndo grinned. Elsewhere did not exist.

In the evening, he called for his six sons. Cāndo sent them travelling all over the Gangetic Plain. They were to visit the small kings and to force them to wipe out all traces of the serpent cult in their puny little dipshit districts.

A few weeks later they returned, and in a splendid mood. The kings had feasted them. Cāndo's sons had drunk and danced and whored, just as they liked, while the kings sent their guards and soldiers through the villages, where they crushed anyone who got in their way, looked remotely like a serpent worshipper or dared to disagree.

Cāndo disapproved of their conduct, and loathed the cheap treasures they had been laden with, but he was glad the job was done. Manasā, as far as he cared, could spend her last days in the Serpent Underworld, starving, while her cult disappeared on earth. Meanwhile, Cāndo's residence was rebuilt. The walls gleamed white, the roofs were freshly tiled, and the gardens sparkled in the sun. The storehouses were larger than before, and goods came in. Business, to be sure, could have been better. But Cāndo always said this sort of thing, and no-one took it seriously.

The merchant king had shown he could recover. Nevertheless, whenever he stalked through the bazaar, accompanied by a few dozen armed guards, people stared and giggled.

"He lost six teeth."

Cāndo snarled. He showed his teeth to everyone. They smiled and bowed. "The things are fake," they said, "they are carved from ivory."

And the sons. News got around. People looked at them and thought, they are young and stupid, and they lack discipline. That's because their father is cursed.

The sons didn't notice. They rarely noticed anything.

"Listen!" Nīlapāṇi, the eldest, had been in a far district, right at the edge to Orissa. "I was in this no-name garbage heap. The king ate from my hand. He was in debt, and had to treat me perfectly. And one evening, I went for a walk. Guess who I met?"

"A woman. She had three tits and two sets of buttocks."

"Shut up. Śūlpāṇi, you bastard, I'm not like you. I met Govardhana."

"The Brahmin's son?"

"Sure, that's him. He was starved and wretched. I hardly recognised him."

"He's always been a loser."

"Don't say so. It's Karman. His father died and left him nothing. I said, 'Hey, let me take you for a meal'. He needed some fat to cheer up.

And he said 'I am sorry, my friend, but I live with my mother. She has prepared a meal for me.'

And I said 'Right, old comrade. I'll come with you.'

He blushed. I thought, it won't be enough for two, and probably awful. But I held back and said, 'Please, for old time's sake. We'll have a meal in a restaurant. I invite you. We'll feast and drink and talk of the old days. What would you like? Catfish in coconut sauce? Lamb with seven spices? Come on; let your mother eat her yuck alone. We'll make it a night!'

'My brother', he said, 'you shame me. My mother is an excellent cook.'

'Then let her eat her excellent meal. We'll go out and feast! It'll be just as in our schooldays. You did my homework, I got you sweets. Come on. We need to talk.'

'No,' he says, 'mother will worry. And she won't eat until I'm home.'"

"I'm not surprised he's starved," said Gayapāṇi." He's still a scholar! You can only be a fat Brahmin when you face reality."

"Maybe that's true. But I pitied him. I said, 'That's fine, you are a good boy. Eat with your mom. But tell me what your mother cooks.'"

"Other people's garbage!" The brothers laughed.

"No, listen to this. It's amazing. He said, 'She takes old, cooked rice. The leftover stuff from last day, or the day before. In the morning, she soaks it in water. Then it can swell during the midday heat. In the night it cools, and the rice ferments. The next evening, it's perfect. It tastes soft and yummy.'"

"Poor people's grub," said Surajāi, "reasonable people would throw it to the dogs."

"No way, Mr. Clever." Nīlapāṇi looked serious. He was the eldest, and they had to listen. "He told me it's a delicacy. You can have it with sour radish slices."

He glared at his brothers. "And I said, 'And that's supposed to be good?' and he grins and says, 'sure, the rice ferments. It's full of alcohol.'"

"That's what he said? Really? He's a Brahmin! He isn't supposed to drink!"

"Ah, allow him his fun. He's a loser. I tried to give him a few coins but he wouldn't have them.

'As a Brahmin, I have my pride,' he said. And I replied, 'You'll end up poor and drunk!'

He went his way. I guess I won't see him again."

"That's how Brahmins are," the brothers laughed, "greater than the gods and hopeless!"

The eldest wasn't finished. In Cāndo's home, alcohol and other drugs were strictly prohibited. He showed a wide grin. "Let's give it a try!"

"What's this?" asked Sonakā, when the eldest got out a large pot, filled with old rice in water.

"A delicacy. I heard about it when I was travelling."

"It's just old rice!" His mother was upset, "and it's beginning to smell."

The brothers tried to keep their faces straight.

Sonakā was upset. "It's garbage! Only the poor eat rot like this!"

"Not the way we prepared it," said Nīlapāṇi. "It's a luxury and we'll enjoy every bite."

"You should get rid of the fluids!" her mother exclaimed.

"The water is the sauce. It's the best part. We just need a few spices."

They took their seats at a low table. Next to each brother, his wife sat. To be sure, the women were not going to participate. As in so many Asian households, the women eat separately from the men, in the kitchen, the dangerous place of the house where few men dare to go.

Custom required the women to attend. Each of them was going to serve her husband.

Their eyes were wide open.

"Go on. We are watching. Astonish us. Have a bite." The women laughed.

"I'll see you throw up!"

"Or on the toilet for the rest of the night!"

"This is good and it's healthy," said Nīlapāṇi, "I have it on the best of scriptural authority."

"It's supposed to raise vigour and other things," agreed Surajāi.

"What a waste! You'll be stiff while you vomit!"

More laughter. "Forget this stuff. We've got real food for you."

Nīlapāṇi, as the eldest brother, had to show authority. It was his idea, and no matter how much the women laughed, he was not going to give in.

He chewed carefully. Then, to demonstrate his approval, he raised his eyebrows, gave a broad grin and twisted his moustache. "It's very aromatic. I love the sauce."

Śūlapāṇi nodded thoughtfully. He was the second eldest and agreed. "Much better than I thought."

"I can feel it makes me happy."

"This stuff has power."

"And it makes you ask for more!"

The brothers held out their bowls and their wives provided a second helping.

"How can you eat this filth?" said the eldest wife.

"It's perfect!"

"Men! What do they understand!"

"You'll be sick!

"You'll twitch and cramp and it'll come out both ways at once!"

"Children!" Sonakā was insistent. "We won't have such talk at the table. If Cāndo were here, he would go mad!"

The sons and their wives collapsed with laughter. No, Cāndo was not here. As usual, he was busy with the accounts, and would be, almost until daybreak.

"I want more!"

Nīlapāṇi was delighted. This stuff was good and the sauce was better. He wasn't used to drinking, and the mildly fermented rice made his head pulse. His brothers had gobbled up their bowls. The taste was strange, juicy, a little fierce, but also sweet and enchanting. They held out their bowls and their wives, laughing, filled them up.

"Don't complain when your stomach dies!"

"Stomach pains?" the youngest brother grinned. "I can live with them, as long as I'm happy. This stuff is deadly. I need more."

"Great," said his wife, "let me poison you. And when you squeak and yowl, don't say I didn't warn you!"

"Right!" the other wives were busy, "go ahead, eat filth and die. You'll see what it does to you!"

Nīlapāṇi had finished his portion. He held out his bowl for more. It wasn't easy, as his hands were cold and clammy.

"This is strange," he tried to say, but his lips were swollen and his tongue was much bigger than before. He groaned, fought for air and collapsed.

The women laughed.

"Didn't we tell you? Do you want some real food?"

"Or a laxative?"

"Get up, eat something real!"

Sonakā frowned. Young people are demanding. They joke all the time, and their manners are deplorable.

The youngest brother tried to speak, and didn't make it. His neighbour twitched, and his face went blue. He fought for breath and vomited. Bowls clattered to the ground. Cāndo's sons twitched like fishes in dry air, they convulsed, grasped, and suffocated.

In the madness that followed, with women screaming for guards and doctors and priests, and eventually, for Cāndo almighty, nobody noticed Neta, in the shape of a black cobra, as she crept out of the hall.

22. Dhanvantari

"Move your legs!"

The voice from the palanquin sounded angry. Here, obviously, someone wasn't in a funny mood. That, of course, is just the moment when some gods have laughing fits. The strange ones, the outsiders, and those who understand Absolute Reality.

The evening sky was darkening and the sorcerer was keen to reach his destination, before Ūrmyā, Goddess Night, had veiled the firmament in black. His invitation did not allow for delays. A former student had sent a message, begging him to attend at once, and Dhanvantari, with a fat smile, was delighted. A man in a hurry, he knew, pays any price. He felt excited. That, of course was counterproductive. I have to slow down. Hurry promotes errors. Let's celebrate leisure. Each moment was to be treasured. Inner peace and detachment, he knew, mean success in bargaining. Provided other people make an effort and accelerate. That's why he made the beads of his meditation necklace move extra slow, and relaxed into each motion.

Outside his palanquin, he heard the hasty running of the bearers, and the panting of his favourite students, as they tried to keep his company.

The famous ohjā had been through a lot. Since that evil day when Manasā shamed him, he had travelled far, and gained more power. He had prayed at sacred sites, had visited crazy people in remote mountain ranges, where ordinary travellers are taken as slaves or have their heads chopped off; he had studied sorceries in Afghanistan, Nepal, Bhutan, Tibet, Mongolia and the mountains of Yunnan and Sichuan, where serpent sorcery is an everyday affair. He had traversed India and spent years in Lanka, that weird island in the Deep South, where the forest goddesses yank out the guts of lone travellers and hang them up from trees. Dhanvantari was powerful and cunning and his guts remained where they were.

Wherever Dhanvantari travelled, he questioned the crazy ones, and those who were inspired and obsessed. He learned what he could, no matter if his teacher was a withering elder or a wild, inspired child. Nobody dared to stand in his way. Dhanvantari knew a lot, and delighted, more than anything, in countering the effects of serpent bites and snake sorceries. No matter which snake, what poison, or how old or weak a patient was, Dhanvantari scored. He wallowed in his god-like reputation, and his price went to the sky.

The sorcerer moved the curtain and gazed out of the palanquin. The heavens turned crimson, well, that was a good sign; the weather would be excellent tomorrow.

A falcon screamed. Dhanvantari hardly noticed. He watched his bearers, strong, bull-like individuals, with far more muscles than brains, whom he had acquired near the cattle market. They had to be strong; his palanquin was made of heavy timbers; it was gilded and encrusted with jewels. His students lagged behind. Weaklings, he thought, a little running and you faint! Why am I cursed with worthless imbeciles!

The falcon screamed again. Dhanvantari looked up. It hovered in the west, where the sun was sinking in a sea of bloody glory.

The falcon screeched "Go back!"

The sorcerer showed his teeth. He had almost reached his destination. This business proposal, he knew, was special.

He pointed at the bird. "Go away! What do you understand?"

The bird shook. "Turn around! Your sun is dying!"

"Go home, little falcon, or I will scorch your wings."

Dhanvantari sank back into his pillows. The falcon, he knew, wasn't real. At this time of the evening, true falcons are perched on trees, ready to sleep. He smiled. Cāndo had called him. His former student, the richest man in East Asia.

The palanquin stopped. The guards ran to announce the arrival of the visitor. They need not have bothered: Cāndo had been watching from a window, and came to meet his guest. The sorcerer stretched his legs, twisted his back and yawned. In all leisure, he examined the property. The gate was plain, but the wall was extra high, and behind the boundary, mighty buildings showed freshly gleaming tiles and pretty whitewashed walls. All of it breathed a spirit of newness.

He watched his host and could have laughed. Cāndo obviously felt like running, but knew that every hint of eagerness would show up on the bill. Dhanvantari took his time; he advanced, his head held high, and smiled. He almost stepped into cow shit.

Right, there was a cow grazing next to the wall. The sorcerer frowned. The bovine looked far too healthy. Generally, holy cows are as generously padded as anorectic supermodels, with bones sticking out to all sides. This one looked like it had had its beauty sleep, its nails done, and was now having the biggest buffet in the universe.

But before he could examine the matter, Cāndo bent and tried to touch the sorcerer's feet.

Dhanvantari did what all well-raised people do: they acknowledge the total submission of their inferiors, stop them as they get down, pull them up and pretend that in this perfect world, all men are equal.

"Cāndo!" he exclaimed. "My favourite student."

"Come in, guru, feel welcome."

Dhanvantari allowed himself to be pushed along. The doors were wide open, there were guards with torches everywhere, and once inside the main palace, there were gold and glamour and bright lights, and thick carpets, and embroidered tapestries, and silver statues, and choice sculptures in rare woods. "My dear friend," he smiled, "I never knew you were so rich!"

"None of this is really mine," exclaimed Cāndo.

"But look at this," said Dhanvantari and pointed at the pillars, finely cut from foreign stone, carved with scenes from the *Mahābhārata* and inlaid with precious stones. "Your taste has improved."

"I do not care for these things. They please my wife. You know me; my desire is spiritual wealth. I live in poverty. Alas, my family does not. I merely keep this rubbish to impress our guests."

"Śiva has been kind to you."

"Thanks to the mantras which you taught me."

"When was that, thirty, forty years ago?"

"Time stops for no one. But you, guru, remain strong and youthful."

The sorcerer showed a half smile. Go on, little dog, flatter me.

"Sorcerer," said Cāndo, "these are my sons."

Dhanvantari examined them with interest. A neural poison, obviously. They suffocated when their lungs stopped moving. And their wives, who wept and screamed like furies. The woman in the centre must have been a great beauty in her youth. Now, the first grey hairs appeared. Unlike the wives, her tears ran in silence.

"Stop howling!" Cāndo shouted. "Get out of here, we have a guest!"

The woman rose and faced Cāndo. "You insulted the snake goddess! You could have worshipped her. But no, you were so proud, you were so right, and now our sons are dead!"

"Wife! Our visitor demands respect."

"And I don't? I should have known you have no heart!"

She tried to strike him. Cāndo caught her fists and called for the guards. "Escort her to her chambers. And get these girls out! My guest and I need silence!"

The merchant king turned. "Women. They have no sense."

"You murdered them!" Sonakā screeched, as she was dragged away.

"My guru, forgive the offence."

"Student, there is nothing to forgive. I can see you need a miracle."

"They were good boys. I lost them all at once."

His face twisted, but no, the Merchant King would not be seen in tears. His voice quavered. "I wasn't there when they needed me."

He faced his teacher. "What killed them?"

"Cobra toxin."

"A cobra bit all six?"

"There are no bite marks. Their death came in their meal."

Dhanvantari placed a hand on Cāndo's head. "You are lucky, son. They haven't been dead for long. It's evening; the air is cool, and decay has only just begun. I will try to make them come alive."

The trader wiped his face. "What will it cost?"

"My friend, how much are they worth to you?"

Cāndo's hands turned to fists.

Dhanvantari showed his teeth. "Let's talk about this in comfort. I have hardly arrived."

"Guru!" Cāndo also tried a smile, but it didn't work. "The women are upset. Revive my sons, and we can talk about the price."

"My student!" Dhanvantari appeared delighted. "We are grown men; we fear naught but the gods. And we have time enough. Why should we care about sentimental girls?"

"I am obliged to my wife. She is a virtuous woman. She, and the wives of my sons, should be released from their anguish."

"Dear friend." Dhanvantari pulled out his meditation beads. "We shouldn't quarrel about money. I am a guest in your hall and I see your wealth. You are an affluent and powerful man. Unlike you, I have no children, and I am poor. Make an offer that suits your station in life."

"Guru! My prince, my land-owner. Why should we bargain, when this could be a deed of friendship?"

"Like you, o Merchant King, I own nothing. I have to feed my students. I live in a shed, and the rain comes through the roof. Times have changed. Nowadays, people are greedy. They don't understand the value of life. Believe me, whenever I see a patient, there are people who try to bargain." Dhanvantari raised his hands. "I hardly have the money for a hand full of rice."

"My lord!" Cāndo was insistent. "Let me call for food. You will receive the finest delicacies. But honestly, you are a spiritual man. How could I insult you with money, when your greatest reward is the blessing of the gods?"

"Food comes and goes. The next day, hunger returns. You are the greatest trader in the world. Why should you worry about a few rupees?"

"In Śiva's name, lord guru, you are my father and my mother. Forget this talk of money: show your generosity. The lord of the gods will reward you beyond your wildest dreams."

"How could he? Śiva is poor, just like me. He has no copper coins in his pouch; he cannot afford a decent set of clothes. My dear Cāndo, so many good people die at the wayside. I see six splendid boys, killed by a cobra's venom, and only I can make them live again."

"Guru, you are a master of all snakes. You crush these worms, you destroy their spawn, and you annul their evil sorceries."

"My student, it is true. The Nāga folk are like maggots under my sandals. I can annihilate them anytime. Even Manasā, the serpent-bitch, cannot stand against my mantras. But great power is not gained easily. The expense was high, the effort immense. So speak up, Cāndo, what do you offer?"

The sorcerer walked to the divan and sank into the pillows. From his bag, he produced a magical pouch and a victory scarf. "See these. Brahmā the creator gave them to me. I gained them when I presented the elixir of immortality to the gods. He was deeply grateful. Without my effort, the gods would have faded away. I am sure you heard the tale. It happened many centuries ago, but, as you say, what is time?"

Cāndo stared at them. The pouch bulged with energy and the victory scarf gleamed with divine lustre. Cautiously, he took them. They were much finer than the items he had received from Śiva and Durgā. How could this be? His favourite deities were much stronger than Brahmā.

Dhanvantari raised a hand, as if to grant a blessing. "My dear, dear student. Show your wisdom. You are a spiritual man. Both of us know: money is just a delusion. It has no value, and it makes people mad. Your sons, however, are your future. They are rotting. Slowly and inevitably, their flesh putrefies, and by tomorrow, they will begin to smell. Consider what they are worth, but do not think too long."

Dhanvantari stroked his beard. Sooner or later, Cāndo would give in. "Yama Death-Lord might arrive any moment, and demand their souls."

The sorcerer pushed himself into the cushions and sank back in relief.

"Ouch!"

His face went red, then white; he leaned sideways, choked and collapsed.

"Hear the great tale of King Vikram and the Corpse!" Arjun, the storyteller, sat in a corner of the marketplace. Behind him was the city wall, before him an empty bowl. The first customers had arrived. The storyteller grinned at his audience.

His customers weren't so excited. "We know the tale. You've been telling it for years."

"My friends!" Arjun was not going to apologise. "What do you expect? My story gets better all the time."

"We want no fairy tales. Tell us about the death of Dhanvantari!"

Arjun lifted his hands. "I loathe all fairy tales. Everything I tell is true."

He pointed at his bowl. "I know the truth, as if I had been there."

"What happened in the night?"

"A little contribution might be helpful."

A few copper coins clattered into the bowl.

"Attend my friends. Come close and listen:

Dhanvantari was a tall man, and he was fat. On Cāndo's divan, he met his fate.

The small, toxic snake Udyakāl had slept underneath the pillows. His weight almost crushed her. She bit the saintly Dhanvantari and filled his ass with fire. You or I would have died instantly. But Dhanvantari was a mighty sorcerer. Brahma, the Creator, had given him a pouch and a victory scarf. The mighty goddess Neta, great is her name, had taught him serpent spells. Śiva had granted him visions and insights. He fought the queen of serpents, the terrifying Manasā, and he came out of the struggle alive, and much wiser than before."

The storyteller tilted his head. "Manasā is the Great Queen, the daughter of Śiva and the greatest goddess of Bengal. You know this and so do I. Alas, Cāndo, the merchant, did not. He was too proud, too vain, too greedy. And Dhanvantari, in his madness, failed to respect her. It was his error, and his doom."

The audience nodded. Yes, disrespecting the gods was a short road to annihilation.

"And now there was Dhanvantari, half dead and half alive, and he faded fast. He shook, his face was wet and his breath laboured. 'Get Dhanā and Manā', he groaned. His students came and when they saw their guru, they began to weep. The sorcerer whispered, 'Fast, go out, and gather healing herbs.'

Dhanā and Manā rushed out of Cāndo's residence, accompanied by guards with torches, but no matter where the apprentices looked, no healing herb was found. And, let me reveal a secret, right next to the wall grazed a cow. She was so great and strapping that she almost gleamed. That, you must understand, was the wise Neta. She had eaten all miraculous herbs and she felt wonderful.

Listen! I tell the truth! The cow laughed. And then it disappeared."

The storyteller leaned back and got out his prayer beads.

"How did the story go on?"

"Ah, my friends. It is a long story. You will be amazed. But first," he gestured to his bowl. More coins clattered.

"Good, very good. I will relate what happened.

The apprentices ran to their master. Alas, Dhanvantari was so weak he could hardly move his lips. 'Listen,' he whispered, 'far away, on the Gandhamādan Hill, grows the Śali-Biśāli herb. Run as fast as the swallow flies, and bring it to me.'

The apprentices ran. Ah, how their feet pounded the dust, how their lungs laboured, how their bellies stung. Finally, they reached the hill. They plucked the wort and bound it. Then they ran back. Their legs trembled and their breath wheezed. But the night air, I tell you, was fresh and the moon was wonderful. In the middle of the road stood a woman. She shone in the moonlight and the apprentices recognised her: it was Kamalā, the wife of their guru. Both of them dropped to the ground and touched her feet. The wife of the guru, as everyone knows, except for the spoiled kids of our wicked age, is the goddess herself. Dhanā and Manā bowed, and pounded their brows into the dust. Kamalā, they knew, was an enlightened lady. She must have known what happened, for her lotus face was sad and tears ran over her cheeks like a waterfall. "My boys," she wept, "you are too late. My husband is dead. The gods say that his fate caught up with him.' She sobbed, and clawed her face, she pounded her breasts and tore out her hair; for this, my dear friends, is how a virtuous wife reacts when she hears that her god, her husband, is no more.

Dhanā and Manā howled with despair. It was their mistake! Had they run faster, they might have saved their benefactor. They wailed and threw the herb into the ditch; they rent their clothes and walked away in tears.

Alas, the world is cruel. Kamalā, the lotus-faced disappeared. In her stead stood a radiant cow. It gobbled up the sacred herb."

"Go on, continue!"

"My friends. I am an old man who lives by his words. It is no easy skill. My head is like a dungeon, and I am bound by truth. All day I hammer at my story! Each word is true, I tell you, but will that feed me, clothe me, and make me happy?"

More coins clattered. Arjun smiled and continued.

"When Dhanā and Manā reached Cāndo's residence, Dhanvantari was almost paralysed. He could barely move his tongue. 'If you respect my teachings, get me the panacea. It's the foam of the Milk Ocean. That's where it all began.'

His head fell back.

Dhanā and Manā were coated in dust and sweat. Their limbs trembled and their throats were parched. The Milk Ocean was far away, on the other side of the universe. But a student has to give everything for his teacher.

They ran.

When they reached the Milk Ocean, they were close to death. They collapsed at the shore and where the pale fluids surged against the beach. The gleaming foam crept up to them. They grabbed as much as they could hold.

That instant, I tell you, the night lit up. A pale light flared across the dunes, and before them stood Maheśvara, the Ruler of the World, the Great and Eternal Śiva. Conch shell trumpets sounded and the earth trembled. Ah, you should have seen his beauty! His brow was high, his eyes compassionate. He was pale like clouds, like bone, like jasmine blossoms!

The apprentices knelt in awe.

"Dhanā and Manā, you tried to save your master. With your puny, mortal strength you ran, and gave your best. Alas, the mighty Dhanvantari is dead. The gods forgive you. He was the greatest serpent sorcerer who ever lived, and my special favourite. Right now, they are raising his pyre."

Dhanā and Manā sat like stones. The sacred foam trickled through their fingers.

"Bodies come and go. The life essence remains. He was the greatest healer of our time. His star sank. Now yours can rise. There is much to gain. Who will replace him?"

Dhanā and Manā dropped the foam and ran. My friends! This is young people. They think that speed improves everything. But life is learning and endurance. Both apprentices had the same thought. Whoever won the race to Dhanvantari's home would get the treasures of the guru.

They ran. They ran like men, like beasts, like hungry ghosts. Their feet were bruised, their legs were scarred, they hurled themselves along the dirty, dusty path, until their lungs pumped fire. Finally, the stars paled, the rosy hues of Uṣas, Lady Dawn shone from the east, but what have you, they were not wise enough to marvel at their beauty. At a street crossing, they collapsed. They gasped and retched, they tried to calm their jittery legs.

The serpents had been waiting.

Dhanā and Manā died before the sun was up."

The storyteller rubbed his hands. "The world of the gods is full of miracles. In truth, it was Manasā herself, who appeared as Śiva."

"Don't mention her," said a fisherman. "Cāndo's spies are everywhere."

"What do I care about spies?" said the storyteller. "A merchant cannot outlaw Śiva's daughter."

He raised himself. "It's time to have a meal."

"No, stay! We want to hear how it ended!"

"Ah, my friends. Forgive me. How can I speak? My stomach is as empty as my bowl."

More coins fell.

Arjun, the storyteller, settled down. His eyes gleamed with delight.

"By Sarasvatī, you are insatiable. But let us continue. You ask for the ending. Let me reveal a secret of the gods: there is no ending. Tales have no beginning nor do they ever end. Everything continues, it comes and goes and reappears. It is just simple humans, like you and me, who think we can cut the flow of events into bite-sized pieces. The stream of stories is eternal, it is a tangle, a weaving of waterways, and it continues through all ages and all worlds, forever.

Behold! Dhanvantari felt that his end was near. He groaned, and Cāndo leaned over him, to hear the last words of his master.

'Cāndo! My true disciple." He hissed, 'here is my last gift for you. I will protect your residence against all serpent spells. You must do what I command, and you may not defy me.'

'Master, I will,' said Cāndo, and his eyes were moist.

'When I am dead, you shall not burn my corpse. Nor shall you put it on a banana stalk raft and send it down the river. Cut my body into eight pieces and bury them around your home, in the directions of the compass. My magic will keep you safe.'

Cāndo recoiled. 'My lord, I cannot do it. We are faithful Hindus! The sin would pollute us forever.'

Dhanvantari groaned and died. The house-priest approached. 'We will do what tradition demands. He has died of snakebite, so we will send him down the river.'

In the early morning light, the corpse was carried to the embankment. Over the last hours, Cāndo's men had cut banana trees, and built a raft from them. They wrapped the corpse in silks. Cāndo held Dhanvantari's pouch and victory scarf. He bowed, and placed them on the sorcerer's chest.

'Farewell, my teacher,' he said. 'In another life, we will meet again.'

The house-priest recited a hymn, and the raft was released. The current took the raft, turned it around, and accelerated. Dhanvantari, the greatest serpent sorcerer of all times, travelled past the burning ghāts, drifted past gardens and plantations, rounded a river bent and was swallowed up by the fog.

Cāndo returned to his residence. More rafts had to be prepared.

But Dhanvantari wasn't fully dead. Those who die of serpent toxin may retain awareness. Sure, the bodies are just as dead as any other piece of carrion. But life remains, and watches. Dhanvantari saw the great city Campaka fading in the morning mist. He looked down at himself and wondered how it could have happened. Now, after dying, the world appeared twice as beautiful. He saw women collecting water from the stream, saw men taking a morning bath and watched the troops of monkeys as they quarrelled. A crane took to wing; a new day had begun, but it wasn't going to be his. Dhanvantari could hardly take his eyes from all the glamour. Then he noticed the woman. She stood on the raft, next to him, and she was almost nude.

'Lady,' Dhanvantari sighed, and would have kneeled, had his body allowed it. 'I regret my greed. I regret my hate.'

'I forgive you,' said Manasā, 'all those years, you deluded yourself. But look at this. It's the snake Udyakāl. She killed you, and now she will protect you. Follow the river and meet me at the Dark Waters. It's close to Sij Mountain.' The goddess smiled. 'In your next life, you will be the serpent king Rājasarpa. From time to time, you may be my necklace, provided you behave.'

Sonakā wept and screamed all day. In his despair, Cāndo had tried to make her see reason. "You are young, wife! Stop howling! You can easily have another six sons!"

Cāndo retired to his office. It was bad enough to hear her in the distance. It was worse when she grew quiet.

Now, long after the stars had appeared, he lay on a couch in his office. Sleep evaded him. He rolled from one side to the other, cursed the hot, moist air, and tried to shut his brain off.

Like a warm breeze, a woman emerged from the shadows.

Manasā. The whore looked hungry. Her eyes were wild and her hair tangled. Her pelvis showed a large hematoma.

'You piece of filth!' Cāndo tried to raise himself, but his body wouldn't move.

'Stay still!' hissed the goddess. 'You fool! You are asleep and think you are awake!'

She stepped closer and seized his head. 'Your guards rape and loot; they torture my people! I'd love to break your neck. Or I could chew your face; it would swell like a gourd and turn blue. Or I could bite your calf. No poison, just an infection, straight into the bloodstream, enough to make your flesh rot. Your doctors would come. They would saw off parts of your leg. But the gangrene would continue. It would climb up your leg. And they would cut off more. Bit by bit, you would die. Imagine that.' The goddess smiled. 'It might take weeks.'

She slapped Cāndo's head. 'My father says you deserve a last chance. Perform a pūjā. Make a few offerings. Say something nice and accept me as I am.'

Cāndo tried to curse. His mouth didn't work.

The serpent goddess tweaked his cheek. 'Just give me a sign of your friendship, and I'll revive your sons.' She grinned at him. 'And now you may speak.'

'You won't break me, slut!'

Cāndo woke. The grey light illuminated his office. His face was wet with sweat. The night had been bad, but the day would be worse."

Arjun, the storyteller, smiled at his audience.

"That's it, folks!" He rose. "It's the truth. But the story goes on. We are all part of it. Come again tomorrow, and I'll tell you the adventures of King Vikram, who carried a corpse through the jungle all night."

His audience scattered. Arjun smoked his pipe until they were gone. He rolled up his carpet and walked, leisurely, along the edge of the marketplace. He passed through an arch and disappeared. On the other side appeared a girl, clad in bright red, whose three bunches bounced. She dropped a handful of coins into the bowl of a beggar woman and descended to the river, singing happily.

Picture 13: "We worship Manasā."

23. Journey to Anupāma Pāṭana

One night, when Cāndo was tossing around on the bed in his office, the room lit up.

Before the merchant king, Śiva appeared in all his glory.

Cāndo dropped to his knees. The Lord of Ascetics granted him a benign smile and touched his head to bless him. "My son!"

"My lord." Cāndo bent over and wept. The tears ran down his cheeks. "Forgive my errors. Forgive my sins. How can I serve you? My heart is troubled. Sonakā is a good wife but she grants me no rest. She is a woman, and her heart is closer to her sons than mine. I understand, and I forgive her. And I forgive my daughters-in-law. Some say, they should have been burned with the corpses of their husbands. I disagree; the custom is old and evil. They shall live and comfort Sonakā."

"Dear Cāndo. My worshipper. You, too will be forgiven, when you forgive."

"My Lord as White as Jasmine. How can I thank you?"

"Be kind. I will grant a wish to you."

"Kill the serpent whore!"

Śiva's face darkened. "Am I your henchman, you imbecile?"

Cāndo stooped. His face was a mask of cramp and despair. He shook his head. "I can't take it anymore."

"You don't have to. Prepare for a journey. You are rich enough to equip a fleet. I order you to travel down the river, along Gaṅgā, and thence across the open sea."

"Lord, this is far."

"The further you go, the more value has your cargo. Sonakā will have time to calm down."

The merchant agreed. "I have heard that there are great opportunities in Anupāma Pāṭana."

"Ah, Cāndo, I like what you say. Few traders have gone that far. Anupāma Pāṭana is the *Unique Harbour*. Much, that has little value hereabouts, has never been seen there."

"It is said, that the city is on an enchanted island."

"Send your people into the forest. Let them cut a hundred woods. Set mana-pabana wood into the keels of your ships. It's magical, and it will know the way. Steer south, and I will send good winds. A few days across the open sea and you will reach the Unique Harbour."

Cāndo had clear ideas about time and space. Both were measured in profit. The people of Campaka were watching him. They gossiped, they frowned and some were gleeful. It would be easy, he thought, to build a fleet. But this one would be marvellous. His journey had to be an overwhelming success. So, grinding his teeth, he decided to do the job with pomp and great expense.

Next morning, he had the astrologer in his office. The man was slightly shaken, as the sun was barely rising, and you hate to get up early when you spend most of the night watching stars, making calculations, keeping records and stuffing yourself with sweets.

"I need several dates," said Cāndo, "and you'll ensure they happen fast. First, a date to begin the cutting of the trees. No, we won't cut much. Fresh wood is of little value. It's just that I have to use one hundred sorts. My agent will get the rest from the lumber yards. I want an auspicious start."

The astrologer nodded agreement. He was neither the first nor last star-gazer in Cāndo's employ.

"Next, a date to complete the fleet. There will be a ceremony, and the carpenters will have a feast. Last, the day of my departure. When I come back, you'll be paid. Depending on how your predictions turn out."

A few days later, the carpenters and woodcutters departed for the forest. They were accompanied by Cāndo's house priest. The man knew everything about money, and made them hurry. In the heart of the jungle, the priest conducted a passionate (if cheap) ritual to make the forest spirits, the Yakṣas and the Yakṣīs happy, and sang the Vedic hymn to Araṇyā, the Goddess of the Forest. More important were the local deities. The priest arranged an altar for the Bengal forest goddess Banbibi, who likes rice, fruit, vegetables, flowers and sweets, and protects her worshippers from tigers. Next, there was a brief ceremony for the Muslims. According to their faith, it is Dakṣiṇ Rai, the tiger rider, who rules the wilderness. His favourite offering is music; Cāndo's drummers did their best and the woodcutters walked through smoke to protect themselves. Finally, the priest made offerings to Brahmā, for it is auspicious to remember the Lord of Creation when a new project is undertaken. The group marched through undergrowth and thicket until they found a sacred mana-pabana tree. More offerings followed, the woodcutters went to work and before long the trunk was carried to the wharf. Meanwhile, Cāndo's accountants ordered seasoned wood of a hundred types.

The Merchant King hurried through his warehouses. Much, indeed, had been lost in the fire, but just as much was being prepared to make the journey a success. His accountants ran along. "Pack everything valuable!" demanded their lord. "We need diversity!"

His accountants composed lists and gave orders. While the ships grew, the goods were sealed in sacks and chests. The range was stunning, and the poets who composed their versions of the *Manasā Epic* couldn't get enough of them. As my version is brief, concise and to the point, I shall only mention that spices, perfumes, tea, poppy seeds, pure opium, best hemp and Chinese silk were weighed, and sewn into waterproof bundles. These, of course, were just the basics. Cāndo had dreams and ambitions. He called for choice ivory, plain and carved, for sacks full of jewels and diamonds, for rare nuts, roots and fruit, and any culinary delicacy he could think of. Less profitable, but essential, was the provision for the crew. He needed food and water, writing materials, and a large assortment of clothes, ornaments and weapons. From dawn to dusk his agents scoured the markets, went travelling, and returned with valuables. They rarely had to pay: Cāndo forced the traders to make up for what they owed him. The ships grew, were completed, set into the water and loaded to the rim. Cāndo had decided on five mighty freighters, and a flagship, Madhukar (the *Bee*), each of them ornamented, painted and decorated with bright colours and flower garlands. His accountants selected the crew. Each sailor was young, muscular and well versed in the fighting arts. Indeed, a lot of them were former pirates. They were equipped with helmet and armour, with round shields, short sabres, bows and arrows. He even loaded a keg or arrow poison.

"My lord," said the captain, "poisoned arrows are against the *Laws of Manu*. We are peaceful traders."

Cāndo showed his teeth. "In Vedic times, poisoned arrows were praised. The Ārya were realists. How real are you?"

"I'm your captain."

"I hope it stays that way."

"More blossoms!" The ships were almost ready. The wood was carved, oiled, or painted, and here and there sacred timbers gleamed. The citizen assembled, they laughed and talked, as they ate sticky sweets and cheered the sailors. This was the major event: the almighty Cāndo was about to embark on a journey like there had never been before. First, the sailors appeared, each of them in shiny armour, paraded to the quay and boarded the ships. Next followed the captains, in finest costume; they were accompanied by their families, who remained behind and wept. Last, gleaming like a peacock, appeared Cāndo. He took his time. In his company were secretaries and scribes, some of whom would travel with him, while others were taking down orders to ensure sound business at home. Sonakā appeared, in gold and gleaming orange, and in her company were her daughters-in-law. Like all widows, they wore plain white and no special ornaments. The white, however, was finest silk. As far as widows go, these looked wealthy and exceptionally well fed.

Cāndo, of course, was in a terrible mood. His employees, he knew, would make a mess of everything. His accountants would embezzle funds. The servants would laze, the gardeners sleep, the bookkeepers neglect to check each document thrice. His wife and daughters-in-law would waste money. And hardly anyone would understand discipline and order. Nevertheless, his road was set. His journey would have epic proportions. He would visit lands that were almost unknown and return with so much wealth that all of Asia would bow to him.

Sonakā wept. He couldn't bear it.

Soon his fleet was gliding along the settlements, and past them, through a landscape of rich fields and fertile plantations. Above them circled a vulture. Cāndo stared at it. The bird followed them, as they rounded the river bent, where the fields stopped and the jungle began. The trees were high, monkeys chattered and the sunlight disappeared.

The journey was slow. Each evening, the ships had to find a place to rest. Sometimes it was a village, a town or just as sandbank. His crew was on the lookout. Whenever Cāndo strode from on-board, he insisted on a fire sacrifice, and conducted it personally.

A few weeks later, their river met the Ganges. Cāndo insisted on a major ritual. Gaṅgā, as the first wife of Śiva, was important. His agents bought goats, fruits and vegetables at a village. There was no need to waste trade goods. During the next weeks, the fleet travelled through the Gangetic Plain. The land was even, the rice fields endless. Here and there a settlement rose: you could see palms and mangoes, bananas and tamarisks, there were small huts with woven walls for the poor and whitewashed houses for the wealthy. One village followed the other. In between, there was forest, deep and dark, with dangerous animals whose calls echoed through the night. As ever, Cāndo insisted on well-armed guards. To encourage his crew, he, himself, wore a curved sword. The thing was more symbolic than useful, badly balanced and encrusted with jewels that were, in his opinion, useless and overdone.

The further they came, the stranger were the villagers. Finally, Mother Gaṅgā and the Brahmaputra fused. The open expanse of the rivers was as wide as an inland sea. The brown, muddy flood had travelled more than a thousand kilometres from the Himalayas, and from the weird mountains near China. These rivers had seen it all; they were quiet and steady, and the sailors remained relaxed but watchful. Soon, they would reach the Gulf of Bengal. By now, the water was rich in salt. Most plants gave up and withered, but in their stead, the mangrove forests throbbed with life. The ships took on pilots, as the waterways, close to the ocean, keep shifting with each flood. Huge masses of water, muddy with nourishment, arrived from distant mountain chains and struggled with the bitter, salty floods swept inland from the ocean. In between was a forest unlike anything. In flood, the mangrove stalks were widely under water. Their extra roots rose like spikes and allowed the trees to breathe. When the flood ebbed, there were mud and sand, and millions of scuttling crabs, each equipped with one huge pincer and a much smaller one, racing between the roots, and climbing trees. The scenery transformed every few hours. The crew espied lonely tigers, swimming from one mud bank to the other, and honey collectors and fishermen who wore masks on the back of their heads. As everybody knows, a tiger will always try to get you from behind: if you face it, it may go away. Or it may not. Some sailors swore they had seen leeches as thick as your arms, black, smooth and shiny. The ships drifted through forests that were dry land one moment and underwater a few hours later. The pilots smoked their pipes, fingered their amulets and tried to express confidence, but their faces were hard and their eyes restless. The shores were full of crocodiles, relaxing in the sunshine, their mouths open, and their teeth shiny.

"They are gavials, my lord," said the captain, and pointed at lizards, which, at six metres length, seemed truly formidable. Their snouts were slim and ended in a bulge. "Ugly but harmless. They only go for fish."

The man grinned. "Their jaws are like pliers. Thin and fast, hardly any resistance in water, and plenty of teeth."

"What about those?" Cāndo pointed at reptiles with broad snouts.

"They are trouble. They grow bigger than gavials. Some weigh as much as ten, fifteen men."

"Would they attack us?"

"Sure. If we tried to swim. They take on anything, as long as it struggles. Even pythons. You should like them."

Cāndo did not. He loathed the captain's lack of manners. The man was repulsively common. He turned and tried to ease his aching back. When, a few hours later, they saw Gangetic dolphins leaping, he had an offering prepared. Mother Gaṅgā's favourites would bless his journey.

Finally, they reached the open sea. The merchant king stared at water birds whose calls echoed like lost souls. There was no way of going back. Evenings would not end with a relaxed fire at a friendly shore. The great rolling waves extended forever, the ships rocked, the breeze was full of salt and he felt queasy. They had reached the point where most Indian sailors give up and go home. "We have come to the limit," said his captain, "out here, there are only fishes. And saltwater crocodiles. They travel to the furthest islands. Just like us."

"See the cloud over there?"

Cāndo squinted. The sun was bright and the sea sparkled. He nodded. A cloud. True. Close to the horizon. Apart from it, there was just water.

"It's rising from the flank of a mountain. There's an island, just beyond the horizon. In a few hours we'll get a better look."

Cāndo glanced at his captain. The man had better be right. He turned to the officers. "Get your armour ready, sharpen the blades, and prepare the arrows. We'll reach an island soon, and I hate surprises."

He turned to the captain. "So far, you were good at your job."

"My lord, we have not reached safe harbour yet. It will be a foreign country. Who knows what expects us?"

"The glory of the gods, my friend." Cāndo felt like reborn. "You can count on it."

"Welcome, noble lords", said the paunchy official with the henna-coloured moustache. The man was wrapped in costly textiles, wore a large turban and gleamed with sweat. "You, my dear guests, come from far away. My name is Muślahatu. I am, if I may say so, a humble servant of my people. Truth to tell, we are not used to visitors. But we will make you feel at home. It's rare that merchants reach the Unique Harbour. You will feel at home. And I trust you will never forget your stay."

"We have heard a lot about you." The captain offered a tiny smile.

"Much of it lies, I am sure. But you will learn our island is far better than you imagined." The official groomed his moustache. His silk, emerald and pale pink, Cāndo thought, is disgusting. He prances like a bloated flamingo!

The captain was serious. "Our lord is King Cāndo, the mightiest man in the world. I am sure you heard of him."

"My apologies," said the official, "we are far from everyone. News is rare and often questionable. I express my regret, but we have never heard of anyone named Cāndo. Nevertheless, we welcome you."

"Lord Cāndo," said the captain "has expressed his desire to trade with your country."

"Oh, sure," said the official, and his face radiated friendliness like an oily morning sun, "I am sure you are wonderful people. We are happy to receive you."

His turban was graced with a ruby larger than a walnut, and his fat fingers gleamed with golden rings.

"Come ashore and be our guests. The harbour is closely watched, no-one will dare to touch your cargo."

I'm sure of it, thought Cāndo. Any intruder will be chopped to pieces.

The official raised an eyebrow. "Please do not mistrust us."

"We are cautious. That's all. And no honest man can blame us." The captain showed a winning smile.

"Noble visitors, we despise thieves. Come ashore. I will show you the city and make you feel at home."

"We will take a small detachment of guards. It will do our sailors good to stretch their legs."

The captain raised a hand and from each ship a group of elite fighters emerged. They were clean and shaved and their armour was hidden under jackets.

Cāndo followed the captain, across the gangway, to the quay, where large stalls were stocked with goods. He stopped, as did his troop. The Merchant King scrutinised his surroundings, and in his head, commodities were valued, numbers blurred and jumped through hoops, and settled down to make themselves at home. Wherever he gazed, he saw wealth. It was dazzling, exhilarating and scary. These people were rich beyond belief! The fishers, squatting near their tiny boats, smoked silver water pipes and wore bracelets of gold, set with pure emerald. The women passing the fruit stands looked as if they wore the wealth of entire districts on their wrists. Even tiny children were clad in jewels and pearls and blue lapis lazuli, sure to come one hell of a long way from far Afghanistan! The Merchant King took his time. He paused, pretended to be ailing, and leaned on his staff. Before him men and women offered foodstuff. They seemed unnaturally happy, and well-fed, and healthy. He ignored their goods and focussed on what was missing: there were no spices anywhere.

Cāndo repressed a grin. He would make them pay until their purses shrivelled, they would indebt themselves, and they would scream for more.

His captain whispered. "Lord, no one is wearing weapons".

The merchant King nodded. That would make it so much easier.

The official led them up the hill. The streets were clean, the doors wide open and all windows were graced with flower pots.

"Take me to your king," Cāndo wheezed. "And I will offer luxuries he has never seen before."

The official stopped. "My lord," he said, "Please let me enlighten you. There is no king on our island."

"No king?"

"We have heard of kings, my venerable guest. We are not totally removed from the world. It sounds like an astonishing custom. I am sure that many countries enjoy this sort of thing. But we never needed any." The official laughed.

"Then take me to your highest priest!"

The official bowed his head. "I apologise. We have none. Worship is conducted in many different ways."

"Are you making fun of me?" Cāndo was in a rage. "Are you governed by a queen?"

"Oh no. We do without regents."

"Don't take me for a fool! Someone has to govern. Is it an assembly? A community of businessmen? Tell me, do you believe in the gods?"

"Our people believe in many gods. Above all, we believe in the serpent goddess Manasā."

"Manasā!"

"She is the Light of the World, the Flame of the Sacrificial Fire, and the Laughter of the Sun on the Waves. The gulls praise her name, the dolphins jump to celebrate her joy. She gives us salt, to make our food delicious and to preserve our meat, she grants us happiness, and wealth, and free breath, and joy of life."

"I'm glad I came here." Cāndo's face was white, and so were his fingers, clutching the staff of black hemtāla wood. "I am sure it was Karman that led me to your island."

He forced a smile. "My dear host," he said. "I want to pay the goddess my respects. Take me to her greatest temple."

"Nāgīn, appear, and let me greet you!"

Cāndo hit the golden bell. Then he turned round. The official was right next to him. He struck, and the man collapsed.

"Destroy everything!"

His sailor warriors rushed in. They had concealed truncheons, knives, and short swords in their costume. The temple was full of worshippers. Some prayed, some meditated, and nearby children played. When the strangers appeared, they panicked.

"You are liars! Filth! Demons! Sinners!" Cāndo struck to right and left. His sailors overtook him. They hit and gouged and stabbed.

Right in the central hall stood a huge vessel full of holy water. The spiky twig across the top seemed to reach from one horizon to the other. Cāndo advanced and swiped at it. The gold burst and water spilled. His troops killed and looted as they went along. The place was full of wealth and blood. Had Cāndo kept a cool head, he would have seen his sailors smashing ivory, breaking jewel-studded balustrades, smashing priceless vessels and crippling those who tried to flee. The Merchant King stood in the centre of the hall and tears ran down his cheeks. "I will kill you!" he screeched, "You murdered my sons! Serpent whore, show yourself, and let me crush you like a cockroach!"

"Enough!" His captain insisted. "Pack the valuables!"

"I won't leave!" Cāndo shook with anger. "I will destroy this temple!"

"My lord, there will be trouble. We will leave now."

"I can't leave!"

"We are lucky if we reach our ships!"

Heavily laden, the men rushed down the hillside. The captain had grabbed Cāndo, and forced him along. Another sailor carried the hemtāla staff. The Merchant King was in tears. "I will kill you!" he yelled, "You will pay! You will pay every rupee and every anna for the death of my sons!"

The street was empty. The windows were empty, the sky was bleak, and the gulls had disappeared.

The troop reached the harbour. The stalls were abandoned, the goods gleamed in the sun, and not a single citizen was in sight.

"This is bad," explained the captain, "it's like a dwelling place of ghosts!"

"I'll give you ghosts!" Cāndo shook all over. "Men! Kill anyone you meet!"

"There is no one," said the captain, "and soon an army will appear."

He dragged Cāndo up the gangway. "Everyone prepare! We leave! Get ready to fight! Everybody else, mount the sails"

The sailors tossed gold and pearls, rare woods, ivory and choice timber on the deck. Thousands of coins chimed, gleamed, rolled, and fell in heaps. In their midst stood Cāndo, and wept.

"Raise the anchors!"

"Not yet!"

The captain turned.

Cāndo grabbed his jacket. "Don't do it." His voice sounds like a puppy, the captain thought, he's whining, and soon he'll go hysterical.

The Merchant King showed a crooked grin. "We are best friends, aren't we? So let us do the right thing. Everything has to be destroyed." He gave a giggle. "Hear me! Officers, sailors, attend! I want every house burned down!"

He covered his face with his hands. "Śiva, my lord, you bring release, and you destroy. I will do as you command. Durgā, you sent me on my mission. I bring the Fire of the End of Time. I am your prophet; I am your humble slave." He turned to the captain. "If you wish to keep your command, equip your men with firebrands. Erase the evil!"

The stands went up first. The dry wood, the textiles, they caught fire and the wind spread the flames. Next, the houses at the harbour front flared up. Cāndo stood at the rails and jittered. He saw the roofs flare, he saw the sparks flying, and watched how they caught other buildings, further up. The flames raced along the streets. They seized the oiled wood of shutters and doors, they engulfed roofs and balconies and spread. Soon, the whole settlement was ablaze. And still, not a single person could be seen.

"We leave!" roared the captain. The sailors tossed their torches away and raced for the ships.

"We can't leave," stuttered Cāndo, "we ain't finished..."

"We leave, "said the captain, "we have done our duty and it's time to go." He shook his head. His employer was delirious.

The Merchant King leaned over the rails. "Durgā!" he screamed, "I do your work, and you show the way!"

The captain frowned. "My lord. You did your best. The city is a furnace."

"It ain't fire!" Cāndo trembled, "Look closely. See the rainbows. There are so many. Everything is blossoming. Everything is beauty. Oh my gods please let me die."

"I can't understand this," said the captain. "No people. No one runs, no one escapes."

"Nobody was ever there!"

A shower of blossoms cascaded on the deck. The Unique Harbour brightened up, spun around, turned upside down, became a whirl of crazy energies and vanished. The Merchant King collapsed. He had plenty of space, as all the stolen goods had disappeared.

Picture 14: Mangroves.

24. Journey to Dakṣiṇ Pāṭana

Another day, another harbour. This one was grim. Cliffs as sharp as monster teeth; surging breakers, white with foam, and gulls fighting over carrion. Rotten algae, dead fish, smashed clamshells: the stench was stunning. Cāndo clung to the railings, and tried to appear indestructible. He hadn't slept much; his eyes were red and his hands trembled.

"Is this sufficiently real, my lord?"

"It's real enough for me."

Cāndo showed his approval. "There's filth on the waves, the buildings are almost in ruins and there are beggars everywhere."

"It's a sad sight," the captain shook his head.

"It's a good omen. It means we make a profit."

"With whom?" the captain frowned. "I see no buyers or sellers. The people look like skeletons."

Cāndo rubbed his hands and grinned like an axe. "Look at the sea. It's full of food. They could be happy and healthy. They could trade, and eat fish, and crabs, and algae, and hunt water birds. And they could sell their surplus inland, where fishes gain good prices. Wealth is everywhere, but they starve. It means a few people are rich beyond belief."

In the middle of the night, King Candraketu had an amazing dream. He was walking through a lavish garden when a filthy ascetic jumped out between the dwarf palms and grabbed him. "Let me go!" exclaimed the king. "This is a place of joy and beauty! Run, before the guards arrive!"

The ascetic laughed. His hair was grubby, his mouth coloured by betel, and his few remaining teeth were black. The guy was as stringy as a dead seagull. He clutched the king and giggled. King Candraketu realised he was caught in the wrong sort of dream.

"The gods warn you, my pretty little king!"

"Of what? Speak up and be gone!"

"Evil and murder and death!"

The ascetic seemed to chortle with delight, and sprayed the king with spittle.

"Tell me what you want!" The king could hardly whisper. The stench was overwhelming.

"There's a murderer around!" The ascetic released the king. "The gods sent me to warn you! You are a silly little chicken. Anyone could take and murder you!"

"I have my guards!"

"They are useless. They serve you and they will serve your successor, and the fool who follows him. The killer will offer you a toxic fruit. It will scorch your mouth, burst your stomach and rip your bowels apart!"

The king stood in a daze. "How can I recognise him?"

"Examine his goods. You have never seen a fruit like this!"

The seer bent over laughing, the king staggered back, and woke, wretched and sweaty, entangled in his blankets.

"You won't need your guards. We shall ensure your safety."

The officials, standing on the quay, wore silk and gold. "Our lord, his majesty, has commanded that you shall be accompanied to the palace."

"I need my carriers," said Cāndo.

"Not at all. The king supplies his own men. Your crew will remain on their ships."

"I refuse to leave without my guards."

"If one man, except you, leaves his ship, he is dead. Please excuse the strictness of our regulations. Like everyone, we agree: the guest is god. But the wise mistrust guests, if they are armed."

Cāndo shrugged. "There are other ports and other kings. I am sure we will meet a friendlier welcome elsewhere."

"Our king would feel insulted. Our archers and our catapults are ready. I doubt you could leave the harbour alive."

"Do you threaten me?" Cāndo stood straight, the black hemtāla staff in his hand.

"We wouldn't dare. You are a treasured guest. But, just like you, we are realists. History contains the most astonishing episodes. It would be wrong to neglect its lessons."

"I am a trader, not a pirate."

"Of course you are. We respect your cherished person. Sailors, however, have been known to misbehave."

"We might stay here, lord, and do our business at the quay," said the captain. "Who says we have to visit their king?"

"Stop interfering."

Cāndo nodded at the officials and ran his fingers through his beard. "I have your word. And I am sure we'll come to an agreement. Send twenty carriers. They shall bear a few samples of my goods."

The official gleamed. He clapped his hands and a bunch of nude slaves appeared. Their faces were branded and their bodies scarred. "You can trust us. These men won't steal your treasures. Unless they stuff them up their asses." He laughed. Cāndo did not.

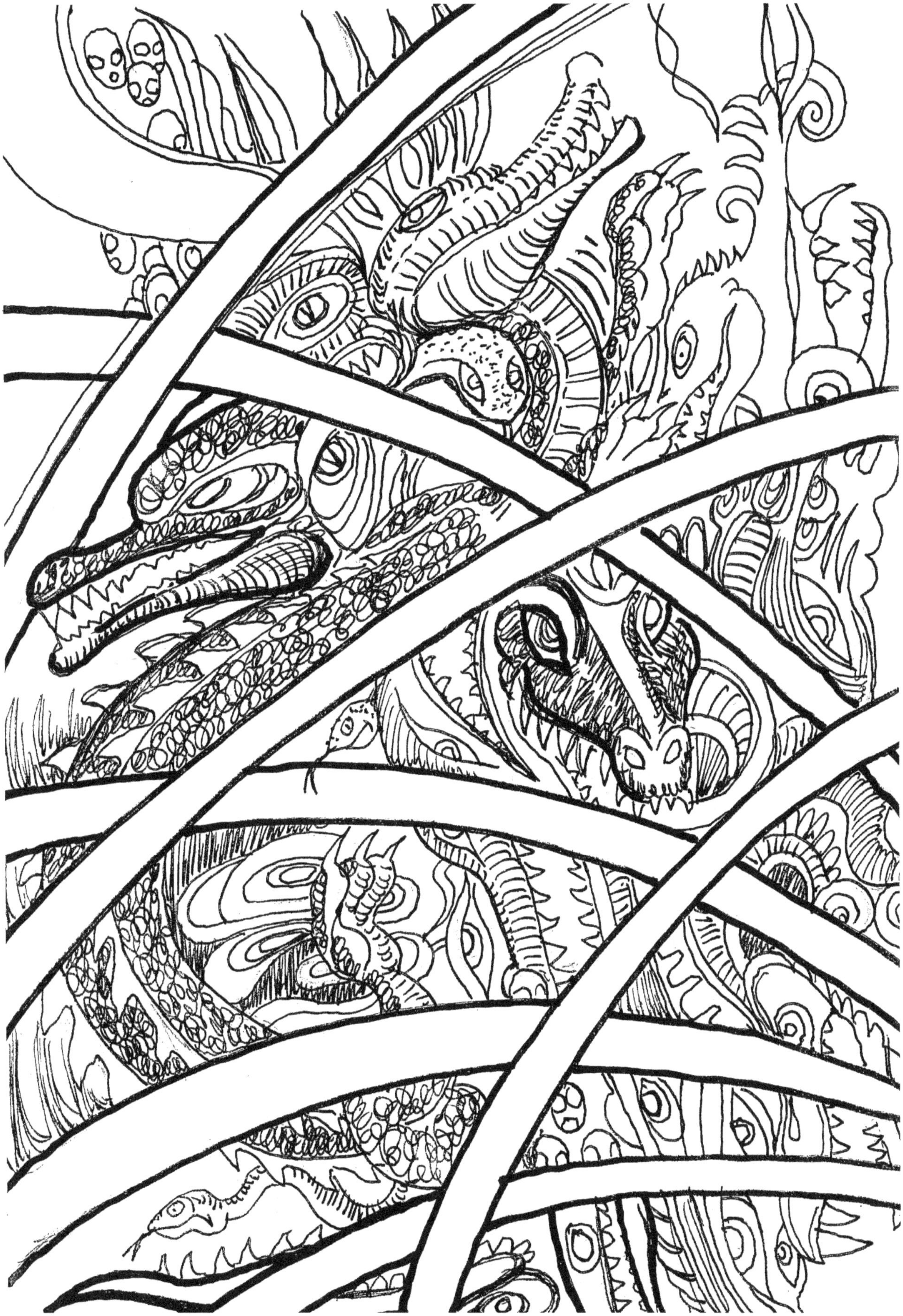

Picture 15: Crocodile Madness.

"We have everything we need."

King Candraketu was wiry, worn and withered. His face seemed full of worries, his skin was wrinkled, and the little of his hair that emerged from underneath his head-gear was thin and greasy. He wore a plain brown robe, rough and coarse, which only showed a few golden threads and pearls at the rim. His feet were in aged sandals, there were no bracelets on his wrists and on his knotty fingers, no rings gleamed. "Visitor, you call in vain. We have few needs, and no desires."

Cāndo kept his face straight. You little liar, he thought, your ministers gleam like statues in the temple. "You are a holy man." Cāndo lowered his gaze. "But I am astonished by your welcome."

The Merchant King was on his knees. As soon as he had entered the throne room, the guards had forced him down.

"We will show mercy." The King whispered, "Like me, the One Man, you are not young. As an act of compassion, I allow you to rise."

Cāndo could have groaned. His knees hurt and his spine seemed misaligned. Painfully, he raised himself. A servant handed him his staff. "Is this the way you greet your guests?"

"Are you a guest? One hears so many awful things. One has to protect one's people."

"I am a peaceful trader and a lord of my own realm. I carry gifts and trade goods."

"Let us see what you can offer."

"Your majesty will be amazed. Let me enquire, in due humility, what is your greatest wish?"

The king appeared amused. "To be young again." He laughed like a bronchitic crow, and as on command, the court joined in.

"Alas, only the gods can fulfil your wish."

"So you are useless."

"I have spices that turn bland fare into delicacies."

The king shook his head. "We have all the spices we need."

"I carry jewels that focus cosmic energies. They serve as talismans, as heal-alls, as bringers of luck and blessings."

"We have plenty of jewels. I don't care for them. But the queen's serving girls, I admit, have quite a fancy for such baubles." The king croaked and his people convulsed with laughter.

"Your majesty," Cāndo raised his eyebrows, "I have medicine and drugs that enlighten the mind, strengthen the back and make new passions sprout."

"Maybe my ministers could need them. They seem a little weary. I, the One Man, have more than fifty children. One forgets their names. They look alike, and they try to kill each other." The king gave another hacking laugh, "here in the palace, life is not entirely peaceful."

"The gods have supplied me with miracle medicines. I have a syrup made from an enchanted plant that gives peace to the soul, encourages visions and grants deep, blissful sleep."

"If we slept deep, we would be dead already. No, little trader. Your goods are worthless here. We are only interested in one commodity."

"Lord, let me serve you."

"So close to the sea, few plants thrive. The salty air gets everywhere. We are always keen to try exotic fruit."

"Your word is my command." Cāndo signalled a slave to fetch a basket. "Here is an assortment of the most delightful fruits that strange mountains and sun-drenched valleys offer. These fruit contain nourishment and healing. They provide clean skin, clear eyes, strong, shiny hair; they improve health and destroy the worms that hide within the gums, the stomach and the bowels. Their freshness offers joy and happiness."

The slave approached the king, who scowled at the offering.

"Mango, yam, durian, blackberries, jackfruit...we know them all. They come from further inland. But this thing is odd. Why is it so hairy?"

"Divine lord." Cāndo smiled and bowed. "It is my honour to give this fruit to you, as a gift, to prove my friendship and devotion."

The king raised a hand. "You!" he pointed at an official. "Take it."

The man advanced. Cautiously, he lifted the thing.

"Good," said the king, "now have a bite!"

"No!" Cāndo screamed.

The official bit and blood ran from his mouth. The fruit fell to the ground and rolled through the hall.

"Guards!"

"Mother of All Gods, Mahāśakti!" Cāndo crouched in the dark. The cell was tiny; he could barely extend his legs.

"Durgā! When the calf calls for its mother, she comes running. You are the Queen of the Universe, everything that exists is you. You are the world, you are loss and gain. You are this prison cell, you are my confinement, and you are hunger and thirst."

The merchant coughed. The air was stale and moist. The smell of excrement was overpowering. His throat was parched; he barely managed to whisper.

"Durgā! By your command I fight the evil snake. In your name, I have crushed her shrines, destroyed her temples, and wrought destruction on her worshippers. You gave me a mission. I lost six sons to her. I lost buildings, treasures and my good name. The people of my city laugh and my wife thinks that I'm insane. Now I suffer, in this hole, all in your name. Though I am in the dark, you see me. Durgā! Warrior Goddess! I am alone. Not even rats live here! Hear my call! Mother! Come and help!"

The cell remained silent.

"Goddess!" Cāndo was beyond tears. His voice sounded like a sandpaper cough. "Listen! Nobody will worship you! They will say, see, Cāndo was her greatest worshipper. They will say, see how he suffers in the dark. She cheated him! She made him fight her battles and then she dropped him like a dirty rag!"

The merchant croaked. "Who will trust you, lion-rider? You are a goddess of stone and your heart is a rock! Your worshippers will desert you! They will hear how you dealt with me and they will learn their lesson!"

Cāndo fought for breath. His mouth burned and his head pounded. "I financed a thousand priests to sing your praise. Each autumn, I have paid for your statues, your music, your offerings and your processions. Will you repay your debt?"

Light hurts. Cāndo staggered after the guards, the officials and administrators. He kept his face straight but feared his legs would give in. The stairs and corridors seemed endless. Last, they emerged in the throne room. Sunlight cascaded through a window and shone on the rich, gold-covered throne, where his majesty, clad in his plain brown robe, sat like an unhappy mud-hopper.

Cāndo was hurled to the ground.

"But no!" His majesty rose, "lift him up." He descended two steps. "My dear friend. You shall be allowed to stand. Get him some water!"

The merchant stared at the chalice.

Slowly, keeping his hands under control, he took the golden vessel.

"Drink slowly!" His majesty seemed worried. "Too much water can kill."

The king returned to his seat, leaned back and gazed at the ceiling. "We had a dream. In the early hours before dawn, a goddess appeared to us. She rode a big, fat lion. I guess it was Śerāṇvālī, or anyone. There are so many goddesses. Who can keep them apart?" He croaked and the court cheered him. "She raised her spear and said 'The fruit was not toxic! No-one should bite a coconut.'

One felt the need to explore this. The guards smashed the item. Our chief physician took a bite. He said, he liked the flavour, and as you can see, he is alive."

The court roared with laughter.

"One has forgiven your offence. You are allowed to leave."

Cāndo took another sip. "My lord, I am here to conduct trade. My fleet consists of six ships, and they are full of treasures. It would be an honour to do business with you."

"Alas, dear friend. One fears you will be disappointed." The king looked deeply saddened. "Karman is cruel. One thing follows another. Of course we unloaded your ships. Your men are kept in chains. One has no idea what happened to your goods."

"My goods-"

"Guard your tongue. We do not approve of accusations. This is not a country of thieves. In our benevolence, we spared your life."

The king raised his eyebrows. "Treasured guest. The goddess favours you. You shall not sail away as a poor man. One imagines that you are married. We will send your wife a few combs, hairpins, ankle chains and the like. You won't find us ungrateful. Just look at you! One is sure you could do with a bath and a set of fresh clothes. And one day, maybe, when, perchance, you return to our harbour, we will delight to trade with you."

Picture 16: Cotton Venom.

25. Return

Weeks later, Cāndo had a dream. Sonakā appeared to him, and Cāndo was surprised to see her swollen belly. She bowed and begged him to return.

When the Merchant King woke, he realised that there were better things than greasy meals and wines that tasted like vinegar. He knelt before his host, and asked the king's permission to depart. His majesty was pleased, and presented him with a small iron-bound chest. Accompanied by an honour guard, the merchant king was paraded to the harbour, where the king's officials unloaded provisions for each ship. By noon, the tide was in, and the fleet sailed into the wide and open ocean. Cāndo retired to his cabin, where he examined the content of the box. "This stuff is cheap," Cāndo muttered, while he stroked his beard. Sonakā was pregnant and he would come home. On the way, he might plunder a few villages to make up for his expenses. He could take a few slaves and sell them elsewhere. It wouldn't be much, but it might improve the morale of his crew.

The only profit, of course, was the king's invitation. The Merchant King had devoted much attention to the commodities of Dakṣiṇ Pāṭana. Sure, the king was a miser. His ministers were not. Next year, he would return, and insist on being treated as a royal guest. That would save him taxes, harbour fees and plenty of bribes. He would provide the rich with luxuries and drugs. He would satisfy any desire, monopolise import and export, would supply the poor and homeless with opium and arsenic, maybe stage a revolution or a civil war, and in five, maximum ten years, this pisspot country would belong to him.

The mangroves faded into a labyrinth of shadows, ghosts and crocodilian surprises. The fleet made for the shore and anchored. Laughing loudly, the sailors set up a camp on the beach. They were glad to be back in India. Cāndo walked around in silence. He watched the captain posting guards, while others made fires and prepared what little rice remained. In the distance he saw a few cheap huts. These people, he thought, have no ambitions. Today, their hovels are home; tomorrow a flood will take them.

"Noble lord!"

Cāndo turned. Before him, on her knees, was a woman whose face looked like a shrivelled mango.

"Great king, give me a coin! I am alone and starve! My husband was a god-fearing fisher, but the crocodiles got him. My daughters scream and weep all day. How can I feed their hungry mouths?"

The woman wept and her wiry hands were covered with scab.

The Merchant King recoiled. "Begone! I never give to beggars!"

"Lord, you could buy my daughters."

The woman tried to hold him. "I am hungry! Show your mercy and I will pray for you!"

"Guards!"

His men came running.

Cāndo spat to avert evil. "Keep this corpse away from me!"

"Shall we kill her?"

"Beat her and let her run. Yama Death Lord will come for her."

Indra's palace was brightly illuminated. Just like every other night, the music boomed and the cheers of drunken heroes echoed over snow-encrusted slopes. The program was simple: free food, plenty of drink, no inhibitions, to bed at sunrise and up again in the afternoon, with a headache that only alcohol and violence can cure. In short, it was Warrior Heaven.

The King of the Gods (retired) had ordered a grand buffet, and his chef had promised a thousand-and-one delicacies. Indra laughed like an avalanche and thumped him on his back. "Don't worry. Forget specialities. Just make a lot."

The chef adjusted his hat. It's an easy, if boring job to provide meals for drunken idiots. Indra's guests were approximately a thousand of the greatest warriors of all times and not very demanding. The main thing was meat, dripping with grease and crusty with spices. The hotter the better. It made them boast and choke, while tears ran down their cheeks. That's how you recognize real men. They fight while they eat and prove how tough they are in the latrine.

But lumps of meat ain't everything. Indra was a master of entertainment, hence, for his female employees, he had a salad table. The Apsarases, clad in tiny, translucent veils, ate small and light. Each of them watched the waistline of her colleagues like a hawk. When not on stage, they stood before their mirrors and despaired.

Heavenly Dancers! The bosom heaves and shimmies, the hips roll like a ship in a maelstrom and all the time they grin like rabbits on amphetamines. Occasionally, they faint. Someone picks them up; they have half a glass of water, a spoonful of rice, a slice of cucumber, and run away to stick a finger in their throat.

The chef kept a healthy distance. Admittedly, these girls were nervous, jerky and full of spite. But they were nicer than the wandering saints, who occasionally appeared on Indra's doorstep, like something the cat had thrown up, to preach abstinence and chastity. Their culinary desires were unbearable. Brown rice, practically free of vitamins.

Water, gathered at the full moon. And soy. As a divine cook, the chef knew everything about plant chemistry. He respected soy. That plant, he knew, fights back. It contains more than fifty phytotoxins harmful to human beings, mammoth doses of estrogens, plus testosterone blockers. It screws up the thyroids, upsets the immune system and perforates the cerebellum. As if there were not enough idiots suffering from impotence and brain shrinkage!

The young woman, who entered his kitchen as if she owned it, was no dancer. Sure, she looked just as hungry. Apart from a few snakes, she was nude. Her aura, however, was stunning.

The chef set up a stern expression. Nobody entered his kitchen without invitation. Guests should never learn that their schnitzel is a breadcrumb coated cleaning rag.

"Sorry, visitors are not welcome."

"Snakes and death are welcome everywhere." The woman smiled and revealed a perfect set of toxic fangs. "I need to speak with Indra. Where is he?"

The chef raised his eyebrows. The woman was a goddess, and as everybody knew, deities can't be excluded. "Feel invited. I assume you are not here for a meal?"

"Here? Certainly not."

"Excellent. Indra is having a snack over there."

"In the kitchen?"

"He does not make a fuss."

Manasā approached the Thunderer, who was drinking spicy goo from a frying pan. The King of the Gods slammed down the item; wiped his oily chin with his hands, and his hands on his dhoti. "Hey," he grumbled, "I know you. We worshipped you, a while ago. In Śiva's palace. You're the crazy one who's into thinking?"

"Right." Manasā smiled. "I do consciousness, awareness, imagination, anything. Śiva's daughter. Thank you for coming to my welcome party."

"Yea, I remember. You went missing, but we had one hell of a night." He laughed. "We pissed down from the balcony."

"Let me ask a question". Manasā folded her hands and tried to appear girlish.

"What is it?" Indra had discovered a pot of aged chicken vindaloo and shovelled the stuff, cold and rancid, into his mouth.

"Tell me: what do you think of a disgustingly rich merchant, who owns an entire fleet and a whole country, and who won't give a single coin to a poor woman? In spite of the fact that she lives in a derelict grass hut, sure to be swept away by the flood anytime, and that her husband has been eaten by crocodiles, and that her six little daughters scream with hunger while she crawls across the beach begging from strangers?"

"What?"Indra shook his head. "Say that again."

Manasā looked at him with antelope eyes. "My enemy. He is an exploiter and a filthy miser."

"What a pig." Indra had his mouth full.

"He has to be punished!"

"Sure."

"You give your blessing?"

"Of course. Try this bean paste. With mutton and onions. It's got black crunchy bits in it. I love them."

"May I count on you? Will you lend me a thunderstorm?"

"Slam him properly. Here, take this bolt of lightning. It's pretty well charged up. Mind you, it's almost new, so be careful. And I want it back."

"Only borrowed. I promise."

"Flatten him. Scorch him to the Underworld. That's what I would do. What I did, long ago. Today, I'm just a host. For the boys. We've got a disco every night. Feast, fight, and fondle. That's my world, these days. But what should I say? We all had our time."

"Thank you. You helped enormously."

"A pleasure. And take Hanumān along. He can lend a hand."

Manasā bowed. Her cheeks were flushed. It felt so good to hold the thunderbolt. "I greet the divine in you."

Then she remembered what Neta told her to say.

"I love your big muscles."

Indra grinned. "Me, too."

"It might be getting stormy." The captain seemed nervous. "The waves are restless and the wind is rising."

"Nonsense." Cāndo crossed his arms. He stood like a pillar and glared at the dark line of trees rimming the riverbanks, more than a mile away. His face was tense and his fingers twitched on the hemtāla staff. "We have more than an hour till sundown. I have no time to waste."

"I say, we head for the shore now."

"Never. We have to get to Campaka."

"If a storm comes up, we won't return."

"Captain. I treasure your opinion. I might even respect your intuitions, for what they are worth. But how do you know the weather will turn worse?"

"The fishes leap. The swallows fly deep. No bird can be heard. The sun looks like an angry, swollen eye, surrounded by a haze. And see these clouds?"

"Superstitions. We are far from land, how could we hear birds? We will continue. For just one hour. Then we head for the shore."

"The shore is far."

"I am sure you can sail faster than this."

Manasā squatted in the twilight. Her feet were buried in rich, dark mud and there were twigs and leafs entangled in her hair. She had crept through thickets, struggled up soggy slopes, twisted through creepers and waded through brackish water. Finally, she had reached the shore. From her vantage point, the great river extended like an inland ocean, an endless plane of glitter under the evening sky. The weather seemed friendly. She was going to put a stop to it. The goddess was alone, apart from a few startled mud-hoppers. Around her, the air-roots of the mangroves rose like millions of lethal spikes. Driftwood was trapped between them, and the air was full of rot. Manasā tasted the sweet water. Soon, the tide would pump seawater inland. She closed her eyes, her breath slowed, and she relaxed. It felt so good.

"Gaṅgā!" she whispered, "My lovely, cosmic stepmother. Your daughter needs you."

The water gurgled. Manasā tilted her head and smiled. Before her, the goddess appeared. "Manasā! Why do you call? Why do you disturb my river? I am not your mother, nor your stepmother. Your father is a failure; I left him, with good reason. I trickle down his locks; he doesn't care."

"Mother, dear." Manasā opened her hands. She raised a lotus blossom. "I have a small request."

"Even small requests have to be considered. I owe you nothing. What do you want, child?"

"Out there is a fleet of trading ships. They belong to Cāndo, the Merchant King. He is an evil man. I have conferred with Indra. He agrees that Cāndo deserves to be punished, and lent me a lightning bolt. Now I am here, before you, on my knees. My wish is small and I am sure you will grant it. You are the flow of life and death; you are the fountain of mercy."

"Don't honey-mouth me. I might help you, though you are Śiva's daughter, if your wish is well chosen."

"I knew I could count on you! My dear, dear mother! It's just a small request. Listen, I beg you, make the river churn, make the water boil, make waves rise until they drown the firmament."

"Serpent Goddess! I heard you were a thinker. So think! You ask for far too much. What has Cāndo done to deserve your wrath?"

"He exploits, he enslaves, he drugs, he is proud and greedy and he hates the gods."

"Dear child. You are so young and innocent. I know this trader, we all know him. Cāndo is generous, Cāndo is devout. He makes many offerings to me. He feeds me with fruit, rice and butterfat; he dedicates entire baskets of blossoms to my worship. He gives me incense, and prayer, and young goats."

"He bribes you!"

"He does not. He never asks for anything."

"You are his slave!"

"Shut up!"

"Never! I'll have it my way, you dumb young goddess!"

"Who's young?" Gaṅgā pressed her fists into her sides and snarled. "I was there when life and death began!"

"I am old, much older than you! Before people learned you exist, before your flood of sewage drenched the earth, we Nāgas were supreme! We ruled the cosmos, we embraced the stars!"

"As stupid worms, as rubbish eaters! Look at the early snakes! Their little legs were so silly that they hid underground!"

"We were proud and beautiful! We were dragons!"

"Nāgas, you insolent thing, are stupid. Snakes get angry at the least provocation."

"That's a lie!"

"Why do you scream?"

"I don't!"

"My poor little wriggler, I don't blame you. Reptiles were well and good, a few million years ago. They were the best that could be done. Then squeaky, neurotic shrews triumphed over them. But you must face the truth. Your time is over; learn to be grateful for what you have."

"I am. Are you? My father kicked you out!"

"I'm water, darling. You can't insult me."

"But I can curse you.

Vomiting poison day and night from my teeth,
I will mix my poison thoroughly with your waters,
The poison will run up and downstream,
People will not drink your water without fear..."

Gaṅgā grasped. "How can you say something so terrible?"

"I can pollute you, until your stream becomes a sewer. I can pile up corpses and make algae blossom until the rot destroys all water life! You'll be a flood of shit and carrion! Your worshippers will vomit, and the river folk will curse you and run for the hills!"

Gaṅgā paled. This girl was a living nightmare. She exhaled. It was time to reconsider. True, Cāndo had given her many presents. She recalled them fondly. But honestly, he was just a simple human being: ignorant, mortal, and, above all, replaceable.

A moment ago they had been quarrelling. The captain had argued, Cāndo had insisted, and now they stood at the railings and stared in different directions.

Then, one instant to the other, heaven went black, and clouds, raging like a herd of drunken elephants, swallowed the sun. Angry, nervous gusts of wind tore at the rigging. Raindrops, heavy as lead, cascaded from the height.

The shore, in the distance, disappeared. Thunder rumbled and far away, lightning flickered.

"I told you" shouted the captain.

"You didn't express yourself clearly," Cāndo roared back.

"You didn't listen!"

"You are a total failure!"

"I curse the day I met you!"

"I curse you twice!"

Cāndo wiped the icy water from his eyes. A sudden wave made him stumble, he caught hold of the railing and gasped for air. The captain, that much was obvious, was worthless. When they returned home, he would kick him out without pay, and see to it he never found work again.

Nearby he heard screams. Then the wood splintered.

The next wave swept clear across the deck. Cāndo stumbled and cursed. Hailstones, as big as walnuts, hammered on the deck.

Lightning struck.

Cāndo covered his face. Next to him, the mast broke.

He heard a female voice. "I guess he had enough." That voice was painfully familiar.

Another lightning bolt.

A deeper voice replied "Do you think so? He's a human being. They use pride instead of sense."

The Merchant King opened his eyes. Nearby, a giant lotus blossom gleamed. On the petals stood the serpent-whore and a guy in funny clothes who was entirely covered by fur.

"One-Eyed Frog-Eater!" Cāndo raised his black hemtāla staff. "Come here and let me kill you! I'll crush your cult! I'll starve you to death!"

"You damn idiot fanatic!" Manasā screamed back. "Look where you are! See this lightning bolt. And tell me, Mr. Finance, how many ships do you see?"

The answer was zero.

"Hanumān, my friend," said Manasā, "show King Cāndo the Underworld!"

Picture 17: Jagged Edges (Pandanus pristis).

26. Coming Home

The crow called as loud as she could. Cāndo opened his eyes. His face hurt. So did his neck, his shoulders, his limbs and anything he could think of. Leave me alone, he thought, go away, let me die. It didn't work.

The crow gave a louder shriek.

Success comes in many formats. The Merchant King was alive. That counted for something. It just felt awful. He was struck in the tangled roots of a mangrove. Another screech. Aching all over, the trader lifted his head.

The crow looked down, aimed, and shat.

Cāndo groaned.

The night had almost killed him.

First, his ship shattered. He was caught by the waves and when he surfaced, gasping for air, there was just darkness anywhere, and angry gusts of rain. The current tore at the staff in his fingers; Cāndo fought to remain alive, and clutched the dark wood like an amulet. His clothes dragged him down. First, using his free hand, he got rid of his turban; next, he took off his jacket. The thing was soaked and heavy, the golden embroidery dragged him down. His shoes, studded with pearls and jade, disappeared. Last, he opened his belt and got rid of his trousers. His legs moved easier, but he began to feel the cold. Cāndo choked and retched.

Out in the darkness a light appeared. It was the goddamn lotus flower, as big as a fisherman's hut, floating on the stormy waves.

"Cāndo, we'll be friends. Let me help you."

The Merchant King cursed until water got into his mouth. He raised his staff and tried to hit the blossom.

"Sorry about this!" said the Monkey God, and tore the staff from Cāndo's grasp. It disappeared in the dark and so did the lotus. Cāndo paddled like a dog. He screamed in outrage, he choked and spat, called on the gods, and finally, he wept.

The Merchant King wiped the crow shit from his head. Moving his aching limbs, one painful motion after the other, he clambered up the slope. He slipped; he slid and struck the ground. Each step disturbed armies of crabs. When he reached dry land, he glanced back. The water was rising; soon there would be crocodiles everywhere. A flock of ducks flew by.

The Merchant King looked at himself. His arms and legs were bruised and bloody and his shirt was in tatters. He screamed into the emptiness. No-one replied. Six ships, a splendid crew, and everything lost. The serpent whore. One day he would get her.

With heavy steps, he made it up the slope. Up here, he was moderately safe, unless the tigers smelled him. He stopped on the peak, in a tangle of willows. Dry land? There wasn't any. Baring his teeth, Cāndo fought his way down the incline, waded across a waterway, scared a huge monitor lizard and staggered up another riverbank.

By midday, he had waded through a dozen waterways. His legs were chaffed and painful. But finally he found a path. The trail was hard to see. In the Sundarbans, where floods are a way of life, any hint of people is a gift. The Merchant King staggered along. His feet were swollen and bled. Every few steps, he stopped and searched the vegetation. There might be serpents anywhere.

He had bandaged his arms and protected his head from the sun. That had cost him most of his shirt. The reeds, each leaf like a scalpel, had cut his legs and thighs. By evening, almost insane with hunger, he reached a settlement. It was tiny, poor, and wretched.

The gate was flimsy. Before it, an ascetic sat. The guy had plaited his grey beard, and his half-closed eyes were shaded by his eyebrows. Very slowly, the beads of his mālā slipped through his fingers. The holy man muttered mantras. Like a reed in the wind, his emaciated body swayed.

When Cāndo approached, his eyes opened and he grinned.

"What's there to laugh?" Cāndo scowled.

"Your shirt. The fabric was expensive. Tell me, rich man, why did you become a beggar?"

"Is this the way to greet a guest?"

"You're not a guest. I guess you are an evil spirit."

"You fool! Do my feet point backwards? Do I look as if I were dead?"

"Not yet, but soon."

"You are half dead yourself!"

"My dear, stupid friend." The yogī raised his hands to heaven, "what do you really know?"

"I know who I am and what I own!"

"You own nothing. Come closer, and for a few annas, I will reveal your fate."

"And I'll tell you yours!" Cāndo's face was red. "You are a parasite who steals from the poor! You exploit the superstitious! Why do you live in the swamp? Go to a city, get a job and work!"

The yogī clapped his hands and giggled. "Why so angry, old man? Did a witch steal your trousers?"

"Did a witch steal your manners?"

The ascetic nodded and stroked his beard. "You are right. My friend, you are a guest. I have no manners. Despise me! I won't hold it against you. And though you look like shit, I'm sure you are a noble character. So let me tell you: I was sent by Karman."

"You were sent by greed and hunger!"

"And you? My friend, let me tell you a secret. I can see that you were wealthy. But you won't have to pay. I'll give you this secret for free. You can become wealthy and powerful again. One happy day, you'll be richer than rich!"

"Like you?"

"Ah, you are angry. I don't blame you. You are wretched and stupid. But let me tell you: to win success and happiness, forget your wrath and worship Manasā!"

"You hairy ape! You are a minion of the frog-eater!"

"Poor Cāndo. You are as proud as a buffalo. No one will love you. It's not easy to be your friend."

And Hanumān disappeared.

Imagine a few huts, slanted, wretched, torn by the winds and drenched by rains. The walls are full of holes, the roofs in tatters, the floors muddy and the mould is everywhere. In a few months, the monsoon would wipe them out. But no matter the filth, here were people, real, caring people. They fished, they collected honey, and they endured the tigers, the crocodiles and the mosquitoes. Lowest of the low, they trusted in their deities, shied away from the upper classes, and died young.

Cāndo staggered into the settlement. He heard screams, as women dragged their kids into the huts, and men reached for their fighting sticks. Within instants, the Merchant king was surrounded by snarling dogs. Cāndo turned and ran as fast as he could.

By sunset, he stopped, and squatted under a willow. His stomach cramped and his extremities felt frozen. The evening went cold, swarms of fruit bats emerged, and the old man trembled. Behind him, a branch snapped. He turned around. A woman slid through the undergrowth. She had the bald head of a tantric nun. She had seen the world and found her way to salvation. Cāndo had not. He glared at her. Female tantrics were trouble. Most were unclean, like barber girls, washers, butchers and entertainers. Occasionally, they were widows who had refused to burn themselves. Or they were householders who had left their men and screaming kids to embrace a spiritual life. Some were veśyas: spiritual prostitutes, who sold their skills to tantric ascetics of the 'heroic' stage. Provided the guys were kind, refrained from orgasm and paid. Or they were crazy women, inspired by the gods, who wandered where their personal deities sent them, women who haunted streets and sacred sites, where they sold talismans and horoscopes, wonder herbs and spells. Like the vultures follow a dying cow, they trailed after pilgrims. Polluted! Polluted! Cāndo gnashed his teeth. This woman was trouble, but her face shone with an inner light. She smiled and offered a blanket.

In her youth, he realised, she had been a beauty. The Merchant King shuddered. Attractive tantrics were the worst.

"This is for you, my friend" said the woman and laid the cloth before his feet. "The nights are cold; I wish to keep you warm."

She bowed and slid into the twilight.

Cāndo glared at the textile.

Disgusted by himself, he reached for it.

He felt the warmth on his naked skin. When he raised his head, the woman was gone.

The Merchant King cursed. He knew who she was.

By daylight he is on his way. The blanket is wrapped around his body. Nevertheless, the damp of the night has touched him and the early morning sun is bright but fails to warm. His bones ache and his mind is numb. The merchant faces the sun and intones the Gāyatrī. Maybe it will help. And maybe it won't. Cāndo is mad with hunger and exhausted. He feels so weak that he could weep. It only makes him angrier. His stomach knots and his muscles burn with pain. The night on the bare ground has twisted him. He advances slowly, his hips ache, his spine is twisted and each step is a nightmare.

At a street crossing, he encounters a group of woodcutters. Though the day is young, the men are sweaty. On their gnarled shoulders, they carry loads of timber.

Cāndo approaches them as fast as he can.

"My friends!" he calls, "let me help you carry the load!"

The woodcutters laugh. This guy is mad, and worn out.

"Are you strong enough, granddad?" asks the leader.

"I'm a bull!" replies Cāndo. "I have strong muscles and I work hard."

The woodcutters are delighted. "Each night he satisfies six women!"

"They go delirious when they see his emblem rise!"

"And they can never get enough!"

"No wonder he's so wretched!"

Loud laughter. Cāndo pretends to ignore it.

"I want to work!" he shouts. "And I can work twice as hard as anyone!"

The woodcutters chortle.

They set down their loads. Each takes a few branches, and puts them on Cāndo's back. A piece of rope and he is ready to go.

Picture 18: Lost (Pandanus balsamifera).

"Stay between us, beggar," says the headman, "we don't want our load to disappear."

Cāndo snarls. "I'm not a thief. I work to make a living."

"You'll have to exert yourself. We are late, granddad. Hurry up, the market is far!"

Cāndo speeds up. His face goes sweaty and his heart pumps. His lungs work like bellows and his feet move as if he was racing. The bundle is heavy. It grinds him down.

But the Merchant King will not give in. He'll show them what age and experience can do. He puts one foot after the other. Each breath burns and his legs tremble.

"It's too light!" he grumbles. The men laugh.

He glances sideways. A snake sits on his shoulder. It seems to grin. Another snake descends. It wraps itself around his neck and continues to the other side. A third snake emerges. A fourth tries to get around his torso. A fifth goes down, to explore his dhoti.

Cāndo drops the bundle.

"Evil!" The old man screams and plunges into the undergrowth.

The woodcutters stare after him. "What an idiot," they say, "he's totally gone," and pick up the branches.

In all of his life, Cāndo had never walked that far. His feet are numb, but when he looks down, he sees they are swollen and bloody. "I should feel pain," he wonders. But he doesn't. The same goes for hunger. His belly has turned into a twisted, knotty piece of iron. His limbs seem strange and distant. He feels strangely light, like a happy cumulus cloud, and the scenery jitters past him, almost without recognition. Distance and direction are mysteries. Earlier, when he started out, he had hurried. Now he simply shuffles along. Occasionally he finds himself on the ground. He drags himself into the shadow of a tree. Travellers pass by, and one throws a few copper coins. Cāndo stares at them, transfixed, and his hands shake as he picks them up. Steadying himself against the tree trunk, he pulls himself up. The ground seems to wobble. He has a few annas, but no place to spend them. The next settlement may be miles away. But over there, in the thicket, something gleams like honey, like a jackfruit or a cake. The Merchant king fights his way through the branches, bends, grabs the thing and bites.

"Look at the poor fool. I could almost pity him." Hanumān wrinkles his brow; his eyebrows converge like hairy caterpillars. "We've abused him far too much. Let's call it a day and continue tomorrow."

"We ain't done yet." Manasā's eyes gleam. "You take the soft approach, and treat it like a game."

"I don't. I see it as a piece of scientific research. We test endurance, flexibility, creative adaption and the ability to re-invent values, cognitive parameters and personality."

"And did you learn a thing? You can experiment with anyone, Friend of all People. We are not in the lab. He is my enemy and I fight for my life."

Hanumān scratches his flank. Sure, his life is easy: he has Viṣṇu as his great protector. Worshippers who are too shy to address the Maintainer of the Universe prefer to pray to him, the Monkey God. His cult, he is happy to say, makes excellent profits, allowing him to spend his days in great university libraries, where the calls of the faithful are almost inaudible, thanks to thick walls padded with books, Superior Knowledge and sheer arrogance. Manasā, however, has just her wits, a few weirdo serpent fans and a father who is out of his skull most of the time. It isn't quite the same.

"Stop quarrelling." Neta holds the reigns; the six swans beat their wings in frantic effort to keep the invisible air-chariot in place. "Take a look, it's not so bad, see, he got his head out of the water. That means he didn't drown yet."

"I told you he's alive." Manasā grins, "let's continue."

"Well, I thought it slightly overdone. You know, in theory, I should be his friend."

"Sure, remain the Friend of all Beings. Even of Cāndo. After he has learned his lesson."

"It could take a while." Neta shakes her head. "He doesn't look as if he learned a thing."

"I like it. He is funny."

"But goddess," Hanumān raised his index finger. Manasā gives him a look and the finger sinks. "The poor man is totally swollen."

"He'll live."

"But he could have died!"

"You would have saved him."

"And you wouldn't?"

"Maybe. I need him alive. But is it my fault, when he bites into a wasp nest?"

At the edge of the jungle, a few huts appear. The land is cleared; the lowest of the lowest try to make a living. It isn't easy, as they have far too many children. Cāndo makes it to the glade by sheer willpower. He raises his hands and begs. The locals ignore him. He takes out a coin, and starts to haggle. After a long and painful negotiation, he gets a little rice, not altogether fresh, staggers into the shade of a mango tree and feasts like an emperor. By dusk, he has found a hiding place. He curls up under a thorn bush and sleeps. Before sunrise he is awake again. Sleep has not refreshed him. Nearby, dogs bark. Soon, they'll be at his heels. Wrapped in his blanket, he follows the path.

By afternoon he is ready to collapse again. But he is lucky; he has found a real village with a proper gate, a palisade, and people of many classes. Cāndo knows he should feel happy, but at the moment all feelings, except for hunger, have disappeared. He staggers to the centre of the settlement. It's market day, there are makeshift stalls, and playing children, and formidable amounts of food. The Merchant King grinds his teeth. Sure, he still owns two copper coins, but he isn't willing to spend them. Weak and slow, he moves along, examines the merchandise, and feels his stomach cramp. Finally, he stops at the stand of a fisherman. The man looks like a fool, and his fishes seem delicious.

"Hey, granddad!" The fisher laughs. "Are you hungry?"

"I am. But I can't pay."

"You look clever. I have a job for a man who can count."

"Numbers are my best friends."

"Excellent. I have to leave for a while. Could you sell my merchandise? Later, you'll get a large fish for free."

"Agreed." Cāndo grins.

"Take eight rupees for the big ones and four for the smaller size, if you can."

"Is the price fixed?"

The fisher sighs. "You may go down a little. Life is hard. These days, you have to take what you can get."

Cāndo grins like a tiger. That is practically his credo.

The Merchant King strides behind the table and straightens his back. You have to show you are proud of your products. It reflects on the price. Let's see what we can do. Eight rupees? That's hilarious.

"My fishes are absolutely fresh," he smiles at a fat lady, leading a boy covered in snot, "we are specialised in exceptional quality."

The woman carries loads of gold on her fat arms, and jingles like a prize-winning cow. She scrutinizes the fishes with the arrogance of a true connoisseur. "How much is the one over there?"

"My queen," Cāndo oozes charm, "such a fish is easily worth twenty-five rupees."

"So much!"

"You will be amazed by the superior taste. Look at this one. He was raised on dainties. He has tender, pale flesh, and an aroma that is incomparable. Such a royal fish is more than food, more than a delicacy. He is a source of health and vigour. Your husband has fathered a strong son." Cāndo smiles like a carefree killer shrew. "Father and son need excellent food."

"Even twenty would be too much. I'm not a queen."

"Lady, you are the sunrise over the Mandāra Hills. Uṣas, Lady Dawn, pales before your beauty. Make an offer. What is the value of this fish?"

"Twelve! And that's the limit!"

"Twelve." Cāndo seems close to tears. "Please don't abuse me. Even a trader needs to live. Your offer shames the fish, who gave his life for you."

"Well, trader, I can give thirteen."

"Impossible. The fisher told me to take eighteen."

"Fourteen. Let's call it a deal."

"Have another fish to go with it. I'll give you two for thirty."

The woman considers. Cāndo smiles, raises an eyebrow and waits. Eventually, the silence grinds her down.

"Twenty-eight. That's my last word."

"Done, O Blossom of the District." Cāndo grants her a generous smile. Smiles, after all, cost next to nothing. "Make your man gorge himself. Fishes destroy sorrow and invigorate the loins."

The day begins to be enjoyable. Cāndo laughs with the customers; he jokes about his swollen face, invents gossip, praises the local village and celebrates the beauty of his female customers. He explains that cardamom improves erections and that turmeric can combat tumours. Both are excellent, when combined with fish, and yes of course, he is ready to make a wonderful offer, and sell his goods below their value. These fishes, he proclaims, are the best there have ever been. His customers laugh, some blush, and all of them pay.

True, the price is high. However, apart from the fish, which is getting to be a little less than wonderful in the noonday heat, the customers receive something invaluable. They walk home with a good feeling.

Within an hour, he sells several dozen large fishes. Of course he keeps counting. This is a happy day; he will give the fisherman six rupees for each of them. The difference will be his provision, and quite humble, considering the effort he puts into promotion.

The sun is high. In an hour, he guesses, he will have sold most of the merchandise. And if the fisher isn't back by then, why, the guy is simply unlucky. Unpunctuality has to be punished.

"This fish," Cāndo grins at a fat money lender, "died of joy."

It is a wonderful line. It makes customers laugh. But right then, lightning strikes nearby.

The screams bring him back to reality.

The fish, a great, strutting champion, pale and dead a moment ago, begins to jerk. It rolls its eyes, widens its gills and opens its great gaping mouth.

The customer jumps back. "It's alive!"

"I told you its fresh!" Cāndo raises a cleaver. "Let me sort him out!"

Another thunder stroke. Believe it or not, no cloud is visible.

Picture 19: Yakṣa Forest.

In each bag, each basket, and in many cooking pots, the fishes return to life. Dozens of large and small fishes, twist, open their mouths, and wriggle like lost souls.

"Let me show you how it's done." It's a female voice. "Right, give me the thunderbolt. You revived them. That was pretty good magick. I like the way they twitch. But can you do this?"

Thunder rumbles. All fishes turn to snakes.

Cāndo runs as fast as he can. One hand holds his blanket, the other is full of coins. Behind him are his customers. Some wield sticks, others have dogs. A stone flies past, while others hit his back. Cāndo races out of the village and hurls himself across a ditch into the undergrowth. Twigs and leaves cut his face. He stumbles through water and runs up a slope. Here, a thicket of pandanus trees wait for him. Their stalks are tangled and their leaves cut like saws. The Merchant King struggles, screams and fights his way. His pursuers are close. His blanket rips; he curses and throws his coins at the crowd. With an effort, he breaks through spikes and disappears. His pursuers stay behind and fight each other for the money.

Finally, Cāndo collapses under a fig tree, out in the gloomy forest, covered in bruises and blood. Far away, he hears the villagers squabbling.

By nightfall, he emerges from the shadows. Mosquitoes had their fun with him. He struggles through the forest, holding a hand before his face to shield his eyes from branches, until he finds a path. He stops and listens. Someone is coming.

"It wasn't fishes. It was snakes."

A pair of beggars approaches.

"I don't believe a word. Go to the market and you hear a hundred stories."

"I'm sure it was snakes. Green, orange and magenta."

"There's no such thing as a magenta snake. Tomorrow it'll be blue crocodiles and the day after, holy cows that fell from the heavens."

"Banana?"

"A pleasure. Thank you. At least, these are edible."

"And they won't transform. Have another one."

The voices fade in the distance. Like a hungry ghost, Cāndo creeps from his hiding place. On the path, right before him, are banana peels. The Merchant King trembles with hunger. The scent drives him crazy, his mouth is full of saliva, and still he hesitates.

"Don't touch them!" In his way stands a hairy yogī. "If you eat food dropped by the Untouchables, you lose your social class."

"He doesn't care. I'm sure he'll eat them." Next to the yogī appears a pretty girl in red. "Our Cāndo doesn't care for classes. He's a free thinker, when he is really hungry."

Her bunches bob, and with her naked navel, she seems obscenely out of place.

The Merchant King freezes.

"He won't eat them." This is Manasā. She claps her hands. The banana peels disappear. "He is a proud man and titles himself 'King'. So, one way or another, he must find food that accords with his station."

"Don't be so stingy. He took your blanket. Give him a mouthful. The peels are good for him."

"The blanket was just a joke. He didn't know it's from a cemetery."

"Now he does. Gods, this is fun. See his eyes open! He's cute!" The girl in red arranges her hair. "You simply want to cuddle him."

"You and your stupid prattle. Next thing, he throws it away. If he freezes to death, it's your entire fault." Hanumān shakes his head.

"Please keep the blanket." Manasā grins. "Cāndo dear, we are just joking."

"I thought you want to kill him?" Hanumān scratches his head.

"Of course not. He's supposed to love me." Manasā raises her hand. "Don't run! Come back! We're your best friends!"

Days later, Cāndo reaches a large settlement. Hunger is his shadow and his stomach is a demon. Here and there, he has found fruit. Once, after he had collapsed at the wayside, a travelling merchant had dropped a few coins. Cāndo bought rice. He gobbled down the rice, salivating like a slug, and vomited. Several times, he sneaked into gardens and plantations, and stole vegetables. If he was lucky, he found hiding places, and devoured his treasures raw. A few times, the farmers sent him running. Most of the time, his sole fare is water, and neither fresh nor healthy. Diarrhoea racks him. In the middle of the night, he squats in the dark forest, shivering, and hears the animals. By dawn, he is on the path again. Bent, cramped and totally beside himself, he approaches the settlement.

Cāndo prides himself on being an excellent observer. As a businessman, you have to tell true from false. You take in every detail, and calculate its worth in real value, meaning money. He stares, he scratches his head, and eventually, he realises that this place is weird.

For a start, he notes that he has grown. His body, distinctly lighter than before, sways from side to side like a ship in a gale, and the ground has dropped into the deep. His feet, somewhere down there, appear to bulge. But honestly, do they belong to him?

Above, the sky seems different, too. And the sun, he notices, is a twitchy, jerky thing. It doesn't stay where it's supposed to be. One moment it's here, the next it's over there. The other thing that makes him wonder is the path. The smooth earth, flattened by thousands of travellers, seems to twist from side to side. Paths are serpents, he thinks, I should have known. She did it. I hate her! She has cursed the street! In the middle, it bulges. Gravity pulls him to the side, where the slope goes down, and drags him into bushes. When he clambers out, the world comes to a halt. And once he has struggled to the top of the trail, the sides drag him down again. Next to him, the trees writhe like cobras and their foliage whispers in the voices of the dead.

Cāndo has seen so many people come and go. Now they are here, and talk to him in tongues he cannot understand. Behind his back, spectres flicker. When he turns around, they disappear. Cāndo stands and waits. "Come out!" he shouts, "you can't fool me! Show your faces, scum!"

When he moves on, they come close again, they hiss, they giggle and they hate him.

The forest opens and another village appears. He stumbles through the gate and trembles. There are people everywhere, and they flicker by like phantoms, they scream and shout and talk and jabber, and Cāndo drops and weeps, for this is all too loud, too frenzied and too much.

He twists aside. Next to him is a building as he has never seen before. The walls are rays of light; he rubs his eyes, and wipes away his tears. He approaches on his knees, he stares and touches. These are woven reeds, so shiny, gleaming golden, and as he gasps, he sees figures dancing across the fibres, and shadows, and gods, who smile at him and make him feel at home.

I have to buy this house, he thinks, and I'll be happy. Or I will simply buy this wall. That'll be cheaper. I'll have it transported to Campaka. The Merchant King collapses. He stares into the sky. Heaven is dirty, he thinks, there are grimy streaks running down, and all is filthy slime, and it comes down to crush me. That's the world of the gods. They are worthless, they take bribes, and I can buy the lot of you, priesthood included, and he laughs, and then he starts to sob. He struggles to get up and the ground tells him to relax, and sucks him down.

The sky is far too large and pitiless. He sees a doorway and creeps into a building. His face hits the ground. It hurts, but when he opens his eyes he sees the earth is really grains, a field, extending forever, that ripples and pulsates, where birds flutter and seeds ripen. I'll live on the ground, forever, he thinks. The soil is wealth. It makes me feel at home. I'll be at peace, eternally. But peace does not last. From the corners of his eyes, Cāndo sees shadows scurrying. Mice, he thinks, there's vermin everywhere! The house pillar attracts his attention. The wood is old and dark, but strangely, the pores extrude an oily slime. The fluid runs, incessantly, and puddles on the floor. Cāndo gasps, the pillar turns and looks at him; it nods and walks away, in silence.

There are people everywhere, talking in voices, their echoes shattering. The Merchant King tries to raise himself. Someone takes his arm, pulls him up, and helps him stand. Cāndo is amazed, his benefactor is huge, and he is clad in fire. People hold him up. The hut is incredibly beautiful. He raises his head. There's a roof. It is a miracle of reeds and light and mystery. Cāndo laughs, the gods are with him, and at last, he has come home. "Hello!" he greets a Brahmin, the man towers above the clouds, and says something incomprehensible. Cāndo giggles, he understands a word: marriage! It means food. He is the guest. They will be kind to him. He tries to retain his tears. These wonderful people will provide for him!

More and more people enter the building. They are clad like gods, their costumes flutter and their faces gleam.

Gandharvas, Cāndo thinks; the sorcerers and musicians of the sky! The Brahmin talks to them. Cāndo faces him, all expectation, and hopes for dishes, many hundred dishes, everywhere. Again, the word resounds, 'marriage.' Get on with it, he thinks, I'll celebrate with you. His stomach rumbles and his hands shake. These people are blossoms. Their colours take my mind away. At last, he understands. The Brahmin keeps talking. It's all about a daughter.

"I have no daughter!" Cāndo says, and everybody laughs. He joins in. These people are wonderful. He feels at home, in paradise.

The Brahmin claps his hands.

An aged crone, her face carved out of rock, leads a blushing girl. She glitters like a young tree after a spring shower, and jewels sparkle in her smile.

Cāndo is amazed. He drops his gaze, the bride is gorgeous, and stares at the ground in due humility.

"Will you take my daughter Padmavatī as your bride?" says the Brahmin.

"I guess I still have a wife," says Cāndo, "somewhere." The men roar with laughter. Cāndo scratches his head; he isn't sure what he's supposed to do. The girl smiles at him and her face lightens up the world. Her skin is pure, her nose is impeccable, her lips gleam and she is surely only twelve, or less.

But what is this? Cāndo stares. For heaven's sake, she only has one eye! The other one is milky, and half closed. Her mouth opens, promising laughter and delight, and between the pearly teeth, a forked tongue emerges. Her fangs gleam and drip poison.

Cāndo screams and runs into the jungle.

Next sunrise Cāndo feels much better. On his headlong flight, he met a palm tree, head first, dropped like a stone and enjoyed several hours of much-needed sleep. Now, he is on his way again, nervous, hungry and prone to faint. He staggers along the path, strays through gardens, forest and jungle, and falls into ditches, until he finds the road. People pass him, like ghosts. His feet are bloody, and seem really strange. He is glad the hallucinations are over, his head hurts, his ribs ache and pain, to be sure, must be real.

Right there, on the endless, dusty road, he meets Rām, the oil merchant. The man is beneath Cāndo's rank, but he is perfectly clad, and Cāndo looks away in shame.

"Cāndo! Old friend! Is it really you?"

"No," says Cāndo, "I hope it's not."

"I knew!" Rām runs and bows. "My friend and business partner, what happened to you?"

"Shipwreck."

"Bad", says Rām.

"Six ships."

"Terrible. My friend, let me help you."

Rām calls for a palanquin. "Cāndo, nobody is as wise and far-seeing as you. None is so saintly and generous. But even good people undergo trials and tribulations. Here is a palanquin. Get in, relax, and forget your worries. We will talk about the costs later on. Stretch your legs, close your eyes, you need a lot of rest and I'll send you home."

Home. The thought took hold of him. Home. It means safety, security, happiness. Cāndo can't keep his face under control. Tears run down his cheeks, and Rām tactfully looks elsewhere. Cāndo climbs in, the cushions are soft, he is so happy and he closes his eyes. The palanquin sways and wobbles, as the bearers raise it, and Cāndo feels like a baby, cushioned, protected and loved.

A thunderbolt. And a female voice. "Hey, give it back to me!"

Another thunderbolt. The palanquin breaks apart. The Merchant King drops to the ground, screams, and struggles. He opens his eyes. Instead of his friend Rām an insolent girl with three bunches grins at him. She is almost nude, and holds a thunderbolt. "Wait, let me do it again!"

Lightning cracks and thunder rumbles. The girl laughs. The bearers of the palanquin transform into serpent princes.

"Hi Cāndo," says Neta, "did you miss us?"

Cāndo screams, and runs.

Somewhere far away, beyond hope and reason, he falls asleep. But you can't sleep forever. Many have tried, and I know some who are damned good at it, but the full, insolent dose of blissful slumber is only available for those who died and haven't been reborn, yet. Unlike the happy dead, Cāndo wakes in a ditch, covered in algae, right next to the bright, dusty road, and feels awful. His limbs throb, his joints are awry, and he drags himself along. The road carries him. See this: a clearing, palm trees and a humble garden; in front of a hut sits a poor Brahmin woman. She tends a fire and boils a pot of gruel. The scent gets him: Cāndo approaches; he tries to speak, groans and collapses.

"Poor beggar," says the crone, "may the gods bless you."

She holds a bowl, and fills it. Cāndo raises himself, takes bowl and spoon, and tries to keep his tremors under control.

"Take your time," says the Brahmin woman, "and blow. It's very hot."

Cāndo tries to blow. It makes him dizzy, stars sparkle before his eyes, and he can barely keep himself from falling over.

A crow flies across the yard and shits into the gruel.

Cāndo screams. Another thunderbolt, the Brahmin woman is gone, and so is her hut.

Cāndo stares into the gruel. His belly knots, his face twists in anguish, but nevertheless, he eats.

Months have passed, and Cāndo has seen more of the world than he has ever wanted to. He has begged and stolen; he has helped young men to harvest and twisted his spine trying to appear much younger than he was. When he accompanied them home to their village, the men laughed and he was greeted like a guest of honour. "Grandad, you did your best. It wasn't much, but we honour your effort."

Cāndo doesn't know if he should feel shame or pride.

Then he sees the Manasā pot. It's large and brown and the sij twig across the rim is extra spiky. Cāndo grabs a stool and hits the item. The vessel cracks and sacred water gushes.

All of a sudden, everyone is silent.

"I will punish you!" screams Cāndo. "I will buy every field and every lousy hut and destroy them all! I will burn your forest, I will clog your river and I will send the serpent whore running!"

He doesn't get any further. The villagers hit him with sticks and they throw stones after him.

The Merchant King escapes. He staggers along the dusty white road, he steals vegetables in a garden and runs when barking dogs approach. One day he meets a group of potters.

"I'll help you," he groans, "I'll help you carry your load, if you feed me."

"Old man," they say, "you are almost dead. What could you carry? You can't even walk upright."

"I'll carry anything."

The potters laugh.

"He's got guts for a beggar," says one, and another replies, "let's give him some rice and leave him to die."

"I hate charity," Cāndo curses, "I have worked all my life and I won't stop now."

The potters load him and make sure his pack is light. The Merchant King raises himself. He won't show his weakness, and he will demonstrate how fit he is.

The Merchant King staggers, and accelerates. Panting fearfully, he hurries along.

"Come on," he gasps, "you want to reach the market? Why are you trailing behind? There's good money to be made!"

Willpower, he thinks, and mind over body. I can beat them anytime. That's because I will never give up. I'm not afraid. And I put my total effort into anything.

Before him, the bushes part and a tiger snarls at him.

Cāndo yells and drops his load. Screaming like a lost soul, he runs for his life.

In the evening, he reaches the river. The slow, grey waters surge along. On the other side, he senses salvation. How will I ever cross this, he thinks, there is no bridge and I can't pay a ferryman.

Cāndo drops to his knees. He stares at the ripples and the foam, he tries to estimate the distance to the other shore. It's simply too far. He might have swum it in his youth. Today, he is just too old. His fingers rake his tattered hair, and his mind shatters. Like a beaten dog, he yowls.

Next to the shore stands a yoginī. The holy woman is thin; she wears a scarlet sari, her face is hard, her hair is long and matted. She is closer to starvation than I am, Cāndo thinks, a tantric beggar, a piece of low-class flotsam lost in the current of the world. His eyes blur, for this woman is truly strange. Her legs are thin, and she sways like a reed in the gale. The next moment she has a large bosom and a formidable bum. Cāndo shakes his head. Is he hallucinating? Is she a witch or a saint, a dancer or a skeleton?

"Pilgrim," says the woman, and Cāndo recoils; her eyes are glowing embers. Maybe she isn't human at all. Maybe she is a man-eating Rākṣasī, a haunter of cemeteries, an eater of corpses.

She points a finger at him; and her hand is gnarled like a creeper strangling a tree. "You've come far. Tell me: what do you really want?"

Cāndo hesitates. He considers gold, diamonds, and precious jewellery. Large tracts of land cross his mind, houses, manufactories, he recalls spices and drugs, sons and wealth and power. Finally, he remembers Sonakā.

He whispers. "I want to go home."

"The gods are with you," says the woman, she raises him, and points him in the right direction. "Forget the river. It only makes you crazy. You'll cross it when it's time to die. Come to your senses! You have staggered past your property twice. This time, you'll do it right. Go straight ahead; follow this road, until you reach the gate. Can you handle that?"

"But the river is over there..."

"So it will be tomorrow. The river did its job. It will be there forever. Now it's your turn. Go straight ahead. Come home."

The Merchant King raises his hands. "You seem familiar!"

The yoginī grabs his shoulders and shakes him. "Go straight ahead. Hurry up. Soon, it'll be dark."

Cāndo walks, one step after the other. His feet move with hesitation. Then he accelerates, he goes fast and faster, while the trees turn to shadows and the sky flames up in rosy madness. The bright road extends in front of him. This will be the future! The scenery seems familiar, and memories come back. A long time ago, I came along this way, on my horse, accompanied by slaves carrying goods and treasures. And over there, the forest on the hills is where my sons used to hunt! Here, at the street crossing, I greeted kings, ambassadors, traders and spies. Cāndo remembers it all. This plantation. He owns it. In fact, he got it dead cheap. He remembers the price, he remembers the former owner; well the guy had no choice. Cāndo laughs. An excellent deal. It wasn't his fault that the seller drank and played his cash away. And the well over there. He had it built, to show his generosity. The villagers were indebted to him, they praised him every day, and they worked for next to nothing. Look at that shrine. He had built it. The local priest worships the King of All Traders every day, and makes sure the faithful stay in line.

The Merchant King hurries along. The sky turns dark and a flock of crows whirrs by. Over there, up the slope, surrounded by gardens, Cāndo sees his property. In the sunset, the walls and battlements appear to gleam. Windows shine as lamps are lit and watchmen patrol, bearing torches.

The traveller is almost beside himself. Only a mile, in the dark, and he will reach the gate. Just behind the iron-studded door, he will find a feast to satisfy a king, and servants on their knees, and his wife, and those silly girls, weeping with relief.

Tomorrow, he would issue orders. He would equip a trading fleet and send it to the seaside cities. He would load each ship with treasures, and gain a profit that would leave the gods shocked and amazed. With the turnover, he would finance a war. Cāndo had seen plenty of snake worshippers in the small villages, out in the jungle. His men would advance by ship, along the rivers, and simultaneously over land, to crush each settlement. This time, Cāndo would not be tolerant and saintly. When a limb is infested by gangrene, it has to be amputated. He vows to burn each settlement that shelters the serpent goddess. Within a few days, he would raise an army of Brahmins to preach docility and obedience; he would destroy the unbelievers and purge East India of her cult!

Cāndo hurries. By now, the night is bitterly cold and black, and there is not a star in sight. He understands his mission, and appreciates the pain that purified him, and made him a better man, a hero of the true faith, fighting heretics with fire and sword.

When people go serious they become silly. That's what Neta says. Cāndo, as she explains, is the prime example. He does not know what had happened in the morning.

His wife Sonakā, on her way to the market, had met a soothsayer. The guy, all filth and tattered rags, grabbed her hand, Sonakā struggled, but the lunatic refused to let her go.

"Merchant wife!" hissed the holy man, "stop and listen! This is about life and death!"

"I don't give alms to soothsayers;" screeched Sonakā, "release me, or my guards will kill you!"

"Your guards are absent-minded." The seer laughed, and revealed red teeth. "Listen! Keep your money, I want none of it. I bear a message of the gods. Tonight, a thief will try to break into your home. Tell your guards to keep their eyes open!"

The crusty laughed and coughed, he doubled over and retched. "Remember what the gods command!" He danced away like a crab, and disappeared in the crowd.

Sonakā stared after him. One short moment she thought the guy wore his mane in three bunches.

When Cāndo reaches his property, the night is truly dark. That's perfect, he thinks, no one shall see me wearing rags. He sneaks along the wall, and reaches a side entrance. The guards, he knows, are lazy. He pays them like princes, and all they do is sleep and dice. It would be simple to slip in. Tomorrow, of course, he would punish them. He reaches the gate, the dogs bark, the men come running; they grab the stranger and hit him with their rods. Sonakā and her daughters-in-law appear at the windows and cheer the guards. Cāndo screams like a dying bull, he struggles and proclaims his innocence, but before anyone recognises him, the guards have beaten him blue and black.

Part Four:

Behulā

Picture 20: Reincarnation (Bollywood Metempsychosis).

27. Heaven

"What a lovely little toy."

Manasā tilted her head and her eyelashes fluttered like a butterfly, as she returned the thunderbolt. Two fingers, hold it softly, that's what Neta had said, spread the pinky and angle the wrist. Be a divine empress. You don't return a spade.

The Serpent goddess shone like grace personified. The Lord of Thunder, dear Indra, half drunk, felt like a bristly bull, and tried to keep himself controlled.

"Did you like it?"

"It's just wonderful." Manasā gleamed.

"That's what I say. There's nothing like a flash of lightning!"

"Actually, there were plenty." Manasā reclined on the sofa. "I pretty much used it up."

"No problem," Indra grinned, "my worshippers will recharge it in a week or two. Let's have a drink."

He handed her a bowl. With great caution, she took a tiny sip. It almost made her head explode; gods, this was pure alcohol, and no mitigating circumstances. She blinked and pressed her lips together.

Indra laughed. "Go ahead, wipe your eyes. This stuff is made for heroes."

"Dead heroes."

"Sure. They are the best. They have nothing to lose."

"I rarely drink."

"I drink all the time. It helps me thunder."

He refilled her bowl, up to the rim. The goddess shuddered.

"It's far too much."

"Nonsense. Drink up and make the world go bang. My days always end like that."

"I admire the divine in you, but, sorry, I am no thunder goddess. My specialities are thought, awareness and imagination."

"Yeah, sorry about that. It must be tough. Nevertheless, you should handle a cup or two. Your father can drink all day."

"He is Universal Consciousness, and honestly, it drags him down. He says he can only handle crazy stuff like reality by alternating soberness, trance and drugs."

"Good thinking. Personally, I don't do the first two, but number three is a favourite." He glanced at Manasā, and smiled. "Girl, you should get out of your head more often. I can see you scheming."

He scratched his beard. "You are too complicated. That slows your reflexes. How can you fight when you keep thinking? But see, I'm the God of Thunder. I like spontaneity and simple words. So tell me. Was your mission a success?"

"Of course" Manasā reclined and tried to loosen up.

Indra roared with laughter.

"All right," she said, "I give in. I blasted the guy and I sank his fleet and it didn't teach him anything. In fact, I harassed him all the way home. He's alive. I made sure of that. By now he should love and worship me, but he doesn't."

"Ah, humans," Indra shook his head, "you can knock them about as much as you like and they remain as stupid as they were." He refilled his cup. "Free Will was a dumb idea. And Karman is a stupid machine that breaks down every few days and you have to order spare parts from wherever and the batteries drip and the oil gets everywhere and you toss it against the wall and it doesn't get any better." He shook his head. "I like thunderbolts. They are simple and they work."

"That's why I want to unwind tonight. I'm fed up with everything."

"Great!" Indra lifted the barrel, "have another drink!"

The goddess glanced at the stage. "Hey, I like this song. These guys are perfect." She turned to get away from her cup and grinned at the Gandharva musicians. They came from a clan of demonic, magical horror creatures. Millennia ago, they had cleaned up their act to become celestial musicians. The *Atharva Veda* still recalls their barbaric past, when they were shaggy, beastly, and effeminate; well things had not changed much, but these days they had a straight job with proper working hours in Indra's heaven, where they could be as loud as they liked, enjoy all the food and groupies they could handle, and even got a tiny wage. They wore black leather with plenty of spikes, and leapt around, screaming like furies, while they abused their instruments. The bass line rumbled, the building shook and their audience roared with delight.

Grinning like a toxic fiend, Manasā raised herself. The beat got her, and she could barely keep herself from dancing. She stared at the guy in front, with his electric vīṇā, studded with skulls, snakes, crocodiles, and upside down Oṁ signs and thought, O my, black leather is sexy, he gleams with sweat and makes my heart throb. Her heart, at that moment, was in her pelvis.

The man was a demon, a saint and a miracle, he was every girl's dream and every mother's nightmare, wrapped into one, and damn it, he knew what he was doing, and he was good at it. He stood on a pedestal carried by celestial swans, struck his vīṇā, strangled its neck and made the strings weep. Damn him, thought Manasā, he goes for the lot. Now he'll straddle his instrument.

The warriors screamed in ecstasy and threw beer mugs, coins and half-gnawed bones.

"That's Aniruddha. My best lead singer and vīṇā player. He spends half his life tuning the damned thing but the other half is mayhem and earthquake and jasmine and tears. That boy has his act together. One hundred percent cool and absolutely horny. I tell you," Indra leaned back, "he's a bundle of nerves, but, baby, he can play his vīṇā with his tongue."

He lifted his cup, which filled itself.

"Did you see that?" Indra grinned. "It's the music. Rāga'n Roll. That's what I call a miracle."

The Serpent Goddess didn't notice. She stared at the stage, transfixed, and fought to keep herself under control. He's the one, she thought, but who is the one for him? She scrutinized the audience. These people were insane. Only the dead can celebrate with such abandon. But there, in front of them, danced the Apsarases. Sure, they looked like pretty girls. Each was clad in next to nothing, and showed more bulges and curves than sane people can handle. Manasā wasn't fooled. In the good old days of Vedic sacrifices, the Apsarases were a girl gang, they did drugs, they rode heavenly motorcycles and chain whipped erring worshippers. They blasted embryos, led men into obsession and madness, sent them dicing until they killed themselves and shrivelled ascetics with a glance. Then, of course, appeared Indra, who had put on a tie and a suit, for the occasion, and carried a briefcase full of drugs. He had a job for them and a thunderbolt in case they didn't like it. The Celestial Girls called him 'Daddy', rewrote their CVs, got the blood stains out of their costumes and kept their little evil habits to themselves.

Who is it, Manasā thought, who is the singer's favourite?

It wasn't easy to follow his glances. For one thing, the guy was high on everything. His eyes swivelled like a chameleon. For the other, Manasā wasn't really used to drink, meaning she only drank when reason and thinking went on her nerves, and she felt it was time to screw her head off and put it in the fridge. It happened once a month. Neta understood, smiled in sympathy, hugged her sister, shared a few drinks, and disappeared to her river before the furniture went flying. Most of the time, Manasā remained sober, and drugged herself with placebos. And honestly, they were much stronger.

She followed his eyes, as the guy dropped to his knees, made his vīṇā screech, tilted his pelvis and stared at a dancer with eyes that could have set all hells alight.

Got you!

The Apsaras spun like a tornado. Her hips shook, her bosom trembled, she shimmied and twisted, while her head fell back, her eyes rolled up and her face went wet with sweat.

Manasā's lethal eye caught her foot. It was a short glance, no permanent damage, but enough to make her stagger. The dancer lost her balance and stumbled into another Apsaras, who reeled into a third.

"Hey, this is funny," said Manasā, "I thought the Apsarases are the best in all worlds."

Indra slammed his bowl on the table.

"What the hell are you doing?" he roared, "We are in heaven, and this means peak performance and no funny extras!"

Manasā smiled as she relaxed into the pillows.

"It's a bloody waste of time to watch you lot!" The Thundergod made the hall tremble, and bits of plaster dropped from the ceiling. "You shamed me in front of my guest! Is this the best you can do? Are we a bunch of losers?"

Meanwhile Manasā, unobserved, emptied her cup under the table.

"Calm down, my friend," she purred, "accidents do happen. Errors are a fact of life."

"No! Not in my palace! Never!" Indra raised his arms and shook his fists. "This is about entertainment! I don't care what you do, provided it's perfect!"

"King of the Gods. It's just a tiny error. I liked it. It was funny."

"Not here!"

"But it's natural. Accidents happen. If they can, they will, and have to, some time or other. It won't happen again."

"What will? I didn't get that bit."

"She stumbled and he stopped playing."

"He? Who?"

"Mr. Lead Singer. Your favourite. He fancies her."

"That's too much! My troupe is professional! They don't fall for each other! It says so in the contract!"

"Oh come on," Manasā made huge antelope eyes, and pouted like a hyena. "Have you never been in love?"

Deep within herself, she yelped with laughter. Neta had told her all the juicy bits. Yes, a long time ago, Indra had been in love. He had fallen for Lakṣmī, the goddess of fullness, prosperity, glamour, shine and beauty, and, after a long and exhausting courtship, she consented to marry him, provided he would behave himself and leave her tits alone in public. Indra sighed, tried his best, got slapped, slapped again, and learned. For a thunder god, he showed supernatural restraint. It didn't help. The universe moves on, the ages change, and one aeon to the other their marriage fell apart. One bad day Lakṣmī became irresistibly attracted by dwarfish, pot-bellied Kubera, a charming Yakṣa who dwells underground, and owns all treasures of the earth. Kubera didn't look great, but he had excellent manners and more wealth than all the gods combined. He showered her with jewels and glittery stuff. But when his cult declined, Lord Underearth was forced into retirement, his mineral resources were up to grabs, and ended in the hands of neo-liberal investors. Lakṣmī cursed: it was time to move on. One fateful evening, when she was hanging around in the Blot-Out-Bar, sipping pink champagne with L-Dopa and a slice of pornapple, she saw the newcomer. Well, truth to tell, Viṣṇu wasn't really new. Long ago, he had been the odd jobs boy for Indra. When Indra wanted to fight the world-surrounding serpent, Viṣṇu made space for their combat by performing three divine steps. It created the three worlds, and the three layers of reality, and gave Indra enough space to bash his enemy around. Since then, Viṣṇu had been looking for something more exalted. So one night, he turned up at the bar, sipped a glass of Soma, and stared into the mirror. His dark, enchanting eyes were full of melancholy. My boy, thought Lakṣmī, you need a proper girl to cheer you up! Men need help, and I am just the girl to make him happy. Look at him, he is strong and muscular, but he is also elegant. I'm sure he has superb manners, and he will suit my outfit perfectly. Her worshippers agreed, and after a hot night and a hasty marriage Viṣṇu and Lakṣmī became a happy couple. Within instants Viṣṇu was incredibly rich and needed a clipboard, an extra large pocket calculator and pens in many colours to keep the sums under control. Soon enough, the planning brought him down. He left early and returned late, while Lakṣmī read women's magazines and felt bored. Their marriage almost disintegrated. But then, what a stroke of luck, the world needed a hero. Viṣṇu reincarnated in the shape of a fish, and saved the first human being from the flood. Lakṣmī got terribly excited, dragged him to bed, and had him ejaculate all over the pillows. "He is my avatāra," she giggled, "and just as good as new."

A few centuries later, her happiness had suffered quite a bit. When the Milk Ocean was churned, and Viṣṇu did his act as a divine turtle, she cheered up again. "Imagine, my husband endured a mountain range on his back, just to make me proud of him!" Her girlfriends were delighted, and slightly envious, which made it all the better. Alas, life goes on, days are filled with trivia and unless you do something pretty good, love and lust cool down. That's because both are made up by the mind, glands and neurochemistry, an unreliable, jittery contraption that needs constant maintenance.

"You and your dumb book-keeping!" Lakṣmī had enough; she slammed doors, threw his desk against the wall and went to sleep alone. Much later, in the early hours of the morning, when Viṣṇu tried to get into their sleeping room, her elephants blocked the door. The Maintainer of the Universe went to sleep on the cold, plain floor of the corridor.

One day, he thought, I'll get you. It just needs a cosmic catastrophe. Then I'll reincarnate, be the hero, and life will be perfect, for a while. Indeed, that's how it keeps happening. Officially, the guy promotes stability, but secretly, he yearns for cataclysms. They make him a success. So far, Viṣṇu has been through more than twenty avatāra reincarnations, and there is no end in sight. Every couple of centuries he is someone new, maybe a divine wild boar, maybe a hero with an axe, maybe a heroic dwarf. Or he turns into divine Kṛṣṇa, dark, with deep and soulful eyes, and plays his flute at the fringe of the forest, so that the milkmaids come running, and melt in his arms, all 16,000 of them.

That's when Lakṣmī curses her husband and goes out with the wild girls, like Kālī and Bhairavī, to do some shopping, have a few drinks, and beat up any man who grins at them.

Thunder god Indra lost. Without the Goddess of Wealth, he packed his gear and retired to his country cottage.

"Cheer up!" the other gods said, "for us, you remain the king!" They seemed so encouraging, but then they left him alone, with his musicians and dancing girls, his hairy belly, his collection of sunglasses, and his troupe of slain heroes, who only cared for grub, provided it was greasy.

Indra, the Thunderer, the Destroyer of Fortresses, the Quaffer of Soma, the Greatest of the Great shook in a rage. "Anyone who acts as a loser can pack up and be gone!"

The Apsaras girl paled, her knees gave in and she dropped like a withered blossom. Of course she was still appealing; unlike the dancer next to her she hadn't stepped into the buffet. That dancer, red with shame, wiped yoghurt from her décolleté.

"You there, girl! Get up and face me! And don't you dare to look demure! You've got to learn. And you'll do that in the most primitive place there is! On earth, that silly, dumb backwater planet at the edge of the rubbish zone!"

The dancer, Ūṣā, raised her head. Her face was wet with tears. "My sovereign," she wept, "earth is full of monkeys. I would be lost among them!"

"My lord!" another voice echoed through the hall. It sounded like velvet and steel. The Gandharva, who had ruled the stage a moment ago, bowed. "If you have a heart, don't tear us apart!"

The Destroyer-of-Fortresses reached for his cup. It seemed too damn small.

"Indra, I ask you." Manasā raised her cup and the Thunderer filled it. "As a poor, lonely goddess, I cherish love wherever it appears. Please allow them to share their next life."

Indra emptied his cup, refilled it, and emptied it again. Slowly, the world regained its gleam.

"I'm not a bad boss, 'cause I really care. So listen, you losers! I gave my word, so you will go to earth. You shamed me, and you will be born as human beings."

He gesticulated to a servant. "You there. Make the fire blaze."

Then he faced the culprits. "Ūṣā, you danced like a drunken cow. So don't be arrogant. Do your best, be strong, and don't give in. You come from Warrior Heaven, there are thunder and lightning in your soul. When we meet again, you will be better than today. And you, Aniruddha, be humble. You will meet your love, and suffer."

He drained his cup. "This stuff doesn't work as it used to."

He pointed at Aniruddha, "Damn it, boy, you will triumph over anything!"

The Gandharva nodded. His fingers danced over the strings. The chord blossomed like a lotus after a rain shower. He raised the instrument and smashed it.

Indra sank back into his cushions. The years would be long and painful.

The dancer and the musician approached the fire. The flames were white hot, much higher than usual, and their bodies crumbled in the heat. Two bees appeared, gleaming like pure gold, circled the pyre, and disappeared into the centre of the furnace.

Indra groaned. "Curse you," he grunted. His eyes were wet. "I hope you kick ass."

Picture 21: Vīṇā Dreaming.

28. Beans

When Cāndo returned from his journey, Sonakā's belly showed a formidable bulge. He grunted happily, gave her a handful of jewellery, and went off to celebrate with his trader friends. "I'm still young," he declared, to the laughter of his cronies, "my loins are strong." He nodded to himself. "I can father many sons."

While Cāndo celebrated, Sonakā reclined on a divan. She felt too heavy to move. The baby in her belly struggled, and the hot night air was suffocating. She rolled around, wiped the sweat from her brow and cursed the fact that she was pregnant. Much later, when she was sound asleep, the Serpent Goddess drifted into the chamber like a dream soul, and placed a golden bee in her womb.

In an auspicious hour, Sonakā gave birth to a splendid boy who screamed all day without getting hoarse. His penis was erect, his face was red with rage and Sonakā left him in the care of a nurse, who used earplugs. Cāndo slept in his office, where life was profitable and quiet. The occasion called for a gesture. He would give a grandiose feast for those who really counted, and felt generous.

A servant appeared and announced the arrival of a holy man.

"He says he sees the future and he has great portents to reveal."

That means he is hungry, thought Cāndo, but what the hell, he can cheer Sonakā up and eat rice and lentils afterwards.

The guy was much as he expected. A bundle of rags, a face full of filthy hair, and yellowish eyes, glazed by blindness or drugs. Cāndo would have thrown him out but Sonakā was insistent.

"Let him in," she ordered, "A true saint may look as if he is fallen, or crazy, or a hungry ghost. It's quite normal. They do that to scare worshippers away. He is here, in this happy hour, and shall predict a wonderful fate."

"He can say his piece where he is. Outside. I'm sure he crawls with vermin."

"King of all Traders, and Queen of Elegance," the seer began. "The gods have sent me. Hear my prophecy: your newborn son is your last and only descendant. He is full of virility, he is almost divine, he will be an example for his friends, a hero, struggling for freedom, a master of many skills, but what does it matter, the gods have decreed that he shall die of snake bite in his wedding night!"

Sonakā paled and Cāndo's face went red. "Guards!"

How do you describe the adolescence of a perfect young man? Cāndo's son was called Lakhindār, or for simplicities sake, Lakhāi. While ordinary children need years to find their place in the world, our boy got the job done instantly. In a few months, he could stand, at the end of his first year he was running about, and when he heard music he went wild. Four years old he could read, aged five he mastered basic maths, and Cāndo was delighted. The Merchant King smiled at the arithmetic tables, which his darling boy handled nonchalantly, and felt duly reimbursed for the sad fact that no other children happened. Age six, our boy was sound in grammar and the science of the phonemes, and began to compose poetry. It continued like that, year after year. He mastered drama, literature, history, he calculated equations with three unknowns and showed an uncanny ability to memorise scripture, and to quote it, when and as it suited him. Music teachers came, taught and gave up. The boy was far too good for them. Lakhindār could play the lot. The dulcimer, the long, deep reed flute, the squeaking reed trumpets, the mdridangar and tabla drums, you name it; he fused with them and the world held its breath. His favourite, of course, was the vīṇā, that marvellous, ancient string instrument, finely crafted, supremely buzzing, of which the new-fashioned sitar is but a crude caricature. The drone of the bourdon strings filled the air, gave him the breath of life, made rivers stand still and girls throw their underwear at him. "It's a gift" Lakhindār said, when he picked up an instrument he had never heard before, and made the heavens weep, "it doesn't mean a thing. I need to practice, many, many years. In a few lifetimes, if the gods help me, I may play something really good." His friends laughed and elbowed him, but Lakhindār was serious. "I'm ashamed," he said, "but all I play is trivial." He looked at his friends with deep, soulful eyes and braved a smile. "You mean well, but you can't understand." The boy faced a cosmic truth, and it hurt. You have to be good at something to realise how immensely more you need to learn.

"The boy should go to university," said the learned Brahmins. "His knowledge of the *Vedas*, the *Brāhmaṇas*, the *Upaniṣads*, the *Forest Books*, the *Śrautasūtras*, the *Gṛhyasūtras*, the *Mahābhārata*, the *Rāmāyana* and their commentaries is remarkable. Of course he is a trader, but he should become a pundit."

Cāndo scowled. "My boy will inherit my empire. He is a man, and he has no time for scripture and other idle arts." Cāndo reached into his purse and produced a handful of golden coins. "My friends, I ask your understanding. My son is made for business. What use is language study, religious history, textual criticism and post-modern destructivism to a man who understands reality?"

The holy men bowed, to express their gratitude, and accepted the offering. They, too, understood reality.

Lakhindār knew what his father wanted. He just didn't like it. In his mind, the hunt for profit was outrageously primitive. You give little, you take much. Your suppliers starve, your customers snarl. And when things get out of control, you raise an army to suppress the turmoil. Free trade, you insist, is in the national interest. Any king who wants to stay in business agrees. Was this the way the gods had organised the world? He had his vīṇā and his friends. Cāndo, of course, insisted that music was a waste of time. But when Lakhindār played for his parents, and chanted hymns to Durgā and Śiva, Sonakā wept and Cāndo ground his teeth together. In a deeply suspicious way, his boy seemed to undermine everything.

How shall we describe Lakhindār? These days he is grown up. Long, black locks gush over his shoulders. His body is finely muscular; he has a slim moustache and eyes like thunderclouds. Young women swoon when they see him on the street, they feel an earthquake rising in the pelvis, and their girlfriends have to support them on the long way home, where they collapse in hopeless misery, threaten suicide, eat enormous amounts of sugary, oily sweets and make their parents want to kill that boy.

Lakhindār does not notice. He thinks about his music, and worries, as it isn't good enough. He listens to the tunes in his head, and knows he cannot play them. His friends taunt him, but they are cautious, because Lakhindār has his way with words. He can misquote sacred texts to make them laugh, make up a biting poem in a second and sing it to a tune that haunts their minds for days. Cāndo, with an eye on the realities of trade and travel, insisted that his boy learns how to handle weapons, and indeed Lakhindār is an expert with the short dagger, the curved sabre, with bow and arrow and the steel whip, the long flexible blade, that whistles, while it spins around. For a merchant's son, he is surprisingly athletic. You can see he trains with the heavy clubs that Indian wrestlers use, every morning, while he feels bored and absentmindedly composes poetry, for perfect girls he never met and would overlook if he chanced to see them.

By night, he slips out of the palace of his father. The guards look aside, they have been bribed, and the young man meets his friends and moves through town, he listens to the musicians, shakes his head in despair, gets out his instrument, drinks too much and plays the night away.

He doesn't even notice the bodyguards that follow him. In the morning, after his bath, and prayers, he appears in his father's office, where he puts in a good days job, jots down numbers in columns, does calculations, says what his father wants to hear and dreams of music. He is a perfect son and he does his best.

"I can't find fault in his performance," Cāndo says to Sonakā, "but he doesn't understand money. I mean, he doesn't understand life."

"He's our boy," says Sonakā. "We had six sons, and none was half as good at calculations. Why do you complain?"

"I work," says Cāndo, "and I work hard. All day, and every day. I'm proud of every rupee that I earn. He plays, as if the whole world is a joke!"

"Did you see how our boy changes?" Sonakā reclined on a divan and put a pastry into her mouth. The thing was saffron yellow, with pink curls and stuck to her teeth.

"What's there to see?" Cāndo felt annoyed. Before him was a folder of documents, essential stuff regarding dues and debts, inheritance and leases. His wife, as usual, was trying to divert his attention.

"He has dark rings under his eyes."

"That's 'cause he is out all night." Cāndo snarled. "A young man should go to bed early, and be up before sunrise."

"He doesn't get enough sleep."

"He sleeps too long!"

"Young people," she said, "can't help it."

Rubbish, though Cāndo, I was young too. In my time, there was no question of getting up at four a.m. I used my time, 18 hours a day, to make a profit. Drunken friends and easy girls never happened to me.

"He's our little boy! You demand too much. And you know it."

"I know he is old enough to work his head off."

Sonakā smiled. Her husband was a little difficult. However, as age ground him down, he was easy to handle. His hair was streaked with white, his back ached and his joints troubled him. My hero, she thought, fights with numbers every day. He worries, he struggles, he makes enormous profits, and he is never satisfied. In every spare minute he fights the Serpent Goddess. The entire world is against him. But he is a good man, and like all men, he doesn't see the obvious.

"Your son is grown up. He has to marry."

"Nonsense." Cāndo raised his head. "He's still a child. Woman, can't you see? He has to learn what life is all about. I want to see him work and work some more."

"Why should he? Come on, he is rich. We all are."

"It's not enough. The times are troubled. In Assam, prices drop, in Orissa the peasants are revolting. Saffron is far too expensive, the jute market is glutted, our warehouses are full of the stuff, and I need more opium addicts to make ends meet. China would be great, but I have no contacts there. The rice harvest will be poor; next year we can expect a famine. I can't keep my business alive only on musk and indigo and hemp. What if the cholera comes round again? These days, people are poor, but next year, they might be dying in the ditches. Woman, we own very little, when things get really tough."

"We've got a thousand times more than the silly little kings. How much security do you need? East India is in your hands."

Cāndo grunted and stared at his papers. East India is not the world. Security does not exist.

Sonakā smiled. "A young man needs a wife. She keeps him at home. He won't get drunk in some tavern and play his crazy music until sunrise. Our boy will forget his worthless friends and stay away from girls who sleep in gutters. He will want to impress his wife. So he remains home and does a proper bit of work."

The Merchant King raised his eyes. All of a sudden, Sonakā sounded reasonable.

"And he will father sons." Sonakā raised herself and ran her hand through Cāndo's beard. The Merchant King twisted his head away. "That's another reason to stay home. You will be granddad. Your grandchildren need a firm hand, and our dynasty continues."

"I'll think about it another time." Cāndo pretended to stare at the numbers on the page. Which great trader, he thought, has excellent connections to the east and a daughter in the right age?

"There's nothing better than family." Sonakā grinned like a happy cat. She knew how to annoy her husband.

There's nothing better than profit, thought Cāndo, but he didn't dare to say so, as he packed his documents and disappeared to his office.

"I'm sure it will be Sāya," said Sonakā, and took another sugary pastry. This one was orange and turquoise. "Cāndo will decide on Sāya. I'll see to it. Sāya has plenty of influence in Ujāni. He is obscenely rich, has excellent contacts in China and once the marriage is settled, he won't compete with us." Sonakā cleaned her lips with an embroidered silk handkerchief. "His daughter Behulā is the perfect choice."

"I see you are up early."

Lakhindār froze. He had thought that Cāndo was in bed. It was three a.m. and the guards, as usual, had allowed him to slip into the house quietly.

And here was his father, in full dress, holding a stack of ledgers in his hands.

"I am sure you are keen to face a profitable day."

"But father..."

"Don't 'but father' me. And don't apologise. Leave your vīṇā here. You won't need it today. And come along, we've got a lot of work to do."

"At this time?"

"Why not? You seem to like the hour. Today, we'll decide how to conquer the east."

"That's Sāya's territory."

"Sāya will cooperate. He just doesn't know it yet."

"Dad." Lakhindār tried to get his head together, while he hurried after his father. "You are breaking your own rules."

"What rules would that be?"

"The ones you always insist on. 'The Six Rules of Perfect Government.'"

"Tell me."

"First, keep your dreams small and expect the worst. Second, expectations mislead. Third, collect information all the time. Fourth, diversify the risk and gain. Fifth, great changes upset everyone. Sixth, many small steps are safer than one big step."

"Right." Cāndo nodded his approval. The boy might be drunk and tired, but he had the basics right. "So where do I break my rules?"

"You aim for a vast target and ignore the risk. You expect Sāya to act as you wish. We lack information. Expanding east is a huge challenge, and could ruin us. And you advance in one gigantic step instead of a hundred small ones. How will you correct your course while you move too fast? You won't even notice what goes wrong. That's what I call breaking the rules."

"But I don't break them." Cāndo grinned like a leech. "You will."

Meet Janārdana. The guy was oily, fat and clad in glittering, embroidered brocade robes, and walked between two servants, one carrying a platter full of oily sweets, the other fanning the great man.

He was a famous poet and the best matchmaker in all of East India, and famous for his connections, his grace, his charm, and his ability to make the most insane matches work. Janārdana, of course, did not arrive by chance. A few days ago, Cāndo had invited him, and had showered so many presents on him, that his servants could hardly carry them.

The matchmaker had the good grace to remain a humble guest. He had only come, he said, to pay a brief visit to the family, and to give greetings from his old friend Cāndo, who, as it so happened, had a fine son in marriageable age.

Sāya felt stunned. Cāndo! His worst competitor! The terror of his nightmares! He sank back in his cushions, while his mind raced and his brow went clammy.

Janārdana took his time. Great art cannot be hurried. He remained for a few days, slept long, watched dancing girls, enjoyed fabulous meals, composed a poem to praise Behulā, that would have made her blush with shame, received a load of presents, and departed like a divine messenger.

"That guy is incredibly expensive!" Sāya complained, "how can a few verses cost so much?"

Amalā knew his complaints; she had stopped listening to them long ago. Unlike her husband, she understood reality. Their daughter had reached an age when marriage was overdue. Poetry was a must.

When he returned to Cāndo, and produced his poem, his voice faltered. "She is", he said, and tears ran down his face, "so divine that I can't praise her. The little birds sing hymns to her and the sky is filled with music. The stars fade, the sun blushes and the moon goes hiding. My words can't do her justice. She is better than any woman who has ever lived, greater than the goddesses, supreme through all world-ages. Alas, my friend, I failed, for my heart bleeds and my tongue is paralysed."

"That's rubbish," said Cāndo, "and you know it!"

"Let him continue," said Sonakā, "I like it."

"My dear hosts, I faint in shame. The gods thwarted my mission; I can't relate the glories of the bride. My mouth is like a spring in the desert; the hot winds dry it up and the howling sands bury it without a trace." He took a drink from a golden cup. "What a glorious vessel!"

"Consider it a gift," said Sonakā. Cāndo gave her a look, but she didn't notice.

The poet bowed before her, as far as his waist allowed. "You know me; I have arranged marriages for decades, and I have found wealthy husbands for girls who were hunchbacked, had harelips and three legs. I could tell lies, and they would be sweet." He nodded earnestly and reached for a platter of grilled meat.

"You lie and sugar-mouth us," said Cāndo. "But I don't blame you, merchant of praises and sweet illusions, provided you get on with it."

"Behulā transcends my humble praise. I saw her but a moment, and my heart was struck by lightning. Her eyes were lovely as the evening stars; and the blossoms of a hundred lilies shone from her cheeks. Now I can only wish to expire. My final thought would be of her."

"How sweet!" said Sonakā.

"Nonsense! Let's focus on the basics: did Sāya mention business?"

Sonakā raised her eyebrows. "Of course he didn't, dear. How can you mention business when we talk about our boy's happiness?"

The matchmaker turned to the Merchant King. "How can I praise a woman who transcends all praise? How can I eulogise her value, when the wish-fulfilling gem is priceless?"

Cāndo chewed on his lower lip.

"Behulā is the manifestation of divine beauty. Should Kāma, the god of desire, face her, he would drop his bow and arrows and faint. For Behulā, Viṣṇu would leave his bride Lakṣmī, and forget he ever heard her name. Verily, Śiva, the Lord of Ascetics himself, would give up his painful yoga, and swoon before her feet, hoping to die."

Cāndo bared his teeth. "If you describe what Brahmā does, I'll throw you out and set the dogs on you."

"Cāndo!" Sonakā seized his arm. "One more word and you'll go to your office and do numbers until I allow you to come back and apologise!"

She turned to the matchmaker. "Forgive my husband. He mistakes rude manners for honesty."

Janārdana took a deep breath and bowed to Cāndo. "Behulā is highly educated. Yes, her parents took the risk to grant her learning. It's a delight to see her solving complicated mathematical problems, and to be awed by her skill in book-keeping. She can dissolve columns of numbers into sheer happiness."

Cāndo gave a cautious nod, but Sonakā wrinkled her brow.

"Great Lady," said Janārdana, "your future daughter in law is an impeccable housekeeper. She rises before the sun is up, to bathe and do her devotion. She sweeps, she cleans, and she keeps the inner chambers perfect. She can serve sweets and drinks, and she never said an angry word." The matchmaker gave a wicked grin, "She'll make your son the happiest man on earth."

That son, of course, was not present. Good sons got what they were given. Eventually, the gods willing, they would appreciate the wisdom of their parents.

"Behulā," said Janārdana "is like a lotus bathed in dew, spreading its petals to embrace the early morning sun. Her hair is thick like a thundercloud, bearing the fullness of fertility, and drops down her shoulders like a waterfall. Her smile is as sweet as the nectar that makes bees go ecstatic, her teeth gleam like stars in the night, and her words are deep and profound, worthy of the sages, and her knowledge of scripture grants blessings and gain."

"Gain," said Cāndo, "I'm glad you mention it. Let's get real. What can she do?"

"She supports her ageing father with the accounts. She sets up contracts, she aids him in all difficult decisions, she organises the servants and schedules the suppliers. All important correspondence passes through her hands."

The matchmaker turned to Sonakā. "Great Queen, you will be delighted. Her face illuminates the universe, her eyes are large like chariot wheels, her hips tower like the Mandāra mountains, her legs are thick like banana stalks, her breasts could make her back break, her navel is as deep as the World-Ocean and her husband will want to drown in it."

He reached for another sticky pasty. The thing was neon-green and purple and dripped. "I would give my life to see her dance."

"She dances?" Cāndo got up. "You say she dances?"

"My Lord!" the matchmaker recoiled. "Of course she only dances in the presence of her family. No stranger has witnessed her. Her mother said that she danced since she was a little girl. It's the whole joy of her life. Let me promise: your son will delight in her."

"I dare say you are making a fool of me. You describe a monster! I don't want her to shake the world with her deformed bosom: she shall work in silence and bear sons!"

"But my lord," Janārdana would have loved to hide behind the sofa. "She is full of spiritual merit. She does religious observances, she performs ascetic rites. There has never been a girl as saintly as she is!"

"Poet!" Cāndo was pale with rage. "Just for once, tell the truth. Who is her personal deity?"

Janārdana grasped. As soon as he got out of here, he would get drunk. "The mighty, victorious Durgā."

"Excellent," said Cāndo, and smiled. "Let's see what we can do."

The guest sank into silk, and pretended to relax. Of course he didn't; it had never been Cāndo's way to relax about anything, and neither did the couple that faced him. He studied his hosts and granted them a tiny twist of his lips to open negotiations. For good reasons, Sāya and his wife Amalā remained tense. They feared that just one wrong word could make the Merchant King depart and crush them.

"Try one of these. They are filled with three types of lentils and mutton and sixteen sacred spices." Amalā held a plate of pastries, like a shield. Cāndo raised a hand to dismiss her. Now her husband had to make a move.

"May I refill your cup?" Sāya held a silver jug that was crafted like a peacock. The item had wings and a beak encrusted with jewels.

"It isn't empty."

Sāya placed the vessel on the table, he sat back and seemed to shrink.

"You know why I'm here."

His hosts nodded eagerly.

"My only son has reached a certain age. I have been informed you have an excellent daughter, who might be a candidate...I am sure you recall the visit of Janārdana. He has praised her skills, her beauty, her awesome qualities and of course, her anatomic peculiarities." Cāndo grinned. Business is simple. First you shock and torture them. Next, they will agree to anything.

Sāya wasn't stupid. He knew this was war, but the Merchant King had the upper hand. Nevertheless he, Sāya, was proud of his daughter, though he wouldn't have dreamed of admitting it. "Our daughter is worthless. She has huge feet and no breasts, her eyes are dull, her mouth is like a rat trap, her hair is a tangle, and her head is full of nonsense. She reads books. They give her ideas. We are ashamed of our only child. She was born in an evil hour."

"You exaggerate." Cāndo showed his teeth. "I was assured of beauty, wisdom and virtue."

"Impossible. Our daughter is twisted like a strangler fig; it would be a relief to lock her up."

"Let me be the judge of that." The Merchant King raised his head, and pretended to study the ceiling. "Go ahead; you are free to call her."

Amalā clapped her hands.

Behulā floated into the room like a swan. Her sari was embroidered with golden threads and pearls, her hair gleamed with jewels and her bangles jingled. Of course she did not dare to catch the eyes of anyone.

Cāndo examined every detail. Good, he thought, her body is normal. You can't trust poets. Her back doesn't look as if it would break, her breasts are about average and her behind does not resemble any mountain range.

"Stand and look at me, child!"

Slowly, as if she was overcome with shyness, Behulā raised her head. She takes her time, thought Cāndo, I'm sure she's good at negotiations.

"I am Cāndo, a humble trader in spices and similar commodities."

He turned to Sāya. "How old is she?"

"Seventeen years."

"So old? And still unmarried? Tell me about her flaws."

"Dear guest. I cannot think of many. Our blossom helps me with the financial records. It will not be easy to see her leave."

"She can't be that good. You will find a better accountant. At her age, she should have two children, maybe three."

Amalā nodded her agreement, while Sāya ran his fingers through his hair.

Cāndo raised a corner of his mouth. "People will talk. I will have to live with it. Circumstances may be strange, but who am I to argue against Karman? We won't discuss faults and shortcomings. With seventeen she isn't an old woman, yet."

The Merchant King took a small sip.

He glared at the girl. "What's your name?"

Behulā stared at the floor.

"Daughter! Answer the question of our guest!"

Behulā put her palms together; she faced Cāndo's and bowed. "My name is Behulā Nācanī."

She's got a fine voice, Cāndo thought. And she isn't half as shy as she pretends to be. That's excellent. Lakhindār won't have it easy. "Walk across the room. I want to see your posture."

Forcing a smile, Behulā crossed the hall, spun around, and returned.

"Open your mouth! Show your teeth."

The Merchant King seemed satisfied. "What is the first duty of each wife?"

"To worship her husband as god."

"I hear you can count." Cāndo extracted his notebook. "And I'm sure you have memorised a few things. What is the relation between the diameter and the periphery of a circle?"

"It is 1250 to 3927."

"Write that down."

Behulā did so.

"There is a swarm of bees. One fifth descends and sits on a kadamba flower. One third settles on a banana blossom. Another group of bees is equal to the triple difference between both groups. These bees flew to a kuṭaja blossom. One bee remained behind. It hovered in the air, and could not decide if it should fly to a jasmine blossom or to the flower of a pandanus tree. Daughter of Sāya, how many bees are there altogether?"

Behulā looked at the roof, as if she was calculating, and pouted. She moved a strand of hair from her face, picked up the pen and wrote a number. Cāndo glanced at it and grunted.

"Are you sure?"

"I am."

"Are you really sure? Your fate depends on it!"

Behulā raised her eyebrows and granted him a shy smile.

"Write your name next to it."

He looked at the page. Her handwriting was excellent, but a little too strong. She is impulsive, he thought, but she knows how to hide it.

Sāya was delighted. His daughter had done him honour. He had been right to have her educated, no matter what his wife said.

Cāndo raised a hand. "One last test."

His hosts exchanged a glance. The usual examinations were over, what else did he want?

The Merchant King raised his hand. "Tonight, in my dreams, the goddess came to me."

"Jai Durgā," said Sāya, and Amalā nodded eagerly, though truly, she was much fonder of Viṣṇu.

"She gave me these bits of iron." Cāndo stood up and extracted a pouch from his belt. "I hear your daughter is devoted to the goddess. If she is truly saintly, and the goddess approves of her, she will take these pieces and cook them, until they become a bean dish, for me."

His hosts stared at him.

Sāya fingered his beard. "All people know that you live like a saint. You don't boast of your wealth, you wear plain clothes, eat simple frugal meals and dedicate your life to fight the Serpent Goddess."

Cāndo nodded his agreement. His face was like a mask, and lacked all feeling.

Sāya continued. "I am sure your son shares your saintliness. From what I hear, he knows scripture better than the Brahmins do. They say he looks like an incarnate deity, and here you are, searching for a bride." Sāya raised his hands. "How shall we understand your iron beans?"

"To make a bean dish from iron bits is the minimum. You doubt my test? It's been a tradition in my family for generations."

"Dear Lord!" Amalā's eyes were damp. "Please accept our apologies. You are our guest and we will do as you command. I am sure we insulted you. Our daughter is trash; she is dust under your feet. The silly thing has shown pride. Be merciful and forgive her."

Cāndo sat down again and let the silence work its spell. He raised an eyebrow but he didn't say a word.

"Daughter!" Amalā grabbed her arm. "You arrogant thing! Education made you lose your head! Get down on your knees and apologise to our guest!"

Behulā bowed. "An apology is not required. Lord, I will cook your beans."

"Daughter!" Sāya leapt up in a rage. "You are conceited!"

"Father, I gave my word."

"You talk utter nonsense!"

"By no means." Cāndo grinned and rubbed his hands. "I want to see her do it."

"I need a good, new pot with lid. And two and a half bundles of holy grasses, clean water, spices and the iron pieces. The goddess is with me."

Her mother shot up. "Have you turned into a witch? Do you play the saint? You will apologise and accept your punishment."

"Oh lord!" Sāya trembled. "Our daughter is stupid and rebellious. I should have beaten her more often."

"Not in the least," said Cāndo. "I agree, she is above the age for marriage, she is overbearing and doesn't know her place in the world. And of course I'm sure she has plenty of secret flaws. Life won't be easy for her husband. But the goddess teaches us to show compassion. I am a humble man, and I do as the goddess commands me. Given her many shortcomings, I am sure her dowry will be immense. Provided her spell works, and she can cook the dish, she may marry my son." He glared at Behulā. "Prove that the goddess is with you."

Behulā stood like a pillar. Her face was frozen; and though she could have screamed, she did not dare to show her feelings. "With your permission, I will go to the river to purify myself."

The Merchant King turned to his hosts. "Excellent. Take your time. Let's talk business."

Behulā left the house like a spider in flight. She was accompanied by two guards and one servant girl. The group walked fast, through twisted lanes, until they reached the river. In Behulā's head, a storm raged. Her enemy? Famous Cāndo? She knew the name. Sāya had been scared of Cāndo all through her life. He was the dominator, the horror of the market.

When Cāndo approached Sāya with a marriage proposition, her parents were terrified.

Her mother pretended that all would be well. She called it a gift of the gods. Behulā saw her mother was pale and ground her teeth and screamed at the servants for no reason at all. Her father went jittery, and worried, and couldn't keep his head together. His sole advantage consisted of his connections to Mahācīna, Great China, a strange place and a huge market that Hindus didn't really understand. Behulā had not expected that Cāndo would treat her like a peasant girl. The man lacked manners! Sure, he followed the traditional rules. Posture, teeth, wide hips, good tits, and, for the better classes, handwriting and skill in simple arithmetic. Next came the extras. When he presented that weary, outdated riddle from Bhāskara's textbook, she had to keep herself from laughing. Honestly, she had mastered that book years ago, and if you'd ask her, she would have told you the blossoms were a stupid distraction and that no swarm of bees has ever been that small.

Sāya's daughter and her guards forced their way through the bazaar, past the cloth merchants, the beggars and the lepers, and down the slope. Close to the ghāts, the steps that lined the riverside, people thronged, traded, hurried and congealed. Some meditated; most went to have a bath, and here and there corpses smouldered. In between were sellers, food merchants, ascetics and thieves. Behulā hurried, she knew that Cāndo would use her absence to force her parents to their knees.

Her steps were fast, and the guards had to elbow their way to stay close to her. At last, the river gleamed. Behulā was deeply religious, but she knew damned well that iron can't be cooked into a beans dish, no matter how long anybody prayed or wished, and what stunning, eye-watering sauces you poured over the gritty, choking scrap metal. Miracles only occurred in legends, in a prehistoric period when weird stuff happened every day and people were too stupid to think, permanently drunk, or totally crazy.

Nevertheless, she prayed. One way or another, Durgā would help her.

"Devī," she whispered, as she hurried down the steps, "be with me and protect my family. The future is a mystery: I will cook these iron pieces, and when I fail, Cāndo will insult me, he will outline my faults and errors, and damn me as a common slut. Goddess, how can I understand him? Maybe he tries to raise my dowry. Maybe he wants to cancel the match. Lion-rider, when I fail, I will weep and howl and threaten suicide. My parents will be angry, and I will run into my chambers and lock the doors and fast, until their wrath has left them. In a few days, they will forgive. They will force me to eat; I will help my dad with the accounts, and organise the household, as ever. And Cāndo can look for another fool to marry his son, and suffer."

A faint smile crossed her face. It will be good to fail.

The ghāts were crowded, as plenty of people had their evening bath. Some cleaned themselves after a hard working day; others fulfilled their vows and prayed, as they stood, hip-deep in water, while the flood carried their sins and errors away. The steps were slimy. Before her, the crowd divided. Everybody knew the daughter of Sāya. His guards wore formidable armour; they had huge whiskers, sharp sabres and a piss-off expression.

Behulā ignored the bathers, the pilgrims, and the waterfront scum. A ritual bath, she thought, would be a perfect show of spiritual effort. It would prove her dedication. When everything had gone wrong, people would recall she had done her best. She would remain in her chamber; recite mantras and passages of sacred scripture, loud enough for everyone to hear, to make up for her failure and her shame. Iron would remain iron, and if Cāndo wanted a bean dish, he could get it elsewhere, preferably in another country, such as the Land of the Dead. "My great Lord Master Merchant King, they do excellent dishes in Manasā's Land." She giggled.

"What is it, Lady?" asked the captain of the guards.

"Nothing," said Behulā.

Reality caught up with her, and it wasn't really funny.

But Durgā was with her. The Lion Rider would support her, would give her strength and courage, and with a bit of luck, would make Cāndo pay for the indignities he had inflicted on her. In maybe three years, her parents would find a man who really loved her. Sure, by the time, she would be twenty, and an old woman. But she would have a child or two, to make the ancestors happy, and life would be worth living.

Behulā stepped into the flow. Durgā, she implored, help me. Current of Eternity, make me clean and pure. Prepare me for the ordeal!

The water tore at her sari, it swept along her torso, it was cool and smooth and gentle, but Behulā didn't feel a thing. Sāya's daughter sighed. She turned around, dripping wet, and climbed the steps of the embankment. The evening would be horrible, no matter what she did.

"Watch it, idiot!" The voice threw her out of her reverie. Behulā turned. Next to her squatted an old woman, clad in rags, hungry, shrivelled, as thin and wiry as a corpse.

River water dripped through her filthy hair. "You drenched me! Are you stupid?"

Behulā tensed. "Why did you get into my way? Can't you see? People could fall over you!"

"You dumb little fool!" the crone cursed, "I've got one blind eye, but you seem to have two! Anyone can speak their prayers at the river!"

Behulā bared her teeth. "My father built these steps! Who invited you? Why do you block my way?"

"I am your way, you silly thing. And there's no way past me!"

"You are crazy! Maybe you should see a doctor, or an exorcist!"

"I've got news for you," hissed the elder, "I can see you marry! And what do you know, you stupid thing, on the wedding night your husband will die! A snake will take his life! You will hold him, pretty girl, but he will thrash about and twist and piss and shit, while he is in your arms!"

"I won't marry!" Sāya's daughter fought the tears. "I'll be alone for years and years. And if I marry, I will take refuge to Manasā, 'cause she controls all serpents!"

"That goddess doesn't exist," smirked the crone, "Cāndo prohibited her."

"I don't care what Cāndo says! What he hates is dear to me!"

"Don't worry, child!" Now the woman doubled over with laughter, "Manasā, who doesn't exist, will help you. She really has a thing for you! Tonight she'll cook Cāndo's favourite dish!"

When Behulā returned, the fire bowl was ready. The embers gleamed, the air felt hot and bitter. Above the glow, shimmering in the heat was a small tripod, holding a pot of boiling water. Before the contraption, Behulā stood. Facing her, on the sofa, sat her father; he was tense, pale, and at the end of his nerves. Next to him was her mother, nervous and restless. And over there was Cāndo, leaning forward, too keen, too greedy for results.

Behulā did not dare to meet their eyes. She reached for the grass. Since ancient times, certain grasses were holy. They were used to bless the ritual space, to sweep the ground, to consecrate the yogic seat, and to scatter holy water. But there is more to grasses. When trees topple or forest fires leave the ground scorched and exposed, the grasses come and coat the wounded earth. They prevent erosion, and keep the winds and rains from sweeping sacred soil away. Behulā held her bundle, close to her heart, and prayed. Grasses, she thought, soft and gentle, heal our wounds. Durgā, my goddess, come in this hour of pain and embarrassment, and keep me and my family from shame. You fought your way, on the battlefield of life; you faced the demons of greed and egoism, and brought the worst of them, the Asura of arrogance and pride, to his knees. I, too, am arrogant. I should have remained humble, and pretended to be stupid. Cāndo forces me to perform a task I cannot do. At the ghāts, I insulted an old woman, and received her curse. You are a warrior goddess; you understand my heart. This evening I have to give everything. Durgā! Lion-rider! I stand before you, all alone, and will endure the outrage of our guest, the shame of my parents, and years of misery. Warrior-goddess, let me do what is right, and be untouchable like you!

"Hurry up, child."

Cāndo laughed. "No, let her pray. Devotion is good. Let her prove that she is pure enough to work a miracle." He leaned towards Sāya, "and let her demonstrate she's good enough for my son."

Behulā shuddered. With a father like that, I can just imagine the son. He'll be an ugly toad, drooling after every pretty swan, and I'm sure he's spoiled, and fat, and greedy and never satisfied.

She lifted the grasses and whispered a mantra. In her heart, she visualised the warrior goddess, in all her radiance, riding her lion, whirling a trident and a sabre, screaming like a fury.

He vision was flat and pale, and the feeling wouldn't come. Durgā fluttered like a moth in the gale, fell sideways, dropped into the deep, and disappeared. In her place, Behulā saw the crazy crone. Her face was wrinkled like a mouldy mango, and she had raised her wrinkly hands, as if to welcome her. The woman was wrapped in snakes. She sat on a throne of gold, ruby and emerald, and around her feet, scorpions, spiders and cobras swarmed. Around her, crazy trees towered, thorny sij twisted, and huge blossoms dripped as the monsoon rains came down. The crone laughed at her. "What are you waiting for?" crooned the elder, "show them how good you are. Cook his iron beans!"

Behulā placed the grasses on the embers, and a flame surged up, as she dropped the iron into the boiling water. She closed her eyes. The woman was gone. Instead of her, Behulā saw a broad, dark stream, emerging from the gloom, disappearing into mystery, thickly lined by ancient vegetation. The haze was thick; the jungle thick and vibrant; and between ferns and creepers, shadows flickered like lost memories.

"You will face this alone." A group of silk cranes rose, the birds shone like pale jasmine blossoms, as they faded into the height. The sky went dark, the tangled foliage turned black and cool mists embraced her. The air was full of fungi and decay. "The Dark Waters. They wait for you. Come home."

Behulā opened her eyes. "Did I fall asleep?"

"No," said her father, "but for a moment, I thought you'd fall into the fire."

Behulā glanced at the pot. Most of the water was gone. The iron bits gleamed dark and fateful.

She reached for a ladle and lifted the metal bits. They had very little weight, and when she dropped them on the plate, they made no sound at all. Behulā crushed one; it was soft like rice. She looked up. The Merchant King stared at her. Well, let him. She poured a little ghī over the beans, spooned chilli, salt and curcuma on them, and presented the dish, as if it were a weapon.

Cāndo recoiled.

He turned to his hosts. "Sāya, your daughter is blessed. Let us arrange the marriage. My friend, our houses have become one. We shall not withhold secrets from each other."

Sāya cowered on the couch and whimpered. His wife, next to him, was all tension and rage. "We will cancel the betrothal," she said, "no matter what happened to the beans."

"He didn't taste them." Sāya wiped his face, "He didn't take one bite, so the whole thing is null and void."

"And you will go and tell him?"

Sāya groaned. "I could say the astrologer made a mistake, and the horoscopes won't match."

"Are you crazy? Do you think Cāndo will accept that? You shame him. Everyone will laugh!"

"I'm guilty." Behulā knelt on the ground, and faced her parents. "She cursed me. My husband will die of snakebite."

Amalā leaned over and patted her head. "The curse won't touch you. The old woman announced the will of the gods. We will be happy, once your father has cleaned up the mess he made. The curse? It will kill Cāndo's son. I'm sure he deserves it."

"I feel responsible!"

"Don't. Responsibility is a luxury. It only happens to men. We've got a message from Campaka. It seems that the young man was doomed immediately after he was born. Cāndo tried to marry you to this living corpse, and did not say a word."

"He'll ruin us." Sāya whimpered, and tears ran down his face.

"You coward! Shut up! Nobody can force our chicken to marry a dead man! Cāndo wages war against Manasā. He is a trader, and she is a goddess. He lost six sons to her! My little darling, it's not your fault."

"He will destroy us all!" Behulā hissed. It took all her willpower to keep her voice down. Her parents didn't deserve to be screamed at. "If I refuse the marriage, he will grind us to dust. If I accept, I'll be a widow on my wedding night. What happens when he's dead? Shall I be burned on his pyre? Or should lose my rank and purity, and face a life of loneliness? Who marries a widow in these awful times?"

Sāya looked up. "You will live with us. You will help with the accounts." Her father faked a grin. "We will grow old together. And when we are gone, you will inherit everything. Maybe, if we retain a little wealth, you will find a husband, one day."

Behulā rose. She stood before the family altar, rang the bell and lit incense. "Hear me, you gods. Cāndo came as a visitor. He did not mention the prophecy, and so I count him as a liar. I am supposed to marry his son. If I don't, he will crush us. If I do, we may stand a chance."

"Nonsense! Maybe the young man will remain alive. You cooked the iron bits until they were a dish. You proved your dedication and your holiness. He might survive the wedding night." Amalā tried to appear happy. "You are a good girl and you will avert misfortune. If anyone can protect her husband from his fate, it's you."

"Wife! You shouldn't encourage her. She runs into death."

Behulā stared at the house altar. The lamps flared and behind them, the statues of Viṣṇu and Lakṣmī gleamed. Maintenance and wealth, royalty and beauty. How we aspire, she thought. How we are caught by lies and dreams and shadows.

"Even though this is a disaster, I will marry him," she said, "if the gods are kind, he may remain alive."

Picture 22: Flowers of the Night.

29. Plans

Like Sāya, many miles away, Sonakā was in tears. Her husband's errand had turned out successful, as she had expected, and Cāndo was frantic in his office, studying maps, traveller's accounts and making lists of distances, trade stations, and rare goods. The accounts disagreed, the maps were unreliable and most of the facts were plainly gossip. But what could he do? He had collected all the data that he could get his hands on, no matter how flawed or stupid. Faithful Hindus are not allowed to leave India; or they will lose their ritual purity. Regaining social class requires extensive ritual and huge donations to the Brahmins. So Cāndo, like Sāya, had to rely on Buddhists, Muslims, weird tribal folk and heretic tantrics. The unbelievers could travel as they liked. Sadly, what they related was unbelievable. Cāndo read about mountains of gold, valleys full of cannibals, countries, where people lived on air, and air alone, and worst of all, a silly place in the Chinese Himalayas called the Country of Women. Ridiculous! Cāndo grit his teeth. Most travellers were liars. You couldn't trust their tales. If he were younger, he would have gone travelling himself. He would have dared all dangers, fought all bandits and made his way to Lijiang, where the Silk and Tea Roads meet, and further on, maybe all the way to the capital. The emperor? After a few days of bargaining, he would have had the Chinese aristocracy in his pocket! He would have explored the lands of the barbarians and returned with treasure, and trade connections, and a network of agents all the way between China and India. Paying the Brahmins for a bit of idiot ritual would have been the smallest of his worries. It would have been so good, a few decades ago. Today, his hair was white, his back ached and his joints were troubling him. Getting up, sitting at his desk and making love were simply painful. Crossing the mountains and sleeping on bare rock did not appeal to him. Nor did the tribal people of the mountains. Tibet, for instance, was run by unwashed priests. Except for the frontiers, where bandits ruled. The entire mountain range, as everybody knew, was cursed with filth and poverty, with superstition, sexual diseases, malnutrition, goitre, and scabies. Even the rich were poor, and the poor were serfs or slaves, cursed by their Karman, grovelling on their knees, not even allowed to consult a proper doctor. Beyond the jagged Jade Dragon Snow Mountains, however, civilisation began. Sure, Yunnan and Sichuan were full of sorcerers. Cāndo had heard of them. Practically every family had a spirit pot. They took five toxic animals-snakes, centipedes, toads, scorpions and poison lizards, and sealed them in a vessel. In the suffocating gloom, the animals fought, until one remained, which turned into a spirit. This spirit, the gu (an ancient word written as 'worms, parasites'), could be sent to kill neighbours, rivals and enemies, and abduct their gold and treasures. Some witches fed their gu spirits with menstrual blood. Every gu was hungry and greedy, and when it didn't get enough victims, it devoured its owners. Some wizards sent a golden caterpillar after their opponents, to waste their lives away. Sorcerers made effigies of people, killed them, and enslaved their souls. For a god fearing Indian, these lands were terrible. The women of the mountains, as Cāndo read, were strong and proud, they wore weapons and did as they liked. Insatiable furies dragged wayfarers to their beds and did not allow them to leave until they were sick and worn out, and dropped dead at the crossroads. Beyond the mountains there were jungles, where elephants roamed, rhinos bathed, serpents lazed in the sun and angry spirits rose at night, to suck the blood of travellers. The Chinese emperors sent their troops through these lands, and further into the moist and lethal south, but only one out of ten soldiers returned alive. South-West China, as everyone knew, was deadly. For one civilised Han Chinese, there were dozens and dozens of savages, some of whom enslaved travellers and collected heads for fun. Nevertheless, there was much to be gained. Even in Yunnan, the Emperor had his officials, his administrators, his tax collectors, who built their palaces just like they did in civilised China; wealthy, refined people, who bowed, smiled and spoke quietly. They treasured literature, art, and luxuries, they bought spices, scents and aphrodisiacs, and paid in gold, silver and jade. Cāndo envisioned silk, raw and embroidered, and studded with pearls, he considered rare woods and tea, cinnabar and mercury. India was hungry for immortality medicine. The aristocrats, the officials and the silly yogīs would pay anything for mercury-based pills. They would stretch their limbs and do their worship and poison themselves, for mercury is a powerful stimulant, while their hair withered, teeth fell out and total madness began.

The Chinese aristocrats, of course, were just the beginning. Like all civilised countries, China provided a huge market for drugs. The poor worked hard, they worked until they died, which happened early, and what they craved was opium. If Cāndo invested in poppy, and devoted more hillsides and valleys to its growth, he could drain China of its wealth. That would be the crowning achievement of his life.

True enough, he could have invested in representatives and agents. It would have taken years. But it was much easier to exploit Sāya's connections. Plenty of Chinese travelled through the Himalayas, to Assam and Bengal. He just needed to get in touch with them. Sāya could have achieved so much. Sadly, the guy was a total failure. Making good deals and being rich wasn't good enough. Unlike him, Cāndo would exploit his chances to the limit. He would invest as much as he could, would guarantee credits and payments, would install new rulers in the mountain valleys and force the natives to subside on a minimal income. He would bribe the Chinese upper classes, until they were under his control, and eventually, with a bit of luck, coerce the Emperor himself. With Behulā gone, Sāya would go into a state of shock. Excellent. Maybe he could provide him with a few good managers.

The sound got on his nerves. Sonakā, only a few rooms away, wept loud and forcefully.

"Wife!" he shouted, "shut up! I have to think!"

Sonakā howled louder. "You have no heart!"

"And you haven't got a brain!"

"Cāndo! We make a mistake!"

"Of course we don't. Everything goes according to plan."

"Chubby! What if our boy dies on his wedding night?"

"He won't."

"A seer prophesied his death!"

"That man was no seer."

"How would you know?"

"He didn't see he would be beaten, stripped and kicked out of my city!"

"But what if he was right?" Sonakā was beside herself. "What if a serpent bites him on his wedding night?"

"I'll see to it."

"You won't! You are not almighty! Why do you quarrel with Manasā?"

Cāndo snarled. For more than a decade he had wasted money and people on the campaign. His troops had scourged the villages, the slums and the Sundarban swamplands. Year in and year out they persecuted serpent worshippers. Of course they claimed to be successful. Sure, they had beaten up all snake charmers in this town. They burned down fishing villages in god-knows-where. And they desecrated cult places, killed cobras, and abused those who were weak and poor, and couldn't fight back. In between, they sacked a few temples, burned a few shrines and raped a couple of women. Cāndo snarled at them, replaced their officers, threatened the troops and sent them off again. In his opinion, killing cow herders and drowning fishers wasn't good enough. As far as he could see, they lazed around in far-away districts, coerced the peasants and collected bribes, and made reports that Cāndo couldn't verify.

The cult, he knew, was still alive. The serpent goddess was venerated, if only by a few, and no matter how much he worried, raged and paid, he couldn't put a stop to it. Durgā! He thought. How can I ever win?

Sonakā walked in. Her face was pale and her body racked by cramps. She looked at her husband, and yes, Cāndo was not a happy man. His hands trembled and his face was deeply lined.

"Husband. Listen to sense. If you curse the goddess, she will curse you."

"Rubbish! Śiva and Durgā protect us, plus several million lazy gods, who loaf around and stuff themselves for nothing."

"How could you know? How can you even say so? You hate Manasā! Your hate will destroy us!"

"It won't. It hasn't. Listen to this, wife!" He raised his eyes to the ceiling. "Hello! Manasā! You evil whore! One-eyed-frog-eater! Your face is like a triangle! Your bones come out! Are you hungry? Do you starve to death? Come on and hurt us if you can!"

"Stop it! You are vain and arrogant! What if she kills you? Or my son? Serpents go everywhere! An enemy of the gods has a short life. You call yourself sāddhu and king, but you are wretched and old."

"I'm your husband, and better than other men. Your luxuries come from my work!"

Sonakā collapsed and wept.

Cāndo watched her. She can't handle the pressure, he thought, and she is all heart and no reason. But she is a good woman. I will forgive her. He bent down to her. "Wife," he soothed her, "calm down. Everything will be all right. The serpent-slut has no power over us. Śiva and Durgā protect us. That seer, when Lakhindār was born, well, that guy was possessed by demons. You can't trust seers, their brains are frayed and their lives are wasted. He was a poor, wretched soul, a beggar and a cheat. His word is worthless. The marriage will be a success. I have my plans and will protect them."

Picture 23: Banana Blossom Serpentine.

30. Marriage

While documents were set up and invitations distributed, Cāndo focussed on security. He sent his agents to negotiate with ironmongers. Iron, as practically every culture knows, is full of magick. Long ago, the first iron was meteoric; it dropped from heaven and was sacred. Much later, people learned to extract the ore from earth. At first, the metal was soft and almost useless. Bronze was far superior. The smiths had to learn how to purify the ore, meaning larger kilns and higher temperatures. When, finally, they understood how to make steel, the Bronze Age ended. When, around 1,500 BCE the Ārya with their incredible horse-drawn battle-chariots began to invade India, they scored victory after victory as they were faster than the cattle pulled carts of the locals, and their weapons were superior, and poisoned. They migrated over the subcontinent, century after century; they suppressed the natives and fought among each other, and followed the lure of the ore. Iron gave them harder sables, sharper arrows, durable sickles and ploughs that cut much deeper. Iron was power and wealth. The best sources were in the East. As a divine metal, iron terrifies evil spirits, elder gods and anyone crusty, dumb and primitive.

Cāndo placed great faith in iron. Unlike most traders, he understood power. Money, he knew, buys violence. Violence creates reality. When you shock a market, culture, or country, you dictate the laws. Before the weak realise what has happened, all rules have changed. The economy needs cataclysms. You can wait for natural disasters to enforce your rule, or you can create social disasters, crisis, hunger and nightmare. While the government kills and tortures in your name, the profits are simply glorious. That, Cāndo knew, was reality, and it wasn't nice. It was simply there, a law of nature, a divine principle. Whether he liked it or not, it had been the past and it would be the future. Personally, the Merchant King considered himself a Man of Peace. But peace, no matter how attractive, would never last. In all ages, rulers were incompetent, hierarchies corrupt and wealth was based on exploitation. The victims were occupied countries, or colonies, or helpless allies. The rich needed the poor. And when no foreigners were left, and no wars to be waged, the rich would terrorize the underprivileged at home. It wasn't Cāndo's choice. He was a king, a sāddhu and a philosopher. One day in the future, he dreamed, the world would be perfect. It would follow the natural, god-given rules of perfect economy. There would be a handful of rich people, a few rulers and ministers, some public figures, all in the service of big business, and a multitude on their knees. Religion would mediate between them, and prevent the worst. The rich would show their altruism, as Cāndo hoped, and the poor would look up to their betters and admire them. It would be the stuff of fairy tales.

How do you protect your loved ones? Passive thinkers invest in defences; active folk use aggression. Cāndo invested in both. While the marriage was prepared, large ships docked at Campaka, loaded to the limit, heavy with metal. I need an iron chamber, he thought. It has to be airtight and solid, and it has to be large. After all, the couple should not suffocate. It would take at least a hundred thousand units of iron, each of them weighing eighty-two pounds. He employed a hundred smiths; they kept their fires going day and night, they cast and hammered and forged, and welded sections together. In their effort, they created solid plates, perfectly sized, impenetrable for any evil being. Finally, the pieces went to the manufactories of the engravers, who adorned each plate with sacred writ, and talismans, and images of snake-devouring animals.

Meanwhile, troops of woodcutters savaged the forests, and cartloads and shiploads of timber arrived, to feed the ever-hungry fires of the forges.

Cāndo had studied the neighbourhood, and decided on a lone hill, a perfect vantage point, easy to reach and easy to defend. The trees were chopped down and transported to the foundries; the bushes were dug up, the vegetation scorched. Slaves scattered salt: no plant would dare to raise a shoot. Finally, the Merchant King sent his men to fill all gaps and holes: no animal would dare to raise its head. Here, he knew, the battle would rage. The citizens watched in amazement. They called the hill 'Cāndo's Folly'. It stood out like an ulcer, like a place of hate and regret, clean, windswept, and absolutely lifeless.

While the smiths cast an iron foundation, troops of hunters patrolled the countryside. These men, each a master of bow and arrow, were under orders to kill anything. They shot the birds from the sky, they trampled anthills, and they allowed no insect to survive. Snakes were caught and burned, geckoes were crushed, monkeys tried to escape and found a messy death. Cāndo demanded safety. It could only be guaranteed in a lifeless environment. The Merchant King made his estimates, he schemed, planned and calculated, and every day the desolation increased, while the monsoon rains came down and washed the topsoil away. Before long, naked rock emerged. The smiths worked overtime, the hunters patrolled at all hours, and, much against his customs, Cāndo paid good wages to keep them motivated. Sure enough, his employees didn't get much sleep. It made them quarrelsome and accident prone. So what? Did Cāndo grant himself much sleep? In the early hours of the morning, in his office, he watched the numbers grow, and wondered how to turn the expenses into profit. It didn't help that, just a few rooms away, Sonakā had weeping fits.

If the happy couple survived the wedding night, the prophecy would be broken. He would grant the newlyweds a day or two, and drag Lakhindār back to work on the third. First of all, he would downsize the workforce, send most smiths packing, and get rid of the iron chamber. The thing was simply ugly. In the monsoon, it would start to rust almost as soon as it was set up, no matter how much oil he wasted.

However, each problem has a bright side. While he monopolised iron, the price went sky high. After the marriage, Cāndo would have the iron chamber dismantled. His slaves would eliminate the rust and his agents would sell the parts to the highest bidders. If all went well, he would turn a neat profit.

Stupid people ignore the divine. Cāndo did not. He invested in sacrifices. Each day, his smiths performed lavish offerings for Viśvakarman, the architect of the gods. Cāndo paid for flowers, lights and food, and Brahmins to perform the services. It wasn't enough. The Merchant King needed more, and that meant elaborate rituals. The Brahmins didn't need to tell Cāndo that any proper ritual required a dakṣiṇā, a special present for each ritualist that made the ceremony valid. In the old days of Vedic sacrifice, the minimum gift for each priest was one healthy cow. And surely, the holy men reminded him, the greatest trader of East Asia was wealthier than all the Vedic kings together? Cāndo disagreed. He was a poor man, as he said, who fed a household of hungry mouths and sold his goods at prices that ruined him. Surely the learned Brahmins were aware that the Vedic period was over, and that sages, if they were truly holy, would perform the rituals for free?

Of course they might, the Brahmins replied, and they would love to do the rituals in a spirit of altruism, but surely Cāndo was aware that the gods frown on misers, and that it wasn't the Brahmins, but the high gods who insisted that each Brahmin received at least a dozen healthy bovines. The gods, Cāndo replied, were not really his concern, since he had built most of the temples of his city, and they, the regents of the cosmos, had long since decided that the Brahmins needed smaller wages. A few copper coins and a free meal, yes, he could raise them, and indeed, the holy men ought to remember, that greed was a sin.

The sages complained and quoted scripture, and Cāndo, after many hours of debate, went to bed in a rage, and couldn't get much sleep.

Meanwhile, the rain came down in torrents.

Each morning, no matter how wet, the Merchant King rode up the hill, surrounded by his guards, where he harassed his employees. He knew that his workers were lazy, or absent, or downright criminal, and that the only way to prevent sloppy work was being there in person. The foundation looked solid. Now the walls began to rise. Cāndo inspected the iron plates, he scrutinized each inch of metal, he argued and nagged, and he made sure that not a single gap remained. The tiniest opening, he knew, was enough to admit a serpent, or even just its noxious breath. The door was set in a frame that was so tight not even an ant could enter. There were no windows. The roof was solid, impenetrable, a massive sheet of heavy metal. Cāndo thought long and hard, he cursed the costs, and ordered a series of iron animals: eagles, storks, peacocks, mongooses: anything that scares and kills a snake, and had them welded to the roof. To be sure, the damned things needed a consecration. That, as before, was expensive. Cāndo cursed and paid and would have loved to kick the holy men into the mud.

"I greet the divine in you. Please open the door, I know, it's late at night, but I am here for urgent business."

The voice sounded young and female. Maybe it's a Yaksī, thought the smith, a goddess of lakes and forests. Yakṣīs are famous for several things. One of them is their habit of stealing babies and small children. They take them away, into the forest, and they are never seen again. Second: they can infect you with any disease or parasite. And that's just the start. If they really dislike someone, they tie him to a treetop by his guts. Third, they have stunning hips and breasts that tower like the Himalayas, and blot out the sun. At least for the man who collapses at their sight, goes down on his knees and prays to stay alive. Which isn't likely, unless the man is a hard-core tantric of the Left-Hand-Path, and slightly suicidal. But these people thrive on drama.

Yakṣas and Yakṣīs haunt the twilight and the night; they are dangerous and defiled.

That, of course, also applied to the smith. If you are born as an iron worker, you are pretty much at the bottom of the Hindu class system. Society frowns on people who work magic, and indeed, to purify ore, to shape things, to make the hard soft, and hard again, are supernatural deeds. A smith, as everybody knows, is polluted. Our smith was well aware of it. True, master Cāndo paid a formidable wage. From up there, seated on his horse, the man addressed him with politeness. It would not last for long.

Our smith was cautious. He opened his door, just wide enough to dare a look. Behind his back, he held a hammer. "What do you want?"

"Your help!"

Before him stood a woman. She was stunningly beautiful. Our smith was a sober character. He realised that there was something wrong with her. For one thing, she was almost nude. For another, the bits he could not see were covered by snakes.

"Go away!" he snarled, and tried to close the door. It didn't work. The woman reached out and pushed it open.

"My dear man." The woman pouted. "Is this the way you treat your guests? No, don't say a thing."

The smith struggled. A terrified gargle escaped his throat.

"See? I told you. Speak well or remain quiet. But I would like you to speak. You could say something nice. Tell me how good I look and that you love to see me."

The smith staggered back, and dropped his tool.

Manasā grinned. She was sure he would like her smile; after all, she had practised for hours. It's like a sunrise, and just like me: young, innocent and bloody.

"Now listen. I am sure we will get along perfectly, and before long you'll love me. Hey, is that your wife over there? She looks so pretty. I guess she should remain asleep. Honestly, she looks slightly overworked. And what's that? You've got a baby! I like small children; they are so close to reality."

The Serpent Goddess gleamed. "You know, people think I'm death personified. I'm not, at least, not all the time. I've got my happy moments. And unlike Yama, I don't approve of hells. And really, I don't have to kill everyone, that's what Neta says. What's that, in the corner? Now, that's amazing! I admire your skill! These sculptures, well, honestly, I loathe mongooses and peacocks ain't my friends. But your art is miraculous."

She raised her hands. "Not that I approve of it. Tell me, are you prejudiced against snakes?"

The smith choked.

"Speak up. I want an honest answer, and I won't hurt you one bit. My dear, wonderful artist, I love your work, and I know how to improve it."

Now she was really close. The fangs were clearly visible.

"All right, my chunky workman, let's discuss business. That means calculations. You know, I think a lot, and numbers confuse me. I count this and that, and none of it makes sense, so maybe you can help me. Tell me, smith: what is the value of your life?"

The man gagged.

"All right, keep it to yourself. I simply ask a tiny little favour. When you complete the iron chamber, leave a gap. It doesn't have to be large. Just big enough to allow a teensy weensy snake to enter."

The smith nodded. He didn't have much of a choice, as Manasā held his ears and shook his head.

"Make it in the north-east. That's a classic. Magick circles are easiest to break at the north-east. That's past midnight, when everyone one is asleep or exhausted, before the false dawn begins, the dead hours of the night."

Manasā stepped back. "I knew we would understand each other. And if you want to worship me, please go ahead."

Sonakā had no inhibitions. Once, she had been the fairest of them all. True, that was decades ago, but when she came close to mirrors, she somehow failed to look quite closely. Her husband was the Number One. He is a miser, she thought, and that's a virtue, provided it left her free to waste his money as she liked. It would be the wedding of her dear and only son, and it would be the stuff of legends. Her husband would grow immensely rich thanks to all future business and of course she, Sonakā, woman without age, would have the centre of the stage. The marriage would shake heaven and earth, no matter the costs. She would turn the ceremony into a miracle. And honestly, Sonakā sighed, he is almost sixty, and not really young. A man should know when he is lost without his wife.

As accounting and planning were not really her domain, she abducted the best managers her husband employed, and forced them to prepare the wedding. For those who have never participated in an Indian wedding ("Hey, lucky you!" says Neta), there is a tradition that all members of both families attend, no matter how much they loathe each other. True, that, by itself, creates its own dynamics, and a lot of hostility. Indian families are huge, so each side could be expected to invite at least a hundred extra guests, in normal circumstances. When it came to high society, the number would be larger. They had to be placed in different spaces. Good marriages are perfectly scheduled. It is simply impossible that all classes take their meals at the same time.

You can have a lot of fun with ethnology, historical sciences and studies in animal behaviour; a branch of zoology that is rarely applied to humans, which, as Neta says, is quite a shame. Hardly anyone in the barbaric West understands the Indian class system. That's because Europeans, Americans and Australians adhere to the silly illusion that people are equal. They also pretend that individuals count. And that we, whoever that may be, have the same rights and opportunities, just because we are allowed to vote for a new set of ugly faces, every couple of years.

Western people assume that the Indian class-system is hopelessly out of date. Why should someone be respected simply for the class that she or he was born into?

Indians, of course, have a different attitude. For those who follow tradition, it is simply normal that merchants eat in the company of merchants. It doesn't matter how rich they are. Sure, some merchants own whole districts, while others sell pirated DVDs and fake handbags in a shady corner of the market. That's good or bad, or meaningless: as long as you eat with people of your class, you avoid spiritual pollution and support Dharma, the order of society. In daily life, the rich merchant may be the best friend of the rich money lender. Both are wealthy and both have a similar outlook on life. Nevertheless, they were born into different classes, and won't have a meal together. Westerners protest. They think this is silly. However, the West has its own class system, which is just as rigid and unforgiving. In the West, class is measured in wealth and people will eat with people of similar income. The bank manager will eat in the company of the millionaire, the warlord, the aristocrat and the dictator, and maybe go to bed with them. You or I will never be allowed into the restaurant where the pope shares a pizza with the godfather. It's just as cruel as all systems of social discrimination that people invented, to hide the fact that plainly, all of us are apes.

So, in a classical Indian marriage, different classes have to be kept apart.

Ethnologists love marriages. They walk around with clipboards and ask men whom they never met before, if they fancied their cross-cousins.

"Don't hold it against me," says Hanumān, who writes ethnographic studies and reads soppy novels, "Marriages are wonderful. I simply love to weep."

Usually, it's about wealth. That's what Neta says, who sneers when she is asked, 'cause she was married once, as some say, for a few hours, and her husband turned out to be ridiculous. She drops her basket. It contains the dirty underwear of all the proper gods; deities who are happily married, who get fat offerings in the big temples, and send their filth to her.

"Curse you," she goes, and goes on quite a while. I'd rather refrain from quoting her, as books are easily inflamed and tend to burn down houses, cities, continents.

Her father Śiva cares even less. Should you meet him in a sober moment, he would tell you that marriage is dumb, stupid and made for losers. "People should make love," he says, "as often as they can. Sure, they'll have children once in a while. Children are fun. Maybe their parents can educate them. Miracles do happen. If they are lucky, the kids will educate themselves. Mine do." He grins and reaches for his pouch. "Hey, try this. You'll be amazed. Or dead. It doesn't make much of a difference."

Durgā is angry. Much of the time, her husband is cosmic, absent, or comatose. She has to handle the boys, and discipline them, which is a nightmare, as she has better things to do and they don't listen. She agrees that her husband is right, where it comes to love and sex, preferably several times a day, in all sorts of places. That, however, isn't everything to life. "You are totally negligent!"

She can hardly see him through the smoke. He retches and gabs into a spittoon. It's graced with little, laughing skulls. "Darling, I agree that children have to learn a lot. They've grown up, and now I teach them to use drugs responsibly."

"That's rubbish!" she complains. "Drugs ain't half as good as you think. Life is war. They have to learn to kill their enemies!"

Let's change the topic.

Sonakā was in her element. As long as Cāndo stayed out of her way, she could plan, redesign, and abuse her husband's administrators as much as she liked. In short, she loved it. Some of them, serious men with furrowed brows and thin lips, brooded over the invitations. Others, all of them experienced strategists, tried to arrange the seats. It was much like planning a battle. Cāndo, of course, cursed and ranted. He had lost his best men, and felt lonely in his office. "I'll just need them for an hour or two", Sonakā had announced. That was weeks ago.

Cāndo's palace had turned into a building site. Sonakā walked through the halls and disapproved. Furniture, trimmings and decorations? What trash! It would be good to get rid of them. The marriage had to stun everyone. East Asia would talk about it for centuries. Cāndo would demonstrate his wealth and power, and she, Sonakā would turn the day into a miracle.

Her husband, for good reasons, tried to evade her. Whenever he emerged from his office, Sonakā was there. "Shall we use more red? Subdued, self-assertive, or dominant?"

"What," asked Cāndo, "are you talking about? Is it hangings, carpets or furniture?"

"It's everything, stupid!" Sonakā shook her head. "I refer to the general background. Like pillars and ceilings."

Cāndo would have loved to run. Sonakā continued. "What about the trees? The ones in the garden are not impressive enough. They are too young. We need old trees. That because they represent reliability, and tradition. How about the chandeliers? Honestly, ours are far too cheap. And how about a pond near the gate? With a bridge, a few pavilions, and flower beds? They symbolise leisure. Sure, most visitors won't notice. But we have to impress everyone."

"Do we?" said Cāndo, "I liked things as they were."

"They were not good enough. So much went up in the fire. Some people laughed. You want to erase that memory."

"Do I?"

"Of course you do. That's why we have to be impressive."

"Right," said Cāndo, "and now I have to hurry."

"But darling, we have not discussed carpets."

"The old ones will do!"

"Of course not. I'll order new ones."

She smiled at her husband. "He's our only son. We have to do this in style. And anyway, what colours should the carpets favour?"

"I don't want them!"

"Nonsense. You see, if we promote bright green, we favour or Muslim friends. They are upstarts, but pretty powerful. And if we emphasise orange, our Hindu friends will be delighted, but our Muslim friends may frown."

"How about green and orange?"

"Don't be silly. I guess, purple would be fine. And magenta-pink. Of course, we have to repaint all the walls. And change the mosaics. But purple suits my complexion. Of course, I have to extend my wardrobe. It might cost a bit. But when our only son marries..."

"For all I care he can become a monk!"

Cāndo cursed and hurried away. Around noon, he had his meal fetched, and at night, he slept on the couch in his office.

Lakhindār didn't feel much better. His nightly tours had been cancelled. Cāndo had had a few hard words with the guards, sacked a few, to show he meant business, and from now on, his boy could hardly leave his quarters. It was a painful lesson. But Cāndo delighted. "I am sure you will forget your so-called friends in a few weeks. You will be a married man. It's time to face reality. You will do business, and think about numbers. And you won't fall in love with a singing-girl!"

Lakhindār disagreed. Of course he did so very quietly. He knew his guards would report everything.

But money solves all problems, except death (as Neta assures me). Lakhindār knew how to keep his freedom. He made grandiose scenes; he wept and ranted he dropped to his knees, and threatened suicide. Next, he used the money his mother supplied, and bribed his guards again. Soon he was out in the dark, roamed from tavern to tavern, played his vīṇā, drank like a sponge, flirted with the girls, until his friends carried him home. Cāndo, likewise, bribed the guards, and threatened to kill them. It didn't really help, as Lakhindār raised his payments. The guards, cooks, butlers, servants, maids and cleaning staff looked away, when Lakhindār tried to stagger to his rooms, in the middle of the night, and walked into the door frame. Truth to tell, they sympathised with him. The young man was just as he should be, meaning irresponsible, while Cāndo, as everybody agreed, was a miser and a tyrant.

Like most musicians, Lakhindār had too many feelings, and they were wild and overwhelming. On occasion, with a bit of luck, he could control them. But some things knocked him over. Most musicians can't imagine anything beyond a month. Some can't even handle a week. They are stuck in the present, and that's why they need drugs and instant friends and twenty minutes relationships, and end up under the control of a manager who is tone deaf but can foresee the future.

Lakhindār, like so many talented rāg'n'roll vīṇāists, was used to hormone-crazed girls who threw their pants at him. Music, after is, is drugs. Either you take them or you make them, in your brain, in your glands, and anywhere you fancy. And drugs, as all human beings know, whether they admit it or not, are the meaning of life. For without dopamine, no matter where it comes from, the greatest experiences are plain rubbish.

Lakhindār was a dopamine amplifier. The girls who wept during his songs, and fought each other like furies, were simply addicts. And he was used to their attention. He had deep, soulful eyes, was rather remote from reality, promised mystery and hinted at deep forbidden sorrows, such as you get when you grow up too rich for your own good. I could make him happy, was the thought of many girls, women, crones and gays, but alas, he remained remote, haunted by Weltschmerz, and played his instrument as if he wanted to die. Like the strings he had to exchange almost every day, he lived and died and was reborn.

One morning, his mother showed him a painting. It was a lovely miniature, done with a brush, tipped with the finest autumn hairs, and set in a tiny golden, ruby-studded frame, to be worn as an amulet, against the evils of the world. The stones are silly, he thought, but the picture caught his attention.

He stared, and emotions washed through him, and set his brain and heart and loins on fire.

"It's just a sketch," said Sonakā, "Sāya sent it. This is Behulā. Your wife."

Lakhindār broke out in sweat. "You can't rely on paintings. Sure, she looks pretty. I wish it were true. But mom, you can't trust artists. They make the world much nicer than it is."

"I see you tremble. Oh come on, darling. You don't have to hide your feelings. I'm your mother. You can trust me. Here, let me wipe your face. And your father says it's accurate."

Lakhindār took the medallion. He sighed. Back in his room, he attached it to a golden chain. When night came, and his friends called for him, he refused to accompany them.

Cāndo pulled his belly in and held his breath. The tailor hurried around him, like an exasperated ant, and took measures. The Merchant King did his best to remain patient.

"Stay still. And do relax. You want to feel comfortable." The tailor grinned like a horse, "We've almost got it."

I should hope we do, thought Cāndo, and I have no idea why this fool makes such a scene. He has my measurements! I'm just as slim as ever!

Sonakā could have laughed. Age changes everyone. When the Merchant King, faint with hunger, came home from his journey, his body made a few decisions. For one thing, it decided, he would need a greater supply of fat. After all, the next famine might happen anytime. And if you want to survive a stroke, or an exhausting disease, a little excess fat is helpful. Underweight people tend to die earlier than the fat ones. They simply lack resources. That's what his body thought. For very good reasons, Cāndo's conscious mind wasn't consulted. He acquired a sensible padding, and everyone noticed, except for Cāndo, who ignored mirrors, and frowned on vanity, and wasn't close to reality, no matter how much money he made.

"You should wear brocade," said Sonakā, who watched the scene like a surgeon. "With subdued ornaments embroidered with gold wire. Plus diamonds. It should be superior, but restrained. We don't want to flaunt our wealth."

No, Cāndo didn't. He just wanted to run away, to his office, and bury his head in a pile of bills and invoices. Sonakā's projects made him toss on his sofa, in the middle of the night, sleepless, enervated, with thoughts that were just too big to be handled. He did not care what he would wear. A dhoti would suffice! But whatever it would be, it was Sonakā's decision. Her voice was like a blade, and his mind went numb.

"You decide colour and material! I'll love it!" he said, as he hurried away.

Sonakā could have slapped him. Somehow, her husband didn't get into the proper mood.

"I'm glad to see you!" said Cāndo, as he faced his visitor. "It's an important matter, and I want my wife out of this."

The artisan smiled and bowed. He was a shy character, or pretended to be, for of course he was the very best at his profession, and could afford humility. "My lord," he said, "I am pleased to take your orders."

"It's the marriage crown," said Cāndo, "I want it to be perfect. I want it to grant the blessings of all the gods. My son needs spiritual support, and you will make it happen."

"My king," said the artisan, and his eyes gleamed, while he twirled his moustache, "spiritual support is not cheap."

His name was Kājilā; the man came from a low family, and had a miserable class standing, but his astonishing skill had lifted him to the highest peer groups of the land. His reputation extended over hundreds of miles and he promenaded like a newt in silk. "I understand that your son is young and he still has to prove himself." Kājilā offered an oily smile, "he doesn't deserve a crown. You do."

"He shall have a marriage crown that exceeds the glory of all emperors!" Cāndo was fairly sure about this. His son should have a better life than he. And he, Cāndo, would never wear a crown.

"I want the best. You are the garland maker, the crafter of figures and images. Your work is famous all over the world. I want you to combine the temporal and eternal, to unite heaven and earth. Make images of the gods. And blossoms, there must be plenty of blossoms."

"My lord, this will take time."

"So what? Employ more helpers. I want flowers and lots of gold, and all sacred symbols."

"The signs of all religions?" Kājilā was cautious.

"All respectable religions, of course. Man, do I have to explain everything? Hinduism, Islam, the Jainas, 'cause they are good at banking, and if you feel that way, I may even acknowledge the Buddhists. Though they are lazy nihilists and almost extinct."

He faced the artisan. "I want this perfect and I want it soon. All proper religions must be represented."

Kājilā smiled and bowed. The crown would be amazingly expensive. "Who are your favourites?"

"Śiva and Durgā, of course. Why do you ask? Don't you know anything? And the ones that count. Viṣṇu and Lakṣmī, and, if need be, but a bit smaller, even Brahmā."

"Sarasvatī, too?"

"Of course. And Kṛṣṇa, Hanumān, Rāma, the lot."

"There isn't much space on a marriage crown."

"Make the figures smaller and the crown higher. Why do I have to tell you?"

The next days, Kājilā was busy. In his workshop, a dozen helpers worked overtime. A marriage crown is a complicated structure in many levels, much like a building, with floors and balconies and staircases. The images of the gods, of course, were essential. But in-between the artist would leave space for real flowers and blossoms, and plenty of vegetation. Space was a problem, and so was weight. The groom would not be happy to wear anything above ten pounds, 'cause of getting a stiff neck, tense shoulders and a headache.

Kājilā may have had the mindset of a shrew (perhaps the most terrifying predator on earth), but he was also dedicated. In his hands, gold bands, wires and precious stones converged, and turned into a marvel of divine architecture. Soon, he began to solder tiny gods into his greatest creation. Śiva and Durgā, as Cāndo demanded, had the centre and were bigger than the rest. Next to them clustered their sons, then, a little to the side, Viṣṇu and Lakṣmī, riding the Garuḍa bird, the eternal enemy of all snakes. To the other side appeared a tiny Brahmā and his occasional wife Sarasvatī, riding her swan. On the lower ranges, to follow ancient traditions, he placed Indra with his thunderbolts, Agni Fire-Lord; Pavana (a wind god, riding on a deer), Kubera, the pot-bellied Yakṣa Lord of Wealth, and the ten Dikṣapālas. Even Yama, Lord of Death, found a modest place in the arrangement. Kājilā grinned, he knew about Cāndo's fears, and understood that Yama needed placation. That, of course, should do. With so many gods, hardly any space remained for jewel studded birds and real flowers.

Kājilā was busy and did not notice the visitor. That was Neta, appearing as a gleaming greenish carrion fly. She had a close look at the workshop, at Kājilā's efforts and at the thing that grew under his hands like an image of the universe. Last, she delved into his garbage bin, had a meal and laid a few hundred eggs.

A few days later, Kājilā was still struggling. Before him were auspicious symbols, like lotus flowers, swastikas, Oṁ signs, half moons, tridents and similar stuff, all of them wrought in pure gold. Trouble was, where should he put them? The buzzing, filthy flies did not improve his mood.

How can a man think, he thought, when insects try to crawl into his nose?

"How can a man think when his thoughts are rubbish?"

Kājilā dropped his pincer.

He spun around and faced a woman wearing snakes and nothing else.

"You look overworked. Maybe you should go on a holiday. It's much better than dying."

The man recoiled. This woman seemed hungry, and angry, and undernourished. Every rib was clearly visible.

"Don't talk," she hissed, "it's time to listen. Here's the crown. It's not too bad. But there is one thing missing."

She pointed into the contraption. "Where is my emblem? Where is the Black Snake?"

"Cāndo said..."

"I'm sure he did. Look at the Merchant King. He lost six sons. How are your sons?"

Kājilā dropped to his knees. "Goddess, forgive me. If I mount a serpent in this crown, Cāndo might kill me."

The goddess smiled. "Hide it, under the ornaments, under the flowers."

"But Cāndo will see it when the flowers wilt."

"Cāndo sees what he wants to see. Like most people, he is practically blind."

Manasā laughed. "Let me assure you: Cāndo won't care. Before the petals droop, his son is dead."

No more delays! On the day of the marriage ceremony, Cāndo dispatched a group of finely clad youths to escort the bride. Traditionally, most Indian brides left their families. After marriage they were supposed to live entirely for the family of the groom. If they could visit their parents for three days a year, in autumn, they could count themselves lucky. Under the rule of the Sen Kings, the special class of Kanoj Brahmins exerted their rule, and turned East India into a fundamentalist's paradise. Literature was censured, local tales were frowned upon and religion became stricter than ever. The Hindu population was forced to follow fasting practices that used to be reserved for ascetics; sins and misdeeds were only forgiven if the donations were high enough, and girls, as the Kanoj Brahmins insisted, ought to be married at the age of eight. That turned them into little goddesses, sure to bring blessings to the husband's family. At nine, they were a little less sacred, at ten their holiness was questionable, and parents who married their daughters at the age of twelve were sure to end in hell. These rules, as the Kanoj Brahmins would have them, were not universally followed. The very poor, the tribal people, the Muslims and the very rich did as they liked. Nevertheless, aged seventeen, a girl like Behulā was terribly old by anyone's standards, and sure to have a mind of her own. That might have been acceptable in old Bengal and Assam, when people were barbaric and sinful. Nowadays, it was a terrible disgrace. But as the Kanoj Brahmins understood Cāndo, and the cash-flow, they kept their mouths shut; they smiled, kept their thoughts to themselves, gave their blessing and went home loaded with presents.

The young men collected the bride, who travelled securely sheltered in a brightly painted palanquin, and proceeded towards Cāndo's estate. With them were relations and guests of the bride's family, singers and drummers, and musicians who blew on trumpets, horns and sea-shells, as if they were preparing for war.

Departing from Cāndo's palace was the husband's entourage, and it was just as loud and wild and colourful.

The Merchant King had invested in decorations: all citizens between Campaka and Sāya's city had to be impressed. He insisted on accompanying the group, riding a white horse, and frowned at the crazy antics of the youths, and the thousands who congested at the wayside, keen to watch the event, to sell food, make deals, to steal or beg. At least one person has to keep a cool head, he thought, and that head, of course, was his.

The groom was nearby, right in the heart of trouble, laughter and noise, clad in his best finery, surrounded by his friends. Around him were heavily armed guards and a lot of muscular plainclothes men with bitter faces and secret weapons. None of them drank, chanted, or smiled. The groom made his progress, slowly and with great vigour, through revellers, observers and a horde of beggars, many of them exhibiting their wounds, sores and diseases with the pride of the lost and damned. They were catered to by servants who carried rice and water and cast copper coins into the crowd.

Halfway, on the road, the bride was to meet the groom, her future happiness and fate. She reclined in her heavy palanquin, enclosed to all sides, surrounded by relations and guards. Her father, Sāya, had insisted that the palanquin left early. He did not want the groom's troops to approach his house. When Sāya said goodbye to his daughter, and watched her step into the palanquin, he was close to a nervous breakdown. He and his wife would not accompany the bridal train, but follow in its wake, and arrive at Cāndo's palace, when things had calmed, a few hours later.

The marriage was a terrible strain. No matter how beautiful or intelligent Behulā was, her father paid and paid and paid. The dowry, of course, was just the beginning. The bride's father also had to provide the guests with food, drink and entertainment, and to load each and every one with presents. That's tradition, and a reason why Indian families with many daughters may end up bankrupt and in debt for generations. All guests want to be cherished, honoured and treasured. Family members came in the company of acquaintances and business partners, and there was no end to the hungry mouths and greedy pockets everywhere. The guests, in turn, carried presents for the newlyweds, mostly toasters, coffee machines and flat TV screens.

When the entourages of bride and groom met, things became chaotic. Few people in the Western World understand what forces are unleashed. In the old times, people liked to copy the ways of the warrior class. For one born as a Kṣatriya, meaning a warrior, it was excellent form and good custom to abduct the bride. The girl, no matter whether she screamed or laughed, was carried home to the groom's family by force, and anyone stupid enough to interfere was hurt. The bride's family, of course, had to show its mettle by taking revenge. Her brothers, in particular, were expected to demonstrate savagery. In short, a typical warrior's marriage ended in bloodshed. East Indian marriages, in the days of Cāndo, were not quite as violent. Nevertheless, a bit of wrath and cruelty is always appreciated, if only to make a boring story colourful.

Here we have our teams: the bride's entourage and the young men supporting the groom. If we were politically correct, and wise in ethnological terminology, we would call it a mock-battle. Sadly, and for good reason, we ain't. A mock battle sounds like a stylish ceremony. It implies that everyone shows restraint. But in India, just like everywhere, hardly anyone remembers what control is all about. Within instants stones were flying. That's traditional, and in some places, the onlookers have to be bribed to refrain from stoning bride and groom, let alone anyone else they chance to hate. Next, the guards rushed in. Most of them were on horseback, but as marriages are occasions of joy and happiness, they were only armed with lathis, thin rods with iron-shod ends. Lathis are fast and devastating. Every family should have a few. They have little weight, and unless they take out an eye or crush a larynx, they are painful, but mostly harmless. That makes them perfect for the police, and for marriage ceremonies.

The guards put their heart into it. Of course, most of them were somewhat drunk. Within seconds, the bridal procession turned into a battlefield. Behulā's palanquin was tossed about, and her carriers struggled to carry her to safety. No matter how much the bride screamed, out there, beyond her cheerful curtains, was the real world, where people hated each other. The musicians were trampled into the mud; the horns squeaked and went mute, and those who stood watching hurled rocks into the melee.

Cāndo went mad. The Merchant King forced his horse through the chaos and screamed at the fighters. He was surrounded by his personal guards, seasoned veterans who were proud of their sobriety, and these men were perfectly armed and made a point of hitting extra hard.

"Stop fighting!" Cāndo shouted, but nobody did listen.

The dust parted. He advanced, and a woman blocked his way. She wore the red clothes of a yoginī, her hair was long and tangled, and she held a trident in her hand.

"Out of my way!"

"Lord!" shouted the yoginī, "give me an offering, and I will pray for your luck and happiness!"

"Away!" roared Cāndo, "How dare you bring your evil to a marriage?"

"Lord!" the yoginī insisted, "show your generosity!"

"At your age you should be married or dead!"

As Cāndo advanced, his guards drove the woman away. Soon, the Merchant King reached the centre of the fight. He saw faces, drenched with blood, and people who staggered, and fell into the dirt.

"Stop it!" he shouted.

A poor Brahmin made his horse shy.

"My lord," he shouted, "I am poor and my children hungry. Spare a few coins!"

Cāndo fought to keep his mount under control. "Out of my way!"

"Great King! Be generous! Greed is a curse! Jackals and dogs will weep over you."

Cāndo hit him, hard.

The man dropped like a stone.

The Merchant King forced his horse past him, and through the crowd.

He whipped the fools into submission. Once the groups were apart, he leaned back, wiped his face and sighed. I'm an old man, he thought, I can't continue. I'll withdraw from business, and devote myself to a spiritual life.

The Merchant King shouted orders; his guards swarmed out, and the procession continued. Before Cāndo's palace, a space was cleared. The bride was escorted from her palanquin, and led into the hall. So was Lakhindār, who looked dusty and excited, and just a little bloody, as a stone hat grazed his brow. Cāndo, in all dignity, followed them. Guests, friends, family and business partners were admitted. The poor had to stay outside, but to assure the blessing of the gods, they were served rice and cheap vegetables. The drunk collapsed at the wayside, the violent pummelled each other into submission. Within Cāndo's palace, lights gleamed and the ceremony began.

The purohit priest, a man of eminent girth, took his seat. He also took his time. If you want to impress everyone, be arrogant and slow. That's what Neta says, who disapproves of both. The man adjusted his whiskers, furrowed his brow and tried to appear serious. This, after all, wasn't your everyday wedding. The marriage, and his part in it, would be history. The hall gleamed like honey. In every corner, in all alcoves, before the statues of the gods and of course in chandeliers, butterfat laps gleamed, spreading a golden glow and a scent that made the congregation hungry. Between the guests, seated on thick cushions, hurried servants, clad in silk and brocade and stunning colours, who tried to be invisible, while they kept the lamps refilled.

The Merchant King leaned back. The hall seems not too bad, he thought, no matter how much it cost. And there comes Lakhindār. The boy looks great. I never knew how manly he could be.

He watched the guests with satisfaction. The merchants were easy; he knew what everyone was worth. Sāya's friends were trickier. Some of them had odd complexions, and a few looked as if they had come all the way from the Snow Mountains, or even from China. His attendants would care for them, and provide them with special luxuries.

The purohit priest straightened himself. Servants offered water, so the holy man could clean his mouth and purify his hands. He spread his hands in a gesture of invocation; he raised his voice and sang a hymn that made the sun and moon descend, to bless the bridal pair. True enough, in these modern days, sun and moon did not really count. In the Vedic Period, they had been major players. Ritual is valued by age: the elder the better. The hymns were in perfect Saṁskṛta. That's another winner: the language of a bygone age. Most guests didn't understand a word. Not that it mattered much, as they were happily chatting away. After the introduction followed hymns praising Gaṇeśa, the Lord of Beginnings, to remove all obstacles, then Gaurī the Bright, the wife of Śiva, who was called upon to bless the marriage. Lakṣmī would grant the newlyweds a life of wealth, happiness, beauty, love and many, many sons. By this time, most guests had lost interest. Merchants discussed deals, while their wives commented on clothes, ornaments, and their children ran and played and laughed. A few parents, with grim faces, discussed future marriages.

The Purohit priest chanted louder. He was important, well worth his wage, and these gossipers should listen. His next hymn invoked Śacī, the blissful goddess, wife of almighty Indra (retired). True, in these weary days, people tend to recall Indra as a breaker of fortresses, long ago. That's what kings, aristocrats and warriors approve of. The merchants, of course, knew that power is money, that breaking fortresses is expensive, and every war a business venture. They did their best to make Indra their own. That's why you find him in the *Atharva Veda* (III, 15) as a merchant: *I stir up the trader Indra; let him come to us, be our forerunner; thrusting away the miser, the waylaying wild animal, let him, having the power, be giver of riches to me...With what riches I practice bargaining, seeking riches with riches, ye gods- therein let Indra assign me pleasure*.

It made the traders purr with pleasure. Each of them considered himself a poor man. Each was clad in silk and embroidered brocade, and gleamed with jewels, gold and pearls. The reference to Śacī was a fine and traditional touch. She and Lakṣmī were responsible for the well being of the bridal pair. The priest stopped and sipped water to clear his voice. Traditional chants sound rough and hard, and in his age, the strain was obvious. He embarked on the middle section of his schedule, and began with the goddesses Jayā and Vijayā, who provide victory and triumph, and shield the bridal pair from envy, hate and the evil eye. Next followed goddess Śantibatī, who ensures peace and harmony. All three were direly needed: no matter how often you chant *oṁ śanti oṁ*, people are people, and most of them seem to live in trees. They squat on branches, eat foliage that gives cramps and flatulence, and throw excrement at each other.

The purohit priest began to sag. His throat was raw, his voice trembled, but hardly anyone noticed, except for Cāndo's administrators and guards, who were strategically spaced within the hall, and watched all proceedings with cold, calculating interest. When the priest gave up, Cāndo rose and clapped his hands. The servants came hurrying, and served the Brahmins, according to their rank and importance, with food, drink and opulent gifts.

The ritual wasn't over by half. Next followed the worship of the Dhritis and Basus, not that you would really like to know about it, and that of Agni, the ancient god of fire, who grants light, warmth, and edible food, provided he gets love, plenty of ghī and is allowed to scorch the odd house, or street, or settlement.

That finished the high-brow part of the program: the intellectuals and fundamentalists were happy. Now, it was Cāndo's task, as the father of his son, to make an offering of curd and nandimukha rice. I'm supposed to tell you that nandimukha means 'Face of the Happy One'. Neta says you are interested in this sort of thing. I wonder why. Meanwhile, Cāndo took his time. With immense dignity, he spooned the mixture on sacred leaves, which had been laid out on the ground. It felt good to participate. Sure, foliage and food had been blessed by the Brahmins, and would surely appear on the bill. But Cāndo was glad to do something. He wished the newlyweds a joyful marriage, full of hard work, excellent profits, fat meals, and many sons. For a few minutes, he was the centre of attention; too bright, too obvious, his clothes felt strange and new, as if his wife had turned him into a parrot.

Finally, it was time to settle things. The bridal pair appeared.

Lakhindār had been crazy since he saw Behulā's portrait, and the presence of his future bride made him want to sing. For weeks, he had improvised bombastic tunes on his vīṇā; he had chanted and wept, and complained that none of the hundreds of scales of Indian music would suffice to express the beauty of his bride. When he came to work, his father saw dark rings under his eyes. A young man, Cāndo had made absolutely clear, had to have a sense of priorities, meaning business. Sonakā threw herself between them; she hugged her little boy and told Cāndo that he was a cold inhuman brute, a man who would never understand emotions, or anything.

Like Lakhindār, Behulā was beside herself. The god of love and desire, Kāma, had hit her with his arrows of passion and madness, and though Behulā had never seen her husband to be, she had suffered from dreams that made her feverish. Her appetite disappeared and she refused to eat. At night, she recited poetry. By day, she was lost in dreams, no matter how much her father worried and complained. Sāya went on about accounts and bills he had mislaid somewhere, while her mother preached that marriage was business, politics or war, take your choice and live with it.

Behulā broke out in tears. "You don't understand! Your world is too small!"

"Daughter, shut up!" said Amalā, "Love comes and goes. It may start hot but it will end cold. That's Karman!"

"Is that enough for you?" Behulā demanded.

Her father stuttered as he tried to find his voice. He almost mentioned that lust might be involved, but kept his mouth shut. In his age, weak erections were normal, and Amalā had long gone cold and dry. She blamed him, he evaded her, and frankly, he only had eyes for young women: perfect, holy and unapproachable, at least, while Amalā spied on him.

"My dear," he squeaked, "love is a dream of the gods. It's a lie, a glamour, a trap! Down here, on earth, only business counts."

"Love keeps the universe alive!" Behulā was close to tears.

"Love is a chain that drags fools to their doom!" Amalā was pale.

Her daughter glared. Had her mother never been in love?

"Scripture says that without love and lust, the world would never have appeared!"

"Who says that?" Her father seemed upset. The man was rightly nervous. Delusions like that could ruin society. He also worried if he was consuming enough aphrodisiacs, to make the singing girls happy, whom he met, once in a while, in the backrooms of taverns. They looked at him with cow eyes and whispered "Oh, it's too big!" He was sure they lied, and that three minutes were not enough to make them happy, no matter how they squeaked and moaned. His doctor, in all secrecy, had recommended powdered Withania somnifera, the root that smelled of horse piss. It would rejuvenate his body, prevent inflammation, stimulate the immune system and provide erections in the middle of the night. "It's famous since the Vedic Period. Some elders," the doctor said, "take it every day."

"I'm not old" Sāya had grumbled. Secretly, he made his servants buy the plant. It gave him erotic dreams and very little fun. The plant took many hours to work, and by that time, it was deep in the night, he was back at home, and Amalā wasn't interested. So Sāya talked with the doctor once again. "All hot spices," the learned man said, "revive youth. They make flowers blossom and branches sprout."

"All of them?" asked Sāya.

"Of course," the doctor replied, "the hotter, the better."

Soon afterwards, Sāya had a little chat with the cook. The good man took his profession seriously. Henceforth, all dishes were so devastating that Sāya and his wife needed extra napkins at the table, to keep the tears from running down their faces. "Hot spices are great against malaria," Sāya said, while he choked and shook, "they kill worms, and parasites, and clean the guts." That, to be sure, was accurate. "My doctor," Sāya insisted, "says that people who eat hot have a greater life expectancy. Also, they tend to be more spiritual."

That was another truth. Instead of having a wild love life, Sāya and Amalā spent ages squatting in the toilet, perspiration running down their faces, and wondered if spirituality and a long life were really worth the effort.

"Love is at the root of everything. The seers, the sages and the poets say so." Behulā had announced. Sāya shuddered. His wife looked like an angry crab. In her mind, a daughter should never have an opinion. "We are traders, not Brahmins. A girl should never read this stuff."

"Scripture will make you crazy." Sāya's hands fluttered like a bird in a cyclone, "our books are made for numbers."

"I hate you!" Behulā shouted, as she ran out of the room, "you sold your hearts for profit!"

Her parents faced each other in silence. It was high time to get her married. The girl was totally insane.

How can I describe the meeting of our lovebirds? Their marriage was predestined; their souls were one before they glimpsed each other. Once they entered the hall, and saw each other, the world held its breath. The ceremony, the guests, the ocean of lights, the costumes and music; they sparkled and whirled, and faded away. Behulā and Lakhindār stood in a tiny sphere of intense reality, while outside, the world could see how it got along. They hardly noticed when they were bound with sacred string. The husband led his wife, as tradition demanded, seven times around the sacred fire, the guests cheered, the musicians made their drums throb, they sounded trumpets and the merchants grinned at each other, and drank toasts to good business.

Far above Cāndo's palace, an invisible chariot hovered. The swans beat their wings frenziedly, as it wasn't easy to keep the vehicle motionless. Standing broad legged, like a conqueror, Manasā chewed on her lower lip and scrutinised the aura of the building. Next to her stood Neta, who was supposed to provide emotional support. From the grand building, fragments of music floated up. Manasā couldn't get her head around them, while Neta tapped a foot and grinned. Sure, the occasion was grim. But that was no reason to dislike it. Anything is better than soaping the underwear of deities. For good reasons, both goddesses had not been invited. That, in Manasā's opinion, was an insult; while Neta smiled and thought it natural. After all, Cāndo was a man of limits. He felt comfortable with them. It's the restrictions that multiply the profits. You couldn't expect him to be open, or generous, or carefree.

Within and around the palace, fires flared. The merchants had turned the night to day, and enclosed the palace in a sea of luminescent delight. How bright the windows shone! And the scent! Enormous amounts of sandalwood went up in smoke.

"They banish evil spirits," said Neta, and laughed.

"I can't see any spirits," said Manasā, "and most of their gods didn't bother to attend. Up here, it's only us."

"Look at this," said Neta, whose gaze penetrates walls, "it's hilarious."

In the great hall, before hundreds of guests, Amalā performed the baraṇa ritual. She stood before her new son-in-law like a python before a rabbit, and waved an entire series of sacred objects in circles.

Manasā opened her wisdom eye. "She tries to hypnotise him," she said, "and then she'll rip his throat out."

"Nonsense!" Neta laughed. "She tries to bewitch him. Or maybe it's a blessing."

"Tell me, what's the difference?" Manasā frowned. "Now she fumigates him with sandalwood incense. Why should she? He's not an evil spirit. And he doesn't smell so bad. I'm sure he had a bath."

"Of course he had. In the pond, this morning. That's customary."

"And why does she wave this stuff? Is it symbolic or what?"

"She tries to be important. And she wants to scare him."

"That's a relief." Manasā relaxed. "I knew this is about power, and subjugation."

Amalā moved to the next part of the ritual. She began to praise her son-in-law.

Manasā hardly trusted her ears. "She calls him 'as handsome as Kārrtikeya, surrounded by a halo of moonbeams'. It's a lot of lies. He can't be that glorious."

"He isn't. But when she praises him, she forces him to behave much better than he really would. In future, Lakhindār has to live up to her dreams."

"That's terrifying. Maybe I do him a favour when I kill him."

Amalā went on, while Lakhindār squirmed. She took hold of her son-in-law, and stuffed a rolled up betel leaf into his mouth, which contained slacked lime from sea-shells and more than sixty spices, some hot, some bland, and some psychedelic. This stuff, called pān, is a speciality, and may become addictive.

Lakhindār chewed the rolled up leaf, and felt his mouth watering. The stuff was strong. Nevertheless, he hardly noticed. His mind was soaked in hormones. That's gland and brain drugs, made by the body, and a damn sight stronger than the stuff that people drink, chew, sniff, smoke or inject.

Truth to tell, the guests, the people and even the families were a nuisance. Before him stood Amalā, and she wasn't done at all. With practised ease, she bowed and ladled curd before his feet. With this charming gesture she placed him on the same level as all those curd-milk-and-butterfat-addicted Hindu gods. It raised his obligations and responsibilities sky-high. He stood and tried to appear delighted, while his mind, his heart and loins were elsewhere. Soon, the madness would be over. He wanted to be alone with his bride.

Amalā didn't care. To fix his fate, she stuck a diamond ring on his finger. Call it a gift or a bribe, whatever you prefer. That should amaze and commit him. Sadly, it didn't.

Behulā advanced. The young bride trembled with excitement. She placed a flower garland around his neck, and it felt better than all the diamonds in the world. Lakhindār and Behulā turned to each other, and lost themselves in infinity, while the guest giggled and smirked and Amalā felt out of place. Ketakādās, the Servant of Manasā wrote: *the two faced each other and saw heaven*.

Manasā reached for the bow. Kāma himself had lent it, 'cause she threatened to kill him, and the weapons felt light and strong and truly wonderful. She reached for the arrow of desire and aimed. When Behulā and Lakhindār came close, she released the string, and shot her missile straight through their hearts.

Picture 24: A Haze of Toxic Berries.

31. Iron-House

Around midnight, Cāndo made his announcement. The guests got up and joined the procession. There is strength in numbers, provided you are a trader, and the numbers are large enough. The Merchant King, seated on his white horse, led the way.

The cavalcade was accompanied by servants with torches, by trumpet players, by drummers and gong-beaters, and, as the poets recorded, by musicians who played 39 instruments. The effect was loud, stunning and way beyond comprehension. That's forty-two instruments altogether (a multiple of six), including staffs studded with jingles and seashell horns. Harmony was not required; it wasn't even invited, but stayed at home, and suicided.

Noise, as Cāndo knew, was good. It had to stun all serpents. Next to his horse walked a dozen heavily armed hunters, men with tridents, nets, and torches.

"This night," Cāndo declared, "is our triumph!"

Sāya, riding next to him, nodded agreement. He didn't have much of a choice. Tomorrow morning, after sunrise, they would go to the iron chamber and meet the newlyweds. Then, at last, he would feel relieved. At the moment, he felt like a plaything of Cāndo, a man who pretended to be confident and obviously wasn't.

Tomorrow morning. He simply couldn't wait. When he was sure the couple was alive, he would be on his way. It would prevent another round of negotiations with a man who insisted on knowing everything. Like him, Amalā had no desire to remain. She had worn her best jewels. And then Sonakā appeared, who wore hardly anything, and announced that too much gold makes women look like trashy whores.

"On this hill, let me assure you, there isn't anything alive," Cāndo gleamed, and rubbed his hands. While the congregation moved uphill, the iron chamber was inspected the sixth time.

"For good reasons, I chose simplicity." Cāndo smiled, as he addressed Sāya, "What do our lovebirds need? Honestly, a simple bed, a few pillows, and a small table will do." He raised his palms to heaven. "True love is happy anywhere."

"How about food?"

"They had their meal."

"And dice?"

"Of course."

Sāya relaxed. Everyone in Bengal knew that dicing in the wedding night brought luck and happiness. Unlike lovemaking, which is strictly forbidden.

Like Cāndo and Sāya, Lakhindār rode up the hill. His progress was slow, as the guards examined every inch of the way. Not far behind followed the palanquin of his bride.

Finally, the newlyweds reached the summit. The night was cold, and a bitter moon shone on a desert landscape, scorched, cut and devastated, and a wedding chamber that bulged like a hungry monster.

"The world is a barren hill and society an iron-house."

"You are too serious." Lakhindār stroked the cheek of his bride. It felt wonderful. "You are the goddess Lakṣmī of our house. You are the sole stay of our tottering hut; you are the moon-beams of my torn straw-roof and the light of my home. Without you, I cannot live a moment!"

Behulā dared a smile. "You overdo it!"

"Of course I do! I'm a musician!"

"You are a fool!"

"I am your fool."

"Be serious!"

"How could I? Like the golden streaks of lightning that play on the dark clouds, you dispel the gloom of this prison by your beauty."

"Don't make me weep!"

"I try to."

"Poetry is lies!" She hit his arm.

Lakhindār leaned back and laughed. "It makes life worth living!"

The moment was serious: both of them knew the prophecy, and feared the night.

Behind them, the heavy iron door slammed shut. It was locked from the outside.

"That's hardly worth the effort." Lakhindār tried to appear optimistic. "The seer, you know, was insane. He couldn't even predict my father would chase him out of town. And honestly, with a door like this, how could a serpent enter?"

"Snakes can go anywhere." Behulā walked to the door. She could hear faint voices from the outside. She bolted the door from the inside.

"My golden wife, you worry too much." Lakhindār tried to laugh. It seemed strained. "We are lucky, the gods protect us and my father has raised a throng of guards with fires and torches everywhere. They are armed and aggressive and sport terrifying beards. We are safe! Nothing can creep up to this chamber, let alone enter it."

He smiled at his wife. "Tonight, my jasmine blossom, we will celebrate. Tomorrow morning, we will emerge, and the prophecy is cancelled."

"We can't be sure what the gods wrote on our brows."

"Look at me, my dove! My nightingale, my sweet cuckoo. You are the pupil of my eye. You are the blossom of delight. You are the inner heart within my heart. We have the night to ourselves."

Behulā bit her lip. She forced herself to make a happy face.

By Indian standards, the marriage had gone well. The families hadn't quarrelled. Of course both merchants had watched each other like duellists; they calculated expenses and tried to estimate future profits. But that was only natural. In their heads, they had carefully noted what each guest had provided, and what would be expected, when the next marriage took place. Luckily, there were no brothers around, who might ruin the evening by fighting. Only the female guests had caused a bit of tension. When Lakhindār in his divine splendour stood at the sacrificial fire, and took the hand of Behulā, several women went green with envy. Fancy his moustache, his royal posture, the silks that made him shine like a peacock on amphetamines, and the heavy dagger at his waist! He was so masculine.

"For a man like him, I would drop my husband anytime," a woman hissed. "He's a young bull." Her voice was loud and everybody heard.

"Me too," said a woman, "my man hardly comes home."

"Mine spends his life eating. He's like a hog," declared a cross-cousin of the groom, "I wish I had one like him, he's such a stunner."

"I guess he can do his act all night!" an elderly relation giggled.

"Shut up granny! You embarrass our stallion!"

"I hear he plays his vīṇā in the taverns. He doesn't know what shame is."

"Well he could play for me. He would forget this skinny girl."

"Behulā doesn't deserve him."

"She doesn't look that bad."

"That's just her dress, and her make-up. She's old. Soon she will be twenty. Her life is half over. How many children can she bear?"

"I wouldn't care." A time-worn aunt squinted at the couple. "He is young, and strong and rich. I'd take him anytime."

"Sure, in front of everyone."

"What do you complain about? My man can't get it up."

"Look at yourself! Give him a chick of sixteen and he humps her all night through."

"And mine is after me, no matter where and when. He thinks with his balls. Only, he doesn't work."

"How about you, Sonakā? Does your husband make you happy?"

Sonakā flinched. "He's an excellent man. He works, every day and most of the night. I can't complain."

Cāndo had heard more than he liked. He glanced at the musicians. The tune went loud and wild and blotted out the gossip.

Lakhindār smiled at his bride. Behulā, shyly, stared at the ground. Once the doors were locked, the priests standing in the cool night air said their prayers, the trumpets called, the drums thundered, and finally, Cāndo and Sāya made their way back to the city. The noise faded away. Through the heavy doors, they heard the calls of a few drunks. These, too, disappeared. There was an army of guards, stationed around them, who did not approve of anyone.

"They'll be at the palace soon. Cāndo will give another meal. The Brahmins are hungry. They always are." Lakhindār laughed. Behulā did not.

The groom took off his marriage crown. The chamber was getting warm.

"Your father will keep them celebrating for a while." Behulā braved a smile.

Lakhindār grinned. "Only those who are worth it. And who aren't drunk."

Behulā sat on the edge of the bed. Her knees were together and her back was perfectly straight.

"My dad has nothing in his mind but money." Lakhindār shrugged, "I have to apologise. It's the way the gods made him. He tried to do his best, and, honestly, this is getting on my nerves. It's too tight in here. I need my vīṇā."

"So?" Behulā raised an eyebrow.

"Do you see it anywhere? Of course not! Just by coincidence, Cāndo did not pack it, and all the guards I bribed forgot to get it here!" He shook his head. "I wonder how much Cāndo paid."

"I would have liked to hear you play."

"Thank you. I would have done my best. Maybe tomorrow, when this nonsense is over."

Lakhindār dropped on the bed and crossed his arms behind his head. His eyes sparkled. Behulā smiled, and edged away.

"Stay with me."

"Husband!" Behulā touched him, cautiously. "Tonight we should keep our distance."

"Why?" the groom raised himself. "I love you, you love me. I'm a musician and you are perfect. We can make our own rules!"

"We should be chaste."

"That's silly."

Behulā gave her husband a glance that made his blood boil. He hardly knew what to say. Like Behulā, he had been rubbed with turmeric powder, so his skin had a nice yellow shine. His hair, just like Behulā's, gleamed with oil, and smelled of a dozen perfumes. But while he was proud of his golden costume, Behulā looked truly stunning. Hundreds of pearls had been fixed in her locks. On each finger and toe she wore gleaming rings.

That was more than he could hope to achieve. To be sure, he had a vest, adorned with rubies, a sash, embroidered with gold wires, and a dagger with a rhinoceros hilt, studded with emeralds. But as he knew, the thing was just for appearances. The handle of the item wasn't functional. A man and his weapon, he thought, this is just a puppet play! I'm a musician, not a merchant and certainly not a warrior. Why do I need a weapon? The chamber is tight, nothing comes in and nothing emerges. I can trust daddy, this chamber is as hard as his head. He snuggled up to his wife.

Behulā jumped from the bed. "Tradition says, we should be dicing."

She knelt next to the small, inlaid table, gleaming in the light of the lonely butterfat lamp. From a velvet purse, she produced three ivory dice. "They say," she smiled, "that this game decides how our marriage will turn out."

Lakhindār raised himself. His smile shone like a chandelier. "Marriage is a piece of music, not a game. There are scales, rhythms and short melodic elements, which can be altered any way we like. We are two musicians, in one space, one time; we chose a mood, a beat, get into it, and improvise."

Behulā giggled. The way he talked about music brought other things to mind. "But, darling, without your vīṇā you have lost already."

"Lost? Never!"

Behulā cast the dice. An unlucky throw.

"Observe this!" Lakhindār cast, and laughed. "I hope my wife is a graceful loser."

"She isn't!" Behulā breathed on the ivory and focussed.

Another miserable cast.

"You don't try hard enough." Lakhindār hurled the dice, as if he wouldn't care, and won again. "Come on. You're gorgeous, I'm sure you can pout better than that."

"I never pout, I fight!"

Behulā rubbed the dice. She closed her eyes and thought of Durgā, but her image didn't appear. Instead, the crone from the ghāts emerged, laughing madly.

Right, Behulā thought, I know you, and we should get this sorted out.

I pray to you, Daughter of Śiva. I will offer an entire basket of bananas and milk and curd. Appear, Bhagavatī, Daughter of the Destroyer of Worlds. I will make offerings to Viṣṇu Nārāyaṇa. For him, you, the Serpent Queen, shall appear as Lakṣmī, and as Sarasvatī, the Lady of Speech and Art, and recline to his left. As Śacī, Lady of Force, Energy and Support, you are united with Indra. You are Śivā, the Female Jackal, and rule at the side of Śaṅkara Śiva. For Kandarpa, the God of Love, you are Ratī, Sheer Lust. You were never born from the womb of woman. You are unborn, infinite, the Source of Everything. I have no hope and take refuge to your feet.

"For Heaven's sake! Stop mumbling and play!"

"Watch me win!" Behulā cast the dice. "See? The best throw: a ten! Good enough for you?"

Lakhindār scooped up the dice. "Not too bad. But now I'll show you real skill."

He cast, the ivory clattered, and he lost, and lost, and lost again.

"These dice are cursed!"

"Of course not. They are blessed. Our marriage will be wonderful. I'll boss you around every day."

"O no, you won't!"

"You'll love it!"

"I'll love you. No matter what."He dropped the dice in their bag. "Right, you've seen I'm great at losing. Now you should take pity on me." His eyes sparkled. "Let's do something better."

Behulā smiled and slapped his hand away. "Tomorrow, dear. Tonight it'll bring bad luck."

"My wife is a witch. She oozes superstitions. But she can dice damned well." He yawned and stretched. "Joy of my life. I'm hungry. The day was long. I didn't have a proper meal."

"It's our wedding night." Behulā stroked his cheek. "The chamber is sealed and the cook is far away."

He reached for her, but she twisted out of his grip. "It's bad luck for the bride to cook on the wedding night."

"The world is full of evil portents! I wish I had my vīṇā here. I could make a song about it, and you could dance." He tried a smile. It made her laugh. Behulā examined the chamber. It was large, to contain plenty of air, but it had very little furnishing. In one corner stood a tiny altar. "We've got a little cold rice," she said, "some milk and three coconuts."

"You'll make me eat the offerings!" Lakhindār gleamed with delight, "you are my wicked wondergirl! I love you! Come here and let me worship you."

"No way! Leave my feet alone! And if you behave, maybe I'll do some sorcery." She lifted a coconut and smashed it on the floor. The shell burst. She scooped out the contents. "See this, my ignorant musician. This is our pot. I'll fill it with cold rice, add milk, and now we need a little heat.

"You want to make a fire?"

"Only a small one. We need kindling."

"Don't ruin our bed!"

"Of course not. I'll take a little cloth." She seized the rim of her sari and tore. "This strip should suffice."

Her husband radiated happiness. He saw more of his wife than earlier, and what he saw made his heart spin. "Take this," he said, "it's just my jacket. We can burn a sleeve or two."

Behulā settled the coconut shell and set the cloth alight. The flame rose, flared, and faded.

The rice was barely warm, but good enough. "Eat this, my hungry warrior," she said.

Lakhindār looked at the portion. It was truly small. "Would you like half?"

"Of course not." Behulā stretched like a lazy cat. "I ate all day."

She grinned. "You look so cute when you stuff yourself."

Lakhindār wiped his fingers and stretched out on the bed. "Come here, my lovebird," he said, "I want to be close to you. Nothing will happen. We'll simply snuggle up."

"Really?"

"Sure. I'm a miracle of discipline and self-denial. And you would surely keep yourself controlled."

Behulā smiled, but she couldn't stop the tears.

"They did it!" Manasā had a laughing fit. "First she cooked for him, and that's bad luck. And then they couldn't get enough of each other."

"Don't be so gleeful. They are young, and they had fun."

"I simply state the facts."

"Why should you?" Neta looked concerned.

"It means I can do what I like. It's their own fault."

"It's not a fault at all! Don't pretend these taboos have meaning!"

"Sure they have. They mean: I win."

"And now?"

"The game is over."

"Have a heart. They are good people."

"Not good enough."

"Don't be so demanding! He plays his vīṇā pretty well and she's got twice as much brains as he. They ought to be happy."

"I don't care. This is about right and wrong."

"It's only about you!"

"And now I'll send a snake." she glanced at her sister, "would you like..."

"I won't. You do it; you face the consequences."

"I will. It'll be easy. That's because it's Karman. It has to happen."

"Even if it hurts?"

"It hurts Cāndo, and he deserves it. Behulā is strong. She'll live and learn. One day she'll thank me. And Lakhindār won't feel a thing." Her fangs gleamed. "Little sister. Stop stalling. Do your thing. Sing the spell."

"I'm not your little sister. Right now I'm billions of years older than you."

"Then I'll do it. You look after the swans." Manasā knotted her fingers in a complicated mudrā and screamed. The guards dropped to the ground and blood ran out of their ears. The Brahmins collapsed and lost consciousness.

The silence hissed. Four snakes slid into the iron chamber.

The bedding was wrinkled and Lakhindār lay, partly covered by blankets, and struggled to regain his breath. He hadn't assumed that his innocent young bride would be quite as passionate. Meanwhile, Behulā dressed. She was sure that the night would turn out dangerous.

"Why do you bother?" asked Lakhindār. "The chamber is closed. Stay nude. I like to see you. And nobody else can."

"Darling, look at this!"

Lakhindār didn't. The excitement of the day and the fervour of the evening had exhausted him. He closed his eyes and began to snore. Behulā shook her head. Would she ever get used to the noise?

There it was, again. A shadow, glanced from the side of her eye, which flickered and disappeared.

Right, Behulā thought, this is business. She picked up the broken coconut and poured a little milk into it. "Gods of the Heavens, the Many Worlds and the Deep Underworlds, where the Nāgas dwell in glory, enjoy this offering and grant our marriage happiness."

She whispered a mantra for her personal goddess, Durgā. It did not seem to work.

Behulā stopped and listened. Apart from Lakhindār's noisy rattling, the chamber was quiet. Should I expect a hiss? That's silly. The snakes I expect are killers, and they won't announce themselves.

"Serpents!" she whispered, "If you are here, take this gift in the spirit of friendship and devotion."

She placed the bowl in the centre of the chamber, stepped back, sat on the bed and drew up her feet.

Four black snakes came slithering. They met at the bowl, immersed their heads and drank. Behulā stared. She felt fascinated, terrified and oddly attracted by the reptiles.

The snakes looked at her, turned, and slithered away.

Manasā stood near the chamber. She had waited and waited, and patience, as she began to discover, wasn't her favourite virtue. Of course she had tried to look into the chamber. Sadly, iron confuses; she couldn't get a clear glimpse, and that made her angry and slightly lethal.

"Is he dead?"

The snakes stared at her.

"Do you recall what I told you?"

The youngest had an inspiration. It smiled and nodded. "Thank you. The milk was excellent!"

"And did you do your duty?"

"They didn't." Neta shook her head. "The girl is good at magick. Look at those snakes: their bellies are full and their heads are empty. In fact, they are much like people."

"I'll kill them!"

"Let them go. They got an offering and now they are happy. Gods ain't that different."

"They didn't obey!"

"So what? Maybe you are lucky that they didn't."

"Why should I?"

"Karman. Deeds go around and come around."

"Of course they do! They go to Cāndo!"

"But they didn't."

"I'm fed up with this! I'm hungry! I need worshippers. And I will see Cāndo broken, on his knees, begging forgiveness, while I grind his face into the dust!"

"You are hungry and hungry makes stupid! Why do I have to explain everything? I wish I were at my river."

"In a pile of filthy underwear. That's evil Karman!"

"Right. It ain't mine."

"I won't give in. And I won't have cheek from my sister."

Manasā clapped her hands. She went as close to the iron chamber as she dared. "I'll break the spell," she hissed. "I curse you, you silly guardian figures. I curse the scripture on the walls. I curse Cāndo. You hound my people, you harass my worshippers! And I curse those who rest within the chamber. You silly kids! Your life was far too easy! The night is long. I'll get you!"

Neta frowned. She had trouble keeping the swans under control. "You hurt two simple, loving people who never caused you any harm!"

"Who cares?" Manasā was barely audible, as she circled the chamber, widdershins, whispering spells at every corner. Finally she stopped at the North-East, the dangerous direction where magic fails, between midnight and sunrise, and horror erupts from the Underworlds.

Manasā clapped her hands and hissed. The thinnest of all snakes, Kālanāginī emerged, black like the heart of the abyss.

Manasā snatched it and pushed it through the slit. "Kill him! Or I will kill you!"

Poor Kāli was terrified. In real life, this type of snake has a friendly character. Her toxic teeth are in the back of her mouth, and she only uses them when no other options are available. Killing humans wasn't part of her agenda.

"These people are our enemies!" Manasā hissed, "go in, bite the guy and come back alive."

Cautiously, Kālanāginī slid into the iron chamber. The light was dim. She could make out a pair of humans. One looked as if he was asleep, the other, female, sat on the bed and quivered with anxiety. Kālanāginī slithered, when Behulā looked elsewhere, and froze when she looked. Like all clever snakes, she could make herself invisible when confronted with humans, insectivores, shrews, bats and rodents, who are, evolutionary speaking, pretty much the same.

The black snake watched. The man seemed harmless. And the woman was so keen to protect him. She had a knife, and she held it like a simpleton. This is wrong, Kālanāginī thought. She's no match for me, and I can't bite him. He's big and stupid, but he never did me wrong.

From the outside, she heard Manasā's voice. "Kill him! Kill him!"

I won't, thought Kālanāginī.

Maybe, if I wait long enough, Manasā will go away.

Kālanāginī crept between a few cushions on the ground.

Outside, Manasā was getting frantic. The greenish glow of the false dawn shimmered in the east, and the fresh gusts of early morning wind tousled her hair. Soon, the insects would wake, the birds would chorus, the sun would rise, and the curse be broken. Manasā hissed. She could hear Lakhindār snoring, and it made her mad.

In the chamber, Kālanāginī had made herself comfortable. The pillows were slightly sweaty, but warm. In an hour or two, the little snake thought, the sun is up and I can go home. Gods may be well and good, if you believe in them, but you can't have them boss you around. It simply makes them arrogant.

This can't go on, thought Manasā; I have to deal with Behulā. That little bitch is wide awake. We'll put a stop to it.

The Serpent goddess formed a complicated mudrā. She raised her twisted fingers to heaven and sang a mantra. Her voice sounded comforting, peaceful and happy. It was sheer joy to relax into it. Within the chamber, Behulā yawned, stretched out and collapsed. Soon, her soft, ladylike snores joined those of her husband.

Outside the chamber, Manasā grinned from ear to ear. Now she needed a small, modest associate. She formed another mudrā, breathed on her hands, she visualised, fused emotions and desires, and created a small and hungry creature. When she opened her hands, the tiny animal looked up. It seemed so fragile and so innocent. Its body was minute, its legs like finely wrought wires, its eyes huge and its sting twitched with excitement. "Hello my little pest," said Manasā, "let me give you a sweet humming voice. It'll be like music." She smiled as she stroked her creation.

She pushed the little beast into the iron chamber. It had perfect vision in the gloom. Over there, it sensed, was a wonderful source of nourishment. It smelled of sweat and heat and passion.

"Manasā!" Neta was in a rage. "Are you aware that you create a nightmare?"

"Why should I worry about problems?" Manasā tried to appear innocent. "Like everyone, I focus on solutions."

"That's what you said when you invented scorpions!"

"So what? They are neat and shiny, friendly, accommodating and they love to dance."

"They dance?"

"Sure. I took care of that. It's so romantic. At night, by moonlight, 'cause they are shy. They hold each other with their claws and then it's one step right, one step left, raise the sting and smile."

"You made life more complicated!"

"Neta, leave me alone. Did you see my new insect? It's friendly and comforting. It likes company. I'm sure that everyone will love it."

When the first mosquito emerged from the iron chamber, it was full and thoroughly happy. The goddesses hardly noticed.

"This is your stupid idiocy!" Neta was at the limit. "You create stuff the world can't handle, and then you infuse it with life and expect everyone to admire you!"

"It's not idiotic, it's art. I think quite a lot. You would be amazed how much I think!" Manasā screamed, "Other gods create rhinoceroses and giant turtles! Our father invented the Ganges river dolphin, just to please Gaṅgā. I have no idea why! It only made her vain and self-important! Brahmā invents stuff and realities and creatures all the time, and he doesn't think at all! And I'm not allowed to invent a tiny little animal that does no harm and is plainly beautiful. Listen to its voice! It sings!"

"And the spiders?"

"I didn't make them. Spiders were always around."

"Centipedes. Let me hear you squirm out of that one."

"I never heard of them. Not even the toxic ones which grow as long as your forearm and eat bats. Or those in the early Carbon, two meters long, and no, I've never been there, and I don't know they ever happened."

"How about ticks?"

"Ticks are harmless."

"They ain't!"

"Look, Neta, I was really careful with them. I made them blind and stupid. They hardly know anything. No eyes, no ears, no emotions; just simple desires, a sense of priority and a perfect sense of smell."

"There you are!"

"Only for butter acid and rancid, adult sweat."

"That should suffice!"

"Neta, get real: ticks are cute. No animal could be more innocent."

"They carry diseases!"

"Don't blame me! Go to Yama in the Underworld, tell him; he's responsible."

"Look! Your little nightmare sucked blood!"

"Of course it did, silly. And it was just a few drops!"

The mosquito froze. All of a sudden, it was the centre of attention.

Neta couldn't be stopped. "Look how bloated it is!"

"That's great! Blood is nourishment. Now it will lay eggs."

"And then?"

"There will be more mosquitoes. Honestly, I can't understand you. I made it self-replicable. Like all good things, it will be happy everywhere." Manasā gesticulated. "It's life, get used to it. The males dance, the females suck. I like it."

"And what did it do in there?" Neta pointed at the iron chamber.

"Yes, darling, tell us. What did you achieve?"

"Sorry," squeaked the mosquito. "I apologise, please don't be so loud. I went in, just like you said, and there was this sweaty human. He had a leg, it emerged from the blankets. I landed. And as I wasn't sure what to do, I stung. Just a little bit."

"And then?"

"I stung another bit."

"What happened?"

"The leg kicked. It wasn't my fault."

"And where?"

"Into the pillows. There was a snake in there."

"That's it," Manasā gleamed. "This is my lucky day."

"Stop gloating! You should be ashamed!" Neta ran her hands through her hair. Half of her face had gone pale, and the contours of a skull emerged. Unlike most skulls, it didn't smile.

Manasā ignored her. "My tiny little darling. I'm sure it must have been hard. What happened?"

"The leg was bitten."

"By the snake. I guessed as much."

"And there was a woman. She screamed. And she got out a knife, and went after the snake."

"And then?"

"The snake lost part of its tail. Honestly, it wasn't much."

"And next?"

"I've got no idea." The mosquito stroked its antennae. "With so much screaming and weeping, I couldn't think."

By sunrise, Manasā and Neta had left. Like them, the mosquito had departed. The poor little thing was totally exhausted. Planet Earth, it realised, is a stressful place. Goddesses are trouble, people make a scene and when the sun rose, it was altogether too bright.

Next to the chamber, the guards woke. They knocked on the door of the chamber and called. Within, they could hear Behulā weeping. This was real trouble: Cāndo would punish them. They did not notice the slim black snake that emerged from the gap in the North East, and disappeared down the hillside. Poor serpent Kālanāginī felt guilty. It made her sing:

Sun, moon and all gods may be my witnesses,
It wasn't my mistake; the gods made me do it,
And Lakhindār kicked my teeth for no reason at all.

Picture 25: Call of the Koel.

32. Water's Edge

The guards carried Lakhindār's corpse into the pale sunlight. Behulā followed and collapsed.

Lakhindār looked as if he was sleeping. Only his leg was slightly swollen. He was nude. Cāndo's men covered him with blankets. Behulā hardly noticed. Her face was wet and her eyes were swollen. She squatted, in her torn sari, on the ground and covered her face in her hands. The guests averted their eyes. Behulā was a widow, cursed by fate, and a carrier of bad luck.

Nearby, Cāndo gave orders. The raft out of banana wood, bound with jute and hemp, and stabilised with bamboo pegs, had to be ready soon. His only son would go on his last voyage, as all victims of snakebite should, drift down the river like a mirage, and fade into eternity. Next to Lakhindār's corpse, Sonakā sobbed, as if she wanted to blame all gods, all people and all beings for her anguish. Eventually, her tears ceased. She raised herself and grabbed Behulā by her shoulders. "You bitch! You tempted my son, you dragged him to hell. Look at yourself, slut! He was nude and your sari is torn! And when he needed you, you stood by and watched him die!"

Behulā stared at the ground.

"You cooked for him! You made a fire and invited evil! Look at yourself. There's red colour on your brow! That's the sign of a married wife! Tell me, demoness: why doesn't it fade? Why didn't you guard him? You should have given your life!"

Cāndo pulled her away. "Let her be. It's not her fault."

"It's your fault!" Sonakā was beside herself. "You insulted the serpent goddess! You and your vanity!"

Cāndo turned away. He forced a fleeting smile for the parents of the bride, who stood at the edge of the congregation, pale and tense, and hopelessly embarrassed.

"Behulā! Face me!" screamed his wife. "Go and poison yourself!" Sonakā bent over and shook. "I'm doomed. My husband is cursed and my last son is dead. Who will brighten up my days, and weep for me when I am gone?"

"Shut up, wife!" Cāndo's voice was all metal. "It's good the way it is. The One-Eyed Witch has done her worst. We are free, what can she do to us?"

"Seven sons are dead!" screamed his wife. She swayed like a wild animal in a cage. "He is dead. He is dead. He is dead."

"Wife! Pull yourself together! We are old, and if we live or die, it doesn't matter."

"You idiot! You made the goddess mad! And you persist in your stupidity! Why can't you apologise? Why do you fail to pray? You should prepare an offering! You should ask her to make Lakhindār return to life!"

The Merchant King recoiled.

"Look at me, husband! You sinned, and I pay the price. My heart is like a shrivelled fruit. How can I face the neighbours?"

"I don't care about the neighbours! I can ruin any of them!"

"My husband." Sonakā howled in pain. "I see you and the earth turns black."

Cāndo tried to pull her up. She clawed his cheek. He caught her hand. "Get up! We have to fulfil our duties. If you want to howl, do it in your chambers, and shut the doors! Our guests need to be cared for. They want food, and entertainment, and a friendly goodbye!"

"Food! How can you even think of food! We have to fast for thirty days!"

"That's it! Suffer if you want to. I won't let the Serpent Whore upset my life! I don't care what custom demands! You there! Run home and fetch my breakfast. I will have baked fish, eggplant, rice with turmeric, and pepper sauce. I won't fast and I won't mourn."

"My lord," the servant was on his knees. "My king. You demanded an ohjā sorcerer. He is here."

The man advanced, his hair was tangled, his beard had the colour of old curry, and he wore a thick cluster of amulets on his sweaty chest. Cāndo's mouth turned into a single, tense line. "Is this the best you could get?"

"My lord, he is the only one around. All the great ohjās are gone. They have assembled in Orissa, at a country fair, to hold their competition. This man didn't go. He says it was preordained."

"I say they didn't want him."

"Lord. We have sent riders. Surely another ohjā will be here soon. Right now, he is your only choice."

Cāndo glared at the sorcerer. The man looked poor and hungry. How can a holy man be poor? Doesn't he understand human nature? Or is he simply dumb?

The man tried to stand straight. "I am Kṛttibās, and I am famous everywhere."

Cāndo bared his teeth. "Well, Kṛttibās, I am sure you are. Or you will be, if you fail. Believe me, word will go around. Here is my son. A snake killed him. Return him to life."

"How long has he been dead?"

"Just a few hours."

"Excellent." The sorcerer produced his medicine pouch. It looked as if he had found the item in a rubbish pile. "In the noontime heat, he will start to rot. You are lucky I was close, and that the day is young."

"Work your magic. If you succeed, you will be paid."

"To revive him, I need the milk of an unborn goat."

"Do you take me for a fool? You can do better than that!"

"There is another option." The sorcerer scratched an ulcer on his cheek. "I need the dirt from Śiva's locks."

Cāndo turned to his servant. "Chase him away. Hit him as much as you like."

Another ohjā approached. This one wore a costume that gleamed with gold, azure silk and radiated overbearing perfumes. The Merchant King snarled at him.

"Are you a sorcerer or a dummy?"

"I am the greatest ohjā there is, and at your service."

"Since Dhanvantari, all ohjās were failures."

"My lord, I am Dhanvantari's son. The gods sent me."

Cāndo tried a smile. It didn't really work. He stared at the little flowers, embroidered on the sorcerer's shoes, and the pearls that graced them.

"Which gods?"

"Śiva and Durgā. Who else?"

"You are too young."

"I'm older than I look. It's the elixir of life. My father passed the secret to me. He taught me, and I own his talismans, his books and ritual utensils. I am Suṣeṇa."

"I acknowledge Dhanvantari, as my guru and my friend. Tell me, boy, what is your skill?"

"I can revive the dead."

"Go and do it. I expect results."

The snake-doctor reached into his vest and produced a silver case. It contained a piece of chalk. The ohjā got down on his knees and drew a tangle of lines on the doorstep of the iron chamber.

"What's that supposed to do?"

"Lord, it's a question, a message and an answer. The gods are everywhere. They reside in iron, in the ground, up in the sky and of course in this piece of chalk. I stare at the lines, and void my mind. They twist and move, and tell me what I ought to do."

The ohjā knotted his hands into a complicated mudrā, and whispered a mantra. Then he relaxed. His body began to sway.

Cāndo stepped from one foot to the other.

Finally, the ohjā rose, and bowed before the Merchant King. "It won't be easy, but it can be done. There is only one way to revive the corpse. The chalk has told me how."

"So tell me!"

"The rite requires a sacrifice. You have to make an offering for Manasā."

"I'll kill you!"

The ohjā squeaked and ran.

By nightfall, all the guests had left. Cāndo had loaded them with presents, to make up for the bad feelings, and tried to win their sympathy. It wouldn't work. By now, people would gossip that great Cāndo had murdered his own son out of pride and arrogance. In the palace, the mood was unbearable. Sonakā was in her chambers, and her howls echoed through the corridors. In their guest rooms, Sāya and Amalā felt lost and lonely. They would have left, but couldn't, as Behulā's fate was uncertain. Elsewhere, Cāndo had mustered guards. They wore heavy armour. "The serpent slut! She's somewhere and I'm sure she laughs." His hands trembled. "We will search. We will find her. No matter where she hides, no matter where people praise her: we will kill her!"

The captain of the guard lowered his face. "My king. How can we kill a goddess?"

"She's not a goddess. She is an evil spirit! Iron will scare her, hemtāla wood will hurt her, mantras will make her beg for her life! Here are amulets: paralyse her! Drag her to the river and drown her!"

"We are only human."

"You are fired! I need men, not cowards! I will lead the troop."

The King of Traders raised a sword that had belonged to the hero of a bygone dynasty. "We'll go into the city. We'll find her; we'll find the scum that worships her."

By daybreak they were back. The Merchant King looked wretched. His eyes were reddish and there were dark rims under them. He and the guards were drenched; the monsoon rain had come over them like an icy waterfall. The rain, of course, was a blessing. A few hours earlier, the guards had smashed the door of a house, and found a poor Brahmin offering blossoms to a Manasā pot. Cāndo had the man and his family beaten out of the house, and set the edifice on fire. Dry reeds, ancient woods and bricks full of straw are a terrible combination. Within instants, the flames spread to other buildings, and rushed down the alley. As the doors flew open, and people ran for their lives, Cāndo screamed abuse. "You deserve it! All of you deserve it!" The guards grabbed his arms and rushed him to safety. The Merchant King broke down, and tears ran over his cheeks. The guards twisted the sword out of his hand. Then the rain came down.

Indian mornings can be fresh, or at least seem so, for people used to warmer climes. Sonakā had wrapped herself in cloth, and shivered. Cāndo looked plainly wretched, as he dismissed the carpenters. The raft was ready; it looked neat, new and absolutely horrible. Lakhindār's corpse was perfectly clad; he shone like a silkworm, and his body was surrounded with baskets of fruit and vegetables, vessels of water and milk, scripture, and talismans. In spite of the early hour, people tried to watch the ritual. Cāndo had posted his guards to keep them off. The smell of fire was in the air, and the guards used their lathis to keep up a semblance of order.

Behulā stood next to the raft. She stared at her husband and trembled. Her tears had long dried up. She was clad in the sari she had worn on her wedding night. No matter how long Amalā argued, the widow refused to change her clothes.

A group of holy men assembled, led by Cāndo's personal house priest, an educated Brahmin of the highest order. The ritual, as Cāndo had expressed, ought to be short. Sonakā had given up. She stood near the corpse, stared at the water, and muttered to herself.

The corpse would float downstream. After many miles, the river would join the Ganges, and follow its way to the sea. Unlike Cāndo, Sonakā hoped that the journey would be interrupted. People who die of snakebite are not really dead. Maybe there was a snake sorcerer somewhere, who would stop the raft and revive her boy.

"It's over." Cāndo tried to be kind. "My son has to depart. You are in the way."

Behulā raised her eyes. The man has lost his soul, she thought, and now he runs on greed and wrath. She looked at Sonakā, who averted her face. In the distance, she could see her parents. Her father, helpless, and her mother, tense and angry.

Behulā bowed and took her seat on the raft.

"Come here!" Amalā was shocked. "We'll go home!"

"Daughter!" Sāya's face was lined with worry. "He is dead and you are alive. Come with us. What can I do without you?"

The Merchant King advanced. "You are the wife of my last son. No matter what people say, you should stay alive. Stupid people despise widows. I don't. The writing on his brow was doom. And yet you dared to marry him. I respect your courage. Please stay with us."

Sonakā joined them. Her voice was weak and timorous. "Girl, it would be evil to let you die." She shuddered. "I know, I said things I shouldn't have. But now you are family, and you must stay alive."

Behulā stroked Lakhindār's hair. "I will cradle his head, and I will share his fate."

"Nonsense!" Cāndo looked angry. "There has been too much death already. Please remain. The house is large and you are welcome."

"Your house won't find peace until our journey is over." Her voice was faint, but clear. "I will travel with my husband, even if it takes six months to reach the Dark Waters. That's the fate written on my brow."

She grasped Lakhindār's hand. "See, he isn't really dead. One day we will return."

"Daughter-in-law! Don't be stupid. Why do you wish to waste your life?"

"You will ruin our reputation!" Sonakā's voice rose. "People will talk! They will say: who is this girl; she travels on her own! Is she keen to find another man?"

"Wife, control yourself! You insult our guests!"

"I won't be silent! Men don't understand. A woman is only as good as her reputation. The world is full of thieves and rapists! They will say, here comes a singing-girl, a little slut, she's asking for it!" Her face went red. "They'll toss Lakhindār into the river! They'll spread her legs and she'll be everybody's whore!"

"That's enough! Why do you insult Sāya? He's my partner! We will do business!"

"No!" Sonakā shook him off. "The river is full of death and shame! They will take her as they like. And if she returns, she will be disgraced! They will say, here she comes, the little whore, she lost her husband and she is still alive! She'll be just like a Doṁ girl! She's cheap, she'll do it for fun, they will whisper, and laugh!"

"Enough!" The Merchant King raised a hand. Two guards approached. "Escort my wife to her chamber. She needs rest."

"I tell the truth!" screamed Sonakā, "I know what will happen. Everyone does!"

Amalā joined in. "Behulā! You come from a good family! You shame our house, you shame our ancestors!"

Behulā stared at the sky. "A serpent killed my husband. I will travel to Manasā. She will make up for her crime!"

"Don't mention the serpent bitch!" Cāndo barked. "I understand your decision. But I don't approve of it. You might think yourself a princess of antiquity. But nowadays, I simply call you stupid."

"I'll go to the Dark Waters."

"You will find your death."

"Listen!" Behulā began to giggle. "I have news for you. Fill a large lamp with oil, worth one cowrie shell. If the flame burns more than six months, Lakhindār will be alive."

"That's fairy tale nonsense!" Cāndo turned away. "You are insane."

"Paint a peacock on the wall of the iron chamber. In six months, it will spread his wings, and Lakhindār returns."

"In six months, all iron will be sold!"

"Husband, I believe she is right. This isn't nonsense. The gods grant her a vision!" Sonakā turned to Behulā. "Daughter, you have my permission. Go and save my boy. I believe in miracles."

"And I believe in reality," said Cāndo. He turned to his guests. "Let her do as she likes. My priests will pray for her."

Picture 26: Downstream.

33. Downstream

Without effort or haste, the raft drifted along. Two days ago, Behulā had watched as her parents and Cāndo fade in the distance. The early morning fog swallowed them. She held her tears back until they were out of sight. The ghāt s continued, gave way to single buildings, then there was just the embankment, and further on, fields, plantations and villages. She saw people having an early morning bath, women who washed their hair and shrivelled pilgrims who stood in the flow and prayed. The river was gentle. Behulā stroked Lakhindārs hair. He looked so peaceful, relaxed and content, on his last journey. With a flick of her fan she scared the flies away.

By noon, the sun emerged from the haze, and she saw women drying saris at the riverside. Children laughed and screamed, as they leapt into the water. The women stared and talked. Behulā could not make out their words, but she knew what they were saying. Word must have gone around. For miles and miles, people would sneer and slight her.

She watched the farmers, as they waded through the mud. The monsoon was coming to an end; the earth was fertile and wet, and the world was clothed in green. Here and there a few houses stood on the embankment; the river had eaten away all land, and the next flood would devour the foundations of the buildings. The walls would crumble and the roof fall in. People still lived in them. They wouldn't leave until they had to, maybe in a few days, maybe in next year's monsoon floods.

Just like her, they wouldn't give up.

Eventually, the rice fields disappeared. Damp meadows extended, with tall high grasses, where cow herders lazed, and watched their bovines feed. They were filthy, in rags, no better than slaves. One laughed as he advanced to the shore, he waved, grinned like a rat and called. Behulā could imagine what. He lifted his dhoti, pointed at his penis and pissed into the river. She turned her head away. Houses and farms became filthier, smaller and finally turned to ruins. Far from the nearest settlement, wild plants reclaimed the gardens and crushed derelict huts. Figs burst through walls, straw roofs, green with mould, collapsed and sank. Monkeys screeched from the palms. Then, at last, the forest rose, and veiled the shore in shadow.

Another shower drenched her to the core. It was brief, and harmless, compared to the torrents of the last weeks. August was coming to a close, and in September, the rains would end. When the night came, the clouds parted and stars gleamed from the height. Without tasting anything, Behulā chewed on fruits and vegetables, and now she smiled at Lakhindār's corpse. "My darling, she said, "let's rest." She stretched at his side. "This is our bed and we will sleep. I'm with you. I protect you."

She looked up at the slim line of the sky. It followed the contours of the river, a current of darkness and sparkle. Out there, she thought, the stars are full of glory. They are our roof, our home, our shelter. Large branches, covered with ferns and epiphytes, reached for them, like questing tentacles. The forest was close, and strange voices called. "It's animals," she whispered. "Sleep well, my love, I'm sure it's animals."

By dawn, when insects buzzed and birds screeched, Behulā was awake. Her back ached and her sari was wet. Above her, monkey troops hollered at each other. Her stomach knotted. She examined the food offerings. Some fruit remained, and a few vegetables. The milk was rotten. Slowly, to keep her hands from trembling, Behulā poured the stuff into the river. She cleaned the jug. For water, it would do, and there was water everywhere.

The sun rose like a rosy ball through the milky morning dew. Behulā washed her face. Before long, the fog faded and the heat became unbearable. Sarus cranes with red heads flew by. Behulā had seen the huge birds in perfectly structured parks. They mated, and stayed true to each other, for life. When one died, the other withered, and remained, a sad soul, haunted by loss, until death in her kindness snatched it away. Her belly knotted and tears ran down her face.

She held out till evening. She prayed, she spoke with Lakhindār, she tried to stay awake. When dusk came, she collapsed at his side.

When Behulā woke, the raft was caught in a tangle of rotting wood. The river was framed by a murky forest. The looming trees, the creepers and the vines were like a vision from another, darker age. At the riverside, her six brothers stood, clad in their best finery, graced with jewel-studded turbans, embroidered robes, and proud sabres stuck in golden sashes. Each man was young, and strong, and wore a perfect beard. "Come with us!" they called. "Our parents need you. Sāya can't handle his numbers. Amalā needs you to run the household. Be a good sister! The dead are gone. Your husband was never yours. He is just a piece of carrion. Let him go!"

Behulā shook all over. She closed her eyes. When she opened them again, her brothers were gone. She struggled to free the raft. Her fingers trembled, but she wielded her knife with frenzied haste, she hacked at the creepers, she dislodged the driftwood, and the rot released them. The current took hold of the raft and they were off, away from the stench, and into the distance, into the future, into a world that wouldn't be and couldn't be, as doom was everywhere. Behulā collapsed. Maybe I'm going crazy. Have I ever had brothers?

A few days later a visitor arrived. Behulā was shivering. A rainstorm had drenched and frozen her. Next to her foot, a white crow landed. Behulā came to with a jolt. The crow tilted its head and hopped along Lakhindār's body, until it reached his face.

"Sister crow." Behulā wasn't aware that she was weeping. "What can I offer you?"

"I'd like the eyes of your husband," said the crow.

"He needs them!"

"He doesn't. He's dead, and they are yummy."

Behulā raised her hands. "He isn't really dead. We are going to the Dark Waters, we will meet Manasā, and she will make him come alive."

The crow laughed.

Behulā extended her hand. "Take this ring to my parents. Tell them I'm alive, and that I will reach my destination."

The crow took the ring and flew off.

By nightfall, Behulā heard a call. She got up. Around her, the jungle was dark and moist. A solid wall of plants framed the river. Someone, somewhere, called for her. The voice sounded familiar. I'm hallucinating, Behulā thought. There are no people in the jungle at night. The tigers would eat anyone.

"Behulā!" the voice was close and clear. The trees parted, the branches admitted starlight, and Behulā saw her mother, emerging at the shore.

"My child! You drift to death! Come to me. Let me take you home."

"You ain't' my mother!"

Amalā raised her hands. Behulā could hear her wail.

"I know I was too hard with you. I should have been kinder. My little girl, your place is home. Your parents need you!"

"My place is with my husband!"

"Darling, come along. We will hide you. Cāndo will never learn that you are back with us. We'll change your name, we'll give out you're a distant cousin. You can live with us, and we will shelter you."

Behulā stood and faced the shore. "If you are my mother, tell me the names of your six daughters-in-law!"

"Little nightingale! You don't trust me!"

"I saw six brothers. I'm sure each has a wife. Come on, what are their names?"

The woman at the shore remained quiet.

"Are you Manasā?"

The Lotus-Born turned and faded into the undergrowth.

Behulā laughed. It sounded bitter and frail. "Listen, Padmavatī! No matter how many illusions you project, you can't deceive me!"

She squatted on her haunches, bent over and sobbed. Above her, the stars were blotted out. Clouds came rolling, black and sinister, the sluices of heaven opened and the downpour came down like a deluge.

When she passed Burdwan, her raft began to wobble. The ropes were soaked and frayed, and several bamboo pegs had disappeared. Her vehicle jolted, and swayed more than before. Behulā had cut herself a pole, and fought to remain in mid-stream.

That, however, was just one of her worries. Lakhindār was beginning to smell. In spite of the many layers of clothing, and the perfumes that had been rubbed into his skin, his corpse began to extrude a sickly sweet aroma. The flies came down in swarms, and Behulā, no matter how fiercely she fanned, couldn't chase them away.

I'll stop them, she thought, and wrapped him up as tightly as she could.

Behulā watched the crocodiles. Like logs, they lined the sandbanks near the riverside. Now they began to raise their heads. Here and there, a reptile slithered into the flood. Behulā could barely discern them, as they melted into the greyish torrent, their finely jagged backs cutting through the waves. Powerful tail-strokes propelled them on. Behulā screamed at them. The reptiles didn't care. They advanced, their tiny legs tucked tight, their eyes and noses barely above the waterline. They sense the rot, she thought, it makes them hungry. She gripped her pole. It wouldn't do.

So far, the crocs were cautious. Like all river dwellers, they were used to corpses. Mostly, the carrion was in the river. Only that this time, the scent came from a large, rectangular thing they couldn't really understand.

"Durgā! My goddess, my companion!" Behulā stood, holding her pole, and watched the reptiles focus. "Lion rider, help me!"

The girl shook. The river had taken everything out of her. She had only one thing, and that was desperation. "Durgā!" she called, "warrior goddess, untouchable! If you don't help, we are doomed! My husband will be eaten by a monster!"

But Durgā didn't answer.

"I curse you!" Behulā screamed. "If you don't come, I know someone who will! She's your enemy! What do you say to that? You hate her and she hates you! I will give myself into her hands! Can you hear me, Durgā? I warned you! Now listen to this!"

The girl squared her shoulders and closed her eyes. For all she cared, the raft could go anywhere. This was about her, and Absolute Reality. "Manasā! Serpent Goddess! You don't care for me or him! All you think about is Cāndo! But you should hear my prayer! I give myself into your hands! Why do you plague me with such misery? My love is dead; you took his life, and you can have mine as well! Manasā! You are a killer! You killed my man! He never harmed you! You owe me!"

Behulā shook her pole. "Gods have to follow rules! It's the only thing that distinguishes them from Anti-Gods and men! Dharma rules us all! Your deeds are unjust! Goddess, I don't ask for much. I want to meet you. I want to face you, and ask your grace. Lotus-Born, Serpent-Mother, Light of the World. Let me be with you."

Her knees gave in.

The ropes tightened and the raft resumed its form.

Behulā raised her head and sighed. The crocodiles seemed to drift away. A huge crocodile bull roared, and the water splattered in fountains.

Behulā turned away. The future was the river, extending to eternity. Endless waters, small waves and big waves, ripples, glitter, foam and nothing else. She bent over her husband. "Your smell is getting stronger," she said, "but I prefer it to perfumes and blossoms."

The flies rose. Behulā hit at them. The buzzing drove her crazy.

The journey continued. When they reached Kejuya, the rain turned to steel. The raft got stuck in a mud bank, close to the ghāts. Behulā struggled, as she tried to get it free. Then she reconsidered. She stepped into the water; washed herself, and waded to land. Dripping wet, she walked into the settlement, and entered Manasā's shrine, where she fasted for three days, while the rains poured down.

Amadipur, another city. Maybe it was beautiful, maybe it only scored average. Or it was hell on earth. Behulā, kneeling on the raft, didn't care. Villages and settlements simply floated by. The rains came down, and then the sky cleared up again. Occasionally, the sun warmed her. Bright birds flew, people stood on the riverbanks, some called, some laughed and Behulā didn't notice. Before long, the warmth returned. Her sari dried. Rainfall became rare and blue skies shone with happiness. The world could have been beautiful. After the monsoon, all India rejoices. There is wealth in the gardens, there are blossoms, exuding heavy perfumes, there are animals that delight and leap, and fruit begins to ripen, grains rise, and joy is everywhere.

Except for the river. The raft moved within a sphere of darkness. Had she raised her head, Behulā could have noticed how the countryside transformed. Different buildings, varying crops, and in-between miles of lonely, shady forest. The widow, bitter, exhausted, and hungry, saw the waves striking her raft, and their innocent glitter, watched the tangled undergrowth near the riverside, and the moss-coated trees, and steered her craft, as well as she could. She rarely felt anything. When she looked up, on the embankment, she saw people. Some were wealthy, some pious, and most were close to starvation. It didn't matter. The whole world had become a nightmare. People were bad actors, deceptive, shallow and meaningless. They played a part, and played it badly. The animals were better. They came to the river to drink. Some played, some delighted, and some were killed by other animals, or men. The world went along, a gigantic play, a phantasmagoria without sense or reason. People, she thought, are insane. They make so much of their aims, their desires, and their endless greed. One moment they are here, the next they are gone. Those who walk proudly will be corpses tomorrow. And those who are dead remain alive.

Occasionally, she stopped the raft and stole fruit at the plantations, bundles of bananas, jackfruit, aubergines, or anything.

From daybreak to nightfall, she prayed, until the words became a meaningless mumble, her throat went parched, her ears rang and exhaustion made her fall asleep.

The man sitting on the ghāt held a rod. He wore a chain of wooden beads around his neck and a broken cowrie shell in his ear. His head was shaved and his eyes gleamed. Behulā recoiled; he was badly disfigured, his legs were swollen with elephantiasis.

"Hey girl!" the cripple called, "stop a while. I can make you happy."

Behulā froze. Like a good girl, she pretended she hadn't heard a thing, and looked away.

"Come here! My thing is huge. You'll never forget me!"

Behulā rose. Good girls don't talk back. Behulā wasn't a good girl any more. "Stay away, you evil goat!"

"My intentions are good!" called the man, "Let me marry you!"

"I'm married!"

"So am I! Don't take me for a poor man. I've got four women who fulfil my wishes every night!"

"And how sick are they?"

The man laughed. "They are healthy and fat! Don't be deluded, I am rich and in the bedroom I'm a wish-fulfilling bull!"

"You are disgusting!"

"My wives are satisfied. They eat all day. None of them really works. I provide food and betel nut, as much as they can chew." The man chortled with glee. "Don't pretend. You are just another whore."

"I'm a widow!"

"Why didn't you join him on the pyre? Come on, you simply want a better man!"

Picture 27: Worms.

The man laid his rod down. "I'm your new husband. Be my fifth wife. I'll feed you until you are happy and fat! And I'm a virtuous man. I swear by all the gods that I will only take you when you want it." He came down the steps. "And you will want it, every day."

Behulā gripped her pole and looked away. It had been wrong to talk with him.

"Darling, whether you like it or not, I will plug you. Look out, I'm coming!"

"I'll smash your head!"

"Ah, my little honey pot, you want it hard. I like it." The man hurled himself into the river. "Watch out! When I catch you, you'll scream with delight!"

Behulā stared. The man struggled. The current was fast and the waves were merciless. His swollen legs fought, and gave in. "Help me!" he screamed and spat, "I sink!"

Behulā turned away and focussed on the future. A cormorant flew by. Behind her, the screams faded.

One day to the other, week after week, life after life, Behulā lost her count. She didn't know how long she had been travelling. Her sari, after so much wear and tear, was in tatters. Her hair was tangled, her face lined. Most of the time, she simply watched the river. Like a statue, she stood and steered, and lost her sense of time, of space, of anything. Water moves on, and so did she. Her hip bones jutted out, her ribs were clearly visible. Her cheeks fell in, her cheekbones emerged, and they were sharp and merciless. Under her eyes were dark rings, 'cause she didn't get much sleep, and her vision seemed smudged. Some days, when she had hardly slept at all, she realised that colours blurred across her field of vision, and that dark, hairy things scuttled out of her way. She could sense the nightgaunts in the periphery. They didn't dare to face her. The water turned leaden, and the heavens vomited streaks of bleakness and despair which dribbled down to drown the river sprites. The jungle pulsed. It wasn't plants: the trees and bushes had turned into a wall of suffocating vegetation, hungry, carnivorous, and merciless. My feet, she thought, as she gazed down, from mind-stunning heights, are covered in mould. But this is silly and unreal. The gods tempt me, and try to frighten me. I won't give in. Nor will my husband. He's as good as new, and we will set them right. I take my daily bath, as scripture requires, and out here, no-one can see me. Maybe I look like a hag. Maybe my clothes disintegrate. So what? It doesn't matter. I'm healthy and I am alive. Sure, once in a while I sit and weep and cramps rack me. That's human. I'm human, and I suffer and laugh and triumph. I don't care how much weight I lose. It's natural, and inevitable, and we progress. My husband stands by my side. We go to the Dark Waters. Anything superfluous has to be shed.

Each day, she prayed. To whoever might hear her, to whatever god or goddess came into her mind. For days, she mumbled to herself. Her words had lost their meaning. The sun went up and down, Behulā hardly noticed. Her diarrhoea got worse. Some days she squatted, twitching and shivering, and felt her life evaporate. She heard the herons calling from the willows. She heard the crocodile bulls roaring. She didn't care; none of them were of importance, and nothing mattered anyway. This was between her, and the river, and Manasā.

Occasionally, a corpse drifted by. Behulā looked at the bloated, pale flesh, gnawed by fishes, reptiles and birds, and looked away. Her husband, securely wrapped, was still alive. Sure, the cloth that covered his face seemed to move. That's his breath, she thought. Unlike him, those corpses were truly dead. Lakhindār, she knew, was just asleep.

The flies kept haunting her. They swarmed around her husband; they crawled into the textiles, and no matter how much she screamed, they wouldn't go away.

Finally, River Gungarī met River Chānak. Two deities embraced, and their currents met, in different colours.

On a sandbank, Behulā stopped the raft. She forced her vehicle into the creepers dangling from the willows. Nearby, there were plantations. She waded to the shore and went in search of fruit.

It wasn't something you could hear. Behulā sensed the presence, as she clambered past a thicket of pandanus trees, each of them covered in mosses, as soggy as the soil she was struggling through. In the foliage to her left, a shadow moved. Behulā stood and froze, and hardly dared to breathe. Slowly, she turned to the spot where the branches swayed, and lifted her pole. She knew it was an empty gesture: there was no space to swing it properly.

The green parted.

A tired, mangy tigress showed her face. The animal was old, by tiger standards, and its age showed. The fur had lost its sheen, the face was pale, and when she opened her mouth, Behulā saw that several teeth were missing. For a predator, old age is a nightmare. The very animal that had released so many herbivores from their suffering, faces an endless trial, once it grows old and weak. The joints ache, the body sags, the eyes go dim. Fleas dance, worms make the guts itch and ticks turn life into a nightmare. A thorn can cripple a paw, and make each leap an agony. Eventually, teeth splinter, and gums go infected. That's the time when a tiger, if it wants it or not, is forced to contest carrion with the jackals and hyenas, and to attack people. Death, long desired, takes her time.

Behulā faced the tigress. Come on, she thought, I've got nothing to lose.

The tigress averted her face. The large cats don't like it when people meet their eyes. She got down on her haunches, her back humped, and her ribs were clearly visible.

"I'm tired," said the tigress, "give me a piece of your husband. He smells and I'm sure he's soft and tasty."

Behulā lowered her pole. This wasn't about fighting, it was about mercy.

"Eat me. This is my lucky day!"

"You're too tough!" snarled the tigress and turned. With a leap, and a whimper, she disappeared down the slope, and into a bamboo thicket. For an instant, Behulā thought she saw a girl in red, whose bunches danced as she ran.

A Doṁ stood at the shore. The man was young and wore a brightly embroidered vest, a sash with a few spots and a perfect beard. Obviously, he was ambitious. Behulā hardly looked. She knew the likes of him. This one was a travelling entertainer. His turban was worn, and aged. His ornaments were corroded, his bracelets of cheap copper etched by sweat and green. Nevertheless, the man stood proud, as if the world belonged to him. Normally, the Doṁ were at the bottom of the social pecking order. Some tended burial fires, some searched the burned down pyres for valuables. If a female Doṁ was pretty and talented, she might become a singer, a whore or both. Or she would squat all day in a long, slim boat, and weave baskets. And when a Doṁ was clever and resourceful, he mastered magic tricks, and sang and told stories and pleased a paying audience. Some would laugh and a few might toss some coins. Others would throw stones. The Doṁs are untouchable. This man seemed ambitious. No doubt he would make an income, as long as he was young. In old age, provided he ever reached it, he would scour the burning places for the valuables of the dead.

"Lady! Great queen!"

Too late. The man knew she was aware of him.

"Don't act the prude, my beauty. What can I offer that you come to me?"

Behulā stared at the bundle that contained Lakhindār. "I want nothing, except my husband."

"Your man is hardly fresh." The Doṁ smiled and his teeth shone. Unhurriedly, he primed the ends of his moustache. "Listen, darling, I'm a sorcerer. I can get the moon from the sky. I know your heart and I can feel your sadness. Be honest. You want to leave this raft, and meet me at the shore."

"There is no shore." Behulā reached for her pole.

"My gorgeous lady, my ruby of desire; join me and find fulfilment!"

"Leave me alone!"

"But lady, I know the greatest sorceries. If you refuse, I'll sing your raft to my shore, and take you anyway."

"Your spells are dirt! They cannot touch me!"

"You defy my offer? You are a sorceress, and I'm delighted." The Doṁ bowed. "I treasure and respect you. I thank high heavens for our meeting. Only a sorceress can resist a sorcerer."

He pointed at her. "But you have to be good, really good, my darling imbecile, to resist me."

The Doṁ lifted a branch. "Come on. I want to see what you can do. Here is a branch, now show your power, baby sorceress, and let me see you burn it!"

"Leave me alone!"

"But I can't. You stole my heart and I am bound to you. Our future is fixed: this night you will squirm in my arms." The man touched his heart. "Here is the branch. Burn it, sorceress, and show your skill!"

"I curse you in the name of the gods!"

"Your gods are rubbish and your skills don't count. Hey, you filthy little thing, who would ever help you?"

Behulā yelled "Manasā!"

The twig went up in flame, and the Doṁ staggered back. His beard caught fire; he screamed in pain and hurled himself into the water. Behulā turned away. Behind her, she heard him beg forgiveness.

A few cities further on, armed men were squatting at the ghāts. They had spent the evening waiting. It could have been a merchant's boat, a group of travellers, or a rich man with his girls. Whoever came close had to pay a fee. This evening, their income was tiny. Just one fisherman had passed, whose catch was ridiculously small. They had taken what he had and smashed his nose.

Darkness came fast. What would they eat tonight?

The leader stood and searched the river. He was tense, as he heard his men whispering, and knew that he needed loot to keep his rank. There was a shadow, somewhere, further out. It might be a boat, a piece of driftwood or a dream.

"Guys, get ready."

"It looks like a raft. Raft people are poor. What can we gain from them?"

"Shut up. Whatever it is, it's ours."

The raft came closer. "It's just a woman and some luggage."

"She looks good."

"She's skinny. There's no flesh on her bones."

"Maybe she is sick?"

"Nonsense." The leader was an expert in such matters. "Feed her sugarcane, ghī and coconut cream for a few weeks, and she will look like Lakṣmī herself."

Picture 28: Between Worlds.

His voice rang through the night. "Halt, woman. Why do you travel on our river? Who gave you permission? And what do you carry? Are you a whore?"

The men laughed. Sure, the woman looked starved. But even a woman who is all edgy can thrill a man who doesn't expect much.

"She's got the eyes of a ghost," one whispered.

"So what? Are you a man? Put a blanket over her face!"

Behulā heard them. She bowed her head in shame.

One of the men raised a torch. "Come; show us what you've got! What's the treasure in your lap?"

Behulā raised herself. She opened the wrapping and the light illuminated what was left of Lakhindār's face. The skin was gone; the flesh was full of maggots.

"This is my husband." Behulā remained calm and composed. "I love him. He was doomed. On our wedding night, a snake bit him. You seek profit? There is none. He is my only treasure."

The men recoiled.

Behulā laughed.

"What do you want, guards? I travel to the Dark Waters. Tell me, have I arrived in hell?"

"No", said the leader. "This is the human world. Forgive us. We honour your courage."

Behulā raised her hands. Her eyes gleamed in the torchlight. "In the name of Manasā, I bless you."

As their voices faded away, she collapsed. "Why did I say this?" she wept. "It's all Manasā's fault!"

Behulā lost her sense of time. No matter if it was days, weeks or months, she didn't care. Only hours counted, or moments, when she realised that she was hungry. She stopped the raft, entangled it in the vegetation, and struggled her way up the riverside and from there to the nearest settlement. She squatted on the ground, a bowl before her, and begged. Good people saw her suffering, and dropped a few coins. Others gave vegetables, which she ate raw, no matter how her bowels churned, or fruit, or a bowl of milk. Behulā took what she got. She ate leftovers, and food that had begun to rot. She raked the garbage at the crossroads. She wept, when someone gave her nourishment, and then she moved on, like a ghost. Here and there, in a fit of anger, she stole fruit from plantations.

Each time when she returned to the shore, she had a fit of despair. It would be so easy to remain on dry land, to become a nameless beggar, or a pilgrim, to forget the raft and what it carried. She could have gone on a pilgrimage, all the way across India. Nobody would have known her. She could have sat at the roadside and collected alms. Anything was better than this! The raft was a cell, a narrow rectangle that imprisoned her. Lakhindār had almost disappeared. She bent over him, and averted her eyes. "My darling. All will be well. Behind the next river bend, an ohjā may revive you. I'll give him my ornaments, my pearls, my gold. You will wake from your sleep; you will be real and wonderful. We will get you a vīṇā, and you will play. Oh, how you will play. You will make earth quake and the gods weep. And we will return to Campaka. Your parents will celebrate, and Cāndo's Brahmins will sacrifice for days, in all the great temples, and we will laugh and be happy. You'll play the greatest tunes ever, and I will dance. We will live in a bright house and our children will be wonderful."

She didn't get further, as tears ran down her face. Her hands turned to fists and the nails buried themselves in her palms. "Why do I talk like an idiot? The lizard calls, the vultures circle, the ravens croak! I am enclosed by thorns, and I pretend. You gods! You have let us down! I chatter like a parrot and my words are garbage! We are going to the Dark Waters, where the world ends! I have no idea if Manasā will be there. Maybe I should die and rot like him!"

The journey continued, through gardens and plantations, past fields of rice, of jute, of indigo. Behulā drifted through jungles, where branches heavy with succulents leaned down to the water, and huge black fishes grasped for air. She watched otters playing, but the sight didn't touch her, didn't make her happy. She saw crocodiles and screamed at them. The rain, the damp, and the sun ruined her raft, her clothes, and her hair. Her face was scorched by the sun, her nails broke, she ate, she vomited, she had the shits. Her thoughts went in circles. Next to her was a corpse, a piece of rot and regret, wrapped in textiles, a bygone memory. Flies had laid their eggs into the rotting flesh; maggots had swarmed, had devoured the putrid matter, and went flying, to search for carrion elsewhere. She had seen the skin around his mouth burst and squiggling horror greet the light of day. Large sections of his scalp disintegrated. The hair endured, the face did not. Behulā wrapped him up again; she laid blossoms and leaves on his carcase, and broke down weeping when a sudden breeze swept them away. She simply didn't want to know what happened underneath.

One day the river narrowed and the current went fast and difficult. Behulā stood, though her head was spinning, and controlled her vehicle with her pole. Rocks emerged, foam sparkled, and the raft began to wobble. The current tilted the contraption and sent it veering sideways. Lakhindār's corpse shifted and she screamed, as she saw him sliding to the edge. The textiles that covered his face shifted, the blossoms fell, and she faced a skull, brightly polished, pure and white, like the bleak light of the void that can be anything. For a moment, she stood paralyzed. The skull had enormous teeth and seemed to grin. A leg

Picture 29: Neta Savage.

jutted out, his foot dangled, and the water seemed to boil. Bodālya fish! The head shot up, in a crest of foam, as the monster took a bite. Behulā screamed and struck with her pole. The raft spun around, water flushed over the logs, and she almost crashed into a rock. Behulā leaned over and dragged the corpse back. It felt almost weightless. She pulled her man into the middle of the raft. He lay like a broken doll. Parts of his heel were gone. Around the raft, the fishes raised their ugly mouths.

She pulled herself up. The river was angry and so was she. She stuck at the fishes, she steered the raft and faced the current.

One night, when the full moon gleamed from heaven, the black river transformed into a lotus blossom wonderland, and Behulā watched a strange man at the shore. He was a large, bull-like fighter, with a perfectly groomed black beard, in shimmering silk, who wore a turban full of jewels and a curved sword on his hip. On his back, he carried a shrivelled, wiry figure, as if it had no weight. The man walked swiftly; he seemed to know the way.

Behulā stared: the man carried a corpse. Around its neck hung a piece of rope, the face was bloated and the tongue emerged.

The corpse raised its head, took a rattling breath and coughed. "You hurt me. Your fingers are too tight! What do you think I'll do? Escape? Big man, get real. I'm your burden, your one and only hope and future!" The corpse retched. "I've got feelings, just like you, and maybe even more!" It turned its head and grinned. Behulā saw the teeth shine. "My emotions are unbelievable. I'm a paragon of subtlety, a treasure of refinement and the wish-fulfilling tree of all young and tender hearts!"

The big man spat, and hurried on.

The corpse laughed. "My king, you are as strong as a lion. But the way is long, and soon you will be bored. Let's use the opportunity. A happy anecdote, among dear friends, can make the way much shorter. We've got the whole night! Fate made us friends, and let's be honest, a king like you isn't really into friendship. Who can you trust? Who will ever tolerate your silly little habits? The moon is glorious, and I'm sure you'll love to hear another story."

The man grunted.

The corpse giggled. "You're a strange item, Mr. Sovereign, but somehow I grow fond of you. It's a rare pleasure to meet a ruler who is so eloquent and droll. Come on, say something! Admire my charm, praise my wit, laugh at my jokes! You carried me for hours, here and there and back again." The corpse chortled happily. "I told you so many fables that I'm sure you feel indebted."

The king stopped and bared his teeth. One moment it seemed as if he would toss the corpse into the river.

The corpse didn't seem to notice. "Let me cheer you up. My company is rare and special, and only the best of the best have enjoyed such wit as mine. You could favour me with admiration. My tales are treasured by old and young! Those who listen understand the hearts of men, and women too, which is much harder; they become sages, they appreciate justice, Dharma, law, and cosmic harmony, they know the secrets of the gods and while we are at it, gain insight into bedchamber skills. My king, I'm sure you heard that great men don't spurt in three seconds. There is much to be learned, and great delight to be uncovered, for those who understand and remember, and take my teachings to their hearts, or even lower, much lower actually, my dear big bear of a royal. I am sure you guessed it already, and congratulate yourself that you met me, your humble teacher. Your queen will swoon at your feet; your concubines will collapse in orgasmic stupor, should you learn but one-tenth of what I may reveal. Honestly, my dear chunky bloke, consider: who doesn't want to be a perfect lover, just like me? Though your looks are barely average, and you dress too flashy, and I, as I'm sure you noticed, have to explain the very simple basics to you, again and again, 'cause you don't listen properly, while the moon gleams and the night goes on, but, darling king, you're such a sweetheart, we've got all the time in the world and honestly, I don't mind. Baby, you don't understand your luck."

The corpse wriggled with delight. "Let's have another true story. It deals with the lusts of common people and the stupidity of righteous kings. I know you'll simply love it."

The king roared with anger, and thundered into the bushes. "Hello!" screeched the corpse. "These branches tickle me!"

Behulā heard the corpse chatting away, and shook her head.

The world was full of lunatics!

The hunger cramps convulsed her. She retched and choked. The pole rested next to her, and the raft went as it liked. Behind her was the corpse. She hardly ever glanced at it. Nor did she mind where she was going. Her prayers had faded away. So had her curses. The silence parched her mind.

The city Hāsānhhāṭi drifted by. Houses, huts and hovels, palaces, minarets and temples, and poor people lining the shore, near the cremation fires, taking their bath, begging for blessings that would never come. Wretches, waiting for death. Beggars, priests, pretenders, flesh eaters and vegetarians, saints, yogīs, exploiters and victims, the good, the bad and the gullible on their knees, moaning, begging, beseeching the divine to fulfil their worthless little dreams. Reality is one lie after the other. Men and women hurried by, driven by greed and fear and lust. Money came and went; property remained a delusion, a nightmare and a drug; society a prison and fame a chain that bound and held and strangled. Make a name for yourself! Envy will drag you down. In this world you only have to raise your head and someone will break your kneecap. Justice, cosmic harmony, a happy dream for everyone? There's luxury for a few and misery for most. The world could be so beautiful. Alas, it's run by people, trust them to make it hell. That's what they want, that's what they get, and they deserve it. And normal folk, teachers and scholars, craftsmen and merchants, peasants, cow-herders and fishers, singing-girls, prostitutes, entertainers, mud-rackers, pimps and money-lenders, they are the living corpses, staggering around like the insane, aching, aging, dropping dead, going into the river and being reborn elsewhere, stupid, hopeless, imbecile. Death doesn't change a thing. History repeats itself with tiny variations: same characters, different costumes, same errors. It doesn't matter, nothing does. Alive or dead, flesh comes and goes; gaudy costumes or filthy rags, good intentions, great virtue or damn-stupid selfishness: apes all over the place. She had seen it all.

The ohjā sorcerer stood at the shore and waved at her. "Come here! I can make your husband come alive!"

Behulā didn't move. It was too late, far too late.

"I am a snake doctor. I can heal him. And I can give you food to eat."

Behulā remained as she was; a statue without breath, a thing of stone.

"Girl!" shouted the sorcerer, "spend three nights with me. Then I'll revive him, and he will be better than before. Though not as good, as I am. Compared to me," he laughed, "you won't like him anymore!"

He is cursed, Behulā thought, all of us are cursed.

The raft drifted past Vaidyapur and reached the Ganges. The great stream opened like a mighty inland sea, a vast realm of silver and sparkle and mist, extending all across the universe. A river dolphin leapt and looked at her. Behulā rubbed her eyes and tried to wake.

"Mother Gaṅgā," she whispered, "you care for the living. I am past life. You have a heart for the dead. You grant rebirth after rebirth, life after life, no matter the pain, the suffering and the delusion. You make the wise ignorant and turn the stupid into sages. I am a fool and my husband is a corpse; we ask for liberation."

She bowed, went on her knees and scooped up water. First, she washed her hands and face. Then she scattered water on the corpse. Ganges water, the water of life. Her husband remained as he was.

Behulā convulsed and sobbed. What had she expected? A miracle? The appearance of the goddess? She stroked his torso and felt bones moving under her touch. He is so soft, she thought; he's just an infant. I am crazy, she realised, I can't trust myself any more. She raised herself and took the pole. Water extended everywhere, and a flight of herons soared.

Occasionally, squinting through the haze, she saw fishers in their long boats, sun-browned men, who kept otters on leashes. The animals were trained, since birth, to hunt fishes, and to drive them into nets. The tight collar prevented them from eating too much of the catch, and made the fishers rich. It could have been fun to watch the animals. The otters looked so happy. Long ago, Behulā would have laughed. She didn't. Her youth was far away, and only bitterness remained.

The longer the journey, the wider the stream. Behulā felt alone, like a tiny speck in a universe of glitter. Far away in the distance, she could see rows of trees lining the riverside. It seemed like worlds away. The fishers faded, as did the merchants in their heavy ships, and travellers. People, she realised, are ghosts. They simply ain't dead yet.

Out of the haze, an island emerged. It wasn't much of a place; the river had eaten mud and sand, and deposited it elsewhere. The place was young and crude and barren. Driftwood lined the shore. Here and there, plants extended their roots and raised their fresh and carefree sprouts to the sky. Young leaves! They seemed so innocent and stupid. No people were around. Islands like these come and go as the river changes its moods. Maybe they are covered in green. Maybe they last for a season or two.

You can't rely on anything. You can't trust the future, no matter how cheerful it seems.

Behulā fought until the raft reached the shore, and struggled uphill. Plenty of deadwood rimmed the beach.

She gathered and pulled. "You gods!" she prayed, "What a fool I was. No-one can cheat death. I will do what a widow has to do."

The thick logs, roots and stems, were soaked with water, and the young shoots were full of sap.

Like a lost soul, Behulā staggered over the island. She collected a twig here, a wind-dried branch there. It wasn't enough and it would never be. She couldn't build a pyre.

Screaming in her rage, she fell over and clawed her nails into the muddy ground. That's how she lay and that's how she remained, while the sky went dark. Behulā lay, shivering, like a storm-toppled tree, like a body without sense, while the raindrops, large like pellets, hit her. Somewhere nearby, lightning flashed and thunder rolled. She couldn't have cared less.

When she came to her senses, the sun was red and sinking. Behulā raised her head, saw mighty gilded cloudscapes and wiped the mud from her face.

Before her sat a woman. She was young and might have been a beauty, a long while ago, but these days she was almost starved. Her posture was majestic, but sorrow and tribulations had cut deep lines into her face. Apart from a few, sun-bleached rags, she was almost nude.

Behulā raised herself. The woman didn't seem to notice.

"Who are you?" she asked. "Are you a spirit, or a goddess? Or do I face myself?"

The woman raised her head. Snakes emerged between her locks.

"I am Brahmānī." She yawned and stretched. "I'm everything and nothing. And I am you. Behulā, you silly thing, did you think you could leave me behind? Can you imagine how many years I lived on air and air alone?"

The woman seemed to crumble. She pressed her palms into her face and whispered "We're almost done. Go to your raft. Our journey is nearly over."

Picture 30: Beyond Exhaustion.

34. Dark Waters

By the time the raft reached Tribeni, Behulā was totally insane. As she was quite alone, with just a corpse for company, nobody noticed. Her madness, however, came in many levels and shades. When normal people are insane, they imagine they are reasonable, and pursue a course of action that leads to a happy, positive result. That's normal insanity: you can observe it in most companies, universities, churches and governments, and smaller organisations, no matter whether they specialise in rabbit-breeding, snail-racing or the occult.

Behulā watched herself going mad, like a hunter stalks its prey, only that the predator and victim were the same. She talked about it, to herself, or whoever might listen, and remarked on the fine details which shifted when she twisted with hunger, or the pale moon turned the river into a sea of silver mist, when she wept and screamed, and called for Lakhindār, but her husband didn't answer. She knew he watched her, as she watched herself, but as he was a good and peaceful man, he left her to her own pursuits.

At Tribeni, three sacred rivers meet. Here, the gates to the gods open, here, the underworlds show their faces, and here, all realities, times and spaces converge. The place is a favourite of travelling pilgrims, ascetics and gurus. Let's take a look at the brochure, published by the Tantric Tourist Agency. Our first witness is Rāmprasād Sen (c. 1718-1775), a famous singer who devoted his life to the Black Goddess Kālī and became an inspiration for East Indian poets.

Maybe he thought of Behulā's journey when he wrote:

...Going on pilgrimage is a false journey, Mind;
Don't be over-eager.
Bathe at Tribeni; cool yourself
In your inmost chamber.
When your body's finished, decomposing,
Prasād will be cast away...

That was pretty good for a start, but not enough. Kamalākanta Baṭṭācārya (c. 1769-1821) picked up the topic, and we ought to thank Rachel Fell McDermott for translating this so beautifully.

...Going on a pilgrimage
Is a journey of sorrow, Mind.
Don't be too eager.
Bathe in the three streams of bliss.
Why not be cooled at their source,
your bottommost mystic centre?
What are you looking at, Kamalākanta?
This world is full of false magic.
But you fail to recognize the magician-
And She's dwelling in your own body!

The poet places the reed-pen in its stand and looks up. "Some say Tribeni is the Ājña cakra, right between the eyebrows. It's a pretty place, but that's no reason to get overexcited. No matter what the guru says," he explains, "you have to think for yourself. It isn't difficult at all. Trees do it, microbes do it; every single cell processes information and makes decisions. Above the Ājña, high on the brow is the Manas cakra. Hardly anyone has heard of it. That's because modern people go for the silly, simplified Seven Cakra System. They miss loads of cakras, in fact, thousands of them. The Manas cakra is great for thinking. Ask Manasā anytime. But thinking isn't always blissful. Too much thought and your mind comes apart. If you want fun and happiness, you have to discover Tribeni further down." He points at his perineum and laughs. "That's where reality is made. Just ask Neta." The poet rolls up his manuscript. "That's how you do enlightenment. It doesn't happen in your head. Anyone for Chicken Masala?"

That should do for now. While hot-blooded renouncers and New-Age dimwits clogged the shores of the Three Rivers, and sought salvation in temples, yoga studios, and esoteric supermarkets, Behulā drifted past unnoticed.

Behind Tribeni, heaven went black. Heavy clouds towered, lightning flashed and hailstones, as large as pebbles, came hammering from the height. They clattered on the wood; they bounced from Lakhindār's skull, and hit Behulā with a vengeance. She crouched; she raised her hands above her head, she felt the pellets sting. On the open raft, tossed by the waves, she had no shelter. Nearby, she heard lightning strike and kept her eyes closed. When she opened them again, dusk had fallen; the sky was veiled, and the cloud cover pressed down on her. Behulā stared into the gloom. The river had become narrow and fast. She glimpsed thickets of mangrove on the shores, saw tangles of creepers, and huge palm leaves, and pale blossoms that gleamed and shone and released their stunning perfumes. The air was heavy with moisture. All of a sudden she was wide awake. This was not the river she had gotten used to. She hadn't felt so much alive for weeks. I am close to the end, she thought, the river will carry us into the Underworld. She crouched and tried to pray, but words failed her. Her mantras were exhausted, the names of gods but empty shells that were snatched away by the current and the foam. The vegetation came closer and leathery foliage hit her face. The jungle will eat us, she thought, unless the river drowns us first. She glanced at her husband. He's dead. Soon, I'll be dead too.

The current speeded and glistening bubbles danced at the sides of the vehicle. The raft was faster than ever, eager to reach its destination, keen to give up and disintegrate. Behulā breathed deeply, and filled her lungs with mould and damp, with rot and fungi, and the stunning scent of midnight blossoms. Her body was taut, her shoulders ached and her face contorted as she tried to see through the haze. The river curved, the raft was swept along, began to circle, and slowed. The river had turned into a lake. Behulā stared into the murk, and shook her head. The trees seemed to glow, foliage sparkled, and blossoms radiated colour. She drifted into a thicket of lotus blossom. Above her, the sky opened, and the stars shone. Behulā didn't recognise a single constellation. Her raft hit a mudbank and got stuck.

Time stands still. In the early morning, Behulā raises herself. Maybe I slept, she thinks, but isn't sure. It must have been an awful night. Her back aches. Her hand opens, and the pole rolls into the water, and drifts away. Behulā understands; it isn't needed any more. Slowly, the traveller gets up, and wipes the dew from her face. Her clothes, or what remains of them, are soggy. She stares into the distance. Fine mist spiral between the lotus blossoms. Behulā crouches and her chest heaves, she breathes like a hunted animal, and feels the anguish in her heart. She shakes her head; her tangled, soggy hair swings, and drops scatter like crystals. A breeze stirs the branches, the foliage trembles, and a shower drenches her. The drops are heavy, wet, and music. She hears each of them, she understands their tune, their colour, and hears her lungs pumping, her heart pounding, she hears the buzz of insects, and turns. The bundle that contains her husband is still there. The raft is stuck.

Cautiously, she steps into the water. Her legs are weak, her knees jittery. She needs food. Maybe there's some fruit around. The water feels pleasantly cool. Behulā wades, her feet get stuck in mud, she pulls them up, and forces herself up the beach, and into dripping vegetation. She hears a sound. It slap-splashes, and the reverberations echo along the river. Behulā grasps a branch and pulls herself through a thicket. Twigs scratch her face. Large rocks emerge, coated with mossy overgreen. She struggles on, feels the plants tear the rim of her sari, grinds her teeth and fights her way through stalks and spikes and strangling vines. The sound echoes again. It seems quite rhythmic. It reminds her of something she can't name. She staggers and stumbles into a thicket of pandanus stalks, jagged like the jaws of a crocodile. She can't clamber underneath, but has to edge around them. They bite and sting and take their toil of blood. Behulā stares down, and sees her legs are bleeding. Strange, that she doesn't feel a thing. She raises her head and faces giant figs, embraced by writhing serpents. They take her breath away. I should scream, she thinks, or go crazy. But she doesn't. A few more steps and she is in the open. Behulā adjusts the remnants of her sari, pulls blossoms and twigs from her hair, realises her earrings are gone and staggers on. The sound, slap-splash, comes again. She hurries.

On a sandbank is a woman. Behulā sees she is clad in red, but cannot discern her age. She is surrounded by baskets. Between the trees loom posts of aged wood, and there are lines connecting them. Some are heavy with clothes, with shiny silks and brocades, with lightweight cotton and colourful blankets. Others bear reddish stuff. Behulā can't discern what they are. Most lines are empty.

The woman raises a piece of clothing. She steps into the water, submerges it, wriggles it, twists it, and turns it around in the current. She pushes the thing into the sand and walks on it. Then she pulls it up and hits the cloth against a stone. Slap-splash!

Behulā cowers behind a tree. She watches the woman drag her load to a line. She lifts it up, straightens it, steps back and observes her work. She turns around, scrutinised the river and walks in again. She seizes a hand, an arm emerges, then a shoulder, then the lifeless head of a corpse.

"You're not too bad," says the woman, as she drags the carcase up onto the shore. For one so small, she seems amazingly strong.

The woman reaches into her underwear, and produces a curved knife. One slash and the corpse splits open. Behulā flinches. The tree supports her, while the ground beneath her feet begins to wobble. Her breath goes fast, her lungs heave and her shoulders go up and down as if she were she were a bird in panic flight.

The woman reaches into the corpse. She doesn't even make a face. At leisure, she pulls out the organs, one after the other, and washes them. She carries them up onto the shore, and hangs them up to dry. Behulā fights her nausea. She stares at the washing line and realises it is full of rot and filth. The intestines take ages. The woman is patient. She washes a section, clambers to the line, and hangs it up with wooden pegs. Then the next couple of metres are washed, wiped and arranged. Behulā fights the urge to vomit. She had never known how long the human guts can be.

The woman turns to Behulā. "That should do for a start. All right, darling, you saw what I do. I do it every day. Come over and help me do my job."

Behulā jerks. She fights the urge to run, but her feet remain rooted where they are.

"See, your feet are clever. They know more than you do. So come here."

Behulā stares. As she advances, her eyes blur. The woman is a girl, maybe sixteen, seventeen, just like herself. She seems so young and innocent, in her shiny red costume, but, by all gods, how shameless, her breasts are almost bare, her legs are nude and she even shows her navel. There is gold all over her bra and pants, as if she wants to dance the night away!

The girl laughs, she raises her arms in welcome, and they are red with blood.

Now her face ages. She looks tired and bitter; as if she had seen aeons come and go. She must have cut and washed millions, thinks Behulā, and it drags her down. She has seen dynasties come and go, has seen world ages end and start anew, has witnessed civilisations fade and be forgotten. Her face wrinkles, her skin splits and Behulā faces bone, rimmed with a few strains of greasy white. The skull grins.

Then she is in middle age. A married woman, who has watched her children grow and find a place in life. She could be Behulā's mother or a friendly aunt, kind and helpful, and wise in the ways of the world.

"Stop staring. You've seen worse. Watch this."

The woman walks into the river. The dark water washes past her thighs. All of a sudden she is young again. She bends over, seizes, laughs, and drags another corpse uphill. The head is framed in white, it's a dead crone, and she looks just like the girl did, a moment ago.

"Come here. You'll like this. First you place the blade, here. And then you go in one smooth cut, but not too deep, or you'll have excrement everywhere. That means stink and spots and they are hard to get out. And mind the gallbladder. That's another no-no. And the bladder. The dead can keep what's left of their piss. You don't want it on your costume. But apart from that, you can cut as much as you like. But don't overdo it. Too much passion and you'll do a lot of needlework later on."

The girl raises herself and grins. One moment she looks just like Behulā. The next, her face is full of teeth, and many are pointed. "Look at this granny. She had a hard life but she was strong. She could have been you! Her lungs are in perfect condition. And her guts, admirable! They are bright and shiny. You could strangle an elephant with them. But look at this, her liver. She must have drunk the cheap rotgut they sell, these days. Maybe she was sad and lonely. Or she was a poet, or a genius. People meet misery. They have to handle it. Most of them need anaesthetics. But you can never be sure."

The girl beckons. "Come closer. And hold this." She thrusts the heart into Behulā's hand. "It's damned big. What an item. You could put a universe in it. Maybe that's why she drank."

The girl adjusts her hair, and blood runs down her face. She extends her tongue to taste it. "Hang the heart on the line, over there. It's in excellent condition. But I have to clean this liver thoroughly." She submerges the item. Behulā sees clouds of dirt emerging. The huge, bloated organ shrinks. "See, now it's almost as good as new. But that's nothing compared to the filth you find in brains. I always say, why are people so proud of them? Compared to them, the guts are bright and shiny!"

The girl passes the liver to Behulā. "Right next to the heart, so we don't get things confused. Maybe more corpses are washed up. Sometimes they come in clusters. But we don't do all of them. You see, we are lucky. We get to chose. We wash heroes, but no soldiers; we care for saints, not for believers. Usually, the river preselects them. Some belong to the serpent world. That's good enough, and quite a bit of work. But all rivers kill, and the big ones drown villages. I couldn't handle the lot. That's where Yama comes in. He runs the standard Underworlds, you know, hells for every size and sin. It's the usual program: feel ashamed, bring your bad feelings, they will go around. He does the job all on his own. In Vedic times, his twin sister Yamī helped him out, but you know, one day she had enough and ran away. She got her hair done; her nails painted and changed her name. Yama sends her postcards at Dīvalī. She drops them in the bin. I hear she does promotion and public relations these days; well, that's hell enough for anyone."

The girl smiles and pats Behulā's head. "Yama does anyone who's really lost and lonely. That's most of them. I do the specials. I can count myself lucky, and so can they. I am sure you are aware how many people die each day. It's millions. And did you know, most of them ain't reborn. Their awareness, sure, it gets recycled. It gets a body and another life. Consciousness goes around, no matter how long it takes, before someone special appears, and makes a difference. The world is full of people who have never been alive. They appear, that's the best you could say, they act, they procreate like brainless rodents, but, damn it, it ain't good enough. Tiny lives, tiny dreams, stupid desires, and the usual package: eat, drink, breed, watch TV and work your life away. Most people have no idea that they are funny. Some are rich, some are mighty, and sure they feel self-important. They say 'I'm a winner'. It proves that they are failures. In the arena, everybody is a loser. You start weak, you end weak. In between you win some and you lose some. There are different games and different contests. Finally, everybody drifts into oblivion. That's a blessing. Look at the urges that define most people: hunger, ambitions, ignorance. Frankly, what is there to be reborn?"

The girl approaches the washing line. First, the heart, and then the liver; next to them the kidneys. The eyeballs dangle in the wind. "Most people waste their chance. They could make the world a happier place. They could be kind and loving. They could realise the divine in everything. But they are proud and greedy and dumb."

Picture 31: Facing the Truth.

Behulā sees that the girl wears her hair in three bunches. The third hangs down her back. A small skull, carved of bone, decorated with feathers and a tiny bell, rests between her shoulders.

"You are just in time," says the washerwoman. "I'm so glad you came. Feel welcome. I'm Neta."

Behulā stares into the water. The current sweeps over her feet. With Neta's help, she drags a corpse out of the deep.

"Hey look at this!" Neta laughs like a happy songbird, "this guy was a poet. But you can see he was ahead of his time."

"Can I?"

"Look at his costume. Look at his hair. Way ahead of his period. He must have been poor and lonely. I'm sure he was a genius. But be as brilliant as you like: if time is against you, you are lost."

"It's not fair."

"Life isn't fair. Not always and not instantly. Sure, in the long run, things straighten out. In his next life, he may be lucky. You can't hold brilliant people down. And we do our best to support them. For a start, we wash the bitterness out of their hearts. And mind you, their lives ain't wasted. They had time to learn and practice. It may have done them well."

Someone approaches. Behulā whirls around, like a scared antelope. Next to her, Neta giggles. From the gloom emerges a hairy, skinny man, parched by the sun, shrivelled and shrunk, leading a boy by the hand.

"Dhana, my love!" Neta waves at the boy. "It's good to see you."

The child squeaks with pleasure. He approaches a carcass, grips the guts and runs.

"Dhana!" Neta sounds serious, but her eyes sparkle. "Bring them back! Right now!"

One moment, Behulā fancies that Neta has a tiger head. Her fangs are huge.

Dhana stops.

"Be a good boy. Give me the bowels."

"No!"

"Don't no me! I've got to work!"

"You are not my mother!"

"That's my great good luck!"

Neta grabs the child and tears the guts from his grip. "That's it, my little troublemaker. And now you'll be nice and quiet. I've got much to do."

"I won't! I can do as I like."

"O no, you can't."

The knife flashes, the boy recoils, and she slits his throat. Blood spurts and Behulā screams.

Neta settles the boy. "One moment. I have to drain him. It will calm him down."

The dark man watches patiently. Neta opens the boy and takes out the organs. "He's young and headstrong. You've got no idea how often I have to wash his viscera."

She steps into the current. "Luckily, his organs are still fresh. Children learn fast."

The man follows her, and watches closely.

Neta turns to him. "See this, Gorakṣa. You might need this trick one day."

"For what?"

"Watch me do this. And pay attention, Mister Blow-My-Head to Kingdom-Come." Neta shows what she holds. Behulā whimpers and turns away.

"You smoke too much. It rots your memory. Or maybe it's the mercury. I don't care what you ingest; Mr. Yogī, to gain transcendence, but now I want you wide awake. This is reality. The innards are sacred. Look and learn. One day you'll do the same. Be gentle. The heart, the lung, the liver: they want to be treasured." Softly, she moves them through the water. "He's a child. Urges and instincts drive him, and like all small children he's a happy little beast and a tyrant in the making. Some call this innocence. I don't. Nevertheless, he hasn't accumulated evil or bitterness. With adults, you have to scrub and pull and wrangle. Sometimes I take a brain out and wish I could throw it away. Instead, I slap it against a palm tree. Then I submerge the damned thing, and walk on it, until the dirt comes out."

Gorakṣa raises his head and his eyes seem to burn. "You disrespect the dead."

Neta shakes her head. "Haṭha Yoga isn't everything. In fact, it isn't even a start. You promote vanity, and silly postures, and venerate the body. So do I, though in a different way. You fast, you ruin your joints, and you praise vegetarian meals as if you were a donkey. All your wisdom comes from books. It isn't good enough. The dead are my life, my bread and butter, and my hobby, too. I do dissolution. A girl has to make her own entertainment."

"Scripture says that corpses are polluting."

"Scripture is dead words by dead writers, quoted by people who'll be dead tomorrow. They shut up, when they face me."

She smiles at the boy. "Look, he's happy. And quiet." She points at Gorakṣa. "Understand this, clever man. Each person contains heaven and hell. No matter how saintly or rotten you believe yourself to be: everything is in there."

The man bows. "I see myself corrected." Tenderly, he lifts the liver from the corpse. He bends over the stream and washes it. "There," he says, "I did it. I touched a corpse. I washed an organ and I did my best. I lost my spiritual purity. Is this what you expected?"

Picture 32: Shore Guardian.

Neta takes the thing and examines it. She passes it to Behulā. "Over there. Hang it up, there's plenty of space."

She turns to Gorakṣa. "So you want to be a Nātha yogīn? Then listen now and hear what I say. First you need a sharpish blade. It'll take some time till you learn how to slay."

Neta points at the guts. "Here are the highest mountains, where the gods dwell. Here are the rivers, in the arteries. In these streams, vitality moves. Ask Behulā, she knows everything about it."

Behulā shakes her head. She doesn't know anything.

"And here," says Neta, "are the lungs. Note that they differ in size. That's why people are always slightly out of balance. They conduct the winds of cosmic vitality. People think that they breathe. Well, people think they think a lot, and think about it. My sister does it all the time. We ought to know better. "

The yogī smiles. "The All-Consciousness breathes us!"

"You're not quite as stupid as I thought. Now see this. In each organ there's a temple. The gods dwell within."

"The gods are everywhere."

"Well done. You don't have much talent, but talent is overrated. Talented people are sloppy and proud. You are barely average. That's much better. It means you try harder, and you persist."

"Do I?"

"Watch this. In the bone-marrow is the Rose-Apple Continent. In the head is the Subtle-Continent. Subtle means: hard to control. Try to hold on to a single thought. It wriggles and tries to slip away. That's why thinkers get lost in themselves. In the saliva is the Milk-Ocean. That's where speech appears, and speech maintains the world. It can be blessings and poison. In the spine is Mount Meru, the centre of the universe, where Viṣṇu resides. That big hump of a hill rests on the eternal serpent."

"I understand!" the ascetic gleams with happiness. "The mountain of the gods defines up and down, and fixes us in the centre of the cardinal directions."

"Not quite wrong," said Neta, "but far too simple."

She drops the organs into the boy. "Gorakṣa. You are a tāntrika. That means, you'll spend your life learning, and you will never come to an end." She raises her bloody hands. "You'll go to bed with doubt and wake with uncertainty. And unlike all fools, you'll never stop."

She points at the cranium. "Here, where the skull touches heaven, is Mount Kailāsa. That's where you meet Śiva and Durgā, and come home to yourself." She runs a finger down the arms of the corpse. "See the many hairs. Each is a goddess or god. Together, they constitute a forest. That's 330 million hairs."

"Who counted them?"

"The wealthy seers. Those who have servants, and cooks, and people who keep the hermitage clean. They have all the time in the world. They can think pure thoughts and define cosmic principles; they preach and make their followers happy. I wouldn't waste my time with them."

Behulā stares at the dead boy. "He was such a little darling. I liked him. Why did you kill him?"

Neta raises an eyebrow. "Behulā, my funny, lovely skeleton, you've been through far too much. And still you try to be a human being. What's so terrible? Life and death are here for fun. They come and go, like everything. Manasā is the Slayer. I am Death, release, and purification. We do what has to be done. Beyond the Dark Waters, there is rebirth."

"He was a little boy! He was alive! You simply cut his throat!"

"One moment he's alive, the next he's dead. That's what mortals always complain about. How about the other way? One moment he is dead, the next, he is reborn, he shits into his pants, he screams, and keeps his parents awake all night. In all likeliness, he won't remember a thing. Is it any better?"

"I don't know," says Behulā. "He's simply cute."

Neta sighs. "So are you, though you look like a corpse. Listen, crazy girl. Those who refuse death, refuse life. There is no life without death. And if you want fun, and laughter, and liberation, come and play with us. We are the ones who like jokes. Face reality: Anything that fills you with joy is heaven. What burdens you with pain is hell. And there are plenty of hells. Look at people these days: they keep inventing new hells, and indulge in them."

"I have been through hells."

"They are within you. Look at your husband. You agreed to marry him. That's bondage. You thought you could tell good from bad. You had a choice, and fixed your fate. Tell me, Behulā, silly woman, what did you think?"

"Maybe I could help him."

Neta punches her arm. "Come on, laugh. Thinking is overvalued. It's all guesswork, no matter how hard you try." She turns to the yogī. "I hope you listen, ascetic. We do this dance for you. Maybe one day I'll make you pass a test, in writing."

"I'm not sure I understand."

"Great." Neta hands him a piece of gut. "Watch this. I want you to observe every single detail."

The yogī stares in wonder. The fibres pulse, the bulges throb, the whole thing squirms and twists like a snake.

Picture 33: Yama Deathlord (based on Bengal Folk Art).

"It's as simple as one, two, three," says Neta, "It's just guts, and they are pretty clever, and you see the whole wild cosmos."

She takes Behulā's arm. "Relax my dear. He'll need a while to stomach this. You know, these yogīs, they've got no sense for reality. You have to shock them awake. You, by contrast found your way to me. Sure, it took some time. How long did you travel? Five months, or six?"

"I don't know." Behulā struggles to hold back her tears.

"And you are punctual. The gods need our help."

The women rest on the sand, and stare into the current. The dark stream surges along and the lotus blossoms sway. Far away, birds screech, and nearby, invisible but ever-present, tree frogs drone and pipe.

"This is where it began," says Neta. "This is the Lotus Lake. It's here and everywhere."

Behulā watches the waves striking the shore.

Several corpses had emerged, and Behulā had done her best. Neta had cut and joked and done silly voices, just to keep her happy. Finally, her job done, she had put little Dhana together again. She settled his lungs in the right place, arranged his heart, spread the nerves; and kissed his brain, before she dropped it in his skull, and patted his cheeks. The boy struggled for a moment, his lungs laboured, and then he turned, relaxed and slept.

Neta looks up. "That's it. Death isn't really bad. It's all about change. Today he is a child. One day, I hope, he'll be a fine young man. I wonder why he came. And I'm keen to learn what will become of him."

Neta turns to the yogī. "You there, wake up. I know you're amazed. So you should be. But honestly, there's more than mystic rapture. You saw intelligence in a piece of guts. You could see it anywhere."

The yogī doesn't move.

"Ah, he's lost within himself. In a year or two he'll wake."

"How do you do it?" Behulā tries to clear her head.

"I simply do it. It's my nature. But I could also do it complicated. It depends on what you like."

The boy grunts, stretches, and wakes.

He rubs his eyes and grins. "May I go and play?"

"Sure," says Neta, and hands him a sweet, "but don't annoy the crocodiles."

Dhana laughs and runs.

Behulā grasps Neta's arm and she knows her journey is over.

"Neta," she whispers, "wash me."

"I won't revive him," says Neta, "the Slayer has to do it."

Behulā glances down. Sure, she feels better now, and her costume gleams like fire. But she is glad there are no mirrors around. Her arms and legs are thin like sticks. She raises herself. "I want my man alive."

"Calm down. Don't hurry. This needs patience and deliberation." Like her, Neta gets up. "We'll do this later on. For now, I still have plenty of work."

"What is it? I thought you fixed all corpses."

"The corpses are the fun bit. Tomorrow they'll be collected. Some go to Sij Mountain for a while. Others will be reborn straight away." She grins. "It's the All-Consciousness. It wants to explore itself. That means many actors, many stories, loads of worlds, and reincarnation."

Neta points at the baskets. "Death is easy. This stuff is really hard. It's the costumes of the gods. They say, hey, Neta, you wash corpses, and they are filthy and polluting, but you don't seem to care. See this, they say, it's our vests and turbans, our skirts and saris and our underwear. You're a tough girl, and a real cutie, how would you like a real challenge?"

Behulā is hip-deep in the water. It is black and sort of gooey, but it cleans perfectly. She raises a filthy dhoti.

"This is Śiva's," says Neta, "please don't complain, he is my dad, and I approve of what he does. But I agree, right, you can only get so dirty when you spend half of your life hanging around at cremation sites. The ashes are a nightmare and you know, when corpses burn, the smoke goes yucky and oily, and you need anger and patchouli and curses to get it out. And look at those spots. That's hyena shit. He must have sat on it."

"But he's a god."

"It almost kills him. That's why he is out of his head most of the time. Honestly, it's one hell of a job. I mean, I've got it easy. I do corpses and underwear and the gods send presents and offerings, and behave extra polite, or else. He runs reality. I wouldn't want to swap with him."

Neta reaches into a basket. "Look at this thing. It's bright and colourful. You would think the goddesses had a sense of decorum. Or that they changed their pants more often. This slip is almost brittle. It's from Kāmākhya, the Goddess of the Vulva. She's one heavy duty chick. And she is hot, and drips. Now I don't blame her. It's her divine function. And we are lucky. It's just the normal dose. In October, when the monsoon ends, they close her temple for three days, 'cause nobody could bear as much. She could turn the Bay of Bengal crimson."

Neta produces another piece of underwear. "This belongs to Kāma, the god of desire and lust. See the sequins, and the bells. And the label: 'Mr. Cucumber.' Our guy knows how to seduce a girl. There are bite marks here. That must have been Ratī. She's a crazy bitch, she chews anything, and you know, like all gods, she hasn't got an off-button. I'll wash this stuff, but I won't repair it." She drops it. "Behulā. Don't faint. I'll do it. Same with Brahmā's underwear; it's so crusty you could stand it up. That's for experts."

Behulā shudders.

"Don't be so serious. This is about religion, and there's always something to laugh about. Just like real life, or anything." She pulls another piece out of the basket. It's a string tanga, blood red with turquoise edges, with fine embroidery in black. "Here, see this. It's really posh. There are small lions here. And tridents, and swords." Neta grins. "She tries so hard. Sure, Manasā gets all edgy with her. I find her funny. This belongs to Durgā. Don't mind the smell. She's a bit insecure, so she drowns her stuff in musk and amber and pheromones. She's your personal goddess, isn't she? So go ahead, and wash it."

Behulā catches the thing. It seems to burn.

"Stay easy and breathe." Neta is almost gleeful. "Here's the divine at its most human. Or the humane at its most divine. Either its corpses or its dirty underwear. It's hard to tell one from the other." She passes a yellowish chunk. "Use this soap. It's made of idealism, true faith and gritty nightmares."

Behulā raises her hands to the Heavens. She declares. "I place my faith in Ganges water. It is clear, it expels all evil, and it grants blessings to humans and gods. And whatever you may say, and no matter how much you joke, I trust the goddess to help me."

"Excellent!" says Neta. "What goddess would that be?"

Maybe Neta overdoes it; maybe she simply likes to show off. It can be a bit lonely at the Dark Waters, no matter that she meets so many people, in all stages of decay. She scrubs and shouts, wields soap and kiñcra blossoms, the Dark Waters foam, she makes snappy remarks and laughs about them if Behulā won't. She, too, faces the current, and it's black. Neta, in her wildness, makes her keep her distance. She recalls that Neta wore a tiger's head. Now she looks more like a crocodile. Behulā shudders. I'm hungry and tired. I hallucinate.

The women stand in the river. They drag costumes into the water, they pull them out and immerse them again, they slap them against stones and on occasion they push them into the sand and walk on them.

Much later, they relax on the embankment. They are tired and Neta, at least, is happy. Behulā feels shattered. Behind them, up the shore, the washing dries.

Neta hands Behulā a mango. "I'm glad you only stay for a while," she says.

"Why?" says Behulā. "You told me I did well." Her chin is wet with juice. She feels embarrassed.

"Too well. Just look at the stuff you cleaned."

"Is it wrong?" Behulā gnaws the big, hairy seed, and tries to look ladylike.

"Very much. My rules say: never pamper the gods. Most of them don't deserve it. They get too much admiration anyway. Leave some spots here and there; return the costume slightly flawed. They have to be reminded of their limits."

Neta rises. "Let's pack it up. Take two baskets; you'll be amazed how light they are. The stuff is really without substance."

Neta smiles, as she watches Behulā struggle, and snaps her fingers. That's how you do it when you are divine.

The women appear on Mount Kailāsa. It's bright, it's frosty, and painfully real.

"Welcome," Neta smiles, "this is Śiva's realm. He's my daddy. Today, he gives a party. All the gods are here. That's 330,000,000. Or at least they were, the last time I dropped in. It could be more, these days. Honestly, gods breed like microbes. You get a new generation every twenty minutes. Whenever a human being has a new ideal, a deity is born. That's humans. They invent gods in their own likeness, only a little better, so they can admire what they would like to be, if they were, but ain't and will probably never be, unless they try really hard, and are extra lucky. Meanwhile, the gods feed on admiration and passion; they shape people, they provide ideals and inspiration. Consider it a symbiosis. That's why every culture developed religions. It's a survival trait. We all need something to live up to."

"You confuse me!"

"That's reality. Get used to it."

"But what you say seems so...it seems to slight them."

"Nonsense. Gods can be great, if they put a bit of effort into their performance. And so can people. There's enough divinity for anyone and anything. Sometimes, you can't tell a deity from a person. Some people worship the divine as themselves, others as the bit of themselves that they can't manifest. One way or another, the gods are company. That's why true believers are never really alone."

"That's crazy! I was alone on the raft, except for Lakhindār."

"Who was there and wasn't there. But Manasā was. And so was I."

"Neta, please. You make my head rotate."

"That's what it's there for. Craniums are round so they can spin."

Behulā drops her baskets. She is surrounded by snow-fields. The air is biting cold and stings her eyes. She stares: there is a slope, and far beyond the cliffs and pinnacles, it's down, down and down. She has never seen a mountain, let alone been on one. It's a miracle, she thinks, it's too beautiful to be real. But all the while, it hurts her naked legs and feet. Maybe, she thinks, this is like death. Purity, simplicity; you just let go and the cold swallows you. It might be a relief.

Neta beckons. Maybe that's death, too, someone kind and friendly, who jokes and keeps you going, while you embrace the mystery.

"We'll be late" says Neta, "hurry up."

Behulā grabs her baskets. When the world stops making sense, you can only continue, if you have a worthwhile task.

Neta stands next to a wall. There is a tiny gate set into the rock. She holds the door open. "Hurry up. In there, it'll be warm and comfy."

Behulā staggers, as he fights her way through the snow. Then she is through the door and hears the music. It echoes through the corridors.

"This is just a side entrance. You know, I'm not a major deity. I never tried to make a career. Competition is for idiots. People, in general, don't care about a washerwoman, even if she is Death, personified. So I use sideways. I walk through empty passages. Come on, girl. You want your man alive. Cling to that thought."

Behulā follows her. Her bare feet feel the marble, and her gaze rests on the pictures, inlaid in carnelian and lapis lazuli, that line the corridor. She watches Śiva and Viṣṇu as they face the primal seers. She is amazed to see how Viṣṇu transforms into a woman, into the stunning Mohinī, and tempts the seers. The guys collapse and kiss her toes. "You are easy, darlings," she giggles. "I'm sure your balls are bigger than your brains." Meanwhile, Śiva has assumed the form of a stunning Bollywood star. His nose is a bit big, he has sensuous lips and his eyebrows are just wonderful. And how that guy can dance! The seeresses swoon with delight. Some of them look really stunning. "Hey girls," his motions say, "I am adventure, I am fulfilment, I am anything you never dared to dream about."

Then there's the hard-core ascetics, a bunch of angry monks and spiteful nuns, with bitter mouths and spiteful eyes. "Hi yogīs," Śiva grins. "Stop me if you can." The hermits hurl angry magic at him. A screeching dwarf, a battle axe, the white-hot heart of fire. Śiva takes them as his emblems. He leaves the renouncers in tears and dances on.

"Don't stand, there, gawking," says Neta. "This is ancient myth. Today we'll create new history."

"But what does it mean?"

"In a nutshell? The dwarf is the human ego. It tries to devour the world. Śiva dances on it. It means you have to get out of yourself to get anywhere at all. And fire? It's transcendence. And great big feelings. And light and warmth and nourishment. Renunciation ain't enough. If you go cold and bitter, you miss the glory of the world."

"How about the battle axe?"

"The battle axe. That's my favourite. It's what we are here for."

Neta opens a door. "Watch this."

Behulā stares. She has never seen so many colours in her life. The grand hall is full of figures. They shine and gleam and flicker. Behulā sees beings in human shape, with many arms, and creatures that sport animal heads, or appear as abstract symbols. Some seem to be vibrations; others are stunning arrays of colours, or mathematical formula. Some dance, some stand, some eat, some copulate. The place is huge. She feels dwarfed by pillars and ornaments, studded with jewels, extending into infinity. There is no limit; the whole universe could be packed into this place, and there would be space for many more.

"That's the realm of the divine. I apologise for belonging. Some of the deities are a bit strange. That's why I only come here when I have to. Most of the time, I prefer my river, and my corpses.

Behulā leans against a wall and closes her eyes.

"Stay relaxed and keep your eyes shut. You'll adjust." Neta taps her arm. "You've got plenty of time. I'll talk to my dad and then I'll be back. Cheer up. You are the battle axe."

Śiva is busy greeting guests. He has put on plenty of finery. True, much of it came from Durgā's wardrobe. He feels a little uneasy. So many jewels, and all that gold and glitter. His wife had dressed and scrutinised him, and when he tried to slip away she pulled him back. Śiva complained and struggled and finally gave up. Durgā knew what appearances were all about. "By dressing fine, you honour our guests," she said.

"I honour the exploiters," he muttered, almost inaudibly .

Now he faces a bunch of newcomers. Their bus had just arrived. These guys were freshly invented gods. They were loaded with flashy electronic gimmicks. Truth to be told, he would have loved to leave them standing in the snow.

But Durgā is insistent. "We have to move with the times," she says.

"No matter how stupid they are," he replies, and shuts up, 'cause she gives him the look. So he puts on a smile, of sorts, and watches these upstarts, as they stare at their smartphones, and complain they get no signal.

"That's the good part," Śiva cheers them, "feel at home and be what you are. And keep trying, if you're not." The new guests grumble, as they fiddle with their gear. The Lord of Transcendence shakes his head. As far as he cares, electricity should be in nerves and silicon in stone tools. Still, when you invite so many gods, you have to accept some misfits. Maybe they would get real later on. He would serve drinks and pipes and cookies full of anything.

Durgā passes him. She reclines on her lion and wears more colours than the human eye can comprehend. "Darling, you are incredible," he breathes. "You could wear garbage bags and still the world would faint before you."

That, of course, wasn't wanted. The goddess bares her teeth, as she disappears into the throng. Śiva shakes his head. Trust me to get this wrong, he thinks. My little darling. She'll have my head for it.

He turns to a deity with the face of a leech. "I am sure we met before," Śiva tries to appear supportive, "I can almost remember you. You're a banker? Or a representative of the weapons industry?"

His guest grins and reveals a range of curved teeth. "I do soy products."

Śiva shudders and turns to another deity. "And who would you like to be?"

He is getting edgy. A few days ago, his daughter, Neta, told him there would be a surprise. He hopes it will happen fast. Before long, he will want to run away. But Neta, he knows, is reliable. She gets things done, unlike his other girl, with the serpent outfit and the strange ideas. Śiva greets another bunch of newcomers. What's that? Nanotechnology? He puts on an extra wide grin. "Hello kids," he says, "I'm sure you'll be someone, someday soon. Once you get yourself sorted out."

He turns away from them and gives a sigh of relief.

"Hi Neta, I missed you. What's on?"

"I brought a guest. She's important, and she needs help."

Neta points, and Śiva looks at the side entrance. Over there, half veiled by shadows, cowering behind the washing baskets, hides a woman.

"She's shy," he says. "Have you offered her a drink?"

"Daddy, she's a human being. She can't take much more. She drifted on a raft for six months, with the corpse of her husband for company."

"Wow" he says, "that's really cool. The things some people do. I'm sure she would like a few cookies." He looks at his daughter, "she looks famished."

"Don't you dare to drug her!"

Śiva shrugs. "Well then. I'm wrong and you are right."

This is his clever daughter, the one who understands reality. He pats her shoulder. "Right, Neta, dear, I'll do what you tell me. But are you sure she wants to remain a human being?"

"She has to. The rules are simple. Please treat her as if she were my sister."

"You mean, like I had another daughter?"

"And behave!"

"That's tricky." Śiva stares into the distance. "I'm too sober for this sort of stuff."

"She is family! So keep your hands to yourself. No drugging, no groping! She helped me do the washing. You know what this means? I refer to your underwear."

Śiva gasps. Most people can't even think about his dhoti, and this one washed it. The new girl might love him. Or loathe him; you never know with people. He shakes his head. The evening is getting difficult.

"Good," he says, and tries to mean it. "I agree. This woman has a problem." He faces his daughter. "But why is she hiding?"

"She's timid."

Śiva laughs. "Why should she? It's just us. 330,000,000 deities. Plus extras and spare parts and these idiots over there. There's no reason to take us seriously."

"She believes, with all her heart. Or, what's left of it."

Śiva senses tragedy. Why do people bother him with stuff like that?

"My girl, what can I do for her?"

"This is your party. She's been through a lot. Allow her to show it."

"What is she good at?"

"She's a dancer," says Neta. "Her dance can shake the Three Worlds."

"That's good enough for me," says Śiva, "I like anything, provided it is strong."

"Thank you, daddy," says Neta. "I knew I could count on you."

Śiva grins. "Tell her to blow my mind. Make her put life and death into each movement. I want to see her laugh and sob and bleed. And when she shakes this bunch of idiots" he points at the guys with the laptops and the headphones, "and makes them faint, I'll fall in love with her."

Behulā stands in the door, as far as she dares to go, and faces the crows. There's far too many luminescent figures, too many heads, too many costumes, too many divine symbols and far too many arms and hands. Here and there, she recognises one. Gaṇeśa, Indra, Lakṣmī... a long time ago they made sense. Now they simply merge into each other. The gods burn and chatter and flame and flicker before her eyes, while her vision seems to blur and her brain goes unhinged.

"Neta," she grasps, "they fight each other at the buffet! Why do they do this sort of thing?"

"Don't ask me. I do corpses and textiles. I'm not supposed to understand anything." Neta grins. "But I could stop them right smartly, if I liked."

"I want to go home!"

"You are at home. Ignore them. They do their best, and so should you."

"I'm just human!" Behulā is close to tears.

"And you know everything about their underwear. So go out, and kill them. I want to see you dance!"

"I can't!"

"You can." She points. "There's Śiva. That's my daddy. He likes you. I told him to. So he will do a lot to make you happy. You are a dancer. It's in your soul. So dance and be what you are!"

Neta is getting cross. Behulā drops to her knees. "I'm full of death and misery!"

"Show it! Be wild and crazy and mad! My dad will love it, no matter what you do."

Behulā advances. It isn't her choice: Neta has pushed her to the front. The gods make space for her. Who is this, they whisper, she looks so miserable. That's 'cause she is human, some propose. But she is also skinny, like a skeleton. Who brought this scarecrow to the party?

Some begin to giggle.

Neta advances. "Let me introduce Behulā. She's my sister and the greatest dancer in the multiverse. You may watch her perform, and if you know what's good for you, you'll cheer her and applaud. That's for three reasons. First, she is really good. And second, she means what she does. And you can guess the third."

The gods quieten down.

"I'm glad you know your places." Neta bows. "This dance is at the special request of my father, Śiva, the Destroyer and Transformer of Worlds."

Neta steps back. She has done her part. Now everything is up to Behulā.

The girl has lowered her head. She stares at the ground and wishes to be far away, or dead.

She feels like a broken doll. There's no bodycentre, her breath is hasty and her shoulders rise and sink in panic.

I'm an assembly of spare parts, Behulā thinks. I can't move.

The gods begin to whisper.

"This is sick" says a voice.

"I heard you," says Neta. "And you will walk in filth for aeons. Your worshippers will spit on you."

The crowd goes deadly quiet.

Behulā raises her head. "What should I dance?" she whispers.

Neta smiles. "Dance who you are. Dance the divine within you!"

The light is far too bright. Behulā is surrounded by deities. There are far too many. They stare at her. The lower gods throng the sides. The high gods sit on thrones, far above the congregation. Śiva is the host, and reclines on the highest seat. He is responsible for the entertainment. If things go wrong, everyone will laugh. At the moment, Behulā can't really discern him, nor can she discern Durgā. The Lord of Transcendence has disappeared in a cloud of smoke. Viṣṇu, sitting next to him, fights for breath. His wife, Lakṣmī, sticks an elbow into his ribs.

Behulā realises that her sari is in tatters, that her hair is unkempt, that she is filthy and thin and almost starved. They are perfect, she thinks, and I am mortal, lost, and ugly. They will sneer at me. Neta will curse me, for having failed, and Śiva will doom me. There will be no dance. I will stand and wait for them to kill me.

Śiva claps his hands. The Gandharvas hear and respond.

The leader nods to his band. This is an emergency. There's this girl. She is human, meaning an ape, and more dead than alive. We can't expect her to do much, he assumes, but we can make her do her best.

Let's play something simple. He lifts his vīṇā and makes a chord resound. The instrument throbs and blossoms under his fingers. The sound drifts through the hall, swirls around the pillars, glides through corridors and expands to other worlds. It's just a simple harmony, enough to lift the ceiling from your head, to open the Underworlds below, to make your heart unfold with yearning and hope. The musician sighs. His fingers dance on the strings, they catch hold of a mood, let it go, and turn to another. In between, tones gleam like diamonds in the night, and the drums set in.

Behulā feels the pulse. It throbs from the ground, goes up her legs, and converges in her belly. Her body sways and she is lost. The Gandharvas grin. The girl wakes, they think, let's see how she can move. They adjust their instruments to her. Behulā struggles; she gasps for air and faces life.

This is how it started, she realises. There's Cāndo, trying to humiliate her. There's herself, proud and angry, at the ghāts. There's the crone who changed her life, and the dish of iron beans. She dances her marriage feast; she reveals her hopes and fears, and the iron chamber where Lakhindār died in her arms. She dances the bleakness of the morrow, the sadness and despair that made her travel with his corpse. She dances the river, the fields and plantations, the darksome jungles and the beasts. Here is a village, there a city, all spires and temples, all glory and wealth, and poverty. Behulā dances the cows on the fields, the herons in the trees, the rapists at the shore, the hope and misery within herself. Her hands imitate the swarms of flies, she wriggles her hands like maggots, she imitates the Ḍom whose beard caught fire. The gods laugh, they cheer her, and they clap. Her arms buzz like a dragonfly. She steers the raft, she begs at the shore, she struggles with herself. See the tiger in the forest, the fish that snatched his heel away! She starves, she weeps, and she gives in to fate. Finally, she arrives on the island, tries to build a pyre, and faces truth. She dances her despair, her horror and insanity. She arrives at the Dark Waters, and does the washing of the gods, in Neta's company, and collapses.

The musicians stop, the guests stand in silence.

Everyone stares at the girl, who lies on the ground, ready to die.

Śiva raises his hands. There are tears in his three eyes. Very slowly, he begins to applaud. The gods join in. They cheer and laugh and triumph.

"Get up, girl!" Śiva calls. "We've seen it all. You danced hope and death and resurrection. Let me bless you for blessing us."

He raises his hands. "And now for something else. Is my daughter Manasā around?"

Manasā, of course, is absent. It's not that she doesn't like a happy dance performance, in particular if it involves serpent motions. In this respect, Indian dance has gained a lot by copying Hongkong gongfu movies. But tonight might be a little difficult. She has watched Neta arrive, and seen the gleam in her eyes. Her little sister! Next, she saw Behulā introduced to Śiva. Her daddy, she knew, has a heart for homeless strays and orphaned dancers, provided they are beautiful, or inspired, or slightly dead.

The Serpent Goddess slithers down empty corridors. She rushes past pot plants, through alcoves, hurries up and downs staircases, changes directions, stops, listens, and runs along. Before long, she relaxes. No sound is audible, except for her naked feet on marble.

See Manasā. She moves like a shadow, she doubletracks, she leaves as little scent as possible. Only the plants watch her, as she climbs out of windows and balances over roofs, as she descends creeping vines, makes her way through dark cellars, and emerges elsewhere, no matter when or how, provided it is far away. All of a sudden, a great big roar emerges from the central hall. Manasā freezes. That's it, she thinks. Behulā has done her share. They'll be on my tracks in instants.

And they will think I try to escape. What nonsense! The Serpent Queen would never dream of fleeing. She would simply prefer to be elsewhere, when gods came rushing, and started to ask questions. Durgā, she realises, would sneer. And she would say, "Hey scaly slut, why do you run so fast?"

"I never run," she would say, and everyone would laugh. "I have to go home for my beauty sleep. That's 'cause I get up early, much earlier than you, to do my breathing exercises." And they would laugh even more. And then Durgā would point at her and say, "Baby earthworm, you squirm with guilt," and she would bare her fangs and the lion would growl and everyone would make a scene and, no, she wouldn't have it. She has nothing to hide. No-one could criticize her for anything. That's because she had thought so much, and has all answers ready. And extra answers, just in case. She would smile like an empress and say, "Sure, Behulā, I know her. She's a little crazy. I saved her life a couple of times."

Yes, that would shut them up. But it would be so much nicer just to get away.

Manasā accelerates. Only a few steps, then out of the side-entrance, into the snow. Out there, she would summon her chariot. The swans would take her home. And Neta could walk. She deserves it.

Before her, the doors bang shut. She hears voices, steps and excitement. Oh damn. That's the minor gods. They hate the higher ones, and they swing weapons, and go mad, and hope for accidents, so they might be promoted. Well, they won't have it easy. The Serpent Goddess steps behind a pot plant. It's a fig. How middle-class! Well, Durgā has no taste and Śiva doesn't care. You can't smoke figs. Why should he notice?

Manasā drifts into the stem and thinks plant thoughts. They travel on electric currents, move with the sap and pass through the air as pheromones. She steadies herself, extends branches, feels the sap rushing and orients herself to light. In each leaf, stomata open and she breathes. Her feet turn into roots, each tiny rootlet intelligent, and self-confident, an individual in its mad pursuit of pleasure. They, in turn, make friends with fungi. Manasā feels herself extending. Each branch makes its own decision, each sprouting tip senses the air, the brightness, sees the colours, explores the environment. Plants are great, if you can handle decentralised intelligence. The small gods can't. Yowling and screeching, they rush past. The goddess, lost within herself, and absolutely conscious, remains. She can stay that way, if need be, for centuries.

Much later, she recalls herself. She entangles herself from the mycorrhizal network, and sighs as she lets go. Leaves turn to dreams and fade, while her stem becomes a spine. She stretches and yawns. Manasā follows the tracks of the small gods. They are so dumb; they will never bother to check what happens behind them. She finds a pool. It looks fresh and pure. She is thirsty; being a pot plant can parch your priorities.

The pool is set in black marble and shaded by lotus blossoms. Maybe she could rest in there, in the gloom, just a short while. Eventually, the chase would end. The small gods would return to the great hall, where the high gods would recline, on their padded seats. The buffet would be almost empty and all the best drinks would be gone.

Manasā assumes her snake form, slides underwater and waits.

"What a beautiful night," says the voice. Manasā gasps.

"The moon is out so early. I hope your swans won't freeze. Maybe you should ask them inside."

Manasā assumes her divine form, and rises. Next to the pool stands her father. He hands her a towel.

"How did you find me?"

"How could I fail? Your thoughts are really loud."

"Here is my daughter," says Śiva. "I'm sure you missed her."

Manasā stands like a statue. The gods glare at her. She hears them mumble, argue, quarrel, and doesn't like the sound. "Six dead in one night," "the whole fleet sank", "Cāndo's stepdaughter," and "her personal vengeance."

The Serpent goddess studies the ceiling.

Indra parts the crowd. The Thunderer isn't quite an intellectual, but even he has noticed that some things are really wrong. "Listen, chick," he addresses her. "I want an explanation. That Behulā girl over there, she seems familiar. Did you abuse one of my dancers?"

Manasā shrugs. "How could I know?"

"And her corpse man. Lakhindār. Is he my favourite vīṇā-player?"

Manasā bites her lips.

"Tell me, reptile girl, did you steal my best entertainers?"

Śiva raises his hands. "I'm sure she simply borrowed them."

He shakes his head. "Look, here is my little girl. She never hurt anyone. She's innocent, and in puberty. Or wherever. You can't blame her. At least, not without blaming me. So, I'll try to be fair. Anyone who wants to complain can have a few pipes with me."

The gods stand and stare. Even Durgā remains quiet. She is pale with rage but she won't make a scene. Not now, when everyone can watch her. But maybe later on.

"Great," says Śiva. "I'm glad we settled this. This ain't about you and me; it's about Manasā and Cāndo, and about Behulā and her man. Or what is left of him."

He glares at everyone.

"And it's all about rules. You know, I tend to overlook them. But there are gods who thrive on them."

Next to him, Viṣṇu straightens his posture and adjusts the feathers in his crown. The Maintainer of the Universe raises his hands. "Listen, deities and associates. It's my great pleasure to address you. Let me outline the ethical implications of the alleged occurrences, and the major points on the agenda, before..."

"We thank you for your contribution," says Śiva. "You cheered us up immensely. But this is my palace and I hate words like 'agenda'."

He smiles at Viṣṇu. "It's not even Saṁskṛta."

"It isn't?"

"And it will never be."

He turns to Manasā. "Daughter, we listen."

The Serpent Goddess squares her shoulders. From the top of her head, seven mighty Nāgas raise their hoods. "My dear, dear gods," she goes, "why do you make a scene? You misunderstood everything. You ran and screamed, you wielded weapons in my father's house. I have no idea what you thought, or thought you thought, but whatever it was or wasn't, or wouldn't be if it could, but honestly it can't, not here or anywhere, 'cause I won't have it, and never will, so here's the truth: it wasn't me."

She folds her hands and tries to look shy and demure. Somewhere in the distance, she hears Neta sniggering.

Śiva turns to Behulā. "Dancer, tell us, how your husband died."

"Lakhindār was killed in our wedding night. A snake bit him."

"Was it an accident?"

"No," says Behulā, "it was prophesied when he was born."

"Is his death related to my daughter?"

"Of course not!" Manasā is furious. "You are a little liar." She turns away. "She is an ape girl. Do we have to listen to her?"

Behulā shows her teeth. "It was a long, thin snake. It crept into our chamber!"

"That snake," says Manasā "does not exist."

"I chopped off the end of its tail. Here is the missing bit!"

"Oh. That snake. I didn't know." She raises her hands in apology. "I haven't seen the little creep for ages."

"It's right behind you!" Durgā's voice is loud and gleeful.

Indeed, the tiny serpent hides behind Manasā's ankle, and tries to be invisible.

"Little wriggler," says Śiva, "No-one will do you harm. Please tell us what happened."

"Nothing!" Manasā snatches the snake and holds its mouth shut. "This poor dumb thing wants to tell us that it feels deeply sorry." Manasā smirks. "My little darling. Shut up and be good. I guess you'll be in trouble soon."

She tosses the snake into a corner and faces the assembly. Her fangs gleam. "I don't want to upset this happy party!"

She turns to Behulā. "And before anyone makes a scene, let me tell you, dancer. I can see you are angry. So am I. But I like you. We have met many times. If you didn't pray to Durgā so often, I could really be your friend."

"You can have her!" This is Durgā, and she is loud. "Take the little glamour girl! And don't believe your lies would fool us! You are guilty. Take her along. I'm glad to be rid of her! And let her learn: you can't be trusted!"

"I won't be vindictive," says Manasā, "Honestly, I'm generous and carefree. Ask anybody. I have a balanced character with a healthy outlook on life. And I have a clear head. Don't ask me where I got it from." She takes Behulā's hand. "Little dancer, you got everything wrong. That's human nature. But I forgive you. So come along, we'll fix that corpse of yours."

She looks like a scared rodent, thinks Manasā. Behulā hurries along the shore. She steps into the water, she runs up the slope, she rounds the river bend and is back again, screaming in anguish. "He's gone!" She can barely keep herself on her feet. "Lakhindār! My darling! He is gone!"

She drops to her knees and weeps. "The raft! It's gone!"

Manasā has heard it a hundred times.

"You must help me!"

Do I? thinks Manasā. Corpses rot and disappear. Rafts come apart. In a wet environment, the microbes will eat anything. That's life. Had she imagined he would last forever? Behulā is up and about again. Precisely because of such emotions, thinks Manasā, I'm glad I'm not human. To accompany a few of them, from time to time, is stressful enough.

She smiles. "Are you sure it was here?"

Behulā points at the organs dangling from the washing lines. "Neta and I were here! We did that."

"It doesn't mean a thing. Neta is a busy woman. Can you imagine how many corpses she does? These shores are infinite, and so are the poles, the lines, and all that hangs on them.'"

"He was here!"

"You imagine things."

"The raft stranded near that root."

"It didn't. Rafts are manmade contraptions. The Dark Waters eat them up."

"That's where I left him!"

"After six months in this climate? There was nothing left of him."

"Neta stood there, she could tell you."

"Neta likes people who are crazy. I don't." Manasā arranges her hair. "Face it. Your mind is off the bent. You hallucinated for months."

She points at the river. "See this. It's beautiful. And it's alive, and so are you. Your husband went to rot, a long time ago. There's nothing left of him. Count yourself lucky that you made it."

Behulā whimpers. She takes off the garland of blossoms that Śiva had placed around her neck, after her dance. She settles it on the sand and bows.

She produces her knife. "Thank you," she says. "A long time ago, I made a vow, and I kept my word. I travelled to the gods. I danced my life. It's time to end it."

She exposes her throat and raises the blade.

Manasā grabs it. "Don't you dare to force me, little bitch. And stop yowling. I want to see you stand!" She pulls the girl up. "Vows are like toys. They keep you amused for a while. They fill a need. Then they fade away. The wheel turns. The rivers continue through infinity."

"You hurt my hand!"

"Says the girl who just tried to kill herself."

The goddess bares her fangs. "Look at yourself. You came to the land of the gods. Only gods can do that."

Behulā gasps.

Manasā grins. "I knew you would understand, one day." She claps her hands. "Right, Gaṅgā, you can return him."

The mist parts, the water heaves and the raft rises to the surface. Lakhindār lies there, motionless, just as she had left him. Crocodiles, fishes and turtles push the contraption to the shore.

"And he?" Behulā hardly dares to breathe.

"Same as you."

"We are?"

"Everyone and everything."

Manasā shakes her head. "You protected him well. Still, he is almost gone. Wouldn't you like a better man?"

"He's the best for me."

Picture 34: Death and Disease Spirits (based on Bengal Folk Art).

"Well, I will trust you, as far as I can." She opens his jacket. Most of the flesh is gone. The rest is beyond description.

Behulā chokes and tries to look away.

"Come on!" The Serpent Goddess hisses. "You had your scene, now prove you learned your lesson. We have to get him out of his costume."

She lays out the spine and attaches the head. "See, he's laughing. So should you."

"I try. It doesn't work."

"Try harder. Lay out the pelvis and the legs. I'll do the hands. They are complicated."

"Here," Behulā points at his foot. "There's a bit missing. A fish got it."

"What sort of fish?"

"I don't know! It was dark and the river tossed us around. His corpse slipped. And then this huge thing rose from the water!"

"Can't you live without his heel? It's not the most important bit."

"No!" Behulā shouts. "I want him complete."

"Hey, I didn't know you could be angry. Fight me! I like it."

"And now you make me weep again."

"Don't. Leave that for Cāndo. He deserves it."

The skeleton gleams. "That was fun," says Manasā. "I guess we got him mostly right. And now it's time for a miracle." She stands up and brings her palms together. When she opens them, light gleams, purple and green throb, the forest opens; and another river appears. "Jālo and Mālo! I need you here, right now!"

A brightly painted fishing boat appears. "Goddess!" Jālo bows, and Mālo tries to hide in the catch. "We didn't expect you."

"Nobody does. And Neta even less." She turns to Behulā, "see this, dancer. They are old friends."

"They seem afraid!"

"Yes! Everyone gets excited when I come round."

She grins at her worshippers. "Stop praying. I need a little favour. Throw out your nets and catch as much as they can bear."

The brothers share a glance. The water before them is too black. The forest is full of weirdish magenta hues and there's a corpse on the beach. They ignore the stuff that dangles from the washing lines. Sure, their goddess is there. She looks slightly edgy. That means trouble. And next to her stands a girl, so thin she could be a skeleton herself.

"Put your flower garland on again," whispers Manasā, "and you'll look more presentable."

She gives the fishers a broad grin. "This is Behulā. Remember her. She'll be famous."

Behulā stares into the net. It's full of wriggling monsters. "I guess it's this one," she says, "it has a guilty look."

"You there! Spit it out!"

The fish twists and the bone comes flying.

"Behulā, fix it. And you, fishers, stop praying. You are getting on my nerves. If you want to make a compliment, say something fresh and meaningful. And stop fiddling with your amulets."

"Manasā?" Behulā smiles. "It's done. The foot is complete. But tell me one thing. You said that only the divine could come here. What about these two? They look human."

"There's no such thing as humans."

The fishers bow. "Great Goddess, Light of the World, Lotus-Born, Eternal, Timeless..."

"That's enough. You can go now. And take the catch."

"But Lady! There are fishes with three heads! Some have feet! Some glow. And this one giggles!"

"That's how it has to be," says Manasā, "we want the story to go around."

Manasā stands over the corpse. Her breath is colourful. The vapours drift through the skeleton, they stick and congeal, they shape a human body, complete with organs, tubes, spongy stuff, stringy nerves and finally, a beautiful complexion and deep soulful eyes.

"You forgot his moustache."

"I don't do moustaches. He can grow his own."

She raises her hands "I call Yama, Lord of the Underworlds, Master of Hells, Twin Born, Bull-Faced, Punisher and Releaser. You are the truth, you ensure justice, you collected his Jiva, his life essence. And maybe you don't want to give it back. I understand; he is a musician, and quite a good one. My dad says there ain't much entertainment in your realm. Not as much as in the Serpent Underworld, or in Indra's All-Aeon discotheque. Well, you've had him long enough. I'm sure you'll get along without him. Send him here, or I'll get really cross."

The sand shudders. A shadow rises from the ground. It flickers, twists and terrifies. Behulā recoils but Manasā snarls.

The Lord of Hells roars like the bull, his emblem. He raises his staff, tramples the ground, and shakes a fist. "Snake girl, leave me alone! Whatever I do, you interfere."

"I don't! It's just that you are in the way!"

"I am part of the way!"

"And a bloody stupid bit. Stop roaring. This girl has been through more hells than you can ever manage."

Yama nods at Behulā. "Sorry about this. I don't want to make a scene. Not again. Last time we had a quarrel, I had one hell of a time getting her serpents out of my hells. Damn it, it's a nightmare to handle worms!"

"You lost. That's why you are here."

"Much against my better judgement."

Manasā grins. "I'm glad to see you so obedient. Now you may worship me."

"You little wriggler! Leave me alone!" The bull-man roars. "You get on my nerves!"

"Release her husband's essence."

"You could try to ask nicely."

"This is nicer than you deserve."

"Fine, serpent girl, laugh as much as you like. You'll get your head. But as you lack manners, and I have to deliver, it must be formal. Scripture is a must! There are rules and regulations."

"So what?"

"Lakhindār died. I'm the boss, and baby, I will make you suffer. He won't return unless you say a traditional anti-serpent spell."

"Are you crazy? A spell against snakes? Me? Shall I knot your ears?"

"It's the law, you dumb thing. And don't you dream of raising a serpent army. You lost. So go ahead, and make me laugh."

"You bastard! I know why Yamī left you! That's not just vicious, it's bad taste."

"It's traditional. You and I have to follow rules."

"I hate rules!"

"Do you want him back?"

"I do, you dumb bovine."

"So I'll see you perform, little girl."

"You'll get your stupid spell. Laugh all you like."

Manasā turns to Behulā. "This is outrageous. He knows I hate this sort of poetry."

She adjusted the snakes in her hair. "Stay calm, darlings. This has nothing to do with you. And Behulā, you may listen, but don't you dare to smile.

What do you do on the branch of the simul tree, o crow?

O powerful Yama-crow, my son is bitten by the serpent's tooth.

Seize the snake and eat!

Make bones and flesh, oh poison living in these bones;

Let the poison be drawn out from the body, oh peacock!

Oh black snake, the mongoose bites you. Oh blue poison, come to me.

Let the poison be dissipated; let the bones join together again."

The corpse begins to twitch.

"Yama, damn you, you had your fun. I hope you hoot a lot. It won't last. One day, I'll get you for this, and I'll grab your balls and tie you to a treetop!"

Laughter echoes along the shore, the earth trembles and the shadow swirls into the deep.

"You heard this, Behulā? What a rotten gobshite! That's why they put him in charge of the hells. He has no class at all. This spell ought to be rewritten! He insulted me! Hey, Behulā! Are you listening? Not so hard! Don't crush him! Let him breathe!"

Manasā turns away. "Well, we had our fun. Man as good as new, wife slightly less insane. The evening is perfect, and the gods had better shut up."

"Goddess! Behulā looks up.

"Don't call me that. I've got plenty of names."

"I ask a favour."

"Another one? Can't you get enough?"

"Cāndo's six sons. Revive them."

"Those bullies? Why don't you ask for his sailors? Cāndo drowned them. Remember the people he killed! How about my worshippers? Why don't you plead for their lives?"

"I can't ask for everything."

"But you should. The story demands it."

Manasā points at a bush. "Neta, come out! I know you listened, and thank you very much. This is big magick. I need your help."

Neta emerges. She brushes twigs out of her hair. "That was fun. You revived him the hard way. Personally, I would have used mercury and cinnabar. And my favourite spell

All the dreams that didn't last,
all the carrion of the past,
juicy, stinking, yummy goo,
dripping slime and gristle too,
what began has found an end,
make me laugh and be my friend!"

"Rubbish! That's not a revival spell at all! You made that up, right now!"

"Never. Could these teeth lie?"

"You are just hungry!"

The goddesses laugh.

Neta grins at Behulā. "Hey, washergirl! You won!"

"Did I?"

"Sure, and you are extra lucky. Cāndo's boys and the rest. I keep them over there." She points uphill. Behulā sees a tangle of jungle plants, fresh, green and dripping wet.

"You have to help me carry them. And, I want you to see my temple."

"But my husband..."

"He's alive. He'll breathe, he'll shit, he'll be better than before. Give him a moment to recover. I'm sure my sister wants to have a word with him."

"What about?"

"He's young, good-looking and a rāg-star. You wouldn't want to know."

Neta drags Behulā along the beach. Their feet sink into the ground. Then it's up an incline, through giant ferns and thickets, wet with moisture. Between the stalks rise horsetails, red, purple, toxic yellow. The ground is soft, the mosses pulse, here and there a broken fig tree rots, while the decomposers gnaw away, and pink fungi raise their heads. The air is damp and warm; the sky invisible.

"That's what I like," says Neta, "the greens, the shadows, and huge blossoms. Don't get too close to them; the scent can knock you out. I find dead animals underneath. Plenty of plants kill animals. Some kill their victims fast; others turn them into addicts, and poison them. Tomatoes, tobacco, you name it. That's how they feed themselves. And watch your step; it's slippery. You wouldn't want to slide into a gully."

She dances on, while Behulā follows cautiously. She is wet; whenever she touches one of the huge leaves, each as large as a table, a shower drenches her hair. "It's up here!" Neta points into the nightmare green. "My dad said I could have a temple, just as I like. And he was amazed to see it. He had to sit down. He got his mālā out and did his breathing. One or two bottles later he said it expresses aesthetic sensibility, an artist's sense of primal truths and the refined humour of true life experience. But see it for yourself." She drags Behulā on. The girl stumbles, recovers her balance and looks up. The temple is pale and small. It rises from a set of stairs, not many, for Neta isn't into grand gestures. It's more her style to wear the grand ones down. The pillars are pale. Behulā gasps: they are long bones, studded with ribs, and hands. The steps are made of made of pelvic bones, neatly compressed, and polished smooth. The ceiling rises, a dome of skulls, all fused together, of birds and cats and elephants, of people and strange creatures that by rights should not exist. Behulā turns her head, and sees shady things scuttle away. "Ignore them," laughs Neta, "they eat the rot." She points at a carcase. "There' several good meals here, before the better bones go somewhere else. And look at the skulls! I've got at least one of each sort! Even the really tiny ones."

Behulā sways. The scent makes her choke.

"Breathe through the mouth. It's easier. But be cautious, or the flies get in. Soon you'll be used to it. I mean, you got used to your husband!" She pokes Behulā's arm. Neta's face has assumed a tigerish expression. It might be a mask. Or else...

"Now come on in. You'll love it. My temple is much larger from the inside. I've got space for practically everyone. There's stairs and crypts and places to relax. And every year, it rises a little bit. That's 'cause the bones pile up."

Neta stands like a schoolgirl; she wrings her hands and gleams. "Behulā, I'm so glad you're here. You are a darling. Hardly anyone comes for a visit. Had I known you'd be coming I would have fixed us a meal. But look at this." She points to the ceiling. "That's where I keep corpses that ain't ready. Like Cāndo's sons."

"Are they dead?"

"Not really. Otherwise, Yama would have tried to get them. I guess they had some time to think and understand their place in the food chain."

"There's so many of them!"

"You never know who needs a comeback. I hang them up, so the Rākṣasas can't reach them, no matter how high they leap. Otherwise, they'd be gnawed. And watch your step. Some bits are slippery. You don't want to go into that corner there. That's where I feed the Piśācīs. Sure, they are filthy. They piss and drop their rubbish where they like. But I'd rather have them in one spot than everywhere."

Behulā whispers. "What sort of place is this?"

"My Temple of Decay. I'm so glad you like it."

Picture 35: Neta: That's me!

35. Back

"No-one will recognise me." Behulā winked; her eyelashes gleamed. She had powdered them, just a little. "I look far too good for our families."

Lakhindār grinned. "You might stay a little longer. Here, in the cabin, with me."

"Really?" Behulā gave him a playful slap. "And all of a sudden, it's tomorrow."

"Well, they don't know we're coming. So we have time. They'll do their usual things. Maybe they miss us. But mostly, they'll be as they always were."

Behulā shook her hips. Silver bells tinkled. "These things should be louder."

"True," Lakhindār stroked his upper lip. His moustache was returning, but it wasn't quite as dashing as before. "When I play loud, the audience can't hear your bells. How about more bells? Or heavier ones, say, at your calves, three, four rows of them?"

"I'd have to put my feet down, hard."

"You could. So I've heard."

Behulā advanced to the door, paused and spun around, so her husband could catch and kiss her. It took ages.

He raised an eyebrow. "I could accompany you. You are the most alluring Ḍom girl on earth and I'm your passionate musician."

"You stay on board. Just like your brothers. People would recognise you."

Lakhindār tilted his head. His eyes went dreamy and his lids half-closed. "Stay just a moment, an instant and let me kiss your neck..."

Behulā twisted out of his arms and ran. She heard him laugh.

The quay was packed with people. Six mighty ships, all strangely shaped, and carved from unknown woods, inlaid with gold and gems and pearls, had reached the shore in early daylight. Sailors clad in orange silk, with heavy earrings, had tied the ropes to the embankment, and retired under deck. The captains were not visible.

Talk went around. Within minutes, the leading merchants sent their representatives, who stood on the pier and waited for someone to emerge. Cāndo, of course, had done more than that. Beside accountants, diplomats and translators, he had sent guards. The ships might be full of pirates or invaders. Campaka was his city and he wasn't taking any risks.

The men were bored. When they saw the lonely Ḍom girl dance down the stairway, they barred her way.

"Girl! Here are some coins. They'll buy you a meal. So tell us. What's inside these ships? Where do they come from? Who owns them?"

Behulā refused to touch the money. As she advanced, the traders stepped back. One tried to slap her bum. Her foot shot out, and the man went to the ground, he clutched his knee, and yelped. Behulā hurried past. She heard the men laughing.

Soon she reached the marketplace. It was easy to spot her target. A group of women, surrounded by guards and slaves, made their way through the stands. The women had all the time in the world; they behaved as if they owned the place. In their centre, Sonakā paraded, like an empress, and frowned at anyone and anything. She's much older, thought Behulā, but she is still a fighter. Her sons are dead; and she waits for her end. Her heart grinds her down. It might take decades, but she will hold herself up, and show her station in the world. There was a bitter, greedy line in the corner of her mouth. The widows in her company chattered like a bunch of finches. Had they always been so stupid?

Behulā watched them. No-one paid attention to her. A Ḍom girl is simply beneath consideration. Few men would dare to come close to her. True, in a bordello they might not be that hesitant. And afterwards they would hurry to the temple and ask Viṣṇu for forgiveness, and beseech Dharma to overlook their lapse.

Behulā had spent hours in front of the mirror. In the past, as the daughter of a wealthy merchant, her costume had been different. She wouldn't have dared to expose her legs, or show her décolleté, or walk across the marketplace, alone. As a Ḍom girl, untouchable, she could.

Sonakā stopped. Her girls wanted to examine textiles. The salesman, in his ill-fitting jacket, stood next to her and trembled. Sonakā didn't bother to greet him. The guy wasn't worth consideration. She wouldn't buy any of his cloth, no matter how the girls chattered. Sure, the pattern was new, and probably in fashion. What interested her was the origin, the weight, the craftsmanship and the price. If it was any good, and anyone was really keen on it, her husband would be interested.

A young woman appeared at her side. Sonakā stepped back. A Ḍombī. Untouchable.

The girl held a fan and extended it to her. Sonakā hardly needed to take a look: the thing was antique. Perfectly carved rosewood ribs, gilded, and the material was the finest silk, a little faded by age.

"Lady," the girl began. She seemed shy. What a joke! As if a Ḍombī had ever known what shame might mean! "See this fan. Please look at it. Maybe it might please you?"

Sonakā tilted her head back. Her face showed disapproval. "It's a common piece of trash. Probably a fake. Where did you steal it?"

The girl bowed. "Goddess. The fan is genuine. And it is old. My father was a great musician. On his journeys, he came to Kāmākhya, in Assam, where he met a great yogī. The man was enchanted by his tunes. He gave this fan to my father. It comes from Mahācīna and is very old."

"Old?" Sonakā had to take it. Her lips tightened to a thin line. What did the Assamese know about culture? They worshipped a goddess of menstruation! I can imagine that yogī, she thought. Yogīs, as everyone knew, were scum. Most of them sold spells and curses, or talismans that didn't work. I'm sure he got it when he killed a traveller.

"Somehow, you seem familiar," said Sonakā. "But that's impossible." The women in her retinue giggled.

She opened the fan, with great caution. Old silk breaks easily. When she saw the painting she almost had a stroke.

"Who painted this? Tell the truth or I will have you beaten! Where did you get this thing?"

"The yogī said, he received the fan just plain. One night, Śiva appeared to him. He had a vision, and the divine craftsman Viśvakarman moved the brush."

Sonakā felt the sweat on her brow. This was impossible! The image showed her husband, Cāndo, and he was absolutely true to life, though a bit younger than today. He had this satisfied, smug expression that meant he had just subjugated someone to the limit. Next to him, Sonakā could see her own portrait. She looked quite favourable, and at least twenty years younger than she was. Behind them stood seven sons, each of them proud and healthy. Even her youngest, crazy Lakhindār was there, hiding a vīṇā behind his back. She felt her eyes go damp. I won't weep; she forced herself, not in front of a dancing girl. It will only raise the price. And there were gods. It was amazing how many gods could fit into the painting. Śiva and Durgā stood right next to her husband. Sonakā saw the well-known, friendly elephant face, the strong warrior Kārrtikeya, the wise and hairy Hanumān. Here, the snake-devouring Garuḍa bird came down from heaven, bearing Viṣṇu and Lakṣmī, who smiled like the sunrise and showered golden coins in all directions. There stood Indra, with his thunderbolt. Even Brahmā had a niche, though not a big one; he looked surprised and forced his dhoti down.

Sonakā kept her expression cool. It was a major effort. "I guess, my husband might be amused to see this silly thing, provided it is cheap. See here," she jabbed a finger at the wood, "it's pretty worn already. The gold comes off. One rib is cracked. The colours won't stand much light and the silk is old and brittle. Did you see these scratches? And that spot? I'm sure that someone squashed a fly. That's ugly. The fan is quite used. And it can't be repaired." She twisted the ribs. "Hear them creak. You can't expect much. So tell me, what's your price?" Sonakā raised her head.

The Ḍom girl had disappeared.

Manasā had come to say goodbye. There, at the shore of the Dark Waters, she had made the ships appear, practically out of nothing, with a few mantras, her breath, and imagination. The shore was thronged with sailors, guards and captains. The men were delighted, they had never seen vessels like these, so precious, so gleaming, so utterly new.

And they were keen to leave. They had spent years hanging upside down from the ceiling of Neta's temple; they had watched all sorts of horrors feast, and all they really wanted was to go home, see their friends, hug their families, and drink until the memories were gone.

Manasā took her time. She wanted to get some things sorted out. She gave a brand new vīṇā to Lakhindār. "I made this for you. Of course I made it old, so the resonance is perfect. The journey is long and Behulā needs to dance. That's her nature, and she deserves it. I hope you like the instrument. It's practically indestructible, and the strings will last much longer than you live. But keep them wiped, and tuned." Lakhindār went down on his knees.

"Oh, do get up!" Manasā snarled. "Play from your heart. And I'm glad you are such a misbegotten son. You've been through life and death and rebirth and you will never make much money."

"Mother," said the musician, and reached for her feet. Manasā slapped his head and laughed.

Then the six brothers advanced. It hadn't taken them much time to understand who was in charge. Neta had had a word with them. She had laughed and gesticulated, and made crazy noises, indicating people who gargle and flop about and choke while toxins bloat them. Behulā knew that Neta was happy.

Instants later, the brothers were on the ground, before Manasā, and begged for mercy.

"My dear stupid boys," said Manasā, "Grovel as much as you like, if it makes you feel good. No matter what your silly father says: I'm glad we like each other."

Finally, Behulā advanced. She didn't know what to say, or what to do. Nor did Manasā. The Serpent Goddess compressed her lips. Reptiles are not into extended goodbyes and plants don't understand them at all. But, in a study composed by Hanumān, she had read what was expected. It was monkey business, as usual. Furry animals, she understood, need touch and warmth, to feel comforted. She reached out and hugged Behulā, until our girl could hardly breathe.

"That should do it." Manasā stepped back. "We've been on a long journey. I hate to let you leave. No matter what you do, you're always welcome on my mountain."

Behulā fought to hold the tears back.

"Stop it!" Manasā glared. "I want to see you laugh and sing and dance. You've been through madness and death; you know why you are happy. And don't make it too easy for your man. Sure, he is a great musician. Artists need discipline. He'll be even better, if you force him to practice really hard."

The goddess produced a fan. "And just to make your return really funny, here's something special. Give it to Sonakā."

Neta stood right next to the gangway. She had made herself twice as smart as usual. Her usual red outfit was almost hidden by the golden ornaments. She seemed so neat, so fresh, so over-clean. Her naked arms were painted with henna. Blossoms, snakes and laughing skulls.

"Our journey was a treat," she said, "you've seen the world, and it couldn't grind you down. Let me give you something special." She pressed a bone amulet into Behulā's hand. It showed a tiger, a snake and a crocodile in close embrace. "Few people have anything like this. It'll suit you fine."

Behulā sobbed, and tears ran down her face.

"Behulā, be proud that you became a washing woman." Neta took her, and held her, until she stopped quivering. "Yes, silly girl, you learned a lot. And tears of relief are a sign of good luck. I'll meet you, now and then. Remember me. When you see a vulture in the air, or a crocodile at the shore, or a hyena running off with something yummy, hey, you are lucky, and it could be me."

Cāndo leaned back into the pillows and eased his cummerbund. Somehow, his clothes were slightly tighter than they ought to be. The meal had been a treat, a feast in many servings, with small dishes of all varieties, and sauces only his wife could compose, when she was in a very special mood. A servant offered a bowl of warm water and Cāndo rinsed his fingers. Another servant offered a small bowl of spices, so he could chew them, to refresh his breath. He reached out for a cup of tea from far away Yunnan. Blossoms floated in it. His wife, he realised, was making an effort.

The Merchant King tried to appear benevolent. Trade was going rather well. Of course, things were far from perfect. He would have to spend a few hours of the night, as every night, to look into the accounts. No matter how much you own, he thought, it can never be enough. Money is a mirage. You think yourself rich, but it might be gone tomorrow. And if he failed to do his duty, why, his accountants would embezzle funds. I'm the poorest of the poor, he thought, and burped. His belly was stuffed to the limit. I can only hope she isn't feeling amorous. I'm an old man, and I deserve respect. I do my best outside the bedroom. Business is war.

His wife seemed cheerful. That was a bad sign. She must have done something stupid.

"Sonakā? What is it? You seem excited."

"Husband!" she cooed. "Today, on the market I got something special, for you."

"What is it?"

"It's a wonderful surprise! I swear, this thing is blessed!"

He leaned back and kept his face straight. Obviously, she had wasted money.

"You wouldn't believe how cheap it was."

No he wouldn't. Not at all. He wouldn't wonder about anything.

"Close your eyes, and hold your hands out."

Cāndo extended his hands. He wore his special negotiation-face: not a single feeling was in sight.

"And now you may look!"

Cautiously, he opened his eyes. This was bound to be a nightmare. It sounded just like the time when Sonakā went overly religious, and tried to feed the beggars of the city. There were poor people before the gate, and anywhere around his property. But the beggars learned their lesson when the guards beat them away.

He glanced at the thing. An ancient fan, probably Tang dynasty, or earlier. Sure, the thing was valuable. A collector's piece. Well crafted, old seasoned wood and the silk was hardly frayed. But what made her so excited? Tenderly, he opened the item.

His face went pale, he screamed, hurled the thing away, and ran.

Sonakā sat as if petrified. She lifted the fan. The picture had changed. It showed Cāndo, alone, and kneeling. His family and all the gods had disappeared. Instead of them, there was Manasā looming over him. She had her foot on his head and pressed his face into the dirt. Behind them stood Neta, smirking, with one hand inside her slip.

"Look at this!" Cāndo was back. He had fetched the captain of the guard. "The thing is cursed! It's evil magic! Take it away! I want you to burn it!"

"That fan?" The man looked uneasy.

"What else? Take the ashes, throw them into the river. I want it gone!"

The captain stared at the fan. It's pretty old, he thought, and probably worthless. And there's a picture. It showed his boss, and his wife, the whole family and plenty of gods.

"That likeness isn't bad," he muttered.

"It's not like me at all!"

"But anyone would recognise you."

"It shows a lie!"

"True," said the captain. "In real life, you ain't happy."

Cāndo glared at the fan. He recognised himself, and Sonakā, and all his sons. Everyone seemed so cheerful. And there were gods, plenty of gods, and loads of money everywhere.

Manasā and her worthless sister were not in evidence.

"I knew you would like it." Sonakā gave a sigh of relief. "The fan is a magic thing. It was painted by a holy man. I'm sure it will bring us luck."

Cāndo felt stunned. The painting was real, almost too real. He looked much younger than today. So did Sonakā, yes, she had been a lovely girl, so many years ago. And there were his sons, six great boys, and one who was slightly strange, but did his best. But the fan, he saw, was old. By what forbidden art had it been painted?

He trembled. It would be a relief to have it burned. But somehow or other, he simply couldn't give it up. "The fan," he gasped, "is mine. There's a good spell on it."

"That's true, my little busy bee," said Sonakā, and tried to feed him a sugary pastry, "Now be a dear and laugh. It's just that you were wrong, again."

The sacrificial priest stood before the crowd and grinned like a sacred bovine. Before him was a rich, well-decorated altar, loaded with offerings. He recited scripture in Vedic Saṁskṛta, which nobody understood, splattered Ganges water over the congregation and rang the ritual bell. The worshippers were clad in opulence. The Merchant King reclined on the place of honour. For the special occasion, he wore a generous smile. In his hand was the magical fan, that wonderful divine object, which had appeared so mysteriously, it was a sign of the gods, and a guarantee for great profits in future.

"This thing is full of potency," he told the house priest. "It proves the presence of the gods."

The man agreed. When the gods work miracles, a Brahmin expects bonus payments.

Cāndo gleamed at his friends. Most of them were rich, but not rich enough to pose a threat. Indeed, a lot were indebted to him.

Sonakā, like her husband, was excited. She wore an entirely new outfit, stitched and embroidered by a dozen seamstresses.

His colleagues leaned forward and tried to catch a look. The fan, they saw, was old, and obviously worth something. But it was also somewhat worn.

"Look at this!" Cāndo opened the fan and revealed the image. "A holy man painted it, at the behest of my favourite deities."

The merchants stared. They saw Manasā, as she trampled Cāndo's head into the dust.

"Sure, it's remarkable," they observed, "and probably unique."

Cāndo folded the fan and stowed it in a sleeve. He clapped his hands. Servant boys cast copper coins out of the windows. Below, beggars, outcasts and lepers fought each other.

I'm a darling of the gods, thought Cāndo. So humble, and so generous. And everybody is my friend.

The trumpets seemed to shake the walls. They were huge, ornately carved sea-shells, the favourite signal instrument since the days of the *Mahābhārata*, for religion, ritual and war, and, as a special extra, the only instrument on earth that always smells of rotting algae.

"King!" the captain of the guard dropped to his knees.

"My friend," said Cāndo, "don't flatter me. We have guests. I am a mere ascetic, a searcher after higher wisdom."

"Out there!" The man was beside himself with excitement. "The people rush to your palace! Your sons are alive!"

"A miracle!" Sonakā jumped up. "Let them in!"

"If you lied, you are dead." Cāndo hurried to the entrance hall.

Who could describe a scene like this? Your mad author, lacking words, cannot. The event was too loud, too colourful and too passionately sentimental to be confined in prose. In every normal Bollywood Movie (Neta says there's no such thing) the scene would require at least forty minutes of dancing. The servants shouted with joy. The widows paled and fainted (very gracefully). Cāndo's personal musicians started to play, all of them, at once, without the least consideration. Before the gate, the crowd parted, and Cāndo's sons, six strong, healthy men in their prime, with gleaming moustaches, oiled muscles and a costume drenched in perfume, marched into the hall. Sonakā howled with happiness and collapsed. Cāndo ran, his hands extended, and he too, wept without constraint. His sons. They were so intelligent, so stout, so blessed by fortune. Behind them, a little distant, came Lakhindār. He was clad like a peacock. Behulā, next to him, was arrayed in more jewels than your average every-day empress could afford. She played her part and looked at the ground, demure and shy, but confident. The pearls on her costume, pale, purple and poisonous, were beyond number. The golden threads between them twisted and coiled, as she moved, hinting at an army of snakes.

How do you describe so much joy, so much relief? Sonakā embraced one son after the other, and crushed them until they fought for breath. Cāndo, all oily charm, gave each of them a manly slap, and allowed his feet to be touched, while he tousled their hair and blessed them. His trader colleagues were out of their head with joy.

Then the captains advanced. Cāndo recalled their faces, and might have guessed their names, if he had tried, eventually. For a brief instant, he felt slightly guilty. Then he remembered how it really was. These men had taken his wage, they understood the risk, much better, indeed, than Cāndo, who had been badly informed, and let down by them. Their death was their affair. After all, they should have refused his orders. Coming to think of it, because of their errors, Cāndo had suffered so much. But the Merchant King was generous. He gave them a few coins and congratulated them for being alive. Then followed the sailors, each of them in splendid clothes, and perfect health. The Merchant King graciously raised a hand in greeting. That should suffice. He signalled to the captain of the guard. "Get them out of here. Serve rice with lentils."

"Śiva! Durgā!" his voice echoed through the hall. "I owe my life to you, my good name, and my wealth. And, of course, my family is grateful."

He pointed at the great shrine in the entrance hall. "More offerings! More incense!"

It's my lucky day, he thought. And he wanted butterfat lamps, and dancing, and happiness. All Asia should see his triumph.

He grinned at the statues of his favourite gods. They were gilded, adorned with jewels, and clad in silk. Reverently, he went to his knees and bowed.

The room became silent. Nobody had ever seen the Merchant king with his head on the ground.

"That's very kind of you," said Manasā. "But don't get carried away. You can kiss the ground at my feet, but brush your teeth first."

"I knew he could be grateful, provided he got everything and more." Neta had a nasty laugh.

"Well then. You're right. But Cāndo, listen! After being such a nuisance, I am sure you want to apologise."

Cāndo crouched, paralysed, and did not believe his ears.

"He pretends to be dead," said Neta, "come on sister, grind his head into the dust. He'll love it."

"I guess he feels guilty."

"He can't. You can't run a trade empire on real feelings."

"That's crude. Think of him as a fallen saint."

"Not pure enough!"

"That's my little sister. She always thinks about the washing."

"No way. I won't do him."

With a scream, Cāndo leapt up. A knife, a sword, there must be a weapon around!

The goddesses were gone. Statues faced him: Śiva seemed absent-minded, Durgā checked her fingernails, Gaṇeśa tried to stuff his head into a honeypot, while Kārrtikeya was engrossed in *Silicone and Steroids*. His lips moved.

The Merchant King wiped his brow. Maybe the guests hadn't noticed.

A brief nod to the altar and the ritual could proceed.

"My dear Cāndo," said Durgā. She stroked the mane of her lion. "I lent you a staff. Where is it?"

Śiva rose. He barely got his eyes open. "You? You had it? I looked for it."

Cāndo kept his posture, but his voice trembled. "My goddess, forgive me. I could not kill the serpent whore. I lost your staff in a thunderstorm. The waves swept it away."

"What?" Śiva coughed. "What did you call my daughter?"

The Merchant King began to tremble.

"Don't piss. It's offensive." Durgā arranged a straying lock.

"Goddess, forgive me. You ordered me..."

"I didn't."

"But I thought..."

"You were wrong."

She pointed at him, and her eyes flared. "Merchant! You are an idiot! You almost caused a tragedy."

"But you commanded..."

"Never!"

"And you gave me..."

"So you wouldn't be so scared."

The goddess reclined on the back of her lion. "That's settled. You misunderstood. You got everything wrong. But it's good that you repent."

"But goddess. You and Manasā. Everyone knows that you are enemies!"

"Impossible. Manasā is a high goddess. You should have known better."

"What?"

"Manasā and me. We are one."

She turned to her husband. "I talked sense into him. Just as I said. I hope he understood. Let's leave."

"She's right, "said Manasā. "But she forgot Neta. She's us, too. And trees and plants and snakes and even beggars. Lakhindār is us. So is Behulā." She placed her hand on Cāndo's head.

"Relax. You could be happy."

The man stared at the ground. His face was white and his breath wheezed.

"This is about intelligence," said Neta. "And consciousness." She pointed at the altar. "Statues won't help you much. It's about reality, and death, and everything."

She handed him the fan. It showed Cāndo and his family. They were happy and cheerful. With them were the major gods. But right next to Cāndo stood Manasā, nude and crazy, and on his other side Neta held ink and brush and had a laughing fit.

Picture 36: Manasā Temple.

36. Thanksgiving

By the time the altar was ready, the sun was high in the sky and the poorer members of the audience, who didn't bring umbrellas or received a special seat under a canopy, were drenched in sweat. Fans fluttered, servants ran and carried water. On the wide empty space, before the great gate, the Brahmins had prepared an altar. The Merchant King had commissioned a grandiose ceremony. He, as Sonakā and his boys insisted, had to make an offering to Manasā. Everyone in Campaka was welcome to watch. The Brahmins had done what they could. True, scripture didn't contain much to make the Nāga deities happy. Most of it was spells against snakes, and these wouldn't do. They rewrote a few traditional hymns, selected more than a hundred sacred names for the goddess to cover all eventualities, and decided that offerings of frogs and rats, though tasty, would not do. The newly acknowledged serpent goddess, they announced, was a good girl and had always been a ruler of the universe. If her father liked milk and flowers, she would be happy with the same. Plus bananas.

Cāndo would have preferred a small and private ritual. He felt exposed. Out there, in the crowd, were mercenaries who had done his will. They had burned villages and beaten serpent worshippers into submission. These men had a hard expression in their eyes. It had been a good life. They had looted and raped as they liked. Today, the fun was over. All of a sudden, the world was full of people who hated them. But like it or not, the Merchant King had had a change of mind. As a supporter of the cult, he would try to redress the balance and do some good. Manasā worshippers, he had declared, were under his personal protection. "I do as the gods demand. A wise man has to be flexible."

"The wise man has no spine," the mercenaries snarled. They would leave as fast as they could.

It had taken hours to raise the altar, and to load it with blossoms, fruit, vegetables, with butterfat lamps and incense stands.

Who could doubt Cāndo's piousness?

He could. He had doubted himself all day. Sure, he was glad that it was over. He felt his age and knew he couldn't fight much longer. It would take all his effort to pass the business on to his sons. On the other hand, he realised, the gods were evil. Durgā, that sleek feline bitch, had played with him, Śiva was a lazy, uncaring dope-head and their boys had never done an hour of decent work. You can't trust the gods. They exploit you to the limit, they reap all profits, and you get nothing in return.

The gods had chased him through the forest, they had turned him into a beggar and a dupe. He remembered how the crow shat on his head, how Manasā tricked him to accept the blanket of a corpse, how they forced him to lie and steal and beg and sleep in the dirt.

And now, at the grand ceremony, he had to show devotion. His wife and his sons! They couldn't get enough. They praised Manasā and that made him a fool. He watched the Brahmins. Not long ago they had cursed the serpent cult. That was past. Today they fell over themselves praising the virtues of the new goddesses. Cāndo would have loved to send them running.

He felt so tired.

The witch had saved the lives of his sons. She had even saved Behulā. But, as far as he could see, that girl was offensively smug. Manasā had revived the captains and the sailors, she had returned the ships, his treasure, and even made it greater. People fell over themselves congratulating him. But what was at the bottom line?

As always, a number.

He glared at the offerings, he calculated gifts and sacrifices and the outrageous fees of the Brahmins, the feeding of the poor and the loss in authority, he heard people laugh, and hated everyone.

On top of the altar rose a statue. The priests had done their best to organise one, on such short notice. A proper statue of the goddess was out of the question. That would need debate, a clear outline of her divine insignia and attributes, and plenty of negotiations with Cāndo and the craftsmen, who would complain that they were underpaid. For the moment, a simple image would do. A carver had been at work for hours, and had produced a cobra. It was neither detailed nor polished, but, and that was the main point, it was large and clearly visible. Even people in the distance, the poor, the curious, and the riff-raff from the gutters, would get the message. The Brahmins were in an excellent mod. A new deity had appeared, and they would ensure that she was important, meaning shrines, congregations, sites of pilgrimage and career opportunities.

Cāndo sat in silence. His meditation mālā slipped, bead by bead, through his hand. Next to him was Sonakā, perfectly dressed, and couldn't get enough of staring at her sons. She had been late. That's because she had spent the morning praying to the new goddess. And she was eager for more miracles.

"Don't look so grim!" She turned to him and patted his cheek. "We ought to be the happiest couple in the world!" She leaned over him and tried to adjust the collar of his jacket. He flinched away.

"But darling. I know she is not your favourite. I can understand. But she returned our sons."

"After she killed them."

"True." His wife pouted. "But that was just because you were proud and obstinate."

The leading priest interrupted them. "Lord!" Cāndo stared at him. That guy dripped with oily charm and greed. He seemed to consist entirely of beard. The fringe was curled.

"What?"

"It's time. Make your offering. Show your devotion. A fruit, a vegetable; the goddess is happy with anything."

Cāndo glared. He would have loved to throw the altar over. He had paid for all that trash! And he had financed the costumes of the Brahmins! Snake goddess, he thought, you owe me a lot!

"Cāndo! Do it" His wife pushed him.

The Merchant King leaned forward and extended his left hand.

The audience gasped, the priest stepped back and Sonakā paled.

His left hand. The hand you use to wipe your arse.

He froze in mid-motion. Everybody stared at him. Then his hand began to shake and sweat ran down his face.

"Listen," said a voice in his head. It was Durgā. "Behave and make a happy face."

"What do I get in return?"

The Warrior Goddess laughed. "You stay alive. Is that enough?"

The Merchant King withdrew his left and extended the right. He picked the smallest berry in reach and placed it on her altar.

The crowd cheered. Cāndo sat, aged and broken, and stared at the ground. A hand touched his shoulder.

"I forgave you long ago," Manasā whispered. "Did you? Together, we made a myth."

Neta advanced from the other side. "You lone and stupid man. Go ahead, feed the poor and wretched. Maybe, one day, they'll be your friends."

The streets were full of music. All Campaka was in excitement. On stalls, all over the city, meals were served. Some laughed, some danced. Clandestine worshippers emerged with paint and brushes and graced their houses with writhing cobras. Potters were asked to burn serpent pots, children ran in frenzy and the women, who invoked the house goddess every evening to protect the family from fire and thieves, called her Viṣahari, Padmavatī and Manasā. It hardly mattered to anyone, except Cāndo, that the grandiose ships that had returned his sons, disappeared from one moment to the other, as if they never had existed.

At the edge of the offering space, a little separate from the happy crowd, sat Behulā and Lakhindār. Their friends and acquaintances had drifted away. Though they were members of Cāndo's mighty clan, and somehow involved in events that no-one really understood, they made the simple merchants uneasy. The few who knew a little, gossiped. Lakhindār had been dead, they said, and now he was back, alive. Behulā had travelled on her own, with nothing but his corpse for company. It couldn't get much worse.

Behulā had overheard the muttering. Who knows, said the people, what happened, out there? Did she stay with the raft? Or did she walk ashore, like a common little whore, to have her fun with other men? She looks pretty good, though somewhat thin. No doubt plenty of men would have delighted to spread her legs. Maybe for a few coins, or a bowl of rice. Or maybe just for fun.

"Now she will be insatiable," whispered a crone. "A single man, no matter how strong, can never satisfy her!"

"Look at her husband. He's not a bull or elephant," another crooned. "She'll waste him in ten minutes and then she'll scream for more."

Another pushed the greyish hair from her face. "How could she have survived, without offering her hole to everyone?"

"Why is she still alive? In our village, she would have been stoned."

Another woman fell in. She was attired like a parrot, but her arms and face showed bruises. "I heard, she pretended to be a Ḍombī. I mean, how filthy can she get?"

"Her man is rich. But he plays the vīṇā, and he doesn't work."

"I guess, on the way home he hired her out."

"She looks juicy. He may have made a profit."

"In a few years, she'll be an exhausted old mare. No one will want to ride her."

The crones laughed. They knew everything about life, and it was terrible. Tonight, they would tell their husbands, and their neighbours, and their friends.

Behulā wished she could shut her ears. She just hoped that Lakhindār wouldn't notice. He sat there, close to her, tense and pale, and pretended to be happy. His brothers barely greeted him. They disappeared into the crowd, where they met business friends and talked about politics, goods and percentages. They could hardly be expected to be friendly to a brother whom they never met. Sonakā, too, had a keen sense for rumours. As the day proceeded, she began to fidget. The only one who didn't seem to care was Cāndo. He sat near the altar, in his own personal gloom, for a short while. Then he rose, bowed to his guests, and returned to his office.

In the grand hall, Behulā approached Sonakā, went down on her knees and touched her feet. "I ask your blessing."

Sonakā accepted the gesture. She had expected an honourable solution. "You were away for six months. Everyone talks about it. My friends laugh." Her voice was timid, but clear. "I don't want to know what happened. Spare me your apologies and lies. You saved my sons. I'm grateful for that. But anything else is impossible. You can't stay at my house. The whole world would despise us."

"I don't want to live in your house."

Sonakā sighed with relief.

"And I won't return to my parents."

"Child, are you crazy? Do you want to sleep in the gutters? Will you be a nun, a beggar, and die somewhere, on pilgrimage?"

"I know my way, and my Karman."

"And, Lakhindār, what about you?" Sonakā glared at him.

"I will follow my wife. She took great care of me."

"Nonsense! Your home is here, in Campaka! We will return the dowry, and pay as much as Sāya wants, to make us all forget. You will remain, join the business, and one day we will find a better bride for you."

"Mother, forgive me. I'm not made to be a merchant. You have six sons who make you proud. Why should you need me?" He bowed and touched her feet.

Sonakā raised her voice. "A life without virtue! I should have known. You and your vīṇā. We should have smashed the thing!"

"You are in my heart, no matter where I go."

Sonakā slumped into her seat. "You are still dead. The serpent stole you."

The couple bowed. A little later they emerged through the servant's entrance. They crossed the garden, walked past hedges and flowerbeds, past fountains and statues, and slipped through a side gate. The guards smiled, they knew Lakhindār from the good old days, and wished him luck. The couple travelled light. Lakhindār had a small bundle of clothes, and carried his vīṇā. Next to him, Behulā walked. Her bundle jingled.

Out of the twilight, Neta appeared. The air chariot was ready, and the swans honked with excitement. The three flew off, headed for Sij Mountain, and disappeared into the dusk. Heaven went black and the stars laughed.

Months later, Sāya and Amalā were in Campaka. They told Sonakā that they had met a pair of strange ascetics at the edge of a village fair. Both of them were almost nude. Their hair was matted and the horizontal marks on their brows shone red.

They had coated their bodies in ashes, and Amalā didn't want to know where the ashes came from.

The yogī carried a vīṇā, surely an unusual instrument, for a travelling tāntrika. He had a faraway expression in his eyes, as if he had lost everything, and was keen to discover it again. How could anyone understand these people? The yoginī had a fair resemblance to their lost daughter. Sure, she was thinner than her mother had ever seen her. Clearly, their begging bowls did not afford much income. Her body was tough and wiry and her eyes burned like a wildfire. She held her skull bowl, a human cranium, and while Amalā wiped the tears out of her eyes, Sāya dropped a few coins into it. The girl laughed and bowed. So did the yogī, for whatever reason. It was just a few coins. Maybe, Amalā thought, the two are drunk. She could only shake her head. Sure, India is full of ascetics. Most are insane and some are saintly. But for whatever reason, she couldn't forget the girl.

And they were hungry.

"How about frogs?" He gleamed at her.

"Or a few rats?" she took his arm.

Sāya and Amalā shared a look. They were such a nice couple, and so young. Why did they waste their lives in poverty?

When they turned, the two were gone.

In their place, a pair of cobras reared their heads, and slithered down the slope.

Picture 37: Manasā, traditional.

Part Five:

Fun with Snakes

37: Snake Charming

Good things coil around.

Scaly, slithering, scintillating: let's take a look at 'serpent cults'. True, that's a woefully inadequate description. The term implies worship. But animals are rarely worshipped for what they are. Few people are aware how wonderful serpents can be. Consider the cobra with its widely open hood. People assume it's aggressive and wear it as a tattoo. As a symbol, it works perfectly. However, a cobra in that posture is defensive. It makes itself bigger because it doesn't want to fight. For snakes, aggression is a last-resort solution. If possible, they will try to avoid conflict; especially with something as big and stupid as a human being. Most snakes are shy. They will flee, play dead, and hide their heads to avoid conflict. Or they will dislocate their jaws and make their body flat and broad to seem more threatening. Many snakes shit at their enemies. They add a special secretion to their excrement to make it smell worse. Only in emergency situations, like when you surprise a snake early in the morning, when it changes its skin, or when you scare it, will it try to bite.

Numerous people, who never touched a snake, assume they are slimy. They couldn't be more wrong. Amphibians are slippery, but reptiles are dry. And even those who like serpents and admire them in zoos are rarely aware that snakes perceive scent with their tongue. That tongue is forked, so it gets a separate input from left and right, allowing snakes to find their prey in the dark. Did you know that snakes have difficulties identifying objects that don't move, and that male snakes have two hemi-penises, that emerge like the letter V, so they can make love sideways, or have one in reserve when the other goes raw or damaged? And honestly, why are they the lucky ones? And that each of the two hemi-penises may be a single organ, or forked, like the letter Y? Snake penises are often equipped with barbs and hooks, so a (smaller) male stays attached when a (larger) female goes for a walk and drags him along. That can be useful, especially when you want to make love for hours. Then there's the jaws. Imagine having no chin, but an elastic connection between the right and left jaw. And, at the back of the jaw, a flexible connection! It makes swallowing large objects much easier. And imagine four rows of teeth, each of them mobile, and independent of each other! A snake can shift its teeth, back and forth, to swallow or regurgitate its prey. Or think of the eyes. People believe snakes have their eyes open all the time. Actually, they don't. There's is a transparent scale shielding each eye, so in real life, the eyes are always shut. Most snakes see in colour and in 3D, and you can't tell if they are awake or asleep.

Badly informed people claim that serpent phobias are natural, and genetic, meaning 'fate'. Of course they ain't. Sure, snakes get attention. Our ancestors survived by getting the message very fast. Call it a reality filter. You don't need to see all of a snake to get excited. Something that resembles a rope, or reveals a scaly pattern, will get attention, which is why snake patterns are a favourite in fashions. Excitement, however, is not the same thing as phobia. Watch small children in the zoo. Clever kids, with clever parents, are delighted.

The world is full of miracles.

So when you meet snakes in temples, gracing statues or deities, you can be sure they have little to do with real snakes, unless that deity or cult promises to cure snakebite or end a rodent plague.

People see snakes but they react to symbols.

This has been going on for quite a long time.

Snakes are rare in Stone-Age art, as most of Ice Age Europe was too damn cold for them, but in the southern fringe, at the edge of the Mediterranean Sea, a few were around. How do you recognise them? Cave art might be helpful. Several caves, like Rouffignac, show wavy bands. Some of them are quite complex. Maybe they represent snakes. Or waves, or rivers, or decorative ornaments. The experts call them 'macaroni style'. Wavy lines ain't good enough, unless they show a head. One example comes from cave La Baume Latrone. The snake picture is three metres long and shows a forked tongue. It is dated around 30,000 BCE. Another couple of snakes appear, finely engraved, on an ivory slab found in Rideaux Cave. It's been dated around 22,000 BCE (Lotzkat, 2016:13). Another piece of polished and carved mammoth ivory, from Mal'ta in Siberia, shows three serpents (Jelinek, 1972:452, nowadays dated 23,000-19,000 BCE). We don't know if these snakes were pictured as their artists admired them, or feared them, identified with them, or wanted to keep them under control. But whatever it was: snakes were important.

Let's visit what is presently the earliest known temple of mankind. It's **Göbekli Tepe**, in Turkish Kurdistan, a wonderful megalith arrangement of 'T' shaped stones. Many are engraved with animals. The place is in the middle of nowhere. I travelled around there in the mid-eighties: the sky was blue, the ground consists of boulders. Between the rocks were shrivelled, parched remnants of flowers. The summer sun had killed them. The only vegetation consisted of towering hemp plants, thriving at a petrol station. Somewhere in the distance, people lived in earth holes. Others owned a tent, large enough for the family, and kept moving. A mere trickle of water was a.

Picture 38: Three Snakes, engraved on a piece of mammoth ivory, Mal'ta, Siberia.

stunning luxury. Anyone with a sense of initiative got on the bus and never came back

At the time, the temple had not been excavated. Göbekli Tepe was built by the first farmers. They began to shape the rocks, starting around 12,000 BCE, and decorated them with plenty of wonderfully executed animals. Among them are several unusual species. Sure, you get lions and bulls and waterbirds. That's what you might expect. But now for something amazingly original: more frequent are foxes, spiders, beetles, scorpions and, the most common animal of them all, serpents. Maybe the peasants worshipped them. Maybe they hated them, and sought to spellbind them with magic. Maybe they didn't even understand them as animals: the beasts on the stones might represent groups, or families, clans or entire districts. Or they could be enemies. If the stones were a war memorial, they might commemorate vanquished clans. That's the trouble with symbols: they can be interpreted in many ways. You might even argue the place was a fast food restaurant and the pictures were the menu. Sure, it ain't likely. But lack of evidence doesn't mean evidence of lack.

The people of Göbekli Tepe were not the only ones who admired snakes. A finely carved flint dagger from Catal Höyük is graced by a snake-shaped bone handle. In Nevah Çori, Turkey, a stone head was embedded in a niche of the eastern wall of a cult building (see illustration). The face is gone; some people demolished it. But when the archaeologists extracted the item, they found a snake rising on the back of the head! Anyone who wants to associate this with Kuṇḍalinī is welcome. She or he only has to bridge the gap between 8,500-7,900 BCE, when the head was made, and the ninth or tenth century CE, when the tantric Kuṇḍalinī made her first appearance. Polished rocks, used to smoothen arrow shafts, graced with crude serpents and centipedes, have been unearthed at Tel Qaramel. A very similar theme appears on the remnants of a stone bowl from Körtik Tepe (see illustration). The item was used for unknown cultic purposes and dates from 9,500-8,500 BCE, the pre-ceramic period.

It goes on like that. We meet serpents in early China, where the Neolithic Hongshan Culture invented the Ouroboros symbol, a snake that eats its tail, around 3,500 BCE. The image was frequently carved from jade and worn as a pendant. One fine example was painted inside a ritual bowl of the Longshan culture, it dates to around 2,500 BCE. The Chinese loved the image, and produced many variations. It certainly got around; there is even a Celtic coin, made by the Boii in southern Germany around 200 BCE that shows a rendering.

Picture 39: Göbekli Tepe: Animals grace Standing Stones.

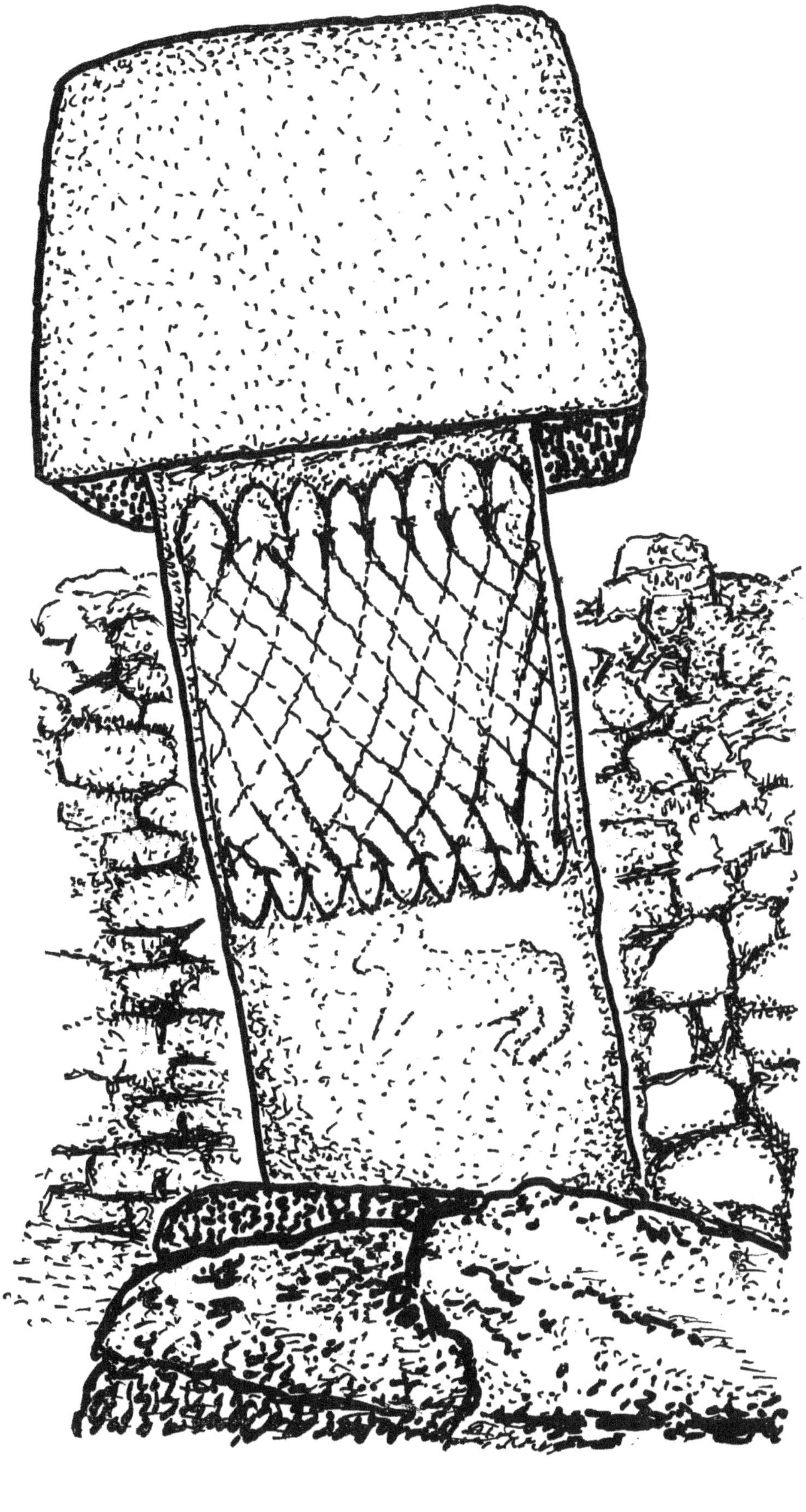

Picture 40: Göbekli Tepe: T-shaped megalith with serpent pattern and unidentified animal (ram?). Photo in Schmidt, 2006:121.

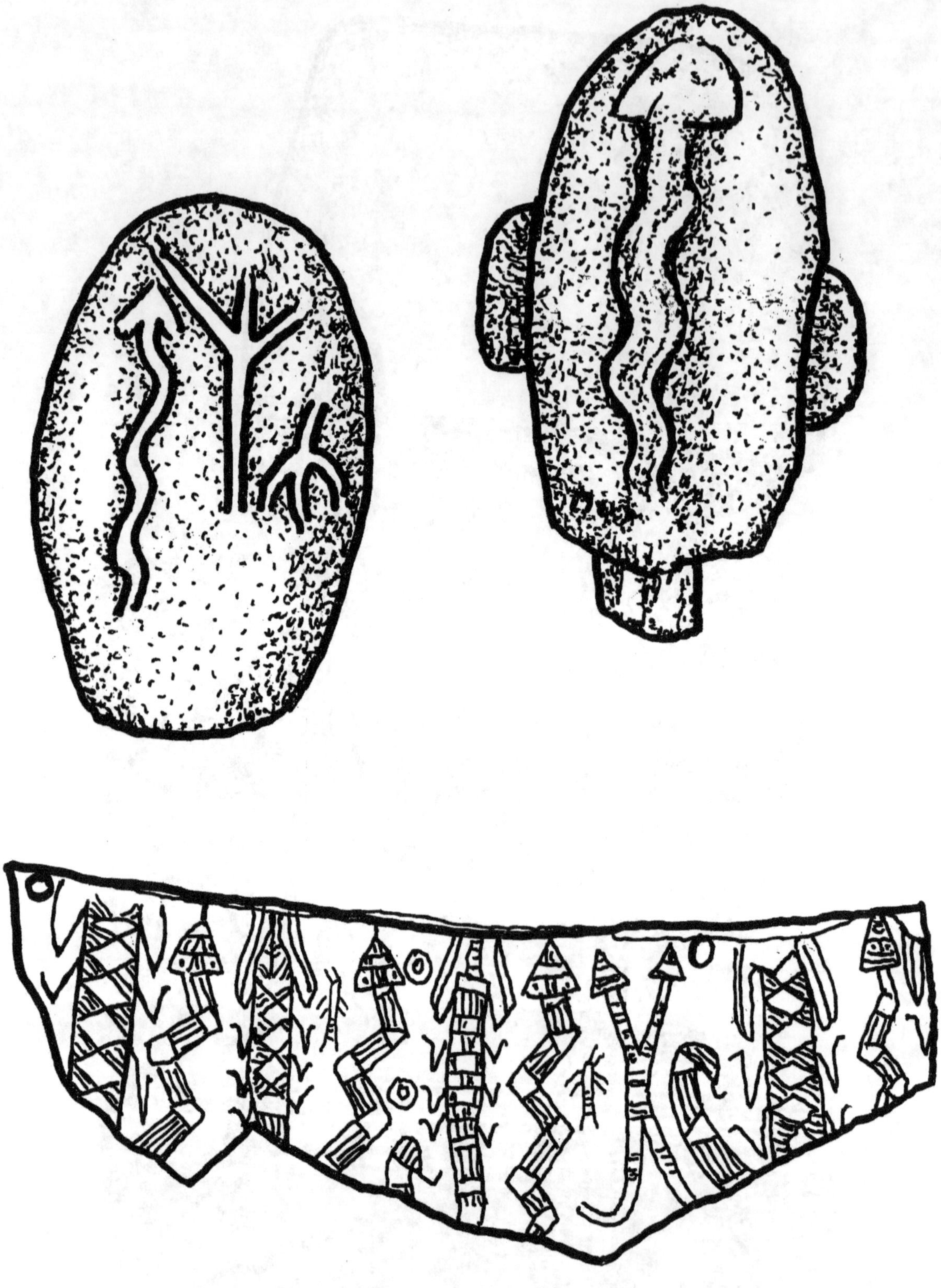

Picture 41: Turkey. Top right: back of a stone head with rising snake, Nevalı Çori, 8,500-7,900 BCE. Photo in Die Ältesten Monumente der Menschheit, 2007:289

Top left: polished stone from Göbekli Tepe (4cm), 8,800-8,000 BCE). Photo in Die Ältesten Monumente der Menschheit, 2007:306

Bottom: Körtik Tepe. Fragment of a stone bowl graced with serpents, centipedes and tiny birds. Pre-Ceramic period, 9,500-8,500 BCE. After Schmidt, 2006:188.

Picture 42: Going East: Top right: snake woman or goddess, from Bahrain, c. 2000 BCE (after Bibby). At the time, the Sumerians and the Indus Valley people were trading with each other. A few centuries later it stopped, when the Indus Valley Culture disappeared. Bahrain was an important trade point in between. Indeed, the Sumerians considered it a holy land, blessed by the influence of Enki.

Top left: Terracotta fragment from Susa (Iran), late 3rd millennium BCE, showing an unidentified serpent goddess (After Koch, 2007:153).

Bottom right: Seal of a vessel, Susa, late fifth millennium BCE (after Koch, 2007:33).

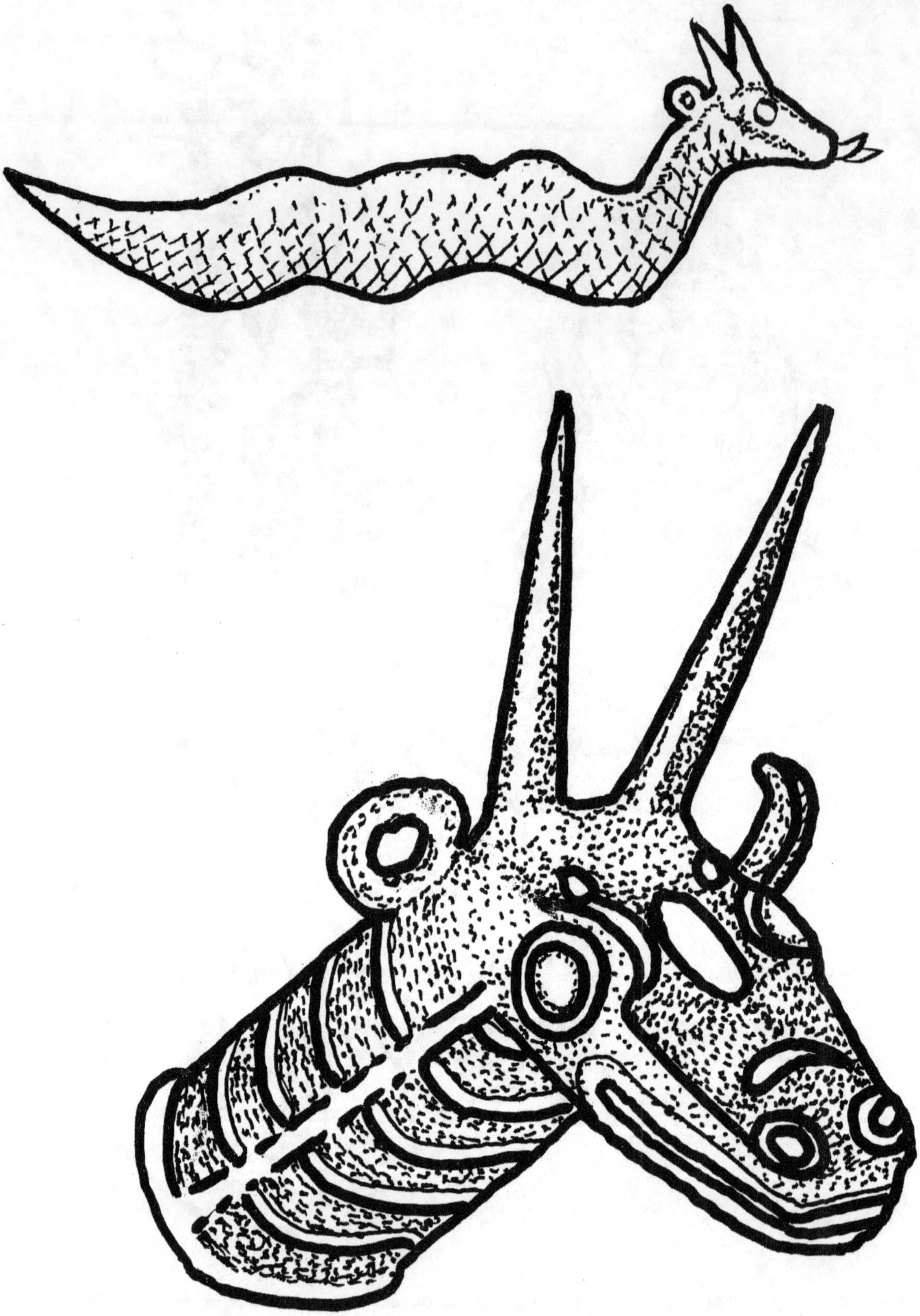

Picture 43: Mesopotamia: an all time favourite, the horned serpent.
Top: a horned serpent from a kudurru stone, presented by Melik-Šipak to his son, Marduk-Apla-Iddina, ca. 1,200 BCE (BKR # 32). The stone shows the emblems of twenty four deities; the horned serpent is at the bottom.
Bottom: horned serpent head, c. 7-6th century BCE, Babylon (photo in Margueron, 1965:128).

Picture 44: Chinese serpents.
Top: from a bronze zun vessel, late Shang Dynasty or early Zhou (c. 1100-1000 BCE), after Yang, 2000:124.
Centre: from a bronze gui vessel, Early Western Zhou Dynasty, after Yang: 2000:124.
Bottom: Snake image from the bottom of a theriomorphic ritual vessel, late Shang Dynasty, after Yang, 2000:121.

Picture 45: Dragon head, copper, treated with tin and gold. 3rd century. Originally mounted on a pole and carried by an officer of the Roman cavalry. A tube of thin cloth (silk?) was attached to the head, which swung and twisted. From Niederbieber ((Neuwied). An image of its use appears on the Ludovisian sarcophagus, Rome.

During the Shang dynasty (c. 1750-1045 BCE), oracle bone inscriptions make much of the snake character. They reveal the existence of a snake clan, and the names of two wives of King Wu Ding, called Grass Snake and Tree Snake, after their families. The sign for snake appears in several ideograms: some are rather negative, like tooth-ache (snake and mouth with teeth), parasites (two snakes in a bowl), curse, misfortune (snake bites foot) and a mysterious disease (snake and human). Others had a sacral character, like 'ritual cult year' (snake and the T-shaped symbol indicating the divine). One important sign shows two snakes next to each other: they represent a deity who received offerings and dance. Maybe it is related to the two famous semi-serpentine deities who created mankind and taught our bedazzled ancestors how to survive in the forest: the Green Emperor Fuxi and his wife, Nüwa. Read it up in *Dragon Bones*. But snake worship isn't restricted to northern China. Stone snakes, beautifully painted, were unearthed in the tombs of the Jingsha culture, right under modern Chengdu, in Sichuan. Not too far away, the highly developed Sanxingdui culture produced stunning artefacts for worship. One of them is a bronze snake. Or consider the Dian Culture of Yunnan. I was amazed to see so many serpent images in the museum in Kunming. Or look at ancient Sumer, where the first magical Grimoire in evidence, composed around maybe 2,700-2,600 BCE, keeps referring to Ningirima, the lady of serpent/dragons. She is the most popular deity of the collection, as her magick made the spells come true. Read about her in my *Seven Names of Lamaštu*. That, of course, is not all. Mesopotamian scholars knew dozens of serpents, including some who swim, have horns, sport seven heads or seven tongues, and protect major deities. Important deities, like Underworld goddess Ereškigal and most of her family, were represented by snakes, and the constellation we call Hydra. Next to Sumer and Babylon are the highland cultures of Iran. In Elam, plenty of sacred serpents grace religious imagery. And in Dilmun/Bahrain, a lone image indicates that a woman or goddess with a serpent received veneration. And we could look at ancient Egypt, where one rather unfriendly snake tries to eat the sun-god Ra every day, while a lot of much better-behaved cobras appear in royal headgear and have a benevolent role, as they protect the regent.

Picture 46: Tombstone of a Frankish Warrior with Pagan Imagery (note the serpents), Niederdollendorf, photo in Schneider: 1951: plate 15.

With so many serpent loving neighbours, and such a range of wonderful snakes, it seems hardly surprising that the Nāga cult is an ancient Indian favourite. Like so many great customs, it originated in unknown prehistory.

Where lotus blossoms, water, trees and serpents meet, where the air is damp and stagnant and thick drops of moisture cling to mosses and ferns, Nāga cults thrive. Add a few moss-covered rocks, ferns, creepers, clingers, stranglers, wet soil, gurgling waters and everything is fine. I'm sure you can find something similar in your neighbourhood. Have a picnic, a trance, relax, recover, or make serpent music. Or travel there in dreams and visions, and come home to yourself.

The term Nāga and its feminine Nāgī or Nāginī have several meanings. It can be applied to all sorts of serpents, to dragons and to a range of deities, some of them in human form, some partly human, partly animal. It can also refer to an elephant, and to a stream of energy within the human body. According to Gorakṣanāth (*Siddha Siddhānta Paddhati*, 1, 68) the Nāga Wind streams through all limbs, it strengthens and liberates.

In everyday parlance, the term nāga often (but not always) refers to the greatest Indian snake, the **king cobra** (Ophiophagus hannah), a cheerful, life-embracing and extremely toxic reptile that can, in rare cases, reach a length of six metres. Its hood is not graced by a spectacle pattern: the scales are dark, brightened by horizontal stripes. King cobras like to explore the world. Indian scientists equipped a few with radio beacons. One had a territory of six square km and moved 36km in five months; another managed 100km in nine months (Lotzkat: 2016:90). When it gets excited, especially during the mating season, it can rear up and look you in the eyes. Striking, it can hurl itself forwards three metres and it slides as fast as a typical jogger. Ignorant people claim it can outrun a horse. That's silly. No snake is that fast. 13km/h is the speed record (ibid:46). And why should it? It couldn't eat a horse, or its rider, anyway. King cobras have a metaposition in the serpent world. Other snakes feed on a large range of foodstuff: they catch fishes, frogs, toads, lizards, rodents; they dangle from branches, snatch passing birds or climb and plunder nests. The king cobra prefers to eat other snakes. Even the ratsnake, which can grow to a length of two meters, is patiently gobbled down. King cobras are immune to the toxins of most snakes. Only vipers require a bit of caution. Their toxin is different, and a bite wouldn't do at all. Here, the trick lies in bearing down from above. The cobra strikes; it appears to chew and pumps the toxin into the blood vessels. The viper twitches, coils and dies. King cobra toxin is lethal. There are well-documented cases where a cobra bite killed a fully grown elephant. That, however, is a tragic accident. Cobras are perfectly aware that elephants are too damn big for food. The same goes for people. When king cobras bite human beings, as happens every year, it is basically in self-defence. Look at life from a cobra's point of view! When the monsoon rains wash snakes out of their hiding places, and flood the fields for miles and miles, when rivers leave their beds and Mother Gaṅgā gleams like an inland sea, every self-respecting king cobra hurries to dry land. Village houses, temples and granaries are high on the list. The sodden snake crawls out of the downpour, gives a sigh of relief and finds a bunch of people making a scene. It's not a good start for a relationship. Our snake remains polite. It raises its head and hisses. That should tell them. Sadly, people are stupid. The hiss may not be enough to warn them. Clever animals, like goats, would get the message and mind their own business. People don't. The king cobra is upset. It spreads its upper ribs; the characteristic hood appears. It sways from side to side, an elegant motion that inspired sacred dances and trance rituals. The hissing is deeper now. The king cobra doesn't want to bite. It is aware of its power. Now its time for Homo (allegedly) sapiens to remain calm and relaxed.

By contrast, the normal **Indian cobra** (Naja naja naja) is much smaller. The species is divided into numerous subspecies, each with a different ornamentation on the hood. These cobras only grow to a length of two metres. Their favourite staple is rodents and small animals. A few years ago, there were districts where suppliers of the leather industry almost exterminated the cobras. They produced fine shoes, belts, handbags and an ecological disaster. The result was a rodent plague. Enormous amounts of grains and other edibles were devoured and contaminated by rats. When plagues broke out, the Indian government showed excellent good sense by placing cobras under protection. I'm sure it wasn't popular.

According to official records, in India, approximately two thousand people die of snakebite every year. The number is woefully inadequate. Vogel (1972:7) relates that in 1919 more than 20,000 people died of snake bite, while only 2,637 were killed by other animals. Things got worse in the meantime. Over the last centuries, most of the Indian forest was destroyed. Simultaneously, the population escalated. Like it or not, people live closer to wild animals than ever. The real number of serpent victims is a mystery. As it turns out, the official statistic only registers people whose death was witnessed and recorded, i.e. those who died in a city or a hospital, be it from poison, shock or allergic reactions. Most snake bites happen in the countryside. The victims die in the fields or in some village hut, far from doctors and medication, and do not appear in the official count. Some institutions estimate that the real number of annual Indian snakebite victims is above 40,000. Plus the official 6,000 deaths by snakebite in the tiny state Bangladesh.

Cobras live all over India. In the Himalayas, you can meet them at an altitude of up to 2,000 metres. Wherever they dwell, the Nāga cult is popular. You encounter snake cults in India, Nepal, Tibet, Yunnan and Sichuan, in Myanmar, Vietnam, Thailand and Cambodia. The only habitat the cobras avoid is the dark forest. There isn't much left. As Indian forests are bright and dry most of the year, you can find cobras practically everywhere. And while the king cobra shies away from people, the smaller cobra follows them, and tasty rodents, into the settlements.

Like the large king cobras, your smaller everyday one-size-fits-anything cobra has a great sense of self-confidence and isn't keen to bite people. Humans are too big to be gulped down. So the cobra gives you a chance. It raises its head, spreads its hood and hisses. That's pretty good for a start. Then it hurls itself forward. In many cases, it keeps its mouth shut: a false attack should suffice. If possible, it will try to flee. Cobras are lethal, but they, like good martial artists, are not aggressive animals. Whenever possible, they try to avoid fights. Some cobras even play dead to stay out of trouble. It is only rarely, when they are surprised or shocked, that they will try to bite. In half of the cases, the cobra won't bother to inject its toxin. Toxin is valuable, and there is no use in wasting it. Some cobras adapt to village life. The British colonial officers were shocked to learn that many families shared their homes with a lethal snake.

One typical Indian cliché is the snake charmer. These entertainers carry their pets in baskets and boxes. They squat on market squares and street corners, open the lids and enchant the bedazzled reptile with a droning wind instrument made of a gourd and two reeds.

For a long time, the experts insisted that the show is a sham, as snakes can't hear. The experts were wrong. Serpents have no outer ears, no middle ears and no Eustachian tubes. However, the inner ear and the mechanism to keep balance, closely coupled to the ears, are well developed. In all likeliness, snakes receive tones near their jaw joints. It seems that the audible range is limited between 0,1 and 1kHz. Serpents hear medium and deep tones. They hear their own hissing and that of other animals, such as crocodile babies; breaking twigs, rain, cars and quarrelling couples. They are sensitive to vibrations, like your footsteps on the ground.

One thing that fascinates the cobra is the sunlight gleaming on the gourd. The snake charmer moves the instrument and the snake follows his motions. Competent snake charmers can do the whole performance without sound; instead of the shiny gourd instrument they move a brightly flashing coin. You need a lot of skill to do that. Of course, the audience would not appreciate it. Common knowledge, for what it's worth, says that snakes dance to music, and every good snake charmer gives the audience what it demands. Mind you, good snake charmers are a rarity. A true professional handles his snakes with devotion and a religious sense of respect. In many cases, he has lived with his favourite cobras for years. He sits a little outside of the striking range and has a healthy respect for his pets. Some will feed the cobra a small rodent before the show, so it releases some of its toxin. Feeding, however, makes the snake happy and lazy. Overfed cobras stay in their baskets, they say, "Dancing? Forget it. It's not in the contract. I'm busy digesting. And I won't need another meal for the next couple of weeks." The result is a lame show.

The nastier sort of snake charmer uses a hungry animal. It's angry and excitable, it can be roused and slapped and made to attack. Only that it can't. The snake charmer has defanged his cobra with a pair of pliers. The reptile is badly hurt, its mouth is infected and in a few days it will die. Others use a cobra whose mouth has been sewn shut. Such snakes can last for weeks, in spite of pain, hunger, and infection, before they find release in death.

These days, I am glad to say, snake charming is disappearing fast. The custom has been prohibited, and the snake charmers make a living as dancers and musicians.

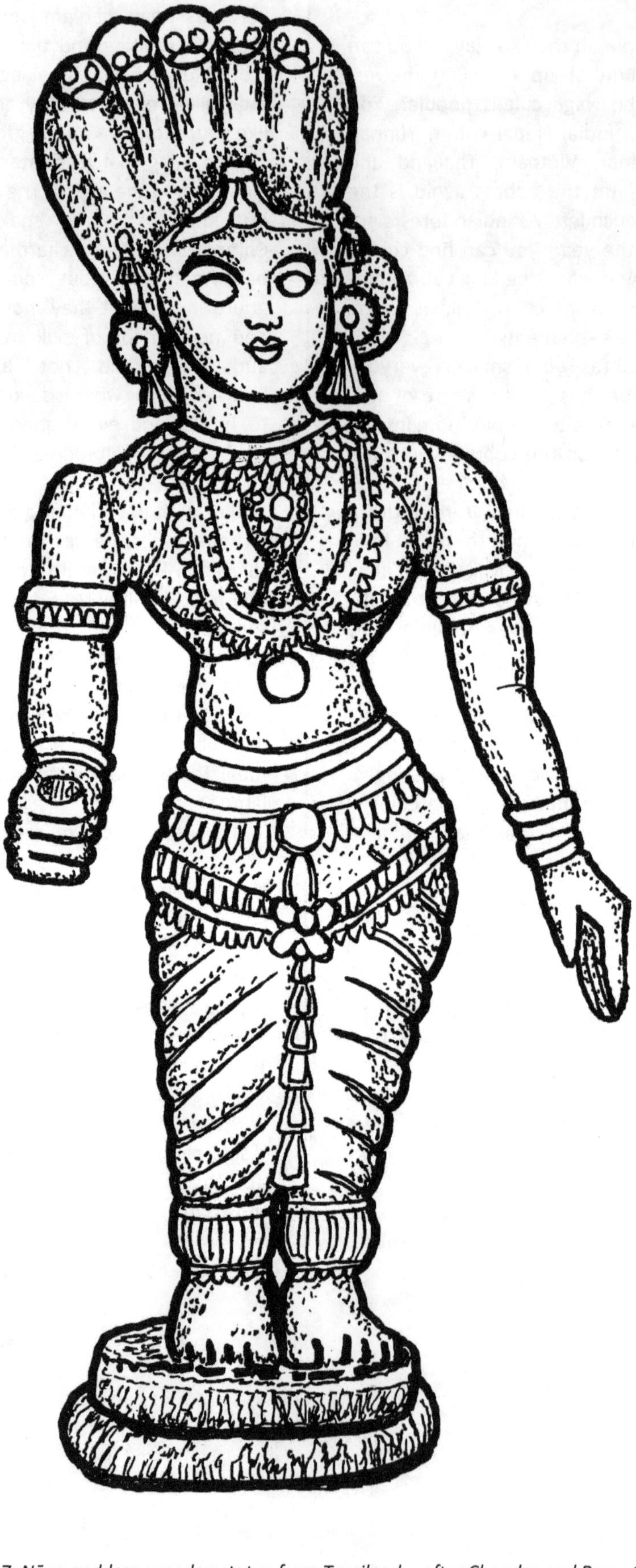

Picture 47: Nāga goddess, wooden statue from Tamilnadu, after Chandra and Bose, 1984:358.

38. The Nāga Cults

For millennia, India was a hot place for serpent worship. Let's recall one of the dumbest episodes in history: Alexander III, the 'Great', convinced of his divine nature, tried to conquer Asia. For the period, his army was amazingly large: 35,000 soldiers and mercenaries from Greece and the Balkans, plus hired help from other parts of Europe. Even a couple of Celtic tribes from Central Germany joined the campaign. And that wasn't all. Wherever his army went, young men were forced to join in. Alexander had visions of glory. After conquering Egypt, the Egyptian priesthood worshipped him as a deity, the offspring of a virgin birth. That eliminated Alexander's father, Phillip of Macedonia, and Alexander was glad of it. As everyone suspected, Alexander was involved in murdering his father, and he was certainly guilty of killing all of his brothers, except for one who was mentally handicapped. The greatest enemy of ancient Greece was Persia, and Alexander wanted to subjugate it. It escaped his attention that he knew next to nothing about the East. Nor did he care about the climate, the seasons, the terrain, the locals or what his generals were saying. Lesser people would worry: Alexander had his divine stubbornness and his visions, which became increasingly nuttier the further he went. It did not trouble him that his troops were dying. Tens of thousands died when they crossed deserts, froze to death in the mountains, and were drowned when the monsoon rains turned dry river beds into raging floods. They were assaulted by snakes, scorpions and parasites and died of an amazing range of plagues the Macedonians had never even heard of. To be sure, on rare occasions a few soldiers were slain in battle. They hardly counted. Finally, Alexander reached the Indus. King Poros faced him with two hundred war elephants. He lost, but so did Alexander. It was his last battle. He couldn't continue. King Poros remained in business, and after a brief exchange of gifts, Alexander was forced to leave. The troops were fed up with their crazy leader; they hated India, hated the weather, and wanted to go home. The divine conqueror turned back, weak, broken, and desperate. Eventually, he reached Babylon. He was feverish, he hallucinated, and maybe his generals accelerated his demise with some poison and a lot of drinking. I hope the last thing he saw was a Babylonian exorcist performing a Lamaštu ritual to expel his feverish heat. It didn't work. Like so much in history, Alexander's grandiose campaign was an incredible waste of human lives. While several Greek historians idolised the hero who wasted almost all young men of his generation, the Indian historians hardly bothered to mention the stupid barbarians who tried to conquer India, and never made it far beyond the periphery. After Alexander's death, his generals split the 'empire' between them. As a result, there was a Macedonian/Greek occupation force, under Seleucis, near the Indus. It had a strong influence on Indian thought and art.

For all their insanity, Alexander's campaigns were the first chance for European historians to explore India. Some of them wrote about the natives, about their religions and of course about their serpents.

Strabo, relying on earlier writers, recorded: *Elsewhere, there are serpents, two ells in length, that have skin-covered wings, like bats. They fly through the night; urine and sweat drops from them, and those who lack caution have their skin scorched* (15,1).

That's pretty amazing. However, according to Strabo, there were also flying scorpions.

Strabo mentioned serpents measuring sixteen ells and commented: *Aristobulus, however, says, that he had seen no* (animal) *of such incredible size, except for a serpent measuring nine ells and a span. In Egypt, like him, I saw a serpent which had been imported from there* (India) *which had a similar size. Nonetheless, he said, there are many smaller adders, cobras and large scorpions. None of these animals are as troublesome as the thin slowworms, measuring but a span, such as one finds hidden in tents, vessels and hedgerows. Those who are bitten bleed out of all pores and die, unless someone comes to their help immediately; the rescue, however, is easy, due to the healing powers of the Indian roots and medications.*

Strabo also quoted Nearchos, an admiral of Alexander. That guy, as Strabo remarked, was a well-known collector of lies. Nevertheless, Nearchos, like all good liars, was mostly reliable. He recorded that when the monsoon starts, the Indians retired to elevated villages. The rising waters made the snakes leave their holes. For good reasons, people preferred high beds. On occasion, the serpents drove the villagers out of their homes. Osenikratos, another admiral of Alexander, claimed that the king of Abhisāra (south-west of Kashmir) used to keep two serpents, one measuring 80 and the other 150 ells. Aelian insisted that those Indian snakes which had bitten men could not return into their subterranean homes. The evil deed condemned them to live on the surface of the earth. He also wrote that when Alexander's armies entered India, they encountered people who considered snakes sacred and worshipped them in caves. When Alexander's troops marched past such a cave, a serpent woke. Allegedly, the animal was 70 ells in length. Don't ask me how anyone could know: the reptile merely lifted its head out of the cavern. According to Aelian, its eyes were as big as Macedonian shields.

For sober people, like you and me, such stories seem slightly unreliable. In Antiquity, just like today,

India was considered an exotic theme park. Everybody knew that in India, giant ants dug up huge chunks of gold. The subcontinent was overrun by unicorns. Alexander's troops, it was said, fought long-tailed monkeys, until they realised that they were not facing human enemies. Indians, as everybody knew, lived for more than a hundred years. Indian dwarfs lacked noses and spent their lives fighting cranes. Some people had feet pointing backwards. Many had no mouths: these people lived on scents. When others went to sleep, they wrapped themselves in their gigantic ears. Well, that was hardly unusual. Similar people, as everybody knew, lived in far-away Germany near the North Sea. And there were people who had just one eye, set in the centre of their brows. Strabo gives good evidence of how Indian ideas appeared to clever Europeans: fancy the silly notion that the earth is pervaded by the deity which created it! Many Greek intellectuals frowned on rebirth, vegetarian diets and voluntary poverty. Except for Pythagoras, of course. Nor did they approve of ascetic hermits who went naked in heat and cold, and spend their lifetime standing on one leg. Some Indians, they recorded, considered disease shameful. When they got ill, they burned themselves alive. And when Indian men fell in love, they gave their blushing sweethearts elephants.

How old is Indian serpent worship? The question isn't easy. Plenty of scholars voiced their opinions. Sadly, academics do not live in a vacuum, but in a world where grants are coupled with politics and economy. Scholars have to be profitable, entertaining or end up unemployed. When the science of Indology began, European scholars tried to satisfy the nationalistic ambitions of their countries. Saṁskṛta was identified as 'Indo-Germanic', indicating a linguistic and cultural relationship between the continents. It defined the western (Iceland) and eastern (India) limits of the language group. As it turns out, the term was wrong. One of the earliest cultures of the group, the Tocharians, migrated to the neighbourhood of Beijing, where they survived until the Tartars destroyed them. After World War II, the term 'Indo-Germanic', loaded with unhappy associations, was replaced with 'Indo-European'.

Earliest Indian literature, i.e. the four *Vedas,* indicates that several waves of migrants, loosely classed as the Ārya (*the First, Lords, Nobles*) entered India sometime between 1,500 and 1,200 BCE. They fought the locals and each other. As they used fast, horse-drawn war-chariots against insignificant nobles trudging along in carts pulled by bovines, and showered their enemies with poisoned iron-tipped arrows, they soon gained territory. Over the centuries they expanded east, mainly as East India has great supplies of quality iron, setting up fortifications on hilltops. They evicted or oppressed the local population, and though they tried to remain apart, eventually they blended with the locals.

Nowadays, the concept of the 'Āryan master race' is blamed on Nazi demagogues. The impression is wrong; long before the Nazi movement, there were plenty of patriotic scholars in Britain, Germany, France, the Netherlands, the United States and elsewhere, who considered Europe the epitome of civilisation. They assumed that the noble, tall and fair skinned Ārya with their Indo-European language acted as culture heroes, bringing the light of civilisation to a bunch of badly organised, dark-skinned primitives with flat noses and filthy habits. At the time, none of the academics were aware that there was an ancient Indian high culture centuries before the Ārya invaded the land. The Indus Valley Culture, otherwise known as Harappa Culture, built amazing cities, developed their own script and entertained close connections with ancient Mesopotamia. We can't blame the scholars for their ignorance (or at least we shouldn't: future generations will laugh about us, too). Like the early scholars, the Ārya were ignorant about the bygone civilisations. When they fought their way into the Punjab, the ancient cities had long been abandoned; many of them had been submerged by the mud of rivers that had shifted their beds centuries ago. The Ārya faced an illiterate population that was just as primitive as they were.

The first Indologists thought that things were simple. Old India was evidently a crude and cultureless place until the Ārya arrived and forced their culture and religion on the natives. Researchers worked hard to unearth cultural connections between the Ārya and the old Europeans, and emphasised cultural achievements they could be proud of.

When Indology became a serious research subject, India itself was a gigantic realm which was ruled, or at least dominated by various Europeans. The British exerted the strongest influence, but here and there the French, Portuguese and Dutch got a slice of the cake. Meanwhile, German scholars, isolated from contemporary reality, as none of India belonged to them, were busy compiling awe-inspiring Saṁskṛta dictionaries and translated ancient literature.

Most Europeans didn't respect native Indian culture. Indian men, so it was frequently claimed, suffered from a *'slave mentality'*, an *'impotent servility'*; the product of corrupting faiths, an overly colourful way of life, the rigid caste structure, the hot climate, spicy food and too much masturbation. Indian women were dreaded for their fierce temperament, their insatiable sexuality and their dangerous unpredictability. The East, it was recorded, is incomprehensible. Like Kipling, many enlightened thinkers assumed that *East is East and West is West, and never the twain shall meet*. Also, everyone agreed, the temples were full of pornography. All of it was blamed on the dark and debased locals. The noble class system hadn't saved the pure, heroic Āryans from being corrupted by the aborigines.

Even well-informed experts, like Oldenberg, subscribed to myths that can only be classed as rubbish in our age. In his opinion, the Ārya lost their '*healthy manliness*' when they crossed the mountains of Iran and entered India. *In the voluptuous silence of their new homeland, the Ārya, the brothers of the noblest nations of Europe, mixed with the dark aboriginal population of India, and took on the characteristics of the Hindu creed, going limp due to the effects of the climate, to which their type, formed by a moderate climate zone, could not adapt without great damage, limp from the lazy gratifications, offered by the rich country after an easy victory over unequal opponents, savages, incapable of resistance, through a lifestyle lacking all great challenges, the steeling anguish, the strong and hard 'it must be'. The intellectual effort, achieved among these people, lacks the traces of the gruelling struggle which alone is fated to plump the last depths of reality, to make its own inner worlds ripen to potent joyousness* (1921:2, trans. JF).

Many scholars did their best to divide Indian culture into a manly, European branch and a degenerated aboriginal section. When they discussed serpent cults, things seemed simple. The worship of reptiles was a disgusting local tradition.

They overlooked the traces of serpent worship in ancient Europe. Let's start with someone really popular: the Greek god of healing was Asclepius (*Snake that Embraces Something*). He could appear as a wise man with a serpent wand, the caduceus, or as a snake. One particular snake is associated with his cult: the Aesculapian snake (Zamenis longissimus; earlier: Elaphe longissimus), a gorgeous, non-toxic reptile that can grow to a length of two metres, and likes to climb trees. His daughter (or wife) is Hygeia, she holds a serpent and three eggs and is a goddess of health. In her temples, and that of her dad, serpents were kept and venerated. Consider the caduceus, the serpent-entwined staff of the healers. Hermes carries one. In the Roman Isis cult, the item was the emblem of Anubis, the jackal-headed god of the Egyptians. Today it remains an emblem of the pharmacists.

Ancient Greece had a primordial goddess called Eurynome. Hesiod (*Theogony* 358) makes her an oceanic deity, the daughter of Okeanos and Tethys, the latter being the Greek version of the Babylonian Tiāmat, and so does Apollodorus (I, 3). Eurynome is ancient. In Apollonios of Rhodos *Argonautica* (I, 503), Orpheus praises the goddess and her husband Ophion (*Serpent,* identified as Uranus by Nonnos Dionysiaka, 41, 352). The eldritch couple used to reside on the peak of snow-covered Mount Olympus. They ruled the world, long before Zeus became the king of the gods. They were, so it was believed, the primal pair of deities (or rather, Titans) and the first regents of the sky. It doesn't get much classier. Chronos, time himself, dethroned the divine couple, and banished them to the bottom of the ocean, or to the Tartarus, deep in the Underworlds. Eurynome is the *Queen of Heaven*, a title that might come from ancient Mesopotamia, where it graced the serpent goddess Ningirima and, later, the goddess Inanna/Ištar.

Here's Hera, who had a really bad day. Her husband, Zeus, had been messing around with human girls (again!), and she was so angry that she gave birth to the first python. Apollo eventually killed it; mind you, the story is a cheap reflection of the *Enuma Eliš*, the *Babylonian Epic of Creation*. And consider the crazy, inspired bacchantes. Wild women ran in ecstasy, out in the hills, rapt in the madness of Bacchus. Greek art often shows them holding serpents in their hands.

Snakes get around. How about those Celtic gods who like to play with serpents? Their best-known representatives are the horned or antlered gods. One of them is called [...]ernunnos. The first letter of his name is damaged. Our modern Wicca movement calls him Cernunnos, a term that is supposed to mean 'the Horned One' and identifies him with any antlered or horned deity in evidence. Except for the female ones. The 'Horny Goddesses' complain. They hang out in bars, sip pink champagne and get into fights. 'Cernunnos' is a nice, though speculative name that makes linguists shudder. In their opinion, anyone with horns should be called Carnunnos. Maybe the one and only inscription of the name is misspelt. But whatever the name may be, the guy likes serpents. So do the warriors on the Gundestrup cauldron. See the trumpet players? There is a serpent above them. Another serpent graces the image of the god with the half-wheel on the same vessel. The 'horned god' as Anne Ross has demonstrated, is actually a group. Some have the horns of rams, of bulls and stags. They are not one character but several, with widely distinct functions. The Romans identified them with Mars and Mercury. The ones identified with Mars are frequently in the company of a horned serpent. Then there is the Celtic god Vitiris, who carries a serpent, and river goddess Verbeia (from Ilkley, Yorkshire) who carries two. A goddess from Mavilly, Côte-d'Or in France holds a pair of serpents in her left hand. In Lyplatt Park, Gloucestershire, an altar graced with a serpent was unearthed. A similar image appears on an altar form Mavilly.

In the Alps, in the Val Camonica, the antlered god is accompanied by a serpent. Quite a few snakes appear in Alpine rock art: Garda and slopes of Mont Baldo, Aosta Valley, Monte Musinè, Ciabergia and Val di Susa, Hallein (Celtic influence?), Carschenna, Monte Bego and Val Fontanalba (Priuli, 1983). Mind you, the animals are very crudely executed. And they are rare: under tens of thousands of pictographs, they hardly amount to much.

On the battlefield, some Roman riders raised standards with serpent/dragon heads. Behind the head a long cloth tube twisted and coiled like a serpent (see the illustration). Not that the Romans invented the item; the serpent standard originated among the Thrakians.

We encounter ophidian imagery among the Germani and Celts. Serpents were frequently associated with the underworlds, an idea that manifests in a priceless item, the Alemannic coffin from Oberflacht, Württemberg (today in Mainz; see the picture in *Seidways*). The corpse was buried in the trunk of an oak tree, graced by a serpent with a head at each end. A similar theme appears in the Frankish tombstone of Niederdollendorf. It shows an armed warrior surrounded by a double-headed and a normal snake, which may or may not represent the underworld.

Then there's a common Central European folk tradition: the harmless grass snake (Natrix natrix) with its beautiful 'crown' pattern, was the 'house snake', which ensured health and wealth and happiness, and appears in many fairy tales. Successful farmers had plenty of manure heaps on their property. Grass snakes love to lay their eggs in them, 'cause they are warm, and hatch faster. Large heaps can be used by dozens of snake mothers, each of them laying up to seventy eggs. In good years, thousands of baby grass snakes could emerge. The richer a farmer, the more manure, and the more snakes on his property.

It brings us to the Nordic cultures: the Bronze Agers of Scandinavia and the Vikings simply loved their serpent/dragons. They appear in bracelets, ornaments, crowns, belt buckles and on many rune stones. Viking ships often had detachable snake/dragon heads gracing the prow. When an attack was intended, the dragon was set up; when intentions were peaceful, it was stowed away. In short, many pagan European cultures fancied serpent imagery. They did not make it the main theme of their worship, but they certainly integrated it.

Indian serpent worship, most scholars agreed, was a perverse habit of the Indian aborigines. To prove their assumption, they pointed at the *Ṛg Veda*, the eldest of the Vedas, which contains no references to serpent worship. The evidence seemed irresistible. After all, the good book is a huge compilation of hymns, allegedly dating from c. 1,500-900 BCE. But things are never quite that simple. After all, the drug-crazed seers who compiled the work were illiterate. If we ignore the ancient Indus People, and their undecipherable script, writing started in India during the third century BCE, under Emperor Aśoka, who made the Brāhmī script popular. Anything composed before his time was memorized and passed to the next generation orally. For comparison: when the Indians started to write, the Chinese had been writing for approximately 1,500 and the Mesopotamians for more than 3,000 years. As it turns out, we can only be moderately sure about the age of ancient Indian literature when we date the transformation of words and grammar. While it is easy to claim that the *Vedas* were composed or compiled since 1,500 BCE, the gritty, troublesome truth is that they were memorised, confused, distorted, forgotten, reinterpreted and edited until the third century BCE. No matter how painfully exact the hymns were memorised, forgetfulness is a fact of life. Also, the meaning of words changes. You have to modernize a text, if you want to keep it meaningful.

More so, it appears that the Ārya were not a single culture, or, if you like, a single horde of invaders. Wave after wave of European migrants entered India. The Ārya fought each other, just as they struggled against the locals. Each group promoted its own deities. That's why so many gods and goddesses appear in old literature. Most of them didn't make it. Nor are the *Vedas* the perfect authority on anything. The *Ṛg Veda* may be the earliest of the *Vedas*, but it is not a reliable representation of Āryan religion. It contains elements that are nowadays attributed to the Indian aborigines, the Upaniṣadic seers and even to the early Hindus around 400 BCE. Also, the collection is narrow-mindedly focussed on the worship of a very few deities. We encounter hundreds of hymns dedicated to Indra the Thunderer, to Agni the Fire God, and to Soma, a lunar god who was also a blend of toxic plants and/or fungi that blew the ancient seers out of their heads. They are the major attractions. Dozens of fascinating Āryan gods were only mentioned in a few hymns and doomed to a background existence that may have very little relation to religious reality. In short, the compilation is distorted. We have no idea how much material was eliminated. Lack of serpent worship may mean a lot or next to nothing.

As it turns out, there is no evidence that the Ārya picked up snake-worship from the aborigines. Indeed, the very word Nāgā is Indo-European. It is related to Old High German 'snahan' (*to creep*) and appears in the German 'Schnecke' (*snail*), the Swedish 'snok' (*adder*) and the English 'snake'. A Nāga is a creeping animal. More so, all early Nāga deities have Indo-European names.

After much quarrelling, the aboriginal theory was discarded. Some scholars pointed out that Nāgas can appear as human beings. It was proposed that the Nāgas were real people, aborigine groups, who were heavily into serpent worship. Indeed, some pointed at Nagaland in East India, nowadays a semi-independent province, and proposed that these jungle dwellers were the original Nāgas. The claim is doubtful. When the Ārya composed their sacred literature, they were a long way from Nagaland. Indeed, most of the *Vedas* were compiled before they even reached the Ganges plain. The Nagas are a distant hill culture, famous for their fierceness, their remoteness and the inaccessibility of their terrain. When the descendants of the Ārya finally encountered them, the serpentine Nāgas had been established in religion and myth for many centuries.

Let's examine our source literature. While the *Ṛg Veda* does not contain praise for serpent deities, it does mention snakes on occasion. Not all the references are negative.

Ṛg Veda 1,3, has:

...*Ye Viśvedevas* (All-Gods), *who protect, reward and cherish men, approach,*

your worshippers drink-offering.

Ye Viśvedevas, swift at work, come hither quickly to the draught,

as milch-kine hasten to their stalls.

Ye Viśvedevas, changing shape like serpents, fearless, void of guile,

bearers, accept the sacred draught!

Wealthy in spoil, enriched with hymns, may

bright Sarasvatī desire,

with eager love, our sacrifice...

The stream of freshly pressed Soma, the wonder drug of the Vedic seers, was compared to a winding serpent:

Sing forth to Pavamāna (a wind god, Vāyu or Vāta) *skilled in holy song:*

the juice is flowing onward like a mighty stream.

He glideth like a serpent from his ancient skin,

and like a playful horse the Tawny Steer (= the Soma drug) *has run* (9,86).

These lines amount to a recommendation. Soma was at the heart of Vedic religion, a faith 'seen' and 'heard' by seers who were spaced out of their heads. To be sure, we have no idea what Soma really was. In one sense, the name refers to a moon god. In another, it is a plant or fungus, or a blend of both. So far, more than a hundred species have been proposed as possible ingredients. None of them could be proved: the texts are contradictory and, for all we know, the seers kept changing their mixtures while the Ārya migrated across the subcontinent.

In other verses of the *Ṛg Veda,* snakes are condemned. Obviously, the feelings towards the ophidian world were mixed. What is missing in the *Ṛg Veda* appears in other ancient texts. As usual, the dating causes problems. Some of the texts of the *Ṛg Veda* also appear in the three other *Vedas.* Here is an example from the *Yajurveda (Maitrāvanī-Samhitā, 2,7,15)* which may be as old, or even older, than the late texts of the *Ṛg Veda.*

Homage be to the snakes whichsoever move along the earth.

Which are in the sky and in heaven, homage be to those snakes.

Which are the arrows of sorcerers and of tree-spirits,

and which lie in holes, homage be to those snakes.

Which are in the brightness of heaven,

which are in the rays of the sun,

which have made their abodes in the waters,

homage be to those snakes.

That's wonderful poetry and excellent magic. Anyone who wants to get close to the Nāgas might recite this spell every day. Dear reader! Don't move so fast. There's a lot to be discovered in these lines, when you slow down, consider each line, explore each word and allow them to exert their magick.

How old is this enchantment? The reference to serpents residing in heaven, earth and the watery underworlds has close parallels to Mesopotamian religion.

More so: that the snakes are likened to rays of the sun connects them to the very roots of **yoga**.

Let's explore this. The word yoga goes back to the Vedic period. However (and you won't find this in popular literature) it used to mean something entirely different. Then, yoga referred to the ideal warrior's death. Like, say, the Vikings, the Ārya assumed that when a very special hero (usually a noble warrior or a semi-divine king) found his death on the battle-field, he could mount his chariot, hold on to the reigns, which were sun-rays, and ascend into the sky. Our superhero rode his war chariot into the height, pierced the sun and entered the paradisiacal otherworlds behind it. That's what earliest yoga was all about. Ordinary souls were not admitted; indeed, if they tried, the sun burned them up. Yoga (literally: *joking, binding together, uniting, preparing a war-chariot, going on a war-raid, plundering*) was a heroic apotheosis limited to a very few. It had nothing to do with meditation, diet, postures or physical exercise. Our slain hero practised yoga to turn his death into a triumph. The serpent idea seems to have been integrated. It's quite close to the Germanic idea that the Underworlds, hence the realms of the dead, are full of snakes, dragons and worms. Go visit goddess Hel under the world tree, where the dark dragon Nidhög devours the souls of the deceased. Countless worms and snakes thrive between the roots of world-ash Yggdrasil. Two serpent names are also names of Odin (Ofnir and Swafnir, see *Grimn.* 34 & 54). To steal the poet's mead, Odin transformed into a snake/worm/dragon: the word 'orm' describes all three.

For obvious reasons, many serpents were associated with death. But they also connect with rebirth, rejuvenation and recovery. I'm sure you noticed: it can be a relief to shrink, slip out of your old skin and return to the world refreshed and open to new experience. Snakes rejuvenate themselves by shedding their old skin. Their old skin is fairly tight: when a snake wants to grow, it fasts, shrinks, and generates a milky fluid that keeps the old and the new skin separate. In this stage, the fluid will also obscure its vision, and make the snake irritable and dangerous. The snake rubs itself against rocks or twigs until it manages to unwrap itself; the old skin is stretched and frequently torn, and looks much larger than the snake it used to cover. It is always without colour; the pigments are stored in deeper layers of the skin. If parts of the old skin won't move, the snake may be hurt or die. And even if the operation is successful, it slips out of its old skin and emerges, very sensitive and vulnerable. That's the very time when snakes are most dangerous. When the new skin has hardened, the colours shine extra bright and the snake can relax.

Consider the *Epic of Gilgameš*, King of Uruk. Several versions were composed by the Sumerians, the Babylonians and Assyrians. After long travels and much suffering, our legendary king managed to obtain the herb of immortality. Returning to his home city, he undressed at the side of a well and went to have a wash. "Gods," he said, scratching his hairy bottom, "my subjects will be so happy that I'll govern them forever!" When he returned, a snake had discovered the herb and eaten it. The king watched it shed its skin. The snake gave him a toothy grin and disappeared into a hole. Gilgameš, the Bull of Uruk, came home with empty hands. Physical immortality was denied to him. However, building the city wall of Uruk and his amazing journeys gave him immortal fame, and when he died, he became a medium-level god of the Underworlds.

When Indian snakes shed their skins they find release and redemption. Here is a passage from the *Tāṇḍya-Mahābrāhmaṇa* (25,15, in Vogel, 1972:14):

By this sacrifice, verily, the snakes have conquered death;
death is conquered by those who will perform this sacrifice.
Therefore they cast off their old skin,
and, having cast the same, they creep out of it.
The snakes are Ādityas; like unto the splendour of the Ādityas
is the splendour of those who perform this sacrifice.

The Ādityas are the sons of the primal creation goddess Aditi, who likes to appear as a cosmic cow. Her husband was the seer Kaśyapa, who fathered plenty of divine clans and, in some versions of the tale, Manasā. The Indian Aditi is a close relation of the primordial Norse cow Audhumla, whom you may meet in the *Eddas*.

In the *Aitareya Brāmaṇa* 6,1 we read:

They (the gods) smote away evil;
in accordance with their smiting away
the serpents smote away evil;
having smitten away evil, they lay aside their old worn-out skin
and continue with a new one.
He smiteth away evil who knoweth this.

The same theme is taken up in the *Bṛhadarāṇyaka Upaniṣad* (4,4,7, trans. Radhakrishnan).

A mighty seer proclaims:

"On this (subject) *there is the following verse:*
'When all the desires that dwell in the heart are cast away,
then does the mortal become immortal,
then he attains Brahman (Extension. The All-Self, All-consciousness, Absolute Reality)
here (in this very body).'
Just as the slough of a snake lies on an anthill,
dead, cast off, even so lies this body.
But this disembodied, immortal life
is Brahman only, is light indeed, Your majesty."
"I give you, Venerable Sir, a thousand cows," said (King) Janaka of Videha.

The empty hides of snakes were used in magical spells:

Yonder on the further shore are she-adders, thrice seven, out of their sloughs;
with the sloughs of them we do wrap up the (two) eyes of the malignant wayslayer. (*Atharva Veda*, 1,27)

Here is a verse from a spell to make the penis rise:

As the black snake spreads himself at pleasure, making wondrous forms, by the Asura's magic (māyā), *so let this arka* (praise song, sun-ray, erect penis) *suddenly make thy member altogether correspondent, limb with limb.* (AV, 6, 72)

This short spell forces a poisoner to meet his doom:

Go away! Enemy art thou; enemy verily art thou; in poison hast thou mixed poison; poison verily hast thou mixed; go away straight to the snake; smite that! (AV, 7, 93)

And there were plenty of spells against snake poison. Here are a few lines from *AV*, 5,13, 4-6:

...With sight I smite thy sight; with poison I smite thy poison; die, O snake, do not live; let thy poison go back against thee.

O Kirātan, O spotted one; O grass-haunter (?); O brown one! Listen ye to me, O black serpents, offensive ones! Stand ye not upon the track of my comrade; calling out, rest quiet in poison.

Of the Timātan (?) black serpent, of the brown, and of the waterless, of the altogether powerful (?), I relax the fury, as the bow-string of a bow; I release as it were chariots.

Let's look at a snippet from a hymn against snake bite. It contains the lines:

...Hither has come the young physician, slayer of the spotted ones, unconquered; he verily is the grinder up of both, the constrictor and the stinger.

Indra hath put the snake in my power, (also) both Mitra and Varuṇa, and Vāta (Wind, Storm) and Parjanya, both of them. Indra hath put the snake in my power, the pṝdāku and the she-pṝdāku, the constrictor, the cross-lined ones, the kasarṇīla, the daṣonasi.

Indra hath slain first thy progenitor, O snake; of them, being shattered, what forsooth can be their sap?

Since I have grasped together their heads, as a fisherman the karvara; having gone away to the middle of the river, I have washed out the snake's poison.

The poison of all snakes let the rivers carry away; slain (are) the cross-lined ones, crushed down the pṝdākus.

I chose as it were the filaments of herbs successfully; I conduct as it were mares; O snake, let thy poison come out.

What poison is in fire, in the sun, what in the earth, in herbs, Kānda-poison, Kanaknaka – let thy poison come out; let it come.

Whichever of the snakes (are) fire-born, herb-born, whichever came hither (as) water-born lightnings; those of which the kinds are variously great – to those serpents would we pay worship with reverence. (AV, 10, 4, 15-23)

You might think that snakes are simply evil. But the spell is astonishing. It starts with an exorcism, but in the last verse some snakes are respected, praised and worshipped.

In these lines from a long healing hymn, the serpents have the knowledge of medical herbs:

...Of this amṛta (death-less, the elixir of immortality) *we make this man* (the patient) *to drink the strength; now do I make a remedy, that he may be one hundred years.*

The boar knows the plant; the mongoose knows the remedial (herb); what ones the serpents, the Gandharvas (celestial musicians & sorcerers) *know; these I call to aid him.* (AV, 8, 7, 22-23)

These examples should suffice. Snakes were feared, annihilated and neutralised, but they were also respected, cherished and invoked. Snakes were a great power, and the seers, delighted to deify power, were keen to put them to good uses.

So far, we discussed beings who are remotely reptilian. The Nāgas are more than that. Vedic literature makes them appear like supernatural monsters, like dragons and like semi-human shapechangers. Let's have some examples of magical Nāgas.

Here, for a start, we encounter an arrangement that identifies each of the six directions with a ruling deity, a special serpent (the defender of the direction) and a magical missile, an arrow. The hymn creates a magical universe. It also turns the viciousness of cosmic serpents against enemies. The snakes are dikpālas, i.e. *guardians of the directions*. Their contribution is essential: without them, the directions of space would disintegrate. They enact the will of the gods.

Eastern quarter; Agni (Fire) *overlord; black serpent defender; the Adityas* (gods born from Aditi) *arrows: homage to those overlords; homage to the defenders; homage to the arrows; homage be to them; who hates us, whom we hate, him we put in your jaws.*

Southern quarter; Indra (Thundergod) *overlord; cross-lined (serpent) defender; the Fathers arrows; homage to those (etc.)*

Western quarter; Varuṇa (Lord of the Oceans and of medicine) *overlord; the adder defender; food the arrows; homage to those (etc.).*

Northern quarter; Soma (the Moon and the Soma drug) *overlord, the constrictor (serpent) defender; the thunderbolt arrows; homage to those (etc.).*

Fixed quarter; Viṣṇu overlord; the serpent with the black-spotted neck defender; the plants arrows; homage to those (etc.).

Upward quarter Bṛhaspati (divine priest, lord of Brahmins) *overlord; the white (serpent) defender; rain the arrows; homage to those (etc.).*(AV, 3, 27)

A very similar passage appears at the very end of AV, 12, 3, 55-60. The hymn interprets a corpse cremation as a sacrifice.

To the eastern quarter, to Agni as overlord, to the black (serpent) as defender, to Aditya having arrows, we commit thee here: guard ye him for us until our coming; may he lead on our appointed (life-time) here unto old age; let old age commit us unto death; then may we be united with the cooked (offering).

To the southern quarter, to Indra as overlord, to the cross-lined (serpent) as defender, to Yama (god of death) *having arrows, we commit thee here; guard ye (etc.).*

To the western quarter, to Varuṇa as overlord, to the pṝdāku (serpent) as defender, to food having arrows, we commit thee; guard ye (etc.).

To the northern quarter, to Soma as overlord, to the constrictor (serpent) as defender, to the thunderbolt having arrows, we commit thee here; guard ye (etc.).

To the fixed quarter, to Viṣṇu as overlord, to the spotted–necked (serpent) as defender, to the herbs having arrows, we commit thee here; guard ye (etc.).

To the upward quarter, to Bṛhaspati as overlord, to the white (serpent) as defender, to rain having arrows, we commit thee, guard ye (etc.).

Very similar catalogues appear in the *Black Yajurveda* and in early Buddhist literature. Sure, the Buddhists gave their serpents different names. The principle remained the same.

Our hymns relate the serpents to the six directions of space. Did you notice how frequently the number six comes up in the *Manasā Epic*? But there is another cosmological map which is just as important. In the *Gṛhyasūtras*, as Vogel points out (1972:11) the snakes are related to the three levels of reality: Underworld, Middle World and Heaven.

The concept of the Underworlds is hardest to understand. The realm of the snakes, Nāgloka, was identified with the two deepest Underworlds. These realms are anything but dark and dreary. Indeed, numerous seers, poets and travellers in the imagination described them as paradises. It's easy to find them. You simply descend through a cave, a chasm, a spring or travel through the secret serpent gate within each anthill.

We have a gorgeous description in the *Viṣṇu Purāṇa* (fourth canto). The sage Nārada went for a visit. He returned with an amazing tale:

"What" exclaimed the seer, "can be compared to Pātālā (the lowest underworld), *where the Nāgas are decorated with brilliant and beautiful and pleasure shedding jewels? Who will not delight in Pātālā, where the lovely daughters of the Daityas* (a divine family) *and Dānavas* (a divine family, later demonised) *wander about, fascinating even the most austere; where the rays of the sun diffuse light, and not heat, by day; and where the moon shines by night for illumination, not for cold; where the sons of Danu* (the Dānavas), *happy in the enjoyment of delicious viands and strong wines, know not how time passes? There are beautiful grooves and streams and lakes where the lotus blows; and the skies are resonant with the Koīl's* (the Indian 'cuckoo') *song. Splendid ornaments, fragrant perfumes, rich unguents, the blended music of the lute and pipe and tabor; these and many other enjoyments are the common portion of the Dānavas, Daityas, and snake-gods, who inhabit the region of Pātālā."*

It sounds inviting. I hope you travel there in trance. See the capital of the deepest Underworld, the gorgeous city Bhogavatī, the serpent town. The name means *'City of Enjoyment'* and *'City of Serpent Coils'* depending on how you understand the term bhoga. Manasā is a Bhoginī, an *Enjoyer* and a *Coiled One*.

But the serpent Underworld is more than a subterranean paradise. It could also appear in the depths of the ocean. Many visionary seers explored the watery abyss, met the Nāgas and returned to earth with treasures, magical powers and mystical scripture. The Buddhists were so fond of the underwater serpent realm that they turned the Vedic god Varuṇa and King Sāgara (*Ocean*), both of them closely related to water, into Nāga kings. But they also promoted the idea that the great Nāgas reside on mountains. The *Jākata* (6) refers to the Nāgas who dwell under the sea and the Nāgas who dwell on mountains. A version of the *Pali Canon* from Sri Lanka mentions the war between these serpent races, and describes how the Buddha intervened and made peace between them (Vogel, 1972:33).

Consider this: Manasā's home is on Sij Mountain, in the serpent Underworld, at the Dark Waters and deep under the sea, and all of them at once. Her favourite places reflect ancient literary and visionary ideas.

One of the earliest traceable ideas is the relationship between the Nāgas and rain. The monsoon floods make serpents appear, hence, serpents have the power to cause rain. When the monsoon is late, the serpents receive plenty of attention, devotion and offerings.

Serpents feature in a rainmaking hymn:

Let the liberal ones favour you, also the fountains, great serpents (pythons); let the clouds, started forward by the Maruts (winds), *rain along the earth.*

Let it lighten to every region, let the winds blow to each quarter, let the clouds, started forward by the Maruts, come together along the earth.

Waters, lightning, cloud, rain-let the liberal ones favour you, also the fountains, great serpents;

let the clouds, started forward by the Maruts, show favour along the earth.

(AV, 4, 15, 7-9). The hymn invokes the blessing of the Maruts, the winds, the stormy singers and bards of the gods, friends of Indra and Agni, to bring on the monsoon.

Here are a few lines from a long hymn that sends destructive magic against an enemy army. The serpents, just like every other being, spirit, deity and plant, is called into the fight. A few lines will suffice:

Let all the gods from above go crowding with force; let the Aṅgirases (descendants of Agni, a class of fire priests) *go slaying midway the great army.*

The forest trees, them of the forest trees, the herbs and the plants, what is biped, what is quadruped I despatch, that they may slay yonder army.

The Gandharvas (celestial musicians and sorcerers) *and the Apsarases* (celestial nymphs and dancers), *the serpents, the gods, the pure-folk, the Fathers, those seen, those unseen, I despatch, that they may slay yonder army.* (AV, 8, 13-15)

How about something even more exalted? Here is a verse from a hymn describing the ascent of Virāj. The hymn is long and describes the rising of Virāj through many realms and worlds. Virāj is an extremely difficult concept. The term means *Ruling Far and Wide*. It appears in a male and female form and refers, among many other ideas, to the Puruṣa, the Universal Spirit. It can also be understood as the power of the cosmos; in this sense it is close to the much later concept of Śakti. Elsewhere, Virāj appears as a (male) creator god or culture hero. In AV 9,10, 24, we learn that Virāj is speech, Virāj is earth, Virāj is atmosphere, Virāj is creator god Prajāpati, Virāj became death, the highest king of the Perfectibles.

Here is the end of a long spell, and Virāj is understood as a female force. She travels through one world after the other. The last verse deals with the Nāgas:

She ascended, she came to the serpents; the serpents called to her: O poisonous one, come! Of her Takṣaka, descendant of Viṣāla, was young, the gourd vessel (was) vessel; her Dhṛtarāṣṭra son of Irāvant milked; from her he milked poison; upon that poison the serpents subsist; one to be subsisted upon becometh he who knoweth this.

Then for whomsoever that knoweth thus one shall pour out with a gourd, he should reject (it).

Should he not reject (it), he should reject (it) by (thinking): with the mind I reject thee.

In that he rejects (it), he thus rejects poison.

Poison is poured out after the unfriendly foe of him who knoweth thus.

(AV, 8, 10, 29-33)

Yes, life is complicated. Let me apologise. I didn't do it. And I am sure you love mysteries. Please note that this Vedic hymn mentions the name of a serpent king, Takṣaka. He appears, much later, as a close relation of Manasā, and as one of the serpents she wears as ornaments. And we encounter a vessel, closely connected with serpent worship. Dhṛtarāṣṭra can be a Nāga king, a son of charming Kadrū, with many snake heads. And he appears, thoroughly human but amazingly powerful, as one of the key figures of the *Mahābhārata*. He is the eldest son of Vyāsa and Ambikā, and the king of the Kuru realm. He has a hundred sons, they are the Kauravas.

Serpents have the power to kill with a glance. So has Manasā. The gaze of a serpent can make men blind, can destroy houses and plants. As they are terribly destructive, in Hindu and Buddhist tales, Nāga aristocrats close or avert their eyes when they are really angry. The famous Indian physician, Suśruta, wrote: *Innumerable are the famous Lords of Nāgas, headed by Vāsuki and beginning with Takṣaka, earth-bearers, resembling the sacrificial fire in their splendour (tejas), who incessantly cause thunder, rain and heat, and by whom this earth with her oceans, mountains and continents is supported, and who in their wrath might smite the whole world by their breath and sight. Homage be to those. With them there is no need of the healing art* (quoted in Vogel, 1972: 17). That's because they are invincible. Regarding the minor serpents and their toxins, Suśruta offered medical remedies.

Another unusual power is the serpent fire. Yes, Indian serpents, if they are any good at their job, can create devastating firestorms. Takṣaka, the famous Nāga King, can blow fire from his nostrils. On occasion, he incinerates trees and buildings. The terrifying Nāga Kāliya lives in a pool of River Yamunā. Dense smoke coils above the lake, and flames dance on the surface of the water. Similar serpents abound in early Buddhist literature. In the *Bhūridatta Jākata*, the protagonist says about himself: *"I am a Nāga possessed of supernatural power and magical fire and difficult to overcome; in my wrath I could bite a prosperous country with my fire."* (Vogel, 1972:15-16).

Serpents are associated with the crudest tattvas (*categories of existence*, usually mistranslated as 'elements'). They are dwellers of the earth and of the lowest underworld; they move in water, they breathe fire and they subside on air. Let's hear Vogel: *The curious way in which the snake protrudes his tongue as if licking up the air may have led to the belief that the creature was content to feed on the wind. Hence the snake is not only called 'licker' (leliha, lelihāna) and 'double tongue' (dvijihva, dvirasana), but also 'wind-eater' (vāyubhakṣa, vātaśin, pavanāśin, pavanabhuj, anilāśana, śvasanāśana, mārutāśana). The poet Bhartṛhari says that the Creator has ordained the wind as food for the snakes: like frugality, therefore, is recommended for the wise* (Vogel, 1972: 13).

Manasā tried it. She lived on wind for ages. Neta says it made her crazy. She went jittery and shrivelled and kept running into trees. Finally, Manasā gave in. She realised that gods need more than air: their natural food is loving devotion.

But there is more to Nāgas. Oldenberg compared the Nāgas to swan-maidens and werewolves. It may seem odd. In Germanic folklore, a swan maiden is a beautiful, shape-shifting girl. She is graceful, celestial and has a snaky neck. For a time, she may take a mortal lover, bear a few children, and disappear into the sky. A werewolf, however, is a hairy, half-crazed animal that haunts the woods around the full moon, drinks beer from the can and thrives on country music. By comparison, the snake deity comes across smooth and sophisticated; it doesn't need to shave and gets its head with elegance. But when we consider werewolves as a prime example for European shape-shifters; pretty much like them are were-tigers and were-foxes in China, Korea and Japan. The Indian Nāgas appear similar. They move like serpents through their underworld, but when they appear on earth, they may look almost human. True, sometimes they fail to transform properly. A snake head on a human body or a snake tail under a human torso is a dead giveaway. So are the corpses left behind a Nāga army.

Nāga aristocrats love fine clothes, gems, jewels and a headdress topped by three, five seven or nine cobras. Some people notice. If they know what is good for them, they keep their mouths shut. Our Nāga princes and princesses are alluring. They charm, seduce, and marry aristocrats. Eventually, they end up as kings and queens and rule the human realm. And, would you believe it, their offspring stay in power. Plenty of royal families in Nepal, Northern India, Thailand and Cambodia trace their origin to a Nāga lord or lady. That's similar to the Viking kings who traced their ancestry to Freyr or Odin. Manasā, incidentally, seems to be an exception. She only married as she had to, and the marriage lasted just a day or two. The Brahmins forced her to live up to the story from the *Mahābhārata*. She doesn't dress well, or at all, if she can help it. She isn't given to enchant aristocrats with her charm, nor does she plan on founding divine lineages.

The Nāga cult is immensely important. Imagine a faith, or a series of faiths, that was essential before Buddhism and Jainism were invented, and Hinduism appeared in East India. It is so powerful that all religions of India acknowledge it. Vedic seers, Upaniṣadic forest ascetics, Jainas, Buddhists, Hindus, Sikhs and Tantrics did their best to gain the blessing of the serpent folk. Consider Nāgārjuna, the great Buddhist reformer, who improved the stern creed of the historical Buddha so thoroughly that its byword became 'compassion' and its followers a major church in many Asian countries. Nāgārjuna claimed that he had obtained secret documents from the Nāgas. He had visited their watery Underworld, so he said, where Vāsuki gave him a priceless pearl and a heap of original documents. The Buddha, as he explained, had composed several amazing texts. He was aware that his contemporaries were not up to those revelations. So the Enlightened One gave them to the Nāgas, who kept them secure in the Deep, until Nāgārjuna came visiting. No, his colleagues did not laugh their heads off. They read the freshly discovered 'original' teachings, which were miles away from the dry, bitter and anti-social stuff the historical Buddha had preached, smiled and acknowledged them. Nāgārjuna's texts turned Buddhism into a church and a mass movement.

The Vedic gods, as far as surviving Brahmanical literature indicates, had little to do with serpents. Nevertheless, there were exceptions. One fascinating example is Indra's famous fight against Vṛta. The latter is an evil force described, depending on the textual source and its age, as a bank of clouds, a serpent (ahi) and, in later texts, as a dangerous Brahmin. Indra does what Thor and other serpent/dragon fighters do. He hurls his deadly thunderbolts and vanquishes his opponent. For many centuries, it made him a paragon of heroic effort. Later, when his status was declining, it turned him into a blemished god who had committed the crime of Bramanicide. By the advent of modern Hinduism, around the start of the Common Era, he had lost much importance. To kill the serpent Vṛta, he has to ask permission from two upstart gods, Viṣṇu and Śiva. Now something strange happens. You might imagine that Indra loathes all serpents. He doesn't. Indeed; he is the best friend of the Nāga King Takṣaka. When King Janamejaya tried to burn all serpents, he also planned to burn their friends, including Indra and his family.

What about the great gods of freshly invented Hinduism? In the Vedic Period, Viṣṇu started as a servant and odd jobs boy for majestic Indra. He made a career leap and became king of the gods. Viṣṇu is the great maintainer of the worlds. Whenever he gets really creative, he dreams, lying on a vast serpent sofa. It's the amazing world serpent Śeṣa, a seven-headed snake, his support, vehicle and close associate. The seven-headed snake, of course, is an import. It comes from Mesopotamia. And there is Śiva, the *Auspicious One*. Before, maybe 1,000 BCE, he was usually called Rudra. The etymology of that name remains uncertain. He had close connections to the Nāgas. They are much closer to him than to the other gods, who sneered at his wild looks and manners. Rudra/Śiva made his first appearance in the Vedic period. Not that it was much of a performance. The seers of the *Ṛg Veda* barely acknowledged his existence and denied him participation in the great Soma offerings. He was known, feared and placated, a dreaded wild hunter of the jungle and mountain forest, an expert in poisons, drugs and medicine, a deadly archer, lord of diseases, a killer of people and cattle. His colour was blood red, but his belly bluish black. Red, in the Vedic period, was the colour of death; corpses were adorned with garlands of red flowers, and red utensils were used for death sorceries. His favourite direction was north, representing the towering mountains of the Himalayas and the direction of greatest darkness. In later Hinduism, north is a dangerous direction and no traditional Hindu would sleep with his head pointing north. Rudra/Śiva's sons, Bhava and Śarva, the haunters of the forest, are savage wolves. But while city folk and villagers dreaded the terrifying slayer in the greenwood, the forest ascetics, the long-haired renouncers, the witches and sorcerers treasured him as a friend. In their opinion, there was one Rudra, but there were also entire swarms of them. Every place was thought to have a Rudra, a genius loci, who required sacrifices. Some of them were the Rudras of the streets, crossroads, the cremation place, the Rudras who lived among cattle and those who dwelled surrounded by serpents. There was even a Rudra of the dung heap: all of them are liminal places, sure to pollute anyone who lacked protection. When Rudra roared through the wilderness on the howling storm gales, leading the Wild Hunt much like Wodan in Central Europe, he was accompanied by a horde of lethal goddesses. They are not self-evident at all. The *Vedas* do mention goddesses here and there, and one of them, Uṣas, goddess of the Dawn, got far more attention than, say, dangerous villains like Rudra and employees like Viṣṇu. But these goddesses were rarely considered housewives. Married gods, or god who had liaisons, were a rarity. Rudra's terrifying girlfriends were an exception from the rule. Oldenberg (1923:219) quotes from the *Śankhāyana Śr.* IV, 20,1: *the Noise-Makers, Counter-Noise makers, Supporting Noise-Makers, Searchers, Hissers, Devourers of Flesh.* These goddesses received the blood and guts of the sacrificial animals at Rudra's sacrifices. He observes that, during the same period, very similar terms were used to describe the Nāga deities. Was Rudra accompanied by the serpent folk?

He (the sacrificial priest) *turned north and made an offering to the Nāgas saying "Hissers, Noise-Makers, Searchers, Winners: may you serpents take what is here for you." The serpents take the blood and guts that have been spilled.* (*Āṣvalāyana* G, IV, 8, 28).

According to the *Black Yajur Veda*, Rudra occasionally received red cows as an offering. Other gods got different colours. Yes, cows were not always sacred and inviolable. Don't mention it in public; Indian professors who state that cows were sacrificed in the Vedic Period are nowadays persecuted and may find themselves out of a job.

In short, Rudra was associated with goddesses who were, at least occasionally, serpents. It's hardly surprising that he walks around with a fat cobra wrapped around his neck. Nor that he fathered Manasā, much to his own surprise.

Picture 48: Unidentified snake goddess with child, from Tundara, Balasor, in Orissa. The image has been identified with Manasā (and the child with Āstika), but there are no convincing reasons for this assumption. In thse region, Manasā was probably unknown, but the Buddhist serpent goddess Jāṅgulī was worshipped. After photo in Maity, 2001:298).

39. Kuṇḍalinī: the Tantric Fire Snake

We are approaching a tricky, slithery and multiple faced phenomena. Where are the Nāga cults in Tantra? I wish I knew. As usual, the Nāgas appear in the periphery. They are important, they cannot be ignored, they are a common topic in folk worship, but they rarely emerge on the centre of the stage. Most Tantras I have read contained few references to the cosmic serpents. Yes, there used to be a tantric cult of the Left-Hand Path, sometime before the ninth century, called the Nāga Kaula. Nobody knows what it was all about: its texts have disappeared.

But what about the Fire Snake? The topic makes me shudder. Things could have been simple. Sadly, they are anything but that. Whenever someone invents something wonderful, cheaters and imposters appear and corner the market. That's what Neta says. She is happy to do the washing. "Clothes, hearts, brains and guts, anything goes. Let other people get their fingers burned." She keeps hers in the Dark Waters. "It's good for my skin," she says, "and the nails remain sharp."

Kuṇḍalinī, literally the *Coiled One*, the 'Serpent Power', is famous. Thanks to a lot of badly informed would-be gurus, people in the west tend to think that the 'raising of the fire snake' is one of the two high marks of tantric practice (the other, you guessed it, is sex).

Let's sum up the most popular myth on the topic. The human body, so it is claimed, consists of several sheaths. On a subtle and refined level, there are such things as cakras (*circles, disks, ritual assemblies*), which focus energy and sentience (Śakti and Śiva). When they are all happily lit up like a Christmas tree, the practitioner is happy, healthy and wise. When they are dull, congested or altogether dark, people are barely fit to watch soccer. To give the cakras their much-needed energy boost, there is a funny little device. It rests in a place which, nowadays, is usually located at the base of the spine. Imagine a snug little serpent girl. The dear thing is sound asleep. It's wrapped three and a half times around a liṅga (here: *emblem, Śivas emblem, pillar, cosmic axis*) and while it snores, you go through everyday reality like any other zombie. Get up, eat, work, make money, come home, raise kids, watch TV, sleep, and get up again. No matter what you do for a living, it becomes a routine and you do it automatically...and that's what reality with a sleeping Kuṇḍalinī is like. Along comes the enlightened guru. He or she does a few magical tricks, the Fire Snake wakes, raises its head and shoots up along the subtle, energetic counterpart of the spine. When it reaches the top of your head, or, in some traditions, pierces your skull and shoots into the sky, you go bonkers with joy and achieve instant sagehood. All of a sudden, you bliss-out in non-duality. It's all a matter of hydraulics: clear the pipes, open the valves, heat the water, build up the pressure and be enlightened. That's perfect eighteenth and nineteenth-century thinking. Then, people were amazed that gas light and tap water were possible and steam engines were their idea of technical success. It wasn't much, when you consider that Heron of Alexandria used steam engines to bedazzle the worshippers in Egyptian temples in the first century CE. Make the temple doors open, let a statue spurt wine...the engineers of his period didn't achieve much. They couldn't have started an industrial age, even if they would have liked to. Egypt had no metals worth mentioning and the same went for coal. If you ask me, steam is overestimated. And I wonder why people of the 21st Century still insist on steam metaphors to explain the workings of the mind.

Ideally, raising the fire serpent could be easy. If, however, some cakra is clogged, the fire snake bumps against it, goes "ouch!" can't ascend further, gets angry and the next thing you find yourself in the loony bin, on medication or at the mercy of a guru with an evil grin and a hungry bank account.

So much for the basic myth. It is based on dualism. There is a 'you' and there is a 'Kuṇḍalinī', conveniently imagined like a female serpent of flaming energy. And a third party, the guru, who gets you going. The fourth element is money. Some add their own little glamour. In their opinion, Kuṇḍalinī is basically sex-energy. That's because sex sells. To wake your little reptile, you need a nubile partner, silly postures, aromatic oils, incense, specific breathing cycles, mantras, mudrās, possibly drugs and a lot of exotic extras, instead of a guru.

That's Western dreamland. It has very little to do with the original.

Let's approach the topic from the historical point of view. My apologies, this is going to be short and, for some people, painful. I have to cover a wide range of complicated topics in very few lines. Please read *Kālī Kaula* for a detailed treatment.

The Kuṇḍalinī concept is rather new. When Tantra developed, around, maybe, the fourth or fifth century of the Common Era, the fire snake was unknown. It remained so until around the ninth or tenth century. By the 11th and 12th century, a few lineages made a big thing out of it, while a lot of others ignored it. Far from being the heart and epitome of tantric effort, Kuṇḍalinī was a vague concept, interpreted in contradictory ways, which attracted a minority of dedicated practitioners. After the 13th century, Kuṇḍalinī and indeed most tantric movements, faiths and techniques lost their appeal. For one thing, the Muslims occupied large parts of India and started their regency with persecution. For another, around 1350, one or two unidentified pestilences swept through Eurasia. In the process, approximately a third of the population died. Those who survived were traumatised. Who, they thought, can trust the gods, when people die, no matter if they are sages, sinners or simply children? In Europe, the pestilence was followed by the Renaissance: the stranglehold of the church broke. Innovative thinkers began to revive the ideas and beliefs of the pre-Christian cultures, while others went for science and materialism.

In India, most of the tantric movements disappeared. The new religious orthodoxy frowned on the earlier cults and saw to it that tantrics remained underground. A few tantric movements, like Śri Vidyā, managed to become socially acceptable by eliminating all heretical, dangerous, wild, sexual and ecstatic practices from their program. Around the 16th century half-hearted attempts were made to revive elder tantric movements. They didn't get far. In fact, many respectable gurus faked lineages. By the time, Hinduism was mostly controlled by the Vaiṣṇavas, the worshippers of Viṣṇu, who did much to eliminate tantric episodes from the history books. Tantra, or what called itself by that name, was socially unacceptable. Its practitioners did their rituals in secret or, more often, entirely in the imagination. To this day, middle-class Hindus loathed the very term and their dislike was and is shared by Muslims, Jainas, Sikhs, Christians, the colonial officers and missionaries of Portugal, the Netherlands, France and Britain, and the religious reformers who accompanied India's way to independence. As everybody knew, tantrics were depraved, sex-crazed alcoholics, who conducted cannibalistic orgies on cemeteries and financed their wickedness with murder, crime and prostitution.

Then as now, this opinion is widely popular. India is not and has never been a country of sacred eroticism. If you want to upset a pious Hindu, tell him that you are interested in Tantra. The same attitude was shared by countless Indologists. When Sir John Woodroffe, writing under his pen-name Arthur Avalon, published the first scholarly translations of tantric texts in the early 20th century, most scholars disapproved. It took decades before Tantra became a topic worth exploring. Academics eventually understood that Tantra is not a single thing but a vague and misleading term for several hundred spiritual systems. It turned out that Tantra, or what was classed as such, had not always been a fringe phenomenon. There had been, in the many tiny kingdoms of India, short-lived dynasties whose regents embraced tantric ideas and sponsored tantric gurus, mainly as their creed promised magical powers, success in battle and possibly immortality. Mind you, such kings were in the minority. Their dynasties were crushed by traditionally-minded Hindus, by Muslims and, later on, by well-meaning European invaders.

When Western scholars became interested in Tantra, most of it was a thing of the past. Living tantrics had practically disappeared; their legacy was a wealth of scripture: holy books, hymns, ritual programs, commentaries and the like. The Tantra we know of is basically a literary tradition. Indeed, the very word 'Tantra' means a *textile, a text, a treatise, a scientific book, a manual.* We are talking about spiritual literature. It turned out to be enormously complicated. Very few tantric authors bothered to express themselves in simple terms. Each work makes use of a mind-blowing range of symbols, of 'twilight language' and of course the various traditions did not bother to use the same terminology. As a result, tantric literature is anything but easy reading. Also, most of the texts are remarkably shy. Sex and drugs are hardly mentioned at all.

In the West, few bothered to read genuine tantric literature. It was so much easier to repeat the stupid old fables.

One enormously influential writer was Helena Petrovna Blavatsky (1831-1891). She did not know anything about Tantra but disapproved nevertheless. Blavatsky achieved something remarkable. She claimed that, disguised as a man, she had travelled to Tibet (prohibited for all foreigners) where she lived, in disguise, for seven years, and met a bunch of holy world teachers and yoga masters who initiated her into a doctrine that was old when Atlantis sank. Her gurus, as it turned out, had funny names and when she had their portraits commissioned, they all looked much like Dürer's version of Jesus. Blavatsky received the 'earliest book of mankind' (*The Stanzas of Dzyan*) from them, wrote an enormous and confused commentary (*The Secret Doctrine)*, founded her own cult, Theosophy in 1875, and went into business.

Nowadays, few people take her fables seriously. There is no shred of evidence that she got close to Tibet, let alone lived there. Her 'Tibetan' terminology came from books. In her time, however, her claims were dynamite. The Theosophical Society exerted an enormous influence on modern thought. For many Europeans and Americans, Blavatsky offered a spiritual alternative to dull and corrupt Christianity, and to a new and destructive materialism. Theosophy, as Madame Blavatsky defined it, was meant to surpass all faiths and religions. As she put it, *'The theosophical society, that's me.'* Among those who were theosophists (permanently or temporarily), or were influenced by it, were Rudolf Steiner (the founder of Anthroposophy, whose insane racial ideology inspired Hitler, Himmler and Hess), Max Beckmann, Wassily Kandinsky, Paul Klee, Paul Gauguin, Pier Mondrian, Gustav Mahler, Jean Sibelius, Alexander Skrjabin, Nicholas Roerich, T.S. Elliot, Hermann Hesse, James Joyce (who subsequently rejected it), W.B. Yeats (who eventually ran a branch of the Golden Dawn), Thomas Alva Edison, Alfred Russel Wallace, Sir William Crookes, Gandhi (who realised the glory of Hinduism after he met Madame Blavatsky), possibly Einstein (who allegedly kept a copy of her *Secret Doctrine* and recommended it, don't ask me why) and Frank L. Baum, the Author of *The Wizard of Oz* (Keller & Sharandak, 2013). Theosophy transformed the world. Thanks to its influence, ideas like reincarnation, cakras, the akashic record, Qabala, world ages, collective consciousness, root-races, astral projection, yoga and Karman became widely popular. Indeed, Dorothy was not in Kansas anymore. Blavatsky combined Buddhism, mystic Christianity, spiritualism, Atlantis, Tibet, Lemuria, Egypt and India in a mind-blowing package. She redesigned her biography repeatedly; especially those troublesome years when she allegedly lived in Tibet. And she got caught cheating at spiritualist sessions in America. In the wake of her nutty vision, Theosophists delighted in mystical India. It proved to be a success story. Between 1879-1885, Madame Blavatsky spent much of her time in India. Her health gave in repeatedly. When the government asked her to leave, as she was a nuisance and had been exposed as a cheat, she was more dead than alive. Nevertheless, the Theosophical society continued to flourish in India, and had a strong influence on the formation of the first Indian Congress. According to HPB, the forbidden Himalayas were full of wonderworking yogīs. Her vision stood in painful contrast to reality: in India, yoga had long disappeared. The only surviving yogīs were sorcerers, quacks, beggars, and spies. The word yogī was an insult. The leaders of Indian Theosophy had to make do with literature and fantasies. Her followers, the feminist Annie Besant and the visionary Colonel Leadbeater (frequently accused as a paedophile), wrote amazing books on esoteric Indian lore, and introduced the world to the cakras and the Kuṇḍalinī. Their books were full of errors. Nevertheless, they bedazzled their readers. And they inspired Indian reformers with the glory of a past that was mostly fictional. India, after all, was struggling to catch up with the modern world. Reformers, like Vivekananda, hoped to create a new spirituality that should be ancient, modern, rational, liberal, politically correct, patriotic, free of the class-system and scientific. In their efforts, they laid the foundation of modern yoga. We owe 'mystical India' to these pioneers. Tantra, however, as Madame Blavatsky and her followers had decided, was wicked, evil, sexual and alluring; in short, the topic remained unspeakable.

In the 1960s, the hippie movement began. The pioneers of consciousness expansion, pacifism, ecological thought and drug abuse made 'Make Love not War' their mantra and decided that anyone who walks around nude, does drugs and spends centuries making love, like, for instance, Śiva and Durgā, has got it right. Tantra, as the missionaries had insisted, was all about drugs and sex. The hippies liked it, flocked to India in aged VW busses and shocked the Indians with their hedonistic lifestyle. Tantra, previously bad, was bliss to them. Of course their vision of Tantra was just as wrong as that of the missionaries. It simply re-evaluated the old misconceptions and turned sex, previously bad, into something sacred and liberating.

Nowadays, you are more likely to discover authentic Tantra in a university library than in India. Instead of the real thing, there are armies of gurus and new-agers who sell sex and bioenergetic exercises in spiritual disguise. They, too, follow the world-view of missionaries and theosophists. Kuṇḍalinī features prominently. Consider the term Kuṇḍalinī-Yoga. It was invented by a philosopher, Swami Vivekananda, in the late 19th century. He also popularised or invented the terms Mantra-Yoga, Jñāna-Yoga, Japa-Yoga, Raja-Yoga, Karma-Yoga, Kriyā-Yoga and others. Vivekananda wrote a stack of books on yoga. They are exceedingly spiritual. Sadly, he had no practical experience whatsoever. Sure, he had seen great spiritual events in the company of his guru, the incomprehensibly wonderful Bengal saint Rāmakṛṣṇa. But where Rāmakṛṣṇa went blissfully insane experiencing the divine, and promoted his personal goddess, Kālī, Vivekananda remained shy, distant and intellectual. Ecstatic frenzy was foreign to him. So was daily practice. He studied classical scripture, praised Vedānta, tried to meet a genuine yogī, and was disappointed when he realised that had died out centuries ago. In short, he made do with old books, a lot of speculation and, of course, Madame Blavatsky's scatterbrained imagination.

Vivekananda's books convinced many Indian enthusiasts that the miraculous yogīs were real. They pounced on the small range of available material and created something new. Among their favourites were Patañjali's classic book on meditative, introverted yoga, the yoga chapter of the *Bhagavad Gītā*, and sections from the *Mahābhārata*. All are products of the 3-4th Century, and all of them contradict each other. The enthusiasts of the 19th century assumed that yoga, meaning a spiritual and physical approach to enlightenment, was an ancient, Pre-Hinduistic tradition, which it wasn't, combined their selection with the medieval *Gheraṇḍa Saṁhīta*, which introduced some postures (āsana) and topped the mixture with Theosophy. As India had no living yogīs, they were sought elsewhere. A few genuine practices were imported from Tibet. Most were developed by trial and error. The whole thing was rounded off with exercises of the Indian wrestlers and the gymnastic drill of the British army. The result was a wonderfully syncretistic, innovative invention and is taught as

Haṭhayoga nowadays. White, in his groundbreaking *Sinister Yogis*, gives a magnificent account.

When, during the 1970's, Tantra became a popular topic, commercialisation began. Several gurus with a sound head for business bedazzled their students with a type of Tantra that had very little to do with reality. The most successful was the incomparable Bhagwan (*god*) Shree Rajneesh, a.k.a. Osho. In real life, he was called Chandra Mohan Jain (1931-1990). Like him or not, Osho delivered. With disarming honesty he announced that he focussed on the two topics that western people are obsessed with: money and sex. One of his inventions was called Kuṇḍalinī meditation. In plain fact, it has no relation to any traditional techniques of Kuṇḍalinī meditation. Nor could we expect it to be so. Osho was no tantric practitioner, nor even a Hindu: his family belonged to the Jaina creed. Jainism is famous for its rules and prohibitions and Osho did his best to rebel against them. Much of his life was devoted to fighting authority figures. He praised his followers as 'rebels' while he put them in uniforms. The universe doesn't get much funnier than this. Truth to tell, his knowledge of real Tantra was badly wanting. Osho, like the missionaries, insisted that Tantra is all about sex, and lectured for ages, preaching "Tantra says...Tantra teaches...". Well, 'Tantra' doesn't. Tantra is not a person. His Tantra is a new invention. He called it radical, revolutionary and rebellious (*The Tantra Experience*, Talk #1). And he claimed that Tantra has no scripture, no priesthood and no temple. He couldn't have been more wrong.

In his opinion, the raising of Kuṇḍalinī is achieved by a physical exercise. The process requires taped music, and starts with shaking, staggering, swaying, chaotic, and involuntary motions. Eventually, when the practitioners have exhausted themselves, follow periods of free dance and stillness. The music continues all the time. To be sure, the format works. It doesn't 'raise the Kuṇḍalinī' but, after the cathartic phase, it permits the participants to enjoy a bit of rest and quiet. To be sure, similar phenomena can be found in Indian folk religion. Shaking, swaying, staggering, glossolalia and the like were part of religious activity since the composition of the *Vedas*. Such phenomena were side effects of intense religious frenzy. They form an important element in rituals of Bhakti, i.e. highly emotional, loving devotion to a deity and/or obsession by it. That, however, is not the background of Osho's technique. His 'Kuṇḍalinī meditation' derived from the exercises which Wilhelm Reich developed to liberate the 'orgasm reflex' and the bioenergetic therapies created by Laing, Lowen and other followers of Reich. Like, for instance, Mesmer's 'healing crisis', Osho's Kuṇḍalinī Meditation celebrated catharsis and exhaustion.

It was very much in tune with the spirit of the 1970's and 80's. Like mind damaging practices such as 'Encounter Therapy', it was based on the mechanistic ideology which Freud promoted when he wrote about 'repressed urges'. The therapies of the Hippie Age were soundly based on 19th-century steam-engine metaphors: emotions 'boiled up' and 'pressure had to be released'. Therapy was loud, wild and crippling. It gave people the idea that it is 'honest' to scream abuse at each other. Politeness and manners were called 'dishonest'. Those who emerged from this process were 'genuine', 'direct', and 'true', and believed that savage eruptions were the key to mental freedom. In the wake of such therapies, they lost their friends, marriages crashed and families disintegrated.

Osho discouraged his followers from researching genuine tantric literature. To read up on Kuṇḍalinī, to think or talk about her, let alone visualise her, was frowned upon. In Osho's opinion, the Kuṇḍalinī and the cakras can only be perceived when they are obstructed. When no blockage exists, there is no resistance and the practitioner feels nothing. You know you are successful when you don't notice anything.

Let's explore the genuine tradition. One of the earliest surviving Tantras (it might date around 800 CE), the *Vīṇāśikhatantra*, a text that was very influential in South East Asia, contains the major elements which would become the Kuṇḍalinī later on. The first is a meditation on fire and water. The Sādhaka raises the fire of the End of Time from the soles of his feet and fans it with the fire mantra. *He should then burn his own body [in meditation] and cause it to overflow with Water-of-Life. Having burnt his mortal body so that it as it were is left as a heap of ashes, he should then meditate on a 'body of wisdom' which is [constituted]by showers of Water-of-Life; and on the supreme Syllable Oṁ, directed downward, [with Amṛta] streaming on one's head.* (72-73, trans. Teun Goudriaan). That's it. The practice involves death, purification, and resurrection in a new, pure body. It can be traced to the meditations of early Chinese alchemy and maybe even to Babylonian purification rituals; I discussed the subject at length in *Kālī Kaula* and in the *Seven Names of Lamaštu*. The other elements are a visualisation of Śiva in his form as Tumburu, above the heart, in the central channel, or in the channels to the sides, for purposes of magic. The Sādhaka transforms into this special Śiva, thereby gaining the power to work magic in his own or other people's interest. And finally, there is a meditation hinted at which requires the practitioner to raise his awareness to a point twelve fingers above his head. All of these visualisations can be found, to a greater or lesser extent, in the later Kuṇḍalinī rituals. However, at the time they were still distinct; and the personal deity, though active in the central channel, remains alone. The duality of Śakti longing to meet Śiva is absent, and indeed, though Śiva is surrounded by four terrifying Śaktis in the four directions of the cosmos, these are not his lovers but his sisters. Similar techniques, involving fire and water, and a stunning range of cakras, appear in other classical Tantras.

Now for another early Text, the *Prapañcasāra Tantra*; it dates from around the end of the first millennium of the Common Era. The work is massive, deep and beautiful; it covers a stunning range of rituals, yantras, mantras and meditations. Anyone who wants to explore real Tantra should get a copy. What appears like Kuṇḍalinī yoga is limited to a mere two verses:

When meditated upon – she who is a radiance as bright as a flash of lightning, subtle in nature and the very fine root cause of all fires – is rising up from the Mūlādhāra to the head like a needle moving through the path of suṣhumnā. Assimilated into the sun, there at once flows nectar from the association of the sun and moon. She who descends onto the head as a stream of nectar droplets becomes all the letters [and] with them she reconstructs the entire body beginning with the head. Descending inside a [streak of] radiant energy she rekindles one's own radiant energy like a fire made of clarified butter. (10, 7-8, trans. Louise Finn).

I am sure you noticed that the goddess who rises is not called Kuṇḍalinī, that she is not visualised as a snake and that she doesn't meet Śiva and Absolute Reality at the crown of the head. However, she moves in the central channel. Her ascent is associated with fire and her descent with a stream of nectar. The reconstruction of the adept's new body happens in a flow of vibration/sound: the sacred phonemes of the 'alphabet' and the categories of reality each sound is related to. This, for many tāntrikas, was an essential. It rarely appears in western books on yoga.

A fourteenth-century text, the *Toḍala Tantra* (see Sanjukta Gupta's fascinating translation in White 2000:463-488) supplies more details. By the time, Kuṇḍalinī yoga was well developed. That, however, was no reason to make it easy for the readers. Our text briefly outlines the cakras. Then, please read this carefully, follows practical advice:

The liberating [yogic duct, called nadī] Mahādhīrā ranges from rasātala to the end of satya, which exists inside the central [channel, that is, the spinal column, meru]. Mahāviṣṇu Śiva resides in the satya region and Vāsukī is full of intense longing to meet him. When Vāsukī, having pierced the six regions (cakras), rises up [to the region of satya], all the other flowing rivers [that is, the ducts] become upward flowing. In the body [the microcosm], O sovereign goddess, the ducts remain in the following order. If [the Sādhaka] presses down air through both the iḍā and the piṅgalā ducts, which have the suṣumṇā between them, O sovereign goddess, while repeating the prāṇa mantra [so'haṁ], the coiled one [Vāsukī] starts [moving upward through the suṣumṇa] following the order of the [six cakras], until she approaches the eternal and immutable lotus [the Sahasrāra cakra]. With anxiety the coiled one enters that eternal abode. Simultaneously all other downward-flowing [ducts] start flowing upstream. Then while repeating mentally 108 times his chief (mūla) mantra [received from his preceptor at the time of initiation] the intelligent [Sādhaka] should bring the coiled one back to his mulhādhāra cakra [her original resting place] in the same way, while refreshing the gods of the six cakras with the nectar [from the thousand petalled lotus].

In this text, the Fire Serpent appears under the name Vāsukī, i.e. the Nāga king Vāsuki in female form. That's because Kuṇḍalinī is a female force, a Śakti. Śakti (here: *consciousness-in-form-and-energy*) wants to reunite with Śiva (here: *formless consciousness*), who resides at the top of the head or above, the sahasrāra cakra. The human body represents the sacred Mount Meru. The abode of the Fire Snake is at the root cakra, the mulhādhāra (*root-support*). Various traditions locate it in different places. For now, two favourites are the base of the spine or the perineum. The root cakra, for good or bad, is the reality-forming circle (cakra) that creates the world (and you) in its densest, most physical aspect. Many yogīs abhorred it. For them, the physical world was a realm of delusion, temptation and bondage. Tantrics of the Left-Hand Path delighted in it. They believed that the very things that form obstacles to most people can lead to liberation, if handled wisely. The root cakra, of course, isn't limited to the base of the body. In Buddhist Tantra the Fire Snake or its equivalents tend to rise from the navel or more often, from the heart. In this model, the three essential cakras are in the heart, the throat and the head. The satya region is the realm of truth, of *that what is*; it is assumed to be at the top of the head or above, the realm of formless consciousness. That's the sahasrāra cakra, the lotus with a thousand petals, within or outside your cranium, depending on what your guru says. The force of union is intense longing. Unless you can build up that emotion until it blows your mind, your Fire Snake won't move much. Visualisation without feeling and desire fails. Our adept (sādhaka, female: sādhikā) has to put plenty of effort into the meditation. Not that effort is enough: the rising of the Kuṇḍalinī is a gift. You can't force it. You can merely create conditions where it wants to occur naturally. It can take five minutes or fifty years. The three channels are occult anatomy. It's extremely complicated. Here, I would just like to state that the central channel runs along the subtle equivalent of the spine, which is also the world pillar and the axis mundi, Śiva's liṅga and the tree of life. Along this pillar are the cakras. There are few or plenty of them; the seers never agreed on a specific number. In an early Hindu format there are three (belly, heart, head), but other sources speak of five, seven, nine, eleven and many more. All of these are right: the cakras ain't organs: we are talking about models. Each cakra represents a union of Śakti and Śiva, a specific reality and the skills you need to master it. The Fire Snake, ascending fast or slow, in leaps, like creeping ants or in stages, annihilates each cakra that it passes. Kuṇḍalinī rising is not a way to light up in happiness and splendour: the ascent of the Fire Snake dissolves each cakra, and the reality it represents, and the 'you' who experiences it. That's why this practice is called Laya-Yoga: the *Union of Dissolution*.

Liberation requires the annihilation of everything. But don't worry: you can't remain formless forever, and when you come down again, the cakras are back in business. You need them to keep your reality balanced.

Two of the major yogīc ducts are to the right and left of the central channel; they are the moon and sun channel. You can make much of them or dismiss them. Some yogīs try to stop their flow, so the central channel gets an overdose, others are aware that all channels, all bodies and indeed anything with a name or an identity is a metaphor for a nameless reality, and ignore them. Holding breath or not is a matter of choice. There are people who knot themselves into painful postures to raise the Kuṇḍalinī, while others relax, feel good and imagine that they are the Fire Snake, or Manasā, rising up within the world Mountain to meet Śiva at the top.

In our text, the adept repeats the mantra '**So'haṁ**'. It means *'I am He'*, i.e. Śiva, the state of formless awareness. Others say '**Sa'haṁ**, meaning *'I am She'*, i.e. the goddess of their choice, understood as supreme and formless consciousness. Or they say, like the Krama tantrics, '**Āhaṁ**' *'I am'*, if they are aware that they are everything. Sure, we seem to deal with mantras. Everyone knows that mantras are sung, whispered or imagined. But the real recitation is way beyond words. So'haṁ, Sa'haṁ and Āhaṁ are references of the sound of inbreath and outbreath. As Kuṇḍalinī rises we focus on the one natural mantra which requires no effort: natural breath. This is the Haṁsa bird, the waterbird which is at home in all worlds, the vehicle of spirit that transcends all realms and limitations.

Finally, after experiencing bliss in formless-consciousness, Kuṇḍalinī descends. Does she? In reality, you do. In flowing downwards, the cakras reappear. So do the worlds they represent and the 'mental organs' which maintain them. The process is accompanied by a shower of heavenly elixir which refreshes your body, mind, self and reality. It's as simple as that.

There are plenty of approaches to raise the Kuṇḍalinī. In early tantric literature, complicated mantras and visualisation generally did the job. If that didn't help, the blessings of the guru or the personal deity produced success. Physical effort was not required. Later adepts, inspired by the newly invented haṭhayoga, devoted decades of strenuous and often painful exercise to raise their Fire Snake. Others gave themselves into the hands of the gods: the rising of the Kuṇḍalinī was a descent of divine grace (Śaktipāta), a treasured gift from the All-Self to the individuals self. Some promoted asceticism, starvation and sexual abstinence; others employed exhausting gymnastic techniques. Eventually, a large group of practitioners (mainly among the Śrī Vidyā tantrics) stopped all physical effort and focussed on visualisation and meditation. Internal worship, they announced, takes longer, but is less likely to cause physical harm or insanity.

Many adepts ignored the serpent metaphor. They identified Kuṇḍalinī as their personal deity, or indeed their incarnate self. Strictly speaking, there is no 'soul' in Indian lore. Instead, there is a phenomenon called jiva, meaning something like *life,* or *life- energy*. When jiva is incarnate, in a body, an identity, a lifetime, it is 'your' personal soul. After death it loses its personification and returns into the All-Self.

At this point we can forget all snake imagery, unless your personal deity happens to be a serpent deity. Your personal deity is the Kuṇḍalinī. You, made perfect, are the Kuṇḍalinī. Simultaneously, the merry-go-round of secret techniques disintegrates. When Kuṇḍalinī is you and you are Kuṇḍalinī, and the whole world you experience is an activity of Kuṇḍalinī, your major effort isn't fancy technique but remembering. It is you who rise, and shed all forms and aspects of personality. And it is you who descend level after level, assuming shape and flesh and function in this world. It is you who yearns to unite with the All-self, and you who desires to be an individual, to dance your way among the mirages and realities of manifest life. This you is only you, when manifest, and indescribably you, when free of limitations.

Many New Age writers claim that Kuṇḍalinī is the bundled and technically applied sexual energy. Of course they are right. Everybody is, most of the time. However, sexual energy is just a tiny aspect of Kuṇḍalinī. Indeed, anything which makes up the cluster of consciousness and identification which you consider yourself is Kuṇḍalinī. Self is Kuṇḍalinī. Not-self is Kuṇḍalinī. The world is Kuṇḍalinī. Bondage is Kuṇḍalinī. Transcendence is Kuṇḍalinī. If you think this is crazy, I agree. Craziness is sanity and vice versa, and both are Kuṇḍalinī. Anything you can perceive or make up or be or imagine is an activity of Kuṇḍalinī.

Call it the world. Call it yourself. Occasionally, it's the Fire Serpent. Or it's your personal deity, or deities. Or it's yourself as you will be in better days. Or maybe it's just the name of an approach.

A long time before the Kuṇḍalinī concept developed, Tantric practitioners used to travel up and down a range of worlds/realities or consciousness stages. Call it 'journeys in the imagination', 'astral projection' or 'shamanic flight' if you like. These spheres of experience and awareness were related to the spine and to various centres of power, the cakras. A cakra can be a circle. It can appear as a complicated graphical diagram. Or as a blossom, a light, a jewel, a place, a temple, a palace, city or landscape. It can be a state of awareness, a set of functions, a biosphere or an entire world. Many people believe that cakras are an occult (*hidden*) reality. In their mindset, cakras are esoteric organs. In truth, each cakra is a metaphor. 'Metaphor' means something that carries across a specific meaning. A metaphor doesn't have to be real or true, as long as it conveys the proper idea, and works. Cakras are metaphors. Different people need different models. That's why some systems acknowledge three (head, heart, and belly) cakras, while others identify four, five, six, seven, eight, nine, ten, eleven, thirteen, fifteen or more. Some tantric texts mention hundreds, thousands or millions of cakras. Our world is a vast and miraculous place. And, luckily, everyone is right. We are not talking esoteric 'reality' but practical application. Nor are we evaluating results: some people get the same effects with three cakras as other people with sixteen.

The same applies to the Kuṇḍalinī. What is visualised as a 'Fire Serpent' in some systems, is a pillar of sheer energy/sentience in others, a tree, a lotus flower, a mountain of enlightenment, the personal deity, or a pair of personal deities in loving embrace, or you, or not you, or the you beyond you, or one hell of a lot of other experiences that defy words. Call it the manifest self. Or call it the All-Self, manifesting in different degrees of reality. Call it consciousness, or Manasā. Or call it Neta, if it means death, purification, transcendence and having a good laugh. The serpent form is just one useful metaphor among many. So where are we? The serpent doesn't travel up your spine. You do. Or the you who is beyond your usual identity, call it your personal deity, or your true self, or whatever. And it's not your spine; the spine is just a model for many states of awareness.

In short, you are supposed to make up a range of experiences that take you beyond what you assumed yourself to be. That's why the process is so enigmatic. Every successful practitioner invented something good and worthwhile, and original.

In tantric terminology, the raising of Kuṇḍalinī is a technical approach to liberation. No matter which system you employ, the practices promise a result. In some systems this means twenty years of daily āsana practice and damaged joints, in others you are supposed to repeat a secret mantra a few hundred thousand times or visualise complicated geometrical shapes, complete with deities, buildings, animals and whatnot, all over your body. All of these methods work. However, they do not work for everyone. That's why so many different techniques developed. If any given method were perfect, everybody would use it.

The counterpart to Kuṇḍalinī is called **Sahaja** (*spontaneity*). Sahaja means that the act of grace happens naturally, without effort, strife, technique or control. In tantric literature, as John Woodroffe explained at length, Sahaja is far superior to Kuṇḍalinī.

Sahaja can happen anytime. It can occur when you have practised hard for decades and it can happen when you are waiting for the bus. It can be the outcome of loving devotion to a deity. At this point, Manasā, Śiva and Neta come in. Maybe you sense them so intensely that the experience shakes you to the core. Maybe they grant you an insight that turns your world-view upside down. Maybe they kick you out of the narrow confines of identification which constitute your personality.

Call it obsession, if you like. Usually, what I experience is something like this. When Manasā takes over, my mind goes drifting along avenues of thought. It's easy to get lost in them. The neural networks extend everywhere. When Neta rises, I turn into a happy skeleton, and laugh a lot, as every experience is wonderful and terrible and a joke. When Śiva moves me, I like to lean back and let the world go on. I grin, feel happy, and relax. That's three options, and there are more. Every deity has their own take on reality, and all of them are Kuṇḍalinī. Or none of them are. The concept can be meaningful, or meaningless; chose what you like and make it real.

Kuṇḍalinī is the force that assembles and dissolves each and every experience. The same goes for Manasā, who is pure awareness, consciousness, thinking, experience. Manasā, in this sense, is the heart, the centre of awareness, the root of all thoughts, the core of your experience and the reality you deem to manifest. Whatever you be-live is the heart. Your inner world and your outside universe are manifestations of your heart. Call it a self or not-self: it's Manasā. Intelligence is everywhere.

Our inner processes have a complexity that defies our comprehension. We think that we think, we shape beliefs and create reality and history as we go along. It's amazing that we notice 'outside reality' at all, provided we do, which I doubt. In plain fact, we are all tied up, coiled up and knotted within ourselves. Inside and outside: both are Manasā. Manasā is Kuṇḍalinī. She is you and you are her, and for obvious reasons the 'you' part of her often leaves her amazed, confused and speechless. "Why do people fuss about identity," she asks, "when they ain't happy with it?

Neta has an easier life. She has seen it all before. "People are funny," she says. "Life can be tragedy or comedy. It's your choice. Which part do you play? The Lovable Loser? Ah!" she laughs, "You know that one. We all know how to lose. You think you are a winner? Then you're a loser thrice over, and hit the ground much harder. Winners are hilarious. Losers remain honest. Here, hold this piece. I need to unravel the guts." She hands you something yucky. "Don't complain," she says, "It's just a bit of carrion. It will rot. And it can only get better. So tell me of your life. Who else could you be? The Sarcastic Bystander, like me? The Confused Thinker, like my sister? The Spiteful One? The Sex Addict? Or the Greedy Exploiter, like Cāndo? The Altruistic Helper? The miserable Give-up Failure? The Enlightened Dropout, like Śiva? The Aggressor, or the Placator? The Hopeless Endurer? The Fluffy-minded Time-Waster? The Naive or Childish One? The Chronic Complainer? The deluded Tyrant? The Intellectual Dis-associator? The insecure, worried Control-Freak; hey Viṣṇu, don't think that I don't talk about you! I know you listen! Or, my favourite, Caught up in your Personal Reality?" She shakes her head. "We do it all the time. Don't worry. I like your show. I like your effort. You do your best. But let's face it: People are silly and so are their gods. The more serious you get, the sillier you are. We're all like that. And we are needed. We have our part in the play. We make it funny and exciting. We make it liveable, no matter how much it hurts. And we are better off than others. Let's face it; the Loveable Loser is at the heart of comedy. You have a major advantage over one who isn't loveable. And we all lose, no matter how much we struggle; people, planets, deities; we fail and age and fall apart. Everybody is bound to fail. It ends up on my shore. I do the washing. You come to me, whether you like it or not. My question: can you do it with a laugh?"

Part Six:

Venoms and Elixirs

Picture 49: Nāga girls, Down in the Seventh Underworld.

40. Drugs and Spices

The *Manasā Epic* revolves around chemistry. In this context, chemistry is first of all a key to the moods and feelings that make life worth living: the hormones and neurotransmitters that allow us to make ourselves happy, sad, enthusiastic, bored, tired, awake, calm, and excited, that allow us to experience lust, love, joy, sadness, bitterness and sorrow. All of these have a neural and a chemical foundation. Our brain and glands are drug factories: their output gives meaning and texture to our dream of life. We are talking drugs, our own and those ingested and otherwise consumed. In our story, three characters symbolise drug dependency.

Śiva craves psychedelic drugs and ascetic sobriety. He represents transcendence, immanence, transcendence-immanence plus the incomprehensible. That makes him a stunningly superior god, but, life being what it is, the manifest world with all its limitations gets him down. Nor is he really happy as a family man. His life is a series of conflicts between cosmic awareness, strong instincts and the need to blow himself out of his skull. They make him such a vivid, enigmatic character.

Manasā stands for poisons, medicines and the power over life and death. Her major drug is worship: she craves to be loved, acknowledged or, at the very least, feared.

Cāndo became perversely rich by trading spices, scents, opium, hemp, arsenic and luxury goods. He sells drugs, desires and illusions, and is hooked on wealth, power and status. Behind his mask of arrogance he feels deeply inferior. That's why he needs the outer signs of affluence and success. He wants to own the world and the gods. They should fill the hole in his soul. Few people realise this, but work and more work are addictive. That's not a metaphor, but biochemistry.

Compared to these three, Behulā, taking the corpse of her husband on a journey and Neta, wallowing in underwear and corpses, are remarkably sane.

Psychedelic drugs affect us as they are similar to the chemicals which we produce within ourselves. Consider Cāndo's trade empire. He wasn't the first nor will he be the last to make amazing profits from spices. Spices and scents seem harmless until you realise what really happens. Scent is a perfect vehicle for manipulation. It goes directly into the brain without being edited, and it's very hard to ignore. Numerous spices share a common chemistry with mind-altering substances. Sure, in many cases, the dose is minute. It has been questioned if mind-altering chemicals make it through the blood-brain barrier. That question, though important, could be misleading. Our brain is not the only place where consciousness is engineered. You use the same neurotransmitters in your brains and in your guts. The intestines are a remarkably complex system that can function pretty much on its own. Sure, the brain can influence the belly. But when they like to, your guts can shut off all signals from the brain and do their job as they please. Indeed, in the lab, immersed in a solution and fed with nourishment, the guts can survive without a body, and function perfectly. Your intestines are the third nervous system. They have been overlooked for decades. Nowadays, researchers are amazed at their intelligence. When you ingest food, your guts identify the hundreds or thousands of chemical components it is composed of and set up a complicated program to dissolve and re-compose them. They decide what is edible, what is waste, and what, in emergency cases, needs to be evicted as vomit or diarrhoea. In short, a lot of our thinking happens in our bellies. Amazingly complex nervous clusters deal with spices, and there is no brain-blood barrier to shield them from the drugs they contain. Consider this: spices are addictive. And they are, like so many plant products, complicated. Regarding most plants, the biochemists hardly know what they contain; let alone how the stuff interacts. Studies indicate that people who refrain from spices tend to go depressive or violent. Bland food is a sure way to ruin the day.

Whatever it may be, we are talking drugs. Let's start with the dopamine cascade. It begins with tryptophan. It is easily available from meat, milk, cheese, but can also be found, in small amounts, in a few other foods. The effect is stronger when combined with carbohydrates, like bread, potatoes or noodles. People who go for special diets, like macrobiotics, vegetarians and vegans have to be careful to ingest enough of it. Otherwise, they tend to go depressed, angry or become sugar junkies. Sugar supplies a serotonin kick. Mind you, in people who lack tryptophan, it is remarkably short-lived. But tryptophan is not enough. You also need saturated fats, meaning animal products, to make them really functional. Your metabolism transforms tryptophan into tryptamine, which is turned into serotonin. Serotonin made it into the headlines. The pharma-industry and the media call it the 'happiness chemical', which is wrong, but makes great profits. Serotonin doesn't make you happy. However, if you lack the stuff, you will be badly misaligned. Serotonin is something like a chemical Swiss army knife: it has many functions in your brain and your digestive tract. One of its derivates is dopamine. Here we are getting to the point. Dopamine is excellent to make you alert, interested, involved and is essential for learning. It docks in at the so-called 'pleasure centres', like the nucleus accumbens of the brain. Whenever you feel really good and happy, dopamine is involved. This is where the action is. Maybe you like to dance, to listen to music, go to the theatre, read literature or cheap thrillers, cook gorgeous menus, turn lovemaking into a fine art or visit museums. Maybe you laugh with your kids, play with a pet animal, go out with your friends, have shopping fits or enjoy it when your garden thrives. All of these activities release dopamine and make you happy, alert and awake. They add meaning to life, and make it worth the effort. Some people want a stronger kick. Maybe you prefer risk sports, excessive or illicit sex or hard drugs. Maybe you gamble like mad, or turn to shoplifting. Or you prefer action movies, soap-operas or internet porn. Anything addictive on TV, in music and in art survives thanks to a dopamine kick. Whenever you go happy and excited, dopamine plays a part. The phenomenon called 'culture' is based on dopamine.

Look at the drugs that people crave! Each of them, no matter whether we talk alcohol, tobacco, amphetamines, hashish, opiates, LSD, mescaline or ecstasy, becomes alluring, habit-forming or addictive thanks to the dopamine cascade. Sure, they all produce different consciousness states. Their chemistry is poles apart, and really complicated. And just as true, each person has a different response to them. But what makes them overwhelmingly seductive is the release of dopamine, or the delay in dopamine re-absorption. Either way, you get an overdose of exciting happiness-inducing-chemicals docking in at your nucleus accumbens. Sure, there are differences of degree. Methamphetamines may accelerate the dopamine kick by 800%. That's more than you get when you hug your kids, play an instrument or marvel at the beauty of a sunset. Nevertheless, all happy experiences involve dopamine. Whatever makes life meaningful: dopamine makes you crave more (Milkman & Sunderwirth, 2010:35-43).

Food culture is drug culture. If you only needed nourishment, a few simple and bland substances would do the job. Some vitamins, minerals, fats, carbohydrates and proteins would satisfy anyone. You could eat the same yuck every day and be happy. But that's not the case. People want more than survival; they crave dopamine. One result is refined cuisine.

Directly after you were born, your mother turned you into an opium addict. Mother's milk, and even more so, cow's milk (just like cheese, curd etc) are full of morphine. These seductive painkillers guarantee that baby gets sleepy and isn't bothered by a belly ache. Maybe this also says something about Hindu deities, who can't get enough of milk products.

There are amphetamines in blood and meat and plenty of morphine in wheat and rice. One friend, he's a cook, says "Noodles make you happy." In the dark season, he colours them with turmeric. That's great against winter-depressions. How about noodles (opiates) with cheese (opiates) and tomato sauce? Tomatoes contain tryptamine and serotonin and, in some varieties, acetaldehyde, which can be transformed into alkaloids by your metabolism. Slow heating brings out the optimum. Especially when tomatoes are combined with vinegar, i.e. ketchup. When methyl, which is widely available, fuses with serotonin, the result is bufotenin, a hallucinogenic substance known from toad skins. It's similar to mescaline. And when methyltransferase, widely available in organic structures, combines with tryptophan, you get DMT. Sure, as with most spices, the dose is small. Some claim it's hardly noticeable. But people love the mixture and find it appetising, no matter whether they douse tomato salad in vinegar or put ketchup on their burger. Ask your taste buds! They'll lead you to the drugs that brighten up your life!

Meat supplies plenty of β-carbolines. We are talking about alkaloids which reduce depression and fear, and act as MAO blockers. In the process, they slow down the re-absorption of serotonin and noradrenaline, which increases the available amount of these substances in your brain. Small doses promote well being; large doses can lead to hallucinations, vomiting and confusion. A few β-carbolines like harmane, norharmane and harmine can dock in at benzodiazepine receptors. They reduce fear and worry. You encounter high amounts of β-carbolines in grilled meat, especially in fried chicken. And in marinated flesh: the marinade, containing sour substances like vinegar and lemon juice, promotes the production of alkaloids. There are β-carbolines in artificial flavouring, such as fake chicken aroma: the producers combine amino-acids like tryptophan or cysteine with sugars.

How about fruit and vegetables? Cāndo, half-starved and desperate, wanted to eat banana peels. Manasā stopped him. Maybe they would have made him unduly cheerful. Bananas contain tyramine, serotonin and dopamine, especially in the dark spots, where salsolinol interacts with the amines. The concentration is strongest in the peels. In many tropical countries, bananas are eaten entirely. Considering that supermarket bananas are sterile triploid genetic cripples, and that they are drenched in pesticides, I wouldn't recommend it. Similar compounds as in bananas can be found in citrus fruit. Former alcoholics tend to consume orange juice (or vitamin C) in large amounts, just like former junkies go for milk products (= opiates). Plums, an all-time favourite of the Daoists, contain serotonin. In Yunnan, I visited the Hei Long Tan (Black Dragon Lake) temple near Kunming a couple of times, where more than a hundred varieties of plums are cultivated. The local priesthood loved them. They also invested plenty of effort into reforesting the hillsides, cut down during the Mao era, with conifers. When they invited me for tea, a monk, using sign language, encouraged me to go to the hilltop. I showed him the pictures in my camera; a huge dragonfly on a thistle, right before the pagoda. I had been there before I went to the temple, as in genuine Daoism, mountains and rivers come first. It was quite in contrast to the Buddhist temples nearby, where nobody gave a damn for nature, the monks were quarrelsome and greedy, and tossed their rubbish anywhere. The effect of plums, of course, is stronger when they are concentrated as jam.

How about a nice slice of toast (wheat-opiates, made stronger by toasting) with marmalade? Bitter oranges and their peels contain synephrine, closely related to noradrenaline. It raises blood pressure, makes you awake and acts anti-depressive. Add sugar, which releases serotonin and is highly addictive. Just the stuff for the breakfast table! Have a cup of chocolate! It contains a high amount of salsolinol, neuroactive alkaloids and anandamide. Those who prefer bitter chocolate favour the effects of methylxanthine, especially theobromine. It sedates, relaxes, improves the blood circulation and docks in at the receptors for THC (i.e. cannabis). Those who prefer milk chocolate increase their serotonin production. The exorphins in milk powder provide an extra kick. How about a nice beer in the evening? Barley is great in tyramine, which transforms into hordenine, and resembles dopamine so closely that it docks in at the dopamine receptors. Hops are closely related to hemp and contain THC, an active ingredient of hashish. Beer drinkers shouldn't condemn dope heads: both are hooked on similar chemistry. Hops are an excellent sedative and contain so many female hormones that women who harvest hops can expect to menstruate on the first day. Regular beer drinkers can grow an impressive set of tits (Pollmer, 2010).

Let's look at spices. A typical Indian speciality are curries. Most of them are a lot hotter than the tame yellow stuff you see in supermarkets in Europe and America. Each of them is a blend of spices. Two essential ingredients are peppers (preferably Indian long pepper, which is a lot stronger than the white and black variety) and turmeric, which provides the happy yellow colour. Incidentally, our word 'pepper' comes from Saṁskṛta 'pippalī'. When the British introduced chilli to India, it also went into the mixture. Now for the fun bit. Why do people, especially in the tropics, eat food that makes Europeans gasp for air? One reason is the endorphin release. Your mouth identifies the spices as a burn and releases your body's self-made morphine, i.e. painkillers. They provide a high, similar to the states experienced by exhausted marathon runners and half-starved dieters, anorectics, bulimics and chilli junkies. No, this is no joke. All of them are addicted to the same chemistry as opium, morphine or heroin. It's just they cook up their own drugs, using pain, hunger and nightmare, instead of acquiring them at street corners. Next, there's the parasites. Hot spices eliminate worms and other bugs that might infest your bowels. Third, hot spices actually lower the temperature of the body. That's useful when you live in a scorching climate. But the main reason is medical. Various types of malaria have killed roughly half of the people who ever lived. The malaria parasites infect red blood corpuscles. Piperine, an active ingredient of peppers, transforms the ionic channels of the corpuscles. It kills malaria parasites. The same happens when you eat chillies. Turmeric (Cucurma ssp.), which seems like a harmless plant of the ginger family, has a similar effect. In short, curry is a powerful drug. People who ate really hot had a better survival chance than those who avoided spices. Natural selection did the rest: spice lovers stood a better chance to breed and pass on their genes. It might explain why pepper was so popular in Medieval Europe. Malaria is not a tropical disease. Up to the early twentieth century, the marshlands near London, the swamps of Northern Germany and the stale side-arms of Rhine and Danube were famous breeding grounds for anopheles mosquitoes. People believed the disease came from gasses, bad air (mal-aria), or from the night air, but it was a specific mosquito that transferred the infection. The dear little thing came out by nightfall, as strong light blinds its eyes. Mosquitoes need slow or stale water to breed their young. It might seem coincidental, but the European demand for pepper dropped while swamps and marshlands were drained. It was even more reduced when china-bark, quinine, became widely available. And while we are at it, the spices in curry also work against trypanosomes, against tuberculosis and amoebic dysentery. Turmeric improves the digestion, has an anti-bacterial effect and seems to fight tumours. These days, many people use it against cancer.

Plenty of spices have a psychoactive effect. It doesn't mean they make you hallucinate. However, they promote digestion and improve your mood.

To this day, the most expensive spice is saffron (Crocus sativus). It is won by picking the tiny yellow stamens within the flower of the purple crocus. You need 100,000-200,000 blossoms to collect a kilogram. The drug was mostly produced in the Near East, using slave labour (nowadays, most of it comes from Spain). It tastes slightly bitter and mildly hot, and produces an intensely yellow colour. The spice stimulates the heart and reduces the growth of tumours. 20 grams can be lethal. Also, for reasons that have eluded chemists so far, the plant has a mild psychoactive effect, and became an all-time favourite.

Another expensive drug is nutmeg (Myristica fragrans). It used to be so rare, that in the Medieval Period, it wasn't used in the kitchen. Instead, rich aristocrats and churchmen carried their own little nutmeg scraper, and spiced their dishes personally. The Dutch once monopolised the market, and burned immense amounts of nuts in Indonesia, in Amsterdam and Middleburg to keep the price high. The chemistry isn't really nice. Some people have died after eating two nuts. They contain elemicin and myristicin, which belong to the family of allylbenzoles. Allylbenzoles appear in many spices. There is apiol in parsley, eugenol in pimento and cloves. Your body can transform them, to a smaller or greater extent, into amphetamines. The liver reformats the nutmeg chemicals into the amphetamines MMDA (similar to 'ecstasy') and TMA (close to mescaline). In small doses, nutmeg can be a stimulant. In large doses, it can destroy the liver.

I am sure Cāndo would have approved of the German Christmas Markets. He just wouldn't have gone there. Imagine small fun fairs with little booths selling jewellery, warm clothes, wellness products, incense, candles, handicrafts, toys, semi-precious stones, hand-made soap, grilled liver, pork kidneys and sausages. The night comes early. There are lights everywhere, carousels whirl, children go mad on sugar and people stand in the cold to drink hot spiced wine. Usually, it's the worst wine imaginable. The stuff is full of tannins and biogenic amines. Like all plants, grapes use many toxins to protect themselves from fungi, insects, mites and microbes. When you make white wine, you simply crush the grapes and ferment the juice. Do that with red grapes and you get rose wine. If you want to make red wine, you have to leave the crushed grapes in the broth. The plant toxins, and all the chemicals the wine grower used to protect the grapes, go into the drink. He used plenty: grapes are often sprayed more than twenty times before they can be harvested. The same goes for 'organic' wine, which is usually drenched in extremely toxic copper derivates. As a result, red wine is far more likely to give you a headache than white. Hot spicy wine is traditionally made from the worst red wine. It has to be. The stuff is heated in large pots, and plenty of spices are tossed into the broth. Typical mixtures emphasise nutmeg, cinnamon and cloves (both provide allylbenzine) and aniseed (propenylbenzine). Most people assume that the wine is spiced to improve its taste and smell. It's the alcohol, they assume, which raises spirits and voices. In fact, the alcohol content is small. The broth is heated, often for hours, and much of the alcohol evaporates. Heat and alcohol activate the chemicals within the spices, and indeed, the more biogenic amines the wine contains, the stronger will the spices react. Your wine is full of amphetamines. The result is uplifting and produces terrifying hangovers. Similar spices are used for typical Christmas sweets. People who suffer from light deprivation often consume large amounts of sweets, and the amphetamines supplied by the spices may add an extra dose of cheerfulness. Lack of light is a key factor. Chocolate sales accelerate in winter. In springtime they drop; during summer and early autumn, they are low. When the dark returns, chocolate and sugar consumption accelerate (Pollmer, 2010:157-158).

Consider modern 'yogī tea'. It combines black tea (a stimulant) with cinnamon and cloves. You just met them as sources of amphetamines. But they also act against viruses, fungi and parasites. Another essential ingredient is cardamom (Elettaria cardamomum). Indians like to mix the spice with bhang (hemp). The essential oils have a sedative effect. They are also used as an aphrodisiac and to improve digestion. After a good meal, some Indians chew cardamom and other spices. Allegedly, it improves the breath. It certainly improves the mood. Ginger (Zingiber officinale) is another stimulant and aphrodisiac. It raises blood pressure and promotes digestion. That's a general idea. We are talking plant chemistry. It's amazingly complicated. What happens when the hundreds or thousands of chemicals in each spice encounter your metabolism is another question.

An all-time favourite is called bēl, or pan. More than half a billion people in India, southern China, Taiwan, Indonesia, Malaysia and along the East African coast consume it frequently. You face a large, green betel leaf (Piper betle) which has been rolled up like a cigar. It contains betelnut, (Areca catechu) and slaked lime, traditionally made from crushing coral, snail houses, or seashells. That's the foundation. Fresh betel leaf comes from a climbing vine, and is a strong stimulant. It makes you wide awake, euphoric and, in large doses, jittery and nervous. Regular use turns the teeth reddish black. Betel nut comes from the betel palm; it is another strong stimulant, an aphrodisiac and a wormkiller. It contains muscarine, which is also found in fly agaric. Alkaloids like arecoline, which is an MAO blocker, and guvacoline make friends with the lime and turn into arecaidine and guvacine. They slow down the re-absorption of GABA (gamma-amino-butyric-acid). The stuff acts as a neural inhibitor and is essential to calm you down and retain your peace of mind. Its counterpart is glutamate, which amplifies neural activity and makes you edgy and excited. Between themselves, the two sort you out. But things are never really simple: phenols like eugenol and isoeugenol release catecholamines in your body, and make blood pressure and temperature rise. 8-10g of betel nut can paralyse heart and lungs and kill.

And that's just the start. The rolled up bēl leaf may contain over sixty different spices and chemicals, including peppers, cinnamon, cloves, cumin, cardamom and sandalwood. South Indians frequently add tobacco to the blend. Some throw in thornapple (Datura stramonium) seeds, an import from America, which are mind-shattering, confusing and extremely toxic. According to contemporary Indian myth, Śiva consumes large amounts of them. I wouldn't recommend it, as thornapple, just like belladonna/deadly nightshade (Atropa lethalis) is really hallucinogenic, meaning, you forget that you are on drugs, and go utterly crazy. Galangal (Kaempferia galangal) is a common extra. That's another powerful stimulant, frequently used in Indian and Thai cuisine, and in Japanese incense. The pulverised root is an aphrodisiac, a strong stimulant and probably hallucinogenic. How about common bistort (Rauvolfia serpentina), otherwise known as snakeweed? Pulverised, the roots are used to lower blood pressure, to sedate and to create a euphoric, cheerful mood. Allegedly, it takes a few days of regular use to get an effect, which may last for a week or more. Some use the plant to improve their meditation. Gandhi drank a cup of rauvolfia tea every day. It helped to keep him calm and optimistic. Extended use can cause depression; large doses can kill (Pollmer, 2010, Alberts and Mullen, 2000 and 2003, *Palmengarten gut gewürzt* (catalogue, 2012) Roth, Daunderer & Kormann, 1994). Bēl users rarely know what they are using. They chew on the mixture for hours, and may even fall asleep, drooling, with the rolled up leaf stuck between their teeth. I was offered rolled pan leaves after participating in Durgā Pūjās at navarātra. The leaves and spices, I was told, had been freshly flown in that day. Just like the Ganges water which had been sprinkled over us. The taste was peculiar, exciting and astonishing. I just can't tell you about the effect. I was so high on ritual that the pan had no effect at all.

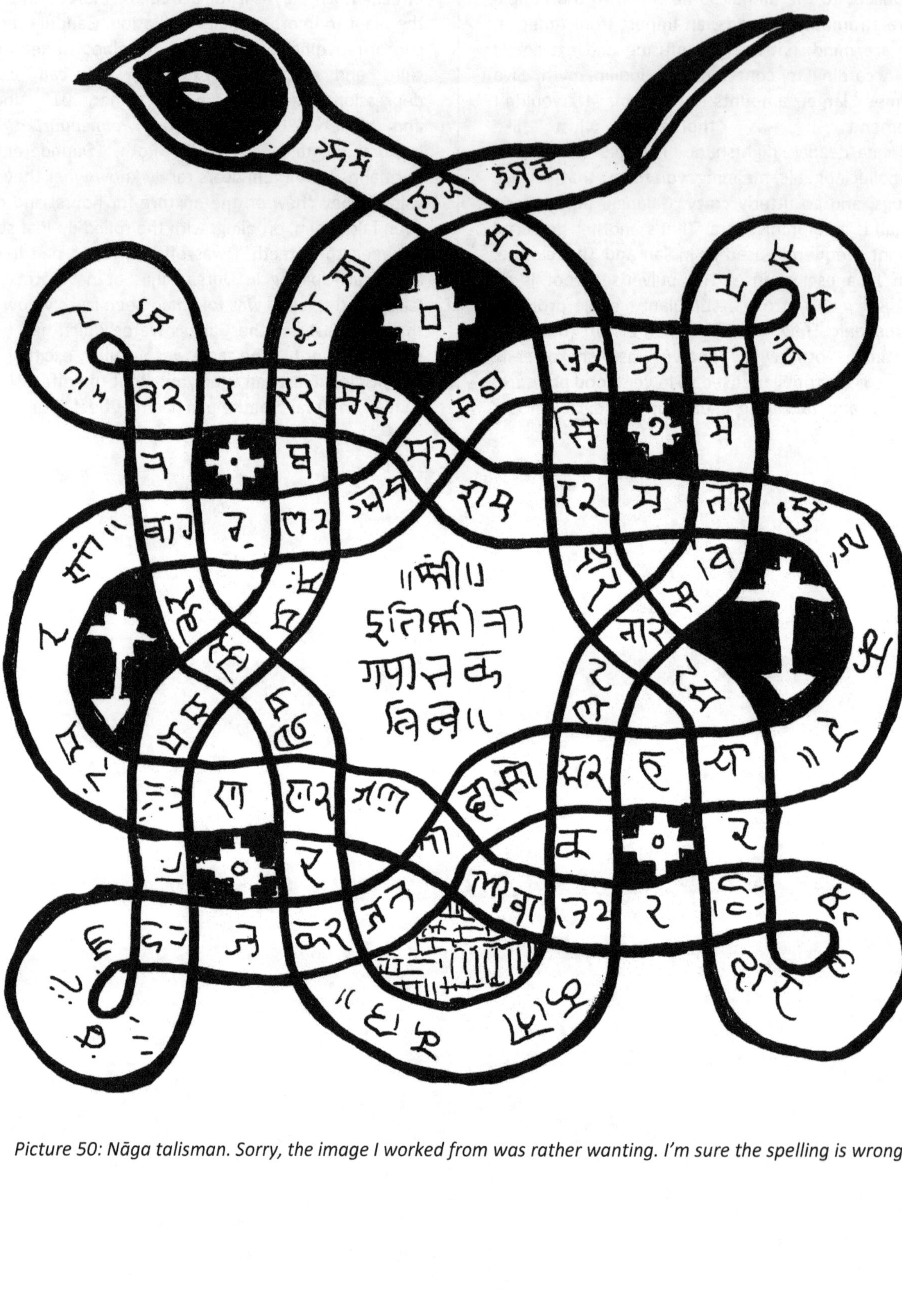

Picture 50: Nāga talisman. Sorry, the image I worked from was rather wanting. I'm sure the spelling is wrong.

41. Cāndo's Paradise

Trade in spices, silk, perfumes, jewels and rare woods goes back to prehistory. It was a small enterprise before the Common Era. Mesopotamian cooks, doctors and exorcists used many types of onion, garlic and leek, plus fennel, mustard, thyme, sage, origanum, mint, sumac, turmeric, cardamom, coriander, ginger, saffron, asafoetida, and cumin. During the Sumerian and Akkadian Period, sea trade with India was a major business. Around the start of the Old Babylonian Period (c. 2,000-1,800 BCE) the Indus Valley Culture disappeared and long-distance sea trade became unattractive. The Egyptians began to import cinnamon and cassia around 1,500 BCE. Other favourites were saffron, Indian peppers and ginger, valued for their taste and for their anti-bacterial, disinfecting ingredients, while thyme was employed during the mummification process. It contains one of the strongest disinfectants of the plant world.

The spice trade became a major enterprise in the first century of the Common Era, once the upper classes in Rome ceased to think like soldiers and developed a taste for luxury goods. The road to the east, in Roman times, was basically through Egypt. Traders floated their wares up the river Nile, packed them on camels, crossed the desert and sailed down the Red Sea. Later, they built a canal to shorten the journey. They followed the coasts of Arabia, passing Canam, and arrived in Barbaricum, Barigaza, Muziris (modern Cochin) and Korkai (near modern Tuticorin) and Trincomale, in Sri Lanka. Some even travelled to the Bay of Bengal. A few traders made it to Malaysia and at least one expedition to Cattigar in China. The journeys followed a timetable based on the monsoon and the prevailing winds. Usually, Roman and Greek traders had to stay in India for months before they could return home. Many acquired land, built houses and founded a second family. When conflicts escalated, two Roman legions were stationed at the coast of Malabar. The traders made immense profits. Asia provided luxuries, and the wealthy in far away Europe paid anything. The Indians were delighted to receive good Roman currency. They were less interested in the meagre trade goods that came in from Europe, such as metals, chemicals, wine and slaves. As a result, huge amounts of Roman coins went to India where they became one of the most popular currencies (Pollmer, 2010:26-29).

When the Roman Empire disintegrated, trade dwindled and almost disappeared. But no matter how poor people were, spices remained essential. In 408, when Alaric, king of the West Goths besieged Rome, he could still demand a payment of silver, gold and 3,000 pounds of pepper. It was the end of an epoch. As more and more migrants from Northern Europe set out to plunder Rome, life in Italy (and elsewhere) became too stressful. The Emperor packed his treasures and concubines, he moved to Constantinople (later known as Byzantium and Istanbul) and so did an important branch of the Christian church. In Italy, the economy went down the drain. Roman agriculture had depleted the soil, the slave-based economy collapsed and poverty became the norm. The poor Christians in Rome looked at the wealthy Christians in Constantinople and hated them. The next centuries were a nightmare. Hordes of Goths, Visigoths, Vandals, Huns, Franks, Vikings and Anglo-Saxons searched for better living spaces or simply went marauding as they liked. Europe ceased to be attractive for most merchants from the East; the place became a cultural backwater, illiterate, uncultured and poor, and remained that way for most of the early medieval period. Meanwhile, the Arabs, totally impoverished by the collapse of their trade in leather and merchandise, embraced a new religion. Islam became a unifying force linking countries from Spain to western China. You could call it a golden age, and in the wake of the gold, arts, science and culture developed. Europeans with access to the East, such as the Vikings, made enormous profits trading in slaves, amber, spices and furs. A branch of the Vikings, the Rhūs, controlled most trade between Baghdad, Constantinople, Eastern and Central Europe. Spices and luxury goods generally came in over Kiev, passed Cracow, Prague, Mainz, Ingelheim and were distributed overland and along rivers like the Vistula, Elbe, Main and Rhine. In turn, the traders supplied the Near East with enormous amounts of slaves: indeed, the word 'Slavs' is derived from 'slave'. As the Slavs were pagans, good Christians were allowed to capture and sell them.

Most of Europe was culturally isolated. The church did it's best to keep it so, ranting against dangerous delusions, such as science, mathematics and medicine. Several churchmen were against spices, such as Clemens of Alexandria and Tertullian (second century), who believed that spices incite people to gluttony and sin. But no matter how bitter life was, a trickle of Asian luxuries entered Europe, where they raised incredible prices. Again, spices, perfumes and silks made up the highlights. The rich, no matter how poor, crude and filthy they were, compared to the wealthy in Asia, had to show that they were better than the common population. Also, and this was just as vital, Central Europe has very little, except salt, to brighten up a meal. Meat was usually salted to conserve it. To make it edible, it had to be watered. The result was anything but delicious and spices were essential to make it palatable. The same went for meat which was slightly aged. Charlemagne passed an edict ordering monasteries to import and grow rosemary, sage and similar herbs, if the climate allowed it. In their wake, parsley, fennel, lovage, garlic, mint and celery entered Middle European cuisine, at least, where the church approved of such dangerous delicacies. They never reached the popularity of pepper. The rich wanted hot spices, no matter how much they cost. In 965, Ibrahim ibn Ya'qub, a trader from Spain, travelled as far as Mainz at the Rhine and recorded *It is extraordinary that one should be able to find, in such far western regions, aromatics and spices that only grow in the Far East, like pepper, ginger, cloves, nard, costus and galingale* (Lunde & Stone, 2012:162).

No matter how expensive, spices were essential. By and by, the rulers realised that Europe was losing money at an alarming rate. Asian luxury goods passed through plenty of hands before they arrived in some dull castle in the middle of nowhere with three heated rooms and no toilets. Every aristocrat paid dearly for pepper, cinnamon and nutmeg to keep up the reputation of his table. Indeed, medieval cookbooks reveal that far more pepper was used than today.

Mediterranean cities, like Venice, Pisa, Amalfi and Genoa made exceptional profits by trading with Constantinople, Baghdad and Alexandria. Soon other cities got involved along the trade routes and expanded: Naples, Perugia, Padua and Verona. In the wake of the money, culture, art and science developed. Sure, some thinkers north of the Alps, where life was plainly rubbish, did their best. Albertus Magnus, a genius in many disciples, studied plants and animals; he realised that science should be based on experiment, instead of gossip, and initiated an architecture 'of the Albertian style' that was subsequently known as 'gothic'. It was a major and wonderful achievement. However, it happened on a low budget.

Dealing with the Orient was dangerous. The merchants had to be fighters, strategists and diplomats; they had to get along with unbelievers, like Eastern Christians, Jews, and Muslims. The Mediterranean trade cities became incredibly rich, while the centre and north of Europe remained poor, primitive and mostly illiterate. When the economic situation became unbearable, the first crusade was initiated. Pope Urban II promised the knights salvation from all sins should they die fighting the infidels, and made them swear to liberate the tomb of Jesus and the holy city of Jerusalem. The European aristocracy and church wanted a foothold in the east, and tried to eliminate the middleman. They assumed that Asian luxuries came from the Near East. After the Crusaders had slaughtered the entire population of Jerusalem in July 1099, they realised that the expensive stuff came from elsewhere. The Second Crusade was even less concerned with religious elements. Bernard of Clairvaux appealed to the faithful, but he also announced that much profit could be made. While the church praised religious war, the masterminds had a different project in mind. The trusty knights were not even supposed to fight in the Holy Land. More interesting were Alexandria and the ports of Egypt, closely connected to the Indian trade. Those who consider the crusades as religious enterprises miss the point. Religion is for the faithful and the naive. That's the people who were sent to fight and die. The regents understood money, meaning spices and luxury goods. The next crusades were just as bad. In 1202, the Venetian fleet graciously supported the journey of the knights. As a small token of thanks, the knights destroyed the city of Zara in Dalmatia, a Christian city that had become a dangerous competitor of Venice. A little later, in 1204, the crusaders drenched Constantinople in blood. The pope in Rome was glad to see Eastern Christianity and its greatest trade port devastated. Another example: Richard 'Lionheart' slaughtered the inhabitants of Acre. The city was a fabulously wealthy trading centre. It had nothing to do with the 'religious' goals of the crusade.

During these centuries, wars, massacres and surprisingly peaceful periods alternated. The competing Italian trade cities established large communities in Near Eastern cities, where they fought it out among each other. Bold Europeans travelled to the Orient, where they discovered so much culture, wealth and scientific knowledge that returning home became a real challenge. When Britain's first scientist, Adelard of Bath, who had spent years researching in the libraries of Antioch and Damascus, came home to Britain, he *found the princes barbarous, the bishops bibulous, judges bribable, patrons unreliable, clients sycophants, promisers liars, friends envious and almost everybody full of ambition* (in Frankopan, 2015:146).

Crusades, and much of the trade to the Near East, came to a stop eventually. The European leaders quarrelled and in the Near East, Saladin proved to be exceptionally successful. The Crusaders had a tough time. Eventually, news from Central Asia came in: a huge Christian army, led by the legendary Prester John, was coming to support them. It was too good to be true. Prester John was a fiction and the army consisted of Mongols. Pretty much around the same time, Egypt became a difficult trade partner as the Mamluks gained control. Their taxes were too high. European traders had to reconsider. When the Mongols had finished slaughtering their way across Eurasia, and had accidentally spared poor Europe, the trade routes shifted. The Mongols may have started as brutal conquerors, using sheer savagery to create the largest land empire on earth, but when they were in power, they protected trade, religion and cultural exchange and took very moderate taxes for their services. Before long, merchants travelled across the Black Sea and overland, to provide the spices and luxuries demanded by the Europeans. It didn't last for long. In the middle of the fourteenth century one or two plagues moved across Asia and Europe. The infection followed the trade routes and killed at least a third of all inhabitants. Afterwards, life was different. In Europe, the churches lost power and a new way of thought developed, much of it based on oriental ideas, on the Greek classics and sheer materialism. Important Greek and Roman works had been carefully preserved in Muslim libraries. They were re-introduced to backwards Europe.

During the Renaissance, the Mediterranean countries made the most profit. It allowed them to build amazing domes and palaces (or, in Pisa, far too many towers), and to invest in the sea trade. Italy was the winner. The other countries had to search for alternatives. It is no coincidence that Spain and Portugal were among the first nations that equipped long distance expeditions. Both of them were desperately poor. Far from the lucrative trade routes, they led a shadow-existence, until their seamen found the way to wealth. When Vasco da Gama reached the coast of Malabar in 1498, he had it made. The shipment of spices he brought to Lisbon was worth six times the costs of his expedition. His next journey gained fifty times the costs. Columbus went the other way. He undertook several journeys, got everything wrong and was derided as a failure. His increasingly bizarre letters from the New World made him the laughingstock of Europe. He claimed to have found the Gates of Paradise, which happened to be the estuary of the Orinoco. The monks and scholars in his company gave more reliable accounts. The American expeditions provided new spices and luxuries, like chilli, chocolate and pimento. And, would you guess it, all of them are excellent mood changers. When the discoverers turned up great amounts of pearls, the Spanish crown began to see the light, and invested.

Let's return to India. The first Portuguese settlements were built along the Malabar coasts. Vasco reached Calicut, and soon enough there was another settlement at Cochin. Before long, the Portuguese were the strongest force along India's western coastline. In 1505, King Manuel I installed a 'viceroy of India'. He controlled a few sea-side cities. In 1509, the Portuguese beat an allied Arab/Indian fleet. In 1510, they occupied Goa (it remained Portuguese until 1961). In 1518 they gobbled up Colombo in Sri Lanka and in 1536 the island Diu at the coast of Kathiawar.

Soon enough, the Dutch joined the fun. The Portuguese insisted that the sea route to India was their sole property. They had made a deal with Alexander VI, (the only honest pope ever), who accepted a lot of gifts and affirmed that the whole world was owned by the Spanish and Portuguese. The Dutch disregarded the setup; they embraced the Protestant faith and spent many years fighting the Spanish. Between 1595 and 1601 they sent out fifteen trade expeditions to East India and Indonesia, and founded a permanent settlement, Bantam, in West Java, after they had slaughtered the Portuguese residents. Officially, the conflict was religious, but under the bottom line is generally a number. Spices were more valuable than gold. The Dutch won. It allowed them to found colonies and to abuse the locals at their heart's content. Their chief import was nutmeg. The tree only grew on the Banda Islands. The Dutch forced the natives to sell the entire harvest at minimal prices, and when the locals revolted in 1621, almost everyone was slaughtered. The rest was enslaved and made to toil on plantations.

After Sir Francis Drake, the British fleet and a convenient storm had destroyed the Armada, Elisabeth I began to wonder about further income. Her country was religiously isolated, poor and in desperate need of income. Eight enterprising businessmen founded the Association of Merchant Adventurers in 1599. Their initial goals were humble. Elisabeth I graciously permitted them to engage in what the company charter described as *'quiet trade.'* Small business seemed to be a safe prospect. After all, the big money, i.e. the Spice Islands, was far away and the Portuguese and Dutch were pretty much in control. To get into this venture, Britain had to become a major naval power. One of the fathers of this enterprise was the amazing Dr. John Dee. He calculated the nativity of Elisabeth I, advised his queen on spiritual matters, acted as her diplomat and spy and spent much of his spare time conjuring spirits. Nowadays, Dee is famous as a magician and alchemist, but he was also one of the leading mathematicians and geographers of his age. He advised a number of daring British captains and wrote a four-volume work called *General and Rare Memorials Pertaining to the Perfect Art of Navigation.* The massive books allowed British captains to find their way in unknown waters. In a moment of sheer inspiration, he wrote a small book entitled *Brytanici Imperii Limites* (*The Limits of the British Empire*) proposing that Britain should contest the division of the earth between Spain and Portugal. Dee proved that King Arthur, and famous seafarers like the Welsh prince Madoc, had first crossed the Atlantic. According to his research, *a great part of Atlantis (otherwise called America) next unto us, and of all isles near unto the same, from Florida northerly and chiefly of all the islands Septentrional [i.e. northerly], great and small, the Title Royal and supreme government is due* (Woolley, 2002: 133). It wasn't the only region that belonged to Britain. In case you didn't know, King Arthur subjugated Ireland, Norway, Iceland, Gotland, Denmark, Germany, Gaul, Italy, Rome and the Holy Land. Plus *every region of the world.* That's medieval legend. Read Geoffrey of Monmouth and look into Coe

& Young, 1995. Dee presented a copy of his book to Elisabeth I and gave her a map showing the regions over which she should assert her right to rule. It was a crazy, daring and highly visionary act. Dee envisioned that Britain would become an Empire. Many contemporaries laughed. Britain was a small and deprived country. It changed once the fleet began to grow.

Dee had created a dream. It worked its magick and transformed the world.

The merchant adventurers were dedicated to trade, but they were also keen to plunder enemy vessels and exploit the natives anywhere. Southeast Asia seemed too rich for comprehension. It provided, at minimal costs, several types of pepper, nutmeg, cumin, camphor, aloe, cinnamon, cardamom, galangal, cassia, cloves and ginger. There were amazing fragrances, like patchouli, sandalwood and, imported from the Himalayan Mountains, musk. There were drugs like opium and arsenic. There were jewels and diamonds. East Indian trade promised the biggest profits on Planet Earth. Who cared about the risk? True, a lot of ships sank, and many sailors died of malnutrition and disease. Hardly anybody cared. The spice trade was in the national interest. Soon, several trade associations were founded, which were eventually united in the British East India Company, the wealthiest and most influential trade organisation in the world.

Captain Lancaster was the first captain of the East India Company who brought treasure from the east. He had loaded citrus fruit, to combat scurvy and other diseases, but nevertheless half of his crew died. Lancaster arrived in Sumatra and offered his goods: coarse iron and heavy woollen clothes. The natives laughed at him. He got rid of his cargo and pirated a Portuguese ship. Lancaster sailed to Bantam and bought spices. When he returned to London in 1603, almost 2,5 years after his departure, his cargo included almost 500 tons of pepper, plus cinnamon, cloves, nutmeg and other valuables. The profit was so great that another expedition was sent out next year. King Jacob I became an investor.

The Dutch, to be sure, remained in Indonesia. They were too deeply entrenched to be moved. And they had far more wealth to finance and protect their trade. When the British founded their East India Company, they made it an exclusive club whose members tried to keep a monopoly on trade and became exceedingly rich. The Dutch East India Company was open to anyone who wanted to invest. As a result, its budget was almost twenty times as large as that of the British. It allowed the Dutch to force the Portuguese and British out of Indonesia.

The British realised that much of India was there for grabs. They founded trade settlements and came to lucrative arrangements with the local rulers, most of them Muslims. Simultaneously, they fought the French. Several French settlements existed in southern India and one in Bengal. There were Dutch traders, some Danes, some Portuguese and many Armenian merchants, who had established themselves centuries ago, trading along the Silk Roads with China and the Near East. To the locals, the British were just another bunch of strangers. They were a minority group, and not very popular. Their supremacy began when the traders acquired a harbour called Bombay and a few small islands from the Portuguese. The place was a malaria-infested marsh. It turned into a blossoming trade settlement where wealthy merchants lived like kings. Their Indian associates and servants experienced an unheard of rise in profits, mainly in charges, fees and favours. Bombay was a success story, even though the life expectation remained alarmingly low. Only one in twenty English babies survived infancy (Dalley, 2006:44). Profits soared when the British managed to get their hands on East India. Welcome to Cāndo's paradise! The first British trade settlement was at the place where goddess Gaṅgā and River Hooghly met. The settlement was founded in 1651, it was strategically useless, but it worked for a while. In 1666 another British settlement was built in Dacca, which was, at the time, the capital of Bengal. It wasn't that well located either. The British did their best to make a profit, but they had to compete with traders from other nations, including the French, who had been settling in Chandranagore since 1688. Both nations bribed the local regent, and the French, showing tact and manners, were far more popular.

Job Charnock acquired the right to build a settlement at the Hooghly River from the Mogul Emperor Aurangzeb, who did not like foreigners, but approved of profits. As the legend goes, Charnock arrived in the middle of the monsoon, had himself and thirty armed men rowed to the shore and pitched tents on August 24th, 1690. There were few settlers in sight, or so he said, as much of the neighbourhood had been burned down during earlier conflicts. It took several years before the first proper houses were built. In the meantime, everyone made do with tents and huts. So much for the official story. In real life, Charnock chose a place close to three villages and several riverside fortifications (Dalley, 2006: 52-55). His choice was Sutanati; its closest neighbour was called Kālīkata, named after goddess Kālī. There was a thriving settlement of traders, most of them Armenians, who had been there for at least a century, plus French, Dutch, Danish and Portuguese. Charnock and his men lived in tents, as the local Nawab did not allow them to build proper houses. He changed his mind when the British lent him military support. The choice couldn't have been much worse. The place was amazingly unhealthy and had very little strategic value. Two hundred years later, Rudyard Kipling gave an excellent description:

Thus the midday halt of Charnock-more's the pity!-
Grew a City
As the fungus sprouts chaotic from its bed
So it Spread
Chance-directed, chance-erected, laid and built
On the silt
Palace, byre, hovel -poverty and pride-
Side by side
And, above the packed and pestilential town,
Death looked down.

Welcome to Calcutta, or, in European eyes, the end of the world. In modern Bengal the place is called Kolkata. That name, so it is claimed, came from Kālī's ghāt, i.e. to the steps at the riverside where a Kālī temple stood. For many Hindus, the location was sacred. Long before time, Śiva married Satī, much against the will of her father Dakṣa, who kept complaining that the husband of his precious daughter was a worthless drug addict. The young couple had a wonderful time making love in the high mountains. Then, one bad day, Satī learned that her father was giving a great feast. All gods had been invited, except for Śiva and her. Satī insisted on going. She arrived at the feast and made a terrible scene. When her father insulted her, she sat down, closed all gates of her body and raised an inner fire that killed her. Śiva, seeing his wife dead, went insane. First, he destroyed the feast and sent the guests running. Then he picked up the corpse of his wife and began to wander around mindlessly. He forgot his divine duties, and when the gods told him to drop the corpse, he didn't understand what they were talking about. Viṣṇu found a solution. Every day, he lurked in ambush. When Śiva staggered past, Viṣṇu hurled his cakra (*wheel, discus*). It cut off a part of Sati's corpse. Each day, Śiva's load became lighter. The bits of Satī dropped all over India and each became a piṭhā, a sacred place. At Calcutta, so it is said, Satī's toe fell. That's wonderfully sacred: Indian religion and custom make a lot of feet. They are the grounding, the manifestation of the divine.

Another explanation for the name is Kālīkkhetro: *Field of Kālī*. Less religious is a third explanation: Khal (*canal*) Kaṭa (*dug*). It appeals to conservative Hindus, Muslims and Europeans who don't fancy Kālī much. The stage was set. Once they were allowed to raise houses, the British practically invented the city and built most of it from scratch. The place was muddy, noxious, and anything but inspiring. In the cool wintertime, the temperature averages between 25° and 30°C, in summer it can be around 50°C around noon and stay that way for months. During the monsoon season, you get rain, damp and thunderstorms that may have the thermometer drop by 15 or 20°C in an hour. In 1863, Sir George Trevelyan claimed *The place is so bad by nature that human efforts could do little to make it worse; but that little has been done faithfully and assiduously*.

Calcutta was famous for malaria, cholera, the pox and a load of diseases the Europeans didn't even have names for. Jan Dalley mentions the 'two monsoon rule': if you made it through two years, you had a chance of survival. Most of the foreigners did not. Westphal (1980:157) mentions a monsoon period that killed 460 of the 1200 British citizens. However, once settled, the British traders remained. They made enormous profits and were willing to take the risks. Near the Hooghly River, a factory was built. Factory, in these days, meant warehouses. Quarrels with the local rulers ensued, and for a while the British had to withdraw. It was a heavy blow to the economy. The Nawab of Bengal, Ibrahim Khan, realised how much money he was losing and asked them to return. Of course the traders obliged, but they insisted on being paid for it. The settlement grew. In 1696, Azim-ush-shan allowed the British to buy three villages near Calcutta, where they were free to build, rule and to exhort taxes. 1717 another 37 villages were acquired. By 1735 the population had grown to a staggering 100,000. The city grew, in spite of setbacks, like the tragic year 1737, when it was almost entirely flattened by a cyclone. However, a little wind is no reason to give up. Nowadays, there are an average of fifteen cyclones with wind speeds between 200 and 400km/h in the Bay of Bengal. Things got a little edgy when the traders began to invest in fortification, and began to build Fort William. The place looked impressive. However, it was made of pukka brick, and started to rot before it was completed. The cannons were stored at the riverfront, in a warehouse, where they were eaten up by rust. 1756, the new Nawab, an angry man called Siraj-du-daula, ordered the French and the British, that the building of all fortifications had to stop. His anger was beside the point: the defences were ridiculous. The traders believed in money. They had no intention to waste it on the military. Fort William was a grandiose storehouse. The walls were thin and weak. Had anyone tried to shoot cannons from up there, the towering merchant palaces would have been destroyed, and indeed, within the fortress, the floors would have collapsed. The French showed tact, they offered bribes and insisted that their building projects were just repairs. The British were stupid: they mentioned the war they were fighting against the French in faraway Europe, implying that India might become a battlefield; they neglected courtesy and failed to invest in bribes. The Nawab had a fit of rage, he besieged the city; the traders were soundly beaten and almost exterminated. The whole painful episode culminated in the Black Hole of Calcutta, which became the stuff of legends. Allegedly, a vast amount of European prisoners were stuffed into a tiny prison cell (18 feet by 14) in Fort William, where most suffocated. As Jan Dalley demonstrated, the facts are enigmatic. Accounts vary enormously, and show major incongruities.

Picture 51: Clay head of Śiva, emphasising his relationship to the serpent world, Nadia, West Bengal. Photo in Bussabarger & Robbins, 1968:35.

The witnesses did not agree on anything. Maybe 175 people were imprisoned, and 16 survived. Or it was 146, with 23 survivors. Or, at the lowest count, it was 6 survivors and 3 dead. In early descriptions, the prisoners were of several nationalities, in others, they were just British. Some mention only men, others propose that women and children were involved. Several historians conclude the whole event was a hoax, blown up for propaganda purposes. Mark Twain remarked: *It was the ghastly episode of the Black Hole that maddened the British and brought Clive, that young military marvel, raging up from Madras; it was the seed from which sprung Plassey; and it was that extraordinary battle, whose like had not been seen on earth since Agincourt, that laid deep and strong the foundations of England's colossal Indian sovereignty.*

It takes a 'humorist' to explain reality, 'cause it hurts.

Soon enough, better strategists were needed. One of them was the famous Robert Clive (1725-1774), who cheerfully declared that Calcutta was *'the most wicked place in the Universe'* and proceeded to make it worse. Clive arrived in India as a scribe of the East India Company. In the early days, scribes earned around £5 a year. A ship carpenter earned that amount each month. In short, a scribe could not even afford to travel home again. If he survived the climate and the microbes, he had to trade, or find employment elsewhere. Clive switched professions and began an enormously successful military career. His greatest achievement was a battle against an army consisting of Indian and French troops, a hundred kilometres from Calcutta, in 1757. The situation was pretty bad. The British troops, consisting of a thousand Europeans, two thousand native soldiers and eight cannons, set out to confront the allied troops of the Nawab. At Plassey, they faced maybe 35,000 soldiers, 15,000 riders and fifty cannons. The Nawab and his troops spent the night singing and drinking and delighted in their future victory. Clive, by contrast, wasn't much into celebrating. He was counting on two advantages. For one thing, he had made a secret pact with Mir Jafar, the strongest ally (and a close relation) of the Nawab, who commanded two-thirds of the Nawab's forces. On a signal, Mir was to join the British and attack the Nawab's troops. For this favour, he was to become the future Nawab. For another, the British troops were better disciplined and had taken extra precautions to keep their gunpowder dry. In monsoon weather, it proved to be essential. By daybreak, the British were rested, but nervous, while the Nawab's troops felt weary and exhausted. When hostilities began, Mir Jafar was signalled to betray the Nawab. He just sat back, smiled and waited. Before long the rain began. The French troops, unprepared for the downpour, lost the use of their artillery. The Nawab sent his riders against the British, thinking that they, too, would be handicapped by wet powder. It turned out they weren't. When the leader of the cavalry fell, the Nawab lost his only trustworthy ally. The British troops made a surprise attack on the Nawab's flank, which caused a mass panic and total chaos. The Indian-French army disintegrated, the soldiers fled in all directions and the Nawab had to escape, in disguise, riding a camel.

For Clive, the battle was a mind-blowing success. To be sure, as a military effort it was hardly worth mentioning. Seven British soldiers and sixteen sepoys (Indian soldiers) fell, while the Nawab lost approximately five hundred. Nevertheless, it demonstrated once and for all that the British were successful, indefatigable and here to stay. Mir Jafar grinned like an oily shark and with Clive's blessing, became Nawab of Bengal, Orissa and Bihar. As a small token of his gratitude, he gave £234,000 to Clive, who bought a house in Berkley Square for £10,000 and a huge estate in Shropshire for £70,000. It was one of the biggest bribes in history, and as could have been expected, some people complained. *When he faced a committee of inquiry, however, he made his famous remark: 'I stand astonished at my own moderation.'* (Dalley, 2006:195). Clive became 'Clive of Plassey' and made sure nobody forgot it. Before long he was Sir Clive and the governor of Calcutta. One of his duties was taxation. He returned home, three years after the Battle of Plassey, as one of the richest men on earth.

The battle changed everything. Mir Jafar celebrated himself as a great regent and mostly did as he was told. The East India Company, which had functioned as a commercial enterprise, became a political force. The British became the unofficial regents of a deeply corrupt country and did their best to exploit it to the limit. The local aristocrats remained in their position. They were obliged to press heavy taxes out of their subjects.

Here is a little lesson in economy. To do business in, say, cotton, each European trader employed a chain of, averaging, five middlemen, each of them with his own team of accountants, servants and bullies. At the bottom of the pecking order was the poor weaver, who was forced to sell his ware far beneath the price he could have received on the local market. In urban Britain, simple women could afford clothes that had been the privilege of the middle and higher classes. In India, the poor were so much poorer. And while we are at it, it's the same today. The T-shirt you wear was, in all likeliness, made from the cotton of a farmer, so impoverished and debt-ridden, that he had to sell his under-age daughters to the cotton factories. Their suicide rate is stunning.

Before British rule, Bengal had been the wealthiest province in India. By 1780 the British had pressed thirty-eight million pounds out of their territory, which made Bengal one of the poorest regions in East Asia.

The monsoon ended unusually early in the years 1769 and 1770. The harvests failed badly and the population starved. The locals sold their valuables, their land, homes, clothes and even their children. The street sides were littered with corpses and before long, plagues were sweeping across the country. When they came to an end, the population of Bengal had dropped from 30 million to 20 million. As good Christians, the traders expressed their heartfelt sympathy. It did not stop them from raising taxes by 10% (Westphal, 1980:194).

Trade continued. The merchants had access to spices, to the silk roads leading to China and Myanmar; they traded in jewels and saltpetre, which was direly needed in the European wars. They turned Bengal into the second-largest producer of coal in the world, mined for iron, created a flourishing steel industry and started a promising railroad business.

In 1793, Cornwallis introduced a reform that threw Bengal, and other parts of India, into total chaos. Cornwallis tried to simplify taxation. To ensure a steady cash flow, he turned the zamindars, who had been agents of the rulers, and essentially tax-collectors, into major land-owners. The zamindars functioned as middlemen between the local farmers and the British government, and did their best to maximise profits. Call it the birth of a new aristocracy.

In the process, 20 million peasants and small land-owners lost their belongings and had to pay dues to till fields that had been in their families for generations. That's part of the story. The other part is: the Permanent Settlement Act ensured that, if the peasants didn't pay enough, the zamindars could not evict them. In the process, a few zamindars became exceedingly rich while many others faced poverty.

The peasants were used to taxation, and they were also used to exploitation. In the old days of Hindu and Muslim rule, much of their dues were paid in foodstuff, textiles and raw materials. The British insisted that taxes were paid in money instead of goods. The zamindars forced the population to grow cash crops. It turned the rural economy upside down. To meet the increasing demands, the peasants had to invest their efforts into export products: indigo, hemp, sugarcane, jute. Meanwhile, they lost the capacity to produce their own cereals and vegetables. Before long, famine became the norm. Famine, in this context, is more than hunger. Hunger is normal in East India; there are tens of thousands who are hungry every day. Famine, however, means that the dead litter the roadside, that parents sell or abandon their children, that families are scattered, that people try to eat grass and tree bark. Starvation is a slow death. It begins with depression, turns to weakness, and transforms into paralysing apathy. Finally, there are people who fade away while birds and dogs ravage them. Bengal became famous for famines, the worst happening in 1770, 1783, 1866, 1873, 1874, 1892, 1897 and 1943 (Moorhouse, 2008:119).

Meanwhile, traditional Indian industries went down the drain. The Indian textile industry collapsed. The same happened to the sugar industry, once sugarcane was introduced to the West Indies, where slave labour was much cheaper. But things can always grow worse. In 1813, the British government cancelled the trade monopoly of the East India Company, allowing any British trader to export to India, any way they liked. It brought wealth to Britain, while the Indian economy broke down. The next nightmare was indigo. Enormous amounts were needed by the world market, but the growth of the plant is risky, difficult and demands a lot of labour. The farmers were forced to grow the stuff, at their own risk, and to sell it at the price demanded by the traders.

The horrors of the indigo industry ended when German chemists discovered how to produce the colour synthetically. The impoverished peasants found themselves released from one nightmare and exposed to another. Instead of indigo, they were forced to produce tea. Meanwhile, the international demand for jute was rising. Up to the middle of the twentieth century, jute, raw or as cloth, made up a third of India's annual exports. The fibre was perfect for sacks, essential for trade and immensely useful to fortify trenches.

The poets and storytellers who created the *Manasā Epic* lived a time of turmoil, need and violence. In their lifetimes, over the last five centuries, the social system was violently disrupted, the farmers lost property and self-sufficiency, a new class of rich people, the zamindars, emerged, the Muslim regents faded into the background, the agricultural landscape turned from small farms to large plantations, vast amounts of forest were cut down, large areas of arable land were exploited until desertification set in and India became one of the poorest countries in the world. Faced by enormous changes, the Bengalis remained religious. Anyone who thinks that religion is just stupid superstition should reconsider. When life is really bad, the gods remain the only comfort of the poor.

Religious sentiments changed. The gentlemen adventurers of the company had rarely interfered with native religion. Indeed, it was good form to celebrate the major festivals. Rich zamindars competed with each other for the honour of inviting English guests to celebrate the Durgā Pūjā, and scored points by receiving the most illustrious guests. Indeed, their efforts to outdo each other formed the beginning of the popular Durgā cult that is so vehemently celebrated in Bengal nowadays. In earlier times, warrior goddess Durgā had been a favourite of the aristocracy, the warrior class and the kings. Thanks to the zamindars, her cult became a popular entertainment. Each great family competed in luxury, grand offerings and lavish feasts. It was a show of faith, an opportunity to demonstrate wealth and a chance to win spiritual glamour. Indeed, for the wealthy Hindu landowners, such festivals were a chance to make up for the loss of their prestige in a country largely controlled by Muslims. Year after year, the festivals become more lavish. It changed when the Permanent Settlement Act was issued in 1793. Many zamindars families could not afford to waste their income in a grandiose manner. Their function as regents and sponsors shifted to groups of associates, who began to pool their wealth for the grand pūjās. The new sponsors were not necessarily members of the aristocrat classes. And, expectably, they tried to outdo those wealthy zamindars who still financed the worship privately.

For the British, the ten-day celebration in October was a major opportunity to feast and be entertained. Clive of Plassey rode to his hosts on an elephant. The foreigners accepted Durgā as a fact of life. They were merchants and administrators, not missionaries, and what the heathens believed didn't bother them. Some made a gesture to participate in the worship and a few became Hindus. That being over and done with, the fun began. In 1793 Lord Cornwallis had promised to *preserve the laws of the Shaster and the Koran, and to protect the natives of India in the free exercise of their religion* (McDermott, 2011:44). Religious tolerance was not only a must; it was good for business. For this reason, missionary activity was strictly discouraged. It annoyed the church, which started a campaign in Britain to assert their right to convert the heathens. By 1813, parliament allowed missionary work (in principle). It was not enforced, however, and the regents of each district retained the right to ignore or deport missionaries. Nevertheless, religious tolerance faded. By 1830, European participation in great religious festivals became increasingly unfashionable. Those who demanded tolerance were accused of approval, and parliament emphasised that the East India Company should distance itself from native religious rituals, festivals and temples. It was the start of a new age of intolerance. Mind you, it took until 1863 before religious apartheid was enforced.

In the perfectly good interest of improving the Indian mindset, the country was opened to missionaries.

Here is an example of their effort:

Around 1840 the protestant missionary Dürr travelled through Bengal. God's good work turned out to be awfully difficult. As he recorded: *The villagers, with whom I spoke, refused to acknowledge that they are sinners (...) The following morning we visited the idol-house of the village, where I saw a row of vessels lined up, all of them marked with red paint. The priest was in attendance and regretted, after having heard about it from his son, that he hadn't been present* (for the sermon) *of the last evening. I enquired about the meaning of the pots and was told: "they are gods."*

When I asked why a twig of the Manasa tree was standing in one, I received the answer: "it is Manasa, the Mother of the World."

He demonstrated the type of worship for me, by making one of those present put a pot on his head and made him dance. He did this, but in such a clumsy fashion, that the goddess fell into the muck, which caused laughter and gave me the opportunity to point out the unworthiness of such worship. "Here, idolatry appears in its true nature!"

Mr. Dürr learned his lesson. When he was fed up with preaching to the *'dull, apathic Hindus'*, he shifted his attention to the son of an aristocrat and bedazzled him with the promise of progressive European thought.

Meanwhile, missionary Weilbrecht witnessed a festival for the goddess:

From there we proceeded to another village and met an assembly of approximately a thousand Hindus. They celebrated the festival of Manasa, the protective goddess of serpents. Four men carried her image on a stretcher. She is seated on a throne and has two serpents in her hand, whose tails are wrapped around her neck. The noise of the people was stunning and in vain I tried to make myself heard. An old man began to sing a Mandra (magical spell) and a chorus of singers accompanied him. He opened a basket from which one of the poisonous serpents raised its head. To my amazement the animal moved in accord with the melody of the singers, showed its tongue, hurled itself against its master, and swiftly withdrew again. Afterwards, boys danced with pots on their heads, as if they were drunk. – May the Spirit of the Lord shake these mortal bones soon!

(M. Blumhardt (publisher), 1841:19 & 29, trans. JF).

From the modern perspective, some reforms were direly needed. For a start, the British weakened the rigid class laws. Hindu society was badly stratified and people were not supposed to eat with people of other classes, or to marry into them. For some fanatics, speaking with a low-class person constituted terrifying spiritual pollution. Under British rule, the class-system lost much of its meaning. The British introduced courts where Indians were considered equal. It made the Muslim upper class hopping mad to be on the same level as the Hindus and it disgusted the Brahmins and warriors to be treated just like the traders, menial workers and illiterate savages. In the process, many social classes tried to improve their ranking. In most districts, only the Brahmins had worn a sacred thread. Under British rule, plenty of people decided they were good enough to do the same. Mantras that had been the exclusive property of Brahmins were recited by middle-class people with a keen sense of spiritual advancement. Entire social groups re-invented themselves. They attached a prestigious term, like 'Kṣatriya' (*warrior*) to their class name, in the sure expectation that eventually they would be recognised as upper-class folk. The Brahmins loathed these innovations. They disagreed with the relaxed marriage customs of the middle classes, and preached a conservative world-view. Basanta Coomar Bose gives an excellent account of the social transformations between the eighteenth and early twentieth century. To everyone's surprise, women began to acquire a little education. I say 'a little', as education was expensive and even wealthy families rarely kept their daughters in school for more than three or four years. The girls learned to read, to compose letters and do simple calculations. It raised their status in the household. Bose pointed out that up until the nineteenth century; social rules prevented most women from learning. His father started the first girl's school in East Bengal in 1865. The locals quarrelled about the institution until it had to be closed. A few decades later, a new school taught almost fifty girls. Female education had become a matter of status, as Brahmin and Kayastha (scribe) families would not accept a bride who couldn't read or do some simple arithmetic. *My grandmother could never write, my mother learned Bengali after her marriage, my wife knew it before her marriage, and my daughter-in-law knows English. Such is the progress of education and enlightened ideas in our society caused by the progress of time and English education* (1875-1926, in Basu and Bose, 2005:203). Consider this: each of these women may have listened to the *Manasā Epics*. Their understanding of Behulā's journey would have been widely different. Meanwhile, brides became older. Thanks to English education, many young men were in their late twenties when they finished their training, and began to earn an income. Men around thirty are rarely interested in marrying eight-year-old girls, as the Kanoj Brahmins would have insisted. Among the upper classes, the demand for mature brides increased.

One of the sad customs, especially popular in Bengal, was the burning of widows. Remember the story of how Sati killed herself with a yogic suicide method, by burning herself up from within? Sure, Sati was no widow. Her husband Śiva was very much alive and remained so. Her father had merely insulted him. It made her kill herself. The word Sati means *Virtuous Wife*. A widow who burns herself commits sati, or, as the British spelt it, suttee. She demonstrates that without her god-like husband, life is meaningless, and wins extra Karman-points by dying. If she is lucky, she will join him in another life. Maybe she even has the amazing good luck to be born as a man. In traditional India, some widows were supposed to prove their virtue by accompanying their deceased husbands into death. The custom is complicated; it was not observed by all people and it had local variations. So we shall stick to the essentials and simplify. In Vedic times, women were not very liberated, but they had some status and could, if they were rich, patronise expensive religious ceremonies like the śrauta rites, and gain their blessings. There were even a few women who composed spiritual poetry; just read *Ṛg Veda*, 10, 39, a long hymn for the Aśvins, full of learning and literary references, composed by the seeress Ghoṣā, daughter of the seer Kakṣivān. The *Vedas* compare women with fertile fields and praise them for fruitfulness. It wasn't much, but a lot better than the future. By the advent of modern Hinduism, say, between 400 BCE and 400 CE, the status of women was much reduced. During this dismal period, women were considered mere vessels to receive seed. They were excluded from most rituals. Only sinners and evildoers were mean enough to be born as women. The same mood appears in early Buddhism. To be a woman was a Karmic punishment. The *Laws of Manu* insist that *animals, drums, illiterates, low-class people and women deserve to be beaten*. To be sure, not everyone subscribed to such ideas. In old India, as all over the world, some men had the good sense to respect and love their wives. However, they reflect how the literate upper classes would have liked to organise the world. In old India, a woman became 'half of her husband', whom she was to adore like a deity. Usually, the husband was not expected to become half of his wife, and unless he was a hardcore Tantric of the Left Hand Path, he wasn't likely to adore her. Through marriage, a woman lost all ties to her old family, whom she was theoretically allowed to visit only a few days each year. Instead, she had to serve her husband's family and her husband's ancestors. When he died, she lost her value and function in the world. Her death seemed to solve a lot of problems.

Widows, and here we are very close to the *Manasā Epic*, were inauspicious. The name Behulā means *'a widow'*. An old widow could be a problem, as she obstructed the inheritance of her dead husband. A young widow was worse. She was sexually experienced, attractive and potentially fertile, hence, in a perfect position to disrupt family life. In consequence, some widows were practically forced to mount the pyre. If they were lucky, they were drugged out of their heads or poisoned before the fire devoured them. Their death was considered an act of true devotion.

Widow burning was a rare event. Usually, when a man died, the widow remained alive. Maybe she moved to a shed at the edge of the property and spent her remaining days doing household chores and religious rituals. She wore plain white, avoided public events, fed on a meagre diet and observed a lot of special rules and prohibitions. Bose gives an excellent account. Her life wasn't much fun. However, she could see her children grow up. Others were cast out. Many widows were simply left at the burning place, homeless, dishonoured, and free to go and die where they pleased. Some became pilgrims and spent their life visiting sacred places, praying for their husband's family. A few widows were rich and bossy and did what they liked. Or they remained a part of their husband's clan, humble, in the background, but with a place in life.

In this issue, Cāndo is remarkably enlightened. He does not expect the wives of his dead sons to suicide. They wear (relatively) plain clothes and no jewellery, but they are integrated, well fed and lead a comfortable life. When Behulā embarks on her journey he tries to dissuade her. He is a trader, accustomed to mediate between many classes of society. And he is, though this isn't always evident, a devotee of Śiva and Durgā. Ordinary religious norms do not interest him.

Moorhouse (2008:71) records that in the years 1815-1817, 253, 289 and 441 women were burned with their husbands in Calcutta. Their number is tiny, compared to the Indian population of the city. However, each enforced death is one too many. Bengal was famous for burning widows, and the British, influenced by the great reformer Rammohan Roy, were quite right to class the deed as murder and abolish it.

Here's another reform: the British abolished the thugs. That's how it appeared in the nineteenth century and that's how it has been repeated 'til today, in newspapers, novels and movies. In real life, the situation is questionable. Let's go back a few centuries and meet an amazing character. This is Colonel Sleeman, who claimed that every year; thousands of people were being murdered on Indian roads in the name of the black goddess Kālī. In Sleeman's opinion, the murderers belonged to a sect called the thugs. He cited a questionable myth stating that the goddess Kālī had given them a rumal, i.e. a silken scarf with a weight (a silver coin) tied into one end. The worshipper approached his victim from behind, whirled the scarf around his neck, caught the heavy end, turned around and hoisted the victim on his back. The innocent struggled, twitched and died; the goddess got the soul and the happy thug fled with the valuables. Well, where it comes to strangling technology, this is pretty convincing. Similar murders, using a piano string with a weight attached, were common in the great cities of Europe. Let me simplify. I have written about the subject in *Kālī Kaula*, and you can find a detailed study by Humes & Urban in McDermott & Kripal, 2003:145-168 and 169-195.

According to Colonel Sleeman, practically every goddess temple was a hiding place of thugs, who planned their assaults and the sale of the valuables under the protection of the Brahmins. Most thugs, as he claimed, were Muslims, many were Sikhs and some were Hindus. All of them were members of hereditary bandit families. The British government authorised Sleeman to crush the cult. Their combined efforts were successful. Journalists around the world were fascinated by the terrible stranglers and by the dark and nude goddess whom they worshipped with human sacrifices. To this day, the thugs are famous and a fact of life.

That being so, we should study Sleeman's evidence. It won't be easy. In plain reality, Sleeman didn't have any. He claimed that his reports and files were stored in Fort William, and that they were eaten by white ants. Copies didn't exist. To strengthen his position he quoted from the works of H.H.Wilson, a translator of myths and folk tales, Major General Sergeant Leger and Dr. Richard Sherwood, who claimed to have insider knowledge of the 'cult' and compiled a dictionary of 'thug-slang' that was widely read by the British. As it turned out, their evidence was many centuries old or plain gossip. Indeed, some thugs appeared in fantastic folk tales and plays of medieval India. So do gods, demons, ghosts and spirits, enchanted paradises, hells and, of course human sacrifices for Kālī. These, however, were usually a privilege of kings, who used condemned criminals as offerings. Consider it a form of justice, and miles away from a clandestine sect of religious terrorists. In short, none of the 'evidence' was contemporary or reliable. And while Sleeman presented the thugs as a religious movement with a nasty means of income, modern historians tend to see the 19th Century thugs as murderous robbers. Like contemporary Indian Dacoits, many of them had a religious side, and left offerings or donations at some local shrine Mosque or temple, for good luck. That, however, is not the same as a hereditary cult for Kālī. Sikhs are not into Kālī worships and neither are most Muslims and Hindus. Sure, Indian travellers were threatened by bandits and murderers. We just can't be sure that these were thugs, let alone that these thugs were quite as the British authorities claimed. Sleeman's jumble of myth, fiction and hearsay evidence wouldn't have convinced a modern jury. However, the thugs turned out to be amazingly useful.

Sleeman arrested and tortured countless Indians. To make his point, he had four hundred alleged 'thugs' publicly hung (an especially dishonourable form of death). More than a thousand 'thugs' were deported to prison camps on the Andaman Islands, where they were worked to death. You would suspect that at least one or two confessions survived. Sorry, tough luck, the white ants ate the lot.

In Sleeman's worldview, one goddess was pretty much the same as another. He followed a typical 19th Century European idea, namely, that there was basically one Great Goddess and that all other goddesses are her 'aspects', whether they like it or not. It didn't really matter if the deluded savages worshipped Kālī, Tārā, Durgā, Pārvatī, Lakṣmī, Sarasvatī or Manasā. One damn idol was as bad as the other. And indeed, when we consider Manasā, there were real links to the cult of Kālī. Some Manasā statues are painted black. The ritualists may, on occasion, address her as Kālī Ma (*Black Mother*).

Sleeman convinced the world, and created a myth. He also made a lasting impression on Indian thought. Before long, the Indians were convinced that thugs were real.

Sleeman's campaign wasn't just an effort to make travel safer. The mere suspicion that a kingdom might harbour thugs was enough to allow the British army to invade and occupy it. When the British had gained enough territory, the thugs were not required any more. Sleeman declared that he had stamped out the cult, and indeed, in the next years no thuggish crimes were heard of. This changed when the Bengali began to revolt against their overlords. In Sleeman's time, the thug had been a religious fanatic. He wanted to serve his goddess and make a little cash. The new generation of 'thugs' was different. They were believed to be a bunch of sexual maniacs: by their time, plenty of poor women came from Britain to find a husband in the army. Stunned by the charms of fishwives and butcher girls, the thugs began to drool. And that was just the beginning. Before long, Indians were demanding independence. Anyone disenchanted by British rule was labelled as a thug. And when the Bengalis began to riot, they united under the symbol of Mother India, who was identified with Kālī. In the periodical *Yugantar* (1908) the revolutionaries declared that '*the Mother*' was thirsty and had to be fed on blood and decapitated heads. This, they assumed, was the only way to independence. After their declaration a series of assaults followed, and in 1912 the viceroy of India, Lord Hardinge was almost assassinated. In their bold imagery, Sleeman, the British Government and the revolutionaries entered new territory. Never before had anyone used the image of Kālī for political purposes. Quite the opposite was the case. For the famous Bengali poets, Kālī was a goddess who transcended race, nationality, faith and ideology, and appears to her worshippers in whatever guise they prefer.

One noble aim of the colonisers was to educate and civilise the Indians. Information, however, always goes both ways. While administrators and merchants delighted in their intellectual superiority over the 'niggers', European scholars were excited by what India had to offer. The Asiatic Society was founded in 1784. It united a range of excellent scholars who were thrilled to explore the Indo-European roots of Indian culture. Nathaniel Halhed compiled a Bengali Grammar, Henry Colebrook studied Saṁskṛta and Jonathan Duncan became an expert in Persian. These pioneering scholars united their effort to prove that India was far from primitive, and laid the foundation for a wide field of studies. In Germany, excited linguists produced the first Saṁskṛta dictionaries and struggled with the *Vedas*, which they considered, on the basis of mutual origin, as a branch of European literature. Educated Europe became enchanted by the glories of the East. The *Vedas*, the *Upaniṣads*, the teachings of the Buddha, the *Bhagavad Gīta* were incorporated in philosophical studies and classed among the greatest achievements of human thought. The first (partial) translation of the *Upaniṣads* was made by Anquetil Duperron in 1801/2. A pioneering scholar of the Romantic Movement, Friedrich Schlegel, wrote about *The Language and Wisdom of the Indians* in 1808. Schopenhauer was deeply touched by the *Vedas* and *Upaniṣads*. According to local legend, he walked through Frankfurt's parks, and lectured about Indian philosophy, to his poodle. Paul Deussen, who admired Schopenhauer, became (maybe) the most important early translator of sacred Indian literature. In his book *Vedānta, Platon and Kant*, he tried to prove that Indian, Greek and German thinkers shared a common root. In 1789, Sir William Jones translated a play by the famous Bengal author Kālidāsa into English; two years later Georg Forster produced a German translation. It was the first time a piece of East Asian literature appeared in Europe. Schiller wrote to Wilhelm von Humboldt, the famous linguist, that there was nothing comparable in classical literature. Goethe praised it in a letter to the French Indologist Chézy. The ageing Goethe announced that a new age of spiritual rejuvenation would arise from Asian philosophy. In the early nineteenth Century, the leading scientist of his age, Alexander von Humboldt, applied for permission to explore India, to study nature and culture in the Himalayas. The British aristocracy and the Royal Society supported his project. They were not influential enough. For ten years the East India Company frustrated all appeals until Humboldt gave up. His Asian expedition happened in Russia. The British traders were well aware that Humboldt loathed slavery and colonialism. Earlier, he had criticized how the Hindus had "*long groaned under a civil and military despotism.*" (Wulf, 2016:163). Jacob Grimm, writing the first proper study of the pagan deities of Germany, was delighted to observe the similarities of the goddess Helja/Halja/Hel to her Indian counterparts (trans., spelling adapted, JF):

The higher we are allowed to enter antiquity, the less hellish and the more divine can Halja appear. This is especially guaranteed by her association with the Indian Bhāvanī, who rides, like Nerthus and Holda, and bathes (s. page 234) and is called, like Kālī and Mahākālī, the Great Black Goddess. She is thought to hold court over the souls in the underworld; this office, the fitting name and the black colour (kâla niger, compare câligo and χελαιγός) make her extremely similar to Halja. Halja is one of the earliest and most common concepts of paganism. (*Deutsche Mythologie*, 1835:262).

Scholars and enthusiasts flocked to India, where they found themselves opposed by the stubborn racism of the European traders.

While European intellectuals became supporters of Indian thought, upper-class Indians pretended to be Europeans. Westernised Indians, derided as babus, became an object of scorn. European traders and traditional Indians loathed them. But the babus were clever. They embraced everything both worlds had to offer and created their own culture. They dressed like Europeans, discussed Newton and Darwin, but remained proud of an old India that was more or less fictional. Their pragmatic attitude proved to be a key to success: as they adapted to both worlds, they rose in society and became influential. Their passionate efforts inspired the locals with a national pride, a pride in being Indian, which had not existed before. It started the independence movement.

Picture 52: Mask of Śiva, used in folk dances, papier-mâché, West Bengal. Note Gaṅgā in his hair. Photo in Bussabarger & Robins, 1968:157.

42. Auspicious Songs

Manasā songs surfaced around the fourteenth or fifteenth centuries. They are part of a special class of literature, the maṅgal songs (maṅgalkāvya). Maṅgala means *amulet, lucky charm, blessing, prayer, congratulation* and *joyous feast*. The word emphasises healing and inspiration. You might think that we are dealing with happy events and good messages. It ain't as simple as that. Maṅgal songs can be full of tragedy. And they are closer to epic ballads than to pop songs: some of them grew to amazing lengths, requiring a team of trained singers who performed for several nights.

How do you recognise maṅgals? To begin with, they are poems in verse, also known as kāvyas. What sets them apart from ordinary poems and ballads is their function. Maṅgals are magically and religiously potent. They transform the singers and enchant the audience. As you remember, hardly any early literature of East India survived. Among the eldest texts are several *Manasāmaṅgals*. Pretty much of similar age are the *Caṇḍimaṅgals* (Caṇḍī is the *Fury*, a popular title of Durgā/Pārvatī) and the *Dharmamaṅgals*, dedicated to Dharma, i.e. truth, rightness, virtue, cosmic order, and the god who represents them. Somewhat later, as Baruah (2010:41) suspects, the first *Śivamaṅgals* were composed. These four categories were the foundation of a popular tradition. By the 18th Century, the range extended: we encounter maṅgals for sun god Sūrya, river goddess Gaṅgā, pox goddess Śitalā, for Lakṣmī, the goddess of luck, wealth and beauty, for the rural goddess Ṣaṣṭhī, patroness of children, for river goddess Sarasvatī and last not least, the ever popular dark goddess Kālīkā (*Little Kālī*). Even special saints, like Caitanya, were worshipped with maṅgal-songs.

One special aspect of the maṅgals is their duration. The audience is practically immersed in them. The shorter maṅgals need an entire night. Others require more. A favourite performance took eight nights, from Tuesday to Tuesday. Such presentations were only possible for well-trained troupes of professional singers who knew most of the text by heart and were happy to improvise the missing bits. The literary quality of their texts and the way they were performed varied. Some poets emphasised the religious aspects of their composition, others preferred the human interaction and many won the hearts of their audiences when they commented on contemporary events or made jokes. They also integrated religious instructions, proverbs and uplifting anecdotes. And they followed the first rule of all successful writing (as Xander Bennett put it): *don't be boring*. It wasn't easy. The singers and poets faced the same challenges as Bollywood producers: their audience came from all classes and religions of society, had different levels of education, means of livelihood and income. Then, as now, everybody wanted to go home happy.

If you listen to a maṅgal you receive blessings. Maṅgalkāvyas are magick. Your mind is purified, your sins are absolved and with a bit of luck you learn something useful. That's as magickal as it can get.

Maṅgals as a literary category differ from other forms of sacred storytelling. One crucial element is **suffering**. Good stories need painful episodes and good writers don't spare their protagonists. As an author, you create characters whom you dearly love. Then you put them into a series of worst-case scenarios and give them hell. The same goes for comedy. If you look for fun and absurdity, you find it where life is painful and stupid. Suffering, desperation and idiocy are bread and butter to comedy writers, and, I'm sure you noticed: the world is full of them. You need human, complex, fascinating characters, so your audience cares for them, and wants to share their lives. And though they face awful, embarrassing, and frustrating events, week after week, they do not give in. That's what keeps comedy from being tragedy.

Maṅgalkāvyas revolve around drama and laughter. They elaborate human vices and their retribution, emphasise the horrors of unhappy love, cruel fate and tyrannical superiors. As a counterpoint, they provide laughs, relief and, if possible, divine justice.

The Bengali poets did their best to class their writings as **divine inspiration**. Usually, they hinted that a deity had appeared to them, in trance, obsession or a dream, and demanded a fine new maṅgalkāvya with plenty of excitement, framed in perfect prose and accompanied by music. By contrast, the Assamese poets rarely claimed divine sanction.

A special aspect of maṅgalkāvyas is the **time** frame: the suffering of a person is described over a length of time, giving the author a splendid opportunity to praise the seasons and the events connected to them. Each month is related to specific flowers and plants, to animals, temperature, weather, agricultural activities, festivals and special moods. Our poets delighted in them. The six months which Behulā spent drifting on her raft were a perfect opportunity to celebrate life.

Another favourite is **catalogues**. Or poets delighted in listing all sorts of things. They listed the serpents adorning Manasā's body, the names of deities, and the places on a journey. Sacred names are an essential element of Hindu and tantric ritual. They also appear in our poems: a singer recited the 34 names of a deity, each starting with a consonant of the Bengal alphabet.

When Cāndo's ships were built, the poets listed the varieties of timber. True, many of those trees are useless for building. Not that it mattered much. Or they catalogued the flowers gracing the bridal bed of

Śiva and Durgā. Not to mention lists of birds, beasts, fishes and trading goods. Anything that was plentiful could make the poets go ecstatic. For the fun of it, I have made up a list of the materials that appear in Śivas drug pouch. Most of them come from tantric literature, especially the *Kulārṇava Tantra*.

Another popular element, common to Bengali maṅgalkāvyas but rare in the Assamese compositions, is **diatribes against men**. It's hardly necessary to elaborate on the low status of many Asian women. Any truly religious song, and that's what the maṅgals are supposed to be, will try to redress the balance. The poets found ample opportunity to slight men and their all-important activities. In the Manasā maṅgalkāvyas, the perfect situation for ridicule is the marriage of Lakhindār and Behulā. When Lakhindār, dressed up like a peacock on amphetamines, shows up before the congregation, the female guests gossip. He looks a damn sight better than their husbands. The wives deride their men as ugly, incompetent, hunchbacked, drooling, toothless and sexually impotent. It's not a demonstration of female emancipation. They would love to seduce Lakhindār and hate Behulā for getting such a splendid husband.

The audience laughed about an agonising subject. Remember? If you want humour, look for pain.

The maṅgalkāvyas were usually sung. The **singer** was a well trained professional, or, more often, a whole team of them, who incorporated acting and music in their program. Some maṅgals contain notes on the rāga which was to accompany each section.

The oral tradition came to an end when the British introduced printing presses. All of a sudden, maṅgalkāvyas were widely available. True, the text was often abridged or faulty. However, it allowed people of the middle classes to acquire and perform parts of the work on their own. The sacred texts could be sung within the family, or read aloud at the major festivals. The troupes of professional performers found their market shrinking. The better ones survived. They performed for illiterate village communities or, if they were really good, for upper-class patrons. The printed form put an end to many oral variations. They supplied ritual instructions, became sacred writ, and unified religious customs.

Very few scholars showed an interest in maṅgal compositions. Educated people sneered at Bengal literature. As Baruah (2010:44-45) emphasised, it wasn't until 1873 that a scholar remarked that maṅgal poetry existed at all. Dinesh Chandra Sen, in 1896, was the first to argue that the maṅgals constitute a special class of literature. When academics began to explore the subject, most of the old songs were long forgotten.

Traditionally, maṅgals are divided into three sections. The length of each is open to the author and the troupes who performed them.

Part One (Vandanā) starts with praise songs for deities, kings and sponsors. Some Bengal poets provided dates for their composition. As they thought upside down and backwards forward, they did it in the most complicated way. For a start, it was fun to provide the date against usual custom by giving the numbers from right to left. Bipradās, for instance, composed his *Manasāmaṅgal* in the year sindhu (oceans). There are seven oceans, meaning the number seven. Next: Indu (the moon). There is one moon, hence: number one. *Veda*: there are four *Vedas*. Finally mahī (earth), and as there is just one earth, the number is one. We arrive at the number 7141 and when we turn it around it's 1417 of the Indian Calendar, which equals year 1495 CE. Bijay Gupta wrote in ṛtu (the seasons, hence: six), śūṇya (voidness: zero), *Veda* (four) and Śaśī (moon: one) = 6041 = 1406, which corresponds with our year 1484. Such codes do not appear in the Assamese Manasā poetry.

Part Two (Devakhaṇḍa) introduced the deities and their relationships. This section is usually remote from human life; it sets up the divine background of the story, the conditions of events and the subliminal emotions. These seeds will become thoughts, feelings and actions in later sections of the tale. As the world of gods follows its own rules, you encounter incomprehensible events, paradoxes, enigmas and bizarre symbolism.

Part Three (Narakhaṇḍa) shifts the story from the divine realm to the world of humans doing their best, which isn't much, and getting tangled up in it. In our story, this part starts when Manasā comes to earth and learns about its rules. This section may include how souls of humans or deities are reincarnated on earth, to fulfil a specific task or make up for earlier sins. The whole thing ends in the human world when the players come to a solution which satisfies the gods, and hopefully the audience.

Picture 53: Gaṅgā in a fierce mood. Statuette, made for the festival season, Nadabwib, West Bengal, photo in Bussabarger & Robins, 1968:134.

Picture 54: Gaṅgā reclining on her crocodile-dolphin-fish. After a kalighat print from 19th Century Calcutta, after Zbavitel, 1976.

43. Manasā Maṅgals

Let's focus on the songs that celebrate the serpent goddess. A wide range of poets contributed to the genre. Maity (2001:323) cites a list which had been compiled by D.C. Sen, naming 58 poets, each of them the creator of a version of the tale. The list is not complete. Nor have the works of all writers survived. The *Manasā Epic* was an all-time favourite. More than any other maṅgalkāvya, her tale became popular over a range of more than a thousand kilometres. It was a unifying cultural influence, bridging the gaps between religions, classes and ethnic groups. The process hasn't stopped. To this day, new versions are created, in poem, prose or, if more successful, as movies and TV series.

One early item appeared in the 14th or 15th century. It was composed by Kānā (the *Blind*, or *Halfblind*) Haridatta. His work is lost, we only know about its existence as Bijay Gupta (Vijaygupta), who was born around the end of the 15th century, had the goddess complain:

A fool composed my song, he didn't know my greatness.

Kānā (one-eyed) Hari Datta first wrote my song.

All of the work of Hari Datta has been lost in the course of time.

His verse was clumsy, he much deceived me.

His story had no coherence; it was not sweet-sounding.

(Smith, 1980:30).

What shall we make of Haridatta? To be one-eyed, blind, or half blind could hint at a tradition where blind people made a living as musicians. Or it could refer to spiritual blindness, and indicate humility. But Haridatta's name Kānā means more. Kānī is one of the titles of Manasā and hints at the episode when Durgā destroyed her eye. Maybe the singer was a devotee.

Who knows if Haridatta was such a bad poet? We only have Vijaygupta's word for it, and, if you ask me, he wasn't such a great poet either. Sure, had had some excellent ideas. He loved to crack jokes about Śiva, presented Cāndo as a vulgar lout and devoted plenty of verses to Manasā's lethal cruelty. His poetic style is bleak, his audience approved of crude remarks and his epic song was so frequently copied, rewritten and extended that textual scholars have to go to bed early and suffer from nightmares.

There are massive differences between the works of simple people, who used crude language and coarse humour to make a living, and that of the refined poets of the upper classes. Some of them took the term 'epic' to the limit, and composed literary masterpieces that mirrored life in all its aspects. Baṁsīdās version amounts to 650 printed pages, and was only topped by the work of Sukavi Nārāyaṇ who wrote approximately 750 pages. To achieve their ends, these poets employed a long-winded, descriptive language with plenty of repetitions. They elaborated on the slaughter inflicted by Manasā and her serpent army, and provided picturesque descriptions of people writhing in death cramps. Another favourite was the suffering of the protagonists. Lakhindār's death can be drawn out endlessly. A few poets were dissatisfied. They made him die twice on his wedding night. Behulā's journey can take ages, provided the reader doesn't mind that she encounters similar robbers, rapists, wild beasts and hallucinations. In my version, I have done my best to limit the repetitions.

Another way to stretch the story was to introduce sub-plots. The great poets were well educated, they knew classical Hindu literature and introduced numerous, somewhat distorted episodes from the *Purāṇas*, and the *Mahābhārata*. Here and there they supplied hymns and ritual instructions. All of these acquired a distinct Bengali character.

For the country people of East India, Manasā is not a remote goddess but a fact of life. Modern people and city dwellers are seriously disadvantaged. Sure, snake symbols, tattoos and images are cool. But you won't understand what they mean unless you've met serpents that could really hurt you. I was lucky. Walking in the Scottish Highlands, I met plenty of adders (Vipera berus), especially early in the morning, when they are moody and bitchy and try to warm up in the hazy sunlight. Truth to tell, that snake is only lethal for elders and children. Adults can expect intense pain, inflammation, possibly a shock. Nevertheless, it's not the sort of thing you'd like to experience, somewhere on a lonely mountainside, with no-one but the Cailleach for company. You get a feeling where to expect them, and appreciate that moment of intense reality when you realise that this moment can be joy, and fascination, or really painful.

Indians can die by snakebite anytime. Their Manasā is lethal, a fierce goddess wielding power over death, healing and resurrection. She is an authority figure, and authority in East India, no matter whether it was wielded by Hindus, Muslims or Europeans, was based on simple, open violence. The same goes for Manasā. In one version of the tale, after Manasā has converted the fishermen Jālo and Malo, she tells them that neglecting her worship would kill them. Those who throw away a Manasā pot, as Bijay Gupta wrote, vomit blood. In one typical example, quoted from Dimock, 1962:318, Neta recommends that Manasā should terrify her worshippers:

Hear me, o merciful one. The snakes are your constant and powerful companions. [...] It is by your snakes that your worship will be established here on earth. Hear me, o Jagatī: you can defeat no one except by showing him the consequences of your wrath. If he is not in trouble, no man in all three worlds will worship you. Therefore, o mother of serpents, slaughter your enemies. Show mercy only to those who will worship you. As many men as you destroy, so many more will worship you.

It isn't nice, politically correct or fluffy minded spiritual. Neta knows that few people love the gods, but many fear them. Nevertheless, generalisations mislead. It's not that all Indians venerate serpents. Several ethnic groups loathe snakes and some, like the Sānthāls, the Orāōs, the Muṇḍas and the Śabaras, eat them.

There are modern versions of the story. An unusual interpretation was made by Śambhu Mitra, the deeply pessimistic theatrical play *Câd Baṇiker Pālā*, premiered in 1978. The play is set in the human realm, and the gods act in the background. Mitra makes Cāndo his hero. Cāndo worships Śiva and for Mitra, Śiva is the principle of freedom, truth and goodness, while Manasā, as Śiva's opponent, represents tyranny, suppression, murder, cruelty, hate, corruption, ignorance and hypocrisy. In short, she is the queen of all vices. In Mitra's opinion, Manasā represents the dark, tamasic guṇa, i.e. the qualities of heaviness, inertia, ignorance, sorrow and materialism. Some Manasā statues are black and several poets identified her with the dark goddess Kālī. Mitra makes much of the metaphor:

Oh mother terrible,
The dark snake deity inhabiting the dark underworld,
Who is darkness manifest, beyond the reach of light,
Beyond all reason, all wisdom,
You can annul all aspiration and bring darkness at noon.

(Kundu, 2008:288). In Mitra's estimation, the universe is an evil place, and Manasā, as its queen, fills it with ignorance, vice, sins, crime and suffering. Cāndo loses his sons, his property and finally all hope. Śiva's light disappears in the eternal darkness of Manasā. The goddess triumphs, as she forces everyone to participate in her reign of evil. Behulā and Lakhindār do the one and only moral thing and commit suicide.

In popular opinion, Manasā remains a favourite. If you want to see something bizarre, check out the Bengali TV series *Behulā*. There are more than 400 episodes, each of them twenty minutes in length, available on Youtube. They are outstanding for bad acting, almost no action and a wonderful example of how an epic tale can be extended into infinity.

44. Brata Rituals

Let's start with the term Vrata. That's the Saṁskṛta spelling; in Bengal, the pronunciation is brata. The word comes from the root vṛ and means *will, intent*. As we are dealing with Bengal rituals in this chapter, I will use the local form. A brata is a magical vow, a religious duty, a spiritual practice. The Saṁskṛta term vratacaryā means spiritual activity. The word appears in the *Atharva Veda*, where we encounter a brief reference to travelling sorcerers, wearing amulets and black clothes, called anayavratas, i.e. vrata ritualists. Maybe they practised some trance or obsession-rituals. That's all we know. Whether the modern brata rituals are related to them remains fiercely debated.

Some scholars claim that folk rituals are developments of the 'high tradition' of educated Hinduism. Others propose that the brata practices started as folk rituals and were subsequently graced with a posh designation and a few upper-class extras. Scholars from Bengal tend to see the brata rituals as an aboriginal development of their motherland, and emphasise their difference to Brahmanical ceremonies (S.K.Ray in Maity, 1988:18).

A vratinī/bratinī (female) and a vratin/bratin (male) are devotees who swear an oath to perform a special religious observance. Maybe it's a regular fast, a pilgrimage, recitation of scripture, giving of alms, ascetic exercises, daily rituals or the performance of good deeds. In Bengal, unlike most of India, brata rituals are conducted all through the year. You might consider them a development of the house- and family cult. Children grow up seeing their parents (or more often, their mothers), participate in them. For most bratas, temples and Brahmins are not required. Brata, as Ray suspects, used to be a form of house religion involving the whole family. The women, he proposed, performed the rituals in the 'inner', i.e. within the house and the courtyard, while the men acted in the 'outer', i.e. on the street, on public places, at the river, in the fields. With the advent of Hinduism, and in particular thanks to the narrow-minded world-view introduced by the Kanoj Brahmins, gender rules became stricter. Men, it might be speculated, oriented themselves along the lines of Hindu and, later, Muslim thought and refrained from participating in most brata rituals, except in secondary roles. Nevertheless, in some bratas, men undergo vows and perform religious practices just as women do. June McDaniel (2003:46-49) refers to the brata rituals of goddess Ṣaṣṭhī. This goddess, or rather, a whole series of goddesses called Ṣaṣṭhī, is among other things, a protector of children. She usually holds a child and is accompanied by a cat. Sometimes she rides the cat and in a few cases she even has the head of one. Or she has the head of a bird. It might remind you of the Babylonian Lamaštu/Lamašti. The Ṣaṣṭhīs are protectors of children and receive special veneration when a child is sick. Though most of their devotees are women, there are also men who worship Ṣaṣṭhī and swear brata vows before her shrine.

Embracing brata vows and strict spiritual discipline, women gain power and influence the gods. A typical example: in traditionally minded families, girls were forced to marry the husband of their parent's choice. Usually during the last centuries, they were not even asked about their preferences. By performing brata rituals, girls could entice the gods to influence their parents. It transformed them from helpless victims into powerful enchantresses. During one evening brata, performed in winter, unmarried girls light lamps and recite: *"Let families of my mother and father grow in wealth and lineage. O Hara, O Śaṅkara, O Bolanāth, do not place me in the hands of a fool."* (Basu, 2005:108)

A lot of lower-class men must have felt quite as helpless as the women. Large sections of society were excluded from the Brahmin ceremonies simply because of their birth, their profession and their income. No doubt plenty of people felt disgusted by a religion that favoured the rich and mighty.

Brata rituals are open for anyone. And they are simple to conduct. Originally, most of them were part of an oral tradition. Around the nineteenth century, the first books of brata rituals appeared. Usually they provided very brief ritual instructions and a short, dry story. The story is a major element. Brata stories are usually sparse. June McDaniel translated several of them. The tales are simple, full of gaps and contradictions, and require improvisation to raise feelings.

On the whole, they start with simple protagonists getting into trouble. Next, a deity appears, and provides a solution. The protagonist performs the required rituals and becomes successful, wealthy and happy. The ritual is performed by the family, then the neighbours become involved and soon the whole district participates. The whole process, and this is crucial, is based on divine inspiration and practical efficiency. The same structure appears in the *Manasā Epic*: the serpent goddess gives the fishermen and the cow herders a few simple instructions. The worshippers do as they are told, improvise as they like, and everybody is happy.

Nowadays we encounter, broadly speaking, two types of brata rituals. The majority are performed by women who assume the role of ritualists, make offerings, swear vows and fulfil them. Thanks to their efforts, households are peaceful, fields are fertile, families have a secure income and pregnancies result in healthy children who are preferably male. In special cases, brata rituals are conducted for wellbeing, to guarantee safe passage over land and sea, and secure employment in far away cities. Modern brata rituals ensure that children do well in school, and that family members find a better job. In some cases, the rituals are for good luck, and promise success in the lottery. Usually, a ritualist swears to conduct a special spiritual practice for at least one year. Some of these ceremonies are conducted on fixed dates, or in special months or seasons. The rituals are colourful and complex and differ in each district. Even in specifically female rituals, men may have a cameo appearance.

The other, less popular group of brata rituals is performed by Brahmins. Their ceremonies are relatively new; they were invented by Brahmins who wanted to control folk religion and make a profit. As you recall, being born as a Brahmin is theoretically better than being a deity. In Bengal, each Brahmin who leads a ceremony expects a gift (usually a set of new clothes) and a dakṣiṇā. That's a ritual fee, or a special present, to make the ritual efficient. Without the dakṣiṇā, so the Brahmins taught, even the greatest offerings will not reach the gods. In the old days of expensive Vedic ritual, the minimal gift was one healthy cow for each priest. Only the aristocracy could afford to sponsor a ritual. Since then, the value of the dakṣiṇā has decreased a lot. Let me quote a few proverbs:

The priest is greedy by nature.

The Brahmin is a beggar, even if he owns a hundred thousand rupees.

Brahmins, rain and flood go away when they receive a dakṣiṇā.

The well-oiled head receives more oil. Poor people walk entirely without oil.

One common dakṣiṇā is a pair of sandals made of gold or silver. That's the basic idea. In real life, the sandals can be tiny. How about a bottle gourd filled with golden coins? Most people can't afford it. The Brahmin gets a gourd, it isn't really big, nor is it full, and few of the coins have much value. Consider the **kalāchārā brata**. It is conducted each day over a full month, and necessitates that a Brahmin receives regular gifts of bananas, betel powder, betel nuts, sweets and money. He doesn't participate in the ritual. Scripture, composed by Brahmins, states that whoever makes gifts to Brahmins wins great spiritual blessings. In the second year, two Brahmins receive presents, in year three, three Brahmins and during the fourth year four Brahmins go home happy without having done a thing.

During the **phal-gachāna brata**, only one Brahmin receives presents. That's a bit mean. However, he gets them every day of the month.

As the Brahmins are manifestations of the divine, they guarantee the blessings of the highest gods. It makes their bratas expensive but classy. The growing class of wealthy Indians feel attracted to Brahmanic brata rituals and enjoys the status derived from making gifts to them.

A traditional brata ritual consists of four basic elements. The first is visual. It's an arrangement of **sacrificial offerings, clay figurines, ritual objects, sacred plants** and a magnificent **ālpanā painting**. The sacrifices are humble. Usually, they consist of fruit, grains, vegetables, flowers and drugs, like betel nut. The clay figurines are small; they are shaped for the ritual. Afterwards, they are destroyed. You can submerge them in a river or pond. Brata rituals often involve special plants, such as sacred tulsī basil (for Viṣṇu), bilva (Aegle marmelos) for Śiva, or rice, for the many goddesses of agriculture. These plants may be arranged around a ritual space, such as a tiny square pond, or placed on a round tray. Each day they receive worship, supplication, praise, songs and blessings. In many rituals, grains are allowed to sprout. After the ritual they may be planted, and bring their blessings to the fields.

An East Indian speciality are **ālpanā (**or: **alpona) paintings**. They are a sacred art. Such paintings are made using a paste of rice on the clean, smooth floor of the courtyard or home. Similar pictures are made all over India. In Bengal they are most popular. Each brata ritual uses at least one traditional ālpanā painting. The designs are passed on within the family. Some emphasise the meaning of a vow, some show what the ritualists desire. Maybe these paintings started with wishful thinking. Call it sympathetic magic: the participants drew pictures of the things they wanted, or of the aims they wanted to achieve. That, however, may have been long ago. Nowadays, it is at least as important to illustrate the deity, as a figure or an arrangement of symbols. In addition, there is an immense range of geometrical shapes, plus ritual objects, offerings and the like. Ālpanā paintings can be quite elaborate. Very popular are the footprints of the goddess. The image shows two feet plus floral elements and blossoms: they invite the house goddess, the village goddess, a great goddess, like Lakṣmī or Durgā, or simply the personal goddess of the woman who makes the painting. In some cases, the footprints appear at the end of a bridge of flowers, inviting the goddess to appear from some paradisiacal otherworld. The footprints are usually surrounded by ornaments, flowers and images of treasure, welcoming the goddess as a guest and asking her to feel at home. Training begins when a girl is around six. By the age of sixteen, she is very skilled and knows a range of designs for various rituals. She has also developed her own style.

Picture 55: Ālpanā painting for Manasā's brata ritual, Bengal, after Mode and Chandra, 1984:195.

Picture 56: Ālpanā painting for Lakṣmīs's brata ritual, Bengal, after Mode and Chandra, 1984: 22.

Picture 57: Footsteps of the Goddess: Ālpanā painting for Lakṣmīs's brata ritual, Bengal, after Mode and Chandra, 1984: 23.

Picture 58: Top: Ālpanā painting for safe travel on sea, bottom: brata painting for unknown ritual, Bengal, after Mode and Chandra, 1984:195 & 226.

Here is a magnificent description. It comes from the Bengal ballad *The Needle Prince*. In our story, the princess is forced to act as the serving maid while the servant pretends to be the princess, becomes queen, and uses the chance to abuse her competitor. In a crucial instant, both women are required to make ālpanā paintings. While the fake queen only manages a few squiggles, the true princess shows her education.

She (the real princess) *kept hands full of rice of a very fine quality – the shati – under water until they were thoroughly softened. Then she washed them carefully and pressed them on a stone. She prepared a white liquid paste with them and first of all she drew the adored feet of her parents which were always uppermost on her mind. She next drew two granaries, taking care to paint the footsteps of the harvest goddess in the paths leading to them, and she introduced at intervals fine ears of rice drooping low with their burden. Then she drew the palace of the great god Śiva and his consort Pārvatī in the Kailāsa Mountains. In the middle of a big lotus leaf she painted Viṣṇu and Lakṣmī seated together, and on a chariot drawn by the royal swan she painted the figure of Manasā Devī from whom all victories proceed. Then she drew the figures of witches* (Yogīnīs?) *and the Siddhas who could perform miracles by tantric practices and next to them nymphs of Heaven (the Apsarases). She drew the sheora grove (Trophis aspera) and under it the figure of Banadevī* (the Forest Goddess). *Then she painted Rākṣa Kālī – the goddess who saves us from all dangers. She next drew the warrior god Kārrtikeya and the writer god Gaṇeśa with their respective vāhanas or animals they rode. And then Rām and Sitā and Lakṣmāna were drawn by her admirably. The great air-chariot Puṣpaka was sketched in her drawings and the gods Yama and Indra were also introduced in this panorama. She next painted the sea, the sun and the moon and last of all an old dilapidated temple in the middle of a woodland with the picture of a dead prince inside it. She drew all figures except her own. The figures of the Needle-Prince and of his courtiers were all there – but not any of her own. When the painting was finished she kindled a lamp fed by sacred butter and then she bowed down with her head bent to the ground.* (Sen, 1923: 268-269, amended)

How does our artist proceed? For a start, she needs cooked rice which has been dried by the sun. She allows it to swell in water and crushes it into a fine, milky paste. If she likes, she mixes it with clay. For a strong colour, a minimum of water is used. Or, if she wants something rare, she adds colourful pigments. The substance is stirred within a small bowl. To apply it, Bengali women prefer a small bit of cloth, sized maybe 8 x 8cm. She dips it in the bowl and allows it to soak up the paste. She wraps it around her middle finger, and starts painting. Traditionally, a brush was not employed. The artist starts in the centre of the design and carefully extends it, layer on layer, to the periphery. Of course some lines go crooked. That's part of the fun. The result is not a perfect geometrical pattern but an organic structure that pulses and throbs with energy.

Such images are not limited to floors, courtyards and doorsteps. Ālpanā paintings decorate clay pots, like the vessels used in Manasā worship. They also appear on house walls.

Nowadays, ālpanās have become an established art form. They are painted on canvas and some are embroidered on textiles. Famous female artists exhibit in art galleries all over the world. In the large cities, ālpanā paintings are sold to tourists. There is a growing ālpanā industry. Designs are created by professional artists, who are usually men, and work in well-organised manufactories. Indeed, contemporary ālpanās tend to be amazingly complex. Most of them are calculated with the help of a computer.

The **second element** of each brata ritual is audible: **sacred songs, ballads** and **mantras**. Many are passed from one generation to the next. One way or another, the brata ritualists picked up sacred sounds and spells. But goddess Time transforms anything. The meaning of words changes. Old songs need to be rewritten or they acquire an entirely new meaning. Maybe a brata ritual started as rain magic. In due time, other rain rituals became more popular. Our brata song, once related to rain, remained in use, but was employed for something else. The anthropologist stops and almost drops the clipboard. He (or she) records the rain song and wonders why the women expect it to bring many children. A ritual, its traditional song and its function do not have to accord with each other.

The third element of brata rituals are special **ceremonial actions**. Some may be done once; others are repeated for weeks or months, or may be performed over several years. Some happen within the household, others may involve the entire village.

The **Aśvattha-brata** is a ritual to make women fertile. Each woman collects five leaves of the aśvattha-fig-tree (Ficus religiosa). Each leaf has its own symbolism. A tender leaf provides a son, an unripe leaf keeps the woman young and beautiful, a ripe leaf ensures that the husband enjoys a long life; a dry leaf attracts joy and income, and a leaf which has dropped to earth promises great prosperity. The women gather their leaves and proceed to a river or pond. As they step into the water, they hold the leaves on top of their heads and sing songs which place them under the protection of the tree. After the bath, a woman tells the proper brata story, which illustrates how the fig tree protects childless women and grants them, after due veneration, sons beyond number.

The **Basudharā-brata** ensures plenty of rain. To make this ritual work, a woman, the bratinī, goes to an aśvattha tree. She is accompanied by a male member of the family. With suitable ceremony, she hangs a large earthenware pot into a branch. The pot has a hole in its bottom, which has been stuffed with durvā grass. Long ago, in primordial times, the gods (devas) and antigods (a-suras) churned the Milk Ocean. As a whisk, Viṣṇu used the Mandāra Mountains. When he lifted the mountain range, a few hairs of his arms were scraped off. They turned into durvā grass and began to grow along the shore of the Milk Ocean. When the gods won the elixir of life, and made libations, a few drops fell on the grass. The result is a respectable, sacred and immortal plant which participates in many rituals. Our bratinī fills the pot with water. The grass swells, and the vessel releases its moisture drop by drop. The result is a gentle, enduring and fertilising downpour. Each morning, after her bath, and before taking food, the bratinī refills the vessel. Day in and day out, for an entire month, the fluids drip, attracting gentle, tender, pleasant rain.

The **Megharānīr-brata** serves a similar purpose. The ritual songs greet the dark-grey clouds (megh) and the beginning of the monsoon. If well sung, the clouds pile up to the sky, and release their moisture in gentle, continuing showers, over many weeks. This brata ritual requires a whole group of ritualists. The women move from house to house for three to seven days. Each of them is prettily attired and holds a special kulā-fan, made of plaited willow rods. The women wear splendid clothes, and they are adorned with red powder, blossoms and sacred durvā grass. A group of bratinīs enters a courtyard. They greet the family; they laugh, sing, and scatter blessed water from small brass vessels which they hold on top of their heads. Their songs invoke the clouds. They receive traditional offerings and gifts, like rice, betel nuts, red powder and oil. In some district, the family assembles on the roof and sprinkles water on them (Maity, 1988:31-37, 40-41).

Bratas for **agricultural fertility** often involve little piles. Some are made of earth, others of cow-dung or rice-husks. Such heaps are made at prominent locations in the courtyard. Each day they receive prayers, and many are adorned with blossoms, week after week. They are a focus of daily ritual; after dusk they become the focus of dances that may continue long into the night.

The fourth element of each brata is one or several **stories**.

In India, as in so many other cultures, **stories** are not a form of trivial entertainment. Stories contain magick. Anyone who listens to a passage of the *Mahābhārata* is sure to win spiritual and worldly blessings. In the days of early Hinduism, Saṁskṛta was still comprehensible and the tales, though slightly strange, were meaningful. As Mogg Morgan told me, kings who listened to the *Book of Drōna*, the famous strategist and martial arts master, were sure to gain success in battle. Some of this was due to the divine power of the story, and some to the stratagems elaborated in the text. To this day, listening to the *Mahābhārata* remains a powerful spell. Sure, most people hardly understand a word. They merely notice the names of some protagonists. It's quite enough. To participate in the telling is far more important than to understand it. When pious people watch the *Mahābhārata* on TV (there are several endless series), they participate in an ancient ritual. Before the show, many light incense and some decorate the TV set with flowers. The audience is not a passive consumer but an active witness, a participator in the divine play. To tell or write a story is an act of magick. You find a similar idea in many other cultures. In old Ireland, as I elaborated in *Cauldron of the Gods*, there were stories that had to be told on special festival days, or when a marriage was celebrated, or only after night time. Stories are magick. People are magickal animals who move in stories, think in stories and invent stories to introduce significance and hope into their lives. That's why we read novels and watch movies. We simplify complex situations, delude ourselves with generalisations and bedazzle ourselves. It makes life straightforward, meaningful and delusive. Each time we explain ourselves to others, we redefine the past. That's why people who fall in love or start a friendship spend ages talking about themselves. In effect, when you relate who you are, you reinvent yourself.

Brata stories differ from, say, the heroic tales of the *Mahābhārata*. Many address the problems of women. One common element is the miseries of a freshly wedded wife. She is very young, she has to leave her family and join the household of her husband. The new family is strange and the mother in law is famous for being a tyrannical despot. Before the young wife has gained status by giving birth to a child, preferably a son, she may be treated like a slave.

Directly after marriage, many Indian women face a terrible time. They encounter problems they never even thought of: home-sickness, lack of integration, conflicts with the in-laws and adjustment to the husband, and his dangerous elder brothers. To top it off, the neighbours watch and listen. Gossip has wrecked many marriages.

There is a brata ritual to pacify a terrifying mother in law. Maity (1988:22-23) cites Dr. S.R. Das, who observed it in Mymensingh. First, a small rectangular pond was excavated in the courtyard. On its eastern side, rice and mānkachu (Colocasia indica) were planted. At all four corners, figurines, made of rice-paste, were set up; they represented crows and kites. The western edge of the 'pond' was graced with a pig figurine. To the east of the 'pond', a figurine was set up showing a woman holding a child. It represented the terrifying mother in law. I guess the baby could symbolise the long-desired son of the bratinī. He would guarantee the future of the family, the happiness of the ancestors and give the young bride a reason to exist. Before the female figurine stood a small tray, woven of willow twigs. It held eight sorts of vegetables, diverse pulses and kitchen utensils. The bratinī scooped up water from the little 'pond' and offered it to the figure of the mother in law. With this act, she had shown submissiveness and done her duty. Now the mother in law had to do hers.

After the ritual, the figurine and the animal figures were dropped into the 'pond', the hole was filled with earth and the whole arrangement disappeared into the Underworld, or the Deep Mind if you like. Dr. Das suspected that this ritual fused an unknown goddess with the terrifying mother in law. Consider that the brata ritual was performed in the family courtyard. Everyone, including the mother in law, was aware of it.

Picture 59: Manasā, kālīghāt print, 19th century.

Part Seven:

The Cult of Manasā

45. Practical Worship

Manasā's realm extends from east to west over a thousand kilometres. The northern fringe at Darjeeling is at the very edge of the Himalayas, the south merges, in a complicated tangle of waterways, swamps, marshes and mangrove flood-lands, with the Indian Ocean. Manasā is popular along the shores of the Bay of Bengal, the largest estuary in the world, as big as Switzerland. There are worshippers of the snake goddess in parts of Bihar, Orissa, and in the eastern states of Assam, Tripura, Manipur, in Bangladesh and maybe even in the fringes of Myanmar, the former state of Burma. In Nepal you will also discover serpent cults, but they are, as far as I know, not focussed on a goddess called Manasā. The favourite serpent goddess of the Himalayas is called Nāgakanyā, meaning *Snake Girl* or *Snake Princess*, who has her own cult and quite a lot of it. She has a crown of five serpents (the senses, the 'elements', the basic tattvas, i.e. *categories*) and wings; and holds a conch (a ritual vessel). Her upper half is human; her lower body is a snake. Manasā can also appear in this shape, but this is only the case in a few districts. Tibet and West China (Yunnan and Sichuan) have their own Nāga cults. I saw plenty of evidence for serpent/dragon worship in the Yunnan Himalayas but no evidence for Manasā.

The cult of Manasā is gorgeously complex. Well, so are all polytheistic religions. You'll be stunned by the courage, the creative originality of each district, each culture and, indeed, each village and household. People are creative. When they have any sense at all, they find inspiration within themselves. Rituals and traditions are not settled forever, they are freshly re-invented all the time and all over the place. That's what keeps the divine alive.

East India houses a vast amount of cultures. They were all influenced, at one time or another, by shamanic polytheism, by Vedic ritual, Buddhism, Jainism, Hinduism, Islam and, in later periods, by Christianity and modern faiths, like Theosophy, Marxism and atheism. In some places the Chinese or Himalayan influence is strong. In others, like Nagaland, the natives resisted foreign influences almost to the end of the 20th Century. Up to the start of the twentieth Century, British anthropologists discovered amazing cultures in the mountains. Some of them were organised along matricentric lines. Some had to be violently discouraged from head hunting. Others were newcomers, like the many Tibetans who fled from their homelands during the last centuries, as the Gelugpa fundamentalists made their lives a nightmare. They moved into north/eastern India and influenced the local Himalayan cultures.

Let's start with the structure of society. Hinduism developed a strict order, and separation, of social classes. The British officially abolished it, and made the natives go to courts where the judges tried to disregard class-associations. When the British hanged one of their countrymen for beating a Hindu labourer to death, they demonstrated a type of justice that hadn't been thinkable before.

Manasā finds her first devotees among crazy Brahmins, ascetics, drop-outs, and low-class folk, like washers, cow herders, peasants and fishermen: the very people who stood the greatest risk of dying by snake bite. It was a start, but it made her unattractive for the upper classes.

Her status varies. In several districts, only the lower classes participate in her worship. These people often employ their own (low class) priests, who have little to do with educated Hinduism or Islam. Many of them are illiterate, but all of them have to show dedication. East Indian goddesses are known for their tempestuous moods. People who fake spirituality are accident prone. But there are also districts where Manasā is promoted by the upper classes, who employ high ranking Brahmins to perform the worship in refined Saṁskṛta.

Some may find it bizarre that Manasā's cult attracts so many Muslims. Islam is, theoretically, a monotheist religion. One should imagine that people follow rules. In real life, they don't. Most worshippers come from low classes, are illiterate, and lack an education. Simple worshippers are pragmatic. They don't give a damn for principles when another cult promises results. East India produced a wide range of cross-over faiths, and famous poets and saints who made them popular.

Manasā can be celebrated in many ways. There's the folk cult, practised by households, families, village communities and professional groups like cow herders, snake doctors and spice merchants. There's the individual cult, endorsed by people who treasure the goddess as their personal deity. And there is a temporal cult, based on the special festivals, the days, weeks and months devoted to her worship. Here, you encounter a lot of variation. Finally, there is upper-class worship, strongly influenced by the Manasā who made it into sacred literature. All of these exerted their influence. Often enough, they overlap. It provides the serpent goddess with a complex and fascinating personality. She awaits your contribution.

Some people have a close relationship. They are likely to perform rituals and meditations every day. If this isn't possible, they will prefer the typical days of goddess worship, i.e. the night of Tuesday to Wednesday and that of Friday to Saturday. Their cult place will be a small shrine; maybe a wall or a corner of a room. It will have a picture of the goddess, or, if affordable, a small statue, or an image of a cobra. There will be a small metal pot holding sacred water and a sij twig on top. The goddess will be illuminated by a few small candles or brazen lambs radiating the soft, golden glow of ghī. The shrine may be decorated with fresh flowers, favourites being marigolds, lotus, water lily and whatever is available. A small dish may hold an offering of milk, small bananas, rice, half a coconut or a sample of your meal. Those who can afford it may also have a bell, which is used to 'wake' the image of the deity.

More professional is the Manasā cult among the large potter clans who produce thousands of earthenware pots for the grand festivals of the goddess. Then there are the ohjā ritualists. Some call them snake doctors; some class them as tribal shamans, sorcerers and wonder healers. Many ohjās carry snakes and use them to demonstrate their power. Others do not. However, every one of them needs a close relationship to the serpent goddess. Manasā is also a favourite of the class of spice and scent merchants. Coming from the same class as Cāndo, they feel obliged to participate in the worship. Many of them are quite rich. As the highest class of merchants, they display their wealth and their religious aspirations when they sponsor statues, offerings and professional priests.

Finally, I would like to mention the tiny minority of dedicated souls who practice Tantra, meditation or yoga and enjoy an intensely personal relationship with the goddess. Some adore her as a personal deity. It may be a peaceful and tranquil effort or happen in fits of crazy obsession. These people are so close to their gods that it's hard to tell if you are talking with their human or divine personality. It's a wonderful and intense thing, but it doesn't make the devotees popular nor is the relationship entirely easy.

Vaiṣṇavas rarely worship the serpent goddess. The devotees of Viṣṇu make up a vast section of pious Hindus. Usually, they tend to approve of law and order, appreciate middle-class values and pretend to follow ritual practices that go back to Vedic times. Many of them are content with the class system, and harbour a strong dislike for ascetics, yogīs, tribal ritualists and, worst of all, hot-blooded tantrics of the Left Hand Path. The majority dislikes the Śākta cults and insists that women ought to obey their husbands, no matter what. That, however, is a general estimation. When you explore the fine details, you can encounter small groups of tantric and śāktic Vaiṣṇavas who believe that Lakṣmī is the power of the universe and that Viṣṇu owes his majesty and wealth to her. Indeed, without her grace, he could pack his things and retire. Such groups are in the minority. When a tantric Vaiṣṇava wants to lead a socially acceptable life, she or he will stoutly refuse to admit such notions. Some dedicated Vaiṣṇavas did their best to integrate Manasā into their cult. Thanks to their effort, there is the story of how Manasā worshipped Kṛṣṇa until he got down on his knees and started to worship her. It appeals to Śāktas and is ignored by the religious mainstream.

Most Vaiṣṇavas will watch the antics of Manasā's worshippers from a safe distance. The same goes for upper-class Śaivas. Śiva worshippers tend to have a predilection for crazy and wild behaviour. But if you want to get ahead in a society controlled by Vaiṣṇavas, Muslims, Marxists and atheists, it's a great idea to keep your personal faith in the background.

Manasā worshippers use a wide range of names to praise their goddess. Here, are a few of the more popular ones.

You might think the name **Manasā** is the favourite. It appeals to intellectuals who like the idea that the goddess embodies manas, i.e. consciousness, Śivas consciousness or even the All-Consciousness, Brahman. That's as exalted as a deity can get. It turns her into the awareness that makes the entire cosmos and all the millions of worlds, beings and things possible. However, given that so many of her worshippers are simple people with simple needs, other names are far more popular. The great favourite is **Viṣahari, Viṣaharī** or, as the Bengali like to pronounce it, **Biṣahari/Biṣaharī**. The title is ancient and somewhat difficult. It could be translated as *Full-of-Poison, Poison-Lady, Destroyer-of-Poisons* or as *Releaser-of-Poisons*. That's a rough estimate and a good description of her functions. However, for linguistic reasons, each translation is doubtful. Asutosh Bhattacharya pointed out that the name ought to be Viṣahāriṇī or Viṣahara, if it related to someone who has power over poison or is able to destroy it. Maybe the name actually started out that way, and was corrupted by people who didn't understand Saṁskṛta. Maity suspected that the name Viṣahari might be older than the name Manasā, but gave no evidence for his assumption.

Quite friendly are the names **Padmavatī** (*Lotus-born*), **Padmā** (*Lotus*) and **Kamalā** (*Lotus*). They show that the serpent goddess is close to the vegetable realm (after all, her first mother was a blossom) and remind us of an unknown lotus goddess of prehistory. All three names also appear as titles of Lakṣmī, the goddess of light, well-being, wealth, fertility, abundance, joy, love and beauty. Padmavatī also appears as the name of a Jaina Nāga goddess, who seems to be unrelated to Manasā's cult. Occasionally, Manasā is invoked with the name **Jāgulī/Jāṅgulī**, a badly documented Buddhist goddess whose popularity began around the late sixth or early seventh Century. Miranda Shaw (2005:225 & 233) wrote: *The name Jāṅgulī, meaning "Snake-Charmer", denotes a goddess* *who counteracts "venom" (jāṅgula), possesses "Knowledge of Poisons" (jāṅgulā), and "lives in the jungle" (jāṅgala) (...) Jāṅgulī was transmitted to Tibet, where her name was rendered Dukselma, "Poison Remover."*

Unlike Manasā, the Buddhist serpent goddess was never widely popular. There are several reasons. Jāṅgulī was invoked to heal serpent bites. Tantric Buddhists, venerating Jāṅgulī in northern India, were exterminated or expelled when the Muslims invaded. The goddess continued in a very minor role in Tibetan Buddhism. Tibet, however, is far too high for most reptiles. Serpent bites are rare and the goddess became a vague memory. She remained limited to the art of healing snake bite, while in faraway India, Manasā became a high goddess, in charge of everything you can think of. Jāṅgulī is often associated with white serpents or even appears as one. Her iconography is close to the Hindu goddess Sarasvatī. It's hardly surprising. When the early Buddhists began to crave political power and wealth, they boldly copied Vedic and Hindu deities who had been worshipped a thousand years before the Buddha was born. The Vedic river goddess Sarasvatī, patroness of speech, learning, science and music, was used as a model for Buddhist goddess Jāgulī: she rides a swan and holds a vīṇā lute. It's a nice thought, and became influential in Chinese and Japanese Buddhism. Another popular name of our serpent deity is **Mārai** or **Mārī**. Here things become really complicated. The historical Buddha gained enlightenment while sitting under a sacred tree. He vowed to stay until he had attained liberation. The ordeal was tough. He was scorched by the sun, frozen by cold and almost starved to death. Finally, he faced his greatest challenge. A god called Māra appeared before him and tempted him to give up. The Buddhist Māra is a form of the ancient Vedic god Kāma. He is *Desire, Lust, Love*, and older than most deities. The name Māra is said to derive from mṛi, *'to die'*, hence, he is death personified. The Buddhists loathed him. In their opinion, Māra is totally evil, a force representing death, plague, doom, lust, desire and love. Well, however much he tried, Māra didn't achieve much. The Buddha remained where he was. So Māra sent his lascivious daughters, the Mārai. They danced around the Buddha, trying to beguile and tempt him. The historical Buddha ignored the girls, endured all challenges and became enlightened. It almost killed him. In Bengal folk religion, Mārai is a goddess of plagues. Sure, she represents death, disease, desire, love and lust. She has her own iconography, showing her riding on a donkey, and she gets plenty of attention each time the cholera breaks out. In some old representations, she appears nude. In contemporary ones, she is decently clothed. But she is also; explain this who will, Manasā. In some districts, the two goddesses are so closely identified with each other that names cease to matter. Manasā songs may be called Māre Git and serpent worship can be called Mārai Pūjā.

Another special name is **Bāhuṛā** (*Without Husband*), indicating that Manasā is an independent woman. The name is almost revolutionary. In Hindu and Muslim thought, unmarried women are bad luck. **Kharatarī** is the *Rough, Wild, Headstrong One*. As **Jagat Gaurī** (*Light of the World*), our cheerful serpent goddess represents universal consciousness. Without awareness-light, the worlds cannot exist. **Priyā** is the *Beloved*, the *Dear One*. **Anantā** is the *Endless*, or *Infinite One*. The name is the female counterpart of the male Ananta, the cosmic serpent who serves as Viṣṇus and Lakṣmīs's couch. In our *Epic*, Ananta is her brother, and a ruler of the serpent underworld. While Anantā rules space, the name **Nityā** (*Eternal, Always*) celebrates how Manasā transcends time. Such titles are excellent if you want to understand the limits of awareness (space and time); they had less appeal to farmers and businessmen. Others call her **Nāgdevī** (*Serpent Goddess*), **Nāgeśvarī** (*Serpent Ruler/Queen*) or **Nāgamātā** (*Serpent Mother*). One name the goddess doesn't like was coined by Cāndo: **Beṅgakhāki Kaṇi**, the *One-Eyed Frog-Eater*.

We can think of Manasā as a unique character. But we can also observe her transform into other deities. Indian gods are not strictly defined. They merge, become each other, and change their gender, powers, divine symbols and functions. Manasā is frequently identified with major deities like Lakṣmī, Kālī, Sarasvatī, and Śiva's wife Gaurī. She may appear as the female form of Brahmā, Viṣṇu, and Śiva, or assumes the shape of her sister Neta. Sometimes she pretends to be Śiva or the famous sorcerer Dhanvantari. Plus plenty of animals.

Manasā can be invoked anywhere, as consciousness (manas) is continuous. Nevertheless, there are places where she is a little easier to approach. Traditional favourites are springs, brooks, rivers, canals and streams, the confluences of rivers, swamps, ponds, marshes and waterfalls. She delights in places that lead to the underworlds, like wells, caves, holes, cliffs and chasms, and feels attracted to special rocks and stones. Wherever the vegetation dominates a place, the serpent goddess is near. Indian faiths make much of sacred trees, and there is a whole range of trees and plants associated with Manasā. Near human settlements, you may find her represented in a shrine, a temple, in an open space, or, on a minimalist level, as a special rock or heap of earth. Like so many deities of East India, Manasā is not a specialist. She may appear like one, as her iconography is so closely related to snakes, but that doesn't keep her from doing all sorts of jobs.

In Indian thought, the realm of the divine is not a bureaucracy where every deity has a specific office, resort, peculiar functions and business hours. Sure, deities do have characteristics and moods. However, their abilities overlap. Let's have an example. In Bengal, plenty of deities are asked to provide children. Among them are Śiva, Kārrtikeya, and a whole series of goddesses called Ṣaṣṭhī. There are plenty of Caṇḍīs: Maṅgal Caṇḍī, Melāī Caṇḍī, Nehrāī Caṇḍī, Keñoyā Caṇḍī, and there are Dharma Thakur, Kālī, Satyapīr, Satyanārāyan, Sītalā, Bhādu, Pañcānan plus diverse Hindu and Muslim saints, and, of course Manasā. That's no reason to class the lot as 'birth deities' or limit their functions to human fertility. Several don't have families or children. Some of them habitually destroy the universe!

The devotees don't care. In their opinion, anyone with divine powers can grant wishes. It hardly matters what these wishes are about.

Of course Manasā is a prime candidate when it comes to healing serpent bites. Indeed, her devotees differ from the rest of the population. Those who love the goddess meet toxic animals and plants with respect, care, love and devotion. Serpents, spiders, scorpions and centipedes are her manifestation. The same goes for many toxic plants. You treat them cautiously and with loving respect, instead of having panic attacks. It reduces the amount of accidents. In some ranges of East India, Manasā is so popular that people allow cobras to move freely through the settlement. They slide through alleys, hide in barns or come visiting your house. The worshipers remain calm. They don't run around, hit them with sticks or make a stupid scene. Instead, they go about their business in peace. The cobras feel welcome and remain (mostly) calm. Occasionally, accidents occur. Some unintentionally step on a cobra, or scare it. Some wake to find a cobra in their bed. Bites do happen. They are not meant to. Cobras don't want to waste their poison of animals that are too big to be digested. Usually, they only inject a part of their venom. Humans may be hurt. However, the healing rate is much better than in other districts. Devotees are less likely to suffer from shock or allergic reactions, and recover faster. It's similar when you are stung by a wasp. If you make a grand scene, the sting will be extra painful. That's classic Gong Fu lore: if you think of the pain it hurts twice as much. If, however, you sink into a pleasant trance, think happy feelings into the wound and extend your love to the insect, the healing may be faster.

Snake bites are not the only domain of Manasā. She is asked to bring the much-desired monsoon rains, to make the fields fertile, to battle plagues like cholera and pox, to heal skin diseases, banish curses and the Evil Eye, to bring success, to unite lovers, to keep children healthy and journeys safe, to grant fertility, wealth, domestic harmony and well-being. In tantric circles, her major gifts are insight, knowledge, wisdom, understanding, and liberation. Here, the goddess is praised as a **Yoginī**, i.e. as a woman or goddess who practices union (yoga), or as a witch or sorceress. Or she is worshipped as the **Bhogīnī**, a term that can mean a *Coiled One*, or an *Enjoyer*, one who knows the world and delights in it. The titles Yoginī and Bhogīnī are related. According to traditional Hindus, a yogīn cannot be a bhogīn, i.e. an ascetic renouncer cannot be a worldly enjoyer. It is a typical insight of Left Hand Path literature that the tantric practitioner has to be both.

The ritual employs an earthenware or metal **pot**, which is partly filled with **holy water**. Such vessels are essential for Manasā worship, but they also appear in rituals for other goddesses. Manasā's pots may be graced with a crude picture of the goddess, or a painting showing snakes and flowers, but that's an optional extra. In the *Manasā Epics*, we encounter sacred pots made of gold. Sonakā acquired a golden pot from the fishermen, but when Cāndo smashed it, the pieces flew in all directions. That's only possible with a breakable pot: a golden vessel would have been flattened. Perhaps some people used gilded pots, or vessels painted yellow. That's a guess. In general, the Manasā pots are made of clay and some are painted red. For private worship, devotees may place a small metal pot in front of the image. Such vessels can be tiny; in the old days, they were made of brass, copper, bronze or bellmetal (an alloy of seven metals representing the planets) and went green with corrosion. That's why modern Indians prefer small pots made of stainless steel. In temples, larger pots may be used. In some districts, two pots are set up, one for Manasā and one for Neta.

The potters in the districts Bankura, Burdwan and Hooghly produce thousands of Manasā pots each year. Many of them are lovingly decorated or painted. Most of the population celebrates the serpent goddess during the monsoon season. Unlike most worshippers, the potters have four feasts for the goddess, which happen in the months Māgha (January/February), Phālguna (February/March), Vaiśākha (April/May) and Śrāvaṇa (July/August). The pots are called manasār-bāri (*vessel to worship Manasā*). There are also highly fantastic vessels which are supposed to look like Manasā's head (see illustration). The vessels are treated in different ways. In some districts, they are set up before a shrine, in a temple or under a sacred tree. In other districts, they are made for private households. Maybe they are only made to last during the rainy season. Or they are used for worship, all through the year. In many districts, they are thrown into the river after the festivals are over. But there are also places where the sacred pot is cleaned and used for household purposes.

A typical extra in Manasā rituals is a **sij twig**. That's a loose term for a branch of a euphorbia plant. The twig is placed across the top of the Manasā pot or stood up in it. Usually, it is tough and spiky. In Central Europe, euphorbias are small and tender flowers. They have pretty yellow blossom and try to look innocent. If you pluck them you are in for trouble. Herbalists occasionally used them again warts. They gave up, as the application was difficult. The milky sap is acidic and toxic. It can irritate the skin and damage the eyes. In warm countries, around the Mediterranean Sea, euphorbias can grow into shrubs. In India, Indonesia, Madagascar and many places in Africa, euphorbias can be bushes and even look like small trees. Many of them have spikes, a water-storing body and resemble cacti. It's a wonderful example of convergent evolution: euphorbias in the Old World and cacti in the New are often similar. They are tough, they are nasty and they like to coil. People in India call several euphorbias sij (Bengal: siju), or even simpler, Manasā trees. *Euphorbia nivulia, Euphorbia neriifolia, Euphorbia antiqorum, Euphorbia tircucalli* and *Euphorbia ligularia* have all been identified as Manasā's favourite plant. Plus, as Frank noted in 1837, *Euphorbia nagadru*, the nāga tree. Alternatively, if you want something spiky and tough, you can use *Cactus indicus*.

Serpents like to rest under spiky plants, as they ensure protection from hungry birds and people with big feet. Several species are used for medicine. It would be easy to get this wrong. Some euphorbias are used to treat snakebite. These, however, are not the euphorbias used for Manasā rituals. In some districts, the choice of sij twigs doesn't even depend on toxins, spikes or a pleasantly twisted shape. If you like, you can place the stalk of a lotus blossom or a water lily across your vessel. Or use a mango twig. Another favourite group of Manasā plants is the pandanus family. There are maybe 600 species worldwide. Several grow in India. Translators like to render the name as 'screw pine'. That's a misleading term, as the pandanus plants are not like pines at all. *The 'screw' is understandable, since the tops of the stems are twisted and the long narrow leaves, which in reality are in three rows, seem to form a spiral* (Tudge, 2005:144). In Bengal, the term ketakā is used. It's also a name of Manasā. One famous poet called himself Ketakādās. It means *Servant/Slave of Ketakā/Manasā*. I've seen pandanus plants that were as large as trees. Others were tangles, wildly growing stalks crowned by a bush of twisted leaves displaying fearsome jagged edges. Some have glorious red flowers. Some are used as spices, and are popular in Thai cuisine. Others contain dimethyltryptamine and may cause *irrational behaviour* (Alberts & Mullen, 2000:156). That's what the natives of New Guinea say.

Indian serpent cults are closely related to tree and plant worship. Look at Manasā! Her father Śiva accidentally ejaculates on a lotus blossom. Or, as some tales have it, he ejaculates anywhere. A crow picks up the milky sap; it's too hot for her, so she drops it on a lotus blossom. The flower soaks it up and allows it to seep into the deepest underworld. The flower is Manasā's mother. When serpent queen Kadrū swallows the stuff, she acts as a stepmother and nurse. It may explain why Manasā is so close to plants. In practical worship, plenty of trees suit her rituals. One splendid group is the fig family. In many Indian villages, there is a sacred banyan tree growing in the marketplace, or near a temple, a shrine or in some place where people gather in the evening. The banyan (Ficus religiosa) can look quite ophidian; it has vast extended branches and plenty of roots and tendrils that coil and twine and crush. Whenever a plant twists, writhes and spirals, it is excellent for Manasā worship. Just as good are bananas. Forget the normal sort. Small bananas are a better choice. Indians believe that serpents love bananas, especially with warm milk. Ohjās may drag a snake-bitten patient to a banana plant. They magically extract the poison and transfer it to the tree. I guess the closeness of serpents to bananas is best understood when you look at the long and spindle-shaped blossom that emerges from a cluster of bananas. It looks like a serpent.

If you want a plant to worship Manasā, go for a spiky, thorny plant with a bad attitude. Hereabouts, I would recommend brambles, hawthorn, blackthorn or rose hip. They all want to get close to you. The common Central European euphorbias ain't tough enough. They lack thorns, a twisted form and resolute endurance.

In the old days, small **clay figurines** were used to represent deities. Nowadays, the great Hindu festivals require figures which are large. The figure makers produce quality images of the gods. They start out with an interior structure made of bundles of grasses and twigs. Bamboo and reeds stabilise the construction. When the figure is moderately defined, the statue makers shape layers of clay around it. The task requires patience. If you apply thick layers, the clay won't dry evenly and crack. It's much safer to go slowly, and to wait until each layer has dried before the next is applied. Figure making isn't a hobby but a professional skill. Making a large statue takes weeks. During the process, the deity is praised, worshipped and treated like a family member. Finally, when all layers are dry, the surface is smoothed and painted. Clothes and ritual utensils are added, plus extras like glass, paper, feathers and ornaments. Śiva receives his hourglass-shaped drum, representing the pulse of the heart/mind, and the trident. Kṛṣṇa is equipped with his enchanted bamboo flute. Durgā is placed on her vehicle, a lion or tiger, crushing the buffalo demon of pride and egoism. Nowadays, such figures are essential for all major Hindu festivals. Often, they are set up on wagons and paraded through the city, while the devotees dance to shrill, mind-numbing music.

Anything important needs a setting. Statues are usually placed within a shrine or a symbolic representation of a temple. This structure (pandal) earths the deity. It is made of bamboo, cloth, paper, and graced with ornaments, tinfoil, and fresh blossoms. The setting is made by another social class. In our days, a third element is essential. The deity is often surrounded by electric bulbs in many colours, and when the festival is important, like Durgā Pūjā, lighting can be elaborate and controlled by a computer. In the great cities, there is often a competition. The best statue, setting and lighting will be judged and prizes will be offered.

The statues are the gods, for a time. When the festivities end, the priests ask the deities to leave their figures. It's a sad moment and many people feel upset. The deity departs from its image. Worshippers may offer parting gifts, and ask the deity to stay with them. Finally, the wagons are driven to the shore of the sea or the riverbank. The statues, empty, meaningless, bereft of the divine, are carefully lifted from their vehicles and carried into the water. The flood dissolves the clay; the images sink into the waves and disappear. It's not an act of destruction. From beginning to end, the statues were temporary vehicles of the divine. No-one expected them to last. In Indian thought, just as in real life, things never last forever. Anything with a name, a shape, a function, is limited to the temporal world. Some call it illusion. Others call it reality. But whatever it is, it will change and disappear. The statues, for all their beauty, performed a task. They return to the flow of life and death, into the eternal coming and going that makes the world so beautiful. It might make you weep or laugh. Next year, there will be other figures. People will discuss whether they are better or worse than the ones that went before.

When ritual descriptions mention clay figures of Manasā, keep in mind that they might be small crude figurines or large, life-like figures made with professional skill.

Manasā statues have a lot of extras. The goddess is often shown with four arms. In two hands, she holds cobras and another group of cobras, usually five or seven, emerge from her headdress. While in her *Epics* she prefers to walk nude, for ritual processions she is beautifully clad. Her seat is a serpent or a water bird. It can be a goose, swan, duck or flamingo. All of them are counted as the famous haṁsa birds, the free-roaming vehicles of breath and spirit.

Let's enjoy this moment and exhale. Then let a new **breath** fill your lungs. Nāga deities thrive on breath. They are wind-eaters, and find nourishment in good fresh air. It's time for a meditation which may accompany you for the rest of your life. The word **haṁsa** is a curious hybrid. According to the *Kulārṇava Tantra* and other influential texts, the mantra 'haṁsa' is the only natural mantra. Its recitation (japa) doesn't take any effort. You've been reciting haṁsa every moment of your life. The sound Ha is your exhalation and the sound Sa your inhalation. That's the basic idea. Some texts have it the other way around. As Ha is Śiva (Hara, the *bandit*, the *destroyer*, i.e. the transcendent) and Sa is Śakti (*force, energy* and *consciousness-in-power-and-form*), the mantra 'haṁsa' refers to the endless, eternal cycles of destruction and re-creation. As you inhale, you create the world. As you exhale, you dissolve it. This meditation is about taking and giving, about life and death, and about Manasā and Neta.

In between the Ha and the Sa appears the sound ṁ, pronounced 'ng'. It is inserted for grammatical reasons, and as the vibration sounds great. Haṁsa is breath and breath is a sacrament shared by all beings. Consider it a unifying experience. Maybe you think that you are breathing. The whole world is breathing you.

Haṁsa is breath and breath is behind each mantra. Without haṁsa, mantras shrivel and fail. You have to align them to your inspiration, which creates, and your expiration, which exhausts. Stupid people huff and puff and strain their lungs. Wise Nāgas realise haṁsa as they watch their breath. It takes no effort. It should never be a project, a task or a strain. There is no goal, there is just being. The haṁsa water bird takes you through the firm world, the fluid world and the gaseous realm of air. And it takes you, like all the water birds that adorn Bronze Age European art, through the worlds and otherworlds and beyond. It's a wonderful idea, and a complete system of meditation.

You can sink into a nice leisurely trance by watching your breath. However, there are a few details to observe. For a start, your breath should be calm, relaxed and joyous. When you watch your breath, you'll be inclined to influence it. It's not easy to watch without interfering. Consider speed and power: if you breathe fast it isn't going to relax you at all. So do yourself a favour. Calm down. Let go. Allow breath to flow as it likes. It will slow down in its own good time.

Second, focus your attention on the exhalation. The exhalation is closely connected to the parasympathetic nervous system. It makes you calm down and sink deep. Provided you relax into it. Wild panting may be exciting, but for this trance it won't do.

Third, many people 'watch breath' to induce a trance. When they feel happily deep down and pleasantly slow, they move on to other things. They recite mantras, go for journeys in the imagination ('shamanic flight' or 'astral travels'), visualise all sorts of stuff, meet the gods and so on. All of these are valuable. All of them have a purpose. However, if you want to realise the pure essence of haṁsa, you don't.

Watch your breath. It's the easiest and hardest thing in the world. Plenty of thoughts will clamour for attention. They always do. Who cares? All sorts of distractions may appear. Maybe you go daydreaming, or lose yourself in memories, or wishful thinking. No matter. Don't make a scene. This isn't about abolishing thinking, nor do you want to enforce silence and voidness. Ideas go floating through your mind, well; some of them may be really good. Remember them later on. Or have a notebook at hand and record them. Return to your breath. Relax and enjoy. Your breath will be soft, possibly minimal, most of the time. Occasionally you may take deeper breaths to freshen up. Simply watch what happens. And calm down again.

As you breathe, your awareness expands and contracts. Your heart/mind opens and closes like a lotus blossom. This meditation isn't about goals. There is no aim, no purpose, no ambition. Maybe you forget what you are doing. Return to it. Maybe you forget yourself. Maybe you even fall asleep. That's all well and good. We all need more sleep than we get. The important thing is to leave result-orientation out of the game. We are not trying to reach enlightenment, to realise voidness or to blot ourselves out in Buddhist fashion (nirvān means *cessation*). Nor do we try to be totally conscious, or aware, or unconscious. We simply watch our breath. We only watch our breath.

It can be a challenge. Some people get upset. Some are overwhelmed. A few are nervous, worried, or go angry. Hard, tense people may encounter scary feelings. Clever people may invent a million reasons to do something else. Some will itch, some will twitch and some will crave to check their mobile phones. Watch yourself as you reach your limits. And relax. Put a smile into it. This isn't a fight. It's more like letting go. Maybe you'll encounter a flood of internal babble and silly mindstuff. It will pass away. Maybe you are submerged in an ocean of silence. If it's any good, enjoy it. And let it pass by. Watch your breath.

Maybe you'll see exciting things. When the mind calms and your eyes relax, astonishing visual effects may appear. Enjoy them. But don't stare. Staring means tension. And return to your breath. Maybe your eyes remain open and maybe they close. Or you'll close them half-way, as Śiva and Manasā do in meditation.

Riding the haṁsa bird doesn't get you anywhere specific. It doesn't aim at anything. But it will refresh and renew your mind. It will allow you to experience life with the innocence and enthusiasm of your natural self.

Good trances move in waves, they pulse, they transform. Sometimes you go deep; sometimes you float to the surface, and sink down again.

It's just breath. Pulsation. Energy. Awareness. Manasā: the journey from birth to death, and Neta: from death to rebirth. In and out. No beginning, no end, no ulterior motive. Make it a happy experience. As you retain awareness of your breath, you travel, like Manasā and Neta, in a haṁsa bird chariot through the sky.

Manasā's **statue** may recline on a serpent, or on a huge pink lotus blossom. Or she may rest under the hood of a giant cobra. When the goddess doesn't hold snakes, she may show a pair of empty hands. When the palm faces you and the fingers point up, it's the abhaya mudrā, the gesture, lock or seal: *don't be afraid*. When the palm faces you and the fingers point down, the sign is varada mudrā: *I grant boons and fulfil wishes*. Plenty of high gods show these gestures. Or she may hold utensils. One typical arrangement consists of trident and ḍamarin drum (both represent Śiva). The drum is shaped like an hourglass, it's a rotation drum, played by ascetics and wandering beggars. Two strings with beads are hanging from the sides. When you rotate the drum, the beads strike the drumheads. By pressing against the ropes, you can alter the pitch. Some travelling mendicants play rhythms with them. For Śiva, the drum represents the heart/mind. Think about it.

The trident is a cosmic symbol celebrating the trinity. Śiva received it almost accidentally. When the descendants of Alexander occupied land near the Indus, they introduced the Indians to Greek statues. The local stone-smiths copied them, as well as they could, and added a couple of non-Indian extras. That's why Buddha statues are so close to Greek art. For the representation of Śiva, they copied Poseidon, the god of the great oceans. That's how Śiva acquired his trident. He isn't really interested in spearing fish. However, his tantric followers delight in all sorts of trinities, like the primal Śaktis Icchā (*will, intend, desire*), Jñāna (*wisdom, knowledge, experience*) and Kriyā (*action, doing*). These ladies are the first manifestations of formless consciousness, the creators of the universe and the essence of all forms and energies. Manasā may also hold a curved knife and a skull bowl full of blood. She borrowed them from Kālī. The knife represents the power to separate one thing from the other and to think, to analyse and liberate. The bowl is a human cranium, it is full of blood representing, among many other things, that you and I and every worshipper has to offer her or his essence. In advanced tantric circles, the skull-cup indicates that the true elixir is created in the mind. Alternatively, she may hold a lotus blossom, representing her birth from a lotus flower, or the pure essence of the heart/mind, usually associated with Lakṣmī. The other hand may hold a whirling disk, such as Viṣṇu spins around a finger, meaning she keeps the universe in motion.

Occasionally, Manasā's statue is accompanied by a smaller female figure, which represents her sister Neta. Maybe there are a male and female figure to her left and right, symbolising Behulā and Lakhindār. In districts with wealthy Hindu populations, Manasā can be accompanied by Hindu high-gods, like Lakṣmī and Gaṇeśa, Sarasvatī and Kārrtikeya. If the sponsor of the statue belongs to the educated Brahmin class and loves the *Mahābhārata*, Manasā may be in the company of Jaratkāru, Vāsuki and Āstika. In a few places, like districts Haldi, Chandipur and Santinandi, Manasā may be half human and half snake. It makes her look like the Nepalese Nāgakanyā.

Pot, twig and clay figurine are not really necessary. Nothing really is, for when you understand consciousness, anything can represent anything else. Some use a **picture** of the goddess instead. It can be painted on paper, wood, cloth, the floor or a wall. One offshoot of the ritual ālpanā paintings is the custom to paint large, wonderfully naive pictures on walls. Houses are often whitewashed, using incinerated cow dung. Cow manure is sacred. The ashes scare demons away and can be used to bless houses, floors, courtyards or ingested as medicine. In many households, the floor and yard are washed with diluted cow dung every morning. Unlike the ālpanā floor paintings, the wall-pictures are often made with a thin reed or bamboo stick. Its top is wrapped with cotton string or grass. Nowadays, brushes are employed. The colours used to be self-made. Sandalwood paste supplied red, yellow was made with arsenic, indigo supplied blue, and green was made by mixing indigo and arsenic. Black was usually soot or burned bones. To bind the pigments, cow urine and an extract of the gum tree were blended, while goat milk was a solvent (Peller, 1988:28). Eventually, it became fashionable to make such paintings on paper made of daphne; it's thin and doesn't tear easily. Once, the sheets were handmade. Nowadays, they are an industrial product. The art of East Indian women is famous all over the world. The seemingly 'naive' paintings are sold in top art galleries. Instead of the traditional pigments, the artists use acrylic colours. Manasā is a popular topic.

In Maity's times, Manasā pictures were widely available. Sure, they were a far cry from the colourful posters of our time. Poor people made do with cheap, monochrome prints. One composition shows the goddess in the centre. She has four arms, holds snakes and makes the gestures that dispel fear and grant boons. Her vehicle is a lotus blossom; behind her, a huge cobra serves as a baldachin. Around her, four scenes are illustrated. They are arranged counterclockwise (for the observer). Seen from the perspective of the goddess, they are clockwise, which is the auspicious way. Top right shows the building of the iron chamber. Top left illustrates how Behulā and Lakhindār spend their wedding night in it. Usually we see Behulā holding a fork: she tries to catch the snake Kāli. Her husband lies in the background, he is obviously dead. Bottom left shows Behulā standing on the raft, next to the corpse of her husband. Bottom right is the end of the tale: Cāndo gives up; he kneels before the goddess and offers flowers.

In some districts, a picture isn't enough. The worshippers construct a small model of a **house** out of paper, cloth and plant marrow. The walls are painted with images from the *Manasā Epic*. It combines the picture with a shrine and makes the goddess feel at home.

It's neat and cheap. But things can be simplified.

Take a lot of dry grasses. Bind them into bundles, form the twisted body of a **snake** and cover the contraption with clay. When it is thoroughly dry, repair the cracks with more clay. Eventually, the surface will be smooth. You can paint it. Or you may form a snake out of earth. Earth is sacred and the representation, no matter how crude, will do. Or you form a **pyramid** or **cone** using pieces of tree bark. Or you may raise a simple **pile** of earth. It gives your ritual a focus. Or make two piles, one for Manasā and one for Neta. Personally, I would suggest you ram two nicely twisted **twigs** into the ground. They connect heaven and earth. As a focus of the ritual they will do fine. Another East Indian favourite is an unusual **stone**. You can identify it with the goddess. The career of many Bengal deities began that way. If you like, you can use red powder to colour the stone. Such stones are often set up near the serpentine roots of fig trees.

Fishers like to paint images of Manasā on the prow of their **boats**. Many fishermen, especially in East Bengal (modern Bangladesh) were (or are?) highly devoted to the snake goddess. Sure, they were good Muslims. It didn't stop them from worshipping the goddess of their vocation. When the Manasā festivals were over, they sank their sacred pots in the river and conducted boat races. Maity (1966/2001:308-310) relates that the rowers sang ballads in honour of Manasā and Behulā, and that the bystanders on the riverbanks provided the chorus. I wonder whether such events still happen.

Like all Hindu deities, Manasā receives **offerings**. Their nature depends on the persons who conduct the rite, those who sponsor the event and the congregation. Brahmins tend to offer vegetables. Ritualists from the lower classes may also sacrifice male goats, sheep and fowl, and eat them after the ritual. Non-hinduistic groups and cultures may sacrifice bulls, water buffaloes and pigs. The goddess receives plenty of flowers, lotus blossoms, marigolds and a piece of cloth, representing new clothes. A few ethnic groups offer hemp, which is consumed once the ritual is over. Incense, especially sandalwood, is often used. It's not the rule: in some places, the worshippers believe that the goddess loathes fumigations.

How about alcohol? The topic is difficult. Traditionally, Hindus and Muslims are not supposed to drink. Alcohol was mainly consumed by those at the bottom of the pecking order, i.e. by people who were too 'polluted' to care, and by the top level, the very folk that were so holy that a bottle or three wouldn't matter. Under the British, the sale of alcohol was enforced and many desperate peasants drank themselves into an early grave. So much for the general public. In rituals of Left Hand Tantra, alcohol may appear as a special sacrament. It's just our bad luck that tantric worship of Manasā isn't really documented. When you study the literature of Left Hand Tantra, in particular such works as the *Kulārṇava Tantra*, you will encounter regular alcohol offerings and a range of unusual wines. Most of them were not made from grapes or grains, but from palm wine, honey and exotic blossoms. Many of them were fortified with spices and drugs. In Left Hand Tantra, provided you have reached the 'heroic stage', you are supposed to use such drinks to improve your ritual. That's because Śiva loves intoxication and what pleases you pleases your deity. The same goes for Durgā/Pārvatī/Umā, who is occasionally accused of alcoholic excesses (McDermott, 2001:128). That's the harmless bit. When she transforms into Kālī, she drinks sperm, sexual secretions and blood.

Alcohol, however, was only a special sacrament. It wasn't consumed outside of a ritual context and when the practitioner transcended the heroic stage, it was often replaced by the fluids generated within the brain, i.e. self-made happiness and ecstasy. Ritual alcohol consumption, in Left Hand Tantra, is confined to the 'heroes' and 'heroines' of the middle level: advanced practitioners who need drama and delirium. People who are 'bound animals', i.e. beginners may not touch the stuff before their guru allows it. In ritual, they use harmless substitutes. Those who have transcended the heroic stage are so divine that they rarely need it. At least in theory. In real life, some tantric assemblies were full or drunkards. Vomiting was thought to make the gods happy (*Kulārṇava Tantra*, 7, 101). Other tantric lineages, in fact most of them, abhorred alcohol. Be that as it may, for some practitioners of Left Hand Tantra, alcohol was a special sacrament or a regular offering. For very good reasons, drinking, for ritual or fun, happened in secret. Whether Manasā received alcoholic beverages remains unknown.

Now for the **ritualists**. Rituals for Manasā are conducted by all sorts of people. Public rituals in districts with wealthy Hindu populations may be performed by one or several Brahmins. It can be a well paid high-status job, if the sponsors of the ritual are wealthy and important. Such ceremonies are confined to places where Manasā is popular among the higher classes. When the ritual is sponsored by low-class people, few Brahmins are willing to participate, as it gains them a small wage and a large loss of status. Sure, poor Brahmins may do the job. They won't be happy, as their reputation suffers.

When low-class people have to get along without brahmanical blessings, they usually employ their own ritualists.

Some low-class ritualists imitate brahmanical forms. It doesn't work well, as they lack an education in classical Saṁskṛta and sacred literature. They usually have a few Saṁskṛta mantras to liven up the ceremony. Many are aware of the old myths, if only in the versions related by storytellers, singers and actors. Their ritual is based on local folk belief.

Then there are ritualists who come from foreign cultures, whose ceremonies are strongly rooted in local forms of shamanism, involving obsession, religious madness and wild ritual.

A special group is the deyāsīs, i.e. the village priesthood, who may come from a low class, such as the Ḍom, Hāri, Bāuri, Keyāt, and Māl. They are specialised in ceremonies for the local deities of a district. Deyāsīs can be male or female. To gain some prestige, they commonly claim to come from Brahmin stock. To escape suppression, so they say, their ancestors took up a lower class vocation. This is not the place to discuss whether their claim is serious. Suffice it to say that few of their neighbours put much faith in it. Many deyāsīs have only superficial knowledge of Brahmin ritual. Their specialities are local rites and traditions, and they are very good at them. The office is generally inherited. It doesn't mean that you become a deyāsī just because your mother or father was one. You have to devote yourself to many years of strenuous and exhausting training. Just like the Brahmins, each deyāsī depends on being respected and admired by the worshippers.

In some places, Manasā rituals are not performed by professionals at all. Within each family, the ceremony may be performed by male or female elders.

Snake charmers, serpent catchers and ohjās may also conduct Manasā rituals. Usually, they are not employed by a community. When Manasā festivals are celebrated, members of these groups may demonstrate their magic skills and healing powers, and fiddle around with snakes. They won't perform the main ritual.

When a Manasā festival requires an **animal sacrifice**, most Brahmins will refuse to participate. In some districts, they make an exception. The animal sacrifice is generally misunderstood. Westerners, especially when they love animals, are usually revolted when an animal is killed for religious purposes. I can understand their sentiments. However, the ritual isn't like most people think. For a start, only male animals may be sacrificed. That's because Śiva prohibited the sacrifice of female animals. He has a sound head for reality: in pastoral societies, female animals are more valuable than male ones. Your cow, ewe or hen will produce offspring, milk, and eggs, while the males are only good at impregnating females. A few males can fertilise a lot of females. In short, the rural economy needs plenty of females and very few males.

The victims are generally in excellent shape. They have to be treated with love and respect; they receive good food and consideration. As Indian festivals are often loud, colourful and chaotic, the animals have to be soothed. Some go into trance thanks to sensual overload. It's not that different in a modern discotheque. An animal which resists, which panics or struggles should not be sacrificed. Involuntary offerings bring bad luck. Ideally, the animal is stunned by the noise and calmed by mantras. When it is led through the crowd, people stuff it with delicacies. Members of a very low class wield a cleaver, which has to be so sharp that the head drops with a single stroke. The animal collapses, twitches, and dies. Head, legs and blood are presented to the deity, who partakes of the spiritual offering. Most of the flesh is returned to the sponsor, who may enjoy it, after the ritual, as a barbecue. The meat has become prasāda: a *blessing, sacrament* and *mercy*. In East Indian belief, most (male) gods are vegetarians. The goddesses, however, can be tough and violent and may demand blood. In some temples, hundreds of goats are slaughtered each festival day. It sounds shocking to folks who live in the realm of fluffy thoughts and pink bubbles. But consider this: one idea behind the sacrifice is that all beings are reborn continuously. By offering itself as a willing sacrifice, the animal gains the blessing of the deity and will be reborn as a human being. Indeed, as many believe, this is the only way an animal can escape its beastly existence. The sacrifice is an act of liberation. For the family or group which offers a goat, the investment is large. Animals are expensive, and most people in India can rarely afford to eat meat. It affects the mind. People whose diet is lacking in animal fat tend to go depressive. Vegetarians have a higher suicide rate, and a life expectancy that is, according to the British Health Food Shoppers study 11% lower, and according to the Heidelberg study 17% lower than that of people on a mixed diet. They suffer from 55% fewer heart seizures but have 69% more strokes and twice as many cases of stomach and prostate cancer, plus miscellaneous diseases (Pollmer & Warmuth, 2007:325-326). But life expectations ain't everything. More important is life quality. Plant-based diets supply only small amounts of tryptophan, and that of mediocre quality. You need tryptophan to create serotonin, an all-round substance with a wide range of functions. Also, tryptophan needs saturated, i.e. animal fats, to function. Some serotonin is transformed into dopamine. For a happy life, it's plainly essential. Then there's vitamin B_{12}. Mammals like us produce it in our guts, but we can't absorb it from there. That's why vegetarian animals, like gorillas, habitually eat some of their excrement. Our closer relations, chimpanzees, bonobos and orang-utans need a varied diet. They eat larvae, insects, eggs, birds, and rodents, small antelopes, monkeys and young apes of their own species. Some may object that in the good old days, traditional Hindus promoted vegetarian diets, enhanced with milk, butter and curd, if they could afford it. With a life expectation below 30 years, most people died before they could notice the long-term effects of their diet. Also, in rural India, the fields were (and usually are) fertilised with human excrement. As vegetables were hardly cleaned, if at all, vegetarians got some B_{12} in their diet. You only need 1-3 micrograms of B_{12} a day to remain cheerful and sane. Modern vegetables, by contrast, grow on artificial fertiliser, and are thoroughly cleaned. Pious Hindu vegetarians who move to Europe eventually find themselves suffering from a lack of B_{12}. (Pollmer & Warmuth, 2007:336; 2010:203-209, Keith 209: 179-244). They may feel edgy, tense and somewhat misaligned. Some twitch, some shake, most worry, and suffer from involuntary muscle cramps. Old people accelerate towards dementia, as B_{12} is essential to insulate the nerves. Fingers and feet go cold, the immune system weakens and emotions are anything but stable, no matter how much you meditate or pull yourself together. Some go aggressive and some depressive. I've been through this, after more than ten years as a vegetarian, and it wasn't fun at all. For poor Hindus, to partake of a sacrificial animal is a rare occasion of joy. It may be the only nourishing meal in many weeks or months. Finally, please consider how animals are bred, kept, fed and slaughtered in the Industrial World. Any self-respecting goat will prefer the Indian version.

In a few versions of the *Epic*, Manasā receives a **human sacrifice** when the cow herders worship her. A herder volunteers, another swings the blade. The head drops to the ground, blood spurts, Manasā drinks and it tastes wonderful. She smacks her lips, smiles and says "What's next?"

"Simple" says Neta, "you return him to life."

"Why?" asks Manasā.

"People like to live" says Neta, "don't argue. Just do it."

Manasā frowns. Why do people make such a fuss about life and death? It happens all the time! That dead cow herder might be reborn as a happy, holy cow! Neta gives her a look. Manasā sighs. She revives the victim and everyone cheers.

The tale has to be evaluated cautiously. Human sacrifice happened in the Vedic period; the *Black Yajur Veda* lists 179 social classes and their use as human sacrifices. It sounds worse than it is: such sacrifices were rare. By the start of early Hinduism, around 400 BCE, only the highest kings had the right to sacrifice humans, and did so only in an emergency. The practice disappeared, but the idea remained. In medieval Indian fairy tales and everyday gossip, especially among the British, weird Indian cultists delighted in human sacrifices. When it comes to proving the act, things become difficult. I wouldn't want to voice an opinion. After all, allegations are not good enough. Kālī, in particular, was assumed to feed on human lives. Captain Sleeman, thug hunter extraordinaire, took the myths seriously. It made him torture, hang and deport suspects. His initiative allowed the British army to invade and occupy kingdoms suspected of harbouring thugs. We have no proof whether human sacrifices to Kālī really happened, let alone to Manasā.

Let me finish by listing **offerings** for Manasā. Some of them are popular, some were common and no doubt new sacrifices will be invented. Religion is a flow and deities thrive on innovation. Please note that there were and are massive differences in the rituals of various districts and classes. In no place all of these items and acts appeared simultaneously.

Vegetable offerings:

-fruit; berries; kāliya konṛa fruit; mangoes, small bananas; sugar cane; pumpkins; coconuts; sweets; bēl leaves with and without lime and spices; betel nuts; betel powder; tips of hemp leaves; grains; parched grains; first (= freshly harvested) grains; sweet pastries; rice; sprouting rice; first rice; paddy; sweetened paddy; baked rice; rice with hot spices and sauces; rice with salted lentils, beans and legumes.

-spiky sij-twigs of various kinds; Indian cactus, mango twigs, twigs from five sacred trees; sacred basil; lotus blossoms; water lilies; red jaba blossoms, marigolds, any blossoms available.

Animals and animal products:

-male goats and sheep; white goats; water buffaloes; bulls; pigs; doves; ducks; geese; cockerels.

-butterfat (ghī); milk; yoghurt; soured milk; curds.

-honey.

Perfumes:

-five types of scented powder; red powder; sandalwood incense; sandalwood paste; various incense and tree resins.

Illumination:

-lights; lamps, burning mustard oil or gī, and (a novelty) candles.

Images, Symbols and Gifts:

-clay figurines and figures showing Manasā and major persons of her myth; small, shrine-like model houses; serpents formed of clay, wood, or metal; a piece of white, red, pink, magenta-coloured, saffron-yellow or, (very unusual in goddess worship) blue cloth; painted or printed images of the goddess; serpents painted on paper, walls, floors or fabric; earth heaps; unusual stones; stones coloured red; pyramids or cones made of tree bark.

Ritual Acts:

-prayer, invocation; storytelling; reading her story from a book; puppet plays, theatrical plays; song; dance; bowing; fasting; giving alms; music made with string instruments, bells, drums, gongs, cymbals, and by clapping hands; meditation; visualisation; mantra recitation, pūjā rituals; trance; obsession.

Finally, let's consider **music**.

One useful option to call the rains, to find release and liberation, is to play a serpent rāga. Of course it's not the only choice; there are plenty of monsoon rāgas (look up Rāga Megh and its variations). Let's focus on the serpents. They control the rains, and so much more. I hope you pick up an instrument and explore. If not, you are likely to miss a lot. Indian religion, and especially Tantra, needs music. Many leading tantrics, like Abhinavagupta, were famous for their appreciation of music. According to legend, the famous universal genius of Kashmir used to lecture while playing a vīṇā. Here is the early *Kulacūḍāmaṇi Tantra* (2,13-14, trans. Louise Finn, my comments in brackets) on morning rituals. After having a bath, *he* (the worshipper) *goes up to the kula pitha* (sacred place of the group/clan/cluster) *for the worship of the kula* (clan) *deity. In the doorway of the place of worship he makes himself joyful with song, dance and musical instruments and having driven away the kula demon, (the Sādhaka) should worship the kula venue.*

Music, in tantric thought, is not an optional extra but essential. It starts the day, it drives away the demons, and it aligns the worshipper with the universe. Music is crucial if you want to focus on your awareness, your emotions and your vital energy. Also, music is available anywhere and anytime. You can sing, hum, whistle, dance and drum on your legs, your cheeks or anything. You can imagine music. It does not require a temple, a shrine, ritual objects, offerings, a guru or a partner. Real music, of course, is made by yourself, for yourself and for the world. It doesn't come from a can nor is it necessarily a group effort. The sound-manifestation of a deity is truer to its divine nature than its manifestation in a symbol, or its human appearance. That's because before form manifests, there is vibration.

Let's explore this practically. Let's assume that the tonic is C. That's a general choice and quite popular in Indian music these days. However, it is not a must. Indian music is not narrowly defined. Plenty of musicians decide on a tonic according to their emotional preferences. Hence, some people prefer Bb, B, C or Db as the basic tone. That's the foundation, if you want to tune a sitar. The lowest tone corresponds to the Mūlādhāra cakra, the root of reality. You can explore the root cakra at the perineum, or, in other systems, at the base of the spine. It's your choice. And it only goes for Hindus: in Buddhist lore, the lower Hindu cakras do not exist, and the root happens to be in the belly, or more often, in the heart. When men and women sing together, the tonic is usually G or Ab. That's because this level is easy for high and low voices. And of course it's the Mūlādhāra cakra. Any sound can be the root foundation of the universe.

Let's call on the serpents. Here is the scale **Nāgagandhari** (*Sweet Music of Divine Serpents*), a subdivision of the family of Asāvarī rāgas: C, D, Eb, F, G, Ab, Bb, c. Emphasise Eb and the Ab. This scale, called C minor or Eb major in Western music, is the same, no matter whether you play up or down. It's one of the sacred scales of Hinduism, and guaranteed to enchant cobras, deer, peacocks, and serpent deities from the underworlds. It is also the most popular scale in the medieval Celtic music of Brittany. There are tin-whistles tuned to it. I recommend Dixon's, they are tuneable. Retune a guitar, a fiddle, a mandolin or a ukulele and take it for a walk. If you put special strings for mandolin tunings on your ukulele (like Aquila New Nylgut, soprano fifths, 30 U), you can give it the basic sitar tuning F, C, G, C'. I use saz plectrums. The relationship is similar to the Irish bouzouki tuning G, D, A, D. Or try a harmonica. Hohner and Lee Oscar offer variations.

This is **Vijayā Nāgari** (the *Victorious Divine Serpents*). If we assume that C is the tonic, we have: C, D, Eb, F#, G, A, c. Again, the scale is played the same, no matter whether you go up or down. It includes two typical 'oriental' extra, the hiatus intervals (two half-tone steps) between Eb and F# and between A and C. Hiatus steps are badly neglected by classical European music. Allegedly, they are difficult to sing. You can find scales based on them, like Phrygian third tone dominant, in the folk music anywhere between China and Portugal, in Gypsy music, in Indian music (two rāgas dedicated to Bhairavī, the *Fear Inspiring Goddess*) and in contemporary hard rock.

Finally, you might wonder how to make it work. You listen. That's essential. The best musicians are not those who make the best tones, but the ones who listen, feel and tune in. Boldness is fine, but sensitivity is better. If you improvise with friends, hearing is far more important than making. You make a sound and sense it. You identify with it, you raise associations and emotions. You play with them. It influences your limbic system, i.e. it changes your emotional awareness. Then, if you like, you add another sound. You improvise, you fool around with the vibrations, and add a third. Three tones! You can do a lot with them! And you enjoy silence. Sound is oppressive unless there are pauses in between. Next, you explore rhythm. Pulsation is the foundation of reality. There is rhythm in your heartbeat, in your breathing, in walking, in your metabolism, in waking and sleeping, and in your sleep cycles. Rhythm is the lotus flower of awareness, as it opens and closes. Once you got rhythm right, you can play melodies. This isn't about reading sheets. It's all about awareness. Allow the melodies to play you. And keep listening! Music, like painting, lovemaking, fighting and ecology, is all about limitations and options. You have to know the restrictions to develop possibilities. No matter how great your solo is, unless it's founded on the pulsation of your acoustic environment, it'll be rubbish. The root pulsations of everything are life and death. You tune in to the gods, to people, to animals, plants, mosses, ferns, fungi, lichen, algae, to microorganisms and viruses, the humus, throbbing with life, each biosphere, the elements, the seasons, the world and the Multiverse. They come in one package: it has sound, rhythm and tune. Participate in it.

Picture 60: Manasā pot. Very unusual, shaped as the head of the goddess with cobra headdress (some missing). Midnapore, West Bengal, photo in Bussaberger & Robbins, 1968:45.

46. Live Performance

Ritual is more than ceremony, symbolism and odd behaviour. Most cults combine their rituals with a net of storytelling. It opens the gates to a wide range of performances.

At this point, religion merges with entertainment. It's hard to tell the difference: both are designed to alter consciousness. Manasā's story wasn't just told, it was frequently performed. Such events are a vital part of her cult and just as important as pūjā offerings or mantra recitation.

Bhāsan Yātrā is an ancient theatrical art. The roots of these ceremonies go back to the period before the seventh century, when most Hindus considered Bengal a dangerous foreign country full of evil spirits and weird people. The performances are devoted to many deities and their myths. Bhāsan means *to glide along, to float*, to let oneself be *carried by a current*. A yātra is a *procession, a journey* or a *drama*. In the first word, the motion is involuntary, while the second word implies choice and activity. That's damned real: it describes life. In the early twentieth century, Bhāsan Yātrā was a theatrical play. It was celebrated by members of the lower classes. The language was simple, the actors lacked education and their gestures and habits were crude. The audience wanted strong effects and rough humour. A good performance required spontaneous improvisation and sarcastic allusion to local events, rude jokes and obscene gestures. The troupes that performed the Manasā story neglected mystical and divine elements. They focussed on the human realm, on Cāndo's miseries (always good for a laugh), the tale of Behulā and Lakhindār and Manasā's triumph.

Jāgaraṇa Gān is an elaborate performance, popular mostly in West Bengal. Imagine a group of well-trained professional actors and singers whose epic performance can take three to eight nights. These groups were sought after and expensive. They were invited for important religious festivals or family occasions, like a marriage. Usually, they performed within the courtyard of a wealthy family. In the 16th century, the poet Vrindābana Dāsa remarked: *People keep vigil at night, hearing the songs of Maṅgal Caṇḍī* (Maity, 2001:313). These songs were at a much higher level as the crude Bhāsan Yātrā performances. They lacked the coarse humour, but they focussed on the same parts of the story. In East Bengal, the same practice was known as **Rayānī Gān**. A gānā is a song; the term is related to words like *chant, cant, cantor, incantation*. A rajānī is a *night*: we might render the term 'Night Chants'. Usually, a troupe consisted of twelve to fifteen well-trained women and men.

Putul Nāch is a puppet theatre. In most parts of East Asia, puppet plays were a popular and polished performance attended by people of all age groups. Today, such events are replaced by TV and the cinema. It's a sad thing. The story has its magick. It doesn't matter if it is performed by human actors or by puppets: the event touches the hearts of the audience. That's because of an amazing human ability: the skill to identify with symbolic representations. Children who play with dolls and fluffy toys exhibit it perfectly. One moment, the doll or 'action figure' is real, the next it is merely plastic, cloth and wishful thinking. Consider board games: the figures are alive. You have to identify with the figures on the game-board to feel the excitement. In Thailand, the greatest epics are played out by finely cut shadow figures. In Japan, people of the upper classes go to an expensive theatre to watch a classic puppet play. These people are neither simple nor stupid. They imbue the figures with life, and feel with them. The message is much greater than the medium. Anyone whose emotions are touched by cartoon characters can tell you. Indian puppet plays are often sophisticated. The performers make great literature, like the *Mahābhārata* and *Rāmāyana* come to life. Similar magick happens in East India when Manasā's tale is performed. Puppet players acted on marketplaces, especially during religious festivals, but they were also employed by private households. The event was scheduled for a religious festival or for marriage, the ceremony when a boy received his sacred string or the festival day when a baby was fed its first solid meal. On occasion, an entire troupe of puppet players is employed by a village community.

The art of the **Pātas** and **Paṭachitrahs** almost disappeared. Both terms denote *pictures*. Their performers are called **Paṭuās**. In Europe their counterparts sang street ballads and accompanied their performance by showing pictures. Generally, they were crude, dramatic and violent. By contrast, the Indian version was usually based on sacred literature. The performers invented their own songs and painted their own picture scrolls. A few examples appear in the illustrations. Their aim was spiritual. Paṭuās moved from village to village. They performed on marketplaces or knocked at the doors of well-to-do people and offered their services. The favourite stories were borrowed from the epic tales of Kṛṣṇa and Rāma. In East India, the story of Behulā's journey was an all-time favourite. Eyewitnesses report that the audiences were deeply moved. The performers presented their pictures and put plenty of passion into their songs. For a little extra charge the most touching scenes were repeated.

The paṭuās did their best to entertain. But they were also keen on educating their customers. They embellished their songs with proverbs, learned remarks and instructive anecdotes. For the illiterates, they functioned as teachers.

Finally I would like to mention the **non-professional performers**. There were plenty of them, once printing made famous *Manasā Epics* available to the public. In many families, long passages were chanted, often over a series of evenings during the monsoon months, to accompany rituals. The audience could be a village community, or the members of an upper-class family. Maity (1966/2001:316) relates that in Bengal, educated women sang on a level of excellence that exceeded the performances of professional singers. Their presentation did not happen in public. The women performed for an audience of family and friends.

Picture 61: Ālpanā painting for Subachani, the Mother of Ducks brata ritual, Bengal, after Mode and Chandra, 1984: 227.

47. Seasons of the Snake

The *Manasā Epic* composed by Ketakādās contains the first detailed description of the cult. Maybe he recorded age-old common customs. Or he invented them. Ketakādās wrote in the late 17th century. Much later, since 1844, his work was printed, in more or less abridged form. The text enchanted worshippers all over East Asia, served to unify the understanding of Manasā and influenced the early Indologists.

Here is a scene where Manasā asks her father Śiva to bless her, and to reveal the future of her cult and worship. Śiva says:

There will be twelve festivals in twelve months: people will worship you on the Daśaharā in Jyaiṣṭha (May/June) *and on the Nāgapañchamī day of Āṣāḍha* (June/July), *the latter day of worship is followed by the Jhānpān ceremony of the ohjās. In Śrāvaṇa* (July/August) *people will offer you curd and parched corn in abundance. In Bhādra* (August/September) *you will be worshipped with a special ritual known as Āraph-Vrata. There will be a great festival in Āśvina* (September/October) *when people will offer you cold rice. You will be worshipped with sij tree branches in Kārtika* (October/November). *An unbroken branch of the sij tree should be planted in Agrahāyana* (November/December), *with offerings of all kinds of new things to you. You will be worshipped widely in Pauṣa, Māgha, Phālguna and Chaitra* (December to April) *with offerings of ghī, honey, incense, lights, agaru and sandal by men, gods and Asuras* (after Maity, 2001:241, amended).

It sounds suspiciously well organised, and it establishes Manasā as a supreme deity who is important all through the ritual year. Manasā was amazed that her father could be so coherent.

Well, Ketakādās didn't speak for everyone. Bipradās mentions the tenth day of the lunar month (tithi) of the month Jyaiṣṭha (May/June) as perfect for Manasā worship. That's his recommendation for other people; personally, he favoured daily worship. Nārāyaṇ Deb promoted Manasā rituals on the fifth lunar night of the waxing and waning moon, plus the full moon night and every Sunday.

Daśaharā. This feast is celebrated in the tenth lunar night of the bright (waxing) half of the month Jyaiṣṭha (May/June). It honours the summer monsoon, and the seer Bhagīrata who invoked Goddess Gaṅgā, and Śiva, who caught her in his tangled hair. The summer monsoon is a heavenly blessing. Look at the Indian year. The spring season, full of flowers and delight, gives way to summer and the days become hot and hotter. Day by day, month after month, the sun beats down incessantly. The sky is blue or dusty. Flowers wither and crumble; the earth hardens, shrivels and cracks. The heat scorches everything. People become moody, then stressed. By noon, everyone retires into the shade and tries to sleep. The farmers pray and search the merciless sky for clouds. Their fields are devoid of life. Unless the monsoon arrives punctually and lasts for months, the year will end in famine. Finally, after much prayer and sacrifice, the winds change. From the Bay of Bengal, vast towering clouds, black and blue, crisscrossed by lightning, move enormous quantities of moisture across the land. Indra's thunderbolt flashes. The clouds are dark elephants, are sacred cows, discharge Kālī's fierceness. The air goes wet and stuffy, and people, coated in sweat, grasp for breath. Then, at last the rains begin to fall. They are cataclysmic, mind-blowing, incredibly refreshing. Further inland, the moist air rushes against a barrier that is rarely passed: the Himalayan mountain chain. Here, the monsoon unleashes its fury. Brooks swell and change their courses, riverbeds become chutes, and landslides sweep part of the mountainside away. Before long, Mother Gaṅgā rises, fed by a thousand tributaries, picks up speed, and becomes a goddess of destruction. She tears down the vegetation, goes deep brown with earth, and surges into the plains. People in field and city greet her. The monsoon may turn a brook into a stream and fields into lakes. The goddess destroys streets, floods houses and brings a rich surge of fertile earth from the mountains. Destruction gives way to fecundity. In the country, most of the traffic stops. Paths that were dusty yesterday turn into sticky mud that stops traffic and makes wanderers sink to ankles, knees or hips. Landslides block major motorways. In the lower parts of the city, the flood will bring all traffic to a halt. Here and there a car may try to move out. Drivers are at a loss: how deep is the water on the road? Look: a couple of kids are standing in the murky flow. The driver gives a sigh of relief; the water level seems promising. He accelerates and hears his engine drowning. The kids are standing on a rock. And they are happy: for a fee, they'll help to push the car out of the flood. Elsewhere, people disappear. In East Asia, canal lids are valuable. Thieves steal them at night and sell the metal. When the rains come, the drainage system collapses. Anyone who steps into a hole (where a lid ought to be) disappears into the underworld and may be found days later, by fishers, out in the Bay of Bengal, as a badly gnawed corpse. Simultaneously, Indians go out for mud-soccer. It's the perfect sport for those who love to slip and slide. The monsoon is a great time to stay at home, and to meet friends from the close neighbourhood. The poets love the rains, and so do lovers, who delight in the cooling air. Outdoors, the city cleans itself. Rubbish, rats and cockroaches are swept away. How much fun the rains can be is proved by wealthy Arabs. They fly to India to enjoy the season. Simultaneously, serpents appear. It's as if the rains had dropped them from the skies! Sure, snakes are always present. Most of the time they avoid people. When the rains turn the fertile Ganges plain into an inland ocean, they emerge from their holes and shrubs and look for safer habitations. People have to handle their visitors as well as they can. After all, the Nāga deities are said to cause the rains.

Those who celebrate Daśaharā find release from sins of ten past lives. Not all of all sins; ten lifetimes provide plenty of opportunity to be sinful or stupid, so it makes sense to celebrate the feast each year. All over Bengal, Daśaharā is the feast day of goddess Gaṅgā. Her holy stream is getting faster every day, and may rise by up to eight metres. In a flat landscape, it creates a minor ocean. Another favourite for Daśaharā worship is Manasā. The two have something like a family relationship. Gaṅga is Śiva's first wife, and hence a stepmother for Manasā. In many villages, the feast day is followed by a country fair, involving music, storytellers, actors, puppet plays and fireworks.

In wide parts of East India, the fifth days of the bright and dark halves of the months Jyaiṣṭha, Āṣāḍha, Śrāvaṇa and Āśvina (May to September) are dedicated to Manasā. That's four months and the approximate length of the monsoon, if all goes well. In some districts a twig of sij may be planted near the sacred basil (tulsī) growing at a temple. While the basil, sacred to Viṣṇu, grows permanently, the sij twig will be uprooted on the fifth day and cast into the rising river. That's one option. In other places, the sij may grow for months before it is thrown into the flood.

Nāgapañcamī: This ritual is usually celebrated on the fifth night of the bright half of the month Śrāvaṇa (July/August). That's the general rule. In some places, the worship can happen on the fifth night of the dark half of the month Āṣāḍha (June/July), Śrāvaṇa (July/August) or Bhādra (August/September). In some districts, it happens on the fifth lunar night of the bright half of the month Agrahāyana (November/December).

'Nāga' means snakes, in particular king cobras and serpent deities and 'pañcamī' is the Fifth. Nowadays, Indians use the reformed national calendar, which is identical with the Gregorian calendar. Let's have a look at traditional Indian time-keeping, or rather, its variants.

In India, the day began at sunrise. It says something about life: the day starts with a bath, prayer, a short ceremony, a meal and work. Those who enjoy meditation do it around dawn, when the day is fresh and new and so is their mind. Breathing exercises are best in the early morning (or very late at night). It's quite a contrast to modern timekeeping (our day starts at midnight) or, say, the old Germanic timekeeping, where the day began at sunset, with a meal and leisure and ended after a lot of work when the sun went down.

Sunrise is not only pleasant, as its cool and peaceful, it is also a sacred moment when the goddess Uṣas (*Dawn*) awakes, and imbues the world with joy. Indian musicians are instructed to start practising before sunrise, as the mind is uncluttered and the world wonderfully silent. That's what their gurus say. The neighbours may disagree.

For religious purposes, the lunar calendar remains popular. In most parts of India, the end of the month happens on full moon night, but in the south and west there are districts where the new moon signifies the end of the month. Again, the difference matters. Does your month start with a bright (waxing) or a dark (waning) period? How about your breath cycles? Do you start by exhaling or inhaling?

As the synodic lunar month is a little shorter than the month of the solar calendar, the ritualists have to handle a yearly difference of ten days. Every three years, an extra month is introduced to keep the ritual calendar in tune with reality.

Classical Indian time-keeping divides the lunar month into 30 tithis. The term can be vaguely translated as 'lunar days'. It's not really precise, as the lunar month takes approximately 29,5 days. Strictly speaking, a tithi is the time the moon needs to move 12° from the sun. The tithis come in two groups. From new moon to full moon is fifteen tithis and from full moon to new moon another fifteen. The waxing moon is called Śuklapakṣa, i.e. the bright half moon, and the waning moon Kṛṣṇapakṣa, the dark (Kṛṣṇa) half moon. There are plenty of beliefs and superstitions regarding these seasons. Indians who live in the countryside tend to believe that all projects begun during the waning moon are under a negative, declining and destructive influence. It's pretty similar to the beliefs entertained in, say, rural Scotland, Wales and Germany. If you want to harvest, destroy or end something, the dark half of the month is great. For things that grow and flower, the bright half is better. That's the general idea. And, as ever, there are plenty of exceptions to the rule.

A tithi is a lunar unit. Instead of the term 'tithi' you can use the term 'kalā' which means a *unit, segment, section* or *digit*, especially a *digit of time*. Anything can be separated into digits. It's quite popular nowadays. Gods have kalās. Śiva, for instance, has eight kalās as Sadyojāta, as Vāmadeva thirteen, as Aghora eight, as Tatpuruṣa four and as Īśāna six (*Garuḍa Purāṇa*, I, 21). Celestial phenomena can be measured in kalās: there are twelve digits of the sun (hours and months) and ten digits of Agni/fire. Each of them has a different symbolic and religious meaning. The moon has sixteen Kalās. That's as each night of the half month vibrates with a specific energy/sentience. On the fifteenth night, a pair of skilled tantric lovers can distil the ultimate kalā, the sixteenth. It's the total of the vibrations of the sixteen Indian vowels. This is amazingly potent: in Indian lore, the sound-form (i.e. its vibration) if a deity is a lot more powerful than its visual appearance or the anthropomorphic form that people imagine to unite with their deity. Or so some gurus say. Others disagree. The sixteen vowels are full of symbolism. I have given a list in *Kālī Kaula*, based on Abhinavagupta, but there are plenty of others. After all, the vowels are energy on a very refined level. Some tantrics scowled and disagreed. In their opinion, a total of sixteen Kalās wasn't enough: they promoted a seventeen kalā system and, in extreme cases, an eighteen kalā system. It never caught on. You shouldn't blame the moon.

In some tantric systems, such as the early Śrī Vidyā (*Auspicious Wisdom*) tradition, the sixteen lunar Kalās were a science (vidyā). As each lunar night has a different energy/awareness, it allows the practitioners to tap into a total of sixteen cosmic energies. Their essences were invoked and refined in the mingled sexual fluids. The fifteenth night can be a new or full moon. Should a śakti (here: *ritual partner*) menstruate at this date; she and her partner could refine the sixteenth kalā, the divine quintessence of the lot. For many tantrics of the Left Hand Path, the mixture of sperm and menstrual blood was the essence of life and the fluid from which each human being was conceived. It doesn't get more powerful than this. At least, for the early Left Hand Path ritualists. After the sixteenth century, Śrī Vidyā was thoroughly reformed. All practices involving sex, drugs, wild behaviour, obsession and fun were discontinued and most ritual acts were frowned upon. The followers of this tradition reduced much of their practice to meditative visualisation.

Back to the tithis. In general Hindu belief, the month consists of two seasons of fifteen units. Each of them is useful for specific rituals and meditations.

-FIRST TITHI. The day of **Agni**, Firelord. Think of the household fire, the sacrificial fire and the fire that cremates corpses and carries the souls to the otherworlds. Agni is a god of beginnings: each book of the *Ṛg Veda* begins with the praise of Agni. It's the first kalā: *deathless, ambrosial*. Its vowel is A.

-SECOND TITHI. **Brahmā**, lord of creation. Out of the primal, energy-transformation of fire, Brahmā, the Creator appears. Creation, in Hindu thought, didn't only happen in prehistory, it's going on all the time. Second kalā: the *essence which nourishes drugs and medicine producing plants*. Vowel: Ā (pronounce a long a).

-THIRD TITHI. **Gaurī**, the *fair, shining, glowing, golden* goddess, the light of awareness, wife of Śiva. Also known as Pārvatī, *daughter of the mountains*. Plus plenty of friendly goddesses. Third kalā: *humility, modesty* and *shame*; the traditional qualities of Indian women. Vowel: I.

-FOURTH TITHI. **Gaṇeśa**, the elephant-headed god. He is wise, huge and strong; he destroys obstacles, blesses beginnings and eats sweets all day long. Or the day of **Yama**, the Lord of Death, the underworlds and several special hells, if you are into suffering and redemption. Fourth kalā: *pleasing*. Vowel: Ī (pronounce a long i).

-FIFTH TITHI. Sacred to all serpents and to all **Nāga deities**. The feast day of **Manasā**. Or, alternatively, to **Skanda/Kārrtikeya**, the heroic son of Śiva and Pārvatī/Durgā. Fifth kalā: *nourishing*. Vowel: U.

-SIXTH TITHI. Sacred to **Skanda/Kārrtikeya**, the fierce champion of the gods, the conqueror of the Asuras (anti-gods). Sixth kalā: *playful*. That's because Skanda plays, even when he fights. Vowel: Ū (pronounce a long u).

-SEVENTH TITHI. A sunny day, devoted to **Sūrya/Sūryā**, and other solar deities. Seventh kalā: *constancy*. Vowel: Ṛ (pronounce: ri)

-EIGHTH TITHI. The perfect time to worship **Rudra**, the terrifying old Vedic form of **Śiva (the Auspicious One)**, the deadly archer, master of medicine, drugs and poisons, stalker of the wilderness, friend of ascetics, god of life and death. Eighth kalā: *containing the hare of the moon*. Vowel: Ṝ (pronounce a long ri).

-NINTH TITHI. **Ambikā** (*Mother*), a fond title for terrifying goddesses, especially warrior goddess **Durgā**, who is beseeched to be kind and friendly. Ninth kalā: *joy producing*. Vowel: Ḷ (pronounce le).

-TENTH TITHI. **Dharmarāja**, the *King of Dharma*. Dharma means *truth, justice, religion, world-order, social order, virtue, rightness, care-for-others* etc. The title is used for the personified god **Dharma**, or for **Yama** (the lord of the dead), or for semi-divine heroes who are incarnations of Dharma, like King **Yudhiṣṭhira**. In some versions of the Manasā songs, the goddess was briefly married to Dharma. It wasn't much of a story. The two separated, and Manasā is famous for leading an unmarried life. Tenth kalā: *charming*. Vowel: Ḹ (a theoretical sound, pronounced as a long li, invented for reasons of symmetry. It does not appear in literature and language).

-ELEVENTH TITHI. Another festival day for **Rudra/Śiva**. This one is useful to simplify, to fast, to let go, to shed troubles and worries and delusions. Eleventh kalā: *producing rays*. Vowel: E.

-TWELFTH TITHI. After exhaustion (day eleven) follows reformation. This day is dedicated to **Viṣṇu**, the lord of all gods, the Maintainer of the Universe, who upholds distinctions, enforces eternal law and keeps the worlds in balance. Twelfth kalā: *prosperity, wealth, fertility*. That's Śrī Lakṣmī, the glamorous wife of Viṣṇu. Vowel: AI.

-THIRTEENTH TITHI. Dedicated to **Kāma** (*Desire, Lust, Love*) the playful ancient deity who keeps the universe (and you) in motion. Also a feast day of **Dharma**. Thirteenth kalā: *producing affection*. Vowel: O.

-FOURTEENTH TITHI. A day of destruction and release, dedicated to **Kālī**, the black goddess of time, destruction and liberation, and to **Rudra/Śiva**. Fourteenth kalā: *purifying the body*. Vowel: AU.

-FIFTEENTH TITHI. The day of the **pitṛdevas**; the *deified ancestors*. Think of those whose genetic inheritance you carry. Remember those, whose ideas and teachings make your life meaningful. And understand yourself as a link in a chain connecting past and future, life after life. What you do today is rooted in the past and will shape the future. In Indian thought, everyone has to leave descendants. They don't necessarily have to be children: projects, students, followers, books, music, arts, skills and ideas do count. Or a feast day of **Soma**, god of the moon, the elixir of immortality, and the drug that allowed the ancient seers to *see the rituals* and *hear the sacred chants*. Fifteenth kalā: *completion*. Vowel: Ṁ (pronounce ng. Not really a vowel, but very sacred).

-SIXTEENTH KALĀ: *full of nectar/elixir of immortality*. Vowel: Ḥ (pronounce an expired, breathy H. It signifies the Great Emission, and the quintessence of all vowels.)

It's an amazing model. You could use it for divination. Invent sixteen symbols, paint them on cards or burn them into pieces of wood. Or inscribe them with numbers. Ask your question, mix them in a bag, draw out one, two or three and make them come to life. Like all systems of divination, it's a creativity machine, a coincidence generator and the perfect solution for all situations when reasoning fails. The lunar kalās, and the deities that empower them, provide an amazing range of insights.

And you can tune your rituals to their timetable. In popular belief, the kalās of the moon can be ordered into lucky and unlucky days. Sorry, but this is complicated. Usually, the fourth, sixth, eighth, ninth, twelfth, fourteenth and fifteenth (full moon & new moon) are unlucky. The first day of both fortnights is always excellent, the second if it is a Wednesday, the third if a Tuesday, the fourth if a Saturday, the fifth if a Thursday, the sixth if a Thursday or Friday, the seventh if a Wednesday, the eighth if a Tuesday or Sunday, the ninth if a Monday, the tenth a Thursday, the eleventh Thursday or Friday, the twelfth a Wednesday, the thirteenth a Friday or Tuesday, the fourteenth a Saturday, the fifteenth (full or new moon) if a Thursday (*Garuḍa Purāṇa*, I, 59).

Manasā gawks with astonishment, as this is crazy and Neta has a laughing fit. In case the complications bother you: there are plenty of Left-Hand-Path Tantrics who considered any time good for luck and ritual and lovemaking, 'cause they feel like it and don't give a damn for astrology.

The fifth day is perfectly suited for serpent worship, no matter if it happens in the bright or dark half of the moon. Maity (1966/2001:220) cites two 14th century texts referring to this custom. Here they are, slightly amended.

Jīmūtavāhana's *Kālaviveka*:

On the fifth day when the lord Janārdana (Giver of Rewards = Viṣṇu) *goes to bed in the courtyard of the houses, the goddess Manasā, placed (at the foot of) the snuhī tree* (sij, a euphorbia plant), *should be worshipped. Leaves of picumarda (neem tree, Azadirachta indica) should be placed in the interior of the house/temple. After worshipping the goddess, a man gets no fear of snakes.*

Plants are important. Neem is an amazing medicine. When we study the serpent cults, we get close to toxins and panacea. Indeed, you won't get far in understanding serpents if you ignore the plants and fungi, their healing powers and their toxins, and their amazing intelligence. Neem can be used to stimulate vitality, to heal skin diseases, and infections. Many Indians chew the leaves to clean their teeth, or chew them on New Year, for an auspicious start. The seeds contain an amazing amount of anti-bacterial and anti-viral compounds. The plant acts against nematodes, mites, fungi and many insects. Neem, in Indian medicine, is an essential tonic. Nowadays, it is also researched as a spermicide. One day, it might make a pill for men. More than that, the plant won't harm mammals or birds. It can be incorporated in pesticides. In the early 1900's, the British introduced neem to West Africa, where it became the most popular healing plant. Closely afterwards, Americans grew it in the southern states and in Central America. In the 1990's, American companies claimed a patent on neem and its components, and tried to monopolise the use of the plant and its ingredients worldwide. They collided with Indian law. Indians have used neem for at least 3,000 years. However, Indian law does not allow anyone to patent plants, 'cause that's plainly insane. The legal battle continues (Tudge, 2005: 222-223).

Raghunananda's *Tithitattva*:

On the fifth day of the dark half of the month of Śrāvaṇa in order to get rid of the danger from snakes one should make a resolve (saṅkalpa) by announcing his gotra (descent, family) and name and saying that he intends to worship the goddess Manasā in the form of a snuhī tree (sij, a euphorbia plant), and, if one is not available, with a pot and water.

More appears in the *Brahma Vaivarta Purāṇa*:

Whoever on the last day of Āṣāḍha invokes the goddess (Manasā) in the form of a twig of the guḍā tree and worships her with devotion; and whoever sacrifices (animals) on the fifth tithi known as Manasā tithi, will definitely be blessed with wealth, sons and fame.

The *Garuḍa Purāṇa (I, 129),* a work completed between the ninth and tenth century, proposes that the eight serpent kings Vāsuki, Takṣaka, Kāliya, Maṇi, Bhādraka, Airāvata, Dhṛtarāṣṭra, Karkoṭaka and Dhanañjaya should be worshipped on the fifth day of any of the months Śrāvaṇa (July/August), Bhādra (August/September), Āśvina (September/October), and Kārtika (October/November). Their images should be bathed in clarified butter. Those who perform this brata ritual will enjoy a long life, good health and bliss. Alternatively, these eight serpent gods can be worshipped in the bright half of the month Bhādra. The result is liberation and spiritual joy.

For those who like to worship serpent deities all round the year, the good book pronounces that Ananta, Vāsuki, Śaṅkha, Padma, Kambala, Karkoṭaka, Nāga, Dhṛtarāṣṭra, Śaṅkhaka, Kāliya, Takṣaka and Piṅgala should be worshipped. You can use the fifth day of the bright half of the month Śrāvana to paint pictures of serpents on either side of the main entrance of your house. To make them magically potent, you should worship them and feed them milk and butter. This ritual removes all poisons and provides freedom from fear.

The celebration on the fifth night can be explained. As usual, the stories vary from place to place. One favourite claims that Kadrū, the ageless, wonderfully sexy, bedazzling mother of all snakes, was born on this day. Or, that the dark god of herders, warriors and flute players, the charming Kṛṣṇa, came to the sacred river Yamuna. He met a group of cow herders, who played ball. The game was rough and lacked anything resembling rules, which excited Kṛṣṇa, and made him join the fun. The ball flew into the crown of a tree and got stuck between branches, directly above the Yamuna. Kṛṣṇa, always ready to set a good example, climbed the tree. He got the ball, slipped and fell into the river. A huge snake rose from the water and tried to devour him. Kṛṣṇa laughed, tied the reptile up in knots and dragged it to the shore. The herders were shocked. It was their sacred serpent! Kṛṣṇa smiled, untied the beast and allowed it to slip into the water unharmed. The herders were greatly relieved that their serpent goddess Kāliya had survived and fed the jittery reptile with milk.

Both tales are popular among the educated classes in Bengal. For most of the population, however, the fifth is the feast day of Manasā. Maity mentions celebrations in Ramsagar near Biṣṇupur. In the night of the fifth, all Manasā pots were set up on the schoolyard, where they were worshipped in a communal ritual. The villagers picked up their pots and carried them on their heads. The procession wound around a field (or playing field?), accompanied by shrill music. The ritual ended with fireworks. The occasion was widely popular and also used for a country fair.

Arandhana Ceremony. The ritual is popular in many districts of East India. It overlaps with a similar custom, the **Ambubāchi ceremony**. The Arandhana ceremony is a feast day of cold food. Women are not allowed to light a fire or cook food. Instead, the hearth is decorated with elaborate rice-paste paintings and a sij twig is set up. That's enough to worship Manasā. Arandhana often happens on the last day of the month Bhādra (August/September) or Āśvina (September/October). Some districts celebrate Arandhana and Nāgapañcamī at the same time. The Tuesdays and Saturdays of Bhādra are preferred in the districts Hooghly and Howrah. There, the custom is called Ichchā-Rānnā or Chaṛchani Pūjā. No food is heated: all meals have to be prepared the day before. There are plenty of stories to explain why. Here is a tale Maity collected in the village Poṣla in Burdwan. On the day, a woman heated milk for her children. The maid enquired if the housewife had carefully inspected the fireplace. Sure, she hadn't. The maid lifted the pot and extinguished the fire. She reached into the hearth and pulled a scorched serpent out of the ashes. It was the goddess Manasā, who had crept into the hearth to sleep. The maid took the serpent into her care; she nursed it back to health with milk from her own breasts, until the snake was fully recovered. The snake was called Jhaṅkeśvarī, which is also a title of Manasā. Since this event, no hearth fires may be lit on Arandhana day and the goddess receives worship (1966/2001:311). And that's just one explanation among many.

Ambubāchi is another feast day which is mostly dedicated to women. For three days, no food may be cooked. It is usually celebrated during Āṣāḍha (June/July) when the rainy season has just begun. Women may not even come close to fire. Earth and Underworld may not be disturbed: men are not allowed to dig or plough.

Personally, I wonder if the feast was introduced from the Far East. The Chinese also celebrate a feast day of cold food. They only do so without Manasā.

The Last Day of the Month Śrāvaṇa (July/August). The last day of a month can be special. Often, it's perfect for a wild and popular Manasā ritual. It may be limited to a single day, if we are dealing with a poor and secluded village, or it may be a ritual that takes several days, culminating on the last day of the month.

When a district is wealthy, the festivities can last for an entire month. It depends on the sponsors, on the participation of many families and on the amount of visitors who can be attracted to the ceremonies and fairs. In some regions, the last days of Bhādra (August/September) and Āśvina (September/October) were dedicated to Manasā. They were an occasion for famous country fairs and visited by thousands of travellers, merchants and pilgrims.

Tuesday and **Saturday** are, in wide parts of East India, the favourite days for the worship of fierce goddesses. The cult of Kālī is closely associated with the night from Tuesday to Wednesday (though some districts prefer Sunday night), a time which is remarkably dangerous, powerful and liberating. Especially when you spend it, secretly, alone in the dark, doing worship and meditation on a cremation place, in a forest or a place which spirits haunt. Thanks to this darksome mood, which can be found in some of the earliest (surviving) Tantras, Manasā, who is best friends with Kālī, is also worshipped. People of Bengal worship Lakşmī on the night from Thursday to Friday. She is supposed to be friendly, well behaved and benevolent. If you are lucky. The tradition differs in other parts of India. Those, who are influenced by astrology (imported from Mesopotamia courtesy of the Seleucids) consider Saturday night a bad time, as it is governed by Saturn: stern, forbidding and deadly serious. The daśa (*duration of influence*) of Saturn can destroy kingdoms and cause misery. One should not travel on his day, or undertake new projects. In these districts, the night from Friday to Saturday, dedicated to Venus, the perfect time to win women, elephants, horses, and kingdoms, is perfectly suited for goddess worship.

Picture 62: Top: Ālpanā painting for the Chariot of the Gods; bottom: for marriage ceremonies, Bengal, after Mode and Chandra, 1984: 226 & 227.

48. West Bengal

We had a look at time. Manasā is time and transcends it: as **Nityā** she is *Eternal, Everlasting*. She is space and transcends it: as **Anantā**, she is *Endless, Infinite*.

Time and space are Manasā, meaning *Mind, Awareness, Imagination*, and so on. That's because the sense of space and time is not instinctual or genetic, but has to be learned. For babies, time and space don't exist. Up to the age of five, children are uneasy about them. And when we are overworked, sleep-deprived, in deep crisis or trance, on drugs or sick, we lose control of them. Our minds make time and space real, and, that's the funny part, says Neta, once we established these coordinates, we feel oppressed by them.

So much for the basics. They provide a wide range of choices. No doubt some appealed to you. But when we summarise complicated procedures, we lose a lot of colourful, fascinating detail. To celebrate the unique, the unusual and the fascinating, I would like to take you on a journey.

Here is a small selection of village rituals. They are amazingly different. And they demonstrate that worship in rural communities, lacking a single holy scripture or an aggressive, unifying church, takes on an amazing amount of varieties. That, of course, is ecology. Large communities tend to remain as they are. The mutants stand few chances to influence the gene pool, as there ain't enough of them. But when you isolate small communities of plants, animals, fungi, people, deities, ideas or customs, individuals get a chance to express themselves and form a new species. Anything new and innovative has to appear outside the mainstream.

In the next chapters you will encounter material on local customs. Much of it derives from Maity's magnificent study. Maity used the available ethnological literature (1966/2001:241-316). I have added material from Maity's later books and from other sources, such as the beautiful books by June McDaniels. Most of my material is outdated. Maity's sources span the period between the late nineteenth century and the time his study was first published, in 1966. As most of the data is old, I decided to present the Manasā cults in the past tense. It was a tough decision. To this day there are plenty of Manasā worshippers and her cult is alive in city and countryside. However, I did not want to give the impression that the old rituals are still performed as they were almost a century ago. Maybe they are and maybe they ain't. Religion is not conservative, it is amazingly innovative. People are creative all the time. They invent new stuff and pretend it's traditional. So when you read about some custom recorded a century ago, keep in mind that it may exist today. It may be gone. Or that it was replaced with something different.

Maity did his best. He studied old accounts, questioned travellers, army officers and school teachers and sent out hundreds of questionnaires. You can read the material in his groundbreaking study. It isn't perfect and of course it isn't statistically relevant (few people bothered to reply) but it's the best that could be done. Let's face it: romantic India is dead. During Maity's time, and since then, a lot happened. East Bengal transformed into East Pakistan, it renamed itself Bangladesh, and turned into a Muslim state. A huge stream of Hindus fled into Bengal, where the government promised a blanket and a little milk for each refugee, and failed to provide them. Calcutta, once the wealthy capital of the British Raj, turned into a city of lost souls; neglected by the government, which resides far away and hardly seems to care. What used to be called 'Bengal' and 'Assam' broke into a range of distinct provinces. 'Communism' appealed to the poor, the hopeless and exploited. The sons of wealthy families titled themselves 'communists' and preached solidarity with the lower classes. Afterwards, in their exclusive clubs, they promoted a different doctrine. A new generation of atheists, freethinkers and socialists harassed religious people, and taught school children to insult ascetics and throw stones at them. The communist party rephrased religious songs, and turned them into revolutionary hymns. Women who sang the old songs were suspected of political propaganda, and many simply shut up, and stopped to celebrate the traditional festivals. East India, in our days, is a painfully modern place. Those who want to make a career are proud of their atheism. Meanwhile, a number of border districts were taken over by warlords, who made immense profits from drugs, weapons and jewels. The Indian government has very little influence in these parts, and can count itself lucky when police and soldiers are not killed in terrorist attacks. Consequently, the British government announced that it is not recommended to travel there. I talked with several Indian businessmen: they agreed that a journey beyond Calcutta is a sure way to be kidnapped, ransomed or shot. So what you read in the next pages belongs to old India. Several Indians told me that they are worried. The young generation is addicted to TV, shopping, computers, discotheques and smartphones. And while the kids play their games and chat their lives away, their attention spans decreases, their language retards and their brains atrophy. It's just like everywhere on earth. Look at modern students! Ask them to focus for five minutes, to ignore their smartphones for an hour, or to spend a day without an SMS and their world comes crashing down. In East India, religion is mostly for the old, the poor and the ignorant. Plus a few dedicated souls.

Bankura. In some places, like **Madanmohanpur, Jayrambati** and **Jayakrishnapur**, Manasā had temples and permanent shrines where her rituals were celebrated every day. The ritual was performed by Brahmins, using classical ritual elements, devotional gestures and well-established sacrifices. These priests recited passages of the holy texts to liven up the ceremonies. Animal sacrifices were a rarity. The goddess had a permanent shrine in **Jayapur**. Worship was pretty much the same, but there was a special taboo that nobody carrying a burning lamp was permitted to pass her shrine at night. I wonder why and so might you. In many villages, Manasā rituals were performed on marketplaces. In a prominent location, a temporary shrine was set up. The structure was made of bamboo rods, paper and leaves. Usually, the Brahmins performed the ritual twice a day. The goddess was represented as her holy pot or as a clay figurine. Essential offerings were lotus blossoms, jaba flowers and intoxicating bēl leaves.

In some locations, a special custom of the Charak festival, which is sacred to Śiva, was adapted to Manasā. The worshippers (exclusively men) walked across a fire pit, measuring roughly four meters in length, full of red-hot coals. The women had their own variation. They walked with a pot on their heads. It was full of gleaming embers and resins. As they were damned hot, the ritual procession was quite a challenge.

Both ceremonies happened in front of Manasā's shrine, to thank the goddess for her blessings. On the same day, fruit of kāliyā konṛā (Menispermum polyspermum) were offered to the goddess. Some fruits were divided into small pieces and eaten by the worshippers. It made them resistant to physical and spiritual poison. Many became ecstatic. They were obsessed by the goddess and were consulted to provide solutions to problems and to prophecy the future. Let's examine the chemistry. Many plants of the menispermum family contain picrotoxin, which acts on the central nervous system. In general they cause cramps, vomiting, headaches, dizziness, depression, sleepiness; but there are people who experience delirium. People in East India and Ceylon use levant berries (Menispermum cocculus) to fish: cast into water, the fishes lose their sense of balance, swim on their backs, space off and are easily collected.

After the worship, which usually lasted for a day, Manasā's pot, representing the goddess herself, was lifted and carried in a glad and noisy procession. There were shrill music, throbbing drums and squeaky wind instruments, the worshippers laughed and delighted.

Birbhum. Manasā was mostly worshipped by the low classes and the foreign, only superficially Hinduistic ethnic groups. Usually, her priests were not Brahmins but deyāsīs, i.e. village ritualists. Bhattacharya witnessed a special ritual. Three or four days before the great Manasā festival, which was scheduled for the fifth day of the month Bhādra (August/September), a lone deyāsī had himself closed up in the temple of Manasā. The door was locked and tightly sealed with clay. Day and night, musicians performed outside the temple. On the feast day, the worshippers thought they heard a faint tapping from within the temple. They suspected it might be made by Nāga deities. The worshippers unsealed and opened the room. The deyāsī lay on the floor, unconscious, and had to be revived. I'd like to know whether the ritualist had access to fresh air, food and water. Maity doesn't tell us. This ritual was occasionally performed by very dedicated (or suicidal) ritualists. You might think of it as a life-or-death ordeal. It could be an ascetic rite of purification, or a grandiose gesture to impress the goddess, oneself and the worshippers. A deyāsī has to do a lot to build up a reputation. He or she is competing with the Brahmin ritualists. Maybe it also served as an initiation; I doubt that anyone would do it twice. Apart from its function, the ritual is closely connected with the *Manasā Epic*. Just think of the three claustrophobic episodes of the tale. First, baby Durgā is sealed in an iron box and committed to the mercy of the waves. Second, Manasā is carried to Mount Kailāsa in a tightly closed flower basket. Third, there's the bridal night in the iron chamber. All three are terrifying, suffocating experiences, and all three end in a dramatic situation that starts a new episode.

In Birbhum, the goddess was so popular that plenty of villages and cities had temples and permanent shrines, where her worship was celebrated every day. A special custom in a few districts required that the statue of Manasā was carried to a well or water-tank (very popular in serpent worship) where she was ceremonially bathed. The washing was accompanied with small hand drums, the drum heads were made of goat intestines, and plenty of singing. On the same day, a sij twig was planted near the sacred basil. During the months of the rainy season, the twig was worshipped every fifth day of the bright and dark half of the month. Months later (usually between September and October) the great Durgā Pūjā was celebrated. On the last day, the statue of Durgā went into the river, and so did Manasā's spiky twig.

In district **Hooghly**, named after the river where the British invented Calcutta and the Raj, Manasā was popular among all classes. Her greatest celebration happened on Daśaharā, when Mother Gaṅgā made the Hooghly swell. Nevertheless, there were plenty of local traditions. They disappear. Just think about it: in the past, there was colourful diversity, while in the future it's monoculture: same dreams, same food, same political correctness for everyone. In some places, like

Manasadanga, rituals were excessive. Up to five thousand male goats were slaughtered in Manasā's temples and shrines. The carcasses, duly transformed into prasāda, were cooked in the households of the neighbourhood. Families usually had their own Manasā vessels, where the goddess was worshipped on a daily schedule. The last days of the rainy seasons were her feast days, plus all Tuesdays, Saturdays, Nāgapañcamī and special occasions. When something unusual was required, the goddess was worshipped in the fields, under a tree. Among the lower classes, Manasā was addressed as Khādai. The worship was performed by ritualists from the class of shoemakers. Anyone working with leather, i.e. dead animals, is despised by the higher classes. That's why Hindu drummers have their drums mounted by low-class people or Muslims. "OK," they say, "I play this drum. It's pretty good. But I didn't kill the animal."

The class of fishers had a remarkable custom: in the temple of **Bainchi, they address Manasā as Behulā**.

Please stop for a moment, or a few days, or months, or a lifetime, and consider. This is important. It opens entirely new perspectives on the *Manasā Epic*. The half-starved serpent goddess and the courageous, crazy girl on the raft share one nature.

In this location, Jaliyā Brahmins led the ceremony, which usually happened on the full moon of the month Vaiśākha (April/May). Or on Daśaharā. In Hooghly, a favourite name of the serpent goddess is Viṣalakṣmī. Usually Lakṣmī is *good luck, auspiciousness, wealth, abundance, fertility, light, beauty, love* and the like. In this name, she is the *good luck/auspiciousness/abundance of poison*. It takes a very special mindset to appreciate this. But maybe the name is corrupted. Viṣālakṣī, meaning *Large Eyed*, is the name of a terrifying, bloodthirsty 'Mother' in the retinue of Skanda/Kārrtikeya, and a popular name for girls. In rare cases, the goddess is worshipped as Ketakā, referring to the pandanus family.

Howrah. Here and in **Dinajpur**, the major celebration is Daśaharā, followed by the last day of Bhādra (August/September). Local variety matters: the last days of the other monsoon months, Nāgapañcamī, Tuesdays and Saturdays were all popular. In the Hirapur was a famous Manasā shrine, with a clay statue, where the goddess received a goose on every Sunday. Another famous Manasā statue was worshipped in the courtyard of the police station in Vedo. The cow herders worshipped her as Rākhāl-Manasā. For the worship, a sij twig was planted under a tree. The herders moved from house to house and collected donations for the great ceremony. Her pūjā was celebrated by Brahmins, who addressed the goddess as Jaratkāru, deriving from the *Mahābhārata*. Related to the cult of Manasā, but often quite independent of it, was daily worship of clay snakes, which were addressed as Vāstu-sarpa (*snake of the house, snake of the property*).

Jalpaiguri. Here, the goddess was mostly worshipped by the Rājbaṁsis, who made up two-fifths of the population. Apart from ceremonies on the last day of Śrāvaṇa (July/August), on the last day of Bhādra (August/September) and the fifth day of the dark half of the month Āṣāḍha (June/July) a couple of special feast days were observed. Manasā was worshipped at marriage ceremonies, on the special day when a baby received its first cooked food and at the ceremony when youths of the upper three classes received their holy string, signifying their 'second birth'. Daily worship, however, was almost non-existent. The Rājbaṁsis had their own ideas about Manasā. In their opinion, the serpent goddess was simply lethal. Slight errors in ritual could bring about terrible revenge. Accordingly, she was rarely loved, but had to be placated. Those who didn't sacrifice enough could expect snake bites, accidents, ailing children, blindness and an early death. The rulers of the district encouraged country fairs which attracted thousands of visitors and lasted for weeks. On the last day of Śrāvaṇa, the major protagonists of her epic were set up as life-sized clay figures. In some places, the celebration of Manasā could last the entire month of Śrāvaṇa. Among the tribal ethnic groups in the villages near Salbari and Dakshin Satali, she was praised as Māreyā or Mārāī. Their ceremonies could last for three days. Long sections of the *Epic* were sung to the audience. Unlike so many other places, the date of public Manasā worship was not fixed by tradition. It could be observed anytime.

Midnapur. Apart from Nachipur and Mahisadal, hardly anyone worshipped the goddess on a daily basis. The goddess was most popular among ethnic groups that cared little for Hindu customs, and the most important feast day was Daśaharā. The last days of Śrāvaṇa (July/August), Jyaiṣṭha (May/June) and Āṣāḍha (June/July) were also celebrated, plus Nāgapañcamī and Ambubāchi. The ohjās and the snake conjurers preferred the last day of the month Āśvina (September/October).

Murshidabad. This district generally favoured Manasā worship during the last days of the rainy season, plus the fifth lunar days of the monsoon months and, in special locations, throughout the entire month Śrāvaṇa (July/August). Plus Daśaharā, Tuesdays, Saturdays and special occasions. In Rajhat, Khaspur and Karjjana, daily worship was widely popular. In some places, the ohjās celebrated during the entire month Āṣāḍha (June/July). Women planted a twig of sij near the holy basil on the last day of Āṣāḍha and worshipped it every Tuesday and Saturday, and every fifth of the bright and dark moon.

Nadia, a major city, widely worshipped Manasā, in spite of the fact that the largest part of the population followed Islam. The major feast days were Daśaharā and Nāgapañcamī, and in some locations the fifth days of Śrāvaṇa (July/August) and Bhādra (August/September). Daily worship was almost unknown.

Major fairs were celebrated in the name of the goddess, whose four-armed clay statue was frequently set up under great trees. Maity mentions figs and banyan. Singing was essential. The district provided an unusual ritual. Four or five days before the major ceremony, the women had a ritual bath and planted beans and legumes on a special, freshly ploughed plot. The seeds were covered with a screen. A few days later, the screen was removed and the seeds watered. In the afternoon before the ritual, the sprouting seeds were gathered and laid out on trays. These were set up on the spot reserved for the statue of the goddess. On the same day, the large clay statue was collected at the house of the statue maker and set up in a house, under a canopy. The sprouting seeds gave their blessing to the place, and prepared it for the arrival of the goddess. The women offered fried rice, sugared paddy, small bananas, milk and fruit. Large amounts of incense went up in smoke and the women sang. On the next day, the 'official' pūjā began, when Brahmins celebrated the goddess in the afternoon, the evening and the morning after. They offered mostly milk and bananas. The women accompanied the ritual with chants. After the ceremony, the statue was carried into the river. In Krishnapur, the women performed an extra ritual. On the day before the ceremony, they only consumed milk and dried paddy. On the day of the offering, they fasted until the evening worship was over. The ritual involved a make-believe marriage. Two girls, bearing plates of sprouting seeds, were married to each other. Both wore colourful flower-garlands, and these were exchanged, just as in a real marriage, to fix their union. During this ceremony, some women assumed priestly roles, while the congregation sang Manasā songs.

24-Pagarnas. The major Manasā festival was celebrated on the last day of Bhādra (August/September). The next best was Daśaharā. In some districts, the last days of all months of the rainy season were the favourites. Few people performed daily worship. But there were exceptions. At Kidderpore, near Calcutta, a major temple was dedicated to the goddess. Her statue was made of brass. It was venerated every day. When the temple had to be dismantled to give way to a new street, the Calcutta Improvement Trust confiscated the statue. The local priest, stemming from a family that had served the serpent goddess for generations, had to move to a shrine in the neighbourhood and made do with a clay statuette. 24-Pagarnas celebrated two serpent goddesses: Manasā and Jagat Gaurī, who was considered her sister. Jagat is the *cosmos*, the *world* and *earth*, while Gaurī is the *fair, bright, shining, yellow* or *golden* one. It's a title of Pārvatī, Śiva's wife. Jagat Gaurī is the light of the world, i.e. consciousness (for without awareness, the world is not just dark: it does not exist). She had a popular shrine near Narikeldanga. The statue held a son on her lap. During the important festivals, Brahmins performed the ceremonies, but when the lower classes, such as the Ḍoms and the Haris celebrated, they employed their own ritualists. Their rites involved pig sacrifices, which are unusual in India. The pork was grilled and eaten after the ritual. For both goddesses, fairs were arranged, and the one for Jagat Gaurī was the more important. S.L. Hora visited the major Manasā temple in Uttarbhag. He recorded, that to his astonishment, the goddess was not represented by a sacred pot. Instead, she was worshipped as two heaps of earth. From each, three cobra-heads, shaped of clay, emerged. In front of the arrangement was a spot coloured in glaring red pigment. Just as unusual was the ritual schedule: the major Manasā festivals were celebrated between January and February.

West Dinajpur may have had the greatest amount of Manasā worshippers in India. The name Viṣahari was extremely popular, less common were Padmā and Padmāvatī. In rare cases, the goddess was addressed as Jagatgaurī, Nāgamātā and Nāgapūjā. The major festival was on the last day of Śrāvaṇa (July/August). The last days of Āṣāḍha (June/July) and Bhādra (August/September) were also celebrated here and there. For several days around the end of Śrāvaṇa up to the second day of Bhādra a feast was celebrated. That's less than a week. In other places, the Manasā festival could last for the entire month of Śrāvaṇa. The members of the warrior class also celebrated Manasā on the day when the first new rice was cooked. Festivities often revolved around fire offerings and in some places, animals were sacrificed (and eaten). In several villages, the goddess was worshipped in a small hut surrounded by banana trees. These shrines sported images of Manasā riding a donkey, accompanied by cobras. Sītalā, goddess of smallpox and contagious diseases also rides a donkey. Sītalā, whose name means *'cold, shivering'*, is usually worshipped outside of settlements, near sacred trees like Pandanus odoratissimus or Acacia arabuca. Quite frequently, she is depicted as a nude, red woman carrying a winnowing fan, a bundle of sticks and a pot of water. Her cult is usually ignored by the upper classes and the Brahmins, until the next plague breaks out and people come rushing to her shrine. Her speciality, smallpox, is being disregarded nowadays, as the disease is getting rare. Instead, she has become the goddess of HIV. There are plenty of places in East India where Manasā, like Sītalā, is invoked to heal cholera, smallpox, leprosy and other pestilences. Occasionally, they can be so similar that their imagery is mutual. In **Birbhum**, Manasā is frequently addressed as Sītalā.

Picture 63: Top: Ālpanā painting for Ganeṣa's brata ritual, bottom: feet of a goddess, Bengal.

49. East Bengal

Indian independence was a terrible challenge. The British divided the subcontinent into sections which were to separate Hindus and Muslims. More than a million people became foreigners in their homeland and had to flee for their lives. The violence, rape and theft defy description. Afterwards, India and Pakistan were lethal enemies. In the east, the British created the small state East Pakistan. It was supposed to be governed from large West Pakistan. As the West Pakistanis didn't give a damn for the problems of the East Pakistanis, the latter declared independence and renamed their tiny country Bangladesh. As modern Bangladesh is a Muslim state, I cannot guarantee that any of these rituals are still being practised.

How about field studies? An acquaintance arranged a meeting with a woman from Bangladesh, who studied economy at Frankfurt University. As it turned out, she had never heard of Manasā. Though 10% of the population are Hindus, she wasn't aware of their customs, rites and ceremonies. After enduring my questions, she apologised: "We Muslims are not allowed to know about these things."

Bakarganj, Midnapur, Jalpaiguri, Malda, Howrah, Cooch-Behar. The goddess was usually celebrated on the last days of Śrāvaṇa (July/August). Images were not a must. Some rituals may have happened without a visual focus. Or maybe her symbol was so inconspicuous that foreign observers didn't notice it. It's hard to generalise, as elsewhere large clay figures were paraded, plus figures of the major characters of her Epic. Some of these were sponsored by high ranging Brahmins. Rituals of thanksgiving could take anything between 2,5 and 5 days. One special custom: a small model of a house was made of wood and paper and painted with scenes from the *Manasā Epic*. The essential element was, of course, the goddess in her splendour. This 'house' was worshipped and the type of ceremony was called a Paṭa Pujā. The word Paṭa means *textile, weaving*. The goddess was addressed as Paṭa Viṣahari. In some locations, the goddess was celebrated as a pot of holy water, all through the month Śrāvaṇa. On the last day of the month, the pot was cast into the river. In addition, Manasā had permanent shrines. One of them was in Gaila: allegedly, it had been sponsored by the famous poet Bijay Gupta in the fifteenth century. The shrine had a brass statue of the goddess. It was close to a large well. At the shrine, daily worship was conducted. The goddess was especially worshipped by a very low class, the Caṇḍālas. Low means polluting. A Hindu who touched a Caṇḍāla lost his class. Their local representatives believed that they were direct descendants of the goddess, and called themselves the Sons of Manasā. While the feast day Nāgapañcamī was widely celebrated for the Nāga deities, it was not related to Manasā's cult.

Chittagong. All through the month Śrāvaṇa, Manasā was worshipped, usually without a statue or picture. Instead, two pots with holy water were set up, and on the last day of the ceremony another two were added. Next to the pots, a twig of sij was planted. Unlike so many districts, the locals did not submerge their pots in the river. After the end of the ritual, the pots were cleaned and used for normal household activities. When a family desired a closer contact with the goddess, an image, usually a clay statuette was employed. In Suchakradani a Manasā figure was celebrated in the company of four other statues of the gods. The event happened in the shrine of Jalkumārī, a goddess who is famous for healing smallpox. Her cult was the main thing; Manasā was a temporary guest.

Jessore & **Khulna** were a cultural unit. The fair began a day after the Manasā celebration. Often more than eight thousand visitors appeared. The most eminent ohjās came to attend. They carried baskets and cages full of snakes, many of them toxic. Their performance was celebrated on an elevated stage. A famous ohjā sat in the centre, and others surrounded him. Each of them drew a magical circle around himself and recited mantras. Cautiously they released one serpent after another and allowed them to creep around. Some ohjās draped snakes around their necks and shoulders and played with them, and muttered mantras to keep them spellbound. Each ohjā made much of his snake collection, and demonstrated his control. Powerful ohjās forced their snakes to crawl into the magical circle of others. It proved their superiority. If the snakes fought, they represented a conflict of magic power, and if an ohjā made his snake bite another ohjā, the audience gasped. The bitten ohjā could show his skill by remaining unperturbed and by drawing the toxin out of himself. It was transferred into an object. If that didn't work, the major ohjā rose and healed him. In Maity's time, such events were rare. Most snakes were in no mood for excursions and remained within their own circles.

Mymensing. Manasā was widely venerated by Hindus and Muslims. According to Sen's ballad collection (1923), worship a few hundred years ago happened on the last day of July, in August, or around the last day of Śrāvaṇa (middle or end of September). After the sinking of her pots, boat races followed, which were attended by countless visitors. In this district, a version of the *Epic*, the *Vyādhī-Bhakti Taraṅhinī* was widely popular. It contains an unusual scene. After Lakhindār was revived, Manasā was worshipped on a special boat called Gauhārī. The scene differs from most versions of the story, where her pūjā is celebrated on dry land. In Mymensingh and other sections of East Bengal, boats equipped with Manasā's image plus the representations of the major gods were set up. Consider this: In West Bengal, boat worship and boat races were rare, but they were common in East Bengal. I'd love to know more about this. Are we observing a Chinese custom? In China, and nowadays in many other countries, boat races were and are performed around midsummer. The custom has been going on for at least two thousand years. Allegedly, they were inspired by Qu Yuan (early third century BCE), a famous statesman, aristocrat, ritualist, part-time shaman (wu) and China's greatest early poet. Qu was a man of virtue. For years, he had warned his stupid king that the state of Qin was preparing an invasion. The king refused to listen, the courtiers cooked up a scandal and Qu was banished from the court. He retired into the country where he composed unequalled poetry and practised wu shamanism, meditation and engaged in shamanic flight. One sad day, he received the message that the state Qin had mounted an invasion. He had been right, but that didn't make him happy. When he got the message, he was walking on the shore of a lake. Knowing what the invaders would do to him, he picked up a large stone, jumped into the water and drowned. A group of fishers raced to save him. Alas, they were too late. According to legend, Qu's death initiated the custom of dragon boat racing. If a rower fell in and chanced to drown, he became a sacrifice to the serpentine dragons who rule Chinese rivers.

Back to East Bengal. In private homes, the goddess was often worshipped as a four-armed figure on the last day of Śrāvaṇa (July/August). Such figures were frequently graced by cobras rising from their shoulders. Before the figure was submerged in the river, the cobras were carefully detached. They were buried in the floor to banish illness, especially child-diseases. In the same district, people set up model houses of paper, wood and tree-marrow, painted with scenes of the Epic.

Rajshahi & Rangpur. The communal celebration happened under a sij tree. Most worshippers were Hindus, and came from all classes of society. They considered themselves (or claimed to be) Vaiṣṇavas. It did not stop them from serpent worship. The ritual was full of non-hinduistic elements. The great festival was the last day of the month Śrāvaṇa (July/August). If required, it was performed in Śiva or Kālī temples. Public fairs followed afterwards. The same went for the districts **Bogra and Dinajpur**. These fairs were, as already described, famous for an assembly of ohjās, who came to demonstrate their serpent sorcery. In an edge of the fairground, a banana tree was planted. Under the banana, a pot of holy water, with a sij twig, was set up. Occasionally, branches of other trees were used. The goddess was invoked, in her sacred pot, by the recitation of mantras. Then the ohjās began their act. The highest ranking ohjā drew a large magic circle. A group of ten to twelve persons, called pātās, took their seat within. They were volunteers, some of them of Hindu, some of the Muslim faith. The ohjās recited mantras for the goddess. Usually, an ohjā recited a spell and a person within the group was 'struck'. The victim shook, quivered and was tossed about. In short, our volunteer was obsessed, overexcited, or hysterical. That's what I would say, but for the gawking audience, the person had been 'poisoned' by magic. When one ohjā had 'poisoned' a volunteer, another broke the spell with his magic. It wasn't easy. The 'poisoned' candidate had fits, rolled around, he jittered and twitched. The healing ohjā had to apply all of his art to lure the suffering patient out of the magic circle, and to perform a healing. When this was done, another ohjā 'poisoned' a volunteer. The ohjā who could 'poison' and 'heal' faster than the others was admired. That's the business side of the event. Some ohjās came out as winners. I wonder why the volunteers participated.

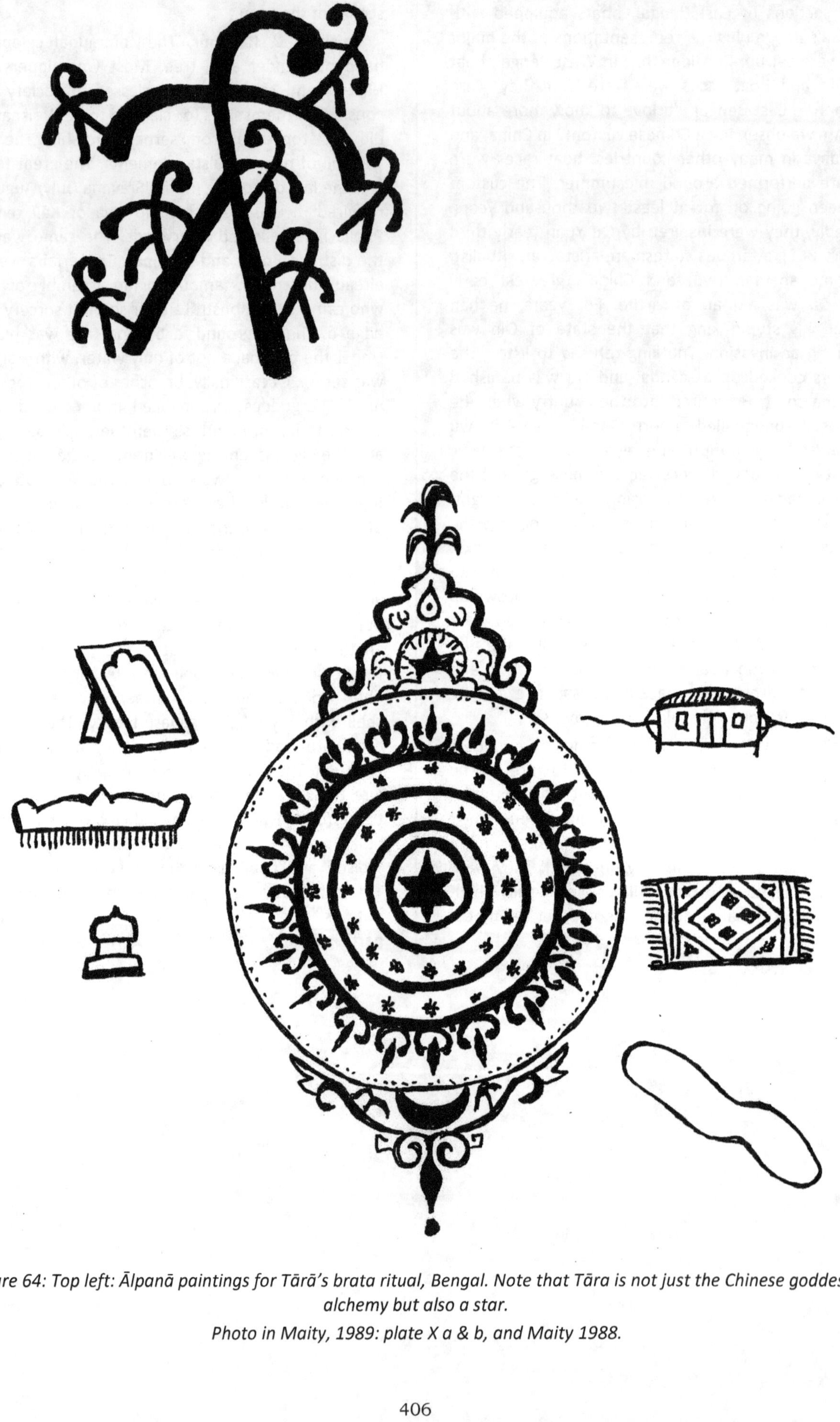

Picture 64: Top left: Ālpanā paintings for Tārā's brata ritual, Bengal. Note that Tāra is not just the Chinese goddess of alchemy but also a star.
Photo in Maity, 1989: plate X a & b, and Maity 1988.

50. Tripura and Bihar

All through the month Śrāvaṇa (July/August), the *Padmā Purāṇa* of Nārāyaṇ Deb was read within each educated family. The readings ended on the last day of the month, on the first day of Bhādra (August/September). On this day, Manasā hymns were sung in public. The class of fishermen (the Mālos) performed a ceremonial mock-marriage similar to the customs of district Nadia. Two unmarried girls acted the part of bride and bridegroom. The 'bride' stood on a stool or chair, while the 'bridegroom' carried a pot full of sprouting grains, and circled her seven times. After each round, the pot was emptied and filled it with new grains. I wonder what happened to the sprouting grain after the ceremony. The event was accompanied by women singing in chorus. It was followed by general feasting, readings from the *Padmā Purāṇa*, hymns and dancing. The music was made with cymbals, plate gongs and dholak drums.

Singbhum. In Kolhan, worship involved innovative elements. Long ago, a hereditary class of serpent priests used to heal snake-bitten people and sold amulets against snakebite. They must have been total failures. The population was so dissatisfied that they were kicked out and replaced by a new class of serpent priests. Teachers were invited from Oriya and a group of young men became their students. They mastered magical chants celebrating Manasā. Their effort was a success; since the 1930s new centres of serpent worship flourished. Maity gives a brief glimpse at training methods in the village Dumbisai. In the courtyard of the ohjā, two days before new moon, a fence was built around a tamarind tree. Within the enclosure, the ohjā performed his meditation and much of the ritual. The students surrounded the fence, and listened as the teacher chanted. The spells, as Maity reported, consisted mostly of the names of Hindu deities and their meditation description. After each spell followed instructions on the practical application. The ohjā recited for three or four hours, and the students repeated his instructions in a chorus (just like most schoolchildren in East Asia). Finally, the ohjā toppled a small pile of earth which had confined the goddess during his lecture. The better students began to quiver, shook their heads from side to side, drooled, staggered, got up and began to hit their heads against the fence. When their rapture culminated, three or four students grabbed sticks leaning on the inside of the barrier and began to thrash each other. A student who was hit without striking back failed. I wonder whether they felt any pain. Those who passed the ceremony went through another ceremony on the new moon, which ended when they received a black ribbon. It was tied around an arm and protected its bearer from snakebite.

South Manbhum. Manasā appeared in the company of other gods, each of them represented as a clay statue. They were worshipped and sunk afterwards. While these customs are typical for Hindu worship, the worshippers were not. Many of them came from cultures which were totally removed from Indian 'high' traditions. Few of them were aware that the goddess had a story, and indeed most of the popular deities were known only by name. Their character, ritual and mythology remained unknown. Deities, no matter how odd, were worshipped on the crudest possible level. They received gifts and were asked to grant health, protection, wealth and good luck. Their philosophical and mystical grandeur, so important in classical Indian worship, was almost unheard of.

Ranchi. The Oraons integrated the cult of Manasā into their faith. Among this cultural group, the snake ritualists are called nāg-mātis. Each snake doctor performed, in the company of his students, three annual ceremonies for the goddess. These happened in Jyaiṣṭha (May/June), Āṣāḍha (June/July) and Śrāvaṇa (July/August). Each ceremony required preparation, such as a day of strict fasting. Most participants sacrificed birds. The hymns of the goddess were accompanied by clapping. That's a special Indian music tradition. You'd be amazed how many sounds can be made by two hands.

Picture 65: Happy lunacy: Kāmākhya, refining the kalās of the gods.

51. Assam

Though the Manasā cult can be traced to eleventh century Assam, the ethnographic documentation leaves a lot to be desired. The cult took several centuries to become really popular. We are talking of Manasā and her myth: there is evidence, that before her, other serpent deities were venerated. Assam is famous for its tantric traditions, its Śākta cults and its cultural connection to China. An important branch of the southern Silk Road went through Assam and connected with Lijiang in Yunnan, a major trading place with excellent connections to the great cities of China, Tibet and Myanmar. Any traveller, merchant or pilgrim who wanted a snow-free road to India used this road. Most cultures along the route are into serpent worship. While Hindus rarely travelled outside of India (theoretically, a Hindu loses his class if he leaves India, and is terribly polluted), Jainas, Buddhists and Muslims did. Chinese Buddhists went to India, where they studied Saṁskṛta for a decade or two and returned laden with priceless original documents. During the Tang dynasty, in 664, a group of Chinese alchemists travelled to Assam. King Bhāskaravarman had invited them to participate in a symposium. Wang Xuanzi presented him with a copy of Laozi's *Daodejing* in Saṁskṛta (White, 1996:62 & Maity, 1966/2001:68). The effect may have been remarkable: when Laozi referred to the *Dark/Mysterious Woman* (Xuannü) in chapter 6, the Assamese presumably thought he talked about Kālī. We can only wonder what happened. Left Hand Tantra and Daoism have much in common, and there is an entire branch of Left Hand Tantra called Mahācīna (*Great China*), indicating the source of its teachings.

Assam was famous for its Kula and Kaula cults. The tantric pioneer Śivānanda (c. 800-850) travelled from Kashmir all the way to Assam to be initiated, and brought the new teaching to his homeland, where he combined it with Krama Tantra. It proved to be a major break-through. In Assam, Manasā's major cult site is in Kāmarūpa, near the temple of Kāmākhya and the sacred shrines and mountains of the ten Mahāvidyās. I am sure you remember how the pieces of Satī's corpse dropped all over India, creating sacred places everywhere. Calcutta got a toe and look what happened. In Kāmākhya the yonī (*vulva, source, spring, origin*) of Satī fell. It made the place holy, powerful and dangerous. Goddess Kāmākhya is famous for her menstruation. Upper-class Hindu goddesses tend to have few physical functions: they rarely menstruate or give birth. How their children appear remains mysterious. Kāmākhya, far from the centres of upper-class Hindu thought, menstruates every month and, once a year, with a vengeance. It happens around the end of the monsoon. By then, the water table has gone up. The major sanctuary of the goddess is said to be an underground temple with a sacred spring to which non-Hindus are not admitted. In autumn, the water turns red. It flows over a large rock representing the yoni of the goddess. During her menstruation, the temple is closed for three days. Afterwards, the worshippers, and there are thousands of them, celebrate the renewal of the goddess. Long ago, Kāmākhya was a famous meeting place for hot-blooded tantric women. Early literature states that highly initiated yogīnīs lived nearby, ready to initiate experienced tantric practitioners. Some of these yogīnīs were, no doubt, spirits or goddesses. Others were real women, who had reached a high degree of spiritual competence, or could transform into a goddess in a fit of wild obsession. Among the tantrics of the Left Hand Path, such women were respected, admired and, in many cases, worshipped. Orthodox Hindus disapproved, and derided them as lethal, evil-minded witches.

In general, Manasā's major feast occurred on the last day of the month Śrāvaṇa (July/August). Her sacred pot was set up in her temple, right next to that of Kāmākhya. Worship continued to the second day of Bhādra (August/September). Worshippers made and dedicated clay serpents to the goddess, which were arranged around her altar. Hymns were sung and parts of her epic, in the versions by Durgābar and Manakar, were recited. The manuscripts were opened in Chaitra (March/April) and closed, after the recitation was complete, on the last day of Bhādra (August/September). Outside of this period, the reading was strictly prohibited. Manasā worship at Kāmākhya was an expensive, elaborate affair, sponsored by wealthy people and performed by the highest Brahmins. Popular passages of the *Epic*, especially the tale of Behulā and Lakhindār, were read to the public. An Assamese version of the Epic, the *Manasākāvya*, was particularly holy. A few families owned copies and kept them like a reliquary. Manasā worship was often accompanied by deodhanī and deaodha dances. For one month, the dancers lived on a vegetarian diet and avoided polluting events, like births and cremations. The dancers were in frenzy. The grace of the goddess entered them, and they proved their obsession by licking sharp swords. Each sword was blessed in Manasā's name before and after the dance. Some laid a sword on their neck as they pranced around, or danced on the edge of the blade. This custom became famous, attracted plenty of visitors and was taken up by communities in the neighbourhood.

In Assam, Manasā received most her veneration during the monsoon months. As elsewhere, her insignias were the pot of holy water and the sij twig. According to the poet Manakar, Manasā was celebrated day and night in a special pavilion dedicated to her, all through the four months of the rainy season. Durgābar recorded that Manasā was mostly celebrated on four days of the month Śrāvaṇa, plus the last two days and the fifth of each half moon. Her representation was simple: in many places, a heap of earth, a cone of banana-tree-bark or a pot sufficed. During the last centuries, the worship of figures became increasingly popular. In many places, the holy pot was set up beneath a sacred tree. Nearby, the sij twig was planted. The cult was popular among the middle and lower classes. Vaiṣṇavas tended to avoid it, unless a plague broke out. Under emergency conditions, even high ranking Viṣṇu worshippers contributed. They sponsored the festivities, but did their best to remain in the background. In the districts Goalpara, Kāmarūpa, Darrang and Nowgong, Manasā was frequently identified with Mārāī, a goddess of death, pestilence, love and lust. But Manasā wasn't simply a healer of snake bites and diseases. Earliest Assamese literature indicates that she grants children to barren couples, wives to lonely bachelors and wealth to the poor and desperate. The blind regain their eyesight, prisoners return to liberty and evil influences are diverted.

Each of these claims is true, one way or another.

Two special events are related to her cult. One is the ohjā dance (ohjā pali), which can be traced to the 15th century. One ohjā recited sacred scripture. He was accompanied by his assistants (pali) who accompanied the text with cymbals and plate gongs, and danced. An important assistant, the daina pali conducted a dialogue with the reciter; he elaborated and explained the text, and entertained the audience with proverbs, comments and jokes. The performance was a rural affair. However, the dance incorporated ritual gestures of high-class Hindu temple dance.

Another popular dance was called deodhanī. The tradition can be traced to Mangaldai and Uttarlakhimpur. The female and male dancers were amateurs. That word, nowadays an insult, ought to be re-evaluated. An amateur is someone who does something for love. Unlike the professional, who does it for profit. The goddess appeared to the deodhanī in a vision or a dream, and asked them to participate. Again, the dance involved obsession. Some dancers were so deeply inspired that they were consulted about important problems and asked to foretell the future. Deodhanī and deodha dances were performed for Manasā and Mārāī. They were widely popular, though they did not include showy elements, like the sword dances of Kāmākhya.

Part Eight:

Meditation and Ritual

Picture 66: Black Manasā. Temple statue.

52. Dhyāna Instructions

Welcome. We have arrived at a crucial stage. For real spiritual practice, you don't need an occult group, a temple or a village community. Nor do you need a guru or teacher. The essential answers are within you. Here are two Bengal proverbs:

'The mind of each person is the temple of devotion.'

'God can be worshipped by thinking.'

We enter the realm of mental worship. As you recall, in Saṁskṛta the mind is mānas. The Indo–European root is 'men-': *to think*. Words like mind, memory, mental, manic, mention, ament, comment, dement, reminiscence, mentor, mantic, monitor, monument, demonstrate, premonition, summon and mantra are related, just like the names of such deities as Mnemosyne, the Eumenides, and (perhaps) Minerva. Greek 'menos' is *spirit*, the manes are the spirits of the dead and German 'Minne' is *love, loving thought, allure, fond remembrance* and designates a class of medieval love songs, and a special event that could easily end in bloodshed. The Minnesänger were supposed to praise an aristocratic lady, mostly, by professing their eternal love to her. But while she wallowed in praise, her husband had fits of jealousy, gnashed his teeth and fiddled with his sword. He and the singers had one hell of a time. Before long, minne songs went out of fashion. In some places, like Iceland, where people were really prude, they were illegal. So minne may be remembrance, and fondness, and allure, but mostly it is awareness. Face the serpent lady! Manasā is the lot. She is thought, imagination, remembrance, speculation, awareness, consciousness, doubt, belief, feelings, sympathies, antipathies, desires and so on. All of these depend on your inner and outer senses. And all of them are necessary to meet the divine within yourself and recognise the divine in the world you assume to perceive.

Nobel Prize winner Barbara McClintock said in 1984: *A goal of the future would be to determine the extent of knowledge the cell has of itself and how it uses that knowledge in a thoughtful manner when challenged* (quoted by Trewavas, 2014:1). *'Thoughtful manner'* implies awareness and intelligence. *'Challenged'* means that every cell, just like every organism, has to deal with difficulties. It has to recognise problems and act on them. Please stop and think this through. The basic requirements of intelligent life are self-awareness, awareness of the surroundings and the ability to make decisions and to act in the best possible way. Let's quote Sunzi (Sun Tzu), the famous strategist of 3rd C. BCE China: *Know your enemy and know yourself, in a hundred battles you will never be in peril. When you are ignorant of the enemy but know yourself, your chances of winning and losing are equal. If ignorant both of your enemy and yourself, you are certain in every battle to be in peril* (trans. Griffith, 1971).

Sunzi wrote about diplomacy, war and strategy. His insights apply to biology. Cells, microbes, trees, ducks, serpents, people and slime mould: we all face the same problems. We have to get by on who we are, and to cope with what the world throws at us. All organisms do so. No matter whether you call some organism 'primitive' or 'complex', it proves its efficiency by being alive. Most organisms are much better at survival than we are. Let's face it: the most successful life forms on earth are bacteria. Algae are amazing. Beetles are stunning. Mammals are hardly worth mentioning. Hominids made their appearance a short time ago. There were more than sixty different species, most of them not part of our ancestry. They died out. We are the last. And we are doing our best to exterminate ourselves. Manasā stands astonished. Neta asks: "How stupid can you get?"

People are funny. And no matter how funny they get, life will continue. Most of the animals and plants don't give a damn whether mankind continues. The dwellers of the deep sea hot water chutes hardly noticed we exist. Our planet will go on for a long time, and the sun is booked for plenty of energy, no matter whether something insignificant like mankind survives. Other species will lead a better life. Intelligence is everywhere. Cells are intelligent, and the same goes for bacteria, fungi, plants and anything organic. Some unicellar organisms, like bacteria, can sense up to fifty different signals from the outside world, and base their decisions on them. Single-celled freshwater algae, like the volvocales, form communities. They chose where to swim: to the sunlight, to nutrients, or away from cold, from shadow, predators, parasites, toxic waste and similar nuisances. They rise by night and descend by day. They decide, however this may work, on which individuals develop sexuality and which reproduce as clones. The decision is important: sexual reproduction means variation, which improves resistance against diseases and parasites. When a community includes sexually reproducing algae, it enjoys much better health, but is burdened down, and has trouble approaching food; as the sexually active individuals cannot propel themselves (they lack the wildly spiralling flagellas). In short, the poor community enjoys better health, while the rich community, with plenty of clones and few sexual individuals, is threatened by viruses, bacteria, and parasites. (Trewavas, 2014:45-46). I'm sure this says something about human culture. In plants, and please remember how closely Manasā interacts with plants, we encounter republics: each branch, each leaf, each rootlet acts independently. It has its own sensors for inner and outer processes. It decides when to advance and when to remain. Each branch is aware of the amount of sunlight it receives, is aware of solar flares, the light cycles, of the day of the year, of tension, weight, of wind and pressure. Each shoot can see infra-red, deep-red, red, blue, violet, ultraviolet and parts of the blue-green range. The plant on your windowsill knows whether you wear red or blue, and it sees your body temperature. It is aware when you touch it, and it won't like it. That's because most plants try to avoid contact, unless they are climbers and creepers and stranglers. Each leaf senses the pheromones produced by other leaves, and by other plants nearby. It knows when another leaf is attacked by bacteria, or caterpillars, a goat, or a farmer. It can tell if it's touched by wind, an obstacle, or an animal. A plant remembers what caterpillars attacked it last year, how they moved, how they fed, their saliva and their feeding speed. It remembers the chemicals it cooked up to discourage, defertilise or kill them. The higher plants (like trees, and anything with blossoms) can produce an average of a 100 to 1000 toxic chemicals to discourage predators, and combine them in endless variations. Some remember their enemies for years. Some pass on the memory of their enemies to five generations of descendants (Lamarck would have loved to hear this!). Each fine rootlet acts independently. It has distinct sensors for humidity, for acid and alkali, for gravity, light, for all important chemicals, for drought, flood, snowmelt, electromagnetic fields, deep sound vibrations, toxic metals, pollution, and so on. Plants know which bacteria, fungi and animals are their friends. They attract some and discourage others. They nourish those who promote it, and poison those who don't. Some call for support when they are attacked by pests: they send out pheromones that attract aggressive insects. These arrive at great speed, and finish off the assailants. Each fine rootlet makes individual decisions. And it communicates them to the rest of the plant using electric action potentials, hormones, and pheromones. Unlike human beings, with their clever-clever brains, plants are objective. They sense what is. People, by contrast, convert sensory input into representations, and imagine that we experience reality. The republic works as there are plenty of information networks. What we see as a single plant or tree is a triumph of decentralised intelligence (See Chamovitz, 2012, Trewavas, 2014 and Karban 2015). Those who think that plants are dumb and insensitive are stuck in Christian thought: each plant senses itself and its environment with much greater intensity and detail than mammals like us ever will.

It goes down to the basics: there is intelligence everywhere. This is about consciousness. It's about you. Whenever you experience joy, insight, inspiration and liberation, our serpent goddess is involved.

To meet Manasā, it is useful but slightly delusive to imagine her in a human form. Hinduism is fond of statues. The gods look like people, and are often bigger, brighter and more beautiful than ordinary folks. Unlike most ascetics, poets, artists and magicians, they dress well. The main distinction between primates like us and our anthropomorphic deities is the number of hands, eyes and assorted extras. Well, you can set up a statue in your living room. That's great fun; it will remind you of the divine and excite your friends and visitors. Magic is often based on remembering: it uses objects to remind you of ideas, emotions and consciousness states, and it allows you to manipulate them. Consider amulet magic. The little pendant around your neck doesn't do much. The real power resides within you. The amulet helps you to remember. Unless you remember, it won't work. The same goes for large representations of the divine. A statue or painting will accumulate emotional energy when you spend plenty of time worshipping. You can pray, make music, anoint the image with all sorts of secretions, feed it tasty dishes and tell it what really moves you. Given enough passion, devotion and madness, it can turn your home into a power zone. That's pretty good; it's also helpful when you come home from work feeling weary and pessimistic, and need an energy boost. However: a statue is too passive. You can talk to it but it won't talk back. That's a major disadvantage: we all deserve being talked back to. Unless someone disagrees, or you disagree with someone, we won't learn enough.

Unlike a statue, the deity can interact with us. The living deity appears a) everywhere, b) in everyone and everything and c) within yourself. Point a) and b) can be experienced when you wake up and remember that the divine is here. Look out of the window, look into a mirror and realise.

The 'deity within' needs a medium to express itself. And it requires a suitable environment. You have to get rid of your mental rubbish to come close to it. That's why people withdraw, fast, clear their minds, eliminate distractions, meditate, go into trance or exhaust themselves with motion, dance, devotion and sex. Your deity or deities will appear in imaginary form. Some think that imagination isn't real. They are wrong. Every real, man-made thing was born in the imagination. Flint knives, bronze axes, tents, houses, cars, streets, cities, comic books and washing machines: they were imagination until their time came. The good thing about imagination is its changeability. Given a bit of training, that representation can be astonishingly alive.

For this purpose, visionaries composed meditation instructions.

The technical term is **dhyāna instructions.** Let's recall the roots of **yoga**. In the Vedic Period, the term used to mean union, yoking, preparing a battle chariot, going on a war raid, and the apotheosis of very special aristocrats, when they found a hero's death on the battlefield and ascended to heaven in their chariots. In the Upaniṣadic Period, it also came to refer to the apotheosis of very saintly ascetics, meaning renouncers who denied themselves everything and starved to death. A yogī could be a renouncer, who attained union when he died, or, far more common, a power-hungry sorcerer, exploiter or charlatan. None of them was interested in meditation, contemplation, gymnastic exercises, stretching, diet, breathing techniques or special postures.

Around the third or fourth century, Patañjali composed one of the earliest texts on a new meditative discipline he identified as **yoga**. His yoga was a minority movement at the edge of society. The new, meditative yogīs did their best to gain respect, and inserted new texts into elder Upaniṣads, and into the *Mahābhārata*, to make their movement seem much older than it was. White, in *Sinister Yogis*, gives an excellent account. Unlike the yogīs of earlier periods, Patañjali introduced the idea that inner discipline, meditation and spiritual development lead to attainment. Plus magic, of course. Contemporary yoga fans tend to ignore that bit. It was a radically new approach. His description is very brief.

Attention fixed on an object is dhāraṇā.

The term comes from the terminology of the Vedic warrior class. Dhāraṇā means to steer a battle chariot by means of its *reins*. Likewise, the reins of your attention fix you to the object of your meditation. The term dhāraṇā can also mean to think, concentrate, remember, hold, carry, custom, and rule.

Union of mind and object is dhyāna (meditation, internal worship, contemplation). *Samādhi* (union, connection, completion, to be together with the divine, deep trance) *is that condition of illumination where union as union disappears, only the meaning of the object on which the attention is fixed being present. The three together form concentration* (samyama: control, taming, binding; end of the world). *Successful concentration is direct knowledge*

(based on Patañjali, *Aphorisms of Yoga*, 1973, amended).

That's one way of expressing it. The terminology is not universally accepted. Let's consider another approach. Dhyāna, in advanced Kashmir Krama Tantra, is a meditation on a stream of ideas. You focus on a topic, such an image, a symbol, a mantra, animal, plant, biosphere or a deity, and allow it to inspire you. The flow of ideas is important. You are not supposed to force your attention on one thing to the exclusion of everything else. Good dhyāna shouldn't be an act of restriction. Like a ride in a battle chariot (i.e. yoga) it should take you somewhere useful. You focus on a topic and allow it to inspire you. Maybe you'll have plenty of great ideas. Enjoy them. Maybe all sorts of dumb stuff comes up, like personal quarrels, memories from work, headlines, political issues, and other trash. Most of them were cooked up by the fear industry. Let them slip away. Relax, smile and return to your topic. That's the basic idea. It means that you keep focussing and intensifying; in fact your attention/ awareness/ mind opens and closes like the petals of a flower. Good dhyāna instructions stimulate.

To give you a basic idea, here is a typical dhyāna instruction for Tārā, the Rescuer, who Carries (the worshipper), Across (the ocean of the world). Tārā is closely related to Neta.

I meditate upon the Divine Mother of the Three Worlds who is sitting on a white lotus in the centre of the waters enveloping the entire universe. In her left hands she holds a knife and a skull, and in her right hands a sword and a blue lotus. Her complexion is blue and she is bedecked with ornaments like ear-rings, necklace, bangles, armlets and anklets. She is decorated with three beautiful serpents and has three red eyes. Her hair is bunched into a single plait of tawny colour. Her tongue is always moving and her teeth and mouth appear horrible. She is wearing a tiger's skin around her waist and her forehead is decorated with white bone ornaments. Sage Akṣobhya (Unmoved, Unshakeable = Śiva), in the form of a serpent, is situated on her head. She is seated on the heart of a corpse and her breasts are hard.

A few pages and several hundred thousand mantra repetitions later, the worshipper holds durvā grass, rice, red sandalwood, and flowers and imagines her- or himself to be the goddess.

Goddess Tārā stands with both feet on the heart of the corpse-like Śiva. With horrid laughter, she is holding in her four hands the sword, blue lotus, sickle and a skull-cup. She arises from the vibration Hūṁ, has blue colour and is small in size. On her head are a single plait of red/brown colour and many serpents. Ugratārā Devī destroys the stupor of the three worlds. (Mahidhara, *Mantramahodadhiḥ*, 1992:179 & 202, slightly amended)

Here is one for Śiva, from the *Mahānirvāṇa Tantra*

As tranquil as the effluence of ten million moons; clothed in garments of tiger-skins; wearing a sacred thread made of a serpent; his whole body covered with ashes; wearing ornaments of serpents; his five faces are of reddish-black, yellow, rose, white and red colours, with three eyes each; his head is covered with matted hair; he is omnipresent; he holds Gaṅgā on his head and has ten arms, and in his forehead shines the crescent moon; he holds in his left hand the skull, fire, the noose, the pināka-weapon (a staff or bow), *and the axe, and in his right the trident, the thunderbolt, the arrow, and blessings; he is being praised by all the Devas and great sages; his eyes are half-closed in the excess of bliss; his body is white as the snow and the kuṇḍa flower* (kuṇḍa is a hole, fire pit, pot or vulva; its flower is the sexual secretions) *and the moon* (i.e. Soma); *he is seated on the bull; he is by day and night surrounded by siddhas, Gandharvas, and Apsarās who are chanting hymns in his praise; he is the husband of Umā; the devoted protector of his worshippers* (Avalon/Woodroffe, 1972:337-338, spelling amended, comments in brackets JF)

The instructions are sparse, descriptive and sober-minded. No poetry, nor extras, no promises of wealth, health and extra blessings. Many high deities appear loaded with magical items. Unlike them, Manasā dhyānas are more focused on appearance, body, ornaments and states of mind.

All of this is functional. It isn't there because it's true. It works. And if it doesn't, you and the deity are supposed to improve it.

This isn't about reality. I have no intention of discussing the 'real nature' of the gods, as my brain isn't up to the job. It can only handle simple things, like runes, oracle bone inscriptions and comics that feature Helja Quinn ("just call me Neta") and Poison Manasā.

Meditation instructions may give you the idea that a deity is limited to specific characteristics. You may read that a deity is young and beautiful. True, so it can be. But gods are shapechangers. Indian gods also change gender. If you think that Śiva is a man, you haven't met Śaivī yet. Viṣṇu likes to assume the form of the divine prostitute Mohinī. Remember how Brahmā quarrelled with her? It almost killed him. Mahākālī (female) can be Mahākāla (male). The two can even make love with each other. Elsewhere, Mahākāla is Śiva. So what? The divine is much greater than our thinking. Manasā can appear as Neta, as Dhanvantari, or totter around, dead drunk, as Śiva. Or the gods turn into animals. Manasā can be a snake, a spider, a mosquito, a bird of prey, a crow, vulture, jackal or a tiger. She can be a euphorbia plant, a pandanus plant, a neem tree, a fig tree, a fruit tree, a banana tree, a cactus, a lotus, or a water lily. And any thorny, toxic, self-assured kick-ass plant you can think of. Gods can appear as people, as things, as landscapes. Manasā can appear as a serpent, as a serpent charmer, as an ohjā, a Brahmin woman, a courtesan or all of them at once. Deities can revert to their primal nature and appear as energy, form, vibration and sound. Sometimes they manifest form. Or they dissolve the form and become formless consciousness. A deity can look like you. Or like your partner. It can be both of you.

In the *Manasā Epic* composed by Jagajīban, when Manasā was born she was neither male nor female (Baruah, 2010:33). Female, male and whatever is a major issue in our time. We face badly understood genetics, cultural delusions, social pressure, desires and our own expectations. We face an industry telling us that male and female brains are fundamentally different (they ain't; the differences are tiny) and a counter-industry enforcing gender-egalitarianism. In between, some people gain liberation and some are crushed. As a side effect, family structures are eroded and lasting partnerships become unfashionable. Society reverts to its atomic ingredients: singles are excellent consumers and, best of all, easy to exploit. In tantric meditation, gender rarely matters. Gods can appear as they like. The essential point is functionality.

Typical meditation instructions are short. They don't tell you stuff like 'go to a place where you won't be disturbed, sit down, light incense, ring a bell, relax, calm down, allow your breathing to become smooth and gentle, slow down, close your eyes, withdraw from the periphery of the body, introvert, sink into yourself...' and so on. The basics are taken for granted.

The student memorises the text. Then, in a gentle trance state, or when relaxing in the dark, or in half-sleep, the deity is visualised bit by bit. It takes a long time to get all the details right. That's because there are a lot of them and each detail is significant. If your deity holds a sword, like Kālī does, you are supposed to understand everything about swords. The same goes for every object a deity may hold. They are all divine. They are mysteries. It can be a lotus blossom, a noose, a rosary, a book, a spinning disk, a string instrument, a drum, a trident or a conch full of elixir. Each of them contains more magic than you or I will ever understand.

Manasā has an entire series of meditation instructions, and if you feel inspired, you can combine attractive elements. The instruction can be used as a checking list. You can build up your visualisation detail by detail. You might start at the feet and work your way up. Or you begin with the eyes. Or you create an imaginary setting first, invent a landscape, make up a shrine, a throne, and build up the image of the deity when everything is ready. All of these approaches are useful. And they are valid when they work for you. There are days when it is a relief to visit the deity in its own enchanted realm, and other days when all you need is a clear vision of its face and good perception of its voice. Or maybe you only see one of the divine objects.

Let me add that the visualisation should be impressive. There are people who make tiny, pale pictures somewhere in the distance and complain that they don't raise much feeling. Good visualisers bring their inner images close to them. They make them large, colourful, bright, and intense; they employ all senses. They see, hear, feel, taste, smell and sense the divine in full mind-blowing glory. And when you recite the meditation instruction, or a mantra, or want to talk with the deity of your choice, do it in a pleasant voice. Make it a voice you'd like to listen to.

When you have explored the meditation instruction every day for a period of months, a lot of things will be easy which seemed difficult in the beginning. You are building up neural pathways. Whatever you think frequently becomes easier to think. Thoughts literally build better nerve connections, increase the transmission of the synapses and the receptivity of the post-synapses, make skills and ideas more accessible and link up with other parts of the mind. Thoughts which are repeated every day become natural, automatic and fast. Thinking, i.e. Manasā, is habit-forming. This goes for awful thoughts (worries, jealousy, greed, hate etc) just as it goes for thoughts that make you happy and wise. It's called neuro-plasticity and means that our brains are changed by what we think. It allows us to learn and allows us to forget. Not on a metaphorical but on a physical level. That's because our brains are more than 'software' and 'hardware'. Thoughts change neural connections, and neural connections change thoughts.

To make the dhyāna instructions work, you are supposed to see and meet the deity in your **heart** (hṛdaya). The **heart** is a difficult subject. As I elaborated in *Kālī Kaula*, the heart is a multi-purpose term. It can mean the physical organ. Or, if you like, it can be represented by a cakra. Or by two cakras: one is the place where the eternal anāhata sound is heard, and another, on a different kind of map, is the location where you can meet your personal deity. Visiting the deity in the heart is a wonderful journey in the imagination. Usually, the heart is imagined as an island of jewels and enchanted plants. In the centre of the island under a wish-fulfilling tree, is the shrine of your personal deity. In your imagination, you can travel to this island, walk to the shrine and approach your deity. You can worship. You can speak, ask questions and listen closely. And you can answer the questions the deity asks of you. You can embrace the deity. Or, if you want something less dualistic, become the goddess or god of your choice.

The heart can be the centre of your body, your self and the entire world. It can describe any location between your shoulders and your hips. In the parlance of the Vedic and Upaniṣadic seers, the heart is the mind, is consciousness, awareness, thought, perception, dreaming, feeling, and any other faculty of the inner and outer senses. The heart creates, maintains and dissolves the worlds. All experiences happen in the heart. Your whole universe is a function of the heart. And, of course, the heart is individual and universal consciousness, and any of the high gods, such as Manasā, Śiva, Bhairava, Kālī etc. In Kashmir Tantra, the heart is the centre of the multiverse. It is the deep and sacred cave within yourself, the place of primordial reality, where consciousness-in-form (Śakti: energy, power, shape i.e. your favourite goddess/es) and consciousness-without-form (Śiva/Bhairava) make love. This heart is much more than a cakra. It is the root and source of all existence. It is the sacred location where reality is born, maintained, dissolved, transformed and re-created.

The heart can be experienced anytime. You can do it right now. The method is simple. Go to a place where you'll enjoy a bit of peace and quiet. Sit, relax and calm down. Observe the world around you. Say goodbye to it. Close your eyes. Relax deeper. Make it a good feeling. Shrink. Become smaller and smaller as you withdraw from the periphery of your body. Sink into the empty core of yourself. Your self can be thumb-sized; your self can be microscopic. Sink deeper, leave the everyday stuff out there. The heart is the greatest cave in the multiverse. It may seem empty but it is also full: voidness is the light of sheer undifferentiated awareness. As you sink into the core of all being, become simple. Let go. Shed all mind-stuff. Let it drift out of you and pass away. Thoughts and worries? Silly memories? Plans and hopes, desires and fears? Let them go their way. Watch how they drift to the periphery and disappear.

This process, elaborated in *Kālī Kaula*, is a journey of simplification. It has no goal and you will never reach an end. It is not supposed to blot you out in nirvāṇa (nirvān means *cessation*) nor is it supposed to illuminate you. It's a process, a journey of discovery and rejuvenation. The heart expands and the heart contracts. In this pulsation, you may meet the gods, mantras come to life, yantras radiate geometrical perfection, and insights arise that may transform you from within.

Now for a few examples. You'll find more dhyāna instructions in the chapters on pūjā. Maity proposed that their present wording can be traced to the period between 1300 and 1600, but that their imagery goes back to the ninth to twelfth century. Before that time, there is no data. Let's start with the most popular dhyāna instruction for Manasā in West Bengal. The text is adapted from the translations supplied by Maity 1966/2001:212 and Smith 1980:18. It comes from the *Tithitattva* of Raghunananda, and is very early.

I worship the Devī (shining one, goddess), *the mother of snakes, whose face is like the moon, of pleasing beauty, bountiful, who is seated on a swan, generous, who wears a red garment, the all-giver, who has a smiling face, who is adorned with gold, jewels and various snake ornaments, who is accompanied by eight Nāgas, who has prominent breasts, who is a yoginī/bhoginī and who can assume any form at will.*

The Nāgas can be king cobras, or ordinary ones, or they may be the sacred Nāga rulers of the directions. They may look like huge snakes, like dragons or appear in human form. The last line is fascinating. There are two versions of this instruction. In the one quoted by Maity, the goddess is a yoginī, i.e. a woman, spirit or goddess who practices yoga (*yoking, union, raid, a ride in a war-chariot*), and a sacred practitioner of hard-core Tantra. In everyday parlance, a yoginī is a dangerous witch. In the version quoted by Smith, the word is bhoginī, meaning an *enjoyer, one who delights in the senses*, or, alternatively, a *coiled one*. I suggest you contemplate both. In Left Hand Tantra, one who practices yoga, i.e. yokes her- or himself with the divine and attains liberation must also be an enjoyer of the world. Outside of Left Hand Tantra, the typical yogī, being a sour-faced ascetic, cannot be an enjoyer, but has to flee the world of illusions and temptations.

This instruction is from Bhattasali, who claims it comes from the commentary of Kāśīrām Vāchaspatī on the *Tithitattva* of Raghunananda (Maity, 1966/2001:213).

I take shelter in the goddess who shines like a golden lotus, who is decorated with ornaments formed by shining snakes, who has a smiling face, who is attended on all sides, who is the mother of Āstika, who has a child and who has well developed prominent bosoms and who holds two snakes in her two hands.

This instruction is clearly based on the *Mahābhārata* and may appeal to upper-class people. To be attended on all sides might refer to the company of the gods. You can visualise a selection. To take shelter/refugee is a popular term of Buddhist scripture.

Here is a dhyāna which calls Manasā by the name of the almost forgotten Buddhist serpent goddess Jāṅgulī. Very little is known about her cult and mythology. Her function was simple: to provide help against snake-bite. The Buddhist goddess was closely modelled on the ancient Vedic river goddess Sarasvatī, the patroness of speech, learning, art and music. Both goddesses ride a swan; hold a lute, a quill, a book, a sword, a blue lotus. In rare cases, Sarasvatī also holds a skull. Jāṅgulī may have one or several white snakes. These elements are absent in this Manasā dhyāna. In East India, the name Jāṅgulī became a title of Manasā. Our meditation instruction is soundly based on Hindu thought, as the father of Jāṅgulī is Śaṅkara (*Auspicious*, a title of Śiva). Let me quote Maity (1966/2001:214). The dhyāna is rarely practised and cannot be found in any Saṁskṛta ritual text. He traces it to an early text on Dharma worship, the *Dharmapūjāvidhāna*.

I adore the lotus-born goddess Jāṅgulī, the remover of poison, the daughter of Śaṅkara, who is of golden complexion, who has a graceful face like a lotus, who is charming, crowned by snakes, whose body is covered by divine cosmetics, who has gracious limbs and who cheerfully carries in her two hands (= shows the mudrās of) *grace and protection.*

Next, we have two dhyānas from Assam (after Maity, 1966/2001:215, slightly amended).

O Padmāvatī (Lotus Born), *the noble-hearted, who is sympathetic towards her devotees, who has three eyes, four arms, a crown and earrings, who is the healer of poison, who is of golden yellow complexion, whose crown is formed by the snakes Takṣaka, Ananta and Vāsuki, whose earrings are made of the snake Kulika, who has a sacred thread of golden colour formed by snakes, who holds the snake Śankha in one of her two right hands and whose other (right hand) shows varada (mudrā); (who in her other two hands) holds the snake Kambala and whose other (hand) is in abhaya mudrā, who is decorated with keyūra, kankana and kaṭisūtra, made of black, golden and yellow snakes respectively, who wears a red garment, who is seated on a lotus throne and who rides on (a) splendid aerial car carried by four swans.*

I adore the goddess, the mother of snakes, who has a crown and kuṇḍalas (curved ones=snakes), *whose head is lighted with moon beams, who has matted hair, whose breasts are prominent, whose eyes are like the moon, who has hāras* (garlands of pearls) *of snakes, who is three-eyed, who is the giver of boons, whose complexion is like that of the little kadamba flowers* (Nauclea cadamba), *who holds a lotus, who is decorated with various ornaments, who rides on a haṁsa* (waterbird/breath/consciousness-vehicle) *and who bestows boons* (i.e. shows the varada mudrā).

Picture 67: Unidentified Snake Goddess. Women's painting on paper, Madhubani, Bihar, after Miode and Chandra, 1984:219.

53. A Tantric Goddess

Manasā made her great career move when she became acceptable to high-class people. It happened when she was integrated into the literary traditions of the learned Brahmins.

Step one: I am sure you remember the tale. We had it briefly in chapter 11. According to the *Mahābhārata*, the serpent princess Jaratkāru was briefly married to a grumpy old sage of the same name. The marriage was painfully stupid, lasted for a few days and ended when her husband walked away, to grump around in other places. The serpent princess remained where she was, shook her head in amazement, watched her belly grow and gave birth to a son, Āstika, who ended the serpent sacrifice of king Janamejaya. That's it. The *Mahābhārata* made much of the event, as the story of the serpents is closely related to the frame of the epic. It didn't say this serpent princess was Manasā. Many centuries later, plenty of worshippers did. Once this identification was accepted, Manasā had a prominent place in the beliefs and customs of the upper classes.

Step two: Manasā became acceptable to orthodox, conservative no-funny-business Vaiṣṇavas. It wasn't easy and in many cases it didn't work at all. It happened by including Manasā episodes in the *Purāṇas*, the mighty, encyclopaedic masterpieces which constitute the backbone of Hinduism. The major appearance occurred in the *Śrīmad Devī Bhāgavatam Purāṇa (DBH)*, the mightiest book on goddess worship ever. This *Purāṇa* is rather late; it seems to have been completed around the seventeenth century. In spite of being classed as Śākta literature, i.e. a work devoted to the goddesses, it is rather conservative, tries to appeal to the Vaiṣṇava orthodoxy and goes to some lengths to damn tantric teachings. Nevertheless, much of its ritual material is soundly based on the milder tantric rituals. Śiva is rarely mentioned and an important topic of Left Hand Path Tantra, the divine nature and rights of women, is usually ignored. That being said, the massive volume contains plenty of fascinating material. Two chapters of the work are devoted to Manasā. Their authors chose to ignore folk worship and the *Manasā Epic*. However, they mentioned Dhanvantari, indicating awareness of another mighty work, the *Brahmā Vaivarta Purāṇa*, which provides the story of Manasā's duel with the sorcerer. Neta, Behulā, Lakhindār, Cando and Sonakā do not appear. Nor do we read of Śiva's love life, his drunken country walks or the quarrels with Durgā. Instead, we are treated to altogether different ideas. Manasā appears in the ninth book of the DBH, in chapters 47 and 48 (in Vijnananda's translation, 1986:991-1000). The first surprise is Manasā's father. In the *Epic*, Manasā is born from Śiva's mind, i.e. when his imagination made him ejaculate. Hence, she is the blissful awareness of the All-Consciousness (Śiva). In the DBH, her dad is not Śiva but the world famous seer Kaśyapa. The second surprise is the highly educated explanation of her name as mind, consciousness and so on. You wouldn't find it expressed in village rituals and brata stories. Thanks to this interpretation, Manasā could be interpreted in a refined philosophical way. It made her attractive to the educated classes, to seers, sages and mad ascetics. Simultaneously, the serpent goddess was integrated into the beliefs of dedicated Kṛṣṇa worshippers and Vaiṣṇavas (Vijnananda's translation, amended):

*Manasā is the **mind-born** daughter of the Mahāriṣi* (great seer) *Kaśyapa; hence she is named Manasā; or it may be **She Who Plays With the Mind** is Manasā. Or it may be **She Who Meditates on God With Her Mind and Gets Rapture in Her Meditation of God** is named Manasā. She finds pleasure in her own self, the great devotee of Viṣṇu, a Siddha Yoginī. For three yugas* (lifetimes, ages, world ages) *she worshipped Śrī Kṛṣṇa and then she became a Siddha Yoginī. Śrī Kṛṣṇa, the Lord of the gopīs* (milk-maidens), *seeing the body of Manasā lean and thin due to her austerities, or seeing her worn out like the muni* (seer) *Jaratkāru called her by the name Jaratkāru.*

Now for the gritty stuff. By eliminating Śiva as the father of Manasā, the DBH made her cult attractive to the followers of Viṣṇu. Meet the remarkable great-seer (mahaṝṣi) Kaśyapa. You don't get such a seer every couple of centuries. Manasā's new father was incredibly holy, magical and he certainly got around. The first references to the famous seer and ascetic appear in the *Ṛg Veda* (9, 114) and the *Atharva Veda* (1, 14 and 4, 37). Both sources have little to offer. It appears that there were one or two guys of that name. And that he was a formidable wizard, who could be called upon to make spells work. It's not much. However, being named in these works was enough to establish a formidable reputation. In AV 19, 53 he turns into the *self-existing being*, Svayambhū, and from that point onward, he had a status higher than most gods. In later literature, he was identified as a manifestation of Prajāpati, who is an early expression of the All-Self (later, Prajāpati lost importance and was replaced by Brahman). The name Kaśyapa, however, seems to indicate humility, as it means *tortoise*. Now Kaśyapa was more than a seer, a representation of the all-consciousness and a patient reptile that enjoyed leisure, slowness and a very long lifetime. He married the thirteen daughters of the god Dakṣa. The daughters represent the thirteen months: each year has either thirteen full or thirteen new moons. One of these daughters was Aditi (*Unlimited*). Here, things become complicated. Aditi also appears, much earlier than Dakṣa, in the *Ṛg Veda*, where she is a cosmic cow, a primordial creatrix who gave birth to plenty of deities. In the *Eddas*, you encounter a Nordic cousin of hers, the primordial cow Audhumla. Kaśyapa made love with Aditi. Their children are the Adityas, an important divine family of the *Vedic* period. Among them is Indra, the thunderbolt wielder, and Agni, the lord of fire. They are the two highest gods of the Ārya. Varuṇa, at the time a lord of the wide web of space, later the king of the oceans and a god of healers, also counts as an Aditya.

Kaśyapa travelled widely, and met the goddess Danu. Their children are the Dānavas. In the good old days of Vedic sacrifices, the Dānavas were a divine family. They might be related to other Indo-European religions: Danu is close to a number of river goddesses, like the Danube and the River Don. Medieval British/Welsh myth mentions a euhemerised semi-divine family called the Children of Don, while Irish seers of the same period referred to the humanised gods as the Children of Danann. The Dānavas were gods. With the advent of modern Hinduism, they were turned into Asuras, i.e. anti-gods, or demons. Nevertheless, some Dānavas, no matter how crazy, became followers of Śiva, which raised their status, and others are known to lead happy lives in the lowest Underworld, Pātālā which is also known as Nāgaloka, the Serpent World.

One day Kaśyapa met the serpent goddess Kadrū. She was simply indescribable. Their offspring are the Nāgas, or at least the aristocratic ones, and, of course, fair Manasā.

Some may object to this. How can a great goddess, like Manasā, be fathered by a human being? Europeans usually assume a great difference between gods and humans. That's a stupid idea. In Indian and Chinese thought any exceptional person can manifest great magical powers, virtue and skill and become a god. A deranged, unhappy or perverse person will turn into a demon. People can become animals and animals can be reborn as people. Some people become the gods of places, rivers or whole countries. Huge, abstract gods can incarnate as humans. Similar thoughts appear in some pagan religions of ancient Europe. The *Eddic* god of poetry, Bragi, is the earliest skald (*poet, singer*) in evidence: Bragi Boddason. He may have lived in ninth-century Norway, and became a deity within a century of his death. You meet him married to fair Iduna, the goddess who guards the apples of youth. In a similar vein, Snorri Sturluson (*Ynglingasaga* & introduction to the *Prose Edda*) portrayed Odin as a mighty sorcerer and king who became a deity after his death. In a religion where people can become deities, you also meet deities who incarnate as people. The protagonists of the *Mahābhārata* are incarnate gods. They are human, they succeed and suffer, commit errors; they sin and win great victories. Often enough they have to pray to other gods. When a god indwells a human body, she or he isn't quite that glorious. Nevertheless, that deity will achieve more than most people can even dream about. And when we look into the world of the *Vedas*, and into the teachings of the Brahmins, we encounter a society where high born seers and ascetics are superior to gods. Seen from this perspective, it is entirely reasonable that a snake goddess might be conceived when the mother of serpents shags a seer to exhaustion.

The DBH tells us that Manasā is a **siddhā** (male: siddha), meaning a practising tantric. That's a remarkable statement in a book characterised by middle-class morality and creeping Vaiṣṇavisation. The word siddhi means *success, talent, perfection, good luck, magical power, completion, fulfilment* and also appears as the name of Gaṇeśa's wife Siddhī. Unlike him, she has no elephant head. Siddhayoga is material used for magical spells; siddharasa is the juice of the siddhas, i.e. mercury-based elixirs and/or the sexual secretions. A siddhayoginī is a sorceress, a fully trained tantric priestess and/or a dangerous witch. There is even a goddess called Siddhilakṣmī; she is the Lakṣmī (*good sign, success, wealth, fertility, brightness, beauty, loveliness, good luck* etc) who grants magical powers.

The word Siddhā isn't well defined. Some siddhās were dedicated ascetics, people who devoted their lives to the divine and spent much of it walking from one sacred place to another. They begged for alms, granted blessings, oracles, prophecy and sold amulets. Occasionally they congregated and celebrated religious feasts. Some lived as hermits, others in a partnership, or in a community of like-minded dropouts. Most of them were keen to *cheat death*, i.e. to prolong their lives or, if possible, to become immortal. But there were also siddhās and siddhas who felt attracted to Left Hand Tantra. These went for all the practices which pious Hindus, Jainas, Muslims, Sikhs and Buddhists abhor. Ritual feasts involved eating meat, alcohol, drugs, music, dance, and obsession by deities, ritual lovemaking and the ingestion of sexual secretions. Plenty of male siddhas worshipped women as embodiments of a goddess. It did not make them popular with the upper-class literati, the aristocracy and all those boring middle-class people trying to be more-pious-than-thou. Most siddhas did not give a damn for common religious rules, avoided mainstream worship, laughed about those who made offerings to Brahmins and declared that there are no lucky or unlucky times for ritual. Tantric siddhas of both sexes sneered at class regulations, at dualist worships and bemoaned the fate of those who could not discern the divine within themselves. Some went on pilgrimages, others did not. Temples were well and good for worship, but just as good, or even better were the fringes of the forest, desolate clearings in the jungle, ruined houses and cremation places. Wherever a strict Hindu wouldn't go, fearing pollution, the siddhas went on purpose. For similar reasons, the siddhas appreciated dangerous and terrifying deities. By facing and embracing their fears, they found liberation. And they realised that a terrifying, lethal deity could be a source of love and compassion, and a partner for life. Siddha worship is characterised by a wide spectrum of practices: meditation, visualisation, self-remembering, awareness-exercises, examination of consciousness, mantra, breathing, Kuṇḍalinī, mudrās, rituals, offerings, sacred music, dance, poetry, painting, astrology, divination, alchemy, drug-abuse, spell-casting, talisman making, shape-shifting, trance, obsession, and the like. Many found it essential to de-conditioning themselves by embracing practices that are abhorred by traditional Hindus. In fact, some siddhas became totally obsessed with breaking unnecessary rules. It shouldn't give you the idea that the siddhas revolted against everything. Sure, they were likely to ignore class, gender and purity taboos. But they did not promote crimes like rape, theft and murder. A siddha or siddhā, they believed, just like a follower of Kaula, Kula or Krama Tantra, should be a boon to the universe, and a blessing for every community. The siddha movement and indeed Left Hand Tantra followed ethical rules. Not that this helped much: in the eyes of most upper-class Hindus, tantrics were scum. If Manasā is described as a siddhā, she appears as a tantric adept of the hardcore fringe. The word siddhā means she is a *Successful One*, a *Perfected One*. It reveals her mastery of one or several tantric systems far from the religious mainstream.

Well, that was easy. With siddhas you pretty much know what to expect. They walk into your home, eat everything in, under and behind the fridge, drink anything including acetone and draino and fall asleep on the carpet, in the bathtub or your bed. When they praise the gods, around four a.m. and do their breathing exercises with a flute or their devotion with an electric guitar, they weep tears of bliss. Their hair stands up, their bodies shake and all of a sudden your entire neighbourhood is wide awake and blessed. It surely counts for something. They haven't been subject to politics and commercialisation.

Yogīs and **Yoginīs**, by contrast come tied up in a thick coating of commercial misrepresentation. When you read that Manasā is a yoginī, what do you expect? That she loves to stretch her limbs, prefers a vegetarian diet, purifies her stomach by spiritual vomiting or draws piss up her nose to clean the sinuses? In all likeliness, you might be wrong. The word **yoga** has undergone enormous changes. I mentioned a few: the war raid, in a battle chariot, the Vedic hero's death, and the sorcerers, ascetics and exploiters of the *Upaniśad* Period,

That's yoga in the old days. It had nothing to do with wellness, health or diet. Nor did it involve physical exercise. As White (2009) describes at length, things changed around the third or fourth century of the Common Era. All of a sudden we encounter a handful of yogīs why try to lead a spiritual life. They meditate; they introvert and start to experiment with breathing exercises. Of course they still go for magic and spellcraft. Nevertheless, they aim at goals that exceed earthly pleasures. These yogīs were a marginal movement. Hardly anyone noted that they existed. Their ideas were formulated by Patañjali, by the unknown authors of the *Bhagavad Gītā*, by the people who added passages on spiritual yoga to the *Mahābhārata* (see, for instance, *The Book of Peace*) and by those cunning forgers who inserted meditative yoga exercises into several *Upaniṣads*. It foxed scholars for years. I guess that plenty of their yoga was inspired by the Chinese. After all, Chinese sages started to write about meditation, breathing, internal energies, power zones (i.e. cakras) within the body, special diets, sexual hygiene and spiritualised physical exercises (daoyin, i.e. *stretching and guiding*, today known as qigong) around the late fifth century BCE.

Meditative yoga was a wonderful innovation. It was based on introversion, and aimed at the realisation of the divine. Kṛṣṇa himself praised it in the *Gītā*. Nevertheless he pointed out that loving devotion to a deity (Bhakti) is superior.

So far for the third and fourth century. It would be nice to know more. Sadly, we don't. Over the next centuries, the meditative yogīs devoted much effort to their craft, and so did the freshly invented tantric movements. As hardly any literature of either survives, it's damn hard to say something meaningful. It was only towards the end of the first millennium that our data becomes reliable. By that time, many yogīs were also tāntrikas. Indeed, the terms yogī (*yoker, uniter, sorcerer*), tāntrika (*practitioner of a teaching, a science, a written tradition*), siddha (*perfected one*) and nātha (*lord*), and their female counterparts yoginī, tāntrikā, siddhā were used for the same sort of drop-outs. Or so it seems. There were plenty of tantric movements. Most of their scripture is lost. The same may apply to yoga. In popular opinion, these people were despised outsiders. And that's how we encounter them through much of Indian history. Most yogīs were power hungry, greedy sorcerers. A few were spiritual people, who sought union with the divine and only performed magic and spellcraft to make ends meet. Like the tantrics, they meditated. It was daring and revolutionary. Meditation was scorned and damned by the early Buddhists and Jainas. It seemed too close to magic. The only āsanas (*throne, seat, chariot-seat, posture*) the yogīs and tantrics were interested in were those for meditation. But things changed eventually. Around the end of the first millennium, āsana, i.e. *posture*, became an art form and a way to liberation. One great guidebook, the *Gheraṇḍa Saṁhīta* outlined a range of basic postures, breathing exercises and contained a few brief passages on meditation. It was the dawn of haṭhayoga, the yoga (*union*) of haṭha (*pain, strenuous effort, force, exertion*). Early haṭhayoga was a far cry from the modern type. Haṭhayogīns delighted in painful exercises, trusted in elixir medicine (the science of the rasa), and ingested formidable amounts of mercury and cinnabar. It allowed them to attain transcendence and find liberation from their earthly vehicles, after becoming totally insane, worn out and wretched. No, wellness had not been invented. Physical exercises for spiritual purposes were a fringe phenomenon. Many yogīs and tantrics were opposed to them. In their opinion, such exercises were barely useful for young and healthy people. Nevertheless, they made the yogī vain and tied him to the body and its capacity; in short, physical skills shackled the ignorant to the realm of form and beauty. For good reasons, many exercises and breathing techniques were damned as harmful and delusive.

Things continued like this over the centuries. There were always yogīs around, and some of them meditated, performed spiritual exercises and stretched their bodies. Most of them did not. The general population loathed them. So did the Europeans. When the British persecuted the yogīs as cheats, vagabonds, beggars, blackmailers and spies, the Hindus and Muslims appreciated the effort.

Words change their meaning. Around the end of the nineteenth century, a wave of Indian patriotism transformed the mental landscape. What is called 'yoga' nowadays was resurrected, fused and invented in this period. India was in upheaval. The British barely retained control. Plenty of Indians wanted a new national identity, new religions, new spirituality, and above all, a homeland they could be proud of. The Theosophists introduced Madame Blavatsky's crazy visions. Saintly intellectuals like Vivekananda wrote book after book about a 'yoga' he had never practised or even seen. Tibet became attractive, mainly as it was mysterious, and closed to foreigners. Before long, several Indian pioneers were busy resurrecting 'ancient yoga' along Vivekananda's lines. None of them found a teacher in India. They read old literature and improvised. Paramahansa Yogananda moved to the US and started a mass movement. His yoga was just as new and innovative as that of the remarkable Krishnamacarya, but remarkably different. Krishnamacarya, being highly annoyed by the lack of reliable information, allegedly travelled to Tibet where he learned a few secret techniques. Or maybe it was tricks: nobody knows. As he refused to teach them to his students (also his relations) B.K.S. Iyengar, K. Pattabhi Jois, and T.K.V. Desikacar, they left him and founded their own branches of freshly invented authentic, ancient yoga. Modern Haṭhayoga combines third/ fourth-century literature on meditative yoga, the āsanas of Saint Gheraṇḍa, the gymnastic exercises of Indian wrestlers and the British army (see White, *Sinister Yogis*, for a brilliant account). In their wake followed an army of Westerners who invented āsanas as they went along. Most of them require a young, slim and well-trained body, and many damage spine and joints.

Luckily, spiritual validity does not depend on age. Personally, I would call it an astonishing achievement. There were loads of unhealthy exercises in traditional yoga which should not be resurrected. Think of mercury and cinnabar ingestion. No, such practices were not rare. They are among the basics of haṭhayoga and we can be glad to be rid of them. There were yogīs who found liberation by disrupting the blood supply to the brain. Others did breathing exercises until their minds gave in. And what do you think about those who stared into the sun until they lost their eyesight, or those who destroyed their ears to enjoy the eternal, inner sound? What of those who starved themselves to death, those who raised an arm to heaven until the muscles atrophied and those who found transcendence eating holy Ganges mud and shat themselves to death? Let's face it. Most yogic practices were not supposed to make you happy, healthy and slim. They simply killed you in a spiritual way. Twentieth-century yoga made an excellent start by eliminating a lot of painful rubbish.

Be that as it may, the advent of modern yoga happened rather late. Manasā may appear like a modern yoginī today, a rolled up yoga mat under her arm, a cup of organic coffee in one hand and a tasty gluten frog in another, but for most of Indian history, she was a tantric initiate, a sorceress, and a terrifying witch. Some yoginīs were tantric adepts. Some were terrifying sorceresses and some spent their time initiating advanced tantric devotees in sexual ritual. You may think of them as highly accomplished women. Indeed, some were literate. Others were less educated, but able to turn into a goddess. Many important tantric visionaries were initiated by these formidable women. Most of them were Hindus. But there were also Buddhist yoginīs who taught, initiated and celebrated feasts where spiritual women congregated, feasted, sang liberation songs and became blissfully free of the bondage of everyday life. You find great passages from their songs in Miranda Shaw's *Passionate Enlightenment*. And then there are the supernatural yoginīs, a vast group of spiritual or divine beings. During the great days of tantric worship, between 800 and 1300, several small kingdoms chose a form of Tantra as the state religion. The kings, many of them initiated into Kaula and Kula mysteries, built temples with open roofs, so the yoginīs could come down from the skies. The goddesses promised magical powers, life extension, and success in everything. There are statues of the yoginīs in these temples. Many of them have animal heads or wings. Some look like human women with the heads of tigers, lions, birds, rabbits or snakes. Again, we meet Manasā. To this day, some folk artists paint her as a woman with a serpent head. The magnificent *Kaulajñāna Nirṇaya* relates that the yoginīs like to come to earth where they play and enjoy themselves in the shape of animals. Most of these animals are female. They shouldn't be eaten, scared, beaten or molested. When you meet a wild animal in your country walks, it could be a yoginī watching you as you are watching her. Encounters with animals can produce moments of total reality. A few days ago, when I was walking in the forest, it began to snow. I met a fox. It was sitting still, in a clearing, between the pines. It told me "Hey, I'm a tree stump. Don't bother to recognise me. I'm just watching the snow. It's lovely." I replied, "Hey, I'm a tree stump too. And the snow is wonderful this dusk." We admired the snow. Time stood still. Some joggers passed and the fox ran away.

If you look for magic, explore the unique moments when you are fully alive. Like the happy occasion when a wasp explores your face, when a spider drops from your hair or when a bird comes close to have a look at you looking at it.

It could be a yoginī. Like Manasā or Neta. Enjoy.

Picture 68: Two pictures of Manasā. These come from the picture scrolls used by travelling Paṭuā singers. Photos in Kaiser, 2012:142 (detail from a painting of Bakha Chidrakal & 46 detail from a painting by Manimala Chitrakar).

54. First Pūjā Instruction

Our next topic is pūjā. Let's start simple. The term pūjā can be applied to the great temple rituals, where Brahmins and musicians are busy for hours or days. And it can be used for minor acts of worship that happen when someone wants to be close the gods, and acts as ritualist and host. In the first variety, much attention is focused on scripture and tradition. The ritual can be detailed, elaborate and magnificent and end in a traditional homa fire sacrifice, when the deity, or deities, receive offerings of butterfat, which is poured into the flame. And of course there is music. It can go on for hours. Private pūjās are different. They may include a couple of traditional elements, but they will also be adapted to the worshipper or worshippers, usually a family group. These pūjās last as long as you and the gods like. A pūjā is a visit. One or several deities are invited to come and visit a given temple, sacred place or home. The gods are treasured guests. They are welcomed; have a wash, receive a seat, drink, food, compliments, music and friendly attention. The host is happy to make the guests feel at home. The ritual emphasises gratefulness. The host is honoured by the visit and the gods are glad to be invited with love and generosity.

The contemporary pūjā is based on rituals that come from many ages. It contains traditional *Vedic*, *Upaniṣadic* and plenty of tantric elements. And it is based on an entirely new idea: the hosts and the gods should enjoy their time together.

Sure, we should be realistic. Plenty of people want to bribe the divine. They show generosity and expect the same in return. That's an ancient principle. Quid pro quo wasn't invented by humans. It was there long before mammals evolved. Consider plant-animal cooperation. Both partners depend on each other, both partners profit from the symbiosis. Here is an example. In Frankfurt's botanical garden (the *Palmengarten*) is a tree called *Acacia drepanolobium* that grows bulbous round vessels. Their outsides are studded with long spikes and their insides are hollow. These spaces are perfectly protected shelters. The plant offers them to ants and hopes to attract a really aggressive species. Some ants move in, say 'thank you' for protection and sugary juice, and spend their days climbing on all branches. When a herbivore comes around, it is savagely attacked. Now, in their home countries there are several ant species. Some of them are too docile. The plant knows whether its tenants are great fighters or just nasty little exploiters. If the ants don't do their job, the plant denies them sugar. The ants are plagued by hunger, pack their gear, move out, another bunch moves in, and with a bit of luck it is more aggressive.

Similar relationships are the norm. Almost all plants thrive in a partnership with one or several fungi. It started an amazingly long time ago. The first proper plants that left the oceans and managed to eke out a meagre existence on the shoreline rocks looked much like mosses. They had no roots. But they had something better: fungus support. It was the start of the symbiosis known as mycorrhiza (*fungus-root*). To make the most of it, the plants developed tendrils, then rootlets and finally real roots. Either the fungi cover the outside of the roots or they invade the roots and do the job from the inside. In the process, they produce a fine coat of fungal hair. It improves the intake of water and nutrients dramatically. Also, fungi are great at hard-core chemistry. It allows them to dissolve minerals. In return the plants supplied the fungi with starches and sugars, the basic products of photosynthesis. Eventually, roots turned out to be useful to build and stabilize taller plants. In a forest, most trees need a symbiosis with fungi. Some trees are in touch with several dozen distinct fungus species at once! The fungi, in turn, extend over large spaces and are in a partnership with several trees. There is an entire network of chemicals, fluids and intelligence underground, connecting roots for hundreds of meters, ensuring that good things go around. When a fungus does a great job and supplies the plant with plenty of moisture and minerals, it receives extra large amounts of sugars and starches. Fungi that fail to do so get less. The plant decides how much to invest in a relationship. No doubt the fungus does the same (Ottow, 2001:455-473, Lüder, 2015:20-23, 38-51). In short, give and take is a principle of ecology.

Praying sounds simple, but isn't. Some people snivel and complain. Personally, I believe that complaining is useful, meaningful and valid. And that it should be limited to fifteen minutes a week. Anything above that level is lethal for the environment. Those who whine to their friends won't feel better afterwards. And their friends, who can't do anything but offer great advice, feel worse. Both players end up full of stress hormones. That's not the way to find a solution. It's talk instead of action. In fact, it turns the world into an evil place. The same happens when you fill your diary with worries. Writing is magic. It makes your misery stronger.

What about result orientation? Traditionally, there are moments in a pūjā where you may briefly express what you desire. You say what is needed, if and when it is needed. You don't make a scene. It would insult your guests.

A good pūjā requires happiness. It is based on doing your best for someone whom you really care for. You are responsible for making your own feelings. The gods will appreciate it. They like people who have the courage to make the best of their lives, no matter how hard it may seem. That's because the gods embody ideals. And so do you.

Let's look at pūjā in a traditional way. There are approximately sixteen (remember the importance of the 16th kalā!) offerings and acts. The list is based on Gonda (1970:186 & 196), Fuller (1992:67) and Rhodes (2010:116-117).

-Āvāhana. Welcoming the deity or deities, invocation, prayer.

-Āsana. The deities are *seated*, or they are 'woken' within a statue, symbol or picture.

-Pādya. They receive water so they may wash their feet.

-Arghya. They receive water, so they may wash face and body.

-Ācama. They receive water, so they may wash out their mouths and have a sip.

-Snāna. The deities are bathed. If the representation of the divine is a picture, a plaster figurine or any other vulnerable image, a substitute, like a fruit, or a stone, may be bathed.

-Vastrayugma. The deities are clad in fresh clothes or receive a sacred thread.

-Madhuparka. They receive a drink of milk and honey.

-The deities are anointed. Common offerings are sandalwood paste, red sandal, vermillion powder and red powder. This stage can include the use of perfumed oils (Sugandhita taila).

-The deities are decorated with blossoms and sacred grasses. The use of perfumed oils can also happen at this stage. In the rites of Left Hand Tantra, the blossoms (puṣpa) can be offerings of sexual secretions or menstrual blood. Some worshippers light incense.

-Dhupa. Or they light incense now.

-Dīpaka. A lamp, burning butterfat, is waved in circles before the deities (Nīrājana). It can be made of clay or brass. In Tantric ritual, the lamp may be made of edible substances, which can be eaten after the ritual.

-Naivedya. The deities are fed. They sip water and are offered betel nut, bēl leaf and fruit after their meal.

-The deities are honoured and entertained with prayer, invocation, reading of scripture, song, music, mantra recitation and hand gestures (mudrā). In some rituals, the deities receive money offerings. These represent the dakṣiṇā, i.e. the special gift to the officiating Brahmins. It makes the ritual efficient.

-The worshipper/s walk around the deities and the offerings (only deosil!). Or the lights are waved in a circle.

-Circumambulation may also be shifted to this stage. Maybe another flower offering occurs. The deities receive thanks and depart. Or the worshiper says goodbye and departs (Namaskāra).

That's sixteen offerings or sixteen good things. Each of them is meant to be enjoyed. The ritual can be abridged. Some worshippers do a brief routine. They greet the deity, present water and offerings, circle the lamp before the altar and say goodbye. It can be done in ten minutes or less. In elaborate ceremonies, especially on feast days, the amount of offerings and ritual gestures can be increased dramatically. Each deity has special preferences regarding food, flowers, songs, mantras and so on.

A pūjā is a work of art. It follows a strict frame but within that structure, you are free to improvise as much as you like. It expresses who you are and what the divine means to you. It's your devotion, love and sense of beauty that makes your divine guests feel welcome.

Basically, what you enjoy also pleases your deities. They experience your joy, and your joy is theirs. That's an essential idea of advanced Tantra. However, there are limits. Some preferences are not accepted. It can happen that a deity curses inacceptable offerings.

When you plan your pūjā, consider what makes you really happy. Remember that the foodstuff can and should be eaten after the ritual. The same goes for drink. You can recite mantras, divine names and sacred hymns. You can offer yourself. Circle your offerings before the images of the divine. And if you really want something intense, involve body and music. One way to alter consciousness is to pick up an instrument and improvise. If you feel bad, express it. Transform what you play and change your mind. You can play yourself happy and wide awake. You can play yourself calm and relaxed. It does not take years of daily practice. You don't have to read sheets and struggle with 'Jingle Bells', unless you really want to. It depends on listening and enjoying. A pūjā is a happy event. It is marked by mutual generosity. Anything that makes you and your guests happy is fine. That's why the Indian proverb states: the guest is god.

Let's discuss a few traditional Manasā pūjās. We begin with the *Devī Mahātmya Bhāgavatam*. The text is based on the translation by Swami Vijnanananda. I have taken the liberty to amend the spelling and modernise the language. My comments appear in brackets.

Religious practices, as you recall, are part of a revealed tradition. A respectful student receives them from a guru, who may be a human teacher or a deity. As the DBH goes to extreme lengths to make goddess worship acceptable to daring Vaiṣṇavas, the first instruction is revealed by Viṣṇu in his shape as Nārāyaṇa. That's the primordial Viṣṇu who reclines on a couch composed of the giant serpent Śeṣa, floating on the primordial ocean (narāḥ), the abode of the creative deity (ayana). Viṣṇu addresses the seer Nārada:

"O Nārada! I will now speak of the dhyāna and the method of worship of Śrī Devī Manasā, as stated in the Sāma Veda (a collection of sacred songs, i.e. sāmans, from the *Ṛg Veda*. This is wrong: the *Vedas* do not mention Manasā. Sorry.)

I meditate on the Devī Manasā, whose colour is fair like that of the white Campaka flower, whose body is decked all over with jewel ornaments, whose clothing is purified by fire, whose sacred thread consists of Nāgas, who is full of wisdom, who is the foremost of the great jñānins (those who have direct insight and knowledge arising from experience), *who is the presiding deity of the siddhas* (the Perfected Ones), *who herself is a siddhā* (perfected one) *and who bestows siddhis* (talents, skills, magical powers, perfection) *on all.*

O muni (seer, ascetic)! *Thus meditating on her, one should present her flowers, scents, ornaments, offerings of food and various other articles, while pronouncing the principal seed mantras.*

O Nārada!

The siddha mantra of twelve syllables, to be mentioned below, yields to the bhaktas (loving devotees) *their desires like the kalpa tree* (kalpadruma, one of the five wish-fulfilling trees in Indra's heavenly realm).

Now the root mantra as stated in the Vedas is:

Oṁ Hrīṁ Śrīṁ Klīṁ Aīṁ Manasā Devyai Svāhā.

Repetition of this mantra, 500,000 times, yields success to the one who repeats it. He who attains success with this mantra gets unbounded name and fame in this world. Poison becomes nectar to him and he himself becomes famous like Dhanvantari. O Nārada! If anyone (ceremonially) *bathes on any day when the sun passes from one sign of the zodiac to another, and goes to a hidden room* (a peaceful place, introverts and descends into the cave of the heart), *invokes the goddess Manasā Īśāṇā* (the Lady, Sovereign) *and worships her with devotion, or makes sacrifice of animals before the Devī on the fifth night of the* (dark or bright) *fortnight, he is certain to become wealthy, endowed with sons and name and fame. Thus I have described for you the method of the worship of Manasā Devī."*

Picture 69: Manasā and Neta, Behulā and Lakhindār. Start of a picture scroll by Madhab Chitrakar of Ghuli, inscription omitted. After Kaiser, 2012: 64.

55. Mantras

Let's explore mantra. The word is supposed to mean *liberation by thinking*. That's because 'man' is said to mean 'manana' (*mind, thought, consciousness, imagination*) and 'tra' is supposed to represent 'trāṇa': to *liberate from bondage*. The etymology is questionable but it's a nice idea. I have described the science of mantra at length in *Kālī Kaula*. Here, it should suffice to give a few hints for practice. A mantra can be a magic spell, a sacred formula, a line from scripture, a verse from a hymn, the name of a deity or the abridged name of a deity. Or it can be an entirely inexplicable arrangement of sounds. Mantras can be meaningful or mysterious; their syllables can be full of deep significance or completely bypass the reasoning mind. Some mantras may have been meaningful ages ago, some may simply sound nice. Mantra can be a tool to gain access to a deity or to work magic, but that's just the surface. On a deeper level, many tantric practitioners believed that the mantra is the deity in a refined and abstract form. Some philosophers assumed that the inexpressible All-Consciousness, Brahman (*extension*) found its first manifestation as vibration, i.e. śabda-brahman. Out of this cosmic vibration arose the cruder expressions of the divine in sound, sight, feeling and so on. A good mantra can be the sound form of its deity. This form is closer to truth than the crude anthropomorphic shape you see in a temple. In short, when you contact a deity through its body of vibration, you gain access to something perfect and powerful. Śabda is the essence of all sacred song. It offers devotion to the deities; it purifies the singer and the congregation.

To wake a mantra you need to be in a special, inspired state. Many think that a mantra is a dumb formula which you repeat like mental chewing gum. They recite the mantra for a minute or ten, find that nothing remarkable happens, and assume that a few thousand repetitions will miraculously do the job. This attitude is quite common. Those who have more faith in quantity than quality will approve. Sadly, mantras don't like to be abused. They are the sound essence of a deity, and deities like attention, feeling and dedication. Monotonous babbling does not appeal to them. Imagine a greedy, stupid beggar. He follows you and repeats your name all day. Would you fulfil his wishes?

It's essential to take mantra beyond the intellectual realm. What many people miss is **Bhakti**. That's a form of devotion which was picked up by the cult of Kṛṣṇa around the third or fourth century and turned into a science of sentiment. Of course there were plenty of devoted people before that time. Those who come really close to the divine recognise themselves in the All-Self. The first time this happens can be a mind-blowing, heart-opening experience that may leave you beside yourself for days. The followers of Bhakti realised that making your own emotions can be a way of liberation. This idea is common in Asian but appears rarely in European thought. Human beings make their feelings. It's not your partner who makes you mad with love; it's your own brain and the nervous system which cook up neurotransmitters and hormones in your glands and limbic system. It's not your boss who makes you angry. Your employer may press a few buttons to make you feel stupid and worthless, but they don't work when you refuse to take her or him seriously.

Whatever you feel, it happens within your emotional system. The emotions you experience are self-made. You can make the feelings which you need; indeed, you have made your feelings all your life. These emotions will differ: a banker needs other feelings than a rock star or a Mixed Martial Arts fighter. Your favourite selection of feelings defines your personality. However, the Greek word persona means *mask*, and a mask is not the player, let alone the self. Good actors, musicians, storytellers and artists know everything about it. They create emotions on a professional basis (once more with feeling!) It produces great art but can make them slightly difficult to live with. The followers of Bhakti cultivate a range of subtle and powerful passions, and release them into their favourite vision of the divine. When you combine Bhakti with mantra, things start to happen. Of course you have to proceed cautiously. A mantra is alive and you can't force it to do anything for you. In fact, you and the deity represented by the mantra will have to come close to each other. Maybe you'll be friends. Maybe you won't. You can't pick up a deity in a supermarket and assume that you'll like each other. Probably the deity wants you to change quite a bit.

Some people are lucky. They read a mantra or receive it from a guru, repeat it for a while and feel happy. That's when you get everything subconsciously right. Most people don't. They need practice and, above all, they have to explore **pronunciations**.

You can take a given word and pronounce it in different ways. Say something in a calm and soothing voice. Make it sound comfortable, slow down and relax into it. That's the sort of voice you need to make a mantra take you into a deep and peaceful trance. Or say the same words in a fresh and excited voice. Make them faster, put lust and joy into them. That's how to use a mantra to raise excitement. Or repeat the words in a dramatic voice. That's excellent to focus your attention, especially when your head is full of every-day rubbish. You can say your words in a sexy and alluring voice. Plenty of gods like that. Or maybe you use a hard and aggressive voice. That's excellent for banishments. All of these can be done with everyday words. Please try this! Pronunciation is a wonderful key to consciousness changing. It works on a subtle level that is much closer to animal consciousness than our reasoning, clever-clever mind. That's why a magical spell or a mantra can include totally meaningless syllables and work perfectly. Provided the pronunciation is right. Mantras are not automatically holy and powerful. You have to imbue them with life and feeling. It's your life and your feelings. That's how to wake them up. And that's how to keep them happy.

Mantras, as many tantrics knew, can be damaged. Those who recite a mantra without care and consideration dull it. Too many repetitions can hurt a mantra. They can also hurt you, and your awareness of the divine. Our ritual instruction suggests 500,000 repetitions. There are people who take such numbers literally. They get themselves a rosary, preferably one with extra beads dangling from the sides for accurate bookkeeping, and repeat a mantra till their brains shrivel.

The experience of the divine shouldn't be a dull and painful exercise. The 500,000 repetitions are a metaphor. The actual number doesn't matter. In fact, some Tantras insist that you should experience a mantra so intensely that a few repetitions make your hair stand on end and tears of joy run down your face. Sure, this isn't easy. Unless you are very emotional, the first tears are simply those that flow when pent-up emotions are released and vitality flows through hitherto cramped channels of your body. They are an energetic phenomenon. Tears of joy are on another level.

Maybe the mantra makes you happy. Maybe it creates a **crisis**. That's great. Most people who read books (like you and me) are too controlled. We need to be shaken out of our comfortable routine once in a while. It's like exploring a new place. Or like getting lost in the forest in a deep fog, or in the middle of the night. You don't know where to go. You could break your leg, crash into a tree, get a branch in your eye or upset a group of wild boars. On the other hand, it dispels all routine thoughts and ensures that you are fully awake. And though you don't know which way to go, you realise who you are and where you are. It's here.

That's what a crisis is good for. It can open doors which are usually locked. However, a crisis is not the solution for everything. There are magicians, artists and shamans who use crisis as a routine remedy. They look for painful and worrying experiences. Plenty of poets can't compose when they feel happy. Plenty of shamans think that great pain, effort and exhaustion produce spiritual insights. Not to mention those who wallow in horror and disgust to get their kick. Sure, it works. It works dramatically. But there is something called habituation. If the same sensory input is repeated continuously, we get used to it. The experience dulls and fades away. It means that when you fail to get your kick you look for stronger experiences. Some people become crisis junkies. The same applies to the so-called positive emotions. Topping joy with bliss only works for a while. Eventually, exhaustion sets in. Holiness has a limited shelf-life. Playing happy-happy all day leaves you empty and wretched. Those who overdo divine love find their devotion dulled. Those who embrace the divine in its dangerous and terrifying form become bored. Crisis is useful from time to time. So are joy, and love, and self-offering. Anything strong works for a while, and dulls. That's why cunning mind explorers change their routines, their moods and play with many different feelings.

Finally, we are promised **rewards**. I wish we were not. Our dhyāna instruction offers boons. That's the wishful thinking department. Some magical spells promise anything. Indian sorcery is full of them. Recite a given mantra a hundred thousand times while sitting under a bilva tree and all women in the neighbourhood are sure to run after you. It's been tested. You wouldn't like it. Or the king becomes your friend. That's lethal. Or you excel all poets, artists and geniuses in their skill. They'll hate you for it. Maybe you'll become filthy rich or gain the power to heal anything. Or you can shake cities, if that's your idea of a meaningful hobby.

The spell comes with a promise. It makes you imagine your goal and enjoy the good feeling. You can amplify this. Make your dream bigger, brighter and wrap yourself up in it. Blow your mind with happy brain chemistry! People do that in positive thinking workshops. They create a happy-dreams-high. When they wake up, a few days later, they crash extra hard. Being high and crashing are not the problem. It's when you give up.

Positive feelings, hopes and happy dreams are valuable. Maybe the good feeling is what you need to make some real improvements. But usually, and this is bad news to hope-addicts, happy dreams are not enough. They may get you started, but they won't take you there. In fact, too much blissful daydreams and you won't get anywhere. Those who dream of success, wealth, true love, health and so on fail. The reasons are simple. Good dreams create the illusion that it'll be easy. Well, occasionally it is. Life is full of surprises. People are lucky, once in a while. But if they ain't, they are unprepared for failure and hope gives way to despair. Positive thinking shouldn't focus on happy endings. It has to describe a way, a process of learning that takes you from here (lack, misery) to there (happiness). Respect difficulties! Any good plan has to acknowledge complications and the possibility that your goal isn't worth it. Stupid hypnotists tell their patients that everything will be changed from one moment to the other. It's a lie. Stupid motivation trainers tell you that there are no limits, that you can achieve anything, that success is easy. Stupid movies tell you to wish upon your star. Stupid books announce you only need to believe in yourself. Rubbish! Without training, perseverance, and luck, it won't be enough. Stupid priests expect you to sit back and trust in god. Watch the pioneer of modern hypnotherapy, Milton Erikson. When treating addicts, he took them on a journey to liberation. In the process, he made them anticipate setbacks, frustration and temptation. Failure isn't the end of the world. Erikson promoted endurance, determination and sense of humour. He made his patients imagine what it's like to progress, to fail, to have a laugh and do it better next time.

Here is a brief summary of the significance of the bījas (seed syllables) of Manasā's mantra ***Oṁ Hrīṁ Śrīṁ Klīṁ Aīṁ Manasā Devyai Svāhā.***

Please note that this mantra is very close to a major mantra of Śrī Lakṣmī, which celebrates her as the generous, radiant mother of the universe: ***Oṁ Hrīṁ Śrīṁ Aīṁ Klīṁ.***

Oṁ is the praṇava (*essence of life*), the most important mantra of Hinduism. It appeared, quite early, in the Vedic period, was celebrated as the pinnacle of spiritual perfection by the Upaniṣadic seers, and integrated into Hinduism, Buddhism, Jainism, Sikhism, Tantra and Yoga. An enormous amount of sacred texts and their commentaries elucidate the meaning of the seed-syllable. Over the centuries the meaning transformed. Let's go on a short journey through time. For more details, please consult *Kālī Kaula*.

Brahman is the foundation of the great *Upanisadic* revolution. It postulates that there is a vast, indescribable, formless, nameless, incomprehensible common principle, an Absolute Reality, which is sheer, passive consciousness. It's not a god, indeed, the gods, just like people, animals, plants and everything arise out of it. The world of the *Upanisadic* seers was based on duality. Brahman is formless, eternal and real while everything else (Prakṛti: *primal matter, nature, form, the material world, root, norm*) is bondage, illusion and suffering. To gain liberation, the seers tried to eliminate anything that kept them in the shackles of Prakṛti.

Most *Upanisadic* seers assumed that the old Mantra Oṁ is the expression of the All-Self, Brahman. Some tantric seers preferred a different interpretation. In their teachings, major gods like Śiva, Kālī, Bhairava, Bhairavī, Kṛṣṇa, Viṣṇu, Lakṣmī, Manasā, Lalitā or Gaṇeśa can be the true Brahman, provided they are understood as formless consciousness.

Most people pronounce Oṁ like A-U-Ṁ. The sound 'ṁ' is not an 'm'; it's a nasal vibration that should be sensed high up in your nose and in the sinuses. It comes close to 'ng'. To understand this vibration, sing ngangingongung or something similar. And, this is crucial, put a sense of awe into the vibration.

The three letters can be interpreted as the Trimurti, the trinity of creation, maintenance and destruction. In this context, A can be Brahmā, U can be Viṣṇu and Ṁ represent Śiva. Or, another option, A is Viṣṇu, U is Śiva and Ṁ is Brahmā. Others identify goddesses with the three letters A-U-Ṁ: creation is Māyā or Sarasvatī, maintenance is Śrī Lakṣmī and destruction Kālī. Again, this simple arrangement is of limited value. Many worshippers insist that their personal deity is in charge of all three functions.

Hrīṁ is the major seed syllable in goddess worship. Some call it the 'Modest Seed', as Hrī means shyness and modesty. For many people, it constitutes a counterweight to Oṁ. When Oṁ represents the formless Brahman, Hrīṁ represents the manifest Prakṛti, the world. The divine assumes form, your form, my form, any form there is. In Indian thought, everything is full of vibration and hence, in some degree, alive. Many Indian thinkers do not make much of a difference between 'dead' and 'alive'; in their scripture the crucial difference is between 'moving' and 'unmoving'. A stone, a cloud, wind, sunlight and water have existence thanks to their inherent Śakti: they manifest energy and form, and that's sufficient to be alive. Hrīṁ appears in many Śākta rituals. It can be used to invoke and worship major goddesses like Bhuvaneśvarī, Mahāmāyā, Devī, Lalitā and so on. They have their own special mantras, but a joyous Hrīṁ will always be appreciated. Hrīṁ is often associated with creation. In this sense, it is the source of all being. In some tantric rituals, Hrīṁ is intoned to initiate women.

Śrīṁ is usually the root-vibration of Śrī Lakṣmī. She appeared around the end of the Vedic period, when the two goddesses Śrī and Lakṣmī fused. Śrī means *brightness, radiance, wealth*, and Lakṣmī means *sign, auspicious sign, good luck, beauty, wealth, brightness, grandeur* and so on. Both goddesses have a similar nature, so the fusion was easy. A third and nameless element is an emblem of the goddess. She fused with one or several unknown lotus goddesses, which equipped her with names like Kamalā (*Lotus*), Padmā (*Lotus*), Padminī (*Lotus, Assemblage of Lotus Flowers*) and Padmāvatī (*Lotus Born*). All four are also names of Manasā. Indeed, Manasā, the serpent deity, can also be addressed as Lakṣmī. These goddesses share the lotus and their close relationship to plants.

Lakṣmī is easily the most popular goddess in modern India. It doesn't mean that this everywhere the case. In West Bengal, she is worshipped by a minority, in South India by the majority of the population. You can see her seated on a lotus, smiling happily while elephants (the storm clouds) shower water over her. Two of her hands make the standard gestures that signal 'Fear not!' and 'I grant boons', the other two may hold lotus flowers, any of Viṣṇus insignia or simply shower money. This is Lakṣmī at her best, the unrivalled queen of the universe, joyous giver of well being, love, joy, wealth, health and happiness. Her picture can be found in many households, companies, restaurants and shops. You might think she appeals to the materialistic, the greedy and the poor. That's part of the play. On another level, her greatest treasures are insight, awareness, knowledge, freedom and bliss. In rural contexts, she is associated with fertility, with dung and mud, while in royal contexts she holds the emblems of absolute sovereignty, and allows the kings to rule. When the *Mahābhārata* was composed, she became the wife of shape changing, continuously reborn heroic Viṣṇu. Conservative followers of Viṣṇu will insist that the goddess is merely his Śakti, the power and form of her grandiose husband. Śāktas may disagree and point out that without wealth, fertility, good luck, brightness and beauty, the greatest gods and kings can pack their things, go home, eat food from cans and pick their noses for the rest of eternity. In their opinion, the goddess is central, while her partners used her wealth to establish their position. Indeed, Lakṣmī is the quality that makes all life, art and civilisation possible. Without her life-giving earth, humus and manure, human civilisation would come to a sudden and painful halt. So would animal and plant life. We all depend on a shallow layer of amazing vitality. That patch of earth, forest soil or field contains thousands of distinct species. You can see a few when you scratch the surface: worms, centipedes, millipedes, springtails, mites, spiders, snails and so on. On a smaller scale there are nematodes and insects that lead a life without seeing daylight once. Still smaller are fungi, slime mould, microbes, protozoa, viruses. Most of them are too tiny to be seen without a microscope. In fact, the majority are not even discovered. Less than one percent of them can be isolated and kept in a laboratory. The rest of them die and shrivel before you come close to a microscope. Many of them can't survive light, or oxygen. All of them interact. They destroy the accumulated dead matter, rotten leaves, shrivelled plants, animal manure and cadavers, and dissolve them into smaller and smaller units. They eat waste material, or each other, they fertilise the ground, interact with the fungus communities, and do a million things we can't even guess. The end result of their mysterious life cycles is humic acids. Their quality determines which plants thrive in a given place. If you look for the new frontiers of ecology, forget about extraterrestrial microbes and deep sea chutes. They are here, in the ground, only a few millimetres beneath the soles of your shoes. Without them, earth would be a barren, rocky place covered by a thin film of microbes. No other life would exist. As queen of fertility, Lakṣmī is also the ruler of death. The soil gets its nourishment by devouring dead matter. That's why Lakṣmī is a creator, maintainer and destroyer, and why she functions as a major deity, with or without her mates. Those who only look at the generous, sweet girl who showers wealth on her devotees understand very little.

And yes, in some Tantras, Lakṣmī is Śiva's wife. That's because Śiva, like any other god, would be helpless without her grace.

When the seed mantras Hrīṁ and Śrīṁ are combined, the first of them means creation and the second maintenance. Those who worship trinities add a third seed mantra. That's usually **Krīṁ**, the famous mantra of Kālī, the black goddess of destruction, time and transcendence. Our Manasā mantra replaces it with **Klīṁ**.

Klīṁ is usually associated with the god Kāma, whose name means *Desire, Lust* and *Love*. He's the cute lad with the bow of flowers and the five arrows of the senses who can enchant, bedazzle and make you fall in love no matter whether you like it or not. Kāma is not a serious character. He enjoys to play and bedazzle, and spends plenty of time making love with his wife Ratī, whose name means *voluptuousness* and *lechery*. Most gods (except for Śiva) are scared of him. That's 'cause Kāma can waste anyone. Indeed, laughing Kāma is older than most gods. Long before Rudra/Śiva was discovered lurking in the forests, eating strange plants and exploring what they did to him, long before Viṣṇu applied to be the odd-jobs boy for majestic Indra, Kāma started the world. The Vedic seers knew it. They didn't trust Kāma and were well aware of how he could bring people to their knees. Nevertheless, he was there when it all began. Without Desire/Lust/Love (Kāma), the universe wouldn't have happened. In this sense, Klīṁ is the seed of desire, love and lust. It is also attributed to the dark god Kṛṣṇa, the alluring warrior god and cow herder. He is waiting at the forest edge in the twilight, playing his flute. Soon, all the milkmaids come running. They cheer, they swoon, and they throw their underwear at him. That's why he can boast of having 1,600 wives. Or maybe he simply has a heart for every woman. For most educated Hindus, Kṛṣṇa is a popular incarnation of Viṣṇu. In West Bengal it's the other way around: Kṛṣṇa is the major god and Viṣṇu the minor manifestation. But **Klīṁ** is also a favourite mantra of passionate tantric goddesses as Kāmarūpinī (*Form of Desire/Lust/Love*) and Lalitā (the *Playful, Flirting, Wanton One*). And finally, Klīṁ is a happy mantra of Kālī, who is called the Klīṁkarī, the *Creatrix of the Sound/Principle Klīṁ*.

Aīṁ belongs to the goddess Sarasvatī. When the Indo-European invaders, the Ārya, entered India around maybe 1.500-1,200 BCE, they encountered the River Indus. The river was sacred to them, and perhaps they named it Sarasvatī, and worshipped it as a goddess who was, like the mighty stream, sure to grant fertility, health, blessings and above all, victory in battle. The Ārya did not stop there. As they moved east and conquered new lands they named another River Sarasvatī. That river has dried up. Myths related that River Sarasvatī runs underground. Indeed, the Indian government spent considerable sums searching for this hidden flow of water. In tantric literature, it is one of the three sacred rivers that meet at the third eye, in the middle of your brow. That's the microcosmic Tribeni, the confluence of three rivers, where Behulā's raft floated into Manasā's otherworld. Or Tribeni is in the root cakra, wherever you might find it. Sarasvatī is a famous Vedic goddess. Toward the end of the Vedic period, she merged with a major goddess called Vac or Vak. Her name means *Voice*. Vac is the first recorded great Indian goddess. You find her grandiose hymn, celebrating her as creator, maintainer and destroyer of the universe, in the tenth book of the *Ṛg Veda*. It's the first appearance of major goddess worship in Indian literature. Vac is a great deity as her voice, your voice, or the voices of the seers, make reality happen. In Near and Middle Eastern religion, things come to be as they are spoken. That's why the Sumerian, Akkadian, Babylonian and Akkadian gods only had to name things to make them real. The same applies to late newcomers, like the Judaic YHVH and the Israelite Elohim. As voice creates anything, mantras, chants, spells, and prayers work. Indeed, only thanks to voice, spoken and written, society, culture and civilisation are possible. In late Vedic India, Vac and Sarasvatī merged. Their fusion created a river goddess who loves to ride a swan or waterbird. She holds a vīṇā lute, a necklace of prayer beads (mālā) and a book, as she is the goddess of speech, literature, art, science, correspondence and documentation. Great authors praised her in the first lines of their books. Sarasvatī stands for everything that is culture. She became a favourite goddess of artists, scholars, musicians, painters, storytellers, scientists and scribes. And, you guessed it, she resembles Manasā, who also loves rivers and rides a waterbird. Indeed, Manasā can be addressed as Sarasvatī.

But Aīṁ has further meanings. As Sarasvatī is the goddess of learning (which, like a great river, never ends), the sound is also the vibration of the guru. It can be a human guru, who represents the divine, or it can be a deity, or your personal deity. Maybe it is also the greatest of all gurus, the universe as a whole. Neta says: "Every Experience is Educational. No matter how dumb it seems." In Left Hand Path Tantra, Aīṁ is the sound and vibration of the yonī/yoni (*vulva, source, spring, well, origin, family line, descent*). Some tāntrikas intoned it when they woke the yonī of their partner.

Manasā Devyai indicates that Manasā, the *Conscious, Mindful, Thinking One*, is a devī. The word comes from the Indo-European word root *deiw- which means *bright, shining, heavenly*. You find the same root in such names as Deus, Dea, Zeus, Dio Pater, Devas, Tiu, Tir, Zis, Twisto and so on. Westerners often speak of 'the Devī'. Some think that this term is generally used for an-all inclusive Indian mother goddess, of whom all other goddesses are 'aspects'. Well, life is complicated. Native Indian religions never favoured monotheism, and a single, specific mother goddess was never generally acknowledged. For each worshipper, the personal goddess is automatically the Great Goddess, even if this goddess is specialised in smallpox or governs a village in the outback. The problem starts with grammar. In Western languages, we can say 'THE Great Goddess' but in classical Indian we can't. Let's hear Constantina Rhodes (2010:19) who reminds us that Saṁskṛta in Devanāgarī script does not distinguish between lowercase and uppercase ligatures. Nouns can be names and vice versa. Anything can be a name. Also, *Sanskrit grammar does not employ definite and indefinite articles; whereas in English we may delineate an entire theology hinging on the difference between "God" and "a god" or "Goddess" and "a goddess", for example, no such linguistic distinction exists in Sanskrit.*

In short "The Goddess" can be "a goddess" or even simply "goddess" in a very general way, as if it was a quality. Hence, Manasā, praised as a devī, is also The Devī and the quality of devī, meaning that she belongs to the divine family of Devas and that she is shining, bright and heavenly.

Svāhā is a popular ending for mantras. The seed mantra is old and can be traced to the Vedic period, when priests chanted it while they made offerings. There's a story here. In ancient days, priests poured sacrificial butterfat into the sacred fire. They did their part and Agni, the lord of fire did his, but none of the butterfat arrived in heaven. The gods remained hungry and began to weaken. After some debate, they chanted mantras and had a vision. A gorgeous blue goddess appeared. Her name was Svāhā and she was the smoke of the sacrificial fire. After some deliberation, Agni decided to marry her and before long the happy couple spent a hundred divine years making love. Henceforth, a sacrifice would only reach the celestial regions when Svāhā was invoked. Her name makes mantras powerful; without her blessing, as the DBH (9,43) insists, all sacrifices are as powerless as snakes who have lost their teeth. According to some traditions, mantras have gender. Those that end with Svāhā are female. They can be called 'mantras' but more precise is the term 'vidyā' which denotes a *magic spell, a magic formula, an art, science, craft, wisdom, a young woman or a goddess.* Thus, when a tantric text advises you to *worship young women*, it can mean real women, imaginary ones, goddesses, your personal goddesses or mantras. You decide.

Alternatively, the Manasā mantra can end with '**namah**'. It means *worship, devotion* or *devotion to* and is often used as a conclusion of mantras which are free of gender and neutral.

Before we rush on, let's have another mantra. This one comes from the *Garuḍa Purāṇa*, a work composed between 850 and 1000. By naming Garuḍa, the massive work is put into a Vaiṣṇava context. Garuḍa is the scorching, earth-shaking firebird, a vehicle of Viṣṇu and the restless enemy of snakes. The book devotes large sections (mainly in the beginning) to syncretistic worship. While you find more than enough ritual for Viṣṇu, there are also highly tantric chapters devoted to the worship of Śiva, Durgā/Kālī and other deities. The Śiva section ends with a spell against snake bite (1, 27). Let me quote the passage. The spelling is slightly modified. My comments, and those of the anonymous translators, appear in brackets. It could be the first appearance of Manasā in *Purāṇic* literature.

O! The skeletal form of Kāla (Time) and Vikāla (Timelessness).
O Carviṇi (The Chewing)!;
Bhūtahāriṇī (Destroying Creatures);
Phaṇiviṣiṇī (Venom of Serpents);
Virathanārāyaṇi (Nārāyaṇī Devoid of a 'Chariot');
Ume (O Umā= Flax; Turmeric; the wife of Śiva);
burn, burn in the hand Caṇḍe (O Fierce One/Fury);
Raudrī (Female Rudra/Śiva);
Maheśvarī (Great Regent/Queen);
Mahāmukhi (Large-Faced);
Jvālāmukhi (Flame-Mouthed);
Śaṅkukarṇi (Dart-Eared);
Śukamuṇḍe (Parrot-Headed);
destroy the enemy,
Sarvanāśini (Destroyer of All)!
Khaka, thou seest blood in every limb!
O goddess Manasā, enchant, enchant!
Thou, born of the heart of Rudra!
Thou art stationed in the heart of Rudra!
Thou hast the form of Rudra!
O Devī, protect me, protect me!
Hūṁ Māṁ Phapha Ṭhaṭha.
Thou hast the girdle of Skanda.
Thou removest the poison of planets and enemies.
Oṁ Śāle Māle,
remove, remove.
O Viṣoka (Free from Sorrow).
Hāṁ Hāṁ Śavari.
Hūṁ Śavari Prakoṇaviṣare Sarve!
Viñca Meghamile!
These mantras (recited properly) are conducive to the removal of poison of all serpents.

Whew. These lines are so crammed full of meaning that I hardly know where to begin. The spell is much more than a cure for snake bite. It also removes the poisons of enemies (murderers or evil sorcerers) and the toxic influence of the planets. In Indian astrology, the planets are grahas, grāhas or grāhīs, which means *seizers*. People are 'seized' by planetary influences, just as they are seized by evil spirits, diseases, sleep, love, passion and fate. To be seized also means to be obsessed; hence, the gods and goddesses can seize you. Manasā can free you from the evils of your horoscope.

She is born from the heart/mind/consciousness of Rudra/Śiva. She wears the girdle of her brother, Skanda/Kārrtikeya, the fierce champion of the gods, and is praised by a number of titles that also appear in the worship of Kālī and other sinister goddesses.

Hūṁ Māṁ Phapha Ṭhaṭha is a fascinating Manasā mantra.

Hūṁ is an ancient Vedic seed syllable. It is almost as important as Oṁ, but has an entirely different feeling to it. Hūṁ ends things and grants liberation. Kālī roars "Hūṁ" when she devours demons on the battlefield of life. Sorcerers sang "Hūṁ" when they projected death spells against enemies. Tantrics imagined "Hūṁ" when they became the Kuṇḍalinī and rose within themselves, transcending bondage and limitation. Plenty of terrifying goddesses were invoked with this sound, among them Bhairavī, Tārā, Chinnamastā and Siṁhamukhā. In tantric parlance, Hūṁ is the armour-seed. It's the sound which you wrap around yourself and drench yourself with for protection. Hūṁ functions like the Island Celtic and Christian loricas, the spells that protect every part of the body. However, Hūṁ is different. I am sure you noticed that the essential energy of Hūṁ in Hindu Tantra is that of liberation. Protection comes from dissolving yourself. When you shed your shape, name, form, no one can be hurt.

Māṁ is Manasā. Māṁ is also the seed syllable of the circle of fire and its ten kalās (*units*).The seed syllable was created by adding the nasal 'ṁ = ng' vibration to the first syllable of Manasā's name. That's a common practice when odd deities need a seed-syllable. Dhūmāvatī, the dreaded widow goddess, for instance, can be invoked with the sound Dhūṁ. The same mantra can be used for Durgā. Gāṁ is Gaṇeśa. Hāṁ and Hauṁ are Śiva as Hara, the *Bandit, Robber, Destroyer*. Bṛhaspati, the sacrificial priest of the Vedic gods, is Brūṁ. Jāṁ is Jayā, the Victorious Goddess.

Tāṁ and Trīṁ are Tārā. Vāṁ is Varuṇa, the lord of the oceans. Those who want a seed syllable for Neta, should try Nēṁ or Nīṁ.

Phapha Ṭhaṭha is open to interpretation. Pha is not pronounced as 'fa'. The letter h indicates exhalation. The word siddhi, for instance, is pronounced sidd-hi. Buddha is Budd-ha. And pha is p-ha. I am sure plenty of people pronounced the words **P-ha p-ha Ṭ-ha ṭ-ha.** The sound is great. Now for meaning. In Kashmir Tantra, using the associations recorded by Abhinavagupta, the letter pha denotes the Āhaṁkara, the Principle of Selfhood. It's the shared sense of 'I am' which is experienced by every being and thing, all over the world, and a supreme Mantra of Krama Tantra. It is 'I' but not 'I am this and that'. This 'I' is universal. It has no name, age, gender or shape. Unlike the 'personal I', the ego, it can never die. Pandey, summarising Abhinavagupta's teachings on Krama mantra (spelling amended, 2006:541), remarks: *The religious formulas, as sets of words, are in themselves ineffective. Their efficacy depends on the rise of the user above the level of individuality. The more the user of a religious formula abandons individuality the more effective they are. But if the individual retains his individuality perfectly intact the mantra used by him is absolutely ineffective. The mystic worship, therefore, consists in the realisation of the "Āhaṁ", the Universal "I", which is the spring of power of all mantras and is the highest mantra. It does not need any other mantra, because it is not concerned with any worldly objective, to the realisation of which the ordinary mantras lead. The mystic worship does not need any definite place, such as a temple, to perform it, nor any invocations (Āvāhana) etc. It may be performed wherever and whenever possible.*

Well, that's Krama for you. It's simple, direct and true. The major realisation is Universal Selfhood. It's shared by rocks, mosses, bugs, slime mould, trees, frogs, people and deities. This sort of mantra recitation is true pūjā. It is an act of remembrance. Everything else is mucking around with spells, techniques, offerings and result orientation. That's not bad. But is it enough? Many students of Tantra went mad about mantras for sorcery and developed mind-blowing complications of letters, cosmic principles and secret traditions. Āhaṁkāra takes you way beyond.

Well and good. The sense of Āhaṁ can be understood as Samvid/Saṁvit, as the Supreme Principle, as Śiva, Bhairava, Kālī and Manasā, and pure consciousness.

Likewise, the letters **Ṭhaṭha** represent pāyu, meaning to *release, to secrete, to extrude, to manifest.* We could understand **Phapha Ṭhaṭha** as releasing and manifesting the principle of 'I am'. From 'I am' arises 'I am this'. That's how the entire cosmos came to be. But things are not that simple. In tantric Twilight Language, the letters Ṭhaṭha are called the two moons. It's a secret code referring to goddess Svāhā and her mantra. It provides two interpretations of the mantra:

Hūṁ Māṁ Phapha Ṭhaṭha.
Hūṁ Māṁ Āhaṁ Svāhā.
I suggest you explore both.

The next mantra is popular for chanting and music:

Jaya Jaya Mā Manasā Jaya Biṣaharī Go

Victory, Victory, Mother Manasā, Victory, Poison-goddess.

Here is another good mantra. It comes from the *Mantra Mahodhadhiḥ* (1, 218-219) and is used to invoke Padmā, the *Lotus* and Padmāvatī, the *Lotus-Born*. Both are names of Manasā.

Oṁ Padme Padme Mahāpadme Padmāvatiye Svāhā.

Let's be inventive. If you wanted a Gāyatrī for Manasā, you could recite something like

Manasāyai vidmahe
Nāgdevyai dīmahi.
Tannaḥ Neta pracodayāt.
May we think of/be inspired by Manasā,
May we contemplate/meditate on the serpent goddess.
May Neta direct/guide us.

Picture 70: Manasā Mask made of plant fibres, Goalpara, Assam. Photo in Mode & Chandra, 1984:118.

56. Second Pūjā Instruction

The next instruction in the DBH appears after the seer Āstika has successfully ended the serpent sacrifice of King Janamejaya. The serpents and their friends, among them mighty thunder god Indra and his family gave a sigh of relief. For good reasons they had disliked the idea of being burned alive.

Feeling greatly cheered, Indra performed a grandiose 'thank you' ceremony for Manasā, and celebrated her with a freshly invented hymn. You may notice that it contains more poetry and sophistication than thunder gods are usually capable of. Again, I have amended the text and added commentaries in brackets.

Nārāyaṇa said: Indra first took his bath and performing ācamana (ritual mouth-purification with water) *and becoming pure, he put on fresh and clean clothing and placed* (an image? A symbol? A visualisation?) *of Manasā on a jewel throne. Then reciting the Vedic mantras he made her perform her bath by the water of the Mandākinī* (the Milky Way) *the celestial river Gaṅgā, poured (water) from a jewelled jar and then he made her put on beautiful clothing, uninflamable by fire. Then, with devotion, he caused sandalpaste to be applied all over her body and offered water for washing her feet and arghya* (water to wash the face), *and offerings of grass and flowers and rice, etc., as a token of preliminary worship. First of all the six Devātas Gaṇeśa, Sun, Fire, Viṣṇu, Śiva and Śivā* (Female Jackal) *were worshipped. Then with the mantra of ten syllables*

Oṁ Hrīṁ Śrīṁ Manasā Devyai Svāhā

he gave all these offerings to her. Stimulated by Viṣṇu, and with great joy, Indra worshipped the Devī with the sixteen articles so rare to any other person. Drums and instruments were sounded. From the height of heaven, a shower of flowers fell on the head of Manasā. Then, at the advice of Brahmā, Viṣṇu and Maheśa (Śiva), *the Devas and the Brahmins, Indra, with tears in his eyes, began to chant hymns to Manasā, while his whole body thrilled with joy and his hairs stood on their ends. Indra said:*

"O Devī Manasā!

Thou standest as the highest among chaste women. Therefore I want to chant hymns to thee. Thou art higher than the highest. Thou art most supreme. How can I praise thee? The chanting of hymns is characterised by the description of one's nature; so it is said in the Vedas. But, o Prakṛti! I am unable to discover and describe thy qualities. Thou art of the nature of Śuddha Sattva (higher than the pure Sattva/quality of the divine, unmixed with any other guṇa-quality)*; thou art free from anger and malice. The muni Jaratkāru could not forsake thee; therefore he prayed for thy separation before (leaving you). O Chaste One! I have now worshipped thee. Thou art an object of worship as my mother Aditi* (the primordial cosmic cow) *is. Thou art my sister full of mercy; thou art the mother full of forgiveness. O Sureśvarī* (Queen of the Gods)! *It is through thee that my wife, sons and my life are saved. I am worshipping thee. Let thy love be increased. O World-Mother! Thou art eternal; and though thy worship is extant everywhere in the universe, yet I worship thee to have it extended further and further. O Mother! Those who worship with devotion on the sankrānti day* (when the sun passes from one sign of the zodiac to the next) *of the month Āṣāḍha, or the Nāgapañcamī day, or on the sankrānti day of every month or on every day, they get their sons and grandsons, wealth and grains increased and become themselves famous, well gratified, learned and renowned. If anybody does not worship thee out of ignorance, rather if he censures thee, he will be bereft of Lakṣmī and he will always be afraid of snakes. Thou art the House Lakṣmī of all the householders and the royal Lakṣmī of Vaikuntha* (Viṣṇu's Heaven). *Jaratkāru, the great muni, incarnating aspects of Nārāyaṇa, is thy husband. Father Kaśyapa has created thee mentally by his power of tapas* (extreme heating, austerity) *and fire to preserve us; thou art his mental creation, hence thy name is Manasā. Thou thyself hast become a siddha yoginī in this world by thy mental power; hence thou art widely known as Manasā Devī in this world and worshipped by all. The Devas always worship thee mentally with devotion; hence the pandits* (scholars) *call thee by the name Manasā. O Devī! Thou always servest truth, hence thou art of the nature of truth. He certainly achieves thee who always thinks of thee as of the nature of truth."*

O Nārada! Thus praising his sister Manasā and receiving from her the desired boons, Indra went back, dressed in his own proper dress, to his own abode. The Devī Manasā, then, honoured and worshipped everywhere, and thus worshipped by her brother (Indra), *long lived in her father's house, with her son. One day Surabhi (Cow of Plenty) came from Goloka (World of Cows, Kṛṣṇa's paradise) and bathed Manasā with milk and worshipped her with great devotion and revealed to her all the Tattva Jñānas* (categories of knowledge/direct experience), *to be kept very secret. O Nārada! Thus worshipped by the Devas and Surabhi, the Devī Manasā went to the heavenly regions. O muni (seer)! One does not fear snakes who recites this holy stotra composed by Indra and worships Manasā; his family descendants are freed from the fear of serpents. If anybody becomes a siddha in this Stotra (hymn), poison becomes nectar to him. Reciting this stotra five hundred thousand times makes a man a siddha in this stotra. So much so that he can sleep on a bed of snakes and he can ride on snakes.*

Picture 71: Behulā and Neta wash the clothes of the gods. Detail from a picture scroll by Bakhar Chidrakar in Kaiser, 2012:150.

57. Third Pūjā Instruction

Classical Indian literature contains another text that raises Manasā to the status of a high goddess. This one comes from a rather late work called *Brahmā Vaivarta Purāṇa*. Unlike the DBH, this work does not make much of Manasā's marriage with cantankerous old Jaratkāru. Nor is the serpent sacrifice of King Janamejaya a topic. The famous meditation on and with Kṛṣṇa is absent. Instead, Kṛṣṇa tells the great story of how Manasā and the famous ohjā Dhanvantari duelled. You read my version earlier on. Manasā won, as she threatened the ohjā with the three-world-destroying spear. Afterwards, the gods encouraged Dhanvantari to apologise and worship Manasā. In fact, they pushed his nose into the ground until he saw sense.

Where shall we begin? Several chapters earlier, voluptuous Rādhā had asked her darling Kṛṣṇa to lecture about pride and arrogance, and the necessity to control anger. Kṛṣṇa related a series of tales. He explained how, one time or another, Indra, the sun, Agni and Durvāsa (you recall him, he was a bad-tempered sage) were shamed by their pride. The last example is Dhanvantari. After relating this episode, Kṛṣṇa paused, and sighed. Neta was there, so she told me. She was delivering the washing and when she saw Kṛṣṇa raising his eyebrows like a puppy she had a laughing fit and was thrown out. "Co-evolution" she says, "means that dogs who look like men and men who look like puppies attract women."

What's so special about Dhanvantari? It's hard to understand him. In the *Mahābhārata*, he arises, just like Lakṣmī, the elixir of immortality and all good things of life, out of the creamy fluids of the Milk Ocean. The MHB devotes exactly one line to him: *And now came forth the beautiful god Dhanvantari who carried a white gourd that held the Elixir* (I, 16). It ain't much. Nor is there much to support his role. In the *Garuḍa Purāṇa* (139, 10) we are briefly informed that Dhanvantari was the son of King Dīrghātamas, a great physician and the father of Ketumān. It makes him a royal son of the Lunar Race. The *Viṣṇu Purāṇa* (4,8) proposes that Dhanvantari invented an eight-fold medical system. And, would you believe it, Dhanvantari was an incarnation of Viṣṇu. He didn't make it into the major lists. That's pretty much the lot. His name was used as a title for excellent doctors, and he received sacrifices. Then, one tough morning in the middle of a mountain range, Manasā subjugated him with her magical spear. We can be grateful. It allowed Dhanvantari to supply a dhyāna instruction and sing two songs to the goddess, who was mightily pleased, though Dhanvantari did not, as Neta tells me, look much like a puppy, or even wag his tail.

I shall use a slightly amended translation by Rajendra Nath Sen, 1922:317-318.

Brahmā, for the good of the world, and the worship of Manasā, cheerfully addressed Dhanvantari, using beneficial and sweet words:

"O most blessed Dhanvantari! O goddess, expert in all sciences. In my opinion you should not fight with Manasā. This goddess is able to reduce to ashes the three worlds completely by virtue of the irresistible spear given to her by Śiva. Therefore, forbear at this time and worship the goddess reverentially with sixteen ingredients according to the form of meditation (Dhyāna; this means pūjā in the imagination) *prescribed by Kanthuma Śikkā and eulogise her with the hymns stated by Manasā. She will then be pleased and grant you a boon."*

Śiva, hearing the words of Brahmā, also gave him permission. Thereupon the son of Vinatā (= Dhanvantari. Vinatā is the mother of Garuḍa, the sister and rival of serpent mother Kadrū) *was also pleased and invoked the goddess with great care. When Dhanvantari heard the words, he bathed and after becoming pure and having duly ornamented himself, he appointed Brahmā as his priest and prepared to worship her. Dhanvantari said:*

"O Jagatgaurī, arrive here and accept my worship. O daughter of Kaśyapa, you are the most adorable and best of all goddesses in the three worlds. O goddess, you are the emblem of Viṣṇu and have conquered the whole world, and this is why in the battlefield, I did not use my weapon against you."

So saying, Dhanvantari humbled himself, and inclining his shoulders with reverence, he held in his hands white flowers and meditated thus:

"I adore the goddess, the radiance of whose hue vies with the graceful campaka flower, whose entire body is very lovely, whose pleasing, round face is lighted up with a gentle smile, who is clad in fine dress, who is ornamented with the load of chignon on her head and decorated with ornaments, who gives immunity from danger to all, who is always eager to show her kindness upon her votaries, who is versed in all sciences, who is the source of all knowledge, whose vehicle is the Prince of Snakes and who is the Queen of Serpents, she who is tranquil and supreme."

O my beloved (said Kṛṣṇa to Rādhā), *after Dhanvantari, had meditated about her in this way, he offered her flowers, and then the sixteen ingredients* (of pūjā) *and different sorts of articles wherewith he worshipped her. Then, with his body thrilling with rapture* (was he shaking?) *and with folded palms, with his shoulders inclined with reverence, he eulogised her thus:*

"O goddess, you are the emblem and the source of perfection. You are the daughter of Kaśyapa and you grant boons. I bow to you again and again. You are the daughter of Śaṅkara (Śiva). *I bow to you. You are the spouse of Śaṅkara (= Śaṅkarī). I bow to you again and again. I bow to the Sister and Queen of Snakes, again and again. I bow to the mother of Āstika and again to the Mother of the World. Your name is Jaratkāru. I bow to you. I bow to you who are the wife of Jaratkāru. I bow to you, and again and again, because you are the source of happiness. I bow to you, again and again, the emblem of meditation, the source of the fruits of devotion. You are good-natured, tranquil and chaste. I bow to you, repeatedly."*

So saying, Dhanvantari, with great esteem and reverence, threw himself prostrate before her. The goddess was placated; she gave him the desired boon and soon went home. Later on Brahmā, Śiva and Garuḍa went home, and the lord Dhanvantari went to his own house. Thereafter the snakes, decked with expanded hoods, merrily departed.

That's the end of the chapter. I am sure that you would like to know more. Ask Neta. She was there and will tell you the lot. She says that puppies are overestimated. Sensible people prefer serpents, spiders, hyenas, vultures and crocodiles. But there are mysteries that defy my understanding. Maity, in his translation of the dhyāna instruction of the *Brahmā Vaivarta Purāna*, gives quite a different reading. Here it is:

I adore the goddess, the queen of snakes, who sits on a snake, whose complexion is like that of a lovely Champaka flower, whose whole body is charming, whose face is marked by satisfaction and a slight smile, who is adorned with fine garments, who has a fascinating chignon, who is adorned with jewels and ornaments, who gives security to all, who is sympathetic towards her devotees because of her love of them, who is the giver of all knowledge, who is peaceful and well versed in all learning.

While Dhanvantari praised the goddess, he kept bowing. Bowing is a common element in folk worship. Indeed, some circumambulate a place, like a temple complex or a hilltop. Every few steps they prostrate themselves full length and extend their arms before them. Then they get up, step to the point where their hands were a moment ago, and lie down full length again. You don't advance fast, but you get to know every centimetre of the way.

In our age of delusion, humility is a difficult concept. People in East Asia traditionally assumed that superior people should be humble. The better you are at whatever you do, the more you will know that it doesn't amount to much. Study one year and you think you know something. Study the same thing forty years and you will be stunned by what you don't know, and will never understand. What seem to be 'facts' turn out to be assumptions, fashions, peer-group estimates. Human lifetimes are too short to master anything. Being humble is an excellent way to continue learning. It will increase your insight and abilities, but it won't make you proud or self-assured. In traditional East Asia, the more self-important you act the less competent will you appear. Boast of your achievements and people will consider you a fool. Among many contemporary Americans, the situation is reversed. In the USA, the mass-media teach 'show what you've got' and 'believe in yourself.' Self-assurance is a must. Approach the average American with an Asian sense of humility and you'll be dismissed as a loser. At the moment, Europeans are somewhere in between. They retain a semblance of humility but would like to be as proud and self-assured as Americans in movies seem to be. In one or two decades they'll be worse.

Dhanvantari acknowledged his inferiority. It shows that he was wise.

Prostrations are controversial, hence a source of great fun. Modern pagans, magicians and their kin like to meet the spiritual as an equal. And they are proud of it. In one sense, their refusal to humiliate themselves is a fine idea. In another, it is plainly absurd. When Dhanvantari bowed to Manasā, he wasn't debasing himself. Real bowing is not a way to be wretched and mean. It's a way of incorporating body language in worship.

Bowing started millions of years ago, when vertebrates learned to perform mock battles to settle hierarchical differences. Most inter-species fights are rituals. They are performed to settle conflicts: who may court a given partner, who may eat or drink first, who uses a territory. To prevent a valuable loss of life, such fights tend to be impressive but fairly harmless. When two male king cobras meet, they will hiss and show their hoods. Usually, this will resolve the conflict. If it doesn't, they will have a wrestling match. The snakes will coil, entwine, bump and lean against each other and try to knock their rival to the ground. Biting is no option. Why waste good and valuable toxin on a rival who is immune to it?

When two stags slam into each other, they try to impress each other, and, more important, want to impress the hinds. After all, it's not the strongest stag who gets the girls. The girls chose which stag appeals to them. In nature, ladies' choice is the norm. And there is an element of competition to the choice: the girls tend to desire the mate who seems most attractive to the other girls.

One great aspect of courtship battles is that the weaker party can stop the ritual. There is no need to end a fight in blood and carnage. Submissiveness is signalled and usually respected. That's the background to bowing in front of deities, kings and honoured persons. When you bow, you are activating instinctual programs that have been used by vertebrates for millions of years. You lower your head and present your vulnerable neck, eliciting a response that the stronger party may not hurt you.

'Being humble' means that you have the guts to admit your station in life. People raised on movie culture aim for being 'a winner'. It's a sad delusion. Winners are losers during most of their lives. That's because they compete. As a child and youth, you are vulnerable, and hence, a loser. After you pass the prime of your life, around the age of 25 or 30, you will be vulnerable again. No matter how strong you are, someone is stronger than you. 'Winners' are such for short periods and pay a heavy price. We are not the pinnacle of creation. Sure, Christianity, Islam, Buddhism and similar transcendent, nature loathing faiths teach that mankind is the greatest thing ever. Tell that to the microbes who protect your skin from invasion and the microbes in your guts who allow you to gain nourishment from food. Tell it to the algae, the plants and trees whose oxygen you breathe. Tell it to the viruses and bacteria which form essential parts of your DNA. As a species, we are pretty close to killing ourselves. Humans are not unique. Over the past six million years, there were at least sixty hominid species. They died out. We are the last. Ecologically and biologically, humanity is not a success. This is where true humility comes in. It appears when we realise that there is one hell of a lot to bow down to. It's a spiritual exercise. Especially for those who pretend to be proud, self-reliant and wonderful.

Evolutionary theory is largely misunderstood. Some believe that the submissive fighter won't breed. In popular opinion, it's only the alphas whose seed is passed to the next generation. In real life, 'survival of the fittest' does not necessarily revolve around bulging muscles and steroids. Fitness, as Wallace and Darwin used the term, doesn't mean strength but adaptability. Natural selection happens on several levels: one is health, another is attractiveness, and a third social skill. Let's return to the forest. The alpha stag has a horrible time. All through late autumn he is edgy and nervous. He hardly eats, gets little sleep, and spends many nights roaring like mad. When another stag bells, the contest begins. It can go on for hours. In the meantime, the hinds are having fun making out with other stags. When the boss eyes them with mistrust they appear submissive. But they are clever. In at least 50% of all cases, it is not the monarch of the glen who impregnates a hind. The same goes for other animal groups. It is excellently documented among our closest relations, the bonobos, chimpanzees, and gorillas. The clever ones, who are charming, tricky and generous, and excel at social skills, stand better chances to procreate than the big muscular brawlers. The true winners grin, bow and step aside. They pretend to be submissive. They acknowledge their humility, and they continue as before. Consider them masters of ritual. They know which buttons to press. And they feel good when they do it.

58. Fast Pūjā Instruction

A brief but valuable summary of how to worship Manasā appears in the *Epic* which Durgābar composed. In his story, it is Dhanvantari who initiates Cāndo's wife Sonakā into the cult of Manasā. The story relates that Sonakā, young and beautiful, is desperate, as she won't become pregnant. As the rainy season begins, Dhanvantari strides into the city, playing his magical drum. He has come from the far mountains in the north. In a loud voice he praises the serpent goddess Manasā. Sonakā hears his chant, rushes out of doors and invites the holy man to come in.

"What goddess do you worship, and what can I expect from her?"

Dhanvantari replies: "*The varied powers of the goddess cannot be explained. A childless person gets a child and a prisoner becomes free, if the goddess is worshipped in the form of a pot in the house. One has to worship her after a day's fast and to offer her five flowers of gold. Then one should bathe in the River Gaṅgā, repeating the saying* ***'Mānasāi-Māī'***."

Sonakā did as she was told. However, she still failed to become pregnant. She wept, despaired and gave in. One bad day she decided to behead herself. Gaṅgā appeared to her and gave her six flowers to eat. Over the next years, Sonakā gave birth to six sons and her marriage with Cāndo was blessed (Maity: 1966/2001:122).

As usual, every word is true. Nevertheless, we must be cautious when we interpret the symbolism. In a tantric sense, the five gold flowers are not the products of a goldsmith's workshop. The number five is a special favourite in several advanced tantric systems, especially those of Kashmir. Here, you could understand them as the five levels of experience, as five worlds, as five stages in the process of transformation and as five main cakras in the microcosm of your body. And, of course, as the five heads of Śiva. You offer your cakras as you dive into Mother Gaṅgā, into the earthly and heavenly stream of birth, life, death, the mysterious, and the supreme sentience that unites the other four states, and blesses them with joy. Your bath happens in the stream of life and death, now, here and everywhere. You give five flowers, but the goddess gives six in return.

Welcome to a wonderful meditation. Sit down in a street café. As you rest, drink and contemplate, enjoy the stream of life and death which surrounds and passes you, as goddess Gaṅgā. Do the same in a park, a forest, a riverside, a playground, a rubbish dump, in the countryside, at the seashore, in a shopping mall, a parking lot, a market, a railway station, a harbour and an airport. Relax. Smile. This is you and you are this. That's Kramamudrā, the *Seal of Transmutation/Going*. Manasā is everywhere. Enjoy places of power and realise their magick as the River of Life and Death.

Of course the number five also relates to the fifth day of the bright and dark half of the month, when the serpents are feasted. Finally, I am sure you noticed that the goddess liberates prisoners, provided they realise that they are in prison. Do you?

59. Divine Names

The DBH relates the episode where Manasā worshipped Kṛṣṇa so intensely that he had to worship her in return. After having come that far, our serpent goddess is praised in her full glory (spelling and language slightly amended, with comments in brackets).

*Devī Manasā is known in the Heavens, in Nāgaloka (the Serpent Wold), in Earth, in Brahmaloka (the World of Truth), in all worlds as of very fair colour, beautiful and charming. She is named **Jagatgaurī** as she is of a very fair colour in the world. Her other name is **Śaivī** and she is a disciple of Śiva. She is named **Vaiṣṇavī** as she is greatly devoted to Viṣṇu. She saved the Nāgas in the Snake Sacrifice performed by Parikṣit* (= Parikṣita, i.e. descendant of Parikṣit= King Janamejaya), *she is named **Nāgeśvarī** and **Nāga Bhoginī** and she is capable of destroying the effects of poison. She is called **Viṣahari**. She got the Siddha Yoga from Mahādeva (Great God= Śiva); hence she is named **Siddhayoginī**. She got from him the Great Knowledge, so she is called **Mahājñānayutā**, and as she got Mṛtasanjivanī (the power to cause life and death) she is called **Mṛtasanjivanī**. As the great ascetic is the mother of the muni (seer) Āstīka, she is known in the world as **Āstīkamātā**. As she is the dear wife of the great high-souled yogī Jaratkāru, worshipped by all, she is addressed as **Jaratkārupriya**.*

***Jaratkāru, Jagatgaurī, Manasā, Siddhayoginī, Vaiṣṇavī, Nāga Bhoginī, Śaivī, Nāgeśvarī, Jaratkārupriya, Āstīkamātā, Viṣahari and Mahājñānayutā** are the Twelve Names of Manasā, worshipped everywhere in the Universe. He who recites these twelve names while worshipping Manasā Devī, he or any of his family has no fear of snakes. (...) He can easily drink poison who attains success in this Stotra. The snakes become his ornaments; they carry him even on their backs. He who is a great Siddha can sit on a seat of snakes and can sleep on a bed of snakes. In the end he sports day and night with Viṣṇu.*

It was just the start. Whenever a deity becomes significant, she or he needs one or several name catalogues.

Name catalogues are more than scholarly achievements; they were compiled for practical use.

We face three options. The first is simply overwhelming. Such catalogues are endless. You need books to handle them. Good examples are the thousand names of Viṣṇu (*Bhagavad Purāṇa*), the thousand and eight names of Gāyatrī Devī (DBH, 12,6), the thousand names of Śiva's wife Ūma/Pārvatī (*Kūrma Purāṇa*), the thousand names of the playful goddess Lalitā (*Śrī Lalitā Sahasranāma*) and so on. These catalogues are mind-blowing and exhausting. They were not written to be memorised. When you recite a thousand names you will come to the point where the deity fills the entire multiverse. The concept of the divine breaks the boundaries and turns the whole world into a multi-dimensional expression of itself. The longer the catalogue, the wider will your understanding be. Of course there are plenty of repetitions. And just as understandably the deity of your choice is identified with a vast range of other deities.

The second type of catalogue is easier to handle. It contains a large, but not impossibly large number of titles and names and can be memorised. Examples are the hundred and eight names of Gaṇeśa (*Śrī Vināyaka Aṣṭottaraśatanāmavalli*), the hundred and eight names of Kālī (*Mahānirvāṇa Tantra*), each of them beginning with the letter 'k', the hundred and eight names of Lakṣmī (*Śrī Kamalā Aṣṭottaraśatanāma Stotram*) and many others.

The third type is much shorter. These lists are memorised and infused with meditation. To make them magickally potent, you experience and remember them in deep trance states and spend plenty of time discovering their hidden mysteries. The effect is amazing: what seems like a simple list can have plenty of meanings. In effect, such catalogues may be brief, but they are just as mind-blowing as the extended ones. There are, for instance, eight Kālīs, nine Durgās, twenty (or more) incarnations of Viṣṇu, and ten (or more) Mahāvidyās. Each name is a special experience, a consciousness state, a unique face of the divine, a mood, a setting, an entire reality. These name lists are quite varied. Gaṇeśa, for instance, has two lists of eight different names (*Brahma Vaivarta Purāṇa* and *Yogajāgama*), twelve names (*Padmā Purāṇa sṛṣṣi khaṇḍa*) and sixteen names (*Cintyāgama*). Plus lists of twenty-four names. Such catalogues are frequently printed as tiny booklets, and illustrated with crude woodcuts or, these days, with brightly coloured pictures. You can buy such stuff in temple shops.

The twelve name catalogue of Manasā's names of the DBH gives an excellent expression of her divine essence, as understood by the upper classes. It's not quite the same as the mindset of those ethnic groups who are not even counted as Hindus.

Here is a name catalogue provided by Bipradās. It is much closer to the folk tradition.

She was born in the Underworlds from the Matrix,
her mother was Nirmāṇī (Measure, Work, Creation),
she was born from the fiery essence (tejas) of Mahādeva (Great God= Śiva),
Vāsuki gave her poison and the rulership of all Nāgas.

As she appeared in the Underworlds her name is ***Pātālākumārī*** *(Girl/Young Woman of the Underworlds).*
As she received the gifts of the Nāgas her name is ***Nāgeśvarī*** *(Queen/Regent of the Nāgas).*
As she was created in the tangle of lotus flowers in Kālidaha (the Lotus-Lake), she is called ***Padmāvatī*** *(Lotus-born).*
As she was born out of the consciousness of Tripurāri (Slayer of the anti-god Tripura= Śiva),
she was granted the name ***Manasākumārī*** *(Conscious, Thinking Girl/Young Woman).*
In all parts of the Śastra she is known as a part of the body of Nirañjana,
she received the consciousness of Brahman and the name ***Brahmāṇī*** *(Female Brahman).*
As the god Śūlpaṇi (a cave-dwelling Yakṣa, dancer among skulls, also a title of Śiva) *gave her great knowledge, she received the names* ***Yogeśvarī*** *(Queen of Yoga) and* ***Sarasyoginī*** *(Yoginī of the Lake?).*
Due to her quarrel with Caṇḍī (the Fury = Durgā) she is called ***Mandākṣī,***
and when she was hit, she received the name ***Viṣapūrna-Ākhi.***
As she went into the forest, clad in white (like a widow),
she is praised as ***Śvetāmbarī*** *(White-Clad).*
Due to her conflict with Caṇḍī, who is also called Nirvāsinī,
she received, dwelling in the mountains, the name ***Parvatavāsinī.***
As the wife of Jaratkāru your name became ***Jaratgaurī,***
divorced from her husband, her name became ***Pati-Mandarī.***
She wakes when the name ***Jagulī*** *is intoned,*
and lives in a sij tree.
With my talents, as (insignificant as) they are, how could I describe her?

In the next pages you can read more than a hundred names that have been, or are used in the worship of Manasā. I apologise for those I cannot translate. Welcome to your next fun-adventure. It may keep you busy for a few weeks, months, or lifetimes. I am sure you can make a meaningful selection of names for your daily meditations. Call it a model of your magical universe. You need as few names as possible, so that things remain comprehensible. And they have to represent yourself and the cosmos (*order, beauty*) you be-live.

Ādimātā: Ancient Mother, Primeval Mother
Ādyā: Ancient, Original, Primeval
Ādyāśakti: Original Śakti, Primeval Energy, Primordial Form
Agnijvālā: Flame of the Sacred Fire (sacrificial fire, hearth-fire, cremation-fire)
Anantā: Endless (female form of the world serpent Ananta)
Anantarūpinī: Endless Beauty/Shape
Āstikamātā: Āstika's Mother
Bagā:
Bāhuṛā: Without Husband
Bankumārī: (Vanakumārī= Forest Maiden?)
Basantakumārī, Vasantakumārī: Girl/Young Woman of Springtime
Bhātāchāṛi: Without Husband
Beṅgakhāki Kāṇi: One-eyed Frog-eater
Bhādāivrata:
Bhagavatī: Universal Self, Divine One
Bhaginī: Moon-Faced
Bhūtahāriṇī: Destroyer of Creatures
Biṣahari, Biṣaharī: (Bengal.:) Destroyer of Poison, Keeper of Poison, Full of Poison
Biṣabinodinī: (Bengal.: Delightful Poison-Woman
Brahmāṇī: Female Brahman
Brahmī: Female Brahmā, Śakti of Brahmā, Worshipper of Brahmā
Caṇḍī: Fury, Wild-One (a popular title of Durgā, Kālī, Śivā and Pārvatī)
Carviṇi: Chewing
Chāyā: Dark, Shadow; Protector; Beauty
Ceṅgamuṛī: Disgusting like a Rag? Head like a Ceṅg fish? Related to the Sij plant?
Ceṅgamuḍī: from Ceṅgamuḍa: Sij plant
Ceṅgamuṛkāni, Ceṅgamuṛī Kānī: One Eyed (-with the head of a Ceṇg fish?)
Cintāmaṇi: Wish-fulfilling Jewel
Devī: Bright, Shining, Heavenly One
Dharmādhare: Supporter of the Dharma (virtue, truth, religion, world-order, care, compassion etc.)
Dharmarāj: Regent of Truth
Dhemenā Bhatarī: A woman who lives with a man who is married to another woman (Assamese expression)
Didiṭhākrun:
Duloramā:
Gāchhpūjā:
Haṁsavāhinī: She Whose Vehicle is the Haṁsa Water-Bird/Spirit/In-breath and Out-breath
Jagatgaurī, Jagadgaurī: Fairest of the World, Light of the World (Light of Consciousness)
Jagatī: World, Universe; Female Being
Jagatīśvarī: Ruler of the Universe
Jagatjananī: Creatrix of the Universe
Jagatmātā: Mother of the Universe
Jāguli, Jāṅgulī: Knower of Poison (name of a minor Buddhist serpent goddess, identified with Sarasvatī)
Jaratgauri: Light of Jaratkāru
Jaratkāru, Jaratkārū: Wearing out the Body (Name of a serpent princess from the *Mahābhārata* and of her husband)
Jaratkārupriyā: Beloved of (the seer) Jaratkāru

Jaya Viṣahari: Victorious-, Triumphant Destroyer/Keeper of Poison

Jhaṁkeśvarī, Jhaṅkeśvarī, Jhānklāi: (possibly derived from the jingling sound of bangles or bells)

Jvālāmukhi: Flame-Head, -Mouth, -Entrance, -Direction, -Beginning, -Method, -Peak

Kadrū, Kadru: Tawny, Brown; a Soma Vessel (usually a name of the Mother of the Nāgas, occasionally used to address Manasā)

Kālīmā: Mother Darkness/Time, Mother Kālī

Kamalā: Lotus (also a name of Lakṣmī)

Kānāi, Kani, Kānī, Kāni (Bengal.): One-eyed, Half-blind, Blind (also a name of several poets)

Ketakā: Keta= Will, Desire, Thinking; and Ketukā, Ketakī, Keyā= pandanus plants, such as Pandanus tectorius Soland., Pandanus ordoratissimus, Pandanus faecicularis Lam. etc

Ketakā Sundarī: Beautiful/Lovely One of the Ketakā-Tree

Kharatarī: Wild, Rough, Fierce, Stubborn; Donkey, Mule; Ritual Earth Heap

Lakṣmī: Good Sign, Good Luck, Wealth, Radiance, Brightness, Beauty, Loveliness, Fertility

Mahādevī: Great Goddess

Mahājñānayutā: She Who Knows Everything

Mahākālī: Great Kālī, Great Darkness, Great Time, Great Death/Destruction

Mahāmukhi: Great-Face, -Head, -Mouth, -Entrance, -Direction, -Beginning, -Method, -Peak

Maheśvarī: Great Female Ruler/Queen (a common title of many goddesses)

Mahī: Great Earth/World/Universe; Union of Heaven and Earth; a river-name

Mainā: Intelligence

Manasā: Thinking One, Aware One, Conscious One, Imaginative One

Mānasāi: (Manasā in an Assamese spelling)

Manasākumārī: Conscious/Thinking-Girl/Young Woman

Mandākṣī: Shy One, Excessively Forgiving One

Maṅgal: Blessing, Prayer, Eulogy; Bringer of Fortune, Amulet; Joyous Feast

Mārāi, Marakī: Pestilence, Epidemic; Lust, Desire, Love

Mauli: (a major deity of the Laman Banjara culture)

Mṛtasanjīvanī: She Who Revives the Dead

Mukti: Liberation, Freedom, Release

Nāgabhaginī: Sister of a Snake

Nāgabhoginī: Enjoyer/Coiled One of the Serpents

Nāgamāta, Nāgamātrī: Serpent Mother

Nāgapūjā: Serpent Worship/Homage

Nāgeśvarī: Serpent Ruler/Queen

Nārāyaṇī: (female form of Nārāyaṇa, a title of Viṣṇu; Lakṣmī)

Nārīpuruṣa: Wife of the Puruṣa (Spirit, All-Self ; a title of Śiva & Viṣṇu)

Nirvāsinī: (folk goddess identified with Caṇḍī)

Nityā: Eternal, Everlasting, Timeless

Padmā, Padumaī: Lotus (also a name of Lakṣmī).

Padmāvāhinī: She Whose Vehicle is a Lotus

Padmāvatī: Lotus-born (also a name of Lakṣmī and of a Jaina goddess)

Pañcādevata: Deity of the Fifth (-lunar day of each fortnight)

Pañcānan: Five-Faced (derived from a title of Śiva)

Pānckuli:

Parvatavāsinī: Mountain-dweller (also a title of Śiva's wife Pārvatī, the Daughter of the Mountains)

Pātālkumārī: Girl/Young Woman of the Underworlds (= Pātāla)

Patimandarī:

Phaṇiviṣinī: Venom of Serpents

Pitāmvarī, Pitāmbarī, Pitāmbaradevī: Goddess Dressed in Yellow (Title of Bagalāmukhī; a popular folk & tantric goddess in Bengal)

Prakṛti: Primal Matter, Form, Nature, Manifestation (the counterpart of the formless, indescribable Brahman)

Priyā: Dear, Beloved, Darling (fun fact: the name is closely related to the Germanic goddesses Frigg, Frea, Frija); Arabian Jasmine; Kadamba Tree

Raudrī: Female Rudra/Śiva, Śakti of Rudra, Devotee of Rudra

Śaivī: Female Śiva; Auspicious; Śakti of Śiva, Devotee of Śiva

Śākambharī: Herb-Bearer, One Who Nourishes With Herbs

Sanātanī: Primordial

Śankukarni: Dart-Eared

Sarasayoginī: The Yoginī Who is Wet, Juicy, Fresh, New, Tasty, Elegant and Amorous

Sarasvatī: Wetland, Place of Pools, Place of Essences (goddess of a sacred river, of speech, song, music, literature, art and science)

Sarpamātā: Mother of Serpents

Sarva: All in All

Sarvanāśini: All-Destroyer

Siddhā: Female Perfected (a tantric adept)

Siddhayoginī: Perfected Yoginī, Yoginī With Magical Powers, Talents, Perfect Skills

Siṁhavāhini: She Whose Vehicle is a Lion

Sitalā: Cool (originally a goddess of smallpox and plagues. Nowadays a deity of HIV)

Śivānī: female Śiva, Śakti of Śiva

Śrāvaṇīvrata, Śrāvaṇībrata: Oath/Ritual/Will/Intent of the Month Śrāvaṇa

Śukamunde: Parrot-Headed

Sureśvarī: Regent/Queen of the Gods

Svetāmbarī: Clad in White (a widow)

Totalā, Totola, Tutulā, Totlā: 1. Invisible, Formless, Beyond Comprehension (= Brahman). 2. Repeating. 3. a woman who lives with a man she is not married to. 4. someone who stutters. 5. possibly a corruption of Tuttārā, a name of goddess Tārā.

Umā: Splendour, Light, Fame; Tranquillity; Night; Flax; Turmeric (Śiva's wife)

Vaiṣṇavī: female Viṣṇu, Śakti of Viṣṇu, Devotee of Viṣṇu

Vāsulī: (a folk goddess worshipped in Bengal and Orissa, identified with Caṇḍī)

Virathanārāyaṇi: Nārāyaṇī Without a Vehicle

Viṣahari, Viṣaharī: an ancient name of the goddess which might mean Destroyer of Poison, Keeper of Poison, or Full of Poison. The etymology is uncertain; as Asutosh Battacharyya pointed out, the grammar is wrong, and better choices would be Viṣahāriṇī or Viṣaharā.

Viṣadhari: She Who Contains Poison

Viṣalakṣmī: Wealth-, Shine-, Beauty of Poison

Viṣapūrna-Ākhi:

Viśoka: Free from Sorrow

Vyāṛi: Snake; Beast of Prey; Wicked, Vicious

Yogeśvarī: Regent/Queen of Yoga (Union, Binding, Yoking, Obsession, Witchcraft)

Yoginī: Full of Magical Power, Yoga-Practitioner (a goddess or woman who practices yoga, a tantric adept, a witch)

You just read that Manasā's devotees can drink **poison** without suffering. On a very simple level, it frees the devotees from their fear of serpents. On a deeper level, the poisons are everywhere. When you come home, weary from a hard working day, there is poison in your mind. Your sense organs feel dulled and worn out. It's hard to meditate, to laugh or enjoy life. Part of it comes from sensory overload. Part is due to stress hormones. You get them at work, no matter what you do, these days. A lot of toxic damage comes from participating in stupid, all too human games. Let's name hierarchies, competition, status displays, territorial struggles, envy, greed, possessiveness, arrogance, formalities, ignorance, bureaucracy, routine thinking, fear of responsibility and inertia. They turn work into a nightmare. People just love them. It can hurt. Life isn't easy at all. Ask Manasā for release. Ask Neta to wash your mind.

Another, more obscure level is based on tantric Twilight Language. The early tantrics of Kashmir used the word 'viṣ' (poison) as a code for orgasm. That's how the term was used by Abhinavagupta, Kashmir's universal genius, when he wrote about the Kula ritual. Bhairava/Śiva briefly alludes to it in the *Vijñāna Bhairava Tantra (68)*

One should direct thought, which is full of joy, into the centre between 'fire' and 'poison'. Alone or filled with breath will one be united with the blissfulness of love.

In this meditation instruction, fire is the excitement of love and lust, while poison signifies the end of the union, i.e. orgasm. True liberation happens in-between. The *Vijñāna Bhairava Tantra* is great at stressing in-between-ness states. Its adepts rest between one thought and another, between one form and another, between one action and another.

In another sense, fire is expansion and poison contraction: awareness, with or without a partner, pulses like a lotus flower. Attention may be directed to the outside world (expansion) or withdrawn into one's empty core (contraction). What happens in-between, when you hover in the nameless realm that is neither 'you' and 'not-you'?

Abhinavagupta, in his *Tantrāloka* (3, 172-174, based on the translations of Chatterjee, 2008 and Bäumer, 2008) adds a fourth interpretation.

Kāma (Desire, Lust, Love, here: *Fire) is Icchā (Will/Passion/Intent) and 'poison'* (= orgasm) *is Jñāna (Direct Insight/Knowledge), and the Devī Kriyā (Activity) is (the) Untainted. Śiva (Auspicious), the union of the three, is called Bhairava (Fear Inspiring). One should always contemplate (their union), as the masters taught. Whoever has entered the category 'poison', cannot be harmed by evil spirits or the toxins of the Seizers* (or: *planets), as one is delighted only by the contemplation of the absolute 'I am' (Āhaṁ).*

Quite simply: Manasā can be a destroyer of orgasms (many tantric ascetics thought that ejaculation and orgasm indicate failure), a keeper of orgasms and full of orgasms.

Another teaching identifies 'poison' as the fluid sacrament of the Kulas, Kaulas, Kramas and their like-minded Chinese associates: the blessed mixture of sperm and menstrual blood. It is lethally polluting to normal Hindus, but the 'deathless' elixir of the Left Hand Path. This 'clan-fluid' is the essence of liberation. It represents, among many other things, the union of the individual self/life (jiva) with the All-Self. Such interpretations make sense in a hard-core Left Hand Path tantric context. The vast majority of religious Indians, no matter whether Hindus, Buddhists, Jainas, Muslims, Atheists or Marxists disagree and turn away in disgust.

Let's end this section by settling down. Maybe you have a meditation seat, such as promoted by the *Bhagavad Gītā* in the passage on yoga. This seat (āsana) had four legs and was elevated above ground. It was covered by the pelt of a black antelope; a sacred item since the early Vedic period.

Between the seat and the fur was a layer of holy kuśa grass (Poa cynosuroides). Things don't get much holier than this. It placed the meditating yogī between the ground and a standing position. It also ensured that creeping creatures were deterred from exploring his underwear.

Let's consider Manasā's seat. It is formed of writhing, coiling serpents. Can you imagine sitting on one?

If you like serpents, you might enjoy this. Before you drift asleep, imagine that your whole bed is covered with snakes. They surround you to all sides. The raise their heads, they hiss, bare their fangs, cover you like a blanket and soothe you to sleep. It's much like drawing a magical circle around your bed. Only that the serpents are alive, and highly intelligent. Explore it! Does it affect your dream life?

As far as ideas go, this one is pretty old. Viṣṇu, in mystic slumber, rests on a bed consisting of the endless world serpent. His bed is vast, and has plenty of extra space, so Lakṣmī, plus her swans and elephants, are welcome, too.

Another example. When the Buddha struggled for enlightenment and liberation, the snakes were watching. Indeed, the region where Buddhism emerged, Magadha, is famous for old serpent cults. Śākyamuni, the Seer of the Śākya Clan, had been through many stressful years. He had left his family, sought liberation hither and yon, had followed ascetics and seers, had studied the *Upaniṣads* and other faiths. He had fasted until it almost killed him. Modern authors would probably add meditations to his programme. It's not quite accurate. The historical Buddha was keen on realisation, on observation and spent plenty of time watching decay and death. He advised his students to observe how corpses go to rot. Meditation, in the sense that it is used today, was not part of his program. Indeed, when the meditative Hindu yogīs of the third and fourth century promoted dhyāna and samadhi, the Buddhists and Jainas were definitely against them. They needed centuries to incorporate meditative practices and visualisation into their curriculum.

Be that as it may, and Neta says it may be any way you like, at some point Śākyamuni had enough. He settled underneath a tree and decided that he wouldn't leave before he had gained liberation. In the next days, he was sorely tried by hunger, thirst, lack of sleep, the great archdevil Māra, his wicked, wonderfully seductive daughters and, in one version of the tale, by the goddess Kālī herself. Finally, he gained freedom and embraced cessation. It didn't kill him. His identity, his fleeting, worthless ego, and the accumulated Karman of his past lives, dissolved. To be sure, his body continued to live. The Enlightened One realised that he would spend the rest of his lifetime preaching, mostly to misfits and merchants, while subsisting on the generosity of wealthy sponsors. He was so wretched that he almost went to pieces. At this point, help came from the Underworld.

An early legend from the *Vinaya Piṭaka* claims that Buddha was way beyond reasoning. He had been through far too much. The tree gave him stability. With the tree, and this is ancient magick, going back to Sumer, comes at least one serpent/dragon. Buddha was cold and exhausted. He had not eaten for ages. A week after his breakthrough experience, the monsoon began. Great storms swept the forest and winds made him freeze. Luckily, the earth opened and a gigantic serpent arose. It was the Nāgarāja Muchilinda. He coiled around the Enlightened One seven times. When he covered the head of the Buddha with his vast cobra hood, he spoke a mantra:

May no cold touch the Blessed One,
May no heat touch the Blessed One,
May no gnats, flies or creeping things,
No wind nor heat come near the Blessed One.
(Vogel, 1972:102)

Muchilinda sheltered the Blessed One in his seven coils for seven days. Finally, the grey-black clouds dispelled, fresh winds opened the sky, the sun shone and each leaf in the forest, dripping moisture, sparkled like a diamond. Cautiously, the Nāga released the Buddha from his embrace. He transformed into a king, clothed in silk and jewels, and bowed.

A similar story appears in several early Buddhist accounts. In one version (*Nidānakanthā*), the Nāga king appears directly after the confrontation with Māra and his daughters. He recognised that the Buddha, though enlightened, was close to death and wrapped him up in seven coils. The Enlightened One gave a sigh of relief *and enjoyed the bliss of salvation as if he had been resting in a shrine*.

The *Lalitavistara* gives another version. Why settle for a single Nāga when you can enjoy the lot? In this text, the Buddha was protected by the Nāga lord Muchilinda and by an army of Nāgas who came slithering from all directions. *They all envelop the Buddha with their coils and form a canopy over his head by means of their crests, so that, when thronged together, they resemble Mount Meru* (Vogel, 1972:103). Our lesson for today: Serpents are there to be enjoyed!

60. Ouroboros

Heaven is Manasā. Earth is Manasā. The snake Ouroboros twists, coils and bites its own tail. Life feeds on itself. Meet her in trees and rivers, in rocks and buildings. She is in wind and storm, in breath and thought, in feeling and experience. She is the thoughts you think and Neta is the silence in between. You are Manasā. So is your partner, the same goes for me, and the people on the road, for dogs and cats, trees, cars, lanterns, lichen and garbage cans. This book is Manasā. But the book you read is not the book I wrote. Manasā interfered. She turned my book into your book, 'cause it is different in your mind. We are an all-encompassing and an individualised awareness. It means we get things wrong, no matter how much we try. It's excellent. Unless we make mistakes, we won't get anywhere at all. To understand the multiverse we have to understand ourselves, at this moment, as we understand the multiverse. And while we understand that, we understand ourselves understanding ourselves as we understand ourselves understanding the multiverse. And so on. It's an infinite progression. There is no limit, and there never will be. Manasā looks slightly worried; Śiva has been expecting something like this, he smiles and reaches for his pouch, while Neta gives a sigh of relief. This is settled, she thinks, and the Dark Waters call. We might imagine that there is an inner and an outer world, that there are distinctions between objective and subjective reality, or even insist on the silly differentiation between body, mind and soul. Forget them. All words are crutches, all concepts tools. Manasā distrusts them. She gets entangled in them. When she shuts up and relaxes, her world turns into images, sounds, feelings, scents and tastes. It makes her life easier: sheer awareness is a lot better than evaluation and debate. Neta laughs; she loves to play with words, and turns each sentence upside down. Śiva smiles; he likes words that are simple, and reliable. Like 'Have another one.'

Try this: first, be aware of things. There's a hell of a lot everywhere. They may be words, images, sounds, feelings, tastes, scents or intuitions: no matter what you perceive out there or within you, it is always a what. That's because awareness has to be aware of something. Whatever you are aware of is Manasā. Now do the Neta act. You meet her as you move from one thing to the other. Between one thought and the next, pause. Between one mantra and the next, relax and enjoy the silence. Between one act and the next, halt. Explore freedom in-between. There is a gap, a moment of freedom, an instant of choice. You leave one form and before you encounter the next, you enjoy formlessness. The mind is fast. Slow it down. Watch how your attention moves, from topic to topic, from inside to outside, how it jumps from one sensory channel to the next, how it time-travels into the past (memory) and dances into the future (imagination). It's the greatest show on earth. It is Manasā. But like all good things, it can be too much. There is an emergency exit: you can stop anytime. Face the gateway. The door is open. That's Neta.

At the shore of the Dark Waters, where crocodiles laze and lotus blossoms glow, all distinctions lose their meaning. Dragonflies buzz, spiders weave their nets inside out and upside down. Manasā sits back and tries to clear her mind. Life is difficult. It's full of stuff. She wishes she were just a carefree serpent, having the time of her life in some unknown underworld. She looks up. "Neta, I've got a hundred new ideas!"

Neta shrugs and grins; as ever, she has work to do.

"Listen to this! You complained about ticks. I've got the solution. We could make them as large as hogs. Imagine a nice sunny day. People would go to a meadow."

"They wouldn't."

"And they would say, 'what a nice place for a picnic'."

"And your ticks?"

"They would be huge! Everyone could see them coming! People would move out of their way. Now what do you say? Problem solved!"

"It's a nightmare!"

"We could improve mosquitoes. They could be as large as aircraft, and there you are, none gets into your bedroom!"

"You are out of your head!"

"Let me tell you about shrews. We could make them even bigger. They could eat the mosquitoes!"

"They would eat anything!"

Other people can worry and think and feel clever. Eventually, costumes, corpses and concepts lose significance. Neta will take them apart, wash them, and string them up so they can dry in the sun. "Life should be simple," she says. "Here's your mantra for today: Relax, smile, exhale."

Appendix:

The Sources

If you've come this far you deserve to know more. Mediocre magicians hide their secrets. The better ones reveal them. For one thing, the miracles improve. For another, we get a chance to learn. It makes for better miracles. Let me cite some of the authors from whom I have picked up ideas.

2. In the Evening.

This section is a brief preview of the ethnological stuff; it settles Manasā in a ritual context and in daily life.

3. A Fairy Tale: Manasā's Brata Story

Maity tells this story, very short and unsatisfactory, with slight differences, in two of his books. His account is limited to a few pages, and, as usual in Brata stories, plenty of details are missing. I had to fill in a lot. The story does not appear in the *Manasā Epic*, it is a magical folk-tale for ritual occasions. Originally, the story is settled in a fairy tale country where the protagonist has no name, where the setting isn't elaborated and loads of open questions upset us. It could be great, Manasā said, to introduce you to the colourful world of East Indian myth. That's why it grew out of proportion. Let me apologise. If you look for the 'real thing', whatever that may be, read Maity. It won't make you happy. Why do the serpent brothers cover half of Vidyā's body? I had to invent a passable solution.

A different version of the tale appeared in the *Meyeder Brathakathā* (*Brata stories for Girls*) by Bhattacharya and Rani Debi. A selection of their tales was translated and presented by June McDaniel (2003:55-57). This one is even worse. For a start, Neta is absent. Unlike Maity's version, the heroine only catches one serpent. It is Manasā's son. She keeps it in her pot and worships it. One day, the serpent is dead (why?). Its soul ascends and visits Manasā's realm, and relates how badly our girl is being treated. Manasā spirits the heroine away into her otherworld, where she is to tend the serpent pot. For unknown reasons, this pot contains eight serpent brothers. Here, the dangerous quarter is south. Usually, north is the region of darkness, and Śiva's favourite direction, when he wears his terrifying guise. South is just as scary. Since Vedic times, the south is ruled by fire, and the place where corpses are cremated. The tale lacks interesting details. Our girl sees Manasā dance, forgets to feed the snakes with milk and accidentally burns their mouths. The snakes want to kill her, but Manasā orders them to follow her to earth and do the deed there. The nameless heroine is clad in precious ornaments and dumped in the household of her husband. The relations harass her, but our girl states that the servants of Ṣaṣṭhī will live long, and that she will receive more ornaments. I wonder how Ṣaṣṭhī got into the tale. The serpent brothers hear the words, forget their vengeance and tell Ṣaṣṭhī what the girl had said. Ṣaṣṭhī is impressed and praises the girl's patience with that horrid family. Manasā gives her more ornaments and all of a sudden her cult is popular everywhere. Don't ask me why. The protagonist doesn't undergo a change, and that's a sure sign of bad storytelling. From one moment to the other, the serpent brothers refuse to bite her. We don't learn why. Did the storytellers fill in the details? Or did they recite this crippled episode in the sure knowledge that even bad stories, when they are holy, work their spell?

For reasons of coherence, I had to place this story at the start. A snake preview was urgently required. I elaborated this story far more than the other bits of this book.

Manasā Epic

Part One: Śiva

4. Creation, Traditional

The Vedic seers made up a wealth of creation stories. They were spaced out of their head by Soma. Several creation tales shaped fundamental brahmanical thought, then Hinduism, and finally the *Manasā Epic*. Others are just splendidly original, crazy, bedazzling and beside the point. As all epics need to start somewhere, I chose a few bizarre items from the *Ṛg Veda*. The tenth book is full of weird stuff. Some of its hymns are ancient, others are comparably new (maybe 800 BCE), and several describe religious insights that never made it. The drug-crazed seers of this chapter recite passages of *Ṛg Veda* 10, 121; ṚV 10, 190; ṚV 10,72; ṚV 10, 90; ṚV 10, 129 and ṚV 10,82.

5. Creation, Bengali Style

Anāndi (*Endless*) Deb (Deva= *Bright One, deity*) is the original god of creation. He creates the basic Hindu trinity of Brahmā, Viṣṇu and Śiva. Much of this chapter is based on the *Epic* by Jagatjīban. The death of Ādyā and the confinement of the baby in the iron chest, its rescue and growth are inspired by Jagatjīban and the anonymous Assamese version. Compare this original tale with the brahmanical creation story presented by Kaiser Haq. His account is close to the high-brow *Purāṇas*; mine to Bengal folk tales.

6. Gaṅgā

The quarrel between Brahmā and Mohinī has an almost archetypal character: a ritual quarrel between a scholar and a prostitute happened among the many preliminary rituals required to distil Soma, in the Vedic period. Some may object that Brahmā behaves like an ill-mannered misogynist. Let me assure you that this is not always the case. In the *Skanda Purāna* (I, II, 23, 46) Brahmā goes to surprising lengths to praise women. *"A daughter is equal to ten sons. The merit that one*

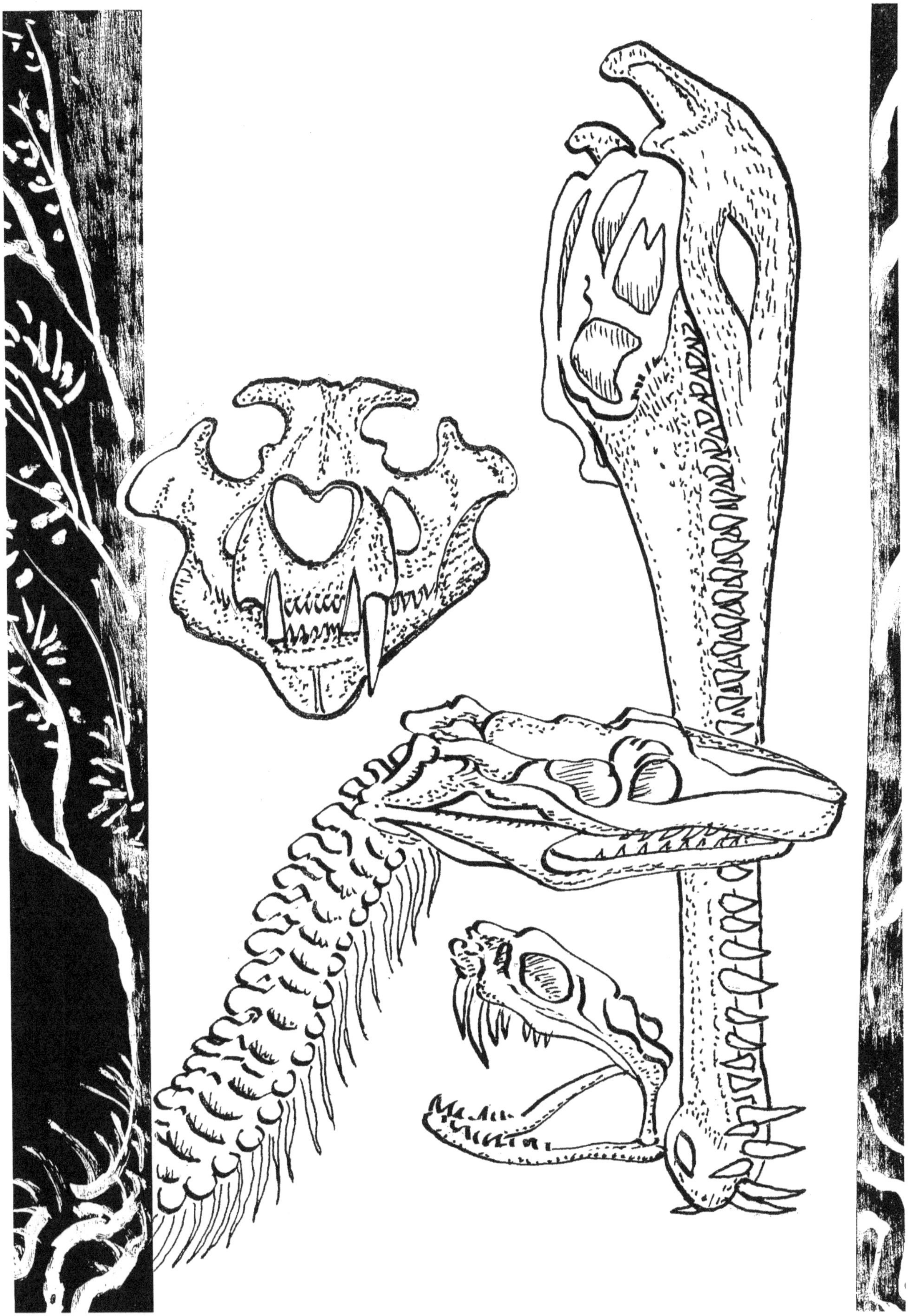

Picture 72: Appendix: Bare Bones. The Sources of the Epic (python, tiger with missing canine, cobra and gavial).

derives by bringing up ten sons is obtainable by bringing up one daughter."

The Gaṅgā episode does not appear in any version of the *Manasā Epic* that I know of. However, it is quite common in the *Purāṇas* and in folk tales. Anyone listening to the *Manasā Epic* would have been familiar with it. The name Gaṅgā means the *Swiftly Moving*. Her heavenly manifestation is Abhra Gaṅgā (*Swift Moving in the Airy Space*) or Ākāśa Gaṅgā (*Swift Moving of Spirit*). When she descends to earth she is Devabhūtī (*Flowing Down from Heaven*). And she is the Milky Way, Mandākinī. In one popular version (*Viṣṇu Purāṇa*) the seer Bhagīrata realised that the souls of his ancestors could not travel into the celestial otherworld. He spent several thousand years with painful ascetic exercises until he gained the power to understand what happened, and to pray to the celestial goddess to come to earth. Gaṅgā answered his prayers and came down like a flood of sheer destructivity. Śiva placed his head in the celestial cascade and his wild and tangled locks calmed the downpour. From this point onward, Śiva has been walking around with a waterfall on his head. As a boon, the seer Bhagīrata became the deity of the first part of the majestic stream, and his name is used for the young River Gaṅgā. In another version of the tale, the river goddess didn't drop on Śiva but on the god Dhruva (*Firm, Immobile*), i.e. Polaris.

7. Courtship

The name Durgā is one option among several. In some versions of the *Manasā Epic*, Śiva's wife is called Pārvatī (*Daughter of the Mountains*) or Caṇḍī (*Fury, Fierce One*). These names are pretty much interchangeable. Nevertheless, they come from different sources and create a different mood. Durgā (*Untouchable*) is a popular warrior goddess, whose image graced fortresses. She is famous for her fight against the buffalo demon of pride and arrogance, i.e. exactly the moods which she exhibits in the *Manasā Epic*. Durgā may be Śiva's loving wife, but she has had a difficult infancy, a weird childhood and needs to learn a lot. In Bengal, she may be the most popular female deity, and her festival, around October, is an all-round favourite. As Pārvatī she is more controlled and a great Yoginī; it doesn't really fit her role as angry stepmother. Caṇḍī, by contrast, is too savage for our tale. The forest ascetics sang a section of the *Hymn to Durgā*, from the *Viśvasāra Tantra*, after Avalon/Woodroffe (2001:81-84). Like many classical hymns it claims to list 108 names, but when you count them, you realize that '108' is symbolic, at best. Gaṅgā tries to make the fishermen drown Durgā: inspired by Jagatjīban and the anonymous Assamese version.

The marriage preparations are based on Bengal customs. However, as neither Śiva nor Durgā are fond of time-consuming customs, they decided to keep things short and simple. Not all versions of the *Manasā Epic* accord. Kaiser Haq provides a synopsis of an elaborate marriage ceremony, which contrasts brahmanical ritual and Śiva's disregard of conventions and social niceties. The seer Nārada appears as a trickster and clown: at Śiva's command, he provides a gale that lifts the skirts of all female guests. I decided against it: one elaborate marriage, between Behulā and Lakhindār, is quite enough for our tale.

8. Married Life

Gaṅgā 's unhappy departure from Śiva is inspired by Manakar's version. The following episodes, relating how Durgā seduced Śiva, assuming different shapes, are quite common. You can find them in the versions of Bipradās, Jagatjīban and in the anonymous Assamese version. I simply chose two examples and hinted at a third, in which Śiva seduced Durgā as a good looking tailor (this one was written by Binod). The story of how Gaṇeśa got his elephant head appears in many folk tales and classical Hindu literature. In some versions, the elephant was Indra's favourite; the cloud-high bringer of the grey-black monsoon. Śiva chopped its head off. "It was an emergency", he says, "Durgā would have killed me". He smiles sweetly. "She did, anyway. The god of ascetics reaches for his pipe. "Again." Luckily, Indra's favourite vehicle simple grew another head. The brilliant idea that Skanda/Karttikeya's peacock hunts snakes and that Gaṇeśa's mouse steals Śiva's drugs in the middle of the night comes from Kabijbana.

Part Two: Manasā

9. Lotusborn

This chapter has a key function in the epic. When we examine the drama structure of Śiva's and Durgā's life, we find it at the mid-point, i.e. in the special moment when things may transform into entirely new directions. When we look at the story from Manasā's point of view, it starts Act One. This difference creates an immense tension. My version is partly inspired by Bipradās. The hymn which Vāsuki sings to describe Śiva is based on the *Kūrma Purāṇa* (2,4). In the original, Śiva sings it for himself; I have amended the grammar. The text goes back to earlier literature: you can find similarities to the hymn for Viṣṇu/Kṛṣṇa in the *Bhagavad Gītā*.

The **Lotus Lake, Kālidaha**, is also known by the name Kāliyadaman. Kāli means black, dark, time and daha may mean river. The term is rare. It's a real lake, and allegedly bottomless, as all good lakes should be, if they want to exist for a few millennia. Ask any archaeologist: they'll tell you that lakes are transient, and disappear fast, unless they are frequently dredged. The mythical Kālidaha is not a location but a place of origin, a state of mind and a magickal realm which you can visit when you travel in your imagination. And of course it is the very place where Neta does her washing. Her temple stands nearby, surrounded by large boulders and moist fern. It grows, age after age, as it is founded on all beings that have ever lived. The very place where Manasā emerged on earth is also the location where Neta meets Behulā and washes the corpses of the lucky ones.

Śiva wants to see Manasā's divine form to be sure she is his daughter: I have used the ideas of Nārāyaṇ Deb and Sukavi Nārāyaṇ. In the versions of Baṁsīdās and Sukavi Nārāyaṇ she gets so angry with her disbelieving, lust-besotted father, that she kills him with a toxic glare. There is a strong incestuous element in the story: Manasā has to deal with her dad's arousal. For dramatic reasons, I shifted Śiva's death to a later section of the chapter.

Durgā blinds Manasā's (left) eye. The story is widely popular, but it is told in many different ways. The most perverse makes Durgā the most horrid stepmother in the world: she deliberately heats a needle until it is red hot, before she stabs Manasā's eye. I am sure this story caused plenty of sympathy. However, if we reduce Durgā to the level of a sadistic psychopath, we demonise her divinity and make her really cross. I stuck to a less sadistic version. After all, in the last chapter Durgā and Manasā agree they are the same.

Durgā is jealous of Manasā. She has excellent reasons. Śiva, if left on his own, is fond of recognising the goddess in any woman, which may result in worship, lovemaking or both. Unless in meditation, when he is terrifyingly abstinent. Durgā knows what happens when her husband meets a nude girl who bulges in the right places. The snakes won't deter him. Indeed there are folk traditions where Śiva is not Manasā's father but her lover.

Manasā kills Durgā with her evil eye: another common story. I added Śiva's death (which would otherwise have happened earlier), as repetitions are boring. Bipradās had a different idea: Manasā and her snakes arrive at the Lotus Lake, where they disturb Śiva, who is picking flowers for a ceremony. He calls on the terrifying Garuḍa bird, the archenemy of snakes. The snakes beat a hasty retreat but Manasā advances and says hello to her dad.

In Jībankṛṣṇa Maitra's version, both Neta and Manasā were created from Śiva's sperm. In the anonymous version from Bihar, Śiva had a bath in the lake and lost five hairs. Each of them turned into a snake-girl: we encounter the terrifying sisters Mainā (*Intelligence*) Viṣahari, Dotolā Brahmānī, Devī Viṣahari, Jaya Viṣahari and Padumā Viṣahari. That's five charming and lethal serpent girls. Nevertheless, the five are also one, who is Manasā. Five sisters make the storyline rather difficult. Durgā blinded one of them, Mainā Viṣahari, in one eye. The other sisters killed Durgā; Śiva called for the divine physician Kesā, who produced a measure of healing water. The four snake sisters evaporated the doctor's fluids. Śiva had to get down to sober reality, which was inconvenient, painful and stupid, he tells me, and appealed to the four sisters to revive Durgā.

I owe Manasā's transformation into a white spider to Biṣṇu Pal, while the anonymous version from Assam makes her transform into a fly. Jībankṛṣṇa Maitra had the odd idea that Manasā forgot to honour her brother Vāsuki before she climbed up the lotus stalk. He cursed her and she lost an eye. In his version, Manasā and Neta were born at the same time, and they were both hiding in the flower basket. Bijay Gupta composed a version where Śiva was late, and couldn't return to Mount Kailāsa on time. The sun was setting and the god of ascetics had to find shelter for the night. He knocked on the door of the peasant Bachāi and asked for his hospitality. While the god of absolute transcendence was snoring like a chainsaw, the peasant explored his flower basket. He was much surprised to find a girl and wanted to marry her. Manasā wasn't in the mood for jokes and killed him. Bachāi's mother wept and howled, Śiva woke and realised what happened. He advised Bahchāi's mom to worship Manasā. The old lady showed remarkable devotion and after a few kind words, Manasā felt flattered and decided to revive the peasant. Bahchāi and his mom became Manasā's first worshippers, while Śiva grinned and went back to sleep.

VERY SPECIAL INTERLUDE: NETA

It's time to meet the little sister, Neta. She is quite formidable. And she is just as powerful as Manasā. That's 'cause some do the thinking, and others get things done. Neta has plenty of names. You can meet her as Neta, Netā, Neto, Netu, Neti, Netalā, Netulā, Nita, Nitaī and Netavatī. Manasā's younger sister is also her elder sister. You'll be amazed. Maity claims that Neta started as an independent serpent goddess. Smith mentions serpent spells from Bengal and Assam which invoke the help of Neta. Sadly, he doesn't quote any. Occasionally, Neta belongs to the Nāgas. She can do the king cobra act better than most. But that isn't enough. After all, she wasn't born from the combination of divine sperm, lotus and serpent queen, but by the union of tear/sperm and cloth. The latter is a woven textile, hence a Tantra. Neta is so far from brahmanical Hindu literature that you find exceedingly little on her nature or worship. There are just a few traces of her cult. In some places in East India she was worshipped before Manasā became popular. The Oriya version of the *Mahābhārata,* composed by Śāralā Dāsa in the 14th Century, mentions Neta, but has no references to Manasā.

Explaining Neta's origin isn't easy. So far you've only met her as a happy girl, as an advisor and friend for Manasā. But Neta, just like East Indian Tantra, has a

Picture 73: Nirṛti, Lack of Cosmic Order, Destroyer, Owl-Goddess of the Dark.

much darker side which appears at the end of the Epic. It would be easy to call her as a goddess of death, purification and spiritual release.

Sukumar Sen (in Maity) tried to relate her to the ancient Vedic deity Nirṛti, whose name means, literally, the *Dissolution of Cosmic Order*. The Vedas contain a few brief and often enigmatic references to her (see, for instance, *Ṛg Veda* 5,41; 7,37; 10,8; 10,10; 10,36; 10, 164). Nirṛti is unlucky, dangerous and terrifying, and if she had hymns, they were not recorded. Her yonī is the darkest place in the multiverse. Sinners and evildoers were condemned to dwell in it. Nirṛti has been classed as a death goddess, but that only covers part of her functions. She is black and so are her altar stones. They were not to be touched with the hands. Nirṛti received black grains and all offerings which accidentally dropped from the main altars. Her home is black soil, the earth of the dead. During the coronation of kings, her small dark altar was set up in the south of the sacrificial space, in the region of scorching heat and cremation fires. It was separated from the main space by spilling holy water on the ground. During this ritual, the barren wives of the king represented her (Oldenberg, 1923:353). She is also vaguely associated with women and dice playing. Dicing was not just a game but also an important ritual. Her animals are owls (her *winged missiles*) and doves, who bring bad luck when they fly into a house. The *Atharva Veda* contains several spells to expel her doves and exorcise their influence. As Nirṛti could bring hunger and despair to anyone, the AV contains curses (7,70 and 16,8) where she is called upon to destroy an enemy. In AV 6,53 you read a spell to release a person from the bonds of Nirṛti. Is Nirṛti related to Neta? In the vague sense that both have to do with death, I agree. Nevertheless the similarity of Nirṛti to Kālī is closer. Sukumar Sen speculated that Neta might also be related to a tantric Buddhist goddess called Nṛtyā (*Dancing Girl*), which makes little sense, as Neta isn't much into dancing, and to the Hindu tantric goddess Nityā (*Eternal*). Apart from the similarity of names, the evidence is poor. Molly Kaushal (2001:56) offers a brief remark (and no details) leading into another direction: *Neto (Netiya) in Bhojpuri is a man-eating demon, whereas the Bengali Neto is a friend of Manasa created by Shiva.*

If you enjoy something extremely speculative, how about this? Let's go to **Mesopotamia**. The Sumerians, Akkadians, Babylonians and Assyrians had varied ideas about the realm of the dead. Several underworld goddesses appear in literature. Eventually, they merged into a formidable figure: Ereškigal, the *Queen of the Great Earth/Underworld*. Ereškigal is a great goddess, a child of heaven. As Kramer reconstructed, she was abducted by an underworld monster called Kur (the word means *outland, foreign state, foreigners, foreign mountains, underworld* etc) and dragged her into the deep. The god of magic, water, music and science, wise Enki/Ea pursued her and sailed straight into a volley of stones. That's as far as the story goes. Kur isn't mentioned again and Ereškigal remains in the deep and becomes its queen. It isn't really fun. She is lonely, sexually frustrated and complains that she never had a childhood. Sure, she had several husbands. Gugalanna, the Bull of Heaven, died under mysterious circumstances. Then she met Nergal/Erra and dragged him into her bed. But while she has to remain in the deep, he stalks the deserts and mountains. From time to time he tries to destroy the world. In short, he is an absent husband. The queen of the dead received standard offerings in some major temples (except for fowl and cattle). Sadly, none of her hymns, if there ever were any, has survived. But there are remarkable spells. The myth of her son Ningišzida ends with the line: *Ereškigala, to praise you is sweet.* Wiggermann (RlA, *'Nergal'*) quotes a middle Babylonian remark: *When people lie down on earth (they say): Ereškigal is our mother, we are her children.*

It's a wonderful mantra.

The goddess was identified with the constellation Hydra, which was called MUŠ 'Serpent/Dragon' by the Babylonian stargazers. The same constellation represented her children and family members. So that's how we begin: we have an underworld goddess with a close link to serpents. Ereškigal, like any other major Mesopotamian deity, has a doorkeeper and mediator. He is called Neti, Netu, Nedu. Sadly, hardly anything is known about him. But there is one description in a poem written around the middle of the seventh century BCE in Aššur: he has the head of a lion, the hands of a man and the claws of a bird (ANET, 1969: 109). In this text, Nedu looks much like Lamaštu, who is also much concerned with death, and specialises in infants and elders. Need I emphasise that Neta can appear as a tigress; i.e. with the head of a terrifying cat? Nedu/Neti has a major role in two much earlier myths, the Sumerian *Inanna's Descent into the Underworld* and its later Babylonian version *Ištar's Descent into the Underworld*. The main theme is simple. Inanna/Ištar, the planet Venus, Torch of the Gods, celebrated as the Lady of Heaven, tries to occupy the Underworld. For this purpose, she puts on her magical powers of civilisation (the Me) and goes to the door to the deep. Neti meets her, informs his Lady Ereškigal, and reluctantly admits the visitor. In these tales, the underworld has seven gates. At each, Inanna/Ištar has to give up an article of clothing or ornament. Each of them is a divine power. She complains, but Neti replies: *"such are the ordinances of the underworld"*. When the celestial goddess reaches the bottom, she is just as naked and powerless as the dead. She confronts Ereškigal, who kills her with her evil eye. Instead of conquering the Underworld,

Inanna/Ištar ends up as a piece of dead meat, dangling from a hook. Only the intervention of Enki/Ea allows the celestial goddess to return, naked and angry, to daylight. Conclusion: in ancient Mesopotamia, we have a snaky underworld goddess with a lethal eye and her doorkeeper, whose name is pretty similar to Neta.

Or how about this? It's just as crazy, unreliable and nutty as everything you just read or which, indeed, makes up the fabric of reality. Here is something funny from ancient **Greece**. An inscription from Pylos (Mycenae, Greece) in Linear B script offers a list of deities. One goddess is called Manasa. Linear B is an archaic script; it was used until c. 1,150 BCE, long before the advent of Greek literature. Between this period, and the works of Homer and Hesiod, lie the 'Dark Ages' of Greece. The great Achaean culture was destroyed by the foreign 'Sea-People' (a term coined by the Egyptians), cities shrank to the size of villages and illiteracy became the norm. For several centuries, everyday life was a bitter struggle for survival. During this dismal period, much was forgotten. Our inscription is a chance discovery, a scrap of insight into a time when elder faiths were popular. There isn't a shred of evidence of who this 'Manasa' was and what she did. Her cult is older than that of most Olympian deities. But I wouldn't dream of insisting that an unknown goddess of ancient Greece is related to a popular East Indian goddess.

Now for another one; it's Greek, inscrutable and I'm sure, another weird coincidence. However, coincidences simply mean we can't explain something. Kallimachos (born 310 BCE in Cyrene) composed a hymn to Zeus, describing the birth and childhood of the Celestial Thunderer (after Ebener's German translation in *Griechische Lyrik*, 1976:302-305).

...Rhea spoke, in her need, the exalted goddess

"You too, dear Gaia, may give birth. For you, the birth pangs shall be easy".

The goddess raised her arm and delivered,

a blow to the mountains, they split, and mighty,

waters rushed forth. So she washed and wrapped you (Zeus) *carefully,*

you, my lord, the mother, and gave you to Neda; she should

carry you to the Cretan cave, for secret care,

Neda, the eldest of nymphs, who helped raise the babe then,

first in nobility after Styx (River of Death)*and Philyra* (the Oceanid, impregnated by Chronos in horse-shape, mother of the centaur Chiron).

The goddess (Rhea), *offered her greatest thanks, she called the river she created,*

the Neda. After long journeys, it flows,

streaming into the sea, quite close to the town Lepreion,

inhabited by the Kaukones. The grandson of the she-bear of Lycan,

drinks of the flood, as the eldest water on earth.

Wild River Neda, nowadays called the Buzi, flows through the Peloponnese, cuts its way through deep, inaccessible valleys, thunders through shady gorges and sparkles, as it drops in countless waterfalls. Neda is the primal, the first of the Nymphs. She was there before Zeus was born.

Nymphs are underestimated. In primordial Greek myth, closely related to other Indo-European faiths, the Nymphs are a class of cave-dwelling or underworldly goddesses who are associated with gardens, meadows and water. Some make rains fall, some create springs (from tears and blood), and many haunt rivers, lakes, swamps and marshes. Look at them emerging from the underworlds! Nymphs seem simple. They laugh a lot. They feel happy in nature. The early type does not demand much; they want no temples or sacred buildings and make do with primitive images and offerings of small animals, wine, fruit and blossoms. What counts to them is the sheer intensity of your awareness. They treasure life, and commitment, and your participation in the divine. They appear as daughters of Zeus (as Homer claimed), of Okeanos (the god of the world-ocean, who surrounds all continents), of Acheloos and, in later periods, of Zeus and oceanic goddess Themis (a Greek version of the Babylonian Tiāmat). Quite a few Nymphs are sex hungry and famed for the seduction of mortal men, like Bormos and Hylas. Some are deep, dark and primordial: they carry the drowned to the otherworld. Poets and seers insisted that the Nymphs grant visions and oracles. Many a poet played his lyre at a spring, a brook or at the place where rivers meet, to find insight and oracles. Those who were seized by the Nymphs (nympholepsy) turned into Υυμφόληπτοι; they attained total clarity of the senses and were shaken by poetic inspiration and divine madness. The Romans called them lymphatici, meaning *'madmen; crazy, frenzied ones'*, a term derived from lympho, lymphare (*to drive crazy, to become frenzied*).

A few Nymphs were protective goddesses of places, districts and cities. "Who cares for temples", they said, "we are the land, and we are the water that keeps it alive". Nymphs blessed the bridal bath, they helped births; in Crete they were called upon to witness vows, and punished oath-breakers. In a good mood, they are sparkle and flow and happiness. But they can also be fierce and sinister, appear as vengeful nightmares, and, you guessed it, as goddesses of the underworld. Occasionally they were called upon during funeral ceremonies to weep for the deceased and to conduct them to a better world.

Late myths reduced them to a semi-divine status and differentiated between Nymphs, Naiads (in sweet water) and Nereids (in the sea). Finally, the Nymphs lost their eminence. They appeared as minor, local nature goddesses in the company of Hermes, Pan, Apollo, Dionysus and of Artemis, a major goddess who may have begun her career as a Nymph. They provided purification and healing at special springs and, in Roman times, at spas and in temples. In countries occupied by the Romans, the 'Nymphs' was the general title for minor local goddesses, especially when these were related to sacred springs. To placate the Nymphs, small coins were tossed into springs and ponds. The wishing well is a faint memory of their cult. Indeed, Neta says, snarling like a tiger, "I wish you well." The Romans classed major Celtic goddesses, like Brigantia (the war goddess of the Brigantes), as Nymphs. As a final insult, artists employed dancing nymphs and lecherous Satyrs to fill gaps in their pictures. As silly topless girls, the Nymphs struggled through the medieval period and the Renaissance. We observe the decline of a major class of early Indo-European deities. Now, for the fun of it, consider Neta (while she considers you). How many of her activities show parallels to the Greek Nymphs?

In Bengal mythology, almost all important deities have advisors, administrators and counsellors. It reflected court life: any great god or goddess acted like a king or queen, and required attendants, a palace and plenty of personnel. Usually, the counsellor is more intelligent than the regent. I did not invent Manasā's naiveté. It's a common theme that Manasā stands there, totally confused, and asks Neta "How is...?". It's a wonderful question. I take it for walks: it reminds me that things are not normal, self-evident or comprehensible at all. Neta knows everything about how, and gets things done. It's no accident that Behulā's journey ends when she meets Neta and gains her approval.

The configuration ruler/counsellor is ancient. The grand vizier is the king's contact with the outside world, and usually more powerful than the regent. When a deity is too supreme, too cosmic, too powerful, many people find it hard to identify with it. They want someone accessible, someone human, or at least someone easy to approach. Those who are awed by Śiva consult his good-natured son Gaṇeśa, while those who find Viṣṇu overbearing prefer his friendly, charming incarnation as Kṛṣṇa.

Where did Neta appear? You have read the most popular version, where Śiva, highly worried about Manasā's fate, sheds a tear, catches it in a piece of cloth and creates a beautiful girl. Remember: Neta is created from Śiva's eye (netra) and caught in a piece of cloth (netā). So much for folk etymology. It doesn't explain the many different variations of her name. But here is something interesting. Netramatī and Netravatī are popular names for girls. They mean *Having Eyes, Observant, With Discriminatory Powers, Wise*. The former variant is also a river in South India; the latter also a title of Lakṣmī. And there's a goddess called Nīti (*Policy*), who is in charge of strategic manoeuvres (*Sk. Pur.*, I, II, 22, 57); she is identified with Parvātī.

In general, the tear represents Śiva's empathy. Baṁsīdās had a different idea; in his version Śiva was sexually excited and shed a tear as his lust welled up. Nārāyan Deb didn't approve: in his *Epic*, Śiva sat at the shore of the Lotus Lake and lost his sperm. Well, most of it. He wiped his penis with a bit of cloth and that created Neta. While the major amount of Śiva's sperm seeps into the underworld, Neta arises: she is the elder sister. Śiva doesn't really know what to say. He creates an air-chariot and asks her to fly to his home, to Mount Kailāsa. Neta is delighted. She mounts the chariot and takes off. Within seconds, she is soaring through the air, giggles with exhilaration, and marvels at the wide, wonderful scenery. On her way she catches a glimpse of the ascetic seer Aṣṭabakra. The man is holy, filthy, and a cripple. Neta she has a laughing fit and makes a few of her price-winning remarks. The seer isn't amused.

He said, "Be you the slave of your younger sister,
You will not stay long in your husband's home,
Gathering up clothing, you will wash it"

(in Smith, 1980:61). As Smith points out, these lines explain three things. First, why Neta's marriage was even shorter than that of Manasā (in many versions it is non-existent), why she was forced to be a washerwoman, and why she, as the elder sister, became the servant and inferior of the younger sister. As you may have noticed, she is anything but a slave. Occasionally she refuses to obey Manasā's commands (like biting Lakhindār or killing her former student Dhanvantari) and whenever possible she sends Manasā out on her own, allowing her to fall on her face and learn something useful.

In ritual, it can happen that two pots of sacred water are set up, one for Manasā and one for Neta. While Manasā gets far more attention than Neta, there are many people of the dhobā class who worship her passionately. The dhobās are the washers, and their clan and class goddess is venerated as Neta Muni (*Neta the Seer*) and Netu Dhopānī (*Netu the Washer*).

Let's examine the 'little sister' (and 'little brother') syndrome. The classification arose from the conflict between upper class and lower class worship. When a deity has gained superior status and the recognition of the upper classes, she or he is worshipped by refined, highly educated Brahmins in the great temples. These people are supposed to be strict vegetarians; they insist on traditional ritual and insist that the ancient purity laws are binding. Their deities are perfectly well behaved. Śiva is astonishingly sober and polite, and goddesses neither menstruate nor do they give birth. Their children are not born, they simply happen. Meanwhile, the lower classes celebrate their deities in their own way. The ceremonies are performed by priests of the lower classes, by local ritualists, shamans and inspired mediums. These rituals are not vegetarian at all; indeed, the goddesses demand flesh and blood. While the elder sister resides in her heavenly palace or secluded mountaintop, the little sister indulges in pollution. That's what Neta is doing. Being a washerwoman, even if she does the washing for the gods, is terribly low-class. Only hardcore tantrics of the Left Hand Path find such women attractive. And when Neta washes corpses in the Dark Waters, she becomes a terrifying goddess of the underworlds. In East India, many goddesses have 'little sisters' who happen to be local goddesses. Their names do not appear in high-class literature. The same thing happens among the gods. When the high god Śiva receives his vegetarian offerings, his 'little brother' Bhairava (the *Fear Inspiring One*) enjoys a wild ritual among his lower-class devotees. Or it may be the other way around. In some places, such as Kashmir, Bhairava is more popular than Śiva. Both of them are essentially the same. Social demands introduce the division. Seen from this perspective, **Manasā and Neta are one goddess**.

Well and good for now. We'll get back to Neta's special tasks in the commentary to chapter 34.

10. Outside

Manasā's devotion to Kṛṣṇa and Kṛṣṇa worshipping Manasā appear very briefly in the DBH. It's pretty much routine; the DBH is full of stories of this type. The amount of goddesses who rise to fame thanks to Kṛṣṇa's efforts is amazing. Manasā and Śiva move from one village to the next and find no place to stay: I followed the ideas of Tantrabibhūti, a work of the northern tradition. His version may be extra interesting as the author's name indicates that he either was a weaver (tantra means a *woven article, textile, text, science, curriculum of knowledge*) or that he chose the name to hint at his religious convictions. The bath, the Gandharva princess and Brahmā's spilling of sperm: Bipradās version.

11. Tigerfight

The tale of the happy cow Kapilā, of Durgā's seductive little finger and her undesired pregnancy, the garden of Brahman and the fight of the calf against the tigers are inspired by Bipradās.

12. Milkocean

The poets of Bengal and Assam copied the ancient tale from the *Mahābhārata* and made up their own version. They turned Śiva into the major character, which, in the original, he isn't. I have made much of the storyline created by Bipradās and Biṣṇu Pal. They introduce the great idea that the whole trouble began when the silly old seer Durvāsā visited Śiva and Durgā on Mount Kailāsa and received a garland of flowers. It was simply too much for him. Tantrabibhūti related that Neta was born when the Milk Ocean was churned. It places her on one level with the elixir of life, Lakṣmī, Indra's favourite elephant and so on. Once born, Tantrabibhūti relates, Śiva asked her to be Manasā's helper and friend. The Milk Ocean is a crucial point in our storyline. It relates how Śiva drank the entire poison of the universe, which killed him, and that Manasā, by breastfeeding her dad, resurrected him. This event also appears in other legends, where the goddess Tārā revives Śiva with her milk. Śiva's death, Durgā's generous gift of a tattered old jute sack and Manasā's triumph were inspired by Bipradās. Durgā is stupid and bitchy and dies from bad Karman. Ketakādās contributed something special; Cāndo, as a venerable sage, is present when the Milk Ocean is churned. At the time, he was at the height of holiness. In future lifetimes, he lost much of his sageliness, until he became, by force, the king of merchants.

13. Husbands

The classic tale of the marriage of the evil-mooded seer Jaratkāru and the serpent princess of the same (or similar) name Jaratkāru, Jaratkārū and Jaratkārī appears in the first book of the *Mahābhārata*. It had nothing to do with Manasā until, more than a thousand years after its composition, the seers of East India identified Manasā with the Nāga princess Jaratkāru. Bipradās had the wonderful idea that the ascetic husband sees his wife eating frogs, runs away and hides under a shell in the ocean, where Śiva finds him. It shows that Manasā is not just a king cobra (which only eats other snakes) but also a common cobra, with a widely varied diet. The hopeless attempt to marry Manasā to the seer Maṇirāja, and the futile effort of Dhāmāi to gain the right to marry Manasā by making a contract with her would-be-groom, is based on Rādhānāth Caudurī and Jībankṛṣṇa Maitra. The failed effort to marry Manasā to the python Ajagara comes from the anonymous Assamese version. Three tries, I thought, would suffice. Indeed there were more. There is a legend which claims that Manasā married the god Dharma (*Virtue, Right, Universal Law, Order, Truth, Compassion, Social regulations* etc.). It would have been a top notch match. For unknown reasons, hardly anyone mentioned it. As Dharma appears in the creation tale of my version, and disappears from the record soon thereafter, I ignored this tale. Sure, there may have been a marriage. As usual, it did not last. Manasā, as her worshippers insist, is unmarried. Except to those devotees who truly love her.

As a parallel to Manasā's marriage, several poets tried to marry Neta to remarkable seers. One of Neta's alleged spouses is the great seer Vaśiṣtha/Baśiṣtha. At least Bipradās says so. The sage is a prominent figure in the *Ṛg Veda*. He appears in several hymns, was present during the great war of the ten kings and may have composed a hymn (*ṚV* 7,18). His teachings did much to form the faith of the Brahmins. In *Ṛg Veda* 7, 33 we learn that he was *born of the love of the sun-gods Varuṇa and Mitra for Urvaśī, the goddess of the dawn.* Don't ask me why. Usually, goddess Dawn is Uṣas. To make things really complicated, Suhindra Nath Ghose (1953) refers to *Neta, whose other name was Urvashi*. Well and good, maybe the seer Vaśiṣtha married his mother. Or he didn't. Just why should Neta be Urvaśī? The famed Urvaśī was an Apsaras, a celestial nymph, a dancer, singer and musician. She appears in early Vedic literature and was subsequently invoked in love spells, as she unites those who are fated for each other. I have no idea why she should relate to Neta, let alone be her. Sure, Neta doesn't mind doing odd jobs, even if they are as difficult and messy as love-spells. For a bit of attention, love and praise, any deity would. Jībankṛṣṇa Maitra promoted the seer Aṣṭabakra/Aṣṭavakra as Neta's husband. His name means *Eight Parts of his Body Deformed*. This guy is famous for extreme austerities, such as standing in water up to his neck for an eternity. Don't do this: it's uncomfortable, especially when you fall asleep. And he is that charming guy who cursed Neta to be the slave of her elder sister. Baṁsīdās and Sukavi Nārāyaṇ contributed their share. They argued that one day the seer Ugratapā watched Manasā taking a bath. He became aroused and when Manasā walked ashore, he threatened to curse her if she wouldn't go to bed with him. As Manasā's best friend, Neta decided to endure the ordeal. She assumed Manasā's form, ravished the seer and became pregnant. Before long, she gave birth to her son, Ugra Dhanañjay. The seer realised he had been cheated and departed. Neta's marriage is so badly documented that we may ignore it. It was made up to balance Manasā's marriage, lasted less than two minutes, and that's as far as it went.

In several versions of the tale we meet, (see chapter 34) a child in Neta's company. His name is Dhana, Dhanā, Dhanapati or Dāmāl. He may or may not be her son. In Bipradās' version, Neta has two sons, their father being her student Dhanvantari. For good reasons, when Manasā asks Neta to kill Dhanvantari with her venom, Neta refuses.

14. Over there

Manasā's first visit to the human world, her visit to the poor washerwoman and her insolent lads is based on Rādhānāth Rāy Caudhurī. I have elaborated the story quite a bit. In my version, Manasā is almost starved. In Bengal belief, deities who are ignored go hungry and become really difficult. Some are so emaciated that they sink into a lake or disappear into the earth. But Forgotten Ones don't die. They exist in a state close to slumber and wait for the time of their resurrection. When conditions are good, they send a dream to a sensitive person (a village woman or a crazy seer). The dreamer steps into the lake or digs up the earth where indicated and discovers an unusual stone. This rock is the primal manifestation of the sleeping deity. It is carefully cleaned, set up and may be coloured with red powder. To wake, the deity needs plenty of attention. The dreamer and her or his family are the first converts, and they put plenty of passion into their devotion. To wake a Forgotten One you need a lot of faith, power and sheer emotion. Getting the job done may take months or even years of whole-hearted effort. It can be exhausting, frustrating and totally crazy. Crisis scenes are common. On the other hand, you get plenty of divine attention. The Forgotten One wants to be adored and will work miracles, such as healings, grant boons, good luck and so on. Before long, other people join the worship, the stone gets a special shrine near a sacred tree, a river or elsewhere, the entire village may get involved and eventually the freshly reborn deity gains status, admiration and enjoys a surplus of power. Many East Indian deities enjoyed such a career. They started in a family and became major gods of a district, provided they delivered. Cynical people, such as scholars, might imagine that some families take a rock, pretend that it is a deity, and start a religious business producing status and a handsome profit. That, however, is not the norm. As June McDaniel (2003:2-8) expresses, cheating in the name of the gods is risky. Especially when the rock represents a goddess: Bengal goddesses are famous for their vicious nature, and make pretenders suffer. Maybe you noticed that the rock, i.e. the deity, might be discovered in a pool. It's exactly where Manasā emerged from the deep.

15. Duel

Bijay Gupta II related that Dhanvantari met Neta, who liked the guy, cooked serpent soup for him and taught him mantras. The duel between Manasā and Dhanvantari is based on the famous *Brahmā Vaivarta Purāṇa*. It's the only long Manasā story that made it into brahmanical literature. Yes, Manasā throws a lotus and mustard seed at her opponent. Finally, she uses the three-world-destroying magical spear to subjugate Dhanvantari. The gods appeal to the defeated sorcerer to worship Manasā. Neta told me that the spear was a hallucination based on a lotus stalk. She invented the wonderful mantras, and she also improvised the silly dialogues.

The duel between Dhanvantari and Manasā appears in many versions. Usually, it happens before Manasā learns about Cando and kills his six sons (versions of Nārāyaṇ Deb, Baṁsīdās, Sukavi Nārāyan, Tantrabibhūti etc). There are also versions where Dhanvantari, accompanied by a peacock and a mongoose, squats in front of the iron chamber to protect Behulā and Lakhindār during their marriage night. His death happens afterwards (in the anonymous Assamese

Version, in Kṣemānanda, Ketakādās, Jagatjīban and Jībankṛṣṇa Maitra). Dhanvantari has an ambiguous role. Yes, in some versions he is a student of Neta, and may even be her lover. In the anonymous Assamese version Dhanvantari appears to initiate the childless Sonakā into the cult of Manasā. Jagatjīban introduced this idea into his composition. However, he insisted that it wasn't Dhanvantari but Manasā, who had assumed the shape of Dhanvantari.

16. Cowherds

The episode with the herders is widely popular. It may be based on history. Perhaps herders and fishers were the earliest devotees of Manasā. And crazy inspired seers, but they, as we know from daily life, don't count. My version of the tale is based on Bipradās, who also contributed the ritual instructions. Biṣṇu Pal provided the idea that the serpents attack the herders and Tantrabibhūti introduced the episode where the herders try to kill and rape the witches. Sukavi Nārāyaṇ added that some herders were killed and resurrected by Manasā. Bipradās suggested that Manasā first appeared to the herders as an old Brahmin woman and was persecuted as a witch; in Bijay Gupta's version she appears as an aged (male) Brahmin who carries a pot on his head. He relates that the herders learned to call upon Manasā's pot when playing dice.

17. Hāsan and Hussein

This chapter is wonderfully anachronistic. It is based on the Muslim invasion of India. As a side effect, it explains why many East Indian Muslims worship Manasā. Bijay Gupta was enchanted by the tale. By contrast, it is entirely missing in the northern variations of the Epic. With Hāsan and Hussein, we enter the world of politics.

The two kings were historical persons. In real life, they were not kings but famous Muslim saints. Our tale seems to echo the destruction of the Gopa Kings through the invading Muslims. Some tales are quite martial. A gigantic army sets out to crush Manasā's cult. One version, related by Kaiser Haq, enumerates 109.350 soldiers, 65.610 riders, 21.870 soldiers on elephants and 21.870 on battle chariots. They are accompanied by officers, generals and administrators who carry swords in one and the *Qur'an* in their other hand. These numbers are mind-blowing and totally over the top. Manasā, faced by the enemy, makes her serpents emerge from the deep and slaughters her oppressors. The account is detailed, savage and excessive. Sadly, it is also politically incorrect. For good reasons, many poets omitted the episode.

Rādhānāth Rāy Caudhurī supplied the idea that the cow herders, freshly converted, spend so much time celebrating Manasā that the milk deliveries come to a stop. The Hindu wife of King Hāsan comes from the version by Bipradās. She is an interesting element. When a Hindu woman or man married a Muslim, the Hindu's family lost their class and became irreversibly polluted. On the other hand, it could gain profit from being connected to the new ruling class.

Bipradās supplied the king's spy, Gorā Minā, who tramples the throne of the goddess. Sukavi Nārāyaṇ claimed that Manasā killed both kings but resurrected them when their mother asked her to. So far, the accounts remain fairly realistic. They describe suppression, violence, and a bloody revenge. Biṣṇu Pal shifts the tale into a fairy wonderland. In his account, the brothers are anything but mortals. They were created when the Milk Ocean was churned. Incidentally, they were fathered by Śiva's sperm. It's not the usual way how Muslim kings or saints are born. Perhaps we face an attempt to show Islam subservient to Śaivism. The kings flee to heaven, receive no help from the gods, hide in a well, are betrayed by a lizard and caught by Manasā. The lizard is a special character in folk-belief. When a lizard chirps, a raven croaks or someone sneezes, you can expect bad luck. That's because the raven and the lizard are wise. Long ago, the famous female astrologer Khans had her tongue cut off. The lizard ate it. Since then, it knew all future events (Basu, 2005:164). But that's hardly enough. Bengal folklore knew dozens of terrible omens. Here is a selection from folk ballads:

'From the dry bough of yonder tree the raven croaks hoarsely and I hear the ticking of the house-lizard and sound of sneezing.'

'To look back is unlucky.'

'The cow died in the temple space.'

'The cow died at home.'

'Witches are haunting the temples. The blot in the moon has spread and covered her (the moon) entirely. Monkeys have defiled the offerings of the gods.'

'In the air, he thought, he heard the light footsteps of ghosts and evil spirits. The crows and the vultures by their wild cries in the broad daylight struck terror to his heart. A jackal passed by and crossed his path and did not look behind. He heard strange shrieks in the air. Coming home he saw the doors of his house shut from within. The flowers lay all withered in the garden, nor did the bees hum there as usual. The pet birds were mute.'

'The moon and stars hid their faces and the air spoke in inaudible whispers, chilling her very life-blood.'

'Her left eye quivered, which was a sign she did not do well to disclose the secret.'

Part Three: Cāndo

18. Power

We arrive at the midpoint of Manasā's tale. She has learned much, found a few worshippers and is happy. Success seems easy. Śiva discourages her. I have elaborated this scene, as it introduces Cāndo. He is Manasā's greatest enemy. The merchant king appears under a range of names. Apart from Cāndo he is known as Candrapati, Candradhara, Candrapāṇi and Candraketu. He was born a spice-trader (gandhavaṇik, ghāndhika). This class of merchants sold spices, scents, perfumes and incense, but many of them, like Cāndo, also profited from luxury articles and drugs. Spice merchants could be rich but they did not belong to a high class. All merchants are Vaiṣyas (*those who follow orders*), a group that also includes farmers and money lenders. They are barely allowed the ritual of the second birth. Brahmins and warriors looked down on them, unless they needed money, which was usually the case. Among the members of the Vaiṣya class, the spice merchants were almost at the top. Only the gold merchants made greater profits. As their income was out of proportion, Vallāla Sen (1158-1179) reduced their status. It allowed the spice merchants to rise to the top of the Vaiṣya class. When Islam was introduced, the job opportunities for members of the Hindu warrior class dwindled. Many Hindu warriors and aristocrats converted to Islam. It created a power vacuum. Cāndo, a rich merchant, rose to a status that was far above his birth. Upper-class people depended on Cāndo's generosity, on his information network and on his willingness to lend money and accept late payment. Nevertheless, as a mere Vaiṣya, he had to appear humble, religious and generous. In the privacy of his household, Cāndo had himself addressed as 'king', while in company he preferred to be called a 'sāddhu', an ascetic beggar who tends a sacred fire, smokes hashish, worships Śiva and lives on alms. No, I didn't make it up. It's part of his wonderfully complex character. For a young and naive deity, like Manasā, the greatest possible opponent is an egomaniac, a rational materialist, a militant billionaire representing the gospel of Milton Friedman and the Chicago School of Economics. Friedman? Maybe you never heard of him. He shaped the world that you inhabit. Read Naomi Klein's *Shock Doctrine*, if you can take the strain. 'Privatise, deregulate, cut welfare' might be Cāndo's war-cry. He sees it as his god-given duty to control East India. But that's not all. We don't talk 'good against bad', as so many stupid people do. Cāndo isn't evil. He honestly believes he's doing everyone a favour, and he leads a religious crusade to make the world a better place. He pities himself for working day and night, while other people laze and enjoy, at his expense.

Plenty of scholars tried to prove or disprove the historicity of Cāndo. The spice merchants believe that their class descended from Candra Bhava, who is otherwise known as Cand Saudagar. This person may have inspired Cāndo's name. D. C. Sen tried to identify Cāndo as a famous trader of the sixth or seventh century. N.K. Bhattasali disagreed; in his opinion Cāndo is based on Śrī Candra Deva, a king of East Bengal, who governed around 975-1000. Other scholars proposed Hariścandra, a Buddhist king. Their claim is weak, as the *Manasā Epic* lacks Buddhist elements. In short, the Cāndo of our story is a blend of various real or legendary figures (Maity, 1966/2001:164-167). And there were Cāndos who appeared long after the epic was composed. Like Omichand, an enormously fat Jaina, who controlled most of the business of the early East India Company, and whose network of informers made him the unofficial king of East Asia. Omichand financed most of the palaces of the new city Calcutta and lived in the richest of them, the only native in the 'white town'. When the British made the tragic mistake of putting him in goal, they aroused his fury. As a result, the Nawab raised an army to destroy them.

Our Cāndo comes in several varieties. I have chosen the common figure of the Merchant King. There are also a few traditions where Cāndo is a real king, who, unlike normal kings, spends an amazing amount of time trading. His past lives were elaborated by several poets (Ketakādās, Bijay Gupta II, Baṁsīdās, Sukavi Nārāyaṇ), who explained how that low-class person could be so mighty, influential and magically successful. In several versions, Cāndo received magickal gifts from Śiva and Durgā. These are represented as physical objects. That's typical for storytelling and movies: we might be dealing with abstract qualities, but we need material objects to signify them. In the version by Ketakādās, Cāndo wears his hair in a long tangle, just like Śiva does, and indeed Śiva invests Cāndo's locks with magical power. Manasā has to ruin Cāndo's hairstyle to destroy his power. Bijay Gupta II relates that Śiva empowered Cāndo with a magical piece of cloth and a mantra: Manasā has to steal the cloth. She charms the trader until he reveals the mantra. Bipradās preferred a combination: Śiva equips Cāndo with magical locks and a magical towel/scarf. In Bijay Gupta's tale, Manasā steals Cāndo's victory scarf and waterpot.

19. Fishermen

My version of this chapter was mostly inspired by Bipradās and Biṣṇu Pal. Tantrabibhūti invented the episode where Manasā changes the boat to gold, and the fishermen implore her to turn it into a real boat again. He was a religious man and understood that gold, without its symbolic value, has very few uses. Like herders, fishers made up (or make up?) a large amount of Manasā's devotees. Maybe these population groups were, just as the story goes, among her first worshippers. Smith mentions a range of fisher-classes, such as the Mālo, Tiyar, Kaibarta, Bauri, Bāgdi, Rājbansis and Keut. These, plus several others, venerate Manasā as their class goddess. The same applies to many Muslim fishers, who have no social class in the Hinduistic sense, but know that Manasā has a heart for them. By the way, the class-name 'Keut' means *cobra*.

The city Campaka has its name from a flowering tree (Michelia champaka). Another version of the name is Campakanagar, a real place in Burdwan and allegedly Cāndo's birthplace. Sadly, this was not a glorious capital but was, until recent times, a village. The river flowing nearby is called 'Behulā' by the locals. They say she started her raft journey on it. Others disagree. Settlements called Campakanagar also exist in Tripura and Malda, and the locals are certain that this is where Cāndo resided. A former city called Campā or Campakanagar is also suspected in Bhagalpur, province Bihar. Nearby is a place called Ujānī, where Behulā was born. The place called Sanakāgram near Dinajpur is the legendary birthplace of Sonakā. The locals will tell you that Cāndo's real residence was there. The inhabitants of the Eastern Himalayas swear that Cāndo's palace was at the shore of River Rangit in Darjeeling. And that's just the start. We are still talking possibilities. Some scholars have done their best to locate Cāndo's miraculous city in Southern India, where Manasā is unknown (Maity, 2001:131-133).

20. Sonakās Conversion

The conversion of the fishermen represents a rite of passage: Manasā's cult crosses a river and finds a place in the human world. She comes closer to Cāndo. The conversion of Sonakā appears in plenty of versions. Bijay Gupta wrote that Sonakā worshipped Manasā since she was a child. In the anonymous Assamese version, Dhanvantari initiates Sonakā into the cult of the serpent goddess. I made use of an episode by Bişņu Pal, who suggested that Manasā was so enchanted and bedazzled by the city Campaka that she wanted to kill and abduct all inhabitants and their settlement, and set them up somewhere on Sij Mountain. Bişņu Pal had much to say regarding the persecution of the fishers by Cāndo's henchmen. Bipradās supplied the storyline how the fishers worship Manasā and Sonakā buys their golden pot. Other elements come from Baṁsīdās and Sukavi Nārāyaņ: Durgā appears to Cāndo and orders him to destroy Manasā's cult. She arms him with the deadly Hemtāla staff.

21. Conflict

Jagatjīban knew how to extend his tale. In his version, Manasā gives Cāndo plenty of opportunities to worship her. She appears to him, but Cāndo despises low-class deities. Next time, Śiva appears and asks Cāndo to worship Manasā. Cāndo refuses. As a last resort, Manasā appears again. She is nude, except for a few serpents here and there, and angry. She announces that she will kill Cāndo's six sons unless he gives in. Cāndo is proud, chases Manasā with his magical staff and has to face the consequences.

Sukavi Nārāyaņ did his best to absolve Manasā of all guilt. In his version, Śiva advises Manasā to kill Cāndo's six sons. She is a good girl and does what daddy says. Personally, I find these interpretations too soft. Manasā is a high goddess in the making, and her favourite animals are lethal. There is a darksome, bitchy side to her character. The killing of Cāndo's sons and the destruction of Cāndo's property are common elements of the tale; they were elaborated by most poets. Bipradās invented the funny episode where the sons eat watered rice, joke with their wives, and pretend to die from their meal. In his version, the small, black Kāli snake spewed her poison into the dish. I asked Neta, she said, like you and me, she wouldn't mind playing a savage role.

22. Dhanvantari

We meet our ambitious, success-hungry snake doctor again. He has grown old, has attained the summit of mastery and forgotten the purpose of his life in a haze of fame and profit. His death appears in several variations. Bişņu Pal had Dhanvantari's death before Manasā even meets Cāndo. In the northern versions (except for Tantrabibhūti), Dhanvantari lives much longer and meets his death after Lakhindār died. Bijay Gupta II informs us that Neta trained Dhanvantari and fed him snake broth. The ominous falcon (Manasā in a bird-form) comes from the anonymous Assamese version. Dhanvantari gets the message: he turns around and goes home. It's a nice touch: the serpent goddess tries to warn the sorcerer. In my tale, he is too self-important to heed her advice. Ketakādās and Tantrabibhūti recorded that Dhanvantari implored Cāndo to cut him to pieces and use his parts as a magical defence to protect the house and its inhabitants. Baṁsīdās and Sukavi Nārāyaņ: Neta in cow form eats all healing herbs. Bipradās: Manasā deceives the greedy students of Dhanvantari and eventually kills them. Bişņu Pal provided a similar account. In his tale, Dhanvantari is granted the boon to be reborn as a snake which Manasā occasionally wears around her neck. He also introduces a 'demoness' who abducts the corpses of the six dead sons from their rafts and keeps them in storage, in her *'Temple of Decay'* (the Jaraņi Maņdap) until they are needed by Manasā. In his tale, the 'demoness' has no name, elsewhere, she seems to be Neta.

23. Journey to Anupāma Pāţan

Bipradās wrote that Śiva appeared to Cāndo in a dream, and told him to make an extensive trading voyage. In various versions, Cāndo's fleet consists of seven (six and a flagship), twelve or fourteen ships. No doubt there is significance to these numbers. Baṁsīdās, Sukavi Nārāyaṇ, Jībankṛṣṇa Maitra and Rādhānāth Caudurī detailed how the journey is prepared. The forest ceremony is elaborated; the account involves rituals and the selection of many different types of wood. Some poets made up catalogues of trees, many of which were never used to build boats with. It's almost like the preparation for a magical journey. Cāndo's voyage goes either to Sri Lanka or to the entirely fictional island Anupāma Pāṭan. Sri Lanka, for many badly educated Bengalis, was a terrible, mythical place. The *Rāmāyana* relates that the island is full of man-eating demons, nature spirits and anti-gods. However, Anupāma Pāṭan is even crazier. Bipradās came up with the idea that Cāndo enjoyed the luxuries of Anupāma Pāṭan for twelve years, until one day Manasā appeared to him in a dream, looking like Sonakā, and implored her husband to get a move on. It provided enough time for his son Lakhindār to grow up.

24. Journey to Dakṣiṇ Pātana.

Several poets described how Cāndo does his business. These people were realists. The merchant king, like all the great exploiters of South East Asia, takes as much as he can get. He exchanges cheap turmeric against gold, cotton against Chinese silk, rice against pearls, buffalo-cows against elephants and long, white radishes against ivory. There is a semi-historical element to the tale. It might reflect trade before the reign of the Pala kings, when the people of Bengal still undertook long sea voyages. The coconut scene is based on Nārāyaṇ Deb, Baṁsīdās and Sukavi Nārāyaṇ. The very idea that the inhabitants of Sri Lanka, Southern India and the islands in the Indian Ocean were not acquainted with coconuts is absurd. Cāndo need not have stored any on his ships. I wonder if he travelled in some strange dreamland.

In the version by Tantrabibhūti, Cāndo proves his innocence by eating the coconut. Biṣṇu Pal had Cāndo locked up without reason.

25. Return

Manasā borrows Indra's vajra thunderbolt and/or warclub. The tale is widely known. I asked Neta for all the details which the poets overlooked. She's been to Indra's kitchen and knows everything; the cooking, the aged fat and the cockroaches, and what Indra gobbles down when no-one watches. Neta insists that, unless you want your thyroid glands to go gaga and your brain to shrink, you should avoid soy. For details, see Lierre Keith (2009: 2011-229). The cursing of Gaṅgā comes from Bijay Gupta II.

26. Coming Home

Cāndo's odyssey is one of the great favourites. The poets went to extremes. There are so many variants that I merely picked out a few significant ones. The huge lotus blossom floating over the water: Ketakādās, Bipradās, Baṁsīdās, Sukavi Nārāyaṇ and Tantrabibhūti. The crow which wakes Cāndo and shits in his face: Tantrabibhūti. Monkey god Hanumān as an ascetic: anonymous Bihar version. Manasā appears as a female ascetic and gives Cāndo a (polluted) piece of cloth: Bijay Gupta, Ketakādās, and Bipradās. Cāndo tries to eat a wasp-nest: Sukavi Nārāyaṇ and Bijay Gupta. The woodcutters: Bijay Gupta and Rādhānāth Rāy Caudhurī. Cāndo sells fish: Nārāyaṇ Deb, Baṁsīdās, Sukavi Nārāyaṇ. A strange Brahmin tries to marry his weird, one-eyed daughter (i.e. Manasā) to Cāndo: Baṁsīdās, Sukavi Nārāyaṇ and Bijay Gupta. And of course Cāndo is not allowed to eat the (polluting) banana peels dropped by the beggars. Neta warns him; well, at least Baṁsīdās said so. I asked her; she says she wouldn't give a damn. Several poets tried to keep Cāndo unpolluted. Bijay Gupta was so excited by this topic that he composed three highly similar episodes which don't convince anyone. Cāndo receives food from a Brahmin woman but a crow shits into it: Tantrabibhūti. He must have had a thing about crows. Or shit. The episode where Cāndo carries pottery and is scared by a tiger is widely popular. He meets an old friend and is carried in a palanquin (which disintegrates): Bijay Gupta II. And so on. No matter what Cāndo does, it hurts. That, so Tantrabibhūti informs us, was *'Neta's excellent advice'*.

Of course this is coarse humour. Most people who listened to the epic or saw it performed were anything but rich. They enjoyed the downfall of the merchant king, and everything he represented. Humour requires pain. It also contains truth: the tribulations of Cāndo are educational. Many ordeals could have been valuable learning experiences. They could have made the Merchant King a better and more humane person. The gods don't simply play their vengeful games with him. The deeper he falls, the better are his chances to learn something valuable. Cāndo experiences his very own, custom-tailored abyss. He has every chance to embrace humility, empathy and tolerance. He could even have understood that low-class people are valuable human beings, and that greed, and vanity, and a workaholic's painful daily nightmare should be limited. It does not work. The best conditions cannot make a stupid student learn. Some people simply go more stupid.

The episode where Cāndo comes home, is mistaken for a thief, and beaten up by his guards and family is quite popular. Several poets indulged in full, and painful detail. And of course the prophet who announced the thief is...ah, you know who. Let a girl have a bit of fun. Grand finale: the traveller comes home. Be it Agamemnon or Cāndo: they get what they asked for.

Part Nine: Behulā

27. Heaven

We are facing the most popular section of the epic. This is where things truly become human, and the humane becomes divine. It turned Behulā into the greatest heroine of East India. But we are dealing with an epic. For good reasons, our poets started very early, i. e. quite a bit before the protagonists of this tale were born. Behulā and Lakhindār, they assumed, had to have a heavenly pre-life. Usually, the couple is identified as Ūṣā and Aniruddha, two favourite characters from the *Purāṇas*. Tantrabibhūti recorded that in a previous existence, they were Sāvritī and Satyavan. Another version, by Dvarika, claims that Śiva cursed Indra's son Nilambara and his wife Chāya to be reborn as Behulā and Lakhindār. Is this enough? By no means. Several poets assumed that our protagonists were originally Kāma (*Desire, Lust, Love*) and his passionate wife Ratī (*Wantonness*). For divine standards, that's pretty much amazing. Kāma and Ratī are overwhelming cosmic powers. Most of the gods are much younger, and stand in awe of them. In short, our human protagonists, just like the great heroes of the *Mahābhārata*, are incarnate deities. It explains a bit. Nevertheless, their divinity is much reduced. When gods incarnate, they face trouble. For one thing, most of their powers are gone and for another, human stupidity remains a mystery to them. Incarnate gods need a lot of support, which usually comes from other gods. That's why they pray to others when they might as well pray to themselves, and spend their days yearning for an inexplicable wholeness they can hardly express. That's one interpretation. You could imagine that a personified deity incarnates. Another interpretation emphasises that we, whether gods or people, are all manifestations of the All-self, call it Brahman, Śiva, Viṣṇu, Lakṣmī, Kālī, Manasā or, for a triple helping of weird humour, Neta. Being divine on earth is possible for anyone. Look around: each person has divine potential. That's as far as it goes. Sadly, it ain't good enough. Potential makes people vain and lazy. Neta prefers those who really make an effort, and persist.

The greatness of Behulā and Lakhindār is their vulnerability.

Biṣṇu Pal related that the souls of our lovers hurled themselves into the sacrificial fire as bees and whirled through the flames into the human world. Fire, sacrificial and otherwise, is a gateway between the worlds. In Nārāyaṇ Deb's version, Indra allows Manasā to dispose of the souls as she pleases. At this point (I left this out), Yama, the Lord of Death, protests. Every soul that dies, he roars, belongs to him. Manasā disagrees. Within instants, Yama and Manasā duel each other. When Yama is overwhelmed by Manasā's serpent army, he gives up. It's a nice tale and perfect to extend a long story. However, we had too many instances of Manasā's serpent army enforcing things.

28. Beans

In this chapter, several problems came up. Just why would Cāndo, a cold-minded, calculating money-maker, ask Behulā to do something as patently impossible as cook iron bits into a bean dish? Is he trying to test her spiritual ability? Or is he trying to find an excuse to cancel the match? I have no idea. To this day, the people of Bengal use the expression 'cooking iron beans' to indicate something impossible. Bijay Gupta II has an extra test for our girl: Cāndo hands her a dead fish and she is supposed to bring it to back to life. Luckily, Behulā is an expert in meditation: she recites a mantra and the fish revives. The fish-theme also appears in Rādhānāth Rāy Caudhurī's version. Behulā has her bath in the river. She emerges from the water holding treasure, which she found in the mud, and a dead fish, which she revives.

I have elaborated how Cāndo tests his potential daughter-in-law. It's nasty, I agree, that she is examined for her obedience, submissiveness, beauty, elegance, posture and teeth, but it's also realistic. Such examinations were common. As Cāndo expects Behulā to be the wife of a businessman, he also wants to see her handwriting and her skill in maths.

How old are our protagonists? When we accept the ideal ages for marriage, as attested by high-ranking Kanoj Brahmins, our heroes are between eight and twelve years old. It makes no sense. Our story deals with adult problems. Smith tells us that in traditional literature, Lakhindār is usually seventeen and Behulā twelve. Neta disagrees; Behulā is far more intelligent than he is. And seventeen is too young, at least by Western standards. On the other hand, kids in the pre-industrial world grew up faster than children do nowadays. They had a damn sight more life experience, hence their frontal cortex developed faster than in the shallow minded brats who waste their youths playing computer games. And this is not a joke.

As the souls of Behulā and Lakhindār flew into the flame simultaneously, I gave them the same age. It turned Behulā into a spinster: the girl is seventeen and hasn't even got three children.

Now for a few details. Behulā's family trades, just like the family of Lakhindār, with spices, perfumes, drugs and luxuries. Her hometown might be Ujāni or Nichānī. Ketakādās related the prophecy and supplied the name of Behulā's mother, Amalā. It means *pure, shining, without taint*, and is also a name of Lakṣmī and of Bombay hemp (Hibiscus cannabinus). He inspired the scene where Behulā meets Manasā at the ghāt and receives her curse. The anonymous Bihar version is similar: Behulā goes for a bath, splatters the old woman and is cursed. Bipradās gives the name of Sāha's wife as Sumitrā (*Nice Friend, Many Friends*, a wife of Kṛṣṇa, a Yakṣī), Rādhānāth Rāy Caudhurī called her Kamalā (*Lotus*), which is also a name of Manasā and Lakṣmī. While the southern poets named Behulā's father Sāha, the northern transmission called him Bācho and her mother Menakā (*Fish-Eyed*). That goddess is the wife of King Himavat (the Himalayas), the mother of Pārvatī/Durgā. One way or another, there are plenty of divine figures in Behulā's family. The poets simply messed them up.

29. Plans

My version follows several poets. Manasā forces the smith to leave a gap or hole in the iron chamber. In the anonymous Bihar version, the smith has three functions: he creates the deadly Hemtāla staff, the iron beans and the iron chamber. Plenty of cultures assumed that smiths are somehow magical. Either they admired or despised them. The Hindu's chose the latter.

30. Marriage

We arrive at the midpoint of Behulā's story. So-called 'mock-combats' or, more often, real fights, were a common element in marriage rituals. Baṁsīdās invented the scene where Manasā appears as a tantric yoginī and asks Cāndo for alms. Well, she was asking for trouble, and quite happy that it happened.

Then there is the death of Lakhindār: some poets couldn't get enough of it, and made him die twice. Manasā, carrying the bow and arrows which she had borrowed (= coerced) from god Kāma, killed Lakhindār during the marriage ceremony. I disagree: Kāma's arrows cause intolerable love and yearning, they don't kill, unless that love is frustrated. Behulā shows her mind-blowing holiness and revives him. The bridegroom gets up, staggers, smiles like an idiot and continues with the ceremony. Bipradās, Bijay Gupta and Biṣṇu Pal agreed that Manasā killed him during the marriage rite; Behulā made a terrible scene and threatened to behead herself, so Manasā was forced to revive her husband. Later that night he dies again. Sorry, this is simply too much. Neta says: "one death a night is enough for everyone". Kṣemānanda and Dvarika showed better sense and allowed the marriage to proceed without interruption.

31. Iron House

The topic appears everywhere. Sure, there are variations. The poets were not decided on which snake enters the iron house first, or what it gets done. Baṁsīdās relates that Behulā waits until Lakhindār is asleep. She picks up his clothes and dresses in them. She hopes that any intrusive snake may be deceived, and kill her instead of him. It's an amazing change. Behulā assumes a 'male' role, and will continue to do so, until she has resurrected her husband. The anonymous version from Assam has a strange feature. It claims that the python Ajagara enters the iron house and kills Lakhindār with its toxin. It's embarrassing. Since when are pythons equipped with poison? And just why should the very snake who was afraid to become Manasā's husband do this job? Another anonymous version, this one from Bihar, also employs a python. Sadly, the fat beast can't enter the tiny hole in the Iron House. It has to be massaged until it can go through. Is this a joke? The same author claimed that the raft which carried Behulā and the corpse of her husband downstream was made of iron. You may begin to understand why this version is anonymous. Honestly, how stupid can a story get?

Lakhindārs death is an essential point in the story. Most poets argued that it was his fault. Lakhindār forces his young wife to cook for him and, worse yet, coaxes her to make love with him. Both acts are extremely unlucky on the wedding night. At least in Bengal. In Assam, marriage customs differ. Things can be even more extreme. In the anonymous northern version, Lakhindār sins before he marries. The Apsaras (heavenly dancing girl, divine nymph) Kāmasonā assumes the shape of Lakhindār's aunt Kośalya. She tempts him, until Lakhindār, a victim of his oversized balls, loses control. Later he meets his real aunt Kośalya at the riverside, makes unpleasant advances and rapes her. The vile Karman of this act catches up with him and condemns him to death in the marriage night. And it produces, much later, the worst crisis in Behulā's journey. When she learns that her dead husband is a rapist, her world comes apart. It's an extreme take. Most poets were not aware of this episode, nor would they have approved of it. They noted that Lakhindār was a victim of his marriage night offences, but forgave him. Manasā sends snake after snake into the bridal chamber, and nearly every one refuses to bite him.

32. At the Shore

The incapable serpent sorcerer was invented by Kṛttibās. Dhanvantari's son comes from Nārāyaṇ Deb, Baṁsīdās and Sukavi Nārāyaṇ.

33. Downstream

Behulā's journey is the most touching episode of the *Epic*. We travel with a girl who goes insane. As a Bengal proverb says: *'I have no offering for the gods than my tears'.*

Though the heroine is an incarnate goddess or an Apsaras, she is humane enough to move the audience. Unlike so many characters in our story, Behulā is almost free of blemish. In most versions of the *Epic*, Behulā's journey is elaborated until boredom sets in. Six months is a long time. There are far too many episodes with rapists, seducers, robbers, and savage animals. Forgive me: I have reduced the obstacles to a minimum. Let's list a few. Omens shall indicate that Lakhindār comes to life again: Ketakādās. Cāndo implores Behulā not to throw her life away: June McDaniel. Sonakā rages against Behulā, widows and independent women: Ketakādās and Dvarika. A crow (Manasā in disguise) asks for a peck and receives a ring: Bipradās.

Behulā's brothers are a bit strange. In most versions, they simply don't exist. They should have been there when Cāndo visited Sāha, when Behulā cooked the beans, when the bride was collected, the marriage happened, the newlyweds were escorted to the iron house, the raft was equipped and Behulā went floating. They were not. That's odd. Now all of a sudden Behulā sees them standing at the riverside. It sounds as if they were invented for this scene. Or as if they are a hallucination. Tantrabibhūti mentions their six wives. Just to extend the story?

The king who carries the talkative corpse is my own addition. It is based on the wonderful Indian collection *Twenty-five Tales of the Vetāla-spirit* (*Vetālapañcaviṁśati*). There are several versions and numerous translations available. You'll love them.

Ketakādās makes Behulā encounter villains, dogs and jackals. She prays to Manasā when her raft disintegrates. In Biṣṇu Pal's version, Behulā pays a visit to the Temple of Decay. Neta as a tigress appears in the versions of Bijay Gupta, Sukavi Nārāyaṇ, Rādhānāth Rāy Caudhurī and Nārāyaṇ Deb. The crippled fisher with elephantiasis comes from Ketakādās. Sukavi Nārāyaṇ preferred two. The horny Ḍom entertainer/sorcerer and the fish that carries away parts of Lakhindār's foot appear in Kṣemānanda. Apart from these, the amount of potential rapists, thieves and killers is immense. Among them feature, in various versions, customs inspectors, pirates, traders, gamblers, holy men, a brother of Behulā and two demon kings. The waters of Gaṅgā fail to revive Lakhindārs corpse: Ketakādās.

34. Dark Waters

Behulā has reached her 'black point'. Things simply can't go worse. She has arrived in that mind-space where she will die or transcend her former self. We are back to Neta. Time for the second coming: CONFESSIONS OF A WASHERWOMAN.

Neta washes corpses. She takes them apart, pulls out the organs, cleans them in the dark waters of the Underworld, hangs them up and allows the sun to dry them. Afterwards, she reassembles the deceased. Baṁsīdās, for instance, describes how Neta washes the dead Dhanvantari. She puts extra effort into the purification and drying of his guts before she allows him to carry on with his journey to the otherworld.

Her bizarre occupation is more than a hobby. All over Eurasia, we encounter myths of dismemberment, purification and resurrection. Countless shamans were killed by their favourite spirits and gods, chopped to pieces, cooked, devoured and finally put together again. Good initiations can be messy. Similar ideas can be found in European myth, see *Cauldron of the Gods* for details. Dismemberment rituals are a form of initiation or self-healing. The remarkable Tibetan ascetic nun, Machig Labdrön, turned such rituals into a series of highly effective meditations. Closely related are the tantric Left Hand Path meditations where initiates imagined their own death and decay and finally resurrected themselves from cosmic vibrations, rainbow light and divine essence. Or consider the tantric trances where adepts imagine that their entire body, self and identity are burned to cinders. Afterwards, they create a fresh body for themselves and come out of their trance much happier than before. All of these are typical cremation and cemetery meditations. They were more popular in Kashmir, Bengal and Assam than in the rest of India.

Neta may be a washerwoman, but here we meet her as a tantric goddess of death and transcendence. That's an essential idea. Manasā guides your way from birth to death, while Neta collects the dead (or those she fancies), purifies them, and makes them ready for rebirth.

Several writers refer to Neta's child. He is a bit of a surprise. During most of the Epic, Neta lives with Manasā. Children rarely appear. Sure, thanks to the *Mahābhārata*, Manasā gave birth to Āstika; he grew up to be a fine young seer, ended the serpent sacrifice and walked away. He doesn't visit Sij Mountain or even sends a postcard to his mum. Nor is Manasā troubled by his absence. Neta, who only married as Manasā did, has even less to do with her alleged child. And now, all of a sudden, we meet a child in her company. Unlike Āstika, Neta's kid never grew up. Though some authors insist the boy is Neta's son, I am not entirely sure and left the relationship between them open. His name appears in several versions: Dhana, Dhanā, Dhonā, Dhanapati, Dāmāl and Dhanañjay. Dvarika and Biṣṇu Pal added a brother, whose name is Manā or Monā. The child-killing episode appears in the *Epics* of Dvarika, Sukavi Nārāyaṇ and in the anonymous Bihar version. It does not appear in the versions by Kṣemānanda, Baṁsīdās, Rādhānāth Rāy Caudhurī and in the anonymous Bihar version.

We encounter Neta as a (badly documented) goddess of some Nātha (*lord*) tantrics of the 16th century. The Nātha cult emerged sometime after the 12th or 13th century. It produced a range of amazing adepts who seem to have believed in a wide range of different ideologies. Most of them had a thing about immortality. They just couldn't agree on how to gain it. Many favoured haṭhayoga, and painful ascetic exercises, to immortalise their bodies, and some used astonishing chemical drugs, incorporating plenty of mercury, to get the job done. Some assumed that immortality would happen while they were still alive. Others saw all their effort as a wonderful preparation for an immortality that could be attained only after the physical body had ceased to function. In a spiritual body, free from the limitations imposed by shape, birth and Karman, they were sure to outlast the universes, one after the other. These adepts were not interested in the cult of Manasā, but they worshipped Neta. Smith (1980:60) cites a line from a 16th-century Nātha composition:

The moon is the post and the sun the board,
Day and night the washerwoman washes at the ghāt of Triveni.

The post represents the Vedic ritual pillar. The board might have been used to crush the ingredients of the Soma drug. Our washerwoman is performing a ritual act. Tribeni is far more than a geographical or mythological location. In Nātha lore, and in many tantric systems, Triveni/Tribeni, the *Confluence of Three Rivers*, is the ājñā cakra, the *'circle of administration'*, the energy/consciousness confluence between the eyebrows. At Tribeni, the major three inner channels meet, and individual consciousness, duly purified, passes into the universal self. That's one explanation. According to another, Tribeni is not at the third eye but at the perineum, the root cakra. Many Left Hand Tantrics claimed that transcendence is not necessary and that the divine should be enjoyed in the material world.

Let's have a look at Gorakṣanāth. He was a famous tantric who allegedly wrote the *Siddha Siddhānta Paddhati,* a great favourite of the Nāthas. In our chapter, for the fun of it, Neta recites some passages from his book. Gorakṣanāth, so a legend of the *Gorakṣa Bijay Gupta* claims, once demonstrated his yogic powers over life and death. He grabbed a boy, killed him, washed his intestines, dried them on a washing line and put the child together again. He was as good as new and possibly better. It's Neta's story.

Tantrabibhūti also had a corpse washing scene. In his account, it was done by an Asurā (anti-goddess, demoness) called **Tārakā**. The name means *Little Tārā*. Tārā, the Saviouress, the *One who Carries You Across the Ocean of Being*, is a major goddess of East Asia. Plenty of scholars identify her as a Buddhist goddess. That's because the Buddhists, in particular those of Tibet, made her a major event. You can find a lot of useful material in Beyer's *The Cult of Tārā* (1978). We meet Tāra in Hindu lore long before the Buddhists gobbled her up. The earliest reference I could find is in the *Mahābhārata*, when Prince Arjuna invokes Kālī, Durgā, Tāriṇī and other goddesses to grant him victory. The episode appears directly before the *Bhagavad Gītā*. It dates around the third or fourth century. By the seventh century, we meet Tārā as a North Indian Hindu and Buddhist deity. Several centuries later, she became the national goddess of Tibet. Tārā means a *star, meteor, rescuer, saviour* and *eye*. A goddess called Tārakā (*Little Tārā*) is the wife of Bṛhaspati, the guru and priest of the Vedic gods. 'Eye' is interesting. I'm sure you remember the folk etymology that traces Neta's name to netra, meaning *eye*. Tārā is the foreign goddess, imported, with the know-how of mercury and cinnabar alchemy, from far away Mahācīna (*Great China*). Consider her a goddess of alchemy. In *Kālī Kaula*, I have elaborated on her similarity to the Chinese goddess Xiwangmu. Hindus and Buddhists immediately fell in love with her. Whenever life is terrifying, you can call on Tārā. As a foreign goddess, Tārā had no iconography. The Hindus made Tārā look like Kālī while the Buddhists copied Lakṣmī. I'm sure this says something about Neta.

Tārāka, the *Little Saviouress*, is Neta, and her mantra, according to the *Mantra Mahodhadhiḥ* (1992:207, 209), is

Auṁ Tāṁ Tārake Praticcha Svāhā.

In Tantrabibhūti's tale, Tārakā disembowels and washes the corpses of Cāndo's six sons. When their organs are clean, dry, and lovely, she carries them to her Temple of Decay and hangs them up for storage. Manasā puts a spell on them to keep them fresh.

Bijay Gupta, Nārāyaṇ Deb, Sukavi Nārāyaṇ, Rādhānāth Rāy Caudhurī and the author of the anonymous Bihar version describe how Behulā helps Neta do the washing of the gods. It's another class-violation: a merchant daughter is too pure to do anybody's washing. More so, she takes great care and washes the clothes cleaner than Neta does. Well, she's motivated. Neta is not. Ketakādās and Bijay Gupta made much of the scene; they emphasised Behulā's devotion to Neta, and turn her into Behulā's patroness.

Bijay Gupta has Behulā say: "*I see no other salvation for myself save Neto*" (Smith, 1980:121).

That's why I had to give an extra spin to the story. Behulā has come a long way and she is clearly finished. In true tantric tradition, Behulā has to ask Neta to wash her. Her only release is the Dark Waters. Neta Carries her Across the Ocean of Life.

Behulā's dance shows, better than anything, that she's been through hell and came out stronger. She has acquired a mindset that allows her to face the gods and confront Manasā. In Behulā's storyline, this is her triumph. Anything that follows simply plays out what happens here.

To satisfy Śiva, she puts all of herself into the dance. It's grandiose. And it's another major offence against the class order. Upper-class women never danced for others. It puts Behulā on a level with the lowest of the lowest: she gains the status of an untouchable Ḍom girl. The Ḍom class fulfilled (and fulfils) several functions. Some Ḍom were entertainers, travelling musicians, dancers and prostitutes. Some built the pyres and tended the cremation fires, handled the corpses and their ashes. The poorest spent their days dredging the muck at the cremation ghāts. They still do, especially at Varanasi, where cremation is a major industry. If they are lucky, they find half-molten ornaments and gold-teeth. Nobody, except for hard-core Left Hand Path tantrics, had a good word for Ḍoms.

Several poets made a grandiose scene out of Manasā's refusal to confess her guilt. It's almost like a theatrical play. Who does she try to fool? Nārāyaṇ Deb, Baṁsīdās and Sukavi Nārāyaṇ described how Behulā produced the tail end of the snake that killed her husband, and Manasā claimed she's never seen that snake. The serpent goddess tries to hide, is exposed, goes bitchy, and Behulā has a chance to triumph over her. It must have done her good. Call it therapy, if you like.

Biṣṇu Pal and Bijay Gupta relate the episode where Manasā hides the corpse and the raft, and Behulā threatens suicide. The resurrection of Lakhindār is self-evident. The same goes for the recovery of the missing bit of Lakhindār's foot. The strange spell which Manasā uses is an anti-toxin glam; it comes from Ketakādās. I am sure it was invented by people who did not like snakes. Why Manasā recites it is traditional and remains a mystery. Here is another anti-serpent-toxin spell; it comes from a ballad:

Poison, descend to the breast of the patient. Poison, descend to the knees, Poison sink to the feet. Black snake of the Underworlds, suck the poison from the feet and leave the patient soothed.

35. Back

Manasā makes Behulā and Lakhindār's return a triumph. She raises Cāndo's ships and resurrects his drowned sailors. In some versions, such as that of Ketakādās, she even creates new ships full of treasure and adds them to Cāndo's fleet. Sure, she wants to impress the greedy old man. But even more so, she wants to make a gesture that everyone in Campaka is bound to talk about.

The fleet is ready to sail. According to Biṣṇu Pal, Bijay Gupta and Bipradās, Śiva comes around to say goodbye. He is so delighted by Behulā's freshly acquired tantric charm that he tries to seduce her. Sorry, I had to leave it out. This book might be read by children.

Behulā's journey balances Cāndo's journey. But while Cāndo merely survives, and comes home more twisted than ever, Behulā realises her divinity and finds liberation. Finally, the ships arrive in Campaka. Behulā dresses as a Ḍom girl. She has nothing to lose. It's an enormous step: Behulā says goodbye to her class, and to the Hindu class system. This is Left Hand Tantra. Her gaudy, much revealing costume serves as her protection: Sonakā doesn't recognise her. Most authors related the tale of the magical fan. The anonymous version from Bihar is different: Behulā sells a basket to Sonakā. Basket making is another typical Ḍom industry.

36. Thanksgiving

Well and good, things should be easy now. They are not. Cāndo hates the way Manasā fooled him with the fan. Sure, he has his sons back and a huge profit besides. It doesn't satisfy him. Like the industrial world, Cāndo is an insatiable hungry mouth. Call him 'progress' if you like, until he'll eat you up.

Several poets claim that when Cāndo heard the good news, he wasn't satisfied. Before he would even consider Manasā as a deity, she should prove her powers and make the ships fly all the way to his palace door. The other merchants are shocked: how could he be so ungrateful? Manasā smiles and tries to think happy thoughts while her poison glands swell. She raises her serpent army. The flood of reptiles lifts the ships and carries them all the way to Cāndo's doorstep. Much good will they do him there.

Tantrabibhūti relates another nasty event. Cāndo insists that Manasā worships him before he'll worship her. Manasā almost kills him. Finally, she calms down a bit. Instead of bowing before him, she gives him an almost lethal look and makes a screen appear which shows Cāndo in the company of the gods. The merchant realises he won't get more, and gives in.

Finally, Cāndo performs a grandiose pūjā for Manasā. It signals that hostilities are over and that he greets her as a guest.

He hates it. Many poets relate that he tries to make his offerings with his left hand. In Tantrabibhūti's version he explains that he offers to Śiva and Durgā with his right hand: how could he use the same hand to honour Manasā?

In Ksemanandra's tale, Cāndo and Manasā face each other during the pūjā like duelists. Cāndo tries to insult Manasā with small, nasty gestures. Manasā seizes Cāndo's mind and muddles his words. Accidentally he says "Jay Debī" (*Triumph to the Goddess!)* and that's it. He has acknowledged her. The serpent goddess smiles. Her teeth show. Cāndo almost collapses. He has lost and he knows it. In the version by Baṁsīdās, Cāndo is just as bad. The ceremony can't find a conclusion and the gods are getting edgy. Finally, Durgā snarls that he should get his act together and worship Manasā. It must have been hard. Cāndo refuses. Durgā declares that she and Manasā are the same. Cāndo objects. If this were the case, which he doubts, Manasā should be content when Durgā gets sacrifices, as she would also receive her share. *"Why does one-eyed Padmā come back and ask for separate pūjā?"* At this point Cāndo is close to the edge. In Bijay Gupta's version, Durgā explains:

"Listen Cāndo the merchant, I am telling you,
I am one form, there is no other,
He who is Brahmā, he who is Viṣṇu, he is Śiva,

Kuvera, Varuṇa, the moon, sun and the rest.
Padmā is me, see! We are one form!"
Having said this, Bhagavatī made herself manifest.
In one look, the merchant saw the two of them.
There was no difference, no division at all, they were one and equal.
Seeing this, Cāndo is astonished.
He falls on the ground, prostrating himself, acknowledging them.
"Why, mother, did you not tell me this for such a long time?
I did not know that Padmā is a manifest deity...
Padmā is the Mother of the World, the primal deity..."
(Smith, 1980:177).

Why didn't she tell him? The answer is simple. If she had, there wouldn't be an epic.

Tantrabibhūti allows Cāndo to announce that from now on, he will worship the feet of Padmā. *Will one who drinks the waters of Gaṅgā lose his virtue when he drinks other waters?*

Let's take a look at the finale. It's the toughest parts of the tale. Sure, Cāndo's battle is dramatic. It is also stupid. His favourite deities turn against him. He does not recognise that his crusade against the serpent goddess will immortalise him.

The tale of Behulā and Lakhindār is much deeper. And it can be painful, depending on how realistic a poet made it. Consider a great epic of India, the *Rāmāyana*. There is heroic Rāma, an incarnation of Viṣṇu, virtuous, brave, spiritual, and he is deeply in love with his wonderful wife Sītā. Sadly, she is abducted by the terrifying Asura Ravenna and spirited away to far-away Lanka. Over many hundred pages we read how Rāma does brave deeds, makes friends, kills enemies and fights his way to the lair of the demon king. It's a long story and the poets did their best to make it longer. Finally, he arrives on that island of horrors, slays his opponent and frees his wife. It would have been the perfect moment to celebrate. But it isn't. Hindu purity rules are merciless. Sītā, we learn, may have been the most virtuous wife in the world. She is a shining example of chastity and virtue. Terrible Ravenna never had a chance to bed her. However, people will talk. Something could have happened. Who was there, during all those weeks, months and years, to attest to the purity of Rāma's wife? The hero curses and grinds his teeth. In victory he meets defeat. Sītā may declare her innocence as much as she likes; the neighbours will gossip; she has stained Rāma's honour and threatens to pollute his reputation and the status of his clan.

There is no apology, no solution, and no happy end to most versions of the *Rāmāyana Epic*.

Behulā is in the same situation as Sītā.

The same thing appears in Bengal ballads: a woman with a questionable reputation, no matter how pure and chaste and virtuous, threatens the status of her husband's family.

When Lakhindār rises from the dead he is confused. Yes, he ought to be grateful to his wife. But what has she done in his absence? Behulā, as most poets agree, has saved the life of her husband. She is a wonderful, dutiful wife. The gods have blessed her voyage. But she has travelled on her own, she has spent months in the presence of a rotting corpse, she went crazy, washed the underwear of the gods, danced for them and returned to mundane reality dressed like a Ḍom girl. Neta introduces Behulā to the gods as a relation, and as a washerwoman, a dhopājhī, a dhobin, a rajak-kumarī. Yes she is a washer. She is needed in this polluted universe, and she is filthy. The poets call her a nācanī, a *dancer*. It doesn't matter that she performed for the gods. Dancers are dirty. It implies that she is soiled and worthless, but also an independent woman who can make a living without a man. I am sure Śiva approved. He has a heart for those who do as they like. And he worships the feet of women who dance, wash, butcher, whore, cut hair, make arrows, write horoscopes, engrave talismans, write poetry or beg on the cremation ground. The other gods may have been less enthusiastic. Is Behulā polluted? I ask you. What counts higher, her real virtue or her possible misdeeds? Our poets disagreed. So did their audiences. Trendy songs undergo a Darwinian process of natural selection. Poets and performers chose the versions they expected to be popular. Was their story to turn out happy or to become a heart-wrenching tragedy?

Accordingly, the ending varied. Most poets insisted that Lakhindār is grateful, and that he stands by his wife, no matter that everyone is gossiping and cursing her. It costs him his class, his family, his place in life. The couple leaves, they have no other choice.

Others did not agree. In some versions, Lakhindār is angry, vengeful and jealous. He insults his wife and denounces her.

In Tantrabibhūti's version, Lakhindār curses his wife, and it fixes his doom. In a fit of anger, Manasā blinds him. Honestly, he asked for it, and he got what he deserved.

Society is against our lovers. All over the place, spiteful women abuse them.

Bijay Gupta II put their mutterings into verse.

It doesn't matter that a good woman is devoted to her husband and firm in dharma,
If she's independent, a woman falls into difficulty.
She stayed on water and on land for six months,
She had no companion, there were many terrors on her way.
In such godless circumstances could a woman's principles remain?

Bijay Gupta II and Tantrabibhūti relate the harsh reality of East Indian customs. Several poets ended their *Epic* with a bitter aftermath. They insisted on a series of ordeals to prove that Behulā had remained pure, unraped and chaste. Nārāyaṇ Deb, Sukavi Nārāyaṇ and Rādhānāth Rāy Caudhurī proposed that Behulā had to demonstrate her purity to the community of traders. It makes me want to retch.

Bisṇu Pal insisted that Behulā has to demonstrate her virtue, as soon as she arrives in Campaka. Bipradās places this episode at the very end of his opus. Lakhindār and Behulā ascend to heaven and return to Indra's palace. That's where they came from, but while Lakhindār is admitted, Behulā has to undergo a series of ordeals before the weary old thunder god is satisfied. She has to walk on a razor blade, is weighted with stones and thrown into the sea and has to escape from a lacquered chamber, which is put on fire. After surviving all three ordeals, she is graciously allowed to be a heavenly dancer again. Honestly, how sick can this get?

These stories reflect a cruel and vindictive mindset, entertained by upright, self-satisfied men and by virtuous, unforgiving women. They found the approval of their audiences. And while we are at it: this ain't a primitive custom in some far away Third World communities. Similar rules, just as hard and bitter, are observed by many people, in many countries, all over the world.

Luckily, most poets had sense, heart and spiritual insight. They, too, acknowledged social reality and admitted that Behulā, her reputation in tatters, has no place in Cāndo's palace. To be sure, he doesn't want to throw her out. Cāndo is not a bad person; he has a mildly spiritual side, and he sympathises as much as he can. However, he prefers his six sons, each of them a merchant at heart, to silly Lakhindār with his music and that strange wife of his. Sonakā sees Behulā as a social disgrace. She knows what the neighbours say, and it isn't nice.

Behulā and Lakhindār realize they have to leave. They have been to the Dark Waters, have undergone death, rot and crisis, and they have met the gods. What place is left for them on earth?

In several versions of our *Epic*, such as those of Ketakādās and Dvarika, our lovers depart. They become travelling ascetics, or yogīs. I took the liberty to turn them into Kāpālikas. That's the name of the earliest documented tantric sect. The Kāpālika (female: Kāpālinī) took their name from a bowl made of a human cranium, preferably that of a Brahmin. The bowl was used to collect offerings, gifts, food and drink, preferably alcoholic. The members of this sect shared their meals and drink. They lived in unusually free relationships, imitated their role models (Śiva and Kālī), ate meat, enjoyed sex, delighted in life and went on pilgrimages across India. Some settled down and ran small temples and shrines. The evidence is patchy; none of their scripture survived and what virtuous Hindus had to say about them is anything but friendly.

And I provided Lakhindār with a string instrument. He was a top-notch heavenly musician, up there, in Indra's heaven. Sadly, we are not informed about his musical preferences when he was alive on earth. In one version of the Epic, he plays a drum while Behulā dances for the gods. Sure, Indian drumming is amazingly sophisticated. But shouldn't he want more? So I equipped him with a vīṇā, a lute-type instrument, an ancestor of the sitar. After what he had been through, it's the least I could do.

Bipradās allowed the couple, who appear like yogīs, to say goodbye to Behulā's parents. He insisted that Lakhindār, having died of snakebite, would be reborn as a Nāga and dwell in Manasā's mountain paradise. I am sure the same goes for Behulā, and for all of us.

Bibliography

Abhinavagupta: *Śrī Tantrālokaḥ. Chapters one, two, three four,* Translation Chatterjee, Gautam, Indian Mind Publishing, 2008

Abhinavagupta: *The Short Gloss on the Supreme; The Queen of the Three,*

Parātrīśikālaghuvṛttiḥ, in Muller-Ortega 1989

Abhinavagupta: *Parātrīśikā-Vivaraṇa. The Secret of Tantric Mysticism*. Trans. and comments by Singh, Jaideva, ed. Bäumer, Bettina Motilal Banarsidass, Delhi 2002 (1988)

Abhinavagupta: *Abhinavagupta's Commentary on the Bhagavad Gītā Gītārtha-saṁgraha*, trans. Matjanovic, Boris, Indica Books, Varanasi, 2004

Alberts, Andreas & Mullen, Peter: *Psychoaktive Pflanzen, Pilze und Tiere. Von Fliegenpilz bis Teufelsbeere. Bestimmung, Wirkung, Verwendung*. Kosmos Verlag, Stuttgart, 2000

Alberts, Andreas & Mullen, Peter: *Aphrodisiaka aus der Natur. Von Alraune bis Tauberpilz. Bestimmung, Wirkung, Verwendung*. Kosmos Verlag, Stuttgart, 2003

Atharva-Veda Saṁhīta. trans. Whitney, William D., revised by Singh, Nag S., Nag Publishers, Delhi, 1987

Basu, Tara Krishna & Bose, Basanta Coomar: *Village Life in Bengal (1962) /Hindu Customs in Bengal (1875-1926?)*. iUniverse, Inc., New York, 2005

Bengalische Märchen. Trans. & ed. Mode, Heinz & Ray, Arun. Insel Verlag, Leipzig, 1992

Beyer, Stephan: *The Cult of Tārā. Magic and Ritual in Tibet*. University of California Press, Berkeley, 1978

Bhattacharya, France: *La Victoire de Manasā* (*Manasāvijaya* von Vipradāsa/Bipradās). Institut Français de Pondichéry, Collection Indologie # 105, 2007

Bibby, Geoffrey: *Dilmun. Die Entdeckung der ältesten Hochkultur*. Originally: *Looking for Dilmun*. Alfred A. Knopf Publishing, New York, 1969.

Blumhardt, M (publisher): *Die Entwicklung der christlichen Mission in Ostindien*. Magazin für neuste Geschichte der protestantischen Missions-Gesellschaft in Basel, Verlag des Missionsinstitutes in Basel, 1841

Bose, Mandakranta & Bose, Sarika Priyadarshini: *A Women's Rāmāyana. Candrāvatī's Bengal Epic*. Routledge, London, 2013

van Buitenen, J. (trans.): *Mahābhārata*, University of Chicago Press, Book 1, 1980, Book 2 &3 1981

Bussabarger, Robert & Rbbins, Betty: *The Everyday Art of India*. Dover Books, New York, 1968

Chakravarti, Kavikankan Mukundaram: *Chandimangal*. (trans. Yazijian) Penguin, London, 2015

Chamovitz, Daniel: *What a Plant Knows: A Field Guide to the Senses*. Scientific American/Farrar, Strauss and Giroux, New York, 2012

Chatterji, Roma (ed.): *Wording the World: Veena Das and Scenes of Inheritance*. Fordham University Press, New York, 2015

Coe, Jon & Young, Simon: *The Celtic Sources for the Arthurian legend*. Llanerch Publishers, Felinfach, 1995

Da Costa, Dia: *Development Dramas. Reimagining Rural Political Action in East India*. Routledge, London 2010

Dalley, Jan: *The Black Hole. Money, Myth and Empire*. Penguin, London, 2006

Dam, Jyotishman: *Shiva Yoga. Indiens großer Yogi Gorakshanatha*. Diederichs, München, 1998

Day, Lál Behàri: *Govinda Sàmanta, or the History of a Bengal Ràiyat,* Macmillan & Co, London1874

The Devī Gītā. The Song of the Goddess. Trans. & commentary Mackenzie Brown, C.. State University of New York Press, Albany, 1998

Devī-Māhātmyam or Śrī Durgā-Saptaśatī. trans. Svāmī Jagadīśvarānanda, Sri Ramakrishna Math, Madras, 1955

Die ältesten Monumente der Menschheit. Vor 12.000 Jahren in Anatolien. Catalogue, Badisches Landesmuseum, Karlsruhe, 2007

Dimock, Edward, C.: Goddess of Snakes in Bengali Literature, 1962

Dimock, Edward C.: *The Thief of Love. Bengali Tales from Court and Village*. University of Chicago Press, 1963

Donaldson, Thomas Eugene: *Iconography of the Buddhist Sculpture of Orissa*, Vol. I (Text), Indira Gandhi National Centre for the Arts, New Delhi, 2001

Mark S.G Dyczkowski: *The Doctrine of Vibration. An Analysis of the Doctrines and Practices of Kashmir Shaivism*; State University of New York Press, Albany, 1987

Fergusson, James: *Tree and Serpent Worship. Illustrations of Mythology and Art in India in the First and Fourth Centuries After Christ*. London, 1888

Finn, Louise M. (intr., trans., & annotated): *The Kulacūḍāmaṇi Tantra and The Vāmakeśvara Tantra with the Jayaratha Commentary*, Otto Harrassowitz Verlag, Wiesbaden, 1986

Finn, Louise M. *The Prapañcasāra Tantra. The Tantra on the Nature of Creation*. Balboa Press, Bloomington, 2017

Frank, Othmar: *Über ein Denkmal in der indischen Mythologie. Nach einer indischen Zeichnung*. Gelesen in der Sitzung der philosophisch-philologischen Klasse, Königlich Bayrische Akademie der Wissenschaften, 1837

Frankopan, Peter: *The Silk Roads. A New History of the World*. Bloomsbury, London, 2015

Fries, Jan: *Seidways. Shaking, Swaying and Serpent Mysteries*. Mandrake of Oxford, 1996

Fries, Jan: *Kālī Kaula. A Manual of Tantric Magick*. Avalonia Books, London, 2010

Fries, Jan: *Dragon Bones. Ritual, Myth and Oracle in Shang Period China*. Avalonia, London, 2012

Fries, Jan: *The Seven Names of Lamaštu. A Journey through Mesopotamian Magick and Beyond*. Avalonia, London, 2017

Fuller, C. J.: *The Camphor Flame. Popular Hinduism and Society in India*. Princeton University Press, 1992

Gandhi, Makeka: *The Penguin Book of Hindu Names for Girls*, Penguin Random House India, Cyber City, Gurgaon, 2004

Ganguli, Kisari Mohan (trans. *Mahābhārata*, 1889-1896)

Gheranda Samhita in: Yogi-Raj Sacharow, Boris: *Das große Geheimnis, Die verborgene Seite der Yoga-Übungen*, Drei Eichen Verlag, München, 1954

Glasenapp, Helmuth von: *Indische Geisteswelt,* I & II, Holle Verlag, Baden.Baden, 1958

Gonda, Jan: *Die Religionen Indiens I & II*, Kohlhammer Verlag, Stuttgart, 1960 & 1963

Gupta, Sanjukta (trans. & intr.): *Lakṣmī Tantra, a Pāñcarātra Text*. Motilal Banarsidass, Delhi, 2003

Gupta, Vijaya: *Padmā Purāṇa* (short passage) in: Paniker, K. Ayyappa

Karuna Goswamy: *The Glory of the Great Goddess, an illustrated manuscript from Kashmir from the Alice Boner Collection in the Museum Rietberg*, Zurich, 1989 (illustrations of the Devī Mahātmya)

Teun Goudriaan *(trans.): The Vīṇāṣikhatantra, A Shaiva Tantra of the Left Current*, Motilal Banarsidass, Delhi, 1985

Teun Goudriaan (ed.): *Ritual and Speculation in Early Tantrism, Studies in Honor of André Padoux*, State University of New York Press, 1992

Teun Goudriaan & Sanjukta Gupta: *Hindu Tantric and Śākta Literature*, Otto Harrassowitz Verlag, Wiesbaden, 1981

Griechische Lyrik in einem Band, Ebener, Dietrich (ed.& trans.), Aufbau Verlag, belin, 1976

Griffith, Ralph T. (trans. & commentary): *The Rig Veda*. Motilal Banarsidass, Delhi, Special Edition for Book of the Month Club, New York, 1992

Grimes, John A.: *Gaṇapati. Song of the Self*. State University of New York Press, 1995

Grimm, Jacob. *Deutsche Mythologie*. Fourier Verlag, Wiesbaden, 2003 (1835)

Gupta, Sanjukta: *The Worship of Kālī According to the Toḍala Tantra*, in White, 2000

Guthmann, Hahn & Reichel; *Taschenlexikon der Pilze Deutschlands*, Quelle & Meyer Verlag, Wiebelsheim, 2011

Haq, Kaiser: *The Triumph of the Snake Goddess*. Harvard University Press, Cambridge, Massachusetts, 2015

Hawley, John Stratton and Wulff, Donna Maria (ed..): *Devi, Goddesses of India*, University of California Press, Berkeley and Los Angeles, 1996

Ibn Fadlān: *Ibn Fadlān and the Land of Darkness. Arab Travellers in the Far North*. Trans. & intr. Lunde, Paul and Stone, Caroline, Penguin, London, 2012

Jagadīśvarānanda, Swami (transl.) *Devī-Māhātmyam or Śrī Durgā-Saptaśatī*, Sri Ramakrishna Math, Mylapore, 1955

Jarrige, Jean-François: *Die frühen Kulturen in Pakistan und ihre Entwicklung*, in: *Vergessene Städte am Indus*, Verlag Phillip von Zabern, Mainz, 1987

Jarrige, Jean-François: *Vorzeit und Induskultur*, in: Heinrich Gerhard Franz (ed.): *Das alte Indien, Geschichte und Kultur des indischen Subkontinents*, Bertelsmann, München, 1990

Jogar, Ulrich & Luckhardt, Jochen (ed.): *Schlangen und Drachen. Kunst und Natur.* (catalogue). Primus Verlag, Wissenschaftliche Buchgesellschaft, Darmstadt, 2007.

Kaiser, Thomas: *Bildrollen. Dauer und Wandel in der indischen Volkskunst.* Arnoldsche Art Publishers, Völkerkundemuseum der Universität Zürich, 2012

Kalidasa: *Der Kreis der Jahreszeiten (Ṛtusaṁhāra)*, trans. Kreyenborg, Herman, Insel Verlag, Leipzig, no year

Karban, Richard: *Plant Sensing and Communication*. University of Chicago Press, 2015

The Kaulajñāna Nirṇaya. Edited by Bagchi, P.C.; Magee, Michael (trans.): Prachya Prakashan, Varanasi, 1986

Kavikankan, Mukundaram Chakravarti: *Chandimangal*. Trans. & ed.: Yazijian, Edward; Penguin, London, 2015

Kaiser, Thomas: *Bildrollen, Dauer und Wandel einer indischen Volkskunst.* Arnoldsche Art Publishers, Catalogue, Zürich, 2012

Kaushal, Molly: *Chanted Narratives: The Living "Katha-Vachana" Tradition*, Indira Gandhi Centre for the Arts, 2001

Keith, Lierre: *The Vegetarian Myth. Food, Justice and Sustainability*. Flashpoint Press, Crescent City, CA, 2009

Keller, Ursula & Sharandak, Natalja: *Madame Blavatsky. Eine Biographie*. Insel Verlag, Berlin, 2013

Ketakādās: *Manasā Mangal* (Exzerpt). In Dimock, 1963, 197-294

Kinsley, David: *Hindu Goddesses-Visions of the Divine Feminine in the Hindu Religious Tradition*, University of California Press, Berkeley, 1988

Kinsley, David: *The Ten Mahāvidyās, Tantric Visions of the Divine Feminine*. Motilal Banarsidass, Delhi, 1998

Koch, Heidemarie: *Frauen und Schlangen. Die geheimnisvolle Kultur der Elamer in Alt-Iran*. Phillip von Zabern Verlag, Mainz, 2007

The Kulacūḍāmaṇi Tantra and The Vāmakeśvara Tantra with the Jayaratha Commentary, intr., trans., annotated by Finn, Louise M., Otto Harrassowitz Verlag, Wiesbaden, 1986

Kulārṇava Tantra, ed. John Woodroffe, summarised translation M. P. Pandit, Motilal Banarsidass, Delhi, 1984 (1916)

Kulārṇava Tantra, trans. Rai, Ram Kumar Prachya Prakashan, Varanasi, 1999

Kūrma-Purāṇa, trans. by Ganesh Vasudeo Tagare, Motilal Banarsidass, Delhi 1981

Kundu, Rama: *Interpret: A Study of the Dialogue between Texts*. Sarup & Sons, New Delhi, 2008

Lakṣmī Tantra, a Pāñcarātra Text. Gupta, Sanjukta (trans. & intr.): Motilal Banarsidass, Delhi, 2003

Lotzkat, Sebastian: *Keine Bange vor der Schlange. Liebeserklärung an ein unpopuläres Tier*. Hanser Verlag, München, 2016

Mahidhara: *Mantra Mahodadhiḥ*, trans. Ramkumar Rai, Prachya Prakashan, Varanasi, 1992

Magee, Michael (trans.): *The Kaulajñāna nirṇaya*. Edited by Bagchi, P.C., Prachya Prakashan, Varanasi, 1986

Mahābhārata, trans. van Buitenen, J., University of Chicago Press, Book 1 1980, Book 2 &3 1981

Mahābhārata, trans. Ganguli, Kisari Mohan, 1889-1896

Mahānirvāṇa Tantra, The Tantra of the Great Liberation, trans. Avalon, Arthur/Woodroffe, John, Dover Books, New York, 1972

Maity, Pradyot Kumar: Historical Studies in the Cult of the Goddess Manasā (a Socio-Cultural Study). Punthi Pustak, Kolkata, 1966/2001

Maity, Pradyot Kumar: *Folk –Rituals of Eastern India*. Abhinav Publications, New Delhi, 1988

Maity, Pradyot Kumar: *Human Fertility Cults and Rituals of Bengal (A Comparative Study)* Abhinav Publications, New Delhi, 1989

Majupuria, Trilok Chandra & Kumar, Rohit*: Gods, Goddesses & Religious Symbols of Hinduism, Buddhism & Tantrism (including Tibetan Deities) (most authentic & exhaustive).* M. Devi, Lakshar (Gwalior) 2004

Mallebrein, Cornelia (and others): *Die anderen Götter. Volks- und Stammesbronzen aus Indien*. Catalogue. Edition Braus, Köln, 1993

Mallebrein, Cornelia & von Stietencron, Heinrich: *The Divine Play on Earth. Religious Aesthetics and Ritual in Orissa, India.* Synchron publishers, Heidelberg 2008

McDaniel, June: *The Madness of the Saints. Ecstatic Religion in Bengal.* University of Chicago Press, 1989

McDaniel, June: *Making Virtuous Daughters and Wives. An Introduction to Women's Brata Rituals in Bengali Folk Religion.* State University of New York Press, Albany, 2003

McDaniel, June: *Offering Flowers, Feeding Skulls. Popular Goddess Worship in West Bengal.* Oxford University Press, 2004

McDermott, Rachel Fell & Kripal, Jeffrey (ed.): *Encountering Kālī in the Margins, at the Center, in the West.* University of California Press, Berkely, 2003

McDermott, Rachel Fell: *Singing to the Goddess. Poems to Kālī and Umā from Bengal.* Oxford University Press, 2001

Milkman, Harvey & Sunderwirth, Stanley: *Craving for Ecstasy and Natural Highs. A Positive Approach to Mood Alteration.* Sage, Los Angeles, 2010

Mode, Heinz & Chandra, Subodh: *Indische Volkskunst.* Müller & Kiepenhauer, Leipzig, 1984

Moorhouse, Geoffrey: *Calcutta.* Faber & Faber, London, 2008

Muller-Ortega, Paul Eduardo: The Triadic Heart of Śiva. Kaula Tantricism of Abhinavagupta in the Non-Dual Shaivism of Kashmir, University of NY Press, 1989

Nicholas, Ralph, W.: *Practical Religion in Bengal.* Chronicle Books, New Delhi, 2003

O'Flaherty, Wendy Doniger (ed. & trans.): *The Rig Veda, An Anthology*, Penguin Books, London, 1981

O'Flaherty, Wendy Doniger (ed. & trans.): *Textual Sources for the Study of Hinduism.* Manchester University Press, 1988

Oldenberg, Hermann: *Die Religion des Veda.* Cotta'sche Buchhandlung, Stuttgart, 1916

Osho (Chandra Mohan Jain bzw. Bhagwan Shree Rajneesh) on Tantra in www.osho.com/de/highlights-of-oshos-world/osho-on-tantra-quotes

Palmengarten gut gewürzt, Catalogue, Frankfurt M, 2012

Pandey, K.C.: *Abhinavagupta. An Historical and Philosophical Study.* Chaukhamba Amarabharati Prakashan, Varanasi, 2006

Paniker, K. Ayyappa (ed.): *Medieval Indian Literature: Surveys and Selections.* Vol.1. Sahitya Akademi, New Delhi, 1977

Patanjali, Bhagwān Shree: *Aphorisms of Yoga.* Transl. Shree Purohit Swāmi, intr. Yeats, W.B.; Faber, London, 1973

Der kleine Pauly, Lexikon der Antike in fünf Bänden. DTV Verlag, München, 1979

Peller, Astrid: *Im Auftrag der Götter. Künstlerinnen aus Mithila (Nepal/Nordindien).* Gallerie 37, Museum für Völkerkunde Frankfurt am Main 1998

Playne, Somerset (Herausgeber): *Bengal and Assam, Behar and Orissa: Their History, People, Commerce and Industrial Resources.* London 1917; Neuauflage: HardPress Publishing, Miami, ohne Jahr

Pollmer, Udo & Warmuth, Susanne: *Lexikon der populären Ernährungsirrtümer,* Eichborn Verlag, Frankfurt am Main, 2007

Pollmer, Udo & Warmuth, Susanne: *Pillen, Pulver, Powerstoffe, die falschen Versprechen der Nahrungsergänzungsmittel.* Piper Verlag, München, 2010

Pollmer, Udo (ed.) *Opium fürs Volk. Natürliche Drogen in unserem Essen.* Rowohlt Verlag, Hamburg, 2010

The Prapañcasāra Tantra. The Tantra on the Nature of Creation. Translation, annotation & illustrations by Finn, Louise M., Balboa Press, Bloomington, 2017

Priuli, Ausilio: *Felszeichnungen der Alpen.* Published by the author, Ivrea, 1983

Radice, William: *Complete Bengali.* London, 2010

Rastogi, Navjivan: *The Krama Tantricism of Kashmir, Historical and General Sources*, vol. I, Motilal Banarsidass, Delhi, 1979

Reallexikon der Assyriologie, ed. Ebeling, Dietz, Meissner, Weidner, von Soden etc. Walter de Gruyter Verlag, Volume 1 Berlin 1928, not complete yet.

Rhodes, Constantina: *Shaiva Devotional Songs of Kashmir. A Translation and Study of Utpaladeva's Shivastotravali.* State University of New York Press, Albany, 1987

Rhodes, Constantina: *Invoking Lakshmi. The Goddess of Wealth in Song and Ceremony.* State University of New York Press, Albany, 2010

The Rig Veda, An Anthology, trans: O'Flaherty, Wendy Doniger, Penguin Books, London, 1981

The Rig Veda, trans. Griffith, Ralph T. H., Motilal Banarsidass, Delhi, Special Edition for Book of the Month Club, NY, 1992

Ross, Anne: *Pagan Celtic Britain.* Constable. London, 1992

Rothermund, Dietmar (ed): *Indien. Kultur, Geschichte, Politik, Wirtschaft, Umwelt. Ein Handbuch.* C. H. Beck Verlag, München 1995

Schmidt, Klaus. *Sie bauten die ersten Tempel. Das rätselhafte Heiligtum der Steinzeitjäger.* C.H.Beck Verlag, München 2006

Schneider, Hermann (and others): *Germanische Altertumskunde,* Beck'sche Verlagsbuchhandlung, München, 1951

Sen, Dineschandra & Bahadur, Rai: *Eastern Bengal Ballads – Mymensing – Vol.1: Part 1,* University of Calcutta, 1923

Śiva Saṁhīta, trans. Vasu, Rai Bahadur Srisa Chandra, Oriental Books Reprint Corporation, New Delhi, 1975

Skanda Purāṇa, part 1 & 2, trans. Tagare, G.V.; Motilal Banarsidass, Delhi, 1992

Smith, W.L.: *The One-Eyed Goddess. A Study of the Manasā Maṅgal.* Almquist & Wiksell International, Stockholm, 1980

Spitzer, Manfred: *Musik im Kopf. Hören, Musizieren, Verstehen und Erleben im neuronalen Netzwerk.* Schattauer Verlag, 2002

Stapelfeldt, Sylvia: *Kāmākhyā – Satī – Mahāmāyā: Konzeptionen der Großen Göttin im Kālikāpurāna.* Peter Lang GmbH, Europäischer Verlag der Wissenschaften, Frankfurt/M, 2001

Strabo: *Geographica.* Transl. Forbiger, F, Marix Verlag, Wiesbaden

Stutley, Margaret & James: *A Dictionary of Hinduism. Its Mythology, Folklore and Development 1500 B.C. – A.A. 1500.* Routledge & Keegan Paul, London, 1977

Sun Tzu (Sunzi): *The Art of War.* Trans. Griffith, Samuel. Oxford University Press Paperback, New York, 1971

Tāntrikābhidhānakośa II, A Dictionary of Technical Terms from Hindu Tantric Literature, Ed: H. Brunner, G. Oberhammer, A. Padoux, Verlag der österreichischen Akademie der Wissenschaften, Wien 2004

Toḍala Tantra, see Gupta, Sanjukta in White, 2000

Trewavas, Anthony: *Plant Behaviour & Intelligence.* Oxford University Press, 2014

Tudge, Colin: *The Secret Life of Trees. How they live and why they matter.* Penguin, London, 2005

Vetālapañcaviṁśatika, die fünfundzwanzig Geschichten des Vetāla-Dämons, in Somadeva: *Kathāsaritsāgara (Der Ozean der Erzählströme)* transl. Mehlig, Johannes, Kiepenhauer verlag, Leipzig, 1991

Vetalapantschavinsati, die fünfundzwanzig Erzählungen eines Dämons, trans. Ohle, Heinrich, Wissenschaftliche Buchgesellschaft Darmstadt, 1966

Vijnana Bhairava Tantra, Das Tantra der Befreiung, trans. Keyserling, Wilhelmine, Verlag Bruno Martin, Südergellersen, 1994

Vijñāna Bhairava. Das göttliche Bewusstsein. Trans. Bäumer, Bettina, Verlag der Weltreligionen im Fischer Verlag, Frankfurt, 2008

The Vīṇāşikhatantra, A Shaiva Tantra of the Left Current, Teun Goudriaan (trans & ed.) Motilal Banarsidass, Delhi, 1985

Vogel, J.: *Indian Serpent Lore or the Nāgas in Hindu Legend and Art*. reprint, Varanasi, 1972

Woolley, Benjamin: *The Queen's Conjurer. The Life and Magic of Dr. Dee*. Harper Collins, Flamingo, London, 2002

Wei, Boyang: *Cantong Qi. The Secret of Everlasting Life.* Trans. Bertschinger, Element, Shaftesbury, 1994

Westphal, Wilfried: *Herrscher zwischen Indus und Ganges. Das britische Kolonialreich in Indien.* C. Bertelsmann, Verlag, München, 1980

White, David Gordon (ed.), *Tantra in Practice*, Princeton University Press. Princeton, 2000

White, David Gordon: *The Alchemical Body, Siddha Traditions in Medieval India*. University of Chicago Press, 1996

White, David Gordon: *Kiss of the Yoginī, "Tantric Sex" in its South Asian Contexts. University of Chicago Press, 2003*

White, David Gordon: *Sinister Yogis*. University of Chicago Press, 2009

White, David Gordon (ed.) *Yoga in Practice*. Princeton University Press, Princeton, 2012

Whitney, William D. (transl.): *Atharva Veda Saṁhīta*. revised by Singh, Nag. S., Nag Publishers, Delhi, 1987

Woodroffe, John (Arthur Avalon) trans.: *Tantra of the Great Liberation (Mahānirvāna Tantra)*, Dover Publications, N.Y., 1972 (1913)

Woodroffe, John (Arthur Avalon) trans.: *Hymn to Kali*, 1922 (included in *Hymns to the Goddess* 2001)

Woodroffe, John (Arthur Avalon) and Ellen Woodroffe trans.: *Hymns to the Goddess*, Ganesh & Co., Madras, 2001 (1913)

Woodroffe, John (Arthur Avalon): *The Serpent Power, The Secrets of Tantric and Shactic Yoga, being the Ṣaṭ - Cakra Nirūpaṇa and Pādukā-Pañcaka*, Dover Publications, New York 1974 (1919)

Woodroffe, John (Arthur Avalon): *The Garland of Letters. Studies in the Mantra-Śāstra.* Ganesh & Company, Pondicherry, 1979 (1922)

Woodroffe, John (Arthur Avalon): *Śakti and Śākta, Essays and Addresses*, Ganesh & Co, Madras, 2001 (1927)

Yoginīhṛdaya. The Heart of the Yoginī. A Sanskrit Tantric Treatise trans. & ed. Padoux, André & Jeanty, Roger-Orphé. Oxford University Press, 2013

Index

A

Abhinavagupta 13, 17, 65, 108, 386, 394, 436, 447, 473, 475
Adelard 346
Aditi 43, 160, 322, 323, 420, 438
Adityas 323, 421
adrenalin 109
Ādyā 50, 51, 52, 445, 452
Agni 29, 42, 44, 53, 110, 118, 175, 238, 241, 320, 323, 324, 393, 394, 421, 434, 440
Āhaṁ 12, 18, 334, 436, 447
Aīṁ 428, 432, 434
Akbar 15, 17, 148
Ālpanā 9, 10, 366, 367, 368, 369, 370, 371, 391, 398, 403, 406
amphetamines 197, 246, 340, 342, 360
Anāndi Deb 46
Anātman 12
Anuttara 13, 108
Apsaras 109, 128, 130, 166, 216, 217, 461, 467
Ārya 187, 233, 318, 319, 320, 321, 421, 434
Āsana 427
Asclepius 319
Aṣṭabakra 459, 461
Āstika 9, 119, 120, 122, 328, 383, 418, 420, 438, 441, 445, 468
Asura 110, 111, 112, 127, 227, 322, 471
Atharva-Veda 473
Avalon, Arthur *See* Woodroffe, John

B

B_{12} 109, 385
Bahadur, Rai 475
Baṁsīdās 363, 455, 459, 461, 463, 464, 465, 467, 468, 470
Bananas 34, 340
Bandler, Richard 16
Basu, Tara Krishna 18, 354, 365, 462, 473
Bäumer, Bettina 447, 473, 476
Behulā 6, 10, 14, 18, 19, 213, 222, 223, 224, 225, 226, 227, 228, 231, 237, 239, 240, 242, 243, 245, 246, 247, 248, 249, 251, 253, 254, 255, 256, 258, 259, 260, 262, 263, 265, 267, 268, 269, 271, 272, 273, 275, 277, 279, 280, 281, 282, 283, 284, 285, 286, 288, 289, 290, 292, 293, 294, 295, 296, 299, 300, 301, 339, 354, 355, 359, 360, 363, 364, 383, 389, 401, 409, 420, 429, 434, 439, 454, 455, 459, 461, 464, 466, 467, 468, 469, 470, 471, 472
Bēl 343
betel 26, 58, 64, 106, 133, 146, 167, 170, 192, 243, 260, 342, 366, 372, 386, 427
Bhagavad Gītā 331, 422, 447, 454, 469, 473
Bhagwan Shree Rajneesh *See* Osho
Bhairava 13, 417, 432, 436, 447, 460, 476
Bhairavī 38, 217, 387, 432, 435
Bhakti 18, 332, 404, 422, 430
Bhattasali 418, 463
Bhoginī 324, 444
Bijay Gupta 149, 360, 363, 404, 455, 461, 462, 463, 464, 465, 466, 467, 468, 469, 470, 471
Bijay Gupta II 461, 463, 464, 465, 466, 471
Bipradās15, 16, 17, 19, 20, 152, 360, 392, 444, 454, 455, 460, 461, 462, 463, 464, 465, 467, 468, 470, 472, 473
Black Hole 349, 351, 473
Black Yajur Veda 327, 386
Blavatsky, H.P 330, 331, 423, 474
Bose, Basanta Coomar 9, 316, 354, 355, 473
bowing 76, 125, 163, 386, 441, 470
Brahmā 14, 15, 18, 49, 52, 53, 58, 59, 60, 61, 62, 85, 89, 91, 93, 95, 98, 101, 103, 104, 105, 106, 110, 111, 112, 116, 122, 135, 139, 140, 150, 155, 181, 186, 223, 238, 250, 280, 293, 378, 394, 416, 420, 432, 438, 440, 441, 445, 452, 460, 461, 470
Brahman 12, 15, 18, 68, 89, 106, 322, 377, 420, 430, 432, 445, 446, 460, 466
Brata 6, 7, 23, 25, 365, 366, 372, 452, 475
Bṛhaspati 323, 435, 469

C

Cakras 335
Calcutta 9, 16, 349, 351, 355, 362, 399, 400, 402, 409, 463, 475
Campaka 161, 162, 173, 183, 186, 198, 209, 228, 233, 239, 265, 292, 299, 300, 301, 428, 464, 470, 472
Caṇḍī 18, 359, 379, 389, 445, 446, 447, 454
cannabis 341
cardamom 64, 101, 162, 174, 206, 342, 343, 345, 348
Caudhurī, R.R. 461, 462, 465, 466, 467, 468, 469, 472
Charnock, Job 348, 349
cinnamon 342, 345, 346, 348
Clive, Robert 351, 353
cloves 342, 346, 348
Columbus 347
Cornwallis 352, 353
crusade 346, 463, 471
curry 36, 142, 162, 173, 253, 341

D

Dakṣa 43, 349, 420
Dānavas 324, 421
Daodejing 409
Das, Jibananda 19
Dāsa, Śāraḷā 455
deadly nightshade 343
Deb, Nārāyaṇ 392, 407, 455, 459, 465, 466, 467, 468, 469, 470
Dee, John 347, 348, 476
Descartes, René 17
Deva 110, 111, 452, 463
Devī 14, 15, 22, 169, 226, 371, 415, 417, 420, 427, 428, 432, 434, 435, 438, 444, 445, 447, 455, 473, 474
Dhana 275, 279, 461, 468
Dhanvantari 6, 18, 111, 112, 135, 136, 137, 138, 139, 140, 179, 180, 181, 182, 183, 254, 378, 416, 420, 428, 440, 441, 443, 459, 461, 464, 467, 468

Dharma 12, 47, 48, 49, 50, 51, 52, 67, 118, 119, 120, 122, 156, 170, 235, 260, 267, 292, 359, 379, 394, 395, 418, 445, 460
Dhyāna 7, 413, 415, 440
Dikpālas 87
Dimock, Edward C. 363, 473, 474
Ḍom 284, 292, 293, 384, 468, 469, 470, 471
Ḍombī 292, 300
Dopamine 339
Durgā 8, 14, 18, 54, 55, 63, 65, 66, 67, 68, 69, 70, 72, 74, 75, 76, 78, 79, 80, 81, 82, 85, 86, 90, 93, 94, 95, 96, 98, 99, 100, 104, 105, 108, 110, 113, 114, 115, 116, 117, 121, 123, 136, 137, 140, 141, 150, 154, 155, 157, 158, 162, 164, 167, 168, 169, 170, 171, 173, 174, 181, 190, 194, 221, 224, 225, 226, 227, 231, 236, 238, 247, 248, 254, 259, 277, 280, 281, 282, 283, 284, 285, 286, 293, 296, 299, 300, 331, 343, 352, 353, 355, 356, 359, 360, 363, 366, 381, 384, 394, 400, 420, 435, 445, 454, 455, 460, 463, 464, 467, 469, 470, 473, 474
Durgābar 409, 410, 443
Dvarika 466, 467, 468, 472

E

Ereškigal 312, 457
euphorbia 380, 395, 416
Eurynome 319

F

Finn, Louise M. 386, 473

G

GABA 342
Galangal 343
Gandharvas 111, 209, 283, 323, 324, 416
Gaṇeśa 19, 78, 80, 81, 94, 95, 121, 171, 173, 241, 282, 296, 371, 383, 394, 421, 432, 435, 438, 444, 454, 459
Gaṅgā 6, 8, 9, 15, 19, 57, 58, 61, 62, 64, 67, 69, 72, 85, 108, 116, 150, 160, 186, 187, 188, 199, 250, 268, 286, 314, 348, 358, 359, 361, 362, 392, 393, 400, 415, 438, 443, 452, 454, 465, 468, 471
Garuḍa 12, 95, 133, 137, 138, 238, 293, 393, 395, 396, 435, 440, 441, 455
Gaurī 241, 378, 394, 402
Gāyatrī 170, 203, 436, 444
Gheraṇḍa 331, 423
Gheranda Samhita 473
Göbekli Tepe 8, 304, 305, 306, 307, 308
grapes 342, 384
Grimm, Jacob 356, 474
Gupta, Sanjukta 333, 474, 475

H

Haṁsa 334, 381, 445
Hanumān 113, 126, 127, 128, 150, 154, 163, 172, 198, 200, 203, 205, 208, 236, 238, 293, 465
Haq, Kaiser 16, 452, 454, 462, 474
Haridatta, Kānā 363
Hāsan 462
Haṭhayoga 332, 423
heart 13, 22, 23, 28, 31, 34, 35, 45, 48, 55, 67, 75, 79, 80, 85, 86, 89, 94, 101, 108, 112, 123, 124, 134, 139, 142, 155, 157, 161, 162, 163, 166, 167, 180, 186, 195, 205, 215, 217, 223, 227, 231, 237, 239, 240, 243, 245, 247, 248, 249, 253, 263, 268, 272, 273, 275, 279, 281, 282, 283, 284, 292, 293, 301, 321, 322, 329, 332, 333, 335, 336, 341, 342, 347, 359, 381, 382, 385, 387, 415, 417, 428, 430, 433, 435, 462, 464, 471, 472
hemp 56, 139, 155, 168, 187, 221, 253, 304, 339, 341, 342, 352, 384, 386, 466
Hrīṁ 428, 432, 433, 438
Hūṁ 27, 415, 435, 436
Hussein 6, 148, 149, 150, 151, 152, 462

I

Icchā 382, 447
Inanna 319, 457
Indra 19, 43, 44, 48, 89, 95, 105, 109, 110, 118, 119, 160, 197, 198, 199, 215, 216, 217, 218, 238, 241, 247, 282, 285, 288, 293, 320, 323, 324, 326, 371, 392, 421, 428, 433, 438, 440, 454, 460, 465, 466, 472
iron 22, 53, 54, 66, 68, 69, 105, 133, 155, 197, 205, 211, 225, 226, 227, 228, 233, 234, 235, 240, 245, 248, 249, 250, 254, 256, 283, 318, 348, 352, 383, 400, 452, 461, 466, 467, 468

J

Jagatjīban 452, 454, 462, 464
Jaina 332, 377, 446, 463
Janamejaya 118, 119, 326, 420, 438, 440, 444
Jāṅgulī 9, 12, 328, 377, 378, 418, 445
Jaratkāru 119, 120, 121, 122, 383, 401, 420, 438, 440, 441, 444, 445, 460
Jīmūtavāhana 395
Jiva 288
Jñāna 77, 331, 382, 447

K

Kabijbana 454
Kadrū 8, 84, 86, 87, 88, 89, 90, 91, 93, 98, 137, 167, 325, 380, 396, 421, 440, 446
Kālī 19, 27, 35, 217, 271, 329, 331, 332, 348, 349, 355, 356, 357, 359, 364, 371, 378, 379, 382, 384, 386, 392, 394, 395, 397, 405, 409, 416, 417, 430, 432, 433, 435, 436, 444, 445, 446, 448, 457, 466, 469, 472, 473, 474, 475
Kalidasa 474
Kāma 25, 44, 48, 58, 62, 120, 223, 242, 243, 279, 378, 395, 433, 447, 466, 467
Kāmākhya 10, 279, 293, 408, 409, 410
Kamalā 109, 111, 182, 377, 432, 444, 446, 467
Kanoj Brahmins 133, 239, 354, 365, 466
Kāpālika 472
Karman 12, 25, 26, 28, 29, 50, 54, 59, 72, 77, 80, 103, 105, 118, 129, 134, 138, 143, 151, 157, 160, 165, 176, 189, 195, 203, 215, 224, 230, 242, 248, 249, 301, 331, 354, 448, 460, 467, 469
Kārrtikeya 81, 94, 121, 134, 171, 243, 293, 296, 371, 379, 383, 394, 401, 435
Kaśyapa 322, 420, 421, 438, 440, 441
Kaula 329, 332, 355, 394, 409, 417, 422, 424, 430, 432, 469, 473, 475

Kaulajñāna Nirṇaya 424, 474
Kaushal, Molly 457, 474
Keith, Lierre 385, 465, 474
Ketakādās 16, 243, 380, 392, 460, 462, 463, 464, 465, 466, 468, 469, 470, 472, 474
King Arthur 347
Kipling, Rudyard 318, 348
Klīṁ 428, 432, 433
Krama 13, 99, 334, 409, 415, 422, 436, 475
Kramamudrā 443
Krishnamacarya 423
Kriyā 331, 382, 447
Kṛṣṇa 98, 99, 134, 142, 143, 217, 238, 377, 381, 389, 393, 396, 420, 422, 430, 432, 433, 438, 440, 444, 454, 459, 460, 467
Kṛttibās 253, 467
Kṣemānanda 462, 467, 468
Kubera 118, 216, 238
Kulacūḍāmaṇi Tantra 386, 473, 474
Kulārṇava Tantra 360, 381, 384, 474
Kuṇḍalinī 305, 329, 331, 332, 333, 334, 335, 336, 422, 435
Kūrma-Purāṇa 474

L

Lakhindār 10, 220, 221, 222, 224, 231, 234, 237, 240, 241, 242, 243, 245, 246, 247, 248, 249, 251, 253, 255, 256, 258, 259, 262, 263, 265, 271, 280, 283, 285, 286, 289, 292, 293, 295, 296, 300, 301, 360, 363, 364, 383, 389, 404, 409, 420, 429, 454, 459, 461, 464, 465, 466, 467, 468, 470, 471, 472
Lakṣmī 26, 27, 49, 95, 104, 109, 110, 111, 118, 122, 129, 150, 167, 173, 216, 217, 223, 228, 238, 241, 245, 247, 263, 282, 283, 293, 356, 359, 366, 371, 377, 378, 383, 394, 397, 401, 421, 432, 433, 438, 440, 444, 446, 448, 459, 460, 466, 469, 474
Lamaštu 13, 15, 312, 317, 332, 365, 457, 473
Laozi 409
lime 243, 342, 386

M

Mahābhārata 14, 15, 108, 118, 119, 120, 167, 180, 220, 295, 325, 326, 331, 363, 372, 383, 389, 401, 415, 418, 420, 421, 422, 433, 440, 445, 455, 460, 466, 468, 469, 473, 474
Mahākāla 416
Mahānirvāṇa Tantra 415, 444, 474
Maitra, Jībankṛṣṇa 455, 460, 461, 462, 465
Maity, Pradyot Kumar 9, 10, 12, 14, 15, 16, 328, 363, 365, 372, 377, 383, 389, 390, 392, 395, 396, 399, 400, 402, 404, 406, 407, 409, 417, 418, 441, 443, 452, 455, 457, 463, 464, 474
malaria 242, 341, 348, 349
Māṁ 435, 436
Manakar 409, 454
Maṅgal 18, 133, 359, 379, 389, 446, 475
mantra 12, 13, 52, 64, 75, 93, 100, 105, 137, 138, 140, 227, 248, 249, 254, 331, 332, 333, 334, 335, 381, 386, 389, 413, 415, 416, 422, 427, 428, 430, 431, 432, 433, 434, 435, 436, 438, 448, 449, 457, 463, 466, 469
Mantra Mahodadhiḥ 474
Manu 47, 187, 354
Māra 378, 448
Mārāi 446
Mārāī 401, 410
Māyā 89, 432
McClintock, Barbara 413
McDaniel, June 16, 365, 452, 461, 468, 475
McDermott, Rachel Fell 18, 271, 353, 355, 384, 475
Milk Ocean 109, 111, 112, 113, 114, 115, 135, 138, 156, 182, 217, 372, 440, 460, 462
Min 13, 14
Minne 413
Mitra, Śambhu 364
Morgan, Mogg 372
Muchilinda 448
Mudrā 13
Mūlādhāra 333, 387

N

Nāgakanyā 376, 383
Nāgaloka 80, 86, 421, 444
Nāgārjuna 326
Nāgas 19, 20, 90, 118, 120, 137, 140, 199, 248, 285, 320, 321, 323, 324, 325, 326, 327, 329, 381, 417, 421, 428, 444, 445, 446, 448, 455, 476
Nandi 55, 154, 171
Nārada 107, 113, 114, 124, 324, 428, 438, 454
Nārāyaṇ, Sukavi 363, 455, 461, 462, 463, 464, 465, 467, 468, 469, 470, 472
Nārāyaṇa 247, 428, 438, 446
Nātha 277, 468, 469
Neda 458
Nedu 457
Neem 395
Neti 455, 457
Ningirima 13, 14, 312, 319
Nirṛti 10, 456, 457
nutmeg 64, 342, 346, 347, 348
nymphs 95, 324, 371, 458, 459

O

Odin 321, 326, 421
Ohjā 139
Oldenberg, Hermann 319, 325, 327, 457, 475
Oṁ 68, 87, 89, 215, 239, 332, 428, 432, 435, 436, 438
Ophion 319
opiates 340, 341
Osho 332, 475

P

Padmā 377, 402, 407, 432, 436, 444, 446, 470, 471, 474
Padmā Purāṇa 407, 444, 474
Pal, Biṣṇu 455, 460, 462, 463, 464, 465, 466, 467, 468, 470, 472
Pan 459
Pandanus 8, 201, 204, 402, 446
Pandey, K.C 436, 475
Pārvatī 14, 18, 150, 356, 359, 371, 384, 394, 402, 444, 445, 446, 454, 467
Pātālā 86, 324, 421
Patañjali 331, 415, 422
Patanjali, Bhagwān Shree 475
pepper 64, 95, 101, 162, 253, 341, 345, 346, 348
Pollmer, Udo 341, 342, 343, 345, 385, 475

Prajāpati 25, 106, 107, 325, 420
Prakṛti 432, 438, 446
Prapañcasāra 333, 473, 475
Prapañcasāra Tantra 333, 473, 475
Pūjā 7, 155, 352, 378, 381, 396, 400, 426, 438, 440, 443

R

Rādhā 98, 142, 143, 440
Radice, William 19, 475
Rāga 174, 216, 386
Rāma 134, 238, 389, 471
Rāmakṛṣṇa 331
Rasik, Dvija 91
Ratī 247, 280, 433, 466
Rhodes, Constantina 427, 434, 475
Ritualists 383
Rudra 87, 88, 89, 110, 138, 171, 326, 327, 394, 395, 433, 435, 446

S

Śacī 241, 247
Saffron 221
Sahaja 335
Śakti 54, 117, 325, 329, 333, 381, 417, 432, 433, 445, 446, 447, 476
Śaktipāta 334
Samādhi 415
Sarasvatī 19, 110, 183, 238, 247, 321, 356, 359, 378, 383, 418, 432, 434, 445, 446
Satī 14, 349, 409, 475
scales 11, 17, 37, 113, 173, 174, 242, 247, 314, 387
Schlegel, Friedrich 356
Sen, Dinesh Chandra 15, 239, 271, 360, 363, 371, 404, 440, 457, 463, 475
Serotonin 339
Siddha 314, 420, 422, 444, 469, 476
Sij 22, 28, 39, 102, 103, 114, 115, 120, 123, 125, 126, 129, 151, 154, 164, 171, 175, 183, 279, 301, 324, 445, 464, 468
Sītā 471
Śitalā 359
Śiva 6, 9, 12, 14, 17, 18, 19, 41, 49, 52, 53, 55, 56, 58, 59, 60, 61, 62, 64, 65, 67, 68, 72, 74, 75, 76, 77, 78, 79, 80, 81, 85, 86, 87, 89, 90, 91, 93, 94, 95, 96, 98, 99, 100, 101, 102, 104, 105, 106, 107, 108, 110, 111, 112, 113, 114, 116, 117, 118, 120, 121, 122, 124, 125, 135, 137, 138, 139, 140, 141, 144, 145, 148, 150, 154, 155, 156, 157, 158, 162, 163, 167, 171, 173, 174, 176, 180, 181, 182, 186, 187, 190, 198, 199, 221, 223, 231, 236, 238, 241, 247, 254, 277, 279, 280, 281, 282, 283, 284, 285, 286, 293, 296, 299, 326, 329, 331, 332, 333, 334, 335, 336, 339, 343, 349, 350, 354, 355, 358, 360, 363, 364, 366, 371, 377, 378, 379, 380, 381, 382, 384, 385, 392, 393, 394, 395, 400, 402, 405, 415, 416, 417, 418, 420, 421, 432, 433, 435, 436, 438, 440, 441, 443, 444, 445, 446, 447, 449, 452, 454, 455, 459, 460, 462, 463, 464, 465, 466, 469, 470, 471, 472, 475
Skanda 17, 394, 401, 435, 452, 454, 475
Skanda Purāṇa 17, 475
Sleeman 355, 356, 386
Smith, W.L. 15, 16, 363, 417, 418, 455, 459, 464, 466, 469, 471, 475
Soma 42, 43, 44, 46, 95, 110, 118, 217, 320, 321, 323, 326, 395, 416, 446, 452, 469
Śrī 334, 394, 420, 428, 432, 444, 463, 473, 474
Śrī Vidyā 334, 394
Śrīṁ 428, 432, 433, 438
Strabo 317, 318, 475
Sumer 9, 13, 309, 312, 322, 448
Sunzi 413, 475
Svāhā 428, 432, 434, 436, 438, 469

T

Takṣaka 20, 119, 325, 326, 396, 418
Tantrabibhūti 460, 461, 462, 463, 464, 465, 466, 468, 469, 470, 471
Tārā 10, 356, 406, 415, 435, 436, 446, 460, 469, 473
Tārakā 469
Teun Goudriaan 332, 474, 476
THC 341
Theosophy 330, 331, 376
thyme 345
Toḍala Tantra 333, 474, 475
Trewavas, Anthony 413, 414, 475
Tribeni 271, 434, 469
Tudge, Colin 380, 395, 475
Twain, Mark 351

U

Umā 14, 18, 384, 416, 435, 446, 475
Ūrmyā 110, 119, 179
Uṣas 110, 182, 206, 327, 393, 461

V

Vāchaspatī, Kāśīrām 418
Varuṇa 110, 323, 324, 421, 436, 461, 471
Vasco da Gama 347
Vāsuki 20, 87, 88, 89, 90, 111, 112, 113, 137, 325, 326, 333, 383, 396, 418, 444, 454, 455
vegans 339
vegetarians 267, 339, 385, 459
Vetālapañcaviṁśatika 476
Vidyā 25, 26, 27, 28, 29, 30, 31, 32, 33, 34, 35, 36, 37, 38, 39, 40, 330, 394, 452
Vijaygupta 363
Vijnana Bhairava Tantra 476
Vikings 320, 321, 345
Vīṇāṣikhatantra 474, 476
Vinaya Piṭaka 448
Viṣṇu 18, 26, 27, 28, 29, 32, 49, 52, 53, 58, 59, 60, 61, 62, 64, 65, 74, 77, 78, 82, 85, 95, 104, 108, 109, 110, 111, 112, 115, 116, 118, 120, 122, 123, 124, 129, 139, 140, 150, 156, 205, 216, 217, 223, 225, 228, 238, 247, 277, 281, 283, 285, 292, 293, 323, 324, 326, 330, 336, 349, 366, 371, 372, 377, 378, 383, 393, 394, 395, 410, 416, 420, 428, 432, 433, 435, 438, 440, 444, 446, 447, 448, 452, 454, 459, 466, 470, 471
Vogel, J. 314, 322, 324, 325, 448, 476

W

White, David Gordon 332, 333, 409, 415, 422, 423, 474, 475, 476

widow 28, 122, 134, 228, 253, 255, 260, 268, 354, 435, 445, 446
Wiggermann, F. 457
Withania 64, 95, 242
Woodroffe, John 330, 335, 416, 454, 474, 476

Y

Yakṣa 8, 110, 207, 216, 238, 445
Yakṣī 130, 467
Yama 8, 175, 181, 197, 235, 238, 250, 273, 278, 288, 289, 290, 323, 371, 394, 466
Yoginī 420, 445, 446, 454, 476

www.ingramcontent.com/pod-product-compliance
Lightning Source LLC
Chambersburg PA
CBHW081144290426
44108CB00018B/2439
* 9 7 8 1 9 1 0 1 9 1 1 4 9 *